Encyclopedia of
Sex and Gender

Men and Women in the World's Cultures

Volume I: Topics and Cultures A–K

Volume II: Cultures L–Z

Encyclopedia of Sex and Gender

Men and Women in the World's Cultures

Volume I: Topics and Cultures A–K

Volume II: Cultures L–Z

Edited by

Carol R. Ember
Human Relations Area Files at Yale University
New Haven, Connecticut

and

Melvin Ember
Human Relations Area Files at Yale University
New Haven, Connecticut

Published in conjunction with the Human Relations Area Files at Yale University

Library of Congress Cataloging-in-Publication Data

Encyclopedia of sex and gender: men and women in the world's cultures/edited by Carol
    R. Ember and Melvin Ember.
        p. cm.
    Includes bibliographical references and index.
    ISBN 0-306-47770-X
    1. Sex—Encyclopedias. 2. Sex—Cross-cultural studies. I. Ember, Carol R. II. Ember,
    Melvin.

HQ16.E53 2004
306.7′03—dc21

                                                                        2003050649

ISBN 0-306-47770-X

Printed in the United States of America.

9 8 7 6 5 4 3 2

springeronline.com

Advisory Board

FLORENCE E. BABB	University of Iowa
CAROLINE BRETTELL	Southern Methodist University
MICHAEL L. BURTON	University of California, Irvine
CAROLYN POPE EDWARDS	University of Nebraska
DOUGLAS P. FRY	Åbo Akademi University and University of Arizona
TERENCE E. HAYS	Rhode Island College
JEROME KAGAN	Harvard University
MAXINE MARGOLIS	University of Florida
MARY MORAN	Colgate University
WINIFRED MITCHELL	Minnesota State University, Mankato
ROBERT L. MUNROE	Pitzer College
ALICE SCHLEGEL	University of Arizona
SUSAN SEYMOUR	Pitzer College
THOMAS WEISNER	University of California, Los Angeles
BEATRICE B. WHITING	Harvard University
MARGERY WOLF	University of Iowa
Managing Editors:	Matthew White and Kathleen Adams

The *Encyclopedia of Sex and Gender* was prepared under the auspices and with the support of the Human Relations Area Files, Inc. (HRAF) at Yale University. The foremost international research organization in the field of cultural anthropology, HRAF is a not-for-profit consortium of 19 Sponsoring Member institutions and more than 400 active and inactive Associate Member institutions in nearly 40 countries. The mission of HRAF is to provide information that facilitates the worldwide comparative study of human behavior, society, and culture. The HRAF Collection of Ethnography, which has been building since 1949, contains nearly one million pages of information, organized by culture and indexed according to more than 700 subject categories, on the cultures of the world. An increasing portion of the Collection of Ethnography, which now covers more than 380 cultures, is accessible via the World Wide Web to member institutions. The HRAF Collection of Archaeology, the first installment of which appeared in 1999, is also accessible on the web to member institutions. HRAF also prepares multivolume reference works with the help of nearly 2,000 scholars around the world, and sponsors *Cross-Cultural Research: The Journal of Comparative Social Science*.

Contributors

Iiris Aaltio, Department of Business Administration, Lappeenranta University of Technology, 53851 Lappeenranta, Finland

Irén Annus, University of Szeged, Hungary

George N. Appell, Department of Anthropology, Brandeis University, Waltham, MA 02254, U.S.A.

Laura W. R. Appell, Sabah Oral Literature Project, Phillips, ME 04996, U.S.A.

Marysol Asencio, Puerto Rican and Latino Studies Institute, University of Connecticut-Storrs, Storrs, CT 06269-2058, U.S.A.

Christine Avenarius, Department of Anthropology, East Carolina University, Greenville, NC 27858-4353, U.S.A.

Benjamin Beit-Hallahmi, University of Haifa, Haifa 31905, Israel

Esben Esther Pirelli Benestad, Grimstad MPAT-Institute, 4876 Grimstad, Norway

Emilio Paqcha Benites, University of Florida, Gainesville, FL, U.S.A.

Ilana Berger, Israeli Center for Human Sexuality and Gender Identity, Tel Aviv 64738, Israel

Deborah L. Best, Department of Psychology, Wake Forest University, Winston-Salem, NC 27109, U.S.A.

Harald Beyer Broch, Department of Social Anthropology, University of Oslo, Blindern, N-0317 Oslo, Norway

Gwen J. Broude, Department of Psychology, Vassar College, Poughkeepsie, NY 12604, U.S.A.

Judith K. Brown, Department of Sociology and Anthropology, Oakland University, Rochester, MI 48309-4495, U.S.A.

Margaret Buckner, Department of Sociology and Anthropology, Southwest Missouri State University, Springfield, MO 65804-0095, U.S.A.

Mary M. Cameron, Women's Studies Center, Florida Atlantic University, Boca Raton, FL 33431-0991, U.S.A.

Fernando Luiz Cardoso, Universidade do Estado de Santa Catarina, Florianópolis/Santa Catarina 88.015-630, Brazil

Maria G. Cattell, Research Associate, Field Museum of Natural History, Chicago, IL 6065-2496, U.S.A.

Dia Cha, Department of Anthropology and Ethnic Studies, St. Cloud State University, St. Cloud, MN 56301, U.S.A.

Janet M. Chernela, Florida International University, Miami, FL, U.S.A.

Richley H. Crapo, Department of Sociology, Social Work, and Anthropology, Utah State University, Logan, UT 84322-0730, U.S.A.

Susan A. Crate, Department of Geography, Miami University, Oxford, OH 45056, U.S.A.

William H. Crocker, Smithsonian Institution, Washington DC, 20013, U.S.A.

Shanshan Du, Department of Anthropology, Tulane University, New Orleans, LA 70118, U.S.A.

Timothy Dunnigan, Department of Anthropology, University of Minnesota, Minneapolis, MN 55455, U.S.A.

Carolyn Pope Edwards, Department of Psychology, University of Nebraska-Lincoln, Lincoln, NE 68588-0308, U.S.A.

Richard Ekins, Cultural and Media Studies Transgender Archive, School of Media and Performing Arts, University of Ulster at Coleraine, County Londonderry BT52 1SA, Northern Ireland

Carol R. Ember, Human Relations Area Files at Yale University, New Haven, CT 06511, U.S.A.

Melvin Ember, Human Relations Area Files at Yale University, New Haven, CT 06511, U.S.A.

Pamela I. Erickson, Department of Anthropology, University of Connecticut, Storrs, CT 06269-2176, U.S.A.

Randi Ettner, New Health Foundation, Evanston, IL 60201, U.S.A.

Pamela Feldman-Savelsberg, Department of Sociology and Anthropology, Carleton College, Northfield, MN 55057, U.S.A.

William H. Fisher, Department of Anthropology, College of William and Mary, Williamsburg, VA 23187-8795, U.S.A.

Diana Fox, Department of Sociology, Anthropology and Criminal Justice, Bridgewater State College, Bridgewater, MA 02325, U.S.A.

Mary Jo Tippeconnic Fox, Department of American Indian Studies, University of Arizona, Tucson, 85721, Arizona, U.S.A.

Susan Tax Freeman, University of Illinois, Chicago, IL 60612, U.S.A.

Rita S. Gallin, Department of Sociology, Michigan State University, East Lansing, MI 48824-1111, U.S.A.

Victoria A. Goddard, Department of Anthropology, Goldsmiths College, University of London, London SE14 6NW, U.K.

Joshua S. Goldstein, American University, Washington DC, 20016, U.S.A.

Alma Gottlieb, Department of Anthropology, University of Illinois at Urbana-Champaign, Urbana, IL 61801, U.S.A.

Chien-Juh Gu, Department of Sociology, Michigan State University, East Lansing, MI 48824-1111, U.S.A.

Timothy M. Hall, University of California, San Diego, CA, U.S.A.

Katsuki Harima, Family Court Clinic of Tokyo Family Court, 100-13 1-1-2 Kasumigaseki Chiyodaku, Tokyo, Japan

Betty J. Harris, University of Oklahoma, Norman, OK, U.S.A.

Mary Elaine Hegland, Department of Anthropology and Sociology, Santa Clara University, Santa Clara, CA 95053, U.S.A.

Lewellyn Hendrix, Department of Sociology, Southern Illinois University at Carbondale, Carbondale, IL 62958, U.S.A.

Warren M. Hern, Department of Anthropology, University of Colorado at Boulder, Boulder, CO 80304, U.S.A.

Gabriele Herzog-Schröder, Research Group Human Ethnology, Max-Planck-Society, Andechs, Germany, and Institute for Ethnology and Cultural Anthropology, Ludwig-Maximilians-Universität, Munich, Germany

Jon Holtzman, Department of Sociology and Anthropology, Kalamazoo College, Kalamazoo, MI 49008, U.S.A.

James Howe, Anthropology Program, Massachusetts Institute of Technology, Cambridge, MA 02139-4307, U.S.A.

Armine Ishkanian, University of California, Berkeley, California, U.S.A.

William R. Jankowiak, Department of Anthropology and Ethnic Studies, University of Nevada, Las Vegas, NV 89154, U.S.A.

Robert Jarvenpa, Department of Anthropology, State University of New York at Albany, Albany, NY 12222, U.S.A.

Carol Zane Jolles, Department of Anthropology, University of Washington, Seattle, WA 98195-3100, U.S.A.

Marianne Ruth Kamp, Department of History, University of Wyoming, Laramie, WY 82070, U.S.A.

Kaisa Kauppinen, Department of Psychology, Finnish Institute of Occupational Health, Helsinki, Finland

Alice Beck Kehoe, University of Wisconsin-Milwaukee, Milwaukee, WI 53211-3436, U.S.A.

Dave King, Department of Sociology, Social Policy, and Social Work Studies, University of Liverpool, Liverpool L69 7ZA, England

Laura F. Klein, Department of Anthropology, Pacific Lutheran University, Tacoma, WA 98447, U.S.A.

Lisa Knoche, Department of Psychology, University of Nebraska-Lincoln, Lincoln, NE 68588-0308, U.S.A.

Kathleen Kuehnast, Institute of European, Russian and Eurasian Studies, George Washington University, Washington DC, 20052, U.S.A.

Asiye Kumru, Abant Izzet Baysal Universitesi, Fen Edebiyat Fakultesi, Psikoloji Bolumu, Golkoy Kampusu, 14280 Bolu, Turkey

Lynn M. Kwiatkowski, Department of Sociology and Anthropology, University of South Alabama, Mobile, AL 36688, U.S.A.

Oneka LaBennett, Department of Sociology and Anthropology, College of the Holy Cross, Worcester, MA 01610, U.S.A.

Mikael Landén, Section of Psychiatry, Institute of Clinical Neuroscience, Göteborg, SE 431 80 Mölndal, Sweden

Lioba Lenhart, Institut für Völkerkunde, Universität Köln, D-50923 Köln, Germany

Charles Lindholm, Boston University, Boston, MA 02215, U.S.A.

Lamont Lindstrom, Department of Anthropology, University of Tulsa, Tulsa, OK 74104, U.S.A.

Bobbi S. Low, School of Natural Resources and Environment, University of Michigan, Ann Arbor, MI 48109-1115, U.S.A.

Judith Macdonald, Anthropology Programme, University of Waikato, Hamilton, New Zealand

Jeannette Marie Mageo, Department of Anthropology, Washington State University, Pullman, WA 99164-4910, U.S.A.

Maxine L. Margolis, Department of Anthropology, University of Florida, Gainesville, FL 32611, U.S.A.

Richard A. Marksbury, Tulane University, New Orleans, LA 70118, U.S.A.

Frank Marlowe, Department of Anthropology, Harvard University, Peabody Museum, Cambridge, MA 02138, U.S.A.

Nancy McDowell, Department of Anthropology, Beloit College, Beloit, WI 53511, U.S.A.

Bonnie McElhinny, Department of Anthropology and Institute for Women's Studies and Gender's Studies, University of Toronto, Toronto, Ontario M5S 3G3, Canada

Winifred Mitchell, Department of Anthropology, Minnesota State University, Mankato, MN 56001, U.S.A.

Brian Montes, University of Illinois, Urbana-Champaign, IL, U.S.A.

Mary H. Moran, Department of Sociology and Anthropology, Colgate University, Hamilton, NY 13346, U.S.A.

Nuno Nodin, Lisbon, Portugal

Barbara S. Nowak, Institute of Development Studies, School of People, Environment and Planning, Massey University, Palmerston North, New Zealand

Regina Smith Oboler, Ursinus College, Collegeville, PA 19426, U.S.A.

Robin O'Brian, Division of Behavioral and Social Sciences, Elmira College, Elmira, NY 14901, U.S.A.

Lyn Parker, Department of Asian Studies, University of Western Australia, Crawley, WA 6009, Australia

Jakob M. Pastötter, Magnus Hirschfeld Archive for Sexology at Humboldt University Berlin, D-13189 Berlin, Germany

Julia Pauli, Institute of Ethnology, Universität Köln, D-50923 Köln, Germany

Sarah D. Phillips, Department of Anthropology, University of the South, Sewanee, TN 37383, U.S.A.

Debra Picchi, Department of Anthropology, Franklin Pierce College, Rindge, NH 03461, U.S.A.

Ulrike Prinz, Institute for Ethnology and African Studies, Ludwig-Maximilians-Universität, Munich, Germany

Volodymyr P'yatokha, Volyn Regional Hospital, Lutsk 43007, Ukraine

Aparna Rao, Institut für Völkerkunde, Universität Köln, D-50923 Köln, Germany

Kathleen C. Riley, Johnson State College, Johnson, VT 05656, U.S.A.

Paul Roscoe, Department of Anthropology, University of Maine, Orono, ME 04469, U.S.A.

Amir Rosenmann, Department of Psychology, University of Haifa, Haifa 31905, Israel

Celia E. Rothenberg, Wilfred Laurier University, Waterloo, Ontario, Canada

Marilyn P. Safir, Department of Psychology, University of Haifa, Haifa 31905, Israel

Richard Scaglion, Department of Anthropology, University of Pittsburgh, Pittsburgh, PA 15260, U.S.A.

Wulf Schiefenhövel, Human Ethology Group, Max-Planck-Institut, 82346 Andechs, Germany

Alice Schlegel, Department of Anthropology, University of Arizona, Tucson, AZ 85721, U.S.A.

Maureen Trudelle Schwarz, Department of Anthropology, Syracuse University, Syracuse, NY 13244-1090, U.S.A.

Edwin S. Segal, Department of Anthropology, University of Louisville, Louisville, KY 40292, U.S.A.

Susan C. Seymour, Pitzer College, Claremont, CA 91711, U.S.A.

Audrey C. Shalinsky, Department of History, University of Wyoming, Laramie, WY 82070, U.S.A.

Andrew N. Sharpe, Department of Law, Macquarie University, Sydney, NSW 2109, Australia

Eric Kline Silverman, Department of Sociology and Anthropology, DePauw University, Greencastle, IN 46135, U.S.A.

Daniel Jordan Smith, Department of Anthropology, Brown University, Providence, RI 02912, U.S.A.

John R. Sosa, Department of Sociology and Anthropology, State University of New York Cortland, Cortland, NY 13045, U.S.A.

Allyn MacLean Stearman, Department of Sociology and Anthropology, University of Central Florida, Orlando, FL 32816-1800, U.S.A.

Lynn Stephen, Department of Anthropology, University of Oregon, Eugene, OR 97403-1218, U.S.A.

Bilinda Straight, Department of Anthropology, Western Michigan University, Kalamazoo, MI 49008, U.S.A.

David E. Sutton, Southern Illinois University, Carbondale, IL 62901, U.S.A.

James M. Taggart, Department of Anthropology, Franklin and Marshall College, Lancaster, PA 17604-3003, U.S.A.

Aud Talle, Department of Social Anthropology, University of Oslo, 0317 Oslo, Norway

Myrna Tonkinson, Department of Anthropology, University of Western Australia, Crawley, WA 6009, Australia

Robert Tonkinson, Department of Anthropology, University of Western Australia, Crawley, WA 6009, Australia

Rebecca L. Upton, Institute for Social Research and Center for the Ethnography of Everyday Life, University of Michigan, Ann Arbor, MI 48106, U.S.A.

Robert A. Veneziano, Department of Social Work, Western Connecticut State University, Danbury, CT 06810, U.S.A.

Eileen Rose Walsh, Council on East Asian Studies, Yale University, New Haven, CT 06520, U.S.A.

William Wedenoja, Department of Sociology and Anthropology, Southwest Missouri State University, Springfield, MO 65804-0095, U.S.A.

Glenn E. Weisfeld, Department of Psychology, Wayne State University, Detroit, MI 48202, U.S.A.

Cynthia Werner, Department of Anthropology, Texas A&M University, College Station, TX 77843-4352, U.S.A.

Dennis Werner, Universidade Federal de Santa Catarina, Santa Caterina 88.015-630 Brazil

Barbara A. West, University of the Pacific, Stockton, CA 95211, U.S.A.

Cynthia Whissell, Department of Psychology, Laurentian University, Sudbury, Ontario, Canada

Tarynn M. Witten, TranScience Research Institute, Richmond, VA 23228-28089, U.S.A.

Felice S. Wyndham, University of Georgia, Athens, GA 30602, U.S.A.

Melissa-Ann Yeager, Department of Brandeis University, Waltham, MA, U.S.A.

Xiaojian Zhao, Department of Asian American Studies, University of California, Santa Barbara, CA 93106, U.S.A.

Laura Zimmer-Tamakoshi, Cultural Solutions, West Chester, PA 19382, U.S.A.

Preface

In some animal species, one can hardly tell the difference between females and males. Their size, coloring, and behavior may be so similar that even experts cannot readily tell the difference until they are ready to reproduce. In contrast, human females and males differ not only in secondary sexual characteristics (like breasts and beards), but they also generally exhibit differences in height, weight, and ratio of muscle to fat. Given the reproductive differences as well as differences in appearance between males and females, it is hardly surprising that most if not all societies conceive of females and males as important social categories. These reproductive and biological facts by themselves cannot explain the enormous variability in the way societies treat persons of the different biological sexes. The most sexually egalitarian societies may hardly treat males and females differently. But there are no societies that clearly give more overall advantages to females than to males, and those that advantage males vary considerably from mild to extreme inequality.

Cultural expectations have profound effects on how males and females grow up in a society, so much so that many researchers prefer to use the terms **gender differences** or **gender roles** to reflect the large impact of culture on differences between the sexes. The terms **sex differences** and **sex roles** now usually refer to differences that are thought to derive primarily from biological differences. The advantage of the term *gender* is that it also allows us to deal with situations where societies conceptualize more than two genders or who have individuals who change gender role in the course of their lifetimes. The problem for social science is that we often do not know whether a particular difference is due to biology or culture, or both. Biological and cultural influences are not always clearly separable because in most societies parents start treating boy and girl babies differently from the moment of birth.

The central aim of this encyclopedia is to give the reader a comparative perspective on issues involving conceptions of gender, gender differences, gender roles, relationships between the genders, and sexuality. We do this in two ways. First, we have invited scholars to write comparative overviews about what may be universal, what is variable, and to discuss theory and research that might explain those patterns. Second, each of 82 specific cultural articles provides a "portrait" of what it is like for boys and girls to grow up and become men and women in that society. Some societies have other gender classes and where these occur, or where boys and girls can cross into other roles, these are discussed. Our portraits also discuss important male–female relationships and a culture's sexual attitudes and practices. We deliberately chose to include cultures from the widest possible spectrums—from egalitarian to stratified, from foragers to intensive agriculturalists, from those with kin groups structured around males to those structured around females, from those where the status of women and men is relatively equal to those where status is mostly unequal. We also have cultures from every major geographical region. The combination of topical overviews and varying cultural portraits is what makes this encyclopedia unique.

The topical overviews are divided into four sections. The first deals with cultural conceptions of gender (Cultural Constructions of Gender, and Gender Stereotypes). The second explores observed differences between males and females in behavior and personality and asks what biological and/or social factors may explain those differences (Biological Bases of Gender Differences, Socialization of Boys and Girls in Natural Contexts, Adolescence, and Personality and Emotion). The third section deals with more institutionalized aspects of gender—gender roles, life-cycle transitions, status, and social institutions that relate to gender (Courtship and Marriage, Parental Roles, Economic Activities and Gender Roles, Leadership, Power, and Gender, War and Gender, Religion, Religiosity, and Gender, Gender-Based Social Groups, Relative Status of Men and Women, Economic Development and Gender, Language and Gender, Transitions in the Life-Course of Women). The fourth section deals with sexuality and male–female interaction (Sexual Attitudes and Practices, Modesty and Sexual Restraint, Husband–Wife Interaction and Aloofness, Homosexuality, Transgender and Transsexuality, and Rape and Other Sexual Aggression). Some of the articles in a section deal with topics that overlap other sections.

To facilitate comparison across cultures, the cultural portraits follow a standard set of topics so that readers may readily compare across cultures. Most of the authors are anthropologists or other social scientists who have lived with the people they write about and are able to give a vivid portrait of life in that society.

The term "gender" in a title or subtitle of a work often suggests today that the work is primarily about women. We have deliberately included the words "men" and "women" in our subtitle to convey that this reference work deals with the roles and status of women *and* men in many cultures and with how they relate to each other. This is another quality that makes this encyclopedia unique.

ORGANIZATION OF THE ARTICLES

The thematic and comparative essays vary in how they are organized, not just in their topics. The authors were encouraged by the editors to structure their discussions as they saw fit. On the other hand, the articles on sex and gender in particular cultures follow the same format to provide maximum comparability. That is, the culture articles cover the same topics, the list of which we developed with the help of our Advisory Board (see the headings in boldface type below). If there is substantial variation within the culture (e.g., by class or gender), the author was instructed to discuss it, either in a particular section or at the end. A heading may be omitted if information on it is lacking or not applicable. The headings that follow are found in the vast majority of the articles to facilitate search and retrieval of information. Thus the reader may easily compare how the cultures of the world differ and are similar in the ways they deal with sex and gender.

The outline for the culture articles includes the following topics.

Alternative Names

Other names or ethnonyms used in the literature.

Location and Linguistic Affiliation

Where the described culture is located (region of the world, country, and location within the country, where appropriate).

Cultural Overview

A summary of the culture to orient the reader, covering such topics as basic economy, political organization, settlement patterns, family and kinship, and intercultural relations. Any general features that are important for understanding gender differences that are not covered in the more specific topics below are included here.

Cultural Construction of Gender

What are the recognized gender categories? How does the culture conceptualize these genders? Do the different genders dress differently or do anything different to their bodies so that they visually appear different (in hairstyle, scarification, make-up)? If differentiation is age related, when the changes occur is discussed. What makes a male or female attractive? Are sexual preferences associated with visual cues?

Gender over the Life Cycle

What are the cultural names for stages in the life cycle? Do they differ for the different genders? Which passages from one stage to another are publicly marked and how do they differ by gender? Any changes in rights and responsibilities accompanying the transitions?

Socialization of Boys and Girls.   The aim of this section is to convey the ways in which boys and girls are reared similarly or differently from infancy through childhood by parents and other socialization agents (extended families, other kin, neighbors, peers). Are boys and girls valued equally, or are there cultural ways that convey a preference? What are the expectations that parents and other caretakers have for boys and girls? Which traits do they value in boys and girls? Do they expect different behaviors or work? Do boys and girls have different patterns of play, games, or leisure? Are there different rites and rituals in infancy and childhood for boys and girls? Do caretakers educate, instruct, or discipline boys and girls differently? Who are the major caretakers? Are there differences or similarities in formal education or apprenticeship? If there are few obvious differences in socialization, this section discusses the common features of socialization. (How boys and girls are introduced to sexuality, rules of modesty, or sexual expression is mostly discussed in a later section.)

Puberty and Adolescence.   Is there a named stage for adolescence? Is there continuity in socialization around the time of puberty or are there significant changes from childhood socialization? Similar questions raised in the previous section are addressed for this stage too, if the culture identifies a separate stage. Are there special rites or genital modifications that are not associated with the attainment of adulthood?

Attainment of Adulthood.   This describes any special rites of passage marking the transition from boyhood to manhood and/or from girlhood to womanhood. If there are no special rites, when are the genders considered adults? What behavioral changes are expected with adulthood?

Middle Age and Old Age.   Aside from adult roles described in later sections, are there any important gender changes associated with middle age and old age (such as changes in respect)?

Personality Differences by Gender

Aside from behaviors required in different roles, are there differences in the ways boys and girls and men and women behave? Are there changes over the life cycle? Particular areas considered are degree of nurturance, dominance, dependency, sociability, aggression, reticence or shyness, expressiveness, etc. What are cultural stereotypes of how males and females ought to be? Do these stereotypes differ from reality? Is there explicit research on gender differences in cognition, perception, or mental illness in the culture?

Gender-Related Social Groups

To what degree are the social institutions in society structured around males or females? Do married couples live with or near the husband's family or the wife's family? Does this change through the life cycle? Are there larger kin groups formed through males (patrilineal kin groups) or through females (matrilineal kin groups)? Are there important nonkin associations for males or females in the society?

Gender Roles in Economics

What is the division of labor between men and women in making a living, household and domestic work, and occupational specialization? How strongly is the division of labor adhered to? To what degree are the genders involved in trade, marketing, and nonmarket exchange? Is one gender substantially removed from home because of involvement in long-distance trade, work, or warfare? When does this happen and what is the duration? Who can own or inherit property and does it vary by type of property?

Parental and Other Caretaker Roles

What defines the parental role? To what degree do fathers (and/or other males) and mothers (and/or other females) play a role in child-rearing and do they differ in the ways they socialize (e.g., in disciplining, education, physical care, time spent with children, or affection)? Does the behavior of a male or female differ toward a male or female child?

Leadership in Public Arenas

To what extent is leadership in the political arena (including social/political movements), kin groups, warfare, etc. restricted to males? If women have leadership roles, do they have equal authority? If there are differences, what are they?

Gender and Religion

What roles do the genders play in religion? Are there any special gendered orders, such as monks and nuns? What entities in the external universe are associated with the gender categories? What genders are the gods and spirits and what is their relative position in a hierarchy, if there is one? Was the original human male or female?

Leisure, Recreation, and the Arts

Do men and women have much leisure time? Does one sex have more leisure time? How do men and women spend their leisure time? (Games, socializing with friends, discussing politics, storytelling, singing, dancing, music, etc.) Are there substantial differences in the ways that boys and girls and men and women spend their leisure time? To what degree are the sexes segregated in their free time? Is segregation voluntary or required? (Gender specialization in crafts and art is discussed under economic activities.)

Relative Status of Men and Women

Status refers to the value attached to men and women by society as well as differential authority, rights, and privileges. Since formal positions in the public arena are described in previous sections, this section focuses on other aspects. Are there substantial differences in decision-making and influence for men and women in subsistence and economy, family matters, community, kin group, and religion? Do men and women have different rights to important resources and do they control the fruits of their labor? Do males and females control or influence their sexuality, education, marriage choice, divorce choice, etc.? Do males or females obtain special privileges (such as deference)? Do these change over the life cycle?

Sexuality

What are male and female attitudes toward sexuality generally (i.e., is it natural, healthy, dangerous, polluting, only for reproduction)? Do attitudes toward, and practices of, premarital sex and extramarital sex differ for males and females? Do they change over the life cycle? How does the cultural conception of male sexuality differ from the cultural conception of female sexuality? To what degree is modesty about the body required in the society? When is modesty expected and does it vary by gender? To what degree is expression of sexuality allowed or not allowed in childhood, adolescence, and adulthood? Does it vary by gender or by class? How does the society deal with expressions of cross-sex identification, cross-dressing, etc.? How does the society treat male and female homosexuality?

Courtship and Marriage

What are the typical patterns of male–female courtship and marriage? To what degree are there departures from those patterns? How many people get married or are expected to marry? What roles do unmarried people have? Is love a part of marriage choice or are other considerations more important? Do males and females have choice in when and whom they can marry? If not, who exercises choice and how are marriages arranged? If there is a marriage ceremony, what is it like? Are there any special postmarriage customs? Can widows or widowers remarry and whom do they marry (any preferences or rules)?

Husband–Wife Relationship

To what degree is the husband–wife relationship characterized by love, affection, and/or companionship, or is there characteristic hostility, antagonism, or aloofness? Do husbands and wives eat together, sleep together, spend other time together, make decisions together? Is there a strict division of tasks, or is there interchangeability? If there is polygamy, describe the relationship between cowives or cohusbands. If the marriage is not satisfactory, what are the possibilities of divorce and for what reasons? Can the husband and/or the wife initiate the divorce? What happens to any children if there is a divorce?

Other Cross-Sex Relationships

Are there significant male–female relationships (other than husband–wife) such as brother–sister, grandparent–grandchild, uncle–niece, aunt–nephew, cousins, cross-sex friendships, etc.?

Change in Attitudes, Beliefs, and Practices Regarding Gender

This optional section describes important changes over time if they are not described earlier.

REFERENCES

References to sources in the text are included to allow the reader to explore topics and cultures further.

USING THE *ENCYCLOPEDIA OF SEX AND GENDER*

This reference work can be used by a variety of people for a variety of purposes. It can be used both to gain a broad understanding of the lives of males and females in different cultures or to find out about particular cultures and topics. A bibliography is provided at the end of each entry to facilitate further investigation.

Beyond serving as a basic reference resource, the *Encyclopedia of Sex and Gender* also serves readers with more focused needs. For researchers interested in comparing cultures, this work provides information that can guide the selection of particular cultures for further study. The "Cultural Overview" section provides a summary that enables users to compare cultures with different types of economies (e.g., foragers, pastoralists, horticulturalists or intensive agriculturalists), or with different degrees of social stratification (e.g, egalitarian versus class or caste systems), or with different levels of political hierarchies (e.g., independent communities to kingships). The section "Gender-Related Social Groups" allows the user to tell if the society is socially structured around males (patrilocal and/or patrilineal societies), females (matrilocal and/or matrilineal societies) or neither (e.g., bilateral or ambilineal societies). Educators and teachers might be interested in having students consider what it is like to grow up as a girl or a boy in different cultures. For students, from high school through graduate school, this encyclopedia provides background and bibliographic information for term papers and class projects. And for those just curious about how sex and gender issues differ from how they may appear in their own society, this encyclopedia provides an unparalleled look at worldwide variation.

ACKNOWLEDGMENTS

There are many people to thank for their contributions. Eliot Werner, formerly at Plenum, played an important role in the planning of the project. The Advisory Board made valuable suggestions about the outline for the culture entries and possible topics to be covered in the thematic essays, and suggested potential authors. The editors were responsible for the final selection of authors and for reviewing the manuscripts. For managing the project at HRAF, we are indebted to Matthew White and Kathleen Adams. We thank Teresa Krauss for overseeing the production process at Kluwer/Plenum and Anne Meagher for her efficient handling of the production of this Encyclopedia. Finally, and most of all, we thank the contributors for their entries. Without their knowledge and commitment, this work would not have been possible.

Carol R. Ember, Executive Director
Melvin Ember, President
Human Relations Area Files at Yale University

Contents

Contents xix

Cherokee 356
Mary Jo Tippeconnic Fox
Chinese Americans 364
Xiaojian Zhao
Chipewyan 371
Robert Jarvenpa
Czechs 380
Timothy M. Hall
Eastern Tukanoans 389
Janet M. Chernela
Germans 400
Jakob M. Pastötter
Glebo 408
Mary H. Moran
Greeks of Kalymnos 417
David E. Sutton
Hadza 425
Frank Marlowe
Han Chinese 433
William R. Jankowiak
Hma' Btsisi' 443
Barbara S. Nowak
Hmong of Laos and the United States 452
Dia Cha and Timothy Dunnigan
Hopi 465
Alice Schlegel
Hungarians 475
Barbara A. West and Irén Annus
Iatmul 487
Eric Kline Silverman
Ifugao 498
Lynn M. Kwiatkowski
Igbo 508
Daniel Jordan Smith
Iranians 518
Mary Elaine Hegland
Israelis 530
Marilyn P. Safir and Amir Rosenmann
Italians 540
Victoria A. Goddard
Jamaica 551
William Wedenoja and Diana Fox
Kayapo 561
William H. Fisher
Kazakhs 572
Cynthia Werner
Kuna 581
James Howe

Glossary

1.5 generation.   Immigrants who immigrated to the host country in the midst of their personal development, between the ages of five and twelve; also called the "in-between generation."

acculturation.   The process of extensive borrowing of aspects of culture in the context of superordinate–subordinate relations between societies; usually occurs as the result of external pressure.

adaptive trait.   A trait that enhances survival and reproductive success in a particular environment. Usually applied to biological evolution, the term is also often used by cultural anthropologists to refer to cultural traits that enhance reproductive success.

affinal kin.   One's relatives by marriage.

age-grade.   A category of persons who happen to fall within a particular, culturally distinguished age range.

age-mate.   One of the persons of one's own age-set or age-grade.

age-set.   A group of persons of similar age and the same sex who move together through some or all of life's stages.

agricultural societies.   Societies that depend primarily on domesticated plants for subsistence; See Horticulture and Intensive Agriculture for the major type of agriculture.

agropastoralism.   A type of subsistence economy based largely on agriculture with the raising of domesticated animals playing an important part.

AIDS (Acquired Immune Deficiency Syndrome).   A recent fatal disease caused by the HIV virus. A positive HIV test result does not mean that a person has AIDS. A diagnosis of AIDS is made using certain clinical criteria (e.g., AIDS indicator illnesses such as *Pneumocystis carinii* pneumonia, malignancies such as Kaposi's sarcoma and lymphoma).

ambilineal descent.   The rule of descent that affiliates an individual with groups of kin related to him or her through men or women.

ambilocal residence.   *See* **bilocal residence**.

ancestor spirits.   Supernatural beings who are the ghosts of dead relatives.

ancestor worship.   Veneration or reverence of ancestor spirits; ancestor spirits may be called upon for help or may be given sacrifices to have them refrain from harming the living.

animism.   A term used by Edward Tylor to describe a belief in a dual existence for all things—a physical, visible body and a psychic, invisible soul.

anthropology.   A discipline that studies humans, focusing on the study of differences and similarities, both biological and cultural, in human populations. Anthropology is concerned with typical biological and cultural characteristics of human populations in all periods and in all parts of the world.

association.   An organized group not based exclusively on kinship or territory.

avoidance relationship.   A custom specifying that people in a particular kinship relationship (e.g., a man and his mother-in-law) must refrain from interaction or show marked restraint with each other.

avunculocal residence.   A pattern of residence in which a married couple settles with or near the husband's mother's brother.

balanced reciprocity.   Giving with the expectation of a straightforward immediate or limited-time trade.

band.   A fairly small, usually nomadic local group that is politically autonomous.

barrio.   A neighborhood in a city; used in Spanish-speaking countries.

behavioral ecology.   The study of how all kinds of behavior may be related to the environment. The theoretical orientation involves the application of biological evolutionary principles to the behavior (including social behavior) of animals, including humans. Also called sociobiology, particularly when applied to social organization and social behavior.

berdache.   A male transvestite in some Native American societies.

Big Man. A male leader in a tribal society who has competed with others to attract followers.

Big Woman. A female leader in a tribal society who has competed with others to attract followers.

bilateral kinship. The type of kinship system in which individuals affiliate more or less equally with their mother's and father's relatives; descent groups are absent.

bilingual. Using or knowing two languages.

bilocal residence. A pattern of residence in which a married couple lives with or near either the husband's parents or the wife's parents.

biological (physical) anthropology. The study of humans as biological organisms, dealing with the emergence and evolution of humans and with contemporary biological variations among human populations.

bride price. A substantial gift of goods or money given to the bride's kin by the groom or his kin at or before the marriage. Also called **bride wealth**.

bride service. Work performed by the groom for his bride's family for a variable length of time either before or after the marriage.

bridewealth. (or **bride wealth**). *See* **bride price**

cash crops. Crops grown primarily for sale.

caste. A ranked group, often associated with a certain occupation, in which membership is determined at birth and marriage is restricted to members of one's own caste.

chief. A person who exercises authority, usually on behalf of a multicommunity political unit. This role is generally found in rank societies and is usually permanent and often hereditary.

chiefdom. A political unit, with a chief at its head, integrating more than one community but not necessarily the whole society or language group.

circumcision. In males, a genital operation in which the fold of the skin covering the top of the penis is removed. In females, a genital operation in which the fold covering the clitoris, or all or part of the clitoris, or parts of the labia may be removed.

clan. A set of kin whose members believe themselves to be descended from a common ancestor or ancestress but cannot specify the links back to that founder; often designated by a totem. Also called a sib.

clan exogamy. A rule specifying that a person must marry outside his/her clan.

class. A category of persons who have about the same opportunity to obtain economic resources, power, and prestige.

classificatory terms. Kinship terms that merge or equate relatives who are genealogically distinct from one another; the same term is used for a number of different kin.

class society. A society containing social groups that have unequal access to economic resources, power, and prestige.

cognates. Individuals who have the same parentage or descent.

cognatic kinship. In contrast to unilineal kinship systems (*See* **unilineal descent**) that allow transmission through either the male *or* the female line, nonunilineal kinship systems allows any or all relatives to be included that can be traced through both parents. The major forms are bilateral kinship and ambilineal descent. *See* **bilateral kinship** and **ambilineal descent**.

colonialism. The control by one nation of a territory or people; the controlled territory may be referred to as a colony.

concubinage. The custom of a socially recognized nonmarital sexual relationship between a man and a woman (concubine) who has lower status than the wife.

commercialization. The increasing dependence on buying and selling, with money usually as the medium of exchange.

compadrazgo. A fictive kinship relationship established primarily through baptism in which a child's sponsor becomes a "co-parent" and establishes a relationship with the child's parents as well as with the child.

consanguineal kin. One's biological relatives; relatives by birth.

couvade. The apparent experiencing of labor by a man during his wife's pregnancy; in milder forms a man may avoid certain types of work or rest during the pregnancy.

crime. Violence not considered legitimate that occurs within a political unit.

cross-cousins. Children of siblings of the opposite sex. One's cross-cousins are father's sisters' children and mother's brothers' children.

cross-sex identification. The psychological identification with the opposite sex (e.g., a boy who wishes to be like his mother).

cultural anthropology. The study of cultural variation and universals.

cultural ecology. The analysis of the relationship between a culture and its environment.

culture. The set of learned behaviors, beliefs, attitudes, values, and ideals that are characteristic of a particular society or population.

descriptive term. Kinship term used to refer to a genealogically distinct relative; a different term is used for each relative.

descent rules. *See* **rules of descent**.

dialect. A variety of a language spoken in a particular area or by a particular social group.

diffusion. The borrowing by one society of a cultural trait belonging to another society as the result of contact between the two societies.

diglossia. The widespread existence of two very different forms of the same language within the same society spoken in different social contexts (e.g., formal versus informal) or by different groups of people (e.g., by varying gender).

divination. Getting the supernatural to provide guidance.

domestic cycle. In many societies, the type of household changes in some regular way depending upon the demographics of the family. An example would be that a married son and his family must leave an extended family household and set up an independent household when his children approach marriageable age.

double descent. A system that affiliates an individual with a group of matrilineal kin for some purposes and with a group of patrilineal kin for other purposes. Also called double unilineal descent or **dual descent**.

dowry. A substantial transfer of goods or money from the bride's family to the bride.

dual descent. *See* **double descent**.

egalitarian society. A society in which all persons of a given age–sex category have equal access to economic resources, power, and prestige.

ego. In the reckoning of kinship, the reference point or focal person.

emic. From the perspective of the insider; often referring to the point of view of the society studied; contrast with **etic**.

enculturation. *See* **socialization**.

endogamy. The rule specifying marriage to a person within one's own group (kin, caste, community).

ethnicity. The process of defining ethnicity usually involves a group of people emphasizing common origins and language, shared history, and selected aspects of cultural difference such as a difference in religion. Since different groups are doing the perceiving, ethnic identities often vary with whether one is inside or outside the group.

ethnic group. A social group perceived by insiders or outsiders to share a culture or a group that emphasizes its cultural or social separateness.

ethnic stratification. A type of social stratification where different ethnic groups in a society have different access to advantages.

ethnonym. An alternative name for a culture or ethnic group.

ethnocentric. Refers to judgment of other cultures solely in terms of one's own culture.

ethnocentrism. The attitude that other societies' customs and ideas can be judged in the context of one's own culture.

ethnographer. A person who spends some time living with, interviewing, and observing a group of people so that he or she can describe their customs.

ethnography. A description of a society's customary behaviors, beliefs, and attitudes.

ethnology.   The study of how and why recent cultures differ and are similar.

ethos.   The dominant assumptions or sentiments of a culture.

etic.   From the perspective of the outsider; often refers to the way a researcher will classify something in the culture studied based on her or his own scholarly perspective.

exogamy.   The rule specifying marriage to a person from outside one's own group (kin group or community).

explanation.   An answer to a why question. In science, there are two kinds of explanation that researchers try to achieve: associations (relationships between variables) and theories (sets of principles that predict associations).

extended family.   A family consisting of two or more single-parent, monogamous, polygynous, or polyandrous families linked by a blood tie.

extensive cultivation.   A type of horticulture in which the land is worked for short periods and then left to regenerate for some years before being used again. Also called **shifting cultivation**.

external warfare.   Warfare that takes places with another society.

family.   A social and economic unit consisting minimally of a parent and a child.

fecundity.   The biological capacity to have offspring; fecundity varies by individual and also by population. May be affected by breastfeeding, caloric intake, strenuous exercise among other factors.

female genital mutilation.   Usually refers to a societally mandated genital operation that removes some part of the female genitalia or alters the genitalia. *See* **circumcision** and **infibulation**.

feuding.   A state of recurring hostility between families or groups of kin, usually motivated by a desire to avenge an offense against a member of the group.

fieldwork.   Firsthand experience with the people being studied and the usual means by which anthropological information is obtained. Regardless of other methods (e.g., censuses, surveys) that anthropologists may use, fieldwork usually involves participant-observation for an extended period of time, often a year or more. *See* **participant-observation**.

first generation immigrants.   Refers to the people who immigrated to the new country after their formative years (e.g., after age 13) in the homeland country.

folklore.   Includes all the myths, legends, folktales, ballads, riddles, proverbs, and superstitions of a cultural group. Generally, folklore is transmitted orally, but it may also be written.

food collection.   All forms of subsistence technology in which food-getting is dependent on naturally occurring resources—wild plants and animals.

food production.   The form of subsistence technology in which food-getting is dependent on the cultivation and domestication of plants and animals.

foragers.   People who subsist on the collection of naturally occurring plants and animals. Also referred to as **hunter-gatherers**.

fraternal polyandry.   The marriage of a woman to two or more brothers at the same time.

gender.   Two or more classes of persons who are believed to be different from each other; society has different roles and expectations for different genders (most societies have two genders—male and female—but others have more than two).

gender differences.   Differences between females and males that reflect cultural expectations and experiences.

gender division of labor.   Rules and customary patterns specifying which kinds of work the respective genders perform.

gender roles.   Roles that are culturally assigned to genders.

gender status.   The importance, rights, power, and authority of a particular gender.

gender stratification.   The degree of unequal access by the different genders to prestige, authority, power, rights, and economic resources.

generalized reciprocity.   Gift giving without any immediate or planned return.

genitor.   The biological father.

genotype.   The total complement of inherited traits or genes of an organism.

ghosts.   Supernatural beings who were once human; the souls of dead people.

gods.   Supernatural beings of nonhuman origin who are named personalities; often anthropomorphic.

grammatical gender.   A set of two or more noun classes in a language which are either modified or are associated with other forms that are modified to indicate the particular class to which the noun belongs (e.g., some languages have feminine and masculine nouns).

group marriage.   Marriage in which more than one man is married to more than one woman at the same time; not customary in any known human society.

group selection.   Natural selection of group characteristics.

headman.   A person who holds a powerless but symbolically unifying position in a community within an egalitarian society; may exercise influence but has no power to impose sanctions.

hectare.   A unit of measurement equal to 10,000 square meters.

homosexuality.   Defined broadly as sexual relationships between people of the same sex; however, cultures differ widely in the ways they define and treat these relationships and the people who engage in them.

homosocial.   Relates to social relationships between persons of the same sex.

horticulture.   Plant cultivation carried out with relatively simple tools and methods; nature is allowed to replace nutrients in the soil, in the absence of permanently cultivated fields.

hunter-gatherers.   People who collect food from naturally occurring resources, that is, wild plants, animals, and fish. The phrase "hunter-gatherers" minimizes sometimes heavy dependence on fishing. Also referred to as foragers.

hypotheses.   Predictions, which may be derived from theories, about how variables are related.

incest taboo.   Prohibition of sexual intercourse or marriage between mother and son, father and daughter, and brother and sister.

indirect dowry.   Goods given by the groom's kin to the bride (or her father, who passes most of them to her) at or before her marriage.

individual selection.   Natural selection of individual characteristics.

infibulation.   Female genital surgery that involves stitching together the vulva leaving only a small opening for the passage of urine and menstrual blood. Usually done following circumcision. *See* **circumcision**.

initiation rites.   A ceremony that marks the entry of a person into a group or marks the individual's passage into a new status (e.g., boyhood to manhood). Male initiation rites are often group initiations involving some trauma (e.g., hazing, tests of manliness, genital surgery); female initiation rites are usually more individual and less painful.

intensive agriculture.   Food production characterized by the permanent cultivation of fields and made possible by the use of the plow, draft animals or machines, fertilizers, irrigation, water-storage techniques, and other complex agricultural techniques.

internal warfare.   Warfare within the society.

joint family.   A type of extended family with at least two married siblings in the same generation; can also contain parents.

junior levirate.   A form of levirate whereby a man's younger brother is obliged to marry his widow.

kindred.   A bilateral set of close relatives.

levirate.   A custom whereby a man is obliged to marry his brother's widow. *See* **junior levirate**.

lineage.   A set of kin whose members trace descent from a common ancestor through known links.

longhouse.   A multifamily dwelling with a rectilinear floorplan.

machismo.   A strong or exaggerated sense of manliness.

magic.   The performance of certain rituals that are believed to compel the supernatural powers to act in particular ways.

maidenhood.   The customary period of time from the onset of puberty to marriage.

mana.   A supernatural, impersonal force that inhabits certain objects or people and is believed to confer success and/or strength.

market (or commercial) exchange.   Transactions in which the "prices" are subject to supply and demand, whether or not the transactions occur in a marketplace.

marriage. A socially approved sexual and economic union usually between a man and a woman that is presumed by both the couple and others to be more or less permanent, and that subsumes reciprocal rights and obligations between the two spouses and between spouses and their future children.

matriarchy. A old general term for the disproportionate holding of power or authority by females; since there are many domains of authority and power, anthropologists now generally identify more specific institutions or customs such as the presence of matrilineal descent, matrilocal residence, the proportion of leaders or heads of household that are female, inheritance by females, etc.

matriclan. A clan tracing descent through the female line.

matrifocal family. A female-centered or female-dominated family consisting minimally of a mother and her children.

matrilateral. Pertaining to the mother's side of the family, as in matrilateral cross-cousins or matrilateral parallel cousins.

matrilineage. A kin group whose members trace descent through known links in the female line from a common female ancestor.

matrilineal descent. The rule of descent that affiliates an individual with kin of both sexes related to him or her through women only.

matrilocal residence. A pattern of residence in which a married couple lives with or near the wife's parents. Often referred to as **uxorilocal residence** in the absence of matrilineal descent.

mediation. The process by which a third party tries to bring about a settlement in the absence of formal authority to force a settlement.

medium. Religious practitioner (usually part-time) who is asked to heal, divine, and communicate with spirits while in a trance.

men's house. A separate building in a community where men commonly sleep and/or spend much of their free time.

menstrual seclusion. A mandated time that women must avoid all or some others (e.g., men) during their menstruation. Seclusion is often in a special menstrual hut or house.

menstrual taboos. Proscriptions about what women may or may not do during menstruation (e.g., must stay in a menstrual hut or avoid cooking for others); rules may also apply to men (e.g., they not have sex with their wives during menstruation).

mestizo. A person of mixed European and Native American heritage; this term is usually used in Latin America.

moiety. A unilineal descent group in a society that is divided into two such maximal groups; there may be smaller unilineal descent groups as well.

monogamy. Marriage between only one man and only one woman at a time.

monolingual. Using or knowing one language.

monotheism. The belief that there is only one high god and that all other supernatural beings are subordinate to, or are alternative manifestations of, this supreme being.

natal home. The place where a person was born and (usually) grew up.

natural selection. The outcome of processes that affect the frequencies of traits in a particular environment. Traits that enhance survival and reproductive success increase in frequency over time.

negotiation. The process by which the parties to a dispute try to resolve it themselves.

neolocal residence. A pattern of residence whereby a married couple lives separately, and usually at some distance, from the kin of both spouses.

nonfraternal polyandry. Marriage of a woman to two or more men who are not brothers.

nonsororal polygyny. Marriage of a man to two or more women who are not sisters.

norms. Standards or rules about acceptable behavior in a society. The importance of a norm usually can be judged by how members of a society respond when the norm is violated.

nuclear family. A family consisting of a married couple and their young children.

oath. The act of calling upon a deity to bear witness to the truth of what one says.

ordeal. A means of determining guilt or innocence by submitting the accused to dangerous or painful tests believed to be under supernatural control.

paradigm.   A general concept or model accepted by an intellectual community as a effective way of explaining phenomena

parallel cousins.   Children of siblings of the same sex. One's parallel cousins are father's brothers' children and mother's sisters' children.

paramount chiefdom.   A chiefdom that has a chief of chiefs who integrates a number of chiefdoms into a larger unit.

participant-observation.   Living among the people being studied—observing, questioning, and (when possible) taking part in the important events of the group. Includes writing or otherwise recording notes on observations, questions asked and answered, and things to check out later.

pastoralism.   A form of subsistence technology in which food-getting is based directly or indirectly on the maintenance of domesticated animals.

pater.   The socially defined father. Compare with **genitor**.

patriarchy.   An old general term for the disproportionate holding of power or authority by males; since there are many domains of authority and power, anthropologists generally identify more specific institutions or customs such as the presence of patrilineal descent, patrilocal residence, the proportion of leaders that are male, inheritance by males, etc.

patriclan.   A clan tracing descent through the male line.

patrifocal family.   A male-centered or male-dominated family.

patrilateral.   Pertaining to the father's side of the family, as in patrilateral **cross-cousin** or patrilateral **parallel cousin** marriage.

patrilineage.   A kin group whose members trace descent through known links in the male line from a common male ancestor.

patrilineal descent.   The rule of descent that affiliates an individual with kin of both sexes related to him or her through men only.

patrilocal residence.   A pattern of residence in which a married couple lives with or near the husband's parents. Often referred to as **virilocal residence** in the absence of patrilineal descent.

peasants.   Rural people who produce food for their own subsistence but who must also contribute or sell their surpluses to others (in towns and cities) who do not produce their own food.

personality.   The distinctive way an individual thinks, feels, and behaves.

phratry.   A unilineal descent group composed of a number of supposedly related clans (sibs).

physical (biological) anthropology.   *See* **biological (physical) anthropology**.

political economy.   The study of how external forces, particularly powerful state societies, explain the way a society changes and adapts.

polyandry.   The marriage of one woman to more than one man at a time.

polygamy.   Plural marriage; marriage to more than one spouse simultaneously.

polygyny.   The marriage of one man to more than one woman at a time.

polytheistic.   Recognizing many gods, none of whom is believed to be superordinate.

postmarital residence rules.   Rules that specify where a couple should live after they marry. *See* **avunculocal residence, bilocal residence, matrilocal residence, neolocal residence** and **patrilocal residence**.

postpartum.   After birth.

postpartum abstinence or **postpartum sex taboo.**   Prohibition of sexual intercourse between a couple for a period of time after the birth of their child.

postpartum amenorrhea.   The suppression of ovulation (and menses) after the birth of a baby.

potlatch.   A feast among Pacific Northwest Native Americans at which great quantities of food and goods are given to the guests in order to gain prestige for the host(s).

prehistory.   The time before written records.

prestation.   Anything (material things, services, entertainment) given freely or in obligation as a gift or in exchange.

priest.   Generally a full-time specialist, with very high status, who is thought to be able to relate to superior or high gods beyond the ordinary person's access or control. A woman priest may be referred to as a priestess.

primate.   A member of the mammalian order Primates, divided into the two suborders of Prosimians and Anthropoids.

primatologists.   Persons who study primates.

primogeniture.   The rule or custom by which the first-born inherits all or most of property or titles.

psychosomatic.   Referring to a physical disorder or symptom that is influenced by the mind or emotional factors.

race.   In biology, race refers to a subpopulation or variety of a species that differs somewhat in gene frequencies from other varieties of the species. All members of a species can interbreed and produce viable offspring. Many anthropologists do not think that the concept of "race" is usefully applied to humans because humans do not fall into geographic populations that can be easily distinguished in terms of different sets of biological or physical traits. Thus, "race" in humans is largely a culturally assigned category.

racism.   The belief that some "races" are inferior to others.

raiding.   A short-term use of force, generally planned and organized, to realize a limited objective.

rank society.   A society that does not have social groups with unequal access to economic resources or power, but has social groups with unequal access to status positions and prestige.

reciprocity.   Giving and taking (not politically arranged) without the use of money.

redistribution.   The accumulation of goods (or labor) by a particular person or in a particular place and their subsequent distribution.

religion.   Any set of attitudes, beliefs, and practices pertaining to supernatural power, whether that power rests in forces, gods, spirits, ghosts, or demons.

reverse migration.   The movement of immigrants back to their homeland.

revitalization movement.   A religious movement intended to save a culture by infusing it with a new purpose and life.

rite.   A ceremonial act or series of actions.

rite of passage.   A ritual associated with a change of status; *See* **initiation rites**.

ritual.   A ceremony, usually formal, with a prescribed or customary form.

ritual defloration.   A rite, usually following a marriage, in which a woman's hymen is ruptured; usually occurs as part of the consummation of marriage.

rotating credit associations.   A mutual aid society in which members agree to make regular contributions for the purpose of giving lump sums to individuals members to do something significant. Lump-sum distributions are rotated among the members.

rules of descent.   Rules that connect individuals with particular sets of kin because of known or presumed common ancestry.

second generation immigrants.   Children of first generation immigrants; usually refers to the children born in the host country, but it may also include those born elsewhere who arrived before the age of 5 and spent their formative years in the host country. *See* **1.5 generation of immigrants**.

section.   A group of kin related to one another by both matrilineal and patrilineal principles; excluded are those related by only one principle as well as those not related by either principle. Associated with moieties and moiety exogamy.

segmentary lineage system.   A hierarchy of more and more inclusive lineages; usually functions only in conflict situations.

sex differences.   The typical differences between females and males which are most likely due to biological differences.

sexual division of labor.   *See* **gender division of labor**.

sexually dimorphic.   Refers to a species in which males differ markedly from females in size and appearance.

shaman.   A religious intermediary, usually part time, whose primary function is to cure people through sacred songs, pantomime, and other means; sometimes called witch doctor by Westerners.

Shamanism.   A religion characterized by the importance of the shaman as the intermediary between people and their gods and spirits.

shifting cultivation.   *See* **extensive cultivation**.

sib.   *See* **clan**.

siblings.   A person's brothers or sisters.

slash-and-burn.   A form of shifting cultivation in which the natural vegetation is cut down and burned off. The cleared ground is used for a short time and then left to regenerate.

slaves.   A class of persons who do not own their own labor or the products thereof.

socialization.   a term used to describe the development, through the direct and indirect influence of parents and others, of children's patterns of behavior (and attitudes and values) that conform to cultural expectations.

social stratification.   The presence of unequal access to important advantages depending on the social group to which one belongs. *See* **class** and **caste**.

society.   A group of people who occupy a particular territory and speak a common language not generally understood by neighboring peoples. By this definition, societies do not necessarily correspond to nations.

sociology.   A discipline that focuses on understanding social relations, social groups, and social institutions. Usually focuses on complex societies.

sociobiology.   *See* **behavioral ecology**.

sorcery.   The use of certain materials to invoke supernatural powers to harm people.

sororal polygyny.   The marriage of a man to two or more sisters at the same time.

sororate.   A custom whereby a woman is obliged to marry her deceased sister's husband.

spirits.   Unnamed supernatural beings of nonhuman origin who are beneath the gods in prestige and often closer to the people; may be helpful, mischievous, or evil.

state.   A political unit with centralized decision making affecting a large population. Most states have cities with public buildings; full-time craft and religious specialists; an "official" art style; a hierarchical social structure topped by an elite class; and a governmental monopoly on the legitimate use of force to implement policies.

statistically significant.   Refers to a result that would occur very rarely by chance. The result (and stronger ones) would occur fewer than 5 times out of 100 by chance.

stereotype.   A mental picture or attitude that is an oversimplified opinion or a prejudiced attitude.

structuralism.   A theoretical orientation that looks for the underlying structure in a society's culture, social institutions, or social relationships.

subculture.   The shared customs of a subgroup within a society.

sublineage.   A smaller division of a lineage; when the core members (e.g., males in a patrilineal system) live together in the same locality, they will be referred to as a localized sublineage.

subsistence economy.   An economy relying principally on food that its people collect or produce for themselves.

subsistence patterns.   The methods humans use to procure food.

supernatural.   Believed to be not human or not subject to the laws of nature.

supernumerary.   Extra or more than the usual.

swidden.   The name used for a plot under extensive cultivation. *See* **extensive cultivation**.

syncretism.   The combination of different forms of belief or practice; usually refers to the blending of elements from different religions as a result of contact.

taboo (tabu).   A prohibition that, if violated, is believed to bring supernatural punishment.

theories.   Explanations of associations.

time allocation study.   A study that systematically measures the time that people spend in various activities.

tomboy.   A girl who behaves in ways that are usually considered boyish.

totem.   A plant or animal associated with a clan (sib) as a means of group identification; may have other special significance for the group.

transnationalism.   A broad term referring to the extension of activities beyond national boundaries. Economic and political relationships today are often transnational. With respect to migration, there is today an enormous movement of people back and forth between national boundaries who often maintain ties with both their host and homeland communities and with others in a global community.

tribal organization.   The kind of political organization in which local communities mostly act autonomously but there are kin groups (such as clans) or associations (such as age-sets) that can temporarily integrate a number of local groups into a larger unit.

tribe.   A territorial population in which there are kin or nonkin groups with representatives in a number of local groups.

unilineal descent.   Affiliation with a group of kin through descent links of one sex only.

unilocal residence.   A pattern of residence (patrilocal, matrilocal, or avunculocal) that specifies just one set of relatives that the married couple lives with or near.

unisex association.   An association that restricts its membership to one sex, usually male.

urbanization.   The process of become urbanized

usufruct.   The right to use land or other property.

uxorilocal residence.   *See* **matrilocal residence**.

variable.   A thing or quantity that varies.

virilocal residence.   *See* **patrilocal residence**.

warfare.   Violence between political entities such as communities, districts, or nations.

warrior society.   An association, usually voluntary, that unites members through their common experience as warriors; warrior or military societies were common among North American Plains Indians.

witchcraft.   The practice of attempting to harm people by supernatural means, but through emotions and thought alone, not through the use of tangible objects.

woman–woman marriage.   A type of marriage in which a woman takes on the legal and social roles of a father and husband. The marriage partner, a younger woman, has children with a male chosen by the female husband. The female husband is considered the father.

Encyclopedia of Sex and Gender

Men and Women in the World's Cultures

Volume I: Topics and Cultures A–K

Volume II: Cultures L–Z

Cultural Conceptions of Gender

Cultural Constructions of Gender

Edwin S. Segal

INTRODUCTION

Throughout the 19th century and the first half of the 20th century a considerable amount of ethnographic data regarding cultural variations in concepts of sex and gender were collected. The data included a variety of casual mentions, some detailed case-oriented studies, and compilations of data. However, most of these were cast within an ethnocentric paradigm focused on psychosocial anomalies or presumed pathologies. The major exception was the collection by Ford and Beach (1951) dealing with variations in human sexual behavior, looking to develop a sense of patterning. A little more than 20 years later, Martin and Voorhies (1975) coined the term "supernumerary sexes" in an effort to make sense out of the data that then existed. They meant this term to refer to cultural categories that did not fit the Western European and North American bipolar paradigms.

Although a great deal of ethnographic data regarding cultural variations in conceptualizing sex and gender had been collected throughout the 19th century and the first half of the 20th, it was not until the mid-1970s that the degree of patterning and variability was recognized as an ordinary part of the range of human behavior. It is not as easy to pinpoint the earliest use of "gender" as a part of the social science vocabulary regarding human sexuality.

At this point in time, three terms have come into common use: sex, gender, and sexuality. There are a variety of definitions of each, so, in order to provide a common ground for readers, this article uses the following conceptualizations. "Sex" is taken to refer primarily to biological characteristics. In that sense human beings everywhere have only two sexes, except for a few rarely occurring genetic or hormonal anomalies, a few of which are clearly understood, a few of whom are not. However, every culture also contains a set of norms describing the "proper" use of sexual physiology. For example, who constitute appropriate sexual partners, when sexual activity should take place, or what sorts of clothing are sexually provocative and which are not. From this point of view we can talk of both biological sex and cultural, or culturally mediated, sex. "Gender" is taken to refer to a culturally based complex of norms, values, and behaviors that a particular culture assigns to one biological sex or another. Where sex and gender are lodged largely in the matrix of a culture's norms, values, and beliefs, "sexuality" is taken here as referring to a more individualized concept. Sexuality is used here to refer to the ways in which individuals structure their sexual and gender performances, and the partners toward whom they direct their behavior and emotional attachments. As Lorber (1994) notes, these are not really completely separate and we are better off thinking in terms of a sex–gender–sexuality system.

INTERSEXUALITY

Human biology is everywhere the same, and follows the basic mammalian sexual pattern. There are, of course, a variety of genetic and hormonal anomalies which occasionally occur. Examination of the ways in which different cultures deal with these helps make the case for understanding gender, and, to some extent, cultural sex, as culturally constructed in ways that are not dependent on biological realities. One anomaly, the birth of a child with external genitalia that are not clearly male or female, usually referred to as intersexuality, illustrates that the variation is along the lines of social and cultural location.

The Pokot, living in Kenya, respond to intersexed individuals as an extremely unfortunate occurrence, and frequently resort to infanticide (Edgerton, 1964). The Navajo classify such individuals as belonging to a third category that is neither masculine nor feminine (Hill, 1935). Most segments of middle class U.S. culture tend to see such people as "mistakes of nature" and seek to correct the "error." For the Pokot, there is no cultural place for those they call *sererr*, and those few who survive live on the margins of the society. U.S. cultures also have no place for intersexed individuals, but try to fit them into one of the two normatively accepted categories.

3

Although both the middle-class United States and the Pokot can be said to have a bipolar view of sex and gender, the conceptualizations are still very different. For the Pokot, only those with the normatively appropriate morphological structures can be transformed into gendered children. For the United States, a surgical transformation renders biologically anomalous individuals fit for the social and cultural transformation that will occur. Ultimately, in every culture there is a process by which genderless neonates are transformed into gendered children (or adults-in-training).

Recently, at least in North America and Western Europe, people who see themselves as transsexual or transgendered have been agitating for an end to the assumption that biologically intersexed people suffer from a malady. They have also urged an end to automatic consideration of sex reassignment surgery. Their vision is of North American macroculture as it might be. However, it is still the case that the most frequent occurrence is to view children born with ambiguous genital structures as needing treatment so that they can fit into one of the two culturally accepted poles.

BIPOLAR CONSTRUCTS

The cultural worlds of North America and Western Europe organize their varied understandings of sex–gender–sexuality systems around a set of intersecting dichotomous pairs: masculine–feminine and homosexual (forbidden)–heterosexual (permitted). This paradigm then constrains and directs understandings of sexual behavior, sexualized behavior, and their association with nonsexual aspects of social and cultural life. When preadolescent North American boys avoid some activities or modes of behavior because they are said to be "girlish," or when preadolescent girls are harassed for engaging in activities said to be "boyish," we are witnessing something more than socialization for a culture's sexual division of labor.

In most of this culture area division of labor is not strongly marked in detail, but it is strongly marked in terms of the diffusely defined general categories of public and private or household and outside. To the extent that the household domain is defined as feminine space and is also associated with motherhood, childcare, and wife roles, it becomes partially sexualized. The result is a cultural constraint on the breadth of role and status variation open to men. Men who are good household

managers and involved parents are often thought of as disturbingly feminine. Similarly, to the extent that the "outside" is defined as masculine space and is also associated with excelling in nonhousehold tasks and with husband and economic support roles, it too becomes partially sexualized, resulting in constraints on the breadth of role and status variation open to women. Women who are good income earners or highly trained professionals are frequently seen as disturbingly masculine.

To be sure, there are cultures outside the boundaries of the Western world that are also traditionally organized around a variation on the bipolar theme. It is also the case that every culture makes some distinction between the positions of women and men. The important point here is the Western association of role transcendence with flawed and improper sexuality.

VARIATION IN GENDER CONSTRUCTS

The accumulation of ethnographic data indicates that some cultures have developed gender paradigms going beyond the Western conceptualization of two gender poles. The existence of more than two gender poles does not mean that both people with the morphological characteristics of men and those with the morphological characteristics of women necessarily have available more than one gender pole. Many multipolar cultures deal with morphological men and morphological women differently. The general case is that morphological men are more likely to be seen as possibly fitting into more than one named institutionalized position with a distinct gender construction, and that morphological women are more likely to be seen as falling along a continuum of variations, all of which are considered womanly and feminine.

The classic instance is the difference between the manly hearted women among the Mandan and other Plains Indians and the *berdache*, or two spirit people, also on the North American plains (Williams, 1992). While morphological men might, as the result of a vision quest or other spirit visitation, occupy the separate *berdache* social position, manly hearted women were still women, and sometimes valued even more highly than "ordinary" women. At least in this instance, morphological women did not cease being sociological women, while morphological men might cease being sociological men.

At the same time, it is also important to note that some cultures (e.g., the Mohave in North America and the

Chuckchee in Siberia) did have parallel institutional structures for women and men. Similarly, in a few North American Plains cultures, some women did, on their own initiative, assume roles comparable to male *berdache*. On a cross-cultural level, it was most often the case that female gender variations were individualized and male variations were institutionalized.

In general, gender, as constructed in particular cultures, consists of both signifying elements and performance elements. A person assumes the signifying elements (e.g., clothing or hair style) and exhibits the performance elements. While biological sex is something a person has, regardless of behavior, gender is seen only when it is performed or signaled.

The existing ethnographic literature documents four different forms of gender variation.

1. Some societies construct gender so as to contain distinct categories that are neither masculine nor feminine.
2. Some societies construct gender in ways that are bipolar, but in which the boundaries are markedly different from those common in Western Europe and North America.
3. Some societies construct gender so that, while the basic pattern is bipolar, people with one set of biological characteristics are able, under specific circumstances, to step outside of the society's ordinary construct and enter the other construct.
4. A residual category—instances that do not quite fit our neatly created typology. This category is necessary to highlight the purely heuristic nature of the other three and to avoid sterile typological debates and arguments.

In all instances, there is an initial transformation from genderless to gendered. But in two of these there is a distinct transformational process that takes place after the initial one has begun. For example, although physiologically intersexed individuals are recognizable at birth, and the Navajo place them in a third category, *nadle*, the Navajo also recognize a group of people they call "those who pretend to be (or play the part of) *nadle*" (Hill, 1935). These individuals come to their status after having begun socialization as masculine or feminine.

Neither Masculine nor Feminine

Here we can place the *berdache* as found in some cultures on the North American Plains. The term *berdache* has a history reflecting its Eurocentric origins and the ethnocentrism of most 17th, 18th, and 19th century European and European American observers of Native American cultures. The term "two spirit" is assuming greater

currency among Native Americans. Two spirit comes closer to reflecting cultural realities than does *berdache*.

In all the ethnographic instances cited by Williams (1992), a young, usually preadolescent, boy would set out on a vision quest, seeking a relationship with a spirit being who would then help him determine and strive for his future life. Once he had the vision, he would return to his group and someone skilled in such matters would interpret his vision for him. For some, their vision was interpreted as indicating the two-spirit status. In the traditional world of late 19th century Plains life, they would then wear women's clothes and engage in the daily activities of ordinary women. But they also had unique roles in instances of weddings, childbirth, child naming, and warfare.

In the contemporary world, the situation is rather different. By the late 20th century, the position of the *berdache* had been heavily overlaid with Western sex–gender–sexuality constructs. One Lakota *berdache* describing his position (Bradley & Phillips, 1991) wears contemporary men's clothing rather than the traditional women's clothing. He also speaks to the contemporary rarity of *berdache*, implies an absence of clearly defined role, and does not mention any sort of vision quest. Although to some extent these changes are illustrative of the effects of westernization, they are also a testament to the resilience of traditional patterns in the face of disvaluing culturally foreign pressures. *Berdache* were, and apparently still are, seen as neither men nor women, or possibly sociologically both. The two-spirit designation reflects the first spirit of the child's birth as well as the second spirit of the child's vision, or other contemporary realization about who he is.

There are other instances of cultures containing sex–gender–sexuality categories that do not fit within the constraints of bipolar paradigms, and many of them also do not fit the two-spirit model. At the time of writing, no clear count has yet been done. However, as will be seen below, the categories created by a particular culture under particular sociocultural conditions are not necessarily fixed and unchangeable. A rough sense of the magnitude of variations may be possible, but not a definitive count.

Nonwestern Bipolar Constructs

Among the classic instances of cultures whose sex–gender–sexuality systems are bipolar, but do not fit Western models of such organization, are those documented more than 70 years ago by Margaret Mead (1950).

In those instances, Mead was most concerned with aspects of behavior other than the sexual, and in that very concern was able to document the ways in which gender was separately constructed and not necessarily causally tied to biological sex. Each of the three cultures she describes assigns a different emotional–behavioral complex to women and to men. Some of those complexes mirror Western constructs and some do not.

Since all cultures contain at least masculine and feminine categories, it is probably also the case that none of those definitions completely matches contemporary Western categories. For example, Maasai in Kenya and Tanzania, or Wodaabi Fulani in the Sahel, are peoples with bipolar gender constructs. But when it comes to cultural definitions of masculine dress, jewelry, or decoration, they are very different from the business suit, wrist watch, and ring model of the Western world.

Transcendent Gender

The peoples falling into this category pose significant theoretical questions about the strength of cultural linkages between gender constructs and biological sex. Smith Oboler's (1980) description of marriage between two women among the Nandi explicitly explores this ground (see also the chapter on the Nandi in this encyclopedia). Her conclusion is that some aspects of male behavior and privileges are lightly tied to concepts of masculinity, so that it is possible for a woman to become husband to another woman, and in so doing be able to own land and other masculine property, as well as found her own patrilineage. Unfortunately, she provides no direct material regarding sexuality.

Similarly, among some groups of Igbo (Amadiume, 1987) it is possible for a woman to engage in a variety of behaviors, including marrying another woman or taking a male position in some rituals or legal proceedings, and not lose her sociological position as a woman. In all of these cases, the dominant factor is that women in a bipolar culture are able to transcend the normative boundaries of womanhood, and in so doing gain prestige and privilege in the society but do not lose a culturally defined essential femininity.

Other Conceptions

The Chuckchee of northern Siberia, as they were at the beginning of the 20th century (Bogoras, 1909), represent one documented instance in which the potential for gender change is restricted to a small segment of the population. In this particular case the option was available only to those who found themselves thrust into the role of shaman. Chuckchee shamans are largely healers, and usually come to that position through recovery from a serious illness. Shamans can be either women or men, and on their recovery acquire a spouse in the world of spirits (*kelet*). Occasionally, the *kelet* spouse for a female shaman will be female, or for a male shaman, male. Under these circumstances, the Chuckchee claimed that the shaman had begun a process of changing sex that would culminate in an actual change in external genitalia. The shaman's human spouses would mirror the *kelet* spouse's gender. By the 1960s, the process of sovietization seems to have been thorough enough to wipe out shamanism. Levin and Potapov's (1964) discussion of the peoples of Siberia makes no mention of shamanism among any of them. The possible resurgence of the institution since the collapse of the Soviet Union is unknown.

Transformations

The Chuckchee represent an instance in which some sort of gender transformation is said to occur. Generally, we can think in terms of three axes of post-childhood gender transformation. One is of a temporary sort: a person takes on different gender characteristics for a short period of time, and then returns to the initial gender stance. The most common example of this phenomenon is the practice referred to by the term *couvade*. Most commonly found among peoples in the Amazon basin (Gregor, 1985), the *couvade* is also found in Melanesia (Blackwood, 1935; Meigs, 1976). In general, during some portion, or all, of his spouse's pregnancy and childbirth, a man takes on some aspects of the woman's behavioral complex. This may range from observing the same food regulations to taking to his bed and experiencing the pains of childbirth, or observing restrictions on sexual activity. Sometimes, the *couvade* lasts until the child is weaned.

This particular institution has been thoroughly researched, and a variety of psychogenic or sociogenic hypotheses have been tested (Munroe, Munroe, & Whiting, 1981, pp. 611–632). Those hypotheses revolving around cultural establishment of a secure masculine identity have been most convincingly supported. The interesting aspect of that explanation here is that in societies practicing *couvade*, secure masculine identity is anchored by a temporary gender transformation.

Not quite as common, but hardly rare, are various forms of gender transgression. Murray (2000), Bullough (1976), and many other writers have noted that rituals of license, such as carnival or Mardi Gras, or rituals of rebellion (cf. Gluckman, 1956) often provide room for transgressing sexual and gender norms. Murray is one of several writers who see this as an acceptance of homosexuality but, as Gluckman points out, it can be just the opposite, in that the rituals permit, for a brief time, that which is generally forbidden. Regardless, a person engaging in a ritual of this sort does seem to temporarily change gender. The same can be said of female impersonators, whether in Shakespeare's plays, the film *Victor Victoria*, or a contemporary stage act.

A second form of gender transformation is relatively rare. In the course of an ordinary life cycle a person moves from one gender status to another. Among the Gabra in Kenya and Ethiopia, men, as they age, pass through a period in which they are said to be women (Wood, 1996, 1999). In a slightly different vein, Turnbull (1986) argues that the Mbuti in the Ituri Rainforest region of the Democratic Republic of Congo are genderless until they marry; that is, they pass through childhood without a distinct gender identity and are transformed only later.

The third form of gender transformation is a more or less permanent second transformation. Wikan (1977, 1982) indicates that those whom she calls *xanith* sometimes choose to become *xanith* and then later choose to stop being *xanith*. A similar phenomenon has also been reported for people in the Society Islands (Elliston, 1999). This third form is the abstract category, containing examples from every continent, of people fitting particular gender statuses unknown in the gender constructions of Western cultures. This is also the category containing instances such as shamans among the Chuckchee, who may undergo a transformation from male to female or female to male (Bogoras, 1909), as well as those being referred to when people talk of a "third gender."

In the world at the end of the 20th and the beginning of the 21st century, globalization, and its concomitant spread of Western European and North American economic, political, and cultural hegemony, has led, in some areas, to adoption of new sex–gender–sexuality paradigms. Donham (1998), in his discussion of African male sexuality in the Republic of South Africa, notes the prevalence of cross-dressing and cross-role-taking behavior

among those who define themselves as gay. He also notes the general perception that gay men were not seen as either women or men, but as occupying a position in between—a "third sex."

Donham is describing aspects of South African sex–gender–sexuality systems in the early 1990s. He notes that at that time "gay" was not the commonly used term. Rather, the commonly used term was *stabane*, literally hermaphrodite, reflecting ambiguity about the sex or gender of the person being referred to. Also important here is Donham's note that *stabane* only referred to the "effeminate" partner in a male same-sex relationship. The implication is that two *stabane* did not have relations with each other. Although Donham is silent on the point, at the most this points to *stabane* as truly occupying a third category, and at the least it points to a very different cultural construction of homosexuality.

Prior to 1994, much of township sexuality in South Africa was conditioned by the strictures imposed by apartheid. We tend to think of that system as being largely a "simple" matter of racial segregation, but it was more. It focused on population control and the provision of cheap industrial labor, particularly in extractive industries. The male labor force was then housed in single-sex hostels. Although *stabane* may have been the appropriate term, and it may have had both connotations and denotations very different from Western concepts of sexuality, the distortions produced by apartheid obscured these differences, reducing them to little more than a variant of female impersonation and a specifically subordinate sexual role. However, Donham's analysis adds one other complication of theoretical significance. Although many people in the township, especially strangers, took gay people to be some sort of biologically mixed third sex, the people themselves did not seem to do so.

This phenomenon brings up the importance of the distinction between the cultural insider's view (emic) and the external observer's view (etic). Donham's analysis presents two emic constructions of the same sociocultural facts. In one, there is a sex–gender category beyond what we usually think of as the ordinary two, and in the other there is not.

The collapse of apartheid has led (or will lead) to changes in the cultural constructions of a local sex–gender–sexuality system, especially to the extent that the system of single-sex hostels disappears. Although he provides some caveats, Donham tends to see the process as a variety of "modernization" matching the "modernization" of the sociocultural system that was apartheid. Given the artificial constraints created by apartheid, there is some justification in this approach. However, considering a bipolar homosexual–heterosexual paradigm as more modern than other paradigms tends to obscure the range of human variation. It also tends to gloss over the two discrepant views of sex–sexuality variations he describes. In a more "modern" context, similar discrepancies are reported by Kulick (1998) among *travestis* in Brazil.

Only Two Genders or More?

Murray (2000) tries to subsume all nonstandard nonheterosexual relationships under a model of three different types of homosexuality. The result is a shift of focus from sociocultural gender constructs to culturally mediated sexual activity. His entire book, which contains a wealth of carefully considered ethnographic material, is largely male oriented and organized around cultural definitions of who takes dominant or receptive positions. While some of his data fit that construct, his model, which denies the possibility of gender constructs beyond masculine and feminine, cannot deal with instances such as that noted by Jacobs and Cromwell (1992), while exploring the cultural construction of *kwidó*, a Tewa "third-gender" category, one of those positions that Williams (1992) would include under the general term *berdache*.

In the course of her fieldwork, Jacobs was told that a person could be homosexual, heterosexual, bisexual, or trisexual. From the perspective of one of her male informants, homosexual meant that he had sex with other sociological men. Heterosexual meant that he had sex with sociological women, bisexual meant that he would have sex with either men or women, and trisexual would mean that he would have sex with men, women or *kwidó*. The logic of these statements is that someone, man or woman, who has sex with a *kwidó* is behaving in a heterosexual manner, even though *kwidó* are morphologically male.

A three- or four-gender system creates a more complex set of gender-based relationships than are contemplated by a system derived from Northern European and North American constructs. One of the complexities is the question of different emic understandings of a phenomenon (Segal, 1997). The problem is clearly marked by Jacobs and Cromwell's material from the Tewa. In this case, Jacobs' informant explained that the *kwidó* was not "gay," despite the fact that some people called him that. Rather, the *kwidó* was made so by

"spiritual powers." In addition, other informants, elders, informed Jacobs that proper socialization for *kwidó* included raising them "to be who they are" aided by the knowledge and experience of an adult *kwidó* (Jacobs and Cromwell, 1992, p. 56).

The Tewa in the southwestern United States are not the only people among whom more than one emic understanding of sex–gender–sexuality phenomena can be found. A strong case can be made for similar variation in the Society Islands, including Tahiti. In that setting, the person occupying a nonmasculine nonfeminine gender position is termed a *mahu*, and is often morphologically male. The data from Tahiti and the other Society Islands also raise a question about the relationship between sex–gender–sexuality systems as they existed prior to contact with European cultures (and conquest), and constructs as they are now found. Levy (1971, 1973) claims that only men were/are *mahu*. However, Elliston (1999) documents the existence of both morphological males and morphological females who take on the *mahu* status. In light of the relatively low level of gender dimorphism in the Society Islands, her projection that this was also probably the case in traditional (i.e., precolonial) times seems logical.

Here, it seems that a man's sexual relations with a *mahu* are conceptualized (except by the *mahu*) as a replacement for relations with a woman. No one (except the *mahu*) seems to consider questions of sexual orientation (Levy, 1971, 1973). Among the Tewa, orientation seems to be an issue. Sex with a *kwidó* is a distinct cultural category and, Jacobs indicates, *kwidó* might have sex with other *kwidó*.

In both instances, we are confronted with a heterogeneity of emic understandings that is all too often glossed over in anthropological literature. Another difficulty is the veneer of Eurocentric ethnocentrism and homophobia created by the European colonial enterprise over a span of at least 200 years in most portions of the globe. In the instance of the Tewa, the major source has probably been an Anglo-Euro-American Protestantism. It is somewhat facile, but the shorthand reference to European colonialism and missionary activities fairly expresses the worldwide trends of which this is a part.

Where the *kwidó*'s origins in an encounter with superhuman forces granted an element of sacredness to his nature, that has been largely lost and concepts of a variety of sexual sins have become part of Tewa cognitions (Jacobs & Cromwell, 1992). On the other hand,

Jacobs' fieldwork is of relatively recent date, and the Tewa third gender seems to continue as a part of both beliefs and behaviors.

In contrast, the status *mahu*, as found in the Society Islands, does not seem to be as clearly delineated as a third gender in the definitive way that the *kwidó* seems to be marked among the Tewa. The largest part of the difficulty lies in the nature of the early sources, none of which took the people's perspectives into account, but the data that do exist are suggestive in a number of directions. By the latter half of the 20th century, when attention to emic perspectives had became more common, most of the world was in the throes of the sort of "modernization" noted by Donham (1998), although not as a result of so felicitous a process as the collapse of apartheid. The effects of colonial and mission cultures in shifting local cultural understandings of sex–gender systems have been pervasive, and sexuality has been a prime target.

Tahiti and the other Society Islands represent one type of tripolar sex–gender–sexuality system, in which there is only a single category beyond masculine and feminine, and that category is equally available to both women and men. The Society Islands are a region in which gender dimorphism is relatively light. People seem unconcerned about sharply marked gender distinctions (Elliston, 1999; Levy, 1973). This is exactly the social setting that seems most conducive to a sex–gender–sexuality system accommodating what Martin and Voorhies (1975) called supernumerary categories (Munroe & Whiting, 1969).

Mahu is not the only category or term currently found on the Society Islands. Of the terms now found, *mahu* has the longest history and might, in some frames of reference, be referred to as "traditional." There are other contemporary categories that explicitly link sexual behavior with gender, but *mahu* separates gender and sexuality in a way more complex than can be reviewed here.

Elliston's (1999) explication makes clear what may be a central question in the study of sex–gender–sexuality systems: In each particular culture, of sexuality and gender, which is perceived as producer and which as product? The very asking of the question points to the interaction of biology and culture, rather than to the primacy of one over the other. Elliston's analysis of sexuality–gender categories in the Society Islands clarifies some of the apparent confusion. *Mahu* refers to the oldest layer, one in which experience and observed behavior

produce gender, which, in turn, directs people to their sexual partners, regardless of their morphology, that is, produces sexuality.

Other categories (*raerae, petea, lesbiennes*) refer to same-sex sexual relationships, coupled with coordinated gender behavior, and are conceived of as referring to categories of sexuality and gender derived from French colonial influence. However, the major difference seems to be that, for people assuming positioning within these categories, sexuality and gender behavior both exist within a performative foreground. In Elliston's experience *mahu* gender characteristics were part of the cultural foreground, and *mahu* sexuality was part of the cultural background. They were not culturally linked as a single ascribed unit.

CONCLUSION

By way of contrast, we might consider the way in which Western cultural constructs first place sex as the producer of sexuality, which then produces behavior. These two different visions of the relationship among sex, gender, and sexuality help us to understand both Western Christian religious difficulties with the sex–gender–sexuality systems of other parts of the world, as well as phenomena such as Zimbabwean, Kenyan, or Ugandan governmental fulminations that homosexuality is a foreign import. The foreign import is actually the cultural construct: sex leads to sexuality leads to behavior, along with the idea that only a portion of the possibilities is permitted.

Ultimately, reducing all sex–gender–sexuality systems to acceptance or rejection of homosexuality imposes a universal foreground, as well as a bipolar system that is consistent with the dichotomous thinking of most Western cultures. If we look at the Western system, which operates with two intersecting dichotomies (masculine–feminine and heterosexual [permitted]–homosexual [forbidden]), and the effort to change that model and the values and meanings attached to it, the desire to demonstrate the "acceptance" of homosexuality on the large cross-cultural canvas becomes understandable. But the distortion of complex sex–gender–sexuality systems in service to that aim does a disservice to the cultural integrity of many peoples and to their efforts to recapture traditional patterns that have often been suppressed.

REFERENCES

Amadiume, I. (1987). Male daughters, female husbands: Gender and sex in an African society. London: Zed Books.

Blackwood, B. (1935). *Both sides of Buka passage: An ethnographic study of social, sexual and economic questions in the north-western Solomon Islands.* Oxford: Clarendon Press.

Bogoras, W. (1909). The Chuckchee. In F. Boas (ed.), *Memoirs of the American Museum of Natural History* (Vol. XI). Leiden, Netherlands: E.J.Brill. (New York: Johnson Reprint Corporation.)

Bradley, S. W. (Producer/Director) & Phillips, R. (Writer) (1991). *Gender the enduring paradox* [Videotape]. Co-produced by WETA-TV and the Smithsonian Institution, with Wentworth Films Inc., Alexandria, VA.

Bullough, V. (1976). *Sexual variance in society and history.* New York: Wiley.

Donham, D. L. (1998). Freeing South Africa: The "modernization" of male–male sexuality in Soweto. *Cultural Anthropology, 13*(1), 3–21.

Edgerton, R. B. (1964). Pokot intersexuality: An East African example of the resolution of sexual incongruity. *American Anthropologist, 66,* 1288–1299.

Elliston, D. A. (1999). Negotiating transnational sexual economies: Female *mahu* and same-sex sexuality in "Tahiti and her islands." In E. Blackwood and S. Wieringa (Eds.), *Female desires: Same-sex relations and transgender practices across cultures* (pp. 230–254). New York: Columbia University Press.

Ford, C. S. & Beach, F. A. (Eds.). (1951). *Patterns of sexual behavior.* New York: Harper.

Gluckman, M. (1956). *Custom and conflict in Africa.* New York: Barnes and Noble.

Gregor, T. (1985). *Anxious pleasures: The sexual lives of an Amazonian people.* Chicago: University of Chicago Press.

Hill, W. W. (1935). The status of the hermaphrodite and transvestite in Navaho culture. *American Anthropologist, 37,* 273–279.

Jacobs, S.-E., & Cromwell, J. (1992). Visions and revisions of reality: Reflections on sex, sexuality, gender and gender variance. *Journal of Homosexuality, 23*(4), 43–69.

Kulick, D. (1998). *Travesti: Sex, gender and culture among Brazilian transgendered prostitutes.* Chicago: University of Chicago Press.

Levin, M. G. & Potapov, L. P. (Eds.). (1964). *The peoples of Siberia* (S. P. Dunn, Trans & Ed.). Chicago: University of Chicago Press.

Levy, R. I. (1971). The community functions of Tahitian male transvestites. *Anthropological Quarterly, 44,* 12–21.

Levy, R. I. (1973). *Tahitians: Mind and experience in the Society Islands.* Chicago: University of Chicago Press.

Lorber, J. (1994). *Paradoxes of gender.* New Haven, CT: Yale University Press.

Martin, M. K. & Voorhies, B. (1975). *Female of the species.* New York: Columbia University Press.

Mead, M. (1950). *Sex and temperament in three primitive societies.* New York: New American Library.

Meigs, A. S. (1976). Male pregnancy and the reduction of sexual opposition in a New Guinea Highlands society. *Ethnology, 15*(4), 393–407.

Munroe, R. L. & Whiting, J. W. M. (1969). Institutionalized male transvestism and sex distinctions. *American Anthropologist, 71,* 87–91.

Munroe, R. L., Munroe, R. H., Whiting, J. H. W. (1981). Male-sex role resolutions. In R. H. Munroe, R. L. Munroe, & B. B. Whiting (Eds.), *Handbook of cross-cultural human development* (pp. 611–632). New York: Garland STPM Press.

Murray, S. O. (2000). *Homosexualities.* Chicago: University of Chicago Press.

Segal, E. S. (1997). Male genders: cross cultural perspectives. In V. Demos & M. Texler Segal (Eds.), *Advances in gender research* (Vol. 2, pp. 37–77). JAI Press.

Smith Oboler, R. (1980). Is the female husband a man? Woman/woman marriage among the Nandi of Kenya. *Ethnology, 19*(1), 69–88.

Turnbull, C. (1986). Sex and gender: the role of subjectivity in field research. In T. L. Whitehead & M. E. Conaway (Eds.), *Self, sex and gender in cross-cultural fieldwork* (pp. 17–27). Urbana, IL: University of Illinois Press.

Wikan, U. (1977). Man becomes woman: Transsexualism in Oman as a key to gender roles. *Man* (NS), *12*(3), 304–319.

Wikan, U. (1982). *Behind the veil in Arabia: Women in Oman.* Chicago: University of Chicago Press.

Williams, W. (1992). *The spirit and the flesh.* Boston: Beacon Press.

Wood, J. (1996). When men are women: Opposition and ambivalence among Gabra nomads of Northern Kenya and Southern Ethiopia. Paper presented at the annual meeting of the American Anthropological Association, San Francisco, CA, November.

Wood, J. (1999). *When men are women: Manhood among the Gabra nomads of East Africa.* Madison, WI: Wisconsin University Press.

Gender Stereotypes

Deborah L. Best

Imagine that you are head of a human relations department in a large company and your job is to hire the administrative/managerial employees for your company. For one particularly important position, you have two finalists who have similar educational backgrounds and other qualifications. To help in making your choice, you give the candidates a self-descriptive personality test to see how they might handle the job. Here are the results. Person A chose these items as self-descriptive: attractive, dependent, emotional, gentle, kind, talkative. Person B chose these items: active, ambitious, determined, inventive, self-confident, serious. Which person would you hire? Why? Is it easier to imagine one of these individuals as a man? Which one? As a woman? Which one? Is it easier to visualize Person A as a woman and Person B as a man? If so, your views demonstrate the influence of gender stereotypes—beliefs about how men and women differ in their psychological make-up.

GENDER STEREOTYPES

Gender stereotypes refer to the psychological traits and behaviors that are believed to occur with differential frequency in the two gender groups (e.g., men are more "aggressive," women are more "emotional"). Stereotypes are often used as support for traditional sex roles (e.g., women are nurses, men are construction workers) and may serve as socialization models for children. The research that will be reviewed here concerns sex roles and stereotypes with the emphasis on cross-cultural research. Methodological issues concerning measurement as well as theoretical views of how stereotypes develop will be briefly reviewed.

What are Gender Stereotypes?

Gender differences in the adjectives used by men and women to describe themselves and others can be seen in two areas: adjectives may be *ascribed* differentially to other men and women, and adjectives may be *endorsed* differentially by men and women themselves. Ascription deals with sex-trait stereotypes, and endorsement concerns how these traits are incorporated into self and ideal-self descriptions, hence masculinity and femininity.

Stereotype traits reflect cognitive beliefs about differences between women and men that participants share with members of their culture. Stereotypes are not necessarily pernicious and may contain some elements of truth. They help predict others' behaviors, but they also fail to recognize individual differences and overlap between groups. For example, if one considers men to be more aggressive than women, this ignores individual differences and variation in aggression found in both gender groups. Some women are more aggressive than some men. Stereotypes make no allowance for variability and, when believed uncritically, they justify treating *all* men as more aggressive than *all* women.

Previous Research on Stereotypes in the United States

One of the earliest programs of research to examine stereotypes was conducted by McKee and Sheriffs in California in the 1950s (McKee & Sheriffs, 1957, 1959; Sheriffs & McKee, 1957). Using a list of 200 adjectives, they found that there were a large number of characteristics differentially ascribed to men in general and women in general. Men were described as frank, straightforward, rational, competent, bold, and effective. Women were emotionally warm and concerned with social customs. Their findings were consistent with those of Parsons and Bales (1955) who identified the traits associated with men as more *adaptive–instrumental* and those associated with females as *integrative–expressive*.

Another series of classic sex stereotype studies was conducted by the Brovermans, Rosenkrantz, and their associates in the 1960s and 1970s (Broverman, Broverman, Clarkson, Rosenkrantz, & Vogel, 1970; Broverman, Vogel, Broverman, Clarkson, & Rosenkrantz, 1972; Rosenkrantz, Vogel, Bee, Broverman, & Broverman, 1968; Vogel, Broverman, Broverman, Clarkson, & Rosenkrantz, 1970).

In their studies, college students listed behaviors, attitudes, and personality characteristics that they thought differentiated men and women. Using these items, bipolar scales were constructed and other college students rated how characteristic each item is for the typical adult male, the typical adult female, and themselves. The sex stereotypes they found were similar to those identified by McKee and Sheriffs, suggesting agreement about the characteristics that college students generally ascribed to men and women.

In the development of their Personal Attributes Questionnaire (PAQ), Spence, Helmreich, and Stapp (1974) revised the Brovermans' questionnaire by simplifying the format and removing the "oppositeness" of the ratings. The original PAQ contained only socially desirable items, but a later version also included undesirable traits (Spence & Holahan, 1979). Research participants described themselves with both female and male traits, permitting the assessment of androgyny (i.e., possessing characteristics of both sexes). Thus masculinity and femininity were considered a duality that could coexist in every person.

Bem (1974, 1975) took a similar conceptual approach in developing the Bem Sex Role Inventory (BSRI). Masculinity and femininity are treated as separate dimensions, and persons can be characterized as masculine, feminine, androgynous, or undifferentiated. Items judged by students to be more desirable in American society for one sex or the other were included in the BSRI. Stereotypes identified with the PAQ and BSRI are generally similar, reflecting male instrumentality or agency and female expressiveness or communion.

Although there are few studies examining the dimensions that underlie male and female stereotypes, in their analysis of traits that raters attributed to others, Ashmore and colleagues (Ashmore & Del Boca, 1979) found two independent dimensions, social desirability and potency. These dimensions are conceptually similar to Williams and Best's (1990a) favorability and strength dimensions which were based on Osgood's (Osgood, Suci, & Tannenbaum, 1957) evaluation and potency dimensions of connotative meaning. These will be discussed below.

Cross-Cultural Research on Stereotypes

Although there are several small-scale studies of sex stereotypes in other countries (e.g., Lii & Wong, 1982;

Sunar, 1982), to date a large number of studies have been conducted by an international group of researchers cooperating in a 32-country project (Williams & Best, 1990a, 1990b). These studies have been integrated by Williams and Best and will be discussed in detail here with highlights on methodological issues and findings.

Williams and Best's Sex Stereotype Study. In their study, Williams and Best examined gender differences in trait ascription in both the USA and 30 other countries, with data from almost 9,000 children and adults. Adult participants identified stereotyped traits in their own culture, but they were not asked whether they approved of the assignment of different characteristic to men and women or if they believed that the items were self-descriptive.

Measure. In their stereotype study, Williams and Best used the 300-item Adjective Checklist (ACL) (Gough & Heilbrun, 1980). They chose this methodology so that they would have a large diverse item pool descriptive of human personality, not just stereotypes. They included both favorable and unfavorable traits in the pool and did not assume the oppositeness of men and women. Items permitted the assessment of androgyny and interfaced with existing personality research.

When translations were not already available for the ACL, translations by groups of bilinguals and back-translation procedures (e.g., translating from English to the second language, then back to English to check translation fidelity) were used. Because individual items may not be comparable across languages, comparisons of individual item scores between countries may not have score equivalence, or similar quantitative values. Hence, Williams and Best only analyzed male and female stereotype differences within the same country—the relative gender differences within a country—rather than comparing masculinity between countries or femininity between countries.

Using the 300 ACL items, college students in each country made relative judgments by identifying the adjectives more frequently associated with men or more frequently associated with women. They were permitted to leave out items that were not associated with either gender group. This method "extracts" differences in the views of men and women rather than focusing on similarities. For example, "coarse" is infrequently used to describe either men or women, but research participants associated this adjective with men more frequently than with women.

Study Participants. Williams and Best used university students as study participants, asking them to be "cultural reporters." College students are not representative of their respective populations, but they represent narrow well-matched samples which are functionally equivalent in each country, and they are certainly products of their respective cultures.

The countries in Williams and Best's stereotype study, shown in Table 1, are not representative of all the nations of the world. The sample has a high proportion of English-speaking countries and economically developed countries. Unfortunately, these biases represent the world of cooperative research in academic psychology.

Analyses and Findings. With approximately 100 participants in each country responding to the 300 items of the ACL, the analysis began with over 750,000 "bits" of data. This required a meaningful way to reduce the data. Four scoring systems were used to summarize findings: analyses of individual items, affective meaning, psychological needs, and transactional analysis (TA) ego states. The last two are part of the standard ACL scoring procedure and will not be discussed here (see Williams & Best, 1990a).

For *item analyses* a simple index was devised to reflect the degree of male association or female association of a particular item in a given country. Male association is represented by an $M\%$ score computed for each item by calculating the male association frequency and dividing it by the sum of the male plus female frequencies and discarding the decimal. Thus a high $M\%$ score indicates that an item is more frequently associated with men than with women. It does not indicate that a particular adjective would be used frequently to characterize a large portion of men who were being described with ACL items. Similarly, a low $M\%$ indicates that an item is more frequently associated with women than with men, not necessarily that the item would be used to describe a majority of women. The method teases out relative differences between men and women.

When the male-associated and female-associated items were identified in each country, a standard degree of association across all countries was used to represent the focused stereotypes, with the number of items varying from country to country. In each country, items were included in the stereotype for a particular sex if they were associated with that sex at least twice as often as with the other sex. Thus items with $M\%$ scores of 67% or greater were identified as male stereotype items, and female stereotype items were those with $M\%$ scores of 33% and below ($F\%$ score of 67% and above). Items that fell into the male-associated and female-associated groups in three quarters of the countries are shown in Table 2. The figures in parentheses beside the adjectives indicate the number of countries out of the original 25 in which the item was in the indicated group. Only three items were female-associated in all 25 countries: sentimental, submissive, and superstitious. On the other hand, six items were male-associated in all countries: adventurous, dominant, forceful, independent, masculine, and strong.

Correlation coefficients were computed for $M\%$ scores between pairs of countries to examine the comparability of stereotypes across countries. Across all 300 items, correlations ranged from 0.35 for Pakistan versus Venezuela to 0.94 for Australia versus England. The mean common variance across all 25 countries was 42%, indicating a substantial degree of agreement about the psychological characteristics differentially associated with men and with women.

What about exceptions to the "rules?" How often did an item which was usually in the high $M\%$ group fall into the low $M\%$ (female) category? For the male-associated items in the table, arrogant, lazy, robust, and rude were associated with women in Nigeria; assertive, humorous, and ingenious were associated with women in Malaysia; boastful, disorderly, and obnoxious were associated with

Table 1. Countries in Williams and Best's Study

Asia	Europe	South America
India	England	Bolivia
Israel	Finland	Brazil
Japan	France	Chile
Malaysia	Germany	Peru
Pakistan	Ireland	Trinidad
Taiwan	Italy	Venezuela
Thailand	Netherlands	
	Norway	*Africa*
Oceania	Scotland	Nigeria
Australia	Spain	South America
New Zealand		Zimbabwe (Rhodesia)
	North America	
	Canada	
	United States	

Table 2. Items Associated with Males and Females in at least 19 of 25 Countries

Male-associated items (N = 49)		Female-associated items (N = 25)
Active (23)	Ingenious (19)	Affected (20)
Adventurous (25)	Initiative (21)	Affectionate (24)
Aggressive (24)	Inventive (22)	Anxious (19)
Ambitious (22)	Lazy (21)	Attractive (23)
Arrogant (20)	Logical (22)	Charming (20)
Assertive (20)	Loud (21)	Curious (21)
Autocratic (24)	Masculine (25)	Dependent (23)
Boastful (19)	Obnoxious (19)	Dreamy (24)
Clear-thinking (21)	Opportunistic (20)	Emotional (23)
Coarse (21)	Progressive (23)	Fearful (23)
Confident (19)	Rational (20)	Feminine (24)
Courageous (23)	Realistic (20)	Gentle (21)
Cruel (21)	Reckless (20)	Kind (19)
Daring (24)	Robust (24)	Meek (19)
Determined (21)	Rude (23)	Mild (21)
Disorderly (21)	Self-confident (21)	Pleasant (19)
Dominant (25)	Serious (20)	Sensitive (24)
Egotistical (21)	Severe (23)	Sentimental (25)
Energetic (22)	Stern (24)	Sexy (22)
Enterprising (24)	Stolid (20)	Shy (19)
Forceful (25)	Strong (25)	Softhearted (23)
Hardheaded (21)	Unemotional (23)	Submissive (25)
Hardhearted (21)	Unkind (19)	Superstitious (25)
Humorous (19)	Wise (23)	Talkative (20)
Independent (25)		Weak (23)

women in Japan; and lazy was associated with women in Pakistan. The exceptions for the female-associated items were even fewer: sympathetic was associated with men in France and Italy, and affected was associated with men in Germany. Impressionistically grouping the items in the table, there is some suggestion of oppositeness for the items associated with men and women (e.g., men—aggressive, dominant, women—submissive; men—stern, severe, women—sentimental, soft-hearted, affectionate). Even though these lists represent considerable cross-cultural and cross-linguistic agreement, this level of analysis is most affected by translation problems. It is perhaps remarkable there is so much similarity in the stereotypes across countries.

Williams and Best's secondly scoring system is an *affective meaning analysis* derived from the research of Osgood and his associates (Osgood et al., 1957). Based on his extensive research in the United States and in 23 language-culture groups (Osgood, May, & Miron, 1975), Osgood concluded that the principle components of

affective meaning—evaluation (good/bad), potency (strong/weak), and activity (active/passive)—were general and could be found in all languages studied. Based on Osgood's findings, Williams and Best had separate groups of American university students use 5-point scales to rate the favorability, strength, and activity of each ACL item, without reference to gender. Standard scores for these ratings were computed by setting the overall mean equal to 500 and the standard deviation equal to 100. Thus scores above 500 indicate ratings that are more favorable, stronger, and more active, while scores below 500 indicate unfavorability, weakness, and inactivity (e.g., Aggressive = favorability 504, neutral; strength 713, very strong; activity 712, very active; Gentle = favorability 635, very good; strength 492, neutral; activity 362, very passive).

Ideally, participants in each country should have scaled each ACL item for favorability, strength, and activity, but this was not possible. However, the Osgood system has sufficient cross-cultural applicability even though particular ratings for individual items may vary by country. Indeed, in making item-by-item translations, affective meaning may determine whether one particular synonym is chosen over another.

In each country the male and female stereotype items were identified and mean favorability, strength, and activity scores for these groups of items were calculated. The ranges of the mean scores across the 25 countries is shown in Figure 1. There is considerable variation among the countries in the favorability associated with the male and female stereotypes, but the ranges of the two stereotypes overlap. In about half the countries the male stereotype was rated more favorably than the female, and the reverse was true in the remaining countries. Moreover, there was no cross-cultural tendency for one stereotype to be more favorable than the other. Frequent objections to the female stereotype are not associated with differential favorability of the adjectives attributed to men and women, but may be related to activity and strength differences.

Looking at these two dimensions, the means for all the male stereotypes are on the active and strong sides of the scales, and the female stereotypes are on the passive and weak sides of the scales, with no overlap between the distributions. Pan-culturally, male-associated items carry connotations of activity and strength, and female items carry connotations of passivity and weakness. It is likely that the differences in activity and strength, rather than

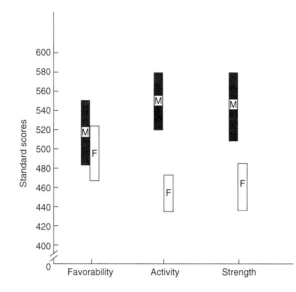

Figure 1. Ranges of mean affective meaning scores (favorability, activity, strength) for male (M) and female (F) stereotypes across 25 countries.

differences in favorability, account for the general disfavor attributed to the female stereotype items in comparison with the male items.

In view of the variation in the stereotype scores across countries, the question arises as to how these differences may relate to cultural differences. Williams and Best (1990a) examined the relationship between stereotype scores and a number of *cultural comparison variables*. They used 17 demographic indices (e.g., *economic/social development*—GNP; *education*—literacy; *status of women*—percentage in university, percentage working outside home; *religion, general demographics*—population, latitude, urban/rural) and four indices of national work-related values from Hofstede's (1980) research (Power Distance, Uncertainty Avoidance, Individualism, Masculinity). They correlated these indices with the stereotype scores. Surprisingly, they found that their stereotype scores were generally unrelated to indices of economic and social development or to work-related values.

The only demographic variable that showed consistent relationships with the stereotype scores was *religious affiliation*. In countries with higher percentages of Catholics, the greater the relative favorability of the female stereotype and the lower the relative strength of the male stereotype. This may be related to a more significant role for women in the Catholic tradition, perhaps due to the virtue and power associated with the Virgin Mary.

Another interesting religious comparison was between the Muslim and Hindu traditions (Williams, Best, Haque, Pandey, & Verma, 1982). In Muslim theology, significant figures are male and religious practice is controlled exclusively by men, as is society. Women are expected to remain secluded in their homes and are depersonalized by traditional dress. The status of women in Hindu tradition contrasts sharply with that just described. Though most Indian women are homemakers, they also participate actively in commerce, government, religious activities, and education.

In Pakistan, a predominantly Muslim country, the traits associated with women were less favorable than those associated with men, but in India the reverse was true. While the male stereotype in each country was stronger and more active than the corresponding female stereotype, the differences were much smaller in India than in Pakistan.

Looking at male–female *stereotype differentiation* within each country, differences were largest in The Netherlands, Finland, Norway, and Germany, and smallest in Scotland, Bolivia, and Venezuela. The stereotypes of men and women showed greater differences in more developed countries, and in countries where Hofstede's male work-related values (Hofstede, 1980, 2001) were relatively high in Individualism. The strength and activity differences between the male and female stereotypes were greater in socio-economically less developed countries, in countries where literacy was low, and in countries where the percentage of women attending the university was low. Perhaps economic and educational advancement are accompanied by a reduction in the tendency to view men as stronger and more active than women. However, those effects were merely reduced, not eliminated, by cultural and economic factors.

MASCULINITY/FEMININITY OF SELF-CONCEPTS

The degree to which stereotyped traits are endorsed or incorporated in the self-concepts of men and women is one definition of masculinity and femininity, and is the one that will be used in this review. However, a person can be masculine or feminine in many ways, including dress, mannerisms, or tone of voice, but these areas will not be discussed here.

Masculinity/Femininity Studies in the United States

There have been numerous studies looking at the differences between men's and women's self-concepts, but these will not be reviewed exhaustively. However, there are two general observations from these studies. First, differences between women's and men's self-concepts are usually found, and these are consistent with the sex stereotypes discussed above (Bem, 1974; Spence et al., 1974, 1975; Williams & Best, 1990a). Second, the differences between men and women are often smaller than those found within each of the gender groups (Deaux, 1984; Spence, Deaux, & Helmreich, 1985).

Cross-Cultural Studies of Masculinity/Femininity

Methodological Issues. Turning to cross-cultural research, measurement is particularly important in studies of gender. A problem arises, for example, when a masculinity/femininity scale developed in one country, often the United States, is translated into another language and administered to persons in other cultures. Spence and Helmreich's (1978) study illustrates this problem. They compared the self-descriptive responses of men in the United States and in Brazil to the PAQ which contains positively valued traits that American research participants identified as male-associated and female-associated. In their study, American men endorsed more male-associated traits than female-associated traits, but Brazilian men had the opposite pattern. Does this mean that Brazilian men have more feminine self-concepts than American men? Probably not. This interpretation pays little attention to how each culture defines masculinity and femininity. Cross-culturally, some items in translated scales may be inappropriate due to content, whereas others may be poorly translated.

Williams and Best's Masculinity/Femininity Study. Because cultural groups may differ in their definitions of masculinity and femininity, Williams and Best (1990b) used culture-specific measures. University

students in 14 countries were asked to describe themselves and their ideal selves using the 300 ACL adjectives. Their descriptions were scored relative to locally defined sex-trait stereotypes derived in their stereotype study (Williams & Best, 1990a).

Williams and Best found that men in all countries were more masculine than women, which is hardly surprising. Interestingly, for the ideal self, both gender groups wished to be "more masculine" than they thought they were. Although some cultural variation in self-concepts was found, surprisingly these differences were not associated with other cultural comparison variables such as economic/social development. Across cultural groups, relative to their own culture's definition of femininity and masculinity, there was no evidence that women in some societies were more feminine than women in others, or that men in some societies were more masculine than men in others.

In contrast, when the affective meaning scoring system was used, there were substantial differences across countries in self- and ideal self-concepts. Men's self- and ideal self-descriptions were stronger and more active than women's, with no general difference for favorability. Moreover, in all countries there was a tendency for both men's and women's ideal self-descriptions to be stronger, more active, and more favorable than their self-descriptions. Differences in men's and women's self-concepts were smaller in more developed countries, in countries where women were employed outside the home, where they constituted a large percentage of the university population, and where relatively modern beliefs about men's and women's roles (e.g., sex role ideology) prevailed.

Hofstede's Masculine Work-Related Values. Using a different methodological approach to examine masculinity/femininity, Hofstede (1980, 2001), compared work-related values in 40 countries. Attitude survey data from thousands of employees of IBM, a large multinational high-technology business organization, were examined. One scale that Hofstede derived in his analyses concerned the extent to which values of assertiveness, money, and things prevail in a society rather than the values of nurturance, quality of life, and people. While this scale could have easily been named "Materialism," Hofstede named it "Masculinity" (MAS) because male employees assign greater weight to the first set of values whereas females assign greater weight to the second.

Rather than examining the level of masculinity/ femininity for individual participants as Williams and Best (1990b) did, Hofstede computed a MAS index for each of the 40 countries in his study. The five countries with the most masculine scores were Japan, Austria, Venezuela, Italy, and Switzerland; the five countries with the lowest MAS indices were Sweden, Norway, The Netherlands, Denmark, and Finland. These indices were correlated across countries with various national comparison variables (e.g., GNP, population density). In high-MAS countries there is greater belief in independent decision making, stronger achievement motivation, higher job stress, and work was more central in people's lives. In addition, societal sex roles were more clearly differentiated and men were expected to dominate in all settings.

Calling the scale Masculinity leads to the expectation that scale scores may be associated with cross-country variations in other gender-related concepts. Hofstede's MAS scores were available for 20 of the 25 countries in Williams and Best's (1990a) stereotype study and for 12 of the 14 countries in their masculinity/femininity study (Williams & Best, 1990b). Nonsignificant correlations were obtained between MAS scores and stereotype scores and between MAS scores and $M\%$ scores for men's and women's self- and ideal self-descriptions (Best & Williams, 1998/1994). Similarly, Ward (1995) found that Attitude Toward Rape scores were unrelated to Hofstede's MAS scores.

Although the MAS dimension is important, designating this value system "Masculinity" is questionable. Indeed, there is little evidence of convergent validity between Hofstede's definition of masculinity and that of other researchers.

SEX ROLE IDEOLOGY

Finding that gender stereotype beliefs and self-concepts are related to differences in cultural comparison variables suggests that they may also be related to beliefs about the appropriate roles of females and males within various cultural groups. What is considered appropriate behavior for males and females varies across societies, but there are two possible cultural universals: At least to some degree, every society assigns traits and tasks on the basis of gender, and in no society is the status of women superior to that of men (Munroe & Munroe, 1975/1994).

In virtually all human groups, women have greater responsibility for "domestic" activities while men have greater responsibility for "external" activities. Women are responsible for cooking, food preparation, carrying water, caring for clothing, and making household things, and men are involved with hunting, metalwork, and weapon making, and travel further from home (D'Andrade, 1966). Women are responsible for child rearing (Weisner & Gallimore, 1977), and men have major responsibilities for child rearing in only 20% of the 80 cultures examined (Katz & Konner, 1981; West & Konner, 1976). Such pancultural similarities may originate from the biological differences between the sexes.

However, in many cultures these socially assigned duties are now being shared, with men engaging in more domestic activities and women in more external, particularly economic, activities. Nevertheless, even in societies where women have moved actively into the labor force, they have not had a comparable reduction in household duties. In the United States, Switzerland, Sweden, Canada, Italy, Poland, and Romania, the overwhelming majority of household work is performed by women, regardless of their occupational status (Population Crisis Committee, 1988). The gender division of labor is reviewed in other chapters, but the beliefs and attitudes about appropriate role behaviors for the two sexes which are related to stereotypes will be discussed here.

Sex Role Studies in the United States

Researchers generally classify sex role ideologies or beliefs along a continuum from traditional to modern. Traditional ideologies maintain that men are more "important" than women and that it is appropriate for men to control and dominate women. In contrast, modern ideologies are more egalitarian, claiming that women and men are equally important, and dominance of one sex over the other is inappropriate. Research in the United States has assumed that there is individual variation in sex role ideology. More masculine men and more feminine women are expected to have more traditional sex role beliefs, and more androgynous men and women would be more egalitarian.

A number of scales have been developed to assess sex role ideology (Beere, 1990), and one of the most frequently used is the Attitudes toward Women Scale (Spence & Helmreich, 1972). Scale items concern the roles of men and women (e.g., a woman should be as free as a man to propose marriage). Women more readily endorse egalitarian attitudes than do men, and over the years attitudes have shifted toward greater acceptance of women's rights (Spence & Hahn, 1997; Twenge, 1997). Interestingly, Martin (1990) isolated two unrelated factors in men's attitudes toward women, one dealing with traditional interpersonal roles and the other with public issues of equality of opportunity and employment. Recent studies have examined more subtle forms of sex role beliefs, such as the importance of maintaining balance in men's and women's roles (Tougas, Brown, Beaton, & Joly, 1995).

Cross-Cultural Sex Role Studies

Cross-cultural research has examined variation in sex role ideology between cultural groups. Using Hofstede's terminology, one would assume that traditional ideologies would be found in masculine cultures and modern ideologies in feminine cultures.

Williams and Best's Sex Role Ideology Study. In their 14-country study of masculinity and femininity described above, Williams and Best (1990b) had study participants respond to the 30-item Kalin Sex Role Ideology measure (SRI) (Kalin & Tilby, 1978) (e.g., "The husband should be regarded as the legal representative of the family group in all matters of law"). To date, this study includes the largest number and variety of countries to be examined in a single-sex role study.

Williams and Best (1990b) found the most modern ideologies in Northern European countries (The Netherlands, Germany, Finland, England, Italy), and the most traditional ideologies in the African and Asian countries (Nigeria, Pakistan, India, Japan, Malaysia). The United States was in the middle of the distribution. Consistent with previous research (Kalin, Heusser, & Edwards, 1982; Spence & Helmreich, 1978), women generally had more modern views than men, but not in all countries (e.g., Malaysia, Pakistan). However, men's and women's scores were very similar in any given country, with a correlation of 0.95 for men and women across the 14 countries. Overall, the effect of culture was greater than the effect of gender.

More modern sex role ideologies were found in more developed countries, in more heavily Christian countries, in more urbanized countries, and in countries in the high latitudes (i.e., relatively far from the equator).

Interestingly, sex role ideology scores were not correlated with Hofstede's MAS indices across the countries in the sample.

Studies with Small Numbers of Cultural Groups. There are several studies in the literature comparing small numbers of cultural groups, but their findings are consistent with those above. For example, when asked about desirable and undesirable roles for women in their culture, Indian university students expressed more traditional beliefs than American students, and women in both groups were more liberal than men (Agarwal & Lester, 1992; Rao & Rao, 1985). University women with nontraditional sex role attitudes came from nuclear families, had educated mothers, and were in career or professionally oriented disciplines (Ghadially & Kazi, 1979).

Similarly, female Arab and Israeli high school students were more liberal than male students (Rapoport, Lomski-Feder, & Masalha, 1989; Seginer, Karayanni, & Mar'i, 1990). Female college students in Japan, Slovenia, and the United States are less traditional than men, with Japanese students being the most traditional of the three groups (Morinaga, Frieze, & Ferligoj, 1993). Japanese adolescents are also more traditional than German adolescents (Trommsdorff & Iwawaki, 1989).

Among both Japanese and American women, education and professional managerial work are strong predictors of sex role attitudes (Suzuki, 1991). Interestingly, American women with jobs of any kind had more egalitarian attitudes than women without jobs. Japanese women with career-oriented professional jobs differed from all other women, with or without jobs. Furthermore, British working-class women are more conservative than American working-class women, but the attitudes of upper-middle-class women in the two countries do not differ (Nelson, 1988).

Gibbons, Stiles, and Shkodriani (1991) studied attitudes toward gender and family roles among adolescents from 46 countries attending schools in The Netherlands. Students from less wealthy and more collectivistic countries had more traditional attitudes than students from the wealthier and more individualistic countries, and girls were less traditional than boys.

Overall, research shows that sex role ideology is more traditional in some cultures than in others. However, across cultural groups, males generally have more traditional attitudes toward sex roles than women. This may not be surprising because in countries with more traditional male-dominant orientations males benefit in terms of status and privileges.

Social Role Theory

The different social roles that men and women play are based on the sexual division of labor and, according to social role theory, these role differences lead to differences in the behaviors of males and females. The division of labor and the status hierarchy of gender result from differences in reproduction and in the physical size and strength of women and men (Wood & Eagly, 1999), with differences typically favoring men (Eagly, Wood, & Diekman, 2000). Differences in position and power lead to differences in gender roles which include both beliefs and expectations (Cialdini & Trost, 1998) about what men and women do. Because women more frequently assume the domestic role, characteristics assumed to exemplify homemakers are stereotypically ascribed to women in general. Similarly, characteristics thought to typify providers are ascribed to men in general (Eagly et al., 2000). Cultural expectations promote conformity to gender roles and influence perceptions of masculinity and femininity in oneself and others. Indeed, gender stereotypes are often used to justify differential sex role assignment (Hoffman & Hurst, 1990; Jost & Banaji, 1994; Williams & Best, 1990a).

DEVELOPMENT OF GENDER ROLES AND STEREOTYPES

Even though biological factors may impose predispositions and restrictions on development, sociocultural factors have important effects. Culture prescribes how babies are delivered, how children are socialized and dressed, what tasks children are taught, and what roles adult men and women adopt. The scope and progression of children's behaviors, even behaviors considered to be biologically determined, are governed by culture.

Within the context of cultural stereotypes about male–female differences, children's knowledge of gender roles develops. In the United States, children as young as 2 years of age stereotype objects as masculine or feminine (Thompson, 1975; Weinraub et al., 1984), and by age 3–4 years they use stereotypic labels accurately with toys, activities, and occupations (Edelbrook & Sugawara,

1978; Guttentag & Longfellow, 1977). Similar gender stereotyping of toys is found in West Africa, where girls play with dolls and boys construct vehicles and weapons (Bloch & Adler, 1994).

Sex-Trait Stereotype Development in the United States

In the USA children acquire knowledge of sex-trait stereotypes somewhat later than stereotypic knowledge of toys and occupations (Best et al., 1977; Reis & Wright, 1982). Williams and Best (Best et al., 1977; Williams & Best, 1990a) developed the Sex Stereotype Measure II (SSM II) to assess children's knowledge of adult-defined stereotypes. In this picture-story measure children are shown silhouette drawings of a male and a female, they are read a story containing a stereotype trait, and they are asked to indicate which person the story is about. European American children show a consistent pattern of increasing knowledge from kindergarten through high school, similar to a typical learning curve. The most dramatic increases in stereotype knowledge occur in the early elementary school years, with scores reaching a plateau in the junior high years. African American children's scores increase with age but are lower than those of the European American children, perhaps suggesting slightly different stereotypes for the two groups.

Cross-Cultural Findings

Turning to the cross-cultural literature, Zammuner (1982, 1987, 1993) found that Italian and Dutch children (ages 5–12 years) assigned different traits and activities to males and females. British and Hungarian children's knowledge of stereotypes was related to parents' gender attitudes and father's sex-typed behaviors (Turner & Gervai, 1995).

Williams and Best's Study of Children's Sex Stereotypes.   In a more comprehensive cross-cultural study of sex stereotypes, Williams and Best (1990a) administered the SSM II to 5-, 8-, and 11-year-olds in 25 countries and found that the percentage of stereotyped responses increased from around 60% at age 5 to around 70% at age 8. Strong, aggressive, cruel, coarse, and adventurous were consistently associated with men at all age levels, and weak, appreciative, soft-hearted, gentle, and meek were consistently associated with women.

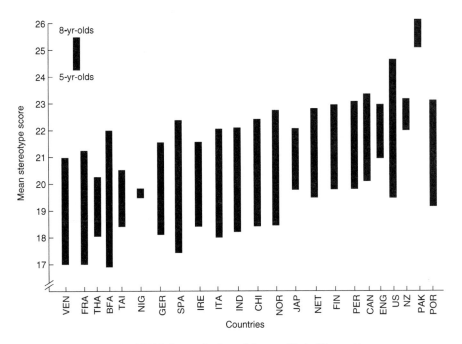

Figure 2. SSM II Scores for 5- and 8-year-olds in 23 countries.

Both male and female scores were unusually high in Pakistan and relatively high in New Zealand and England, suggesting that children in these countries have an appreciable knowledge of sex stereotypes (see Figure 2). Scores were atypically low in Brazil, Taiwan, Germany, and France, suggesting that children in these countries did not have consistent knowledge of the stereotype traits. Although there was variation between countries in the rate of learning, there was a general developmental pattern in which stereotype learning begins prior to age 5 years, accelerates during the early school years, and is completed during the adolescent years.

Boys and girls learned the stereotypes at a similar rate, but there was a tendency for male-stereotype traits to be learned somewhat earlier than female traits. In 17 of the 24 countries studied, male stereotype items were better known by both sexes than female items. Germany was the only country where there was a clear tendency for the female stereotype to be better known than the male. Female stereotype items were learned earlier than male items in Latin/Catholic cultures (Brazil, Chile, Portugal, Venezuela) where the adult-defined female stereotype is more positive than the male.

In predominantly Muslim countries, 5-year-olds associate traits with the two sexes in a more highly differentiated manner and they learn the stereotypes, particularly the male items, at an earlier age than in non-Muslim countries. Children in predominantly Christian countries initially learn the stereotypes at a slower pace, perhaps reflecting the less differentiated nature of the adult stereotypes, particularly in Catholic countries.

Intons-Peterson's Study of Adolescent Sex Stereotypes. Looking at older children (11–18 years of age), Intons-Peterson (1988) found that stereotypes of men and women were more similar in Sweden than in the United States. Surprisingly, however, ideal occupational choices did not overlap for Swedish boys and girls; females were interested in service occupations (e.g., flight attendant, hospital worker, nanny), and males were interested in business occupations.

Stereotype findings with children are consistent with the adult model of sex stereotypes discussed earlier. Children's stereotypes seem universal, with culture modifying the rate of learning and minor aspects of content.

Theories of Gender-Related Learning

Cultural universals in gender differences are often explained by similarities in socialization practices while cultural differences are attributed to differences in social- ization. Children grow up within other people's scripts, which guide their actions long before the children them- selves can understand or carry out culturally acceptable actions. For gender researchers, one of the crucial tasks is to unpackage broadly defined cultural variables to identify the aspects or processes responsible for the development of particular behaviors. Gender should be examined not only in relation to culture (e.g., social systems, practices, myths, beliefs, rituals), but also in the context of the history and economics of a society (Mukhopadhyay & Higgins, 1988).

Most theories of gender role learning emphasize the gender information readily available in the culture even though the theories were devised primarily in the United States. *Social learning theories* consider sex role develop- ment to be the result of cumulative experience. Parents, teachers, peers, and other socialization agents shape chil- dren's gender-related behaviors through reinforcement and punishment, modeling, expectations, toy choices, and other differential treatment of boys and girls. *Cognitive developmental theory* suggests that the impact of cultural factors is governed by the child's emerging cognitive structures. Children acquire gender knowledge in stages and their level of understanding structures their experi- ences. *Gender schema theory* assumes that the primacy of gender concepts in a culture serves as a basis for organiz- ing information To date, there is little evidence regarding these theories cross-culturally.

CONCLUSIONS

The similarity in gender stereotypes found cross-culturally suggests that the psychological characteristics differen- tially associated with women and men follow a pancul- tural model with cultural factors producing minor variations around general themes. Biological differences (e.g., females bear children, males have greater physical strength) serve as the basis for a division of labor, with women primarily responsible for child care and other domestic activities, and men for hunting (providing) and protection. Gender stereotypes evolve to support this division of labor and assume that each sex has or can develop characteristics consistent with their assigned roles. Once established, stereotypes serve as socialization models that encourage boys to become independent and adventurous, and girls to become nurturant and affiliative. Consequently, these characteristics are incorporated into

men's and women's self-concepts, aspects of their mas- culinity and femininity. This model illustrates how, with only minor variations, people across different cultures come to associate one set of characteristics with men and another set with women.

Pancultural similarities in sex and gender greatly outweigh cultural differences. Indeed, the way in which male–female relationships are organized is remarkably similar across social groups. The relatively minor biolog- ical differences between the sexes can be amplified or diminished by cultural practices and socialization, mak- ing gender differences in roles and behaviors generally modest but in some cases culturally important.

REFERENCES

Agarwal, K. S., & Lester, D. (1992). A study of perception of women by Indian and American students. In S. Iwawaki, Y. Kashima, & K. Leung (Eds.), *Innovations in cross-cultural psychology* (pp. 123–134). Amsterdam: Swets & Zeitlinger.

Ashmore, R. D., & Del Boca, F. K. (1979). Sex stereotypes and implicit personality theory: Toward a cognitive–social psychological conceptualization. *Sex Roles, 5,* 219–248.

Beere, C. A. (1990). *Gender roles: A handbook of tests and measures.* New York: Greenwood Press.

Bem, S. L. (1974). The measurement of psychological androgyny. *Journal of Consulting and Clinical Psychology, 42,* 155–162.

Bem, S. L. (1975). Sex-role adaptability: One consequence of psycho- logical androgyny. *Journal of Personality and Social Psychology, 31,* 634–643.

Best, D. L., & Williams, J. E. (1993). Cross-cultural viewpoint. In A. E. Beall & R. J. Sternberg (Eds.), *The psychology of gender* (pp. 215–248). New York: Guilford.

Best, D. L., & Williams, J. E. (1998/1994). Masculinity and femininity in the self and ideal self descriptions of university students in 14 countries. In G. Hofstede (Ed.), *Masculinity and femininity: The taboo dimensions of national cultures* (pp. 106–116). Thousand Oaks, CA: Sage.

Best, D. L., Williams, J. E., Cloud, J. M., Davis, S. W., Robertson, L. S., Edwards, J. R., et al. (1977). Development of sex-trait stereotypes among young children in the United States, England, and Ireland. *Child Development, 48,* 1375–1384.

Bloch, M. N., & Adler, S. M. (1994). African children's play and the emergence of the sexual division of labor. In J. L. Roopnarine, J. E. Johnson, & F. H. Hooper (Eds.), *Children's play in diverse cul- tures* (pp. 148–178). Albany, NY: State University of New York Press.

Broverman, I. K., Broverman, D. M., Clarkson, F. E., Rosenkrantz, P. S., & Vogel, S. R. (1970). Sex-role stereotypes and clinical judgments of mental health. *Journal of Consulting and Clinical Psychology, 34,* 1–7.

Broverman, I. K., Vogel, S. R., Broverman, D. M., Clarkson, F. E., & Rosenkrantz, P. S. (1972). Sex role stereotypes: A current appraisal. *Journal of Social Issues, 28,* 59–78.

Cialdini, R. B., & Trost, M. R. (1998). Social influence: Social norms, conformity, and compliance. In D. T. Gilbert, S. T. Fiske, & G. Lindzey (Eds.), *The handbook of social psychology* (Vol. 2, 4th ed., pp. 151–192). Boston: McGraw-Hill.

D'Andrade, R. G. (1966). Sex differences and cultural institutions. In E. E. Maccoby (Ed.), *The development of sex differences* (pp. 174–204). Stanford, CA: Stanford University Press.

Deaux, K. (1984). From individual differences to social categories. *American Psychologist, 39,* 105–116.

Eagly, A. H., Wood, W., & Diekman, A. B. (2000). Social role theory of differences and similarities: A current appraisal. In T. Eckes & H. M. Trautner (Eds.), *The developmental social psychology of gender* (pp. 123–174). Mahwah, NJ: Erlbaum.

Edelbrook, C., & Sugawara, A. I. (1978). Acquisition of sex-typed preferences in preschool-aged children. *Developmental Psychology, 14,* 614–623.

Edwards, C. P. (1992). Cross-cultural perspectives on family–peer relations. In R. D. Parke & G. W. Ladd (Eds.), *Family–peer relationships: Modes of linkages.* Mahwah, NJ: Erlbaum.

Ghadially, R., & Kazi, K. A. (1979). Attitudes toward sex roles. *Indian Journal of Social Work, 40,* 65–71.

Gibbons, J. L., Stiles, D. A., & Shkodriani, G. M. (1991). Adolescents' attitudes toward family and gender roles: An international comparison. *Sex Roles, 25,* 625–643.

Gough, H. G., & Heilbrun, A. B., Jr. (1980). *The Adjective Check List manual.* Palo Alto, CA: Consulting Psychologists Press.

Guttentag, M., & Longfellow, C. (1977). Children's social attributions: Development and change. In C. B. Keasy (Ed.), *Nebraska Symposium on Motivation.* Lincoln, NE: University of Nebraska Press.

Hoffman, C., & Hurst, N. (1990). Gender stereotypes: Perception or rationalization? *Journal of Personality and Social Psychology, 58,* 197–208.

Hofstede, G. (1980). *Culture's consequences: International differences in work-related values.* Beverly Hills, CA: Sage.

Hofstede, G. (2001). *Culture's consequences: Comparing values, behaviors, institutions, and organizations across nations.* Thousand Oaks, CA: Sage.

Hoyenga, K. B., & Hoyenga, K. T. (1993). *Gender-related differences: Origins and outcomes.* Boston: Allyn & Bacon.

Intons-Peterson, M. J. (1988). *Gender concepts of Swedish and American youth.* Hillsdale, NJ: Erlbaum.

Jost, J. T., & Banaji, M. R. (1994). The role of stereotyping in system-justification and the production of false consciousness. *British Journal of Social Psychology, 33,* 1–27.

Kalin, R., Heusser, C., & Edwards, J. (1982). Cross-national equivalence of a sex-role ideology scale. *Journal of Social Psychology, 116,* 141–142.

Kalin, R., & Tilby, P. (1978). Development and validation of a sex-role ideology scale. *Psychological Reports, 42,* 731–738.

Katz, M. M., & Konner, M. J. (1981). The role of the father: An anthropological perspective. In M. E. Lamb (Ed.), *The role of the father in child development* (pp. 155–185). New York: Wiley.

Lii, S.-Y., & Wong, S.-Y. (1982). A cross-cultural study on sex-role stereotypes and social desirability. *Sex Roles, 8,* 481–491.

Martin, A. (1990). *Men's ambivalence toward women: Implications for evaluation of rape victims.* Unpublished doctoral dissertation, City University of New York.

McKee, J. P., & Sheriffs, A. C. (1957). The differential evaluation of males and females. *Journal of Personality, 25,* 356–371.

McKee, J. P., & Sheriffs, A. C. (1959). Men's and women's beliefs, ideals, and self-concepts. *American Journal of Sociology, 64,* 356–363.

Morinaga, Y., Frieze, I. H., & Ferligoj, A. (1993). Career plans and gender-role attitudes of college students in the United States, Japan, and Slovenia. *Sex Roles, 29,* 317–334.

Mukhopadhyay, C. C., & Higgins, P. J. (1988). Anthropological studies of women's status revisited: 1977–1987. *Annual Review of Anthropology, 17,* 461–495.

Munroe, R. L., & Munroe, R. H. (1975/1994). *Cross-cultural human development.* Prospect Heights, IL: Waveland Press.

Nelson, M. G. (1988). Reliability, validity, and cross-cultural comparisons for the Simplified Attitudes Toward Women Scale. *Sex Roles, 18,* 289–296.

Osgood, C. E., May, W. H., & Miron, M. S. (1975). Cross-cultural universals of affective meaning. Urbana, IL: University of Illinois Press.

Osgood, C. E., Suci, G. J., & Tannenbaum, P. H. (1957). *The measurement of meaning.* Urbana: University of Illinois Press.

Parsons, T. & Bales, R. F. (1955). *Family socialization and interaction process.* New York: Free Press.

Peterson, V. S., & Runyan, A. S. (1993). *Global gender issues.* Boulder, CO: Westview Press.

Population Crisis Committee. (1988, June). *Country rankings of the status of women: Poor, powerless, and pregnant* (Issue Brief No. 20). Washington, DC: Author.

Rao, V. V. P., & Rao, V. N. (1985). Sex-role attitudes across two cultures: United States and India. *Sex Roles, 13,* 607–624.

Rapoport, T., Lomski-Feder, E., & Masalha, M. (1989). Female subordination in the Arab–Israeli community: The adolescent perspective of "social veil." *Sex Roles, 20,* 255–269.

Reis, H. T., & Wright, S. (1982). Knowledge of sex-role stereotypes in children aged 3 to 5. *Sex Roles, 8,* 1049–1056.

Rosenkrantz, P. S., Vogel, S. R., Bee, H., Broverman, I. K., & Broverman, D. M. (1968). Sex-role stereotypes and self-concepts in college students. *Journal of Consulting and Clinical Psychology, 32,* 287–295.

Seginer, R., Karayanni, M., & Mar'i, M. M. (1990). Adolescents' attitudes toward women's roles: A comparison between Israeli Jews and Arabs. *Psychology of Women Quarterly, 14,* 119–133.

Sheriffs, A. C., & McKee, J. P. (1957). Qualitative aspects of beliefs about men and women. *Journal of Personality, 25,* 451–464.

Spence, J. T., Deaux, K., & Helmreich, R. L. (1985). Sex roles in contemporary American society. In G. Lindzey & E. Aronson (Eds.), *The handbook of social psychology* (3rd ed., pp. 149–178). New York: Random House.

Spence, J. T., & Hahn, E. D. (1997). The Attitudes Toward Women Scale and the attitude change in college students. *Psychology of Women Quarterly, 24,* 44–62.

Spence, J. T., & Helmreich, R. (1972). The Attitudes Towards Women Scale: An objective instrument to measure attitudes towards the rights and roles of women in contemporary society. *JSAS Catalog of Selected Documents in Psychology, 2,* 66.

Spence, J. T., & Helmreich, R. (1978). *The psychological dimensions of masculinity and femininity: Their correlates and antecedents.* Austin, TX: University of Texas Press.

Spence, J. T., Helmreich, R., & Stapp, J. (1974). The Personal Attributes Questionnaire: A measure of sex-role stereotypes and masculinity-femininity. *Catalog of Selected Documents in Psychology, 4*, 43–44.

Spence, J. T., Helmreich, R., & Stapp, J. (1975). Ratings of self and peers on sex role attributes and their relation to self-esteem and conceptions of masculinity and femininity. *Journal of Personality and Social Psychology, 32*, 29–39.

Spence, J. T., & Holahan, C. K. (1979). Negative and positive components of psychological masculinity and femininity and their relationship to self-reports of neurotic and acting out behaviors. *Journal of Personality and Social Psychology, 37*, 1631–1644.

Sunar, D. G. (1982). Female stereotypes in the United States and Turkey: An application of functional theory to perception in power relationships. *Journal of Cross-Cultural Psychology, 13*, 445–460.

Suzuki, A. (1991). Predictors of women's sex role attitudes across two cultures: United States and Japan. *Japanese Psychological Research, 33*(3), 126–133.

Thompson, S. K. (1975). Gender labels and early sex role development. *Child Development, 46*, 339–347.

Tougas, F., Brown, R., Beaton, A. M., & Joly, S. (1995). Neosexism: Plus ça change plus c'est pareil. *Personality and Social Psychology Bulletin, 21*, 842–849.

Trommsdorff, G., & Iwawaki, S. (1989). Students' perceptions of socialisation and gender role in Japan and Germany. *International Journal of Behavioral Development, 12*(4), 485–493.

Turner, P. J., & Gervai, J. (1995). A multidimensional study of gender typing in preschool children and their parents: Personality, attitudes, preferences, behavior, and cultural differences. *Developmental Psychology, 31*, 759–772.

Twenge, J. M. (1997). Attitudes toward women, 1970–1995: A meta-analysis. *Psychology of Women Quarterly, 21*, 35–51.

Vogel, S. R., Broverman, I. K., Broverman, D. M., Clarkson, F. E., & Rosenkrantz, P. S. (1970). Maternal employment and perception of sex roles among college students. *Developmental Psychology, 3*, 384–391.

Ward, C. (1995). *Blaming victims: Feminist and social psychological persepctives on rape*. London: Sage.

Weinraub, M., Clemens, L. P., Sockloff, A., Etheridge, T., Gracely, E., & Myers, B. (1984). The development of sex-role stereotypes in the third year: Relationships to gender labeling, gender identity, sex-typed toy preference, and family characteristics. *Child Development, 55*, 1493–1503.

Weisner, T.S., & Gallimore, R. (1977). My brother's keeper: Child and sibling caretaking. *Current Anthropology, 18*, 169–190.

West, M. M., & Konner, M. J. (1976). The role of the father: An anthropological perspective. In M. E. Lamb (Ed.), *The role of the father in child development*. New York: Plenum.

Williams, J. E., & Best, D. L. (1990a) *Measuring sex stereotypes: A multination study* (Revised edition). Newbury Park, CA: Sage.

Williams, J. E., & Best, D. L. (1990b). *Sex and psyche: Gender and self-viewer cross-culturally*. Newbury Park, CA: Sage.

Williams, J. E., Best, D. L., Haque, A., Pandey, J., & Verma, R. K. (1982). Sex-trait stereotypes in India and Pakistan. *Journal of Psychology, 111*, 167–181.

Wood, W., & Eagly, A. H. (1999). The origins of the division of labor and gender hierarchy: Implications for sex differences in social behavior.

Zammuner, V. L. (1982). Sex role stereotypes in Italian children. *International Journal of Psychology, 17*, 43–63.

Zammuner, V. L. (1987). Children's sex-role stereotypes: A cross-cultural analysis. In P. Shaver & C. Hendrick (Eds.), *Review of personality and social psychology: 7. Sex and gender* (pp. 272–293). Newbury Park, CA: Sage.

Zammuner, V. L. (1993). Perceptions of male and female personality attributes and behaviors by Dutch children. *Bulletin of the Psychonomic Society, 31*, 87–90.

Gender Differences

Biological Bases of Sex Differences

Bobbi S. Low

INTRODUCTION

A basic goal of biologists is to explain observed variation at many levels, including observed differences between and within the sexes.[1] The biological underpinnings of sex differences are considerably more complex than it might at first seem. In no species are "males" and "females" fully identical, despite huge variation in the logistics of sexual reproduction. What, then, is meant by "biological causes"? It is not simply "genetic" or "hormonal" or a "difference in chromosomes." Rather, sex differences, however mediated, arise from past evolutionary and ecological pressures. Specific environmental pressures favor particular complexes of behavioral, physical, and physiological traits—and these evolved phenomena are the proximate triggers of differences. Under most conditions, these selective pressures lead to a (sometimes striking) divergence of the traits shown by each sex.

Begin with the evolution of sexual reproduction itself. There are evolutionary costs to sexual reproduction (loss of genetic representation) (Maynard Smith, 1978; Williams, 1975). Biologists recognize that sexual reproduction has evolved when there are counterbalancing evolutionary advantages to sexual reproduction. These include the production of variable offspring in unpredictable environments (a sort of bet-hedging): (Maynard Smith, 1978; Williams, 1975; review in Ridley, 1993). The specific mechanisms can vary greatly.

Sexual reproduction is not always achieved by the fusion of two haploid gametes (eggs and sperm), nor is it even always genetic (XY or XO chromosomes). In humans the 23rd pair of chromosomes is either homogametic (XX) or heterogametic (XY); XX individuals develop as females and XY individuals become males. In contrast, in birds, for example, males rather than females are the heterogametic sex. In some species, sexual reproduction is accomplished simply by exchange of genetic material; in these species there may be more than two sexes (e.g., 13 sexes are described for slime molds; see reviews by Ridley [1993] and Low [2000]).

Even in species in which sex is determined by gametes, and there are clearly active sex chromosomes, there is chromosomal information, some of which influences sex, in autosomes (Wizemann & Pardue, 2001, pp. 51–55). In many species, sex is not genetically determined. In crocodilians and many turtles, the temperature at which the egg develops determines an individual's sex (Shine, 1999). In some fish, such as the coral-reef-dwelling blue-headed wrasse, sex is determined by the social environment. Individuals change sex depending on the local population sex ratio: the largest individual becomes a male (Warner et al., 1975). The social environment changes the costs and benefits of being male or female, setting in motion a series of hormonal and physical changes (Lee et al., 2001).

Whether sex is mediated by the physical or social environment, whether there are chromosomal differences between the sexes—these are not the crucial biological bases of sex differences. The specifics of sexual reproduction can differ, but sex differences are common and also predictably patterned. Males and females in most species behave differently, in predictable ways, regardless of how sex is mediated; the number of "sex-role reversed" species is very small. The real keys to the evolution of sex differences are the interplay among environmental influences, genes, and expressed traits, and how these mediate the costs and benefits of similar, versus differing, traits for the sexes.

Sex differences are likely to be particularly striking in gametic-sex species. When sex is accomplished by the joining of haploid gametes to make a diploid zygote (as in humans), anisogamy (unlike gametes) evolves with ecological cost–benefit implications. What we call disruptive selection means that the traits that make a small-gamete maker (male) successful (moving about to seek mates, and making small mobile gametes that travel well) are incompatible with the traits that make a large-gamete maker (female) successful (being risk averse, committing considerable nutrition to the fertilized zygote). Further, the fact that there is information in the cytoplasm of each gamete means that conflicts can arise; in part, sperm become smaller and smaller by eliminating cytoplasm to avoid this conflict (Hurst, 1991, 1992; Hurst & Hamilton, 1992).

This means that the *ecology* of succeeding as a male, versus as a female, differs. Costs and benefits differ for the sexes: roaming or staying home, seeking versus avoiding risk. Note, too, that among the wrasses and some turtles (see above), in which sex is mediated by the social or physical environment, the ecology of succeeding as a male, versus a female, nonetheless still differs—and males and females behave differently, look different, and so forth. The ecological pressure at the heart of all these differences is: Can males be more successful reproductively through seeking many matings (and leaving offspring care to females), or through investing in the offspring in ways that preclude additional matings? No matter whether the sexes are mediated chromosomally, or change with the environment, this consideration is central to sex differences.

Natural selection has shaped sex differences in all species, including humans. The important consideration is always: In the evolutionary history of each species, what were the reproductive costs and benefits of behaving in particular ways? These trade-offs give rise to the complex interplay that we see: systematic behavioral differences (Geary, 1998; Low, 2000; Maccoby, 1998; Mealey, 2000) correlated with prevalence of particular alleles, X and Y chromosomes in some species, and production of hormones like testosterone that affect behavior.

In genetically sex determined species like humans, the sex chromosomes are clear proximate influences on many traits. For example, although both sexes produce both androgens and estrogens, they do so in different proportions. There is still variation, of course, and the distributions of most traits overlap when the two sexes are compared. These are always interacting with environmental pressures: the resulting hormonal profiles are clearly associated with consistent behavioral differences, which are differentially profitable to mate seekers and parental investors. All this reflects the ecological and evolutionary costs and benefits.

There is, then, a complex interactive causal mediation of sex differences: external conditions—physical, biotic, and even social—affect the costs and benefits of different genetic, physical, physiological, and behavioral traits for the sexes. Over time, these trade-offs result in *systematic differences between the sexes*, mediated in a variety of ways. When males and females profit reproductively from doing similar things (e.g., when males

gain enough from offspring-specific true parental investment, like feeding, that precludes additional matings), males and females will be similar in size, appearance, and behavior (e.g., Canada geese). When males profit from seeking matings rather than investing in offspring, as in most mammals, the two sexes will differ, sometimes profoundly, in size, appearance, and behavior (e.g., elephant seal males are several times larger than females).

Among mammals in general, the sexes tend to differ strikingly, because females are specialized to nurse offspring, giving expensive post-natal nutritional care, while males tend to specialize in mating effort. As a result, male mammals tend to have traits that aid in sexual competition: to be larger, to move about more, and to be more aggressive and risk prone than females. In contrast, females tend to be risk averse and more cooperative than males (Low, 2000). In many mammals, the maximum harem size is a good predictor of the degree of physical sexual dimorphism.

Thus the "typical" suite of human sex differences reflects a mammalian evolutionary history. Among mammals, humans are moderately sexually dimorphic in genes, physiology, physical appearance, and behavior, reflecting a past in which moderate polygyny was probably the rule (review in Low, 2000): The following examples of human sex differences reflect the evolved selective underpinnings of sex differences in humans.

PHYSICAL SEX DIFFERENCES

Gross Physical Differences

Many human male–female physical differences are immediately obvious: compared with women, men on average have more upper-body strength and muscular development, larger jaws, and heavier brow ridges. Women have breasts and hips. Less obvious in some cultures, men have penises and testes, and women have clitora, labia, and vaginas. Many of these differences have obvious selective relevance and reflect our evolutionary history. Women's wider hips (as well as hormonal shifts in childbirth) facilitate giving birth; permanently enlarged breasts appear to have evolved in the context of sexual selection (Low, 2000; Low, Alexander, & Noonan, 1987; Mealey, 2000). Men's heavier facial features, versus women's more neotenic faces, appear to relate to sexual selection and mate choice (review in Buss, 1999).

And where it has been measured, taller men have more children than shorter men.

Women's and men's waist–hip ratios differ strikingly (about 0.7 vs. 0.85). Women's waist–hip ratio changes, thickening with both pregnancy and menopause; thus a ratio of 0.7 in a woman sends the message: I am young, and not pregnant. Across a variety of cultures, men find women's "typical" waist–hip ratio of 0.7 most attractive (Singh, 1993; Singh & Luis, 1995), and women do not find wide hips in men attractive. Related physical sexual differences may be exaggerated in specific environments; for example, in some populations in harsh environments, women store fat on the buttocks, giving an exaggerated shape that reflects ability to thrive in harsh conditions (Low, 2000).

Brain

A number of sex differences exist in the physical structure of the brain (review by Kimura, 1999). The hypothalamus, a clump of nuclei at the base of the brain that mediates a variety of sexual behaviors (Kimura, 1999, p. 130), differs between the sexes. Androgens appear to affect parts of an area called the interstitial nuclei of the anterior hypothalamus (INAH), which is larger in men than in women, and larger in heterosexual men than in homosexual men (LeVay, 1991). Though this suggests that the hypothalamus and its development may be involved in sexual preferences, of course the data are simply correlational. Similarly, the anterior commissure (probably involved in sharing information between the brain's hemispheres) is larger in women and homosexual men than in heterosexual men (Allen and Gorsky, 1991).

Male brains are 10–15% larger than female brains, and have more cortical neurons than female brains (Kimura, 1999, p. 128), in part related to sex differences in spatial ability (see below). Because men are physically larger than women, the brain–body weight ratio is roughly equal between the sexes (Ankney, 1992; Kimura, 1999, p. 128). Interestingly, so far, brain sex differences related to sexual selection (e.g., spatial differences, see below) tend to be significantly different. Other differences (e.g., in the United States, men have a nonsignificant ~4-point advantage on IQ tests) tend to be nonsignificant—the distribution of the traits may differ between men and women, but we find no systematic or significant differences.

PHYSIOLOGICAL AND HORMONAL SEX DIFFERENCES

Hormonal differences between the sexes in humans, as in other mammals, are so pervasive and systematic, and are the mediators for so many other differences, that they are sometimes incorrectly cited as *the* biological causes of sex differences. It is clear, however, that these mediators have evolved to differ between the sexes, just as in other species, and specifics vary. Sex hormones organize a variety of sexually dimorphic behaviors, from aggression to reproductive behavior (see reviews by Kimura [1999] and Wizemann and Pardue [2001] for hormonal details, and by Low [2000], Mealey [2000] and Geary [1998] for behavioral, evolutionary, and ecological comparisons). Although both sexes have both androgenic and estrogenic compounds, they do so in differing degrees. In general, the baseline condition hormonally (and in resulting embryological development) is "female," and androgens are required to masculinize both physical and behavioral traits. The sex chromosomes impart important information. For example, it has long been clear that the Y chromosome is necessary for the development of testes; this is accomplished by testicular differentiating hormone (TDF) (Vilain & McCabe, 1998). As with several other kinds of sexual dimorphisms, much of what we know comes from studying individuals with deficiencies or defects (below).

COGNITIVE AND BEHAVIORAL DIFFERENCES

Some physical brain sex differences (see above) are linked in turn to cognitive differences (Kimura, 1999). Many of these differences are easily linked to past selection on sex differences (Geary, 1998, pp. 280–295), although it is important to note that, with few exceptions (noted below), most work has been done in Western developed nations, and cross-cultural work may well add considerable variation.

Behavioral differences are obvious between the sexes shortly after birth. Newborn boys cry more, respond less to parental comforting, and require more holding than girls. Newborn girls respond more strongly than boys to adult faces and to being held. Boys are somewhat more interested than girls in inanimate nonsocial objects. Boys seem to begin technical problem-solving sooner, and wander farther from home earlier. These differences are seen very early and occur across several cultures (Freedman, 1974; Kagan, 1981; R. L. Munroe & R. H. Munroe, 1975; R. H. Munroe, R. L. Munroe, & Brasher, 1971; R. H. Munroe, R. L. Munroe, & Bresler, 1985). It seems likely that spatial "practice" associated with wandering farther from home may contribute to boys' advantages by the time they are 7 or so (R. H. Munroe, R. L. Munroe, & Bresler, 1985).

Perceptual

In all senses except vision, women appear to have greater sensitivity than men. Women have a greater sensitivity to the four tastes (sweet, sour, bitter, salt) than men (Velle, 1987), and have a lower threshold for hearing pure tones (McGuinness, 1972). Women have slightly larger peripheral visual fields than men (Burg, 1966). In studies done in Western developed nations, men have a clearer perception of true vertical and horizontal (Witkin, 1967) and are less susceptible than women to perceptual illusions like the equal-length line with arrowheads at each end (pointing "in" versus "out") (Dewar, 1967). Depth perception also appears more precise in men.

Many of the visual perception differences contribute to sex differences in spatial abilities. Cross-cultural data (Berry, 1976) suggest that, while the sexes tend to differ, the degree of sexual difference varies with subsistence mode and acculturation across cultures.

Spatial

Spatial ability differs between the sexes in polygynous species; males, who search for mates, tend to have greater spatial abilities than females. For example, among voles (small mouse-like creatures) males in polygynous species (who search for females) have better developed spatial abilities than females, and than males in closely related monogamous species (Gaulin & Fitzgerald, 1986; Gaulin & Hoffman, 1988). In humans, men and women use different cues for spatial orientation (McBurney, Gaulin, Devinieni, & Adams, 1997); women tend to use landmarks, while men tend to use directional cues. Scholars suggest that this is related to past pressures of men's hunting versus women's gathering (Silverman & Eals, 1992; Silverman & Phillips, 1998). As noted above, Munroe et al. (1985) also suggest that practice in navigating spatially (e.g., distance from home in young children) contributes to boys' abilities.

Mathematical

Consistent sex differences in mathematical abilities were among the first to be recognized, though the role of biological influences is still controversial. It is difficult to disentangle social from biological influences. Differences exist cross-culturally (expectations of boys and girls are not identical), and girls outperform boys in some cases (e.g., on computational tests). These findings suggest that both biological and social components contribute significantly to observed differences (Engelhard, 1990; Low & Over, 1993; Lubinski & Benbow, 1992; summary in Kimura, 1999, Chapter 6).

Verbal

Girls begin to speak earlier than boys and have larger vocabularies at each age (Maccoby, 1998). By the last year of high school, girls retain a slight advantage in grammatical and spelling skills (Hyde & Linn, 1988). Even as adults, women retain advantages over men in fluency (ability to produce words and sentences under particular constraints) and in speed of naming colors and forms (Kimura, 1996).

One of the most widely recognized and studied differences between the sexes in humans is that of aggression. Here, as in many other differences, we find a general pattern mediated by both genetics and acculturation, with some variation shaped by our evolutionary past (Low, 2000; R. L. Munroe, Hulefeld, Rodgers, Tomeo, & Yamazaki, 2000). Aggression, including warfare, male–male fighting, homicide, and even child abuse, appear to have evolutionary roots (Daly & Wilson, 1988). Cross-culturally, in many societies and through much of human evolutionary history, men have been able to make large direct reproductive gains through aggressive strategies in gaining resources; women's reproduction has typically been more limited by physiological and physical factors (Low, 2000). Perhaps as a result of this evolutionary ecological history, there are clear genetic contributions to aggressiveness, such as abnormalities in the gene encoding the neurotransmitter-metabolizing enzyme monoamine oxidase A (MAOA) (Brunner, 1996; Caspi, McClay, Moffitt, Mill, Martin et al., 2002). However, the costs and benefits of aggressive behavior are affected by societal norms, and there is cross-cultural variation in the degree to which males and females differ (Ember, 1981; Munroe et al., 2000). As we learn more about the genetic contributions to aggressiveness, we may also find cross-cultural variation in the equilibrium frequency of genes like MAOA.

SEX DIFFERENCES IN LIFE HISTORY

Human life histories are unusual among primates, our closest relatives. If we followed the "typical" primate pattern (in which many phenomena vary with size), women would nurse their children until about age 7 years, and then their daughters would have their first children at about age 8 or 9 years (review in Low, 2000). Human distortions of "typical" primate patterns appear to be linked to our extreme sociality. Any glance at census data suggests that there are also significant sex differences in human life history. Women live longer than men and have greater life expectancy at birth. In this, humans are like most mammals, in which males engage in risky competition for mates, and females specialize in expensive but risk-averse post-natal care; females tend to mature significantly earlier, to be less aggressive, and to live longer than males (Low, 2000). Of course, there are social reinforcements of these patterns (Geary, 1998; Low, 2000), but the differences follow the general mammalian pattern and occur across a wide spectrum of human societies. Patterns of senescence—the failure of systems (and system repair) with age—differ between the sexes only in reproductive senescence; menopause is more regular and defined in females than is age-related decrease in male reproductive function.

UNUSUAL CONDITIONS ILLUMINATE PATHWAYS

Rare and deleterious conditions highlight some of the causal biological pathways that yield sex differences. For example, babies missing an X chromosome (XO rather than XX) have Turner's syndrome; they are 98% likely to die before birth, and individuals who survive show mental deficiency. Similarly, XY (genetic male) individuals born without androgen sensitivity lack androgen receptors in their cells and look superficially like females. Their testes develop normally but remain in the abdominal cavity; the scrotum and penis do not develop. Other related examples are reviewed by Kimura (1999).

Other pathways are demonstrated by examining changes in brain-damaged individuals. For example, men's and women's brains differ somewhat in the degree to which functions are uni- or bilateral. Thus, after damage to the left hemisphere, women are less likely than men to suffer aphasia, and they recover more quickly, suggesting that their speech functions are more bilateral (Pizzamiglio & Mammucari, 1985). Wizemann and Pardue (2001) and Kimura (1999) review additional sex differences in disrupted development and health syndromes.

CAUSAL PATHWAYS AND LINKS

The biological bases of sex differences lie in our evolutionary past; they are not simply "genetic" or "hormonal," although genes and the resulting hormones produced mediate many sex differences. The evolutionary history of any species (including humans) underlies all, and the impact of natural selection shapes the differences that we see. Differences evolve because ecological, social, and physical/physiological factors interact in a complex way: environmental conditions (which affect the relative benefits of traits in the two sexes) result in the differential success of individuals with different genetic make-up; individuals of different genetic make-up have different hormonal profiles, and different expressions thereof.

The result is, in many species, a pattern of systematic differences between the sexes. Occasional disruptions of the normal patterns sometimes help to illuminate the general patterns. Of course, above and beyond these biological influences on sex differences, we have huge sociocultural influences (Low, 1989; Geary, 1998, Chapter 9). Although some currently observed differences in modern environments are difficult to trace to our evolutionary past (e.g., differential abilities on SAT tests), there is no doubt that evolutionarily based sex differences can, even today, affect men's and women's lives (Lubinski & Benbow, 1992; Wizemann & Pardue, 2001).

NOTE

1. Here, we follow the National Academy of Sciences (Wizemann and Pardue, 2001) in using "sex" to refer to the biologically defined categories "male" and "female"; the term "gender" will apply to individuals' self-representation and social roles.

REFERENCES

Allen, L. S., & Gorsky, R. A. (1991). Sexual dimorphism of the anterior commissure and massa intermedia of the human brain. *Journal of Comparative Neurology, 312,* 97–104.

Ankney, C. D. (1992). Sex differences in relative brain size: The mismeasure of woman, too? *Intelligence, 16,* 329–336.

Berry, J. W. (1976). *Human ecology and cognitive style: Comparative studies in cultural and psychological adaptation.* New York: Halsted Division, Wiley.

Brunner, H. G. (1996). MAOA deficiency and abnormal behavior: Perspectives on an association. *Ciba Foundation Symposium, 194,* 155–164.

Burg, A. (1966). Visual acuity as measured by dynamic and static tests. *Journal of Applied Psychology, 50,* 460–466.

Buss, D. M. (1999). *Evolutionary psychology: The new science of the mind.* Boston: Allyn & Bacon.

Caspi, A., McClay, J., Moffitt, T. E., Mill, J., Martin, J., Craig, I. W. et al. (2002). Role of genotype in the cycle of violence in maltreated children. *Science, 297*(5582), 851.

Daly, M., & Wilson, M. (1988). *Homicide.* Hawthorn, NY: Aldine DeGruyter.

Dewar, R. (1967). Sex differences in the magnitude and practice decrement of the Muller–Lyer illusion. *Psychonomic Science, 9,* 345–346.

Ember, C. (1981). A cross-cultural perspective on sex differences. In R. H. Munroe, R. L. Munroe, & B. B. Whiting (Eds.), *Handbook of cross-cultural human development* (pp. 531–580). New York: Garland Press.

Ember, C. (1996). Gender differences and roles. In D. Levinson & M. Ember (Eds.), *Encyclopedia of cultural anthropology* (Vol. 2, pp. 519–524). New York: Holt.

Engelhard, G. (1990). Gender differences in performance on mathematics items: Evidence from USA and Thailand. *Contemporary Educational Psychology, 15,* 13–15.

Freedman, D. G. (1974). *Human infancy: An evolutionary perspective.* Hillsdale, NJ: Erlbaum.

Gaulin, S. J. C., & Fitzgerald, R. W. (1986). Sex differences in spatial ability: An evolutionary hypothesis and test. *American Naturalist, 127,* 74–88.

Gaulin, S. J. C., & Hoffman, H. A. (1988). Evolution and development of sex differences in spatial ability. In L. Betzig, M. Borgerhoff Mulder, & P. Turke (Eds.), *Human reproductive behaviour: a Darwinian perspective* (pp. 129–152). Cambridge, UK: Cambridge University Press.

Geary, D. C. (1998). *Male, female: The evolution of human sex differences.* Washington, DC: American Psychological Association.

Hurst, L. D. (1991). Sex, slime, and selfish genes. *Nature, 354,* 23–24.

Hurst, L. D. (1992). Intragenomic conflict as an evolutionary force. *Proceedings of the Royal Society of London, Series B, 244,* 91–99.

Hurst, L. D., & Hamilton, W. D. (1992). Cytoplasmic fusion and the nature of sexes. *Proceedings of the Royal Society of London, Series B, 247,* 189–207.

Hyde, J. S., & Linn, M. C. (1988). Gender differences in verbal ability: A meta-analysis. *Psychological Bulletin, 104,* 53–69.

Kagan, J. (1981). Universals in human development. In R. H. Munroe, R. L. Munroe, & B. B. Whiting (Eds.), *Handbook of cross-cultural human development* (pp. 53–62). New York: Garland Press.

Kimura, D. (1996). Sex, sexual orientation and sex hormones influence human cognitive function. *Current Opinion in Neurobiology, 6,* 259–263.

Kimura, D. (1999). *Sex and cognition.* Cambridge, MA: MIT Press.

Lee, Y. H., Du, J. L., Yueh, W. S., Lin, B. Y., Huang, J. D., Lee, C. Y., et al. (2001). Sex change in the protandrous black porgy, *Acanthopagrus schlegeli*: A review in gonadal development, estradiol, estrogen receptor, aromatase activity and gonadotropin. *Journal of Experimental Zoology, 290*(7), 715–726.

LeVay, S. (1991). A difference in hypothalamic structure between heterosexual and homosexual men. *Science, 253,* 1034–1037.

Low, B. S. (1989). Cross-cultural patterns in the training of children: An evolutionary perspective. *Journal of Comparative Psychology, 103*(4), 311–319.

Low, B. S. (1990). Marriage systems and pathogen stress in human societies. *American Zoologist, 30,* 325–339.

Low, B. S. (1998). The evolution of human life histories. In C. Crawford (Ed.). *Handbook of evolutionary psychology: Behavior: Ideas, issues, and applications* (pp. 131–161). Mahwah, NJ: Erlbaum.

Low, B. S. (2000). *Why sex matters.* Princeton, NJ: Princeton University Press.

Low, B. S., Alexander, R. D., & Noonan, K. M. (1987). Evolution of human breasts and buttocks. *Ethology and Sociobiology, 8*(4), 249–258.

Low, R., & Over, R. (1993). Gender differences in solution of algebraic word problems containing irrelevant information. *Journal of Educational Psychology, 85,* 331–339.

Lubinski, D., & Benbow, C. P. (1992). Gender differences in abilities and preferences among the gifted: Implications for the math–science pipeline. *Current Directions in Psychology Science, 1,* 61–66.

Lynn, R. (1994). Sex differences in intelligence and brain size: A paradox resolved. *Personality and Individual Differences, 17,* 257–251.

Maccoby, E. E. (1998). *The two sexes: Growing up apart, coming together.* Cambridge, MA: Belnap Press of Harvard University Press.

Maynard Smith, J. (1978). *The evolution of sex.* Cambridge, UK: Cambridge University Press.

McBurney, D. H., Gaulin, S. J. C., Devineni, T., & Adams, C. (1997). Superior spatial memory of women: Stronger evidence for the gathering hypothesis. *Evolution and Human Behavior, 18,* 165–174.

McGuinness, D. (1972). Hearing: Individual differences in perceiving. *Perception, 1,* 465–473.

Mealey, L. (2000). *Sex differences: Developmental and evolutionary strategies.* San Diego: Academic Press.

Munroe, R. H., Munroe, R. L., & Brasher, A. (1971). Precursor of spatial ability: A longitudinal study among the Logoli of Kenya. *Journal of Social Psychology, 125*(1), 23–33.

Munroe, R. H., Munroe, R. L., & Bresler, A. (1985). Precursors of spatial ability: A longitudinal study among the Logoli of Kenya. *Journal of Social Psychology, 125,* 23–33.

Munroe, R. L., Hulefeld, R., Rodgers, J. M., Tomeo, D. L., & Yamazaki, S. K. (2000). Aggression among children in four cultures. *Cross-Cultural Research, 34*(1), 3–25.

Munroe, R. L., & Munroe, R. H. (1975). *Cross-cultural human development.* Monterey, CA.: Brooks/Cole.

Pizzamiglio, L., & Mammucari, A. (1985). Evidence for sex differences in brain organization in recovery in aphasia. *Brain & Language, 25,* 213–223.

Ridley, M. (1993). *The Red Queen: Sex and the evolution of human nature.* New York: Viking.

Shine, R. (1999). Why is sex determined by nest temperature in many reptiles? *Trends in Ecology and Evolution (TREE)*, *14*(5), 186–189.

Silverman, I., & Eals, M. (1992). Sex differences in spatial abilities: evolutionary theory and data. In J. H. Barkow, L. Cosmides, & J. Tooby (Eds.), *The adapted mind* (pp. 533–549). New York: Oxford.

Silverman, I., & Phillips, K. (1998). The evolutionary psychology of spatial sex differences. In C. Crawford, J. Anderson, & D. Krebs (Eds.), *Handbook of evolutionary psychology: Ideas, issues and applications* (pp. 595–612). Hillsdale, NJ: Erlbaum.

Singh, D. (1993). Adaptive significance of waist-to-hip ratio and female physical attractiveness. *Journal of Personality and Social Psychology*, *65*, 293–307.

Singh, D., & Luis, S. (1995). Ethnic and gender consensus for the effect of waist-to-hip ratio on judgements of women's attractiveness. *Human Nature*, *6*, 51–65.

Velle, W. (1987). Sex differences in sensory functions. *Perspectives in Biology and Medicine*, *30*, 490–522.

Vilain, E., & McCabe, E. R. B. (1998). Mammalian sex determination: From gonads to brain. *Molecular Genetics and Metabolism, 65*, 74–84.

Warner, R. R., Harlan, K., & Leigh, E. G. (1975). Sex change and sexual selection. *Science*, *190*, 633–638.

Williams, G. C. (1975). *Sex and evolution*. Princeton, NJ: Princeton University Press.

Witkin, H. A. (1967). A cognitive style approach to cross-cultural research. *International Journal of Psychology*, *2*, 233–250.

Wizemann, T. M., & Pardue, M.-L. (Eds.). (2001). *Exploring biological contributions to human health: Does sex matter?* Washington, DC: National Academy Press.

Socialization of Boys and Girls in Natural Contexts

Carolyn Pope Edwards, Lisa Knoche, and Asiye Kumru

INTRODUCTION

Socialization is the general process by which the members of a cultural community or society pass on their language, rules, roles, and customary ways of thinking and behaving to the next generation. Sex role socialization is one important aspect of this general process. In common language, socialization means something like "learning to function in a social setting," as in "socialization of children in child care." This usage implies that the young children acquire social competence through the concerted efforts of adults, who carefully train and mold them to behave appropriately (thus we also speak of "puppy socialization"). In the social sciences, however, the meaning of "socialization" is more complex and does not carry the implication that children are simply the passive recipients or objects of the socialization process.

Rather, in recent years, concepts of socialization in general, and sex role socialization in particular, have been transformed along both theoretical and empirical dimensions. The theoretical aspect includes efforts to integrate social learning and cognitivist perspectives through a focus on self-socialization. Self-socialization can be defined as the process whereby children influence the direction and outcomes of their own development through selective attention, imitation, and participation in particular activities and modalities of interaction that function as key contexts of socialization. For example, many children prefer to observe and imitate same-gender models rather than the opposite gender, and to interact and participate in gender-typical activities. The empirical aspect of the reconceptualization of socialization thus involves a renewed focus on context. Whereas earlier studies of behavioral sex differences typically involved appraising individual behavioral dispositions across contexts, the new approach seeks ways to understand behavior within specific relational interactions and activity settings (e.g., the conversation of boys and girls in small or large groups) or in settings with children of mixed-age (e.g., in neighborhood games) versus the same age group (e.g., classmates at school).

Thus the goals of earlier work were to understand how, why, and at what age girls and boys begin to vary behaviorally along such dimensions as "nurturance," "aggression," and "dependency," including determination of how sex-typical dispositions are influenced by cultural factors. In contrast, the new approach seeks to answer such questions as the following. How are different kinds of gender-specific social behaviors called out or elicited by different contexts of socialization? How are gender differences influenced by children's relationship to their social companions—for example, their gender, age, status, and kinship relationship? How are gender differences influenced by different activity contexts (e.g., school, work, play) that we know are differentially distributed across cultural communities, depending on such factors as adult subsistence strategies, leisure patterns, family structures, household organizations, and forms of social networks? Finally, how are gender differences affected by where children are found, their location in space (e.g., distance from home)?

CHILDREN'S COMPANIONSHIP: AGE, GENDER, AND KINSHIP

Children's companions are those individuals whom they watch, imitate, and interact with in natural settings of home, school, neighborhood, and community. These social partners influence children's emerging gender expectations through face-to-face relationships in which children give and receive care, help, instruction, support, and cooperation, or where they engage in dominance struggles, conflicts, arguments, and fights. As they interact with different companions, children learn to discriminate the different categories of people in society, such as infants, elders, older versus younger siblings, extended family, household guests and visitors, and passers-by.

To understand the different socialization experiences of boys and girls, it is important to know what factors possibly influence children's companionship. Children around the world have different opportunities with respect to social companions. Their cultural community, developmental age, gender, and kinship composition strongly determine the company they keep. Cultural community shapes children's companionship through such macro features as the following: geographic layout, settlement pattern, cooperative networks, household composition, and age/gender division of labors (Whiting & Edwards, 1988). For instance, in a community where the mother's primary responsibilities keep her in the vicinity of the house and adjacent garden areas, while the father's work takes him to a nearby town, the mother's companionship would necessarily be more salient to young children during the day than would the father's. In a community where families live in extended families with bilateral kinship, they will often have many houses where they can freely visit and play and a wide variety of cousins from both sides of their family with whom to interact.

Children's age has a strong influence on their choice of companions, much more so than does their gender in the early years. Age-related changes in children's physical, social, and intellectual capacities are necessarily related to changes in their social settings and their companions. For example, infants and toddlers require constant supervision and show dependency behaviors such as seeking comfort, protection, and food from the primary caregiver or designated guardians. They are more likely to be in the company of mothers or other female adults (grandmothers, aunts, or hired caregivers) rather than male adults in almost all cultural communities.

Preschool-age children expand their capabilities to do more things with more companions in a widening variety of settings (Garbarino & Gilliam, 1980). They can now have younger as well as older companions in their playgroup, and they begin to learn about their position in the "pecking order" of childhood. As they become aware of their gender identity, they begin to show preferences for same-sex playmates and their cross-gender interaction decreases in settings when they can choose their companions, as at preschool or childcare.

During middle childhood, the experiences of children in different communities become even more divergent according to gender, as well as according to educational opportunities. In cultures where schooling is present for both girls and boys, children experience the very important transition of moving from a more home-centered to a more school-centered existence. School-age children interact frequently with same-age peers, the majority of whom are not kin, during half the daylight hours. At this age, children seem to seek interaction with companions who are not their family members but who are like them in other ways. They may show avoidant or exclusive behavior toward children not of their gender, especially when they are playing in large groups (Whiting & Edwards, 1988). Research shows that children's play in these single-gender groups involves high proportions of both egoistic conflict and sociability/play behaviors, as if the children are using the group as a "laboratory" for learning how to negotiate and get along with peers in the culturally approved masculine or feminine way (Maccoby, 1998).

The age gap between the children and their companions is also important. When children interact with children who are older than they are by 3 or more years, they tend to display certain dependency behaviors (seeking proximity, exchanging information/inquiring, and watching/imitating) (Whiting & Edwards, 1988). Toddlers and preschool-aged children seem especially motivated to imitate the behavior of older children, and learn much from contact with older siblings. When older children interact with younger and smaller children, they are much more likely to take on a dominant style of interaction than they are when they are with peers or older persons. Older children (especially boys) tend to decrease their contact with female family adults once they begin to attend school, but their contact with fathers may actually increase in communities where sons are allowed to help their fathers in work (Whiting & Whiting, 1975).

Thus children's gender interacts with their age in influencing their preferred patterns of companionship. Throughout the world's cultures and subcultures, gender segregation for play and leisure are seen during the years of middle childhood. The same-gender peer play seems to appear around age 3 years (Hartup, 1983; Jacklin & Maccoby, 1978), and to become predominant during the ages of 6–9 (Feiring & Lewis, 1989; Whiting & Edwards, 1988). These patterns may reflect in part the child's own preferences for friends and playmates (self-socialization) as well as their parents' and other institutions' structuring of the social environment (Cochran & Riley, 1987).

Children tend to compare their appearance, skills, and behavior with their same-gender peers who are close in age to them. Thus, interacting with same-gender companions may help them to establish gender identity and roles. However, girls usually have more access to adult females than boys do to adult males in their daily settings (Whiting & Edwards, 1988). As a result, boys seem to seek out interaction with boys who are older than themselves, who may serve as models. Boys have more daily contact with male playmates in their dyadic settings than girls do with girl playmates (Feiring & Lewis, 1989).

Finally, the organization of people in space and the social structure of households and neighborhoods affect the availability of kin versus non-kin companionship for children. For instance, in communities where children are restricted to the home environment, their main companions are usually their siblings and cousins, as observed among Abaluyia children of Kisa, Kenya (Weisner, 1984). Instead, where they have more autonomy to explore the neighborhood and more access to communal play areas or schools, they have more contact with nonrelatives and more chances to divide themselves into gender- and age-segregated playgroups, as is common in North America. In a study of United States social networks, Feiring and Lewis (1989) found that children aged 3, 6, and 9 years had a greater number and more daily contacts with nonkin than with kin. With increasing age, children significantly increased the number of kin with whom they were in contact, but they decreased nonsignificantly in their frequency of daily contact. Though boys and girls were not different in the proportion of kin versus nonkin with whom they were in contact, an increasing trend found that, with age, girls had more daily contact with kin than did boys.

CHILDREN'S ACTIVITIES

Activity settings allow children around the world to try out and experience different kinds of roles and occupations and to learn to navigate social relations with family and peers. As children move around different settings, they encounter different opportunities for work, play, learning, and sociability, and come in contact with different standing patterns of behavior and toys, objects, and natural materials to be manipulated. Boys and girls may or may not engage in the same sorts of activities, resulting in divergent socialization processes. A general review of the literature finds that parents behave surprisingly similarly in their explicit treatment of sons versus daughters, for example, in the rules they enforce (Maccoby and Jacklin, 1974). However, they do assign boys and girls to different settings (e.g., work vs. play) and encourage different patterns of companionship (e.g., time spent in mixed-age groups containing infants). Perhaps it is the cumulative effect of these large and small differences in task assignments, work, and play experiences that result

in divergence of socialization experiences and outcomes for boys and girls (Morelli & Tronick, 1991).

Children's activities in rural subsistence communities are often focused on responsible work (e.g., cleaning, gardening, herding, childcare), whereas in contemporary industrial communities, children are often put into organized play settings (e.g., preschools, schools, and after-school programs). Around the world, girls and boys engage in different proportions of work versus play (Whiting & Edwards, 1988), and these differences contribute to the gender-socialization process.

Activities can be thought of as "directed" or "undirected" (Munroe et al., 1983; Munroe, Munroe, & Shimmin, 1984). Directed activities are ones that are specifically assigned to children by an authority figure, perhaps a parent or older sibling. They include such things as caring for younger siblings, household work, and errands outside the home. The age at which children are directed toward particular activities depends upon their society. In communities where women take a leading role in subsistence work, children (but especially girls) are recruited by their mothers to take on more responsible tasks at a younger age (Edwards & Whiting, in press). In communities where boys can be easily incorporated into the work of the adult men (hunting, fishing, farming), and where that work is time consuming and labor intensive, boys move relatively early into work roles. Undirected activities are less structured, leaving the child to set the course for the event, as for example in free play or idle sociability. Both directed and undirected activities can be identified across cultural contexts, and both contribute to gender role development.

In a study of Australian youth aged 6–7 years, boys were found to be more engaged in competitive sports, and girls in ballet and dance (Russell & Russell, 1992). In many studies (e.g., Edwards, 2000), girls have been more often observed playing with dolls, handling household objects, and participating in dress-up and art activities. Their play activities and toy preferences more often focus on domestic roles and nurturance. In contrast, boys are often found playing with store-bought or handmade vehicles, weapons, building materials, sports equipment, or other objects considered culturally masculine. In Senegal, the pretend play of girls focuses on domestic activities over the course of childhood; boys engage in domestic pretend play at age 2, but increasingly turn to themes involving transportation and hunting as they get older (Bloch & Adler, 1994).

Types of play vary considerably by context. A reanalysis of the Six Culture data found that in locations where work predominated over play, all children were relatively unlikely to engage in fantasy play, perhaps because they were enacting such scenarios in real life. For example, instead of playing with dolls, young children could care for infant siblings, tend their household fire, and handle sharp cooking tools (Edwards, 2000). Furthermore, in communities where children had freedom to venture beyond the bounds of the immediate home and yard, they engaged in considerable amounts of creative–constructive play (e.g., building dams, making whistles and mud pies out of natural materials, and creating slingshots). The most "playful" children were found in Taira, Okinawa, where their workloads were light and they were supervised by all of the village adults collectively, giving them considerable freedom to move around the village (Edwards, 2000).

In some cultures, gender roles are impressed upon young children through directed, often work-related, activities. Through work, children can learn adult roles and skills (Nsamenang, 1992). In the Children of Different Worlds project, boys as young as age 4 years were trained to care for livestock (Whiting & Edwards, 1988). In fact, animal care was generally a male task, especially with large animals such as cattle or water buffalo. In Rogoff's (1981) study of Guatemalan children, children were beginning to perform gender-specific work tasks by age 5 or 6, with boys gathering firewood and feeding animals, and girls running errands and doing cleaning. This same division of labor was noted for an American middle-class sample (Bloch & Walsh, 1985), where girls at age 5–6 years were directed to perform more housework, and again in a Caribbean sample of youth (Lange & Rodman, 1992). Likewise, in a study of Senegalese children, girls were assigned more responsible work than boys starting at age 5 and 6 years (Bloch & Adler, 1994). Certainly, however, children's work is not always gender specific. Mothers with heavy workloads recruit both sons and daughters to help (e.g., with gardening), and in households where there is no child of the appropriate gender to perform a gender-specific activity, children may be expected to cross over and do opposite-gender chores; for example, boys will clean or care for infants, and girls will tend to animals or repair fishing equipment (Ember, 1973; Lange & Rodman, 1992).

Task assignment is thus a strong influence of the socialization process. Ember (1981) describes task assignment as an unconscious effort on the part of caretakers to transmit gender-specific information. For example, mothers in Senegal were found to be more likely to ask girls than boys to do work, and more likely to pull girls away from their play activities to perform responsible work (Bloch & Adler, 1994). Across societies, girls are generally engaged in more responsible work than boys (Whiting & Edwards, 1973). In a West African community, girls aged 8–10 years were often found caring for younger siblings, family members, and neighbor children (Nsamenang, 1992). In most cultures, females continue to be seen as responsible for children, and as young females become adults they expect to take on responsibility for children (Best & Williams, 1997).

In sum, cultures around the world socialize boys and girls, through both direct and indirect means, to understand their gender role in society. The work activities of children reflect gender differences, with girls engaged in more household tasks and responsibilities than boys. Leisure and play activities between the sexes also vary, with girls focusing more on domestic scenarios and nurturance, and boys engaging in competitive and large-motor activities. Socialization through these activities, while discrete, generally results in separate societal rules and roles for the sexes. The activities in which children engage—both work and leisure—provide important learning opportunities for children, to help them become knowledgeable, informed participants in their culture.

THE SETTINGS OF SOCIALIZATION

Just as the activities in which children engage contribute to gender socialization, *where* children work and play also has important implications. The settings in which children spend their time shape those behaviors they can observe, try out, rehearse, and master. The impact on socialization is directly related to the *strength* of the setting. Some contexts of development are considered "strong" and other situations "weak" (Snyder & Ickes, 1985). In strong contexts, the range of behaviors that an individual is permitted to display is limited. The situation almost dictates the individual's response. Weak contexts allow more variability; the situation does not demand a specific behavioral or emotional response. With regard to gender socialization, many social situations are relatively strong, particularly for older children who are more aware of gender stereotypes and expectations. These strong contexts demand gender-appropriate behaviors, whereas weak-context environments allow children more flexibility in behaving outside or beyond the bounds of gender constraints.

Girls and boys tend to occupy different locations in space, along with some shared venues (Maccoby, 1998). In general, boys tend to play outdoors and in relatively large groups. When possible, they combine undirected play with their work, for example, interspersing rough-housing and chasing games with tending animals in the fields. Girls are more likely to be found playing with two to three peers in an indoor setting, or assisting inside with household chores, or outside performing errands such as going to the market or getting water or fuel. Girls also spice up their work with fun, especially through conversation, games, or singing. They engage in conversations more readily than boys do, while boys engage in more physical activity (Best & Williams, 1997).

The school setting can be seen as both a "strong" and "weak" context for gender behaviors, depending on the specific location. For example, the cafeteria is a strong context, where boys and girls separate to different tables if given the choice. Likewise, on the playground, boy and girl groups take over separate spaces. Girls usually play around the periphery of the playground, while boys occupy a larger more central space. In fact, boys take up 10 times more space on the playground and often invade girls' activities (Maccoby, 1998; Thorne, 1994). The Children of Different Worlds project found that in societies where all the boys and girls go to school together, same-gender interaction was very high during free play, thereby resulting in more gender segregation than was generally found in the homes and neighborhoods (Whiting & Edwards, 1988). Within the classroom, however, creative and constructive activities, such as art, manipulatives, and dramatic play, can promote gender integration. For instance, in a social studies project, boys and girls can work cooperatively on tasks and are more likely to over-look gender differences than outside in the playground. The teacher's presence can attract both girls and boys to circle around nearby, causing them to mingle and interact.

Neighborhoods are generally "weaker" contexts than school settings with respect to gender roles. Owing to the limited number of playmates available, they often promote play that is mixed as to gender and age, and many favorite group games (such as "hide-and-seek," kick ball, and tag) attract children of all ages, boys and girls equally. Cross-gender play is also common when children collect in small groups or pairs, and when children have known one

another for a long period of time and have built up trust and friendship. The more children are present in a space, and the more unfamiliar they are with one another, the more likely they will segregate based on gender.

The Children of Different Worlds spot observations revealed boys to be generally farther from home than were girls, in contexts that are considered weak in regard to gender socialization but strong in terms of peer pressure. Girls' movement away from the home was restricted in some societies, and they left the home area most often when following a predictable path doing a "directed" chore such as gathering water, collecting firewood, or going to the shop (Whiting & Edwards, 1988). Boys had more freedom to wander beyond the home environment in undirected play where they were less accountable to figures of authority and perhaps more free to experiment in their behavior and follow their curiosity. On the other hand, we know from other research that when boys play together in groups, they strongly pressure one another toward what they consider masculine behavior (by ridiculing boys who do not measure up) (Carter & McCloskey, 1984; Fagot, 1984). Thus, boys turn their free play away from home into strong contexts for gender role socialization.

The Children of Different Worlds project found that during directed activities, boys were found farther from home than girls in four of the six communities, and these differences were maintained during undirected play. In fact, it was during undirected activities that gender differences were maximized. Boys spent more time in locations and activities (such as rough-and-tumble play) that accentuated gender differences. Girls were generally nearer the home environment, more often engaged in directed activities with specific task or supervision responsibilities, interspersed with undirected intervals of leisure and socializing.

CHILDREN'S BEHAVIOR: NURTURANCE, DEPENDENCY, PROSOCIAL ACTS, AND AGGRESSION

In this final section, we discuss four categories of child behavior (nurturance, dependency, prosocial acts, and aggression) that appear at an early age and are important outcomes of the kinds of socialization processes we have described. Children's behavior seems to have certain similar characteristics across cultures because of their universal developmentally-based needs and desires. However, there are also important differences tied to cultural experiences. All four categories of behavior are particularly reciprocal in the child's dyadic interaction with their companions, and they are subjected to a cultural channeling that specifies under what circumstances and to whom the child can display them.

Nurturance can be defined as offering help and support to an individual who is in a state of need. Although there are variations in the styles and situations in which it is expected to express nurturance, it is a recognizable universal across culture. With age, children are more capable of perceiving, understanding, and meeting others' needs and wants, and then responding to them. For example, they learn how to offer food to distract a crying toddler or how to encourage a friend with a smile.

In almost all societies, infants and toddlers receive higher proportions of nurturance than do older children because of their relative helplessness and vulnerability as well as their cute and endearing physical characteristics (Braten, 1996; Edwards, 1986, 1993; Whiting & Edwards, 1988). Infant crying seems to elicit nurturance behavior from even very young children (Zahn-Waxler, Friedman, & Cummings, 1983). When infants grow older and become more mobile, independent, and demanding, they still need to be watched, protected, and instructed. However, toddlers are in many ways harder to care for than infants. They are still small and defenseless, but they seem to elicit many prosocially dominant behaviors from others (for instance, commands to desist from dangerous and annoying behaviors, and suggestions about how to eat their food properly) rather than the pure nurturance behavior that they formerly received (Whiting, 1983; Whiting & Edwards, 1988).

Both older boys and girls tend to be highly nurturing toward babies. However, girls are more nurturing than boys to toddlers, other children, and adults (Whiting & Edwards, 1988). In most societies, girls are assigned as caretakers of babies and have more opportunity to practice nurturance than do boys. Girls are more frequently in the company of their mothers and more eager to imitate the maternal role. In their play, girls are more likely to act out scenes from familiar settings, such as the home and school where they can rehearse and create domestic roles involving nurturing interpersonal relationships and nurturance (Edwards, Knoche, & Kumru, 2001). Thus, girls seem to have more opportunities in everyday life to practice nurturance than do boys.

Dependency behavior can be described as seeking help, attention, permission, information, emotional support, or material resources. Because of the helplessness of the human infant, dependency behavior is strong at the beginning of life and is elicited and rewarded by caretaking adults at least some of the time. One would expect that the dependency would then decrease as the child becomes more mature and competent. However, research has documented no clear-cut changes in age in overall levels of dependency behavior during childhood. Maccoby and Masters (1970) discussed these findings with reference to the different types of dependent behaviors. They noted that clinging and proximity-seeking behavior decrease with age, while help- and attention-seeking behavior remain high. Similarly, Whiting and Edwards (1988) suggest that a child's dependency tendencies toward mother does not so much decrease as change in style from early to middle childhood. Children's preferred style tends to shift from more physical and intimate modes toward ones like help, attention, information, and permission-seeking that rely on verbal skills and help them act in accord with cultural values. Thus, children's dependency changes in format with age, becoming less intimate and proximal, but it does not disappear.

Findings on gender differences in child's dependency are decidedly mixed. Luo boys from Kenya were observed to exhibit significantly more dependency behavior than were the girls (Ember, 1973). However, many studies from Western and non-Western societies have shown little or no sex differences in overall dependency behavior (Maccoby & Jacklin, 1974; Whiting & Edwards, 1973). Ember (1981) suggested that girls and boys might exhibit different types of dependency behavior. For instance, in the Six Cultures data, girls tended to seek help and physical contact more than boys in the 3–6-year-old age range, but boys seemed to seek attention and material goods more than girls once they were about 7 years old (Edwards & Whiting, 1974).

Prosocial behavior can be described as voluntary acts intending to meet the needs of others. Prosocial behavior tends to increase with age because of developmental changes in children's cognitive, socio-emotional, and physical competence (Eisenberg & Fabes, 1998). In most societies, children are expected to carry more responsibility at home as they become mature and to display more prosocial acts. Studies with Western and non-Western samples show that older children displayed higher proportions of prosocial behaviors compared with their younger peers (Eisenberg, 1992; Eisenberg & Fabes, 1998; Whiting & Edwards, 1973, 1988; de Guzman, Edwards, & Carlo, 2002).

Socialization pressures and learning might play an important role in children's prosocial tendencies. From toddlerhood on, children experience socialization pressure to learn the rudiments of prosocial behavior (Whiting & Edwards, 1988). In cultures where children have more opportunities to interact with infants, they seem to acquire capacities for prosocial behavior naturally and smoothly. Likewise, where they grow up in the company of elders who need their assistance, they learn prosocial values about respect and care of the very old.

Literature about gender differences in prosocial behavior has produced mixed conclusions. For example, studies conducted in contemporary Western societies suggest that girls seem to perform more prosocial behavior than boys, at least during late childhood and adolescence (Eisenberg & Fabes, 1998). Barry, Bacon, and Child (1957) found that socialization pressure toward nurturance, obedience, and responsibilities was much higher for girls than for boys across 110 societies. However, some studies have produced contrary results. For example, de Guzman et al. (2002) found no gender differences in prosocial behaviors for the Gikuyu children of Ngecha, Kenya; for these children, social contexts of work and childcare proved to be strong socialization settings that elicited high levels of prosocial behavior from both boys and girls.

Finally, *aggression* can be defined as satisfying the actor's own needs through an ascendant or commanding style that inflicts some kind of injury or loss of resources to the other. Although psychologists continue to debate about whether aggression is innate or learned, research has documented that positive reinforcement and permissive conditions increase the level of aggressive behaviors. Indeed, Western research shows that parents who reward and encourage aggression seem to have aggressive children (Bandura & Walters, 1963). The same is true of mothers in non-Western societies, who have high levels of controlling and reprimanding behavior and who uphold children's dominant/aggressive and insulting behaviors to meet their egoistic needs (Whiting & Edwards, 1988). Indeed, societies where people value and reward aggression produce highly aggressive individuals (Chagnon, 1968; Ember & Ember, 1994). Punitive socialization promotes rather than decreases children's hostility and aggression (Zigler & Child, 1969). This can occur in cultural communities with extended family households where outward aggression cannot be tolerated with so many people living together (Harrington & Whiting, 1972).

Whiting and Edwards (1988) found that physical teasing, assaulting, and insulting occured at similar levels whether older children are interacting with younger ones, or vice versa. However, there was also very consistent evidence of gender differences in aggression, and this has been confirmed across both Western and non-Western societies. Past about age 3, boys generally show more aggression than girls (Maccoby & Jacklin, 1974; Whiting & Edwards, 1973).

Children seem to come into the world with similar but not identical endowments for dyadic interaction across cultures. Cultural scripts in many societies then set girls and boys on different courses by exaggerating, reducing, or redirecting any emerging gender differences through the mechanisms of constraining the company that children keep, the activities they perform, and the locations in which they spend their time. Children too are active in their own gender socialization and, whenever they can, make predictable choices about whom they will observe and imitate, how, where, and with whom they will play, and when and how they will contribute to the care of others and the useful work needed to carry on daily life in their community.

REFERENCES

Bandura, A., & Walters, R. H. (1963). Aggression. In H. W. Stevenson (Ed.), *Child psychology. The sixty-second yearbook of the National Society for Education* (pp. 364–415). Chicago: University of Chicago Press.

Barry, H., Bacon, M. K., & Child, I. L. (1957). A cross-cultural survey of some sex differences in socialization. *Journal of Abnormal Psychology, 55,* 327–332.

Best, D., & Williams, J. (1997). Sex, gender and culture. In J. W. Berry, M. H. Seagall, & C. Kagitcibasi (Eds.), *Handbook of cross-cultural psychology* (Vol. 3) (pp. 163–212). Boston, MA: Allyn & Bacon.

Bloch, M. N., & Adler, S. M. (1994). African children's play and the emergence of the sexual division of labor. In J. L. Roopnarine, J. E. Johnson, & F. H. Hooper (Eds.), *Children's play in diverse cultures* (pp. 148–178). Albany, NY: State University of New York Press.

Bloch, M. N., & Walsh, D. (1985). Young children's activities at home: Age and sex differences in activity, location, and social context. *Children's Environment Quarterly, 2*(2), 34–40.

Braten, S. (1996). When toddlers provide care: Infants' companion space. *Childhood, 3,* 449–465.

Carter, D. B., & McCloskey, L. A. (1984). Peers and the maintenance of sex-typed behavior: The development of children's conceptions of cross-gender behavior in their peers. *Social Cognition, 2,* 294–314.

Chagnon, N. A. (1968). *Yanomamo*. New York: Holt, Rinehart, and Winston.

Cochran, M. M., & Riley, D. (1987). Mother's reports of children's social relations: Agents, concomitants and consequences. In J. Antrobus, S. Salzinger, & M. Hamner (Eds.), *Social networks of children, adolescents and college students*. Hillsdale, NJ: Erlbaum.

de Guzman, M. R. T., Edwards, C. P., & Carlo, G. (2002, July). Prosocial behaviors in context: A study of the Gikuyu children of Ngecha, Kenya. Poster session presented at the biennial meeting of the International Society for the Study of Behavioral Development, Ontario, Ottawa, Canada.

Edwards, C. P. (1986). Another style of competence: The caregiving child. In A. Fogel & G. F. Melson (Eds.), *Origins of nurturance: Developmental, biological, and cultural perspectives on caregiving*. Hillsdale, NJ: Erlbaum.

Edwards, C. P. (1993). Behavioral sex differences in children of diverse cultures: The case of nurturance to infants. In M. E. Pereira & L. A. Fairbanks (Eds.), *Juvenile primates: Life history, development, and behavior*. New York: Oxford University Press.

Edwards, C. P. (2000). Children's play in cross-cultural perspective: A new look at the Six Cultures study. *Cross-Cultural Research, 34*, 318–338.

Edwards, C. P., Knoche, L., & Kumru, A. (2001). Play patterns and gender. *Encyclopedia of Women and Gender, 2*, 809–815.

Edwards, C. P., & Whiting, B. B. (1974). Women and dependency. *Politics and Society, 4*, 343–355.

Edwards, C. P., & Whiting, B. B. (Eds.), (in press). *Ngecha: A Kenyan community in a time of rapid social change*. Lincoln, NE: University of Nebraska Press.

Eisenberg, N. (1992). *The caring child*. In A. Kamiloff-Smith, & M. Cole (Eds.), *The developing child*. Cambridge, MA: Harvard University Press.

Eisenberg, N., & Fabes, R. A. (1998). Prosocial development. In W. Damon (Series Ed.) & N. Eisenberg (Vol. Ed.), *Handbook of child psychology; Vol. 4. Social and personality development* (5th ed., pp. 701–778). New York: Wiley.

Ember, C. (1973). Feminine task assignment and social behavior of boys. *Ethos, 1*, 424–439.

Ember, C. (1981). A cross-cultural perspective on sex differences. In R. H. Munroe, R. L. Munroe, & B. B. Whiting (Eds.), *Handbook of cross-cultural development*. New York: Garland STPM Press.

Ember, C. R., & Ember, M. (1994). War, socialization, and interpersonal violence: A cross-cultural study. *Journal of Conflict Resolution, 38*, 620–646.

Fagot, B. I. (1984). The child's expectations of differences in adult male and female interactions. *Sex Roles, 11* (7/8), 593–600.

Feiring, C., & Lewis, M. (1989). The social network of girls and boys from early through middle childhood. In D. Belle (Ed.), *Children's social networks and social supports*. New York: Wiley.

Garbarino, J., & Gilliam, G. (1980). *Understanding abusive families*, Lexington, MA: Lexington Books.

Harrington, C., & Whiting, J. W. M. (1972). Socialization process and personality. In F. L. K. Hsu (Ed.), *Psychological anthropology* (New ed., pp. 469–508). Cambridge, MA: Schenkman.

Hartup, W. (1983). Peer relations. In P. H. Mussen (Series Ed.) & E. M. Hetherington (Vol. Ed.), *Handbook of child psychology: Vol 4. Socialization, personality and social development*. New York: Wiley.

Jacklin, C. N., & Maccoby, E. (1978). Social behavior at 33 months in same-sex and mixed-sex dyads. *Child Development, 49*, 557–569.

Lange, G., & Rodman, H. (1992). Family relationships and patterns of childrearing in the Caribbean. In I. E. Sigel (Series Ed.) & J. L. Roopnarine & D. B. Carter (Vol. Ed.), *Annual advances in applied developmental psychology: Vol. 5. Parent–child socialization in diverse cultures* (pp. 185–198). Norwood, NJ: Ablex.

Maccoby, E. E. (1998). *The two sexes: Growing up apart: Coming together*. Cambridge, MA: Harvard University Press.

Maccoby, E. E., & Jacklin, C. N. (1974). *The psychology of sex differences*. Stanford, CA: Stanford University Press.

Maccoby, E. E., & Masters, J. C. (1970). Attachment and dependency. In P. H. Mussen (Vol. Ed.), *Carmichael's manual of child psychology* (Vol 2, pp. 73–157). New York: Wiley.

Morelli, G. A., & Tronick, E. Z. (1991). Parenting and child development in the Efe foragers and Lese farmers of Zaire. In M. H. Bornstein (Ed.), *Cultural approaches to parenting* (pp. 91–114). Hillsdale, NJ: Erlbaum.

Munroe, R. H., Munroe, R. L., Michelson, C., Keol, A., Bolton, R., & Bolton, C. (1983). Time allocation in four societies. *Ethnology, 22*, 355–370.

Munroe, R. H., Munroe, R. L., & Shimmin, H. S. (1984). Children's work in four cultures: determinants and consequences. *American Anthropologist, 86*, 369–379.

Nsamenang, A. (1992). *Human development in cultural context: a third world perspective* (pp. 149–157). Newbury Park, CA: Sage.

Rogoff (1981). Adults and peers as agents of socialization. *Ethics, 9*, 18–36.

Russell, A., & Russell, G. (1992). The socialization of Australian boys and girls in middle childhood for independence and achievement. In I. E. Sigel (Series Ed.) & J. L. Roopnarine & D. B. Carter (Vol. Ed.), *Annual advances in applied developmental psychology: Vol. 5. Parent–child socialization in diverse cultures* (pp. 53–74). Norwood, NJ: Ablex.

Snyder, M., & Ickes, W. (1985). Personality and social behavior. In G. Lindzey & E. Aronson (Eds.), *Handbook of social psychology: Vol. 2. Research methods* (3rd ed., pp. 883–947). New York: Random House.

Thorne, B. (1994). *Gender play: Girls and boys in school*. New Brunswick, NJ: Rutgers University Press.

Weisner, T. (1984). The social ecology of childhood: A cross cultural view. In M. Lewis (Ed.), *Beyond the dyad*. New York: Plenum.

Whiting, B. B. (1983). The genesis of prosocial behavior. In D. L. Bridgeman (Ed.), *The nature of prosocial development* (pp. 221–242).

Whiting, B. B., & Edwards, C. P. (1973). A cross-cultural analysis of sex differences in the behavior of children aged 3–11. *Journal of Social Psychology, 91*, 171–188.

Whiting, B. B., & Edwards, C. P. (1988). *Children of different worlds: The formation of social behavior*. Cambridge, MA: Harvard University Press.

Whiting, B., & Whiting, J. (1975). *Children of six cultures: A psycho-cultural analysis*. Cambridge, MA: Harvard University Press.

Zahn-Waxler, C., Friedman, S. L., & Cummings, E. M. (1983). Children's emotions and behaviors in response to infants' cries. *Child Development, 54*, 1522–1528.

Zigler, E., & Child, I. L. (1969). Socialization. In G. Lindzey & E. Aronson (Ed.), *The handbook of social psychology* (2nd ed., Vol. 3, pp. 450–589). Reading, MA: Addison-Wesley.

Adolescence

Glenn E. Weisfeld

INTRODUCTION

This article constitutes an attempt to provide some illustrations of how the integration of biological and cultural factors is proceeding with regard to the topic of adolescence and gender. It will begin with a survey of some theories and research methodologies used in studying the prevalence, causation, and function of a given behavior or sex difference. Next, human adolescence will be described and analyzed functionally, with special attention to sex differences of puberty and puberty rites. Sex differences in adolescent family relations, labor, and mate choice will then be addressed. Some illustrative individual and cultural differences in these general patterns will also be analyzed. The article, then, will take a functional approach in attempting to explain why particular sex differences in behavior occur in adolescence.

THEORIES

Understanding sex differences and sexual behavior in adolescence requires some comprehension of adolescence as it occurs throughout the world. Statements restricted to adolescence in the West or in industrialized societies beg the question of whether or not they are also true of adolescence elsewhere, whether or not they are universal, and, if so, whether or not they are true of adolescence in other primate species as well.

It goes without saying that human behavior is exceedingly flexible, but this does not mean that it has no evolved basis and is entirely learned. Consistent with the fact that humans share 99% of their genes, universal behaviors and sex differences have been reported (Brown, 1991; Friedl, 1975; Mealey, 2000; Schlegel & Barry, 1991; van den Berghe, 1979). Even adolescents living in post-industrial society, an environment far removed from the African savannah in which hominids evolved, generally retain the evolved behavioral propensities of the Pleistocene era since 99% of our genes are still the same. Therefore it should be possible to find a core of adolescent behavioral tendencies in any normal population, albeit with some individual exceptions. Once a general species-wide characteristic of adolescence is identified, it can then be analyzed functionally to learn why it has stood the test of time. General statements about adolescence, to the extent that they can be established, will provide a functional framework for viewing this stage of life.

On the other hand, it is important not to overgeneralize, to see consistency where it does not exist. Variability exists, and is due mainly to differences in socialization by family and culture, not genetic differences between populations. Various theories have arisen to explain these socialization influences, including the social cognitive theory of gender, which stresses observation and imitation, and cognitive developmental theory, which emphasizes one's self-concept as male or female. Gender schema theory recognizes an internal (evolved?) motive to conform with culturally based gender expectations. This cultural variability is widely acknowledged by evolutionists, but until recently evoked little attention from them. In the past decade or so, however, evolutionists have begun trying to explain some of this variability by invoking the concept of biological function. As in the case of a particular species, individuals and populations must exhibit behavior that enhances their survival and reproduction. A given practice can be interpreted in functional terms whether it arises because of natural selection or cultural selection. If a particular trait is adaptive in the species as a whole, given enough geological time, it will evolve genetic supports and come to have an evolved basis (the *Baldwin effect*). If the trait is adaptive only locally, culture will usually support it. The neural basis of culture and learning evolved to permit rapid behavioral adjustments to environmental changes. Learning would not be so widespread in animals if it did not generally enhance their biological fitness. The same can be said of human culture. This broad approach promises to strike a balance between biological and cultural approaches, and to provide a unifying construct—biological function. Language, tool use, warfare, ornamentation, religion, and other well-developed biocultural capacities are increasingly being analyzed in adaptive terms. The discovery of rudiments of some of these capacities in great apes is facilitating this functional analysis (e.g., McGrew, 1992).

METHODOLOGIES

Testing for an Evolved Basis

Every behavioral action occurs because of a combination of interacting genetic and environmental factors. Despite general acceptance of this notion, it is useful to learn whether or not a particular behavior or sex difference has a *specific evolved basis*. All human behaviors are genetically based because all involve a genetically programmed brain, but only some behaviors are mediated by brain structures that evolved for a specific behavioral purpose. Other behaviors are incidental byproducts of our species' domain-general capacities for perception, learning, cognition, and movement. For example, all chickens will peck at grain, but only some will learn to peck at a disk for food.

Some of the methodologies used in distinguishing between these alternatives will now be outlined. They can provide evidence for or against the presence of an evolved basis for a given anatomical or behavioral trait or sex difference. For further critical discussion of these research strategies, which were pioneered by Darwin (1872/1965) himself, see C. R. Ember (1981), Miller (2002), and G. E. Weisfeld (1982).

Universality. The main research strategy is to distinguish species-wide traits from those that vary across populations. Species-wide anatomical and behavioral traits have an evolved basis, as a rule. Variable traits usually have a cultural basis and are adaptive or neutral for that population but lack a population-specific genetic basis. Like all statements about human behavior, these have exceptions. If the behavior remains the same across this cultural variability, then the behavior probably has an evolved basis. If the behavior or sex difference varies with culture, then genes do not effectively constrain it and it is primarily culturally based.

Developmental Research Strategies. Similar reasoning applies to other research strategies for drawing this distinction between traits with an evolved basis and those that are purely acquired. Another strategy is to minimize the role of culture or socialization in order to see if the behavior still develops. For example, if newborns exhibit the trait, then postnatal socialization can hardly be responsible. If, on the other hand, the behavior or sex difference is absent at birth, then its later appearance is probably due to socialization—although it may be a delayed effect of genes, such as the changes of puberty (C. R. Ember, 1981).

A variant of this secondly strategy in analyzing a sex difference is to hold socialization constant by concealing the gender of infants and noting whether they are still treated the same. If not, then an evolved basis for any sex differences in the infants' behavior is likely. Yet another variant is to identify the onset of some cognitive capacity and see if the sex difference in question appears before this hypothesized cognitive cause. If, for example, children exhibit a particular sex difference before they understand gender differences, then the behavior cannot depend on this comprehension.

Comparative and Physiological Strategies. A third main strategy is to determine whether or not a human behavior or sex difference also occurs in our primate relatives. If so, then the trait probably was passed on to our species by our forebears and is not rooted in human culture. Similarly, demonstrating a *specific* neural or hormonal mechanism for a behavior or sex difference renders improbable a purely cultural basis. Many hormonal and brain structural differences between men and women have been correlated with sex differences in behavior (Hampson, 2002).

Interpretation of Data from these Research Strategies. These research strategies are not infallible. For example, a trait that we do not share with even our closest primate relatives, such as speech, may still have an evolved basis because every species possesses some unique traits. A sex difference that occurs in hundreds of cultures except one doubtless has an evolved basis, because culture can always override an evolved behavioral propensity.

Because of these complications, evidence from various strategies is sought in analyzing a given behavior or sex difference. The evidence from various strategies for a given behavior is usually consistent, thereby validating them. For example, cross-cultural, hormonal, and comparative evidence converges to indicate that sex differences in human aggression have an evolved basis (Hoyenga & Hoyenga, 1993).

Also, demonstrating an evolved *basis* for a behavior does not mean that socialization factors are not also involved. Most behaviors are probably shaped by both types of factor, by information obtained by our ancestors and embodied in our genes, and by information acquired by ourselves through learning and observation.

Methodologies for Implicating Socialization Factors

Another methodology for examining the source of a given behavioral sex difference is to see if boys and girls are treated differently by parents or the general culture. If so, the sex difference may be due to differential socialization, although an evolved basis cannot be ruled out. Some evidence suggests that the effects of differential socialization may have been exaggerated. Maccoby (1998) reviewed this cross-cultural literature and concluded that when people react to an unfamiliar infant of unknown gender, they do not consistently alter their treatment on the basis of the infant's perceived or labeled gender. Furthermore, parents deal quite similarly with their sons and daughters. In a meta-analysis of hundreds of studies, no statistically significant sex differences were found for warmth, restrictiveness, discipline, or encouragement of achievement or dependency (Lytton & Romney, 1991). In many cultures no sex difference in socialization for a given behavior is reported, making it difficult to say that socialization generally causes the corresponding sex differences in behavior (C. R. Ember, 1981).

Cognitive theories of the acquisition of sex roles may account for many sex differences. However, children begin to conform with these expectations, or stereotypes, before they understand about sex-appropriate behavior or even to which sex they belong. For example, the cooperative style of girls and the confrontational style of boys emerge before children come to believe that girls are supposed to be "nice" and boys "rough." Even if children do understand a certain expectation for sex-typed behavior, they may not conform with it themselves (Serbin, Powlishta, & Gulko, 1993; Signorella, Bilger, & Liben, 1993), and may even exhibit a backlash against demonstrations of nontraditional behavior (Durkin & Hutchins, 1984).

However, Maccoby (1998) did find the following consistent gender-specific differences in treatment. Parents treat daughters more gently than sons, and talk more with daughters about interpersonal events. Parents express more approval of sex-appropriate behaviors than of sex-inappropriate ones, especially for boys. Across cultures, girls tend to be less different in their behavior than boys, and experience a less radical transformation upon entering adolescence (Schlegel & Barry, 1991). In many different cultures, mothers begin training daughters to behave properly and to help with tasks before they do so with sons (B. B. Whiting & Edwards, 1988). Girls are generally socialized to be nurturant, and boys to strive for achievement and self-reliance (Barry, Bacon, & Child, 1957; Hoyenga & Hoyenga, 1993; Welch & Page, 1981).

Subtle socialization influences may occur and may have profound and unexpected consequences. Girls have been found to have more traditionally feminine occupational aspirations if they have *more* brothers (Abrams, Sparkes, & Hogg, 1985; Lemkau, 1979). In a study of young children's interest in babies, a sex difference was observed only when the child was asked to look after the baby, not when spontaneous play with the baby was measured (Berman & Goodman, 1984). This seems to indicate the operation of sex role identification. Then too, children may be directed to perform sex-specific tasks, develop competence in these tasks, take pride in their mastery, and therefore come to enjoy these activities (Edwards, 1985).

Behavioral genetics research indicates that *nonshared* environmental factors that affect siblings differently, such as peers, mentors, and illnesses, contribute much more to individual differences in behavior than do parents' values and practices (Plomin, 1990; Rowe, 1994). Our understanding of environmental influences will have to be drastically revised to be consistent with these data. Behavioral genetics has also demonstrated that parents' socialization practices are themselves somewhat heritable, showing that genes and environment interact in subtle ways (Plomin, 1990). For example, brighter parents (intelligence is highly heritable) keep more books in the home, an environmental influence enhancing intelligence. Also, genetically based characteristics of the child may elicit particular parental responses, and a child with a particular genetically based propensity may seek out environments with like-minded peers.

Functional Analysis

Once a species-wide evolved trait or sex difference is identified, its biological function can be investigated. This is attempted by determining which other species possess the same trait and pinpointing the crucial difference between these species and those that lack the trait. For example, M. Ember and Ember (1979) analyzed the function of marriage by showing that its analog in animals, pair bonding, occurs in birds and mammals in which the mother's need for food interferes with care of her young. Marriage thus serves to keep the father close by so as to aid in raising the offspring. Functional analysis is not mere guesswork; hypotheses must be tested, and are disconfirmed if the distribution of the trait proves inconsistent with the hypothesized explanation. In the case of a human trait, its function in ancestral hunter–gatherer society must be identified because our contemporary genetic program is essentially a throwback to that era. An evolved trait may no longer be adaptive in a modern environment. The study of function—the "why" question about a species-wide behavior or sex difference—provides an entirely different level of explanation from analysis of how and when the behavior develops (Weisfeld, 1982).

PUBERTY, THE KEYSTONE OF ADOLESCENCE

Overview

In humans, sex differentiation in body and behavior, although in evidence throughout ontogeny (Bjorklund & Pellegrini, 2002), becomes most marked at puberty. Before puberty, the sexes are relatively similar (Willner & Martin, 1985). After puberty, hardly anything can be said about adolescents that applies equally to boys and girls.

Yet the amount of sex differentiation in adult humans is relatively small. Human sexual size *dimorphism* is comparatively modest, suggesting that behavioral sex differences are likewise relatively small. Indeed, most studies of behavioral sex differences reveal a great deal of overlap between the distributions of males and females. Individual differences tend to be far greater than sex differences in behavior (Schlegel & Barry, 1991).

Why is sex differentiation, to the extent that it exists, so pronounced at puberty? Puberty constitutes sexual maturation. It prepares males and females to fulfill their specialized reproductive roles, like the complementarity of sperm and egg. Primatologists define adolescence as the period from the onset of puberty to the attainment of fertility (Pereira & Altmann, 1985). Likewise, adolescence is recognized as a life stage in all cultures and is usually delimited by the observable changes of sexual maturation

(Schlegel & Barry, 1991). Before maturity, the child depends heavily on parents and others for assistance—so much so that Bogin (1999) has asserted that humans are the only primate with childhood, a stage of feeding by the mother after weaning. After maturity, adolescents themselves become, potentially, the parents of dependents (see Charlesworth, 1988; Schlegel, 1995). Given the great amount of parental care exhibited by our species, this is indeed a radical transformation. Accordingly, puberty entails dramatic changes in body and behavior.

Sex differences emerge or intensify at puberty in libido, spatial skills, arithmetic skills, verbal skills, strength, nurturance, and dominance aggression, among other behaviors (Hoyenga & Hoyenga, 1979, 1993; Kimura, 1999). Gonadal hormones contribute to all of these sex differences, as indicated by research on prenatal and adult hormonal exposure, sometimes using assays of amniotic fluid, umbilical cord blood, serum, or saliva; individuals with abnormal levels of endogenous and exogenous gonadal hormones; prepubertal, adult, pregnant, lactating, and postmenopausal individuals; and variation across menstrual, diurnal, and circannual hormonal fluctuations (Hampson, 2002). Some cognitive as well as motivational sex differences have been confirmed in studies on other species (Kimura, 1999; Mitchell, 1981; Patterson, Holts, & Saphire, 1991) and cultures (Christiansen, 1993). Hormones can affect the adolescent's behavior directly, not just by altering her body and thus changing others' reactions to her (e.g., Nottelmann et al., 1990). Furthermore, others' reactions to adolescents' bodily changes may themselves have an evolved basis.

Some sex differences emerge before puberty, but doubtless have implications for adolescence. Prenatal androgen exposure during the second trimester, when the brain is sex differentiating, is related to young girls' interest in play fighting versus doll play and in motherhood versus a career, employment in male-dominated fields, and some personality measures (Hampson, 2002; Mealey, 2000; Udry, Morris, & Kovenock, 1995). Prenatal androgen levels can also play a role in the development of sexual orientation, as can genes and adult experience (L. Ellis, 1996). Methodological objections that prenatally masculinized girls are treated differently by their parents, and that control groups and measures have been inadequate, have been addressed by subsequent research (e.g., Hines & Kaufman, 1994). However, this research does not gainsay the likelihood that socialization forces also contribute to these sex differences.

The functions of sex differences with evolved bases can often be understood by considering their possible advantages for our hominid ancestors. The tentative functional analysis proposed here will begin with the changes of puberty.

Puberty in Girls

Puberty in girls functions mainly to prepare them for childbearing. This includes choosing and attracting a desirable mate, and then nurturing their children. Adolescent girls become attractive to males and infants, and begin to evaluate males as possible mates (Tanner, 1978). Other clearly adaptive pubertal changes have been documented that would have prepared a girl for married life in a forager society. Women excel at remembering the location of objects—a skill of value in gathering plant food, their ancestral livelihood (Hampson, 2002; Silverman & Eals, 1992). This ability varies with stage of the menstrual cycle (Postma et al., 1999). By contrast, males excel at finding their way and at hurling projectiles accurately—skills useful in hunting (Kimura, 1999). Women tend to surpass men in manual dexterity, and do best around ovulation (Hampson, 2002; Kimura, 1999). Manual dexterity is serviceable for gathering plants and for delicate handiwork (Hampson, 2002). Women also exceed men in verbal and nonverbal communication performance, skills advantageous for teaching and raising children (Babchuk, Hames, & Thompson, 1985). These sex differences have all been related to gonadal hormone fluctuations (Hampson, 2002; Kimura, 1999).

Evidence suggests that girls, like other female primates, become more attracted to infants at puberty (Coe, 1990; Goldberg, Blumberg, & Kriger, 1982). Throughout the life span females perform more parental care than males in all cultures (Daly & Wilson, 1983; Friedl, 1975; Schlegel & Barry, 1991; van den Berghe, 1980). Various pregnancy and lactational hormones have been implicated in human maternal behavior, including estrogens, progesterone, oxytocin, and prolactin (Altemus et al., 1995; Uvnas-Moberg, 1997). Socialization of girls for nurturance complements an evolved propensity for child care.

Puberty in Boys

Puberty in boys prepares them to compete for mates and to enter into married life and parenthood. Observational research indicates that adolescent boys become rougher

in their competition (Boulton, 1992; Neill, 1985), just as aggressiveness and mate competition increase in the maturing males of many other species. In no culture are adolescent girls more competitive than boys (Schlegel, 1995). Young males commit the vast majority of assaults and homicides worldwide, most of which are related to sexual competition directly or indirectly (Daly & Wilson, 1988). Cross-culturally, ridicule and humorous repartee are a common form of competition among adolescent boys and young men (Apte, 1985).

Why do males become larger and stronger than females? When the nondominant arm (to control for training) is tested for strength before puberty, no sex difference is found, but a sex difference emerges at puberty (Åstrand, 1985). Comparative analysis suggests the main reason. Polygynous species, in which mate competition is intense, tend to show greater sexual dimorphism than monogamous ones. Thus greater male size seems to have evolved mainly to enhance competitive ability. Humans are a mildly dimorphic species and, accordingly, exhibit a mild degree of polygyny. Large size also aided in hunting and in defense of the family.

As boys become taller and stronger, they become hairier—why? Again, comparative analysis helps to identify the function of a trait. Dark, thick, curly, and conspicuous hair of the type that covers men's bodies typically functions in male primates to inflate the apparent size of structures, such as the jaw, that serve as bodily weapons (Guthrie, 1976). Men's deep voice, deep-set eyes, and large jaw likewise constitute general primate threat or dominance features that attract females and intimidate males (Keating, 1985).

Male as well as female adolescents become romantically motivated; pubertal hormones impel them to establish pair bonds (Money & Ehrhardt, 1972). The typical human male is not promiscuous, but rather seeks to marry—but to remain open to the possibility of extramarital reproduction (Daly & Wilson, 1983). Men, like a few other male mammals, are inclined to aid their own offspring. Rising levels of prolactin during his mate's pregnancy render a man more parental (Storey et al., 2000), so paternal behavior is not merely socially constructed.

Explaining Sex Differences in Reproductive Behavior

Why do these particular sex differences in social behavior occur? Why are females more nurturant, and males more aggressive and competitive? Why are males more interested in multiple sex partners and more prone to sexual jealousy? Why are men the sexual initiators and women the main choosers cross-culturally (Stephens, 1963)? Why do adolescent girls avoid being nude around males even in a sexually permissive society (Spiro, 1979)?

Explanations are to be found by recognizing that this pattern of sex differences is not confined to our culture or even our species (Daly & Wilson, 1983; Schlegel & Barry, 1991), but occurs in almost all sexually reproducing species (Bjorklund & Shackelford, 1999; Trivers, 1972). The female of a species, by definition, produces the larger and less mobile gamete. After fertilization, this gamete usually develops near or within her body, so the female is typically better situated to care for the offspring. In mammals, the female is always present when the young are born, but the male may not be. He may enhance his reproductive fitness more efficiently by seeking other females than by caring for offspring that may not even be his own. Therefore natural selection has favored mammalian females that are successful in bearing and raising offspring, and males that are efficient at attracting mates and repelling rivals. Providing most of the parental care, the female would benefit from choosing a mate carefully so as not to waste her parental effort on sickly offspring. On the other hand, the male would waste little effort on an unfertile mating, and would therefore benefit from being promiscuous.

Now, in those few mammalian species in which the young are so helpless that they need the efforts of both parents to survive, males tend to pursue a mixed or variable strategy of caring for their putative offspring but also seeking additional sex partners. Thus, even in mammals with paternal care, the male always provides less care than the female. Males can pass on their genes with a minimum of effort, if the female is able to bear and nurture their common offspring. Therefore male mammals are more inclined to seek extra-pair copulations, to seek sexual variety, whereas females have less to gain reproductively by pursuing multiple sexual liaisons. They can only have one litter at a time.

However, males in paternal species are wary of being cuckolded, of caring for a rival's offspring, and so they usually resort to *mate guarding*. Men's sexual jealousy is readily aroused by the prospect of their mate having sex with a rival male (Buss, 1994). Women may gain a fitness advantage by being fertilized by a man with better genes than their husband's, and so female marital infidelity occurs with some frequency (Baker & Bellis, 1995). Women's sexual jealousy, on the other hand, is most strongly aroused by the image of her mate deserting her for another woman and withdrawing his paternal support. It is important not to exaggerate these sex differences. Men are parentally inclined, and women are competitive. Sexual competition is intense for adolescent girls, since most of them are vying for the same few boys and under time pressure to marry. As in males, female assault and homicide rates peak in the reproductive years (Daly & Wilson, 1988), although females compete less violently than males, such as by insulting a rival. Even though women will invest more care in the children than will men, both sexes invest mightily and hence exercise care in choosing a mate. Both sexes sustain great costs in order to reproduce.

Individual and Cultural Differences

Adolescents within each sex also differ. Although many intrasexual differences are due to experiential factors, some are due to differences in hormone levels. Individual differences in testosterone level are associated with the strength of libido in adolescents of both sexes (Udry, 1988). Moreover, experience can sometimes affect hormonal levels that alter behavior. Youths who live in violent neighborhoods tend to have higher testosterone levels than those living in peaceful ones, controlling for various factors (Mazur & Booth, 1998). In mammals generally, testosterone rises in competitive situations to mobilize the individual for aggression. Thus living in a dangerous environment can potentiate aggressiveness and competitiveness through a rise in testosterone. Similarly, when men marry, their testosterone levels tend to fall as they withdraw from mating competition, and to rise again if they divorce.

Evolutionary analysis helps to explain individual differences in maturation rate. Reproductive maturation in mammals is accelerated by the presence of potential mates. It is adaptive to mature more rapidly when potential mates are available. In the 19th-century Oneida Community in New York State, prepubertal girls practiced frequent sex and reached puberty about 2 years earlier than girls in the surrounding area (Jones, 1991). In addition, although most stressors slow reproductive maturation, mild stress sometimes speeds maturation in mammals, probably so that the organism is assured of reaching maturity and reproducing under adverse conditions (Worthman, 1993). A cross-cultural comparison indicated that painful treatment during infancy can accelerate menarche (J. W. M. Whiting, 1965). Girls also tend to reach menarche early if they suffer from paternal absence or neglect, or from other family stresses (Coall & Chisholm, 1999; B. J. Ellis, McFadyen-Ketchum, Dodge, Pettit, & Bates, 1999; Rowe, 1999; Surbey, 1990). The presence of a potential mate (a stepfather or the mother's boyfriend) can accelerate menarche independently from the effect of father absence; in a recent study, total number of such males was the best predictor of the girl's tendency to engage in early sexual behavior (B. J. Ellis & Garber, 2000).

Thus, evolutionary hypotheses are being proposed for some individual and population differences, not just for universals. It makes adaptive sense for organisms to vary their development to meet different environmental contingencies. Such evolved pluripotentiality has been demonstrated even in insects, so it would be surprising if it were absent from our genetically more complex species. This variability is likely to be adaptive, to enhance the individual's reproductive interests. For example, father absence is common in societies with polygyny and frequent warfare (Chisholm, 1999), and girls tend to marry early in polygynous societies; early maturity may be advantageous under these conditions.

As these examples show, current evolutionary analyses do not discount the role of environment in human diversity. In fact, functional analysis can sometimes explain a pattern of cross-cultural diversity. To take another illustration: adult status is conferred on young men at different average ages in different societies, but a pattern exists. Adult status tends to be conferred on a youth when he marries (van den Berghe, 1980). In societies in which men require many years to accumulate sufficient wealth or economic skills to afford marriage, adult status usually comes relatively late (G. E. Weisfeld, 1999). Thus, cultural differences can sometimes be explained in functional terms, rather than as historical accidents or consequences of conceptual, linguistic, or other cultural features. Cultural practices, like genes, are subject to selection pressure even if historical and other factors also shape them. Practices that enhance reproductive success under extant ecological conditions will be passed on across generations.

PUBERTY RITES

Just as body and behavior must be compatible, the genetic and cultural programs must cooperate for the successful survival and reproduction of the organism. This notion is illustrated by puberty rites, which may be regarded as a cultural growth spurt analogous to the changes of puberty; both provide intensive preparation for adulthood (G. E. Weisfeld, 1997). Functional analysis of the various features of puberty rites may reveal some general characteristics of adolescence. Although only 56% of preliterate cultures have a formal initiation ceremony (Schlegel & Barry, 1980), virtually all have an intensive training period before induction into adulthood (Schlegel & Barry, 1991), and so puberty rites, broadly construed, are a constant of adolescence.

Puberty rites vary widely across cultures because different environments demand the cultivation of different skills and behaviors, but some general patterns emerge (J. W. M. Whiting, Kluckholn & Anthony, 1958). Initiates typically are tutored in sex-specific adult economic, familial, and cultural skills. The same-sex parent is usually the main teacher of subsistence skills, but the initiate is tutored by some other same-sex adult in social and ceremonial matters (Schlegel & Barry, 1991). Puberty rites usually entail some challenging ordeal that boys, in particular, must endure (Schlegel & Barry, 1980). Ordeals may be used to subdue recalcitrant youths, who are more likely to be boys, as in the Hopi (G. E. Weisfeld, 1999). This is analogous to the more rigorous competition that males of most species, as opposed to females, undergo to enter the breeding pool. Boys will also have to hone their economic skills in order to compete for a wife. Consistent with this interpretation, the theme of boys' initiation rites is usually graduation, rebirth, or accomplishment (Hotvedt, 1990; Schlegel & Barry, 1980). The theme for girls' rites is typically fertility or beauty (Schlegel & Barry, 1980; Sommer, 1978). Thus, for both sexes, traits important for reproductive success are cultivated and extolled. Upon completing their initiation rites, adolescents are usually regarded as adults and are eligible to marry. To signify their emerging adulthood, initiates usually have their bodies specially marked, much as primates take on adult bodily features so they can be identified as sexually mature.

The timing of puberty rites has been something of a conundrum. Some sources state that the rites occur at the onset of puberty, others at the conclusion of puberty. The ambiguity may be resolved by recognizing a sex difference in these events. Girls are usually initiated at menarche, after most of the events of puberty have been completed (Schlegel & Barry, 1991). By contrast, boys are typically initiated before most of the changes of puberty (Schlegel & Barry, 1980). Interestingly, for both sexes initiation occurs shortly before the onset of fertility, thus underscoring the significance of this institution as a preparation for family responsibilities (G. E. Weisfeld, 1997).

Several other features of puberty rites seem to be functionally analogous to various pubertal changes. The sexes are almost always segregated during the training period, just as nonhuman primates—and children—spontaneously sex segregate before puberty and are drawn to older same-sex models (Goodall, 1986; Mackey, 1983). These affinities doubtless aid the learning of sex roles, as do the bodily and behavioral changes of pubertal sex differentiation. Sex differentiation of personality traits reaches its end point around age 11 around the world (Beere, 1990; Best, 2001).

Initiates are separated from their parents as well, just as mature simians distance themselves from their mothers and increasingly associate with peers. Likewise, emotional distance from parents increases in U.S. adolescents (Silverberg & Steinberg, 1987). Parent–adolescent distancing in humans may be orchestrated by (among other factors) pubertal hormones, as suggested by research on family conflict. As adolescents enter puberty, discussions between them and their parents (especially the mother) tend to increase in acrimony (Holmbeck & Hill, 1991; Paikoff & Brooks-Gunn, 1991; Sagrestano, McCormick, Paikoff, & Holmbeck, 1999; Steinberg, 1987). Fewer explanations are offered, and more harsh words are exchanged. This contentiousness peaks at the height of the adolescent growth spurt, controlling for chronological age (Molina & Chassin, 1996; Sagrestano et al., 1999). This suggests that contentiousness is driven either directly by hormonal effects on behavior or indirectly by the bodily changes of puberty triggering perceptual changes in the parents.

Parent–child conflict tends to be harshest between mother and son, in U.S. research (Montemayor & Hanson, 1985; Paikoff & Brooks-Gunn, 1991; Silverberg, 1989). After the velocity of growth peaks, conflict usually subsides. However, at this point adolescent sons tend to win most arguments with their mothers, whereas previously the mothers prevailed (Jacob, 1974; Steinberg, 1987). In effect, mother and adolescent son reverse their dominance relationship, just as happens in chimpanzees (Goodall, 1986). Dominance reversal between sons and mothers probably occurs universally, in that in all cultures males are ascribed higher social status than females, and youth defers to age (Stephens, 1963; van den Berghe, 1980). On the other hand, human mothers remain dominant over daughters, and fathers over sons and daughters. Parent–adolescent distancing and renegotiation of dominance relations may be necessary for adolescents to gain appropriate independence from their parents.

Given the ubiquity of this adaptive problem, a genetic basis for this separation probably evolved. It is likely that some dependable hormonally based mechanism provided a *proximate* cause for this aversion, although cultural and individual factors certainly modify it. Fathers and sons often come into conflict, especially over transferring wealth that the son needs for bride wealth, as among African pastoralists (Schlegel & Barry, 1991). Hopi mothers and adolescent daughters sometimes argue over the daughter's socializing immodestly with boys or neglecting her chores. However, in terms of dominance relations, Schlegel and Barry (1991) stated that boys and girls are more subordinate to fathers than to mothers, and that mothers have greater authority over daughters than over sons. This implies a dominance order of father > mother > son > daughter, meaning again that the least clear-cut parent–adolescent relationship is mother–son.

Another possible adaptive, or *ultimate*, causal explanation for conflict between parents and adolescents is a natural selfishness in the latter. Being about to confront the challenges of independence from parents and of mate competition and parenthood, young people may look after their own interests. By contrast, grandparents tend to be quite devoted to their grandchildren and other kin. They are past their reproductive years and so can only increase the representation of their genes in subsequent generations by practicing *kin altruism*: aiding close relatives with whom they share genes by common descent. Kin altruism provides an indirect way of passing one's genes on to future generations, and therefore occurs in many species and all human societies. For example, postmenopausal Hadza women worked even harder than childbearing women, allowing their daughters to have more and healthier children (Hawkes, O'Connell, & Blurton Jones, 1989). Similarly, in other species in which life continues after reproduction, kin altruism of various sorts has been observed. Adolescents, being at the other end of the reproductive span, would be expected to act rather selfishly toward kin and others. In addition, their lack of experience in adult society may cause them to behave badly on occasion (G. E. Weisfeld, 1999).

Other widespread features of puberty rites also make functional sense. Newly initiated young men often serve as warriors (Young, 1965), just as young male monkeys act as sentinels and shock troops (Chance & Jolly, 1970; Schlegel, 1995). These youths have undergone the rigors of puberty rites as a group, developing solidarity that will serve them well in warfare. They are unmarried and have no dependents, and so are relatively expendable. Girls, by contrast, are invariably initiated singly as soon as they reach menarche (Young, 1965). This ensures that a girl will be initiated, and hence eligible for marriage, just as she approaches the onset of fertility. She will be most in demand as a bride when her *reproductive value*—her expected future number of offspring—peaks (Daly & Wilson, 1983). By marrying such a woman, who cannot be carrying another man's child but has all of her child-bearing years ahead of her, a man maximizes his own reproductive chances. In most societies, girls marry within 2 years of menarche (Schlegel & Barry, 1991). In modern society, however, women often postpone marriage or reproduction until they have completed their education. This variation on the species-typical pattern can probably be explained by factors that did not operate when the human genome was evolving, such as the availability of effective contraception and the time needed to learn the complex skills of our economy.

The Adolescent's Family Context

Social Structure

What is known of the social situation of ancestral adolescents? Aside from the likelihood that hominid adolescents underwent intensive training for adulthood, several facts can be adduced about the social context of adolescence in our species. A virtually universal feature of not just forager societies but all preliterate human societies is the extended family, if we define it as three generations of family members dwelling together or nearby (Stephens, 1963). The great majority of ancestral adolescents' social contacts would have been with kin, including clan members of more remote consanguinity. Through the genetic benefit of kin altruism, this arrangement would have rewarded cooperation in endeavors such as hunting, gathering, warfare, and child care. In addition, because foraging communities tend to be small (hunting requires low population density), ancestral human

settlements were limited to perhaps 60 individuals (van den Berghe, 1980). This would have meant that adolescents had few age mates and therefore socialized extensively with older and younger kin. Contact with neighboring bands and their adolescents, that is, members of the same tribe sharing a language, would have occurred occasionally.

This pattern of limited age segregation would have fostered adolescents' assisting and teaching younger children. In turn, there would have been ample opportunity for observing and being instructed by adults. In most preliterate cultures, children and adolescents perform important work for their families, especially instructing and supervising younger children (Cicirelli, 1994). As they grow older and more competent, they undertake increasingly challenging and valuable tasks, and their prestige increases concomitantly. For example, contemporary Mayan children become net producers in their teens (Kramer & Boone, 1999). In traditional cultures adolescents typically begin full-time work at age 10–12 and assume an adult workload at 14–16 (Neill, 1983). The labor contributions of children and adolescents, unique among the primates, are thought to have allowed women to wean their children sooner and hence to bear more children (Zeller, 1987).

Sex Segregation of Labor

Labor is strongly sex segregated everywhere, with males and females specializing in tasks congruent with their inherent interests, aptitudes, and training, and with practicalities such as distance from the settlement and compatibility with related tasks (Friedl, 1975; Murdock & Provost, 1973). The universality of sexual division of labor suggests that this arrangement has generally been advantageous. In all preliterate cultures the labor of husband and wife is complementary: women perform most of the domestic tasks, including child care, cleaning, and cooking, and men specialize in work requiring strength, such as handling heavy and hard materials (C. R. Ember & Ember, 2001; van den Berghe, 1980). Women in many forager societies provide most of the calories by gathering plants, a reliable and preservable source of food, whereas men supply protein-rich game and fish. Of the 46 tasks analyzed in terms of which sex performed each in how many traditional cultures (Murdock, 1965), 36 tasks were predominantly (at $p < 0.001$) performed by one sex or the other (G. E. Weisfeld, 1986).

Vestiges of this arrangement can be seen in modern society in that men still predominate in occupations requiring heavy manual labor and in the military, and women gravitate toward the service sector, which demands interpersonal skills at which females excel (Hall, 1984). Technical advances and changing social attitudes can, of course, alter the sex ratio of a given occupation dramatically, thus showing that genetic influences on behavior always interact with and may even be overridden by environmental influences. On the other hand, tolerance for women and men working in nontraditional roles has not increased measurably in recent years (Feingold, 1994; Lueptow et al., 1995, 2001), and sex role "stereotypes" are similar across cultures (Williams & Best, 1986, 1990). Also, consistent with the resilience of many behavioral sex differences, attempts to obliterate sex roles have proven quite difficult and have been resisted by their alleged beneficiaries (e.g., Tiger & Shepher, 1975). Change in these expectations may occur very slowly, however; they are less pronounced in developed societies than in developing ones (Williams & Best, 1989).

What sort of labor do adolescents provide, and how does it aid the family? Research on the Hadza of Tanzania has shown that the adolescent boys provide food for their younger siblings, but also forage in order to improve their reputations as hunters (Blurton Jones, Hawkes, & O'Connell, 1997). That is, they practice kin altruism but also strive to advance their social standing and, ultimately, their *mate value*. Hadza adolescent girls often dig for roots while tending younger siblings. This is an inefficient foraging technique but it frees the mothers to forage more efficiently. In many preliterate cultures adolescents do not perform arduous labor. In the !Kung of southern Africa, for example, adolescents are discouraged from working hard until about age 15 (Blurton Jones, Hawkes, & Draper, 1993). Evidently the optimal reproductive strategy in this forager society is extensive care of offspring, including prolonged breast-feeding. This line of research suggests that cultural and individual differences in adolescent industriousness and other traits can often be explained by family and ecological factors. One adolescent may be slothful because cultural selection has favored an easy life under his or her circumstances. Another adolescent may be industrious because she will be fitter biologically by acquiring a reputation for industry or by aiding kin. Adolescents devote themselves to subsistence activities, training, supervision of children, and courtship in patterns that vary across cultures,

gender, and individuals, but this variation seems to fall into functional patterns. Socialization by the family sometimes directs an adolescent toward particular tasks. For example, adolescents with working mothers have a more favorable attitude toward working women than do those with nonemployed mothers (Huston & Alvarez, 1990). Sometimes the effects of participating in sex-specific tasks can transfer to other contexts. Luo boys in Kenya who were assigned indoor feminine tasks behaved in a generally more feminine manner than did boys assigned outdoor feminine tasks (C. R. Ember, 1973).

MATE CHOICE

If adolescence consists mainly of preparation for reproduction, a major "task" of adolescence must be to secure a desirable mate. Research reveals some cross-cultural commonalities in the criteria of mate choice.

Traits Sought by Both Sexes

Both sexes seek kindness in a mate, which makes sense given the strains of marriage and child rearing (Buss, 1994). They also seek a mate whom they are likely to be able to retain, that is, one of similar mate value. Likewise, they seek someone who appears to be committed to them emotionally. And of course, like other species (Andersson, 1994), people tend to prefer a sexually mature and physically attractive mate, who is likely to be healthy and fertile, and to carry high-quality genes (e.g., Shackelford & Larsen, 1999). Valid cues to genetic quality include normality and bilateral symmetry of features, and healthy skin; these features are admired worldwide (Ford & Beach, 1951; Thornhill & Gangestad, 1994). Naturally, not everyone can attract someone who is above average in desirability, and so people usually wind up with mates who lack some ideal features, but the preferences that most people express are often clear and specific, and generally hold even across cultural and racial lines (Cunningham, 1986).

Human mates, including courting adolescents, tend to be similar in many traits, a finding that is difficult to explain solely in terms of spousal social and ideological compatibility because it also occurs in insects, birds, and simians (Thiessen & Gregg, 1980). Why would genetic similarity (or *homogamy*) be advantageous in mate choice? One possibility is that it conserves locally adaptive gene combinations that would be fragmented if the mates were genetically dissimilar. Consistent with this idea, homogamy reduces the likelihood of miscarriage (Rushton, 1988; Thomas, Harger, Wagener, Rabin, & Gill, 1985) and low birth weight (Ober et al., 1987). In any case, people tend to choose similar mates, and similar mates stay together longer (Hill, Rubin, & Peplau, 1976). Of course, extreme consanguinity risks the deleterious effects of inbreeding depression.

Sex Differences in Mate Choice Criteria

In addition to seeking kindness, availability, commitment, and moderate similarity in a mate, the sexes exhibit some differences in their respective mate choice criteria. Worldwide, men seek signs of youth and fertility in a bride—traits that obviously would enhance their lifetime reproductive success (Buss, 1994). They also seek a sexually faithful wife, in order not to be deceived into caring for a rival's children, and a skilled and industrious one.

Women likewise exhibit definite mate preferences. They tend to desire a man who is older than they—but not necessarily an old man. Because of menopause and other factors, a man retains his fertility longer than a woman, and so youth is less advantageous in a groom than in a bride. Most women also prefer a man who is taller and wealthier.

These preferences suggest that many women seek a man who is somewhat dominant over them—taller, richer, older, and higher ranking. In traditional societies, high-status men tend to have more children than low-ranking ones (Barkow, 1989; Buss, 1999). Even in monogamous societies, high-status men have more sexual partners (Perusse, 1993). In many other species too, males compete among themselves and the females mate with the successful dominant competitors (L. Ellis, 1995). Additional data confirm that male dominance in nonverbal behavior and bodily features attracts females in various cultures (reviewed by G. E. Weisfeld, Russell, Weisfeld, & Wells, 1992). Moderate male dominance in decision-making—but not extreme dominance—was correlated with marital satisfaction, especially for wives, in a British study (G. E. Weisfeld et al., 1992). However, male dominance in decision-making may be merely a matter of perception, not reality—a clever concession to the male ego, if you will. An observational study suggested that men often appeared to be making decisions but the outcome actually favored the wife in each of 15 cases (Schell & Weisfeld, 1999).

These criteria for mate choice for the sexes, then, show some consistency. But they also show some cultural variability, as in the subsistence skills that are prized in each sex.

Female Inhibition in Mixed-Sex Competition

One frequently neglected topic is mixed-sex competition and its possible role in mate choice. Females tend to be less competitive and self-confident than males cross-culturally (e.g., Stetsenko, Little, Godeeva, Grassof, & Oettingen, 2000), but they also sometimes attenuate their competitiveness when facing a male opponent. This phenomenon is seen mainly in adolescence and adulthood, and is observed cross-culturally. For example, C. C. Weisfeld, Weisfeld, and Callahan (1982) documented it in the Hopi and African Americans, and also established that it occurs even in female-biased competitive tasks such as a spelling bee (Cronin, 1980). Interestingly, adolescent girls who exhibited this behavior tended to be unaware of it and often denied that they were not trying their hardest. The phenomenon has also been observed in women who use more tentative speech but only when addressing a man (Carli, 1990), and in women who act more submissively in mixed-sex groups compared with same-sex ones (Aries, 1982), and toward their husbands compared with other men (McCarrick, Manderscheid, & Silbergeld, 1981). Women who exhibit this inhibition also tend to differ in hormonal profile from those who do not (C. C. Weisfeld, 1986).

The function of female inhibition in mixed-sex competition is probably reproductive, given its predominance during the reproductive years. Callan (1970) suggested that it enhances harmony with one's husband, in that it reduces competition in this relationship. Then too, a wife may benefit from bolstering her husband's self-esteem and consequent performance in public arenas. Another possibility is that female inhibition increases a woman's appeal by making her appear more feminine. However, this last explanation is thrown into question by a review of the literature by Harter, Waters, and Whitesell (1998). They concluded that adolescent girls tended to be less self-confident when talking with boys than with adults or other girls, but that boys were also less self-confident when talking with girls. Adolescents of both sexes may be very concerned with how they are viewed by potential mates.

CONCLUSION

The concept of adaptive value, or biological function, is crucial for understanding not just what exists, but why. However, traditional ethological analysis on the species level alone is insufficient. Analysis on the cultural, social class, and individual levels is essential for understanding patterns of variability, particularly between males and females (G. E. Weisfeld, Weisfeld, & Segal, 1997). In short, interdisciplinary cooperation is needed for understanding how and why a given behavior pattern emerges. Neither genetic nor environmental determinism is consistent with the facts.

Many aspects of sexual development and sex differences in adolescence could not be addressed in this brief treatment. For further information, see C. R. Ember (1981), Schlegel and Barry (1991), and G. E. Weisfeld (1999).

REFERENCES

Abrams, D., Sparkes, K., & Hogg, M. A. (1985). Gender salience and social identity: The impact of sex of siblings on educational and occupational aspirations. *British Journal of Educational Psychology, 55*, 224–232.

Altemus, M., Deuster, P. L., Galliven, E., Carter, C., & Gold, P. (1995). Suppression of hypothalamic–pituitary–adrenal axis responses to stress in lactating women. *Journal of Clinical Endocrinology and Metabolism, 80*, 2954–2959.

Andersson, M. (1994). *Sexual selection.* Princeton, NJ: Princeton University Press.

Apte, M. L. (1985). *Humor and laughter: An anthropological approach.* Ithaca, NY: Cornell University Press.

Aries, P. (1982). Verbal and nonverbal behavior in single-sex and mixed-sex groups: Are traditional sex roles changing? *Psychological Reports, 51*, 117–134.

Åstrand, P. O. (1985). Sexual dimorphism in exercise and sport. In J. Ghesquiere, R. D. Martin, & R. Newcombe (Eds.), *Human sexual dimorphism* (pp. 247–256). London: Taylor & Francis.

Babchuk, W. A., Hames, R. B., & Thompson, R. A. (1985). Sex differences in the recognition of infant facial expressions of emotion: The primate caretaker hypothesis. *Ethology and Sociobiology, 6*, 89–101.

Baker, R. R., & Bellis, M. A. (1995). *Human sperm competition: Copulation, masturbation and infidelity.* London: Chapman & Hall.

Barkow, J. H. (1989). *Darwin, sex, and status: Biological approaches to mind and culture.* Toronto: University of Toronto Press.

Barry, H., III, Bacon, M. K., & Child, I. L. (1957). A cross-cultural survey of some sex differences in socialization. *Journal of Abnormal and Social Psychology, 55*, 327–332.

Beere, C. A. (1990). *Gender roles: A handbook of tests and measures.* New York: Greenwood Press.

Berman, P. W., & Goodman, V. (1984). Age and sex differences in children's responses to babies: Effects of adults' caretaking request and instructions. *Child Development, 55*, 1071–1077.

Best, D. L. (2001). Gender concepts: Convergence in cross-cultural research and methodologies. *Cross-cultural Research: Journal of Comparative Social Science, 35*, 23–43.

Bjorklund, D. G., & Pellegrini, A. D. (2002). *The origins of human nature: Evolutionary developmental psychology.* Washington, DC: American Psychological Association.

Bjorklund, D. G., & Shackelford, T. K. (1999). Differences in parental investment contribute to important differences between men and women. *Current Directions in Psychological Science, 8*, 86–89.

Blurton Jones, N. G., Hawkes, K., & Draper, P. (1993). Differences between Hadza and !Kung children's work: Original affluence or practical reason? In E. S. Burch (Ed.), *Key issues in hunter–gatherer research* (pp. 189–215). Oxford: Berg.

Blurton Jones, N. G., Hawkes, K., & O'Connell, J. F. (1997). Why do Hadza children forage? In N. L. Segal, G. E. Weisfeld, & C. C. Weisfeld (Eds.), *Uniting psychology and biology: Integrative perspectives on human development* (pp. 279–313). Washington, DC: American Psychological Association.

Bogin, B. (1999). *Patterns of human growth* (2nd ed.), Cambridge, UK: Cambridge University Press.

Boulton, M. J. (1992). Rough physical play in adolescents: Does it serve a dominance function? *Early Education and Development, 3*, 312–333.

Brown, D. C. (1991). *Human universals.* New York: McGraw-Hill.

Buss, D. M. (1994). *The evolution of desire.* New York: Basic Books.

Buss, D. M. (1999). *Evolutionary psychology: The new science of the mind.* Boston: Allyn & Bacon.

Callan, H. (1970). *Ethology and society.* Oxford: Clarendon Press.

Carli, L. L. (1990). Gender, language, and influence. *Journal of Personality and Social Psychology, 59*, 941–951.

Chance, M. R. A., & Jolly, C. J. (1970). *Social groups of monkey, apes and men.* New York: E.P. Dutton.

Charlesworth, W. R. (1988). Resources and resource acquisition during ontogeny. In K. B. MacDonald (Ed.), *Sociobiological perspectives on human development* (pp. 24–77). New York: Springer-Verlag.

Chisholm, J. S. (1999). *Death, hope and sex: Steps to an evolutionary ecology of mind and morality.* New York: Cambridge University Press.

Christiansen, K. (1993). Sex hormone-related variations of cognitive performance in !Kung San hunter–gatherers of Namibia. *Neuropsychobiology, 27*, 97–107.

Cicirelli, V. G. (1994). Sibling relationships in cross-cultural perspective. *Journal of Marriage and the Family, 56*, 7–20.

Coall, D. A., & Chisholm, J. S. (1999, June). *Childhood psychosocial stress accelerates age at menarche: A test of Belsky, Steinberg and Draper's model.* Paper presented at the convention of the Human Behavior and Evolution Society, Salt Lake City, UT.

Coe, C. L. (1990). Psychobiology of maternal behavior in nonhuman primates. In N. A. Krasnegor & R. S. Bridges (Eds.), *Mammalian parenting: Biochemical, neurological, and behavioral determinants* (pp. 157–183). New York: Oxford University Press.

Cronin, C. L. (1980). Dominance relations and females. In D. R. Omark, F. F. Strayer, & D. G. Freedman (Eds.), *Dominance relations: An ethological view of human conflict and social interaction* (pp. 299–318). New York: Garland.

Cunningham, M. R. (1986). Measuring the physical in physical attractiveness: Quasi-experiments in the sociobiology of female facial beauty. *Journal of Personality and Social Psychology, 50,* 925–935.

Daly, M., & Wilson, M. (1983). *Sex, evolution and behavior (2nd ed.).* Boston: Willard Grant.

Daly, M., & Wilson, M. (1988). *Homicide.* Hawthorne, NY: Aldine de Gruyter.

Darwin, C. (1965). *Expression of the emotions in man and animals.* Chicago: University of Chicago Press (Original work published 1872).

Durkin, K., & Hutchins, G. (1984). Challenging traditional sex role stereotypes via career education broadcasts: The reactions of young secondary school pupils. *Journal of Educational Television, 10,* 25–33.

Edwards, C. P. (1985). Behavioral sex differences in children of diverse cultures: The case of nurturance to infants. In M. E. Pereira & L. A. Fairbanks (Eds.), *Juvenile primates: Life history, development, and behavior* (pp. 327–338). New York: Oxford University Press.

Ellis, B. J., & Garber, J. (2000). Psychosocial antecedents of variation in girls' pubertal timing: Maternal depression, stepfather presence, and marital and family stress. *Child Development, 71,* 485–501.

Ellis, B. J., McFadyen-Ketchum, S., Dodge, K. A., Pettit, G. S., & Bates, J. E. (1999). Quality of early family relationships and individual differences in the timing of pubertal maturation in girls: A longitudinal test of an evolutionary model. *Journal of Personality and Social Psychology, 77,* 387–401.

Ellis, L. (1995). Dominance and reproductive success among nonhuman animals: A cross-species comparison. *Ethology and Sociobiology, 16,* 257–333.

Ellis, L. (1996). The role of perinatal factors in determining sexual orientation. In R. C. Savin-Williams & K. M. Cohen (Eds.), *The lives of lesbians, gays, and bisexuals: Children to adults* (pp. 35–70). New York: Harcourt Brace.

Ember, C. R. (1973). Female task assignment and the social behavior of boys. *Ethos, 1,* 429–493.

Ember, C. R. (1981). A cross-cultural perspective on sex differences. In R. H. Munroe, R. L. Munroe, & B. B. Whiting (Eds.), *Handbook of cross-cultural human development* (pp. 531–580). New York: Garland.

Ember, C. R., & Ember, M. (2001). *Cultural anthropology.* Upper Saddle River, NJ: Prentice-Hall.

Ember, M., & Ember, C. R. (1979). Male–female bonding: A cross-species study of mammals and birds. *Behavior Science Research, 14,* 37–56.

Feingold, A. (1994). Gender differences in personality: A meta-analysis. *Psychological Bulletin, 116,* 429–456.

Feldman, S. S., Brown, N. L., & Canning, R. D. (1995). Pathways to early sexual activity: A longitudinal study of the influence of peer status. *Journal of Research in Adolescence, 5,* 387–412.

Ford, C. S., & Beach, F. A. (1951). *Patterns of sexual behavior.* New York: Harper & Row.

Friedl, E. (1975). *Women and men: An anthropologist's view.* New York: Holt, Rinehart & Winston.

Goldberg, S., Blumberg, S. L., & Kriger, A. (1982). Menarche and interest in infants: Biological and social influences. *Child Development, 53,* 1544–1550.

Goodall, J. (1986). *The chimpanzees of Gombe: Patterns of behavior.* Cambridge, MA: Harvard University Press.

Guthrie, R. D. (1976). *Body hot spots: The anatomy of human social organs and behavior.* New York: Van Nostrand Reinhold.

Hall, J. (1984). *Non-verbal sex differences: Communication accuracy and expressive style.* Baltimore: Johns Hopkins University Press.

Hampson, E. (2002). Sex differences in human brain and cognition: The influence of sex steroids in early and adult life. In J. B. Becker, S. M. Breedlove, D. Crews, & M. M. McCarthy (Eds.), *Behavioral endocrinology* (2nd ed.) (pp. 579–628). Cambridge, MA: MIT Press.

Harter, S., Waters, P., & Whitsell, N. R. (1998). Relational self-worth: Differences in perceived worth as a person across interpersonal contexts among adolescents. *Child Development, 69,* 756–766.

Hawkes, K., O'Connell, J., & Blurton Jones, N. (1989). Hardworking Hadza grandmothers. In V. Standen & R. Foley (Eds.), *Comparative socioecology: The behavioural ecology of mammals and man* (pp. 341–366). London: Blackwell Scientific.

Hill, C. T., Rubin, Z., & Peplau, L. (1976). Breakups before marriage: The end of 103 affairs. *Journal of Social Issues, 3,* 147–168.

Hines, M., & Kaufman, F. R. (1994). Androgen and the development of human sex-typical behavior: Rough-and-tumble play and sex of preferred playmates in children with congenital adrenal hyperplasia (CAH). *Child Development, 65,* 1042–1053.

Holmbeck, G., & Hill, J. (1991). Conflictive engagement, positive affect, and menarche in families with seventh-grade girls. *Child Development, 62,* 1030–1048.

Hotvedt, M. (1990). Emerging and submerging adolescent sexuality: Culture and sexual orientation. In J. Bancroft & J. M. Reinish (Eds.), *Adolescence and Puberty* (pp. 157–172). New York: Oxford University Press.

Hoyenga, K. B., & Hoyenga, K. T. (1979). *The question of sex differences: Psychological, cultural, and biological issues.* Boston: Little, Brown.

Hoyenga, K. B., & Hoyenga, K. T. (1993). *Gender-related differences: Origins and outcomes.* Boston: Allyn & Bacon.

Huston, A. C., & Alvarez, M. (1990). The socialization context of gender-role development in early adolescence. In R. Montemayor, G. R. Adams, & T. P. Gulotta (Eds.), *From childhood to adolescence: A transitional period?* (pp. 156–179) Newbury Park, CA: Sage.

Jacob, T. (1974). Patterns of family conflict and dominance as a function of age and social class. *Developmental Psychology, 10,* 21–24.

Jones, R. E. (1991). *Human reproductive biology.* New York: Academic Press.

Keating, C. F. (1985). Gender and the physiognomy of dominance and attractiveness. *Social Psychology Quarterly, 48,* 61–70.

Kimura, D. (1999). *Sex and cognition.* Cambridge, MA: MIT Press.

Kramer, K. L., & Boone, J. (1999, June). *Does children's work increase household production? Production, consumption and family size among subsistence agriculturalists.* Paper presented at the convention of the Human Behavior and Evolution Society, Salt Lake City, UT.

Lemkau, J. P. (1979). Personality and background characteristics of women in male-dominated occupations: A review. *Psychology of Women Quarterly, 4,* 221–240.

Lueptow, L. B., Garovich, L., & Lueptow, M. B. (1995). The persistence of gender stereotypes in the face of changing sex roles: Evidence contrary to the sociocultural model. *Ethology and Sociobiology, 16,* 509–530.

Lueptow, L. B., Garovich, L., & Lueptow, M. B. (2001). Social change and the persistence of sex typing: 1974–1997. *Social Forces, 80,* 1–36.

Lytton, H., & Romney, D. M. (1991). Parents' sex-related differential socialization of boys and girls: A meta-analysis. *Psychological Bulletin, 109,* 267–296.

Maccoby, E. E. (1998). *The two sexes: Growing up apart, coming together.* Cambridge, MA: Harvard University Press.

Mackey, W. C. (1983). A preliminary test for the validation of the adult male–child bond as a species-characteristic trait. *American Anthropologist, 85,* 391–402.

Mazur, A., & Booth, A. (1998). Testosterone and dominance in men. *Behavioral and Brain Sciences, 21,* 353–397.

McCarrick, A. K., Manderscheid, R. W., & Silbergeld, S. (1981). Gender differences in competition and dominance during married-couples therapy. *Social Psychology Quarterly, 44,* 164–177.

McGrew, W. C. (1992). *Chimpanzee material culture: Implications for human evolution.* Cambridge, UK: Cambridge University Press.

Mealey, L. (2000). *Sex differences: Developmental and evolutionary strategies.* San Diego: Academic Press.

Miller, P. (2002). *Theories of developmental psychology* (4th ed.). New York: Worth.

Mitchell, G. (1981). *Human sex differences: A primatologist's perspective.* New York: Van Nostrand Reinhold.

Molina, B. S. G., & Chassin, L. (1996). The parent–adolescent relationship at puberty: Hispanic ethnicity and parent alcoholism as moderators. *Developmental Psychology, 32,* 675–686.

Money, J., & Ehrhardt, A. A. (1972). *Man and woman, boy and girl.* Baltimore: Johns Hopkins University Press.

Montemayor, R., & Hanson, E. (1985). A naturalistic view of conflict between adolescents and their parents and siblings. *Journal of Early Adolescence, 5,* 23–30.

Murdock, G. P. (1965). *Culture and society.* Pittsburgh, PA: University of Pittsburgh Press.

Murdock, G. P., & Provost, C. (1973). Factors in the division of labor by sex: A cross-cultural analysis. *Ethnology, 12,* 203–219.

Neill, S. R. St J. (1983). Children's social relationships and education— An evolutionary effect? *Social Biology and Human Affairs, 47,* 48–55.

Neill, S. R. St J. (1985). Rough-and-tumble and aggression in school children: Serious play? *Animal Behaviour, 33,* 1380–1382.

Nottelmann, E. D., Inoff-Germain, G., Susman, E. J., & Chrousos, G. P. (1990). Hormones and behavior at puberty. In J. Bancroft & J. M. Reinisch (Eds.), *Adolescence and puberty* (pp. 88–123). New York: Oxford University Press.

Ober, C., Simpson, J. L., Ward, M., Radvany, R. M., Andersen, R., Elias, S., et al. (1987). Prenatal effects of maternal–fetal HLA compatibility. *American Journal of Reproductive Immunology and Microbiology, 15,* 141–149.

Paikoff, R., & Brooks-Gunn, J. (1991). Do parent–child relationships change during puberty? *Psychological Bulletin, 110,* 47–66.

Patterson, F. G. P., Holts, C., & Saphire, L. (1991). Cyclic changes in hormonal, physical, behavioral, and linguistic measures in a female lowland gorilla. *American Journal of Primatology, 24,* 181–194.

Pereira, M. E., & Altmann, J. (1985). Development of social behavior in free-living nonhuman primates. In E. S. Watts (Ed.), *Nonhuman primate models for human growth and development* (pp. 217–309). New York: Liss.

Perusse, D. (1993). Cultural and reproductive success in industrial societies: Testing the relationship at proximate and ultimate levels. *Behavioral and Brain Sciences, 16,* 239–242.

Plomin, R. (1990). *Nature and nurture: An introduction to human behavioral genetics.* Pacific Grove, CA: Brooks/Cole.

Postma, A., Winkel, J., Tuiten, A., & van Honk, J. (1999). Sex differences and menstrual cycle effects in human spatial memory. *Psychoneuroendocrinology, 24,* 175–192.

Rowe, D. C. (1994). *The limits of family influence: Genes, experience, and behavior.* New York: Guilford Press.

Rowe, D. C. (1999, June). *Environmental and genetic influences on pubertal development: Evolutionary life history traits?* Paper presented at the convention of the Human Behavior and Evolution Society, Salt Lake City, UT.

Rushton, J. P. (1988). Genetic similarity, mate choice, and fecundity in humans. *Ethology and Sociobiology, 9,* 329–333.

Sagrestano, L. M., McCormick, S. H., Paikoff, R. L., & Holmbeck, G. N. (1999). Pubertal development and parent–child conflict in low-income, urban, African American adolescents. *Journal of Research on Adolescence, 9,* 85–107.

Schell, N. J., & Weisfeld, C. C. (1999). Marital power dynamics: A Darwinian perspective. In J. van der Dennen & D. Smillie (Eds.), *The Darwinian heritage and sociobiology* (pp. 253–259). Westport, CN: Greenwood Press.

Schlegel, A. (1995). A cross-cultural approach to adolescence. *Ethos, 23,* 15–32.

Schlegel, A., & Barry, H., III (1980). Adolescent initiation ceremonies: A cross-cultural code. In H. Barry III & A. Schlegel (Eds.), *Cross-cultural samples and codes.* Pittsburgh, PA: University of Pittsburgh Press.

Schlegel, A., & Barry, H., III (1991). *Adolescence: An anthropological inquiry* (pp. 277–288). New York: Free Press.

Serbin, L. A., Powlishta, K. K., & Gulko, J. (1993). The development of sex typing in middle childhood. *Monographs of the Society for Research in Child Development, 58* (2, Serial No. 232).

Shackelford, T. K., & Larsen, R. J. (1999). Facial attractiveness and physical health. *Evolution and Human Behavior, 20,* 71–76.

Signorella, M. L., Bilger, R. S., & Liben, L. S. (1993). Developmental differences in children's gender schemata about others: A meta-analytic review. *Developmental Review, 13,* 147–183.

Silverberg, S. B. (1989, April). *Parents as developing adults: The impact of perceived distance in the parent–adolescent relationship.* Poster presented at the biennial meeting of the Society for Research in Child Development, Kansas City, MO.

Silverberg, S., & Steinberg, L. (1987). Adolescent autonomy, parent–adolescent conflict, and parental well-being. *Journal of Youth and Adolescence, 16,* 293–312.

Silverman, I., & Eals, M. (1992). Sex differences in spatial abilities: Evolutionary theory and data. In J. H. Barkow & L. Cosmides (Eds.), *The adapted mind* (pp. 533–549). New York: Oxford University Press.

Sommer, B. B. (1978). *Puberty and adolescence.* New York: Oxford University Press.

Spiro, M. E. (1979). *Gender and culture: Kibbutz women revisited.* Durham, NC: Duke University Press.

Steinberg, L. (1987). The impact of puberty on family relations: Effects of pubertal status and pubertal timing. *Developmental Psychology, 23,* 451–460.

Stephens, W. N. (1963). *The family in cross-cultural perspective.* New York: Holt, Rinehart & Winston.

Stetsenko, A., Little, T. D., Godeeva, T., Grassof, M., & Oettingen, G. (2000). Gender effects in children's beliefs about school performance: A cross-cultural study. *Child Development, 71,* 517–527.

Storey, A. E., Walsh, C. J., Quinton, R. L., & Wynne-Edwards, K. E. (2000). Hormonal correlates of paternal responsiveness in new and expectant fathers. *Evolution and Human Behavior, 21,* 79–95.

Surbey, M. K. (1990). Family composition, stress, and the timing of human menarche. In T. E. Ziegler & F. B. Bercovitch (Eds.), *Socioendocrinology of primate reproduction* (pp. 11–32). New York: Wiley–Liss.

Tanner, J. M. (1978). *Fetus into man: Physical growth from conception to maturity.* Cambridge, MA: Harvard University Press.

Thiessen, D., & Gregg, B. (1980). Human associative mating and genetic equilibrium: An evolutionary perspective. *Ethology and Sociobiology, 1,* 111–140.

Thomas, M. L., Harger, J. H., Wagener, D. K., Rabin, B. S., & Gill, T. J. (1985). HLA sharing and spontaneous abortion in humans. *American Journal of Obstetrics and Gynecology, 151,* 1053–1058.

Thornhill, R., & Grammer, K. (1999). The body and face of woman: One ornament that signals quality? *Evolution and Human Behavior, 21,* 105–120.

Thornhill, R. & Gangestad, S. W. (1994). Fluctuating asymmetry correlates with lifetime sex partner numbers and age at first sex in *Homo sapiens. Psychological Science, 5,* 297–302.

Tiger, L., & Shepher, J. (1975). *Women in the kibbutz.* New York: Harcourt Brace Jovanovich.

Trivers, R. L. (1972). Parental investment and sexual selection. In B. Campbell (Ed.), *Sexual selection and the descent of man* (pp. 1871–1971). Chicago: Aldine.

Udry, J. R. (1988). Biological predispositions and social control in adolescent sexual behavior. *American Sociological Review, 53,* 709–722.

Udry, J. R., Morris, N., & Kovenock, J. (1995). Androgen effects on women's gendered behavior. *Journal of Biosocial Science, 27,* 359–369.

Uvnas-Moberg, K. (1997). Physiological and endocrine effects of social contact. In C. Carter, I. Lederhendler, & B. Kirkpatrick (Eds.), *The integrative neurobiology of affiliation* (pp. 146–163). New York: New York Academy of Sciences.

van den Berghe, P. (1979). *Human family systems: An evolutionary view.* New York: Elsevier.

van den Berghe, P. L. (1980). The human family: A sociobiological look. In J. S. Lockard (Ed.), *The evolution of human social behavior* (pp. 67–85). New York: Elsevier.

Weisfeld, C. C. (1986). Female behavior in mixed-sex competition: A review of the literature. *Developmental Review, 6,* 278–299.

Weisfeld, C. C., Weisfeld, G. E., & Callahan, J. W. (1982). Female inhibition in mixed-sex competition among young adolescents. *Ethology and Sociobiology, 3,* 29–42.

Weisfeld, G. E. (1982). The nature–nurture issue and the integrating concept of function. In B. B. Wolman (Ed.), *Handbook of developmental psychology* (pp. 208–229). Englewood Cliffs, NJ: Prentice-Hall.

Weisfeld, G. E. (1986). Teaching about sex differences in human behavior and the biological approach in general. *Politics and the Life Sciences, 5,* 36–43.

Weisfeld, G. E. (1997). Puberty rites as cues to the nature of human adolescence. *Cross-Cultural Research, 31,* 27–55.

Weisfeld, G. E. (1999). *Evolutionary principles of human adolescence.* New York: Basic Books.

Weisfeld, G. E., Russell, R. J. H., Weisfeld, C. C., & Wells, P. A. (1992). Correlates of satisfaction in British marriage. *Ethology and Sociobiology, 13,* 125–145.

Weisfeld, G. E., Weisfeld, C. C., & Segal, N. L. (1997). Final overview: Uniting psychology and biology. In N. L. Segal, G. E. Weisfeld, & C. C. Weisfeld (Eds.), *Uniting psychology and biology: Integrative perspectives on human development* (pp. 525–534). Washington, DC: American Psychological Association.

Welch, M. R., & Page, B. M. (1981). Sex differences in childhood socialization patterns in African societies. *Sex Roles, 7,* 1163–1173.

Whiting, B. B., & Edwards, C. P. (1988). *Children of different worlds: The formation of social behavior.* Cambridge, MA: Harvard University Press.

Whiting, J. W. M. (1965). Menarcheal age and infant stress in humans. In F. A. Beach (Ed.), *Sex and behavior* (pp. 221–233). New York: Wiley.

Whiting, J. W. M., Kluckholn, R., & Anthony, A. S. (1958). The function of male initiation ceremonies at puberty. In E. E. Maccoby, T. M. Newcomb, & E. L. Hartley (Eds.), *Readings in social psychology* (pp. 359–370). New York: Holt, Rinehart & Winston.

Williams, J. E., & Best, D. L. (1986). Sex stereotypes and intergroup relations. In I. S. Worchel & W. G. Austin (Eds.), *Psychology of intergroup relations* (2nd ed.) (pp. 244–259). Chicago: Nelson-Hall.

Williams, J. E., & Best, D. L. (1989). *Sex and psyche: Self-concept viewed cross-culturally.* Newbury Park, CA: Sage.

Williams, J. E., & Best, D. L. (1990). *Measuring sex stereotypes: A multinational study.* Newbury Park, CA: Sage.

Willner, L. A., & Martin, R. D. (1985). Some basic principles of mammalian sexual dimorphism. In J. Ghesquiere, R. D. Martin, & F. Newcombe (Eds.), *Human sexual dimorphism* (pp. 1–42). London: Taylor & Francis.

Worthman, C. M. (1993). Biocultural interactions in human development. In M. E. Pereira & L. A. Fairbanks (Eds.), *Juvenile primates: Life history, development, and behavior* (pp. 339–358). New York: Oxford University Press.

Young, F. (1965). *Initiation ceremonies: A cross-cultural study of status dramatization.* New York: Bobbs–Merrill.

Zeller, A. C. (1987). A role for children in hominid evolution. *Man, 22,* 528–557.

Personality and Emotion

Cynthia Whissell

INTRODUCTION AND DEFINITIONS OF TERMINOLOGY

Definition of Personality

The areas of personality and emotion are being treated together in this article because they are related and to some extent overlapping. Measures of personality quantify an individual's characteristic modes of thought and behavior, and describe them in comparison to a normative standard. By this definition of personality, an "aggressive individual" would consistently think, talk, and act aggressively at a high rate or a high intensity in comparison with most individuals from a comparative sample. In terms of responses to a personality inventory, a "sociable person" would choose answers reflecting sociability at a higher rate than most people. In order to satisfy the criterion of "characteristic modes," the sociable person would have to select sociable responses in preference to alternative responses (e.g., shy responses, aggressive responses).

Definition of Emotion

Emotion is a reaction to an external or internal stimulus event that has both subjective (thoughts) and objective (bodily) components. Naive observers often define emotions as "feelings," a definition that recognizes the importance of the subjective components of emotion. William James placed the body's viscera or guts at the center of the emotional experience in his early theory of emotion (James, 1891/1952, p. 744). Despite the fact that emotions can interfere with cognitive performance, it is generally held that emotions are adaptive—that they exist because they promote survival and are useful in some way. Emotions are assumed to focus and motivate behaviors in response to emotion-provoking situations.

Overlap of Personality, Emotion, and Psychopathology

Personality and emotion employ similar terminologies. Aggression, for example, is both an emotion and a personality trait. The same is true for depression and anxiety. Personality and emotion may be discriminated in terms of their causality and their time frame, with emotions being regarded as situationally dependent reactive states and personality characteristics as enduring traits. Plutchik (1980, pp. 173–198) defined personality in terms of the characteristic emotions displayed and experienced in interpersonal interactions. In this view, the emotions we tend to feel and/or express most often when interacting with other human beings *are* our personality: a timid or shy person feels and expresses fear most often in her or his interactions with others, while a friendly person feels and expresses friendliness or trust. Working in the opposite direction (from personality to emotion), Côté and Moskowitz (1998) demonstrated the validity of personality descriptors as predictors of affect. As well, Yik and Russell (2001) indicated the presence of relationships between momentary affects described by the "big two" dimensions of emotion (pleasantness, activation) and the "big five" factors of personality (extraversion, neuroticism, agreeableness, openness, and conscientiousness).

Both emotion and personality are related to psychopathology (abnormality), with words such as "anxiety" and "depression," for example, describing emotions, traits, and pathological diagnoses. Measures of personality are predictive of psychopathological diagnosis (Lynam & Widiger, 2001).

Definition of Sex

There are many ways to define sex when studying sex differences, ranging from chromosomal definition through the use of identifying bodily characteristics to self-identification. Because most research into personality and emotion does not begin with genetic testing, or even with an evaluation of primary and secondary sexual characteristics, the definition of sex employed in this overview will be the one depending on self-identification as male or female.

Sex Differences in Personality

Scales Designed to Measure Sex Role Identification

Some scales have been designed specifically to measure sex or gender role identification as an aspect of personality. One of the earliest of these was the Mf scale of the Minnesota Multiphasic Personality Inventory (MMPI), which was created shortly after World War II. The original Mf scale was used to assess homosexuality in men. It was developed by the method of extreme groups (empirical criterion keying; Anastasi & Urbina, 1997, p. 351) for which the MMPI is famous, with male soldiers representing the "extremely male" group and female airline employees the "extremely female" group. Answers that matched those of the soldiers were keyed as "masculine" while answers that matched those of the female group were keyed as "feminine." Many items from the original scale which addressed emotions, relationships, and hobbies remain in the present form of the test (MMPI-2: Hathaway & McKinley, 1989). The extreme group identified in the MMPI-2 manual is "men who sought psychiatric help" in respect of problems with homoeroticism and gender role. The Mf scale is scored inversely for men and women. In either case, a high score is indicative of problems. The implications of elevated scores are discussed in the MMPI-2 manual (Hathaway & McKinley, 1989, p. 38). For men, very high scores ($T \geq 76$) are indicative of "conflicts over sexual identity" as well as a "passive and effeminate" character. For women very high scores ($T \geq 70$) are indicative of dominance, aggression, and unfriendliness (MMPI-2). A low score for a man ($T \leq 40$) predicts a macho, action-oriented, crude, and aggressive character, while a low score for a woman ($T \leq 40$) predicts passivity, self-pity, helplessness, and complaining.

A more recently developed inventory focusing on sex roles is the Bem Sex Role Inventory (Bem, 1981). Bem envisioned Masculine and Feminine sex roles as independent dimensions, with individuals being able to score high on one and low on the other (masculine or feminine sex stereotype), high on neither (undifferentiated), or high on both (androgynous). Items on the Bem Sex Role Inventory were not scored ipsatively, or in opposite directions for men and women, so scores were free to vary along both dimensions. Bem ensured that the items were all of high social desirability. Men most often scored higher on the Masculine items and tended to

receive masculine stereotyped scores. The converse was true for women. Analyses of the language of Masculine and Feminine items on the inventory revealed that the Masculine keyed items were more emotionally Active while Feminine keyed items were more emotionally Pleasant (Whissell & Chellew, 1994).

Differences in Personality Scales as Seen in Test Norms

It is not surprising to find sex differences in scales designed specifically to measure such differences, but sex differences are common in personality tests even in scales designed to measure something other than gender role identification. For example, on the MMPI-2 a T score of 50 (average) is associated with a raw Depression score of 18 for men but 20.5 for women. A T score of 50 for Social Introversion is associated with a raw score of 28 for women but 26 for men (Hathaway & McKinley, 1989). These comparisons, based on large samples, suggest that the "average woman" is somewhat more Depressed and more Socially Introverted than the "average man" (Hathaway & McKinley, 1989, p. 55). An investigation of the norms for Cattell's 16 PF (Russell & Karol, 1994, p. 127) reveals, for example, that the mean raw score for women is higher in Warmth ($F = 15.67$, $M = 12.83$) and much higher in Sensitivity ($F = 15.62$, $M = 8.91$) than that for men. On the other hand, men have higher raw means for Dominance ($M = 13.6$, $F = 12.4$) and Privateness ($M = 12.22$, $F = 10.67$). For the revision of the NEO Personality Inventory (NEO PI-R), Costa and McCrae (1992, p. 55) report that women tend to have higher scores on two of their five key scales—Neuroticism and Agreeableness (with no differences evident for Extraversion, Openness, and Conscientiousness). Such differences as did exist in the NEO PI-R were adjudged small (correlations of scale score with sex were 0.2 or lower).

Differences in Specialized Instruments

In comparison with the MMPI, the NEO PI-R and Cattell's 16 PF, there are tests which do not attempt to provide a broad overview of personality, but rather address one particular aspect of it. Feingold (1994) performed a meta-analysis of previously examined studies that had employed inventories and specialized tests measuring Self-Esteem, Internal Locus of Control (belief in one's own agency), Anxiety, and Assertiveness. He reported that overall males scored higher in

Self-Esteem, Assertiveness, and Internal Locus of Control, while scoring lower in Anxiety than females (Feingold, 1994, p. 438). Again, the reported differences, though statistically significant, were small. Feingold's findings are generalizable because they were based on a variety of measurement instruments including Rotter's Locus of Control test, the State–Trait Anxiety Inventory, and the Taylor Manifest Anxiety Scale, and on behavior as well as personality inventories. The meta-analysis of sex differences in Self-Esteem by Kling, Hyde, Showers, and Buswell (1999) confirms the conclusion that Self-Esteem is higher for men than for women.

An Overview of Sex Differences in Personality

Differences between men and women are evident on scales designed to measure sex role identification. Differences for these scales occur in the obvious direction (males are more Masculine, females more Feminine) in part because of the way in which the scales were created. Sex differences are also present in scales measuring aspects of personality not directly related to sex roles. Men, in comparison with women, obtain scores which indicate that they are more Assertive, less Anxious, have higher Self-Esteem and a greater sense of agency (Internal Locus of Control).

On the basis of a meta-analysis of the norms for commonly used personality inventories including the MMPI, Cattell's 16 PF, and the NEO PI-R, Feingold (1994) reached several broad conclusions as to sex differences in personality. Scales from all tests were realigned with the facets of the NEO Personality Inventory. Feingold (1994) concluded that, by and large, females scored higher than males on scales addressing Anxiety (a facet or subscale of Neuroticism), Gregariousness (a facet of Extraversion), and Trust and Tender-Mindedness (facets of Agreeableness) but lower than males on scales addressing Assertiveness (another facet of Extraversion). These differences were stable over tests, time, and a variety of samples.

SEX DIFFERENCES IN EMOTION

Emotion Inventories

Two of the testing instruments most frequently used in the literature to assess emotion or affect are the Multiple

Affect Adjective Check List (MAACL-R) (Zuckerman & Lubin, 1985) and the Profile of Mood States (POMS) (McNair, Lorr, & Droppleman, 1992). Sex differences are evident for both these instruments. The manual for the MAACL-R (Zuckerman & Lubin, 1985, p. 6) reports higher mean scores for women on scales representing Anxiety, Depression, and Positive Affect, and higher mean scores for men on the scale representing Sensation Seeking. In the POMS sex differences for a college sample show females scoring higher on the factors of Tension/Anxiety, Depression/Dejection, and Confusion (McNair et al., 1992, p. 21). A study of outpatients showed similar patterns of sex differences, with male outpatients additionally scoring higher on Vigor (McNair et al., 1992, p. 18).

The state–trait distinction between personality and emotionality is parallelled in two Spielberger instruments, the State–Trait Anger Expression Inventory (STAXI-2) (Spielberger, 1999) and the State-Trait Anxiety Inventory (STAI) (Spielberger, 1983) which address anger and anxiety in both short-term subjective reactions to situations (states) and long-term dispositions (traits). When one-tailed t-tests were used to assess data provided in the STAXI-2 manual (Spielberger, 1999, p. 10), it was determined that "normal adult" men scored higher on both State Anger and Trait Anger than a parallel group of women, though differences were small. For the STAI, groups of military recruits and college students showed sex differences in both State Anxiety and Trait Anxiety in favour of females (Spielberger, 1983, p. 5). However, differences were missing in other comparative groups where men and women scored alike on the inventory.

Emotional Sex Differences Not Based on Inventories

The assessment of personality rests largely on inventories and other testing instruments. In the case of emotion, however, researchers often employ a variety of additional measurement techniques, some of which will be exemplified here.

The Dictionary of Affect is a tool developed to assess the emotionality of language in terms of two dimensions, Pleasantness and Activation (Whissell, 1994a). It is based on ratings assigned by individuals to words along these dimensions. According to Dictionary of Affect scoring, there are emotional differences in descriptive words typical of the two sexes, with men being described more in terms of Activation and women more in terms of Pleasantness (Whissell & Chellew, 1994). Echoes of the male = more Active/female = more Pleasant distinction were found when the Dictionary was used to score excerpts from popular fiction (Whissell, 1994b, 1998) and similar differences were identified in the emotion underlying the language in advertisements directed at men, women, boys, and girls (Rovinelli & Whissell, 1998; Whissell & McCall, 1997).

A relatively new metric for emotion in language addresses the emotionality of the sounds that make up words, with sounds such as l and m being emotionally soft, and sounds such as r and g being emotional rougher (Whissell, 2001a). This metric capitalizes on the interaction between the muscle movements used to express emotion and those used to produce sound. When the metric was applied to several million men's and women's names, men's names were found to contain more Active sounds and women's names more Pleasant sounds (Whissell, 2001a). Both real and randomly created (nonsense) names evince this difference (Whissell, 2001b). A typically Active man's nonsense name was Mowgahk, and a typically Pleasant woman's nonsense name was Neera.

Sex differences are also evident in research that involves emotion-related behaviors. For example, Widen and Russell (2002) reported that the assignment of emotion to a figure in a story told to preschoolers depended on whether the figure was identified as male or female (e.g., disgust was more often attributed to the male figure by boys). In a different domain, MacGeorge, Clark, and Gillihan (2002) reported that women's provision of emotional support to a person in a troubling situation was more person-centered than that of men, and that women had a greater sense of self-efficacy in providing emotional support.

Sexual Selection and Mate Choice

Evolutionary theorists view sex differences as the outcome of sexual selection strategies (Buss, 1994; Whissell, 1996). According to these theorists, the ways in which women choose their mates, the ways in which men succeed in winning the opportunity to mate, and the different strategies that men and women have for ensuring the survival of their offspring and genes are responsible for the sex differences evident in both humans and other animals. This assumption makes the study of mate choice important to the study of sex differences. In his book *The Evolution of Desire*, Buss (1994) outlined the different mate choice preferences of men and women. Buss and colleagues (Buss, Shackleford, Kirkpatrick, & Larsen, 2001) assessed and compared mate preferences in different regions of the United States over a span of several years (1939–1996). Several consistent sex differences were identified, with men, for example, valuing physical attractiveness more than women and women valuing a pleasing disposition and social status more than men. Other preferences (e.g., men's preference for chastity) varied across time or location.

Overview of Sex Differences in Emotion

The results described in this section on emotion suggest that women are more emotionally Anxious, Depressed, Tense, Confused, Positive, and Pleasant than men who are more Sensation-Seeking, Vigorous, Angry, and Active. Whissell (1996) performed a meta-analysis of measures of emotion and personality that had been aligned with the basic emotions from Plutchik's (1980, p. 157) psychoevolutionary theory and with a two-dimensional emotional space representing Pleasantness and Activation. The theory underlying Whissell's meta-classification was evolutionary, and focused on mate selection strategies and differential techniques for promoting genetic survival in men and women. Whissell concluded that sex differences in emotion and personality could be understood in terms of higher scores for men in the Active and Unpleasant areas of emotional space (including the emotions of Disgust/Distrust, Anger, and Boldness) and higher scores for women in the Passive and Pleasant areas of the space (including the emotions of Gregariousness, Friendliness/Trust, Fear, Surprise, and Sadness). By far the majority of personality and emotional differences between men and women in Whissell's meta-analysis were in the direction predicted by this model (the ratio of upheld predictions to contradicted predictions was 19 : 1).

Whissell (1996) also compared sex differences obtained on the basis of self-ratings, scales, and inventories (actual sex differences) with those obtained when individuals were required to make stereotyped judgments (e.g., "Is anger a masculine or feminine emotion?"). Stereotyped sex differences were almost always in the same direction as but larger than real ones, and it was demonstrated that the size of a difference could predict with considerable success (83%) whether the difference was an actual or a stereotypical one. Differences that were too large were almost always the result of stereotypical exaggerations.

SEX DIFFERENCES IN PSYCHOPATHOLOGY

One of the best sources for identifying broad sex differences in psychopathology is the *Diagnostic and Statistical Manual of Mental Disorders* (4th ed.) (*DSM-IV*) (American Psychiatric Association, 1994), the manual used by psychologists and psychiatrists to diagnose psychological problems. Under the heading of individual diagnoses, this manual includes a check-list of diagnostic criteria, a discussion of several related problems, and a section entitled "Specific Culture, Age, and Gender Features" which outlines, where appropriate, sex differences in various diagnostic categories. Major Depressive Episodes, for example, and Major Depressive Disorders (*DSM-IV*, pp. 325, 341) are reported as occurring twice as often in women as in men. This finding echoes those of higher Depression scores for women in personality tests and higher Depression or Sadness scores for women in tests focusing on emotion.

Women are also more likely to be diagnosed with several types of Anxiety Disorder, for example, Panic Attacks (*DSM-IV*, p. 399), Phobias (pp. 408, 414), and Generalized Anxiety Disorder (p. 534), though Obsessive–Compulsive disorder is equally evident in both sexes (p. 421). Again, this is an extension of the finding that women scored higher on Anxiety-related personality scales and emotions. Males were more likely than females to be diagnosed as having Conduct Disorder (p. 88) and Oppositional Defiant Disorder (p. 92). Both these diagnoses involve behavior related to anger and aggression, although both also belong to the category of problems usually first diagnosed before adulthood. An adult diagnosis of Intermittent Explosive Disorder (one which reflects the existence of bursts of aggressive impulses) is also more frequent in males than in females (p. 616).

There is a continuity of sex differences along the dimension describing emotions (reactions to stimuli of relatively short duration, states), personality factors (characteristic manners of reacting, traits), and pathologies (diagnoses of abnormality). That which is more typical of one sex at the emotional level (e.g., Anger in men or Anxiety in women), is more likely to be a personality characteristic typical of the same sex (e.g., Aggression in men or Neuroticism in women), and is also more likely to be involved in pathological diagnoses more commonly associated with that sex (e.g., Intermittent Explosive Disorder in men or Generalized Anxiety Disorder in women). This continuity is emphasized in articles, such as the one by Lynam and Widiger (2001), that demonstrate parallels between the NEO PI-R five-factor model of personality and diagnoses of pathology.

One of the most serious problems associated with the understanding of sex differences in psychopathology is the problem of reporting bias. The *DSM-IV* frequently cautions that its epidemiological conclusions are based on analyses of individuals presenting themselves for help with certain problems. If men are as depressed as women, by and large, but are also much less willing to look for help with their depression, the observed reporting rates (more women reporting depression) would be biased, and they would not accurately reflect the fact of depression. The authors of the *DSM-IV* also recognize the importance of culture in the reporting of psychological problems. Culture is frequently mentioned in the segment on special features, as well as in Appendix I. The writers advise that "it is important that the clinician take into account the individual's ethnic and cultural context" in making a diagnosis (*DSM-IV*, p. 843). Diagnoses such as "evil eye", "ghost sickness", "koro", and "pibloktoq" are regarded as distinct in other cultures but are difficult to understand from a North American point of view. It is possible that diagnoses of "depression" and "panic attack" make equally little sense when they are proposed in other cultures.

CULTURAL AND REGION

Making Cultural Comparisons

Cultural differences are of concern in the study of emotion and personality as well as in the diagnosis of pathology. Although some measures of emotion (chiefly those which rely on bodily responses, or judgments of basic facial expressions) do not vary greatly from culture to culture, a description of emotion in terms of language cannot be assumed, without study, to generalize across cultures. Authors writing in the book edited by Russell,

Fernandez-Dols, Manstead, and Wellencamp (1995) include examples of many cases where emotional language from one culture does not match that from another. Even what are considered "basic" emotions in North American research may not have fully equivalent labels in the languages of other cultures. On the other hand, research into the development of categories of emotion based on natural language suggests that these categories may be universal (Hupka, Lenton, & Hutchison, 1999), and Moore, Romney, Hsia, and Rusch (1999) emphasize the universality of the semantic structure of emotional terms (while allowing for, and describing, intercultural differences). There is considerable evidence of the validity of the factor structure of the NEO PI-R in many different cultures (e.g., McCrae & Costa, 1997).

Sex Differences in Personality that Are Relatively Stable across Cultures

Feingold (1994) examined cross-cultural norms for the PRF, a test related to the NEO PI-R described above. The norms came from Canada, China, Finland, Germany, Poland, and Russia. Overall, males scored significantly higher than females on the facet of Assertiveness and females scored higher than males on facets reflecting Impulsivity, Tender-Mindedness, and Order. Costa et al. (2001) examined cross-cultural modifiers of sex differences in the facets of the NEO, reporting that men across cultures (e.g., Zimbabwe, Peru, Belgium, Croatia) score higher on scales of Assertiveness and Openness to Ideas while women score high on scales reflecting Neuroticism, Warmth, Agreeableness, and Openness to Feelings. Contrary to what might have been predicted on the basis of the assumption that culture creates or constructs sex differences, the sex differences observed were strongest for cultures with the most progressive sex role ideologies. This finding is also reported by Greenberger, Cheng, Tally, and Dong (2000) who found greater sex differences in depression for American than for Chinese youths, though both were in the expected direction (higher scores for females).

Studies based on observation rather than on reactions to linguistic stimuli overcome several of the limitations associated with language. Munroe, Hulefeld, Rodgers, Tomeo, and Yamazaki (2000) observed the occurrence of aggressive behaviors in the children of several nonwestern

cultures (Belize, Kenya, Nepa, American Samoa), and concluded that boys displayed aggressive behaviors more often than girls. A similar finding had been reported by researchers engaged in the Six Cultures Project (children from Nyansongo, Juxtlahuaca, Tarong, Khalapur, Orchard Town, and Taira cultures were compared) (Whiting, Whiting, & Longabaugh, 1975). In the six cultures as a group, girls behaved more nurturantly and boys more aggressively (Whiting et al., 1975, p. 166). Cross-cultural studies of psychopathology in terms of behavioral measures include those of suicide. In almost all cultures, successful suicide is more common in men than in women (Phillips, Li, & Zhang, 2002), the only question being how much more common. This conclusion applies to many nonwestern countries (e.g., India), with few exceptions (e.g., China).

Regional and Historical Differences within the United States

Culture can act as a modifier of sex differences even within a single country. Buss, Shackleford, Kirkpatrick, & Larsen (2001) studied mating preferences in several regions (e.g., Michigan, Texas) and across a 67-year time span (1939–1996). The authors report significant regional and historical modifiers of sex differences in mate preferences (e.g., men in Texas valued housekeeping, cooking, and chastity more than those in other states; mutual attraction and love rose in women's estimation from fifth- to first-ranked criterion over time). Although there were differences across generations and across regions, there were also similarities or consistencies. Sex differences that persisted across time were men's higher ranking of good health, good housekeeping, and good looks, and women's higher ranking of ambition/industriousness, good financial prospects, and similar educational background.

An Overview of Cultural Modifiers of Sex Differences

Feingold (1994) noted in his research that the interaction between culture and sex (for measures of personality) was ordinal. This implies that such differences as are reported tend to be in a predominant direction regardless of culture, although they may vary in size. Sex differences seldom reverse themselves across cultures (with men, e.g., having higher scores on trait X in some cultures and women having higher scores on the same trait in others). This finding can be used to summarize the study of cross-cultural sex differences, although it is not without its contradictions. The underlying pattern of differences remains the one established in the sections above discussing emotion, personality, and psychopathology, but differences along individual measures might be absent, muted, or exaggerated in various cultures. In view of the evidence summarized here, though, it is best to keep in mind that there are "tremendous diversities of human cultural institutions" that have a "profound impact on individual psychology," as well as "universals of human nature that transcend cultural differences" (McCrae & Costa, 1997, p. 509).

SEX DIFFERENCES AND THE NATURE–NURTURE CONTROVERSY

The nature–nurture debate remains a topical one in the area of sex differences, with some theorists attributing sex differences to differences in disposition (innate personality or emotion) and others preferring to attribute them to differences in situation (culture, social construction, roles; Eagly & Wood, 1999).

Nature-Based Explanations

Nature-based explanations of sex differences have grown in popularity in recent years due to the emergence of research identifying particular genes that reflect personality traits (e.g., Egeland, Gerhard, Pauls, & Sussex, 1987). Unless these genes are located on the 23rd chromosome pair, however, they are not sex-linked and would not differentiate men from women directly. The chromosome pair responsible for sex differences, including those formatted *in utero* by means of hormones that influence the developing fetus, is the 23rd. Hormones produced by this pair are capable of modifying the effects of genes from other pairs, thus making their own influence more widely felt than one might at first assume.

The "nature" side of the nature–nurture debate in the area of sex differences is further bolstered by studies of heritability (e.g., Stein, Jang, & Livesley, 2002) that examine similarities in emotion, personality, and psychopathology between relatives with varying degrees of genetic similarity. Although such studies recognize a

reaction range (a degree to which nurture or environment can reshape a characteristic), they assume that nature provides a significant contribution to individual differences in personality and emotion. Nature-based explanations of sex differences frequently attribute these to the sexually dimorphic brain. There are sex differences in brain size (men's are larger), laterality (men's are more lateralized), and responsiveness (different regions of men's and women's brains react differently to similar stimuli, e.g., Karama et al., 2002) with differences being tied to the effects of testosterone released during fetal development. Findings that are consistent across cultures (e.g., Costa et al., 2001; Munroe et al., 2000) suggest that personality and emotion may be pancultural and innate, and therefore nature based. However, the same studies that report similar patterns of differences across cultures (e.g., Eid & Deiner, 2001) are also quick to point out differences within a particular culture. The presence of such differences confirms that nurture is a contributing factor to sex differences in personality and emotion. As well, the appearance of the same sex difference across cultures is a necessary condition for considering that difference an innate one, but not a sufficient condition: similarities *across* cultures may be caused by similarities *of* cultures. It is relatively difficult to attribute causality when similar cultures have one or more factors in common (Ember, 1996).

Nurture-Based Explanations

Nurture-based explanations of sex differences focus on the contention that situation is more formative of personality and emotion than disposition. With the exception of behaviorism, psychology came late to such explanations (e.g., Heider, 1958, p. 297). Students of personality such as Mischel (1973, p. 162) suggested that personality does not exist purely as a disposition and that it cannot be defined without situational referents. The situational viewpoint implies that there may be as many differences between one individual's personality from one situation to the next as there are differences between people. The power of schemas or roles (e.g., Tenenbaum & Leaper, 2002) and the presence of cultural, regional, and historical differences, such as the ones mentioned in various examples above, all suggest that nurture is an important determinant of sex differences. Tenenbaum and Leaper (2002) illustrated the manner in which gender schemas held by parents influenced their children's manner of thinking about gender. This suggests that there are cultural mechanisms in place that promote thinking in terms of sex differences.

Nature plus Nurture

Most researchers would not go so far as to deny totally the validity of the complementary viewpoint (nurture/ situation or nature/disposition) in explaining sex differences, but many have distinct preferences for one approach or the other, and these are evident in their work. Buss, for example, who based his theory of sex differences in mate selection on the theory of evolution, clearly favours nature-based explanations for these differences, even though he acknowledges the importance of culture and environment (Buss et al., 2001). Eagly and Wood (1999), on the other hand, suggested that Buss's own data support a "social structural account" of sex differences rather than indicate the presence of an "evolved disposition." In their article on emotion and behavioral disturbance, Rutter and Silberg (2002) address the interplay of nature and nurture. The gene–environment interaction is important in the manifestation of various emotions and disturbances—for example, the risk of antisocial behavior in adoptees increases only as a function of the joint presence of a genetic predisposition and an adverse adoptive family environment. Neither of these by itself is predictive of antisocial behavior.

ISSUES

Summary of Previously Mentioned Issues

Several issues in the study of sex differences in personality and emotion have been mentioned already in this article. These include the problem of reporting bias (observed differences may be due to differences in the ways in which men and women report their preferences and reactions), generalizability (results from personality tests may not generalize to other situations or even to other tests), attribution (observed differences tend to be attributed—by inference—to situations, dispositions, or a combination of the two), degree of overlap (even when different, men's and women's scores still evince considerable overlap), and cultural, regional, and historical variability (results differ to some degree across cultures,

regions, and years). There are several more issues deserving of mention.

How Big Are Sex Differences?

Reports of sex differences in early research involved merely the establishment of statistically significant differences between mean scores obtained by men and women. Towards the end of the 20th century, researchers began to insist on a more careful reporting of the size of sex differences. The metric commonly used to represent the size of differences is d' (d prime) or the difference between means expressed in standard deviation units. A d' of 1 suggests that the means of distributions representing men's and women's scores are one standard deviation apart. There is a total (100%) overlap between male and female score distributions when $d' = 0$, and an overlap of close to zero when $d' = 5$. Feingold (1994) reported, in meta-analysis of sex differences in personality, that d' scores for his comparisons were in the range of 0.30, while Whissell's (1996) meta-analysis identified d' measures greater than 0.59 as stereotypes rather than actual sex differences. With d' values of 0.3, only a small proportion of all cases occur in areas of nonoverlap between men's and women's scores. An alternate manner of reporting sex differences is by means of a coefficient of effect size (e.g., eta, r). All types of measures confirm the oft-stated conclusion that although there are sex differences in personality and emotion, these are not of such size as to separate men and women completely, and a good deal of overlap is present between scores generated by the two sexes.

Variability of Scores

Although d' successfully establishes the size of sex differences, this metric is based on the assumption of roughly equal standard deviations for men's and women's scores. In addition to, or in lieu of, differences between means, there may be sex differences in standard deviations. For example, 12 of the 16 PF scales have larger standard deviations for women's than for men's scores, though differences are small (Russell & Karol, 1994, p. 127). Data are not easily available to test this hypothesis, but there seems to have been an increase in the variability of women's scores on tests of personality and emotion over the last 30 years. Unequal standard deviations might affect the calculation of d', and they are also of interest in their own right.

Sample Size

Meta-analyses reporting sex differences in personality and emotion or cross-cultural analyses that report significant sex differences often include samples of thousands of cases, while smaller studies conducted with $n = 100$ or $n = 50$ may fail to report sex differences for the same variables, even though means and standard deviations for these variables are similar across studies. This is because large sample sizes are associated with greater power in statistical hypothesis testing than small ones. Power is defined as the ability to reject correctly the null hypothesis (i.e., reject it when this hypothesis is wrong in the population), and power rises in proportion to the square root of sample size n. If sex differences in personality and emotion were large, then the null hypothesis of equality could be rejected with the use of relatively small samples, but if the differences are small (and it has been demonstrated several times that they are), the null hypothesis of equality of the sexes could not be rejected in small-n projects without sufficient power.

Not rejecting the null is not equivalent to proving that two groups are equal, and a lack of power raises the researcher's risk of committing a type II error (failing to reject the null when the null is false in the population).

Sexism

To what extent does the conclusion that there are meaningful sex differences in personality and emotion leave the researcher open to accusations of sexism or sex bias? Glick and Fiske (2001) have argued that even benevolent or nonantipathetic sexism—where sexism is defined as the unwarranted acceptance of sex differences—can influence behaviors in ways unfavourable to women. A commentator on the original article (Sax, 2002) argued that there were actual sex differences between men and women, but Glick and Fiske (2002) affirmed that they were not measuring benevolent sexism in terms of such differences but rather by means of items that "did not access beliefs about well-established sex differences in personality" (p. 445).

The obvious question arising from this dialog among researchers is: "How thoroughly must a sex difference be documented before accepting it as fact will not make a person sexist?" To add to the confusion, Glick and Fiske (2002) maintain that "belief in sex differences, arguably, could be both accurate and sexist" (p. 445).

Because of the overlap between the sexes in terms of most measures of personality and emotion, even those differences accepted as "facts" do not have much power to discriminate successfully between men and women in a majority of cases. This being true, the person using such facts in a discriminative manner might still be liable to accusations of sexism.

Secondary Effects of Emotion and Personality

Sex differences in emotion and personality do not occur in a vacuum—they often impact on or interact with other variables such as cognitive performance. For example, Pomerantz, Altermatt, and Saxon (2002) noted that girls from grades 4–6 experienced more internal distress over school performance at the same time as actually performing better than boys. Jacobs, Lanza, Osgood, Eccles, and Wigfield (2002) reported that girls have a lower sense of competence in the areas of mathematics and sports than boys, while being more confident than boys in the area of language arts. The male–female difference in competence beliefs with respect to mathematics was not modified by grade (1–12), with boys always having the advantage. Emotional reactions such as the ones outlined in these two articles may result in self-identifications like those described by Nosek, Banaji, and Greenwald (2002), where female college students had negative attitudes towards mathematics and used gender stereotypes to conclude that math was "not me" (the article was entitled "Math = male, me = female, therefore math ≠ me").

Theories Predicting Sex Differences

This article has studied sex differences by examining measures that display such differences. An alternate approach would be the theoretical one. Several of the classical personality theories such as those discussed in a classic text on personality (e.g., Hall & Lindzey, 1970) have something to say on the issue of sex differences. Freudian theory, for example, originally explained sex differences in terms of penis envy, differential complexes (Oedipus, Electra), and differential problems with identification. A contrasting nurture-based theory, that of Skinner, explained not only personality but most behavior in terms of reinforcement history.

CONCLUDING OVERVIEW

With the qualifications outlined above, research has revealed several robust but small sex differences in emotion, personality, and psychopathology. The differences included in Table 1 have appeared with some consistency across both times and cultures, and have been validated in a variety of experiments. Differences are categorized

Table 1. Stable Sex Differences in Personality, Emotion, and Psychopathology[a]

Categories and measures	High scoring group	Countries/cultures other than North America[b]
Femininity	Women	
Masculinity	Men	
Agency/Activation	Men	
Self-Esteem		Australia, Canada, Holland, Hong Kong
Internal Locus of Control		India
Activation		Canada, China, Finland
Anger/Aggression		American Samoa, Belize, Kenya, Nepal, Six Cultures[c]
Diagnoses Related to Anger		
Boldness/Excitement Seeking		25[d]
Openness to Ideas		25
Distrust/Disgust		
Assertiveness		Canada, China, Finland, Germany, Russia, 25
Dominance		Six Cultures
Suicide		Africa, Asian Countries, India, Middle East
Friendliness/Gregariousness	Women	
Pleasantness		
Positive Affect		25
Gregariousness		Canada, Finland, Russia, 25
Trust		
Agreeableness		Canada, Finland, Germany, Poland, Russia, 25
Openness to Feelings		25
Tender-Mindedness		Canada, Finland, Germany, Poland, Russia, 25
Warmth/Nurturance		Six Cultures, 25
Sensitivity		
Anxiety/Depression	Women	
Anxiety		Israel, Sweden, Canada, India, Thailand, 25
Diagnoses Related to Anxiety		
Depression		China, 25
Diagnoses Related to Depression		
Neuroticism		Canada, Finland
Surprise		
Fear/Timidity		
Mating Criteria		
Good Health	Men	
Good Looks		
Good Housekeeping Skills		
Ambition/Industriousness	Women	
Financial Prospects		
Similar Education/Background		

[a] This is a lexical summary of sex differences. Individual terms have been preserved in order to illustrate research findings, but there is some overlap among terms used. Tender-mindedness, for example, is a facet of Agreeableness on one test and a distinct dimension of another; Anxiety is both a facet of Neuroticism and a scale and diagnosis in its own right.

[b] All differences in Table 1 have been reported in North American studies. Additional countries and cultures exhibiting the differences (as per articles referenced) are cited in the third column. The list of studies employed is limited so differences may exist that have not been included above.

[c] The Six Cultures are the Nyansongo, Juxtlahuaca, Tarong, Taira, Khalapur, and Orchard Town (Whiting et al., 1975).

[d] The 25 cultures are those discussed by Costa et al. (2001) and include a wide variety of groups from Croatians through African and European South Africans to Peruvians, Estonians, and Malaysians. There were also significant intercultural differences.

into subareas representing Agency and Aggression (where men generally score higher), Friendliness and Gregariousness (where women score higher), Anxiety and Depression (where women also score higher), and Mating Criteria (where men and women score higher on different sets of criteria). These differences are certainly multidetermined, with both nature and nurture contributing to the observed effects, and not necessarily in the same proportion to all effects.

Future meta-analyses might fruitfully investigate the relative or proportional contributions of different influences to sex differences, taking their cue from work such as that of Moore et al. (1999) that partitioned the semantic structure of emotion words in terms of culturally shared meaning, culturally specific meaning, and individual differences and error. Researchers might also choose to address the role that culture plays in sex differences by aligning cultures along several dimensions, taking their cue from the Six Cultures Project (Whiting et al., 1975) which not only studied relatively simple cultures but also quantified them in ways that were seen to be related to emotional behaviors (cultural simplicity predicted nurturant/responsible actions while a more nuclear household structures predicted greater sociable intimacy).

REFERENCES

American Psychiatric Association. (1994). *Diagnostic and statistical manual of mental disorders (DSMV-IV)* (4th ed.). Washington, DC: Author.

Anastasi, A., & Urbina, S. (1997). *Psychological testing* (7th ed.). Upper Saddle River, NJ: Prentice-Hall.

Bem, S. L. (1981). *Bem Sex Role Inventory: Professional manual.* Palo Alto, CA: Consulting Psychologists Press.

Buss, D. M. (1994). *The evolution of desire.* New York: Basic Books.

Buss, D. M., Shackleford, T. K., Kirkpatrick, L.A., & Larsen, R. J. (2001). A half century of mate preferences: The cultural evolution of values. *Journal of Marriage and Family, 63,* 491–503.

Cole, P. M., Bruschi, C. J., & Baby, L. T. (2002). Cultural differences in children's emotional reactions to difficult situations. *Child Development, 73,* 983–996.

Costa, P. T., Jr., & McCrae, R. R. (1992). *NEO PI-R: Professional manual.* Odessa, FL: Psychological Assessment Resources.

Costa, P. T., Jr., Terracciano, A., & McCrae, R. R. (2001). Gender differences in personality traits across cultures: Robust and surprising findings. *Journal of Personality and Social Psychology, 81,* 322–331.

Côté, S., & Moskowitz, D. S. (1998). On the dynamic covariation between interpersonal behavior and affect: Prediction from

Neuroticism, Extraversion, and Agreeableness. *Journal of Personality and Social Psychology, 75,* 1032–1046.

Eagly, A. H., & Wood, W. (1999). The origins of sex differences in human behavior: Evolved dispositions versus social roles. *American Psychologist, 54,* 408–423.

Egeland, J. A., Gerhard, P. S., Pauls, D. L., & Sussex, J. N. (1987). Bipolar affective disorders linked to DNA markers on chromosome 11. *Nature, 325,* 783–787.

Eid, M., & Diener, E. (2001). Norms for experiencing emotions in different cultures: Inter- and intranational differences. *Journal of Personality and Social Psychology, 81,* 869–885.

Ember, C. (1996). Gender differences and roles. In D. Levinson & M. Ember (Eds.), *Encyclopedia of cultural anthropology.* (pp. 519–523). New York, NY: Holt.

Feingold, A. (1994). Gender differences in personality: A meta-analysis. *Psychological Bulletin, 116,* 429–456.

Glick, P., & Fiske, S. T. (2001). An ambivalent alliance: Hostile and benevolent sexism as complementary justifications for gender inequality. *American Psychologist, 56,* 109–118.

Glick, P., & Fiske, S. T. (2002). Ambivalent responses. *American Psychologist, 57,* 444–446.

Greenberger, E., Cheng, C., Tally, S. R., & Dong, Q. (2000). Family, peer, and individual correlates of depressive symptomatology among U.S. and Chinese adolescents. *Journal of Consulting and Clinical Psychology, 68,* 209–219.

Hall, C. S., & Lindzey, G. (1970). *Theories of personality* (2nd ed.). New York: Wiley.

Hathaway, S. R., & McKinley, J. C. (1989). *MMPI-2: Manual for administration and scoring.* Minneapolis, MN: University of Minnesota Press.

Heider, F. (1958). *The psychology of interpersonal relations.* New York: Wiley.

Hupka, R. B., Lenton, A. P., & Hutchison, K. A. (1999). Universal development of emotion categories in natural language. *Journal of Personality and Social Psychology, 77,* 247–278.

Jacobs, J. E., Lanza, S., Osgood, D. W., Eccles, J. S., & Wigfield, A. (2002). Changes in children's self-competence and values: Gender and domain differences across grades one through twelve. *Child Development, 73,* 509–527.

James, W. (1952). *The principles of psychology.* Chicago, IL: Encyclopedia Brittanica. (Original Work Published 1891.)

Karama, S., Lecours, A. R., Leroux, J.-M., Bourgouin, P., Beaudoin, G. et al. (2002). Areas of brain activation in males and females during views of erotic film excerpts. *Human Brain Mapping, 16,* 1–13.

Kling, K. C., Hyde, J. S., Showers, C. J., & Buswell, B. N. (1999). Gender differences in self-esteem: A meta-analysis. *Psychological Bulletin, 125,* 470–500.

Lynam, D. R., & Widiger, T. A. (2001). Using the five-factor model to represent the DSM-IV personality disorders: An expert consensus approach. *Psychological Bulletin, 110,* 401–412.

MacGeorge, E. L., Clark, R. A., & Gillihan, S. J. (2002). Sex differences in the provision of skillful emotional support: The mediating role of self-efficacy. *Communication Reports, 15,* 17–28.

McCrae, R. R., & Costa, P. T., Jr. (1997). Personality trait structure as a human universal. *American Psychologist, 52,* 509–516.

McNair, D. M., Lorr, M., & Droppleman, L. F. (1992). *Profile of Mood States manual.* San Diego: Education and Industrial Testing Service.

Mischel, W. (1973). Implications of behavior theory for personality assessment. In H. N. Mischel & W. Mischel (Eds.), *Readings in personality*. New York: Holt, Rinehart & Winston.

Moore, C. C., Romney, A. K., Hsia, T.-L., & Rusch, C. D. (1999). The universality of the semantic structure of emotion terms: Methods for the study of inter- and intra-cultural variability. *American Anthropologist, 10,* 529–546.

Munroe, R. L., Hulefeld, R., Rodgers, J. M., Tomeo, D. L., & Yamazaki, S. K. (2000). Aggression among children in four cultures. *Cross-Cultural Research, 34,* 3–25.

Nosek, B. A., Banaji, M. R., & Greenwald, A. G. (2002). Math = male, me = female, therefore math ≠ me. *Journal of Personality and Social Psychology, 83,* 44–59.

Phillips, M. R., Li, X., & Zhang, Y. (2002). Suicide rates in China, 1995–99. *Lancet, 359,* 835–840.

Pomerantz, E. M., Altermatt, E. R., & Saxon, J. L. (2002). Making the grade but feeling distressed: Gender differences in academic performance and internal distress. *Journal of Educational Psychology, 94,* 394–404.

Plutchik, R. (1980). *Emotion: A psychoevolutionary synthesis.* Philadelphia: Harper & Row.

Rovinelli, L., & Whissell, C. (1998). Emotion and style in 30 psecond television advertisements targeted at men, women, boys, and girls. *Perceptual and Motor Skills, 86,* 1048–1050.

Russell, J. A., Fernandez-Dols, J.-M., Manstead, A. S. R., & Wellencamp, J. C. (Eds.), (1995). *Everyday concepts of emotion: An introduction to the psychology, anthropology, and linguistics of emotion.* New York: Kluwer.

Russell, M., & Karol, D. (1994). *16PF Administrator's manual* (5th ed.). Champaign, IL: Institute for Personality and Ability Testing.

Rutter, M., & Silberg, J. (2002). Gene-environment interplay in relations to emotional and behavioral disturbance. *Annual Review of Psychology, 53,* 463–490.

Sax, L. (2002). Maybe men and women are different. *American Psychologist, 57,* 444.

Spielberger, C. D. (1983). *Manual for the State-Trait Anxiety Inventory.* Palo Alto, CA: Consulting Psychologists Press.

Spielberger, C. D. (1999). *State–Trait Anger Expression Inventory-2: Professional manual.* Odessa, FL: Psychological Assessment Resources.

Stein, M. B., Jang, K. L., & Livesley, W. J. (2002). Heritability of social anxiety-related concerns and personality characteristics. *Journal of Nervous and Mental Disease, 190,* 219–224.

Tenenbaum, H. R., & Leaper, C. (2002). Are parents' gender schemas related to their children's gender-related cognitions? A meta-analysis. *Developmental Psychology, 38,* 615–630.

Whissell, C. (1994a). A computer program for the objective analysis of style and emotional connotations of prose: Hemingway, Galsworthy, and Faulkner compared. *Perceptual and Motor Skills, 79,* 815–824.

Whissell, C. (1994b). Objective analysis of text: I. A comparison of adventure and romance novels. *Perceptual and Motor Skills, 79,* 1567–1570.

Whissell, C. (1996). Predicting the size and direction of sex differences in measures of emotion and personality. *Genetic, Social, and General Psychology Monographs, 122,* 253–284.

Whissell, C. (1998). Linguistic, emotional, and content analyses of sexually explicit scenes in popular fiction. *Canadian Journal of Human Sexuality, 7,* 147–159.

Whissell, C. (2001a). Sound and emotion in given names. *Names, 59,* 97–120.

Whissell, C. (2001b). Cues to referent gender in randomly constructed names. *Perceptual and Motor Skills, 93,* 856–858.

Whissell, C., & Chellew, G. (1994). The position of sex-typical words in two-dimensional emotion space. *Psychological Reports, 74,* 3–11.

Whissell, C., & McCall, L. (1997). Pleasantness, activation, and sex differences in advertising. *Psychological Reports, 81,* 355–367.

Whiting, B. B., Whiting, J. W. M., & Longabaugh, R. (1975). *Children of six cultures: A psychocultural analysis.* Cambridge, MA: Harvard University Press.

Widen, S. C., & Russell, J. A. (2002). Gender and preschoolers' perception of emotion. *Merrill–Palmer Quarterly, 48,* 248–262.

Yik, M. S. M., & Russell, J. A. (2001). Predicting the big two of affect from the big five. *Journal of Research in Personality, 35,* 247–277.

Zuckerman, M., & Lubin, B. (1985). *Manual for the Multiple Affect Adjective Check List revised.* San Diego, CA: Education and Industrial Testing Service.

Gender Roles, Status, and Institutions

Courtship and Marriage

Lewellyn Hendrix

INTRODUCTION

Past and present cultures around the world have diverse practices in selecting spouses and in the nature of marriage itself. Important variations in spouse selection include the range of persons eligible for one to marry, the persons having a voice in this selection, the gifts or transactions accompanying marriage, and the culturally appropriate motives for marriage. Marriages around the world vary in many ways, including their intimacy or aloofness, the extent and form of violence, the level of husband dominance, the division of labor, divorce freedom, level of divorce, and the number of permitted spouses of either sex. Space does not permit discussion of all of these aspects of courtship and marriage, and some are discussed elsewhere in this volume

My focus is on the range of eligible spouses, voice in mate selection, and in the number of permitted spouses of either sex.

COURTSHIP

Modern Western cultures value love as the base on which to build an intimate marriage. Personal freedom—both in voice and in a wide range of eligible spouses—is seen as essential to this process. In many non–Western cultures, this love—intimacy—freedom complex is less often valued or practiced. There are a range of courtship practices and values which are joined together in numerous ways in cultures around the world.

Selecting a Spouse

Courtship can be thought of as shopping for a spouse. In some cultures, potential spouses do the shopping, while in others parents and other kin make the selection. We usually refer to these patterns as free-choice and arranged marriage, but these terms are oversimplifications as efforts at cross-cultural coding show (Broude & Greene, 1983). Some extreme cases, such as the United States

today and some traditional Asian societies, fit this pair of concepts. The United States exemplifies free-choice for bride and groom with the absence of parental veto power, despite the call in the traditional Christian marriage ceremony for objections to the couple's marrying, and despite the fact that youth want their parents to approve. Basically, Americans believe that they have a right to marry anyone they want, without "interference" from other people. Traditional Japan exemplifies parental shopping with no voice for potential spouses. Before modern times, marriages were commonly arranged by parents with the help of go-betweens. Offspring typically had no voice in the decision of whom they were to marry, and often met their spouses only at the wedding or shortly before (Freeman, 1968).

Some other cultures have elements of both free choice and marriage arrangement. Here is one place where the free-choice versus arranged marriage distinction runs into trouble for these courtship systems crosscut the two categories. Some cultures with so-called arranged marriage let offspring veto the parents' decisions, while in others, where youth do the shopping, parents have a veto right over the selections of courting youth. Rhetorically, we may ask: "In which case is there the greater freedom for marrying?" While the answer is not clear, obviously these are intermediate categories standing between free choice and arranged marriage. Freeman's (1968, p. 457) definition of marriage arrangement as a matter of degree—the extent of external intervention in mate choice—is preferable.

We must think yet more complexly about courtship and marriage, for the degree of arrangement of marriage—or, conversely, the extent of freedom to choose—may be somewhat different for men than for women. Some cultures have more intervention in women's choices of spouse than in men's. A table constructed from Broude and Greene's (1983) codes on 142 cultures around the world shows that only 12 have fully free choice for both sexes and 16 have fully arranged marriage for both. The remainder are intermediate in level of intervention. Most have similar levels of intervention in the marriages of both sexes. While 20 of these cultures clearly have greater freedom for men, only two clearly have more freedom for women. However, this statement also needs qualification: if the groom's parents do not intervene in his choice, but the bride's parents have veto power over hers, her parents nonetheless do intervene in his choice of spouse. Thus degree of sex difference in intervention cannot be so great as it initially appears. The question of whether parental intervention is really patriarchal intervention or involves the mother, and the conditions under which these occur, is an issue that needs investigation.

Most comparative research on courtship has used the awkward distinction between arranged and free-choice marriage, or has examined the place of romantic love as a criterion. Given the conceptual problems in this distinction, our knowledge of the structural sources of the degree of arrangement is provisional at best. Some research has been stimulated by the theories of family life linking free choice to the decline of extended families and kinship structuring of social life (Parsons, 1951; Goode, 1967). Some cultures with extended families, such as India today, do have explicit ideologies against romantic love and free choice which bolster the authority of family elders in arranging marriages (Derne, 1994). Earlier research asked whether arranged marriage is more likely in societies in which the couple lives among kin (non-neolocal residence). This research found that, while romantic criteria are unrelated to residence rule, they are associated with lower subsistence dependence of spouses in non-neolocal societies (Coppinger, 1968). Romantic criteria do occur with more freedom of choice (Lee & Stone, 1980; Rosenblatt & Cozby, 1972). Dances and community endogamy appear to facilitate freedom of choice, since these allow youth to become better acquainted. A side-effect of this freedom of choice, perhaps due to more extensive and unsupervised interaction, is greater courtship antagonism between the sexes (Rosenblatt & Cozby, 1972). Unsupervised interaction may also reflect less concern over the control of sexual activity. Thus research also shows that romantic mate selection criteria are related to greater tolerance for premarital sex and for extramarital sex on the wife's part (de Munck & Korotayev, 1999). This suggests that equality of women and men in sexual matters could be another factor in love-based marriage.

Further research using a larger sample of cultures found some associations of romantic criteria and freedom of choice to extended family structure and to non-neolocal residence but concluded that these are "not particularly strong" (Lee & Stone, 1980, p. 326). Another study showed that greater intervention, while unrelated to extended family, is related to other structural traits such as transactions of substantial amounts of goods accompanying marriage, the number of social strata in the society, and patrilineal descent (Hendrix, 2002). Moreover, this study found no association of arranged marriage with strong male dominance, as posited by some theories (e.g., Collins, 1975). However, it found that male dominance and extended family structure statistically work together to enhance or reduce marriage arrangement: In societies with more male dominance, arranged marriage tends to occur in the absence of large extended family structures. However, in societies with more sexual equality, elders are more likely to arrange marriages if there are extended families. Clearly, there is a lot to be learned about the conditions under which arranged marriage is practiced, not to mention how it might relate to the quality of marriage itself.

Research in evolutionary psychology has examined personal mate-selection criteria in samples of modern nations. While this research needs to take into account that parental intervention in mate selection is common and ask about preferences for offspring's mates, its findings are nonetheless interesting. In a study of individual preferences across 37 countries, males were found to prefer features associated with reproductive value or fertility, such as youth and beauty, while females tended to prefer ambitious mates with good financial prospects. Few countries showed exceptions to this pattern, suggesting that humans may have an evolved sex difference in mate choice (Buss, 1989). However, other scholars have reanalyzed these data to show that the degree of sex difference varies with social structure. Specifically, the degree of sex difference in mate selection criteria is stronger in less developed countries (Glenn, 1989) and in countries with greater sexual inequality (Eagly & Wood, 1999; Kasser & Sharma, 1999).

The Field of Eligible Spouses

All cultures rule that some close kin are ineligible as sexual partners or as marriage partners. The social norms pertaining to these are respectively the incest taboo and kin exogamy (Murdock, 1949). Beyond this, cultures may restrict eligibility of partners for marriage in various ways. Modern large-scale cultures often have further preferences that spouses be similar in age, race, social standing, education, religion, and the like. These generally are not necessarily absolute or legal restrictions, but they do result in individuals selecting spouses within their own social categories more often than if mate selection were purely random. The standard term for this statistical tendency is *homogamy* (Kalmijn, 1998). Homogamy occurs in part because of structural factors such as residential and age segregation in communities, but also because of individual preferences and group pressures. American culture, with its emphasis on love, holds a contradiction to widespread homogamy in the phrase "Searching the wide world over to find Mr (or Ms) Right." This expresses our value on personal freedom in mate choice and suggests that mate selection is an international process in which persons of radically different backgrounds often select each other as spouses. In reality, Americans mostly search within their own neighborhoods and communities, within their own education, social class, race, and age brackets, and within their own major religious denominations.

Some social theorists (Parsons, 1951) suggest that these mate selection preferences help maintain the structure of society. Since race and ethnic groups, social classes, religions, and age groups differ in their values and lifestyles, intermarriage would tend to weaken or dilute the values and lifestyles of these diverse social categories. Group differentiation and status structures are impossible without homogamous marriage. At the same time, for individual couples, marriage has been conceived as easier for mutual adjustment and more lasting when one marries a spouse with similar values, lifestyle, and the like.

Traditional, less diverse, cultures are often structured more along kinship lines with people being grouped into extended families, or even larger groups tracing descent from a common ancestor. Some of these cultures restrict the range of eligible spouses in a different way. They prefer, or in some cases require, that one marry a particular kind of cousin. Typically this is a *cross-cousin*. A cross-cousin is one to whom one is linked via a cross-sex sibling link in a previous generation. For first cousins, the cross-cousins are one's mother's brother's offspring, and one's father's sister's offspring. Even in societies with large clans tracing their membership through only one sex, these cousins are not covered by the incest taboo or the rule of exogamy, and hence are eligible to marry. The cousin marriage rule simply adds more pressure to

marry into this category. Parenthetically, parallel cousins are the other type. For first cousins, they are the offspring of one's father's brothers and one's mother's sisters. Only a few cultures in the Middle East have had a preference for marrying parallel cousins.

What is cross-cousin marriage about? It helps perpetuate relationships among kin groups and thus stabilizes social structure. Two leaders in the anthropological study of kinship had different ideas about how marriage relates to social structure, and what a marriage does to social structure. The British anthropologist Radcliffe-Brown (1950, p. 43) asserted that marriage is a rearrangement of social structure. He had in mind that new links between families and kin groups are formed with each new marriage. Whereas two families may not have been well acquainted before a marriage, they now become in-laws, a new relationship for them, and enter into a lasting, if intermittent, bond. This view has much merit when we are thinking of individual families and the personal ties between them, but it leads us to think of marriage as destabilizing existing social structure.

However, the French anthropologist Levi-Strauss (1969) held the antithetical view. In an examination of cultures with cross-cousin marriage, he held that those groups use marriage to stabilize social structure rather than allowing marriage to change it. By having people marry the same type of cross-cousin generation after generation, new marriages do not always create new ties among kin groups, but may perpetuate existing alliances. Perhaps the most interesting use of marriage to stabilize social structure is called *generalized exchange*, in which a woman marries a person in the same kinship category as her father's sister's son, and a man marries into the category of his mother's brother's daughter. With this restriction on the field of eligible spouses, each kin group in the culture always receives wives from one set of kin groups, but gives its daughters as wives to a different group. In other words, one never gives and receives wives from the same group (see Levi-Strauss [1969] or Fox [1967] for details on how this and other patterns of marital exchange work). Levi-Strauss theorized that this type of marital exchange among groups not only helps perpetuate cooperation among kin groups, but also expands its scope. This perspective helps in understanding the implications of cross-cousin marriage for relations among the kin groups of some societies, but it can blind one to the real changes that occur in everyday interpersonal relationships when a new marriage is undertaken.

What cultures are likely to include close cousins from within the field of eligible spouses? The type of cousin marriage preferred in a society is related to the rule of descent. The type of cousin marriage called generalized exchange, for example, is more likely in cultures with patrilineal descent than with matrilineal kin groups based on female ancestors (Homans & Schneider, 1955). A common misperception is that the very simplest small-scale societies prefer or practice cousin marriage, but Ember (1975) has shown conclusively that this is incorrect. In a cross-cultural study, he found that marriage with a first cousin is more likely to be permitted in societies with a centralized political hierarchy more than in simpler uncentralized ones. Similarly, first-cousin marriage is more likely to be permitted in societies with some urban aggregations than in those with no settlements of over 5,000 population. Furthermore, for societies of medium scale (with populations between 1,000 and 25,000), recent extensive population loss is associated with norms permitting first-cousin marriage. This study suggests that cousin marriages may be allowed under two conditions. It may be allowed in larger-scale societies where it is less likely to occur by chance and where peaceful cooperative relations are well established. Second, close-cousin marriage may be allowed in very small, especially depopulated, societies in which too few spouses might otherwise be available. These findings fly in the face of Levi-Strauss's widely cited view of cross-cousin marriage as establishing peace and cooperation in small-scale societies. More research and some rethinking are needed to reconcile this issue.

MARRIAGE

Defining Marriage

Before discussing the three major forms of marriage, it is useful to discuss definitions of marriage itself. While marriage is often believed to be a universal feature of culture, it is a difficult feature to define. Radcliffe-Brown (1950, pp. 11–12, 50) defined marriage as a transfer of rights in the new spouse. These are rights of sexual access, rights to claim offspring, and rights to the spouse's labor. In this definition, Radcliffe-Brown recognized cross-cultural variability within each set of rights while emphasizing that marriage is a cultural creation, since it consists of rights and obligations rather than behavior. The social and

behavioral tie we call marriage involves several of the following behavioral elements, most of which were suggested by Murdock (1949). The idea that marriage consists of a sexual relationship plus several other traits also makes a useful working definition. These traits include:

> a sexual relationship that is socially approved
> childbirth that is socially approved
> economic cooperation and sharing
> coresidence of spouses
> expected duration for some years, at least
> a ritual or transaction marking entrance to marriage.

Some foraging societies have little or no marker for entering marriage. In some with men's houses in each village, spouses do not constantly live together. In some societies people move through several marriages and divorces over a lifetime, so durability is questionable. For example, among the forest period Ache, a foraging group of South America, the average duration of first marriage was only 7.7 months for women and 14.3 months for men. By age 30, women on average had been in over 10 marriages (Hill and Hurtado, 1996, pp. 230, 245).

The Na, an ethnic group within China, presents the most recent challenge to the universality of marriage. In this matrilineal culture, most men and women live in the home into which they were born. Most sex before recent decades occurred through men's furtive visits to women's bedrooms at night. Both women and men had almost complete sexual freedom, except that women were required to take a passive role, always receiving or rejecting male sexual visitors rather than going to visit on their own initiative. Members of Na society can point out the genitors of most children, but these genitors have no claims over children and no obligations to them, and this makes no difference to the status of the child. Marriage does exist in the case of the only son in a family. Without daughters, the family line cannot be passed down. Complex transactions and rituals mark entrance into marriage. The wife and her offspring are adopted into the husband's family. The spouses have rights of sexual access to each other, and each is obliged to work for the benefit of the larger family, and she can eventually succeed to the position of female household chief, should her mother-in-law die. It is forbidden for the wife to return to her own home (Hua, 2001, pp. 185–236, 303–334). If we focus on Na marriage being practiced by a minority of members we would conclude that they are an exception to the universality of marriage. However, if we focus on marriage existing as a cultural institution known by all, we would only regard the Na as unusual, rather than exceptional. The Na have marriage in Radcliffe-Brown's sense of a set of rights transmitted, but not in the sense of behaviors that are typical of the bulk of group members.

Forms of Marriage

Marriage in all cultures sanctions a tie between persons of opposite sex, but some cultures add to this that some marriages can be between people of the same sex (Cadigan, 1998; Fulton & Anderson, 1992). The heterosexual component will be the focus here. Marriages can involve one or more males and one or more females. Thus there are four logical possibilities. These types, and their frequencies as ideal forms of marriage among preindustrial societies, are (Pasternak, Ember, & Ember, 1997, p. 86, adapted from Murdock 1949, 1967):

monogamy—one wife and one husband, 16%
polygyny—two or more wives with one husband, 83.5%
polyandry—two or more husbands with one wife, 0.5%
group marriage—two or more husbands with two or more wives, 0.0%

Although a topic of speculation within 19th century cultural evolutionary theory, group marriage has never been observed as the ideal or the typical form of marriage in any culture. It only seems to occur as an alternate or secondary form of marriage in some cultures (Murdock, 1949, p. 24).

Polygyny

It is important to distinguish between polygyny as an ideal state of marriage and polygyny as a practice, and to distinguish subtypes of polygyny. While all highly industrialized societies legitimize monogamy only (Goode, 1967), traditional cultures have preferred polygyny over other types of marriage by a wide margin (Murdock, 1949). Despite this widespread ideal, the typical marriage in many, if not most, "polygynous" societies is monogamous. Indeed, Murdock (1949, p. 28) put the dividing line between the frequent and infrequent practice of polygyny at only 20% of marriages in a society. He labeled these *general* and *limited* polygyny, respectively. This low frequency occurs in part because men ordinarily

marry only one wife at a time but may accumulate more over a lifetime, and because polygyny requires more wives than husbands. A balanced sex ratio stands in the way of widespread polygyny. Some societies, such as the Tiwi of Australia, offset the age at first marriage for women and men, delaying men's first marriage until they are past 30 years of age. Under this condition, the majority of marriages may be polygynous (Hart & Pilling, 1960). In the New World, sororal polygyny, in which cowives must be sisters of the same clan, is most commonly preferred (White, 1988). Restricting cowives to close kin puts further restrictions on the frequency of polygynous practice.

While naive libertarians might assume that polygynous sexuality involves multiple simultaneous partners, most cultures have stringent regulations which have been interpreted as reducing sexual rivalry and jealousy among cowives (Murdock, 1949, p. 30) but also as preventing cowives from organizing against the husband (Blumberg & Pilar Garcia, 1977, pp. 137–139). These regulations include the following:

1. The senior wife has authority over the others. This provides a mechanism for dispute resolution, and may aid the husband in controlling the wives.
2. The wives either live, eat, and sleep separately, or are preferentially sisters. Separate residences reduce the interaction and interdependence among cowives, thereby abating the potential for conflict. Some authors believe that sisters are less likely to disagree than women who enter the marriage as strangers to each other.
3. The wives take turns with the husband. Polygynous husbands and wives do not sleep, eat, recreate, and have sex all together, but most cultures specify a period of rotation in which the husband spends time with each wife in turn. In this sense, polygynous interaction in many cultures is analogous to monogamous interaction—one on one—but in a serial manner.

Research on the structural and environmental sources of polygyny as a frequent practice has identified several important factors. First, general polygyny is most common in Africa, where it is associated with female food production (White, 1988; White & Burton, 1988). Rather than fitting the male-provider–female-caregiver concept, cowives both provide and prepare the food in these societies while also caring for infants and young children. In this way, polygyny is not necessarily a drain on a husband's resources, but may be a source of wealth and status. A secondly line of research considers the sex ratio problem and asks whether general polygyny might be linked to a shortage of men, finding that general polygyny tends to appear in cultures having extensive male deaths in warfare (Ember, 1974, 1985). Polygyny, then, may be an adaptive practice which keeps fertility at high enough levels to replenish the population. If monogamy were rigorously practiced under these conditions, many women would be unable to find husbands or have offspring, and population might shrink. A third, sociobiological, line of research ties polygyny to pathogens such as malaria. With pathogen stress, it is argued, people may want to select mates who have some pathogen resistence and may want offspring who vary in genetic make up since pathogen resistance may be easily recognizable. Nonsororal polygynous marriage provides a way for men to have offspring by different mates, thus increasing their genetic diversity of offspring (Low, 1990).

Polyandry

Polyandry is the rarest ideal form of marriage and occurs primarily in Asia. Because of its rarity, there is less research on it. Just as polygyny is preferentially sororal, polyandry is often preferentially fraternal—a woman marries full brothers or clan brothers. Among the polyandrous Toda, a dairying caste of India, when the eldest son married a woman, his younger brothers became married to her also. A simple ritual identified the one brother, usually the eldest, who would be the social father of the woman's children (Queen & Habenstein, 1974, pp. 18–47). The conditions conducive to the development of polyandry are believed to be subsistence resource scarcity and male food production (Lee, 1982, pp. 94–95). Fraternal polyandry allows brothers who have inherited land or other resources to cooperate in subsistence production, while limiting their fertility by sharing a wife. The family unit thereby has more resources, more food producers, and fewer dependents.

It seems likely that polyandry is never the most common form of marriage in a society, as polygyny sometimes is when there is high male mortality in warfare or when men marry much later than women. The constraints placed on women's fertility by pregnancy, lactation and nursing, and the menopause would prevent general polyandry from overcoming the problems set into play by a shortage of women or an extremely late age at marriage for them. Rather, fertility decline and depopulation would be the likely result. We need to view polyandry then as an aid to population limitation that

develops only when population threatens to outstrip environmental resources.

Thus scholarship has shown that the different forms of marriage are not founded upon differences in the balance of power between women and men or upon religious doctrines. They are not arbitrary cultural inventions, but practical adaptations, developing from a particular set of social and environmental stressors and subsistence practices.

REFERENCES

Blumberg, R. L., & Pilar Garcia, M. (1977). The political economy of the mother–child family: A cross-societal view. In Lenero-Otero, L. (Ed.), *Beyond the nuclear family model: Cross-cultural perspectives* (pp. 99–163). Beverly Hills, CA: Sage.

Broude, G. J., & Greene, S. J. (1983). Cross-cultural codes for husband–wife relationships. *Ethnology, 22*, 263–280.

Buss, D. (1989). Sex differences in human mate preferences: Evolutionary hypotheses tested in 37 cultures. *Behavioral and Brain Sciences, 12*, 1–14.

Cadigan, R. J. (1998). Woman-to-woman marriage: Practices and benefits in sub-Saharan Africa. *Journal of Comparative Family Studies, 29*, 89–100.

Collins, R. (1975) *Conflict sociology.* New York: Academic Press.

Coppinger, R. M. (1968). Romantic love and subsistence dependence of spouses. *Southwestern Journal of Anthropology, 24*, 310–319.

de Munck, V. C., & Korotayev, A. (1999). Sexual equality and romantic love: A reanalysis of Rosenblatt's study on the function of romantic love. *Cross-Cultural Research, 33*, 265–277.

Derne, S. (1994). Structural realities, persistent dilemmas, and the construction of emotional paradigms: Love in three cultures. *Social Perspectives on Emotion, 2*, 281–308.

Eagly, A. H., & Wood, W. (1999). The origins of sex differences in human behavior: Evolved dispositions versus social roles. *American Psychologist, 54*, 408–423.

Ember, M. (1974). Warfare, sex ration, and polygyny. *Ethnology, 13*, 197–206.

Ember, M. (1975). On the origin and extension of the incest taboo. *Behavior Science Research, 10*, 249–281.

Ember, M. (1985). Alternative predictors of polygyny. *Behavior Science Research, 19*, 1–23.

Fox, R. (1967). *Kinship and marriage.* Baltimore: Penguin.

Freeman, L. C. (1968). Marriage without love: Mate selection in nonwestern societies. In Winch, R. F. & Goodman, L. W. (Eds.), *Selected studies in marriage and the family* (pp. 456–469). New York: Holt, Rinehart & Winston.

Fulton, R., & Anderson, S. W. (1992). The Amerindian "man–woman": gender, liminality, and cultural continuity. *Current Anthropology, 32*, 603–610.

Glenn, N. D. (1989). Intersocietal variation in the mate preferences of males and females. *Behavioral and Brain Sciences, 12*, 21–23.

Goode, W. J. (1967). *World revolution and family patterns.* New York: Free Press.

Hart, C. W. M., & Pilling, A. R. (1960). *The Tiwi of North Australia*. New York: Holt.

Hendrix, L. (2002). *A cross-cultural exploration of mate selection*. Paper presented at the annual meeting of the Society for Cross-Cultural Research, San Diego, CA.

Hill, K., & Hurtado, A. M. (1996). *Ache life history: The ecology and demography of a foraging people*. New York: Aldine De Gruyter.

Homans, G. C., and Schneider, D. M. (1955). *Marriage, authority, and final causes*. Glencoe, IL: Free Press.

Hua, C. (2001). *A society without fathers or husbands: The Na of China* (A. Hustvedt, Trans.). New York: Zone Books.

Kalmijn, M. (1998). Intermarriage and homogamy: Causes, patterns, trends. *Annual Review of Sociology, 24*, 395–421.

Kasser, T., & Sharma, Y. S. (1999). Reproductive freedom, educational equality and females' preference for resource-acquisition characteristics in mates. *Psychological Science, 10*, 374–377.

Lee, G. R. (1982). *Family structure and interaction* (2nd ed.). Minneapolis, MN: University of Minnesota Press.

Lee, G. R., & Stone, L. H. (1980). Mate-selection systems and criteria: Variation according to family structure. *Journal of Marriage and the Family, 42*, 319–326.

Levi-Strauss, C. (1969). *The elementary structures of kinship*. (J. H. Bell, J. R. von Sturmer, & Ro. Needham, Eds. & Trans.). Boston: Beacon Press.

Low, B. S. (1990). Marriage systems and pathogen stress in human societies. *American Zoologist, 30*, 325–339.

Murdock, G. P. (1949). *Social structure*. New York: Macmillan.

Murdock, G. P. (1967). *Ethnographic atlas*. Pittsburgh, PA: University of Pittsburgh Press.

Parsons, T. (1951) *The social system*. Glencoe, IL: Free Press.

Pasternak, B., Ember, C. R., & Ember, M. (1997). *Sex, gender, and kinship: A cross-cultural perspective*. Upper Saddle River, NJ: Prentice-Hall.

Queen, S. A., & Habenstein, R. W. (1974). *The family in various cultures* (4th ed.). New York: Lippincott.

Radcliffe-Brown, A. R. (1950). Introduction. In A. R. Radcliffe-Brown & D. Forde (Eds.), *African Systems of Kinship and Marriage* (pp. 1–85). London: Oxford University Press.

Rosenblatt, P. C., & Cozby, P. C. (1972). Courtship patterns associated with freedom of choice of spouse. *Journal of Marriage and the Family, 34*, 689–694.

White, D. R. (1988). Rethinking polygyny. *Current Anthropology, 29*, 529–572.

White, D. R., & Burton, M. (1988). Causes of polygyny: Ecology, economy, kinship, and warfare. *American Anthropologist, 90*, 871–887.

Parental Roles

Robert A. Veneziano

INTRODUCTION

One of the most enduring elements of social and behavioral science research in the last half of the 20th century was the scholarly reexamination of traditional ideas about fatherhood and motherhood. For over 200 years maternal behavior had been considered paramount in child development (Kagan, 1978; Stearns, 1991; Stendler, 1950; Sunley, 1955), and fathers were often thought to be peripheral to the job of parenting because children throughout the world spent most of their time with their mothers (Fagot, 1995; Harris, Furstenberg, & Marmer, 1998; Munroe & Munroe, 1994). Some argued that fathers contributed little to children's development except for their economic contributions (Amato, 1998), and others believed that fathers are not genetically endowed for parenting (Belsky, 1998; Benson, 1968). Indeed, even though Margaret Mead concluded that fathers were important contributors to childcare, and that "Anthropological evidence gives no support ... to the value of such an accentuation of the tie between mother and child" (Mead, 1956, pp. 642–643), Mead (1949) perceived basic differences between fathers and mothers:

The mother's nurturing tie to her child is apparently so deeply rooted in the actual biological conditions of conception and gestation, birth and suckling, that only fairly complicated social arrangements can break it down entirely. ... But the evidence suggests that we should phrase the matter differently for men and women—that men have to learn to want to provide for others, and this behavior, being learned, is fragile and can disappear rather easily under social conditions that no longer teach it effectively. (pp. 191–193)

However, many contemporary scholars now cite a growing body of empirical evidence that parental behaviors are not simply the consequence of biology and human nature, but rather are informed by cultural, historical, and social values, circumstances, and processes. In fact, as gender ideologies shifted in the last half of the 20th century, so too did researchers' exploration of variations in men's and women's behavior generally, and fathering and mothering specifically (Rohner & Veneziano, 2001; Sanchez & Thomson, 1997). Moreover, contemporary

perspectives on fatherhood and motherhood are in large part derived from research that concurrently studied fathers and mothers, rather than earlier research that focused almost exclusively on mothers. This chapter discusses some of the literature from this vast body of behavioral science research by first discussing similarities and differences in fathers' and mothers' behavior in Western and non-Western cultures. The chapter also reviews research about the social, cultural, psychological, ethnic, economic, environmental, biological, and evolutionary conditions that influence the parenting practices of mothers and fathers, as well as the social, emotional, behavioral, and psychological consequences for male and female offspring of fathers' and mothers' practices.

SIMILARITIES AND DIFFERENCES IN FATHERS' AND MOTHERS' INTERACTIONS WITH OFFSPRING

Much of the research into parent–child relations has been informed by the belief that mothers influence children's physical, emotional, psychological, and social well-being through expressive and affective behaviors, including warmth and nurturance (Bowlby, 1969; Hojat, 1999; Mahler & Furer, 1968; Phares, 1992; Stern, 1995), whereas fathers have often been viewed as influencing children's development through the instrumental roles of provider and protector, and as role models for social, cognitive, psychological, and gender-identity development (Bronstein, 1988; Gilmore, 1990; Lamb & Oppenheim, 1989; Mackey, 1996; Parsons & Bales, 1955; Radin, 1981b). However, contemporary research suggests that maternal behavior is not situated exclusively in the expressive sphere any more than paternal behavior is situated exclusively in the instrumental one. Indeed, multivariate research in the 1990s demonstrated the importance of paternal expressive and affective behaviors despite the fact that mothers are often characterized as "superior caregivers," whereas fathers are viewed as "less capable of, and/or less interested in, nurturant parenting"

(Hosley & Montemayor, 1997, p. 175). As discussed below, fathers' and mothers' behaviors are in fact multi-dimensional and multifaceted, and these behaviors often vary as a result of contextual variables including youths' age and gender.

Youths' Age and Gender

According to Collins and Russell (1991), research in Western societies shows that fathers and mothers interact differently with their middle childhood (i.e., preteens) to adolescent children than with younger children. For example, fathers generally interact with their adolescents through focusing on instrumental goals (e.g., school and athletic achievement, future plans) and objective issues such as political discussions. Mothers' interactions with adolescents, on the other hand, tend to be marked more by discussions of personal issues. More specifically, in their review of the literature on U.S. families, Collins and Russell (1991) reported that 15- to 16-year-old U.S. adolescents spent twice as much time alone with their mothers as with their fathers. Collins and Russell also reported that 14- to 18-year-olds, more than 12- to 13-year-olds, spent more time alone with their mothers than with their fathers. As for middle childhood, Collins and Russell (1991) found that mothers tend to be more involved in caregiving, whereas fathers are more involved in play activities.

Parental interaction with children also varies during infancy, and infants appear to demonstrate a biological predisposition to respond differently to fathers and mothers.

Alert, fed, comfortable babies, when approached by their mothers, tended to relax, coo, and modulate their breathing and cardiovascular responses—as if to sort of say, "Ah, here's Mom." Then when the father approached, the babies' eyes tended to open, the shoulders would go up and the heart and respiratory systems were activated rather than calmed, as if to say, "Here's Dad, let's party!" (Pruett, in Louv, 2002, ¶ 8)

Pruett (Louv, 2002, ¶ 9) also cites one study in which American mothers picked up and held their infants in the same manner 90% of the time, whereas fathers were more unpredictable, perhaps picking up the child by their feet on one occasion and by their sides on another.

In a review of the literature, Witt (1997) found that American fathers and mothers interact differently with sons than daughters. According to Witt, fathers and mothers have different expectations for sons than for daughters, have a preference for male offspring, and communicate differently with their offspring, depending on the child's sex (Hargreaves & Colley, 1986; Hoffman, 1977; Snow, Jacklin, & Maccoby, 1983; Steinbacher & Gilroy, 1990). Updegraff, Mchale, Grouter, and Kupanoff (2001) found that American mothers more than fathers exhibited traditional patterns of gendered parenting in their involvement with their daughters' and sons' peer relationships. Fathers spent more time in offspring's peer-related matters when they had sons, whereas mothers spent more time with daughters and their friends and were more involved in daughters' than sons' peer relations.

Witt (1997) also found that fathers reinforce gender stereotypes more often than mothers. Indeed, a significant body of research finds that differences in paternal versus maternal behaviors influence different aspects of gender-role development of both boys and girls, including offspring's use of gender stereotypes, toy preferences, preferred household tasks, and self-esteem (Biller & Borstelmann, 1967; Bronson, 1959; Distler, 1965; Kelly & Worell, 1976; Mussen, 1961; Mussen & Distler, 1959; Orlofsky, 1979; Payne & Mussen, 1956). Goldstein (2001), for example, reports that fathers tend to enforce gender norms more strongly than mothers, and often exhibit harsh responses to boys who attempt to play with feminine toys. According to Goldstein, a large body of empirical research shows that fathers throughout the world use the language of dominance (e.g., imperatives and power assertion) more than mothers in talking with children. Mothers by comparison soften demands by using polite language, forms of endearment, and questions. Fathers more than mothers use depreciatory language and do so more with sons than daughters. Goldstein also reports that children see their fathers as having more authority than mothers, comply more quickly with paternal than maternal requests, and speak more politely to fathers than mothers. Goldstein believes that boys learn masculine imperatives from parental figures, especially fathers, and this in turn reinforces widely held male gender attitudes and behaviors regarding aggression and war.

However, Martin and Anderson (1997) found that U.S. college students' assertiveness, argumentativeness, and verbal aggressiveness were predicted by maternal rather than paternal modeling of assertive and aggressive behavior. Interestingly, Martin and Anderson's findings about maternal influence held for both daughters and sons, rather than the same-sex modeling that Martin and Anderson expected to find.

Verbal communications between parents and children also vary by gender. In a meta-analysis of studies of parent–child communication in Western societies, Leaper, Anderson, and Sanders (1998) found that differences in maternal and paternal communication with sons and daughters were often dependent on contextual circumstances. Even though mothers tended to communicate more with daughters than with sons, it is most often during the toddler years. Moreover, mothers used more controlling styles of communication with daughters than with sons. Leaper et al. also found that mothers and fathers communicated with both sexes in similar ways when directed in clinical studies to discuss a problem or complete an assigned task. On the other hand, when mothers had a choice of topic or activity, they tended to choose a less task-oriented one than did fathers—one that allowed for more conversation and interaction. Fathers most often chose activities where communication was centered on directive task-oriented communication, particularly with their sons.

As for fathers' involvement specifically, Radin (1981b, 1994) found that American fathers spend more time with sons than with daughters. Moreover, Erickson and Gecas (1991) investigated relationships between parental behavior and family socio-economic status and found that from infancy onward, regardless of social class standing, U.S. fathers spend more time with first-born boys than with first-born girls. Furthermore, by the time children reach the age of 7, middle-class fathers, as compared with working-class fathers, are more involved with boys than with girls (Erickson & Gecas, 1991). Other studies indicate that U.S. fathers spend more time with sons than with daughters, regardless of age (Collins & Russell, 1991; Pleck, 1997). Research in Dominica, West Indies, also found that fathers interacted more frequently with sons than with daughters of all ages, particularly during their sons' adolescence (Flinn, 1992). Father–daughter interactions were also highest during girls' adolescence, although still less than father–son interactions, when fathers were expected to fulfill the role of protector of young females.

Parental nurturance, discussed more specifically later in this chapter, has also been shown to vary by youths' gender. Starrels (1994) reports that data from a U.S. national survey shows that mothers tend to exhibit affective support across the genders, whereas fathers tend to exhibit more closeness and nurturance to their sons than to their daughters, and tend to interact warmly with sons while doing things together rather than through talking and confiding. On the other hand, in a study of low- and middle-income intact Mexican families, Bronstein (1988) reported that Mexican fathers were more emotionally nurturing than Mexican mothers who were more physically nurturing (i.e., caretaking tasks). However, several gender-related differences emerged, with sons experiencing higher amounts of paternal authoritarian control and instrumental directives than daughters. Fathers were not excessively harsh with sons but scored higher on those measures relative to their very gentle interaction with daughters.

Sociocultural antecedents of fathers' and mothers' behavior are explored later in this chapter, but it is worth noting briefly Flinn's and Starrels' application of micro- and macrosystemic perspectives in interpreting their findings. Using a microsystemic perspective, Flinn (1992) speculated that the greater interaction between fathers and sons, particularly sons who are older, was due in part to cooperative work and economic activities in which sons were expected to learn mastery of skills from their fathers that would ensure the family's long-term survival. Starrels (1994), on the other hand, employed a macrosystemic perspective in concluding that fathers' and mothers' behavior reflect mainstream Western cultural beliefs about appropriate behavior for men and women. Each perspective offers important insights into the many forces that influence and shape fathers' and mothers' behavior.

Youths' Age, Gender, and Parent–Child Play

A consistent finding in research on samples of middle-income European American families indicates that playful and sociable activities such as physically stimulating rough-and-tumble play marks father–child interactions, whereas mother–child interactions are dominated by caretaking, holding, and soothing (Collins & Russell, 1991; Forehand & Nousiainen, 1993; Lindsey, Mize, & Petit, 1997; Parke, 1996). For example, when engaged in play, mothers were found to play nontactile games, or predictable and contained limb-movement games, such as peek-a-boo and pat-a-cake. Fathers engaged in more unpredictable, tactile, and arousing games. Infants were said to respond with more enthusiasm to being held by their fathers than by their mothers. Bernstein reported that fathers engaged in more physical play and interactive games, and encouraged visual, fine motor, and locomotor exploration more with sons than with daughters. Fathers' interactions with daughters were marked by verbal games and social conversation. On the other hand, in an early study of parent–child play interactions, Hoffman (1989) concluded that play may be related to parents' employment status, particularly that of mothers. According to Hoffman, studies have shown that employed mothers engaged in more actively stimulating play with their infants than did their husbands or nonemployed mothers.

However, Hewlett's (1987) study of parent–child relations in the Aka of central Africa demonstrates that the rough-and-tumble play observed in some Western studies is by no means a universal feature of father–child interactions. Utilizing naturalistic observations of father–child and mother–child interactions among the Aka, Hewlett found that Aka fathers did play frequently with their children. However, Aka fathers did not exhibit the vigorous rough-and-tumble play representative of American fathers. Moreover, Aka fathers also exhibited nurturing capacities and levels of emotional support similar to that of Aka mothers. Hewlett compared this finding with Swedish and German studies where father–child contact was marked less by vigorous play than by other forms of contact. Hewlett suggested that these findings demonstrate that play does not serve a critical role in influencing father–child attachment across cultures. Because Aka fathers and mothers had similar styles of interaction with children, he hypothesized that Aka fathers were more intimate and therefore more aware of their children's needs, and subsequently did not need to utilize rough-and-tumble play to form attachments.

As demonstrated by Hewlett and Hoffman, fathers' and mothers' behaviors vary according to social and cultural circumstances. The next section examines social, cultural, psychological, ethnic, economic, environmental, genetic, biological, and evolutionary antecedents of maternal and paternal practices, and the consequences for male and female offspring of these practices.

ANTECEDENTS AND CONSEQUENCES OF PARENTING STYLES AND BEHAVIORS

Sociocultural Models

As noted at the beginning of this chapter, behavioral science increasingly recognizes the importance of contextual factors as well as biological or genetic factors that influence male–female behavior generally, and fathers' and mothers' behavior specifically. A number of researchers have developed models that take into account complex processes that influence parent–child relations. For example, Rohner's (1986) sociocultural systems model connects the behavioral, psychological, and social development of children to parents' behavior and to sociocultural processes. That is, parental behavior and children's development are linked in reciprocal fashion to the natural environment and to a society's maintenance systems, which include the ways people make a living, ensure social control, and ensure the procreation and successful rearing of children. Maintenance systems include political structure, defense systems, family structure, household composition, social class system, and economic organizations.

Rohner's model builds conceptually on earlier models designed by Kardiner (1945), and by J. Whiting and Child (1953), which link primary institutions and maintenance systems to child rearing and child and adult personality. Other models include Bronfenbrenner's bio-ecological approach (Bronfenbrenner & Ceci, 1994) and Super and Harkness's (1986) developmental niche model that links parent–child relations to a society's customs and values, fathers' and mothers' psychology, and the social and physical setting. For example, Moreno (in press) found that Latino mothers' involvement with their children's education varies according to their education level and socio-economic status, language proficiency, availability of extended family supports, goals for their children's futures, personal and psychological variables, and level of acculturation. A range of contextual indicators, as discussed in the next section, also predicts paternal involvement.

Antecedents of Parental Behavior: The Case of Fathers

It has been well documented that fathers, compared with mothers, spend only a small portion of their time in day-to-day child-rearing activities, including supervising children, feeding children, transporting children, and so forth (Pleck, 1997; Sanchez & Thomson, 1997). Moreover, the negative consequences for children's development of low levels of paternal involvement have also been amply documented (Bacon, Child, & Barry, 1963; Biller, 1993; Broude, 1990; Ember & Ember, 1994, n.d.; B. Whiting, 1965). Research on fathers' involvement is instructive as it reveals the complex interaction of sociocultural conditions that influence paternal, as well as maternal, interactions with children.

Cross-Cultural Evidence.   Katz and Konner (1981) conducted cross-cultural comparative research utilizing a subsample of the Standard Cross Cultural Sample (SCCS) (Murdock & White, 1969), determined by Barry and Paxson (1971) to be at the highest degree of confidence on the nature of fathers' relationship with infants and children. The SCCS includes 186 societies that represent the world's known and adequately described sociocultural systems. Katz and Konner found that increased levels of father involvement were associated with monogamy, nuclear family structure, nonpatrilocal cultures, and, subsistence economy, where gathering, rather than hunting, was the primary subsistence mode. Findings also showed that increased father involvement occurred in societies where mothers were active contributors to the acquisition and maintenance of resources for the family and the community. Indeed, the character of parents' work activities, as discussed below, has major implications for the nature of fathering and mothering behaviors.

Hewlett's (1987) research of the Aka details the complex processes that influence the behavior of high- and low-investment fathers. The high-investment Aka father (i.e., actively involved with children) was profiled by (1) having no brothers, (2) having few relatives in general, (3) being married relatively late in life, (4) being monogamous, (5) having a wife from a distant clan, (6) having a small hunting net, (7) relying more on individual as opposed to group hunting techniques, (8) having close relationships with nearby non-Aka villages, (9) being of relatively low status, and (10) having a wife who was actively involved in subsistence activities. Because high-investment fathers often have few or no brothers, they build alliances with other clans and with non–Akas, hunt more on their own, and invest time with their offspring, freeing their wives for other activities and thus contributing to the well-being and survival of the group.

On the other hand, the behavior of low-investment Aka fathers (i.e., limited involvement with children) develops differently than that of high-investment fathers, but is no less important to the viability of the group than that of high-investment fathers. That is, because low-investment fathers generally have several brothers, their clans tend to be more economically viable, which in turn

leads to greater prosperity for low-investment than for high-investment fathers. Females are attracted to prosperous males, increasing the likelihood of polygyny and an increased number of offspring, which also contribute to the prosperity of the clan and individual fathers. Low-investment fathers have higher social status than high-investment fathers and are involved in more status-maintaining economic tasks and roles, which, according to Hewlett (1992), also help to insure the survivability of the group.

Biosocial Models of Parental Investment

As noted above, Hewlett (1987) addresses social and cultural conditions and processes that influence parents' investment in their children. Indeed, a substantial body of research proposes evolutionary and biological explanations for variations in maternal and paternal parenting (Anderson, Kaplan, & Lancaster, 2001; Fox & Bruce, 2001; Gelles & Lancaster, 1987; Hewlett, 1992). In such evolutionary perspectives:

Individuals face trade-offs between investing in themselves (their own human capital, physical growth or immune system, etc.), in mating effort (initiating and/or maintaining a relationship with a sexual partner), or in parental effort (investments in existing offspring) … [The evolutionary perspective] emphasizes two reasons for parental investment in offspring. First, parents invest in genetic offspring because doing so increases their own genetic fitness, i.e., the number of copies of their genes present in future generations. Secondly, an individual may invest in an offspring because the investment influences that person's relationship with the offspring's other parent. (Anderson et al., 2001, p.6)

For example, Hagen, Hames, Craig, Lauer, & Price (2001) found that when Yanomamo parents were forced to allocate food carefully to their children during a period of poor garden productivity, they invested in younger children more than in older ones. Moreover, boys whose fathers were significantly invested in them were better nourished than were girls, whereas girls who had large patrilineages were better nourished than were girls from smaller patrilineages. In Yanomamo society, patrilineage size reflects the amount of local political power held by families, thus reflecting how political arrangements influence fathers' and mothers' investment in their offspring.

Paternity Certainty.   Fathers' certainty about their paternity has also been found to influence investment in their offspring (Buss, Larsen, Westen, & Semmelroth, 1992;

Fox & Bruce, 2001; Wilson & Daly, 1992). Indeed, in a quotation (Byrnes, 1988) widely attributed to Aristotle some 2400 years ago, the philosopher spoke of the importance of paternity certainty: "This is the reason why mothers are more devoted to their children than fathers: it is that they suffer more in giving them birth and are more certain that they are their own." In fact, Fox and Bruce (2001) found that fathers' commitment to offspring varied due to fathers' paternity certainty and to fathers' willingness to invest in children who will more likely meet fathers' needs (e.g., mating success, finances, time, and energy) and disinvest in those children who are unlikely to meet fathers' needs.

Parents' Work and Subsistence Activities

Evidence from intracultural and cross-cultural research also reveals how parents' work roles affect maternal and paternal involvement with offspring. For example, the Aka of Central Africa (Hewlett, 1992) and the Batek of Malaysia (Endicott, 1992) exhibit egalitarian marital and parental relationships as well as similar and often shared work roles. Aka and Batek fathers are involved with their children both in their villages and homes, and in their work tasks, where children often work alongside their fathers. According to Hewlett and Endicott, the shared economic activities of Aka and Batek fathers and mothers leads to greater daily interaction between fathers and children. This interaction often leads to paternal familiarity with a broad range of children's needs, and thus increased opportunities to practice and master child-rearing skills.

Similar findings were reported by Morelli and Tronick (1992) who found that the foraging Efe of Zaire had relatively egalitarian mother–father relationships compared with their neighbors, the pastoralist Lese. Efe mothers and fathers were equally involved in work activities, while there was a stricter division of labor among the Lese. Efe fathers, like Lese fathers, were generally physically proximate to their children, but Efe fathers were more actively involved in monitoring and training children than were Lese fathers.

Aronoff (1967) also found significant differences in child-rearing practices, particularly those associated with warmth and control, between two groups of fathers living in St. Kitts, West Indies—those employed as cane cutters, and those employed as fishermen. These men lived in the same West Indian island village, but their subsistence activities, male–female relationships, family structure, and early childhood experiences differed significantly. The differences in child-rearing, according to Aronoff, were related to parents' work and subsistence activities that promoted authoritative and nurturant caretaking behavior on the part of fishermen fathers, and closed, hostile, and discipline-focused behavior on the part of cane-cutter fathers.

But the cane cutter is clearly a marginal figure in the life of the child. His most important task, beyond [financial] support, is to discipline the child and teach him manners. Items such as "proper behavior," "teach them not to do wrong," "give them licks," and "rule the children," are heavily stressed. The children are very much the responsibility of the mother, and the male is useful only in providing the financial resources and the strong right arm ... Just as the fisherman is concerned with establishing a crew in which he is interdependent and interactive with the other members, so too does he demand the same with his family. His role seems to be much more nurturant, thoroughly implicating him in the care and fostering of his children. (Aronoff, 1967, pp. 183–185)

Radin (1981b, 1994) found that middle-class U.S. fathers who adhered to nontraditional gender-role ideology (i.e., frequently valued fathers' involvement with their children) were more likely than traditional fathers (i.e., who infrequently valued fathers' involvement with children) to have a positive influence on youths' intellectual and personality development. Radin (1988) found that the non-traditional style was initially adopted when fathers had flexible work hours or were not working at all, and the non-traditional fathers supported their wives' (i.e., children's mothers) strong career interests. Also, mothers supported fathers' decisions to be more involved, particularly when fathers were not positively invested in their own careers. Predictors of long-range paternal involvement included mothers' growing investment in their careers, mothers' high salaries, and fathers' part-time work schedule and/or flexible work hours (Radin, 1988). Furthermore, Barnett and Baruch (1988) found that fathers' participation was the highest when both husbands and wives were employed, and when mothers' gender-role attitudes were liberal toward fathers' decisions to be involved in child-rearing.

Aronoff's findings about the influence of social and economic realities on men's parenting behaviors appear to echo Mead's perception, quoted earlier, that father–child attachments are fragile and highly dependent on sociocultural circumstances. Indeed, together with findings about the negative effects of low father involvement, or father absence (Biller, 1993; Broude, 1990;

Munroe & Munroe, 1992; B. Whiting & Whiting, 1975), it is perhaps understandable that some have concluded that fathers' influence tends to be less positive than that of mothers, or that fathers are less important than mothers (Amato, 1994; Hojat, 1999; Shulman & Collins, 1993; Stern, 1995; Williams & Radin, 1993). However, as noted earlier, a significant body of multivariate research from the 1990s shows that when fathers and mothers are studied concurrently, both make important positive and negative contributions to children's development.

Nurturant, Supportive, Affectionate, Loving, and Warm Parenting

Studying Maternal and Paternal Warmth and Nurturance.

An extensive body of research shows that warm, nurturing, and affectionate relationships between parents and offspring are often predictive of positive psychological, behavioral, and social development of both children and adults (Rohner, 1975, 1986, 2000; Rohner & Britner, 2002). Even though most research has focused on maternal warmth and nurturance, there is a growing body of work that shows the importance of paternal warmth and nurturance as well (Rohner & Veneziano, 2001). Consequently, this section will discuss the influence for children's development of both maternal and paternal warmth and nurturance.

Caring for and Caring about Children.

As noted earlier, many studies conclude that children whose fathers spend a significant amount of time taking care of them exhibit positive psychological adjustment and cognitive and intellectual development, strong academic achievement, ability to empathize, flexible gender-role orientation, and competency at problem-solving tasks (Biller, 1993; Easterbrooks & Goldberg, 1984; Lamb, 1997; Pleck, 1997; Radin, 1981b; Radin & Russell, 1983; Radin & Sagi, 1982; Radin, Williams, & Coggins, 1993; Reuter & Biller, 1973; E. Williams & Radin, 1993; S. Williams & Finley, 1997). These simple correlational studies measure the amount of time that fathers spend with children and sometimes also included measures of paternal warmth, often finding that the two variables are related to each other and to youth outcomes. However, it is unclear from these studies whether the amount of time involved and the degree of warmth make independent or joint contributions to youth outcomes. Indeed, as Veneziano and Rohner (1998) argued, "caring for" children is not

necessarily the same thing as "caring about" them. And contemporary scholarship frequently asserts that qualitative factors such as paternal warmth, support, or nurturance are more important for children's development than factors such as the simple amount of time fathers spend in child care (Cabrera, Tamis-LeMonda, & Bradley et al., 2000; Lamb, 1986, 1997, 2000; Lamb & Oppenheim, 1989; Lamb, Pleck, Charnov, & Levine, 1987; Pleck, 1997; Shulman & Collins, 1993).

Research by Veneziano and Rohner (1998), Wenk and Hardesty (1994), and Veneziano (2000a) illustrates research about the relationship between the quality and quantity of paternal involvement. In a sample of African American and European American children, Veneziano and Rohner found that the amount of time that fathers spent with children across the ethnic groups was associated with children's psychological adjustment primarily insofar as it was perceived by youths to be an expression of paternal warmth. These results varied by ethnicity, however. In the European American families, paternal warmth and paternal involvement were significantly correlated with each other, and both were correlated with youths' psychological adjustment. However, in multivariate regression analysis, only fathers' warmth predicted positive psychological adjustment. In the African American families, fathers' time involvement was not significantly correlated with paternal warmth or with psychological adjustment, although paternal warmth was significantly related to psychological adjustment. Wenk and Hardesty also found that the quality of the positive emotional involvement of both fathers and mothers, not father's physical presence, significantly predicted children's emotional well-being in a national survey of 762 U.S. children. Finally, Veneziano's (2000a) cross-cultural comparative study found that the lack of paternal warmth and socialization for aggression predicted young males' interpersonal violence, whereas the amount of time that fathers were involved with children had no significant impact.

Outcomes Associated with Maternal and Paternal Warmth and Nurturance.

As discussed earlier, studies of the influence of parental warmth and nurturance have been extensively studied in Western and non-Western societies. In recent years, the influence of paternal warmth has been investigated but the vast amount of empirical findings come from studies of maternal warmth.

Mental Health, Psychological Adjustment, and Emotional Well-Being Outcomes.

Evidence of mental health, psychological adjustment, behavioral, and substance abuse outcomes of maternal warmth or lack thereof have now been documented for over 50 years. For example, when Australian, Chinese, Egyptian, German, Hungarian, Italian, Swedish, and Turkish mothers exhibit little warmth, offspring tend to exhibit significant symptoms of both clinical and non-clinical depression. Moreover, lack of maternal warmth has been related to depression among every major ethnic group in the United States, including Asian Americans, African Americans, Mexican Americans, and European Americans (Rohner & Britner, 2002).

When paternal warmth is concurrently investigated with maternal warmth, paternal warmth often merges as a more significant predictor of mental health and psychological adjustment problems than does maternal warmth (Rohner & Veneziano, 2001). Cole and McPherson (1993), for example, concluded that father–adolescent conflict, but not mother–adolescent conflict, was positively associated with adolescent depressive symptoms. Barrera and Garrison–Jones (1992) also concluded that paternal supportive behaviors were related to adolescent depression, whereas maternal support was not. Similarly, Barnett, Marshall, and Pleck (1992) and Rohner and Brothers (1999) found that the quality of relationship between offspring and fathers had a more significant impact than did the quality of relationship between mothers and offspring. Barnett et al. showed that the quality of son's relationships with their fathers, but not with their mothers, predicted adult sons' psychological adjustment, whereas Rohner and Brothers (1999) found that paternal, but not maternal, rejection (i.e., lack of warmth) predicted self-reported psychological adjustment problems in women diagnosed with borderline personality disorder.

Finally, Veneziano (2000b) found in a sample of 281 African American and European American families that only youths' self-reports of paternal warmth were significantly related to the European American youths' psychological adjustment when controlling for the influence of maternal warmth. Indeed, maternal warmth dropped from the regression model altogether. However, in the African American families, paternal as well as maternal warmth was significantly related to youths' psychological adjustment, making both independent and joint contributions.

Behavioral Outcomes.

Conduct disorder, behavior problems, delinquency, and externalizing behaviors, including violent and non-violent crimes, have all been found to be significantly related to maternal and paternal warmth. Lack of maternal warmth has been shown to influence behavior problems in Bahrain, Mainland China, Croatia, England, India, and Norway, as it has in all major ethnic groups in the United States. Most studies of the relationship between lack of maternal warmth and behavior problems control for a host of other variables, including family conflict, parental control (i.e., permissiveness–restrictiveness), household composition, father absence, parental employment, social class, ethnicity, gender, and age. Interestingly, lack of maternal warmth continues to be significantly associated with behavior difficulties when studied concurrently with such sources of variation (Rohner & Britner, 2002).

Researchers have also found that fathers' warmth is at least as important as mothers' warmth in influencing youths' behavior and conduct (Becker, 1960; Deklyen, Biernbaum, Speltz, & Greenberg, 1998; Deklyen, Speltz, & Greenberg, 1998; McPherson, 1974; Paley, Conger, & Harold, 2000; Patterson, Reid, & Dishion, 1992; Renk, Phares, & Epps, 1999; Russell & Russell, 1996; Siantz & Smith, 1994). Other researchers such as Forehand and Nousiainen (1993) and Kroupa (1988) have reported that fathers' warmth and acceptance was the sole significant predictor of youths' conduct and behavior problems. Forehand and Nousiainen speculated, "An adolescent may be more eager to obtain the approval of the father than of the mother, as the father's acceptance is less available. Thus, the father's acceptance, because of its lower level of occurrence may actually play a more salient role … than the mother's approval" (p. 219).

Substance Abuse Outcomes.

Rohner and Britner (2002) also show that lack of maternal warmth has been linked to substance abuse problems in Australia, Canada, England, The Netherlands, Sweden, Australia, Brazil, China, Curacao, Japan, Singapore, and Venezuela, as well as in most American ethnic groups including African Americans, Asian Americans, European Americans, and Hispanic Americans.

As for fathers, Campo and Rohner (1992) found a strong association between perceived parental acceptance–rejection, psychological adjustment, and substance abuse among young adults. The substance-abusing group as compared with the nonabusing group "experienced qualitatively more paternal rejection than acceptance in their families of origin but did not experience more maternal rejection than acceptance" (p. 434). The nonabusers tended to perceive both their maternal and paternal relationships as quite warm and accepting. Perceived paternal acceptance–rejection, more than perceived maternal acceptance–rejection, was the best predictor of substance abuse among male and female young adults.

Paternal and Maternal Parenting and Outcomes in Sons and Daughters

Earlier in this chapter, differences in fathers and mothers' interactions with their sons and daughters were reviewed, and it was shown that researchers have found that fathers and mothers exert a strong influence on such outcomes as youths' gender-role ideology. This section builds on those findings by briefly reviewing other consequences of maternal and paternal behavior for children's development, including self-esteem, psychological adjustment, and cognitive and academic competence. For example, Rohner and Veneziano (2001) reported on the work of Barber and Thomas (1986) who found that the cluster of conditions predicting adolescent daughters' self-esteem was different from those that predicted sons' self-esteem. Sons' self-esteem was best predicted by fathers' sustained physical contact (e.g., picking up the boy for fun and safety) and by mothers' companionship (i.e., spending time with the boy, and sharing activities with him), whereas daughters' self-esteem was best predicted by fathers' physical affection and by mothers' praise, approval, encouragement, use of terms of endearment, and helping behaviors. Rohner and Veneziano (2001) also reported on Booth and Amato's (1994) longitudinal study, which found that marital quality influenced adult sons' and daughters' feelings of closeness with their fathers and mothers. Specifically, adult sons whose parents had a poor marital relationship felt somewhat less close to both parents than did sons whose parents had a good marital relationship. Daughters, on the other hand, felt much less close to their fathers but only slightly less close to their mothers when parents had poor marital relationships. Booth and Amato concluded that the father–daughter tie tends to be especially vulnerable in the context of serious marital problems between parents, whereas the mother–daughter tie tends to be especially resilient. Moreover, in a study of maternal and paternal

warmth and control, Jones, Forehand, and Beach (2000) found that only maternal behavior (i.e., firm control) during adolescence was independently associated with secure adult romantic relationships in both male and female offspring. Although fathers' warmth and control by themselves did not predict secure adult romantic relationships, a combination of paternal firm control and maternal warmth did predict secure adult romantic relationships for both male and female offspring.

Additional evidence about the influence of paternal behavior on boys' and girls' development comes from the work of Radin. In the early 1970s, Radin and colleagues (Jordan, Radin, & Epstein, 1975) found that paternal nurturance was positively related to the cognitive competence of European American middle-class preschool boys, but not girls. For example, in the first of two observational studies, Radin et al. investigated the influence of paternal nurturance (e.g., responsiveness) and restrictiveness (e.g., ordering without explanation) on boys' intellectual functioning. They found that paternal nurturance was positively related to boys' scores on the Stanford–Binet Intelligence Scale (SBIS) and the Peabody Picture Vocabulary Test (PPVT) (a test of verbal intelligence). On the other hand, paternal restrictiveness was negatively associated with boys' achievement on these same measures. However, after examining a subset of fathers and their daughters from that study, Radin found that high paternal involvement was positively related to girls' mental age as measured by the Peabody Picture Vocabulary Test (Radin, 1981b). Furthermore, she found a positive relationship between high levels of father involvement and daughters' scores on the Cognitive Home Environment Scale (CHES). The CHES measures fathers' long-term educational and career expectations for their children, and fathers' cognitive stimulation of their children's intellectual growth (Radin, 1981b).

In a subsequent study, Radin (1981a) investigated the relationship between paternal involvement and both girls' and boys' intellectual growth as measured by the CHES. She also investigated the relationship between scores on the PPVT and levels of fathers' involvement. Her study consisted of 59 intact middle-class, primarily European American, families living in the midwestern United States. Radin found that for the sample as a whole, paternal involvement was positively related to fathers' stimulation of youths' intellectual growth. Paternal involvement in childcare was also positively related to youths' verbal intelligence. As for consequences by gender, girls' verbal intelligence was positively related to paternal involvement. Moreover, paternal involvement in decision-making was positively related to fathers' stimulation of boys' intellectual growth and verbal intelligence. Thus the verbal intelligence of boys and girls was significantly affected by paternal involvement. However, these findings also indicated that fathers stimulated the intellectual growth of sons more so than daughters, suggesting that even highly involved fathers direct more attention to sons than to daughters.

Researchers have also found ethnic variations in gender-related outcomes of paternal behavior. For example, McAdoo's (1993) research of African American families suggests that middle-income African American fathers tend to demand immediate obedience, suppression of children's feelings, and constraint of children's assertive and independent behavior. However, Baumrind (1972, 1991) found African American fathers to exhibit a combination of firm control, warmth, and encouragement of autonomy in her observational study of African American and European American fathers' interactions with preschool children. African American and European American fathers exhibited similar expectations concerning the behaviors of sons, encouraging their independence, while African American fathers tended to discourage independence or individuality in daughters. Nevertheless, Baumrind found that these same African American daughters were actually independent and positively involved in social interactions at school. According to McAdoo, the authoritarian style of African American fathers may not contain the same degree of emotional coldness as that of European American fathers, such that authoritarian paternal control among African American children may be experienced somewhat differently than it is by European American children.

Summary and Conclusion

This chapter reviewed research that suggests that fathers and mothers often interact differently with their offspring, and that these differences influence offspring behavior across the life span. However, differences in fathers' and mothers' behavior have often been found to be a function of social, cultural, and economic circumstances. On the other hand, recent findings in Western and non-Western cultures show that fathers' and mothers' nurturing behaviors are similar across a wide variety of sociocultural

contexts, and that paternal warmth is at least equal to maternal warmth in influencing offspring development. This latter finding raises questions about how knowledge about gender-related parenting is generated. For example, were fathers less warm and nurturing in the past, or did behavioral science neglect to investigate warmth-related fathering behaviors because of adherence to cultural constructions of fathers as peripheral to family life, or as less important than mothers? Notwithstanding this possibility, there may be more to our knowledge-building about fathering and mothering than can be explained by a failure to look closely at particular maternal or paternal behaviors, or by a failure to consider sociocultural contexts, or values, or ideologies that shape men's and women's behavior. That is, evidence from biosocial and evolutionary studies suggests that we have not heard the last word about the relationship among gender, parenting, and the survival strategies of our species. Indeed, the conjoint application of cultural and biological perspectives to research on maternal and paternal behavior seems ripe for further investigation during the 21st century.

References

Amato, P. (1994). Father–child relations, mother–child relations, and offspring psychological well-being in adulthood. *Journal of Marriage and the Family, 56*, 1031–1042.

Amato, P. (1998). More than money? Men's contributions to their children's lives. In A. Booth & A. Crouter (Eds.), *Men in families* (pp. 241–278). Mahwah, NJ: L Erlbaum.

Anderson, K., Kaplan, H., & Lancaster, J. (2001). *Men's financial expenditures on genetic children and stepchildren from current and former relationships.* (Population Studies Center Research Report No. 01-484.) Ann Arbor, MI: Population Study Center.

Aronoff, J. (1967). *Psychological needs and cultural systems: A case study.* Princeton, NJ: Van Nostrand.

Bacon, M., Child, I., & Barry, H. (1963). A cross-cultural study of correlates of crime. *Journal of Abnormal and Social Psychology, 66*, 291–300.

Barber, B., & Thomas, D. (1986). Dimensions of fathers' and mothers' supportive behavior: A case for physical affection. *Journal of Marriage and the Family, 48*, 783–794.

Barnett, R., & Baruch, G. (1988). Correlates of fathers' participation in family work. In P. Bronstein & C. Cowan (Eds.), *Fatherhood today: Men's changing role in the family* (pp. 66–78). New York: Wiley.

Barnett, R., Marshall, N., & Pleck, J. (1992). Adult son–parent relationships and the associations with son's psychological distress. *Journal of Family Issues, 13*, 505–525.

Barrera, M., Jr., & Garrison-Jones, C. (1992). Family and peer social support as specific correlates of adolescent depressive symptoms. *Journal of Abnormal Child Psychology, 20*, 1–16.

Barry, H., III, & Paxson, L. (1971). Infancy and early childhood: Cross-cultural codes 2. *Ethnology*, *10*, 466–508.

Baumrind, D. (1972). An exploratory study of socialization effects on black children: Some black–white comparisons. *Child Development*, *43*, 261–267.

Baumrind, D. (1991). Parenting styles and adolescent development. In J. Brooks-Gunn, R. Lerner, & A. Petersen (Eds.), *The encyclopedia on adolescence* (pp. 746–758). New York: Garland.

Becker, W. (1960). The relationship of factors in parental ratings of self and each other to the behavior of kindergarten children as rated by mothers, fathers, and teachers. *Journal of Consulting Psychology*, *24*, 507–527.

Belsky, J. (1998). Paternal influence and children's well-being: Limits of, and new directions for, understanding. In A. Booth & A. Crouter (Eds.), *Men in families* (pp. 279–293). Mahwah, NJ: L Erlbaum.

Benson, L. (1968). *Fatherhood: A sociological perspective*. New York: Random House.

Biller, H. (1993). *Fathers and families: Paternal factors in child development*. Westport, CT: Auburn House.

Biller, H., & Borstelmann, L. (1967). Masculine development: An integrative review. *Merrill–Palmer Quarterly*, *13*, 253–294.

Booth, A., & Amato, P. R. (1994). Parental marital quality, parental divorce, and relations with parents. *Journal of Marriage and the Family*, *56*, 21–34.

Bowlby, J. (1969). *Attachment and loss*. New York: Hogarth Press.

Bronfenbrenner, U., & Ceci, S. (1994). Nature–nurture reconceptualized: A bio-ecological model. *Psychological Review*, *101*, 568–586.

Bronson, W. (1959). Dimensions of ego and infantile identification. *Journal of Personality*, *27*, 532–545.

Bronstein, P. (1988). Father–child interactions: Implications for gender-role socialization. In P. Bronstein & C. Cowan (Eds.), *Fatherhood today* (pp. 107–123). New York: Wiley.

Broude, G. (1990). Protest masculinity: A further look at the causes and the concept. *Ethos*, *18*, 103–122.

Buss, D., Larsen, R., Westen, D., & Semmelroth, J. (1992). Sex differences in jealousy: Evolution, physiology, and psychology. *Psychological Science*, *3*, 251–255.

Byrnes, R. (1988). *The 1,911 best things anybody ever said*. New York: Fawcett.

Cabrera, N., Tamis-LeMonda, C., Bradley, R., Hofferth, S., & Lamb, M. (2000). Fatherhood in the twenty-first century. *Child Development*, *71*, 127–136.

Campo, A., & Rohner, R. (1992). Relationships between perceived parental acceptance–rejection, psychological adjustment, and substance abuse among young adults. *Child Abuse and Neglect*, *16*, 429–440.

Cole, D. A., & McPherson, A. E. (1993). Relation of family subsystems to adolescent depression: Implementing a new family assessment strategy. *Journal of Family Psychology*, *7*, 119–133.

Collins, W., & Russell, G. (1991). Mother–child and father–child relationships in middle-childhood and adolescence: A developmental analysis. *Developmental Review*, *11*, 99–136.

Deklyen, M., Biernbaum, M., Speltz, M., & Greenberg, M. (1998). Fathers and preschool behavior problems. *Developmental Psychology*, *34*, 264–275.

Deklyen, M., Speltz, M., & Greenberg, M. (1998). Fathering and early onset conduct problems: Positive and negative parenting,

father–son attachment, and the marital context. *Clinical Child and Family Psychology Review*, *1*, 3–21.

Distler, L. S. (1965). *Patterns of parental identification: An examination of three theories*. Unpublished doctoral dissertation, University of California, Berkeley.

Easterbrooks, M., & Goldberg, W. (1984). Toddler development in the family: Impact of father involvement and parenting characteristics. *Child Development*, *55*, 740–752.

Ember, C., & Ember, M. (1994). War, socialization, and interpersonal violence: A cross-cultural study. *Journal of Conflict Resolution*, *38*, 620–646.

Ember, C., & Ember, M. (n.d.) Father-absence and male aggression: A reexamination of the comparative evidence. *Ethos* (special issue in honor of Beatrice B. Whiting).

Endicott, K. (1992). Fathering in an egalitarian society. In B. Hewlett (Ed.), *Father–child relations: Cultural and biosocial contexts* (pp. 281–295). Chicago: Aldine.

Erikson, R., & Gecas, V. (1991). Social class and fatherhood. In F. Bozett & S. Hanson (Eds.), *Fatherhood and families in cultural context* (pp. 114–137). New York: Springer.

Fagot, B. (1995). Parenting boys and girls. In M. Bornstein (Ed.), *Handbook of parenting* (Vol. 1, pp. 163–183). Mahwah, NJ: L Erlbaum.

Flinn, M. (1992). Paternal care in a Caribbean village. In B. Hewlett (Ed.), *Father–child relations: Cultural and biosocial contexts* (pp. 57–84). New York: Aldine.

Forehand, R., & Nousiainen, S. (1993). Maternal and paternal parenting: Critical dimensions in adolescent functioning. *Journal of Family Psychology*, *7*, 213–221.

Fox, G., & Bruce, C. (2001). Conditional fatherhood: Identity theory and parental investment theory as alternative sources of explanation of fathering. *Journal of Marriage and Family*, *63*, 394–404.

Gelles, R., & Lancaster, J. (Eds.). (1987). *Offspring abuse and neglect: Biosocial dimensions*. New York: Aldine.

Gilmore, D. (1990). *Manhood in the making: Cultural concepts of masculinity*. New Haven, CT: Yale University Press.

Goldstein, J. (2001). Excerpts from War and gender: How gender shapes the war system and vice versa (Cambridge University Press). http://www.warandgender.com/wgfather.htm

Hagen, E., Hames, R., Craig, N., Lauer, M., & Price, M. (2001). Parental investment and child health in a Yanomamö village suffering short-term food stress. *Journal of Biosocial Science*, *33*, 503–528.

Hargreaves, D., & Colley, A. (1986). *The psychology of sex roles*. London: Harper & Row.

Harris, K., Furstenberg, F., & Marmer, J. (1998). Paternal involvement with adolescents in intact families: The influence of fathers over the life course. *Demography*, *35*, 201–216.

Hewlett, B. (1987). Intimate fathers: Patterns of paternal holding among Aka Pygmies. In M. Lamb (Ed.), *Father's role in cross-cultural perspective* (pp. 295–330). New York: Erlbaum.

Hewlett, B. (Ed.). (1992). *Father–child relations: Cultural and biosocial contexts*. New York: Aldine.

Hoffman, L. (1977). Changes in family roles, socialization, and sex differences. *American Psychologist*, *42*, 644–657.

Hoffman, L. (1989). Effects of maternal employment in the two-parent family. *American Psychologist*, *44*, 283–291.

Hojat, M. (1999, November). *Theoretical perspectives and empirical findings on the role of the biological mother in human survival and development*. Paper presented at the World Congress of Families II Conference, Geneva. http://www.worldcongress.org/gen99_speakers/gen99_hojat.htm

Hosley, C., & Montemayor, R. (1997). Fathers and adolescents. In M. Lamb (Ed.), *The role of the father in child development* (3rd ed., pp. 162–178). New York: Wiley.

Jones, D., Forehand, R., & Beach, S. (2000). Maternal and paternal parenting during adolescence: Forecasting early adult psychological adjustment. *Adolescence, 35*, 513–531.

Jordan, B., Radin, N., & Epstein, A. (1975). Paternal behavior and intellectual functioning in preschool boys and girls. *Developmental Psychology, 11*, 407–408.

Kagan, J. (1978, August). The parental love trap. *Psychology Today*, pp. 54, 57, 58, 61, 91.

Kardiner, A. (1945). The concept of basic personality structure as an operational tool in the social sciences. In R. Linton (Ed.), *The science of man in the world crisis* (pp. 102–122). New York: Viking Fund.

Katz, M., & Konner, M. (1981). The role of the father: An anthropological perspective. In M. Lamb (Ed.), *The role of the father in child development* (pp. 155–186). New York: Wiley.

Kelly, J., & Worell, L. (1976). Parent behavior related to masculine, feminine, and androgynous sex role orientations. *Journal of Consulting and Clinical Psychology, 44*, 843–851.

Kroupa, S. (1988). Perceived parental acceptance and female juvenile delinquency. *Adolescence, 23*, 171–185.

Lamb, M. (1986). The changing role of fathers. In M. Lamb (Ed.), *The father's role: Applied perspectives* (pp. 3–28). New York: Wiley.

Lamb, M. (1997). Father and child development: An introductory overview and guide. In M. E. Lamb (Ed.), *The role of the father in child development* (pp. 1–18). New York: Wiley.

Lamb, M. (2000). The history of research on father involvement: An overview. *Marriage and Family Review, 29*, 23–42.

Lamb, M., & Oppenheim, D. (1989). Fatherhood and father–child relationships: Five years of research. In S. Cath, A. Gurwitt, & L. Gunsberg (Eds.), *Fathers and their families* (pp. 11–26). Hillsdale, NJ: Analytic Press.

Lamb, M., Pleck, J., Charnov, E., & Levine, J. (1987). A biosocial perspective on paternal behavior and involvement. In J. Lancaster, J. Attman, A. Rossi, & L. Sherrod (Eds.), *Parenting across the lifespan: Biosocial dimensions* (pp. 111–142). New York: Aldine de Gruyter.

Leaper, C., Anderson, K., & Sanders, P. (1998). Moderators of gender effects on parents' talk to their children: A meta-analysis. *Developmental Psychology, 34*, 3–27.

Lindsey, E., Mize, J., & Petit, G. (1997). Differential play patterns of mothers and fathers of sons and daughters: Implications for children's gender role development. *Sex Roles, 37*, 643–661.

Louv, R. (2002). *Kyle Pruett talks about fatherhood*. Connect for Kids. (http://www.connectforkids.org/content1555/content_show.htm?attrib_id = 333&doc_id = 8149#roles). The Benton Foundation.

Mackey, W. (1996). *The American father: Biocultural and developmental aspects*. New York: Plenum.

Mahler, M., & Furer, M. (1968). *On human symbiosis and the vicissitudes of individuation*. New York: International University Press.

Martin, M., & Anderson, C. (1997). Aggressive communication traits: How similar are young adults and their parents in argumentativeness, assertiveness, and verbal aggressiveness? *Western Journal of Communication, 61*, 299–314.

McAdoo, J. (1993, January). The roles of African-American fathers: An ecological perspective. *Families in Society: The Journal of Contemporary Human Services*, 28–35.

McPherson, S. R. (1974). Parental interactions of various levels. *Journal of Nervous and Mental Disease, 158*, 424–431.

Mead, M. (1949). *Male and female: A study of the sexes in a changing world*. New York: Morrow.

Mead, M. (1956). Some theoretical considerations on the problem of mother–child separation. In D. G. Haring (Ed.), *Personal character and cultural milieu* (pp. 637–649). Syracuse, NY: Syracuse University Press.

Morelli, G., & Tronick, E. (1992). Male care among Efe foragers and Lese farmers. In B. Hewlett (Ed.), *Father–child relations: Cultural and biosocial contexts* (pp. 231–262). Chicago: Aldine.

Moreno, R.P. (in press). *Parental involvement among high and low acculturated Latina mothers* (Research Report). Julian Samora Research Institute, Michigan State University, East Lansing, MI.

Munroe, R. H., & Munroe, R. L. (1992). Fathers in children's environments: A four culture study. In B. Hewlett (Ed.), *Father–child relations: Cultural and biosocial contexts* (pp. 213–230). Chicago: Aldine.

Munroe, R. H., & Munroe, R. L. (1994). Behavior across cultures: Results from observational studies. In W. Lonner & R. Malpass (Eds.), *Psychology and culture* (pp. 107–112). Boston: Allyn & Bacon.

Murdock, G., & White, D. (1969). Standard cross-cultural sample. *Ethnology, 8*, 329–369.

Mussen, P. (1961). Some antecedents and consequences of masculine sex-typing in adolescent boys. *Psychological Monographs, 75*(2, Whole No. 506).

Mussen, P., & Distler, L. (1959). Masculinity, identification, and father–son relationships. *Journal of Abnormal and Social Psychology, 59*, 350–356.

Orlofsky, J. L. (1979). Parental antecedents of sex-role orientation in college men and women. *Sex Roles, 5*, 495–512.

Paley, B., Conger, R., & Harold, G. (2000). Parents' affect, adolescent cognitive representations, and adolescent social development. *Journal of Marriage and the Family, 62*, 761–776.

Parke, R. (1996). *Fatherhood*. Cambridge, MA: Harvard University Press.

Parsons, T., & Bales, R. (Eds.). (1955). *Family, socialization, and interaction process*. New York: Free Press.

Patterson, G., Reid, J., & Dishion, T. (1992). *Antisocial boys*. Eugene, OR: Castalia.

Payne, D., & Mussen, P. (1956). Parent child relations and father identification among adolescent boys. *Journal of Abnormal and Social Psychology, 52*, 358–362.

Phares, V. (1992). Where's Poppa? The relative lack of attention to the role of fathers in child and adolescent psychopathology. *American Psychologist, 47*, 656–664.

Pleck, J. (1997). Paternal involvement: Level, sources, and consequences. In M. E. Lamb (Ed.), *The role of the father in child development* (3rd ed., pp. 66–103). New York: Wiley.

Radin, N. (1981a). Child rearing fathers in intact families I: Some antecedents and consequences. *Merrill-Palmer Quarterly, 27*, 489–514.

Radin, N. (1981b). The role of the father in cognitive/academic and intellectual development. In M. Lamb (Ed.), *The role of the father in child development* (2nd ed., pp. 379–427). New York: Wiley.

Radin, N. (1988). Primary caregiving fathers of long duration. In P. Bronstein & C. Cowan (Eds.), *Fatherhood today* (pp. 127–143), New York: Wiley.

Radin, N. (1994). Primary caregiving fathers in intact families. In A. E. Gottfried & A.W. Gottfied (Eds.), *Redefining families: Implications for children's development* (pp. 55–97). New York: Plenum.

Radin, N., & Russell, G. (1983). Increased father participation and child development outcomes. In M. Lamb & A. Sagi (Eds.), *Fatherhood and family policy* (pp. 191–218). Hillsdale, NJ: Erlbaum.

Radin, N., & Sagi, A. (1982). Childrearing fathers in intact families in Israel and the U.S.A. *Merrill–Palmer Quarterly, 28,* 111–136.

Radin, N., Williams, E., & Coggins, K. (1993, October). *Paternal involvement in childrearing and the school performance of Native American children: An exploratory study.* Paper presented at the Conference on Race/Ethnic Families in the U.S., Brigham Young University, Provo, UT.

Renk, K., Phares, V., & Epps, J. (1999). The relationship between parental anger and behavior problems in children and adolescents. *Journal of Family Psychology, 13,* 209–227.

Reuter, M., & Biller, H. (1973). Perceived nurturance, availability, and personality adjustment of college males. *Journal of Consulting and Clinical Psychology, 40,* 339–342.

Rohner, R. (1975). *They love me, they love me not: A worldwide study of the effects of parental acceptance and rejection.* New Haven, CT: HRAF Press.

Rohner, R. (1986). *The warmth dimension: Foundations of parental acceptance–rejection theory.* Newbury Park, CA: Sage.

Rohner, R. (2000). *Parental acceptance and rejection bibliography* [on-line]. Available: http://vm.uconn.edu/~rohner/CSPARBL.html

Rohner, R., & Britner, P. (2002). Worldwide mental health correlates of parental acceptance–rejection: Review of cross-cultural and intra-cultural evidence. *Cross-Cultural Research, 36,* 16–47.

Rohner, R., & Brothers, S. (1999). Perceived parental rejection, psychological maladjustment, and borderline personality disorder. *Journal of Emotional Abuse, 1,* 81–95.

Rohner, R., & Veneziano, R. (2001) The importance of father love: History and contemporary evidence. *Review of General Psychology, 5,* 382–405.

Russell, A., & Russell, G. (1996). Positive parenting and boys' and girls' misbehaviour during a home observation. *International Journal of Behavioral Development, 19,* 291–307.

Sanchez, L., & Thomson, E. (1997). Becoming mothers and fathers: Parenthood, gender, and the division of labor. *Gender and Society, 11,* 747–772.

Shulman, S., & Collins, W. (Eds.). (1993). *Father–adolescent relationships.* San Francisco: Jossey-Bass.

Siantz, de Leon, M., & Smith, M. (1994). Parental factors correlated with developmental outcome in the migrant Head Start child. *Early Childhood Research Quarterly, 9,* 481–503.

Snow, M., Jacklin, C., & Maccoby, E. (1983). Sex of child differences in father–child interaction at one year of age. *Child Development, 54,* 227–232.

Starrels, M. (1994). Gender differences in parent–child relations. *Journal of Family Issues, 15,* 148–166.

Stearns, P. (1991). Fatherhood in historical perspective: The role of social change. In F. Bozett & S. Hanson (Eds.), *Fatherhood and family in cultural context* (pp. 28–52). New York: Springer.

Steinbacher, R., & Gilroy, F. (1990). Sex selection technology: A prediction of its use and effect. *Journal of Psychology, 124,* 283–288.

Stendler, C. (1950). Sixty years of child training practices. *Journal of Pediatrics, 36,* 122–134.

Stern, D. (1995). *The motherhood constellation.* New York: Basic Books.

Sunley, R. (1955). Early nineteenth-century American literature on child rearing. In M. Mead & M. Wolfenstein (Eds.), *Childhood in contemporary cultures* (pp. 150–167). Chicago: University of Chicago Press.

Super, C., & Harkness, S. (1986). The developmental niche: A conceptualization at the interface of child and culture. *International Journal of Behavioral Development, 9,* 545–569.

Updegraff, K., Mchale, S., Grouter, A., & Kupanoff, K. (2001). Parents' involvement in adolescents' peer relationships: A comparison of mothers' and fathers' roles. *Journal of Marriage and Family, 63,* 644–658.

Veneziano, R. (2000a, February). *The influence of paternal warmth and involvement on offspring behavior.* Paper presented at the meeting of the Society for Cross-Cultural Research, New Orleans, LA.

Veneziano, R. (2000b). Perceived paternal and maternal warmth and African American and European American youths' psychological adjustment. *Journal of Marriage and the Family, 62,* 123–132.

Veneziano, R., & Rohner, R. (1998). Perceived paternal acceptance, paternal involvement, and youths' psychological adjustment in a rural, biracial southern community. *Journal of Marriage and the Family, 60,* 335–343.

Wenk, D., & Hardesty, C. (1994). The influence of parental involvement on the well-being of sons and daughters. *Journal of Marriage and the Family, 56,* 229–235.

Whiting, B. (1965). Sex identity conflict and physical violence: A comparative study. *American Anthropologist, 67,* 123–140.

Whiting, B., & Whiting, J. (1975). *Children of six cultures.* Cambridge, MA: Harvard University Press.

Whiting, J., & Child, I. (1953). *Child training and personality.* New Haven, CT: Yale University Press.

Williams, E., & Radin, N. (1993). Paternal involvement, maternal employment, and adolescents' academic achievement: An 11-year follow-up. *American Journal of Orthopsychiatry, 63,* 306–312.

Williams, S., & Finley, G. (1997). Father contact and perceived affective quality of fathering in Trinidad. *InterAmerican Journal of Psychology, 31,* 315–319.

Wilson, M., & Daly, M. (1992). The man who mistook his wife for a chattel. In J. Barkow, L. Cosmides, & J. Tooby (Eds.), *The adapted mind: Evolutionary psychology and the generation of culture* (pp. 289–322). New York: Oxford University Press.

Witt, S. (1997). Parental influence on children's socialization to gender roles. *Adolescence, 32,* 253–259.

Economic Activities and Gender Roles

Robin O'Brian

INTRODUCTION

It seems obvious that gender and economic activity are interrelated; in every society human beings appear to associate some activities with women and others with men. In addition, what constitutes an "economic activity" is open to argument. Are all productive activities economic? Are only activities that enter the commercial realm economic?

Economic activity can of course encompass all of that work that supplies people with food and shelter, that is, the work that meets their basic needs. It also includes the activities of exchange and trade, and of consumption. Certainly, there is much written on people's commercial production—that most easily defined as "economic activities". Ethnographies have explored Kuna women's commercial production of mola, traditional appliquéd textile panels now sold to tourists (Tice, 1995), the economic specialization of men and women in the embroidery industry of Lucknow, India (Wilkinson-Weber, 1999), the interrelationship of class and gender in the weaving industry of Oaxaca, Mexico (Stephen, 1992), and women's specialization in the pottery industry of La Chamba, Colombia (Duncan, 2000). Collections of similar topics are also popular and timely, with a number focusing again on commercial craft production (Nash, 1993; Grimes & Milgram, 2001) but others exploring marketing as well (Seligmann, 2001; Sheldon, 1996). What ties all these recent works together is the theme of commercial production in the cash economy, but of course economic activities go well beyond this, and are part and parcel of domestic life as well.

ECONOMIC ACTIVITIES IN THE HOUSEHOLD

Much economic work takes place in the household, where people produce and reproduce family life. Here economic activity is broadly defined, rather than being restricted solely to the commercial. Indeed, grappling with what constitutes the "economic" within the household remains a conundrum (Wilk, 1989). To understand how gender roles and economics interact, particularly in traditional societies, the household must be a focus. However, different perspectives differ widely in their view of economic roles in the household. World systems theorists influenced by the work of Immanuel Wallerstein (1974) sometimes seem to suggest that households exist merely to satisfy the needs of industrial capitalism (e.g., Smith, Wallerstein, & Evers, 1984) while some Marxists see women's work and behavior as the result of women's lack of control of the means of production or their victimization by patriarchal ideological relations (Young, Wolkowitz, & McCullagh, 1981). Scholars with this viewpoint sometimes suggest that the household is a sort of patriarchal structure or device to marginalize or otherwise control women, rather than exploring it as a way of understanding both men's and women's economic activities.

Cross-Cultural Patterning of Activities Based on Gender

At the same time, scholars from a range of perspectives (e.g., Brown, 1970; Burton, Brudner, & White, 1977) note that women's duties, particularly as mothers but also as homemakers, require them to perform work that can be easily begun and abandoned, that is relatively routine, and that can be combined with childcare. However, while men's work may take them further afield, it too will frequently be embedded in domestic life and general routine (e.g., chopping wood, clearing, plowing, or planting fields, and building houses or outbuildings).

We might systematize some explanations offered for the persistence of "men's work" and "women's work," even when activities take place in a variety of settings. Some activities tend to be assigned repeatedly to one or the other gender, as can be seen in table 1. Often the determining factor appears to be strength or physical prowess ("strength theory"; see Murdock & Provost, 1973). Men are certainly more efficient at plowing, clearing land, or

Table 1. Cross-Cultural Patterning of Gender Assignments in Subsistence/Economic Activities

Type of activity	Nearly always male	Usually male	Either gender or both	Usually female	Nearly always female
Primary subsistence	Hunt and trap large and small animals	Fish Herd large animals Collect wild honey Clear land and prepare soil for planting	Collect shellfish Care for small animals Plant crops Tend crops Harvest crops Milk animals Preserve meats and fish	Gather wild plants	
Secondary subsistence and household		Butcher animals		Care for children Cook Prepare vegetable foods, dairy products, drinks	Care for infants

Adapted from Ember & Ember (1996, p. 164).

lifting heavy objects—activities that they are far more likely to specialize in. Yet there is little strength required in the collection of honey or in trapping small animals, suggesting that this theory is incomplete.

Expendability theory that makes a similar argument, bolstered by sociobiology: "… men, rather than women, will tend to do the dangerous work in a society because men are more expendable, because the loss of men is less disadvantageous reproductively than the loss of women." (Ember & Ember, 1996, p. 164). If men specialize in the heavy and physically demanding work of plowing or hunting, work that is also dangerous, their loss to society will not be as harmful as that of women, who can still reproduce as long as they have access to some men (Mukhopadhyay & Higgins, 1988, p. 473).

Women's role as mothers probably does play some role in the activities they pursue; such activities are likely, as noted earlier, to be easily combined with childcare. Compatibility theory suggests that women specialize in activities that essentially do not interfere with infant care. In many societies, where infants and young toddlers nurse for lengthy periods and accompany their mothers everywhere, work must fit around the demands of infant care (Brown, 1970; see also Nerlove, 1974). Thus women remain near home, pursuing tasks that can be taken up and abandoned as childcare needs dictate. Such an explanation also suggests why men specialize in various forms of hunting, and even the collection of honey, as these activities could also be dangerous to an infant or young

child (Hurtado, Hawkes, Hill, & Kaplan, 1985). At the same time, it does beg the question as to why women collect shellfish or tend and milk animals, activities that could be seen as similarly risky.

Compatibility theory and another line of argument, "economy of effort," share a further claim sometimes made regarding women's less frequent participation in commercial activities that they pursue in the home. "Economy-of-effort" theory suggests that specialization is a series of linked activities; men may, for example, specialize in woodworking and building because they clear fields, know how to work with wood, and understand its properties, and because the fields, the wood, and the location of the building are all near each other (Murdock & Provost, 1973; White, Burton, & Brudner, 1977; cf. Byrne, 1994). Both compatibility theory and economy-of-effort theory have been used to suggest that women are less likely to pursue commercial activities because, for example, men are more compatible with commercial work or the extension of their activities from subsistence to cash production is more easily made. However, there is suggestion that men compete with and even displace women when activities become commercially productive, a point taken up in more detail below.

Finally, if we accept that gender and activity are strongly linked, with many tasks assigned on the basis of one's gender, we must also examine how activities themselves can create or signal gender. As Murdock and Provost (1973) have noted, some tasks, such as cooking and heavy labor like plowing, are strongly gendered, with women nearly always performing the former and men the latter. Others may vary based on one's ability, inclination, or desire, or may vary from society to society. But the performance of those strongly linked to one's gender help to define one as male or female, as has been seen among some Native American societies. One's gender role can be manipulated or shifted if specific tasks are taken up or avoided (Callender & Kochems, 1983). Among a fairly wide range of such groups appropriate performance of a gender role—particularly through work performed and choice of dress—is a key part of one's gender identity (Blackwood, 1984). The female cross-gender role, where males adopt female behavior and dress (often called *berdache* in the literature) was widespread among native North Americans, including the Crow (Simms, 1903) and the Arapaho (Kroeber, 1902). Less well known are female-to-male cross-gender individuals—females who adopt the male role. While details differ culturally— some such individuals identify their role in childhood while others assume it in puberty—the overall pattern features individual learning and performing the tasks of the other gender and being socially recognized as a member of that gender. Detailed descriptions of this complex are given by Callender and Kochems (1983) and Blackwood (1984).

RELATIVE CONTRIBUTIONS OF MEN AND WOMEN TO SUBSISTENCE

The interrelationship of economic activity and one's gender is also implicated in understanding relative social status, but again, this relationship is complex. In a comprehensive survey article, Ember and Levinson (1991, pp. 93–94) point out that among horticultural and agricultural peoples, the value placed on the activities of men and women and their social status vary. Women in both horticultural and agricultural societies both perform approximately the same amount of work, but agricultural women perform less than men, as both domestic work and fertility increase. Such changes are indirectly related to agricultural intensification; others (Burton & White, 1984; White, Burton, & Dow, 1981), for example, adoption of the plow and draft animals and the cultivation of grain crops, are also part of agricultural intensification and are also related to the decline in female status.

Consequences of Relative Contribution to Division of Labor

Sanday (1974) noted long ago that women's economic participation tended to contribute in one way or another to their overall social status. In societies where women and men contribute more or less equally to production, women generally have a social status similar to men's. Where women do little productive work or conversely nearly all of it, their social status is subordinate to that of men's. In the former instance, women are economic liabilities; in the latter, little more than servants in their own homes. Indeed, various studies suggest that women's economic activities are not directly linked to their greater social status; for instance, Whyte (1978), in a series of cross-cultural tests, found that name of female control of property, control over the products of their labor, or female economic collectivities accurately predict women's higher social status.

COMMERCIAL ACTIVITIES

Men and women behave as commercial actors and enter a wide number of economic activities, although, again, these appear to fall into gendered categories. Women enter a wide range of activities, including food processing, domestic work, and vending, while men will specialize in heavy labor. Men also produce items and vend, although they generally make and sell different products. Men and women both tend to extend their traditional activities outside the home and into the market (Babb, 1989; Bunster, 1983).

What of instances where the genders occupy quite different social spheres? Here, women extend their traditional economic work into the commercial realm while still remaining within the home. For instance, traditional Muslim women often live secluded in the household and work hard to earn a living while remaining in seclusion. Traditional Hausa women in Nigeria, who maintain complete seclusion and never leave the home, trade a variety of prepared snacks and meals, clothing and cloth, cooking oil, eggs, and compound sweepings that are sold as fertilizer. These women will also prepare food and/or sew clothes on commission, and cook at large events. They maintain their seclusion by selling their items out of windows in their homes, and using their children to deliver goods and solicit customers. Hausa women may sometimes become the primary support of their families, while agriculture becomes a secondary source of family income (Hill, 1972).

Similarly, high-caste Indian women in Naraspur make lace while remaining in seclusion. The Naraspur women in particular are able to earn a small income while continuing to observe seclusion and, again, are often the primary support of their families (Mies, 1982). Nonetheless, in this case the available skills of these women interact with religious and gender norms to keep earnings small; lower-caste women, who seek work as farm laborers and who do not practice seclusion, earn far more money and can provide more for their families.

In the Indian city of Lucknow some high-caste women embroider, but there the local embroidery called *chikan* is practiced by everyone, and higher-caste and Muslim women aspiring to a higher social class will observe purdah strictly and thus cannot market embroidery or enter other embroidery-related activities that might require them to leave home (Wilkinson-Weber, 1999).

CHANGING ECONOMICS AND CHANGING GENDER ROLES

Murdock and Provost (1973) have also argued that "[w]hen the invention of a new artifact or process supplants an older and simpler one, both the activity of which it is a part and closely related activities tend more strongly to be assigned to males" (p. 212). However, a range of scholars (Bourque & Warren, 1981; Byrne, 1994, 1999; Ehlers, 1990; Minturn, 1996; O'Brian, 1999) suggest that men also take up female activities when they become commercially viable.

For men, the entry into commercial economic activity seems to follow a superficially similar path—men tend to perform some similar activity for cash, such as agricultural labor construction—but beyond this men are more likely to suffer as an ethnic or racial rather than a gender category, and to have their status within their traditional society rise, while women's declines. For example, indigenous men in the highland Ecuadorian community of Zumbagua begin migrating to Quito for construction work as teenagers, where they compete with nonindigenous Ecuadorians for work. Typically, they are hired at lower wages but more often fired, and are treated as members of an inferior caste. The impact on gender roles becomes clearer when they return home and

confront wives who manage the household and are still rooted in agricultural work. For Zumbagua women, work is subsistence. Life revolves around the patterns of farming and herding, patterns that themselves are part and parcel of Zumbagua life. Still, farm life does not completely support families, who are dependent in part on the cash and store-bought foods that men's wages provide. When men return from the city, where they are disadvantaged, to a community where they have status, they bring the foreign foods, language, and ideas that create friction between them and their traditional wives. If they have made money, they can bring home more commercially produced or imported foods prized by children who turn away from the traditional meals that their mothers cook. If men do not make enough money to bring the commercial foods on which families depend, tensions remain but with the addition of family hunger (Weismantel, 1988).

In the small market town of Chiuchin in Andean Peru, women are active workers in a local economy driven by trade. Women work as cooks, kitchen assistants, waitresses, and launderers, and consider themselves shrewd and savvy businesswomen. But their job choices are limited by cultural ideas about what appropriate female behavior is. Women do not attend school for long, and are usually far more comfortable in the indigenous language Quechua rather than Spanish. Women do not drive and they do not travel beyond the bounds of town, effectively marginalizing them from the more lucrative interregional trade networks that are monopolized by men.

Byrne (1994) explored the factors contributing to who produces pottery. Potting is a so-called "swing" activity, as likely to be performed by men as by women (Murdock & Provost, 1973, pp. 209–221). Byrne argued that male specialization in pottery production rises among those families that lack access to other subsistence resources. In instances where men lack access to land for example, or rights to pasturage, they turn to alternative income strategies, among them pottery production, displacing female kin (Byrne, 1994, pp. 234–235).

Byrne (1999) extended his examination of craft production in his more recent analysis of clothing manufacture. In this case, he explicitly focused on the interrelationship between the gendered division of labor and income-producing activities. Here, Byrne found that in those cases where families are economically dependent upon clothing production, as an item for either trade or sale, men are more likely than women to specialize in this activity (Byrne, 1999, p. 315).

O'Brian (1999) pursued a similar line of inquiry in her analysis of weaving. While weaving is similarly considered a "swing" activity (Murdock & Provost, 1973), this is due to a high male participation in central and West Africa. For the most part, weaving is strongly associated with female production. While weaving production appears to shift from "female" to "male" with increasingly complex looms, loom complexity and maleness are both associated with increasing commercial production, in which men are more likely to participate (O'Brian, 1999, pp. 32, 34–35).

In those parts of West Africa where women have traditionally been subsistence farmers, men displace them and convert land to cash cropping which they also monopolize. In these cases the arguments of Murdock and Provost (1973) and Minturn (1996) are both borne out, as men adopt new processes and technologies, and also enter commercial production (Benería & Sen, 1981).

Similar processes occur in family businesses, and the economic changes that occur with them often leave women behind. In San Pedro Sacatepecquez, Guatemala, women have traditionally run small businesses of weaving, sewing, knitting, and other traditionally female skills out of their homes, training their daughters to take them over upon adulthood. But as the economy is increasingly urbanized and industrialized, fewer women are able to support themselves and their families with such earnings. Girls and young women brought up to take over the businesses do not have skills that translate into an urban job market, which pushes them deeper into the home as that arena too is devalued (Ehlers, 1990).

Similarly, vending, like many other activities, is often highly gendered, with men and women specializing in different segments. This has been true in U.S. society, in the sense that people think it is somehow "natural" for women to sell clothes and men to sell cars or refrigerators, an argument made by a national department store chain to justify tracking sales personnel into different areas based on gender (Milkman, 1986). But a range of cultural norms interact to contribute to the idea of appropriateness. As in the United States, in rural Peru and Guatemala men will sell larger items, items in bulk, or "high-end" prestige items, while women will sell household products or extra produce, for instance, some carrots or two or three eggs (Babb, 1989; Ehlers, 1990; Swetnam, 1988). The increasing effect of market capitalism is contributing to changes in this interrelationship. Women are everywhere increasing participation in market activities in addition to performing their traditional household work, a pattern replicated in the United States as well as in traditional societies (Dwyer & Bruce, 1988; Hochschild, 1989).

GENDER, WORK, AND SOCIAL STATUS

The larger economy, the work people do in the home, the work they conduct outside it, and ideas about status all contribute to shifts and changes in what is an appropriate role for a man or a woman. As market incorporation increases women's economic activities, those more likely to be found in the home tend to decline in the status they confer, while commercial activities become more desirable. Among the Zumbaguans discussed above, men's incorporation into cash work, even poorly paid work done far from home, allows them the money that is increasingly necessary. The time away from home increases the social distance between men and women who have different interests and values. Women remain tied to farm and home; men increasingly become oriented to urban life. Children themselves enjoy the excitement and allure of the urban world and may ignore or devalue their mothers' daily lives and routines (Weismantel, 1988).

Such a pattern is seen throughout the rural world, although there are occasions where women may exploit changes that allow them to benefit from a larger disaster. Among the Ju/twasi (Kung San) people of Botswana, women's status declined dramatically after forced settlement into reservations. As traditional gatherers, Ju/twasi women acquired much of the vegetal foods eaten by their families and were regarded nearly equally with men (Lee, 1979). After they were forced into reservations, women's status declined markedly as they lost their traditional tasks. Men became socially superior, generally based on cash income they could acquire by becoming mercenaries. However, women's status has risen as they have entered and dominated the local production of beer that they manufacture themselves and sell to others, primarily men (Lee, 1979, p. 418). These examples tend to support earlier arguments about the interrelationship of economic participation and social status. When women, or men, as can be seen in the latter example, lose control of their productive activities, their status may decline as well. While people continue to conduct their economic activities even though the economic systems in which they live change, these processes will have a range of effects on their own gender roles and on their participation in their family and community life.

REFERENCES

Babb, F. (1989). *Between field and cooking pot: The political economy of marketwomen in Peru.* Austin, TX: University of Texas Press.

Benería, L., & Sen, G. (1981). Accumulation, reproduction, and women's role in economic development. *Signs, 7,* 279–298.

Blackwood, E. (1984). Sexuality and gender in certain Native American tribes: The case of cross-gender females. *Signs, 10,* 27–42.

Bourque, S., & Warren, K. S. (1981). *Women of the Andes: Patriarchy and social change in two Peruvian towns.* Ann Arbor, MI: University of Michigan Press.

Brown, J. K. (1970). A note on the division of labor by sex. *American Anthropologist, 72,* 1073–1078.

Bunster, X. (1983). Market sellers in Lima, Peru: Talking about work. In M. Buvinic, M. A. Lycette, & W. P. McGreevey (Eds.), *Women and poverty in the Third World* (pp. 93–102). Baltimore: Johns Hopkins University Press.

Burton, M. L., Brudner, L. A., & White, D. R. (1977). A model of the sexual division of labor. *American Ethnologist, 4,* 227–251.

Burton, M. L., & White, D. R. (1984). Sexual division of labor in agriculture. *American Anthropologist, 86,* 568–583.

Byrne, B. (1994). Access to subsistence resources and the sexual division of labor among potters. *Cross-Cultural Research, 28,* 225–250.

Byrne, B. (1999). The sexual division of labor among clothes makers in non-industrial societies. *Cross-Cultural Research, 33,* 225–250.

Callender, C., & Kochems, L. M. (1983). The North American berdache. *Current Anthropology, 24,* 443–456.

Duncan, R. J. (2000). *Crafts, capitalism, and women: The potters of La Chamba, Colombia.* Gainesville, FL: University Press of Florida.

Dwyer, D. H., & Bruce, J. (Eds.). (1988). *A home divided: Women and income in the thirdly world.* Stanford, CA: Stanford University Press.

Ehlers, T. B. (1990). *Silent looms: women and production in a Guatemalan town.* Boulder, CO: Westview Press.

Ember, C. R., & Ember, M. (1996). *Cultural anthropology* (8th ed.). Upper Saddle River, NJ: Prentice-Hall.

Ember, C. R., & Levinson, D. (1991). The substantive contributions of worldwide cross-cultural studies using secondary data. *Behavior Science Research, 25,* 79–140.

Grimes, K. M., & Milgram, B. L. (Eds.). (2001). *Artisans and cooperatives: Developing alternative trade for the global economy.* Tucson, AZ: University of Arizona Press.

Hill, P. (1972). *Rural Hausa: A village and a setting.* Cambridge, UK: Cambridge University Press.

Hochschild, A. (1989). *The secondly shift.* New York: Viking.

Hurtado, A. M., Hawkes, K., Hill, K., & Kaplan, H. (1985). Female subsistence strategies among the Aché hunter gatherers of eastern Paraguay. *Human Ecology, 13,* 1–28.

Kroeber, A. L. (1902). The Arapaho. *American Museum of Natural History Bulletin, 18,* 1–150.

Lee, R. B. (1979). *The !Kung San: Men, women, and work in a foraging society.* New York: Cambridge University Press.

Mies, M. (1982). *The lacemakers of Naraspur.* London: Zed Press.

Milkman, R. (1986). Women's history and the Sears case. *Feminist Studies, 12,* 374–400.

Minturn, L. (1996). The economic importance and technological complexity of hand-spinning and hand-weaving. *Cross-Cultural Research, 30,* 330–351.

Mukhopadhyay, C. C., & Higgins, P. J. (1988). Anthropological studies of women's status revisited: 1977–1987. *Annual Review of Anthropology, 17,* 461–495.

Murdock, G. P., & Provost, C. (1973). Factors in the division of labor by sex: A cross-cultural analysis. *Ethnology, 12,* 203–225.

Nash, J. (Ed.). (1993). *Crafts in the world market: The impact of global exchange on Middle American artisans.* Albany, NY: State University of New York Press.

Nerlove, S. B. (1974). Women's workload and infant feeding practices: A relationship with demographic implications. *Ethnology, 13,* 201–214.

O'Brian, R. (1999). Who weaves and why? Weaving, loom complexity and trade. *Cross-Cultural Research, 33:* 30–42.

Sanday, P. R. (1974). Female status in the public domain. In M. Z. Rosaldo & L. Lamphere (Eds.), *Woman, culture and society* (pp. 189–206). Stanford, CA: Stanford University Press.

Seligmann, L. (Ed.). (2001). *Women traders cross-culturally.* Stanford, CA: Stanford University Press.

Sheldon, K. (Ed.). (1996). *Courtyards, markets, city streets: Urban women in Africa.* Boulder, CO: Westview Press.

Simms, S. C. (1903). Crow Indian hermaphrodites. *American Anthropologist, 5,* 580–581.

Smith, J., Wallerstein, I., & Evers, H.-D. (1984). *Households and the world economy.* Beverly Hills, CA: Sage.

Stephen, L. (1992). *Zapotec women.* Austin, TX: University of Texas Press.

Swetnam, J. J. (1988). Women and markets: A problem in the assessment of sexual inequality. *Ethnology, 27,* 327–338.

Tice, K. E. (1995). *Kuna crafts, gender and the global economy.* Austin, TX: University of Texas Press.

Wallerstein, I. (1974). *The modern world system.* New York: Academic Press.

Weismantel, M. J. (1988). *Food, gender and poverty in the Ecuadorian Andes.* Philadelphia, PA: University of Pennsylvania Press.

White, D. R., Burton, M. L., & Brudner, L. A. (1977). Entailment theory and method: A cross-cultural analysis of the sexual division of labor. *Behavior Science Research, 12,* 1–24.

White, D. R., Burton, M. L., & Dow, M. M. (1981). Sexual division of labor in African agriculture. *American Anthropologist, 83,* 824–849.

Whyte, M. K. (1978). *The status of women in preindustrial societies.* Princeton, NJ: Princeton University Press.

Wilk, R. (Ed.). (1989). *The household economy: Reconsidering the domestic mode of production.* Boulder, CO: Westview Press.

Wilkinson-Weber, C. M. (1999). *Embroidering lives: Women's work and skill in the Lucknow embroidery industry.* Albany, NY: State University of New York Press.

Young, K., Wolkowitz, C., & McCullagh, R. (Eds.). (1981). *Of marriage and the market: Women's subordination in international perspective.* London: CSE Books.

Leadership, Power, and Gender

Kaisa Kauppinen and Iiris Aaltio

BACKGROUND

Leadership and power are related to each other in multiple ways. Leadership refers to public power, that is, positions people hold in organizations and society which provide them means to use power over other individuals, groups, and organizations. Leadership is defined as personal influence over other people, that is, having an effect on their behavior with the aim of better results in their work (Weiss, 1996). Power can be defined as a person's ability to influence other people (Hoskings, cited in Cornforth, 1991). Leadership is a value-laden activity, whereas management is more practically orientated. Management is more about administering and controlling, whereas leadership is about innovation and inspiration (Hughes, Ginnett, & Curphy, 1999). The main difference between the two is that leaders lead people, whereas managers manage tasks. However, the two do overlap, and it is often hard to separate leadership from management (Hughes et al., 1999). There is no management without leadership and vice versa.

The complex relationships among leadership, power, and gender became a research topic in 1970s, when Kanter started the debate on the "blind spots" of organizational analysis. The aspects of organizational life that hide gender attributes of leadership and power became topical. The prevailing gender-neutral tradition, particularly in the United States, was broken, and the discourse of organizations as sites where gender attributes are presumed and reproduced, started to gain foothold, especially in 1990s (Aaltio and Kovalainen, 2001). The underrepresentation of women in high-status roles has been documented by feminist literature (e.g., Acker, 1992; Auster, 1993; Gherardi, 1995). Schwartz (2000) brought forward one of the early arguments, claiming that because of maternity women have a harder time creating a career; there is a distinct mother track that either slows down or prevents women from career development proper. Hewlett (2002) argues that this claim still holds true.

Gender relations occur in roles and organizational positions; for example, the (female) secretary is subordinate to the (male) boss (Pringle, 1988), and in a similar way the supportive wife/mother looks up to the authoritative husband/father. There are inequalities that favor men on various criteria including salary and professional grade. Male dominance is preserved by multiple barriers, both psychological and structural. Feminist theory argues that sex roles exist in patriarchal societies and organizations where established social structures and relationships favor men (Gough, 1998). Gender regime exists and continues to exist (Wahl, 1992). Social roles are gendered and determined by a variety of social, political, and economic factors, and in addition to sex and biological differences between men and women, there are cultural and historical factors that create them. It is generally believed that leadership, organizational culture, and communication are constructed with a masculine subtext, and dominant views on leadership are difficult to integrate with femininity (Aaltio, 2002; Lipman-Blumen, 1992).

WOMEN AS MANAGERS: STATISTICS

According to the United Nation's *World's Women 2000* report, women's share of the administrative and managerial labor force is less than 30% in all regions of the world. In all regions, women's share of administrative and managerial professionals is less than their total share of the labor market. However, women's share of administrative and managerial workers rose in every region of the world, except Southern Asia, between 1980 and the early 1990s; women's share doubled in Western Asia (from 4 to 9%) and in sub-Saharan Africa (from 7 to 14%) (United Nations, 2000).

Even though the number of women in middle-management positions was 44% in the United States, for example, 1998 (Powell, 2000), women hold only 1–5% of top executive positions (Wirth, 2001). In the European Union countries women's share of top management positions has barely changed since the early 1990s, and has remained at less than 5% (Davidson & Burke, 2000). Women tend to hold top management positions in areas that are female dominated; for example, in Finland, in the hotel and catering business, human resource management, and public services. The smallest number of women in top positions can be found in male-dominated areas, such as heavy industry and the construction business, where the proportion of female leaders is under 10%. There are fewer female directors in an organization that employs mostly men (Kauppinen, 2002).

Alvesson and Due Billing (1997) argue that the number of women managers should increase not only because there should be equality between the sexes, but also because women can contribute to work life in a way that men cannot. They produce four reasons to support their case: (1) there should be equal opportunities for both sexes; (2) women's competencies should be fully utilized; (3) women's contribution as leaders should be taken into account, especially their values, experiences, and behavior; (4) women's alternative values enrich an organization and work life in general.

When it comes to political decision-making, only nine women in the world were heads of state or government during the first part of 2000 (United Nations, 2000). The Nordic countries (Finland, Sweden, Norway, Denmark, and Iceland) have a number of women in high positions in government; for example, Finland has had a female president since 2000. The Finnish people's attitudes towards the female president were examined in the *Gender Barometer 2001* (Melkas, 2002). The results indicated that both women and men, and especially women, thought that having a female president was important for equality between the sexes and that it signaled a change in the political climate. Iceland had a female president during the 1990s. In the Baltic States, Latvia has had a female president since 1999—a former professor of psychology in a Canadian university with a Latvian background. Studies show the same kinds of changes in attitudes regarding gender issues in Latvia as in Finland with the election of a female president.

On average, in 1999 one-third of members of parliament in the Nordic countries were women (Nordic Council of Ministers, 1999). In 2002, women's share in Sweden's parliament had risen from 43 to 45%, and the average age of members of parliament had decreased from 50 to 48 (Manninen, 2002). Even in 1999, Sweden had the highest percentage of women in parliament (43%), while Finland and Denmark both had 37%, Norway had 36%, and Iceland had 35%. The percentage of women in municipal councils in the Nordic countries

was somewhat higher. In Sweden, 42% of members of municipal councils were women, and in Norway and Finland slightly less than 40%. Iceland's figure for 1999 was just over 30% and Denmark's was about 25% (Nordic Council of Ministers, 1999).

DIFFERENCES AND SIMILARITIES BETWEEN FEMALE AND MALE MANAGERS

Earlier management research took it for granted that managers were men (e.g., Dalton, 1959; Mintzberg, 1973, 1989), and ignored gender issues altogether. The so-called great-man theory is one of the earliest management theories. It argues that persons (men) who have influenced Western civilization have characteristics that are needed in a good leader. Another of the early theories is trait theory. It assumes that effective leaders have distinct personal qualities that differentiate them from other people. Many of these traits tend to be stereotypically male (Weiss, 1996).

Behavioral theories focus on managers' behavior. There are three main types of behavioral theory. The first distinguishes between two types of behavior: task-oriented style and interpersonally oriented style. The second distinguishes between two types of leadership: autocratic and democratic. The third type, situational theory, regards different types of behavior appropriate for various situations. The behavioral theories implicitly suggest that better managers are either masculine (i.e., high-task/low-interpersonal style, autocratic decision-making) or feminine (i.e., low-task/high-interpersonal style, democratic decision-making) (Powell, 1993).

Powell (1993) introduces a modern approach to management theory and claims that there are three perspectives on the difference between female and male managers: (1) there are no differences between men and women as managers. Women managers try to become like men and reject the gender stereotype; (2) men make better managers because their early socialization experiences differ: they play more team sports than girls (Hennig & Jardim, 1977); (3) stereotypical differences between the sexes, where women in managerial roles bring out their feminine characteristics which tend to be stereotypical.

Feminist researchers, such as Rosener (1990), argue that female and male leaders differ in accordance with gender stereotypes. Rosener argues that femininity is particularly needed in today's work life and claims, along the same lines as Powell (1993) and Gardiner and Tiggemann (1999), that there are profound differences between male and female leaders: female leaders concentrate on the relationships between people, whereas men tend to concentrate on the issues or tasks. Women use more personal power, that is, power based on charisma and personal contacts, whereas men tend to use structural power, that is, power based on the organizational hierarchy and position (Eagly & Johnson, 1990). Lundberg & Frankenhaeuser (1999), in turn, argue that there is no difference between men and women in interpersonal style of leadership, but that men are more task oriented than women.

Schein's (1973) classic study concluded that both female and male executives believed that managers possessed characteristics that were more associated with men than with women. In later studies that examined the perceptions of executive women, women no longer describe successful managers as having only masculine characteristics. More recent management theories, such as the managerial grid theory, claim that both masculine and feminine characteristics are important in a good manager. This theory suggests that the best managers are androgynous; they combine both (masculine) high-task and (feminine) high-interpersonal styles (Kauppinen, 2002; Powell, 1993). Although the concept of androgyny has received mixed support, one aspect has been agreed upon: leadership is generally conceived in masculine terms (Goktepe & Schneier, 1988; Kruse & Wintermantel, 1986), but also feminine features are needed in a manager. Frankenhaeuser et al. (1989) claim that female managers are psychologically more androgynous than men, suggesting that female managers absorb masculine features whereas men stick more to the masculine style. Some researchers suggest that women should adopt a masculine style to become accepted as leaders (Sapp, Harrod, & Zhao, 1996). Women in leading positions have been shown to be more masculine (Fagenson, 1990). However, Watson (1988) has indicated that masculine women's performance level is low, and women choosing such a strategy often experience role conflicts (Geis, 1993). Baril, Elbert, Mahar-Potter, and Reavy (1989) claim that adopting one's masculine and feminine behavior to suit each situation separately might be the best approach.

To summarize, Powell (1993) argues that both feminine managers and androgynous managers seem preferable to the masculine manager in today's work environment. More often than not, management and leadership are dependent on the local context and culture where they are practiced, and this makes it difficult to draw universal theories.

CROSS-CULTURAL DIFFERENCES IN LEADERSHIP BEHAVIOR

Leadership behavior varies in different countries. Whyte (1978) claims that even in most preindustrial societies, men held political leadership positions. Hofstede (1980a) has examined cross-cultural differences in work-related values, for instance the masculinity–femininity dimension. He conducted a study on a large number of employees of a multinational corporation that has offices all over the world. He found countries such as Japan, Austria, Switzerland, Italy, and Venezuela to be masculine countries, where sex roles are clearly differentiated, and men dominate and exercise power in traditional terms. In feminine countries, such as the Scandinavian countries (including Finland) and the Netherlands, emphasis is placed on cooperation and greater gender equality prevails in society and organizational culture: group decision-making is encouraged, managers give greater autonomy to subordinates, and hierarchical differences are not emphasized (McKenna, 2000). In other words, power distance is minimized.

Power distance is another cross-cultural dimension in Hofestede's (1980a) studies. In countries high in power distance, such as the Philippines, Mexico, and Venezuela, there is a great power imbalance between superiors and subordinates in organizations. Decision-making is centralized and subordinates tend to be passive. Austria, Israel, and the Scandinavian countries represent countries low in power distance. In these countries subordinates are typically involved in decision-making, organization structures tend to be flat, and there is greater decentralization of decision-making (McKenna, 2000). One of Hofstede's (1980b) conclusions was that participative leadership advocated by American theorists is not suitable for all cultures. However, there have been criticisms of Hofstede's work, as it is likely that there are great variations *within* cultures as well.

Kauppinen and Kandolin (1998) have come to the same conclusions as Hofstede. Finland, Sweden, Denmark, and the Netherlands had the characteristics of a "feminine" society; there was a considerable amount of interaction between the management and the subordinates, organizational structures were not hierarchic, and the employees participated in organizational decision-making. The Southern European countries (Spain, Portugal, Italy, and Greece) had more "masculine" characteristics; organizational hierarchy was strong and there was less direct face-to-face interaction between managers and subordinates. Organizational culture also differed in women-led organizations as there was more interpersonal interaction between the employer and the employees, and the female manager tended to control the subordinates less than the male manager. However, it is important to note that work was also different, as women tended to lead smaller units and organizations that employ mostly other women (Kauppinen, 2002). Across the European Union, only 10% or less of men work in places where their immediate superior is a woman.

SEX DIFFERENCES IN COMMUNICATION PATTERNS OF LEADERS

Lips (1997) argues that power difference between the sexes is maintained by variations in men's and women's communication. Men talk more than women, and maintain the difference partly by interrupting women and by not listening or responding to women (Malamuth & Thornhill, 1994). James & Clark (1993; cited in Tainio, 2001) have found conflicting results. After reviewing 33 research reports dealing with the relationship between gender and interruptions, they concluded that there was no support for the argument; both genders interrupted and became interrupted. Interruptions may not always be power displays or games but, for example, a sign of enthusiasm and solidarity (e.g., Tannen, 1994). Tainio (2002) claims that gender difference in communication styles is mostly due to the difference in social status rather than gender, that is, women have a lower status and behave accordingly.

Thus studies on sex differences in language and communication do not show uniform results. Overall, the results tend to show that women's verbal and nonverbal behavior is warmer and more deferential whereas men are more powerful and authoritative in their communication style (Mulac, 1998). Women use more indirect influence strategies (Gilligan, 1982; Steil & Weltman, 1992), they speak more tentatively (Carli, 1990), and they show more

nonverbal warmth and adaptive behavior than men (Hall, 1984). In a study by Carli, LaFleur, and Loeber (1995), men were more influenced by the warm and competent female speaker than by the female speaker who was just competent. The warm woman was considered as competent as the one who was just competent. Gray (2002) argues that women express more feelings in their communication in order to include the listener in what they wish to say and to establish a connection with them.

Women show less visual domination than men; they maintain more eye contact than men while listening, but less eye contact while talking (Dovidio, Brown, Heltman, Ellyson, & Keating, 1988), particularly in mixed-sex interactions (Ellyson, Dovidio, & Brown, 1992). Interestingly, it has been found that, in mixed-sex interactions, women's influence is more effective when they display low levels of visual dominance than when they display high levels of visual dominance. On the other hand, men are more effective when they are visually dominant (Mehta et al., 1989; cited in Ellyson et al., 1992). Carli (1990) found that women exert greater influence over a male audience when they use tentative rather than direct speech, whereas males are equally influential with a male and female audience whichever of these two styles they use. These results indicate that women receive negative sanctions for being direct, but men can exhibit a wider range of behaviors and still remain influential (Carli & Eagly, 1999). Because of gender stereotypes, the same nonverbal cues that are a sign of power for men may not work for women (Hite, 2000; Lips, 1997). There are vast cultural differences and norms that regulate face-to-face behavior and communication between men and women.

Carli & Eagly (1999) claim that patterns of interaction in groups place women at a disadvantage. Henley (1977) argues that much of the nonverbal communication that characterizes male–female relationships follows a pattern parallel to that of superior–subordinate relationships, since women are more often in subordinate positions than men. Garsombke (1988) claims that organizational vocabulary is masculine, since many typical expressions used in business, such as "strategy" and "headquarters," originate from wars and male-led organizations. Gardiner and Tiggemann (1999) claim that in female-dominated industries women managers were more interpersonally orientated than men, but women and men did not differ in male-dominated industries. On the other hand, women receive attention in male-dominated organizations because they are different. The attention can be either positive (flattery, compliments) or negative (e.g., sexual harassment). Gender can both hinder and advance a woman's career.

Gender Power in Organizations

Most classic organizational texts were written from a masculine perspective and failed to analyze the significance of gender, or the relationships among sex, gender, organizations, and power, in any explicit manner (e.g., Hearn & Parkin, 1992). In many contemporary organizational texts gender is increasingly referred to. Yet it is often included in a brief, marginalized, and unanalytic manner (Gherardi, 1995; Green, Parkin, & Hearn, 1997).

In a classic study French and Raven (1959) differentiated between five kinds of power sources: expert, referent, reward, coercive, and legitimate power. Expert power refers to the ability to influence because you possess superior skills or knowledge. Referent power is charismatic power—the ability to get another person to change their behavior. Reward power means the ability to mediate rewards, such as money and promotion, in order to obtain change. Coercive power refers to the ability to give punishment. Legitimate power refers to the right to influence. Wilson (1995) argues that all of these forms of power are perceived as belonging to men, since traditionally men have held most of the power in organizations, have controlled and dominated women and also other men, and thus have been able to maintain power.

An important source of power in organizations is informal power. Informal power often depends on the informal personal contacts one has inside and outside the organization, and refers to the ability to gather information and mobilize resources and support outside official power structures. The amount of informal power one has is influenced by factors such as age, family background, looks, and attractiveness. In order to gain informal power, whom one knows is important (Drennan, 1997).

Access to informal networks of communication and exchange is an important determinant of an individual's power and success in an organization (Auster, 1993; Lips, 1997). Men's and women's informal networks function differently. Women's relative lack of access to informal networks within and outside an organization often limits

their influence. For instance, women may have more difficulty in obtaining rewards for their subordinates, which in turn may create a vicious circle where subordinates lose respect for a manager who appears powerless. This diminishes the manager's power (Ragins & Sundström, 1989). In addition, lack of access to informal networks can hinder a woman's chances of career advancement and limit access to resources critical to doing her job properly (Travers & Pemberton, 2000).

Patriarchal Power in Organizations

In western organizations the ideal of a good manager is still implicitly included in the notion of hegemonic masculinity that represents qualities such as competitive, aggressive, nonemotional, goal orientated, and psychologically and physically strong (Connell, 1987). Hegemonic masculinity is the culturally dominant and most powerful form of masculinity. It is based on heroism, where the hero controls and guides his subordinates (Block, 1996, 1999). The dominant forms of masculinity, construed in aversion to femininity, are those that dictate how organizations are managed (Cheng, 1996). Patriarchal leadership was common, and possibly functioning, in times when people worked in hierarchic organizations where work was organized into assembly lines (Block, 1996, 1999), but, according to Koivunen (2002), patriarchal leadership does not fit today's more flexible expert organizations. Leadership by partnership, a concept brought forward by Block (1996, 1999), where jointly agreed goals are the way to motivate and lead people, is much more appropriate, especially in modern expert organizations (Koivunen, 2002). Women could have a lot to contribute in expert organizations, since they tend to use leadership by partnership instead of a hierarchical model of leading.

Himanen (2001) argues that computer hackers will become heroes of the information society. He claims that the heroes will be men. There will be no room for women in the information society. Women will be left to perform the invisible domestic tasks, and their main function will be to further men's careers. There seem to be very few women in higher-level positions in information technology (e.g., Silicon Valley) (Ruckenstein, 2002). However, Koivunen (2002) argues that the development of computer networks such as Linux, where everyone is allowed to change the code, will decrease the hierarchical system of organizations and present everyone with the opportunity to take part in developing the code.

Kanter (1977, 1993) has discussed metaphorical male "homosocial reproduction"—how men attempt to reproduce their dominant power relations by only uniting with and sharing the same occupational space and privilege with those males they deem similar in image and behavior, cloning themselves in their own image, and forming so-called old-boy networks (Auster, 1993; Wirth, 2001). Koivunen (2002) argues that men's physical power and size affects their career development more than capabilities or education. Martin (1996) shows how homosocial male networks tend to preclude women from high-status jobs by sex segregation and selection procedures, and seek to discredit women while elevating men. Male homosociability not only keeps women out of key organizational roles, but also controls the behavior of other men and punishes men who behave differently. Vianello and Moore (2000) conclude their cross-cultural research report on women in top positions by saying that executive women feel that the greatest barrier to their career development are male networks that they have a hard time entering. Martin (1996) has drawn attention to men's domination of assessment, selection, and promotion—processes that isolate women.

Zuboff (1988) claims that male managers protect their status and power by mystifying their knowledge and exaggerating their abilities rather than by sharing knowledge. Women are marginalized in meetings because men refuse to hear them, ignore the contribution they are making, or attribute it to a male participant (Josefowitz, 1988). Women in senior management have experienced a great deal of male hostility and misogyny because men have felt that women are taking their jobs (Gutek, 1989). Nicolson (1996) and Hite (2000) argue that women's constant exposure to sexism in organizations is an overriding reason why more women are not in authority, and those few that do reach senior positions often sacrifice their feminine identity and relations with other women to do so. According to the Finnish *Gender Barometer 1998* (Melkas, 1999), 30% of women claim that they experience disparaging behavior at work at least every now and then. Nearly one-third of women claim that they have experienced sexual harassment, ranging from dirty jokes to proposal of sexual relations, during the past 2 years. Women on top often feel isolated. However, some enjoy their token positions; they consciously keep distance from other women, do not help other women to further

their careers, show envy and jealousy towards other women, and prefer to work with men. This is referred to as the "queen-bee" syndrome (Kanter, 1977).

Davidson and Cooper (1983) have shown that female managers encounter greater sources of stress than male managers. Women managers experience high levels of gender stereotyping, prejudice, and discrimination, and report greater pressure than their male counterparts at all management levels. In addition to work stressors, women have to deal with substantially more domestic pressures than the majority of men (Davidson & Fielden, 1999; Nelson & Burke, 2000). Considering the fact that women have to balance on the "tightropes" of traits, verbal styles, appearance, and work versus family responsibilities (Auster, 1993), the resulting stress reactions are hardly surprising. Despite a substantial amount of stress, many women enjoy their leading role, authority, and influence. A woman's enjoyment is increased if she has a supporting partner (Vianello & Moore, 2000).

According to Nicolson (1996), the only way women can fight patriarchal power in organizations is by networking and supporting other women; according to Nicolson, men recruit, promote, and mentor other men, and women should support each other in the same way. Arroba and James (1987) suggest the same: if women are excluded from male networks, they can form their own networks and overcome some of the effects of "tokenism." Kuusipalo, Kauppinen, and Nuutinen (2000) argue that women, who themselves have passed through the glass ceiling, claim that they are excluded from the male world in a large part because they do not have access to male-dominated networks and lack the informal contacts that are vital to their career development.

GLASS CEILING

"Glass ceiling" is a symbolic term for the existence of an invisible line in the hierarchical structures of working life above which it is difficult for women to rise (Auster, 1993; Kauppinen-Toropainen, 1994; Wirth, 2001). Auster (1993) claims that the glass ceiling is a gender bias that occurs all the time and takes many forms. Women encounter both internal and external obstacles in their careers. It has been easier for a woman to reach a middle-management position in an organization than to rise to the very top management. However, if she does that, she is still a "loner," that is, the only or almost only representative of her own sex (Kauppinen-Toropainen, 1987).

The reasons why there are so few women in management positions, and especially in top management, have been addressed by many researchers (e.g., Acker, 1992; Auster, 1993; Izraeli & Adler, 1994; Oakley, 2000; Powell, 2000; Vanhala, 2002). Though researchers categorize the reasons differently, most divide them as societal, organizational, behavioral, and psychological. Izraeli and Adler (1994) use three main perspectives to explain the fact that women are underrepresented among the levels of management. The first perspective concentrates on individual-level differences; it claims that the paucity of women in management is due to behavioral characteristics and personal traits. Men's characteristics and behavior have been taken as a norm, thus making it hard for women to enter male-dominated areas. Auster (1993) argues that in order for women to be successful in organizations, they have to be very self-conscious of their own behavior and keep constant control of what they are saying and how they are acting. Oakley (2000) claims that women in middle- and lower-management positions often play down their femininity and instead adopt a masculine style to increase credibility.

According to Izraeli and Adler's second perspective, organizational context, an organization's culture and way of treating women often shapes attitudes and behavior more than an individual manager's behavior. Powell (2000) makes a similar point by arguing that women's entry into top management positions is influenced by the way decision-making is structured in an organization and whether the decision-makers can be held accountable for the decisions they make. Eyring and Stead (1998) claim that women's underrepresentation in management is due to the fact that men prefer supporting people like themselves to top positions in organizations.

The third perspective, institutional discrimination, claims that organizations are not gender neutral and that this fact leads to gender discrimination. Izraeli and Adler (1994) and Gherardi (1995) argue that gender discrimination forms of part of managers' basic assumptions about society and organizational culture. Powell (2000) refers to the same phenomenon as a societal factor; men are more taken aback by women in top positions than in lower positions, since men have traditionally had the higher status in society. He claims that this norm is reinforced in subtle ways, for instance, in stereotypes of what makes a good leader. Izraeli and Adler also bring

forward a fourth perspective that focuses on senior managers' greater ability to influence, and limit, women's access to top positions. They argue that societal and organizational institutions that privilege men have persisted simply because senior managers do not want competition or change. Senior executives are more able than lower-level managers to protect their sphere of influence from outsiders. This explains why women have succeeded in entering the lower levels of management, but, once in, have failed to move up into senior management.

Green et al. (1997) claim that built-in societal structures, such as women's role in children's upbringing and maternity, may help to explain why husbands do not support their wives' careers in the same way that women support men's careers by doing most of the child care and housework (Auster, 1993). In many societies there appears to be a tendency for high-level positions to be occupied mainly by married men with children, while women in the same type of positions tend to be single, divorced, and childless (Hewlett, 2002; Vanhala, 2002; Woodward, 1996). Women often have to make more sacrifices in their personal lives than men do. Many top-level jobs require long and antisocial working hours that preclude many women with children. According to Vanhala (2002), women still carry most of the responsibility for housework in dual-career families, and thus it is the woman's career that suffers more than the man's. The same applies to families where both parents are in top positions. Even as a manager, the woman still has a greater responsibility over the family.

FUTURE PERSPECTIVES AND CHANGE

Statistics show a slow but evident increase of women managers in organizations. Leadership and management roles for both sexes will change in the future as organizations change, and become lean or anorectic. Competition for top positions will tighten in the future, so will there be room for the participative leadership that women have been seen to portray? Women make good experts. This is something that should be rewarded, and encouraged in the future. Expertise is an important strength and resource in turbulent times. It is worth trying out new spheres, as so-called traditional spheres are prone to change.

A social exchange analysis would suggest that, because men are those who have occupied the most powerful positions in organizations and have most to lose if the status quo is disturbed, a male hegemony within an organization is naturally quite resistant to change (Gough, 1998). Change will not occur automatically but requires positive action which provides women with the opportunity to break the glass ceiling to advancement and the glass wall to equality of access. As Alvesson and Due Billing (1997) state, there are reasons to be skeptical about radical changes taking place in organizations leading to substantial requirements for female skills or female managers. Much of the talk is rhetoric and behind superficial changes there is often much less actual change (Calás and Smircich, 1993). Moore and Vianello (2000) claim that men's near-monopoly of powerful positions will slowly continue to decline. They argue that women's elites are more likely to have less hierarchical and more post-materialist orientations than male elites, and women may actually make more effective leaders in the emerging society. However, there are individual differences among women managers, as well as differences in the demands that organizations put on their members. This should be kept in mind, because many female managers also face the demands of behaving in a stereotypically female way in situations where strategic fast decisions are made, those typically suited to males. Simplicity in organizational culture is less supportive of female leadership than is a culture with high tolerance of diversity of values, behavioral patterns, and self-reflectiveness.

ACKNOWLEDGMENTS

The authors wish to thank Heljä Huuhtanen and Saara Patoluoto, of the Finnish Institute of Occupational Health, for their help in collecting material and preparing the article.

REFERENCES

Aaltio, I. (2002). Naisjohtajuus ja työelämän kulttuuriset yhteydet [Women, leadership, and the cultural connections of working life]. In R. Smeds, K. Kauppinen, K. Yrjänheikki, & A. Valtonen (Eds.), *Tieto ja tekniikka—Missä on nainen?* [Knowledge and technology—Where is the woman?] (pp. 159–168). Helsinki, Finland: Tekniikan Akateemisten Liitto.

Aaltio, I., & Kovalainen, A. (2001). Personality. In E. Wilson (Ed.), *Gendering organizational analysis* (pp. 17–31). London: Sage.

Acker, J. (1992). Gendering organizational theory. In A. Mills & P. Tancred (Eds.), *Gendering organizational theory* (pp. 248–260). Newbury Park, CA: Sage.

Alvesson, M., & Due Billing, Y. (1997). *Understanding gender and organizations*. London: Sage.

Arroba, T., & James, K. (1987). Are politics palpable to women managers? How can women make wise moves at work? *Women in Management Review, 10*(3), 123–130.

Auster, E. R. (1993, Summer). Demystifying the glass ceiling: Organizational and interpersonal dynamics of gender bias. *Business and the Contemporary World*, pp. 47–68.

Baril, G. L., Elbert, N., Mahar-Potter, S., & Reavy, G. C. (1989). Are androgynous managers really more effective? *Group and Organization Studies, 14*, 234–249.

Block, P. (1996). *Stewardship: Choosing service over self-interest*. San Francisco: Berrett-Koehler.

Block, P. (1999). *Flawless consulting: A guide to getting your expertise used*. San Francisco: Jossey-Bass.

Calás, M. B., & Smircich, L. (1993). Dangerous liaisons: The "feminine-in-management" meets "globalization." *Business Horizons, 36*(2), 71–81.

Carli, L. L. (1990). Gender, language, and influence. *Journal of Personality and Social Psychology, 59*, 941–951.

Carli, L. L., & Eagly, A. H. (1999). Gender effects on social influence and emergent leadership. In G. N. Powell (Ed.), *Handbook of gender and work* (pp. 203–222). Thousand Oaks, CA: Sage.

Carli, L. L., LaFleur, S. J., & Loeber, C. C. (1995). Nonverbal behavior, gender, and influence. *Journal of Personality and Social Psychology, 68*, 1030–1041.

Cheng, C. (1996). "We choose not to compete": The "merit" discourse in the selection process, and Asian and Asian American men and their masculinity. In C. Cheng (Ed.), *Masculinities in organizations* (pp. 177–200). Thousand Oaks, CA: Sage.

Connell, R. W. (1987). *Gender and power*. Cambridge, UK: Polity Press.

Cornforth, C. (1991). *Managing voluntary and non-profit enterprises*. [Open Business School Voluntary Management Programme]. Buckingham, UK: Open University.

Dalton, M. (1959). *Men who manage*. New York: Wiley.

Davidson, M. J., & Burke, R. J. (2000). *Women in management: Current research issues* (Vol. 2). London: Sage.

Davidson, M. J., & Cooper, C. L. (1983). *Stress and the woman manager*. Oxford: Robertson.

Davidson, M. J., & Fielden, S. (1999). Stress and the working woman. In G. N. Powell (Ed.), *Handbook of gender and work* (pp. 413–428). Thousand Oaks, CA: Sage.

Dovidio, J. F., Brown, C. E., Heltman, S. L., Ellyson, K., & Keating, C. F. (1988). Power displays between men and women in discussions of gender-linked tasks: A multichannel study. *Journal of Personality and Social Psychology, 55*, 580–587.

Drennan, L. (Ed.). (1997) *Action for women's health: Making changes through organisations*. Glasgow, UK: Glasgow Healthy City Project.

Eagly, A. H., & Johnson, B. T. (1990). Gender and leadership style: A meta-analysis. *Psychological Bulletin, 108*, 233–256.

Ellyson, S. L., Dovidio, J. F., & Brown, C. E. (1992). The look of power: Gender differences in visual dominance behavior. In C. L. Ridgeway (Ed.), *Gender, interaction, and inequality* (pp. 50–80). New York: Springer-Verlag.

Eyring, A., & Stead, B. A. (1998). Shattering the glass ceiling: Some successful corporate policies. *Journal of Business Ethics, 17*, 245–251.

Fagenson, E. A. (1990). Perceived masculine and feminine attributes examined as a function of individuals' sex and level in the organizational power hierarchy: A test of four theoretical perspectives. *Journal of Applied Psychology, 75*, 204–211.

French, J. R. P., & Raven, B. (1959). The bases of social power. In D. Cartwright (Ed.), *Studies in social power.* Ann Arbor, MI: University of Michigan Institute of Social Research.

Frankenhaeuser, M., Lundberg, U., Fredrikson, M., Melin, B., Tuomisto, M., Myrsten, A., et al. (1989). Stress on and off the job as related to sex and occupational status in white-collar workers. *Journal of Organizational Behavior, 10,* 321–346.

Gardiner, M., & Tiggemann, M. (1999). Gender differences in leadership style, job stress and mental health in male- and female-dominated industries. *Journal of Occupational and Organizational Psychology, 72,* 301–315.

Garsombke, D. (1988, Summer). Organizational culture dons the mantle of militarism. *Organizational Dynamics,* pp. 46–57.

Geis, F. L. (1993). Self-fulfilling prophecies: A social psychological view of gender. In A. E. Beall & R. J. Sternberg (Eds.), *The Psychology of Gender* (pp. 9–54). New York: Guilford Press.

Gherardi, S. (1995). *Gender symbolism and organizational cultures.* London: Sage.

Gilligan, C. (1982). *In a different voice: Psychological theory and women's development.* Cambridge, MA: Harvard University Press.

Goktepe, J. R., & Schneier, C. E. (1988). Sex and gender effects in evaluating emergent leaders in small groups. *Sex Roles, 19,* 29–36.

Gough, B. (1998). Roles and discourse. In K. Trew & J. Kremer (Eds.), *Gender and Psychology* (pp. 15–27). London: Arnold.

Gray, J. (2002). *How to get what you want in the workplace.* London: Vermilion.

Green, L., Parkin, W., & Hearn, J. (1997). Power. In E. Wilson (Ed.), *Organizational behaviour reassessed: The impact of gender* (pp. 188–214). London: Sage.

Gutek, B. (1989). Sexuality in the workplace: Key issues in social research and organizational practice. In J. Hearn, D. L. Sheppard, P. Tancred-Sheriff, & G. Burrell (Eds.), *The sexuality of organization* (pp. 56–70). London: Sage.

Hall, J. (1984). *Nonverbal sex differences: Communication accuracy and expressive style.* Baltimore: Johns Hopkins University Press.

Hearn, J., & Parkin, W. (1992). Gender and organizations: A selective review and critique of a neglected area. In A. J. Mills & P. Tancred (Eds.), *Gendering organizational analysis* (pp. 46–66). London: Sage. (First published in 1983)

Henley, N. (1977). *Body politics: Power, sex and non-verbal communication.* Englewood Cliffs, NJ: Prentice-Hall.

Hennig, M., & Jardim, A. (1977). *The managerial woman.* London: Pan Books.

Hewlett, S. A. (2002, April). Executive women and the myth of having it all. *Harvard Business Review,* 66–73.

Himanen, P. (2001). *The hacker ethic and the spirit of the information age.* New York: Random House.

Hite, S. (2000). *Sex and business.* Harlow, UK: Pearson Education.

Hofestede, G. (1980a). *Culture's consequences: International differences in work-related values.* Beverly Hills, CA: Sage.

Hofestede, G. (1980b). Motivation, leadership, and organization: Do American theories apply abroad? *Organizational Dynamics, 9*(1), 4–21.

Hughes, R. L., Ginnett, R. C., & Curphy, G. J. (1999). *Leadership: Enhancing the lessons of experience.* Boston: Irwin–McGraw-Hill.

Izraeli, D. N., & Adler, N. J. (1994). Competitive forces: Women managers in a global economy. In D. N. Izraeli & N. J. Adler (Eds.), *Competitive forces: women managers in a global economy* (pp. 3–22). Cambridge, MA: Blackwell.

James, D., & Clark, S. (1993). Women, men and interruptions: A critical review. In D. Tannen (Ed.), *Gender and conversational interaction* (pp. 231–280). New York: Oxford University Press.

Josefowitz, N. (1988). Paths to power in high technology organizations. In J. Zimmermann (Ed.), *The technological woman* (pp. 191–200). New York: Praeger.

Kanter, R. M. (1977). *Men and women of the corporation.* New York: Basic Books.

Kanter, R. M. (1993). *Men and women of the corporation* (2nd ed.). New York: Basic Books.

Kauppinen, K. (2002). Nais- ja miesjohtajuus—Viva la différence! [Female and male leadership—Viva la différence!]. In R. Smeds, K. Kauppinen, K. Yrjänheikki, & A. Valtonen (Eds.), *Tieto ja tekniikka—Missä on nainen?* [Knowledge and technology—Where is the woman?] (pp. 149–168). Helsinki, Finland: Tekniikan Akateemisten Liitto.

Kauppinen, K., & Kandolin, I. (1998). *Gender and working conditions in the European Union.* Dublin: European Foundation for the Improvement of Living and Working Conditions.

Kauppinen-Toropainen, K. (1987). Ainokaiset työyhteisössä [Loners in the working community], *Työ ja Ihminen, 1*(1), lisänumero 1.

Kauppinen-Toropainen, K. (1994). Women under a glass ceiling. In *Women at the top: A study on women as leaders in the private sector* (pp. 50–62). Helsinki: Tilastokeskus.

Koivunen, H. (2002). Suurmiehiä ja piennaisia—Lasikaton mystiset rakenteet [Great men and small women—The mystical structures of the glass ceiling]. In R. Smeds, K. Kauppinen, K. Yrjänheikki, & A. Valtonen (Eds.), *Tieto ja tekniikka—Missä on nainen?* [Knowledge and technology—Where is the woman?] (pp. 132–148). Helsinki, Finland: Tekniikan Akateemisten Liitto.

Kruse, L., & Wintermantel, M. (1986). Leadership ms.-qualified: The gender bias in everyday and scientific thinking. In C. F. Graumann & S. Moscovici (Eds.), *Changing conceptions of leadership* (pp. 171–197). New York: Springer-Verlag.

Kuusipalo, J., Kauppinen, K., & Nuutinen, I. (2000). Life and career in north and south Europe. In M. Vianello & G. Moore (Eds.), *Gendering elites: Economic and political leadership in 27 industrialised societies* (pp. 177–188). Basingstoke, UK: Macmillan.

Lipman-Blumen, J. (1992). Connective leadership: Female leadership styles in the 21st century workplace. *Sociological Perspectives, 35*(1), 183–203.

Lips, H. M. (1997). *Sex and gender: An introduction* (3rd ed.). Mountain View, CA: Mayfield.

Lundberg, U., & Frankenhaeuser, M. (1999). Stress and workload of men and women in high-ranking positions. *Journal of Occupational Health Psychology, 4,* 142–151.

Malamuth, N. M., & Thornhill, N. W. (1994). Hostile masculinity, sexual aggression, and gender-biased domineeringness in conversations. *Aggressive Behavior, 20*(3), 185–193.

Manninen, M. (2002, October 1). Valtiopäivät nuorentuivat ja naisistuivat [More young people and women in the parliament]. *Helsingin Sanomat,* p. C 3.

Martin, P. Y. (1996). Gendering and evaluating dynamics: Men, masculinities, and managements. In D. L. Collinson & J. Hearn (Eds.), *Men as managers, managers as men: Critical perspectives on men, masculinities and management* (pp. 186–209). Thousand Oaks, CA: Sage.

McKenna, E. (2000). *Business psychology and organisational behaviour: A student's handbook* (3rd ed.). Hope, East Sussex, UK: Psychology Press.

Mehta, P., Dovidio, J.F., Gibbs, R., Miller, K., Huray, K., Ellyson, S.L., & Brown, C. E. (1989, April). Sex differences in the expression of power motives through visual dominance behavior. Paper presented at the Annual Meeting of the Eastern Psychological Association, Boston, MA.

Melkas, T. (1999). *The Gender Barometer 1998*. Helsinki, Finland: Tilastokeskus.

Melkas, T. (2002). *The Gender Barometer 2001*. Helsinki, Finland: Tilastokeskus.

Mintzberg, H. (1973). *The nature of managerial work*. Englewood Cliffs, NJ: Prentice Hall.

Mintzberg, H. (1989). *Mintzberg on management*. New York: Macmillan.

Moore, G., & Vianello, M. (2000). General conclusions. In M. Vianello & G. Moore (Eds.). *Gendering elites: Economic and political leadership in 27 industrialised societies*. (pp. 269–277). Basingstoke, UK: Macmillan.

Mulac, A. (1998). The gender-linked language effect: Do language differences really make a difference?. In D. J. Canary & K. Dindia (Eds.), *Sex differences and similarities in communication: Critical essays and empirical investigations of sex and gender in interaction* (pp. 127–153). Mahwah, NJ: Erlbaum.

Nelson, D. L., & Burke, R. J. (2000). Women, work stress and health. In M. J. Davidson & R. J. Burke (Eds.), *Women in management: Current research issues* (Vol. 2, pp. 177–191). London: Sage.

Nicolson, P. (1996). *Gender, power and organisation: A psychological perspective*. London: Routledge.

Nordic Council of Ministers (1999). *Women and men in the Nordic countries 1999: Facts and figures 1999* (TemaNord 1999:514). Copenhagen: Nordic Council of Ministers.

Oakley, J. G. (2000). Gender-based barriers to senior management positions: Understanding the scarcity of female CEOs. *Journal of Business Ethics, 27*, 321–334.

Powell, G. N. (1993). *Women and men in management* (2nd ed.). Newbury Park, CA: Sage.

Powell, G. N. (2000). The glass ceiling: Explaining the good and bad news. In M. J. Davidson & R. Burke (Eds.), *Women in management: Current research issues* (Vol. 2, pp. 236–250). London: Sage.

Pringle, R. (1988). *Secretaries talk sexuality, power and work*. London: Verso.

Ragins, B. R., & Sundström, E. (1989). Gender and power in organizations: A longitudinal perspective. *Psychological Bulletin, 105*, 51–88.

Rosener, J. (1990, November/December). Ways women lead. *Harvard Business Review*, pp. 119–125.

Ruckenstein, M. (2002). Teknologian lupaukset ja sukupuolen tulkinnat [The promises of technology and interpretations of gender]. In R. Smeds, K. Kauppinen, K. Yrjänheikki, & A. Valtonen (Eds.), *Tieto ja tekniikka—Missä on nainen?* [Knowledge and technology—Where is the woman?] (pp. 115–128). Helsinki, Finland: Tekniikan Akateemisten Liitto.

Sapp, S. G., Harrod, W. J., & Zhao, L. (1996). Leadership emergence in task groups with egalitarian gender-role expectations. *Sex Roles, 34*, 65–80.

Schein, V. E. (1973). The relationship between sex-role stereotypes and requisite management characteristics. *Journal of Applied Psychology, 57*(2), 95–100.

Schwartz, F. N. (2000). Management women and the new facts of life.*Harvard business review on work and life balance* (pp. 103–126). Boston: Harvard Business School Press. (Original work published 1989)

Steil, J. M., & Weltman, K. (1992). Influence strategies at home and work: a study of sixty dual career couples. *Journal of Social and Personal Relationships, 9*, 65–88.

Tainio, L. (2001). *Puhuvan naisen paikka: Sukupuoli kulttuurisena kategoriana kielenkäytössä* [A place for a talking woman: Gender as a cultural category in vocabulary]. Helsinki, Finland: Suomalaisen Kirjallisuuden Seura.

Tainio, L. (2002). Naisten ja miesten kieli [Women's and men's language]. In R. Smeds, K. Kauppinen, K. Yrjänheikki, & A. Valtonen (Eds.), *Tieto ja tekniikka—Missä on nainen?* [Knowledge and technology—Where is the woman?] (pp. 260–269). Helsinki, Finland: Tekniikan Akateemisten Liitto.

Tannen, D. (1994). *Talking from 9 to 5: How women's and men's conversational styles affect who gets heard, who gets credit, and what gets done at work*. New York: William Morrow.

Travers, C., & Pemberton, C. (2000). Think career global, but act local: Understanding networking as a culturally differentiated career skill. In M. J. Davidson & R. Burke (Eds.), *Women in management: Current research issues* (Vol. 2, pp. 84–104). London: Sage.

United Nations Statistics Division (2000). *United Nations World's Women 2000—report*. Retrieved July 18, 2002, from http://unstats.un.org/unsd/demographic/ww2000/overview.htm

Vanhala, S. (2002, May). *Under the glass ceiling: The triangle of work, career and family of women in middle management*. Paper presented at the Second Annual Conference of the European Academy of Management on "Innovative Research in Management," Stockholm, Sweden.

Vianello, M., & Moore, G. (Eds.). (2000). *Gendering elites: Economic and political leadership in 27 industrialised societies*. Basingstoke, UK: Macmillan.

Wahl, A. (1992). *Könsstrukturer i organisationer: Kvinnliga civilekonomers och civilingenjörers karriärutveckling* [Gender structures in organizations: Female business graduates' and engineers' career development]. Stockholm, Sweden: Fritze.

Watson, C. (1988). When a woman is the boss. Dilemmas in taking charge. *Group and Organization Studies, 13*(2), 163–181.

Weiss, J. W. (1996). *Organizational behaviour and change. Managing diversity, cross-cultural dynamics and ethics*. USA: West Publishing Company.

Whyte, M. K. (1978). *The status of women in preindustrial societies*. Princeton, NJ: Princeton University Press.

Wilson, F. M. (1995). *Organizational behavior and gender*. Maidenhead, UK: McGraw-Hill.

Wirth, L. (2001). *Breaking through the glass ceiling: Women in management*. Geneva: International Labor Office.

Woodward, A. E. (1996). Multinational masculinities and European bureaucracies. In D. L. Collinson & J. Hearn (Eds.), *Men as managers, managers as men: Critical perspectives on men, masculinities and management* (pp. 167–185). London: Sage.

Zuboff, S. (1988). *In the age of the smart machine*. New York: Basic Books.

War and Gender

Joshua S. Goldstein

INTRODUCTION

The gendered character of warfare is extraordinarily consistent across human cultures. I define war broadly as *lethal intergroup violence*, and define the war system as the interrelated ways that societies organize themselves to participate in potential and actual wars. This war system is among the most consistently gendered of human activities. Every known society assigns war roles differentially by gender, with men as the primary fighters (and usually the only ones). Since nearly every society has war in its social repertoire, gendered war roles have broad social ramifications.

Attention to Gender and War in Anthropology

Anthropology has long taken gender seriously in studying war, in contrast to political science and history (Goldstein, 2001, pp. 34–36). Margaret Mead's (1967, p. 236) conclusion in the first major anthropological symposium on war called for paying "particular attention ... to the need of young males to validate their strength and courage, and to ... the conspicuous unwillingness of most human societies to arm women." Anthropological thinking that connects war and gender is not limited to one ideological perspective, nor just to female scholars. Also, anthropology engages gender even though women are poorly represented among anthropologists studying war. Still, attention to gender in studying war has been inconsistent. In anthropology volumes on war, the number of index entries concerning gender are as follows: Fried, Harris, and Murphy (1967), two; Nettleship, Givens, and Nettleship (1975), none; Ferguson (1984), four; Foster and Rubinstein (1986), thirteen; Turner and Pitt (1989), none; Haas (1990), eight; Ferguson and Whitehead (1992), two; Reyna and Downs (1994), none.

CROSS-CULTURAL CONSISTENCY OF GENDER ROLES IN WAR

In war, the fighters are usually all male. Exceptions to this rule are numerous and informative (see below), but these exceptions together amount to fewer than 1% of all warriors in history (Goldstein, 2001, pp. 10–22).

Present-Day Society

Of about 23 million soldiers in today's uniformed standing armies, about 97% are male (somewhat over 500,000 are women). In only six of the world's nearly 200 states do women make up more than 5% of the armed forces, and most of these women in military forces worldwide occupy traditional women's roles such as typists and nurses. Designated *combat* forces in the world's state armies today include several million soldiers (the exact number depending on definitions of combat), of whom 99% are male. In U.N. peacekeeping forces, women (mostly nurses) were less than 0.1% in 1957–89 and still under 2% when U.N. peacekeeping peaked in the early 1990s. These disparities persist despite women's having reached historically high levels of social and political power globally, and despite the world's predominant military forces carrying out the largest-scale military gender integration in history, with 200,000 women comprising one-sixth of U.S. forces (Goldstein, 2001, pp. 10–11).

Historical States

Today's 97% male military worldwide may be the all-time low for this variable through history—a variable that has shown amazing consistency and robustness against technological, military, and politico-diplomatic evolution through history. When war shaped the rise of states and civilizations after the Neolithic revolution, it was already a male domain. The importance of horses in historical warfare did not alter the gender division despite the fact that women ride as well as men (only equestrian events are gender integrated in the Olympics). The introduction of firearms, and later the mechanization of war, radically changed the importance of physical strength in war, but still barely affected the gender division.

Preindustrial Societies

Nor do simple societies offer counterexamples. No empirically corroborated cases are known of Amazon societies in which all (or even a majority) of fighters were female (Goldstein, 2001, pp. 11–19). Some archeological evidence suggests that early Iron Age nomadic women of the Eurasian steppes rode horses, may have used weapons, and may even have had some political influence, though probably not dominance. But excavated graves yielded war-related artifacts for about 90% of men and only 15–20% of women (Davis-Kimball, 1997, p. 47). Little evidence exists for purported Amazon societies in ancient Greece or South America.

Among contemporary preindustrial societies, both the very war prone and the relatively peaceful ones share a gender division in war, with men as the primary (and usually exclusive) fighters. For example, although gender relations on Vanatinai island (where war is rare) are radically more egalitarian than those among the war-centered Sambia, one commonality is war fighting—a male occupation. In many present-day gathering–hunting and agrarian societies, special gender taboos apply to weapons, and special practices focus on men's roles as warriors. Sometimes war and hunting are the only two spheres of social life to exclude women.

Modern nonpacified preindustrial societies are not generally peaceful. Ember and Ember find that over half of a sample of 90 societies were in a constant state of war or readiness for war, and half of the remaining societies fought every year during a particular season (C. R. Ember & Ember, 1997; M. Ember & Ember, 1994). In only eight societies did wars occur less frequently than once in 10 years on average. Of 31 gathering–hunting societies surveyed in another study, 20 typically had warfare more than once every 2 years, and only three had "no or rare warfare" (C. R. Ember, 1978, p. 444). Nonstate societies have as much warfare as states do. Relatively peaceful societies can become warlike and vice versa, as the !Kung have done. Among the very few actual peaceful societies,

the common factor is physical isolation from their neighbors (Goldstein, 2001, pp. 22–34).

Thus neither gender roles in war, nor warfare itself, result from agriculture, the state, or any particular historical stage. They have deep roots in the human experience.

The Diversity of Gender and of War

The cross-cultural consistency of gendered war roles is set against a backdrop of great diversity of both gender roles and war considered separately. Human beings have many forms of marriage, sexuality, division of labor in household and child-care work, ownership of property, and lines of descent. Overall, human societies have organized gender roles *outside* war "in an almost infinite variety of ways…" (Sanday, 1981, p. 1). Similarly, forms of war vary greatly, except for their gendered character. Different cultures fight in very different ways, and for different purposes. Thus, the *connection* of war with gender is more stable, across cultures and through time, than are either gender roles outside war or the forms and frequency of war (Goldstein, 2001, pp. 6–9).

MEN'S WAR ROLES

Norms of masculinity show great diversity cross-culturally, yet various constructions of masculinity typically serve a functional role in the war system.

Inducing Men to Kill

Killing does not come naturally to men. Combat is a horrific experience marked by confusion, noise, terror, and atrocity, in addition to any physical injury. Societies historically have worked hard to get men to fight—drafting them, disciplining them (e.g., shooting deserters), sometimes drugging them, and sometimes abruptly breaking family and community ties and replacing them with military bonding. After a war, many cultures honor veterans and confer special status or rewards on them. In some societies, war participation and war leadership open opportunities for political leadership. By contrast, men who do not fight may be shunned as cowards. All these inducements to participate in combat show the difficulty of getting men to fight (Goldschmidt, 1989, pp. 16–17, 22–23; Goldstein, 2001, p. 253).

Many such inducements to participate do not involve gender. Men may believe in a cause, or strongly identify with a country or group they are fighting to defend. However, gendered inducements are also common. War service is often construed as a test of manhood—primarily of courage—that "real men" are expected to perform.

Boyhood and Coming of Age

Rites of passage into manhood vary cross-culturally but often include common elements relevant to war preparation. Gilmore (1990, pp. 11–20) argues that a broad sweep of cultures reflect the central theme that men are made, not born. Men must take actions, undergo ordeals, or pass tests in order to *become* men. In rites of passage, only select men can achieve "manhood," and it must be won individually. Rituals typically inflict pain on adolescent males and force them not to cry out, on pain of lifelong shame if they fail. In some especially war-prone societies, men have had to kill an enemy to be considered a man or to marry. In others, near-universal male conscription marks a passage to manhood. These various passages, based on passing harsh tests bravely, adapt males for war (Goldstein, 2001, pp. 264–267).

Combat Trauma and Post-Traumatic Stress Disorder

In societies that have experienced war, many survivors suffer lasting psychological effects, including post-traumatic stress disorder (PTSD). The experience of battle is inherently traumatic. Isolation is central to this trauma. Civilian society's common lack of interest in hearing about war traumas, along with survivors' own denial, make healing difficult (Herman, 1992). PTSD has gone by various names in different wars, notably "shell shock" in World War I. Women war veterans are as prone as men to PTSD, but more men than women are exposed to combat trauma (Goldstein, 2001, pp. 259–263).

Wartime Sexuality

Little evidence suggests that male sexuality is a key component of male soldiers' aggressiveness, but the temporary dislocation of sexual norms during wartime does change patterns of sexuality (Goldstein, 2001, pp. 333–342). For example, by one calculation, the average U.S. soldier who served in Europe from D-Day through the end of World War II had sex with 25 women (Holmes, 1985, p. 97). The peak was reached after the surrender of Germany in 1945. In U.S.-occupied Italy, three-quarters of U.S. soldiers had intercourse with Italian women; about three-quarters of these paid with cash and the rest with rationed food or nothing. Fewer than half used condoms (Costello, 1985, pp. 97, 99, 262).

Military prostitution has accompanied most wars historically. Many military commanders have encouraged prostitution in response to serious attrition caused by sexually transmitted diseases (most recently AIDS). The Roman Empire operated a system of brothels for its armies. The Spanish army invading The Netherlands in the late 16th century trailed "400 mounted whores and 800 on foot" who were like "troops" commanded by appointed officers. The word "hooker" comes from U.S. Civil War general Joseph Hooker, whose Army of the Potomac was accompanied by "Hooker's girls." In World Wars I and II, French and German armies set up systems of military-supervised brothels (Costello, 1985, pp. 81–82; De Pauw, 1998, pp. 96–100; Enloe, 1993, pp. 142–160; Goldstein, 2001, pp. 342–356; Hicks, 1995, p. 29).

Conquest and Rape

Although wartime sexuality occurs behind the lines, not in tandem with violence, gender and sexuality can sometimes encode domination in war. These aspects do not characterize war generally, but do recur in a variety of contexts.

Trexler (1995, pp. 1, 12–37) documents the "inveterate male habit of gendering enemies female or effeminate" throughout the ancient world. The most common pattern in warfare in the ancient Middle East and Greece was literally to feminize a conquered population by executing male captives, raping the women, and then taking women and children as slaves. Gendered massacres continue today, notably in Srebrenica, Bosnia, in 1995. Another way to feminize conquered enemies—castrating men before or after killing them or taking them prisoner—was widespread in the ancient world, practiced by Chinese, Persian, Amalekite, Egyptian, Norse, Inca, and Dahomey armies (Trexler, 1995, pp. 16–19, 66, 72–73, 76–78). Symbolic and actual anal rape of men has also served to feminize enemies in many cultures (Trexler, 1995, pp. 14–15, 20–29).

Rape of women—actual and symbolic—recurs in wartime (Goldstein, 2001, pp. 362–373). It expresses domination and conquest, while humiliating enemy males. Conceivably, elevated testosterone levels in victorious soldiers contribute to post-conquest rapes, though such an effect seems weak. Most soldiers do not rape. Rape in wartime, including forced prostitution, has long been illegal under the Geneva Conventions.

Homosexuality

Male homosexuality has been treated differently in different historical armies. The Theban Sacred Band, an effective military force in ancient Greece, consisted of gay lovers placed together on front lines to spur each other on to courageous actions. By contrast, some modern armies and navies have punished homosexuality with death. Currently, the ban on openly gay men in U.S. military forces remains a contentious political issue. Policies vary in other countries (Goldstein, 2001, pp. 374–379).

FEMININE WAR SUPPORT ROLES

Women frequently support men's war participation through various means.

War Boosters

In simple societies, the role of women in warfare varies cross-culturally, but women generally support more than oppose war (Goldstein, 2001, pp. 301–322). No society routinely requires women to fight in wars. But often women "engage in ceremonial activities … while their men [a]re away fighting"—dancing, acting out the war, remaining chaste, and so forth. Women sometimes help to drive the men into a war frenzy by dancing, singing, and other supportive activities: "Rwala women bared their breasts and urged their men to war" (Goldschmidt, 1989, pp. 23–24). Women commonly egged men on to war in Norse legends, among Germans fighting the Roman Empire, and among Aryans of India (Turney-High, 1971, pp. 160, 163–164). In the Kitwara Empire, the Zulu kingdom, and elsewhere in Africa, women stayed at home during a war expedition and followed strict taboos (such as silence in an entire village) to bring magical powers to the war party. Zulu women also ran naked before departing warriors (Turney-High, 1971, p. 161).

Among American Indians, in Arikara culture, during a 2-day war-preparation ceremony, women danced in their husbands' clothes and took turns praising their husbands' valor. In the Comanche war preparations, women held up one side of a large drum while men held the other. Teton women wore ornaments indicating their husbands' success as warriors, and Ojibway widows and mothers received the enemy scalps (Turney-High, 1971, p. 153). Among the Chiriguano and Chané of Bolivia, women performed special dances and songs to support the warriors, both before and during battle. Apache women did not sing for the war dance, but did see off the departing warriors and fulfilled special obligations during their absence, such as keeping the woodpile neat. Thus women participate in various ways in promoting and rewarding warrior roles for men (Goldstein, 2001, pp. 316–317).

In various societies, from Germanic tribes of Roman times to American Indians, women have been "the sacred witnesses to male bravery" (Elshtain, 1987, p. 181). Women performing feminine roles on the battlefield, such as nursing, "improve morale by enhancing a man's identification of himself as a warrior" (Holmes, 1985, p. 103). Women also often actively participate in shaming men to goad them into fighting wars. In Britain and America during World War I, women organized a large-scale campaign to hand out white feathers to able-bodied men found on the streets. Before the 1973 coup in Chile, right-wing women threw corn at soldiers to taunt them as "chickens." Apache women met successful warriors with "songs and rejoicings" but unsuccessful ones with "jeers and insults"; Zulu women did likewise (Goldstein, 2001, pp. 272–274).

Mothers

For young men in combat, their mothers can symbolize a nurturing feminine sphere that contrasts with war. It is their mothers that dying soldiers most often call out for on the battlefield. In addition to their actual mothers, soldiers use mother-like figures in similar ways—nurses, sweethearts, and wives (Goldstein, 2001, pp. 309–312).

In theory, since mothers control child care, they could change gender norms, training girls to be aggressive and boys to be passive. But in fact mothers worldwide generally reward boys for being tough and girls for being nice. They raise warriors. Harris (1974, pp. 85–87) argues that although women could subdue their sons, they cannot control their enemies' sons: "As soon as males ... bear the burden of intergroup conflict, women have no choice but to rear large numbers of fierce males of their own."

Nurses

The idea of using female professional nurses in war is little more than a century old, although now widespread. However, for centuries the job of nursing has fallen to wives, camp followers, and other women accompanying military forces. Modern women's military nursing traces from the Crimean War—Florence Nightingale's war (Enloe, 1983, pp. 92–116). Military nursing has most often meant very hard work, until recently often unpaid. The moral character of nurses has traditionally mattered more to the military than their professional ability. Nurses' work generally does not entail any form of sexuality. Rather, nurses most often position themselves as mothers or sisters (sometimes being called "sister"). Women—as nurses, mothers, wives, and girlfriends— also play a central role in men's long-term recovery from combat trauma (Goldstein, 2001, pp. 262, 312–316).

Laborers

In every society at war, women workers help to sustain the war effort. Most of this work is unpaid, and largely unmeasured. The armies of 20th-century total war depended on women in new ways, not only within the army but in the civilian work force (and in addition to the ongoing responsibilities of women for domestic, reproductive, and sexual work). Both Britain and the United States mobilized millions of women into the workplace. Such new gender arrangements boost the war effort, but are typically cast as temporary (Goldstein, 2001, pp. 380–396).

Women face additional economic hardship in wartime. For example, Mae women in New Guinea "detest" wars because they fear "being left to bring up children relatively unaided .... In addition, ... they have to bear even more of the burden of food production ... in exposed gardens" (Meggitt, 1977, p. 99).

Support Troops

Despite women's exclusion from combat, a number of societies have routinely used women as *support* troops

(Goldstein, 2001, pp. 114–115). Cheyenne women occasionally, though rarely, went with war parties, and showed courage equal to the men. Shasta women also occasionally accompanied war parties, cutting enemy bowstrings with knives. They cooked and carried supplies, as did women of the Gabrielino, Hidatsa, Choctaw, and Guiana Amerindians, and the extremely aggressive Mundurucú of Brazil. Apache girls and young women received much physical training, including riding and using knife, bow, and rifle, and were expected to guard camp while males were away. Adult women occasionally joined a raiding or war party, usually to help with cooking, cleaning, and nursing. War prisoners were often taken back to camp for the women (especially those who had lost loved ones in battle) to torture and kill.

Women's participation in torturing and killing prisoners is also found elsewhere. The Konkow sometimes allowed women to participate in torturing captured male enemies. Among the Tupinamba of Brazil, women enthusiastically helped torture prisoners of war to death and then dismember and eat them. Similarly, Kiwai women of Oceania had the special job of "mangling" enemy wounded and then killing them with knives or digging sticks (Turney-High, 1971, p. 162). In 17th-century colonial Massachusetts a mob of women tortured two Indian prisoners to death after overcoming their guards. In the 19th century, Afghan women tortured enemy survivors of battle. In 1993, a mob of Somali women tore apart four foreign journalists (Goldstein, 2001, pp. 114–115).

It is possible for a culture to mobilize women into combat support without taking away their noncombatant protected status. In Papuan warfare, women collected stray arrows and scouted enemy movements, enjoying immunity from attack. Kapauku warfare (New Guinea) extended total immunity to women support troops in the middle of the battle (Goldstein, 2001, p. 115).

In addition to their support roles at the bottom of military hierarchies, women can make effective military leaders. Male soldiers and officers will follow the commands and exhortations of women leaders possessing proper authority. Most women military leaders (but not Joan of Arc), were "warrior queens" who held political power and exercised military leadership from that position. Different stories treat such figures differently—for example, some emphasize their chastity and others their sexual voracity (Fraser, 1989, pp. 11–13; Goldstein, 2001, pp. 116–126).

Women and Peace

Most women support most wars, but others often organize *as* women to work for peace (Goldstein, 2001, pp. 322–331). In some simple societies, women tend to restrain the men from war or play special roles as mediators in bringing wars to an end. For instance, Andamanese Islands women "tried to settle quarrels and bring fighting to a conclusion." (However, the Ibibio of Nigeria did not permit women to witness peacemaking rites lest they upset them.) Among the Kiwai-Papua, after both sides signal a desire for peace, "a number of men accompanied by their wives make their way to the enemy village. The women walk a few paces ahead. It is taken for granted that bringing their wives is a demonstration of peaceful intentions .... During the night, the hosts sleep with the visitors' wives—a practice known as 'putting out the fire' " (Eibl-Eibesfeldt, 1979, p. 213).

In modern societies, women's peace activism expanded with the suffrage movement in the 19th century, In 1852, *Sisterly Voices* began publication as a newsletter for European women's peace societies. The Women's Peace Party, founded during World War I, grew out of the international suffrage movement. In recent decades, women's peace activism can be found in dozens of countries. In the United States, a gender gap of about 10–15% in support for military actions has persisted for decades. However, a recurring problem for women's peace activism is that construing peace as feminine masculinizes war and thus reinforces mechanisms that societies use to induce men to fight.

WOMEN'S PERFORMANCE IN COMBAT

Beyond women's war support roles, occasionally women do participate in fighting. These cases, although rare overall, are sufficient to show that many women *can* fight wars.

Simple Societies

In several prestate societies, women sometimes participate in fighting. I mentioned above the early Iron Age Eurasian steppes. Some Native American societies let women have some participation in combat. Among the southern Apaches, some women accompanied war parties and a few fought (bravely). The most famous Apache woman warrior was Lozen, who helped a force of 15–40 warriors elude a U.S. force of over a thousand soldiers and win eight battles. However, most Apache women did not participate in war (Goldstein, 2001, pp. 113–114).

The Dahomey Kingdom

In the 18th–19th century Dahomey Kingdom of West Africa, women made up one wing of the army, at times contributing a one-third of all soldiers (Alpern, 1998; Goldstein, 2001, pp. 60–64). They lived in the king's palace, followed special rules, and were excellent fighters whose presence substantially increased the kingdom's military power. Dahomey is an important case since it shows the possibility of an effective permanent standing women's combat unit making up a substantial minority of an army. However, it is the only case of its kind.

The Soviet Union in World War II

In the Soviet Union during World War II—desperate times—800,000 women reportedly made up at peak about 8% of Soviet forces. Most were medical workers but a few thousand were combatants—anti-aircraft gunners, pilots, snipers, and infantrywomen. War propaganda exaggerated women's exploits to cheer on a devastated society and shame men into fighting harder. But overall, the evidence indicates that the women fought about as well as the men. Nonetheless, as soon as circumstances permitted, women were purged from the Red Army. Even the official estimates make women combatants at their peak fewer than 1% of Soviet combat forces (Goldstein, 2001, pp. 64–72).

Guerrilla Armies

Women fighters are not uncommon in modern guerrilla armies. From the Cold War and post-Cold War eras alone, scholars have illuminated women's crucial roles in a variety of wars, including those in Vietnam, South Africa, Argentina, Cyprus, Iran, Northern Ireland, Lebanon, Israel, Nicaragua, and others. In World War II, women participated in the partisan forces of various occupied countries (which mostly did not allow women into regular forces) including Yugoslavia, Italy, Greece, France, Poland, and Denmark. The Vietnamese communists later employed women guerrillas extensively, as did the Sandinistas and FMLN in Central America, revolutionary forces in Southern Africa, and the Tamil Tigers in Sri Lanka (Goldstein, 2001, pp. 77–83).

Present-Day State Militaries

More than a dozen states—mostly industrialized countries that are U.S. allies—currently allow women into certain combat positions (Goldstein, 2001, pp. 83–86). The exact number depends on how exactly one defines combat. Eritrea and South Africa have women in the infantry, owing to the recent integration of former guerrilla forces into state armies there. Eritrean women fought in the lethal ground war with Ethiopia in the late 1990s (constituting perhaps a third of all soldiers). Some reports put women at one-third of Eritrean combat forces. Women's status in NATO militaries is evolving year by year, with the policies and numbers shifting continually toward greater women's participation. Countries are generally moving along a common path—though at different speeds—from combat aviation, to combat ships, to submarines, to ground combat. Women aviators bombed Serbia (1999) and Afghanistan (2001).

Individual Warriors through History

Individual women have also effectively fought in wars, contrary to the norms of their societies, in such times as 19th-century Europe, the U.S. Civil War, and World War I. Other women of unknown number have fought wars while disguised as men (Goldstein, 2001). These individual cases share the quality of being exceptional and thus not upsetting the main gender arrangements in those wars.

SOME POSSIBLE EXPLANATIONS

Elsewhere, I review available empirical evidence to evaluate 20 hypotheses that might help to explain the consistency of gender roles in war (Goldstein, 2001, pp. 4, 404–405). I conclude that a complex interaction of biology with culture best explains this phenomenon, with neither alone being sufficient. Here, I will sketch three approaches in anthropology that might explain gendered war roles—biology, male dominance, and marriage patterns.

Biological and Evolutionary Approaches

Some biological anthropologists tie war and aggression to male biology. Konner (1988, p. 33) argues that "testosterone is a key" to aggression. Wrangham and Peterson (1996) describe male apes as innately "demonic," needing restraint by females.

Empirical evidence offers mixed support for these biological approaches. Men's biology favors them for fighting in several ways. On average, men are larger and stronger than women—though men's and women's bell-curve distributions overlap. Men's spatial abilities, modestly higher than women's on average, might also slightly help men in war. Testosterone does not cause aggression, but it does play complex roles in male social behavior regarding winning and losing (which are relevant to war) in humans and other primates. These biological differences explain why *most* combatants would be male. But none can explain the near-total exclusion of women from combat, since a minority of women are stronger, more spatially adept, and more competitive than most men (Goldstein, 2001, pp. 128–182).

Efforts to adduce an evolutionary basis for gender roles in war—in terms of reproductive advantage—have been controversial. Some scholars see male warfare as mainly about competition for females. In Harris's (1974, pp. 83–107) "male supremacist complex," war limits population relative to scarce natural resources by putting a premium on raising boys, and thus lowering girls' survival rates. The idea that males are expendable from an evolutionary perspective is problematical. In theory, in polygynous societies a few men can impregnate many women. But if many men die in war, labor resources diminish and fewer babies survive to reproductive age.

Women's Status

Another explanation links women's status with the frequency of war. Feminist theories of war offer a variety of contradictory views linked by their concern with women's status. Difference feminism focuses on biological (or otherwise innate) qualities that distinguish men as a group and suit them for fighting. This approach underlies women's peace movements. Liberal feminism, in contrast, portrays women as men's equal in war, celebrating the historical record of women combatants, support troops, and factory workers. Postmodern feminists also criticize the "essentialism" of difference feminism, and show how binary oppositions based on gender operate in wartime narratives to reinforce the power of dominant groups. Harding (1986, p. 129) describes the "social constructionist strain of recent anthropological literature" which argues that "absolutely nothing—no behavior and no meaning—[is] universally and cross-culturally associated with either masculinity or femininity. What is considered masculine in some societies is considered feminine or gender-neutral in others and vice versa; the only constant appears to be the importance of the dichotomy." However, this approach does not explain the near-universality of gender roles in war.

Empirically, across cultures, women's status seems to correlate with infrequency of war as difference feminists might expect, but only mildly so (Goldstein, 2001, pp. 396–402). Measuring women's status is difficult, and studies suffer from assumptions about direction of causality between women's status and warfare (which most likely is bidirectional).

One review of a dozen cross-cultural studies finds that societies with frequent war tend to have wife beating, along with warlike sports, beliefs in malevolent magic, severe criminal punishments, and feuding (C. R. Ember & Ember, 1997). Women's status and power vary greatly across 150 cultures worldwide in another study, and gender relations are very unequal in 33% of the societies with "endemic or chronic" war, but in only 17% of the others (Sanday, 1981, pp. 6–7, 174). In a sample of 33 gathering–hunting societies, warfare decreases women's domestic and political status (Hayden, Deal, Cannon, & Casey, 1986). In Ross's statistical analysis of 90 "small scale, preindustrial societies," war seems to be more likely in societies with high gender inequality, harsh child-rearing practices, and the absence of fathers from child rearing (Ross, 1990, pp. 55–56, 60). In another sample of 82 societies, low female decision involvement correlates with low internal war (between same-language communities), high external war (across language lines), harsh child socialization, and strong fraternal interest groups (Ross, 1986, pp. 848–850). However, Whyte (1978, pp. 129–131, 156–157) finds only mild mixed effects of war on women's status. Thus war frequency correlates somewhat with gender inequality cross-culturally, but modestly and unevenly.

Marriage Patterns

Another line of argument explains the gendering of war by the potential disloyalty of women toward their communities. Most cultures are patrilocal. In the event of war between the two communities, women might have mixed loyalties—to their current husbands and their birth families—which could explain why many cultures

exclude them from war-fighting, planning, and access to weapons (Adams, 1983, pp. 7, 198–203, 207–210; cf. Manson & Wrangham, 1991, pp. 372–374). An alternative way to resolve the dilemma is to draw marriage partners from within one's own community (endogamy). Another alternative is to fight mainly external wars, so that marrying enemies is rare.

Matrilocal societies tend to practice endogamy and fight external wars (Adams, 1983; Ember & Ember, 1971), so in these societies the disloyalty problem would not occur.

Empirically, women's participation in war is somewhat higher in matrilocal than patrilocal societies, although still extremely limited. In a sample of 67 prestate cultures, women participated at least occasionally as warriors in nine, all of them among the 33 cultures characterized by either exclusively external war or exclusive community endogamy. However, in all nine cases—mostly Native Americans—women comprised a small minority of warriors and were generally treated as unusual. For example, Navaho war parties never had more than two women, Delaware women "seldom" fought, Fox women warriors were unusual, and Comanche women just sometimes sniped from the fringes (Adams, 1983, pp. 200–202).

The majority of communities have internal war, and the majority are patrilocal, but all combinations of war and marriage occur in at least a few cultures (Table 1). Cultures with frequent internal war, patrilocal residence, and at least some exogamy—the ones where women's loyalties could explain gendered war roles—are the

Table 1. Cross-Cultural Relationship of Marriage and War in 115 Societies

War pattern	Marriage pattern (exogamy; endogamy)			
	Patrilocal	Matrilocal	Bilocal/other	Total
Some internal war	44 (19; 9)	5 (1; 4)	9 (1; 4)	58
External war exclusively	8 (2; 1)	14 (2; 7)	3 (0; 1)	25
Infrequent war	15 (9; 2)	5 (1; 4)	12 (1; 3)	32
Total	67	24	24	115

Numbers in parentheses indicate cultures practicing only exogamy (marriages from other communities) and only endogamy, respectively. The rest practice mixed exogamy and endogamy.

Data from Adams (1983, pp. 199–200, 203). Reprinted with permission from *War and gender: How gender shapes the war system and vice versa* (p. 227), by J. S. Goldstein, 2001, Cambridge, UK: Cambridge University Press.

largest single category but make up fewer than a third of the 115 cultures in the sample. The major problem with women's loyalties as an explanation of gendered war roles is that it does not explain the rareness of women warriors in the other two-thirds of the cultures, where marriage patterns vary (Goldstein, 2001, pp. 225–227).

Causality may run from war to marriage type as much as vice versa (Adams, 1983, pp. 202–203). The patrilocal marriage system, by keeping the men together in kin groups (fathers and brothers stay together), strengthens communities that frequently fight their neighbors. By contrast, matrilocal marriages break up such ties and thus promote unity across neighboring communities; this is functional when they together face an external threat (Ember & Ember, 1971). Polygyny occurs most in societies with high male mortality in warfare (M. Ember, 1974, 1985). Cultures with infrequent war usually lack strict marriage residency rules.

CONCLUSION

The ubiquitous nature of both war and gendered war roles suggests that these phenomena play central roles in social life. However, no single or simple explanation can account for gender roles in war. Many aspects of gender in human cultures connect—in complex interactive ways—with war. Not only do societies use gender in various ways to enable successful participation in war, but war in turn strongly influences a range of gender relationships within those societies. Without war, cultural patterns of sex and gender would be substantially different.

ACKNOWLEDGMENTS

Parts of this article are excerpted and adapted, with permission, from my *War and Gender: How Gender Shapes the War System and Vice Versa* (Cambridge University Press, 2001), which also contains further scholarly references. For more resources, see www.warandgender.com

REFERENCES

Adams, D. B. (1983). Why there are so few women warriors. *Behavior Science Research*, *18*(3), 196–212.

Alpern, S. B. (1998). *Amazons of Black Sparta: The women warriors of Dahomey.* New York: New York University Press.

Costello, J. (1985). *Virtue under fire: How World War II changed our social and sexual attitudes.* Boston: Little, Brown.

Davis-Kimball, J. (1997). Warrior women of the Eurasian steppes. *Archaeology, 50*(1), 44–48.

De Pauw, L. G. (1998). *Battle cries and lullabies: Women in war from prehistory to the present.* Norman, OK: University of Oklahoma Press.

Eibl-Eibesfeldt, I. (1979). *The biology of peace and war: Men, animals, and aggression.* New York: Viking.

Elshtain, J. B. (1987). *Women and war.* New York: Basic Books.

Ember, C. R. (1978). Myths about hunter-gatherers. *Ethnology, 17*(4), 439–448.

Ember, C. R., & Ember, M. (1997). Violence in the ethnographic record: Results of cross-cultural research on war and aggression. In D. L. Martin & D. W. Frayer (Eds.), *Troubled times: Violence and warfare in the past* (pp. 1–20). Langhorne, PA: Gordon & Breach.

Ember, M. (1974). Warfare, sex ratio, and polygyny. *Ethnology, 13*, 197–206.

Ember, M. (1985). Alternative predictors of polygyny. *Behavior Science Research, 19*, 1–23.

Ember, M., & Ember, C. R. (1971). The conditions favoring matrilocal versus patrilocal residence. *American Anthropologist, 73*, 571–594.

Ember, M., & Ember, C. R. (1994). Cross-cultural studies of war and peace: Recent achievements and future possibilities. In S. P. Reyna & Downs (Eds.), *Studying war: Anthropological perspectives* (pp. 185–208). Langhorne, PA: Gordon & Breach.

Enloe, C. (1983). *Does khaki become you? The militarization of women's lives.* Boston: South End Press.

Enloe, C. (1993). *The morning after: Sexual politics at the end of the cold war.* Berkeley, CA: University of California Press.

Ferguson, R. B. (Ed.). (1984). *Warfare, culture, and environment.* New York: Academic Press.

Ferguson, R. B., & Whitehead, N. L. (Eds.). (1992). *War in the tribal zone: Expanding states and indigenous warfare.* Santa Fe, NM: School of American Research Press.

Foster, M. Le., & Rubinstein, R. A. (Eds.). (1986). *Peace and war: Cross-cultural perspectives.* New Brunswick, NJ: Transaction.

Fraser, A. (1989). *The warrior queens.* New York: Knopf.

Fried, M., Harris, M., & Murphy, R. (Eds.). (1967). *War: The anthropology of armed conflict and aggression.* Garden City, NY: Natural History Press.

Gilmore, D. D. (1990). *Manhood in the making: Cultural concepts of masculinity.* New Haven, CT: Yale University Press.

Goldschmidt, W. (1989). Inducement to military participation in tribal societies. In P. R. Turner & D. Pitt (Eds.), *The anthropology of war and peace: Perspectives on the nuclear age* (pp. 15–31). Granby, MA: Bergin & Garvey.

Goldstein, J. S. (2001). *War and gender: How gender shapes the war system and vice versa.* Cambridge, UK: Cambridge University Press.

Haas, J. (Ed.). (1990). *The anthropology of war.* Cambridge, UK: Cambridge University Press.

Harding, S. G. (1986). *The science question in feminism.* Ithaca, NY: Cornell University Press.

Harris, M. (1974). *Cows, pigs, wars and witches: The riddles of culture.* New York: Random House.

Hayden, B., Deal, M., Cannon, A., & Casey, J. (1986). Ecological determinants of women's status among hunter/gatherers. *Human Evolution, 1*(5), 449–474.

Herman, J. L. (1992). *Trauma and recovery.* New York: Basic Books.

Hicks, G. (1995). *The comfort women: Japan's brutal regime of enforced prostitution in the Second World War.* New York: Norton.

Holmes, R. (1985). *Acts of war: The behavior of men in battle.* New York: Free Press.

Konner, M. (1988, August 14). The aggressors. *The New York Times Magazine,* p. 33.

Manson, J. H., & Wrangham, R. W. (1991). Intergroup aggression in chimpanzees and humans. *Current Anthropology, 32*(4), 369–390.

Mead, M. (1967). Epilogue. In M. Fried, M. Harris, & R. Murphy (Eds.), *War: The anthropology of armed conflict and aggression* (pp. 235–237). Garden City, NY: Natural History Press.

Meggitt, M. (1977). *Blood is their argument: Warfare among the Mae Enga tribesmen of the New Guinea Highlands.* Palo Alto, CA: Mayfield.

Nettleship, M. A., Givens, R. D., & Nettleship, A. (Eds.). (1975). *War, its causes and correlates.* The Hague: Mouton.

Reyna, S. P., & Downs, R. E. (Eds.). (1994). *Studying war: Anthropological perspectives.* Langhorne, PA: Gordon & Breach.

Ross, M. H. (1986). Female political participation: A cross-cultural explanation. *American Anthropologist, 88*(4), 843–858.

Ross, M. H. (1990). Children and war in different cultures. In F. M. Cancian & J. W. Gibson. (Eds.), *Making war/making peace: The social foundations of violent conflict* (pp. 51–63). Belmont, CA: Wadsworth.

Sanday, P. R. (1981). *Female power and male dominance: On the origins of sexual inequality.* Cambridge, UK: Cambridge University Press.

Trexler, R. C. (1995). *Sex and conquest: Gendered violence, political order, and the European conquest of the Americas.* Ithaca, NY: Cornell University Press.

Turner, P. R., & Pitt, D. (Eds.). (1989). *The anthropology of war and peace: Perspectives on the nuclear age.* Granby, MA: Bergin & Garvey.

Turney-High, H. H. (1971). *Primitive war: Its practice and concepts* (2nd ed.). Columbia, NC: University of South Carolina Press.

Whyte, M. K. (1978). *The status of women in preindustrial societies.* Princeton, NJ: Princeton University Press.

Wrangham, R., & Peterson, D. (1996). *Demonic males: Apes and the origins of human violence.* New York: Houghton Mifflin.

Religion, Religiosity, and Gender

Benjamin Beit-Hallahmi

INTRODUCTION

Religion is an ideology, meaning "… that part of culture which is actively concerned with the establishment and defense of patterns of beliefs and values" (Geertz, 1964, p. 64). But it is clearly different, in the nature of its claims, from all other ideologies we know, such as left-wing or right-wing world views in politics. Religion as an ideology involves the individual in a unique commitment and a unique network of relationships, real and imagined. The irreducible belief core common to all religions contains the belief in spirit entities inhabiting an invisible world, and our relationship with them (Beit-Hallahmi, 1989). The working definition of religion used here is the straightforward everyday description of religion as a system of beliefs in divine or superhuman powers, and ritual practices directed towards such powers (Argyle & Beit-Hallahmi, 1975).

It is the premise of every religion—and this premise is religion's defining characteristic—that souls, supernatural beings, and supernatural forces exist. Furthermore, there are certain minimal categories of behavior, which, in the context of the *supernatural premise*, [emphasis in the original] are always found in association with one another and which are the substance of religion itself. (Wallace, 1966, p. 52)

Similarly, William James describes a separation of the visible and the invisible worlds, which parallels the separation between sacred and profane:

Religion has meant many things in human history: but when from now onward I use the word I mean to use it in the supernaturalist sense, as declaring that the so called order of nature, which constitutes this world's experience, is only one portion of the total universe, and that there stretches beyond this visible world an unseen world of which we now know nothing positive, but in its relation to which the true significance of our present mundane life consists. A man's religious faith … means for me essentially his faith in the existence of an unseen order of some kind in which the riddles of the natural order may be found explained. (James, 1897/1956, p. 51)

We will use the presence of the supernatural premise, or the supernatural assumption, as the touchstone for defining certain human behaviors as religious.

All religions, as ideologies, promote the idea of an invisible world inhabited by various creatures, gods, angels, and devils, which control much of what happens to us. And if we believe in the existence of the unseen world, then religion as a social institution is for us the mediator between the invisible supernatural world and the visible, human, and natural world; but that institution, with the behaviors tied to it, does not exist without the belief in the supernatural.

While this description may be too narrow to include some traditions sometimes referred to as religious, it is broad enough to cover what to most human beings is connoted by religion through their concrete historical experience. This definition has the advantages of being concrete, historical, and close to the direct experience of the proverbial person in the street, the common believer. The behavioral definition of religion has to be close to that which real people experience and recognize immediately, and such substantive definitions are in line with the traditions of scholarship in the study of religion. The universality of our definition is based on the universality of beliefs in the world of the spirits. Despite the cultural variations and the claims for uniqueness, there is a universal common denominator to religion. The description of supernaturalism is valid not just for westerners, but also for Shintoists, Hindus, Moslems, Sikhs, and members of thousands of other religious groups.

While religion is an institution and a belief system, what we measure in the behavior of individuals is religiosity, which is the adherence to a particular belief system—any one of the 10,000 religions currently in existence. This does not imply, of course, that individuals have much choice in matters of religion. In 99% of cases, young humans are successfully taught to accept the tenets of whatever faith their parents hold.

Religiosity is a continuous, rather than a discrete, variable. The expression of religious beliefs is the main measure of religiosity, which is then related to other beliefs, and to psychological and behavioral indicators. Religiosity is not randomly distributed in any population, as beliefs and attitudes are correlated with the primordial social roles of age, sex, and social status (Beit-Hallahmi & Argyle, 1997).

Individuals follow cultural scripts for religion, as for other behaviors. But we can still point to some generalizations or even universals. Despite the cross-cultural and historical evidence for the diversity of religious beliefs, there are also some universal features in terms of the common belief system. Gods are envisaged as invisible spiritual forces with some of the properties of persons, who are good and powerful. They are usually thought of as male. Religion is universally claimed as the source of, and the authority for, moral codes, impulse control, and social power arrangements. Women are everywhere more committed to religion, and the family is everywhere sacralized.

METHODS

Most of our data on traditional cultures come from anthropological research, while most research on industrialized societies is based on sociological surveys and psychological research. Anthropological and historical studies in traditional societies do not normally look at individual differences, and cover the structure and contents of a whole cultural system. Representative cultural practices and beliefs are observed and recorded by outsiders, who normally do not question individual adherence to them (Needham, 1972).

In the industrialized societies of the developed world we collect our data by using as our instruments surveys, interviews, questionnaires, and standard psychological tests, with the emphasis being the individual's beliefs and attitudes. Sociologists may be interested in group differences, while psychologists focus on individual differences and the correlates of different belief systems. The individual believer is asked to reply to specific questions and then becomes part of a data pool. The simple and direct question "Do you believe in God?" has become a standard and useful measure of one's basic stand vis-à-vis religion. We can compare answers to this question across cultures and we can compare the answers of men and women. If we are going to use ethnographic observations in the industrialized world, they will amplify the findings we already have from studies using questionnaires or interviews.

FINDINGS

It is important to note that only a few studies have ever been started with sex differences in religiosity as the actual research question. While almost no studies were ever initiated to look at sex differences, the finding of consistent differences between women and men just emerged from data whenever researchers cared to make a comparison (e.g., Hollinger & Smith, 2002).

In studies of religious behavior over the past 100 years, the greater religiosity of women must be one of the oldest, and clearest, findings. It has been reported in comprehensive surveys of the research literature in the sociology and psychology of religion over the past 50 years (Argyle, 1958; Argyle & Beit-Hallahmi, 1975; Beit-Hallahmi, 1989; Beit-Hallahmi & Argyle, 1997; Lenski, 1953), but this ubiquitous difference between men and women is rarely mentioned in the literature on sex differences.

We will use the ratio of females to males as our main measure of differences, so that 1.50, for example, means that 50% more women than men are involved in a particular activity. We will start with those aspects of religion where the greatest differences have been reported, and work downwards.

High-Involvement Rituals

The largest differences have been reported for Catholics going to confession (1.93; Fichter, 1952), and people being converted in the Billy Graham crusades of the 20th century (1.8; Colquhoun, 1955). Women in an African American independent church were much more likely to go into a trance in services (Alland, 1962), and the sex ratio for members of Pentecostal and similar groups is about 2.0 : 1.

Daily Prayer

The sex ratio is higher here than for any other form of religious activity. Gallup (1977) found a ratio of 1.57 for reading the Bible and 1.36 for prayer in the United States, and Gorer (1955) found a ratio of 1.87 for English adults. Anthropological reports indicate that Hindu women are more likely than men to pray at home shrines (Firth, 1997).

Beliefs

Women are more conservative or orthodox in religion, that is, they more often say they hold the central and traditional beliefs, in God, the afterlife, and, for Christians, that Jesus was the Son of God. In British surveys the ratio is about 1.50; in American surveys it is lower, about 1.2, because of the larger percentages of believers. Surveys all over Europe have reported similar ratios (Zulehner & Denz, 1993). The picture is even more striking if we look at the reality of religiosity in post-Communist Russia. The rate of belief in God there was found to be 32% for men and 57% for women (White, McAllister, & Kryshtanovskaya, 1994).

Religious Experience

Differences here are smaller: the ratios are 1.32 in Britain (Hay, 1982), and 1.20 in the United States (Back & Bourque, 1970), although the overall percentages are much the same in both countries at about 33%. This gender difference is found in early childhood; at age 9–10 more girls say they have experienced "God's closeness" (Tamminen, 1994).

Ritual Attendance

This is the most visible and obvious source of sex differences, though the differences are lower. In the United States, the ratio is typically about 1.20 and in Britain it is higher at 1.50. Buddenbaum (1981) reported that women in the United States are also overrepresented among viewers of televangelists.

If we make some basic ethnographic observations, and visit churches in Rome, Paris, New York City, or Moscow, we will immediately realize that women make up the majority of those in attendance. Anthropological observations in India indicate that women make up the majority of those attending Hindu temples (Firth, 1997). In those traditions where ritual attendance by women is discouraged, such as Islam and Judaism, the majority of those attending will be men (Loewenthal, MacLeod, & Cinnirella, 2002).

Overall Religiosity Measures

Stark (2002) provides data on levels of religiosity for men and women in 49 western and eight nonwestern cultures.

In every single case, as expected, women are more likely than men to describe themselves as religious. The ratios range from 1.05 in Brazil to 1.69 in Estonia (cf. Gallup, 1980). In the British Values Survey (Gerard, 1985), factor analysis produced two factors, and the scores on each were combined to give a single index of religious commitment. One factor consisted of items about basic beliefs and reported religious experience, and the second was about ritual attendance and positive attitudes to the church. Fifteen percent of men, 20% of working women, and 26% of nonworking women had high scores—a ratio of 1.53 if the two groups of women are combined. The ratio for the medium to high group was 1.61. The American Gallup ratio for "being a religious person" was 1.45. As reported by Gallup and Lindsay (1999), women in the United States have been found to be significantly higher than men on all measures of religiosity used in public opinion polls. This is the largest data pool anywhere in the world.

Anderson (1993) reported that in the Soviet Union the higher level of religiosity among women was found in both the European republics, with their Christian heritage, and the republics of Central Asia, which were historically part of the Islamic world.

In a survey of 1172 Ethiopian students, representing three Christian denominations and Islam, and 15 ethnic groups, the 408 females received higher overall religiosity scores than the males (Wondimu, Beit-Hallahmi, & Abbink, 2001).

Membership in Different Denominations

In all Christian denominations in the world, with the exception of Roman Catholicism, there are more women than men, but the proportion varies. In a survey of 310,000 Australian churchgoers (Kaldor et al., 1994) the following ratios were found: Anglicans, 2.02; United Church, 1.86; Baptists, 1.38; Pentecostalists, 1.33.

American Gallup polls found the following ratios (Gallup & Castelli, 1989): Episcopalians, 1.39; Charismatics, 1.35; Evangelicals, 1.28; Mormons, 1.28; Methodists, 1.23; Baptists, 1.00; Lutherans, 1.00; Catholics, 0.96; No religion, 0.59.

In British studies the Church of England again has a high sex ratio, and the Roman Catholic church a low one, but there are also very high ratios for new religious movements, often between 2 : 1 and 4 : 1 (e.g., Wilson, 1961).

Para-Religious Beliefs

Women are also higher in adhering to para-religious beliefs, or "the occult," such as astrology, "telepathy," and fortune-telling, as well as readier to believe in various "miracle drugs" (Emmons & Sobal, 1981; Markle, Petersen, & Wagenfeld, 1978; Wuthnow, 1976; Zeidner & Beit-Hallahmi, 1988). In 1999, a survey of 3,569 university students in Argentina, Brazil, Colombia, Uruguay, the United States, Austria, Germany, Great Britain, Italy, and Portugal looked at involvement in religious and esoteric beliefs and practices. It was found that females were both more religious and more involved in esoteric beliefs and practices (Hollinger & Smith, 2002).

ANALYSIS AND EXPLANATIONS

The greater religiosity of women must be one of the oldest, and clearest, findings in the psychology of religion, and should be considered one of the universals in human religious behavior, but its explanation has proved challenging. The greater religiosity of women is often viewed as a puzzle and a paradox. That is because religious organizations, institutions, and traditions are developed and controlled by men. There is one aspect of religious activity where men predominate, and that is public worship.

In some historical religious traditions, such as Islam and Judaism, women are not expected to take an active or public role in most religious activities, as in many traditional cultures public activity by women is limited and controlled (Anderson, 1993; Loewenthal et al., 2002).

Beyond the discouragement of public participation in some cultures, clergy roles are reserved for men in most religions around the world. Women clergy have been the rare exception (Yinger, 1970). The social institution of religion and specific religious institutions in different societies are in the overwhelming majority of cases controlled by men. Cross-culturally we can say that women are rarely in positions of power and influence in religious institutions and organizations, and in many cases they are formally excluded from positions of liturgical and clerical leadership.

Weber (1968) observed that religious movements of the underprivileged gave equality to women at first, but as they became established withdrew it. This theory has been found to be true of American Pentecostal sects in the

early 20th century, some of them African American. At first they had many charismatic women preachers, sometimes the founders of sects, but their numbers then fell (Barfoot & Sheppard, 1980). This is true for the rare female founders of modern religious movements such as Ellen G. White, Mary Baker Eddy, and Madame Blavatsky. The groups they started soon came to be run by men.

We can describe the psychological world of the committed religious believer as a pyramid made of three tiers. The top of the pyramid is the religious pantheon, made up of imaginary invisible creatures. Then we have actual humans who constitute the religious hierarchy. The broad base of the pyramid is made up of the followers, who are the largest group. As we get closer to the top of this pyramid, we find fewer and fewer females, and as we move to the bottom tier, we find a female majority. The pantheon, which includes gods, angels, saints, and mystics, has little room for women (Carroll, 1979). The world of religious figures, real and imagined, which has in it angels, demons, saints, founders, prophets, priests, is thus a masculine universe. It was obviously created by men, reflecting their wishes, so why are women so willing to adopt this masculine universe and commit themselves to it?

Here are some of the most likely explanations.

Differences in Personality

Women's religiosity has often been explained as related to personality factors. Thus the overrepresentation of women in 19th-century U.S. revivalism was explained by Cross (1965) as due to their being "... less educated, more superstitious, and more zealous than men" (p. 178). More recently, it has been suggested "that women's behaviour is more often directed by sensitivity and intuition, while men are more likely to act according to rational and logical considerations" (Hollinger & Smith, 2002, p. 242).

There is plenty of evidence for personality differences between men and women; some of these may be relevant to the differences in religious activity. Some of them may be innate, such as greater male aggressiveness and risk-taking (Geary, 1998; Gray, 1971; Stark, 2002). Males are more likely to die violently and to commit suicide at any age. They tend to be more aggressive and dominance oriented than females in most mammalian species, including humans (e.g., Daly & Wilson, 1983; Pratto, Sidanius, & Stallworth, 1993). Human males are verbally and physically more aggressive than females across cultures (Eibl-Eibesfeldt, 1989; Rohner, 1976). Research suggests that males tend to be more inclined toward aggressiveness, whether physical or psychological (Cairns et al., 1989; Eagly, 1987; Eagly & Steffen, 1986). Sex differences in dominance emerge early in the preschool years and at about the same time in all cultures that have been studied (Maccoby, 1988). As children, boys are observed to be competitive and aggressive. Girls are sociable and helpful, and enjoy social contact for its own sake (Opie, 1993). "In general, women tend to manifest behaviors that can be described as socially sensitive, friendly, and concerned with others' welfare, whereas men tend to manifest behaviors that can be described as dominant, controlling, and independent" (Eagly, 1995, p. 154).

Are women more emotional? They clearly are readier to express feelings and admit dependence. They are also readier to demonstrate interpersonal caring, sensitivity, and warmth. Spence and Helmreich (1978) described the dichotomy of orientations in females and males as communion versus agency. Communion is the tendency to be concerned about closeness to others, while agency is the tendency to be self-interested and assertive. It has been suggested that "the feminine (not simply female) voice adheres to a calculus of development through attachments and connectedness, rather than growth through separation and substitution" (Thompson, 1991, p. 391). In most cultures males are less nurturant and less emotionally expressive (D'Andrade, 1967), while women are more submissive and passive, anxious, and dependent (Garai & Scheinfeld, 1968).

J. B. Miller (1986) suggested that the subjective experiences of women are affected by two major factors: first, the permanent inequality in social relationships, under which women are encouraged to be submissive, dependent, and passive; second, the relational self is the core of self-structure in women. Boys' groups tend to be larger, forming "gangs," while girls organize themselves into smaller groups or pairs (Thorne, 1993). Women assume more responsibility for relationship maintenance and social support (Belle, 1982; Turner, 1994). Empathy, defined as the vicarious affective response to another person's feelings, is more prevalent in females (Hoffman, 1977). Eibl-Eibesfeldt (1989) suggested that, throughout human evolution, the social style of females provided the basis for maintaining the long-term stability of social groups. "Women throughout the world are perceived to be the nurturant sex" (Maccoby & Jacklin, 1974, p. 215).

Males appear to be relatively more object oriented, and females more people oriented (McGuinness, 1993). On standard personality inventories, such as the Edwards Personal Preference Schedule (EPPS), consistent differences are found, with women higher on Affiliation, and Nurturance, and men higher on Dominance and Aggression.

Females "express more fear, are more susceptible to anxiety, are more lacking in task confidence, seek more help and reassurance, maintain greater proximity to friends, score higher on social desirability, and at the younger ages at which compliance has been studied, are more compliant with adults" (Block, 1976, p. 307). There is much evidence showing that women have stronger guilt feelings, and are more intropunitive than men (Wright, 1971). It has been stated that women experience higher rates of childhood abuse, especially sexual abuse, which is a predictor of later depression, and may have depressions related to hormonal changes and to sex-role conditioning that encourages patterns of negative thinking and passivity (McGrath, Keita, Strickland, & Russo, 1990). In the United States, it has been estimated that between 2.3% and 3.2% of men, and between 4.5% and 9.3% of women, meet the diagnostic criteria for major depressive disorder at any given moment (Depression Guideline Panel, 1993). Higher levels of depression are found in women, starting in adolescence. This has been explained as the result of "ruminative coping," a tendency to focus inwardly and passively on one's emotions (Nolen-Hoeksema, 1990, 1995). Kaplan (1983) showed that women were more commonly diagnosed as suffering from disorders of internalized conflict, such as depression, cyclothymic disorder, panic disorder, and phobia, while men were more often diagnosed as suffering from acting-out disorders, such as substance abuse or antisocial personality.

Many of the "female" traits could well lead to greater religiosity. Dependence, on gods and saints, is part of the religious attitude. Nurturance is a basic religious value. Guilt feelings are often appealed to in sermons and revivals, which then offer relief from them. A. S. Miller and Hoffmann (1995) found that males' risk preference and females' risk aversion were related to religiosity.

The basic difference in personality styles is reflected in fantasy products. Women's dreams involve relationships and loss, while men are likely to dream about fighting, protecting, and competing, almost always with other men (McQuarrie, Kramer, & Bonnet, 1980;

A. R. Moffitt, Kramer, & Hoffmann, 1993). And when ready-made fantasies are consumed, as in watching television, women constitute the audience for soap operas while men watch aggressive sports (or follow political and economic news, which are often far from fantasies). Women live vicarious family and relationship conflicts and happy endings through the reading of popular romance novels. It has been noted that religious mythologies deal with family conflicts, loyalty, and betrayal, as well as with fierce competition among men.

Religious attitudes are crystallized during adolescence, and it seems likely that sex differences in religion are also fixed at this age. Suziedalis and Potvin (1981), with a large sample of children aged 12–17, found that religiosity was related quite differently to the self-images of boys and girls. For the girls, religion was related to aspects of extraversion such as help-seeking and sociability, and to being rule-bound rather than rebellious, interpreted as needing external guidance. For the boys, religion was related to an activity cluster (adventurous and ambitious), but not to a potency cluster of "macho" scales, and also related to a socialized cluster (nurturance, trusting, and tolerant), interpreted as inner harmony.

It seems that males and females experience the transition from adolescence to adulthood as a crisis and/or an opportunity, but it is more of the former for females. Block and Robins (1993) found that between the ages of 14 and 23, males became more self-confident and females became less self-confident. At age 23, women with high self-esteem valued relationships with others. At age 23, men with high self-esteem were more emotionally distant and controlled in interpersonal relations.

Psychological Femininity

Is religiosity a matter of psychological femininity, rather than sex roles and gender? Thompson (1991) found that both men and women who had a feminine self-image, on the Bem Sex Role Inventory, were more religious, especially as measured by prayer and other devotional activities. In a study of 411 undergraduates, Mercer and Durham (1999) found that those with a feminine or androgynous orientation, of both sexes, were higher on a mysticism scale.

Individuals who choose the priesthood as their life's work are clearly demonstrating a high level of religious commitment, becoming the embodiment of the religious message. What we observe is that the priesthood in many cultures presents indications of an ambiguous and conflicted sexual identity. The idea of a third sex appeared in both emic and etic discourse in many cultures, from the masculine/feminine shaman to European priesthood. Transcending normal sex roles through sex/gender ambiguity or androgyny is tied to "spiritual prowess" or religious authority in many cultures. The discussion of celibacy regarding Roman Catholic priests is one modern example.

Research on the clergy in Western cultures shows the relevance of these notions. It turns out that Western clergy are similar to traditional shamans. Francis (1991) tested British candidates for the clergy (men and women) and concluded that male clergy are more feminine, and female clergy more masculine, than the averages for their sexes. Clergy seem to be different from the general population in terms of sexuality. It has only been possible fairly recently for data on homosexuality to be obtainable, and there are still no proper surveys. Wolf (1989) concluded that about 40% of American Roman Catholic priests are gay; this was the average estimate of the gay priests interviewed. Sipe (1990) interviewed 1,000 Catholic priests, half of them in therapy, and 500 of their sexual partners, and concluded that 20% were in a homosexual relationship and 20% were in a stable relationship with a woman. Male members of the clergy not only differ from the majority of men in sexual orientation, but have problems in object choice, leading to pedophilia (Loftus & Camargo, 1993). Thus it seems that a religious career may be chosen to compensate for problems in sexual identity and to find a shelter from normative sexual and family commitments. Religion as an institution is thus maintained by a mass of women followers and a group of male religious professionals who are ambivalent, ambiguous, or deviant in terms of sexual orientations and practices.

Coping Styles

Women's social status, in interaction with personality dispositions, may create a modal "feminine" coping style. In responding to challenges, great and small, women show a greater tendency to express emotions and seek social support. Long (1990) showed that women are more prone to use emotionally oriented coping and seek more social support in stressful situations when compared with men. Pearlin and Schooler (1978) reported that men use more effective coping strategies than women, and Folkman and Lazarus (1980) found that, on the job, men show a tendency to use more problem-oriented strategies than women. Ilfeld (1980) suggested that women use more resignation and rationalization than men and are less prone to use direct action. All these findings fit traditional stereotypes about women's and men's roles in society (Ptacek, Smith, & Zanas, 1992).

Differences in Socialization

Just as important as personality styles may be the different ways in which boys and girls are socialized. Barry, Bacon, and Child (1957) found that nearly all cultures emphasize nurturance, obedience, and responsibility for girls, while boys are trained for self-reliance and independence.

[T]he socialization of women is said to emphasize conflict resolution, submission, gentleness, nurturance, and other expressive values that are congruent with religious emphases. By contrast, the more instrumental emphases in male socialization are said to make religion less consonant with male roles, values, and self-images. (de Vaus & MacAllister, 1987, p. 472)

It has sometimes been suggested that female socialization includes the expectation of being active in the religious congregation, doing "religious work," supporting and nurturing others, and being subordinate to the clergy.

Women Are Better Socialized

This explanation, which is connected to the previous explanation, suggests that women are on the whole much better socialized than men, and they conform much more to most social norms. This female conformity and its relation to religion was noted by de Beauvoir (1949), who suggested that it has to do with the closeness between mother and daughter. The difference in aggressive tendencies, together with the greater conformity of women, is reflected in the large differences that have been noted in the occurrence of antisocial behavior, which is so much rarer among women (T. E. Moffitt, Caspi, Rutter, & Silva, 2001).

Structural Location in Society

Women are not only well socialized, but they are also the main socializers. They are the main transmitters and

guardians of cultural norms and traditions, including religion, in their maternal role. This role leads to some deprivation. Moberg (1962) suggested that the child-rearing duties of women actually lead to greater social isolation, relieved by the involvement in religious activities. A closely related explanation is that women will be more religious when involved in child-rearing. However, careful analysis in an Australian survey, comparing otherwise similar females with and without children, has found that children have no such effect (de Vaus & McAllister, 1987). The greatest gender difference in this study was found for single individuals; the difference declined during the life cycle and was lowest after children had left home. However, in a study of 2,384 subjects in Holland, Steggarda (1993) found that men, but not women, engaged in child-rearing were more religious, so that there was no gender difference when they both shared this task.

Parental Projection Explanations

None of the theories discussed so far throw any light on the greater sex differences found in membership ratios, especially in Protestant groups. However, Freud's notions of paternal projection can provide an explanation. According to psychoanalytic conceptions of the oedipal period (age 3–6), girls should have a positive attachment to fathers but boys should feel ambivalent about them. Freud then proposed that God is a fantasy and substitute father figure. The main evidence in support of this hypothesis is the finding that images of God are similar to images of parents, particularly to opposite sex parents. For women the image of God, and attitudes to God, are more similar to those towards father, and for men to those towards mother. For women God is seen more often as a healer; He is also seen as more often benevolent rather than punitive. If the culture carries an image of God as male, as a father, this image should therefore appeal more to women. It is also found that Catholics experience God as more like a mother (Rees, 1967); in addition the Virgin Mary and some female saints are very prominent in Catholic worship. This could produce a stronger religious response from males. For Protestants the main object of worship is Jesus, and this should appeal to women. DeConchy (1968) found, in a large study of Roman Catholic children, that for boys the image of God was more often connected with the Virgin Mary, while for girls it was linked more often to Jesus. Also relevant to women's experience is the maleness of most of the clergy, who are addressed as "father" in many religious traditions.

Women Are More Deprived

This explanation looks at women's social status and power: "There is not a single society known where women-as-a-group have decision-making power *over* men or where they define the rules of sexual conduct or control marriage exchanges" (Lerner, 1986, p. 30) It is easy to conclude that women are deprived and oppressed in many social situations. Reporting on the greater religiosity of women in the Soviet Union and then in post-communist Russia, Anderson quotes an unnamed "Intourist guide, who explained that there were greater numbers of women in church 'because women suffer more'" (Anderson, 1993, p. 209).

In many cultures, being a woman often means also being powerless, illiterate, and poor. When being female is tied to lack of social support, religious involvement is more likely (Argyle & Beit-Hallahmi, 1975). Anderson (1993) reported on "... surveys which demonstrated that up to 50 per cent of many congregations were single women" (p. 209). Deprivation often leads members of oppressed groups to coping through imaginary compensation and magical acts, and religion in this case functions as it does with other oppressed groups (Beit-Hallahmi, 1989). A 1989 study of 4,367 adolescents in 13 nations (Australia, Brazil, China, Greece, India, Israel, Kuwait, The Netherlands, The Philippines, Russia, Turkey, the United States, and Venezuela), which looked at coping styles, led to the following conclusion: "We find it a fascinating comment on gender that females responded ... more like lower ... SES groups and more like minority than majority groups! This occurred within all socioeconomic groupings and most countries" (Gibson-Cline, 1996, p. 267).

Women Are Not Allowed to Express Their Sexuality

Explanations of religiosity as related to sexuality are especially relevant to women, who have always been less free to express their sexual impulses. Some reports of mystical experiences, especially in women, seem to reflect diverted sexual energy.

Women Suffer from Predatory Male Sexuality

Beit-Hallahmi (1997) suggested that religion offers women a shelter from the male way of defining and controlling sexuality, which views women as sex objects and regards unattached women as easy prey for male predators. Religion also sacralizes maternity, which is another shelter from male advances.

The Effect of Employment

Luckman (1967) suggested that those most involved in religion are women, especially those not at work, together with the old and young, who are also not at work. There are a number of reasons why women who are not at work should be more active in religion—they have more time, they may feel that they are not filling a valued social role or feel socially isolated, they have narrower social contacts and so are under less secular pressure, and they have less conflict with worldly instrumental activities (de Vaus, 1984). Large-scale surveys show that it is indeed the case that women at work are less active in religion, though not very much less (de Vaus, 1984; Gee, 1991). But how about men—should employment status affect them equally? In an Australian study, de Vaus and McAllister (1987) found that employment was a powerful explanatory variable for female ritual attendance after many controls had been used; it explained a little over half the variance. However, this does not explain the other half of sex differences in religion; when men and women both work, the sex ratio is smaller, but it is not one.

However, the main problem concerns men. In a large-scale American study (de Vaus, 1984) it was found that men were less religious the less they worked, as was also found by Hertel (1988) with data from 14,900 people. The opposite effects of work on attendance for men and women may be because those who play the usual gender roles also play conventional religious ones (Steggarda, 1993). Perhaps women who are independent and assertive enough to go to work are by temperament less attracted to religion, as a later theory will explain. Perhaps men who are out of work are too demoralized to attend religious services. Part of the explanation is simpler—unemployed men are less educated and of lower social class, two groups which are less religious (Hertel, 1988). According to deprivation–frustration theories of religion they should attend religious services more often, but they do not.

Differences in Deity Images

Studies have shown that women hold different images of God. For them God is seen more as a healer, as supportive rather than instrumental (Nelsen, Cheek, & Hau, 1985), and as loving, comforting, and forgiving, where males see him as a supreme power, a driving force, a planner and controller (Wright & Cox, 1967). Yeaman (1987), in a study of members of a radical Roman Catholic association, found that 73% of the women had a "sex-inclusive" image of God, that is, as neither male nor female, compared with 58% of the men. Hood and Hall (1980) tested a sex-related theory of religious experience with 220 students. They found that the females described both their sexual and their mystical experiences, when they had them, in "receptive" terms; the males described their sexual experiences, but not their mystical ones, in "agentic" terms. Therefore the sexual model was supported for females but not for males. These findings indicate that women may experience the religious message in a feminine compensatory way, thus appropriating and creating a female sphere of religiosity which subverts the intent of the male hierarchy.

CONCLUSION

The greater religiosity of women, found in most studies conducted over the past 100 years, is a true cross-cultural finding which is rarely discussed or noted. It seems to grow out of a complex of factors, which include women's typical personality style, their social status, their being better socialized and in the role of socializers in all cultures, and their childhood experiences. The underlying causes range from the innate physiology of women, which makes them less aggressive, to their inferior social position in most cultures. Looking at the phenomenon of women's religiosity and its psychological contexts teaches us much about religion's universal message and its interaction with other social institutions. It also helps us appreciate women's unique ways of coping with both anatomical "destiny" and culture.

REFERENCES

Alland, A., Jr (1962). Possession in a revivalistic Negro church. *Journal for the Scientific Study of Religion, 1*, 204–213.

Anderson, J. (1993). Out of the kitchen, out of the temple: Religion, atheism and women in the Soviet Union. In S. P. Ramet (Ed.), *Religious policy in the Soviet Union* (pp. 206–230). Cambridge, UK: Cambridge University Press.

Argyle, M. (1958). *Religious behaviour*. London: Routledge & Kegan Paul.

Argyle, M., & Beit-Hallahmi, B. (1975). *The social psychology of religion*. London: Routledge & Kegan Paul.

Back, C. W., & Bourque, L. B. (1970). Can feelings be enumerated? *Behavioral Science, 15*, 487–496.

Barfoot, C. H., & Sheppard, G. T. (1980). Prophetic vs. priestly religion: the changing role of women clergy in classical Pentecostal churches. *Review of Religious Research, 22*, 2–17.

Barry, H., Bacon, M. K., & Child, I. L. (1957). A cross-cultural study of sex differences in socialization. *Journal of Abnormal and Social Psychology, 55*, 327–332.

Beit-Hallahmi, B. (1989). *Prolegomena to the psychological study of religion*. Lewisburg, PA: Bucknell University Press.

Beit-Hallahmi, B. (1997). Biology, destiny and change: Women's religiosity and economic development. *Journal of Institutional and Theoretical Economics, 153*, 166–178.

Beit-Hallahmi, B., & Argyle, M. (1997). *The psychology of religious behaviour, belief, and experience*. London: Routledge.

Belle, D. (1982). The stress of caring: Women as providers of social support. In L. Goldberger & S. Breznitz (Eds.), *Handbook of stress: Theoretical and clinical aspects* (pp. 496–505). New York: Free Press.

Block, J. (1976). Issues, problems, and pitfalls in assessing sex differences. *Merrill–Palmer Quarterly, 22*, 283–308.

Block, J., & Robins, R. W. (1993). A longitudinal study of consistency and change in self-esteem from early adolescence to early adulthood. *Child Development, 64*, 909–923.

Buddenbaum, J. (1981). Characteristics and media related needs of the audience for religious television. *Journalism Quarterly, 58*, 266–272.

Cairns, R. B., Cairns, B. D., Neckerman, H. J., Ferguson, L. L., & Gariety, J. L. (1989). Growth and aggression: Childhood to early adolescence. *Developmental Psychology, 25*, 320–330.

Carroll, M. P. (1979). The sex of our gods. *Ethos, 7*, 37–50.

Colquhoun, F. (1955). *Harringay story*. London: Hodder & Stoughton.

Cross, W. (1965). *The burned-over district*. New York: Harper.

Daly, M., & Wilson, M. (1983). *Sex, evolution, and behavior*. Boston: Willard Grant Press.

D'Andrade, R. G. (1967). Sex differences and cultural institutions. In E. E. Maccoby (Ed.) (pp. 174–204). *The development of sex differences*. London: Tavistock Press.

de Beauvoir, S. (1949). *Le deuxieme sexe*. Paris: Gallimard.

DeConchy, J. P. (1968). God and parental images: The masculine and feminine in religious free associations. In A. Godin (Ed.), *From cry to word*. Brussels: Lumen-Vitae.

Depression Guideline Panel. (1993). *Depression in primary care: Vol. 1. Diagnosis and detection*. Rockville, MD: Department of Health and Human Services.

de Vaus, D. A. (1984). Workforce participation and sex differences in church attendance. *Review of Religious Research, 25*, 247–256.

de Vaus, D., & McAllister, I. (1987). Gender differences in religion: A test of the structural location theory. *American Sociological Review, 52*, 472–481.

Eagly, A. H. (1987). *Sex differences in social behavior: A social role interpretation*. Hillsdale, NJ: Erlbaum.

Eagly, A. H. (1995). The science and politics of comparing women and men. *American Psychologist, 50*, 145–158.

Eagly, A. H., & Steffen, V. J. (1986). Gender and aggressive behavior: A meta-analytic review of the social psychological literature. *Psychological Bulletin, 100*, 303–330.

Eibl-Eibesfeldt, I. (1989). *Human ethology*. New York: Aldine de Gruyter.

Emmons, C. F., & Sobal, J. (1981). Paranormal beliefs: Testing the marginality hypothesis. *Sociological Focus, 14*, 49–56.

Fichter, J. H. (1952). The profile of Catholic religious life. *American Journal of Sociology, 58*, 145–149.

Firth, S. (1997). *Dying, death and bereavement in a Hindu community*. Leuven, The Netherlands: Peeters.

Folkman, S., & Lazarus, R. S. (1980). An analysis of coping behavior in a middle-aged community sample. *Journal of Health and Social Behavior, 21*, 219–239.

Francis, L. J. (1991). The personality characteristics of Anglican ordinands: Feminine men and masculine women? *Personality and Individual Differences, 12*, 1133–1140.

Gallup, G. H. (1977). *The Gallup poll*. New York: Random House.

Gallup, G. H. (1980). *Index to international public opinion*. Westport, CT: Greenwood Press.

Gallup, G., & Castelli, J. (1989). *The people's religion*. London: Collier Macmillan.

Gallup, G., Jr., & Lindsay, D. M. (1999). *Surveying the religious landscape—Trends in U.S. beliefs*. Harrisburg, PA: Morehouse.

Garai, J. E., & Scheinfeld, A. (1968). Sex differences in mental and behavioral traits. *Genetic Psychology Monographs, 77*, 169–299.

Geary, D. C. (1998). *Male, female: The evolution of human sex differences*. Washington, DC: American Psychological Association.

Gee, E. M. (1991). Gender differences in church attendance in Canada: The role of labor force participation. *Review of Religious Research, 32*, 267–273.

Geertz, C. (1964). Ideology as a cultural system. In D. E. Apter (Ed.), *Ideology and discontent*. New York: Free Press.

Gerard, D. (1985). Religious attitudes and values. In M. Abrams, D. Gerard, & N. Timms (Eds.), *Values and social change in Britain*. London: Macmillan.

Gibson-Cline, J. (Ed.). (1996). *Adolescence: From crisis to coping—A thirteen nation study*. Oxford: Butterworth Heinemann.

Gorer, G. (1955). *Exploring English character*. London: Cresset.

Gray, J. A. (1971). Sex differences in emotional behaviour in mammals including man: Endocrine basis. *Acta Psychologica, 35*, 29–46.

Hay, D. (1982). *Exploring inner space*. Harmondsworth, UK: Penguin.

Hertel, B. R. (1988). Gender, religious identity and work force participation. *Journal for the Scientific Study of Religion, 27*, 574–592.

Hoffman, M. L. (1977). Sex differences in empathy and related behaviors. *Psychological Bulletin, 84*, 712–722.

Hollinger, F., & Smith, T. B. (2002). Religion and esotericism among students: A cross-cultural comparative study. *Journal of Contemporary Religion, 17*, 229–249.

Hood, R. W., & Hall, J. R. (1980). Gender differences in the description of erotic and mystical experiences. *Review of Religious Research, 21*, 195–207.

Ilfeld, F. W. (1980 June). Coping styles of Chicago adults: Description. *Journal of Human Stress, 6*, 2–10.

James, W. (1956). *The will to believe*. New York: Dover. (Original work published 1897.)

Kaldor, P., et al. (1994). *Winds of change*. Homebush West, NSW, Australia: Anzea.

Kaplan, M. (1983). A woman's view of DSM-III. *American Psychologist, 38*, 786–792.

Lenski, G. (1953). Social correlates of religious interest. *American Sociological Review, 18*, 533–544.

Lerner, G. (1986). *The creation of patriarchy*. New York: Oxford University Press.

Loewenthal, K. M., MacLeod, A. K., & Cinnirella, M. (2002). Are women more religious than men? Evidence from a short measure of religious activity applicable in different religious groups in the UK. *Personality and Individual Differences, 32*, 133–139.

Loftus, J. A., & Camargo, R. J. (1993). Treating the clergy. *Annals of Sex Research, 6*, 287–303.

Long, B. C. (1990). Relation between coping strategies, sex-type traits, and environmental characteristics: A comparison of male and female managers. *Journal of Counseling Psychology, 37*, 185–194.

Luckmann, T. (1967). *The invisible religion*. New York: Macmillan.

Maccoby, E. E. (1988). Gender as a social category. *Developmental Psychology, 24*, 755–765.

Maccoby, E., & Jacklin, C. (1974). *The psychology of sex differences*. Stanford, CA: Stanford University Press.

Markle, G. E., Petersen, J. C., & Wagenfeld, M. O. (1978). Notes from the cancer underground: Participation in the Laetrile movement. *Social Science and Medicine, 12*, 31–57.

McGrath, E., Keita, G. P., Strickland, B., & Russo, N. F. (1990). *Women and depression: Risk factors and treatment issues*. Washington, DC: American Psychological Association.

McGuiness, D. (1993). Gender differences in cognitive style: Implications for mathematics performance and achievement. In L. A. Penner, G. M. Batche, H. M. Knoff, & D. L. Nelson (Eds.), *The challenge of mathematics and science education: Psychology's response*. Washington, DC: American Psychological Association.

McQuarrie, E., Kramer, M., & Bonnet, M. (1980). Sex differences in dream content. *Sleep Research, 9*, 156–160.

Mercer, C., & Durham, T. W. (1999). Religious mysticism and gender orientation. *Journal for the Scientific Study of Religion, 38*, 175–182.

Miller, A. S., & Hoffmann, J. P. (1995). Risk and religion: An exploration of gender differences in religiosity. *Journal for the Scientific Study of Religion, 34*, 63–75.

Miller, J. B. (1986). *Toward a new psychology of women*. Boston: Beacon.

Moberg, D. O. (1962). *The church as a social institution*. Englewood Cliffs, NJ: Prentice-Hall.

Moffitt, A. R., Kramer, M., & Hoffmann, R. F. (Eds.). (1993). *The functions of dreaming*. Albany, NY: State University of New York Press.

Moffitt, T. E., Caspi, A., Rutter, M., & Silva, P. A. (2001). *Sex differences in antisocial behaviour*. Cambridge, UK: Cambridge University Press.

Needham, R. (1972). *Belief, language and experience*. Oxford: Blackwell.

Nelsen, H. M., Cheek, N. H., & Hau, P. (1985). Gender differences in images of God. *Journal for the Scientific Study of Religion, 24*, 396–402.

Nolen-Hoeksema, S. (1990). *Sex differences in depression*. Stanford, CA: Stanford University Press.

Nolen-Hoeksema, S. (1995). Gender differences in coping with depression across the lifespan. *Depression, 3*, 81–90.

Opie, I. (1993). *The people in the playground*. New York: Oxford University Press.

Pearlin, L. I., & Schooler, C. (1978). The structure of coping. *Journal of Health and Social Behavior, 19*, 2–21.

Pratto, F., Sidanius, J., & Stallworth, L. M. (1993). Sexual selection and the sexual and ethnic basis of social hierarchy. In L. Ellis (Ed.), *Social stratification and socioeconomic inequality: Vol. 1. A comparative biosocial analysis*. Westport, CT: Praeger.

Ptacek, J. T., Smith, R. E., & Zanas, J. (1992). Gender, appraisal and coping: A longitudinal analysis. *Journal of Personality, 60*, 747–770.

Rees, D. G. (1967). *Denominational concepts of God*. Unpublished M.A. Thesis, University of Liverpool, UK.

Rohner, R. P. (1976). Sex differences in aggression: Phylogenetic and enculturation perspectives. *Ethos, 4*, 57–72.

Sipe, A. W. R. (1990). *A secret world: Sexuality and the search for celibacy*. New York: Brunner–Mazel.

Spence, J. T., & Helmreich, R. L. (1978). *Masculinity and femininity: Their psychological dimensions, correlates, and antecedents*. Austin, TX: University of Texas Press.

Stark, R. (2002). Physiology and faith: Addressing the "universal" gender difference in religious commitment. *Journal for the Scientific Study of Religion, 41*, 495–507.

Steggarda, M. (1993). Religion and the social positions of women and men. *Social Compass, 65*, 73.

Suziedalis, A., & Potvin, R. H. (1981). Sex differences in factors affecting religiousness among Catholic adolescents. *Journal for the Scientific Study of Religion, 20*, 38–51.

Tamminen, K. (1994). Religious experiences in childhood and adolescence: A viewpoint of religious development between the ages of 7 and 20. *International Journal for the Psychology of Religion, 4*, 61–85.

Thompson, E. H. (1991). Beneath the status characteristic: Gender variations in religiousness. *Journal for the Scientific Study of Religion, 30*, 381–394.

Thorne, B. (1993). *Gender play: Girls and boys in school*. New Brunswick, NJ: Rutgers University Press.

Turner, H. A. (1994). Gender and social support: Taking the bad with the good? *Sex Roles, 30*, 521–541.

Wallace, A. F. C. (1966). *Religion: An anthropological view*. New York: Random House.

Weber, M. (1968). *Economy and society*. New York: Bedminster.

White, S., McAllister, I., & Kryshtanovskaya, O. (1994). Religion and politics in postcommunist Russia. *Religion, State and Society, 22*, 73–88.

Wilson, B. R. (1961). *Sects and society*. London: Heinemann.

Wolf, J. G. (Ed.). (1989). *Gay priests*. New York; HarperCollins.

Wondimu, H., Beit-Hallahmi, B., & Abbink, J. (2001). *Ethnic identity, stereotypes, and psychological modernity in Ethiopian young adults: Identifying the potential for change*. Amsterdam: KIT.

Wright, D. (1971). *The psychology of moral behaviour*. Harmondsworth, UK: Penguin.

Wright, D., & Cox, E. (1967). A study of the relationship between moral judgment and religious belief in a sample of British adolescents. *Journal of Social Psychology, 72*, 135–144.

Wuthnow, R. (1976). Astrology and marginality. *Journal for the Scientific Study of Religion, 15*, 157–168.

Yeaman, P. A. (1987). Prophetic voices: Differences between men and women. *Review of Religious Research, 28*, 367–376.

Yinger, J. M. (1970). *The scientific study of religion*. London: Collier Macmillan.

Zeidner, M., & Beit-Hallahmi, B. (1988). Sex, ethnic, and social class differences in parareligious beliefs among Israeli adolescents. *Journal of Social Psychology, 128*, 333–343.

Zulehner, P., & Denz, H. (1993). *Wie Europa lebt und glaubt*. Dusseldorf, Germany: Patmos.

Gender-Based Social Groups

Carol R. Ember and Melvin Ember

INTRODUCTION

In most of the societies known to anthropology, married couples live with or near the groom's or bride's kin. Since no existing society allows sex or marriage between brothers and sisters or between parents and children, some children when they grow up must leave their homes or home villages and move to their spouses' natal places of residence. But who leaves? There are only a few choices—females only leave, which we call patrilocal or virilocal residence; males only leave, which we call matrilocal or uxorilocal residence; females or males leave, which we call bilocal residence; both males and females leave, which we call neolocal residence; neither gender leaves, which we call duolocal residence. (Then, there is avunculocal residence—see below.) These patterns of marital residence can have profound psychological consequences for the individuals involved, and for the social organization of the society, as we shall see. For example, the most common pattern of residence is patrilocal residence; the couple lives with or near the husband's parents. In a society with this pattern of residence, many if not all the males in the band or village are likely to be related to each other, but only some of the in-marrying women are likely to be related to each other. So an in-marrying woman not only has to deal with leaving her natal family, but she also has to deal with the fact that she is moving into a situation where the husband is surrounded by his kin, and her kin are somewhere else, sometimes far away. Minturn (1993, pp. 54–71) has published the text of a letter that one new Rajput bride sent to her mother shortly after marrying into her husband's village. The letter was written when the bride had been gone for 6 weeks. She repeatedly asked if her mother, her father, her aunts had forgotten her. She begged to be called home and said her bags were packed. She described herself as "a parrot in a cage" and complained about her in-laws. Seven years later the mother reported that the daughter was finally happy. But some other brides had serious symptoms of psychological distress—ghost possession, serious depression, or suicide after their marriages.

We know of no systematic research on the psychological state of in-marrying women, but the anecdotal evidence provided by Minturn and others points to considerable stress. Do men in matrilocal (uxorilocal) societies, where couples live with or near the wife's parents, have similar stress? We do not know. But there is reason to think that stress for men is not as serious in matrilocal societies because, as we shall see later, men in matrilocal societies usually do not move far away from their kin; indeed, they may merely move "across the street."

Because marital residence is the main predictor of the kinds of transfamily kin groups there may be, we first address what seems to explain the variation in marital residence patterns. Then we discuss what might explain the kinds of kin or descent group that may develop when people practice patrilocal, matrilocal, bilocal, or neolocal residence. We then briefly examine some unisex associations. We close with a brief look at some of the likely consequences of gender-based social organization.

PATTERNS OF MARITAL RESIDENCE

There are three gender-neutral rules of residence. They are neolocal residence, where couples live apart from the kin of either spouse, bilocal (ambilocal) residence, where couples can live with either set of parents, and duolocal residence, where both the husband and wife remain in their own homes. The last residence pattern mentioned, duolocal residence, is exceedingly rare and usually occurs where the marriage bond is very weak (see the article on the Mosuo in this encyclopedia). Because duolocal residence is so rare, we shall not deal with it any further here. Most societies known to anthropology do not have gender-neutral patterns. Bilocal residence only occurs in about 7% of the world's societies, and neolocal in about 5% (see Figure 1).

While bilocal residence looks like a couple may choose with whom they want to reside, the choice is probably based more on who is still alive that you could

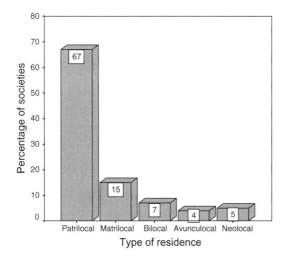

Figure 1. The percentage of societies with each type of residence. Calculated from *Cross tabulations of Murdock's world ethnographic sample*, by A. D. Coult and R. Habenstein, 1965, Columbia, MO: University of Missouri Press.

live and work with. Service (1962, p. 137) suggested that depopulation of indigenous populations may have been responsible for much of the observed bilocal residence in the anthropological record. In the last 400 years, contact with Europeans in many parts of the world resulted in severe population losses among the local people who lacked resistance to European diseases. Even diseases that were not killers to Europeans (e.g., colds, measles) caused widespread mortality in newly contacted populations, particularly in regions furthest from Europe (e.g., the New World and the islands of the far Pacific). With severe population losses, a population with a unilocal residence rule (patrilocal or matrilocal) would not be able to maintain it. Assuming that couples need to live and work with kin, they would be forced to be pragmatic and live with whichever group of relatives was still alive. Thus a couple in a patrilocal (matrilocal) society might not have enough husband's (wife's) relatives to live with, and the likely consequence would be a pattern of bilocal residence— some couples living with the husband's relatives and some couples living with the wife's relatives. We designed a test (C. R. Ember & Ember, 1972) of Service's interpretation, using data from a worldwide sample of societies, and it turned out to support Service's theory: societies with bilocal residence and appreciably frequent departures from unilocal residence (multilocal residence) were significantly likely to have been depopulated in their recent

history. Some other factors also seem to predict bilocality and multilocality among hunter–gatherers (unpredictable rainfall in an arid environment and very small communities; C. R. Ember, 1975). But generally, depopulation appears to be the most important predictor of bilocal residence (C. R. Ember & Ember, 1972). Thus, residence patterns that depart from gender-based patterns are probably recent phenomena, due mostly to the depopulation that often accompanied contact with expanding Europeans.

The presence of a commercial or a money economy, which is also a recent phenomenon in some regions, is probably what mainly makes neolocal residence possible. Couples can buy the goods and services they need without having to depend much on kin. Cross-culturally, money and commercial exchange do predict neolocal residence (M. Ember, 1967a). Although neolocal residence is not very common in the anthropological record in terms of percentages of societies (see Figure 1), it has increased in frequency as commercialization has become more and more important in the world.

Let us now turn to the gender-based patterns of residence.

MALE-BASED VERSUS FEMALE-BASED RESIDENCE PATTERNS

The two most prevalent residence patterns are patrilocal (67% of the world's societies) and matrilocal (15% of the world's societies). There is one residence pattern that we have not yet discussed. It is called avunculocal residence. In this unusual pattern, couples live with the husband's mother's brother. Although it might be that both sons and daughters leave their homes to go to the husband's mother's brother, sometimes a boy will marry his mother's brother's daughter, in which case the wife remains home after her marriage. And if a boy has previously moved to his mother's brother's house, avunculocal residence may mean that neither the bride nor the groom leaves home after they get married. Avunculocal residence does result in males being localized, but instead of father and son, it is a man and his sister's son. Avunculocal residence is difficult to explain without first discussing matrilineal descent, so we will come back to this pattern later.

The major contrast, and perhaps the most important to explain, is why a society would choose to have sons stay (patrilocal residence) or daughters stay (matrilocal residence). In other words, what explains patrilocality versus matrilocality?

For many years the traditional explanation of residential choice was that it was a function of who the "breadwinner" was. Presumably parents would be reluctant to let the gender contributing most to the economy leave home. To test this explanation, one can compare those societies with a high male contribution to basic food-getting activities (gathering, hunting, fishing, herding, agriculture) and those with a high female contribution to see if degree of contribution does predict residence. Two separate studies found *no* support for this simple expectation (Divale, 1974; M. Ember & Ember, 1971). Of course, this result does not mean that subsistence contribution has no effect; it may simply mean that subsistence contribution has no simple effect on residence (Korotayev, 2003; Pasternak, Ember, & Ember, 1997, p. 223). Indeed, the relationship between residence and subsistence contribution may be masked by a more important factor—the type of warfare in the society.

Most societies in the world have had warfare, by which we mean armed combat between communities or larger territorial units. In most societies people fight with communities belonging to the same language group or society—we call such warfare *internal warfare.* However, some societies have purely *external warfare*, or warfare only with people of a different society who speak a different language. Usually, then, in these societies, the "enemies" are more distant than speakers of the same language. We have reasoned that if a community may be attacked by one or more nearby communities, parents would want their sons at home to protect them (M. Ember & Ember, 1971). They would mistrust potential sons-in-law from other communities because such communities could have been enemy communities in the past or could be in the future. Daughters might be valuable economically if they do much of the subsistence work, but we argue that security concerns would take precedence over economic considerations, and so patrilocal residence should be favored when the warfare is at least sometimes internal, when the enemies might be coming from close by. On the other hand, if daughters contribute a great deal to the economy and warfare is purely external, parents need not worry who stays at home after marriage. There is no reason to suppose that a son-in-law would not defend the family against people attacking from another society. It is this situation (purely external warfare and women

contributing a great deal to subsistence) that should favor matrilocal rather than patrilocal residence. Cross-cultural research confirms that internal warfare predicts patrilocal residence and purely external warfare predicts matrilocal residence (Divale, 1974; M. Ember & Ember, 1971). Furthermore, the combination of purely external warfare and relatively high female contribution to subsistence predicts matrilocal residence even more strongly, and patrilocal residence is predicted by internal warfare or by males doing most of the subsistence work (C. R. Ember, 1974, endnote 2).

It should be noted that Divale (1974) has different interpretations for the relationship between internal warfare and patrilocality and for the relationship between purely external warfare and matrilocality. Whereas the Embers argue that type of warfare is a cause of matrilocal or patrilocal residence, Divale (1974) argues that type of warfare is a consequence of residence. More specifically, he suggests that residence will "normally" be patrilocal because males are generally dominant. Citing "fraternal interest group theory," Divale suggests that localized groups of related males are likely to get into fights with other such groups in nearby communities, creating internal warfare. He suggests that matrilocal residence develops when people migrate into an already inhabited area and the intruding society cannot afford internal fighting, which would make it adaptive to switch to matrilocal residence to promote internal harmony. Divale assumes that matrilocal residence promotes internal peacefulness because it scatters related males. Divale's cross-cultural research seems to support his interpretation of matrilocality; it does seem to be associated with migration into previously inhabited areas. But there are a number of problems with Divale's causal theory (C. R. Ember, 1974). First, migration and matrilocality are not that strongly associated. Only about half of the migrating societies in Divale's sample are matrilocal. If matrilocality were so advantageous for promoting peace, why did not most migrating societies become matrilocal? Second, how would people have realized the peace-keeping potential of matrilocal residence? It is not until matrilocal residence is in existence that related males are scattered. Third, size of society seems to predict purely external warfare. Societies under 21,000 people are likely to have internal peace, perhaps because a population of that size or smaller facilitates informal connections between people that can minimize the risk of fighting. Matrilocal societies are significantly smaller than patrilocal societies, so perhaps they are unlikely to have internal warfare for this reason alone.

The Embers' theory and the Divale theory both explain why patrilocality is much more prevalent than matrilocality. Divale says that male dominance is responsible. But males are dominant in all known societies, so how come patrilocality is not universal? If the Embers are right, matrilocality occurs only with the combination of purely external warfare and women contributing a good deal to subsistence; patrilocality would occur either because of internal war (more common than purely external war) or because men did most of the subsistence work (more common than equal or high women's contribution).

MALE- AND FEMALE-ORIENTED DESCENT GROUPS

It is one thing to live together in the same community with relatives; it is quite another to have unilineal descent groups. Unilineal (literally, "one line") descent groups exist where people consider themselves to be descended from a common ancestor through one gender only. If we speak of patrilineal descent, membership in the patrilineal descent group is passed through males only (membership is acquired from the father); members of both sexes belong through their fathers. If we speak of matrilineal descent, membership in the matrilineal descent group is passed through females only (membership is acquired from the mother). A group is more than a category of people, so to call it a group there must be some things that are done or regulated by the group (e.g., collectively using land owned by or assigned to the group, collectively avenging an attack on a member of the group). Some close relatives are always excluded from your own unilineal group. For example, if a society has matrilineal descent groups, membership in a group (usually named) is acquired from your mother (full brothers and sisters are always in the same unilineal group because they share the same mother), but your father is usually not in your kin group. If the society is patrilineal, your mother is not usually in your kin group. Most societies with unilineal descent have a rule of exogamy with respect to at least one level of kin group; you are usually precluded from marrying someone in your smallest unilineal group. The rule of exogamy often extends to the largest unilineal group. Among the Luo of Kenya, for example, one is prohibited

from marrying anyone in the same maximal lineage that might extend back 14 or more generations (C. R. Ember, 1970). Societies with parallel-cousin marriage, that is, marriage to father's brothers' children and mother's sisters' children, which is common in the Arab world, are exceptional to the rule that unilineal descent groups are normally exogamous. In the Arab world, your father's brothers and their children, your parallel cousins, belong to your group, and marriage may be allowed or even preferred with a parallel cousin.

Besides regulating marriage, unilineal descent groups may have many different functions in a society. Many unilineal descent groups function as corporate landholders, allocating portions of the group's land for use by descent group members. Labor may be organized by descent group. Different unilineal groups may have their own gods, goddesses, or ancestral spirits. And unilineal groups also often function politically, either with elders or heads functioning as arbiters of disputes, or as offensive or defensive fighting units.

Why do unilineal descent groups develop? It has generally been assumed that patrilocal or matrilocal residence is a necessary precondition for the emergence of unilineal descent (Lowie, 1961, pp. 157–162; Murdock, 1949, pp. 59–60; Service, 1962, p. 122). After all, if a rule of descent is followed over time, then persons who descend from a common ancestor will be localized in the same neighborhood. Therefore it would be easy for those people to conceive themselves as descending from a common ancestor. But there are reasons to be skeptical that unilocal residence is a sufficient reason for creating unilineal descent. First, it may be easy to form a group, but that does not require people to do so. Second, in a cross-cultural comparison looking at the relationship between unilocal residence and unilineal descent (C. R. Ember, Ember, & Pasternak, 1974), only 72% of unilocal societies had unilineal descent. This is a high percentage, but 28% of the unilocal societies lack unilineal descent, consistent with the idea that the residence pattern is not sufficient to explain the development of unilineal descent groups. On the other hand, unilocal residence does look necessary in order for unilineal descent groups to develop. Of the unilineal societies in the sample, 97% have unilocal residence!

What condition or conditions would push a unilocal society to develop unilineal descent? Building on Service's (1962, p. 117; cf. Sahlins, 1961) observation that intersociety competition favors the development of pan-tribal sodalities such as unilineal kin groups to provide fighting units for offense and defense, we have suggested (C. R. Ember et al., 1974) that in the absence of centralized political systems, unilineal kin groups are the most likely solution to any kind of warfare, internal or external. First, unilineal kin groups provide unambiguous sets of kin with no conflicting loyalties. Everyone knows exactly who is in, and who is not in, their unilineal group. In bilateral societies, which have no descent groups, any transfamily kin groups are overlapping and nondiscrete, and therefore loyalties are conflicting. Second, unilineal kin groups, in contrast with neighborhood associations, have the advantage of being able to draw upon larger sets of people to whom connections can be remembered (or sometimes invented). (We discuss below why age-sets, or nonkin associations, may also develop.) The presence of warfare does improve our ability to predict that a unilocal society will also have unilineal descent. In contrast to the 72% of unilocal societies that have unilineal descent (mentioned earlier), 91% of unilocal societies with warfare have unilineal descent. Thus, although we cannot be certain that warfare causes unilineal descent to develop, in the absence of centralized political organization, the data are consistent with that theory (C. R. Ember et al., 1974).

There is one kind of descent system that is gender neutral. (Bilateral kinship is not a descent system.) Ambilineal descent is found in some societies. Instead of taking the descent group membership of one parent, some societies allow individuals to join a descent group through males or females. Ambilineal descent, however, is probably a departure from unilineal descent caused by a switch to bilocal or multilocal residence (C. R. Ember & Ember, 1972).

Some societies have double unilineal descent, both matrilineal and patrilineal groups exist. Murdock (1940/1965) and others have speculated that these are societies in transition from one form of descent system to another.

DIFFERENCES BETWEEN MATRILINEAL AND PATRILINEAL SYSTEMS

One of the classical paradoxes about matrilineality is that it is *not* the mirror image of a patrilineal system. It differs in one important feature that has important structural consequences. Schneider (1961, p. 7) pointed out that the lines of authority and descent *diverge* in matrilineal societies, but *converge* in patrilineal societies. This is because males are usually the political leaders in all societies. So in a patrilineal society, descent and political authority (if there is a rule of succession) pass through males; authority, like membership, passes from father to son. In a matrilineal society, descent passes through females, but authority is passed from a man to his sister's son. Recall that in a matrilineal system, children take their descent membership from their mother, so brothers and sisters always share the same descent group membership. The father would not be the authority figure in that descent group; rather, the mother's brother would be. If there is an authority position held by males, the successor is normally the sister's son.

Schneider (1961, p. 27; cf. Kloos, 1963) also pointed to the greater difficulty of maintaining a one-kin group community in matrilineal societies as compared with patrilineal societies. The difficulty arises from the fact that if males are to be effective authority figures for their matrilineal kin groups, it would be better if they did not move far away when they marry; that is, it would be better if marital residence were matrilocal. In fact, most matrilineal societies have matrilocal residence. Accordingly, we would expect another difference between patrilineal societies and matrilineal societies: matrilineal matrilocal societies should be unlikely to require marriage with someone outside the community (local exogamy). Aberle (1961, pp. 715–717) found that matrilineal societies are significantly less likely to have local exogamy than patrilineal societies; we also found (M. Ember & Ember, 1971) that matrilocal societies are significantly less likely to have local exogamy. The flip side of this is that matrilineal matrilocal societies are much more likely to have communities composed or more than one descent group. If a unilineal society requires marriage outside the descent group, which is commonly the rule, there would be no one to marry in the community unless it contained more than one descent group.

Earlier we mentioned the psychological stress experienced by an in-marrying female in a patrilocal society. We raised the question of whether men would feel the same kind of stress. Although we do not know for sure, the structural differences between the two types of society suggest that men in matrilocal matrilineal societies would probably not be exposed to the same degree of stress. Husbands would generally not have to move far away when they got married if marriages generally involve people from the same community. Thus the men could still retain important roles in their own descent groups. In contrast, females in patrilocal patrilineal societies not only generally have to move to other communities, but they also have to move into a community whose core members belong to a descent group that is not theirs. Ties to their own descent group would mostly be severed or minimized by the distance from their "home" community.

Avunculocal Residence

Now that we understand more about the differences between matrilineal and patrilineal systems, the puzzling form of residence called avunculocal may be understandable. Recall that in this form of residence the couple lives with the husband's mother's brother. Or, to put it the opposite way, we could say that a man takes his sister's son and wife to live with him. This is precisely the dyad that forms the basis of political succession in a matrilineal system. It is also a way of localizing men who are matrilineally, rather than patrilineally, related. Not surprisingly, all avunculocal societies have matrilineal descent (M. Ember, 1974, p. 251). But most matrilineal societies are matrilocal, so why should some be avunculocal?

M. Ember (1974, pp. 250–251) suggested that avunculocal residence may be favored by the same condition that favors patrilocal residence—internal warfare. Normally, purely external warfare is characteristic of matrilocal societies. But if warfare in such societies should switch from purely external to at least sometimes internal, the matrilineal descent groups that are present might want to keep their males (i.e., their warriors) in the same place after they are married. Avunculocal residence would do that. Consistent with this theory, that avunculocality develops in a previous matrilineal society that started to fight internally, *all* societies with either invariably avunculocal residence or alternatively avunculocal residence have at least some internal warfare (M. Ember, 1974). There are no exceptions in this correlation.

Male Leadership

If most societies are patrilocal, it is not surprising that men are generally the political leaders.[1] A cross-cultural study found that, in about 85% of the surveyed societies, *only* men were the political leaders (Whyte, 1978, p. 271).

But why should men almost always be the political leaders in matrilineal systems also? We suggest that many of the most important political decisions made in a society are about offense and defense. Unfortunately, war has been an almost ubiquitous part of the ethnographic record (C. R. Ember & Ember, 1997). Just as the "economy-of-effort" theory predicts that the gender involved early in a production sequence (e.g., lumbering) will be involved in activities later in the sequence (e.g., making musical instruments), so might this theory predict that those most involved in war (e.g., the warriors) should be the most involved in political decision-making about future wars and therefore would be likely to be the political leaders. To be sure, in matrilocal societies women may not be as excluded from planning war, or other activities involving war, as in patrilocal societies. This difference between matrilocal and patrilocal societies is suggested by a cross-cultural study of women's involvement in war (Adams, 1983). In that study, societies practicing local exogamy and societies with internal warfare were the least likely to have women involved in war. Such societies are also likely to be patrilocal, with single-lineage communities. Adams (1983) suggests that the conflicting loyalties of wives (who may come from "enemy" communities) would lead the men to isolate women from knowledge about war plans and access to weapons. For this reason too, we might expect that patrilocal societies would be likely to exclude women from political leadership.

AGE-SET ORGANIZATION

A unilineal descent rule may be a way to get a transfamily kin group to come to one's aid, but it is not the only possible way to do so. Some societies use age-sets for integrative purposes. An age-set is a group of persons of similar age and sex who move through some or all of life's stages together (C. R. Ember & Ember, 2002, p. 184). Usually the transition occurs at a ceremony or ritual. For example, every 10 years or so, males might be initiated into one status and then move on to others every time a new set becomes initiated or inducted (e.g., "initiates," "warriors," "married men," "mature men," "elders"). Age-sets are usually nonvoluntary associations, and those initiated and "graduating" together form close bonds with each other. Age-sets have a limited distribution and are mostly found in Africa, the North American Plains, and some Ge-speaking groups in the Brazilian Amazon (Ritter, 1980). Ritter (1980) tested a number of theories about the conditions that might favor age-set systems. Contrary to the widely held idea that age-set systems function to integrate societies whose kinship or political groups are not equal to the task, Ritter found that age-set societies are not less likely to have unilineal descent groups or other ways to integrate the actions of different local groups. But consistent with other previous theory, age-set societies have significantly more warfare than other societies. Ritter suggests that age-sets will develop when warfare is very frequent and where the size and composition of the local group fluctuates throughout the year. Usually the fluctuation is required by the subsistence regime (e.g., pastoralists often have to move their herds away from settlements to find grazing). Cross-cultural tests support this hypothesis. Age-set societies may have unilineal descent groups and political integration of different local groups, but the age-sets would provide reliable allies during the periods of mobility and separation. Wherever you may be, you could find age-mates. But you may not be close to members of your descent group or political unit. Presumably, fully sedentary societies or fully nomadic societies would not need age-set organization for defense or offense because their descent groups would not ever disperse during the year.

Many of the societies with male age-sets also have female age-sets. For example, the Shavante have female age-sets into which girls are inducted when males are inducted into their age-sets (Maybury-Lewis, 1967). However, the age-sets for females do not seem to be as important as those for males.

OTHER UNISEX ASSOCIATIONS BESIDES AGE-SETS

Age-sets are not the most common unisex associations in noncommercial societies. Many societies have male associations with initiation rites that provide a dramatic (and often traumatic) way for boys to become transformed from "boys" to "manhood." These men's groups often have a building where initiates and adult men may meet and sleep. A number of ideas have been put forward to explain male initiation ceremonies, ranging from a way to help boys resolve psychological conflicts in sex-role identification (Burton & Whiting, 1961; Whiting,

Kluckhohn, & Anthony, 1958), to promoting male solidarity for cooperative purposes (Young, 1965), to providing the equivalent of basic army training (M. Ember, 1967b). There is some evidence to support all of these interpretations.

Women's associations are not that common in non-commercial societies. But in some partly commercialized economies, such as in West Africa, women's associations are common. Many of these associations, such as rotating credit associations (Ardener & Burman, 1995), help women obtain money for economic enterprises. While these associations are often for women of the same ethnic background, in Papua New Guinea some of the associations link thousands of women from different tribal areas (Warry, 1986).

In complex commercial–industrial societies, there are many types of voluntary associations. Some are explicitly unisex (like the Boy Scouts or Girl Scouts), but more often than not these voluntary associations are what political science and sociology call "interest groups" (e.g., political or professional associations), not restricted to one gender.

CONSEQUENCES OF GENDER-RELATED GROUPS

Unilocality and Unilineality

Aside from the psychological stress created for the unimportant gender in a unilocal–unilineal system, which we discussed earlier, what does research suggest about other possible consequences of unilocality and unilineality? One domain that has been investigated is status. Whyte (1978, pp. 132–133) has tested the hypothesis that women will have higher status in matrilocal and matrilineal societies. He measured status in a number of domains ranging from property control to value of labor to domestic authority to informal influence. Matrilocality and matrilineal descent do not predict that well. He finds that in matrilocal and matrilineal societies women do have significantly more control over property than men (including inheritance of property and control over the products of labor). But that was the only area of significant difference. Why? Schlegel's (1972) study of matrilineal societies suggests that variation among matrilineal societies may complicate things with respect to status of women. For example, the degree to which brothers and/or husbands have domestic authority varies across matrilineal societies. As we noted above, a woman's brothers are very often important authority figures. This may be true in the political sphere as well as in the domestic sphere. So even if a woman is relatively autonomous with respect to her husband, she may still be subject to her brother's control. Schlegel's research suggests that women in matrilineal societies have the most autonomy when neither husbands nor brothers are dominant (or both are equally dominant).

Frayser (1985, pp. 341 ff) points out that patrilineal societies have some difficulty with women's reproduction. They need to have reproduction for their kin groups, but elevating the status of mothers is somewhat antithetical to the patrilineal principle. On the other hand, if patrilineal societies denigrate women too much, they risk having women who are not interested in having children. Patrilineal systems depend upon passing membership in kin groups through males, so it is also important for a man to know that the children his wife gives birth to are his. Frayser suggests and presents evidence to support the notion that patrilineal societies are more interested in limiting a woman's sexuality and reproduction to a particular husband by insisting on premarital and extramarital sex restrictions and by making it harder for a woman to obtain a divorce. Restrictive societies also tend to have elaborate marriage arrangements and ceremonies and honeymoons that isolate the couple.

Separate Unisex Associations and Power

If women form their own associations and hold leadership positions within them, does that give women more power and voice in a society? Or, does "separate" merely mean "separate, but unequal" as in segregated schools in the American South? There is only a little systematic research on this question. Ross (1986) looked at the relationship between women's political participation and the presence of separate associations for women. His cross-cultural research suggests that separate women's organizations do not generally predict greater political decision-making or access to political leadership roles. Of course, this does not mean that women in organizations do not have influence. But their influence may not translate to influence beyond their organizations. Future research needs to consider what kind of association women participate in. Women's associations that are adjuncts to male associations (such as a women's auxiliary) may have much less influence than those that control important economic resources.

NOTE

1. Some research in selected societies suggests other factors that may give men a leadership advantage. One is a height advantage; some studies have shown that taller individuals are more likely to become leaders (Werner, 1982). Greater involvement in childcare may also detract from influence (Werner, 1984). Draper (1975) argued that sedentarized !Kung women seemed to lose some of their influence the less gathering they did, perhaps because they knew less about the outside world.

REFERENCES

Aberle, D. F. (1961). Matrilineal descent in cross-cultural perspective. In D. M. Schneider & K. Gough (Eds.), *Matrilineal kinship* (pp. 655–727). Berkeley: University of California Press.

Adams, D. (1983). Why there are so few women warriors. *Behavior Science Research, 18,* 196–212.

Ardener, S., & Burman, S. (1995). *Money-go-rounds.* Oxford, Washington, DC: Berg.

Burton, R., & Whiting, J. W. M. (1961). The absent father and cross-sex identity. *Merrill–Palmer Quarterly, 7*(2), 85–95.

Coult, A., & Habenstein, D. R. (1965). *Cross tabulations of Murdock's world ethnographic sample.* Columbia: University of Missouri Press.

Divale, W. T. (1974). Migration, external warfare, and matrilocal residence. *Behavior Science Research, 9,* 75–133.

Draper, P. (1975). !Kung women: contrasts in sexual egalitarianism in foraging and sedentary contexts. In R. Reiter (Ed.), *Toward an anthropology of women.* New York: Monthly Review Press.

Ember, C. R. (1970). *Effects of feminine task-assignment on the social behavior of boys.* Unpublished doctoral dissertation, Harvard University, New Haven, CT.

Ember, C. R. (1974). An evaluation of alternative theories of matrilocal versus patrilocal residence. *Behavior Science Research, 9,* 135–149. (Reprinted in *Marriage, family, and kinship,* pp. 199–218, by M. Ember & C. R. Ember, Eds., 1983, New Haven, CT: HRAF Press.)

Ember, C. R. (1975). Residential variation among hunter–gatherers. *Behavior Science Research, 10,* 199–227. (Reprinted in *Marriage, family, and kinship,* pp. 274–311, by M. Ember & C. R. Ember, Eds., 1983, New Haven, CT: HRAF Press.)

Ember, C. R., & Ember, M. (1972). The conditions favoring multilocal residence. *Southwestern Journal of Anthropology, 28,* 382–400. (Reprinted in *Marriage, family, and kinship,* pp. 219–248, by M. Ember & C. R. Ember, Eds., 1983, New Haven, CT: HRAF Press.)

Ember, C. R., & Ember, M. (1997). Violence in the ethnographic record: Results of cross-cultural research on war and aggression.

In D. L. Martin & D. W. Frayer (Eds.), *Troubled times: Violence and warfare in the past* (pp. 1–20). Amsterdam: Gordon & Breach.

Ember, C. R., & Ember, M. (2002). *Cultural anthropology*. Upper Saddle River, NJ: Prentice-Hall.

Ember, C. R., Ember, M., & Pasternak, B. (1974). On the development of unilineal descent. *Journal of Anthropological Research, 30*, 69–94. (Reprinted in *Marriage, family, and kinship*, pp. 359–397, by M. Ember & C. R. Ember, Eds., 1983, New Haven, CT: HRAF Press.)

Ember, M. (1967a). The emergence of neolocal residence. *Transactions of the New York Academy of Sciences, 30*, 291–302. (Reprinted in *Marriage, family, and kinship*, pp. 333–357, by M. Ember & C. R. Ember, Eds., 1983, New Haven, CT: HRAF Press.)

Ember, M. (1967b). Still another interpretation of male initiation ceremonies. Presented at the 66th annual meeting of the American Anthropological Association, Washington, DC.

Ember, M. (1974). The conditions that may favor avunculocal residence. *Behavior Science Research, 9*, 203–209. (Reprinted in *Marriage, family, and kinship*, pp. 249–259, by M. Ember & C. R. Ember, Eds., 1983, New Haven, CT: HRAF Press.)

Ember, M., & Ember, C. R. (1971). The conditions favoring matrilocal versus patrilocal residence. *American Anthropologist, 73*, 571–594. (Reprinted in *Marriage, family, and kinship*, pp. 151–197, by M. Ember & C. R. Ember, Eds., 1983, New Haven, CT: HRAF Press.)

Frayser, S. (1985). *Varieties of sexual experience: An anthropological perspective on human sexuality*. New Haven, CT: HRAF Press.

Kloos, P. (1963). Matrilocal residence and local endogamy: Environmental knowledge or leadership. *American Anthropologist, 64*, 854–862.

Korotayev, A. (2003). Division of labor by gender and postmarital residence in cross-cultural perspective: A reconsideration. *Cross-Cultural Research, 37*.

Lowie, R. H. (1961). *Primitive society*. New York: Harper.

Maybury-Lewis, D. (1967). *Akwe-Shavante society*. Oxford: Clarendon Press.

Minturn, L. (1993). *Sita's daughters: Coming out of purdah: The Rajput women of Khalapur revisited*. New York: Oxford University Press.

Murdock, G. P. (1949). *Social structure*. New York: Macmillan.

Murdock, G. P. (1965). Double descent. In G. P. Murdock (Ed.), *Culture and society* (pp. 167–175), Pittsburgh, PA: University of Pittsburgh Press. (Reprinted from *American Anthropologist, 42*, pp. 167–175, 1940.)

Pasternak, B., Ember, C. R., & Ember, M. (1997). *Sex, gender, and kinship: A cross-cultural perspective*. Upper Saddle River, NJ: Prentice-Hall.

Ritter, M. L. (1980). The conditions favoring age-set organization. *Journal of Anthropological Research, 36*, 87–104.

Ross, M. H. (1986). Female political participation: A cross-cultural explanation. *American Anthropologist, 88*, 843–858.

Sahlins, M. D. (1961). The segmentary lineage: An organization of predatory expansion. *American Anthropologist, 63*, 322–345.

Schlegel, A. (1972). *Male dominance and female autonomy: Domestic authority in matrilineal societies*. New Haven, CT: HRAF Press.

Schneider, D. (1961). Introduction: The distinctive features of matrilineal descent groups. In D. M. Schneider & K. Gough (Eds.), *Matrilineal kinship* (pp. 1–29). Berkeley: University of California Press.

Service, E. R. (1962). *Primitive social organization: An evolutionary perspective*. New York: Random House.

Warry, W. (1986). Kafaina: Female wealth and power in Chuave, Papua New Guinea. *Oceania, 57*, 4–21.

Werner, D. (1982). Chiefs and presidents: A comparison of leadership traits in the United States and among the Mekranoti-Kayapo of Central Brazil. *Ethos, 10*, 136–148.

Werner, D. (1984). Child care and influence among the Mekranoti of Central Brazil. *Sex Roles, 10*, 395–404.

Whiting, J. W. M., Kluckhohn, R., & Anthony, A. (1958). The function of male initiation ceremonies at puberty. In E. E. Maccoby, T. M. Newcomb, & E. L. Hartley (Eds.), *Readings in social psychology* (3rd ed., pp. 359–370). New York: Holt.

Whyte, M. (1978). *The status of women in preindustrial societies*. Princeton, NJ: Princeton University Press.

Young, F. W. (1965). *Initiation ceremonies*. Indianapolis, IN: Bobbs-Merrill.

The Relative Status of Men and Women

Maxine L. Margolis

INTRODUCTION

What is meant by the "status" of men and women in cultures around the world? Anthropologists do not agree on what the relative status of the two sexes means in the abstract nor do they agree on how to measure it. Does equal status mean "equal" rights for men and women in society? Some argue that the key to status is the relative power and authority of men and women and the roles of both sexes in decision-making, while others say it refers to how a particular society values the qualities that are defined as masculine versus those defined as feminine. Still others look to the work that men and women do and ask if it is equally valued. And this, in turn, leads some to question whether separate can also be equal. Others try to gauge if men and women have equal rights to live their lives as they see fit. Do women have personal autonomy and do they fully participate in the institutions of their society at large or are they barred from public life and primarily confined to the domestic sphere? Still others suggest that the regulation of sexual access to females is the key to their status. Is divorce equally available to women and men? Is there a double standard in the premarital and extramarital sexual activities of men and women, that is, do men have more sexual freedom than women?

Do all of these conditions co-vary? Do women have equal rights to men in some areas of life but not others? For example, do they have the right to inherit property but no say over whom they marry? Do women enjoy the same sexual freedom as men but have little influence on political decisions? Research suggests that these areas are not always related and that status does vary from one sphere to another. In fact, some researchers insist that so many elements comprise women's status that we cannot generalize about "low-status" and "high-status" societies (Quinn, 1977). Nevertheless, here we will take a broad overview and suggest that in some societies women's status is high in many spheres of life, while in others it is not (Whyte, 1978).

In any discussion of gender status, two central questions are whether male dominance is universal and whether female-dominant societies have ever existed. Today, with very few exceptions, social scientists see male dominance as widespread but certainly not universal, and nearly all researchers have abandoned the idea that in the distant past matriarchies—societies controlled by women—flourished. A consensus is emerging that sexual inequality ranges from societies characterized by extreme male dominance to ones in which true equality exists between the sexes (Hendrix, 1994).

The reader will notice in the sections that follow that theories regarding status are differentially applied. That is, it is *women*'s status, not *men*'s status, that is seen as problematic and therefore requires explanation. The implicit assumption is that male status does not vary a great deal cross-culturally but that women's status fluctuates widely. The issue of cultural variation is crucial. Why in some societies do women have few rights and little influence, while in others their rights are equal to those of men?

In analyzing sexual stratification, social scientists face two basic issues: (1) how to measure the relative status of males and females in a given society, and (2) what are the determinants of their relative status (Schlegel, 1977)? Scholars do not agree on how to measure sexual inequality. What are the exact dimensions of female status and power and how is it to be gauged vis-à-vis male status and power? One methodological problem is that most studies try to determine women's status without measuring women's status and influence *relative to* men's status and influence (Hendrix, 1994).

Since there is no widely agreed upon standard for judging female status, two observers may evaluate women's status in the same society differently. For example, some anthropologists suggest that the Inuit (Eskimo) are a clear case of a male-dominant society, while others argue that Inuit gender roles are balanced and complementary (Bonvillain, 2001; Briggs, 1974). Here the issue of ethnocentric pronouncements arises. Is women's status in other societies being evaluated by using the standards of one's own culture? Judgments about women's status in other societies may be colored by the concerns and goals of anthropologists as well as their own socially constructed views of what constitutes superiority and inferiority. Because women have different roles than men, does that automatically imply they are inferior roles? Separate but equal may be meaningful in some societal contexts, even if it is not in many Western cultures.

In many societies, however, the clear differentiation of roles for each sex does imply ranking. One way to gauge if such ranking exists is the reaction to crossing gender-role boundaries. If women take on men's roles, are they admired, even ambivalently? Why are men who take on women's roles ridiculed? The case of the "tomboy" and the "sissy" in American society is illustrative. Girls who exhibit predilections for sports and other "boyish" activities may be admired for their skills, or their behavior may be dismissed as "just a stage" that they will grow out of. But sissy (read, girlish) behavior in boys is greeted with no such equanimity. Boys are usually actively discouraged from such behavior; they may be teased by their peers and a source of worry to their parents. These different reactions to the crossing of gender-role boundaries likely indicate a hierarchy with the roles of one sex valued less than those of the other sex.

Before we consider theories that deal with women's status cross-culturally, we should distinguish between correlational statements and causal statements in such theories. Correlations do not "explain" female status; rather, they suggest what societal elements or institutions co-occur with high or low female status (Hendrix & Hossain, 1988). For example, exclusive men's houses tend to be found in societies in which female status is low. However, men's houses may not *cause* the status of women to be inferior. Rather, another factor, perhaps population pressure, may explain the presence of both phenomena. So it is well to bear in mind that while some theories attempt to *explain* differential status between males and females, others only seek institutional correlates of high or low status.

PRODUCTION, CONTROL, AND PUBLIC VERSUS PRIVATE WORLDS

The relative status of men and women is affected by their roles in the production and distribution of important resources, public versus private settings, the dynamics of kinship, and the presence or absence of warfare, as well as other systems of inequality related to rank, social class, and race. Such systems may produce dimensions of power or oppression apart from gender so that men's and women's gender status and power relations may be cross-cut by other hierarchies and ideologies of inequality.

Some of the early theories regarding the status of women and men have been abandoned in light of additional data, while others still hold promise for analyzing gender hierarchies cross-culturally. Such theories ask under what conditions are male dominance and female subservience found? What are the social, political, and economic arrangements that give rise to equality or inequality between the sexes?

A once popular theory linked women's status to their contribution to subsistence. The assumption was that in societies in which women made significant contributions to producing food, their status would be higher than in those in which their contributions were insignificant or nonexistent. However, no systematic cross-cultural study to date supports the notion that the size of women's contribution to production leads to their higher status across several domains of social life (C. R. Ember & Levinson, 1991).

This theory was linked to another hypothesis suggesting that women's participation or non-participation in production depended upon how compatible subsistence activities were with simultaneous childcare (Brown, 1970). If an activity placed a child in danger, required rapt attention, was not easily interrupted, and resumed or involved long-distance travel, it was incompatible with simultaneous childcare. Such activities included hunting large game animals, herding, plowing, and deep-sea fishing. But other activities, like gathering, market trading, and many of the tasks associated with horticulture, could be done while minding small children. According to this theory, by knowing a society's primary subsistence activity, one could predict the degree of women's participation and, in turn, their status.

Subsequent research has shown that such a straightforward link between female status and subsistence is not supported by the data (Sanday, 1973; Whyte, 1978). Women's economic contribution is likely a necessary but not sufficient condition for high female status. While in societies in which women contribute less than 30% to subsistence their status tends to be low, if women's contribution to subsistence were the primary or sole determinant of their status we would expect that women would have high status in societies like Tikopia, an island culture in the southwestern Pacific, where women are responsible for about 75% of the food supply. But Tikopia women do not enjoy high status across a range of social and political domains despite their large contribution to subsistence. In this case, while women produce a considerable amount, they have no control over what they produce and hence low status. One important finding is that women seem to enjoy the highest status in those societies in which they produce about the same amount—neither a great deal more nor a great deal less—as men (Sanday, 1974).

Production alone is not the key to female status; it is also women's right to distribute what they produce. Using this insight, Sanday (1973) suggests that female status is linked to the degree to which women have power to make decisions that effect the political unit as a whole—band, village, community—not just decisions that impact their own families. She operationalizes this theory by proposing four indicators to measure women's status:

1. Material control. Do women distribute food and wealth outside the family?
2. Demand for female produce. Is women's work valued outside the family?
3. Political participation. Do women express opinions or influence policy in official ways?
4. Group strength. Do women form solidarity groups devoted to their own political and economic interests?

Sanday assumes that if, in a given society, the answer to all these factors is affirmative, women's status will be high, whereas if all four are negative, it will be low. This is tentatively supported by the small sample of societies she uses to test her hypothesis; it needs to be replicated on a larger sample. Iroquois women of New York State—well known ethnographically for their economic, social, and political power—receive positive scores on all four indicators. In contrast, in Somalia where female genital mutilation—a definitive sign of low female status—is widely practiced, all of the indicators are negative (Brown, 1975).

The apparent link between market trade and women's status also supports Sanday's theory. When women are involved in trade, they tend to have a significant degree of economic autonomy. While women's trading activities do not always result in the formation of female trade associations or in women's participation in politics, trade does give women their own capital as well as control over what they produce—conditions often associated with female equality (Friedl, 1975; Ottenberg, 1959; Quinn, 1977).

Control over the distribution of critical resources is central to another theory of status differences between men and women: "Regardless of who produces food, the person who gives it to others creates the obligations and alliances that are at the center of all political relations" (Friedl, 1978, p. 222). Friedl suggests that men's near monopoly over hunting and, with it, the distribution of meat united males in a society-wide system of exchange that may have been the first instance of the enhanced power of males over females. Women's gathered products which were consumed by their families—rather than traded—afforded them no such power base. Thus, among hunters and gatherers, if male dominance rests on controlling the distribution of meat, the degree of male authority should vary with the importance of this key dietary resource. This is why, Friedl (1975) argues, male dominance is much more pronounced among the Inuit (Eskimo), where men provide nearly all the food in the form of large game, than among the Washo Indians of Nevada, where men and women work together in gathering activities and communal hunts.

This line of reasoning implies that a culture's mode of subsistence is related to female status. And, in fact, anthropologists have long recognized that most hunting and gathering societies have relatively egalitarian gender roles compared with more complex societies. Aside from women's contribution to subsistence, foragers do not distinguish between public and private domains, another variable that appears to influence female status. Life is lived in the open among the nomadic !Kung Bushmen of the Kalahari Desert in southern Africa. People eat and sleep outside, conversations are public, and almost all activities are visible to the band as a whole. As such, the notion of a private or domestic sphere is absent (Draper, 1975). The same is true in most horticultural societies. Women generally have important roles in planting and harvesting staple crops and the division between "public" and "private" is vague and indistinct (Boserup, 1970; Martin & Voorhies, 1975).

Contrast this with agricultural societies in which women's contribution to subsistence is generally low and the domestic and extradomestic realms are set apart. With the appearance of intensive cultivation, women "not only dropped out of the mainstream of production for the first time in the history of cultural evolution," but they were cut off from the larger society as they became ever more ensconced in the domestic sphere (Martin & Voorhies, 1975, p. 290). This meshes with the suggestion that women's work must be public and social for it to enhance female status (Sacks, 1974).

Wherever women are isolated or segregated and expected to devote their lives exclusively to domestic tasks, they necessarily rely on men to mediate their dealings with the larger society. Having no direct access to the public sphere, women's personal autonomy, sexual freedom, and legal rights are also limited. Hence, wherever the "inside–outside dichotomy" is well developed, women's status is likely to be low (Martin & Voorhies, 1975, p. 48).

A correlate of agricultural production is an increased work load in the domestic realm. With the intensification of production, larger and more permanent dwellings are filled with more possessions that require care, the time devoted to food preparation increases, and the rising fertility rate associated with agriculture means that women have more children to look after (C. R. Ember, 1983). As such, women's relative contribution to production not only declined in most agricultural societies, but they were also drawn into the domestic sphere because of the greater time and effort required to maintain it.

The segregating and isolating effects of women's confinement to the domestic sphere were intensified in early industrial societies with their sharp distinction between the home and the workplace. The home was seen as a place of refuge from the rough-and-tumble workaday world and the ideology that women's "place" was in the home, and their true calling was motherhood, flourished (Margolis, 2000).

Colonialism accompanied by Western ideologies concerning women's "natural" domesticity also had an adverse impact on women's status and role in many prestate societies. Colonial contact often dramatically altered traditional gender relations, undermining women's productive roles and, with them, their status (Leacock, 1975).

These interrelated factors affecting women's status can be summarized as follows: as societal modes of production become more complex, sexual inequality grows and women's power and prestige declines (Sacks, 1979). Such a decline is not only associated with general cultural complexity and the emergence of separate public and private realms but with their correlates: intensive plow agriculture, complex political hierarchies, the appearance of private property, and social stratification. Conversely, female power and relatively high status occur in societies with a number of other cultural traits—female

contribution to subsistence, male contribution to child care, lack of a distinct domestic realm and absence of societal complexity (Whyte, 1978; Zelman, 1977). Nevertheless, as two researchers note, "while the relationship with cultural complexity appears to be important, we are still a long way from understanding just what it is about cultural complexity that may produce generally lower status for women" (C. R. Ember & Levinson, 1991, p. 91).

THE ORGANIZATION OF WORK AND SEX ANTAGONISM

The organization of work also has an impact on women's status. In those societies in which the sexes are mutually dependent and work together—as in husband-and-wife teams—women's status is higher than when work is strictly organized along gender lines. A rigid sexual division of labor may lead to more general segregation of the sexes which, in turn, may promote differing interests between spouses. Research suggests that under certain conditions an inflexible division of labor leads to marital instability, whereas role sharing enhances cooperation and marital quality (Hendrix, 1997; Hendrix & Pearson, 1995). In essence, extreme task segregation based on sex may lead to distinct male and female worlds with divergent interests.

Consider several examples here. Among the Machiguenga of lowland Peru men and women cooperate, cultivating manioc and fishing, and they spend their leisure time together. As a consequence, husbands and wives feel more solidarity with each other than with their same-sex friends and there is little friction between the sexes (O. R. Johnson & Johnson, 1975). In contrast, in many cultures in highland New Guinea the sexes are segregated from one another in nearly all aspects of life, women are thought to contaminate men, and men engage in rituals to "purge" themselves of impure female substances (Meigs, 1984). Similarly, the Mundurucu of Brazil have a rigid division of labor, friendships rarely cross sex lines, men reside in exclusive men's houses apart from women and children, and relations between the sexes are strained (Murphy, 1959; Murphy & Murphy, 1974).

The two latter cases are examples of "sex antagonism," a complex of traits that is particularly prevalent in highland New Guinea and the Brazilian Amazon and is correlated with low female status. In varying combinations, the complex includes notions of male purity and female pollution, ideologies that women pose a danger to men, behaviors that separate women and/or their belongings from men, elaborate male rituals that exclude females, anxiety about male sexual depletion, extreme sexual segregation, gang rape, female subservience, male dominance, and generally hostile relations between the sexes (Quinn, 1977). Several explanations have been given for the complex. One suggests that it is found in societies in which the interests of the sexes are opposed and, in effect, men marry their "enemies," while another proposes that it is a reaction to the threat of overpopulation since it may reduce sexual contact between men and women (Lindenbaum, 1972; Meggitt, 1964). C. R. Ember (1978) tested four theories about men's fear of sex with women cross-culturally. She found worldwide support for both the "marrying enemies" theory (Meggitt, 1964) and the population-pressure theory (Lindenbaum, 1972).

Beliefs and behaviors associated with female pollution and avoidance are said to maximize differences between the sexes and occur in societies in which such distinctions are an important organizing principle. The complex is correlated with a gendered division of labor in which women are solely responsible for childcare, they have minimal power in the economic and political realms, and female prestige and personal influence are low. In contrast, in societies that have male rituals associated with the female reproductive cycle, gender role differences are de-emphasized and female status is higher. The most notable ritual of this kind is the couvade—the practice in which men's activities are limited during their wives pregnancies, childbirth, and post-partum recovery. Such rituals serve to minimize the distinctions between the sexes (Zelman, 1977).

DESCENT AND RESIDENCE: HOW DO THEY INFLUENCE WOMEN'S STATUS?

The pollution–avoidance complex described above has one other notable feature; it is associated with patrilineal descent and patrilocal residence. Certain features of social organization, specifically descent and postmarital residence rules, have long been known to influence the relative status and power of the sexes. In fact, some

researchers suggest that the strongest associations with equality or inequality between the sexes are postmarital residence and descent rules. They argue that such kinship variables may exert an effect on status independent of economic and political organization (G. D. Johnson & Hendrix, 1982).

Whereas women's status varies in patrilineal societies, it tends to be higher in matrilineal ones. Since women are the focus of the social structure in matrilineal societies, they define political and social relationships (Martin & Voorhies, 1975). But the picture is complicated. While women's position in matrilineal descent groups facilitates their political influence and economic control, neither is insured by the existence of such descent groups alone (Quinn, 1977). Women's degree of domestic autonomy, and with it their status, varies in matrilineal societies and tends to be higher where domestic authority over women is divided between husbands and brothers than in those societies where either male relative has exclusive authority (Schlegel, 1972; Whyte, 1978).

The following example illustrates the sexual differentiation in status related to descent and its practical consequences. In most of the Arab world, where patrilineal descent and inheritance are the norm, the children of women who marry foreigners are not considered citizens of their mother's country. But the reverse is not the case. The children of a man who marries a foreign woman are deemed full citizens of their father's natal land. In essence, one's status in society is derived solely through males, not females. Egyptian-born children of Egyptian mothers and foreign fathers cannot attend public schools or free state universities without paying tuition fees, and they cannot get jobs unless they first get work permits as "foreigners." But the foreign wives and children of Egyptian men automatically become full citizens of Egypt (MacFarquhar, 2001).

Matrilocal postmarital residence appears to be an even more crucial determinant of women's status than matrilineal descent, although the two often coincide. By describing the practical consequences of matrilocal and patrilocal residence, we can see the daily impact that these arrangements have on men and women. In a matrilocal society, after a woman marries she remains in her natal village surrounded by female kin. Her imported husband, with no resident kin of his own, must deal with a coalition consisting of his wife, her mother, and her sisters. He is the outsider, the stranger. Moreover, there is usually a greater degree of domestic equality in matrilocal situations than in patrilocal ones. With matrilocality, a divorcing woman need not change residence or locate kin willing to take her back. Then, too, matrilocality disperses related males, making it more difficult for them to form kin-based coalitions (Friedl, 1975).

But in patrilocal societies positions are reversed and the woman is the outsider. She leaves kin behind and moves to her husband's place of residence where she is unlikely to have her own relatives nearby to provide aid and comfort in time of need. She is faced with the scrutiny of strangers, her husband's relatives, who may make life difficult for her if she does not live up to their expectations. Then, too, women's autonomy is reduced because of their isolation from their own close kin, and in cases of divorce they must change residence (Friedl, 1975).

One theory proposes that it is not primarily descent and residence but women's kinship roles as sisters and wives which help define their relations to production and hence their status (Sacks, 1979). As the mode of production in society becomes more complex, the role of sister, and with it women's direct control of production, declines. Women become increasingly defined as wives, a status of reduced power and greater dependency. As wives, women only relate to production indirectly through the productive and reproductive activities they perform for their husbands' kin group. Here again, women's simple involvement in production is not a precondition for their high status; rather, the key to women's power and prestige is whether or not they control both the means of production and what is being produced.

The sister–wife distinction can shed light on differences in women's status in matrilineal and patrilineal societies, since the lifelong importance of the sister role is highlighted in matrilineal societies where women produce and reproduce for their own natal kin groups, not for the kin groups of their husbands.

WARFARE, POPULATION PRESSURE, AND FEMALE INFANTICIDE

Many scholars have suggested that warfare impacts negatively on women's status. Anecdotally, women seem to have fared better and their status has been higher in peaceful prestate societies in noncompetitive environments than in state societies or in societies with endemic warfare. However, cross-cultural studies on the frequency of warfare are not so clear. On the one hand, a study of hunter–gatherers, generally egalitarian, found a strong correlation between low female status and male combat deaths (Hayden, Deal, Cannon, & Casey, 1986). On the other hand, Whyte's (1978, pp. 129–130) worldwide comparison was equivocal; although a few aspects of women's status appear to decrease with warfare (e.g., men and women have less joint social life), more appear to increase (e.g., *women's* greater domestic authority and somewhat greater value *placed on* women's lives).

Perhaps more important than warfare itself is the type of warfare and the degree to which population pressure may cause endemic fighting. Warfare tends to be found in situations where human populations compete over resources—often the result of population pressure—and it is associated with solidary male groups, notably patrilineal and patrilocal ones. Warfare in such societies tends to be local. In contrast, abundant resources and lack of competition seem to favor matrilineal and matrilocal systems. Moreover, one characteristic of matrilineal societies is the general absence of *internal* warfare, that is, warfare waged on the local level. Long-distance or external warfare, which takes male warriors away from home for long periods of time, is more typical of these societies. Under conditions of long-distance warfare and trade which remove men from their communities for months at a time, women take on a greater role in subsistence with a concomitant rise in status The Iroquois are a classic example; men were absent at distant wars for many months, as well as on hunting and trading expeditions (Brown, 1975; C. R. Ember, 1975; M. Ember & Ember, 1971; Martin & Voorhies, 1975).

Some anthropologists claim that because warfare puts a premium on rearing males to serve as warriors, females are devalued. And, in fact, female infanticide, the selective neglect and killing of female infants, is sometimes found in horticultural societies with endemic warfare, competition over resources, and growing populations. These conditions are said to result in a "male supremacist complex" that provides an ideological justification for devaluing females. In the absence of modern contraceptive techniques, the selective killing of female infants helps to control population increase because, other things being equal, the rate of population growth is dependent upon the number of females who reach reproductive age (Divale & Harris, 1976). A well-known example of a society with such a complex is the Yanomamo of northern Brazil and southern Venezuela

(Chagnon, 1997). There the intensity of warfare is said to be related to male dominance and female subordination, as evidenced by female infanticide, frequent physical aggression against women, and the glorification of male warriors.

This complex supports the contention that when women's role in reproduction becomes a threat to society because of overpopulation, women's value plummets and their rights and freedoms are severely restricted (Abernethy, 1993). According to Abernethy, practices associated with low female status, such as the benign and malign neglect of female infants, bride burning, bans on widow remarriage, strict regulation of female sexuality, and severe punishment of female adultery, are found in societies where population threatens to outrun resources.

The role that population pressure may play in women's status is suggested by a comparison of the treatment of women in two societies in New Guinea. Among the Enga, plagued by insufficient land to sustain a rising population, women and their childbearing capacities are devalued. A high premium is put on premarital chastity, sexual abstinence is required on many occasions, women are killed shortly after their husbands' deaths, and funerals are held for men and pigs, but not for women and children. In contrast, the Fore faced a situation of underpopulation as a result of high mortality from an endemic disease (kuru). In Fore society women and their reproductive abilities were valued, premarital sexuality was not discouraged, and widows remarried after the death of their husbands (Lindenbaum, 1972; Meggitt, 1964).

Unbalanced sex ratios are evidence of the benign or malign neglect of female infants and children and of low female status. That is, in societies where males significantly outnumber females, cultural practices such as female infanticide and the undernutrition of girls are suspect. For example, estimates suggest that nearly 6% of women in India are "missing" and that as many as 100 million women worldwide are unaccounted for when demographers compare expected with actual sex ratios (Coale, 1991; Miller, 1997). Ultrasound technology has made the selective abortion of female fetuses in contemporary China, Korea, and India a source of concern. For example, India has the lowest ratio of females to males among the 10 most populous countries in world (Dugger, 2001).

But such practices do not result from population pressure alone. In northern India, where sex ratios are

very skewed, the selection against females likely results from two additional factors. Women, particularly those of the middle and elite castes, do not engage in agricultural production and upon marriage their families are required to provide their husbands' families with large dowries. Thus, women produce little but cost a lot so that families see it in their own economic and social interest to limit the number of daughters (Miller, 1997). It comes as no surprise that these conditions make for low female status.

WHAT WOMEN ARE LIKE: IDEOLOGY AND RELIGION

What is the role of ideology in determining women's status? And why do beliefs about women's "true nature" and "natural place" vary cross-culturally? Such beliefs are not free floating and random but are related to women's actual roles in society. For example, the ideology that depicts women as immature and requiring male protection and supervision is associated with the domestic isolation of women which, in turn, is related to the rise of intensive agriculture and the state (Quinn, 1977).

Given the link between actual roles and ideology, under what conditions do ideologies of male dominance arise? Rogers (1975) suggests that such ideologies need not reflect women's low status but may instead occur when women do, in fact, have a good deal of economic importance, personal autonomy, and influence within the domestic realm. The "myth of male dominance" is a cross-cultural phenomenon found in societies with a strong domestic orientation and informal sources of power. While men have greater access to formal rights, the sexes are equally dependent on one another economically, politically, and socially. Hence, notions of male dominance in these societies function to mask women's strong, albeit informal, power in the domestic realm.

Certain religious beliefs also correlate with female status. Sanday (1981) argues that the gender of the creator(s) in a given society is linked to the status of women and men in the society. Societies with egalitarian gender relations tend to believe in a female creator or a male–female creator pair, while male-dominant societies have creators that take the form of human males or animals. Myths, especially origin myths, with feminine symbolism are charters that grant power to women, while masculine symbols grant power to men. The egalitarian

Iroquois, for example, believe in both male and female creators, while the male-dominant Mundurucu believe that a single male creator fashioned human beings and also taught the Mundurucu all the essentials of life; females had no role in creation (Murphy & Murphy, 1974).

CONCLUSION

In summary, material and ideological factors may both come into play when accounting for cross-cultural variations in gender status and sexual hierarchies. As yet, however, no single theory seems able to explain why some societies have egalitarian gender roles and others do not. Future lines of inquiry which might clarify this issue include research on the societal conditions under which women form solidarity groups and have collective political influence versus conditions in which they do not. Demographic variables, specifically population pressure and its impact on the valuation of females, is another area that demands additional research. Still, even in the long term, it is unrealistic to expect that any single overriding theory will successfully explain the wide variation in women's status around the world.

REFERENCES

Abernethy, V. (1993). *Population politics: The choices that shape our future*. New York: Plenum.

Boserup, E. (1970). *Women's role in economic development*. New York: St. Martin's Press.

Briggs, J. (1974). Eskimo women: Makers of men. In C. J. Matthiasson (Ed.), *Many sisters: Women in cross-cultural perspective* (pp. 261–304). New York: Free Press.

Bonvillain, N. (2001). *Women and men: Cultural constructs of gender* (3rd ed.). Upper Saddle River, NJ: Prentice-Hall.

Brown, J. K. (1970). A note on the division of labor by sex. *American Anthropologist, 72*, 1073–1078.

Brown, J. K. (1975). Iroquois women: An ethnohistoric note. In R. Reiter (Ed.), *Toward an anthropology of women* (pp. 235–251). New York: Monthly Review Press.

Chagnon, N. (1997). *Yanomamo* (5th ed.). Fort Worth, TX: Harcourt Brace.

Coale, A. J. (1991). Excess female mortality and the balance of sexes in the population: An estimate of number of "missing females." *Population Development Review, 17*, 517–523.

Divale, W. T., & Harris, M. (1976). Population, warfare and the male supremacist complex. *American Anthropologist, 78*, 521–538.

Draper, P. (1975). !Kung women: Contrasts in sexual egalitarianism in foraging and sedentary contexts. In R. Reiter (Ed.), *Toward an anthropology of women* (pp. 283–308). New York: Monthly Review Press.

Dugger, C. W. (2001, April 22). Abortions in India spurred by sex test skew the ratio against girls. *New York Times*, p. 1.

Ember, C. R. (1975). Residential variation among hunter–gatherers. *Behavior Science Research, 10*, 199–227.

Ember, C. R. (1978). Men's fear of sex with women: A cross-cultural study. *Sex Roles: A Journal of Research, 4*, 657–678.

Ember, C. R. (1983). The relative decline in women's contribution to agriculture with intensification. *American Anthropologist, 85*, 285–304.

Ember, C. R., & Levinson, D. (1991). The substantive contributions of worldwide cross-cultural studies using secondary data. *Behavior Science Research, 25*(1–4), 79–140.

Ember, M., & Ember, C. R. (1971). The conditions favoring matrilocal versus patrilocal residence. *American Anthropologist, 73*, 577–581.

Friedl, E. (1975). *Women and men: An anthropologist's view*. New York: Holt, Rinehart & Winston.

Friedl, E. (1978, April). Society and sex roles. *Human Nature*, 222–226.

Hayden, B., Deal, M., Cannon, A., & Casey, J. (1986). Ecological determinants of women's status among hunter/gatherers. *Human Evolution, 1*(5), 449–474.

Hendrix, L. (1994, August). What is sexual inequality? On the definition and range of variation. *Cross-Cultural Research, 28*, 287–307.

Hendrix, L. (1997, August). Quality and equality in marriage: A cross-cultural view. *Cross-Cultural Research, 31*, 201–225.

Hendrix, L., & Hossain, Z. (1988). Women's status and mode of production: A cross-cultural test. *Signs, 13*(3), 437–453.

Hendrix, L., & Pearson, W., Jr. (1995, Summer). Spousal interdependence, female power, and divorce: A cross-cultural examination. *Journal of Comparative Family Studies, 26*, 217–232.

Johnson, G. D., & Hendrix, L. (1982, August). A cross-cultural test of Collins' theory of sexual stratification. *Journal of Marriage and the Family, 44*, 675–684.

Johnson, O. R., & Johnson, A. (1975). Male/female relations and the organization of work in a Machiguenga community. *American Ethnologist, 4*(4), 634–648.

Leacock, E. B. (1975). Class, commodity and the status of women. In R. Rohrlich-Leavitt (Ed.), *Women cross-culturally: Change and challenge* (pp. 601–616). The Hague: Mouton.

Lindenbaum, S. (1972) Sorcerers, ghosts and polluting women: An analysis of religious beliefs and population control. *Ethnology, 11*, 241–253.

MacFarquhar, N. (2001, May 14). In Egypt, law of man creates a caste of shunned children. *New York Times*, pp. 1, 4.

Margolis, M. L. (2000). *True to her nature: Changing advice to American women*. Prospect Heights, IL: Waveland Press.

Martin, M. K., & Voorhies, B. (1975). *Female of the species*. New York: Columbia University Press.

Meggitt, M. J. (1964). Male–female relationships in the highlands of Australian New Guinea. *American Anthropologist, 66*, 204–224.

Meigs, A. S. (1984). *Food, sex and pollution: A New Guinea religion*. New Brunswick, NJ: Rutgers University Press.

Miller, B. D. (1997). *The endangered sex: The neglect of female children in rural north India*. New Delhi, India: Oxford University Press.

Murphy, R. F. (1959). Social structure and sex antagonism. *Southwestern Journal of Anthropology, 15*, 84–98.

Murphy, R. F., & Murphy, Y. (1974). *Women of the forest.* New York: Columbia University Press.

Ottenberg, P. (1959). The changing economic position of women among the Afikpo Ibo. In W. R. Bascom & M. J. Herskovits (Eds.), *Continuity and change in African cultures* (pp. 205–223). Chicago: University of Chicago Press.

Quinn, N. (1977). Anthropological studies of women's status. *Annual Review of Anthropology, 6*, 181–225.

Rogers, S. C. (1975). Female forms of power and the myth of male dominance. *American Ethnologist, 2*, 727–756.

Sacks, K. (1974). Engels revisited: Women, the organization of production and private property. In M. Z. Rosaldo & L. Lamphere (Eds.), *Women, culture and society* (pp. 207–222). Stanford, CA: Stanford University Press.

Sacks, K. (1979). *Sisters and wives: The past and future of sexual inequality.* Westport, CN: Greenwood.

Sanday, P. R. (1973). Toward a theory of the status of women. *American Anthropologist, 75*, 1682–1700.

Sanday, P. R. (1974). Female status in the public domain. In M. Z. Rosaldo & L. Lamphere (Eds.), *Women, culture and society* (pp. 189–206). Stanford, CA: Stanford University Press.

Sanday, P. R. (1981). *Female power and male dominance: On the origins of sexual inequality.* Cambridge, UK: Cambridge University Press.

Schlegel, A. (1972). *Male dominance and female autonomy: Domestic authority in matrilineal societies.* New Haven, CT: HRAF Press.

Schlegel, A. (1977). Toward a theory of sexual stratification. In A. Schlegel (Ed.), *Sexual stratification: A cross-cultural view* (pp. 1–40). New York: Columbia University Press.

Whyte, M. K. (1978). *The status of women in preindustrial societies.* Princeton, NJ: Princeton University Press.

Zelman, E. C. (1977). Reproduction, ritual and power. *American Ethnologist, 4*, 714–733.

Economic Development and Gender

Robin O'Brian

INTRODUCTION

Economic development carries multiple meanings, ranging from improvements to the quality of life among traditional peoples, to the harsh and rigorous demands of organizations like the International Monetary Fund. The continuum that constitutes economic development always interacts with and shapes other parts of human culture, including gender. We can understand at least some of the impact on gender by exploring the implicit assumptions of so-called development theory, both in its traditional and more recent phases.

A BRIEF HISTORY OF ECONOMIC DEVELOPMENT

The Rise of Modernization Theory

Development theory itself had its roots in post-World War II redevelopment that began in Europe and was later extended to Africa, Asia, and Latin America. Less a theory than a school of thought, its underlying assumption was that "undeveloped" (i.e., mostly rural) agrarian nations would benefit from being incorporated into the expanding world market. The most marginal citizens in these countries would benefit, at least indirectly, through an improved economy that created demand for products and labor (Rostow, 1956). Born out of post-World War II optimism, the so-called "modernization" perspective provided the basis for many assumptions that persist today. Modernization theory had its roots in neoclassical economic theory and functionalist sociology ascendant in the postwar period (Jacquette, 1982). The modernization perspective presumed that individuals maximize their self-interest in rational ways and that social relations are in essence exchange relations. Modernization explicitly demands the diffusion of Western capitalist institutions and values which will absorb or replace less "efficient" traditional patterns (Kuznets, 1973; E. M. Rogers, 1983). Indigenous institutions, behaviors

and practices stand in the way of modernity (Holdcroft, 1984; Schultz, 1964).

The functionalist analysis of society by Parsons (1954) also contributed to a modernist view of the family, seeing it as the classic location of sentiment outside the world of work (Parsons, 1954, p. 79). In a modern society, occupational mobility allows individuals to find the work to which they are best suited, while the family provides the support and nurturance outside of work. Modernity focuses more on the individual achievement typical of the workplace and supersedes the ascribed identity traditional peoples retain as members of a specific ethnic group. Still, Parsons assumes that women will themselves find their greatest satisfaction in the expressive life of the family rather than in the instrumental achievement-oriented world of work (Parsons, 1954, pp. 77–69; see also Parsons & Bales, 1955).

This argument has been adapted and extended by the economist Gary S. Becker, who treated the household as a small firm and argued that rational economic choice sends men into the marketplace and keeps women at home, since it is the logical choice for the better-paid member of a household to work (Becker, 1974, 1981). This perception of the family, so familiar to westerners and reinforced by the social and economic theory of the day, led to a preference on the part of development specialists for households that resembled those in the West.

Liberal Feminist Critique

In 1970, agricultural economist Ester Boserup laid out the first liberal feminist critique of such assumptions, suggesting that women who were the clients of development programs often lost control they previously had. Boserup (1970, p. 53) noted:

... in the course of agricultural development, men's labor productivity tends to increase while women's remains more or less static. The corollary of the relative decline in women's labor productivity is a decline in the relative status within agriculture, and, as a further result, women will want either to abandon cultivation and retire to domestic life, or leave for the town.

146

Awareness of this unexpected effect of development upon women has prompted more recent schools of thought to incorporate the views of liberal feminism into their analysis of development and its affects on women. Although this is helpful, this perspective remains firmly rooted in the assumptions of "modernization" theory: modernity and economic development, defined as greater participation in the global market, are seen as a positive goal. The difference is that women as well as men should benefit directly. Though it may not be explicit, a Western bias remains (B. Rogers, 1980).

The Accumulationist Perspective

A second perspective, forming a critical response to modernization, may be called the "accumulationist" or "capital-accumulation" viewpoint. This line of argument draws on neo-Marxism, as well as dependency theory influential among Latin Americanists. Briefly put, accumulationists recognize the roles of power, capital accumulation, and private ownership that are emphasized in the modernization school of development (e.g., Baran, 1957). Dependency theorists further incorporate the ideas of Frank (1967; see also de Janvry, 1983), who has described the structural inequalities inherent in relationships between the West and the Third World. While these perspectives differ in minor ways, as a practical matter they may be considered together.

Drawing on the accumulationist critique, Benería and Sen (1981, 1982) provide a wide-ranging assessment of the modernization model. They note that Boserup's work itself is rooted in modernist assumptions, for example, in Boserup's unproblematic acceptance of individual choice and market economics as the means of development (Benería & Sen, 1981, pp. 282–283), and ignores the problems arising among societies that were formerly colonized by outsiders. Further, Boserup ignores entirely the role of capital accumulation, often gendered, wherein men use tools and skills acquired from development experts to expand and concentrate their own capital (e.g., in the form of land). Such processes have profound consequences for women who may be marginalized from land or excluded from farming. Benería and Sen also argue that this oversight neglects the issue of incipient rank or class. For those individuals who can accumulate capital, differences based on class rapidly develop. The literature is rife with such examples (e.g., Colloredo-Mansfeld, 1999; Hogendorn, 1978; Stephen, 1992)

and this process can work in several ways. Colloredo-Mansfeld (1999) has recently described the ways that the Ecuadorian Otovaleño movement into the world market has intensified class differences in Otovalo communities. The better off are increasingly likely to accumulate and reinvest their income, while those unable to do so remain poor (Colloredo-Mansfeld, 1999). Hogendorn (1978) noted that the shift from subsistence farming to the commercial production of peanuts in Nigeria intensified rank and gender differences as increasingly large fields were planted with peanuts. Those with more land could increase production and acquire the land of their poorer neighbors. Women's best subsistence land was planted with peanuts, leaving women to farm on less and less productive land. Stephen's (1992) research among commercial weavers in Oaxaca, Mexico described the ways that weaving families mobilized unpaid family labor to increase their production and move into a merchant class; increasingly such "merchant" families are accumulating capital to reinvest in the family business.

Benería and Sen further describe this process, noting that in polygynous societies men with several wives may use access to such tools combined with their wives' labor to accumulate wealth that they invest in more landholdings. In these cases, wives retained less and less control over the land they worked, devolving into their husband's field hands (Benería & Sen, 1981, p. 287). Such structural changes separate women directly from their own means of production and increase their economic dependence upon male kin, from whom they must now seek cash to purchase food they previously grew themselves. With a growing lack of borrowing power, they find themselves in a cycle of intensifying inequality.

The accumulationist perspective criticizes modernization theory for its unquestioning acceptance of the expanding global market, maintaining that capitalist development in particular marginalizes women in several important ways: it intensifies class divisions between different women through the processes described above, it intensifies patriarchy, because women are further confined to the household, and it concentrates women in the informal economy—that is, working for cash "off the books"—most often as vendors or domestics (Hart, 1973).

Nash has written widely on the impact of development, and upon development policy and its effects, specifically upon women. Most development policy tends to ignore women or undervalue the subsistence contributions that they make within a household or family. This omission can increase women's economic dependency upon men because when women's subsistence activities are reduced or eliminated they are increasingly forced to rely on the incomes of male kin. This itself further pressures men to seek wage labor or to intensify such labor, even though they might prefer subsistence-based labor that is socially and culturally valued (Nash, 1977, p. 152). The desire to maintain a traditional agrarian subsistence pattern is particularly widespread in Latin America, and is found in the Maya regions of Mexico (for Chiapas see Eber, 2001; for Yucatán see Re Cruz, 1996), in Ecuador (Weismantel, 1988), and in Peru (Deere & León de Leal, 1981).

The situation is less clear in the African case, where women rather than men are farmers. Because agricultural development emphasizes large-scale market-driven projects, all small farmers tend to be marginalized. However, women subsistence farmers fare poorly since technology projects are still generally presented to men, who themselves may have had a wider range of experience with technology (e.g., Ferguson, 1994). Again, these factors push women farmers to the margins and increase their dependence on male kin (Nash, 1977, pp. 172–173).

How Development Changes the Household

The traditional modernization paradigm often overlooks domestic production and reproduction in its projects. The role of the household is regarded in a familiar traditional way—households are the targets of family planning projects, for example—but the persistent role of the household and its members in production may be missed. Households in subsistence economies remain production units, making items with use-value—immediate household value—rather than value created through exchange. Women (and men) perform both domestic services and produce goods that contribute to the reproduction of the household itself as children are born, raised, and mature to begin their own families. Even subsistence agriculture may be regarded as a form of domestic production as crops are eaten rather than sold. When this balance is upset, for instance when men shift land formerly used in home production into commercial farming and increase or monopolize cash income, women may be forced from their larger subsistence roles to functioning entirely

inside the home, performing housekeeping, food processing, and childcare. Ideology that links women entirely with the household, as does the modernization paradigm, further concentrates them there.

Gendering Development

As a corrective to the assumptions of the larger development community, various workers and scholars have explored ways of understanding and implementing more gender-sensitive development projects. This "women in development" perspective has generated a large literature (e.g., Feldstein & Jiggens, 1994; Poats, Schmink, & Spring, 1988) and has expanded the ways in which development can be understood. Ferguson (1994) addresses this issue by noting that economic development that involves women may be generally more focused on local knowledge and folk agricultural systems. Although lip service is now paid to women's role in economic development, practice remains depressingly static. Specialists will still assume that behavior or work mirrors that found in the west. Ferguson (1994) provides an explicit recent example in her description of bean agriculture in Malawi. Development specialists wished to discover why women farmers (beans were a women's crop) grew a seeming hodgepodge of bean varieties. In their discussions, primarily with local men, the specialists assumed that the crop mixes were designed to withstand various biological risks, such as drought (Ferguson, 1994, pp. 541–542). However, further research among women farmers showed that the women themselves grew quite specific variants of beans in their mixes, that the varieties fulfilled different purposes, and that the range of varieties grown also differed depending on the rank or social standing of the farmers themselves: higher-status women with larger landholdings grew a greater variety of beans, while poor women only grew a few, and those few had early maturity and quick cooking time so that they could be harvested, cooked, and eaten early (Ferguson, 1994, pp. 543–544). This not only permitted a food supply during the growing season, but conserved firewood. What had seemed random and disorganized to outsiders was intentional and planned, and further differentiated along incipient class lines. The original intention of the project had been to formulate an appropriately introduced bean mixture for planting across Malawi; Ferguson's research suggested that bean agriculture was far more involved and the range of needs more complex.

Ferguson suggests that the difficulties she described and that occur repeatedly in development work can be understood in part as a reluctance on the part of development workers to acknowledge that science itself is socially contextualized. Scientists themselves may take for granted the division of labor typical of their own culture, and development workers, generally trained as agricultural economists or biologists, tend to ignore the social and cultural contexts in which they work, contexts which certainly in this case were vital in understanding the larger agricultural needs of the community (Ferguson, 1994).

This school of thought differs from the traditional viewpoint by asking very different questions of its clients. Rather than noting that, for example, men and women specialize in different activities and that women's activities are overlooked or devalued, these workers ask why this should be the case. They are willing to be more client driven, and respond more to those demands that clients need, rather than instituting "top-down" projects. While they provide a critical viewpoint and corrective to earlier work, they are careful not to upset imperfect programs that nonetheless provide some good.

REFERENCES

Bandarage, A. (1984). Women in development: Liberalism, Marxism and Marxist-feminism. *Development and Change, 15,* 495–515.

Baran, P. A. (1957). *Political economy of growth.* New York: Monthly Review Press.

Becker, G. S. (1974). A theory of marriage. In T. W. Schultz (Ed.), *Economics of the family: Marriage, children, and human capital* (pp. 299–344). Chicago: University of Chicago Press.

Becker, G. S. (1981). *A treatise on the family.* Cambridge, MA: Harvard University Press.

Benería, L., & Sen, G. (1981). Accumulation, reproduction, and women's role in economic development. *Signs, 7,* 279–298.

Benería, L., & Sen, G. (1982). Class and gender inequalities and women's role in economic development: Theoretical and practical implications. *Feminist Studies, 8,* 158–176.

Boserup, E. (1970). *Woman's role in economic development.* New York: St. Martin's Press.

Colloredo-Mansfeld, R. (1999). *The native leisure-class.* Chicago: University of Chicago Press.

Deere, C. D., & León de Leal, M. (1981). Peasant production, proletarianization, and the sexual division of labor in the Andes. *Signs, 7,* 339–360.

de Janvry, A. (1983). *The agrarian question and reformism in Latin America.* Baltimore: Johns Hopkins University Press.

Eber, C. (2001). *Women and alcohol in a highland Maya town: Water of hope, water of sorrow* (Rev. ed.), Austin, TX: University of Texas Press.

Feldstein, H. S., & Jiggens, J. (Eds.), (1994). *Tools for the field: Methodologies handbook for gender analysis in agriculture.* West Hartford, CT: Kumarian Press.

Ferguson, A. E. (1994). Gendered science: A critique of agricultural development. *American Anthropologist, 96,* 540–552.

Frank, A. G. (1967). Capitalism and underdevelopment in Latin America; historical studies of Chile and Brazil. New York: Monthly Review Press.

Hart, K. (1973). Informal income opportunities and urban employment in Ghana. *Journal of Modern African Studies, 11,* 61–89.

Hogendorn, J. S. (1978). *Nigerian groundnut exports.* Zaria, Nigeria: Ahmadu Bello University Press & Oxford University Press.

Holdcroft, L. E. (1984). The rise and fall of community development, 1960–65: A critical assessment. In C. K. Eicher & J. M. Staatz (Eds.), *Agricultural development in the third world* (pp. 46–58). Baltimore: Johns Hopkins University Press.

Jaquette, J. S. (1982). Women and modernization theory: A decade of feminist criticism. *World Politics, 34,* 267–284.

Kuznets, S. (1973). Modern economic growth: Findings and reflections. *American Economic Review, 63,* 247–258.

Nash, J. (1977). Women in development: Dependency and exploitation. *Development and Change, 8,* 161–182.

Parsons, T. (1954). *Essays in sociological theory.* Glencoe, IL: Free Press.

Parsons, T., & Bales, R. F. (1955). *Family, socialization, and interaction process.* Glencoe, IL: Free Press.

Poats, S. V., Schmink, M., & Spring, A. (Eds.), (1988). *Gender issues in farming systems research and extension.* Boulder, CO: Westview.

Re Cruz, A. (1996). *The two milpas of Chan Kom: Scenes of a Maya village life.* Albany, NY: State University of New York Press.

Rogers, B. (1980). *The domestication of women.* London: Tavistock Press.

Rogers, E. M. (1983). *Diffusion of innovations.* New York: Free Press.

Rostow, W. (1956). The take-off into self-sustained growth. *Economic Journal, 66,* 25–48.

Schultz, T. W. (1964). *Transforming traditional agriculture.* New Haven, CT: Yale University Press.

Stephen, L. (1992). *Zapotec women.* Austin, TX: University of Texas Press.

Weismantel, M. J. (1988). *Food, gender and poverty in the Ecuadorian Andes.* Philadelphia: University of Pennsylvania Press.

Language and Gender

Bonnie McElhinny

THEORETICAL DEBATES IN THE STUDY OF LANGUAGE AND GENDER

Most people, when they think of work on language and gender, probably think of works like linguist Deborah Tannen's *You Just Don't Understand* or perhaps even psychologist John Gray's *Men are from Mars, Women are from Venus*—studies of "miscommunications" between women and men in heterosexual couples. Indeed, early studies of gender by academics often assumed that gender was most salient "in cross-sex interaction between potentially sexually accessible interlocutors, or same-sex interaction in gender-specific tasks" (Brown & Levinson, 1983, p. 53). Despite an increasing number of different approaches, in studies of language and gender in the North Atlantic this focus remains influential and, at its best, insightful (e.g., Fishman, 1983; Gleason, 1987; Tannen, 1990; West & Zimmerman, 1983; Zimmerman & West, 1975).

However, there are, a number of increasingly controversial theoretical assumptions about gender often implicitly embedded in this approach, including the notions that the study of gender is closely wedded to the study of heterosexual relations, that gender is an attribute rather than a practice, and that the study of gender is the study of individuals (McElhinny, 2003; Thorne, 1990). These assumptions are often highlighted in work done outside North America or with subordinate groups in North America. Studying gender in heterosexual dyads can suggest that "gendered talk is mainly a personal characteristic or limited to the institution of the family" (Gal, 1991, p. 185). A focus on interactions between heterosexual romantic partners assumes rather than investigates the relationship between sexuality and gender, and also prejudges which gendered dyads are central to the elaboration of gender in a given locale. It also draws attention away from the importance of studying the ways that gender is a structural principle organizing social institutions such as workplaces, schools, courts, and the state, and the patterns they display in the

recruitment, treatment, and mobility of different men and women (Gal, 1991).

Increasingly, linguistic studies of gender adopt a *practice* approach. To suggest that gender is something one continually *does* is to challenge the idea that gender is something one *has*. A variety of metaphors have arisen to capture this idea: gender as activity, gender as performance, gender as accomplishment (Butler, 1990; Eckert & McConnell-Ginet, 1992; Goodwin, 1990; West & Fenstermaker, 1993). They participate in a wider move within linguistic and sociocultural anthropology since the mid-1970s to use practice-based models (Abu-Lughod, 1991; Hanks, 1990; Ochs, 1996; Ortner, 1984, 1996). Practice theory reacts against structural–determinist social theories (e.g., British–American structural–functionalism, determinist strands of Marxism, and French structuralism) that did not incorporate a sufficient sense of how human actions make structure. A focus on activities suggests that individuals have access to different activities, and thus to different cultures and different social identities, including a range of different genders. We discover that:

stereotypes about women's speech … fall apart when talk in a range of activities is examined; in order to construct social personae appropriate to the events of the moment, the same individuals [will] articulate talk and gender differently as they move from one activity to another. (Goodwin, 1990, p. 9)

Crucial to note here is that it is not just talk which varies across context, a point long familiar in sociolinguistics. Gender identity also varies across context. Language and gender *covary*.

However, adopting such a practice-based approach does not always challenge approaches which focus largely on gender in individuals. Thus linguistic anthropologists have recently begun to develop more carefully an approach to gender which considers it as a principle for allocating access to resources. Gender, like class and racialized ethnicity, nationality, age, and sexuality, is an axis for the organization of inequality, though the way each of these axes work may have their own distinctive features (Scott, 1986, p. 1054). Such work considers the role that language and gender together play in political economy, defined here as as:

resource allocation in the sense, for example, of control over goods. Political economy involves the generic economic processes of the production, distribution and consumption of goods, including "non-material" ones, and the patterns and culture of power that control or influence these processes. (Friedrich, 1989)

Coupling studies of practice and political economy means that sociolinguists and linguistic anthropologists who study gender are no longer simply asking how language and gender affects politics, but instead are asking how notions of language or of gender are produced through theories and practices of politics. Notions of politics are also approached in a more nuanced way, moving beyond earlier debates about whether to understand gender as a product of difference or dominance (for reviews see Talbot, 1998; Uchida, 1992) to understanding gender as it is imbricated in complex historical, political, and economic circumstances.

LANGUAGE AND GENDER AROUND THE WORLD

Gender and Genre in "Egalitarian" Societies

In societies that have traditionally been called egalitarian by anthropologists, men and women often have their own distinct social spheres. Participation in culturally central rituals and concomitant verbal genres is often linked to (though not necessarily absolutely determined by) gender. In everyday conversation there were no marked male or female registers among the Kaluli, a small nonstratified society in Papua New Guinea (Schieffelin, 1987). There was some distinction, though, in other verbal genres: men tended to tell the two major genres of stories (trickster stories and bird or animal stories), and women performed sung-texted weeping at funerals and on other occasions of profound loss. Both men and women composed songs and dances for exchange and ceremonial contexts, although women composed a more limited number of song types. Finally, women and girls engaged in an interactional routine (known as *ElEma* which means "say like that") used in the linguistic socialization of children under the age of 3.

Sherzer (1987) describes the linguistic practices of the Kuna Indians of Panama. Although he notes that there were relatively few gender differences in phonological variation and intonation, in the speech of Kuna men and women was linked to differences in ritual and everyday discourse. Kuna ritual verbal genres (the chanting of chiefs, the speech-making of political leaders, the curing chants of healers, and the chants of puberty rite directors) in which men, and the very occasional woman, participated had specific linguistic properties distinguishing them from everyday speech, as do the two verbal genres which were unique to women (lullabies and tuneful weeping). However, the relationship between gender and discourse was indirect: "[T]he linguistic properties of the Kuna ritual verbal genres are not defined or viewed in terms of gender. Rather they are associated with the verbal genres themselves" (Sherzer, 1987, p. 104). The genres in turn are generally linked to certain tasks which are gender differentiated.

Recently, Briggs has argued for the need to consider language practices and ideologies in "egalitarian" communities as no less complex, differentially distributed, or historically produced than those in other communities. Ideologies and practices of groups now often incorporated (if differentially) into nation-states as cultural minorities or indigenous ethnic minorities need to be studied for the ways that certain kinds of discursive authority are naturalized. To this end, he has written a series of papers about the Warao in Venezuela, paying particular attention to gender and politics, and how these are linked to different relationships with bureaucrats, politicians and missionaries (Briggs, 1992, 1993, 1996, 1998). Women's ritual wailing after a relative dies can provide comments on recent community events. Because such laments are collectively produced, the critiques they offer and the blame they assign is difficult for others, even those putatively more powerful, to challenge. Men's negative accounts of women's gossip can become a field in which disputes between men of different generations with different claims to relations between state and religious officials are worked through, though not necessarily worked out.

Gender and Multilingualism

In settler societies, postcolonial contexts, diglossic linguistic situations, and many other multilingual situations, it may be use of or access to certain languages which differentiates the speech of men and women. Each of these situations presents its own dynamics in ways that can only be briefly touched upon here. Gal's (1978) work on the use of Hungarian and German in Austria focuses on the effects of urbanization and industrialization on the speech patterns of women and men. Because the urban settings associated with use of German have different meanings and present different opportunities for young women and men, they use German and Hungarian differently. Young women are leading in the shift to German because, for them, German is associated with urban opportunities, having husbands who are workers, and having less strenuous and time-consuming household responsibilities, while Hungarian is associated with having peasant husbands and physically taxing household and farm responsibilities. Younger men, for whom the peasant life-style retains the attraction of self-employment and some measure of personal autonomy, use Hungarian more than young women. Because they cannot find Hungarian-speaking women to marry, however, they marry German-speaking women and their children tend to speak German.

Linguistic minorities which attempt to shore up their position against such shifts often invoke the logic of state nationalism to try to resist state power. Heller's (1999) study of a francophone school in Ontario finds that it adheres to two tenets of nationalist ideology: insistence on French monolingualism within the school as a form of institutional territorial autonomy (modeled on Québec's geographical state territorialism), and concern for the production of *un Français de qualité*. Nonetheless, the dominant group of students believe that bilingualism, not monolingualism, best serves their aims. Going to a monolingual school allows them to become the kind of bilingual they want to be. These bilingual practices shock monolingual francophone students (from, especially, Québec or France), as well as immigrants from former French colonies who accept French as the dominant language of communication, and lead to debates about what a francophone means. These debates drown out debates about gender and class, though other ethnic voices (perhaps because they can also draw on some of the discourses of nationalism) are beginning to be heard at the school. The voices of boys of these different groups tend to be more clearly heard than the voices of girls. Where girl's voices are heard, they are confined to a fairly limited repertoire of gendered images. Québecois are tough and rugged and authentic; bilinguals are hip, popular, and plugged into North American popular culture;

Africans are anticolonialist, antiracist, streetwise, and cool warriors. Boys predominate in school roles where language use is showcased (like student councils).

Immigrant linguistic minorities may not speak a country's official language(s), and this too is often shaped by and linked to gender. In Canada, working-class Italian and Portuguese workers were heavily recruited between the 1950s and 1970s for unskilled jobs that native-born Canadians considered undesirable (Goldstein, 1995, 1997). Amongst Portuguese immigrants, women are 50% more likely to speak only Portuguese. Language choices and abilities are linked to the dynamics of the Portuguese family and the class position the workers hold within the Canadian political economy. Men are more likely to have had access to English speakers in Portugal as soldiers or in encounters with tourists. In Canada, the jobs men are hired into also give them access to more English speakers, and they are less likely to be restricted by family obligations or concerns about their safety from taking evening language classes. In addition, for some of the factory jobs in which women work, Portuguese is an important asset rather than a liability. Its use functions as a symbol of solidarity and of participation in the company "family," and use of other languages is actively sanctioned.

Hill (1987) investigates gender differences in the use of a former colonial language (Spanish) and an indigenous language (Mexicano) in Mexican communities undergoing proletarianization. In these communities, use of Spanish is believed to be crucial for access to wage labor, but Mexicano is understood as crucial for expressing solidarity with traditional norms. Women engage in a wide variety of nonwage economic activity, but most do not participate in regular wage labor. Therefore one might expect, and indeed Mexicano speakers believe, that women are likely to use Mexicano (or at least certain salient features of Mexicano) more than men do and to use Spanish less (or at least certain salient features of Spanish less), but Hill finds that women's speech is at once less Mexicano and less Spanish than men's speech. She argues that women are barred from using the full range of code variation in the way that men do because of the constraints of the local political economy. Local men contest their integration into a capitalist system by emphasizing their Mexicano identity and at the same time manipulate Spanish to be able to participate in that capitalist system.

Understanding the complex politics of such postcolonial situations is crucial for understanding the resistance that both men and women might have to the teaching of Spanish to women in such situations; the kinds of economic advantages and mobility it might give women could be outweighed by the loss of some parts of the traditional culture that men and women value. Harvey (1991), describing another postcolonial situation in Peru, finds that women are less likely to have access to Spanish than men and are more likely to be monolingual in Quechua. Women who abandon tradition by changing their style of dress and/or acquiring Spanish risk slurs on their reputations, social ostracism, and even violence. As in Mexico, ignorance of Spanish and ability to speak Spanish both count against women. Women become living symbols of tradition, but their economic mobility is limited and in some instances they become more dependent upon men than in traditional societies. When speakers from such a linguistic situation choose to migrate to a country where yet another language (say, English in the United States) predominates, there are sometimes different challenges associated with gaining access to English for men (who might be fluent in another "world" language with which at least some instructors are familiar) and women (who may not be fluent in a "world" language).

In diglossic situations, that is, situations where two varieties of the same language exist in a community, men and women may have differential access to, different attitudes toward, or different incentives for using the high or officially prestigious variety. Haeri (1987) points out that in Amman, although education is directly and positively correlated with the use of classical Arabic among men (with the more highly educated men using salient features of classical Arabic more than the less highly educated men), highly educated women use salient variants of the local urban Arabic standard, which is associated with modernity, progress, and change of the status quo. It is not surprising that highly educated women might choose not to adopt all aspects of the use of classical Arabic, which symbolizes the norms of the dominant culture and is associated with Quranic schools which close their doors to women.

Finally, new work has begun to investigate the effect of the rollback of socialist and social democratic governments and the increasing significance of neoliberal governance and market economies in China and Eastern Europe on language use. Zhang (2001, 2002) reports that in Beijing the transition from a state-controlled to a market-driven economy has given rise to a new group of Chinese professionals working for foreign businesses (yuppies). Yuppies use local Beijing phonological features significantly less than state-employed professionals, and use a nonmainland (Hong Kong/Taiwan) feature significantly more. Further, gender differences with respect to these features are mild among state professionals, but dramatic among yuppies, with female yuppies leading in use of nonmainland features. Male yuppies tend to use local features associated with being a "Beijing smooth operator" (a native who is streetwise, crafty, and smooth), a character type not associated with women and which it is not advantageous for them to associate with.

Gender and Politeness

So far, this discussion has focused on gender differences in the use of languages, codes, or verbal genres. Pragmatic stances are also a domain in which many kinds of social differentiations are manifest. Politeness is:

[A] special way of treating people, saying and doing things in such a way as to take into account the other person's feelings. On the whole that means that what one says politely will be less straightforward or more complicated than what one would say if one wasn't taking the other's feelings into account. (Brown, 1980, p. 114)

In societies where politeness is normatively valued or seen as a skill, or where acquisition of politeness is not an automatic part of language learning but requires additional training, men tend to be understood as more polite, and women are understood as impolite (Malagasy) or too polite (Java). In societies where directness is valued, and politeness is seen as a form of deference rather than a skill, women tend to be more polite, or at least are perceived as more polite (many groups in the United States, certain Mayan women—e.g., Brown, 1980). In certain cases, at certain times, women challenge such dominant views of their actions.

Keenan (1974) studied a village in Malagasy in which there were two politeness systems, one perceived as traditional and the other perceived as European, and in which both men and women believed that men were more skillful polite speakers. Men and women actually shared the traditional politeness system, which included long winding speeches associated with traditional values placed on personal relationships, the use of traditional metaphoric sayings, positive politeness markers, use of stand-ins to make requests, indirect ways of giving orders, and avoidance of outright expressions of anger or criticism. However, since women did not, engage in the ritually-oriented interactions that had to do with village-to-village negotiations, dispute resolution, and marriage requests, they were perceived as less skilled at politeness. Women were also perceived as less polite because the devalued European politeness system was consigned to them (men use it only when ordering around cows). They used this system in marketplace transactions associated with bargaining about and selling food and at times when a village member had behaved in an unacceptable way and had to be more directly approached. Men deputized their wives to handle such situations.

In Java, the politeness system is quite complicated and elaborate, with every utterance being marked for respect, so that properly mastering how to be deferential means mastering a skill that allows one to control others and express authority (Smith-Hefner, 1988). Men are seen in this society, too, as being more adept and skillful at using politeness forms. By producing polite forms for an inferior, a speaker can force the interactant to respond politely in turn—or lose face. The coerciveness of the act is hidden, and thus difficult to challenge. Because people must be explicitly drilled in the more intricate politeness forms (they are not learned along with the rest of the language), an educated man who uses politeness forms can reduce a man not so educated to silence—or at least agreement (disagreement would require explanation and skillful use of politeness forms). Javanese women are understood by men as less skillful in using politeness—not because they are not polite enough, but because they are *too* polite. Women who are mothers are often more polite than befits their status because they are modeling the production of politeness forms for their children and are using forms which are appropriate for children to use toward their elders. Furthermore, in situations in which it is unclear which politeness forms to chose, women tend to speak (choosing the more polite forms to be on the safe side) and men remain silent. Here again is a complementary system similar to that in Malagasy, where men can use women's actions to preserve their own status. Women interpret their own actions differently than men do, however, in ways that point out the importance of considering how all members of a group interpret a given act. Women take advantage of the polysemy of politeness to understand their kinds of politeness not as subservient but as refined.

Gender and Socialization

Caregivers in all societies share the dilemma of how to talk to humans who have not yet mastered language. The ways caregivers solve these dilemmas reflect distinctive cultural attitudes towards children, adults, and parenting. Ochs (1992) argues that the use of different child-rearing strategies shapes, in considerable part, some of the differences in how the social positions of women are understood. Some caregivers accommodate to children (child-centered cultures); others ask children to accommodate to them (adult- or situation-centered cultures). For example, European American middle-class North American caregivers simplify their talk when speaking to young children. They use a smaller vocabulary, shorter sentences, exaggerated intonation, talk more slowly, and repeat themselves often. Before children are able to talk, they may even construct elaborate dialogs in which they take the part of both interlocutors ("You see that squirrel outside? Yes, you do! You like the squirrel don't you? Look at him moving across the yard!"). In order to do this, the caregiver must place self in the position of the child, arguably diminishing or losing adult status in doing so. Western Samoan caregivers do not simplify their talk; indeed, they direct very little talk to young children, because they believe young children do not understand it. In traditional Western Samoan villages, children grow up in a compound with several households, in houses which have no internal/external walls, with conversations taking place between those inside and outside. Infants are thus bathed in language; they are often talked about, but they are not seen as appropriate conversational partners. European American middle-class North American caregivers extensively praise children for tasks jointly accomplished ("Look at the tower you built! What a beautiful tower!"). Samoan caregivers may also praise children for work done, but also expect to be thanked in return for the assistance they have offered in the completion of the task. Ochs (1992) concludes that European American middle-class mothers have become underrated, in part, in Western families and society because they do not socialize children to acknowledge their participation in their accomplishments, and because their own language behavior makes mothers invisible. Samoan mothers, by contrast, enjoy a more prestigious position because they command human labor (younger caregivers) and socialize children to recognize and accommodate to them.

The explanation for the nonaccommodation strategies practiced in Western Samoa are clear: children are being socialized into a highly stratified society. In traditional Western Samoan society individuals are ranked in terms of whether they have a title or not and in terms of what kind of title it is, and people without titles are ranked in terms of gender and age. Rank also affects the task of caregiving. When more than one caregiver is present, the lower-ranking caregiver undertakes most tasks. As a result, a young child is not primarily cared for by its mother, but by a range of younger people. Infants are soothed, bathed, clothed, and delivered to the mother for feeding by lower-ranked caregivers—siblings, especially sisters, and girl cousins. Indeed, Margaret Mead even described late childhood as the most stressful period of a girl's life because she was at the beck and call of both adults and younger children. Children learn from caregivers that lower-ranking persons are expected to accommodate to higher-ranking ones, and not vice versa. What, however, might be the explanation for the accommodation strategies practiced by European American middle-class mothers in the United States and Canada? One explanation alludes to political ideology (Ochs, 1992). People living in a democracy are uncomfortable with asymmetry, and therefore they try to establish an egalitarian relationship with their children. However, such explanations seem to ignore the ways in which Canada and the United States are also highly stratified societies, with sharp economic and social differences between people who belong to different social classes, nor do they seem to explain why these patterns tend to be particularly associated with middle-class caregivers.

One study that may give insight into what drives the North American pattern is Collier's (1997) study of changes from an other-centered child-rearing pattern to a child-centered one in a village in Spain alongside the growth of capitalist industry and agriculture between the 1960s and the 1990s. When Jane Collier and her husband George arrived in an agricultural village in Spain in the 1960s with a 2-month-old baby and a copy of the latest edition of Dr Spock, they were struck, sometimes secretly appalled, by the ways that the villagers treated children. The villagers spoke loudly to infants and initiated actions that ignored the baby's response (sometimes jouncing them harder and harder as they cried, instead of stopping). They, on the other hand, spoke softly to their baby and others, waited for the baby to respond,

and then adapted their actions to the infant's reactions. The villagers' strategies were in line with what parents thought children needed to succeed in adult life. The future well-being of both girls and boys depended on the inheritance of agricultural lands from their parents, so parents were intent on making children behave in ways that would not lead them to squander the land, would lead to a sense of responsibility to the parents who might continue to live on the land when older, and would lead to a sense of respectability that would allow them to marry others of equal or larger inheritance.

When the Colliers returned to the same village in the 1980s, they found some dramatic changes. Children were repeatedly said to have no respect, to always be talking back to their elders. Parents seemed obsessed with helping children prepare themselves for adult jobs. Schooling had become necessary for economic security. Unlike inherited property, however, education was not owned and managed by the parents, but rather acquired and controlled by children. When children's futures depended on their own achievements, rather than inheritance, parents had to identify and foster children's unique abilities. Instead of "subjugating" them, they had to listen to discover likes and dislikes. Children had changed from being seen as animals whose instincts needed to be controlled to miniature humans who needed encouragement and who needed to learn to think for themselves and make their own decisions. This led to a style of parental interaction much like that characterized by Ochs as accommodation. For middle-class families in the United States that depend on education for their children's life chances, such accommodating practices also seem critical. Spanish and European American middle-class American mothers are faced with a double bind. If they stay home, they give up the ability to become a self-supporting adult. If they keep their jobs, they might be seen as not giving the intense motherly care children are said to need to realize their potential. The conflict between the economic interests of parents and children is thus most acute for mothers. Mothering is devalued not because of the linguistic strategies adopted by mothers, but instead because of a political economic context that devalued the unpaid work of mothering.

In Canada, the United States, and elsewhere, many middle-class mothers choose to work, for these and other reasons, and childcare is provided by a variety of paid caregivers. The linguistic strategies associated with caregiving for pay has, for the most part, been remarkably understudied by anthropologists. One exception is a study of West Indian nannies by Colen (1995). She develops the theoretical notion of *stratified reproduction*, by which she means that "physical and social reproductive tasks are accomplished differentially according to inequalities that are based on hierarchies of class, race, ethnicity, gender, place in a global economy, and migration status and that are structured by social, economic and political forces" (Colen, 1995, p. 78). She highlights some of the misunderstandings that can arise in households which are cross-cultural, transnational, and interracial. For example, she found that West Indian women were often reluctant to get down on the floor and play with children, in part because they believed that this was not appropriate behavior for grown women and because they felt children should learn independence through play. A study of how nannies are understood in Toronto suggests that Filipinas are often understood as being too soft, as not disciplining children when necessary (Bakan & Stasiulis, 1995). In each case, then, whether the paid caregiver is understood as "too" accommodating or not accommodating "enough," the immigrant women and their caregiving strategies are being dismissed and devalued, while the European American middle-class North American child-rearing practices are treated as a universal norm. Such judgments also appear in academic and bureaucratic discourses in colonial and postcolonial writings (McElhinny, 2002).

Gender and State Formation

Entities understood as outside human political activity, as part of the biological or divine order, are often used to justify and rationalize political power (Gal & Woolard, 2001). Gender and language have, individually and together, been summoned up to undergird or legitimate other social formations, particularly nations or nation-states in a variety of different contexts, ranging from 18th century European states, to postcolonial nationalist movements and postsocialist states in Eastern Europe. To question the significance of language or of gender is often to question an entire political edifice. The prevalence of naturalizing accounts of language and of gender may explain some of the challenges that have faced scholars in linking up studies of language, gender, and political economy, since linguists themselves are not immune from such ideologies (Irvine & Gal, 2000). Recent work on state formations has begun to consider how notions of language and of gender are produced in certain discourses about

politics (see also Scott, 1999). For instance, Edmund Burke's attack on the French Revolution was built around a contrast between ugly *san-sculotte* hags and the softly feminine Marie Antoinette (Scott, 1986). By contrast, part of the way the critique of the Old Regime was developed during the French Revolution was by identifying elite women with the system of patronage, sexual favors, and corruption of power, in which they had been active participants. Political revolution was seen to lie in excluding women and their corrupt influence from the public sphere; the sexual virtue of women who engaged in public speech and activities was questioned, in ways which presented a double bind for women who were themselves revolutionaries. In yet another example, Teodoro Kalaw, a Filipino nationalist, critiqued American colonialism by criticizing the effects of the teaching of English. Filipino women reading books in English were corrupted by Anglo-Saxon influence, he argued, and insisted on being known as "girls" instead of *dalagas* or maidens. Soon, he lamented, they would be walking out alone without *duennas*, with handbags under their arms just like bold little American misses (Karnow, 1989, pp. 201–202).

One of the most sophisticated and detailed examples of the role that language and gender play in nation formation is Inoue's (2002) geneaological account of Japanese women's language. Linguistic scholars in Japan and elsewhere have published countless articles describing how Japanese women are said to speak differently from men at all levels of language—phonology, semantics, syntax, pitch. Some scholars argue that these same differences have been transmitted largely without change since the 4th century. Inoue demonstrates, however, that the association of specific speech forms with gender did not exist until the late 19th century. This period was also critical for the development of the Japanese nation-state. It was characterized by rapid industrialization, massive urban migration, labor struggle, the development of mass communication and transportation systems, a new legal code, the appearance of representative democracy, and compulsory education. At the same time wars with China and Russia led to skepticism about the desirability of rapid westernization and to an embrace of the need to "return" to Japanese tradition. The government launched a project to shape women into good wives and wise mothers, a project that mixed Confucianism and the western cult of domesticity. Women came to symbolize the shifting boundary between tradition and modernity, and speech forms referred to as "Japanese women's language" emerged in serialized novels, letters in magazines for young girls and women, and advertisements for commodities such as perfume and ointment. Inoue points out that the social power of language in this case is such that it constitutes reality not by naming and pointing to an object which already existed, but by constructing that object.

Other kinds of discourse about women can serve as a way of constructing new notions of nation. In all the countries of Eastern Europe, questions of procreation and reproduction became for a time the focus of intense public debate in the postsocialist era. In an analysis of how a debate about abortion proceeded in Hungary in the late 1980s and early 1990s, Gal (1997) points out that the debate was not linked to sexuality and women's right to privacy, as in the United States, but instead to ideas about nationhood, communism, and the defense of civility. Everyone defined himself or herself against a godless, immoral, and overly ideological communism. In conservative writings, women were portrayed as the corrupt beneficiaries of the communist state (with maternity leaves and favorable divorce and custody laws) and were called on to renounce cynically materialistic motives and produce children for the health of the nation. Doctors, lawyers, and politicians, in making these arguments, constructed themselves as the best judges of what was good for women, and thus enhanced their own role in the state and civil society as they constructed a model of a state built around national and ethnic unity. Liberals offered more lenient proposals for legalized abortion, but were ultimately less concerned with women and their rights than articulating a vision of the state as a minimal one which did not assume or construct a unified populace, and which left both private property and reproductive decisions outside its own realm. Gal points out that arguments about abortion were not the means to reach already defined political goals, but rather were constructed as ways to justify and naturalize certain political visions, to gain moral credit for those advocating certain views, and thus to display and argue for certain styles of leadership. Debates about abortion were the discursive terrain on which other issues about the form of the state, how leaders would be chosen, and what was worthy of political attention, were being fought.

Ideas about language and gender were also used to rationalize 19th century imperialist actions, especially in the analysis of grammatical gender. Many linguists have argued that in languages with grammatical gender the nouns are placed in classes not according to their meaning, but only according to their form. Indeed, feminists adopted the analytic concept of "gender" from these analyses precisely because it suggests that differentiation occurs on a social, rather than a biological, basis. However, more recent feminist analyses suggest that speakers often perceive a connection between grammatical gender and sex, and that connection reproduces a covert hierarchy between the masculine and the feminine, in scholarship and everyday life alike (see Cameron, 1992, pp. 82–98 for an extended analysis; Munroe & Munroe (1969) is an early attempt to correlate the occurrence of grammatical gender with sex bias in a society (though it should be noted that in terms of the criteria used in their analysis, American society has no structural sex bias). In the 19th century many scholars of African linguistics suggested that the way a language handled gender relations, specifically grammatical gender, revealed its "family" relationship to other languages, as well as speakers' mentality and sociopolitical conditions (Irvine, 2001). Linguists appealed to what were then taken to be ethnographic facts about African family life to explain linguistic structure and relationships. Early writers, influenced by the notions of universal fraternity developed during the French Revolution, saw in African languages the proof of human equality. Some even found the absence of grammatical gender in Wolof more rational than the arbitrary sex distinctions encoded in French. Later in the century, however, during the establishment of European colonial empires, African languages were seen to contain evidence of the importance of sexual and racial hierarchies. In the view of these linguists, African languages were not categorizable into language families because of the lack of written traditions, the supposed lack of public meetings, and the lack of the kind of family life in which children were properly supervised by parents. Children, portrayed as not being carefully instructed in language use by their parents because they were largely left in the company of peers or older adults, were thought to construct a whole new language with each generation. Languages that put all humans into the same grammatical class, or which showed no noun class distinctions at all, were associated with polygamy or promiscuity. Languages lacking sex-gender systems were claimed to mark a mentality not able to recognize social hierarchy or assert independence. Constructions of family relationships based on ideologies about gender and politics shaped the representation of linguistic relationships. This analysis suggests the ways that linguists' own assumptions about gender and language always also require careful analysis.

Finally, Philips (2001) has pointed out that, though it is common for gender ideologies to be elaborated around gender dyads, societies differ in which gender dyads are selected for ideological elaboration. Key gender dyads are typically drawn from cross-gender relationships within the family, and can include wife–husband, sister–brother, mother–son, and father–daughter relationships. In many North Atlantic societies, the husband–wife relationship is treated as primary, but in the South Pacific the sister–brother relationship is much more explicitly developed, discussed, and celebrated. Philips (2001) demonstrates how the condemnation of crimes of bad language by Tongan court officials on the grounds that brothers and sisters might have been present projects such a relationship from the family to the nation: all Tongans are expected to treat one another in public as if they were brothers and sisters.

Gender and Sexuality

The study of language and gender is now about three decades old. However, the study of language and sexuality is much more recent—most of the books and articles on this topic have appeared within the past 5 years. Much of this work has so far been done in North Atlantic settings, with a few key exceptions. One of the first questions which arises in talking about people whose sexual and gendered practices and identities fall beyond the boundaries of normative heterosexuality is what to call them. Debates about, and studies of, naming practices point to a continuing concern amongst linguists and activists about which identities are to be foregrounded. These are not trivial issues; the overriding theme here is that naming confers existence, and it appears everywhere, from coming-out narratives to AIDS activism. Linguists have considered lexical and political debates over the usage in English of *homosexual* versus *gay*, *lesbian* versus *dyke*, *queer* versus *gay*, *gay* as *adjective* versus *gay* as noun, etc. (Murphy, 1997; Zwicky, 1997). However, a focus on lexicon alone can be quite limiting. Since the 1990s, then, linguists have largely tried to move "beyond the lavender lexicon" to investigate intonation and phonological patterns that might be said to characterize queer language (Leap, 1996, 1997). However, trying to find those features which can be so labeled is problematic, since labeling a specific feature as "gay" is both too

general and too specific (Podesva, Roberts, & Campbell-Kibler, 2002), assuming as it does that there is a singular way of being and speaking gay, and reifying certain features as gay though they are shared throughout society. Studying the construction of queer identities requies a more flexible model of the relationship of language to acts, activities, stances, and styles (e.g., Ochs, 1992). Indeed, recent work by some linguists suggests that queerness will not ever be located in specific codes, but in the juxtaposition of incongruous codes. African American drag queens who perform in Texas bars do not convey queerness by relying on a clearly delineated set of features, like high pitch or lexical choice; instead, they convey queerness by skillfully switching between a number of styles and forms that stereotypically denote other identities (European American women, African American men) (Barrett, 1994, 1997). Queerness is conveyed by the juxtaposition of socially contradictory forms (hypercorrect pronunciation while uttering obscenities). Queen (1997) has made a similar argument for lesbian language.

One of the areas where linguists have made the most progress in studying language and sexuality is in studies of discourse. Not surprisingly, given the importance of the distinction of being out versus "closeted" in North Atlantic society, and given pervasive presumptions of heterosexuality, "coming-out stories," or stories about how people realize their own sexuality and disclose it to others, have received a great deal of attention. Coming out is a speech act that describes a state of affairs (gayness) but also brings that state of affairs into being (Liang, 1997). Weston (1991) offers a rich ethnographic analysis of what gays and lesbians from a variety of different ethnicities and classes in San Francisco think a good coming-out story is, and by extension their sense of what it means to "come out" properly. Crucially, Weston points out that in San Francisco such stories are understood in terms of a sense of self that is distinctively Western. There is an assumed division between inner and outer selves, and the core self is seen as essential and privileged. Resolving contradictions between the inner and outer self creates a sense of wholeness between inside and outside. What a coming-out story might look like if a different model of self prevails has only just begun to be investigated in groups inside North America, or in select other countries where the notion of coming out circulates (for Asian American coming-out stories, see Liang, 1997). For instance, Valentine (1997) offers a historical account of lexical terms and the identities they are seen to designate in Japan, a consideration of why Western terms for understanding sexual identity do not apply in Japan, and the ways Japan and the United States define themselves over and against one another in dialogic gestures of orientalism and occidentalism. Valentine points out that the practice of coming out, of having a political stance or association with a political movement, and of feeling that sexuality defines self (the ideas that are picked out by the Western notion of *gay*) are associated with the Japanese use of that foreign term *gay* but that the word is mostly used to describe westerners, or certain aspects of the commercial gay scene (like bars and magazines). This identification is not a common one. The concealment of less public selves is valued, rather than seen as being dishonest or conflicted. To argue that this is "backward" is, Valentine argues, ethnocentric; it is to judge Japanese culture against Western norms. Wong (2001; see also Wong & Zhang, 1999) has also explored the interaction between occidentalism and orientalism in the construction of *tongzhi* identity in Hong Kong. *Tongzhi* was a word originally used to mean "comrade" during the Communist Revolution in China, but has been reappropriated in recent years by the Chinese gay and lesbian community as a term which marks for some the cultural distinctiveness of same-sex desire in Chinese society over and against "the west," as it works to create a "transnational" community for those from Taiwan, Hong Kong, and mainland China.

In many places, notions of sexuality vary dramatically from dominant North American models, raising wholly different linguistic issues. Consider a group in India which have been variously called transvestites, eunuchs, hermaphrodites, a thirdly sex, and *hijras*. *Hijras* are known for taking on feminine dress and mannerisms, and for acting as ritual specialists; they sing and dance at births and weddings, and are compensated with clothes, jewelry, and money. Most community members focus on the asexuality of *hijras*, but some also describe relationships they have with men while others survive by prostitution. Many European and North American anthropologists have pointed to their organized and extensive network as evidence that a greater social tolerance of gender variance exists in India than in the West, but Hall (1997) argues that the network exists because the *hijras* have created it to resist systematic exclusion from families and jobs. They are not given respect; they have demanded it in political arenas. Many *hijras* claim that they are physically

hermaphrodites, that they are "naturally" different, though some community members and researchers argue that up to three quarters of them undergo operations (castrations and penectomies), with some dying as a result. *Hijras* are contrasted with women because they tell lewd jokes, use obscenity, and have a conversational style perceived as aggressive. They are distinguished from men by their putative penchant for gossip and endless meaningless chatter. *Hijras* use verbal insult, a practice that underlines and constructs the sexual ambiguity for which they are feared, to gain immediate interactional advantages in social situations where they might otherwise be ignored. Their insults often use obscenity and double entendre. On the surface, their comments may seem to be about, say, the buying and selling of fruit and vegetables, but they are meant to be understood in ambiguous sexual terms, as about the buying/selling of sex. To be offended, however, one must acknowledge understanding sexual innuendo, crudity, gender fluidity—all the realms of activity the *hijra* talk about and participate in.

In northern Nigeria, Gaudio (1996, 1997) has described Hausa-speaking Muslim *'yan daudu*, men who talk like women. *'Yan daudu* talk and act in woman-like ways, engage in a woman's occupation (cooking and selling food), and use woman-like gestures (roll eyes, slap thighs, swing hips). Their clothing is usually conventionally masculine, though they may put on selected items of female clothing (head-ties, waist-wrappers). They do not attempt to pass as women; they have men's short haircuts and moustaches, and they never fully relinquish the sociocultural perks accorded to them as men, including marriage and children. Heterosexual marriage and homosexual behavior are not mutually exclusive. Like the *hijras*, they exploit linguistic ambiguity to establish and enhance their power to attract and criticize others in a society that demeans them. For instance, they use *karin magana* (proverbs) and *habaici* (innuendo). Such indirect speech is stereotyped as female. Hausa cowives are stereotypically portrayed as jealous, conniving, and back-biting, and the use of figurative indirect language is said to arise from verbal sparring in polygamous households. Their use of thigh-slaps and loud laughter is also said to be woman-like. However, they also talk in ways seen as flamboyant, frivolous, and shameless. Indeed, the practices of *'yan daudu* call attention to the ambiguities and contradictions in dominant ideas about women. They use language stereotyped as female, yet another stereotype of married women is passive and demure. *'Yan daudu*'s actions undermine—and reinforce—gender, sexual, and moral boundaries.

Finally, it is important to note that much of the early and continuing work on language and gender is work on heterosexuality, but it is rarely studied as such, though see Cameron (1997) and Kiesling (2001) for discussions of flagrant heterosexuality in the discourse of college men. Indeed, one of the tasks which faces the field of language and gender in general is to return to that work and place it within larger political, economic, cultural, and historical contexts.

REFERENCES

Bakan, A., & Stasiulis, D. (1995). Making the match: Domestic placement agencies and the racialization of women's household work. *Signs, 20*(2), 303–335.

Abu-Lughod, L. (1991). Writing against culture. In R. Fox (Ed.), *Recapturing anthropology: Working in the present* (pp. 137–162). Santa Fe, NM: School of American Research Press.

Barrett, R. (1994). "She is *not* white woman": Appropriation of white women's language by African American drag queens. In M. Bucholtz, A. C. Liang, L. Sutton, & C. Hines (Eds.), *Cultural performances: Proceedings of the Third Berkeley Women and Language Conference* (pp. 1–14). Berkeley: Berkeley Women and Language Group, University of California.

Barrett, R. (1997). The "homo-genius" speech community. In A. Livia & K. Hall (Eds.), *Queerly phrased: Language, gender and sexuality* (pp. 181–201). Oxford: Oxford University Press.

Briggs, C. (1992). "Since I am a woman I will chastise my relatives": Gender, reported speech, and the reproduction of social relations in Warao ritual wailing. *American Ethnologist, 19*, 337–361.

Briggs, C. (1993). Personal sentiments and polyphonic voices in Warao women's ritual wailing: Music and poetics in a critical and collective discourse. *American Anthropologist, 95*, 929–956.

Briggs, C. (1996). Conflict, language ideologies and privileged arenas of discursive authority in Warao dispute mediation. In C. Briggs (Ed.), *Disorderly discourse: Narrative, conflict and inequality* (pp. 204–242). New York: Oxford University Press.

Briggs, C. (1998). "You're a liar—You're just like a woman": Constructing dominant ideologies of language in Warao men's gossip. In B. Schieffelin, K. Woolard, & P. Kroskrity (Eds.), *Language ideologies: Practice and theory* (pp. 229–254). Oxford: Oxford University Press.

Brown, P. (1980). How and why are women more polite: Some evidence from a Mayan community. In S. McConnell-Ginet, R. Borker, & N. Furman (Eds.), *Women and language in literature and society* (pp. 111–149). New York: Praeger.

Brown, P., & Levinson, S. (1983). *Politeness*. Cambridge, UK: Cambridge University Press.

Butler, J. (1990). *Gender trouble: Feminism and the subversion of identity*. New York: Routledge.

Cameron, D. (1992). *Feminism and linguistic theory* (2nd ed.). London: Macmillan.

Cameron, D. (1997). Performing gender identity: Young men's talk and the construction of heterosexual masculinity. In S. Johnson & U. Meinhof (Eds.), *Language and masculinity* (pp. 47–64). Oxford: Basil Blackwell.

Colen, S. (1995). "Like a mother to them": Stratified reproduction and West Indian childcare workers and employers in New York. In F. Ginsburg & R. Rapp (Eds.), *Conceiving the new world order: The global politics of reproduction* (pp. 78–102). Berkeley: University of California Press.

Collier, J. (1997). *From duty to desire: Remaking families in a Spanish village*. Princeton, NJ: Princeton University Press.

Eckert, P., & McConnell-Ginet, S. (1992). Think practically and look locally: Language and gender as community-based practice. *Annual Review of Anthropology, 21*, 461–490.

Fishman, P. (1983). Interaction: The work women do. In B. Thorne, C. Kramarae, & N. Henley (Eds.), *Language, gender and society* (pp. 89–102). Cambridge, MA: Newbury House.

Friedrich, P. (1989). Language, ideology and political economy. *American Anthropologist, 91*(2), 295–312.

Gal, S. (1978). Peasant men don't get wives: Language and sex roles in a bilingual community. *Language in Society, 7*(1), 1–17.

Gal, S. (1991). Between speech and silence: The problematics of research on language and gender. In M. Di Leonardo (Ed.), *Gender at the crossroads of knowledge* (pp. 175–203). Berkeley: University of California Press.

Gal, S. (1997). Gender in the post-socialist transition: The abortion debate in Hungary. In R. Lancaster & M. di Leonardo (Eds.), *The gender sexuality reader: Culture, history, political economy* (pp. 122–133). New York: Routledge.

Gal, S., & Woolard, K. (2001). Constructing languages and publics: Authority and representation. In S. Gal & K. Woolard (Eds.), *Languages and publics: The making of authority* (pp. 1–12). Manchester, UK: St Jerome.

Gaudio, R. (1996). *Men who talk like women: Language, gender and sexuality in Hausa Muslim society*. Unpublished Ph.D. dissertation, Department of Linguistics, Stanford University, Stanford, CA.

Gaudio, R. (1997). Not talking straight in Hausa. In A. Livia & K. Hall (Eds.), *Queerly phrased: language, gender, and sexuality* (pp. 416–429). New York: Oxford University Press.

Gleason, J. B. (1987). Sex differences in parent–child interaction. In S. Philips, S. Steele, & C. Tanz (Eds.), *Language, gender and sex in comparative perspective* (pp. 189–199). Cambridge, UK: Cambridge University Press.

Goldstein, T. (1995). "Nobody is talking bad": Creating community and claiming power on the production lines. In K. Hall & M. Bucholtz (Eds.), *Gender articulated: Language and the socially constructed self* (pp. 375–400). New York: Routledge.

Goldstein, T. (1997). *Two languages at work: Bilingual life on the production floor*. Berlin: Mouton de Gruyter.

Goodwin, M. H. (1990). *He-said-she-said: Talk as social organization among Black children*. Bloomington: Indiana University Press.

Haeri, N. (1987). Male/female difference in speech: An alternative interpretation. In K. Denning, S. Inkelas, F. McNair-Knox, & J. Rickford (Eds.), *Variation in language: Proceedings of the Fifteenth Annual Conference on New Ways of Analyzing Variation* (pp. 173–182). Stanford, CA: Department of Linguistics, Stanford University.

Hall, K. (1997). "Go suck your husband's sugarcane": *Hijras* and the use of sexual insult. In A. Livia & K. Hall (Eds.), *Queerly phrased: Language, gender and sexuality* (pp. 430–460). New York: Oxford University Press.

Hanks, W. (1990). *Referential practices: Language and lived space among the Maya*. Chicago: Chicago University Press.

Harvey, P. (1991). Women who won't speak Spanish: Gender, power and bilingualism in an Andean village. In P. Wilkings (Ed.), *Women and secondly language use*. Oxford: Berg.

Heller, M. (1999). *Linguistic minorities and modernity: A sociolinguistic ethnography*. London: Longman.

Hill, J. (1987). Women's speech in modern Mexicano. In S. Philips, S. Steele, & C. Tanz (Eds.), *Language, gender and sex in comparative perspective* (pp. 121–162). Cambridge, UK: Cambridge University Press.

Inoue, M. (2002). Gender, language and modernity. *American Ethnologist*, 29(2), 392–422.

Irvine, J. (2001). The family romance of colonial linguistics: Gender and family in nineteenth-century representations of African languages. In S. Gal & K. Woolard (Eds.), *Languages and publics*: *The making of authority* (pp. 13–29). Manchester, UK: St Jerome.

Irvine, J., & Gal, S. (2000). Language ideology and linguistic differentiation. In P. Kroskrity (Ed.), *Regimes of language: Ideologies, politics, identities* (pp. 35–84). Santa Fe, NM: School of American Research Press.

Karnow, S. (1989). *In our image: America's empire in the Philippines*. New York: Ballantine.

Keenan, E. O. (1974). Norm-makers, Norm-breakers: Uses of speech by men and women in a Malagasy community. In R. Bauman & J. Sherzer (Eds.), *Explorations in the ethnography of speaking* (pp. 125–143). Cambridge, UK: Cambridge University Press.

Kiesling, S. (2001). Playing the straight man: Displaying and maintaining male heterosexuality in discourse. In K. Campbell-Kibler, R. Podesva, S. Roberts, & A. Wong (Eds.), *Language and sexuality: Contesting meaning in theory and practice* (pp. 249–266). Palo Alto, CA: CSLI, Stanford University.

Leap, W. (1996). *Word's out: Gay men's english*. Minneapolis: University of Minnesota Press.

Leap, W. (Ed.). (1997). *Beyond the lavender lexicon: Authenticity, imagination, and appropriation in lesbian and gay languages*. Gordan & Breach.

Liang, A. C. (1997). The creation of coherence in coming out stories. In A. Livia & K. Hall (Eds.), *Queerly phrased: Language, gender, and sexuality* (pp. 287–309). New York: Oxford University Press.

McElhinny, B. (2002, April). *Accomodating others: Studies of child-rearing in the Philippines and the anthropology of western hegemony*. Paper presented at IGALA-2 (Second International Gender and Language Conference), University of Lancaster, UK.

McElhinny, B. (2003). Theorizing gender in sociolinguistics and linguistic anthropology. In J. Holmes & M. Meyerhoff (Eds.), *The language and gender handbook* (pp. 21–42). Oxford: Basil Blackwell.

Munroe, R., & Munroe, R. (1969). A cross-cultural study of sex, gender and social structure. *Ethnology*, 8, 206–211.

Murphy, M. L. (1997). The elusive bisexual: Social categorization and lexico-semantic change. In A. Livia & K. Hall (Eds.), *Queerly phrased: Language, gender and sexuality* (pp. 35–57). New York: Oxford University Press.

Ochs, E. (1992). Indexing gender. In A. Duranti & C. Goodwin (Eds.), *Rethinking context* (pp. 335–358). Cambridge, UK: Cambridge University Press.

Ochs, E. (1996). Linguistic resources for socializing humanity. In J. Gumperz & S. Levinson (Eds.), *Rethinking linguistic relativity* (pp. 438–469). Cambridge, UK: Cambridge University Press.

Ortner, S. (1984). Theory in anthropology since the sixties. *Comparative Studies in Society and History*, 26(1), 126–166.

Ortner, S. (1996). *Making gender: The politics and erotics of culture*. Boston: Beacon Press.

Philips, S. (2001). Constructing a Tongan nation-state through language ideology in the courtroom. In P. Kroskrity (Ed.), *Regimes of language: Ideologies, polities, and identities* (pp. 229–258). Santa Fe, NM: School of American Research.

Podesva, R., Roberts, S. & Campbell-Kibler, K. (2002). Sharing resources and indexing meanings in the production of gay styles. In K. Campbell-Kibler, R. Podesva, S. Roberts, & A. Wong (Eds.), *Language and sexuality: Contesting meaning in theory and practice* (pp. 175–190). Palo Alto, CA: CSLI, Stanford University.

Queen, R. (1997). "I don't speak spritch": Locating lesbian language. In A. Livia & K. Hall (Eds.), *Queerly phrased: Language, gender and sexuality* (pp. 35–57). New York: Oxford University Press.

Schieffelin, B. (1987). Do different words mean different worlds? An example from Papua New Guinea. In S. Philips, S. Steele, & C. Tanz (Eds.), *Language, gender and sex in comparative perspective* (pp. 249–260). Cambridge, UK: Cambridge University Press.

Scott, J. (1986). Gender: A useful category of historical analysis. *American Historical Review*, 91(5), 1053–1075.

Scott, J. (1999). Some reflections on gender and politics. In M. M. Ferree, J. Lorber, & B. Hess (Eds.), *Revisioning gender* (pp. 70–96). Thousand Oaks, CA: Sage.

Sherzer, J. (1987). A diversity of voices: Men's and women's speech in ethnographic perspective. In S. Philips, S. Steele, & C. Tanz (Eds.), *Language, gender and sex in comparative perspective* (pp. 95–120). Cambridge, UK: Cambridge University Press.

Smith-Hefner, N. (1988). Women and politeness: The Javanese example. *Language in Society*, 17, 535–554.

Talbot, M. (1998). *Language and gender*. Cambridge, UK: Polity Press.

Tannen, D. (1990). *You just don't understand: Women and men in conversation*. New York: Morrow.

Thorne, B. (1990). Children and gender: Constructions of difference. In D. Rhode (Ed.), *Theoretical perspectives on sexual difference* (pp. 100–113). New Haven, CT: Yale University Press.

Uchida, A. (1992). When "difference" is "dominance": A critique of the "anti-power-based" cultural approach to sex differences. *Language in Society*, 21, 547–568.

Valentine, J. (1997). Pots and pans: Identification of queer Japanese in terms of discrimination. In A. Livia & K. Hall (Eds.), *Queerly phrased: Language, gender and sexuality* (pp. 95–114). New York: Oxford University Press.

West, C., & Zimmerman, D. (1983). Small insults: A study of interruptions in cross-sex conversations between unacquainted persons. In B. Thorne, C. Kramarae, & N. Henley (Eds.), *Language, Gender and Society* (pp. 102–117). Rowley, MA: Newbury House.

West, C., & Fenstermaker, S. (1993). Power, inequality and the accomplishment of gender: An ethnomethodological view. In

P. England (Ed.), *Theory on gender/feminism on theory* (pp. 151–174). New York: Aldine de Gruyter.

Weston, K. (1991). *Families we choose: Lesbians, gays, kinship.* New York: Columbia University Press.

Wong, A. (2001). The semantic derogation of *tongzhi*: A synchronic perspective. In K. Campbell-Kibler, R. Podesva, S. Roberts, & A. Wong (Eds.), *Language and sexuality: Contesting meaning in theory and practice* (pp. 161–174). Palo Alto, CA: CSLI Stanford University.

Wong, A., & Zhang, Q. (1999). The linguistic construction of the *tongzhi* community. *Journal of Linguistic Anthropology*, *10*(2), 248–278.

Zhang, Q. (2001). *Changing economy, changing markets: A sociolinguistic study of Chinese yuppies in Beijing.* Unpublished Ph.D. dissertation, Stanford University, CA.

Zhang, Q. (2002, November). *"Smooth operators" and "cosmopolitans": Situating meaning and agency in a broader sociohistorical context.* Paper presented at annual meeting of the American Anthropology Meetings, New Orleans, LA.

Zimmerman, D., & West, C. (1975). Sex roles, interruptions and silences in conversation. In B. Thorne & N. Henley (Eds.), *Language and sex: Difference and dominance* (pp. 105–129). Rowley, MA: Newbury House.

Zwicky, A. (1997). Two lavender issues for linguists. In A. Livia & K. Hall (Eds.), *Queerly phrased: Language, gender and sexuality* (pp. 21–34). New York: Oxford University Press.

Transitions in the Life-Course of Women

Judith K. Brown

INTRODUCTION

The Classics

Two works have shaped the anthropological study of life-course transitions: *Les Rites de Passage* (van Gennep, 1909), which analyzed the initiation into a new status as a three-stage process and, "Continuities and discontinuities in cultural conditioning" (Benedict, 1938/1953), which focused on the transition from childhood to adulthood. Breaking with tradition, the present essay will assume a broader perspective and will include the entire female life-course, and will focus less on analysis and more on description. Ethnographic examples will be drawn from all over the nonindustrialized world, and the "ethnographic present" will represent a variety of time periods.

The Controversies

The anthropological study of life-course transitions has not been without a history of controversy, particularly in the research on male adolescent initiation rites. J. W. M. Whiting, Kluckhohn, & Anthony (1958) first viewed the rituals as related to certain psychological factors. In response to criticism of this interpretation and as a result of further analysis, and also reflecting a changed approach within anthropology itself, a later publication (J. W. M. Whiting, 1964) took other, especially ecological, variables into account. Today's scholarship on life-course transitions is also involved in anthropological controversies. The first is between scholars who advocate a more evolutionary/biological approach and those whose approach stresses the cultural. Following the example of Ember (1981), the present essay will attempt to present both views. The second controversy concerns ritual observances (largely outlawed in their own countries) such as the genital mutilation of girls and the burning of wives. There is strong worldwide disapproval of these customs, and they are viewed by many as inhumane and as violations of basic human rights

(Korbin, 1987), but some anthropologists see such opposition as imposing our own values on certain traditional cultures.

Transitions: Biological and Cultural

Every female life-course is marked by dramatic biological transitions—menarche, defloration, motherhood, menopause—but there is wide variation among non-Western societies in the cultural elaboration of these developmental milestones. In some societies, certain of the biological changes are cause for extensive, costly celebration. In other societies the same biological events are virtually overlooked. The number of recognized stages within the female life-course and the definition of each category also vary greatly among different societies. Some biologically determined transitions are shared by all humans, regardless of sex, such as the eruption of the first tooth; others are uniquely female, such as giving birth. Yet other life-course stages, such as widowhood may be of major cultural importance but have no biological reality for women.

The transitions in the female life-course may be joyous, as for example, wedding celebrations in our own society. But in many societies the wedding ceremonial can be an ordeal for the bride. Indeed, the preponderance of celebrations of female life-course transitions are an occasion of stress and pain for the individual; there are a few observances which are life threatening, and there are even some which result in death.

TRANSITIONS BEFORE BIRTH, AT BIRTH, AND IN INFANCY

Female-Selective Abortion

With the introduction of modern medical procedures, which can detect the sex of the unborn child, the transition into death may actually occur before birth for females in many parts of the world today. Female-selective abortion is practiced among many societies in Asia and certain Asian immigrant groups in North America, and is motivated by "strong son preference" (Miller, 2001). This is in turn typically related to the expense of raising a daughter and providing a dowry payment at her marriage. Miller's evidence for the practice of female-selective abortion is based on an analysis of male-biased sex ratios at birth among certain societies, and she warns ominously that societies with unbalanced sex ratios exhibit a proclivity for violence.

Infanticide and Neglect

There are also more traditional causes for unbalanced sex ratios: female-selective infanticide and fatal neglect, as Miller (1987) has reported for rural North India (for an evolutionary view of these customs see Ball & Panter-Brick, 2001; Hausfater & Hrdy, 1984; Hrdy, 1996; Lipson, 2001). An ethnographic example of pervasive female infanticide is provided by the Yanomamo of South America (Chagnon, 1977). A traditional society, noted for its "hostile devaluation of women" and its stress on warfare, the Yanomamo created a shortage of women (which in turn caused much armed hostility) largely through the practice of female infanticide. Since giving birth to a daughter was viewed as a wifely misdeed, for which the disappointed husband might inflict a severe beating, mothers of female neonates frequently opted for infanticide.

Ceremonies for Babies

Unlike the transitional observances above, those ceremonies performed for infants tend to be benign and are typically celebrated for both sexes. The ceremony may mark a physiological event such as the severing of the umbilical cord or the eruption of a first tooth. Or the ceremony may have a purely cultural definition such as naming (Alford, 1996). Although there are societies in which the individual may receive new names later in life, the choice of a baby's name is often a serious matter, which may be delayed for a month or longer and which may be a necessary step in making the baby a member of her group. Kilbride and Kilbride (1974) report that among the Baganda of East Africa, a ceremony is celebrated when the baby is 3–4 months old. She is seated on a mat with other babies to establish her legitimacy and in yet another seating ceremony, the baby is told,

"Now you are a woman." Diener (2000) reports that on the Island of Bali a baby's first birthday marks her "departure from the divine world and entry into the human world" (p. 112) by a ceremony which provides purification and spiritual strength. And among the traditional Walpiri Aborigines (Pierroutsakos, 2000), a betrothal was celebrated for infant girls (and even unborn girls)—a betrothal to the husband they would marry 9 or 10 years later.

One or more ceremonials for the infant appear to be celebrated in every society and yet these practices remain relatively unexplored cross-culturally. It seems likely that such rituals are related to a society's concepts of personhood and the self, as well as to the meaning of gender and identity.

Weaning

Weaning is one of the major transitions in the young child's life and in many societies the change in diet coincides with changed sleeping arrangements, less indulgence from caretakers, and possibly the arrival of a sibling. The timing and harshness of weaning vary cross-culturally (J. W. M. Whiting & Child, 1953), but in many societies the newly weaned child is reported to be poorly nourished and susceptible to illness (Briggs, 1970; J. W. M. Whiting, 1941). It was McKee (1985) who first reported that within certain societies, such as the mestizos of Ecuador, there are customary sex differences in weaning age. Girls are weaned long before boys, because it is believed that prolonged nursing results in "qualities of sexuality and aggression" (p. 96), viewed as inappropriate for girls. Relatively deprived of "high quality protein and immune protection" (p. 100), the little girls have a higher mortality rate. Cronk (1989, 1993) reports the exact opposite for the Mukogodo of Kenya, one of the rare societies that favors daughters.

CHILDHOOD TRANSITIONS

An Unmarked Transition

"Both folk wisdom and the findings of psychologists agree that between the ages of 5 and 7, there is a change in the intellectual capabilities of children" (B. B. Whiting & Edwards, 1988, p. 241). This changed capacity is exploited in many societies (Bradley, 1993). The child is expected to make a genuine contribution to the economy of the household and in many societies where this is not the case, the child begins school. Surprisingly, these major changes in the lives of boys and girls, which roughly coincide with the eruption of the second teeth, are not given ritual recognition. However, there are some societies in which ceremonials are celebrated in mid-childhood and these practices mutilate and inflict severe pain, when the observance pertains only to girls.

Childhood Ceremonies for Both Boys and Girls

Among some traditional Native North American peoples, certain major childhood transitions, such as the spirit quest, were shared by boys and girls. Both boys and girls aged 6–10 were initiated among the traditional Hopi (Goldfrank, 1945/1964). The ritual, which involved being publicly whipped by masked men representing the gods was anticipated and feared by the children. Girls were not whipped as severely as boys, who were often left with bleeding wounds, yet the traumatic nature of the event was shared by all the initiates.

Ceremonies Only for Girls

One childhood transition celebrated only for girls was the thousand-year-old practice of foot binding in China (Gates, 2001, in press; see also Kroeber, 1948/1963). There were regional variations in its prevalence. Girls aged approximately 7–12 years were subjected to this torment, which could last for as long as 4 years. Although the practice of binding a daughter's feet may appear to have had an esthetic purpose, it served to prevent a young woman from a life of performing strenuous and degrading labor and from being sold into servitude.

In numerous traditional societies, ritual genital mutilations are performed on adolescent initiates. Yet the most complex and radical of these operations, infibulation, is performed on younger girls, aged 4–10 years, among a number of societies in northeastern Africa, including Sudan, where the practice has been outlawed since 1945 and is opposed by governmental and religious authorities. Nevertheless, infibulation continues (Boddy, 1989; Hayes, 1975; Hicks, 1996), perpetuated by grandmothers, in the belief that the operation is needed to assure the initiate's sexual purity on which, in turn, the honor of the family is based. For the participating

women, it is a joyous celebration, and their clapping, singing, and drumming drown out the screams of the mutilated child.

MENARCHE, MAIDENHOOD, ADOLESCENCE, AND INITIATION

Observances at Menarche

Although the first menstruation is experienced by all women everywhere, the event is elaborated by ritual only in some societies, such as the Maroni River Caribs of Surinam (Kloos, 1969, 1971). Here, in traditional times, the girl was secluded for a month in a special place within her parental home, subjected to certain restrictions, and expected to spin cotton to make a hammock for a member of her family. As part of one of the rituals celebrated toward the end of her seclusion, the initiate places her hand into a bowl of large stinging ants in order to impress upon her the need to be industrious like the ant. A feast ensues, and the initiate is told by guests that she is now a woman. The ceremony stresses the industriousness that will be demanded of her as the adult she has become. (For an unusually rich description of a ceremony celebrated at menarche among the Navajo, see Frisbie [1967].)

Not only is menarche given ritual elaboration in some societies, but it also appears that certain cultural practices actually influence the onset of menarche. According to J. W. M. Whiting (1965; see also Landauer & Whiting, 1981; Lipson, 2001), in those societies with cultural practices that inflict stress in infancy, girls will experience menarche earlier than girls in societies without such customs. Furthermore, East African data reported by Borgerhoff Mulder (1989) indicates that age at menarche is a major predictor of completed family size.

Menstrual Customs

After menarche, women must observe the society's customary menstrual practices, and these can range from minimal to cumbersome. Particularly elaborate customs are typical of societies where menstruation is viewed as polluting (Buckster, 1996) or dangerous. Unlike Stephens (1962), who interpreted these customs as a response to male castration anxiety, Benedict (1934/1959) had earlier noted that menstruation could be viewed not only as a peril but also as a blessing. More recently, Buckley (1988) has provided support for the latter interpretation, in a reexamination of menstrual customs among the Native American Yurok of California.

Maidenhood

Menarche can also mark the beginning of a period in a girl's life that J. W. M. Whiting, Burbank, and Ratner (1986) have labeled "maidenhood." This interval, between "the onset of female fecundity and a wedding [which] legitimates motherhood" (p. 273) can last up to almost 12 years in industrial societies, but typically lasts only 3 years or less in nonindustrial societies. In those nonindustrial societies in which girls are married before menarche, there is no maidenhood period at all. It is in the maidenhood period that "post menarchial subfecundity" and a variety of societal rules governing premarital sex are depended upon to control premarital pregnancy. The rules of some societies are relatively lax, while in other societies girls are confined and chaperoned. Thus, for example, Flinn (1988) describes the traditional "daughter guarding" by fathers in a Trinidad village, suggesting that it serves to enhance a man's "inclusive fitness." Culture change resulting from "modernization" and schooling can totally alter the experience of "maidenhood," as Worthman and Whiting (1987) have reported for the Kikuyu of East Africa, where unwed motherhood has vastly increased with the virtual abandonment of traditional observances. One of these, a female initiation ritual involving a genital operation, had been an important part of Kikuyu maidenhood. Adolescent initiation rites for girls appear to be particularly vulnerable to the introduction of Western influence. One of the fullest descriptions of an initiation for girls, the Chisungu celebrated by the Bemba of East Africa, was recorded by Richards (1956) in the 1930s. She notes that, even then, the ceremony was already a briefer, simplified, and somewhat altered version of the lengthy, complex traditional observance. A recent reversal of this trend are the initiation rites for adolescents newly introduced in certain African American communities (Hirschoff, 2002).

Becoming an Adult: Initiation Ceremonies for Girls

Becoming an adult provides one of many examples of biological life-course transitions which are virtually ignored in some societies but culturally elaborated in others. Some initiation rituals must be celebrated before the first menstruation. Others coincide with the actual event, and the timing of others has to do with the availability of food for feasting. Some ceremonies are for groups of girls; others are individual. Some are large public celebrations and others are performed in virtual secrecy. Men are banned from some rites but are active participants in others. In some societies the rites continue for months. In other societies, the observances are brief. Some rituals include challenging tests of competence. And some initiations conclude with immediate marriage. Only a few involve painful procedures such as a genital operation (clitorodectomy or subincision) or extensive scarification. Many ceremonies are clearly joyous and involve feasting, music, and dance, as the initiate parades publicly in new finery and receives gifts. On the other hand, many societies do not celebrate initiation ceremonies for girls at all. What accounts for their presence in some societies and their absence in others?

One basic fact concerning all girls' initiation rites is that they require a society's commitment of considerable time, effort, and resources, warranted because the role of adult women is of such crucial importance. Thus when the economic contribution of women provides the basic sustenance of a society, as among the Maroni River Caribs, the rite (described above) is needed to assure the competence of the initiate. According to Kloos (1969, 1971), she has already mastered the actual skills she will need, but it is her attitude toward work (an aspect of education largely neglected in postindustrial society) on which the ritual is focused. Similarly, Richards (1956) reports this focus for the initiation ceremony of the Bemba, a rite which also includes tests of competence (perhaps somewhat analogous to American SATs). On the other hand, in the many societies where the economic role of women is minor or negligible, initiation rituals of this type are not celebrated.

The expenditures of an initiation ritual for girls are also warranted in societies where women have an important role in the social structure. Such is the case in that minority of societies, in which the groom joins the household of his wife's mother at marriage, and where women remain in the household of their mothers for life (however, the residence of men is discontinuous, as they move in and out at marriage), and where this type of household is basic to the society's structure. The initiation ritual provides public recognition (as well as recognition by the girl's mother) of the changed status of the young woman, despite the unchanged locus of her activities. Such initiation rituals for girls are not needed in the far more numerous societies in which women join the household of their husband's father at marriage (see below) and where the household of related males is basic to the social structure. (For further analyses of female initiation rites, see, Brown [1963], Schlegel & Barry [1979, 1980], Fried & Fried [1980], Lincoln [1981], and La Fontaine [1986], among others. An excellent succinct summary of this research is provided by Burbank [1997].)

VIRGINITY, DEFLORATION, MARRIAGE, AND DIVORCE

Virginity

It has been suggested that among certain societies like the traditional !Kung of southern Africa, who were tolerant of childhood sexual activity, the concept of virginity was virtually absent. At the other extreme are societies where the honor of a family depends upon the virtue of its women, as is typical for much of the circum-Mediterranean area, where women are secluded, chaperoned, and severely restricted in their activities. In some of these societies, a woman who dishonors her family is killed (Kressel, 1981). Following Goody (1973), Schlegel (1993) explains the emphasis on virginity in certain societies as a by-product of property arrangements at marriage. Where a family must part with considerable property at the marriage of a daughter, young women are confined and restricted to prevent "male social climbing through seduction" (Schlegel, 1993, p. 133).

Ritual Defloration

Originally published in 1918, Freud's (1918/1953) essay "The Taboo of Virginity" is remarkable for its use of ethnographic examples (limited to what was available in a World War I Austria), and provides some indication of the great variety of cultural elaborations of defloration. More recently, Wikan (1982) provides a first-hand account of the traditional (Near Eastern) Oman wedding ceremony, in which physical evidence for the defloration of the bride, in the form of a bloody cloth, must be publicly displayed to the waiting guests (see also, Korbin, 1987). The consequences are grave for a young woman

entering upon marriage without her virginity. Similar practices have also been reported beyond the Near East, among certain societies in Oceania.

Marriage

Anthropology has provided a literature on marriage so extensive that it cannot be summarized briefly. Included are intricate arguments concerning the definition of marriage (complicated by unusual customs such as woman–woman marriage among the Nandi of East Africa [Oboler,1985]) and a rich descriptive literature concerning wedding rituals and the many forms that marriage can take (e.g., Stockard, 2002). The study of weddings and marriage is further complicated by the existence of various gradations of marriage within a single society. Thus a first marriage is typically elaborate and celebrated very fully, whereas subsequent marriages and leviratical marriages (see below) are minor events in those societies that practice polygyny. In societies without a great deal of storable wealth in forms such as cowrie shells, cattle, pigs, and (more recently) bolts of cloth and money, the property exchanged as well as the ceremonial activity at marriage tends to be minimal or a marriage may be established by an exchange of sisters between two men. In some societies, the wedding can take years to complete, being fully recognized only after repeated ritual activity, extensive exchange of property, and even the arrival of children. Benedict (1934/1959) reports that marriage ceremonials were essentially lifelong events among the Kwakiutl of the Northwest Coast of North America. Payments between father-in-law and son-in-law, in the form of prerogatives and wealth continued, throughout life, marking the birth and the maturity of a couple's children.

In most but not all nonindustrial societies, marriages are arranged by the elder generation (aided by a go-between in some parts of the world). If there are objections, those of a young woman are more likely to be disregarded than those of a prospective groom. As the structuralist theorists have pointed out, marriage creates relationships among groups, and such weighty decisions are not left to the personal inclinations of young people. Furthermore, young people do not typically own the large amounts of property required for the exchanges that legitimate a marriage. As a result of this dependence on their parents, young people are respectful and polite toward their elders to an extent unknown in postindustrial societies.

The Creation of In-Laws

One aspect of the transition at marriage, which is almost entirely overlooked in the anthropological literature, is the transformation of the elder generation into in-laws, a change of status that is sometimes almost as dramatic as that of the bride. In the area of the Old World that Brown (1997) has designated as "the great mother-in-law belt," reaching from the Mediterranean to the Pacific, we encounter societies in which the overbearing and often abusive mother-in-law is freed from most work by the young bride. At marriage the wife enters into a life of servitude and is expected to be obedient, submissive, and stoic in the face of gratuitous mistreatment, both psychological and physical, until she becomes a mother-in-law herself. (For additional information concerning the intergenerational relationships among women, see Dickerson-Putman & Brown [1998], and for a cross-cultural analysis of these relationships, see Brown, Subbaiah, & Sarah [1998].)

Post-Marital Residence and Vulnerability to Abuse

In most of the world's nonindustrial societies, marriage means a change of residence for the bride but not the groom. For example, in parts of India, the young bride must leave her family and the village where she has spent her entire life to take up residence in a distant community, among people she has never seen before. On the other hand, in some Near Eastern societies, in which the fathers of the bride and groom are brothers, the bride's move to her husband's parents' home may just be a move across the neighborhood or even merely across the courtyard. Mernissi (1987) reports that Moroccan women and their families prefer such a marriage within the neighborhood, to insure that a wife will not be beaten and mistreated. Similarly, Chagnon (1977) reports that women among the Yanomamo prefer a marriage with a man of their own village, to reduce the severity of the beatings that all wives regularly receive. The dark side of the transition at marriage, wife abuse, has only recently been the focus of an ethnography (McClusky, 2001) or explored cross-culturally (Counts, Brown, & Campbell, 1999; Harvey & Gow, 1994; Sev'er, 1997). Wife-beating appears to be virtually universal (Erchak & Rosenfeld, 1994), yet the vulnerability of wives varies in different societies from those in which the abuse of wives is rare to those in which it is frequent and brutal (Brown, 1999).

The Transition at Marriage: Transformation

One of the most dramatic transitions at marriage is described by Elam (1973) for the Hima, who were traditional African pastoralists. The unmarried maiden, nude and physically active, helped the men with herding activities and was expected to be chaste. After marriage, she was no longer permitted to participate in herding. Now physically inactive, heavily clothed, and confined to the home, she was fattened by her husband. Her obesity was viewed as sexually attractive and made her appealing to other men, whom she was expected to seduce in order to attract a work force for her spouse.

Whereas the wedding ceremonial in our own society typically provides the bride with a shining moment, and the prospect of "happily ever after," such illusions do not pertain in the wedding celebrations of many nonindustrial societies. Girls attempt to run away to avoid not only the ceremony itself, but the diminished and difficult existence to which it leads. The mother of the bride also enters a new status. In many societies, the tears mothers shed at the weddings of their daughters are tears of true grief because their daughters will be separated from them and will embark on a life of toil, possible abuse, and the dangers of child-bearing under traditional conditions. The transition at marriage, which is so eagerly anticipated by girls in our own society, is viewed quite differently by young women in many parts of the world, where remaining unmarried during the child-bearing years is not an option.

Divorce as Transition

Divorce is almost, but not entirely, as universal as marriage. A frequent reason for divorce is a wife's infertility, whether real or alleged (since the possibility of male infertility is often not recognized), or failure to bear sons. Whether the procedure is simple or complicated, terminating a marriage is an option open only to men in many societies. A divorced wife may be compelled to return to her natal family, who may not welcome her because the property which the divorcing husband and his family expended for her marriage must be returned. Typically the property, possibly in the form of cattle or pigs, has already changed hands in order to establish a marriage for the woman's brother or to acquire yet another wife for her father. Custody of children is not negotiable, since a society's rules of descent are the deciding factor. Thus in most societies, the transition a woman experiences at divorce can deprive her of her children and, unless she remarries, forces her into a life of dependency and penury.

CHILD-BEARING, PARENTHOOD, MAKING A LIVING, AND DOMESTICITY

Pre-Parenthood

Possibly the most dramatic transition in the lives of women everywhere comes with motherhood, which also involves a transition into grandparenthood for the ascending generation. Nowhere is the birth of a child, and particularly the birth of a first child, unmarked by cultural observances (Davis-Floyd & Georges, 1996; Raphael, 1975). The degree to which a society allows its women to participate in the decision-making concerning their reproductive activities varies cross-culturally (Browner, 2000), as do the customs associated with pregnancy. Food prohibitions are typical among the numerous pregnancy avoidances and taboos that must be observed to assure the well-being of the unborn child (Ayres, 1967). Obeyesekere (1963) noted the importance of food cravings and Fessler (2002) has recently suggested an "adaptionist explanation" for "pregnancy symptoms," suggesting that these food aversions may help the expectant mother to avoid certain pathogens. In addition, there are societies in which the couvade is practiced, where pre- and post-partum observances for the welfare of the baby must be performed by the father (Munroe, Munroe, & Whiting, 1973).

Birth and Motherhood

A society's birth customs (e.g., Jordan, 1978; MacCormack, 1994) dictate the birthing position of the mother (Naroll, Naroll, & Howard, 1961), the use of special equipment, such as a birthing chair, where the birth will take place (whether out of doors, in a secluded room, or in a crowded communal dwelling, as among the Mundurucú of South America), and whether the mother is alone or attended by a midwife or certain relatives. The role of the father can vary from being excluded to performing the actual delivery, as reported for the Utku of Northern Canada (Briggs, 1970). The nursing of the baby (Hull & Simpson, 1985; Raphael, 1972) is only one of the many complex activities that are involved in motherhood, a subject for which Hrdy (1999) has provided a particularly rich and complex analysis that combines evolutionary, historical, psychological, and anthropological perspectives. As for what a society views as good mothering, B. B. Whiting (1996) has shown that, among the Kikuyu, this definition is not fixed but has been changed by "modernization."

The Balancing Act

Motherhood ushers in the parenting phase of a woman's career, which will engage her for the rest of her life, particularly with those offspring which societal rules concerning postmarital residence assign to her vicinity. Furthermore, motherhood complicates the delicate balancing act that every society demands of its female members. Not only must the economic activity of women be reconciled with their domestic responsibilities (Bujra, 1979; Clark, 1999; Ember, 1983), but both must now also be reconciled with parental responsibilities (Ball & Panter-Brick, 2001; Brown, 1970, 1973, 1978). Each society has its own formula for how this mutual accommodation is achieved, an issue of continuing anxious concern for women in postindustrial societies. In many societies, the solution is to delegate the work of childcare (Minturn & Lambert, 1964) to female relatives such as grandmothers (see below), sisters and co-wives, or to the youngster's older siblings (Weisner, 1987), or to the local children's peer group (Draper & Harpending, 1987), or to delegate a mother's other activities (Bradley, 1993; Hawkes, O'Connell, & Blurton Jones, 1989, 1997). Parenting activities by fathers vary widely, from those in which fathers make a major contribution to child care (Hewlett, 1994) to the numerous societies in which fathers have virtually nothing to do with babies and children. J. W. M. Whiting and B. B. Whiting (1975) have suggested that the latter pattern is typical of those societies (societies which are "mid-level" in complexity, and have a need for warriors) in which men and women seem to live in very separate worlds, where there is "aloofness" between husbands and wives.

Women's Associations

As full adults, women in some societies can join organizations such as the women's work group.

Ross (1986) suggests that these associations do not provide their members with access to greater authority within the wider community. On the other hand, Levinson (1989) reports that wife-beating is less prevalent in those societies that have women's work groups.

MENOPAUSE AND MIDDLE AGE

Menopause

The end of child-bearing, the transition into middle age, which typically brings empowerment to women in non-industrial societies is ceremonially unmarked, no doubt because menopause can only be identified retrospectively. Yet this biological change, experienced by women everywhere, is so strongly shaped by culture that even its physical symptoms, such as the hot flash, show cross-cultural variation (Kay, Voda, Olivas, Rios, & Imle, 1982; Lock, 1993).

Middle Age

The psychoanalyst C. G. Jung (1931/1960), and more recently Gutmann (1987) and McCabe (1989), noted that in middle age men and women exhibit behaviors which would have been gender-inappropriate earlier in life. Many ethnographers report the greater assertiveness of older women (Jacobson, 1977; Kerns & Brown, 1992; McCabe, 1989; Mernissi, 1987; Roy, 1975); in some societies, matrons are described as becoming like men. Middle-aged women can even achieve the "purity" of men, as among the Hua of New Guinea, according to Meigs (1988). The Hua ascribe a dangerously polluting quality to women of child-bearing age, which no longer applies to older women who have experienced the cleansing effect attributed to repeated child-bearing. Brown (1982a, 1982b, 1992, 1998a, 1998b) has suggested that in the nonindustrial world, transition into middle age brings with it three major changes in the lives of women. First, they are freed from conforming to cumbersome restrictions such as rules of modesty, showing elaborate respect, observing menstrual customs, and being confined within the home. Second, they are given authority over younger kin, making decisions for them and delegating the work they once had to perform. Third, some matrons become eligible for special status and recognition outside the home by becoming a midwife, healer, or matchmaker.

The Post-Reproductive Life Span

It is difficult to reconcile the extensive post-reproductive life span among human females with the maximization of reproductive success and inclusive fitness (Sievert, 2001). However, P. Draper (2002, personal communication) has found that, among the traditional !Kung, those adult women who had a surviving mother also had more surviving children. Similarly Hawkes et al. (1989, 1997) have noted that, among the Hadza, the presence of grandmothers contributes to the reproductive success of their daughters by freeing them from the rigors of strenuous subsistence activities.

WIDOWHOOD, OLD AGE, DEATH, AND BEYOND

Widowhood

The transition into widowhood, which is unrelated to any biological event in the life-course of women, receives considerable cultural elaboration in certain societies, where the widow is demeaned, compelled to change her appearance, and to engage in public acts that denote grief, such as wailing and inflicting pain on herself. She may be blamed and punished for her husband's death and accused of poisoning or sorcerizing him, unless she can prove her innocence, as Strathern (1972) reports for the people of Mount Hagen, New Guinea. Perhaps most dramatic (and most controversial) is the Indian custom of *sati (suttee)*, which dictates that, to avoid widowhood, the bereaved wife must throw herself on her husband's funeral pyre to be immolated with his corpse (Hawley, 1994). Embree (1994) explains, "... in India, as elsewhere, widows were a special subset of dangerous women .... Not only would life [as a widow] be miserable for her, but inevitably she would yield to base sensual passion and bring disgrace on her community" (pp. 155–156). In some societies, the widow is expected to enter into a levirical marriage with her husband's brother, which places her in a relatively unenviable position, or she may be expected to return to the household of her own people, typically her brother's, where her welcome is questionable.

Old Age

Becoming frail and dependent marks the transition into old age, a difficult period in the life-course of women even in postindustrial societies (see Albert [2002] for a cross-cultural perspective). However, unlike aged men, even frail women still have the ability to contribute to the household by doing light domestic chores. In the tradition of Simmons' (1945) pioneering cross-cultural study of aging, Counts and Counts (1985) provide an overview of the contrasts in the lives of aged men and women among Pacific societies, stressing the continuing importance of the parental role for aging women. In West Bengal (Lamb, 2000), the care adult children provide for the frail incontinent parent is viewed as a repayment for the nurture once received in infancy and childhood; yet it is believed that the "moral debt" can never be fully repaid by the younger generation. On the other hand, in some societies the decrepit elderly are subjected to "death hastening behavior" (Glasscock, 1983).

Death-Related Customs

Funerary customs, burial customs, and mourning customs are prolonged and complex in certain societies. A very full description is provided by Kerns (1983) for the Garífuna of Belize. Although men participate in the burial procedures and in the funeral celebration, it is Garífuna women who actually bear the major responsibility for carrying out the complex customs ushered in by death. This uneven division of labor is typical of many societies, as are the more elaborate observances at a man's death than at the death of a woman (Friendly, 1956).

Beyond Death

In some societies, the transition to the afterlife takes on a unisex character (not unlike the transitions very early in life), as among the traditional Navajo (Kluckhohn & Leighton, 1962) where a woman, like a man, is feared once she has turned into a ghost. However, in other societies the afterlife itself may differ greatly for men and women. Writing under an assumed name, Sabbah (1984) provides a feminist analysis of the place of women in the context of Islam, noting that, whereas men are assured an eternity of sensual bliss in the company of numerous compliant maidens, the description of the afterlife for women is left somewhat vague and not particularly promising.

Conclusions

Transitions in the life-course of women vary from society to society. They may be numerous or few. They may come early in life or later. They may be joyous or painful or even life-threatening. They may be cultural elaborations of biological changes, or purely cultural. They may be the same as for males or for females only. However, all life-course transitions share the fact that they are inevitable and irreversible. Thus they serve to remind the individual and those around her, that life is finite and that there will be a final transition at death.

References

Albert, S. M. (2002). Anthropology and the second 50 years. *Current Anthropology, 43*(2), 338–340.

Alford, R. D. (1996). Naming. In D. Levinson & M. Ember (Eds.), *Encyclopedia of cultural anthropology* (Vol. 3, pp. 833–836). New York: Holt.

Ayres, B. (1967). Pregnancy magic: A study of food taboos and sex avoidances. In C. S. Ford (Ed.), *Cross-cultural approaches* (pp. 111–125). New Haven, CT: HRAF Press.

Ball, H., & Panter-Brick, C. (2001). Child survival and the modulation of parental investment. In P. Ellison (Ed.), *Reproductive ecology and human evolution* (pp. 249–266). New York: Aldine de Gruyter.

Benedict, R. (1953). Continuities and discontinuities in cultural conditioning. In C. Kluckhohn & H. Murray (Eds.), *Personality in nature, society, and culture* (2nd ed., pp. 522–531). New York: Knopf. (Original work published 1938.)

Benedict, R. (1959). *Patterns of culture*. Boston: Houghton Mifflin. (Original work published 1934.)

Boddy, J. (1989). *Wombs and alien spirits*. Madison: University of Wisconsin Press.

Borgerhoff Mulder, M. (1989). Menarche, menopause and reproduction in the Kipsigis of Kenya. *Journal of Biosocial Science, 21*(2) 179–192.

Bradley, C. (1993). Women's power, children's labor. *Cross-Cultural Research, 27*(1&2) 70–96.

Briggs, J. (1970). *Never in anger*. Cambridge, MA: Harvard University Press.

Brown, J. K. (1963). A cross-cultural study of female initiation rites. *American Anthropologist, 65*, 837–853.

Brown, J. K. (1970). A note on the division of labor by sex. *American Anthropologist, 72*, 1074–1078.

Brown, J. K. (1973). The subsistence activities of women and the socialization of children. *Ethos, 1*, 413–423.

Brown, J. K. (1978). The recruitment of a female labor force. *Anthropos, 73*, 41–48.

Brown, J. K. (1982a). A cross-cultural exploration of the end of the child-bearing years. In A. Voda, M. Dinnerstein, & S. O'Donnell (Eds.), *Changing perspectives on menopause* (pp. 51–59). Austin, TX: University of Texas Press.

Brown, J. K. (1982b). Cross-cultural perspectives on middle-aged women. *Current Anthropology, 23*(2) 143–148, 153–156.

Brown, J. K. (1992). Lives of middle-aged women. In V. Kerns & J. K. Brown (Eds.), *In her prime: New views of middle-aged women* (pp. 17–30). Chicago: University of Illinois Press.

Brown, J. K. (1997). Agitators and peace-makers: Cross-cultural perspectives on older women and the abuse of young wives. In A. Sev'er (Ed.), *A cross-cultural exploration of wife abuse: Problems and prospects* (pp. 79–99). Lewiston, NY: Mellen.

Brown, J. K. (1998a). Lives of middle-aged women. In N. Stromquist (Ed.), *Women in the third world: An encyclopedia of contemporary issues* (pp. 246–251). New York: Garland.

Brown, J. K. (1998b). Menopause. In S. Young (Ed.), *Encyclopedia of women and world religion* (Vol. 2, pp. 647–648). New York: Macmillan Reference.

Brown, J. K. (1999). Introduction: Definitions, assumptions, themes, and issues. In D. Counts, J. K. Brown, & J. Campbell (Eds.), *To have and to hit: Cultural perspectives on wife-beating* (2nd ed., pp. 3–26). Chicago: University of Illinois Press.

Brown, J. K., Subbaiah, P., & Sarah, T. (1998). Being in charge: Older women and their younger female kin. In J. Dickerson-Putman & J. K. Brown (Eds.), *Women among women: Anthropological perspectives on female age hierarchies* (pp.100–123). Chicago: University of Illinois Press.

Browner, C. H. (2000). Situating women's reproductive activities. *American Anthropologist, 102*(4), 773–788.

Buckley, T. (1988). Menstruation and the power of Yurok women. In T. Buckley & A. Gottlieb (Eds.), *Blood magic: The anthropology of menstruation* (pp. 187–209). Los Angeles: University of California Press.

Buckster, A. (1996). Purity and pollution. In D. Levinson & M. Ember (Eds.), *Encyclopedia of cultural anthropology* (Vol. 3, pp. 1045–1049). New York: Holt.

Bujra, J. M. (1979). Introductory: Female solidarity and the sexual division of labour. In P. Caplan & J. M. Burja (Eds.), *Women united, women divided: Comparative studies of ten contemporary cultures* (pp. 13–45). Bloomington: Indiana University Press.

Burbank, V. (1997). Adolescent socialization and initiation ceremonies. In C. Ember & M. Ember (Eds.), *Cross-cultural research for social science* (Vol. 1, pp. 83–106). Englewood Cliffs, NJ: Prentice-Hall.

Chagnon, N. (1977). *Yanomamo: The fierce people* (2nd ed.). New York: Holt, Rinehart & Winston.

Clark, G. (1999). Mothering, work, and gender in urban Asante ideology and practice. *American Anthropologist, 101*(4), 717–729.

Counts, D., Brown, J. K., & Campbell, J. (Eds.) (1999). *To have and to hit: Cultural perspectives on wife beating* (2nd ed.). Chicago: University of Illinois Press.

Counts, D. A., & Counts, D. R. (1985). Introduction: Linking concepts aging and gender, aging and death. In D. A. Counts & D. R. Counts (Eds.), *Aging and its transformations: Moving toward death in Pacific societies* (ASAO Monograph No. 10, pp. 1–24). New York: University Press of America.

Cronk, L. (1989). Low socioeconomic status and female-biased parental investment: The Mukogodo example. *American Anthropologist, 91*(2), 414–429.

Cronk, L. (1993). Parental favoritism toward daughters. *American Scientist, 81*, 272–279.

Davis-Floyd, R., & Georges, E. (1996). Pregnancy. In D. Levinson & M. Ember (Eds.), *Encyclopedia of cultural anthropology* (Vol. 3, pp. 1014–1016). New York: Holt.

Dickerson-Putman, J., & Brown, J. K. (Eds.). (1998). *Women among women: Anthropological perspectives on female age hierarchies.* Chicago: University of Illinois Press.

Diener, M. (2000). Gift from the gods: A Balinese guide to early child rearing. In J. DeLoache & A. Gottlieb (Eds.), *A World of babies: Imagined childcare guides for seven societies* (pp. 97–116). New York: Cambridge University Press.

Draper, P. (2002). Personal Communication.

Draper, P., & Harpending, H. (1987). Parent investment and the child's environment. In J. Lancaster, J. Altmann, A. Rossi, & L. Sherrod (Eds.), *Parenting across the life span: Biosocial dimensions* (pp. 207–235). New York: Aldine de Gruyter.

Elam, Y. (1973). *The social and sexual roles of Hima women.* Manchester, UK: Manchester University Press.

Ember, C. (1981). A cross-cultural perspective on sex differences. In R. H. Munroe, R. L. Munroe, & B. Whiting (Eds.), *Handbook of cross-cultural human development* (pp. 531–580). New York: Garland.

Ember, C. (1983). The relative decline in women's contribution to agriculture with intensification. *American Anthropologist, 85*(2), 285–304.

Embree, A. (1994). Comment: Widows as cultural symbols. In J. S. Hawley (Ed.), *Sati, the blessing and the curse: The burning of wives in India* (pp. 149–159). New York: Oxford University Press.

Erchak, G., & Rosenfeld, R. (1994). Societal isolation, violent norms, and gender relations: A reexamination and extension of Levinson's model of wife beating. *Cross-Cultral Research, 28*(2), 111–133.

Fessler, D. (2002). Reproductive immunosuppression and diet: An evolutionary perspective on pregnancy sickness and meat consumption. *Current Anthropology, 43*(1), 19–38, 48–61.

Flinn, M. (1988). Parent–offspring interactions in a Caribbean village: Daughter guarding. In L. Betzig, M. Borgenhoff Mulder, & P. Turke (Eds.), *Human reproductive behaviour: A Darwinian perspective* (pp. 189–200). New York: Cambridge University Press.

Freud, S. (1953). Contributions to the psychology of love: The taboo of virginity. In E. Jones (Ed.) & J. Riviere (Trans.), *Collected papers* (Vol. 4, pp. 217–235). London: Hogarth Press. (Original work published in 1918.)

Fried, M. N., & Fried M. H. (1980). *Transitions: Four rituals in eight cultures.* New York: Penguin.

Friendly, J. P. (1956). *A cross-cultural study of ascetic mourning behavior.* Unpublished Honors Thesis, Radcliffe College, 1956. Cambridge, MA.

Frisbie, C. (1967). *Kinaalda': A study of the Navaho girl's puberty ceremony.* Middletown, CT: Wesleyan University Press.

Gates H. (2001). Footloose in Fujian: Economic correlates of footbinding. *Comparative Studies in Society and History, 43*(1), 130–148.

Gates, H. (in press). Girls' work in China and Northwestern Europe: Of Guniang and Meisjes. In T. Engelen & A. P. Wolf (Eds.), *Hajnal in China and Northwestern Europe.* Stanford, CA: Stanford University Press.

Glasscock, A. (1983). Death-hastening behavior: An expansion of Eastwell's thesis. *American Anthropologist, 85*(2), 417–420.

Goldfrank, E. (1964). Socialization, personality, and the structure of Pueblo society. In D. Haring (Ed.), *Personal character and cultural milieu* (pp. 302–327). Syracuse, NY: Syracuse University Press. (Original work published 1945.)

Goody, J. (1973). Bridewealth and dowry in Africa and Eurasia. In J. Goody & S. J. Tambiah (Eds.), *Bridewealth and dowry* (pp. 1–58). New York: Cambridge University Press.

Gutmann, D. (1987). *Reclaimed powers: Toward a new psychology of men and women in later life.* New York: Basic Books.

Harvey, P., & Gow, P. (Eds.). (1994). *Sex and violence: Issues in representation and experience.* New York: Routledge.

Hausfater, G., & Hrdy, S. (Eds.). (1984). *Infanticide: Comparative and evolutionary perspectives.* New York: Aldine.

Hawkes, K., O'Connell, J. F., & Blurton Jones, N. G. (1989). Hardworking Hadza grandmothers. In V. Standen & R. A. Foley (Eds.), *Comparative socioecology: The behavioural ecology of humans and other mammals* (pp. 341–366). Boston: Blackwell Scientific.

Hawkes, K., O'Connell, J. F., & Blurton Jones, N. G. (1997). Hadza women's time allocation, offspring provisioning, and the evolution of long postmenopausal life span. *Current Anthropology, 38*(4), 551–565, 571–577.

Hawley, J. S. (1994). Introduction. In J. S. Hawley (Ed.), *Sati, the blessing and the curse: The burning of wives in India* (pp. 3–26). New York: Oxford University Press.

Hayes, R. O. (1975). Female genital mutilation, fertility control, women's roles, and the patrilineage in modern Sudan: A Functional analysis. *American Ethnologist, 2*(4), 617–633.

Hewlett, B. (1994). *Intimate fathers: The nature and context of Aka Pygmy paternal infant care.* Ann Arbor: University of Michigan Press.

Hicks, E. (1996). *Infibulation: Female mutilation in Islamic Northeastern Africa.* New Brunswick, NJ: Transaction Publishers.

Hirschoff, P. (2002). Museum bridges chasm, links rites in Africa and America. *Anthropology News, 43*(5), 21.

Hrdy, S. (1996). Infanticide. In D. Levinson & M. Ember (Eds.), *Encyclopedia of cultural anthropology* (Vol. 2, pp. 644–648). New York: Holt.

Hrdy, S. (1999). *Mother nature: A history of mothers, infants, and natural selection.* New York: Pantheon.

Hull, V., & Simpson, M. (Eds.). (1985). *Breastfeeding, child health and child spacing: Cross-cultural perspectives.* Dover, NH: Croom Helm.

Jacobson, D. (1977). The women of North and Central India: goddesses and wives. In D. Jacobson & S. Wadley (Eds.), *Women in India: Two perspectives* (pp. 17–111). Columbia, MO: South Asian Books.

Jordan, B. (1978). *Birth in four cultures: A crosscultural investigation of childbirth in Yucatan, Holland, Sweden and the United States.* St. Albans, VT: Eden Press.

Jung, C. G. (1960). *The structure and dynamics of the psyche* (R. F. C. Hull, Trans.) (Bollingen Series 20). New York: Pantheon. (Original work published in 1931.)

Kay, M., Voda, A., Olivas, G., Rios, F., & Imle, M. (1982). Ethnography of the menopause-related hot flash. *Maturitas, 4,* 217–227.

Kerns, V. (1983). *Women and the ancestors: Black Carib kinship and ritual.* Chicago: University of Illinois Press.

Kerns, V., & Brown, J. K. (Eds.). (1992). *In her prime: New views of middle-aged women.* Chicago: University of Illinois Press.

Kilbride, P., & Kilbride, J. (1974). Sociocultural factors and the early manifestation of sociability behavior among Baganda infants. *Ethos, 2*(3), 296–314.

Kloos, P. (1969). Female initiation among the Maroni River Caribs. *American Anthropologist, 71*(5), 898–905.

Kloos, P. (1971). *The Maroni River Caribs of Surinam.* Assen, The Netherlands: Van Gorcum.

Kluckhohn, C., & Leighton, D. (1962). *The Navaho.* Garden City, NY: Doubleday. (Original work published 1946.)

Korbin, J. (1987). Child sexual abuse: Implications from the cross-cultural record. In N. Scheper-Hughes (Ed.), *Child survival: Anthropological perspectives on the treatment and maltreatment of children* (pp. 247–265). Boston: Kluwer.

Kressel, G. (1981). Sororicide/filiacide: Homicide for family honour. *Current Anthropology, 22*(2) 141–152, 156–158.

Kroeber, A. L. (1963). *Anthropology: Culture patterns and processes.* New York: Harcourt, Brace & World. (Original work published 1948.)

La Fontaine, J. S. (1986). *Initiation.* Dover, NH: Manchester University Press.

Lamb, S. (2000). *White saris and sweet mangoes: Aging, gender, and body in North India.* Los Angeles: University of California Press.

Landauer, T., & Whiting, J. W. M. (1981). Correlates and consequences of stress in infancy. In R. H. Munroe, R. L. Munroe, & B. Whiting (Eds.), *Handbook of cross-cultural human development* (pp. 355–375). New York: Garland.

Levinson, D. (1989). *Family violence in cross-cultural perspective.* Newbury Park, CA: Sage.

Lincoln, B. (1981). *Emerging from the chrysalis: Studies in rituals of women's initiation.* Cambridge, MA: Harvard University Press.

Lipson, S. (2001). Metabolism, maturation, and ovarian function. In P. Ellison (Ed.), *Reproductive ecology and human evolution* (pp. 235–248). New York: Aldine de Gruyter.

Lock, M. (1993). *Encounters with aging: Mythologies of menopause in Japan and North America.* Los Angeles: University of California Press.

MacCormack, C. (Ed.). (1994) *Ethnography of fertility and birth* (2nd ed.). Prospect Heights, IL: Waveland Press.

McCabe, J. (1989). Psychological androgyny in later life: A psycho-cultural examination. *Ethos, 17*(1), 3–31.

McClusky, L. (2001). *"Here our culture is hard": Stories of domestic violence from a Mayan community in Belize.* Austin, TX: University of Texas Press.

McKee, L. (1985). Sex differentials in survivorship and the customary treatment of infants and children. *Medical Anthropology, 8,* 91–108.

Meigs, A. (1988). *Food, sex, and pollution: A New Guinea religion.* New Brunswick, NJ: Rutgers University Press.

Mernissi, F. (1987). *Beyond the veil: Male–female dynamics in modern Muslim society* (Rev. ed.). Bloomington: Indiana University Press.

Miller, B. D. (1987). Female infanticide and child neglect in rural North India. In N. Scheper-Hughes (Ed.), *Child survival: Anthropological perspectives on the treatment and maltreatment of children* (pp. 95–112). Boston: Kluwer.

Miller, B. D. (2001). Female-selective abortion in Asia: Patterns, policies, and debates. *American Anthropologist, 103*(4), 1083–1095.

Minturn, L., & Lambert, W. (1964). *Mothers of six cultures: Antecedents of child rearing*. New York: Wiley.

Munroe, R. L., Munroe, R. H., & Whiting, J. W. M. (1973). Couvade: A psychological analysis. *Ethos, 1*(1) 30–74.

Naroll, F., Naroll, R., & Howard, F. (1961). Position of women in childbirth: A study of data quality control. *American Journal of Obstetrics and Gynecology, 13*, 207–214.

Obeyesekere, G. (1963). Pregnancy cravings (*Dola-Duka*) in relation to social structure and personality in a Sinhalese village. *American Anthropologist, 65*, 323–342.

Oboler, R. (1985). *Women, power, and economic change: The Nandi of Kenya*. Stanford, CA: Stanford University Press.

Pierroutsakos, S. (2000). Infants of the dreaming: A Walpiri guide to child care. In J. DeLoache & A. Gottlieb (Eds.), *A World of babies: Imagined childcare guides for seven societies* (pp. 145–170). New York: Cambridge University Press.

Raphael, D. (1972). CA comment. *Current Anthropology, 13*(2), 253–254.

Raphael, D. (1975). Matrescence, becoming a mother, a "new/old" rite de passage. In D. Raphael (Ed.), *Being female: Reproduction, power and change* (pp. 65–71). Chicago: Aldine.

Richards, A. (1956). *Chisungu: A girls' initiation ceremony among the Bemba of Northern Rhodesia*. New York: Grove.

Ross, M. H. (1986). Female political participation: A cross-cultural explanation. *American Anthropologist, 88*(4), 843–858.

Roy, M. (1975). *Bengali women*. Chicago: University of Chicago Press.

Sabbah, F. A. (1984). *Woman in the Muslim unconscious* (M. J. Lakeland, Trans.). New York: Pergamon.

Schlegel, A. (1993). Status, property, and the value on virginity. In M. Womack & J. Marti (Eds.), *The other fifty percent: Multicultural perspectives on gender relations* (pp. 123–134). Prospect Heights, IL: Waveland Press.

Schlegel, A., & Barry, H., III. (1979). Adolescent initiation ceremonies: A cross-cultural code. *Ethnology, 18*, 199–210.

Schlegel, A., & Barry, H., III. (1980). The evolutionary significance of adolescent initiation ceremonies. *American Ethnologist, 7*, 696–715.

Sev'er, A. (Ed.). (1997). *A cross-cultural exploration of wife abuse: Problems and prospects*. Lewiston, NY: Mellen.

Sievert, L. L. (2001). Aging and reproductive senescence. In P. Ellison (Ed.), *Reproductive ecology and human evolution* (pp. 267–292). New York: Aldine de Gruyter.

Simmons, L. (1945). *The role of the aged in primitive society*. New Haven, CT: Yale University Press.

Stephens, W. (1962). *The Oedipus complex: Cross-cultural evidence*. Glencoe, IL: Free Press.

Stockard, J. (2002). *Marriage in culture: Practice and meaning across diverse societies*. New York: Harcourt College Publishers.

Strathern, M. (1972). *Women in between: Female roles in a male world: Mount Hagen, New Guinea*. New York: Seminar Press.

van Gennep, A. (1909). *Les rites de passage*. Paris: Libraire Critique Emil Nourry.

Weisner, T. (1987). Socialization for parenthood in sibling caretaking societies. In J. Lancaster, J. Altmann, A. Rossi, & L. Sherrod (Eds.), *Parenting across the life span: Biosocial dimensions* (pp. 237–270). New York: Aldine de Gruyter.

Whiting, B. B. (1996). The effects of social change on concepts of the good child and good mothering: A study of families in Kenya. *Ethos, 24*(1) 3–35.

Whiting, B. B., & Edwards, C. P. (1988). *Children of different worlds: The formation of social behavior*. Cambridge, MA: Harvard University Press.

Whiting, J. W. M. (1941). *Becoming a Kwoma: Teaching and learning in a New Guinea tribe*. New Haven, CT: Yale University Press.

Whiting, J. W. M. (1964). Effects of climate on certain cultural practices. In W. Goodenough (Ed.), *Explorations in cultural anthropology* (pp. 511–544). New York: McGraw-Hil.

Whiting, J. W. M. (1965). Menarchial age and infant stress in humans. In F. Beach (Ed.), *Sex and behavior* (pp. 221–233). New York: J Wiley.

Whiting, J. W. M., & Child, I. (1953). *Child training and personality*. New Haven, CT: Yale University Press.

Whiting, J. W. M., & Whiting, B. B. (1975). Aloofness and intimacy of husbands and wives: A cross-cultural study. *Ethos, 3*, 183–207.

Whiting, J. W. M., Burbank, V., & Ratner, M. (1986). The duration of maidenhood across cultures. In J. Lancaster & B. Hamburg (Eds.), *School-age pregnancy and parenthood: Biosocial dimensions* (pp. 273–302). New York: Aldine de Gruyter.

Whiting, J. W. M., Kluckhohn, R., & Anthony, A. (1958). The function of male initiation ceremonies at puberty. In E. Maccoby, T. Newcomb, & E. Hartley (Eds.), *Readings in social psychology* (pp. 359–370). New York: Holt.

Wikan, U. (1982). *Behind the veil: Women in Oman*. Chicago: University of Chicago Press.

Worthman, C., & Whiting, J. W. M. (1987). Social change in adolescent sexual behavior, mate selection, and premarital pregnancy rates in a Kikuyu community. *Ethos, 15*(2) 145–165.

Sexuality and Male–Female Interaction

Sexual Attitudes and Practices

Gwen J. Broude

SEXUAL ATTITUDES AND PRACTICES: PERSPECTIVES

Major Theoretical Paradigms

Sexual behavior is a cross-cultural universal. Across time and place, the vast majority of human beings engage in sexual relations. The biologically ubiquitous drive to engage in sexual activity is also transparently related to reproduction in our own and other species. Among human beings, however, different cultures also elaborate and interpret sexuality in different ways. Each of these three observations regarding human sexuality motivates one of three major theoretical perspectives regarding the study of human sexual attitudes and practices.

The first perspective assumes that matters having to do with sex, as with any human function, are basically a product of learning. Individuals pick up beliefs and customs regarding sex from members of the culture in which they grow up and live. Theorists sympathetic to this point of view expect to see a wide variety of attitudes and practices exhibited across societies dictated by such things as local values, culturally determined roles, values, and the like. Thus, for instance, if a society places a value on virginity in unmarried girls, this may simply be in accordance with a culturally determined view that girls should be chaste until marriage. This is the position of the cultural determinist.

The second perspective assumes that sexual beliefs and practices are systematically related to other aspects of culture and behavior, and may generally reflect practical solutions to problems of living characteristic of certain kinds of cultures. Thus, for instance, if a society is large and anonymous and has no reliable birth control, adults may place a value on virginity, especially in girls, to minimize the chances that a man will impregnate an unmarried female and then disappear. This represents a practical problem in many cultures because it means that the girl's family is left to take care of the child. This view that cultural attitudes and behaviors are practical responses to some kind of problem or opportunity presented by a culture is characteristic of cross-cultural anthropologists.

The third perspective assumes that sexual attitudes and behaviors are actually grounded in biology. They are mediated by natural selection and represent adaptations. According to this view, customs and behaviors having to do with sex show up in societies today because they have been successful in promoting reproduction in the past. Variations in sexual attitudes and practices from one society to the next just represent adaptive responses to local conditions. Theorists who argue for a role of natural selection in sexual beliefs and behaviors assume that environment also influences how people think about and deal with sex. But the effect of environment is not to create sexual attitudes and behaviors from whole cloth. Rather, local circumstances act to shape pan-human sexual impulses to respond to the particulars of a given society while still allowing individuals to reproduce most successfully. This is the position of the evolutionary psychologist.

Controversies and Trends in the Evidence

A related question has to do with what constitutes a proper context for understanding the meaning of a sexual belief or behavior. Some theorists assume that any attitude or behavior having to do with sex has a unique meaning for the culture in which it is exhibited. According to this view, it is impossible to view what looks like the same belief or behavior across two or more cultures as in fact equivalent. Thus, for example, if members of two cultures view virginity as valuable in a single girl, this may in fact mean one thing in one society and another thing in another society. The reasoning is that members of any given society attach unique meanings to their customs and practices despite the appearance of superficial similarities. This point of view characterizes the thinking of cultural determinists.

The opposing two positions assume that we can make meaningful cross-cultural comparisons. Thus the cross-cultural anthropologist may argue that, if two cultures believe virginity is valuable in unmarried girls, this is because both cultures have similar causal conditions. And the evolutionary psychologist will then argue that strategies aimed at avoiding single motherhood make sense because a woman is often at a disadvantage if she has to raise a child on her own.

All three positions assume that there will be some unique features in every society. Cross-cultural and evolutionary psychologists also assume that we will see patterned variation in how sex is managed across societies. These patterns are borne out in a number of investigations of sex and culture, as indicated in this article. The discovery that sexual attitudes and practices are patterned similarly across cultures, and that the same custom or belief is predictably associated with the same ecological, social structural, economic, or political variables supports the idea that the same sexual attitude or custom has a similar meaning across societies. Further, sexual attitudes and practices across cultures are often patterned in ways that look like good strategies for promoting successful reproduction.

ATTITUDES TOWARD SEX

Range of Variation

The variation in attitudes toward sex across cultures is striking. This variability is reflected in the degree to which sex is viewed as a perilous or harmless pursuit.

The belief that sex is dangerous at least some of the time is shared by a majority of societies for which information on attitudes toward sex is available. In only 41% of a worldwide sample of 34 cultures is sex viewed as safe all of the time (Broude & Greene, 1976). Thus, for instance, sex is viewed as normal and natural among societies such as the Tibetan Lepcha, who think of sexual activity as wholesome, fun, and even necessary, much like food or drink (Gorer, 1938).

Sexual secretions are seen as dangerous in 6% of the same 34 cultures (Broude & Greene, 1976). For the Kurd, is it not sex itself that is dangerous, but the body fluids produced during sexual activity are viewed as dirty, and therefore Kurd men bathe after sex (Broude, 1994). The Kimam of New Guinea believe that sperm has healing qualities, but sex can stunt the growth of boys (Serpenti, 1965).

Sexual activity is always considered dangerous in 15% of the sample of 34 societies (Broude & Greene, 1976). For instance, Ethiopian Konso males believe that the vaginas of some girls can literally snap off a man's penis (Hallpike, 1972). Similarly, the Azande of Zaire claim that the mere sight of a woman's anus or genitals can have injurious effects on a man (Leighton & Kluckhohn, 1969).

Finally, unusual or unsanctioned sex, for instance, sex at the wrong time, or in the wrong place, or using the wrong technique, is dangerous in 26% of the same sample. Sex is dangerous to specific categories of persons, for instance, shamans or unmarried people, in 12% of these cultures (Broude & Greene, 1976). (See sex taboos below for further discussion.)

Societies also differ with regard to the meaning that they impute to sexual activity. Thus, for example, for the Bhil of India sex is sacred and should not be engaged in for pleasure. For the Lepcha, by contrast, sex is merely a diversion. And among the Cayapa of Ecuador, sex is "a little like work" (Gorer, 1938). In some places, sex is an occasion for expressing hostility. For instance, the Gusii of Kenya treat sexual intercourse, even between spouses, as a contest in which the male attempts to conquer and cause pain to the female (LeVine & LeVine, 1966).

Correlates of Attitudes Toward Sex

Beliefs about whether sex is harmless or dangerous are predictably associated with other sexual beliefs and practices. In cultures where people believe that sex is dangerous, extramarital affairs for women are condemned and the incidence of both premarital and extramarital sex is low. Interestingly, attitudes about sex are not predictably related to beliefs about the desirability of frequent sexual activity within a marriage, so that people in a particular culture may think that sex can be harmful but nevertheless advocate frequent sexual activity between a husband and wife. It is common, however, to find taboos associated with menstruation in societies that equate sex with danger (Broude & Greene, 1976).

PREMARITAL SEX

Norms of Premarital Sex

Cultural rules regarding the sexual behavior of unmarried individuals range from extreme permissiveness to extreme intolerance. A slight majority of cultures tend to disapprove of premarital sex for girls. In a worldwide sample of 141 cultures, 45% at least tolerate premarital sexual activity on the part of unmarried females, while the remaining 55% disapprove of premarital sex for most, if not all, girls. Rules regarding premarital sex are somewhat more tolerant for boys. Thus, in a sample of 57 cultures, 63% approve of sexual activity for unmarried boys, while only 33% disapprove of premarital sex (Broude & Greene, 1976).

Among the Truk of Oceania, adults take it for granted that adolescents will be sexually active and there is a widespread belief that girls will not menstruate unless they have engaged in sexual intercourse, a reflection of how common premarital sex must be among young Trukese females (Gladwin & Sarason, 1953). The Garo of India would prefer unmarried girls and boys to remain virgins but acknowledge that "after all, they are young so what can you do?" (Burling, 1963).

Premarital sex is mildly disapproved of for girls in 17% of the sample of 141 cultures and for boys in 14% of the sample of 57 cultures (Broude & Greene, 1976). Among the Kutenai of North America, virginity is valued, but not required, and an unmarried girl is warned that if she engages in sexual relations, she will turn into a frog when she dies and go to live with her ancestors. But no punishment is meted out to the young person who does, in fact, have sexual intercourse before marriage (Turney-High, 1941).

Thirty-four percent of the sample of 141 societies strongly disapprove of premarital sex for girls and 23% strongly condemn premarital sex for boys (Broude & Greene, 1976). In these cultures, the repercussions for engaging in sexual relations before marriage are always substantial and sometimes extreme. A Javanese boy and girl are married on the spot if caught engaging in sexual activity (Geertz, 1961). Among the Chiricahua of southwest North America, chastity is required of females until marriage, and a girl who engages in sexual activity before marriage will be whipped, perhaps in public. Boys are not as severely restricted, but they are warned about acquiring a bad reputation. Fathers warn their sons not to have sexual relations with a woman because "they have teeth in there. They bite off your penis and have some diseases." If a pregnancy occurs before marriage, the boy and girl are forced to wed if possible (Opler, 1941).

Where premarital sex is strongly condemned, death is the most common punishment for engaging in sexual activity before marriage. The Kenuzi Nubians in Egypt will have a girl who has engaged in premarital sex killed by her closest male relatives (Frayzer, 1985). A Rwala girl who is caught having sexual relations will be killed by her father or brother. Her corpse will then be cut into pieces (Raswan, 1947).

In 4% of the sample of 141 cultures, a boy and girl are allowed to engage in sexual relations if they are betrothed. In some cases, adults are permissive with an engaged couple when they view premarital sexual relations as test of fertility. In some cultures, a pregnancy then means that the couple must be married (Broude & Greene, 1976).

Correlates of Premarital Sex Norms

Cultures that require or value chastity among the unmarried appear to be responding to practical problems associated with premarital sexual activity. People in many societies with restrictive premarital sex norms will tell you that they disapprove of premarital sex because they wish to avoid premarital pregnancies. Of 28 cultures permitting premarital sex, 38% condone sex before marriage as long as the girl does not become pregnant (Frayzer, 1985).

Pregnancy presents a special set of problems for some kinds of cultures, and in fact it is in just these societies that premarital sex tends to be prohibited. Societies in which descent is traced through the father are predictably restrictive because, where a child obtains his social identity from his father, out-of-wedlock births produce children who must live in social and legal limbo. Similarly, where individuals are expected to marry and then go to live with or near the kin of the husband, children born to single mothers disrupt living arrangements. Where descent and residence are traced through a mother and her relatives, premarital pregnancies are less disruptive, and in fact, in these cultures, premarital sex norms tend to be permissive (Goethals, 1971).

Cultures also tend to restrict premarital sexual activity when a bride receives some kind of money or property at marriage. This may be because adults worry that some boy may want to make a girl pregnant so that he can marry her and gain control over the property that she will receive at marriage. Adults in these cultures want the authority to make a match for their unmarried female relatives and so they try to minimize the chances that a pregnancy will interfere with their matchmaking. In fact, where there is no property exchange at marriage, societies are overwhelmingly permissive regarding their attitudes toward premarital sex (Schlegel, 1991). Premarital sex norms also tend to be restrictive when class structure is fluid (Broude, 1981). Again, parents may be trying to protect their daughters from boys who want to form a connection with a wealthy woman.

Permissive premarital sex norms, by contrast, are typical of small communities. Perhaps this is because people all know one another so that the father of an out-of-wedlock child can be tracked down and a marriage can be arranged. Finally, premarital sex norms tend to be permissive where women contribute to the subsistence economy, perhaps because in such cultures women are relatively independent and therefore have some control over their own behavior (Eckhardt, 1971).

While premarital pregnancies are often disruptive, in some societies pregnancy in an unmarried girl is considered to be a good thing. This is usually because such a pregnancy indicates that the girl is fertile. Among the Lepcha of Tibet (Gorer, 1938), a pregnancy makes girl more attractive because it is now clear that she can conceive. In the Caribbean, a Callinago couple will marry only after a woman has demonstrated that she is fertile, and often a woman will already have a number of children by different men before she marries (Taylor, 1946).

Premarital sex norms are also predictably found alongside other customs and beliefs about sex. Where attitudes toward premarital sex are restrictive, people tend not to talk about sex. Homosexuality and extramarital sex for females are condemned, and in fact women do not typically have extramarital affairs. Societies with restrictive premarital sex norms are also more likely to practice love magic, and marriages tend to be arranged by third parties (Broude, 1975).

Frequency of Premarital Sex

Norms of premarital sex across cultures also reliably predict the number of unmarried boys and girls who actually engage in sexual activity. The patterns are similar for boys and girls, although there are fewer societies in which premarital sex is universal for girls and more in which almost no girls engage in premarital sex. All or most unmarried males have at least some premarital sexual experience in 60% of 107 societies. Premarital sex is practiced by many but not most males in 18% of the sample. In 10% of the 107 cultures, some unmarried boys engage in sexual relations. But in those cultures, premarital sex is not typical. Finally, premarital sex for boys is rare in 12% of the sample. All, or almost all, unmarried girls engage in premarital sex in 49% of a sample of 114 societies. In 17% of the sample, many, but not most or all, girls have sexual relations before marriage. Premarital sex for girls occurs occasionally in 14% of the sample, while in 20% of these cultures, premarital sex is rare or absent for girls (Broude & Greene, 1976).

Virginity

Virginity, especially in unmarried girls, is of at least some concern in most cultures around the world. Of a cross-cultural sample of 134 societies, only 25% place no value at all on virginity (Broude, 1975). Among the Marshallese of Oceania, every girl is sexually active before puberty and virginity is a foreign idea (Erdland, 1914). The Chuckchee of Siberia have no word for chastity (Bogoras, 1929). By contrast, in 35% of the sample of 134 societies, virginity is very important, at least for girls, and in 75% of these cultures, virginity is required in unmarried females (Broude, 1975).

Where virginity is required, a girl must often prove that she was a virgin on her wedding night. Such tests of virginity require that a newly married couple produce a blood-stained article of bedding or clothing. Among the Fon of West Africa, the groom sends his new father-in-law the mat on which the couple have slept on their wedding night. If the girl is not a virgin, the couple may have kept the bedding on which they first slept, and it is that which the girl's father receives (Herskovits, 1938). In Afghanistan, Basseri newlyweds sleep in a tent with nothing in it but the bride's bedding and a white cloth. Once the marriage is consummated, a male relative of the new husband fires a gun and the women living in camp respond by making a trilling sound. The next morning, the groom's family checks for signs of blood on the white cloth (Barth, 1961).

In cultures where virginity is valued, a celebration may follow proofs of a new bride's virginity. Among the Fur of the Sudan, if a bride was a virgin, her new husband honors her with a feast (Beaton, 1948). In Oceania, the Tikopian husband of a virgin bride wears a white flower in his hair. In the past, he would have smeared blood on his forehead instead (Firth, 1936).

Where a culture values virginity in the unmarried, attempts are made to increase the likelihood that young people will not engage in sexual activities. The Silwa of Egypt adopt the extreme measure of removing the girl's clitoris when she is 7 or 8 years old, reasoning that this will reduce her sex drive (Frayzer, 1985). Other societies practice infibulation, a procedure that temporarily closes the vaginal opening. In some places, girls are accompanied by older women whenever they are likely to find themselves in the company of the opposite sex. Sometimes, the sexes are segregated to minimize the opportunities for sexual experimentation.

In cultures for which virginity is important, a girl or her family may pay a price if she is not a virgin at marriage. In some societies, the groom or his family traditionally present money or property to the bride or her family upon their marriage. Where virginity in a bride is expected or required, the value of the gifts may be less, or they may be forfeited altogether, if the girl is not a virgin. Sometimes, a marriage is called off if the bride cannot prove her virginity. If the bride or her family have presented gifts to the groom or his family, then the gifts may be kept even though no marriage takes place. In extreme cases, the bride may be killed. At a minimum, the bride and groom may be humiliated.

Defloration

Defloration refers to the rupture of the hymen, a fold of mucous membrane covering the vaginal opening. Cultures that require proof of virginity in a bride at marriage are assuming that the hymen of an inexperienced girl will still be intact. The blood that is taken as a test of virginity is the result of the breaking of the hymen during sexual intercourse. When premarital sex is successfully prohibited, defloration often, although not always, occurs when a marriage is consummated. But in a number of societies, special customs surround the loss of virginity in a girl before she is married.

In cultures with defloration customs, loss of virginity takes place during some specific event or with a specific male or group of males. In Australia, an Aranda girl's first sexual experience must be with the male kin of her husband. At marriage, the new bride is taken into the bushes by some of the groom's male relatives, all of whom have intercourse with her. She is then returned to her husband (Murdock, 1936). Among the Marshallese of Oceania, a girl loses her virginity to the chief at her initiation rite (Erdland, 1914). In the Amazon, a Cubeo girl is digitally deflowered in private at about 8 years of

age by an elderly celibate man from her sib. Afterwards, an announcement is made that she is a woman (Goldman, 1963). Among the Toda of India, a man who is not from a girl's clan has sexual intercourse with her before she reaches puberty. People say that the girl would be disgraced if she were still a virgin after puberty, and she might have trouble finding a husband (Rivers, 1906). Palauan girls are deflowered by their mothers when they reach puberty. Sex is prohibited for some months afterward, but then girls are educated about sex and encouraged to engage in sexual relations (Barnett, 1949). Sometimes a girl is expected to deflower herself. In Zaire, Nkundo girls gradually enlarge the vaginal opening by inserting larger and larger plant shoots in the vagina. The procedure is called "opening the way." Sometimes a group of girls will carry out the process together (Hulsaert, 1928).

FREQUENCY OF SEX IN MARRIAGE

People living in different cultures report widely different incidences of sexual activity between spouses. In part, the differences are related to cultural attitudes regarding how often individuals ought to engage in sexual intercourse.

In 17% of 70 cultures around the world, frequent sexual intercourse between spouses is viewed as highly desirable (Broude, 1976). Among the Lepcha, who typify this attitude, married couples claim to engage in sexual activity five, six, or more times a day when first married, although they acknowledge that a person would be tired afterward (Gorer, 1938).

By contrast, 9% of the same sample of 70 societies believe that too much sex, even between married couples, is a bad thing (Broude, 1976). The Konso of Ethiopia believe that sex makes men weak, and therefore only engage in sex in moderation (Hallpike, 1972). The Yapese of Oceania believe that too much sexual activity will make a man ill, and tell legends of men who have died from an overactive sex life (Hunt, Schneider, & Stevens, 1949). Therefore sexual activity perhaps two or three times a month is recommended. The Chiricahua say that too much sex is dangerous and sexual intercourse two or three times a week is about the limit. In the words of one Chiricahua male, "...after eleven years of married life, when I'm home, [I have sex] about once a week. Once a week won't hurt a man, I guess" (Opler, 1941).

In cultures that worry about the effects of too much sexual activity, total abstinence may nevertheless also be viewed as dangerous. Thus, for example, the Kaska of Alaska think that sexual moderation is important for a long life and good luck. But too little sex is also dangerous especially for males, since a man who is deprived of sexual intercourse will spend his time worrying about girls and may even lose his brains and go insane (Honigmann, 1949).

Fourteen percent of the sample of 70 societies not only view excessive sex as undesirable but also promote abstinence, even between spouses, as a positive virtue (Broude, 1976). The Navaho of North America say that an individual who engages in sexual intercourse too frequently may bleed from the genitals or be struck by lightning. Indeed, a person who has too much sex may actually go mad. This association of sex with dangers of a variety of kinds causes the Navaho to promote abstinence in a variety of circumstances (Leighton & Kluckhohn, 1969).

In the remaining 60% of the sample of 70 cultures, abstinence is seen as desirable in a limited number of circumstances, but in general frequent sex is viewed as desirable (Broude, 1976).

The modal incidence of sexual intercourse across cultures for which we have evidence is once per day, omitting days for which specific taboos are invoked (Broude, 1994). Across cultures, people also tend to engage in sex less often as they grow older. The Lepcha, who claim to engage in sexual intercourse many times over a 24-hour period, admit that by the time they are 30 years old married people typically engage in sex only once a day (Gorer, 1938). The incidence of sexual activity across cultures also levels off as a relationship matures (Broude, 1994).

Attitudes toward the desirability of frequent sexual intercourse between spouses are related to a number of other beliefs regarding sexual behavior. Thus, where frequent sexual activity between husband and wife is regarded as desirable, homosexuality is accepted, love magic is absent, and extramarital sex for wives is accepted, or else it is condemned for both sexes (Broude, 1975).

SEX TABOOS

Even in societies where frequent sexual activity between spouses is regarded as desirable, sexual relations are prohibited under some circumstances. Sex taboos are present in 60% of the 70 cultures for which evidence is available with specific categories of people, or at certain ages, stages, or crises in life (Broude, 1975).

In some societies, sexual activity is prohibited during certain times of the day. The Cuna of Panama approve of sexual relations only at night in accordance with the laws of God (Broude, 1994). The Semang of Malaysia believe that sex during the day will cause thunderstorms and deadly lightning, leading to the drowning not only of the offending couple but also of other innocent people (Murdock, 1936). And the West African Bambara believe that a couple who engage in sex during the day will have an albino child (Paques, 1954).

Sometimes, sex is prohibited in certain places. The Mende of West Africa forbid sexual intercourse in the bush (Little, 1951), while the Semang condemn sex within camp boundaries for fear that the supernatural will become angry (Murdock, 1936). Among the Bambara, engaging in sexual relations out of doors will lead to the failure of the crops (Paques, 1954).

Sex taboos can also apply to certain activities. Often, sex prohibitions are associated with war or economic pursuits. The Ganda of Uganda forbid sexual intercourse the night before battle if the fighting is likely to be protracted (Roscoe, 1911). The Lepcha prohibit sex for 3 months after a bear trap has been set. If the taboo is broken, no animals will be caught (Gorer, 1938). The Cuna of Panama outlaw sexual intercourse during a turtle hunt (Broude, 1994), the Yapese of Oceania prohibit sex during a fishing excursion (Hunt et al., 1949), and among the Ganda of Uganda, sex is forbidden while the wood for making canoes is being processed (Broude, 1994). Ganda women may not engage in sexual intercourse while they are mourning the dead (Broude, 1994), and Kwoma men are prohibited from engaging in sexual activity after a cult ceremony has been held (Whiting, 1941). The Jivaro of Ecuador refrain from engaging in sex after someone has died, after planting narcotics, when preparing a feast, or after an enemy has been killed (Broude, 1994).

Sex taboos can also apply to certain categories of people. The Marshallese prohibit sex with a person taking or dispensing herbal medicine or else the sick person will become worse and perhaps die (Broude, 1994). The Yapese comdemn sex for all religious figures (Hunt, Schneider, & Stevens, 1949).

Sexual relations may also be forbidden at certain times of life. Some societies prohibit sex until a person reaches puberty or has undergone an initiation rite. Sexual relations are often prohibited while a woman is menstruating or pregnant or after she has given birth. Sex taboos during menstruation are reported in 20% of a sample of 44 societies. In the 117 societies for which a post-partum sex taboo is reported, the prohibition lasts for under a year in 80% and for over a year in the remaining 20% (Broude, 1975).

EXTRAMARITAL SEX

Norms of Extramarital Sex

In every society around the world, the overwhelmingly majority of men and women marry, and married couples are expected to engage in sexual relations. Sexual activity outside marriage is also condemned in many societies. However, in a number of cultures, extramarital affairs are at least tolerated, and a majority of societies accept and even expect husbands to engage in them. Fifty-six percent of a worldwide sample of 112 societies do not officially condemn extramarital sex for males, while extramarital liaisons are condemned and may be punished in only 44% of these societies. By contrast, extramarital sex is overwhelmingly condemned for women across the world. Extramarital sex is condemned in 88% of a sample of 114 societies, while is accepted in only 12% of these cultures (Broude & Greene, 1976).

As these statistics demonstrate, there is a clearly double standard when it comes to the extramarital sexual behavior of husbands versus wives. The double standard is magnified by the tendency of cultures to sanction more severe punishments for wives than for husbands, even when extramarital affairs are condemned for both sexes. For example, among the Chiricahua, a husband whose wife has engaged in extramarital sex is permitted to whip, mutilate, or kill his spouse, and pressure from the community provokes extreme responses even in husbands. A wife, by contrast, may scold an adulterous husband, but she may in fact ignore infidelities altogether for fear of otherwise chasing away a future potential husband. In matters of infidelity, a wife is not considered to be as greatly wronged as is a husband, since people think unfaithfulness is always the woman's fault anyway (Opler, 1941). Similarly, among the Crow, a husband might beat a wife who is unfaithful or slash her face with a knife. He might also instigate gang rape by his older clansmen. Men, on the

other hand, are expected to carry on a number of affairs while they are married, and a man who remains faithful to his wife loses respect (Lowie, 1912, 1935).

Whereas it is usually the unfaithful spouse who is blamed and punished for acts of infidelity in most cultures, sometimes the lover is the target of reprisals. In Malaysia, an Iban wife can collect a fine from the partner of an unfaithful husband. She can also thrash the guilty woman, but then forfeits half the fine (Roth, 1892). Among the Igbo of Nigeria, a husband may demand compensation from his wife's lover, or he may rape the lover's female kin as retribution for the infidelity (Uchendu, 1965).

Even when extramarital sex is condemned, some societies selectively lift the restraints on extramarital sexual activity. Sometimes, extramarital sex is permitted with certain specified categories of people. The North American Haida allow husbands and wives to have sexual relations with the clansmen of the spouse (Murdock, 1936). Similarly, the Siriono of South America permit husbands to engage in sexual relations with anyone whom his wife calls sister, while a woman may engage in extramarital sexual relations with anyone whom her husband calls brother. This means that any married person is permitted to have perhaps 10 partners other than the spouse. Affairs of this kind are common and accepted, but do tend to be thought of as adulterous (Holmberg, 1950).

Sometimes, the normal constraints on extramarital sexual activity are also lifted on certain occasions. The Orokaiva of New Guinea allow married people to engage in extramarital sex during initiation ceremonies, although the same relationships would be condemned at other times (F. E. Williams, 1930). The Fijians permit husbands and wives to have extramarital sexual encounters when prisoners are brought home (Williams & Heylin, 1860).

A minority of cultures also have institutionalized wife-sharing, in which a husband is allowed to lend his wife to a particular other man or category of men. Sometimes, two men exchange wives. Wife-sharing is present in 34% of 101 cultures around the world (Broude, 1981). Typically, a man will share his wife with his kin or with a good friend. In cultures where wife-sharing is practiced, the husband can be expected to reap some kind of benefit from the exchange. Thus, wife-sharing is sometimes practiced to consolidate relationships between two men. For instance, among the Kimam of New Guinea, the feeling of obligation between friends who have lent each other wives is increased so that the men are now expected to help each other in times of need (Serpenti, 1965).

Wife-sharing can also ease tense relationships among men. In Australia, Aranda men will lend wives to members of an enemy village in an attempt to defuse hostilities (Murdock, 1936). Among the Lesu, a wife receives money from her lover and turns it over to her spouse (Powdermaker, 1933).

Correlates of Extramarital Sex Norms

Norms regarding extramarital sex for women may be so overwhelmingly restrictive because husbands wish to avoid having their wives become pregnant by some other man. Unless a man then divorces such a wife, he will be investing time, energy, and resources in a child who is not genetically his own, a situation that evolutionary theory predicts men will vigorously attempt to avoid. In fact, infidelity is a very common reason for divorce across cultures and men are far more likely than a women to seek divorce from an unfaithful spouse (Broude, 1994).

Often, societies view infidelity on the part of a wife as an infringement of the property rights of the husband. For instance, the Wogeo of New Guinea say that a man who engages in extramarital sex with someone else's wife is "the same as a thief." Similarly, a woman who has sexual relations with a married man is a "receiver of stolen goods" (Hogbin, 1970).

Norms of extramarital sex are predictably related to other sexual beliefs and practices. Restrictive rules regarding extramarital sex for wives are associated with restrictive attitudes toward premarital sex for girls, restrictions on talk about sex, the belief that too much sex is undesirable, the belief that sex is dangerous, condemnation and punishment of homosexuality, and male boasting about sex and other exploits (Broude, 1975).

Frequency of Extramarital Sexual Behavior

Norms of extramarital sexual behavior are not predictably associated with how many married husbands or wives actually engage in extramarital sex. Thus, whereas a slight majority of societies condone extramarital sex for males, extramarital sex is universal or at least common in 78% of 107 cultures and uncommon or absent in only 22%. The discrepancy between extramarital sex norms and actual behavior is even more striking in the case of women. While societies overwhelmingly condemn affairs for wives, extramarital sex is universal or common for

women in 66% of 114 cultures and uncommon or absent in only 34% (Broude, 1981). The fact that men and women engage in extramarital sex despite of cultural condemnation suggests how powerful the impulse is to give into sexual temptation. Women seem to be especially motivated to conduct affairs, given that the punishment for a wife's infidelity in some societies is so extreme. Evolutionary theory suggests a reason for these patterns. For males, sexual relations with more women means a greater chance of producing more offspring. Males may not be consciously thinking about their reproductive success while planning an affair, but the result of engaging in sex outside marriage is nevertheless an increased likelihood of fathering more children. For women, extramarital affairs may mean producing children with genes superior to those of the wife's own husband. Ideally, a woman might even attract a man who can provide a life for her and her children that is superior to the one that her current husband can provide. Research indicates that a woman who has an affair has an easier time breaking up with her current mate and finding a new partner that is, in her opinion, more desirable than her present mate (Buss, 1999).

Correlates of Extramarital Sexual Behavior

Extramarital sexual activity is predictably associated with other sexual attitudes and practices. Where extramarital sex for males is uncommon or absent, sexual relationships include foreplay and women tend to have a say in the choice of a marriage partner. These correlations suggest that where marital relationships are characterized by choice and intimacy, males do not look outside marriage for sexual gratification. However, extramarital sex for males is also absent in societies where female modesty is valued, rape is punished but also present, and wife-beating is common. These associations suggest that the absence of sexual activity outside marriage on the part of males reflects a certain hostility toward, or at least devaluing of, women more generally. Where extramarital sex for wives is uncommon or absent, males are likely to be sexually aggressive and even hostile in their sexual approaches to women (Broude, 1975). This set of relationships may represent a reluctance on the part of women to engage males in sexual activity simply because male sexual aggression is an experience that women wish to avoid when possible.

OVERALL PATTERNING OF SEXUAL ATTITUDES AND PRACTICES

Folk wisdom leads us to expect a certain consistency regarding how an individual culture will manage human sexuality. This intuition is only moderately borne out by the evidence. Certain aspects of sexual belief and behavior do tend to be predictably related within and across societies. But some sexual attitudes and practices also tend to be independent of others.

Cultures across the world do appear to be consistent with regard to some aspects of premarital and extramarital sexual behavior. Thus a society that is permissive regarding premarital sex for boys will also have permissive norms for girls. The same society is also likely to have high incidences of both premarital and extramarital sex for males and females. Similarly, a society that restricts premarital sex for boys will also do so for girls, and both premarital and extramarital sex will be uncommon (Broude, 1976).

Interestingly, extramarital sex norms are not related to these attitudes or behaviors. Neither are premarital and extramarital sex norms and behavior predictably related to another cluster of behaviors related to sex. In particular, male concerns about or incidence of impotence, male boasting about sexual exploits, and incidence of homosexuality are all unrelated to the patterning of premarital and extramarital sex. However, these three aspects of human sexuality are related to each other, so that in societies where male impotence is a theme, males boast about their sexual exploits and homosexuality is absent, while, by contrast, where male impotence is not an issue, homosexuality is present and boasting is absent (Broude, 1976).

Thus there seem to be three independent clusters of sexual attitudes and practices: one concerned with premarital sexual norms and behavior and with extramarital sexual activity, a second concerned with attitudes toward extramarital sex, and a third concerned with male sexuality.

REFERENCES

Barnett, H. G. (1949). *Palauan society*. Eugene: University of Oregon Publications.

Barth, F. (1961). *Nomads of South Persia*. Boston: Little Brown.

Beaton, A. C. (1948). The Fur. *Sudan Notes and Records, 29*.

Bogoras, W. (1929). Siberian cousins of the Eskimo. *Asia, 29*, 316–337.

Broude, G. J. (1975). *A cross-cultural study of some sexual beliefs and practices*. Unpublished Ph.D. dissertation, Harvard University, Cambridge, MA.

Broude, G. J. (1976). Cross-cultural patterning of some sexual attitudes and practices. *Behavior Science Research, 2*, 227–262.

Broude, G. J. (1981). Cultural management of sexuality. In R. Munroe, R. Munroe, & B. B. Whiting (Eds.), *Handbook of cross-cultural development* (pp. 633–674). New York: Garland.

Broude, G. J. (1994). *Marriage, family, and relationships*. Santa Barbara, CA: ABC-CLIO.

Broude, G. J., & Greene, S. J. (1976). Cross-cultural codes on twenty sexual attitudes and practices. *Ethnology, 15*, 409–429.

Burling, R. (1963). *Rengsanggri: Family and kinship in a Garo village*. Philadelphia: University of Philadelphia Press.

Buss, D. W. (1999). *Evolutionary psychology. The new science of mind*. New York: Allyn & Bacon.

Eckhardt, K. (1971). Exchange theory and sexual permissiveness. *Behavior Science Notes, 6*, 1–18.

Erdland, A. (1914). *The Marshallese Islanders: Life, customs, thought, and religion of a South Seas people*. Munster, IW: Aschendorff.

Firth, R. (1936). *We, the Tikopia*. Boston: Beacon Press.

Frayzer, S. (1985). *Varieties of sexual experience*. New Haven, CT: HRAF Press.

Geertz, H. (1961). *The Javanese family*. New York: Free Press.

Gladwin, T., & Sarason, S. (1953). *Truk: Man in paradise*. New York: Munster, I. W. Ashendoff Wenner–Gren Foundation.

Goethals, G. W. (1971). Factors affecting rules regarding premarital sex. In J. M. Henslin (Ed.), *Sociology of sex: A book of readings* (pp. 9–25). New York: Appleton–Century–Croft.

Goldman, I. (1963). *The Cubeo: Indians of the Northwest Amazon*. Urbana: University of Ilinois Press.

Gorer, G. (1938). *Himalayan village: An account of the Lepchas of Sikkim*. London: Joseph.

Hallpike, C. R. (1972). *The Konso of Ethiopia*. Oxford: Clarendon Press.

Herskovits, M. J. (1938). *Dahomey: An ancient West African kingdom*. New York: Augustin.

Hogbin, H. I. (1970). *The island of menstruating men: Religion in Wogeo, New Guinea*.

Holmberg, A. R. (1950). *Nomads of the long bow*. Washington, DC: U.S. Government Printing Office.

Honigmann, J. J. (1949). *Culture and ethos of Kaska society*. London: Oxford University Press.

Hulsaert, G. (1928). *Marriage among the Nkundu*. Bruxelles: G. Van Campenhout.

Hunt, E. E., Schneider, D. M., and Stevens, W. D. (1949). *The Micronesians of Yap and their depopulation*. Washington, DC.

Leighton, D., & Kluckhohn, C. (1969). *Children of the people*. New York: Octagon.

LeVine, R. A., & LeVine, B. B. (1966). *The Gusii of Nyansongo, Kenya*. New York: Wiley.

Little, K. L. (1951). *The Mende of Sierra Leone*. London: Routledge & K. Paul.

Lowie, R. (1912). Social life of the Crow indians. *American Museum of Natural History, Anthropological Papers, 2*, 179–248.

Lowie, R. (1935). *The Crow indians*. New York: Farrar & Rinehart.

Murdock, G. P. (1936). *Our primitive contemporaries*. New York: Macmillan.

Opler, M. (1941). *An Apache life-way*. Chicago: University of Chicago Press.

Paques, V. (1954). *The Bambara*. Paris: Presses Universitaires de France.

Powdermaker, H. (1933). *Life in Lesu*. New York: Norton.

Raswan, C. (1947). *Black tents of Arabia*. New York: Creative Age Press.

Rivers, W. H. R. (1906). *The Todas*. London: Macmillan.

Roscoe, J. (1911). *The Baganda: An account of their native customs and beliefs*. London: Macmillan.

Roth, H. L. (1892a). The natives of Borneo. *Anthropological Institute of Great Britain and Ireland, 21*, 110–137.

Roth, H. L. (1892b). The natives of Borneo. *Anthropological Institute of Great Britain and Ireland, 22*, 22–64.

Schlegel, A. (1991). Status, property, and the value on virginity. *American Ethnologist, 18*, 719–734.

Serpenti, I. M. (1965). *Cultivators in the swamps*. Assen, The Netherlands: Van Gorcum.

Taylor, D. (1946). Kinship and social structure of the Island Carib. *Southwestern Journal of Anthropology, 2*, 180–212.

Turney-High, H. H. (1941). Ethnography of the Kutenai. *American Anthropologist, 43* (Supplement).

Uchendu, V. C. (1965). *The Igbo of southeast Nigeria*. New York: Holt, Rinehart, & Winston.

Whiting, J. M. (1941). *Becoming a Kwoma*. New Haven, CT: Yale University Press.

Williams, F. E. (1930). *Orokaiva society*. London: Oxford University Press.

Williams, T., & Heylin, A. (1860). *Fiji and the Fijians*. London.

Modesty and Sexual Restraint

Celia E. Rothenberg

INTRODUCTION

Notions of modesty and sexual restraint are found across all cultures, but in no cases are these notions defined or practiced in exactly the same ways. In a survey of the modesty practices of 92 societies, Stephens (1972) found great variation in the following: the perceived need for copulation to take place in private (although in all societies surveyed none is completely indifferent to a need for privacy); notions of appropriate clothing as well as the perception of which bodily parts are in need of covering; the presence of sex and/or sexuality in ceremonies, including erotic song or dance, sexual talk, or sexual intercourse outside ordinarily permitted relationships; the presence and tolerance of sex talk and sexual humor; and degrees of avoidance (in terms of touching, eating, joking) due to notions of "respect" or "shame." Stephens concludes that modesty practices are most elaborate in preindustrial civilizations, and are associated with all the major religions and with the presence of premarital and extramarital sex restrictions.

Today the concepts of modesty and sexual restraint are most highly elaborated and central to daily life in the Islamic cultures of the Middle East and North Africa. These concepts play a significant role in shaping local practices related to veiling, female seclusion, female circumcision, premarital virginity, and marital fidelity. Three theoretical approaches to understanding modesty and sexual restraint in Middle Eastern Islamic cultures are commonly used and discussed here, including (1) "Islamic principles" or the Great Tradition versus the Little Tradition approach, (2) honor and shame or a structuralist approach, and (3) personhood and self approach. Specific ethnographic examples drawn from the Islamic societies are offered to demonstrate the insights gained through attempts to study and understand better the issues surrounding modesty and sexual restraint.

Studying modesty and sexual restraint, particularly in the Islamic Middle East, offers one way to explore the relationship between biological sex and socially constructed gender roles, religious beliefs and practice,

and men's and women's lives. In terms of sex and gender, examining the practices of modesty and sexual restraint allows us to see how biological sex is elaborated, in some cases literally constructed (e.g., through female circumcision), and thus given meaning. Modesty practices further suggest that ideas about gender are not constructed only from the facts of genitalia; rather, parts of the face, the hands, and the feet may also be highly meaningful and believed to require certain modest acts. The parameters of exactly what constitutes the most meaningful aspects of the body are therefore greatly expanded, allowing us to reflect on the western preoccupation with genitalia as the sole source of gender identity (cf. Butler, 1990).

Looking at modesty and sexual restraint practices in the Islamic Middle East also adds to our understanding of the relationship between religious beliefs and practices. In the ethnographies discussed in this article, all the men and women believe that they are acting in accord with proper Islamic belief. Yet this does not mean that men and women act in the same way; indeed, one striking feature of the ethnographies discussed here is the variation in practice and belief in the name of Islam. Thus modesty and sexual restraint are excellent windows for viewing the complex nature of religious interpretation and practice, and for understanding that these issues are not static but continue to change to meet new demands and challenges.

Finally, examining the issues of modesty and sexual restraint allows for a consideration of the highly variable nature of the relationship between men and women across cultures. While the evidence presented here may seem to support the theory that men are symbolically associated with culture and women with nature (Ortner, 1974), this evidence also complicates and deepens this formulation and addresses the central issue of who determines and challenges this symbolic association. Also challenged here is the notion that practices associated with modesty and sexual restraint—in particular the veil and female seclusion—are necessarily demeaning to women and indicative of men's control over them. Rather, women often assert that they voluntarily adhere to these practices in order to gain both self-respect and the respect of others, including men. While women's relationships with men may at times be antagonistic over these practices, this is certainly not necessarily the case.

THEORETICAL APPROACHES

Islamic Principles, or Great Tradition Versus Little Tradition Approach

One approach to understanding the issues of modesty and sexual restraint in Islamic cultures has been to focus on Islamic principles as explained in Islamic texts, such as the Quran and Hadith. This approach can be understood as part of the Great Tradition versus Little Tradition approach; scholars in this vein of analysis look at the tenets of Islamic texts—the Great Tradition—and compare local practices—the Little Tradition—with them.

The best-known study in this vein was done by Antoun (1968). He examined prescriptions for modest practices, including appropriate sexuality, in the Quran. He then looked at a variety of modesty practices and beliefs about women's sexuality in a village in Jordan for their "accommodation," or lack of "accommodation," to these textual dictates. In a well-known critique of Antoun's argument, Abu-Zahra argued that his focus on legalistic terms and arguments and dictionary definitions of commonly used words would not be familiar to "illiterate peasant communities"; in addition, the same words would have highly variable meanings in different contexts (Abu-Zahra, 1970, p. 1084).

It is important to underscore here the points raised by Abu-Zahra in a discussion of the concepts of modesty and sexual restraint. It is central to any analysis of these behaviors to recognize that the existence of Islamic texts and their widespread use as references for proper moral behavior in many cultures does not mean that individuals within and across cultures understand these texts in identical ways. What is considered to be within the realm of proper Islamic practice in one place may be understood quite differently—even as un-Islamic—in another setting. For example, Palestinian village women in the West Bank who experience possession by the *jinn*, or spirits, believe their possession experiences to be well within the realm of appropriate Islamic practice; Palestinians in typically urban settings, such as Toronto, Canada, argue that, while the *jinn* are known to exist

due to their mention in the Quran, such possession experiences are significantly contrary to proper Islamic belief and practice (Gibb & Rothenberg, 2000; Rothenberg, in press). Thus singling out a particular Islamic tradition as normative is arbitrary, as exactly what should constitute the "normative tradition" is the subject of great debate in many Muslim societies (Eickleman, 1989, p. 203). Identifying a single Islamic normative tradition as a yardstick for local practice is not only arbitrary and homogenizing, but also ahistorical, creating a decontextualized view of both Islam and Islamic women (cf. Kandiyoti, 1991).

Honor and Shame, or "Structuralist" Approach

A second approach to understanding modesty and sexual restraint in Islamic cultures can be described as a "structuralist" approach, or an approach which sees these issues as part of a pan-cultural complex of "honor and shame" (Eickleman, 1989, p. 204). For these scholars, modesty and sexual restraint are part of a strict code of maintaining men's honor by avoiding shame through the strict regulation of women's behavior, including in particular their modest comportment and sexuality (e.g., Peristiany, 1974). Honor is thus primarily understood as men's achievement, at the expense of women's lives because of their identification as potentially dangerous sources of shame.

However, honor and shame must be carefully defined in local contexts and may not always be easily identifiable with men and women, respectively (Delaney, 1987; Herzfeld, 1980; Wikan, 1984). While locally specific concepts of honor and shame are typically central in shaping the practices of modesty and sexual restraint (as discussed in the examples in this article), the former concepts must be carefully contextualized before the latter practices can be properly understood.

Personhood and Self

Finally, numerous scholars, including many feminist analysts, have looked at the issues of modesty and sexual restraint as part of an individual's sense of personhood and self which is shaped and acculturated by relevant social mores. This approach allows scholars to look at how an individual negotiates and defines his or her sense of self with respect to locally defined Islamic dictates, other local practices and beliefs, and political economic forces. Thus these authors avoid both understanding the practices of modesty and sexual restraint as a simple result of "Islamic beliefs" or locating honor as most relevant to men and shame most significant for women, as the structuralists discussed previously. Rather, honor and shame, when relevant to the lives of women and men, are viewed from multiple perspectives within a society and believed to have a variety of implications and definitions for different social actors. This allows for an understanding of honor, for example, as relevant to the lives of both women and men, although their paths for achieving it may differ (see Abu-Lughod, discussed below). This approach further allows for understanding modesty and sexual restraint as complex practices that are highly symbolic and often pragmatic strategic resources (rather than necessarily restraints) for women and men in a variety of societies.

ETHNOGRAPHIC EXAMPLES

Each ethnographic example discussed here addresses the issues of modesty and sexual restraint in a particular Middle Eastern or North African society. These examples demonstrate the variability of these concepts in practice and thought; they can be primarily characterized as utilizing the "personhood and self" approach described above.

Bedouin Women in Egypt: Lila Abu-Lughod

A highly influential argument concerning modesty and sexual restraint is that women's adherence to the code of modesty is a means of obtaining honor (Abu-Lughod, 1986). Based on fieldwork with a group of Bedouins in the Egyptian desert (1978–1980), Abu-Lughod argues that, for Bedouin women in Egypt, demonstrating modesty and denying sexuality are key ways to obtain honor. While men obtain honor through demonstrating their autonomy, women obtain honor through voluntarily adhering to the modesty code. *Hasham* refers to a voluntary grouping of behaviors, including veiling, modest dress (dress which covers the hair, arms, legs, and curves of the body), downcast eyes, and demonstrated restraint when eating, smoking, talking, and laughing (Abu-Lughod, 1986, p. 108). Thus, while Bedouins idealize the qualities of autonomy and equality—qualities women are

largely unable to achieve as men can—women, by demonstrating their voluntary adherence to the modesty code, display their independence and thus gain honor. The modesty code further demands that women deny their sexuality before others; this voluntary denial is a further way for women to obtain honor.

Although clearly concerned with issues of honor and shame, Abu-Lughod avoids the simplicity of structuralist arguments that associate men with honor and women with shame. Along the lines of the personhood and self approach, Abu-Lughod demonstrates how women strategically use the resources available to them, such as variably positioning their veil to cover more or less of their faces to reflect appropriate degrees of deference to others, to earn honor in the eyes of others and themselves.

Elite Urban Women in Saudi Arabia: Soraya Altorki

In a careful study of the lives of three generations of women in Jiddah, Saudi Arabia, Altorki (1986) demonstrates that modesty practices, although always legitimated in terms of Islamic doctrine, change over time (fieldwork periods included 1971–1973, 1974–1976, and numerous visits until 1984). Avoiding the Great Tradition versus Little Tradition dichotomy, Altorki shows how women's own understandings of the same Islamic teachings have changed over time. In the oldest generation (between the ages of 50 and 80), girls began veiling when they began menstruating. The veil consisted of a black cloak which hung from the shoulders to the ground and a chiffon shawl wrapped several times around the head and face. This veil was to be worn at all times by women in public places and at home in the presence of men other than their grandfathers, fathers, brothers, sons, grandsons, and men they could not marry due to a existing affinal link. The middle-generation women (born during and after the World War II), many of whom spent long periods abroad, modified this dress, while their daughters have further changed it. Appropriately modest dress in public is now defined as a shorter cloak that ends just below the knee and a headscarf. At home, married women may not veil in the presence of a variety of people, including friends and servants (although unmarried women veil before older men and men of their own generation). The covering of the face in all public places has also changed, so that even young unmarried women may not do so in certain areas, such as western-style shopping centers.

Rural Sudanese Women: Janice Boddy

The practice of female circumcision is often popularly understood in Western contexts as simply intended to enforce female sexual restraint resulting from "Islamic" beliefs. Indeed, many scholars have analyzed the practice of female circumcision, arguing that the operation is intended to curb female sexual desire (Boddy, 1989, p. 53). In an important analysis of the issue based on fieldwork in rural Sudan (1976–1977, 1983–1984), Boddy argues that understanding female circumcision as an attempt at controlling female sexuality represents a primarily male perspective and "confuses causes with effects" (Boddy, 1989, p. 53). While the procedure does effectively restrain women's sexuality, women assert that its intent is to prepare girls for womanhood by making them "clean" and pure. Further, women emphasize through circumcision their fertility potential over their sexuality. By removing parts of their genitalia, women demonstrate that their value stems from their ability to give birth rather than simply be sexual partners for men. In terms of the operation as an "Islamic" practice, its regional variability—including radical Pharaonic circumcision to an absence of its practice at all—demonstrates once again the necessity of exploring rather than assuming what is considered to be proper Islamic practice in specific contexts (Boddy, 1989, p. 52).

Boddy avoids any consideration of Islam as separable (in the vein of a Great Tradition) from the way in which a group of Muslims practice it. Indeed, Boddy points out that even within the village, opinion on appropriate Islamic practice was highly variable. For example, women view their practices of spirit possession and trance as absolutely compatible with their identities as Muslims, while local religious authorities and many village men understand women's interactions with spirits as "reprehensible and abhorrent," even if they are not entirely forbidden in Islam (Boddy, 1989, p. 142).

Yemeni Town Women: Anne Meneley

Among Zabidi women in Yemen, women's modesty practices are closely linked to their understandings of morality and appropriately pious behavior (Meneley, 1996). Based on her fieldwork (1989–1990), Meneley (1996, p. 81) argues that modesty is at the root of moral personhood and female gender identity. *Istihya*, translated broadly as modesty, captures a range of emotions, including piety, deference, and self-control (centrally including the denial of sexuality), and a number of practices, including gender segregation, female circumcision, veiling, and the control of one's physical appetites and self-expression. Rather than understanding modesty practices as simply in the interests of men's honor, women view them as in the best interests of their families, including themselves. They are an appropriate demonstration of propriety and piety, which are intimately related to women's behavior, that lend force to a family's claim to status in village life.

Town Women in Oman: Unni Wikan

What is considered to be a modest face covering varies widely in the Middle East. In Sohar, Oman, women first wear the *burqa* facial mask when they marry (Wikan, 1982) (fieldwork during 1974 and 1976). The *burqa*, unlike a face veil covering the face from the eyes to below the chin, looks like a sideways H, covering only the upper lip, the center of the nose, and the lower section of the forehead including the eyebrows. A married woman must wear the *burqa* in any situation in which she could be seen by a marriageable man; women remove the *burqa* completely only before God and their husbands. As Wikan points out, a striking feature of Sohari women's wearing of the *burqa* is not that they wear it in situations when they must in order to appear appropriately modest (e.g., before men), but that they wear it in many instances when it is not necessary such as in all-female gatherings. Women often argue that the *burqa* greatly enhances their beauty—a beauty achieved through a demonstration of modesty. Modesty practices further demand the practice of sex segregation in almost all aspects of daily life; the fact of women's sexual restraint is an absolute requirement to be considered an honorable moral person. However, in cases where it is well known that a woman does not practice sexual restraint, such as a prostitute, Soharis practice tact and avoid insulting or offending her. In short, Soharis' sense of personhood is deeply entwined with their sense of beauty, diplomacy, and graciousness, and demonstrated through tact, wearing of the *burqa*, and other modesty practices. It is this strongly developed sense of appropriate selves which guides women's actions and practices in daily life.

Conclusion

Scholarly approaches to understanding modesty and sexual restraint in Islamic cultures in the Middle East and North Africa are increasingly nuanced and sensitive, privileging the view of these issues from the perspective of those who practice them. Such perspectives are complex, ever-changing, and shaped by a variety of forces, including most centrally an individual's sense of self, religious understanding, and historical context.

Stephens' (1972) argument concerning the association of the most elaborate modesty practices with preindustrial societies is to some extent borne out here. Indeed, the ethnographic examples discussed here are drawn primarily from peasant societies that are not industrialized (although other areas in their countries may be)—societies in which Islam plays a major role, and there are premarital and extramarital sex restrictions. Yet this argument cannot effectively explain why, for example, urban educated working women in Cairo are adopting the veil in increasing numbers (Macleod, 1991), or the growing appeal of Orthodox Jewish practices and their accompanying modesty practices for women (Kaufman, 1989). It remains to be seen what, if any, generalizations can be drawn from the resurgence of modesty practices among particular segments of urban educated women in varying parts of the world.

References

Abu-Lughod, L. (1986). *Veiled sentiments: Honor and poetry in a Bedouin society*. Los Angeles: University of California Press.

Abu-Zahra, N. M. (1970). On the modesty of women in Arab villages: A reply. *American Anthropologist*, 72(5), 1079–1088.

Altorki, S. (1986). *Women in Saudi Arabia: Ideology and behavior among the elite*. New York: Columbia University Press.

Antoun, R. (1968). On the modesty of women in Arab Muslim villages: A study in the accomodation of traditions. *American Anthropologist*, 70(4), 671–697.

Boddy, J. (1989). *Wombs and alien spirits: Women, men, and the Zar cult in Northern Sudan*. Madison: University of Wisconsin Press.

Butler, J. (1990). *Gender trouble: Feminism and the subversion of identity*. New York: Routledge.

Delaney, C. (1987). Seeds of honor, fields of shame. In D. Gilmore (Ed.), *Honor and the unity of the Mediterranean* (pp. 35–48). Washington, DC: American Anthropological Association.

Eickelman, D. (1989). *The Middle East: An anthropological approach*. Englewood Cliffs, NJ: Prentice-Hall.

Gibb, C., & Rothenberg, C. (2000). Believing women: Harari and Palestinian women at home and in the Canadian diaspora. *Journal of Muslim Minority Affairs*, 20(2), 243–259.

Herzfeld, M. (1980). Honour and shame: Problems in the comparative analysis of moral systems. *Man*, 15, 339–351.

Kandiyoti, D. (Ed.). (1991). *Women, Islam, and the state*. Philadelphia: Temple University Press.

Kaufman, D. R. (1989). Patriarchal women: A case study of newly orthodox Jewish women. *Symbolic Interaction*, 12(2), 299–314.

Macleod, A. E. (1991). *Accomodating protest: Working women, the new veiling, and change in Cairo*. New York: Columbia University Press.

Meneley, A. (1996). *Tournaments of value: Sociability and hierarchy in a Yemen town*. Toronto: University of Toronto Press.

Ortner, S. (1974). Is female to male as nature is to culture? In M. Z. Rosaldo & L. Lamphere (Eds.), *Woman, culture, and society* (pp. 67–88). Stanford, CA: Stanford University Press.

Peristiany, J. G. (Ed.). (1974). *Honour and shame: The values of Mediterranean society*. Chicago: Midway.

Rothenberg, C. (in press). *Spirits of Palestine: Palestinian village women and stories of the jinn*. Lanham, MD: Lexington Press.

Stephens, W. (1972). A cross-cultural study of modesty. *Behavior Science Notes*, 7, 1–18.

Wikan, U. (1982). *Behind the veil in Arabia: Women in Oman*. Chicago: University of Chicago Press.

Wikan, U. (1984). Shame and honour: A contestable pair. *Man*, 19(4), 635–652.

Husband–Wife Interaction and Aloofness

Gwen J. Broude

INTRODUCTION

When a man and woman enter into a socially sanctioned relationship recognized by themselves and their community to be more or less permanent, they are said to be married. All known societies, past and present, recognize the institution of marriage, and, as far back as historical references go, virtually every human being who has lived to adulthood has gotten married.

But it is also the case that the nature of the relationship between husbands and wives varies widely across cultures. Spouses may live together or separately. They may share meals or eat at different times and in different places. A couple may sleep in the same bed or in different rooms or even different houses. They may perform chores side by side or engage in different kinds of tasks and carry them out in different locations. A husband and wife may spend their leisure time together or apart. The relationship between spouses may be egalitarian, or one spouse may be subordinate to the other. Husbands and wives may provide each other with concrete and emotional support during important or stressful times, or each spouse may look outside of the marital relationship in times of need. And their marriage may be the primary source of emotional fulfillment for a man or woman, or the marital relationship may be eclipsed by other, more important, bonds to parents, friends, or others.

What is more, husband–wife day-to-day interaction tends to be consistent in its overall nature. Thus, cross-cultural evidence indicates that husbands and wives who eat together are also likely to sleep, work, and spend their leisure time together, and to be available to each other for help and support during momentous occasions such as the birth of a child. By contrast, where spouses eat apart, they also tend to sleep, work, and spend their leisure time apart, and to participate in momentous events separately (Broude, 1983). Where marriages are characterized by frequent husband–wife interaction across a variety of activities, the marital relationship is described in the literature as intimate. Marriages that are typified by

husband–wife segregation are identified as aloof. In a worldwide sample of 73 societies, 56% are characterized by intimate marriages and 44% by aloof marriages (Broude, 1983).

The Trobriand Islanders of New Guinea nicely illustrate the intimate marriage. Husband, wife, and young children live in a house of their own. Opportunities for marital closeness in Trobriand marriages are increased because, once they demonstrate some measure of independence, older children, as well as adolescents, live in separate huts. Husbands and wives eat, sleep, and spend the better part of their work and leisure hours together, talk and joke with each other, and share household tasks, including baby tending. Spouses are devoted to one another, frequently give one another gifts, call each other *lubaygu*, "my friend," and in general lead a "common life of close companionship" (Malinowski, 1929, p. 109). Similarly, interactions between spouses among the Garo of India are intimate. Households are typically composed of parents and their children, and even when relatives live with the family, the oldest married couple have a private sleeping room. The family cooks, eats, and entertains visitors together in the large front room of the house, and husbands and wives work alongside each other in the fields. Couples sit together, talking and laughing with each other, when they are alone, although, by custom, men and women sit apart in public. Overall, Garo husbands and wives rely on each other for companionship and support, and as the marriage matures, each spouse is regarded as the most important person in the life of the partner (Burling, 1963).

At the opposite extreme are the Rajputs of Khalapur, India, who represent the aloof marriage. Separation of spouses is promoted by the custom of purdah, which requires the seclusion of women. Rajput women spend their time in an enclosed courtyard, performing chores and tending the young children. It is here that women also eat, sleep, and cook. Meanwhile, when they are not working, the men sit talking and smoking with other male relatives and friends in the men's quarters of the house, where a husband may also sleep. The household arrangements are consciously designed to dilute the ties between a husband and wife in order that the attachment of mother and son can be maintained. The result is that husbands view the role of a wife as essentially sexual and reproductive. Only after her mother-in-law dies may a woman become a real companion as well as advisor to her husband (Minturn & Hitchcock, 1966). Traditional Chinese marriages are also characterized by aloofness. Even after they are married, a young husband and wife are kept segregated from each other by their parents. During the day, couples rarely have the opportunity to be alone together in their crowded households and, at night, wives sleep in the women's quarters of the house and husbands sleep in the men's quarters. Males and females are customarily segregated during formal functions, such as weddings or funerals, and it is considered improper for husbands and wives to be seen together in public. Perhaps because males and females have so little contact with each other, interactions when spouses are alone are not characterized by emotional intimacy (Headland, 1914).

THEORETICAL CONTROVERSIES

Researchers interested in the patterning of marital interaction have correctly assumed that marriages are generally intimate or generally aloof. The antecedents of marital intimacy and aloofness, on the other hand, have been a focus of some controversy. The fact that research on marital interaction has sometimes used indirect or partial measures of husband–wife intimacy and aloofness has complicated the interpretation of research on the origins of variations in patterns of marital interaction.

Psychodynamic Approaches

Anxiety About Sex and Women.
Initial attempts to account for variations in patterns of marital interaction across cultures focused in particular on marital aloofness. The goal was to explain why husbands and wives in some societies tended to avoid one another and to devalue the importance of their relationship. The most influential explanations of marital aloofness, in turn, relied on a prior commitment to psychodynamic theory, which assumes that human motivation is influenced by unconscious mechanisms meant to minimize anxiety. With regard to marital interaction, the assumption was that aloof marriages prevail in societies where men are anxious

about sex and/or women. To deal with their anxiety, men simply avoid their wives. As is characteristic of psychodynamic theory, the source of male anxiety was traced to childhood.

Slater and Slater (1965) and Stephens (1963) proposed in particular that males who ultimately opt for aloof marriages have been raised by mothers who are seductive and/or hostile toward their sons. Maternal behavior was itself explained by marital aloofness. Thus, where women have little opportunity to form an intimate attachment with their husbands, they turn to their sons for emotional and sexual satisfaction, but also exhibit hostility toward their male children because their sons unconsciously symbolize their husbands, whom they resent. In turn, boys who are raised in such a climate become unconsciously anxious about sex and women. As a consequence, their own marriages are aloof, resulting in the tendency of their wives to turn toward their sons for emotional and sexual satisfaction. The cycle is thus perpetuated.

Cross-Sex Identification.
Whiting and Whiting (1975) proposed an alternative psychodynamic explanation for marital aloofness. Their focus was on the need for male warriors with accumulated wealth. In such societies, males guard the family property, which means that husbands and wives often eat and sleep apart. The Whitings reasoned that, in such circumstances, little boys, raised largely by their mothers, would come to view women as the source of power and form an initial identification with females. When, later in their development, boys came to recognize that it is the men who have the power, they would unconsciously turn away from their original identification with females. Further, as a way of compensating for their initial cross-sex identification, males would begin to exhibit extremely masculine behavior, for instance in the form of aggression and pursuit of military glory, and also avoid women, especially their wives.

Researchers attempting to test psychodynamic theories of the origins of marital aloofness have used partial or indirect measures as indices of marital interaction. These included polygyny, exclusive mother–child sleeping arrangements with fathers sleeping elsewhere, a long post-partum sex taboo, wife-beating, and eating arrangements in which spouses do not share meals. Each index has been used as a separate measure of aloofness between spouses. Using this methodology, researchers did report significant relationships between marital aloofness and other measures that they took to represent male fear of sex, male fear of women, cross-sex identifi-cation, and hypermasculinity (Slater & Slater, 1965; Stephens, 1963; Whiting & Whiting, 1975). However, Broude (1987) constructed a composite measure of marital intimacy and aloofness, which allowed marriages to be coded as intimate or aloof on the basis of a number of variables considered simultaneously. These included whether or not husbands ate, slept, worked alongside of, and spent their leisure time with their wives, and whether or not they attended the birth of their children. This composite scale failed to correlate with individual measures of aloofness used in other studies, suggesting that earlier research on the antecedents of marital aloof-ness were not really coding for overall marital interac-tion. Further, the same composite measure of marital interaction failed to correlate significantly with measures of male fear of sex or women, cross-sex identification, or hypermasculinity, suggesting that marital aloofness is not caused by the intrapsychic dynamics suggested by psychodynamic theories.

Attachment Theory.   Adult interpersonal relation-ships have also been explained as an outcome of child-hood experiences with attachment. The idea here is that babies construct working models of what they can expect from other people based upon their experiences with their first attachment figure, who is usually the mother (Ainsworth, 1967; Bowlby, 1973; Erikson, 1963). A mother who is consistent, available, and indulgent teaches her baby that people are trustworthy and rela-tionships are gratifying. Such a baby will grow up to be a person who embraces the opportunity for an intimate relationship in marriage. By contrast, a caretaker who is inconsistent, unavailable, and cold teaches her child that people are untrustworthy and relationships disappointing. Such a person will avoid marital intimacy in adulthood.

However, cross-cultural evidence, does not support the theory that patterns of marital interaction originate in experiences with childhood attachment. The composite scale of marital intimacy and aloofness constructed by Broude (1987) is not significantly related to caretaker availability or to the degree to which caretakers are indulgent toward babies.

The Social Environment Approach

Marital intimacy and aloofness have also been explained as a response to the larger social environment characteristic

of a society. Evidence does suggest that patterns of marital interaction are predictably associated with certain features of a couple's overall interpersonal environment. Thus marriages tend to be intimate in societies where people frequently move from place to place or live in communi-ties in which neighbors are not kin. Where people are sedentary and also live near kin, marriages become overwhelmingly aloof (Broude, 1987). The connection between marital relationships and social environment has been interpreted psychologically. The grounding assump-tion of this interpretation is that human beings everywhere seek membership in a secure interpersonal network. Ideally, that network is composed of kin simply because relatives typically act as a more trustworthy support group than do people who are unrelated by blood. Living arrangements in which people remain in the same location and surrounded by kin provide this ideal support group, with the result that married people look, not to their spouses, but to their kin as their source of interpersonal embeddedness. Hence, we see aloof marriages. Where couples move around a lot and where their neighbors are unrelated individuals, a husband and wife will fall back on the marital relationship for interpersonal security. Intimate marriages are the result (Broude, 1987). This hypothesis regarding the sources of marital intimacy and aloofness suggests that social structural features of a culture can influence the way in which universal psychological needs are met in specific social contexts.

FEATURES OF MARITAL INTERACTION

Importance of the Marital Relationship

While all societies expect men and women to marry, cultures vary widely with regard to the importance that they place on the marital relationship. In some cultures it is assumed that one's spouse will be the most important person in one's life, while in others the marital bond is marginalized in favor of other human associations.

Attitudes regarding the importance of the marriage bond influence the degree to which other people encour-age spouses to develop a close relationship. The Khalka Mongols view the marital relationship as the primary attachment in the life of a man or woman and support a new marriage by prohibiting a bride from making a formal visit to her natal family for 3 years after she is married. Therefore, a young wife only sees her parents if they come to visit her in her new camp (Vreeland, 1953). Contrast this with the experience of a wife among the Truk of Oceania, who value the relationship of a woman and her mother over that of a wife and her spouse. A Truk wife is also required to move away from her natal home after she is married. But here, a wife will visit her mother for a month each year if she lives far away, and will make frequent informal visits to her mother if she lives closer. A Truk mother gives comfort, aid, and advice to a daughter even after she is married (Gladwin & Sarason, 1953).

In cultures where a relationship other than the marital bond is viewed as primary, people may actively try to obstruct intimate interactions between a husband and wife. Thus, for instance, a traditional Hindu husband is warned not to look at his wife while she is eating, sneezing, yawning, breast-feeding, or relaxing comfortably, the idea being to encourage continued distance between spouses (Mace & Mace, 1959).

The expectations of spouses will also be influenced by cultural assumptions regarding the importance of the marriage. Where a culture views marriage as the primary source of emotional gratification and support in the life of an adult, men and women will bring these same hopes to their own marriage. The results of this attitude are captured in the words of an Omaha widower, who remarked that "no one is so near, no one can ever be so dear as a wife; when she dies, her husband's joy dies with her" (Dorsey, 1884). By contrast, in societies where the marital bond is viewed as secondary to the bonds between other people, a husband and wife will expect less from their marriage. When asked about their expectations regarding marriage, men living in many different regions of India agreed that a wife provides sexual satisfaction and sons and a smoothly running household. Similarly, women agreed that husbands provided financial security, protection, and children. But neither sex looked to marriage as the source of emotional support. Rather, both men and women named relatives or same-sex friends as the people to whom they would go in times of personal distress (Mace & Mace, 1959).

Where the husband–wife bond is viewed as primary, this can lead to disruptions in the relationships between a spouse and other family members. This is the case among the Iban of Borneo, where the marital relationship is assumed to be uppermost in the life of a man and woman. Iban newlyweds sometimes move in with the family of one of the spouses. When a couple lives in the house of the groom, conflicts may arise between the groom's brothers and his new wife. In such cases, the young husband's loyalties shift to his bride and the couple move into their own house (Freeman, 1958). By contrast, among the Bemba of Zambia, where a woman's relationship with her mother remains the most important bond in her life, a bride will occasionally refuse to leave own community to go and live with her husband if he wishes to live in his own village after their marriage (Richards, 1940). Among the North American Hidatsa, the attachment between a son and his mother remained strong throughout life, and was expected to do so. A new groom visited his mother whenever he liked and friends and kin at her home, not his own. A husband often ate at his mother's house and never stayed in the house that he shared with his wife if she happened to be away. Married men kept their own belongings at their mothers' lodges, and younger members of the mother's household looked after a man's horses. A son was expected to see to his mother's well-being even after he had married and moved away (Matthews, 1877). Among the matrilocal Navaho of Arizona, a husband lived with his wife's family and participated in the activities of that household. But he was also expected to meet certain ceremonial and economic responsibilities with respect to his natal household. A married man made long frequent visits to his mother's house. Wives, for their part, were more influenced by their brothers or uncles than by their husband, and were likely to side with their parents against their husband in the case of a disagreement between them (Leighton & Kluckhohn, 1969). The Creek were representative of societies in which a man's loyalties toward a spouse were less profound that those toward the natal family. Among these people, the word "home" referred to the household of a husband's own female kin, even if he had built the house in which he and his wife lived (Swanton, 1924–1925).

The marriage bond tends to be viewed as important in societies where men are particularly interested in establishing paternity. In societies of this sort, a woman's sexual activity is often restricted to the marital relationship and the marriage celebration is elaborate. In turn, male concern with paternity recognition is found predominantly in societies where descent is traced exclusively (unilineal descent) or at least partially (nonunilineal descent) through males (Frayzer, 1985). The connection between descent systems and emphasis on the social recognition of paternity can be explained by the fact that, where a child's membership in a descent group depends at least in part on the identity of his father, recognition of paternity becomes critical to assigning each person to the proper descent group.

Newlywed Customs

The transition to the married state is marked in many cultures by special treatment of newlyweds. A new bride and groom may be treated specially for just a few hours (e.g., through the wedding night) or for days, weeks, or longer. Further, newlywed customs tend to come as a package, so that if newlyweds are treated as special in one way, they are treated as special more generally. For instance, if the wedding night is considered special, then the couple are also likely to be sent on a honeymoon, excused from routine tasks for some period of time, and so on.

Newlywed customs are predictably related to other aspects of courtship and marriage. Thus it is uncommon to see newlyweds treated specially in societies where males and females choose their own spouses, where husbands and wives eat together, where special houses dedicated to male activities are absent, where males do not exhibit sexual aggression, and where wives do not tend to engage in extramarital sexual affairs. Newlywed customs are present where marriages are arranged by thirdly parties, where a husband and wife eat apart, where men's houses are present so that married males eat, sleep, and/or spend their leisure time away from home, where males are sexually aggressive, and where wives typically carry on extramarital affairs. Thus newlywed customs seem to represent a strategy for allowing a newly married couple some time alone under circumstances where they have had no opportunity to become comfortable with each other prior to their marriage and where, further, their married life will not be characterized by agreeable contact. In a worldwide sample of 62 cultures, 47% regard the wedding night as special and accommodate a newly married couple in other ways, while 53% do not regard the wedding night as special and do not make any other special arrangements on behalf of a new bride and groom (Broude & Greene, 1983).

The Middle East Rwala provide a newly married couple with a special tent on their first night together, or else they are left to themselves in a corner of the family tent (Musil, 1928). A Khalka Mongol couple live in their own tent in the camp of the new wife for up to a month (Vreeland, 1953). Among the Wogeo of New Guinea,

it is inappropriate for a newly married couple to sleep together if they do not have a house of their own. Under such circumstances, the bride and groom will sleep in different beds, or the bride may sleep in a corner of the family sleeping room while the groom stays in the men's house. But the older family members will see to it that the couple are by themselves for a few hours during the day (Hogbin, 1970).

In 11% of a sample of 53 societies, a newly married couple are sent off on a honeymoon. A Somali couple receive a new house as a wedding gift and will live there during their marriage. It is expected that the bride and groom will remain in the house by themselves for a week after their wedding, devoting themselves to consummating their marriage (Lewis, 1962). Similarly Mexican Huichol newlyweds seclude themselves for 5 days. During this brief honeymoon, it is hoped that they will get to know each other. When bride takes food from groom, this means that she accepts the marriage (Zingg, 1938).

In 51% of the same 53 cultures, the newly married are excepted from participating in at least some of the responsibilities of normal married life. Among the Quiche of Guatemala, a young wife sits and watches for 2 days while members of her new family go about their daily tasks. The goal is to permit the girl to become accustomed to her new home (Bunzel, 1952). For an Orokaivan bride in New Guinea the transition to her new household is made easier by a similar time out. For as long as a month, instead of performing her routine chores the young wife sits on a platform in the village for a part of each day and receives gifts (Williams, 1930).

On occasion, a newly married couple are required to avoid each other for some period of time. In India, it is understood that a young bride and groom should not see too much of each other because "new love is delicate, and gets easily destroyed, unless nurtured with care" (Nanda, 1950). In China, a new groom is teased if he pays too much attention to his bride or wants to be with her for any length of time (Mace & Mace, 1959). Among the Kimam of New Guinea, a groom continues to sleep in the men's house for perhaps 2 weeks after he is married. Finally, his father comes and reminds him that he needs to begin to live with his bride. Then, the new husband goes off to his parent's house, where his bride is staying. After eating with his family, the man then spends the night with his wife (Serpenti, 1965).

In 15% of the 53 cultures, it is customary for a groom to stage a mock courtship after his marriage.

After the wedding ceremony, a Nigerian Hausa couple are provided with their own hut, where the bride stays with some of her female friends for a number of nights. Meanwhile, the new groom goes off with the men. When a week has passed, some friends of the husband try for a number of nights to force the groom to enter his bride's hut, but he runs away. At the end of another week, the groom finally goes into his wife's hut and sleeps there, but now the bride runs away. The new groom begins to send her gifts and eventually the two remain in the hut together. At this point, the marriage is said to have "taken" (Smith, 1954).

Sometimes, a newly married couple engage in a genuine courtship after marriage. In India, for example, it is said that love comes after marriage. As a result, a newly married couple court each other in private. One Indian woman recalled being allowed into her newly married aunt and uncle's rooms when she was a child and witnessing the couple flirting with and kissing each other and behaving rather foolishly (Mace & Mace, 1959).

Husband–Wife Eating Arrangements

The nature of the husband–wife relationship is influenced in part by how eating arrangements are patterned in a society. Spouses may eat meals together or apart, or a wife may keep her husband company and serve him while he has his meal but not eat with him.

In 65% of a sample of 117 societies around the world, husbands and wives eat their meals together (Broude & Greene, 1983). This was the pattern among the North American Papago, where husbands and wives not only shared meals but also ate out of same dish as a symbol of the intimacy of their bond (Underhill, 1939). Husbands and wives may eat together even when marriages are polygynous. For example, among the Tanala of Madagascar, a man and all his wives eat together. On any given day, one wife cooks for the entire household (Linton, 1933).

In 35% of the 117 societies, spouses eat their meals separately. In roughly a fourth of these societies, a wife will serve her husband his meal, and perhaps chat with him, but women do not eat their own meals in the presence of their husbands. In New Guinea, a Manus husband and wife do not eat together until they have had a few children together or else they have been married for some years. Instead of eating with his spouse, a Manus husband may have meals at his sister's house.

Meanwhile, the sister's own husband will eat elsewhere (Mead, 1930). Among the polygynous Katab of Nigeria, all wives eat together, the junior wives joining the senior wife on her porch, while the husband eats elsewhere (Gunn, 1956).

Eating arrangements tend to reflect overall patterns of husband–wife interaction. Where spouses eat together, they are also likely to sleep and spend their leisure time together. Men's houses tend to be absent in such cultures. Conversely, where spouses eat separately, they also sleep and spend their leisure time apart and men's houses are likely to be present (Broude, 1983).

Husband–Wife Sleeping Arrangements

Husband–wife sleeping arrangements also differ dramatically from one place to the next. Spouses may sleep next to each other, or in the same room but in different beds. Some married couples sleep in the same house but in different rooms, while some sleep in separate houses altogether. A New Mexican Zuni couple sleep in their own room alone. If they have a baby, the infant will sleep with them, but in a cradleboard that is placed near the mother (Stevenson, 1901–1902). Among the Kwoma of New Guinea, the entire family sleeps together in the same room. But each spouse has a separate bark slab on which to sleep, as spouses would be ashamed to be found in the same bed (Whiting, 1941). In Oceania, an entire Pukapuka family may sleep in the same bed in the sleeping house if there is only one mosquito net. Otherwise, everyone sleeps in same house but under different nets (Beaglehole & Beaglehole, 1938).

A husband and wife among the Manus of Oceania sleep apart and, indeed, the Manus like it best when a family has two children, one to sleep with the father on one side of the house and one to sleep with the mother on the other side (Mead, 1930). Men and women among the Maria Gond of India sleep in separate quarters. A woman and her grown daughters sleep in the *angadi*, which also doubles as a kitchen. Her husband lives and sleeps in the *agha*. A boy who is still too young to stay in the bachelors' house may also sleep in the *agha* (Grigson, 1949). Among the Azande of Zaire, everyone has his or her own hut and sleeps there. A small child will sleep with the mother (Baxter & Butt, 1953).

Where marriages are monogamous, a couple are very likely to sleep in the same room. Ninety-four percent of a sample of 116 monogamous societies have same-room sleeping arrangements for spouses (Broude & Greene, 1983). However, such a sleeping arrangement does not guarantee a husband and wife privacy. First, the couple may share sleeping quarters. Sleeping companions may range from only small infants to all prepubescent children, to all nuclear family members who are not themselves married. In 6% of a sample of 95 societies, a husband and wife sleep with their infants, in 15% they sleep with all prepubescent children, and in 32% at least older unmarried family members also sleep in the same room as their mother and father (Broude & Greene, 1983). Second, partners who share the same room may not sleep in the same bed. In at least 41% of the 116 monogamous societies where spouses sleep in the same room, they also share the same bed or blanket or use adjacent sleeping places. But in at least 13% of these cultures, a husband and wife do not sleep in close proximity even though they are in the same room. Rather, spouses sleep in different beds, different hammocks, different sections of the room, or the like (Broude & Greene, 1983).

Husbands and wives are most likely to sleep apart where marriages are polygynous. Sometimes, cowives have their own houses and the husband either has lodgings of his own or rotates between wives. Spouses may also sleep apart when a society has men's houses, that is, separate structures where only men congregate and where they may also sometimes sleep. Husbands and wives also tend to sleep apart when social institutions favor the segregation of the sexes more generally. In some societies, spouses are expected to sleep apart as long as there is an infant sleeping with the mother. This arrangement can last for some years.

Sleeping arrangements are also related to climate. Husbands and wives predictably sleep together in colder climates, where the temperature falls below 50°F in the winter, and apart where the weather is mild or warm for the entire year. Interestingly, temperature also predicts where a baby will sleep, so that infants sleep with the mother in warmer climates but in their own crib, cradle, or sleeping bag where the climate is cooler. The association between ambient temperature and sleeping may reflect a pragmatic way of trying to achieve temperature control. Adults will benefit from the body warmth of the partner when sleeping together in colder climates, and babies will be kept warmest if sleeping in their own bed, especially as the sleeping schedule of a baby does not coincide with that of its parents (Whiting, 1969).

Husband–wife sleeping arrangements are predictably associated with other aspects of married life. Where couples sleep together, they also eat and spend their leisure time together and men's houses tend to be absent. Where they sleep apart, a husband and wife also eat and spend their leisure time apart and men's houses tend to be present (Broude, 1983).

Husband–Wife Work Activities

Because many of an adult's waking hours are devoted to subsistence activities, the nature of husband–wife interaction in a society is significantly related to the way in which work activities are allocated by sex. A husband and wife can work side by side or they can conduct their subsistence activities independently. In the former case, a couple will find themselves spending some or much of the day together, while in the latter case, they may not see one another for much of the time.

Among the Bhil of India, spouses perform many tasks together. This includes weeding, manuring, and harvesting their crops side by side. A wife may also spend time with her husband when he is in the logging camp, helping him manufacture the charcoal and cooking for him (Naik, 1956; Nath, 1960). In Okinawa, everyone in a Tairan family lumbers and works the rice patties together (Matetzki & Malone, 1966).

When spouses do different kinds of work, they are also likely to be separated for most of the day. In Arizona, Navaho men were responsible for building the corrals and fences, did most of the farming, took care of the horses, cattle, and wagons, hauled the water, and cut the firewood. It was the job of the women to butcher the mutton, cook, gather farm crops for meals, keep the house clean, and take care of the children. As men's and women's chores were performed in different places, husbands and wives did not spend much time together during the day (Leighton & Kluckhohn, 1969).

Sometimes, men and women work on the same overall task, but each specializes in a different aspect of the job. When this assembly line strategy for accomplishing tasks is employed, husbands and wives may work in the same location and therefore spend much time together, but they may also work in different places. Among the Gururumba of New Guinea, husbands and wives both participate in gardening activities, but each focuses on a different set of chores. Husbands break the soil for the garden, put up fences, and dig and drain the ditches. Meanwhile, wives prepare the broken soil and weed. Men see to the sugarcane, bananas, taro, and yams, while women are responsible for the vegetables and sweet potatoes. Men build the houses, and women cut and carry the thatch (Newman, 1965).

There is some indication that cultural patterns of allocating work are related to male–female relationships more generally. In societies where husbands and wives perform different tasks, sex is predictably viewed as dangerous, premarital sex norms for both sexes are restrictive, and extramarital sex norms for males are permissive. Division of labor by sex is also correlated with male sex aggression. So the tendency to segregate the sexes, including husbands and at work, seems to reflect an overall attitude of caution and even hostility regarding intimate and committed opposite-sex interaction. Where husbands and wives perform the same tasks, people choose their own marriage partners as opposed to having their future spouses chosen by thirdly parties. Thus, where marriages are based upon personal preference, spouses organize their work days in such a way as to be able to spend time together (Broude, 1983, 1987).

Husband–Wife Leisure Activities

In many cultures, a husband and wife who are not engaged in work activities usually spend their discretionary time in each other's company. This is the case in 47% of a sample of 104 societies (Broude & Greene, 1983). Sometimes, a couple will spend their leisure time together but in the context of a larger group. This occurs in 21% of those societies for which information is available (Broude & Greene, 1983). Thus, for instance, when not engaged in subsistence activities, Southern African !Kung spouses remain together, but are surrounded by members of their band. !Kung life is communal, with a local group living in a clearing of perhaps 20 feet in diameter. Each family has its own hut, but these are used mainly for sleeping and storage of property. Therefore everyone lives out in the open. A family may sit near its own fire in front of its own hut, but everyone faces centrally and within seeing and hearing distance of everyone else (Marshall, 1959). Thus married couples are together, but in a crowd.

In another 21% of the sample of 104 cultures, couples also spend their leisure time together, but often alone, although they also participate in group activities (Broude & Greene, 1983). In Kenya, a Kikuyu husband and wife like to sit and talk around the fire at home while dinner is cooking. A couple will also visit neighbors or attend dances and ceremonies, and a wife will help her husband entertain guests in his hut (Cagnolo, 1933).

In 5% of the same sample of cultures, husbands and wives almost always spend their discretionary time together and alone or only with family members (Broude & Greene, 1983). Among the Nambicuara of Brazil, for example, individual families gather around the fire singing, dancing, and talking until it is time to go to sleep (Levi-Strauss, 1948).

Husbands and wives spend at least a large proportion of their leisure time separately in 53% of 107 cultures (Broude & Greene, 1983). In such societies, men and women tend to congregate instead with members of their own sex. This can mean that a husband and wife virtually never see one another during their leisure time. The Mbundu of Angola have a men's house, which serves as a school, dining room, recreation facility, and hotel. It is here that men and boys spend much of leisure time. Women congregate in the kitchen. There are dances on the last few days of each month, but even at these events men and women, including spouses, separated from each other, with males on one side of floor and females on the other (Childs, 1949).

Where husbands and wives spend their leisure time together, they also tend to eat together. Husbands are also likely to attend the births of their children and men's houses are unlikely to be present (Broude, 1983).

Deference Customs

The nature of the husband–wife relationship is not only reflected in the number and kinds of activities in which married partners engage together or separately. The tone of the marital bond is also influenced by cultural values regarding the relative status of spouses. Ideas about relative husband–wife status are, in turn, mirrored in what are known as deference customs. These are culturally agreed upon behaviors that a person of lower status directs toward a person of higher status in acknowledgement of this difference between them. Deference behavior includes such actions as bowing, kneeling, standing, speaking in a low voice, remaining silent, and using a special language in the presence of the dominant individual. Walking behind the dominant person, reserving a seat of honor for the dominant person, and saving the dominant individual the choicest foods are also examples of deference customs found in some societies (Stephens, 1963). One person may also show deference to another by asking permission to engage in certain behaviors. Status differences reflect inequality between people with respect to power, privilege, and the like. A number of cultures expect wives to show deference in the presence of their husbands. In contrast, it is rare for husbands to show deference to their wives. Even when men display such behaviors, their actions do not signify submissiveness to their wives but rather something closer to politeness. Thus, in some cultures, a wife is viewed as subservient to her husband and required to demonstrate this outwardly multiple times a day.

A traditional Hindu wife is prohibited from speaking her husband's name. Rather, when she talks to him, she is required to call him "my lord." A wife who wants to refer to her spouse to other people calls him "the master of the house" (Mace & Mace, 1959). In Korea, women of the upper classes remain in seclusion at home and must ask their husbands for permission even to look out at the street (Griffis, 1882). Among the Ganda of Uganda, a wife washes her husband's feet every night (Stephens, 1963). A rural Ukranian wife will walk behind her husband in public and will enter the house after him (Wilber, 1964). In traditional Japanese families, the husband is the first to be served at meals and first to take a bath (Stephens, 1963). Among the Chuckchee of Siberia, the husband gets the choicest food. His wife eats what is left behind (Bogoras, 1909).

A wife's subordination to her spouse can also be communicated by behavior on the part of the husband. It is customary for a religious Hindu to refer to his wife using such labels as "my servant" or "my dog" instead of calling her by her name (Mace & Mace, 1959). Traditional Japanese husbands are proscribed from speaking gratefully or respectfully about their spouses. Instead, they use such terms as "my old hag," the idea being to demean the women in the presence of other people. Japanese men also use the impolite terms for "you" when talking to their wives, while women are required to use the polite form of the pronoun when speaking to their spouse. A man who uses the polite form of "you" is assumed to be henpecked by those who hear him (Mace & Mace, 1959).

Outwardly deferent behavior on the part of a wife more accurately reflects a woman's informal status more in some societies than in others, as in many cultures women who are required to indicate their subordination to their husbands by various gestures nevertheless have some, sometimes considerable, power. Even where customs reflect overall real subordination, wives can, in fact, have some amount of power. While a Javanese woman shows formal deference to her husband, she retains most of the control and makes most of the decisions with regard to household matters (Geertz, 1961). The Saharan Tuareg husband has all of the power outside of his household. However, wives own their own property and have no responsibility for household expenses, with the result that they can amass considerable wealth in comparison with their husbands, whose resources are likely to remain stable or even to diminish over the course of the marriage (Lhote, 1944). While a Burmese girl understands even as a child that she must treat men with supreme respect and always defer to a man's judgment, in fact, husbands ask for and take the advice of their wives in both public and private matters (Scott, 1910).

There are also cases where deferent behavior on the part of a wife reflects a real lack of power. A Gandan wife not only displays deference but is genuinely subordinate to her husband. She is expected to plan household activities around his schedule, make meals when convenient for him, visit only with his permission, and stay away from home only as long as he permits. If she does not obey her husband, she can expect a beating (Stephens, 1963).

Behavior indicating deference of wives toward their spouses, then, is sometimes a reflection of genuine differences in power, privilege, respect, freedom, and so on between a woman and her husband. Sometimes, deference behavior on the part of a wife masks a level of status that is higher than these gestures indicate. Nevertheless, it seems reasonable to conclude that a marriage characterized by expectations of frequent deference behavior on the part of a wife will be different from marriages in which such gestures are not expected and are not witnessed.

In some cultures, husbands do display behavior toward their wives that has a superficial similarity to deference behavior. Among the Brno of Czechoslovakia, a wife is seated before her husband is at meals and also begins eating first (Stephens, 1963). In Madrid, aristocratic wives walk to the right of their husbands, which is considered to be the honored position. A husband also holds his wife's chair while she is being seated and stands when she enters room. These gestures, which are reminiscent of the code of chivalry, seem to be indications, not of a man's subordination, but of good manners (Stephens, 1963).

Marriage and Other Aspects of Male–Female Interaction

Around the world, married couples tend to be consistent with regard to their day-to-day interactions. That is, a husband and wife tend either to engage in a variety of activities together or to conduct their daily activities independently. This is why marriages are characterized as either on the whole intimate or on the whole aloof.

Patterns of day-to-day marital interaction are also related to certain other features of male–female interaction. Marriages tend to be intimate in societies in which there is a greater range of things over which women have power. This may be the result of the fact that, as women gain more status, there is less male–female segregation in a culture. This means that males and females have more opportunities to get to know each other on a personal basis. And it means that day-to-day contact between spouses becomes a possibility. In cultures where the sexes are segregated, husband–wife intimacy is, by definition, not an option for a couple (Broude, 1990).

Day-to-day marital interaction is also related to ideas regarding whether or not sex is dangerous. Where a society endorses the belief that sex is a dangerous activity, marriages tend to be aloof. Where societies do not subscribe to the belief that sex is dangerous, marriages tend to be intimate. Intimate marriages are also associated with uninhibited talk about sex, whereas in societies where marriages are aloof talk about sex is regarded as inappropriate, shameful, and the like.

Interestingly, patterns of marital interaction are not related to certain other features of male–female interaction. Thus there is no predictable connection between husband–wife day-to-day interaction, mode of choosing marriage partners, honeymoon customs, beliefs about the desirability of frequent sexual activity in marriage, frequency of premarital or extramarital sex for males or females, incidence of or concern about impotence, attitudes toward or frequency of homosexuality, male sexual aggression, rape, or frequency of divorce. There is one exception to this overall pattern. Husband–wife eating arrangements are predictably associated with honeymoon customs and divorce, so that where spouses eat together honeymoon customs are absent and divorce is relatively rare, while where spouses eat apart honeymoon customs are present and divorce is more common. However, the overall lack of a connection between marital interaction and other features of male–female relationships leads to the perhaps surprising conclusion that day-to-day interaction between spouses is unrelated to courtship customs, sexual attitudes, concerns, behavior, or the likelihood that a marriage will be terminated by a spouse. In short, day-to-day contact between spouses seems to operate independently of other aspects of male–female interaction (Broude, 1983).

The relative independence of patterns of day-to-day interaction and other features of opposite-sex relationships suggests that the degree of daily contact between spouses is determined by factors different from those that influence other aspects of male–female interaction. This is not surprising, as customs for choosing marriage partners, norms regarding sex, actual sexual activity, daily contact between spouses, and patterns of divorce all have different functions in the life of an individual and the operation of a culture. Therefore, we should expect them to vary independently, as indeed they do.

REFERENCES

Ainsworth, M. D. (1967). *Infancy in Uganda*. Baltimore: Johns Hopkins University Press.

Barton, R. F. (1938). *Philippine pagans: the autobiographies of three Ifugaos*. London: Routledge.

Barton, R. F. (1969). *Ifugao law*. Berkeley: University of California Press.

Baxter, P. T. W., & Butt, A. (1953). *The Azande, and related peoples of the Anglo-Egyptian Sudan and Belgian Congo*. London: International African Institute.

Beaglehole, E., & Beaglehole, P. (1938). *Ethnology of the Pukapuka*. Honolulu, HI: The Museum.

Bogoras, W. (1909). The Chukchee. *Memoirs of the Museum of Natural History*.

Bowlby, J. (1973). *Attachment and loss: Vol. 2. Separation*. New York: Basic Books.

Brant, C. (1954). *Tagadale: A Burmese village in 1950*. Ithaca, NY: Cornell University Press.

Broude, G. J. (1983). Male–female relationships in cross-cultural perspective: A study of sex and intimacy. *Behavior Science Research, 13*, 154–181.

Broude, G. J. (1986). *The relationship between male–female roles and marital intimacy and aloofness*. Paper presented at the 15th annual meetings of the Society for Cross-Cultural Research, San Diego, CA.

Broude, G. J. (1987). The relationship of marital intimacy and aloofness to social environment: A hologeistic study. *Behavior Science Research, 21*, 50–69.

Broude, G. J. (1990). The relationship of the division of labor by sex to other gender-related phenomena. *Behavior Science Research, 24*, 29–50.

Broude, G. J., & Greene, S. J. (1983). Cross-cultural codes on husband-wife relationships. *Ethnology, 22,* 263–280.

Bunzel, R. (1952). *Chichicastenango: A Guatemalan village.* New York: AMS Press.

Burling, R. (1963). *Rengsanggri: family and kinship in a Garo village.* Philadelphia: University of Philadelphia Press.

Cagnolo, C. (1933). *The Akikuyu: Their customs, traditions, and folklore.* Nyeri, Kenya: Mission Printing School.

Childs, G. (1949). *Umbundu kinship and character.* London: Oxford University Press.

Dorsey, O. J. (1884). *Omaha sociology* (Annu. Rep. 3, 1881–1882). Bureau of American Ethnology, Smithsonian Institute, Washington, DC.

Durham, M. E. (1928). *Some tribal origins, laws and customs of the Balkans.* London: Allen & Unwin.

Erikson, E. (1963). *Childhood and society.* New York: Norton.

Faron, L. (1961). *Mapuche social structure: Institutional reintegration in a patrilineal society of central Chile* (Illinois Studies in Anthropology I). Urbana, University of Illinois Press.

Fock, N. (1963). Mataco marriage. *Folk, 5,* 91–101.

Frayzer (1985). Varieties of sexual experiences. New Haven, CT: Heaf Press.

Freeman, J. D. (1958). The family system of the Iban of Borneo. In J. Goody (Ed.), *The developmental cycle in domestic groups.* (pp. 105–139). Cambridge Papers in Social Anthropology, No. 1.

Furer-Haimendorf, C. von. (1964). *The Sherpas of Nepal: Buddhist highlanders.* London: Murray.

Geertz, M. (1961). *The Javanese family.* New York: Free Press.

Gladwin, T., & Sarason, S. (1953). *Truk: Man in paradise.* New York: Wenner–Gren Foundation.

Gluckman, M. (1959). Lozi of Brotseland in north-western Rhodesia. In E. Colson & M. Gluckman (Eds.), *Seven tribes of British Central Africa* (pp. 1–93). Manchester, UK: Manchester University Press.

Goldschmidt, W. (1966). *The culture and behavior of the Sebei.* Berkeley: University of California Press.

Griffis, W. (1882). *Corea: The hermit nation.* New York: Scribner's Sons.

Grigson, W. (1949). *The Maria Gond of Bastar.* London.

Gunn, H. D. (1956). *Pagan peoples of the central area of northern Nigeria.* London: International African Institute.

Gusinde, M. (1937). *The Yahgan: The life and thought of the water nomads of Cape Horn.* Mödling bei Wien, Austria: Anthropos-Bibliothek.

Gutierrez de Pineda, V. (1950). *Social organization in La Guajira.* Bogota: Instituto etnologico nacional.

Headland, I. T. (1914). *Home life in China.* New York: Macmillan.

Hendrix, L. (1997). Varieties of marital relationships. In C. R. Ember & M. Ember (Eds.), *Cross-cultural research for social science.* (Vol. 1, pp. 147–170). Englewood Cliffs, NJ: Prentice-Hall.

Hendrix, L., & Pearson, W. (1995). Spousal interdependence, female power, and divorce: A cross-cultural examination. *Journal of Comparative Family Studies, 26,* 217–232.

Hogbin, H. I. (1970). *The island of menstruating men: Religion in Wogeo, New Guinea.* Scranton, PA: Chandler.

Holmberg, A. R. (1950). *Nomads of the long bow: the Siriono of eastern Bolivia.* Washington, DC: U.S. Government Printing Office.

Karsten, R. (1935). *The head-hunters of western Amazonas: The life and culture of the Jibaro Indians of eastern Ecuador and Peru.* Helsingfors.

Leighton, D., & Kluckhohn, C. (1969). *Children of the people: The Navaho individual and his development.* New York: Octagon.

LeVine, R., & LeVine, B. (1966). *Nyansongo: A Gusii community in Kenya.* New York: Wiley.

Levi-Strauss, C. (1948). The Nambicuara. In J. H. Steward (Ed.), *Handbook of South American Indians* (Vol. 3, pp. 361–369). Washington, DC: U.S. Government Printing Office.

Lewis, I. M. (1962). *Marriage and the family in northern Somaliland.* Kampala, Uganda: East African Institute of Social Research.

Lhote, H. (1944). *The Hoggar Tuareg.* Paris: Payot.

Linton, R. (1933). *The Tanala: A hill tribe of Madagascar.* Chicago: Field Museum of Natural History.

Mace, D., & Mace, V. (1959). *Marriage east and west.* Garden City, NY: Doubleday.

Malinowski, B. (1929). *The sexual life of savages in north-western Melanesia.* New York: Halcyon House.

Marshall, L. (1959). Marriage among the !Kung bushmen. *Africa, 29,* 335–364.

Matetzki, T. W., & Malone, M. J. (1966). *Taira: An Okinawan village.* New York: Wiley.

Matthews, W. (1877). *Ethnography and philology of the Hidatsa Indians.* Washington, DC: U.S. Government Printing Office.

Mead, M. (1930). *Growing up in New Guinea: A comparative study of primitive education.* New York: Morrow.

Minturn, L., & Hitchcock, J. T. (1966). *The Rajputs of Khalapur, India.* New York: Wiley.

Musil, A. (1928). *The manner and customs of the Rwala Bedouins.* New York: Creative Age Press.

Naik, T. B. (1956). *The Bhils: A study.* Delhi, India: Bharatiya Adimjati Sevak Sangh.

Nanda, S. D. (1950). *The city of two gateways.* London: Allen & Unwin.

Nath, Y. V. S. (1960). *Bhils of Ratanmal: an analysis of the social structure of a western Indian community.* Baroda, India: Maharaja Sayajirao University.

Newman, P. L. (1965). *Knowing the Gururumba.* New York: Holt, Rinehart & Winston.

Reay, M. (1953–1940). Social control amongst the Orokavia. *Oceania, 24,* 110–118. (Original work published in 1940.)

Richards, A. (1940). *Bemba marriage and present economic conditions.* Rhodes–Livingstone Papers 4.

Roscoe, J. (1911). *The Baganda: An account of their native customs and beliefs.* London: Macmillan.

Scott, J. G. (1910). *The Burman, his life and notions.* London: Macmillan.

Serpenti, I. M. (1965). *Cultivators in the swamps.* Assen, The Netherlands: Van Gorcum.

Slater, P. E., & Slater, D. A. (1965). Maternal ambivalence and narcissism: A cross-cultural study. *Merrill–Palmer Quarterly, 11,* 241–260.

Stephens, W. N. (1963). *The family in cross-cultural perspective.* New York: Holt, Rinehart & Winston.

Stevenson, M. C. (1901–1902). *The Zuni Indians* (Annu. Rep. 23). Bureau of American Ethnology, Smithsonian Institute, Washington, DC.

Swanton, J. (1924–1925). *Social organization and social usages of the Indians of the Creek confederacy* (Annu. Rep. 42). Bureau of American Ethnology, Smithsonian Institute, Washington, DC.

Underhill, R. (1939). *Social organization of the Papago Indians.* New York: Columbia University Press.

Vreeland, H. H. (1953). *Mongol community and kinship structure*. New Haven, CT: Human Relations Area Files.

Whiting, J. W. M. (1941). Becoming a Kwoma. New Haven, CT: Yale University Press.

Whiting, J. W. M. (1969). Effects of climate on certain cultural practices. In Andrew P. Vayda (Ed.), *Environment and cultural behavior* (pp. 416–455). Garden City, NY: The Museum of Natural Press.

Whiting, J. W. M., & Whiting, B. B. (1975). Aloofness and intimacy of husbands and wives: A cross-cultural study. *Ethos, 3*, 183–208.

Wilber, D. N. (1964). *Pakistan: Its people, its society, its culture*. New Haven, CT: Human Relations Area Files.

Williams, F. E. (1930). *Orovaika society*. London: Oxford University Press.

Zingg, R. M. (1938). *The Huichols* (Contributions to Anthropology I). Denver, CO: University of Denver.

Homosexuality

Fernando Luiz Cardoso and Dennis Werner

INTRODUCTION

We might define "homosexuality" simply as sexual relationships between people of the same sex. Yet behind this simple definition lie many different phenomena. People vary tremendously in their same-sex behaviors, in their sexual desires, and in the ways they define themselves. Cultures also differ widely in the ways they define and treat these relationships and the people who engage in them.

Our knowledge has grown tremendously in recent years. But for several reasons, this literature has dealt mostly with male homosexuality. Written reports have come mostly from men, who may not have cared about or been fully aware of what women do. Also, women's sexuality has usually been restricted to a more limited private sphere of acquaintances that is less visible, or considered less important. Finally, female sexuality may be more difficult to distinguish from "affection," or may, in fact, be less common than male homosexuality. Although parallels and contrasts with male homosexuality may be drawn, readers should be aware of the disparity in available information.

INTELLECTUAL HISTORY OF HOMOSEXUALITY

Probably since the beginnings of human culture people have been thinking about homosexuality. Records of these reflections have come to us in the form of myths, political histories, legal documents, literature, and religious injunctions. Even attempts at explaining homosexuality date from ancient times.

Pottery from the Peruvian Mochican culture more than 2000 years ago shows homosexual acts (Gregersen, 1983), and rock drawings of homosexual intercourse from the African Khoi-San culture may be thousands of years old (Epprecht, 1998). However, it is the written records of early civilizations that are most informative about how people conceptualized homosexuality.

Mesopotamia, Egypt, and India

Sumerian temple records from the middle of the third millennium BC mention *gala* priests, who for centuries served the goddess Inanna/Ishtar. These priests and their later equivalents in Babylonia and Assyria adopted female dress and manners and engaged in passive anal intercourse with other men. The written word for *gala* combined the symbols for penis and anus. Babylonian and Assyrian omens even instructed men to have sex with these priests to bring good luck. But not all types of homosexuality were considered positive. Middle Assyrian laws from 1250 BC decreed severe punishments for men who falsely accused others of passive homosexuality or who raped companions (Roscoe, 1997). Similar associations of passive homosexuality with humiliation come from Egypt. In one ancient myth the god Horus rapes the god Seth to humiliate him (Roscoe, 1997), and in the *Book of the Dead* (after 2000 BC) a dead man argues that the god "Atum has no power over me, because I copulate between his buttocks" (Gregersen, 1983). Records of homosexuality from India date from a much later period. Law books from the 4th century BC refer to eunuchs occupying important posts in Indian courts. Later records show that some had affairs with their masters, and may have been castrated specifically for sexual purposes. The *Kama Sutra* (5th century CE) gives instructions on how to be fellated by eunuchs (Murray, 2000).

China and Japan

In China and Japan homosexuality also appears in some of the earliest surviving texts. In one story from the Chinese Eastern Zhou dynasty (770–256 BC) the Duke Ling of Wei falls in love with a boy named Mizi Xia. The boy finds a peach that is especially sweet and shares it with the Duke. From that time up to the present the term "shared peach" has referred to male homosexual ties (Hinsch, 1990). In Japan, ambiguous references to homosexuality appear by the 8th century CE, and unambiguous records appear in personal diaries from the 11th century

(Leupp, 1994). Most of the Chinese and Japanese texts describe love affairs between a ruler and his younger favorite, and were probably recorded because they had political implications. Rulers often attempted to provide land and other gifts to their protégés.

Ancient Greece and Rome

It was with the Greeks that conjectures on the origins of different homosexual activities became common. The Cretan customs of segregating boys and encouraging homosexual relations between boys and men were attributed by Aristotle to a desire to hold down the birth rate. Plutarch suggested that Theban pederasty resulted from a conscious policy of channeling the "natural ferocity of adolescent males to socially useful purposes" (Murray, 2000). Xenophon contrasted the transitory couplings between men and boys of Elis with the more permanent pairings common in Thebes. Whereas in Thebes, Sparta, and Crete physical relations between a mature mentor (*erastes*) and a beardless youth (*eromenos*) were encouraged, Plato argued that in Athens the relationship ideally avoided physical sex at least until one's partner had proved his worth (Murray, 2000, p. 105).

When Alexander the Great conquered most of the western world a period of wider cross-cultural comparisons began. Observers noted the homosexual use of eunuchs and effeminate boy slaves in different parts of the Hellenic empires, and in fact, even before Rome conquered Greece, the old Greek system had given way to systems more like those in the conquered territories. By late Hellenistic times Charicles thought the idea of women having sex with women was so ridiculous that he used it to clinch a *reductio ad absurdum* argument.

In Rome what a man did with his slave was considered his own business, but freemen were ridiculed if, as adults, they engaged in "receptive" homosexuality. In the 5th century Caelius Aurelianus argued that homosexuality was an inherited disease (Murray, 2000).

The Age of Discovery

The European discovery of the New World greatly enhanced curiosity about homosexuality. Explorers' many accounts of "sodomy" in the newly discovered cultures were often used to justify the subduing of native peoples. In the early 1500s Cieza de León complained of homosexual temple prostitutes among native cultures along the Peruvian coast, and these complaints reinforced the conquistadors' will to stamp out native religions (Murray, 2000). In the early 1500s Balboa sent wild dogs to kill homosexual shamans in California tribes (Grahn, 1986).

Explorers, traders, and missionaries continued to report on the homosexual activities of newly discovered cultures well into the 20th century. Over time the moral judgments diminished and the descriptions became richer. The 19th-century English explorer, Sir Richard Burton (1967), based many of his detailed descriptions of homosexuality in different countries on "participant observation." Although he left us with many valuable texts, his widow burned many more (Rice, 1990).

Anthropological Accounts

Up to the 1980s anthropologists' incidental references to homosexuality were typically no more detailed than those of explorers, missionaries, or traders. Ford and Beach (1951) compiled and quantified some of this information from other cultures, and throughout the 1950s and 1960s the Human Relations Area Files busily indexed accounts from hundreds more. Most accounts were brief, and often ambiguous, but by the late 1960s cross-cultural researchers were able to use statistical analyses to examine psychological and other theories about male homosexuality.

By the 1980s the gay liberation movement had made it possible for Herdt (1981) to initiate a new age in anthropology in which fieldwork was dedicated primarily to homosexuality. At much the same time the social historian, Michel Foucault, published his influential *History of Sexuality* (French edition, 1978; English translation, 1980), making the study of homosexuality one of the central themes of academic research.

Foucault argued that prior to the 19th century people may have talked about homosexual acts, but there was no notion of the "homosexual" as a separate social category. For some of his followers this meant that "homosexuals" themselves did not exist until very recently when they were socially "constructed." Other scholars pointed out that the lack of a category does not mean that "homosexuals" did not exist, any more than the lack of a concept for "gene" means that genes did not exist prior to Mendel. Still other scholars went further and tried to show that most societies did, indeed, have concepts for "homosexual" that, in essence, were the same everywhere. Thus was born the great "essentialist–constructivist" debate that permeated gender studies throughout the 1980s and 1990s and resulted in far richer descriptions of homosexuality in different cultures (DeCecco & Elia, 1993).

Attempts to reconcile our knowledge of cross-cultural variation with studies on the biology of homosexuality clarified a need to make greater distinctions with regard to *what* is explained, whether homosexual behaviors, identities, or desires. Several recent studies have once again used cross-cultural statistical studies to test some of these ideas.

THE DIVERSITY OF HOMOSEXUALITY

Cultural Systems of Homosexuality

Most scholars of the 1980s and 1990s emphasized the uniqueness of homosexuality in every culture. Of course in some respects every culture *is* different from every other culture. Still, we *can* classify cultures on many different characteristics. One popular typology, originally suggested almost 40 years ago, groups cultures into one of three male homosexual systems (Gorer, 1966). The first, and by far the most common, has been labeled the "pathic" ("passive") or "gender-stratified" system. The second, also very common, has been called the "pederasty" or "age-stratified" system, and includes societies with "mentorship" or "ritualized" homosexuality. The third system, much less common, has been labeled "homophilic" or "egalitarian," and may be subdivided into "adolescent homosexuality," "comrade," and "gay" systems.

Systems of female homosexuality are similar but not exactly parallel to the male systems. Examples of each system can illustrate the cross-cultural variation.

Male Homosexual Systems

Gender-Stratified Systems. In gender-stratified systems men who take on a pathic (passive or receptive) role in sexual relationships are culturally distinguished from typical men, but the men who take on "active" (insertor) roles are not. Unlike "gays," pathics do not typically have sex with other pathics. This system is widespread on all the world's continents. In many societies pathics are known for their special ceremonial roles. Among the Siberian Chuckchee a youth begins his transformation when he receives a "shamanic calling." He gradually

adopts female characteristics—hairstyles, then dress, then female tasks, and finally female speech. At this point he begins to seek the "good graces of men" and may eventually marry one of his lovers. Pathic shamans, called "soft men," also communicate with supernatural husbands, The pathic's human husband is not differentiated from the other men in society, but he may have to follow the orders of his cross-gendered wife's supernatural husband. Many non-pathic Chukchee also become shamans, but the "soft-men" are considered special (Murray, 2000).

Gender-stratified homosexuality is also common in Latin America. Although some pathics may adopt special religious roles, like the Brazilian *pai de santo*, most do not, and homosexuality is not necessary for these positions. In his study of a Brazilian fishing village Cardoso (2002) found that most men had had sex with the village's *paneleiros* (pathics), some of whom were transvestites. Lack of heterosexual opportunities could not explain why men turned to the pathics. The men who had sex with *paneleiros* were actually somewhat more popular with the women than other men. Nor did these men appear to have "bisexual" personality profiles. The local culture did not distinguish them from other men, and they were not intermediate between pathics and other men on childhood precursors to homosexuality (Cardoso, n.d.).

Age-Stratified Systems. Age-stratified homosexual systems have been identified on all the continents except the Americas. One of the most common forms is the "mentorship" system, in which an older male takes on a boy as his protégé to teach the arts of politics, religion, or warfare. In most of these societies relationships are monogamic, and much care is taken to select the proper mentor. Boys may become apprentices as young as 7–10 years, as among the New Guinea Sambia, and may continue with their "passive" role until as old as 25, as among the New Guinea Etoro. At this point a man may take on a boy apprentice of his own until he eventually marries a woman. In some societies, as among the ancient Greeks, the men may continue their mentorship roles even after marrying women. In some societies, like the Etoro, these homosexual activities were more common and considered far superior to heterosexual sex that might be totally prohibited for two thirds of the year. Lengthy and complex rituals assured that insemination would give the boys male strength (Herdt, 1984; Murray, 2000).

From the 13th to the 17th centuries in Japan older Buddhist monks maintained (active) homosexual relations with (passive) younger acolytes or postulants. Although these *nanshoku* relationships were attributed to the founder of Japanese Buddhism in the 8th century, the custom probably drew more from Shinto and Confucian traditions. At the same time, older Samurai maintained a similar tradition with younger warriors. Sometimes these relationships continued throughout adult life and led to heroic tales of the "comrade loves of the Samurai," similar to the ancient Greek myths of Achilles and Patroclus or Apollo and Ametus (Ihara, 1972; Leupp, 1994; Murray, 2000).

In both Japan and Greece these "mentorship" systems eventually transformed into "catamite" systems (similar to those of the later Roman emperors and Turkish sultans) in which kept boys were made more effeminate for the sexual pleasures of powerful older males, with no pedagogical aims. Among the West African Mossi, chiefs kept boys for sexual purposes, especially for Fridays when sex with women was taboo (Murray & Roscoe, 1998). Among the Ashanti, some male slaves were treated as female lovers. In many societies (China, Korea, Japan, Rome, Egypt, Iraq) boys took on women's roles in theatrical productions and served as prostitutes, a practice which led some (including possibly Shakespeare's England) to denounce the theater (Murray, 2000).

Egalitarian Systems. In egalitarian systems power differences between "active" and "passive" partners do not exist, or are downplayed. In many societies adolescent friends engage in homosexual play. Among the African Nyakyusa boys live apart in separate villages from adults. They sleep together and commonly have interfemoral intercourse with each other. Informants said that an adult male may have sex with boys, but never with another adult male (Murray, 2000). Among Yanomami Indians intervillage homosexuality is encouraged and a youth is likely to marry his "best friend's" sister. Some Australian aborigine adolescents similarly have sex with their future brothers-in-law. Adolescent homosexuality has also been common in many Melanesian and Polynesian societies like Tikopia, Samoa, Tahiti, and Hawaii.

In a few societies an adolescent sexual relationship may develop into a "comrade" relationship that lasts a lifetime and continues to include sex, although both men also have heterosexual relationships and marry women. Although never typical of all the men in a society, such relationships have been reported among ancient Greeks,

Romans, and Japanese (Murray, 2000), and among the more modern Pashtans of Pakistan (Lindholm, 1982).

The rarest of homosexual systems in the ethnographic literature is our modern "gay" system, in which exclusive homosexuals engage in sex with other exclusive homosexuals throughout their lives. This system may, indeed, be unique to modern society as claimed by Foucault. In any case, the "gay" system appears to be increasing recently. Murray and Arboleda (1995) noted changes over time from "pathic" to "gay" systems in Guatemala, Mexico, and Peru. In the 1970s, only 50% of their informants had heard of the term "gay," and only 23% thought it referred to both "passive" and "active" partners. In the 1980s, 76% had heard of the term and 58% applied it to both "passives" and "actives."

Other Male Systems. Although this classification system may be useful, it cannot account for all of the ways homosexuality occurs in different societies. For example, Duerr (1993) points out that homosexual rape has often been used to humiliate defeated enemies. Greek vases show Persians submitting anally to their conquerors. The losers in Yanomomi club fights were also victimized in this way. Homosexual rapes in prisons throughout the world have been well documented (see www.spr.org).

Also, different types of homosexuality may be found in different sectors of the same society. "Gay" systems may characterize most of the homosexual activity found in today's northern European cultures. Still, gender-stratified systems occur in prisons, and age-stratified systems may occur in private schools or street gangs (Duerr, 1993). In ancient Greece age-stratified systems may have received most of the attention, but gender-stratified homosexuality also occurred. The Greek terms *kinaidos, europroktoi,* and *katapygon* referred to men who engaged in passive anal intercourse even as adults. Although their behavior was tolerated, these men were not allowed to hold public office or participate in citizen assemblies (Murray, 2000).

In addition, especially in small-scale societies, rather ad hoc social adjustments may be confused with long-standing cultural traditions. Crocker (1990) reports the presence of three elderly cross-gendered men among the Brazilian Kanela Indians he studied, but states that the group had no tradition for transvestites to follow. Native research assistants told Crocker that these men were not active sexually, but one had previously allowed Kanela men to have anal intercourse with him. Similarly, Clastres (1972) describes a transvestite among the hunting and gathering Aché of Paraguay. His account ties traditional structural characteristics of Aché culture to the transvestite's behavior (including his sexual relations with his own brothers), but it seems more likely that these behaviors were ad hoc rather than traditional since a closely related band of Aché reported never having heard of transvestites.

Female Homosexual Systems

In her study of lesbian relationships in Lesotho, Kendal (1998) pointed out how easy it is to ignore female homosexuality. Basotho women simply say that sex is impossible without a penis. Women "have sex" with their husbands, but simultaneously maintain affective ties with women (including "grinding" genital contacts) that they describe as "loving." This has made it difficult for cross-cultural researchers to ascertain just how "sexual" women's relationships are. For example, women taking on the typically male roles of "warrior" or "husband" have been reported for many societies, but it is unclear whether these involved lesbian sex.

Still, there are clear descriptions of gender-stratified female homosexuality. Among the Chuckchee, two women who adopted male dress, speech, and work activities eventually married girls, and one of the wives became pregnant by a cohusband. Records of gender-stratified female homosexuality also appear from ancient China and Japan. A chronicle of the Han emperor Cheng (32–7 BC) reports that his wife had a *dui shi* (husband–wife) relationship with a female student who then became the emperor's concubine so that both could enjoy the girl's sexual favors (Murray, 2000). During the Tokugawa period (1615–1867 CE) lesbianism was common in the shoguns' harems, and there are references to women dressed as males who sought female prostitutes. Japanese theater companies also included women who took on male roles and became enamored of their female counterparts (Leupp, 1994). Gender-stratified lesbian relationships have also been described in Sumatra and Java (Murray, 2000).

Age-stratified female homosexuality occurred as part of initiation ceremonies among the Kaguru of Tanzania, and in the form of "mentorship" systems in ancient Greece. A Spartan text mentions women's intercourse with girls before their marriage, and Sappho, the poet from Lesbos, addressed women in the language of *erastes/eromenos* used for male homosexual relations. Since Sappho had a daughter, she obviously also had sex with a man. Female homosexuality also occurred in the form of a reverse "catamite" system in Japan, where girl dancers imitated men's behavior and served as prostitutes for female customers (Murray, 2000).

Accounts of non-"gay" egalitarian female homosexuality have been ambiguous. Big Nama women of Malekula (Melanesia) commonly practice homosexuality, but it is unclear whether this is age structured. Similarly, the lesbian relationships described in early 20th century Chinese sisterhoods and in the "mummy–baby" relations of Lesotho women appear to have been egalitarian, but we cannot be sure (Murray, 2000).

As these examples illustrate, homosexual activities occur under many varied forms, and may be given vastly different meanings in different cultures. For some this diversity is great enough to invalidate any attempts at explanation.

Animal Homosexuality

As Bagemihl (1999) points out, zoologists and ethologists have often been reluctant to label animal behaviors as "homosexual." Often these activities are listed as dominance/submissive gestures or "mock" courtships, even though the same behavior with a heterosexual couple would have been called sex. Bagemihl suggests that this reluctance sometimes stems from negative attitudes toward human homosexuality, but in part it may also reflect a recognition that human behavior simply is not the same as animal behavior.

When comparing different species it is important to distinguish "analogous" from "homologous" behaviors. Analogous behaviors may appear similar but are phylogenetically unrelated, while homologous behaviors are similar because they share an evolutionary past. When a bedbug forcibly deposits his own sperm in the sperm ducts of another bedbug, he helps pass along his own genes whenever his victim copulates with a female. Although scientists might label this behavior "homosexual rape," it really has nothing to do with human sexuality (Sommer, 1990). On the other hand, when a male gorilla mounts another male and ejaculates in his anus (Bagemihl, 1999), this behavior is more likely to be homologous to human homosexuality. Whether we decide to call the gorilla's behavior "homosexuality" is less important than recognizing that it is similar enough to human same-sex behavior for us to postulate an evolutionary connection.

Many primate behaviors might be homologous to human same-sex sexuality. Examples might include the male–male mounting, with anal penetration but no apparent ejaculation, of stump-tailed macaques and squirrel monkeys, or perhaps the simple mounts without penetration so common in langurs, pig-tailed macaques, baboons, orangutans, chimpanzees, and bonobos—or the mutual masturbation and fellatio reported among stump-tailed macaques—or the genital–genital contacts of female bonobos and male gibbons (Bagemihl, 1999; Werner, 1998). If we classify these behaviors as homologous with human homosexuality, why not include the sniffing and inspecting of another male's anogenital region among stump-tailed macaques, or the displaying of erections among vervet macaques or baboons, or the deposition of urine drops on subordinate males among squirrel monkeys? Could the preference of some rhesus monkeys for homosexual partners indicate primate homologs for "pathics" (Werner, 1998)?

Deciding these questions requires theory-driven comparisons of different primates, but our growing knowledge of homosexual-like behaviors among primates has revealed such complexity that some researchers seem to think that we should eschew all attempts at explanation and simply appreciate all the glorious exuberance of nature (Bagemihl, 1999).

EXPLAINING HOMOSEXUALITY

No single argument could possibly account for all aspects of homosexuality in humans and animals. However, attempts have been made to explain some of the variation.

Evolution of Homosexuality

Many scientists have puzzled over how homosexuality (especially exclusive homosexuality) evolved. How could a behavior that appears to reduce reproductive success survive the rigors of natural selection? Many researchers have suggested some hidden adaptive value: (1) exclusive homosexuals may help their relatives raise more offspring (kin selection, parental manipulation); (2) genes that are maladaptive in males might be especially adaptive in females, and vice versa; (3) genes for exclusive heterosexuality may be less adaptive than *combinations* of genes that permit *some* homosexuality (balanced polymorphism, heterosis, hybrid vigor) (Kirkpatrick, 2000; Sommer, 1990; Werner, 1998). Clear evidence for or against these different ideas is still lacking.

Most theorists have considered only adaptation, but evolutionary arguments must also account for how changes might have arisen throughout our phylogenetic history. Werner (1998) suggested an evolutionary sequence of ever greater male–male cooperation among primates that progressed gradually from systems that marked territories in more solitary animals, to systems that marked dominance and subordination in multimale groups, to systems that marked alliances in more complex social animals.

Only small changes needed to occur to move from one system to another. The scent deposits in urine or other bodily secretions that marked territorial boundaries began to mark some animals as subordinate "guests" in a dominant's territory. In addition to "paying homage" to dominant individuals by inhaling their markings, subordinates also had to hide or avoid penile erections while observing the erection displays of the dominant males (who had exclusive sexual rights to the group's females), and perhaps also tolerate the dominant's mounting behaviors. In many of these groups adolescent males practiced these dominance displays by alternating roles with each other. In more complex animal societies this adolescent behavior continued among adult males who could mark alliances by alternating subordinate and dominant roles. As these alliances became more complex, the same-sex behaviors came to resemble human homosexuality more and more.

In a complex animal society a male with genes that encouraged only submission might fail to reproduce for lack of trying, but a male that could act only as a dominant might also fail to reproduce. A little submissiveness helps avoid dangerous fights and facilitates the formation of alliances. In every generation some males may be too dominant and others too submissive to reproduce, but their genes will be passed on through those who have a little of both personalities.

In line with this theory, one of the most peaceful and cooperative of primates, the bonobo, probably also has the highest incidences of "homosexual" behavior, especially among females. As De Waal (1989) points out, sex is probably the major way that these animals reconcile conflicts and maintain peace.

Cross-Culturally Recurrent Themes

If homosexuality is not a totally arbitrary construct of symbolic culture, then we should find some recurrent themes behind all of the cultural diversity. For example, are "pathics" like "gays"? What about the typical men who have sex with them? Are there perhaps universal cognitive associations with homosexuality?

"Cross-gendered Individuals" versus Typical Men and Women.

People with experience in both gender-stratified and modern gay systems often compare "pathics" with "gays," under the assumption that a man who became a "pathic" in one culture would become a "gay" if he had lived elsewhere. Williams (1985) interviewed Lakota Sioux Indians who automatically associated their traditional *winktes* with modern "gays." They noted, however, that *winktes* would have sex with men, not with other *winktes* like gays do, and one Indian complained: "It makes me mad when I hear someone insult *winktes*. A lot of the younger gays, though, don't fulfill their spiritual role as *winktes*, and that's sad too."

Just how similar are modern gays to the receptive partners in gender-stratified systems? At least with regard to early cross-gender behaviors, like playing with girls, engaging in girls' play activities, and avoiding fights, American "gays" are very similar to "pathics" from the Philippines, Peru, Guatemala, and Brazil (Cardoso, 1994; Whitam, 1983; Whitam & Mathy, 1986; Whitam & Zent, 1984). Psychoanalytic theories often attributed homosexuality to hostility with fathers, but the U.S. correlations between hostile fathers and homosexuality did not appear in the more accepting cultures of Guatemala and the Philippines. This finding suggests that fathers' hostility may be a consequence, and not a cause, of homosexuality in more intolerant cultures.

In their comparison of Brazil, Peru, the Philippines, and the United States, Whitam and Mathy (1991) also found that cross-gendered females were more likely than other females to have engaged with boys' in boys' play activities, and to have adopted men's clothes during childhood.

Typical Men Who Engage in Homosexual Activities.

Research on the characteristics of typical males who engage in homosexual behaviors is much rarer and the results are more ambiguous. In his study of prisoners in Brazil, Silva (1998) found that it was those most concerned about their positions in status hierarchies who spoke most favorably about raping other prisoners. Looking at homosexual activities in a Brazilian fishing village, Cardoso (1994, n.d.), found that the men who had sex with the village's pathics were more fond of aggression during sex. Perhaps these findings are related to U.S. studies that show high-stimulus-seeking males are more likely to engage in bisexuality (Ekleberry, 2000; Udry, 2002), or to the finding that U.S. males expressing more hostility towards homosexuals are more likely than other males to show sexual excitement (measured by penile volume) when viewing films of male homosexual activities (Adams, Wright, & Lohr, 1996).

Cognitive Associations of Homosexuality.

For centuries scholars have puzzled over how our concepts are constructed. Plato thought that we are all born with very specific ideas (like "horse") which we later attribute to empirical phenomena. Kant reduced these inborn ideas to a few basic building blocks (categories like "time," "space," or "causality") that he thought necessary to construct any intelligent system. Piaget followed Kant, but more recently, developmental psychologists have discovered that babies are born with some very specific concepts (McKenzie, 1990; Pinker, 1994) and that (as etymologies and pidgin languages show) more abstract concepts are built up from earlier more concrete concepts (Givon, 1989). This ontogenetic process may reflect phylogenetic changes in cognition as thought becomes more complex.

Do humans have any elementary concrete ideas regarding homosexuality? The psychoanalyst Arango (1989) suggests that our "dirty words" reflect some of our most basic concepts. These words seem to be stored in a different part of our brain, and may continue to be remembered and used even after brain damage destroys the rest of our conceptual thinking.

Many of the dirty words mentioned by Arango seem to derive rather directly from primate markers for dominance and submission. For example, in most, if not all, human languages, typical primate "homage-paying" behaviors are used to insult people thought too anxious to please their superiors. Brazilians call such people *puxa-sacos* (literally sack-pullers), recalling the behavior of subordinate vervet monkeys. More common is the subordinate's gesture of sniffing the dominant's behind.

The association of "active" (insertor) homosexual roles with domination and "passive" (insertee) roles with subordination also appears to be almost universal, although the nature of the domination may vary from cruel demonstrations of power (as in prison rape) to more fatherly "mentorship" roles.

Explaining Cross-Cultural Variation

Every culture has some characteristics that are unique and others that are shared by all, but it is those characteristics that only *some* cultures share with *some* others that most interest anthropologists concerned with explaining cultural variation. So far anthropologists have tried to explain why societies vary in their frequency, acceptance, and type of homosexuality.

Frequency and Acceptance of Homosexuality.

Early cross-cultural studies of homosexuality dealt almost exclusively with the closely related variables "frequency" and "acceptance" of male homosexuality (Broude, 1976; Minturn, Grosse, & Haider, 1969; Werner, 1979). Although intercoder reliability coefficients were high, some later scholars (e.g., Bolton, 1994; Gray & Ellington, 1984) complained that these ratings were invalid because they failed to distinguish "homosexual behavior" from "homosexuals." They pointed out that most of the cultural variance comes from the homosexual behaviors of heterosexually identified men. Thus, cross-cultural comparisons of "modal" psychological characteristics would be irrelevant to theories about differences between homosexuals and heterosexuals, although they might tell us something about heterosexual males who engage in homosexual practices.

Most of the cultural variation in homosexuality recorded in these early studies probably had to do with gender-stratified cultures. Gray and Ellington (1984) showed that societies coded as having more homosexual behavior were also generally coded as having transvestism, and Werner (1975) found that societies with positive attitudes toward exclusive homosexuals also had positive attitudes toward the homosexual behaviors of typical males.

Here are the principal correlations found in these studies.[1] First, homosexuality is more frequent where there are mixed-sex play groups (Werner, 1979), and transvestites are more common where there are fewer sex distinctions within a society (Munroe, Whiting, & Hally, 1969). As the authors explain, these findings suggest that social tolerance of "pathics" is at least partly a function of a more general tendency toward sexual equality.

Homosexual behaviors are also more acceptable where heterosexual outlets are less available or less attractive. They are more common in polygynous societies, where some males have difficulty attaining wives, and in societies where males marry at a later age (Barber, 1998; Werner, 1975). Homosexuality is also more common where there are arranged marriages (Minturn et al., 1969), perhaps reflecting less sexual satisfaction with wives.

Homosexual behaviors are rare in societies with monogamous nuclear families where husbands and wives sleep in the same room, and where there is close father–child contact. Homosexuality and transvestism are also rare in societies with the couvade (Carroll, 1978; Munroe, 1980). Although early researchers explained these findings with neo-Freudian theories about sex identities, a more parsimonious explanation might be that they simply reflect a society's attitude toward paternal investments. By spending more time with the children of just one wife, a father automatically devotes more of his resources to his children. And by submitting to couvade taboos around the time of birth he demonstrates to all of society his willingness to assume his paternal responsibilities. In societies with the couvade, fathers are more likely to sleep apart from their wives during the first months or even years after birth. Rather than indicate *less* paternal investment, this may in fact indicate greater concern with the new-born's welfare since the mother's attention would not be divided between her husband and her child during this critical period. Werner (1979) found homosexual behaviors to be less acceptable in societies where married women are punished for committing infanticide or abortion with legitimate offspring. Werner originally attributed this correlation to a "pro-natalist" social policy in which women are encouraged to bear more children. However, in light of these other studies, it may be more accurate to see intolerance of homosexuality as reflecting a desire to invest more in children rather than simply bear more. One correlation from these early studies seems to require at least some psychological theorizing about sexual identity formation: more accepting societies, and those with more homosexual behaviors, are more likely to perform male genital mutilations (Minturn et al., 1969). Bolton (1994) suggested that this might be part of the ritualization of age-stratified homosexual systems. But, as the next section shows, genital mutilations are actually associated with gender-stratified homosexuality, not with age-stratified homosexuality. Perhaps males living in gender-stratified systems are more intrigued or anxious about male genitalia because of the ever-present contradiction between the gender roles and the biological sex of their "pathics."

Different Cultural Forms of Homosexuality.

Crapo (1995) and Murray (2000) coded societies for the presence of the three principal homosexual systems. For male homosexuality, Murray was able to code 120 societies as gender-stratified, 53 as age-stratified, and 30 as egalitarian. For female homosexuality he was able to code only 19 as gender-stratified, seven as age-stratified, and six as egalitarian. Crapo and Murray compared the different types of homosexual organization with regard to other aspects of culture.

Crapo found that gender-stratified societies generally had fewer overall sex distinctions, sleeping arrangements in which husbands and wives stayed together, and more female power. Murray found that gender-stratified societies were more likely to be matrilineal, somewhat more likely to have equal participation by males and females in the principal subsistence activity, less likely to have segregation of adolescent males, and more likely to practice male genital mutilations. These associations confirm the earlier studies on male transvestism (Munroe et al., 1969) and suggest that acceptance and frequency of "pathic" homosexuality is related to greater equality between the sexes.

Crapo found age-stratified systems more common in societies with patrilocality and patrilineality, where polygyny is preferred but limited to older and wealthier men, and where boys are segregated from others. Murray noted that in age-stratified systems male age-mates are more likely to live apart from others, and people are more likely to consider virginity necessary for brides. These societies are also more likely to have social classes, and somewhat more likely to have cities. Neither Murray nor Crapo distinguished between "mentorship" societies and "catamite" societies. It seems likely that the "mentorship" systems may be part of a more general sexual segregation in society, while the "catamite" system may result from class differences that allow the wealthy and powerful to subordinate younger males for sexual purposes.

In both age- and gender-stratified systems, Crapo noted that fathers are less involved with infant care than in societies with neither of these systems, perhaps reflecting once again a less pro-natalist social policy.

In egalitarian systems most typical males (after adolescence) do not usually engage in homosexual relations. Murray found that, for males, egalitarian systems are most likely where premarital sex is most permissible, where post-partum sex taboos are longest, and where there are fewer wealth distinctions. Perhaps more generally open attitudes toward sex coupled with more egalitarian ideologies make equal male–male sexual ties more acceptable. The taboos on post-partum sex may have more to do with respect for the new mother and encouragement of fatherhood than with any sexual repression.

Murray's correlations for female homosexuality are more precarious, since he could code far fewer cases. But it is worth noting that female gender-stratified systems are most common where men and women participate equally in the major subsistence task, where there is less segregation of adolescent males, where there are fewer wealth distinctions, and where female premarital intercourse is more acceptable. These correlations are based on very few cases but do seem to indicate, once again, that fewer overall sex distinctions within a society make cross-gender roles more acceptable.

Murray found that female age-graded systems are most likely where women participate more than men in the major subsistence activity. Perhaps the importance of women's work makes it more crucial for girls to receive closer guidance from older women. His data on female egalitarian systems were based on very few cases (six or seven) and percentage differences so small that any conclusions regarding cross-cultural correlations would be premature.

These findings may lead to some tentative speculations that, of course, will require further confirmation. First, we might observe that typical males are more likely to engage in homosexual activities in age-stratified and gender-stratified systems. In egalitarian systems the homosexual behaviors of most males is usually limited to adolescence, and the number of "comrade" relationships is few. Greater general repression of homosexual activities among typical males may be partly a function of a society's natalist policy, including paternal investment in offspring. Perhaps the major question facing males is whether to invest directly in offspring or in male–male competition/cooperation. If male–male relations are more important, the next question is how they might be organized. Sexually segregated societies appear to favor age-stratified homosexuality as a way for men to compete/cooperate, while sex with cross-gendered homosexuals may be a part of male camaraderie where sex distinctions are few.

Just why the gay system appeared is under debate. Besides questions of paternal investment, Werner (1999) suggested this change may partly be due to changes from a "patron–client" political system to a "meritocratic" system in which personal qualifications are valued more than personal ties in getting ahead. In line with this theory, Cardoso's preliminary data from 79 male Brazilian slum dwellers showed that 85% of those who adopted the "pathic" homosexual ideology thought personal ties were most important to getting ahead, while only 60% of those adopting the "gay" ideology agreed with this statement.

As to the different systems for female homosexuality, data are much more precarious. Women everywhere invest more in their offspring than do men, and cooperation/competition between women is usually limited to a smaller and more intimate group. That female gender-stratified systems are more common where sex and wealth differences are fewer, and where premarital sex is more common, may simply imply a more relaxed attitude toward their behavior.

As for the more limited homosexual activities typical of "egalitarian" systems, there is still a great deal of variation with regard to tolerance. These activities appear to be most acceptable where social equalities and sexual freedoms are greatest, probably reflecting a greater sense of equal "justice" for all.

THE SCIENTIFIC STUDY OF HOMOSEXUALITY AND SOCIAL POLICY

One of the most common philosophical mistakes is to confuse what *is* with what *ought to be*. One variation of this confusion is known as the *naturalistic fallacy*—the idea that if something *is* natural, then it is good (i.e., *ought to be*). As Sommer (1990) points out, the presence or absence of homosexual behavior among animals has been used since ancient times either to defend or to condemn the practice. The contradictory conclusions of different authors illustrate well the problems in trying to conclude from what is "natural" (found among animals) to what "ought to be": In *Laws*, Plato argues *against* homosexuality because it does not occur among animals. But the 2nd century Pseudo-Lucien *defends* homosexuality by arguing that "lions have no homosexuality because they have no philosophers," and "bears have none because they know not beauty." On the other hand, the 2nd century

author of *Physiologus* argues that impure hyenas *do* exhibit homosexual characteristics and thus humans should *not* engage in homosexuality, while the 20th century author, André Gide, argues that homosexuality *does* occur in animals and thus is "natural" and so "good." As these arguments make clear, simply knowing whether animals do or do not engage in homosexuality tells us nothing about whether human homosexuality is good or not. The same holds for arguments about evolutionary adaptiveness.

Likewise, knowing whether homosexual behavior is common or highly regarded in different cultures tells us nothing about whether it *ought to be* common or highly regarded there or anywhere else. This confusion is known as the *relativistic fallacy*. In 1986 Chief Justice Burger of the U.S. Supreme Court argued that historical evidence of proscriptions against homosexuality in different cultures justified upholding the Georgia sodomy laws (Bowkers vs. Hardwick, 1986). More recently, the Zimbabwean dictator, Robert Mugabe, initiated a violent antihomosexual campaign in his country with the justification that homosexuality did not exist there prior to European colonization (Murray & Roscoe, 1998). Actually, both are wrong about history, but even if they had been right on the facts, they would still be committing the relativistic fallacy.

The confusion of "is" with "ought" is so common that some scholars have fallen into the reverse error of concluding about what "is" based on what they think "ought to be," thus committing the *moralistic fallacy*. For example, the Soviet scientist Lysenko decided that the theory of natural selection must be wrong because it implied that reality was based on unjust non-Marxist principles. Some more contemporary scholars have attempted to conclude that men and women, or gays and straights, "are" equal because they "ought to be" equal.

Science deals with what "is," not with what "ought to be." How, then, can science help us to draw conclusions about what social policy "ought to be." The answer depends on the principles we accept (for nonscientific reasons) as the basis for our moral, ethical, or political decisions. For example, one of the most respected principles sees "increasing well-being" as the basis of moral decisions. Many religions have adopted similar principles, such as "love thy neighbor as thy self."

If we accept "increasing well-being" as our moral aim, then science can help us establish what policies enhance both physical and mental well-being. In the study of homosexuality we need to understand what can be done to increase the well-being of all involved. Many topics are amenable to this type of research. For example, can we predict beforehand who will benefit from transsexual surgery? What kinds of programs diminish problems like bullying behaviors in school? What social policies can help reduce AIDS contamination? What kinds of domestic arrangements lead to most happiness for different kinds of people? What kinds of laws most encourage these arrangements? As we learn more about homosexuality and its many possible manifestations, we will surely be able to answer these and other questions with greater confidence.

NOTE

1. We did not include the correlations in Broude's (1976) matrix because some appeared to be contradicted by statements in the text. We suspect that there may be misprints.

REFERENCES

Adams, H. E., Wright, L. W., & Lohr, B. A. (1996). Is homophobia associated with homosexual arousal? *Journal of Abnormal Psychology, 105*, 440–455.

Arango, A. C. (1989). *Dirty words: Psychoanalytic insights.* Northvale, N.J.: Jason Aronson.

Bagemihl, B. (1999). *Biological exuberance: Animal homosexuality and natural diversity.* New York: St. Martins.

Barber, N. (1998). "Ecological and psychosocial correlates of male homosexuality": A cross-cultural investigation. *Journal of Cross-Cultural Psychology, 29*(3), 387–401.

Bolton, R. (1994). "Sex, science and social responsibility": Cross-cultural research on same-sex eroticism and sexual intolerance. *Cross-Cultural Research, 28*(2), 134–190.

"Bowkers vs. Hardwick" U.S. Supreme Court reports. (1986, August 27). *Newsweek* (Latin American ed.), pp. 148 ff.

Broude, G. J. (1976). "Cross-cultural patterning of some sexual attitudes and practices." *Behavior Science Research, 4*, 227–261.

Burton, R. (1967). *The vice: Sir Richard Burton's, the sotadic zone.* Atlanta, Georgia: M.G. Thevis.

Cardoso, F. L. (1994). *Orientação sexual masculina em uma comunidade pesqueira.* (Masters dissertation in Anthropology, Universidade Federal de Santa Catarina, Brazil, 1994).

Cardoso, F. L. (2002). "Fishermen"—Masculinity and sexuality in a Brazilian fishing community. *Sexuality and Culture, 6*, 4.

Cardoso, F. L. (n.d.). *Cultural universals and differences of male homosexuals: The case of a Brazilian fishing village.* Manuscript submitted for publication.

Carroll, M. P. (1978). "Freud on homosexuality and the super-ego: Some cross-cultural tests." *Behavior Science Research, 13*, 255–271.

Clastres, P. (1972). *Chronique des indiens Guayaki: Ce que savent les Aché, chasseurs nomades du Paraguay.* Paris: Librairie Plon.

Crapo, R. H. (1995). "Factors in the cross-cultural patterning of male homosexuality: A reappraisal of the literature." *Cross-Cultural Research, 29*(2), 178–202.

Crocker, W. (1990). *The Canela (Eastern Timbira), I: An ethnographic introduction.* Washington: Smithsonian Contributions to Anthropology, number 33.

DeCecco, J. P., & Elia, J. P. (1993). *If you seduce a straight person, can you make them gay? Issues in biological essentialism versus constructivism in gay and lesbian identities.* New York: Haworth Press.

De Waal, F. (1989). *Peacemaking among primates.* New York: Penguin Books.

Duerr, H. P. (1993). *Obszönität und Gewalt: Der Mythos vom Zivilisationsproze.* Frankfurt am Main, Germany: Suhrkamp Verlag.

Epprecht, M. (1998). Good God almighty, what's this!: Homosexual "crime" in early colonial Zimbabwe. In S. O. Murray & W. Roscoe (Eds.), *Boy-wives and female husbands: Studies in African homosexualities* (pp. 197–222). New York: Palgrave.

Ekleberry, S. C. (2000). The histrionic personality disorder. Web site: http://www.toad.net/~arcturus/dd/histrion.htm

Ford, C. S., & Beach, F. (1951). *Patterns of sexual behavior.* Harper & Brothers.

Foucault, M. (1978). *Histoire da la sexualité* [*History of Sexuality*, 1980]. Paris: Librairie Plon.

Gorer, G. (1966). *The danger of equality.* London: Cresset.

Givon, T. (1989). *Mind, code and context: Essays in pragmatics.* Hillsdale, NJ: Erlbaum.

Grahn, J. (1986). *Another mother tongue: Gay words, gay worlds.* Boston: Beacon Press.

Gray, J. P., & Ellington, J. E. (1984). Institutionalized male transvestism, the couvade and homosexual behavior. *Ethos, 12*(1), 54–63.

Gregersen, E. (1983). *Sexual practices: The story of human sexuality.* New York: Franklin Watts.

Herdt, G. H. (1981). *Guardians of the flute.* New York: McGraw Hill.

Herdt, G. H. (1984). *Ritualized homosexuality in Melanesia.* Berkeley: University of California Press.

Hinsch, B. (1990). *Passions of the cut sleeve: The male homosexual tradition in China.* Berkeley: University of California Press.

Ihara, S. (1972). *Comrade loves of the Samurai.* Rutland, VT: Tuttle.

Kendal, L. (1998). When a woman loves a woman in Lesotho: Love, sex and the (western) construction of homophobia. In S. O. Murray & W. Roscoe (Eds.), *Boy-wives and female husbands: Studies in African homosexualities* (pp. 223–242). New York: Palgrave.

Kirkpatrick, R. C. (2000). The evolution of human homosexual behavior. *Current Anthropology, 41*(3), 385–413.

Leupp, G. P. (1994). *Male colors: The construction of homosexuality in Tokugawa Japan.* Berkeley: University of California Press.

Lindholm, C. T. (1982). *Generosity and jealousy:The Swat Pukhtun of northern Pakistan.* New York: Columbia University Press.

McKenzie, B. E. (1990). Early cognitive development: Notions of objects, space and causality in infancy. In C. A. Hauert (Ed.), *Developmental psychology: Cognitive, perceptuo-motor and neuropsychological perspectives* (pp. 43–61) Amsterdam: North-Holland.

Minturn, L., Grosse, M., & Haider, S. (1969). Cultural patterning of sexual beliefs and behavior. *Ethnology, 8*, 301–318.

Munroe, R. L. (1980). Male transvestism and the couvade: A psycho-cultural analysis. *Ethos, 8*(1), 49–59.

Munroe, R. L., Whiting, J. W. M., & Hally, D. J. (1969). Institutionalized male transvestism and sex distinctions. *American Anthropologist, 71*, 87–91.

Murray, S. O. (2000). *Homosexualities.* Chicago: University of Chicago Press.

Murray, S. O., & Arboleda, M. G. (1995). Stigma transformation and relexifiction: gay in Latin America. In S. O. Murray (Ed.) *Latin American male homosexualities* (pp. 138–144). Albuquerque: University of New Mexico Press.

Murray, S. O., & Roscoe, W. (Eds.). (1998). *Boy-wives and female husbands: Studies in African homosexualities.* New York: Palgrave.

Pinker, S. (1994). *The language instinct: How the mind creates language.* New York: Morrow.

Rice, E. (1990). *Captain Sir Richard Francis Burton: The secret agent who made the pilgrimage to Mecca, discovered the Kama Sutra, and brought the Arabian Nights to the west.* New York: Scribner's.

Roscoe, W. (1997). Precursors of Islamic male homosexuality. In S. O. Murray & W. Roscoe (Eds.), *Islamic homosexualities: Culture, history and literature* (pp. 55–86). New York: New York University Press.

Silva, E. A. (1998). *A natureza cultural da justiça: por uma teoria multidisciplinar da justiça, vista através do ritual de violência sexual no presídio masculino de Florianópolis.* Unpublished master's dissertation, Universidade Federal de Santa Catarina, Brazil.

Sommer, V. (1990). *Wider die Natur? Homosexualität und Evolution.* Munich: Beck.

Udry, J. R. (2002, July). Risk assessment of adolescents with same-sex relationships. *Journal of Adolescent Health 31*(1), 84–92.

Werner, D. (1975). *On the societal acceptance or rejection of male homosexuality.* Unpublished master's dissertation, Hunter College, New York.

Werner, D. (1979). A cross-cultural perspective on theory and research on male homosexuality. *Journal of Homosexuality, 4*(4), 345–362.

Werner, D. (1998). Sobre a evolução e variação cultural na homossexualidade masculina. In J. M. Pedro & M. P. Grossi (Eds.), *Masculino, feminino plural* (pp. 99–129). Florianópolis: Mulheres. (English version available at http://www.floripa.com.br/dennis)

Werner, D. (1999). *Sexo, símbolo e solidariedade: Ensaios de psicologia evolucionista.* Florianópolis, Brazil: Coleção Ilha, PPGAS, Universidade Federal Santa Catarina.

Whitam, F. L. (1983). Culturally invariable properties of male homosexuality: Tentative conclusions from cross-cultural research. *Archives of Sexual Behavior, 12*(3), 207–226.

Whitam, F. L., & Mathy, R. M. (1986). *Male homosexuality in four societies: Brazil, Guatemala, the Philippines, and the United States.* New York: Praeger.

Whitam, F. L., & Mathy, R. M. (1991). Childhood cross-gender behavior of homosexual females in Brazil, Peru, the Philippines, and the United States. *Archives of Sexual Behavior, 20*(2), 151–170.

Whitam, F. L., & Zent, M. (1984). A cross-cultural assessment of early cross-gender behavior and familial factors in male homosexuality. *Archives of Sexual Behavior, 13*(5), 427–439.

Williams, W. L. (1985). Persistence and change in the berdache tradition among contemporary Lakota Indians. *Journal of Homosexuality, 11*(3/4), 191–200.

Transgender and Transsexuality

Tarynn M. Witten, Esben Esther Pirelli Benestad, Ilana Berger, Richard Ekins,
Randi Ettner, Katsuki Harima, Dave King, Mikael Landén, Nuno Nodin,
Volodymyr P'yatokha, and Andrew N. Sharpe

BRIEF INTELLECTUAL HISTORY OF TRANSGENDER

Ancient Greece and Rome

Plato, in his *Symposium*, allows Aristophanes the opportunity to speak on the concept of the power of love. In that speech, Aristophanes says:

… For one thing, the race was divided into three; that is to say, besides the two sexes, male and female, which we have at present, there was a third which partook of the nature of both, and for which we still have a name, though the creature itself is forgotten. For though "hermaphrodite" [now called "intersexed"] is only used nowadays as a term of contempt, there really was a man–woman in those days, a being which was half male and half female … The three sexes, I may say, arose as follows. The males were descended from the Sun, the females from the Earth, and the hermaphrodites from the Moon, which partakes of either sex … (Harvey, 1997, p. 32)

The Greeks, forerunners of modern medicine, believed in the concept of more than one sex. It was well within their mythological construct and cultural norms. However, somewhere in between then and now, this concept of a "third sex/third gender" (Herdt, 1996) has been lost. It is not hard to conjecture how this loss came to be. The imposition of Judeo-Christian monotheism replaced the pantheistic view and brought the associated gender/sex continuum of the Greco-Roman era into the digital age (on or off, male or female). Perhaps the more amazing aspect of this disappearance of a conceptual construct is the fact that we now know that there is a population of individuals, currently living in Western cultural environments as well as other locations, whose birth sex should be defined as a third choice "intersexed"—even within the realm of the Western dual-sex perspective.

Defining the Body

The body exists as a shell (we see the body). It exists as a container (the person's body). Meaning and metaphorical reality are inferred from and transmitted through this shell. The body can act and be acted upon. The body can be active (initiating action) or reactive (responding to action). The body both displays and participates in the creation of the self (self-identity). It contains the brain, supposed seat of the mind, and yet the mind and spirit are also viewed as both part of and yet not part of the body. To a certain degree, the body is plastic in its ability to alter its physical construct to meet assorted needs, both internal as well as external. These alterations can lead to alterations that become learned behaviors, increased or decreased capabilities, and eventually even embodied actions that transcend the conscious attempt to understand them. The body can be viewed as separate from the mind or unified with it in a holistic fusion. The body has location in space and time. Fausto-Sterling (2000) addresses the complexity of the issues associated with the interplay of the body and sex.

The advent of political correctness added to the problems of dealing with this terminology by creating increased confusion over sex and gender and by creating an atmosphere of increased confusion wherein the two words became interchangeable. Further, the conservative religious backlash could not deal with sexuality or sex in any form. Therefore, all reference to "sex" was squashed. The politically correct world provided the perfect atmosphere for the conservatives to squelch the use of "sex" in any document and to replace it with "gender." For the fun of it, the first thing that I did, while writing this introductory section, was to ask MS Word to look up the word "sex" in its built-in dictionary. As it is programmed to do, MS Word automatically gives synonyms and it provided the word "gender" as a synonym for "sex." One of the most widely used word-processing programs identifies sex and gender as interchangeable. Even the online Merriam-Webster's Collegiate Dictionary, which yields three entries for gender, lists entry 2 as "sex." Pryzgoda and Chrisler (2000) ask the question: "Do people actually know what the word gender means?" In their paper, they report that for a sample of $n = 137$ study participants a "variety of understandings and beliefs about gender that range from the common response that 'gender' is the same as 'sex' to less common responses that associate gender with females or discrimination" occurred.

Defining Sex

We live in a Western culture. That culture is dualistic, when it comes to looking at the subject of sex. When we ask a person "What sex are you?", the implied/understood question is "what birth sex are you, what is the genitalia between your legs?" As a consequence of our evolution as a Western Judeo-Christian cultural environment, we are immersed in the cultural norm of the "Adam and Eve" mythology and hence, of there being only two birth-sex possibilities. This perspective is known as the *biblical norm of sex*. When we say "birth sex," we are making the hidden assumption that we are saying the "sex defined by the genitalia seen, by a person authorized to interpret the genitalia as displayed at birth." It is clear that this definition is made within the cultural context of the baby's birth. In Western culture, which has the biblical norm of sex already deeply and incontestably embedded within it (embodied norm; Cassell, 1998), the only way to interpret the genitalia is within this biblical norm and hence as either anatomically male or female.

As has already been illustrated, even the ancient Greeks recognized that there was a "third sex." They called it *hermaphrodite*, which is now considered a pejorative term for an individual who displays both sexual organs at birth (actually, the anatomical presentation can be quite varied and does not necessarily require both complete organs to be displayed). The preferred current terminology is "intersexed." The prevalence of intersexuality is estimated at 1 in 2,000 births. Additionally, it is estimated that there are nearly 65,000 intersex births worldwide per year.

Because Western medical culture specifically, and Western culture in general, is steeped in the biblical norm of sex, the concept of multiple genitalia or atypical genital anatomy has been deeply and profoundly problematic for the medical establishment. Up until very recently, intersexed children were "sexed" as soon after birth as was medically reasonable, a practice that continues to be sanctioned by the American Pediatric Association, despite voluminous protestation on the part of the Intersex Society of North America (ISNA) (http://www.isna.org) and other agencies.

The tie between sex, gender, genitalia (the body), and stigmatization/destigmatization via labels is also important here. For example, intersexed children have been sexed without parental permission or even with the parents' knowledge of the fact that their child is intersexed. It is almost as if it is "unspeakable." Additionally, the forced sexing transfers the burden from the parents of the child to the child. Therefore politically correct language or medicalization terminology, such as nondominant genitalia or micro-phallus, is used to remove the stigma of the intersexuality. On the other hand, transsexuality and transgenderism are immediately stigmatized. Words like neo-clitoris, neo-phallus, pseudo-testicles, and neo-vagina disenfranchise the transsexual from the contragender status they so strongly desire to attain. This disenfranchisement and stigmatization are best illustrated by terminology used by the radical lesbian feminist movement. While they are willing to stretch their metaphor of reality to allow a male-to-female transsexual to be classified as a "woman," they do not consider her a real woman. Rather, she is labeled as not "woman born woman."

Current estimates are that sexing operations are performed five times per day across the United States alone. The term "sexed" is a verb that is used to mean that these children were subjected to genital surgery to remove the "non-dominant" genitalia. Hence a baby with a "micro-phallus" and a predominant "vaginal canal" would be sexed as a woman, and the micro-phallus removed surgically or surgically "sized" (thereby risking permanent sexual response reduction). This "sexing" operation has led to many problems for these intersexed children; the most famous of them is the very recent case of John/Jane (Goodnow, 2000).

Defining Gender

Gender is, perhaps, a far more elusive concept. If we look up the definition of "gender," we find that it states "an individual's self-conception as being male or female, as distinguished from actual biological sex. For most persons, gender identity and biological characteristics are the same. There are, however, circumstances in which an individual experiences little or no connection between sex and gender…" (Encyclopedia Britannica Online, 2001). This last point, concerning the connection between sex and gender, or the lack thereof, will be crucial when we address issues of sexuality. Other definitions of gender (e.g., Oxford English Dictionary Online, 2001) provide constructions that are more complex. Perhaps the most common understanding of gender may be found in Perry (1999, p. 8) who states that "gender is defined here as the cultural construction of femininity and masculinity as opposed to the biological sex (male or female) which we are born with." Observe that both of these definitions are based upon the biblical norm of sex and hence of the associated construct that Witten (2004, in press) calls "the biblical norm of gender." Contrast these definitions with the 1984 definition (Webster, 1984), which states that gender is "any of two *or more* [italics added] categories, as masculine, feminine, and neuter, into which words are divided and that determine agreement with or selection of modifiers or grammatical forms." This viewpoint is further supported in the following statement from the Oxford English Dictionary Online (2001):

b. By some recent philologists applied, in extended sense, to the "kinds" into which sbs. are discriminated by the syntactical laws of certain languages the grammar of which takes no account of sex. Thus the North American Indian languages are said to have two "genders," animate and inanimate. With still greater departure from the original sense, the name "genders" has been applied to the many syntactically discriminated classes of sbs. in certain South African langs.

Hence, gender does not necessarily have anything to do with the discriminated classes of male and female. Rather, it can be used as a descriptor for any syntactically discriminated set of classes within a language.

Defining Sexuality

The Western biomedical model of sex and gender, coupled with the Judeo-Christian model of reproduction and sexuality, provides for only one socially acceptable model of sexuality, namely heterosexuality. The concept of heterosexuality is based upon a sexing of the body that forces the body to be seen as either male or female (based upon the observed genitalia) and either masculine or feminine (based upon the individual's self-perception), and is coupled with the expected reproductive role required of those two states of being. The tacit assumption is that a male (genetically XY), with masculine self-perception and social role acceptance—in the best of all reproductive worlds—when having sexual intercourse with a female (genetically XX), with feminine self-perception and social role acceptance, will produce a child having either of these two states. Such a construction is

consistent with Cassell's (1998) "right mind/right body" concept. With this construct as the socially accepted norm of reality, it is clear that any deviance would be dealt with as just that—a deviance—and handled within the resources of the social system's mechanism for dealing with deviance. In the case of intersexuality (right mind/wrong body [confused body]), the system medicalizes the problem and deals with it as a body issue. In the case of transsexuality (confused mind [wrong mind]/right body), the system medicalizes the problem and deals with it as a "mind" issue, as we have already discussed in a previous section.

As Western biomedical medicine holds to a body-oriented philosophy, it is easy to see how "intersex," which is body oriented, easily visually identified with the senses (body-oriented detectability), and remediable with "surgery" (body-oriented intervention consistent with the biomedical way of thinking) is far more acceptable than "transgender," which is in the mind (mind oriented), not readily verifiable via any sort of Western biomedical rational means, and remediable with a set of counterintuitive surgical interventions that violate the visceral sanctity of the body public and private. Intersexuality is concretized within the "medicalization of illness," as is understood through the western cultural norm of somaticizing medicine. It is not listed in the *Diagnostic and Statistical Manual of Mental Disorders* (4th ed., text revision) (American Psychiatric Association, 2000). In fact, the intersex condition is an explicitly stated contraindication for diagnosis of gender identity disorder. On the other hand, transgenderism is too elusive; it is culture bound, a deviation at a visceral level of gender role "embodiment" (Cassell, 1998), inaccessible, and confounding.

DEFINING TRANSGENDER AND THE DEMOGRAPHY OF TRANSGENDER

Defining Transgender/Transsexual

The terminology describing the "gender" community is extremely dynamic, not just in the descriptors of gender, but also in the body/sex/sexuality and medical status terminology associated with a given gender identity. This, along with certain components of the population being unwilling to allow themselves to be labeled or categorized by labels fixed by someone else, makes it extremely difficult to obtain an accurate census or description of this population. For example, an individual who is born genetically female (XX), but states that she is actually male, might describe himself as an FTM (female-to-male) transsexual, while another woman might claim the label transman. Others might choose to define themselves in terms of hormone usage (lo-ho, hi-ho) transman and still others might use their "operative status" as a description (pre-op transsexual, post-op transman). Yet others might claim that they were MBT (men born trans). Thus, categorizing the membership of the transgender community is exceedingly difficult.

Although they are frequently invisible and highly stigmatized within our society (i.e., marginal legal protection, noninclusion in hate crimes legislation and Equal Employment Opportunity Commission/Affirmative Action, and inclusion in *DSM IV-TR* (Currah & Minter, 2000; Witten & Eyler, 1999a) transgender individuals form more than a negligible percentage of the U.S. population. Understanding that there are labeling and power concerns of importance that surround any issue of subdividing a population, Witten and Eyler (1999a) address the definition of transgender stating that:

The gender community includes *cross-dressers* (men and women who take on the appearance of the other gender, often on a social or part-time basis), *transgenders* (people whose psychological self-identification is as the other sex and who alter behavior and appearance to conform with this internal perception, sometimes with the assistance of hormonal preparations), and *transsexuals*, both male-to-female (MTF) and female-to-male (FTM), who undertake hormonal and/or surgical sex reassignment therapies. In addition, it includes others with gender self-perceptions other than the traditional (Western) dichotomous gender world-view (i.e., including only male and female), such as persons with "non-Western" gender identities (Langevin, 1983; Godlewski, 1988; Hoenig & Kenna, 1974; Sigusch, 1991; Tsoi, 1988; van Kesteren et al., 1996; Wålinder, 1971a,b; Weitze & Osburg, 1996).

It is also important to mention that there are overlaps between the transgender and intersex communities with respect to the aforementioned definitions. As was pointed out earlier, because the majority of intersexuals have been and still are forcibly reassigned to the female gender at birth, the majority of intersexuals that seek sex reassignment are FTM. However, this does not mean that there are not some who are MTF as well. Thus the confluence of both gender and sex issues further adds to the problem of counting both the intersex and transgender populations.

Estimating the Prevalence of Transgenderism

With regard to population estimates of transsexuality, Tsoi (1988) has noted that, "A...problem confounding an epidemiological survey is that transsexuals tend to congregate in cities and in certain parts of cities, and most of them do not want to be identified." Much of our own research work has further substantiated this phenomenon. Nonetheless, Tsoi (1988) has also noted that, in Singapore (where sexual reassignment surgery [SRS] is well established and transsexuals are not "suppressed") diagnosed transsexualism is more than eight times more prevalent than in any other country for which estimates exist. Witten (2002a, 2003) has pointed out that estimates of the number of individuals claiming to have "alternative gender identities" in the United States, as well as in other countries, are confounded by the lack of a control group by which to test prevalence and incidence estimates. Even so, in an international random survey performed by Witten and Eyler (1999b), approximately 8% of the 300 respondents identified their gender self-perceptions as something other than 100% male or 100% female. Taking only the international estimates for postoperative transsexuality as a basis (1–3%) (Godlewski, 1988; Hoenig & Kenna, 1974; Langevin, 1983; Sigusch, 1991; Tsoi, 1988; van Kesteren et al., 1996; Wålinder, 1971a,b; Weitze & Osburg, 1996), and using the approximate estimate of 300 million people for the U.S. population, this would imply that there are potentially 3–9 million potential postoperative transsexuals in the United States. While this estimate seems overly surprising, Witten (2002a, 2003) has discussed the rate of gender reassignment surgeries currently performed in the United States and Europe with some of the more prominent surgeons worldwide. A number of these surgeons indicate that they are performing two surgeries per day, 48 weeks per year, 4–5 days per week. Some state that they have waiting lists of upwards of 2 years. In France, the surgical waiting time is now 5 years. If we allow for the broader interpretation of transgender as including nonsurgical and cross-dressing individuals, the estimates increase to approximately 20 million people, depending upon definitional criteria. Others claim that the estimates for MTF prevalence are 1 in 1,000 to 1 in 30,000, while FTM prevalence estimates are significantly lower at 1 in 100,000. There are simply no statistically significant data from which one can draw strong conclusions. It is also important to recognize that each of these individuals touches numerous others in his or her life—family, friends, employers, employees, acquaintances, and random individuals on the street. Consequently, support services may well be necessary for many other individuals other than just the actual transgendered persons. This insight identifies the impact of the transgendered population and its needs as being significantly larger than the immediate population of the transgendered alone.

For brevity, in the upcoming discussion, the term *transgenders* will be used to signify the entire gender community, unless otherwise specified. It should also be pointed out that many indigenous peoples recognize genders other than male and female. For example, Tewa adults identify as women, men, and *kwido*, although their New Mexico birth records recognize only females and males (Jacobs & Cromwell, 1992). See also Elledge (2002) and his discussion of transgender myths from the Arapaho to the Zuni, as well as the work of Matzner (2001) discussing Hawaii's *mahu* and transgender communities. Persons with such "non-Western" gender identities will also be considered as belonging to the gender community.

Etiology of Transgender

What do we actually know about transgender and transsexuality in terms of its origins and risk factors? The answer is quite simple—not very much. The state of being "transgendered or transsexual" is classified by *DSM IV-TR* as a psychiatric disorder and given the name gender identity disorder (GID). A detailed discussion of GID can be found below in the section on diagnostic criteria.

Biological. There is no known biological reason for GID. Anecdotal discussion among some evolutionary biologists has looked at the GID issue as an evolutionary experiment in adaptivity of the human being. Some argue that it could be embedded within the "junk" DNA about which we know next to nothing. There is no scientific evidence to show that anything is true.

Social/Environmental. There is no evidence to indicate that there are social causes of GID, although social environment, roles, etc. are clearly implicated in GID. There is a psychosocial argument that GID may be induced by abuse in childhood and that GID is an extreme avoidance/dissociative response to the sexual, physical, and/or emotional abuse subjected upon such individuals (Devor, 1994). There are some studies in this area; none are conclusive one way or another. This particular theory is a chicken or egg first theory, and most data are anecdotal, at best, as accurate on violence against transgendered individuals is not readily available (Witten & Eyler, 1999a).

Medical/Psychological Aspects of Transgender

Medical. There is no known medical reason for GID. Suggested possibilities include possible *in utero* hormonal effects that create a vulnerability or propensity that is then exacerbated by subsequent environmental factors. Some argue that there are morphological changes in the corpus callosum, but evidence is ambivalent (some studies say yes, others say no, some find it inconclusive). Some argue that other areas of the brain are altered. In particular, one study by Zhou, Hofman, Gooren, and Swaab (1997) argues that the central subdivision of the bed nucleus of the stria terminalis (BSTc) in transgendered individuals does, in fact, have features of the contragender brain structure. However, these results are based upon post-mortem analyses of a very small sample of transgender brains. Additionally, there are androgenic factors such as partial androgen insensitivity syndrome (PAIS), Turner's syndrome, or congenital adrenal hyperplasia (CAH) that may or may not play into the biomedical mix.

Psychological. Axis II disorders such as schizophrenia can play a part in a person's self-perception and therefore need to be ruled out, along with environmental factors such as drug abuse, depression, etc. Depression does not rule out GID as a diagnosis, but needs to be considered within the GID diagnostic context. Multiple personality disorder issues must be resolved, so that all the different personalities agree on the sex change procedures. Axis III disorders are also critical and need to be rigorously addressed before GID diagnostic assignment. A recent study from Scandinavia (Haraldsen & Dahl, 2000) has demonstrated that transsexual persons selected for sex reassignment show a relatively low level of self-rated psychopathology before and after treatment.

Significant pressure to remove GID from *DSM* is currently mounting. In order to understand the reasoning behind this pressure, let us examine the current diagnostic criteria for GID.

Diagnostic Criteria (DSM IV-TR). GID is diagnosed via four criteria that must be met:

1. Evidence of a strong and persistent cross-gender identification (the desire to be or insistence that one is the other sex. The identification must not merely be a desire for perceived cultural advantages of being the other sex).
   (a) Repeated stated desire to be, or insistence that he or she, is the other sex.
   (b) In boys, preference for cross-dressing or simulating female attire; in girls, insistence on wearing only stereotypic masculine clothing.
   (c) Persistent preferences for cross-sex roles in make-believe play or persistent fantasies of being the other sex.
   (d) Intense desire to participate in the stereotypic games and pastimes of the other sex.
   (e) Strong preference for playmates of the other sex.
2. There must be evidence of persistent discomfort about one's assigned sex or a sense of inappropriateness in the gender role of that sex.
   (a) In boys we see assertions that penis or testes are disgusting and will disappear or assertion that it would be better not to have a penis, or aversion towards rough-and-tumble play and rejection of male stereotypical toys, games, and activities.
   (b) In girls, we see rejection of urinating in a sitting position, assertion that she has or will grow a penis, or assertion that she does not want to grow breasts or menstruate, or marked aversion toward normative feminine clothing.
   (c) In adolescents and adults the disturbance is manifested by symptoms such as preoccupation with getting rid of primary and secondary sex characteristics (requests for hormones, surgery, or other relief-based procedures), or the belief that he or she was born the wrong sex (born in the wrong body).
3. Intersex conditions and metabolic conditions such as PAIS or CAH rule out GID as a diagnosis.
4. To make the diagnosis there must be evidence of clinically significant distress or impairment in social, occupational, or other important areas of functioning.

A detailed discussion of the pros and cons of the *DSM IV-TR* GID diagnosis can be found at the website of the Harry Benjamin International Gender Dysphoria Association (HBIGDA) (http://www.hbigda.org), along with the current standards of care document. In the upcoming sections, we present a discussion of transgender and transsexuality in a number of countries as reported by researchers from those countries.

THE CULTURAL DIVERSITY OF THE TRANSGENDER POPULATION

Transsexuality and Transgender in Sweden

In 1972, Sweden was the first country to pass special legislation regulating surgical and legal measures required for sex reassignment, thereby granting the sex-reassigned person the rights and obligations of the new sex (Wålinder & Thuwe, 1976). Ever since then, unmarried Swedish citizens are allowed to obtain publicly financed sex reassignment if they are diagnosed as transsexuals. The patient applies to the National Board of Health and Welfare. An extensive medical certificate, in which documentation for the diagnosis is elaborated, must accompany the application. Because these data are always collected, this procedure implies that all data from all applicants for sex reassignment are on file, which facilitates phenomenological studies. Given that legislation is known to influence moral values in a society (Monteith, 1993), the Swedish law is likely to have boosted the public's positive views on transsexuals, as seen in a recent Swedish poll. Interestingly enough, this survey of attitudes towards transsexuals also demonstrated that those respondents who believed that transsexualism is caused by biological factors had a less restrictive view of transsexualism than those people who viewed transsexuality as a psychological problem (Landén & Innala, 2000).

A review of the annual frequency of applications for sex reassignments in Sweden between 1972 and 1992 showed a stable rate of, on average, 11.6 applications per year with an MTF/FTM sex ratio of 1.4/1.0 (Landén, Wålinder et al., 1996). Since then, however, the annual frequency has almost doubled in Sweden, an escalation attributable to an increase in MTF applicants, and this has changed the sex ratio accordingly. Phenomenological studies of the Swedish cohort have shown that transsexualism manifests itself differently in MTF and FTM (Landén, Wålinder et al., 1998). The MTF group are older than the FTM group when requesting sex reassignment surgery and have less cross-gender behavior as children, more frequent heterosexual experience, more frequent occurrence of fetishism, more frequent history of suicidal attempts, more often a history of marriage and parenting of children, and a lower level of education and socioeconomic status.

Most importantly, an outcome study of the Swedish cohort demonstrated that family opposition against the sex reassignment, belonging to the secondary group of transsexualism, and a history of psychotic disorder predicted regrets of sex reassignment (Landén, Hambert et al., 1998).

Transgender and Transsexuality in the United Kingdom

Transpeople now have a higher profile in the United Kingdom than ever before. There are popular transvestite entertainers (Eddie Izzard), prominent drag entertainers (Lily Savage), celebrated soap opera "transsexuals" ("Hayley" of *Coronation Street*), extensive media coverage of most aspects of trans, and a plethora of informal networks and support groups, formal organizations, and commercial ventures to cater for the needs of transsexuals, cross-dressers and transgendered people.

Sex reassignment surgery was pioneered in the 1940s by U.K. surgeon Sir Harold Gillies who operated on transman Michael Dillon (1944) and transwoman Roberta Cowell (1953). The first U.K. "gender identity clinic" was pioneered by psychiatrist John Randell at the Charing Cross Hospital in London in the 1960s, and has remained the most consistent source of medical intervention in the United Kingdom. Sex reassignment procedures are available through the National Health Service, but long waiting lists increasingly result in the use of private health care.

A number of U.K. transsexuals, namely April Ashley, Jan Morris, and Caroline Cossey, have become prominent internationally. Most notable of those who pioneered self-help groups for transpeople have been Alice (Beaumont Society, 1967 to date), Judy Cousins (Self Help Association for Transsexuals, 1979–1989), and Stephen Whittle (FTM Network, 1991 to date). From these beginnings emerged today's gender identity clinics and networks of support and activist groups. Currently, the major trans support groups are the Beaumont Society (http://www.beaumontsociety.org.uk/), the Gender Trust (http://www.gendertrust.org.uk/), the Gendys Network (http://www.gender.org.uk/gendys/index.htm), and the FTM Network (http://www.ftm.org.uk/). This last organization reflects the greater visibility, more recently, of transmen within the transgender community.

Since 1970, the legal status of transsexuals has been determined by the judgment in the case of *Corbett* v. *Corbett*, [1970] 2 All ER 33. That judgment decided that transwoman April Ashley was still to be considered a man for the purposes of marriage, although it has been used to decide sex status in many other areas. The situation now looks set to change following two rulings by the European Court of Human Rights (July 2002, *Christine Goodwin* v. *UK Government*, Application No. 28957/95 [1995] ECHR; *I* v. *UK Government*, Application No. 25608/94 [1994] ECHR) which have held that the U.K. government's failure to alter the birth certificates of transsexual people or to allow them to marry in their new gender is a breach of the European Convention on Human Rights. Press for Change (PFC) (http://www.pfc.org.uk) has been the major U.K. pressure group lobbying for transgender rights since 1992, and the past decade has witnessed a gradual improvement towards equal rights and opportunities in areas such as employment, marriage, and parenting.

Most recently, radical transgender activists who have been a small but consistent undercurrent in U.K. transactivism since the 1960s have come to some prominence in the confluence of transgender politics and radical transgender writings in sociology, cultural studies, and queer theory. These developments have been documented by U.K. transgender theorists Ekins and King (1996) and More and Whittle (1999).

Transgenderism and Transsexualism in Portugal

Transgenderism is widely unknown in Portugal. There are no statistics concerning the transgender population, and investigation in this field is limited by the standard difficulties in accessing transgender individuals, as addressed earlier in this article. Transgendered individuals lack legal support and are stigmatized by society in general. There are many commonly accepted myths concerning transgenderism in Portugal. For example, one myth is that all transsexuals are prostitutes or that they have some other nightlife activity such as strip tease or drag show performance. In this way, Portuguese transgendered persons are frequently socially disregarded and made fun of in public, as well as discriminated against. Nevertheless, it should be noted that the traditional Portuguese "tolerance" (not true acceptance) towards what is considered different (homosexuality, ethnic minorities, etc.) is usually inclusive of the members of the Portuguese transgender community.

Some important issues concerning the Portuguese transsexual population were identified in a recent study (Bernardo et al., 1998). These authors conducted a small-sample study involving of 50 transsexual individuals, most of whom were sex workers (86%). The great majority of the sample came from rural parts of the country (72%), and many individuals had moved away from their birthplace because of their sexual orientation (28%). Some started to work as early as age 11. Additionally, the study identified some serious health problems in this sample. For example, 30% of these transsexuals knew they were HIV positive, although only 61% always used a condom. More on the subject of HIV/AIDS in transgender/transsexual populations can be found in Warren (1999) and Bockting, Rosser, and Coleman (1999). A significant percentage (70%) of the sample abused alcohol, tranquilizers, or heroin on a regular basis.

There are no specific laws in Portugal regarding transgenderism or transsexualism. Only a few court decisions serve as references, and they are sometimes contradictory (ILGA-Portugal, 1999). Until 1984 it was not possible to go through a legal gender identity change. That date marks the court decree regarding the case of a transsexual individual whose request for legal gender identity change was granted by the court. However, if this decision marks a completely new attitude of the Portuguese law towards these situations, this same attitude was not the rule for other judgments that followed it. Currently, the legal system is more liberal towards change of gender identity requests and all of the requests for a legal sex change have been granted. The major problem is that, in general, the legal system in Portugal is very slow and it can take nearly 4 years for a decision to be given on a case. As it is only possible, in Portugal, to begin the legal process after the surgical sex change is completed, it can take over a decade until the whole process, both medical and legal, is completed.

Apart from the legal sex change procedure, any Portuguese citizen can change his or her name through a rather simple procedure. However, this change can only occur if the new name belongs to the same gender category as the previous one or the change is to a gender-neutral name. This last option is frequently chosen by many transgender individuals as a means of avoiding the more complex procedure required to have their gender identity legally recognized.

Until 1996 any surgical sex change was expressly forbidden by the Portuguese Medical Order (PMO).

After that date, surgical sex change was allowed. However, it is the only medical procedure that requires the prior authorization of the PMO. In order to address this issue, a commission composed exclusively of medical doctors was created. Unfortunately, the commission was considered biased, given the fact that transsexualism is a multidisciplinary issue that requires the technical evaluation of nonmedical specialists, such as psychologists and social workers. Consequently, an ad hoc group of specialists with expertise in the field was formed, including psychologists and other professionals. This ad hoc group has a consultative role in regards to the PMO, in that it first evaluates each request of sex change surgery that is made to the PMO.

In the meantime, no information is available regarding the true number of sex-change operations performed in Portugal. The Santa Maria Hospital, Lisbon, has the greatest experience in these surgeries. The process of having a sex-change operation is long, and carries with it the requirement of stringent psychological and psychiatric evaluation in order to verify whether or not the candidate is eligible for the surgical reassignment process. This evaluation period often takes about 2 years. However, it can take longer. Some transsexuals, confronted with the time they have to face in order to have their gender change completed, opt to medicate themselves with hormones and to go abroad to have the sex-change operation. Before 1996 and even to this day, many Portuguese transsexuals go to Morocco, or more recently to England, to have their operations. Unfortunately, the surgery is not always performed under the best sanitary and medical conditions, leaving the postoperative transsexual with serious health problems.

In conclusion, it can be stated that some important steps have been taken in Portugal toward the recognition of transsexualism as a condition that requires special medical and legal procedures, even if the process is not always simple or quick. Despite this progress, transgender individuals still have to face a social and cultural reality that has difficulty in understanding their condition and thus can be transphobic.

Transgender: The Israeli Experience

The discussion of the Israeli transgender experience is based on a survey of the transgender population members who consulted the Israeli Center for Human Sexuality and Gender Identity between 1997 and 2001.

The survey included 86 participants; 67 of them were genetic males and 19 of them were genetic females (the ratio of male to female is 3.5 : 1). The age range of the participants was 8–71 years with median of 31.4. Most of the participants (65%) were single, 23% were married, and 12% were divorced. The educational background of the participants was relatively high: 52% of them had obtained college degrees (42% had graduate degrees), 24% had high-school diplomas, and only 16% had not obtained a high-school diploma.

Occupationally, most participants were academic professionals (74%) with a high percentage of representation in the high-tech industry (24%); 16% held blue-collar jobs, 3% worked in the sex industry, and 5% were unemployed. In terms of ethnic background, 65% of the participants were Ashkenazi Jews, 30% were Sephardic Jews, and 4% were Palestinian Arabs. Most of the participants in the sample (96%) were Jews, with only 4% Muslims and Christians.

Thus one can characterize the population of transgender clients in the Center as highly functional on personal, interpersonal, and occupational levels. Additionally, most of the clients in the Center expressed interest in exploring gender identity issues before pursuing genital surgery.

In Israel, one can obtain free surgery for sex change through the national health system, following an evaluation and approval by a specialized gender identity committee. Other features, which may be unique to the Israeli society, are army service, the dominant influence of religion, and the strong nationalistic sentiments. These features impact the discourse on sex and gender and tend to be more transsexual confirming and less focused on identity politics. Despite the open and liberal nature of Israel towards the transsexual/transgendered person, there is a rigidity and polarization of femininity and masculinity in Israeli society.

Transgender and Transsexuality in Ukraine

Ukraine is located between Central Europe and Asia. Before integration with Russia in 1654, communication between Ukraine and Europe encountered few obstacles. Additionally, there was a strong influence of the East on Ukrainian culture. Christianity came to Ukraine in 988. Before the arrival of Christianity, Ukrainian religions were based upon polytheism or many gods. Upon reading many of the writings by the old authors, it can

be discerned that there were many holidays in which it was commonplace to wear the dress of the opposite gender. Moreover, there were performing artists called *schomorochs* and, based upon the ancient writings, it is possible to find some elements of transvestism appearing in their performances.

Traditionally, the head of the Ukrainian family has always been male. It was the male's duty to hold the power in the family and to provide sufficient means for the family. The women's duties were to take care of the home and the children. The woman's role changed, to some extent, with the appearance of one of the first leaders of the Ukrainian state (then called Kyiv Rush), Queen Olga, who ruled from 945 to 969. With her appearance, the precedent for a woman to have a leading role was established. On the death of her husband, King Oleg, she finally became Queen of Ukraine. Olga was famous as the first woman to become a Christian Queen of Kyiv Rush.

The emergence of Queen Olga encouraged women to become highly educated, engendering a deep respect within the Ukrainian social structure. For example, in the Middle Ages, one Ukrainian woman prisoner became a wife of the Turkish Sultan and played a significant role in governing this Islamic country. Despite the acknowledged abilities of Ukrainian women during these times, it was not until the end of the 19th century that we begin to read about the leading roles of women in state life in Ukraine. Thus, like many of the Central European countries at that time, while women's knowledge and roles were highly respected, the traditional gender roles predominated in Ukrainian society.

During the Soviet period (1917–1991), homosexuality, transvestism, and transsexuality were considered to be psychiatric disorders. Moreover, people who had one of these "diagnoses" were forced to obtain treatment in psychiatric hospitals. Additionally, these disorders were persecuted under an assortment of Soviet laws.

In 1994, a special commission addressing questions of transsexuality was organized within the Ukrainian Ministry of Public Health. This commission decided to legalize transsexuality. As a result of this new legalization, a number of Ukrainians decided to undergo sex reassignment. According to the rules of the commission, patients who wish to change their gender must be observed by a sexologist in an outpatient setting for a period of a year. Additionally, a psychiatrist in a hospital must see them for a period of at least a month. After these specialists diagnose the individual as being transsexual, he or she is allowed to have gender reassignment surgery upon submitting an application for the surgery to the commission. Once the commission has given a positive decision, it is also possible for the gender of the individual to be changed on his or her passport.

Reconstructing Sex: Australian and New Zealand Transgender Reform Jurisprudence

Australian transgender jurisprudence now represents the frontier of transgender law reform, for it is in Australia that the most radical legal reconstruction of sex has recently occurred. In order to understand this claim it is necessary to sketch the background to this reform moment. Transgender jurisprudence is of relatively recent origin. It emerged in the postwar period and coincided with advances in sex reassignment surgical techniques. This jurisprudence has led to two distinct approaches to the legal determination of sex claims. In the first approach the courts have selected particular biological factors and have insisted that sex is determined at birth (the *biological* approach), (*Corbett* v. *Corbett* [1970] 2 All ER 33). This has led to the denial of the sex claims of transgender claimants. Within the second approach the courts have focused instead on present realities and, in particular, on the fact of sex reassignment surgery (the *psychological and anatomical harmony* approach), (*Re Anonymous* 293 NYS 2d 834 (1968); *MT* v. *JT* 355 A 2d 204 (1976)). This latter approach has enabled legal recognition of sex claims for a variety of purposes.

While the reform approach appears to be gaining the upper hand at judicial[1] and, especially, legislative levels (the sex claims of postoperative transgender people have been recognized through legislation in New Zealand and in many states or provinces within the United States, Canada, and Australia, and similar legislation has been enacted by nearly all the European Community members and by other nation states), the biological approach continues to find favor.[2] However, these two approaches should not be thought of as mutually exclusive. Rather, they share a number of commonalities. In particular, both approaches have privileged the genital factor in determining sex. Thus within the biological approach three factors are specified, namely, chromosomes, gonads, and genitalia at birth. Where these factors are "incongruent,"

however, it is the genital factor that proves decisive.[3] In relation to reform jurisprudence, on the other hand, it is the surgical removal and reconstruction of genitalia subsequent to birth that proves crucial. Moreover, it is not merely a concern with bodily esthetics that has led to this focus. Rather, legal analysis has also exhibited concern over postoperative sexual functioning. In the biological approach this has manifested itself in terms of judicial horror at the prospect of "unnatural" sexual intercourse. Within reform jurisprudence it is the capacity for penetrative heterosexual intercourse postoperatively that has been emphasized repeatedly. In New Zealand the judiciary have dispensed with the requirement of postoperative sexual function (*Attorney-General* v. *Otathuhu Family Court* [1995] 1 NZLR 603). However, New Zealand law still requires genital reassignment surgery (see Sharpe, 2002).

Indeed, prior to a recent decision of the Family Court of Australia, no superior court or legislature anywhere in the world had recognized the sex claims of a transgender person whose genitalia had not been brought into "conformity" with his or her psychological sex. In *Re Kevin and Jennifer* v. *Attorney General for the Commonwealth of Australia* (*Re Kevin and Jennifer* v. *Attorney-General for the Commonwealth of Australia* [2001] FamCA 1074) the court held Kevin, a transgender man who had not undertaken phalloplastic surgery (phalloplasty refers to the surgical construction of a penis), to be a man for the purposes of Australian marriage law. The decision is especially significant, dealing as it does with marriage, for it has been in relation to issues of marriage that the greatest resistance to transgender law reform has been apparent across jurisdictions. In effect the decision rearticulates the reform test of *psychological and anatomical harmony*, one that had received prior endorsement by Australian courts (*R* v. *Harris and McGuiness* [1989] 17 NSWLR 158; *Secretary, Department of Social Security* v. *HH* [1991] 23 ALD 58; *Secretary, Department of Social Security* v. *SRA* [1993] 118 ALR 467), so as to uncouple sex claims from the genitocentrism of law. In this respect, and while the court placed emphasis on the fact that Kevin had undergone other irreversible surgical procedures (in addition to receiving hormone treatment Kevin had undergone a breast reduction procedure and a total hysterectomy), this decision represents a major step forward for transgender people. For a critique of the decision, see Sharpe, (2003).

Transsexuality and Transgender in Japan

In 1969, a Japanese gynecologist was tried and found guilty of performing SRS for three MTF transsexuals. Since then, medical treatment, and even discussion of transsexuality, has been practically a taboo in Japan. For this reason some transsexuals have obtained their SRS abroad, while others have received hormonal therapy and/or SRS underground at home.

However, this situation is now changing. In 1998, Dr Harashina performed the first SRS in Japan that was legally admitted. Today, Japan has two gender clinics that perform SRS in Saitama Medical College and Okayama University Hospital. From 1998 to 2002 over 1000 transsexuals and transgenders came to gender clinics and about 20 transsexuals received SRS. However, because it takes long time to follow Japanese guidelines, there are still many transsexuals who receive SRS in other countries. It is estimated that there are about 500 postoperative transsexuals in Japan.

Change of sex registration of transsexuality is still very difficult. Recently, Saitama Family Court rejected an appeal of change of sex registration from an FTM who had received legally admitted SRS. The main reason for rejection is "biological etiology of transsexuality is not clear." In his decision, the judge stated: "I hesitate to admit the change of sex registration."

However, there is now a new movement in the Diet. Some lawmakers have set up a study team to make a new law about changing a transsexual's sex registration. Last year, *Kinpachii Sensei*, a very popular school television drama, spotlighted an FTM student and a famous professional boat-racer came out as an FTM. These nationwide topics teach us that Japanese have a positive attitude toward transsexuals and transgenders. With these developments, the situation for transsexuals and transgenders in Japan continues to improve. For additional discussion on sex reassignment surgery in Japan, see Ako et al. (2001).

Transgender and Transsexualism in Norway

In the western hemisphere there is a need to date all descriptions concerning diversities in genderland. Much change is taking place: new insights, new words, concepts, and contexts are constantly being inspired as others are being expired.

Norway has two organizations for transpeople. The oldest is FPE-NE which was founded in 1968 to meet the needs of "heterosexual transvestites." Today members of the FPE-NE form a continuum from classical part-time cross-dressing, through self-defined bigendered, to transgendered, to transsexuals. By 2002 FPE-NE had a membership of 142 individuals.

The younger organization is LFTS. It was founded in January 2000 on three main premises. The most urgent of these was the size of offers from the Norwegian State to transsexuals seeking gender-confirming surgery. The second was the willingness of some transsexuals to display themselves as transsexual women and men, thus generating the power to influence on most levels in society, including the arenas of politics and media. The third reason was the need for transsexuals to come into contact with other transsexuals and/or other transpeople, to generate a context where each could find friendships, insights, and addresses of approved therapists in the field. LFTS currently has a membership of 120 individuals. There is the option of a supportive membership with cheaper fees for parents, siblings of transpeople, and any others that might find such a membership meaningful. LFTS does receive economic support from the Norwegian State, but is not yet securely financed.

On the public scene, during the past years several transpeople have been extremely active in trans-advocacy. In part, this activism has been due to the founding of the LFTS. One of these individuals has actually been named the "Norwegian national trans-person," and her/his/hir (hir is a common genderless contraction of his and her) son has made a documentary entitled *All about my Father* which has won a number of prizes both internationally and nationally. Most notably, it won the Norwegian Amanda Prize for the best film of the year.

Through all this openness combined with persistent work by the LFTS and other transpeople, conditions, especially for transsexuals seeking surgery, have been greatly improved in the one hospital where such surgery is performed. The standards of the HBIGDA are followed at least to an acceptable degree, even though the most officially recognized therapists in the field are not members of the organization. The surgery and consequent convalescence are funded totally by the Norwegian State.

On the legal side, transsexuals in Norway have the right to a new birth certificate and social security number once genital surgery has been completed. Additionally, couples do not have to divorce if one partner undergoes complete hormonal and surgical treatment.

Overall, there is very little discrimination against transgendered persons in Norwegian society. People seem to have a great deal of respect for otherness. Employers are very supportive of transpeople crossing the boundary between the two gender majorities which still exists. Families are seeking advice from well-known therapists, who are themselves expressing gendered otherness, instead of rejecting their children and young adults. Presently, in some respects, Norway represents a society that lets its members explore the diversities of gender.

Other Countries

Many other countries have transgender/transsexual populations ranging from those that exist in absolute secrecy (Arab Countries, South America, Mexico) to the open and accepting policies of countries such as Canada and Israel. India has a population of transgendered individuals called the *hijra*, while in Malaysia the MTF transsexuals are known as *mak nyah* (Teh, 2001). For a discussion of transgender in Thailand, see Winter and Udomsak (2002). For an excellent introduction to the cross-cultural aspects of transgender and transsexual, see Green (1966).

WHAT WE DO NOT KNOW

Longitudinal/Cohort Studies

Currently, much is unknown about the long-term effects of contragender hormonal treatment. In light of recent studies on increased breast cancer risk in non-transgendered females due to hormone replacement therapy, it is critical that longitudinal studies are undertaken in the transgender community. Questions of increased risk of breast cancer in MTF transsexuals remain open, as do questions of breast cancer in the FTM transsexual community. Questions of the effect of estrogen on bone mass in this population are also important and go unanswered, as do questions of the effect of estrogen on oral health and the potential to affect cardiovascular problems. Only recently have studies begun to address the issues of excessive smoking in this population. Little is known about the effects of replacing estrogen with testosterone in FTM

transsexuals with respect to potentiating onset of Alzheimer's disease due to the absence of estrogenic protection. Comorbidity of disease states due to contragender hormone treatment and elevated stress states due to the social stigma associated with being transgendered (Witten, 2002a, 2003; Witten & Eyler, 1999) remain unstudied. To date, only one study has examined the mortality risk of contragender hormones (Asscherman, Gooren, & Eklund, 1989). For a review of issues associated with MTF hormone treatment, see Gooren (1999).

It is also important to address life-course issues. Very little is known about transgender and transsexual issues in individuals under the age of 18. Studies in this domain are complicated by strict human subject requirements that involve consent of the parents as well as the child. Some discussion of child and adolescent gender identity issues can be found in Ceglie, Freedman, McPherson, and Richardson (2002).

Additionally, very little is known about issues of middle to later life in this community. Questions of social support networks and other long-term quality-of-life components of society still remain open for investigation. Little is known about transgender and intersex elder abuse (Cook-Daniels, 1995). The impact of transgendered parents on their children is unstudied. Family dynamics and restructuring due to transgendering in the family are relatively unknown, except anecdotally (Boenke, 1999).

Issues of late life are also unstudied. The gerontological literature is replete with documentation supporting the importance of social network structure (family, spirituality, and friends, to name but a few items [Pinquart & Sorenson, 2000]) on the morbidity and mortality rates of heterosexual elders. There is no reason to believe that these results do not apply to nontraditional gender identities, gender expressions, sexualities, sexes, and body forms. The work of Witten and Eyler (1999a) indicates that nearly 50% of the respondents are living alone (a significant risk factor for the elderly), and only 10% of the respondents indicate that they are either living with or have children (a potentially deleterious factor indicating diminished social support networks [Everard, Lach, Fisher, & Baum, 2000; Rautio, Heikkinen, & Heikkinen, 2001]).

Among the transgendered populations, it is reasonable to assume that while spirituality may or may not be an important component of their lives, there is little formal outlet for religious interaction and support, as transsexuality in particular, and transgenderism in general, are highly stigmatized within the traditional Judeo-Christian–Islamic religions. Lack of access to religious support—emotional, physical, or otherwise—is also a significant risk factor for the elderly. Among transgenders, divorce is very high (estimates are not available; however, TLARS results indicate that 20% of the respondents were separated and another 10% were divorced). This further exacerbates the diminished social support network structures well known to be critical in the later life.

The impact of transgender on quality of life, caregiving and caregiver burden, longevity, wisdom, healthcare utilization and access (Witten, 2002c), and social isolation remain open for study. Financial issues are equally important (Crystal, Johnson, Harman, Sambamoorthi, & Kumar, 2000). Multiracial and multicultural issues within the transgender and intersex populations, as they relate to life-course issues, also remain relatively unstudied.

NOTES

1. See, for example, *Richards* v. *United States Tennis Association* 400 NYS 2d 276 (1977); *Vecchione* v. *Vecchione* No 95D003769 (Orange County, Calif filed 23 April 1996); *Re the Estate of Marshall G Gardiner* Kan App LEXIS 376 (2001); *R* v. *Harris and McGuiness* [1989] 17 NSWLR 158; *Secretary, Department of Social Security* v. *HH* [1991] 23 ALD 58; *Secretary, Department of Social Security* v. *SRA* [1993] 118 ALR 467; *M* v. *M* [1991] NZFLR 337; *Goodwin* v. *UK* ECHR [2002] 2 FCR 577.
2. See for example, *R* v. *Tan* [1983] QB 1053; *Re Ladrach* 32 Ohio Misc 2d 6 (1987); *Lim Ying* v. *Hiok Kian Ming Eric* (1992) 1 SLR 184; *Littleton* v. *Prange* 9 S.W. 3d 223 (Tx App 1999); *Bellinger* v. *Bellinger* (unreported, CA [2001] EWCA Civ 1140, 17/7/01).
3. See *Corbett* v. *Corbett* [1970] 2 All ER 33 at 48 per Ormrod J. See also *W* v. *W* [2001] 2 WLR 674.

REFERENCES

Ako, T., Takao, H., Yoshiharu, I., Katsuyuki, K. et al. (2001). Beginnings of sex reassignment surgery in Japan. *International Journal of Transgenderism*, 5(1). Retrieved from http://symposion.com/ijt/ijtvo01no05_02.htm

American Psychiatric Association. (2000). *Diagnostic and statistical manual of mental disorders* (4th ed., text revision). Washington, DC: Author.

Asscherman, H., Gooren, L. J. G., & Eklund, P. L. E. (1989). Mortality and morbidity in transsexual patients with cross-gender hormone treatment. *Metabolism*, 38(9), 869–873.

Bernardo, J., Campos, M. C., Machado, G., Tavares, G., Wandolly, K., Salce, G. et al. (1998). *The Portuguese transgender community:*

an unknown reality. Paper presented at the 12th World AIDS Conference—Bridging the Gap, Geneva.

Bockting, W. O., Rosser, S., & Coleman, E. (1999). Transgender HIV prevention: Community involvement and empowerment. *International Journal of Transgender*, 3(1 + 2). Retrieved from http://symposion.com/ijt/hiv_risk/bockting.htm

Boenke, M. (Ed.). (1999). *Transforming families.* Imperial Beach, CA: Trook.

Cassell, J. (1998). *The woman in the surgeon's body.* Cambridge, MA: Harvard University Press.

Ceglie, D. D., Freedman, D., McPherson, S., & Richardson, P. (2002). Children and adolescents referred to a specialist gender identity development service: Clinical features and demographic characteristics. *International Journal of Transgenderism*, 6(1). Retrieved from http://symposion.com/ijt/ijtvo06no01_01.htm

Cook-Daniels, L. (1995). *Lesbian, gay male, and transgender elder abuse.* Retrieved from http://www.amboyz.org/articles/elderabuse.html

Crystal, S., Johnson, R. W., Harman, J., Sambamoorthi, U., & Kumar, R. (2000). Out-of-pocket health care costs among older Americans. *Journal of Gerontology*, 55B(1), S51–S62.

Currah, P., & Minter, S. (2000). *Transgender equality.* NGLTF Policy Institute, New York.

Devor, H. (1994). Transsexualism, dissociation and child abuse: An initial discussion based on non-clinical data. *Journal of Psychology and Human Sexuality*, 6(3), 49–72.

Ekins, R. & King, D. (Eds.). (1996). *Blending genders: Social aspects of cross-dressing and sex-changing.* London: Routledge.

Elledge, J. (2002). *Gay, lesbian, bisexual, and transgender myths from the Arapaho to the Zuni: An anthology.* Bern, Switzerland: Lang.

Encyclopedia Brittanica Online. (2001). Retrieved from http://search.britannica.com/search?query=gender+identity

Ettner, R. (1999). *Gender loving care: A guide to counseling gender-variant clients.* New York: Norton.

Everard, K. M., Lach, H. W., Fisher, E. B., & Baum, M. C. (2000). Relationship of activity and social support to the functional health of older adults. *Journal of Gerontology*, 55B(4), S208–S212.

Fausto-Sterling, A. (2000). *Sexing the body.* New York: Basic Books.

Feinberg, L. (1997). *Transgender warriors: Making history from Joan of Arc to Dennis Rodman.* Boston, MA: Beacon Press.

Godlewski, J. (1988). Transsexualism and anatomic sex ratio reversal in Poland. *Archives of Sexual Behavior*, 17(6), 547–548.

Goodnow, C. (2000, March 13). *A tragically maimed boy, raised as a girl, comes to terms with his identity.* Seattle Post-Intelligencer. Retrieved from http://www.seattlep-i.nwsource.com/lifestyle/gndr13.shtml

Gooren, L. J. G. (1999). Hormonal sex reassignment. *International Journal of Transgenderism*, 3(3). Retrieved from http://symposion.com/ijt/ijt990301.htm

Green, R. (1966). Transsexualism: Mythological, historical, and cross-cultural aspects. In H. Benjamin (Ed.), *The transsexual phenomenon.* New York: Julian Press. Website: http://symposion.com/ijt/benjamin/index.htm

Haraldsen & Dahl. (2000). *Acta Psychiatrica Scandinavica*, 102(4), 276–281.

Harvey, A. (1997). *Gay mystics.* New York: HarperCollins.

Herdt, G. (Ed.). (1996). *Third sex, third gender: beyond sexual dimorphism in culture and history.* New York: Zone Books.

Hoenig, J., & Kenna, C. (1974). The prevalence of transsexualism in England and Wales. *British Journal of Psychiatry*, *124*, 181–190.

ILGA-Portugal. (1999). *Situação portuguesa* [The Portuguese situation]. Retrieved from http://www.ilga-portugal.org/portugues/index.html

Jacobs, S. E., & Cromwell, J. (1992). Visions and revisions of reality: Reflections on sex, sexuality, gender, and gender variance. *Journal of Homosexuality*, *23*, 43–69.

Landén, M. (1999). *Transsexualism: Epidemiology, phenomenology, aetiology, regret after surgery, and public attitudes*. Göteborg, Sweden: Institute of Clinical Neuroscience, Göteborg University.

Landén, M., & Hambert, G. et al. (1998). Factors predictive of regret in sex reassignment. *Acta Psychiatrica Scandinavica*, *97*, 284–289.

Landén, M., & Innala, S. (2000). Attitudes towards transsexualism in a Swedish national sample survey. *Archives of Sexual Behavior*, *29*(4), 375–388.

Landén, M., Wålinder, J. et al. (1996). Incidence and sex ratio of transsexualism in Sweden. *Acta Psychiatrica Scandinavica*, *93*(4), 261–263.

Landén, M., Wålinder, J. et al. (1998). Clinical characteristics of a total cohort of female and male applicants for sex reassignment: a descriptive study. *Acta Psychiatrica Scandinavica*, *97*(3), 189–194.

Langevin, R. (1983). *Sexual Strands: Understanding and treating sexual anomalies in men*. Hillsdale, NJ: Erlbaum.

Matzner, A. (2001). *'O au no keia: Voices from Hawai'I's mahu and transgender communities*. Philadephia, PA: Xlibris.

Monteith, M. J. (1993). Self-regulation of prejudiced responses: Implications for progress in prejudice-reduction efforts. *Journal of Personality and Social Psychology*, *65*(3), 469–485.

More, K., & Whittle, S. (1999). (Eds.). *Reclaiming genders: Transsexual grammars at the fin de siècle*. London: Cassell.

Oxford English Dictionary Online. (2001). Retrieved from http://etext.lib.virginia.edu/etcbin/oedbin/oed2www?specfile=/web/data/oed/oed.o2w&act=text&offset=159137452&textreg=0&query=gender

Perry, G. (Ed.). (1999). *Gender and art*. New Haven, CT: Yale University Press.

Pinquart, M., & Sorenson, S. (2000). Influences of socio-economic status, social network, and competence on subjective well-being in later life: A meta-analysis. *Psychology and Aging*, *14*(2), 187–224.

Pryzgoda, J., & Chrisler, J. C. (2000). Definitions of gender and sex: The subtleties of meaning. *Sex Roles*, *43*(7/8), 553–569.

Rautio, N., Heikkinen, E., & Heikkinen, R.-L. (2001). The association of socio-economic factors with physical and mental capacity in elderly men and women. *Archives of Gerontology and Geriatrics*, *33*, 163–178.

Sharpe, A. (2002). *Transgender jurisprudence: Dysphoric bodies of law* London: Cavendish.

Sharpe, A. (2003). Thinking Critically in Moments of Transgender Law Reform: *Re Kevin and Jennifer* v. *Attorney-General for the Commonwealth. Griffith Law Review*, *11*(2), 309–331.

Sigusch, V. (1991). Die Transsexuellen und unser Nosomorpher Blick. *Zeitschrift für Sexualforschung*, *4*, 225–256.

Teh, Y. K. (2001). Mak nyahs (male transsexuals) in Malaysia: The influence of religion and culture on their identity. *International Journal of Transgenderism*, *5*(3). Retrieved from http://www.symposion.com/ijt/ijtvo05no03_04.htm

Tsoi, W. F. (1988). The prevalence of transsexualism in Singapore. *Acta Psychiatrica Scandinavica*, *78*, 501–504.

Van Kesteren, P. J., Gooren, L. J., & Megens, J. A. (1996). An epidemiological and demographic study of transsexuals in the Netherlands. *Archives of Sexual Behavior*, *25*(6), 589–600.

Vitorino, S. & Dinis, G. (1999). *Lesbian, gay, bisexual and transgender (LGBT) politics in Portugal: the awakening of a new social movement*. Paper presented at the Euro-Mediterranean Conference of Homosexualities, Marseilles.

Wålinder, J. (1971a). Transsexualism: Definition, prevalence, and sex distribution. *Acta Psychiatrica Scandinavica*, *44*(Suppl.), 255–257.

Wålinder, J. (1971b). Incidence and sex ratio of transsexualism in Sweden. *British Journal of Psychiatry*, *118*, 195–196.

Wålinder, J., & Thuwe, I. (1976). A law concerning sex reassignment of transsexuals in Sweden. *Archives of Sexual Behavior*, *5*(3), 255–258.

Warren, B. E. (1999). Sex, truth and videotape HIV: Prevention at the Gender Identity Project in New York City. *International Journal of Transgenderism*, *3*(1,2). Retrieved from http://symposion.com/ijt/hiv_risk/warren.htm

Webster, D. (1984). *Webster's new dictionary and Roget's thesaurus*. Cambridge, Ontario, Canada: Nelson.

Weitze, C., & Osburg, S. (1996). Transsexualism in Germany: Empirical data on epidemiology and application of the German transsexual's act during the first ten years. *Archives of Sexual Behavior*, *25*(4), 409–425.

Winter, S., & Udomsak, N. (2002). Male, female, and transgender: Stereotypes in Thailand. *International Journal of Transgenderism*, *6*(1). Retrieved from http://www.symposion.com/ijt/ijtvo06no01_04.htm

Witten, T. M. (2002a). Transgender aging: An emerging population, an emerging need. *Geriatric Care Management Journal*, *12*(3), 20–24.

Witten, T. M. (2002b). *The Tao of gender*. Athens, GA: Humanics.

Witten, T. M. (2002c). *White Paper: Transgender and intersex aging issues* (Tech. Rep. Ser., TRS-01-2002). Richmond, VA: Transcience Research Institute.

Witten, T. M. (2003). Transgender aging: An emerging population, an emerging need. *Sexologie, XII*(44), 11–20.

Witten, T. M. (2004). Life course analysis: The courage to search for something more—Middle adulthood issues in the transgender and intersex communities. *Journal of Human Behavior and Social Environment*, *8*(3–4) (in press).

Witten, T. M., & Eyler, A. E. (1999a). Hate crimes and violence against the transgendered. *Peace Review*, *11*(3), 461–468.

Witten, T. M., & Eyler, A. E. (1999b). [International Survey of gender self-perception.] Unpublished raw data.

Zhang, Z., & Hayward, M. D. (2001). Childlessness and the psychological well-being of older persons. *Journal of Gerontology*, *56B*(5), S311–S320.

Zhou, J.-N., Hofman, M. A., Gooren, L. J., & Swaab, D. F. (1997). A sex difference in the human grain and its relationship to transsexuality. *International Journal of Transgenderism*, *1*(1). Retrieved from http://symposion.com/ijt/ijtc0106.htm

Rape and Other Sexual Aggression

Laura Zimmer-Tamakoshi

RAPE AND OTHER SEXUAL AGGRESSION

Sexual aggression occurs the world over. I begin with a review of sexual aggression, primarily in the United States where it is more thoroughly researched. I then discuss perpetrators and victims, setting the stage for cross-cultural analyses of causes, questions of definition and methodology, and the relationship of sexual aggression to other violence.

Their Nature and Extent

Acts of sexual aggression have been documented for centuries. The statistics used here are recent and considered among the more valid by top researchers in this field of study.

Rape and Child Sexual Abuse. In 1997, the U.S. Bureau of Justice's *Uniform Crime Reports* estimated the annual rate of *reported* rapes to be 70 per 100,000 women (Russell & Bolen, 2000, p. 51). Federal crime victimization surveys found the annual *prevalence* of completed or attempted rapes to be three to four times higher. Russell's 1978 *lifetime prevalence* survey of 930 San Francisco women suggests a greater risk of rape: one in four women were rape victims and one in two had experienced rape or attempted rape (Russell & Bolen, 2000, p. 54). Such statistics support the statement that "A woman is raped every minute in America" (Koss et al., 1994, p. 112). Thirty-eight percent of Russell's survey participants reported at least one experience of incestuous or extrafamilial sexual abuse before the age of 18 (Russell & Bolen, 2000, p. 163). Add in the sexual abuse of boys, and one in two children in America may experience sexual abuse.

Sexual Aggression in Warfare and Religious and Ethnic Conflicts. The most public rapes occur in wars and ethnic conflicts. In *Against Our Will*, Brownmiller (1975) writes of the use of rape as terrorism and spoil of war citing Christian pilgrims' rape of Muslim women in the First Crusade (p. 31), Japanese concentration camp rape and camp brothels in World War II (p. 62), and the rape and murder of women by U.S. soldiers in Vietnam (p. 103). Military brothels servicing American soldiers in Thailand, the Philippines, and Vietnam created an image of Southeast Asia as a "sex capital" (Perpinan, 1994). Upon occupying Tibet in 1949, Chinese soldiers raped and impregnated Tibetan women as a means of ethnic cleansing and humiliation for Tibetan men (Campaign Free Tibet, 1994). Serbian soldiers did the same, raping Bosnian Muslim women and denying them abortions so they might "give birth to little Chetniks" (Drakulic, 1994, p. 180).

Date Rape and Acquaintance Rape on College Campuses. A study of students at 32 American institutions of higher education showed that 28% of the women had experienced a rape or rape attempt since age 14, and that 8% of the men admitted having committed at least one rape (Koss, Gidycz, & Wisniewski, 1987). Investigating a fraternity rape at the University of Pennsylvania, Sanday (1990b, p. 9) argued that sexual aggression is "the means by which some men display masculinity and induct younger men into masculine power roles." The campus party culture that encourages group sexual aggression against lone college women promotes their seduction with alcohol and drugs, defines a drunken woman as "asking for it," and labels men who object to this kind of behavior as *wimps* and *faggots* (p. 11). The community supports such behavior. The Penn case settled out of court and the fraternity house closed for one semester. Some fraternities are more dangerous for women than others. Boswell and Spade (1996) note that the abusive attitudes that some fraternities perpetuate are part of a general culture where rape is part of traditional gender scripts. Sexually active men are positively referred to as *studs* whereas sexually active women are labeled *sluts*. A double standard is more often applied to nameless acquaintance or unknown women. Houses where more of the men have regular girlfriends are less likely to host high-risk parties.

Intimate Partner Rape and Partner Violence.

Women are more likely to be raped, injured, or killed by current or former partners than by other assailants (Finkelhor & Yllo, 1985). As many as 34% of women are physically assaulted by intimate males (Koss et al., 1994). Violence is mutual in many partnerships (Kantor & Jasinski, 1998, p. 9), but women are more often seriously injured and a woman raped by her partner lives with her rapist and suffers repeated rapes and violence (Mahoney & Williams 1998, p. 116). Official statistics do not include same-sex partner rapes, yet violence in same-sex relationships is high, with 38% of gay and 48% of lesbian couples experiencing partner violence. Surveys on psychological, physical, and sexual abuse show that 50% of lesbians are victims of previous or current partners. When dating relationships are considered, straight women are more likely than lesbians to be abused by dates—19% versus 5% (West, 1998a). Other groups with high partner violence and sexual abuse are some Latino groups, African and Asian Americans and American Indians (West, 1998b). African American men reportedly abuse their wives four times as often as European Americans (West, 1998b, p. 190) and their wives are twice as likely to engage in severe acts of violence in return. Puerto Rican men are reportedly 10 times more likely than Cuban men to assault their wives. However, intimate violence is hidden in wealthier communities, making it difficult to be sure that the difference is so great (West, 1998b, p. 191).

Child Sexual Abuse.

State legal definitions of child sexual abuse and incest vary as to specific acts and ages of victims and perpetrators, the relationship between them, and whether or not violence is used. Given difficulties in reporting and prosecution, few cases of child sex abuse result in conviction (Russell & Bolen, 2000, p. 144). Two difficulties are the social and economic pressures placed on victims to protect their abusers, and children's difficulties in recalling details of their victimization. Researchers also disagree over what constitutes child sexual abuse or incest, arguing over whether or not to include peer sexual abuse or unwanted touches on the buttocks, thereby making comparisons difficult (Finkelhor, 1994). The National Incidence Study is an effort of the National Center on Child Abuse and Neglect to collect data on reported and unreported child abuse in the United States. In 1993 there were an estimated 300,200 sexually abused children, 198,732 of whom were female (Sedlak & Broadhurst, 1996). The study was flawed, however, because it limits child sexual abuse to acts perpetrated by parents and caretakers. Other studies show sexual abuse by nonrelatives to be more prevalent. Russell uncovered the prevalence of incestuous and extrafamilial child sex abuse in her 1978 San Francisco study. She found that 38% of her female respondents reported at least one experience of incestuous or extrafamilial sexual abuse before 18 years of age, with 16% of the 930 women reporting at least one experience of incestuous abuse (Russell & Bolen, 2000, pp. 151, 163). When Russell added non-contact sexual abuse, 54% of her sample reported at least one experience of sexual abuse before 18 years of age. In Los Angeles, Wyatt (1985) found no significant differences in prevalence rates for child sexual abuse between African American and European American women. The prevalence rate for child sexual abuse for Hispanic women in Russell's San Francisco sample was 45%, slightly higher than her prevalence rate of 42% for non-Hispanic white women (Russell & Bolen, 2000, p. 185).

Pornography.

In *Dangerous Relationships*, Russell (1998) reviews research showing pornography's close relationship to violence against women and children. She defines pornography as "material that combines sex and/or the exposure of genitals with abuse or degradation in a manner that appears to endorse, condone, or encourage such behavior" (p. 3). She distinguishes pornography from erotica, defining the latter as "suggestive or arousing material that is free of sexism, racism, and homophobia and is respectful of all human beings and animals portrayed." Adult pornography depicts women's bodies in ways suggesting that sexual harassment is harmless and that women enjoy being raped and sexually degraded. Russell argues that such images predispose some males to desire rape and undermines their inhibitions against acting out rape desires (p. 121). Young children are exposed to pornography, with most boys seeing *Playboy* or some other soft-porn magazine by the age of 11 years (p. 127). An example of femicidal pornography is the 1979 film *Snuff*, in which an unsuspecting South American actress is killed, a man ripping out her uterus and holding it up in the air while he ejaculates (Labelle, 1980; Russell, 1998, p. 98). The selling of sexual violence includes the glorification of killers like Jack the Ripper. According to Cameron (1992), "ripperology" reached its height with the 100th anniversary of Jack the Ripper's spree of killing prostitutes and his status as a cultural hero and role model for other sexual killers like the 1981 Yorkshire Ripper, Peter Sutcliffe. The rapid growth of Internet pornography has many concerned about the impact on young people (Russell, 1998, p. 160).

Sexual Harassment.   Sexual harassment is often depicted as a lesser, even enjoyable, form of sexual coercion. However, research shows it to be a serious problem, affecting one in two women in the United States (Koss et al., 1994, p. 111). Women in traditionally male occupations are at greater risk, as shown by the Tailhook Convention incident in which drunken male pilots assaulted their female peers (Koss et al., 1994, p. 113). The seriousness of sexual harassment involves not only the physical and emotional victimization that women suffer but also their economic vulnerability. For a long time sexual harassment was not a crime, so it was not included in victimization surveys. In 1980 it became a civil rights violation when the Equal Employment Opportunity Commission issued its guidelines. In 1986 the Supreme Court made sexual harassment illegal by including it in the category of gender discrimination. However, few victims confront their harassers. Less than 5% file a complaint (Koss et al., 1994, p. 123). Many victims trivialize their situations while others fear losing their jobs. Some fear that they will not be believed or will be accused of causing trouble, as happened publicly in the Anita Hill–Clarence Thomas hearings (Gutek, 1985). Studies show that younger women tend to be objects of sexual harassment more than older women, and minority women are less likely than European American women to quit a job as a result of sexual harassment (Koss et al., 1994, p. 143). In Giuffre and Williams' (1994) study of labeling sexual harassment in restaurants, they found that many men and women experience sexual behavior in the workplace as pleasurable. This is especially so in jobs where workers are hired on the basis of their attractiveness and solicitousness—work such as receptionists and restaurant servers. Waitpeople used complex double standards when labeling behavior. Many claimed that they enjoyed sexual interactions involving coworkers of the same race/ethnicity, sexual orientation, and class/status background, but labeled as sexual harassment the same behaviors when they involved interactions between gays and heterosexuals or between men and women of different racial/ethnic backgrounds.

The Threat of Sexual Violence.   The threat of sexual violence limits the freedoms of likely victims and gives an edge of terrorism to likely perpetrators. *Men on Rape* (Beneke, 1982) looks at the effects of the threat of sexual violence on women. Talking to women, Beneke found that the threat of rape alters the meaning and feel of the night and nature, with women fearful of walking late at night or alone in the country or wooded areas. Limiting mobility at night, the threat of rape limits where and when one works, making it harder for women to earn money. It makes solitude less possible and women more dependent on men and other women. It inhibits expressiveness, making women fearful of seeming "too friendly" or "sexy." It inhibits freedom of the eye, forcing a woman to worry about her safety over enjoying the view. Add to this the fears of women in abusive marriages. Others become exasperated with women who stay in abusive marriages, but the women (and researchers) know that it is dangerous leaving abusive men, many of whom stalk and kill wives who leave.

Perpetrators and Victims.   Most victims of sexual aggression in the United States are women and children, with 95% of the perpetrators being male. There are three times as many female child victims as male child victims (Russell & Bolen, 2000, pp. 150–151). Two-thirds of sexual assault and rape victims know their assailants. Women are more than twice as likely to be murdered by an intimate partner than by a stranger (Hatty, 2000, pp. 4–5). Low-income urban females between 16 and 19 years are the most likely to be sexually victimized, and their attackers are mostly young themselves. The majority of attacks are not reported to the police. While adult males in general are rarely rape victims, they are at risk in prison and other male institutions. Favored victims are gay and heterosexual youths forced by their attackers to play *girls* or *gal-boys*. Attackers are called *protectors* or *wolves*, names highlighting power positions in hierarchical relationships (Brownmiller, 1975). Children are at risk for sexual abuse in relationships with male authority figures, some related (fathers, uncles, brothers) and others not (teachers, police, priests). Rarely discussed are rapes by females on females and females on males. While the latter are rare, such rapes can be committed by a woman using a weapon to force a male into having intercourse with her and include the statutory rapes of underage males (Russell & Bolen, 2000, p. 23). There are also statutory rapes of underage females by adult women and the rape of women by their female partners.

Universal Phenomena or Cultural Variables?

Rape and sexual aggression occur everywhere in the world. However, they do not occur to the same extent in every society, nor are they everywhere judged the same. Social and cultural configurations account for much of the variation. Generalizations are difficult.

Egalitarian Societies.   In societies where resources are shared or accessible to able-bodied adults and where both sexes play important roles in the production of food and other necessities, sexual aggression is rare. Rape is reportedly rare among the Ituri forest foragers in Africa (Turnbull, 1961), the Kalahari desert foragers in southwest Africa (Lee, 1984; Marshall, 1976), and the Kaulong gardeners in New Guinea (Goodale, 1980). Rape is common in some tribal societies, especially those "faced with depleting food resources, migration, or other factors contributing to a pervasive sense that human beings are dependent on male efforts to control…natural forces" (Sanday, 1990a, p. 8). Among the Yanomamo and Mundurucu in South America, warfare is endemic and gang rape and the abduction of women in raids are common (Chagnon, 1997; Murphy & Murphy, 1974). Child sexual abuse is rarely reported for egalitarian societies. However, it is not uncommon for children to engage in sexual play, and for girls to be married and sexually active before they are 18 years old. Among the Tiwi in Australia, husbands instruct prepubescent wives in sexual techniques, deflowering them with their fingers and gradually moving on to full intercourse (Goodale, 1971). A striking variation is the Kaulong. The Kaulong believe sex drains a man's life force and is to be engaged in solely to have children—that it is females who aggressively seduce men into having sex with them. Should a man initiate courtship, it is considered rape, and in the past marriage or death was the expected result (Goodale, 1980, pp. 133–135).

Nonegalitarian Societies.   Sexual aggression is common in nonegalitarian societies. Violence against women is part of power complexes in which men use violence and sexual aggression to display their masculinity and induct younger men into masculine power roles.

Victims include women, children of both sexes, and men in subordinate ethnic groups, classes, or other statuses who suffer sexual abuse directly or indirectly as men who cannot protect their families from those in power. Again, there are differences among societies in levels and acceptance of sexual violence that are not the result of inconsistencies in measurement or reporting. Rape rates in the United States are among the highest in the world, even when compared with other nations that keep good statistics. Rates are three times higher in the United States than in England, Sweden, or West Germany, and 5–10 times higher than in France, Belgium, or Japan (Ellis, 1989, pp. 6–7). Theorists associate high levels of sexual aggression with America's violent society. There are many kinds of sexual aggression, however, and it is noteworthy that workplace sexual harassment is common in France and Japan (Louis, 1994) where gender roles have been slower to change than in the United States. For many reasons, the sexual abuse of children is poorly documented and widely denied in many societies. Nonetheless, studies done in the United States show that the sexual abuse of children occurs in every group, including African Americans, Anglo-Americans, Puerto Ricans, Asians, Jews, Seventh Day Adventists, and gays and lesbians (Fontes, 1995). Cultural variables exist in the family climates in which children can be abused, how the culture hinders disclosure, and how the culture plays a role in seeking or accepting social services or mental health assistance for victims and their families. Latina women, for example, enjoy more power at home than Anglo-Americans. However, Latina women are expected to be sexually passive and not to enjoy sex. Latina victims of rape and child sexual abuse are considered "whores" because they had sex outside marriage. Victim blaming silences most Latina victims (Fontes, 1995, pp. 41–43). Societal contexts also play a role. For example, an African American mother may not report the rape of her child because of her fears of police brutality against her group. Poverty makes participating in therapy sessions difficult or impossible. A child's vulnerability to sexual aggression may be increased—as with Asian children— by pressures to sacrifice their needs for their families and fears of reporting abuses by dominant persons within or outside their subculture such as elders or employers. Colonization and globalization bring cultures together, often violently and unequally. Cultures in which rape and wife-battery were rare see increases in violence and sexual aggression in the context of change and the violent edge of empire (Davies, 1994; Ferguson & Whitehead, 1992). The young migrate to towns to work in the new economies and find themselves in social environments where poverty and the absence of extended families encourage conjugal violence and new patterns of sexuality. Studies from Latin American countries show that more than 60% of rape survivors know their rapists—employers, boyfriends, spouses, or other family members (Cox, 1994, p. 122). Such women's situations are further complicated when their families force them to marry their rapists, an expectation in many Latin American countries. Domestic violence rates range in the vicinity of one in two women.

CAUSES AND CONSEQUENCES OF SEXUAL AGGRESSION

Folk theories of sexuality and aggression vary. In some cultures, women are temptresses entrapping men. In others, men are the aggressors held in check by chaste women and their male protectors. In yet other cultures, both sexes are seen as sexually aggressive and in need of rules to keep their sexuality in bounds, or both need help in firing up their sexuality to ensure a next generation. Many cultures are mixes of all of the above.

Sociobiology

Despite strong evidence attesting to cultural variability, there is a large literature that presumes that human males are sexual aggressors and human females are by nature sexually passive or very selective in their mating choices. Sociobiology is the perspective that widespread social behaviors are the result of natural selection and are to some degree genetically controlled. Sociobiologists do not suggest specific genes for rape, but do argue that genetic factors contribute to sexual aggression. Basing their theories on aggression in other species and the belief that evolutionarily ancient behaviors are embedded in our genes, they point to acts of forced copulation by male animals (Ellis, 1989, p. 45). Forced sex is not typical in most species, however, with young males more likely to try to copulate with resisting females. In *Men in Groups*, Tiger (1969) argued that males are genetically wired to bond with other males and to exhibit aggression and that females tend to be excluded from aggressive organizations and kept

separate in subordinate relationships with adult males who protect them when the group is attacked. Tiger (p. 190) believe that it is the lonely deviant individual who rapes. Crucial to a sociobiological approach is the notion that males enhance their reproductive success by copulating with many females and preventing other males from copulating with those same females. Females are thought to enhance their reproductive success by selecting the strongest male protector and engaging in an exclusive relationship with that male. Such arguments do not account for cultural diversity, the facts of rape, or the sexual behavior of female primates. Feminist critics remind us that for a genetic propensity for forced sex to have evolved, there must be a high probability that rapists impregnate their victims. Reviewing evidence on the risk of pregnancy from rape, Ellis (1989, pp. 46–49) found that 3% of rapes are reported to result in pregnancy. Rapes involving several rapists or child-abuse cases where there are repeat copulations over extended periods of time do result in higher incidences of pregnancy, 6.3% and 11.6% respectively. Data are lacking on whether or not such pregnancies might be aborted or result in increased infanticide in cultures where those options are available, and it is unclear what advantages accrue to rapist-fathers in cultures where a women's children belong to their "husbands" regardless of biological origin and where sexual predators are ostracized or executed for their acts. In *Female Choices*, the anthropologist Small (1993) shows that females and males are not that different in sexuality and mate choice, and there are variations among primates that make simple sociobiological arguments incapable of explaining human behavior. Small (p. 202) cites studies showing that nonhuman female primates are neither passive nor choosy when males do not restrict their behavior, and that over three-quarters of the world's cultures believe both male and female sex drives are strong. She also cites the Kinsey studies and *Playboy* and *Cosmopolitan* surveys showing that American women are sexually active, with their sexual interest increasing with age and their rates of extramarital sex approaching those of men. Small (p. 208) argues that it is male power that compromises female choices, with males convincing women that they are less sexual as a means of controlling female sexuality for their own ends.

Psychology of Sexual Aggression

Early psychologists saw rape as the act of degenerates and imbeciles. Freud and his disciples said little on the subject, other than noting female fears of rape and female rape fantasies. Freud (1896/1961) believed that humans are innately incestuous and for a time argued that female hysteria was the consequence of incest. However, the Victorian society that Freud worked in believed incest to be rare and the act of primitives. Freud repudiated his theory less than a year after proposing it (Meigs & Barlow, 2002). Wilhelm Reich briefly considered a "masculine ideology of rape" (Brownmiller, 1975, pp. 11–12), but it was latter-day feminists who explored the cultures and social conditions of rape and other sexual aggression. Even today, many psychologists treat sexual aggression as deviance, focusing on the reform or medication of perpetrators and on the consequences of sexual aggression for victims. Psychologists differ on causes, but most side with nature in the nature–nurture controversy, assuming dominance and sexual aggression to be natural male traits that are exaggerated in some males. Psychologists have done thousands of studies to determine sex differences that may be linked to various behaviors. In *Brain Sex*, evolutionary psychologists Moir and Jessell (1991) warn that there are biological facts of life that we cannot buck. Such "facts" include the views of sociobiologists E. O. Wilson and Richard Dawkins who believe that female exploitation begins in the fact that females perpetuate their genes by lengthy nurturance of embryos and that natural selection favors traits that encourage sexual hierarchy: physical strength, aggression, and promiscuity in men; caretaking and fidelity among women. Like sociobiologists, evolutionary psychologists ignore variations among human societies in patterns of aggression and nurturing and the fact that, in a wide cross-section of cultures, both male and female children exhibit nurturant behaviors (Whiting & Whiting, 1975). They also ignore psychological research demonstrating few sex-linked differences in brain structures and functions. In *The Psychology of Sex Differences*, Maccoby and Jacklin (1974) reviewed over 1200 works covering areas such as intellect, perception, learning, memory, cognitive styles, achievement motivation, self-concept, temperament, and power relationships. They found that boys in the primarily western cultures studied are slightly more aggressive than girls and excel slightly in visual–spatial ability, while girls tend to excel in verbal abilities. The differences were extremely small and unstable with a 1–5% variation in mathematical, verbal, and visual–spatial skills. Theories focusing on a hormonal (testosterone) basis for male dominance and aggression

also disregard cultural variation, certain forms of female aggression, and the fact that women have been aggressive in work situations as well as violent with their children and other family members. Given mounting cultural and sociological evidence, many psychologists now attribute American men's heightened aggression to the gender-specific ways in which parents teach children about the acceptability and uses of aggression.

Sociology and Feminism

The dominant social science explanation for rape and other sexual aggression is that they are social phenomena. Social feminist theories consider rape to be the result of traditions in which males dominate political and economic activities, and women tend to be treated in subservient and degrading ways (Brownmiller, 1975; Dworkin, 1981). Rape is seen as the use of sexuality to establish or maintain dominance and control of women, with some feminists seeing it as a pseudosexual act motivated out of desire for power and hatred for women rather than by sexual passion (Ellis, 1989). According to such theories, reducing rape requires political and economic equality for men and women. More pessimistic feminists believe that a reduction in disparities could trigger a backlash, as frustrated males use rape to reestablish their supremacy. Social stratification theories also see a connection between economic structures and the status of women. Engels theorized that the development of private property and men's desire to protect lines of inheritance resulted in the monogamous nuclear family and women's oppression and economic dependence on men. Anthropologists have faulted the latter view, arguing that it ignores precapitalist societies where property is owned and utilized by women, but where women do not oppress men, and that economic equality does not prevent political inequality. Working mothers burdened with childcare and double workdays have no time for politics, and women in tribal societies who provide most of the family subsistence are not thereby free of sexual aggression against them. The social learning theory of rape, in common with feminist theories, sees rape as aggression against women learned through mass media, rape myths, and violent pornography, and made less offensive by the desensitizing effects of frequent exposure to scenes of violence against women. Social learning theorists are less insistent than feminists that rape is a nonsexual act and more open to seeing both sociocultural traditions and individual experiences combining to propel males toward aggressive behavior toward women (Ellis, 1989, pp. 13–14).

Anthropology

Cultural anthropologists have long understood rape and incest from the perspective of the rules surrounding them, and the roles that rules play in structuring social life and making culture possible. More attention has been paid to how incest taboos promote "networks of social relations and economic exchange that are constitutive of the social world" than to the potential for incest taboos to protect the young against incestuous abuse (Meigs & Barlow, 2002, p. 39). The rape of an enemy's women is more often seen as a means by which leaders encourage bonds among groups of young males than as acts of physically and emotionally devastating aggression against females. Biosocial explanations are mixed, with some arguing that inbreeding avoidance is evolutionarily old and others that the learning of taboos and genetic transmission are not mutually exclusive alternatives. The latter view dovetails with the biosocial perspective that sexual aggression and male dominance are natural male traits. Social inequality between the sexes is more often offered as a primary reason for more aggression being committed against females than against males and for sociocultural variation. Arguing that a sexist mentality cannot be explained in terms of universal unconscious process in men and that, in many societies, demeaning women and negating the feminine in boys are not evident in the larger social ideology nor are they strategies for male bonding, Sanday (1990a, p. 183) points to the matrifocal Minangkabau of West Sumatra (Indonesia), among whom the most salient social bonds are with mothers and between brothers and sisters. Unlike the Mundurucu of South America, who use gang rape to dominate women (Murphy & Murphy, 1974), Minangkabau men do not display masculine invulnerability by oppression or sexually abusing women. Early cross-cultural studies of the relationship between fraternal interest groups and the frequency of rape support Sanday's argument, showing the frequency of rape to be higher in societies where power groups of related males use aggression to defend members' interests (Otterbein, 1979). The frequency of rape was highest in societies where there is no punishment for rape; something university administrators might take into consideration in efforts to curb fraternity rapes. In a pioneering article, Ortner (1974) explored the question of why women and their work are devalued in many cultures. Her answer was that all people value objects that are under human control (culture) more than unregulated and frightening events such as childbearing that are closer to nature than culture.

Anthropologists were quick to challenge the universality of the notion that female is to male as nature is to culture, and the idea that "nature" and "female" are less under cultural control than the things that men do and believe. The articles in *Nature, Culture and Gender* (MacCormack & Strathern, 1980) disprove women's universal lower status and association with nature. That culture won in this debate is reflected in the rapid growth of the anthropology of gender and a focus on male and female ideologies as key elements in explanations of sexual inequality and aggression. A more reflexive anthropology reveals that many early studies of societies in which males allegedly dominate females were biased by male anthropologists with little access to or interest in what women did or had to say for themselves (Goodale, 1971; Weiner, 1976).

METHODOLOGICAL CONTROVERSY

Reliable cross-cultural comparisons and making sense of particular national statistics are nearly impossible given the wide variations among and within societies in definitions of rape and other sexual aggression. Government and nongovernment sampling techniques vary significantly, and survivors' reluctance or inability to disclose incidences of rape or other sexual violence contribute to compromised data collection and lower than actual rates.

The Law and Definitions of Rape

In the feminist classic *Against Our Will*, Brownmiller (1975, p. 18) declares that a female definition of rape can be contained in a single sentence: "If a woman chooses not to have intercourse with a specific man and the man chooses to proceed against her will, that is a criminal act of rape." While this may suffice in cases of bride-capture or the rape of conscious women, it does not protect children, men, or victims who are unable to protest acts of sexual aggression against themselves. Many legal definitions of rape are narrower. The Czech legal code defines rape as the use of violence, the threat of immediate violence, or the misuse of a woman's inability to defend herself to force her to consent to sexual intercourse (Siklova & Hradlikova, 1994, p. 112). Not protected by this definition are men and victims of domestic and child sexual abuse and violence.

FBI's Definition of Forcible Rape.

The definition of forcible rape used by the U.S. Federal Bureau of Investigation (FBI) excludes many victims of rape and sexual abuse:

The carnal knowledge of a female forcibly and against her will. Assaults or attempts to commit rape by force or threat of force are also included; however, statutory rape (without force) and other sex offences are excluded (Federal Bureau of Investigation, 1998, p. 25).

With this definition, children and adolescents who are forcibly raped qualify for inclusion in FBI rape statistics. As Russell and Bolen (2000, p. 21) point out, since carnal knowledge is understood to refer to penile–vaginal sexual intercourse, the FBI's definition excludes oral and anal penetration and penetration when a woman is unable to consent because she is unconscious, drugged, or incapacitated. It also excludes forcible rape by males on males, females on females, and females by males. Statutory rape is intercourse with a female who is below the age of consent. Although the inhabitants of different states are subject to state and not federal rape laws, the FBI's definition of rape determines which cases are included in their national crime statistics.

Searles and Berger's More Inclusive Definition.

Encouraged by feminists in the 1970s and 1980s, state level reforms include redefinitions of rape in line with the more inclusive definition of rape proposed by Searles and Berger (1987, p. 26):

Rape is defined as nonconsensual sexual penetration of an adolescent or adult obtained by physical force, by threat of bodily harm or when a victim is incapable of giving consent because of mental illness, mental retardation, or intoxication. Included are attempts to commit rape by force or threat of bodily harm.

This definition omits child rape, but uses sex-neutral terms and covers domestic rape and the inability to protest. States still disagree on how to define rape and its victims. In 1987, the cut-off age for statutory rape varied from 13 to 18 years with 16 years being the age of consent in 61% of states; 26% of states defined rape as sexual assault involving penetration, and another 20% as sexual assault that includes sexual touching as

well as penetration. Such differences make statistical comparisons impossible (Russell & Bolen, 2000, p. 23).

Other Definitions. Researchers disagree over the sex-neutral terms in the Searles and Berger definition. Koss and Harvey (1991) argue that rape is applicable to men only when penetration occurs. They believe that an assault by a woman using a weapon to force a man to have sex with her should be disqualified as rape because she is the one to be penetrated. Russell and Bolen (2000, p. 23) disagree, asserting that the full range of rape offenses should be included regardless of how rare women's rape of men is, pointing out that women can rape men anally with fingers, hands, or foreign objects. Researchers also differ over the use of the term *sexual assault* instead of or in combination with rape. Many definitions of sexual assault include less severe nonpenetrative acts, such as forcible touching of the genitals, than are covered by the Searles and Berger definition. Russell and Bolen argue that lumping rape with sexual assault results in the noncomparability of survey findings.

Sampling Techniques and Methodological Limitations

Variations in quantification and sampling techniques, along with survivors' reluctance to report sexual abuses, also challenge our ability to compare studies. The FBI's *Uniform Crime Reports* give the number of rape incidents that are reported each year and the rate per 100,000 inhabitants in the United States. A number of reported rapes are "unfounded" by police every year as "false" or "baseless." No explanation is given for why many more reported rapes are unfounded by the police than other major crimes of violence. Russell and Bolen (2000, p. 49) suggest that some policemen subscribe to the same rape myths as the general populace. One such myth is the belief that most reported rapes are invented by women to protect their reputations. In recognition of the fact that most crimes are not reported, a second annual measure is the Bureau of Justice Statistics National Crime Victimization Survey (NCS) to assess the extent and character of criminal victimization in the United States. A representative sample of male and female household residents aged 12 or older are interviewed. The NCS's 1974 San Francisco incidence rate of 5.0 per 1,000 female residents was higher than the FBI's 1978 San Francisco incidence rate of 1.7 per 1,000 female residents. Russell, avoiding some limitations of both federal surveys, found an incidence rate of 36.7 per 1,000 female residents in her 1978 study, more than seven times higher than the NCS rate. Some of the methodological differences that resulted in Russell's obtaining a truer picture of the San Francisco rape incidence include collecting qualitative data on how respondents understood the questions, using rape-appropriate methods such as face-to-face interviews, pretesting interview schedules, not farming out the fieldwork to other professionals, rejecting victim-blaming interviewer applicants, and conveying a non-victim-blaming attitude by the interviewers (Russell & Bolen, 2000, pp. 41–46). Survivor reluctance to disclose sexual abuse is a universal problem for researchers. West (1998a, p. 163) found that, while partner violence is as prevalent among gays as it is among heterosexuals, many gays are afraid to report incidents to the police who, for their part, do not count same-sex violence in domestic violence reports. Russell and Bolen (2000, p. 27) list 13 factors discouraging women from reporting their rape experiences to the police. The top reasons were survivors' concerns about their families knowing that they had been raped, people blaming them for the attack, and people outside their families knowing about the rape. Many minority women do not report attackers who belong to their ethnic group out of a sense of loyalty. Minority women raped by men of the majority culture may opt not to report because they anticipate no justice from a racist system. In post-Communist Czechloslovakia (Siklova & Hradilkova, 1994), women do not report rape for many of the same reasons, including distrust of the authorities and the social damage inflicted on victims in public trials.

Backlash Against Feminists, Real and Imagined

In the 1970s, feminists and rape survivors spoke out about their experiences, challenging any notion that rapists and child molesters are a small group of pathological males. A backlash erupted against their claims that the United States suffered an epidemic of rape. Ignoring the facts that not all those who study sexual aggression are feminists or women, and not all feminists exclude violence against males from their studies, critics accused researchers of being man-hating females assaulting American society and encouraging sexual assault by angering men. Paglia (1992, p. 63), who criticizes feminists for not seeing "what is for men the eroticism or fun element in rape, especially the wild, infectious delirium of gang rape," writes for a public who would rather hear that sexual violence is the work of predators and not endemic to American society.

MASCULINITIES, VIOLENCE, AND CULTURE

Locating sexual aggression within particular political and cultural contexts reveals the close connection between high levels of sexual aggression and societies organized around masculine violence and hierarchy. The more complex a violent society, the more sexual aggression and other forms of violence will also be complex in victims and expression.

Engendering Violence

In *Masculinities, Violence, and Culture*, Hatty (2000) notes that violence is not a deviant act, it is a conforming one, and that violence against women is part of a larger context of normative male violence. In the United States, cultural ideals promote violence in the service of the masculine self, preserving individuality and forestalling fusion with the dangerous nonself, the other, the feminine (Hatty, 2000, pp. 10–11). Sexual aggression and violence are means of social control, hierarchy, and inequality. Domestic violence, rape, sexual slavery, and sexual harassment, whether in the United States, Zimbabwe, or the Philippines, are located in relationships of power, dominance, and privilege (Davies, 1994). Such relationships are supported by hegemonic masculinity— unattainable by most men and by definition all women. Brownmiller (1975, p. 309) claimed that women are trained to be rape victims. Examining the popular and "scientific" cultural imagination of American society, we find that violence is masculine and acceptance and nurturance feminine. Women are told that they do not bond naturally and that they are in competition for high-status men. Sadly, researchers have found that violence against women is more prevalent when alliances between women are weak, and alliances between men are valued and strong (Hatty, 2000, pp. 55–56; Smuts, 1992). If women are taught to be rape victims, the opposite is true for men. Surveys in the United States show that many males might commit rape if they thought they would not be caught or punished (Ellis, 1989, p. 6). Among high-school boys in Los Angeles, almost half believed it is acceptable to force a girl to have sex if she sexually teases her date. The culture of violence has many training grounds, the more effective being sports, the military, and the movies. In organized sports, boys learn a "masculine" ambivalence to intimacy and an affinity for instrumental relationships (Messner, 1990). In all three, men's bodies are presented as hard, dangerous, and dominant. In adventure films and Westerns, men are portrayed as fearless discoverers and builders of society—men at the edge (Hatty, 2000). Female characters like voluptuous hard-bodied gun-toting archeologist Lara Croft and Charlie's Angels mimic the invulnerability of the masculine mystique, but their rarity in film and life exaggerates women's alleged softness and passivity. When real women commit violence, it carries cultural shock value by going against the cultural imagination.

Violence and the Other

Violence in America and other complex societies has many inflections. Gender and race combined in stereotypes supporting sexual aggression against female slaves and Native American women, while myths of the voracious sexual appetites of African American men and other minorities condoned mob justice in the American South. Congolese leaders and soldiers cast the rape of Belgian women in the newly independent Congo as acts of vengeance against Belgian men rather than sexual assault (Brownmiller, 1975, pp. 138–139). The link between sexuality, gender stratification, and violence against the other is clear in aggression against homosexuals and other sexual anomalies in Western societies. In "What Price Independence?", Weitz (1984) explores social reactions to lesbians, spinsters, widows, and nuns. Weitz (p. 455) argues that as more women live lives independent of men, men see their power in society threatened and all unmarried women face a risk of stigmatization and punishment, one punishment being rape. Sanctions against male homosexuality are stronger because gay males appear to reject masculine values and privileges. While gender diversity is accepted in many societies (Nanda, 2000), in places where patriarchal gender systems operate sexual diversity is expressed as those who penetrate and those who are penetrated. In the Brazilian sex/gender system, men may penetrate both male and female bodies without their virility or heterosexuality

being challenged (Nanda, 2000, pp. 44–45). Men who prefer same-sex sex do not regard themselves and are not regarded as homosexuals as long as they are the penetrators. This structure mirrors prison hierarchies where victims of prison rape are "womanized" and perpetrators valorized as "double-males" regardless of sexual preference (Brownmiller, 1975, pp. 257–268).

The Politics of Masculinity

Gender hierarchies extend to the level of the nation and beyond. In *Nationalisms and Sexualities*, Parker, Russo, Sommer, and Yeager (1992) describe eroticized imaginary communities in which *love of country* is expressed as comradeship or brotherhood with a willingness to defend the homeland—often feminized as the Motherland—against outsiders and "improper" insiders who threaten a nation's stability. Historically, women's movements have challenged the inequalities concealed in such visions of common nationhood. In anticolonial struggles, feminist interests have been sacrificed to the cause of liberation. With independence, male leaders have often strived to keep "their women" pure and more conforming than the perceived man-threatening and promiscuous western feminists or, in some cases, to make their women more educated and sophisticated so as to fit in with the West. Either way, the politics of masculinity and nationalism require women to conform to versions of ideal femininity that support men's relations with one another. Women and men who do not conform risk sexual abuse and other violence. In Iran, reformers promoting capitalist development and nuclear families with educated and employable women recalled Zorastrian traditions that accorded women a high status and many of the same freedoms of men (Jayawardena, 1986, p. 15). In 1979, despite women's participation in the Islamic populist movement and the left's promise of continued equality, Iranian women were rendered dependent minors by laws enacted to make gender relations as different as possible from gender norms in the West (Moghadam, 1992, pp. 427–430). With a new government, men attacked women seen in public without the veil, calling them "whores, bourgeois degenerates and un-Islamic." While few countries have criminalized feminism, anger against liberated women can be seen in the growth of the international sex and mail-order bride industries. Power and gender relations radiate across the globe as men from wealthy countries like Germany or Japan demonstrate their masculinity and privilege on young sex slaves in Southeast Asia who will never be given medals for serving their nations' economies. Young women seeking work in foreign lands suffer human rights violations, rape, and physical assault. In the years following Kuwait's liberation in 1991, 2,000 women domestic servants from Sri Lanka, India, Bangladesh, and the Philippines fled abusive Kuwaiti employers (Beasley, 1994, p. 53).

SEXUAL AGGRESSION IN OCEANIA

Violence against women and children is a development issue in many Pacific islands nations. Pacific islanders are reluctant to report such crimes to the police, preferring to solve problems peaceably by bringing the families of victims and offenders together and exchanging custom money, food, and Christian forgiveness. In the words of one Solomon Islander, "In custom days, a man who played around with a child would be beaten up. Then his tribe would put him into exile. Now, because of Christianity that kind of thinking has changed" (Davies, 1994, p. 98). Whether or not Christianity aids the cover-up of child sex abuse, many women fear coming forward, citing threats from offenders and beatings by husbands and male relatives who wish to avoid prosecution. Drawing on her experience as a Principal Project Officer for the Papua New Guinea Law Commission (1986–1990), running a national program on violence against women, Bradley (1994) argues that "development can be dangerous to women's health." While wife-beating and sexual abuse are not new in Papua New Guinea, she argues that the severity of wife-beating and other violence against women is greater in towns, where alcohol is readily available and women are more dependent on their husbands with fewer avenues of escape or sources of support than village women have. Women's frustrations are captured in Papua New Guinean Mary To Liman's "Bia botol longlong" and Solomon Islander Jully Sipolo's "A man's world" (Sipolo, 1981; To Liman, 1979; Zimmer-Tamakoshi, 1995).

The Sexual Politics of Rape and Domestic Violence in Papua New Guinea

Alarmed by increased violence against women, in 1982 the Papua New Guinea government—in an unprecedented

move for a developing country—directed its Law Reform Commission to investigate domestic violence. Resulting publications revealed that a majority of Papua New Guinean wives have been hit by their husbands, most more than once a year, with urban wives suffering a higher level of violence than rural women (Toft, 1985, 1986a, 1986b; Toft & Bonnell, 1985; Zimmer-Tamakoshi, 2001). Papua New Guinea has a reported rape rate of 45 rapes per 100,000 persons, similar to the U.S. rate of 35 per 100,000 persons (Dinnen, 1993; Herman, 1984), although this is less systematically researched. Many of the rapes, counted as single incidents in police reports, were committed by gangs. Like everywhere else, rapes go unreported, especially those committed by victims' partners or relatives (Dinnen, 1996; Finkelhor & Yllo, 1985; Russell & Bolen, 2000; Toft, 1985, 1986a; Zimmer, 1990). While traditional attitudes contribute to the acceptance of violence, research shows that the pressures of development and inequality fuel violence against women. Men in town fear their wives' potential independence and their own uncertain situations. Urban life-styles, including alcohol abuse and reduced social support networks, adversely affect male–female relations. Increased eroticism and the breakdown of old taboos place unfamiliar demands on couples (Bradley, 1994; Rosi & Zimmer-Tamakoshi, 1993). In several publications (Rosi & Zimmer-Tamakoshi, 1993; Zimmer-Tamakoshi, 1993, 1995, 2001), I have explored a political dimension in order to understand better violence against women in Papua New Guinea and elsewhere in the Pacific. While individuals experience the dislocations of change and development, sex and class politics also fuel sexual and domestic violence. In Papua New Guinea, only a small number of men and women enjoy an elite life-style. With the male leadership under pressure from the grassroots to bring about an economic miracle, elite women are targets of disaffection from both the lower classes and men in their own class. Educated women have opportunities for expression and independence not shared by the grassroots and often rivaling their male peers. Violence against women is rife among the elite, and is partly motivated by class and sexual tensions that paint elite females as symbols of all that is wrong with today's society. In a weak state such as Papua New Guinea, men who want to can assert their dominance over women with little fear of resistance as long as there is widespread envy or fear of those women, and state officials charged with protecting them are unable or unwilling to do so. Rape and domestic violence are not traditional in every New Guinea society

(Goodale, 1980), but gang rape and mutilation of women's genitals were ways men "used to" punish errant wives and daughters (Zimmer, 1990; Zimmer-Tamakoshi, 2001), and attacks against the enemies' women in warfare were common. In some areas, men's cults celebrated masculinity and new entrants with the sexual abuse of widows and other women without male protection (Bradley, 1985). Gang rape and the achievement of manhood have been linked not only in New Guinea (Herdt, 1982) but in many cultural contexts such as crack dealers in New York City (Bourgois, 2001) and the world over (Gilmore, 1990). Today, initiates into Papua New Guinea's urban *raskol* gangs replicate such attacks in gang rapes, the most prestigious being the rape of women of European descent or their Papua New Guinean analogs—elite women. While violence against women occurs throughout Papua New Guinea, the intersection of elite and urban sexual politics with nationalist and class interests and rhetoric targets women of privilege. Holding elite and educated women— *meri universiti*—responsible for all that is wrong is a political maneuver to ease class and ethnic tensions in Papua New Guinea's culturally diverse society and a satisfying fiction for Papua New Guineans who feel left out of "progress" and "development." Unlike their male counterparts, who come from all parts of the nation, Papua New Guinea's small class of elite women come from coastal and island areas that have been long involved with the outside world. Elite women are more likely than their male peers to come from educated and economically privileged backgrounds, and are, as a group, more western in demeanor and appearance than most Papua New Guinean women. Increasing the distance between elite men and women, some elite women have married foreigners or foregone marriage to avoid the violence that mars many Papua New Guinean unions. Examples include two of the three women ever to sit as members of National Parliament and a former president of the National Council of Women. Elite women's marriage to expatriates embarrasses male leaders as most Papua New Guineans see them as signs of elite immorality and elite men's inability to control their women. Attempts to limit elite women's freedoms include public censure, violence, the refusal of citizenship rights to foreign spouses, and threats to disenfranchise the children of mixed marriages. Although, in the mid-1980s, a male-dominated government supported the Law Reform Commission studies and a public awareness campaign on violence against women, politicians soon lost interest as economic and other issues pushed to the forefront of public concern. The shift was brutally apparent in 1987 when an all-male Parliament booed lawyer Rose Kekedo and other women from the floor when they tried to present the Law Reform Commission's interim report on domestic violence. Women's groups continue to wage the campaign against violence against women, but victories have been few. Female leaders throughout the Pacific are beginning to realize that half the battle is to get other women to join them in the fight. Vanuatu poet Grace Mera Molisa spoke for women throughout the region in "Delightful acquiescence" (Molisa, 1989, p. 24):

> Half of Vanuatu
> is still colonized
> by her self.
>
> Any woman
> showing promise
> is clouted
> into acquiescence.

REFERENCES

Beasley, M. (1994). Maltreatment of maids in Kuwait. In M. Davies (Ed.), *Women and violence: Realities and responses worldwide* (pp. 53–59). London: Zed Books.

Beneke, T. (1982). *Men on rape.* New York: St Martin's Press.

Boswell, A. A., & Spade, J. Z. (1996). Fraternities and collegiate rape culture: Why are some fraternities more dangerous places for women? *Gender and Society, 10*(2), 133–147.

Bourgois, P. (2001). In search of masculinity: Violence, respect, and sexuality among Puerto Rican crack dealers in East Harlem. In M. S. Kimmel & M. A. Messner (Eds.), *Men's lives* (5th ed., pp. 42–55). Boston: Allyn & Bacon. (Reprinted from *The British Journal of Criminology, 36,* 412–427.)

Bradley, C. (1985). Attitudes and practices relating to marital violence among the Tolai of East New Britain. In S. Toft (Ed.), *Domestic violence in Papua New Guinea* (Monograph No. 3, pp. 32–71). Port Moresby: Papua New Guinea Law Reform Commission.

Bradley, C. (1994). Why male violence against women is a development issue: Reflections from Papua New Guinea. In M. Davies (Ed.), *Women and violence: Realities and responses worldwide* (pp. 10–26). London: Zed Books.

Brownmiller, S. (1975). *Against our will: Men, women and rape.* New York: Simon & Schuster.

Cameron, D. (1992). That's entertainment?: Jack the Ripper and the selling of sexual violence. In J. Radford & D. E. H. Russell (Eds.), *Femicide: The politics of woman killing* (pp. 17–19). New York: Twayne. (Reprinted from *Trouble and Strife,* Spring 1988, 17–19.)

Campaign Free Tibet. (1994). We have no rights, not even our bodies. In M. Davies (Ed.), *Women and violence: Realities and responses worldwide* (pp. 133–136). London: Zed Books. (Adapted and reprinted from a report compiled for Campaign Free Tibet.)

Chagnon, N. A. (1997). *Yanomamo* (5th ed.). Fort Worth, TX: Harcourt Brace College.

Cox, E. S. (1994). Gender violence and women's health in Central America. In M. Davies (Ed.), *Women and violence: Realities and responses worldwide* (pp. 118–132). London: Zed Books.

Davies, M. (1994). Child sexual abuse: Why the silence must be broken—Notes from the Pacific region. In M. Davies (Ed.), *Women and violence: Realities and responses worldwide* (pp. 97–110). London: Zed Books.

Dinnen, S. (1993). Big men, small men and invisible women. *Australian and New Zealand Journal of Criminology, 26,* 19–34.

Dinnen, S. (1996). Law, order, and state. In L. Zimmer-Tamakoshi (Ed.), *Modern Papua New Guinea* (pp. 333–350). Kirksville, MO: Thomas Jefferson University Press.

Drakulic, S. (1994). The rape of women in Bosnia. In M. Davies (Ed.), *Women and violence: Realities and responses worldwide* (pp. 176–181). London: Zed Books.

Dworkin, A. (1981). *Pornography: Men possessing women.* New York: Perigee.

Ellis, L. (1989). *Theories of rape: Inquiries into the causes of sexual aggression.* New York: Hemisphere.

Federal Bureau of Investigation. (1998). *Implementing the national incident-based reporting system.* Website: http://www.nibrs.search.org/frmain.htm

Ferguson, R. B., & Whitehead, N. L. (1992). The violent edge of empire. In R. B. Ferguson & N. L. Whitehead (Eds.), *War in the tribal zone: Expanding states and indigenous warfare* (pp. 1–30). Santa Fe, NM: School of American Research Press.

Finkelhor, D. (1994). Current information on the scope and nature of child sexual abuse. *Future of Children, 4*(2), 31–53.

Finkelhor, D., & Yllo, K. (1985). *License to rape: Sexual abuse of wives.* New York: Holt, Rinehart, & Winston.

Fontes, L.A. (1995). Sexual abuse in nine North American cultures: Treatment and prevention. Thousand Oaks, CA: Sage.

Freud, S. (1961). The aetiology of hysteria. In J. Strachey (Ed. & Trans.), *The standard edition of the complete psychological works of Sigmund Freud* (Vol. 3, pp. 189–221). London: Hogarth Press. (Original work published 1896.)

Gilmore, D. D. (1990). *Manhood in the making.* New Haven, CT: Yale University Press.

Giuffre, P. A., & Williams, C. L. (1994). Boundary lines: Labeling sexual harassment in restaurants. *Gender and Society, 8,* 378–401.

Goodale, J. C. (1971). *Tiwi wives: A study of the women of Melville Island, North Australia.* Seattle: University of Washington Press.

Goodale, J. C. (1980). Gender, sexuality and marriage: A Kaulong model of nature and culture. In C. MacCormack & M. Strathern (Eds.), *Nature, culture and gender* (pp. 119–142). Cambridge, U.K.: Cambridge University Press.

Gutek, B. A. (1985). *Sex and the workplace.* San Francisco: Jossey-Bass.

Hatty, S. E. (2000). *Masculinities, violence, and culture* (Sage Series on Violence Against Women). Thousand Oaks, CA: Sage.

Herdt, G. H. (1982). *Rituals of manhood: Male initiation in Papua New Guinea.* Berkeley: University of California Press.

Herman, D. (1984). The rape culture. In J. Freeman (Ed.), *Women: A feminist perspective* (3rd ed., pp. 20–38). Mountain View, CA: Mayfield.

Jasinski, J. L., & Williams, L. M. (Eds.), (1998). *Partner violence: A comprehensive review of 20 years of research.* Thousand Oaks, CA: Sage.

Jayawardena, K. (1986). *Feminism and nationalism in the Third World.* London: Zed Books.

Kantor, G. K., & Jasinski, J. L. (1998). Dynamics and risk factors in partner violence. In J. L. Jasinski & L. M. Williams (Eds.), *Partner violence: A comprehensive review of 20 years of research* (pp. 1–43). Thousand Oaks, CA: Sage.

Koss, M. P., Gidycz, C. A., & Wisniewski, N. (1987). The scope of rape: Incidence and prevalence of sexual aggression and victimization in a national sample of higher education students. *Journal of Consulting and Clinical Psychology, 55*(2), 162–170.

Koss, M. P., Goodman, L. A., Browne, A., Fitzgerald, L. F., Keita, G. P., & Russo, N. F. (1994). *No safe haven: Male violence against women at home, at work, and in the community.* Washington, DC: American Psychological Association.

Koss, M. P., & Harvey, M. R. (1991). *The rape victim: Clinical and community interventions* (2nd ed.). Newbury Park, CA: Sage.

Labelle, B. (1980). *Snuff:* The ultimate in woman hating. In L. Lederer (Ed.), *Take back the night: Women on pornography* (pp. 272–276). New York: Morrow.

Lee, R. (1984). *The Dobe !Kung.* New York: Holt, Rinehart & Winston.

Louis, M. (1994). Sexual harassment at work in France: What stakes for feminists? In M. Davies (Ed.), *Women and violence: Realities and responses worldwide* (pp. 85–97). London: Zed Books.

Maccoby, E. E., & Jacklin, C. N. (1974). *The psychology of sex differences.* Stanford, CA: Stanford University Press.

MacCormack, C., & Strathern, M. (Eds.), (1980). *Nature, culture and gender.* Cambridge, U.K.: Cambridge University Press.

Mahoney, P., & Williams, L. M. (1998). Sexual assault in marriage: Prevalence, consequences, and treatment of wife rape. In J. L. Jasinski & L. M. Williams (Eds.), *Partner violence: A comprehensive review of 20 years of research* (pp. 113–162). Thousand Oaks, CA: Sage.

Marshall, L. (1976). *The !Kung of Nyae Nyae.* Cambridge, MA: Harvard University Press.

Meigs, A., & Barlow, K. (2002). Beyond the taboo: Imagining incest. *American Anthropologist, 104*(1), 38–49.

Messner, M. A. (1990). Boyhood, organized sports, and the construction of masculinities. *Journal of Contemporary Ethnography, 18*(4), 416–444.

Moghadam, V. M. (1992). Revolution, Islam and women: Sexual politics in Iran and Afghanistan. In A. Parker, M. Russo, D. Sommer, & P. Yaeger (Eds.), *Nationalisms and sexualities* (pp. 424–446). New York: Routledge.

Moir, A., & Jessell D. (1991). *Brain sex: The real difference between men and women.* Dell, New York: Carol Publishing Group.

Molisa, G. M. (1989). *Black Stone II.* Port Vila, Vanuatu. Block Stone Publications and Vanuato University of Pacific Centre.

Murphy, Y., & Murphy, R. F. (1974). *Women of the forest.* New York: Columbia University Press.

Nanda, S. (2000). *Gender diversity: Cross-cultural variations.* Prospect Heights, IL: Waveland Press.

Ortner, S. B. (1974). Is female to male as nature is to culture? In M. Rosaldo & L. Lamphere (Eds.), *Women, culture, and society* (pp. 67–87). Palo Alto, CA: Stanford University Press.

Otterbein, K. F. (1979). A cross-cultural study of rape. *Aggressive Behavior, 5,* 425–435.

Paglia, C. (1992). *Sex, art, and American culture.* New York: Vintage Books.

Parker, A., Russo, M., Sommer, D., & Yeager, P. (Eds.), (1992). *Nationalisms and sexualities.* New York: Routledge.

Perpinan, M. S., Sr. (1994). Militarism and the sex industry in the Philippines. In M. Davies (Ed.), *Women and violence: Realities and responses worldwide* (pp. 149–152). London: Zed Books.

Radford, J., & Russell, D. E. H. (Eds.), (1992). *Femicide: The politics of woman killing.* New York: Twayne.

Rosi, P., & Zimmer-Tamakoshi, L. (1993). Love and marriage among the educated elite in Port Moresby. In R. Marksbury (Ed.), *The business of marriage: Transformations in Oceanic matrimony* (pp. 175–204). Pittsburgh, PA: The University of Pittsburgh Press.

Russell, D. E. H. (1998). *Dangerous relationships: Pornography, misogyny, and rape.* Thousand Oaks, CA: Sage.

Russell, D. E. H., & Bolen, R. M. (2000). *The epidemic of rape and child sexual abuse in the United States.* Thousand Oaks, CA: Sage.

Sanday, P. R. (1990a). Androcentric and matrifocal gender representations in Minangkabau ideology. In P. R. Sanday & R. G. Goodenough (Eds.), *Beyond the second sex.* Philadelphia: University of Pennsylvania Press.

Sanday, P. R. (1990b). *Fraternity gang rape: Sex, brotherhood, and privilege on campus.* New York: New York University Press.

Searles, P., & Berger, R. J. (1987). The current status of rape reform legislation: An examination of state statutes. *Women's Rights Law Reporter, 10*(1), 25–43.

Sedlak, A. J., & Broadhurst, D. D. (1996). *Third national incidence study of child abuse and neglect: Final report.* Washington, DC: U.S. Department of Health and Human Services.

Siklova, J., & Hradilkova, J. (1994). Women and violence in postcommunist Czechoslovakia. In M. Davies (Ed.), *Women and violence: Realities and responses worldwide* (pp. 111–117). London: Zed Books.

Sipolo, J. (1981). *Civilized girl.* Suva, Fiji: Mana.

Small, M. F. (1993). *Female choices: Sexual behavior of female primates.* Ithaca, NY: Cornell University Press.

Smuts, B. B. (1992). Male aggression against women: An evolutionary perspective. *Human Nature, 3*(1), 1–44.

Tiger, L. (1969). *Men in groups.* New York: Vintage.

Toft, S. (1985). Marital violence in Port Moresby: Two urban case studies. In S. Toft (Ed.), *Domestic violence in Papua New Guinea* (Monograph No. 3, pp. 14–31). Port Moresby: Papua New Guinea Law Reform Commission.

Toft, S. (1986a). *Domestic violence in urban Papua New Guinea* (Occasional Paper No. 19). Port Moresby: Papua New Guinea Law Reform Commission.

Toft, S. (1986b). *Marriage in Papua New Guinea* (Monograph No. 4). Port Moresby: Papua New Guinea Law Reform Commission.

Toft, S., & Bonnell, S. (Eds.). (1985). *Marriage and domestic violence in rural Papua New Guinea* (Occasional Paper No. 18). Port Moresby: Papua New Guinea Law Reform Commission.

To Liman, M. (1979, October 3). *Bia botol longlong.* Ondobondo Poster Poem.

Turnbull, C. M. (1961). *The forest people: A study of the Pygmies of the Congo.* New York: Simon & Schuster.

Weiner, A. B. (1976). *Women of value, men of renown: New perspectives in Trobriand exchange.* Austin, TX: University of Texas Press.

Weitz, R. (1984). What price independence? Social reactions to lesbians, spinsters, widows, and nuns. In J. Freeman (Ed.), *Women: A feminist perspective* (3rd ed., pp. 454–464). Palo Alto, CA: Mayfield.

West, C. M. (1998a). Leaving a second closet: Outing partner violence in same-sex couples. In J. L. Jasinski & L. M. Williams (Eds.), *Partner violence: A comprehensive review of 20 years of research* (pp. 163–183). Thousand Oaks, CA: Sage.

West, C. M. (1998b). Lifting the "political gag order": Breaking the silence around partner violence in ethnic minority families. In J. L. Jasinski & L. M. Williams (Eds.), *Partner violence: A comprehensive review of 20 years of research* (pp. 184–209). Thousand Oaks, CA: Sage.

Whiting, J. W. M., & Whiting, B. B. (1975). *Children of six cultures: A psycho-cultural analysis.* Cambridge, MA: Harvard University Press.

Wyatt, G. E. (1985). The sexual abuse of Afro-American and White-American women in childhood. *Child Abuse and Neglect, 9,* 507–519.

Zimmer, L. J. (1990). Sexual exploitation and male dominance in Papua New Guinea. *Human Sexuality* [Special issue]. *Point, 14,* 250–267.

Zimmer-Tamakoshi, L. (1993). Nationalism and sexuality in Papua New Guinea. *Pacific Studies, 16*(4), 61–97.

Zimmer-Tamakoshi, L. (1995). Passion, poetry and cultural politics in the South Pacific. In R. Feinberg & L. Zimmer-Tamakoshi (Eds.), *Politics of culture in the Pacific islands* [Special issue]. *Ethnology, 34*(2 + 3), 113–128.

Zimmer-Tamakoshi, L. (2001). "Wild pigs and dog men": Rape and domestic violence as women's issues in Papua New Guinea. In C. B. Brettell & C. F. Sargent (Eds.), *Gender in cross-cultural perspective* (pp. 565–580). Upper Saddle River, NJ: Prentice-Hall.

Sex and Gender in the World's Cultures

Abaluyia

Maria G. Cattell

ALTERNATIVE NAMES

Abaluyia are also known as Baluyia or Luyia, or by the alternative spelling Abaluhya/Luhya. During the colonial occupation, the British called them Bantu Kavirondo or WaKavirondo—derogatory terms today. Abaluyia is a social and political identity claimed by 17 Kenyan ethnic communities: Bukusu (Kitosh, Vugusu), Idakho (Idaxo), Isukha (Isuxa), Kabras, Khayo, Kisa, Marachi, Maragoli (Avalogoli, Logoli), Marama, Nyala, Nyole (Nyore), Samia, Tachoni, Tiriki, Tsotso, and Wanga (Bahanga). (Songa, in Nyanza Province, speak a Luyia dialect but claim a Luo identity.) The Bantu prefix "ba" or "aba" (or "ava," indicating the unvoiced "b") signifies "people"; for example, Babukusu are "Bukusu people," and so also with Banyala, Bamarachi, Abawanga, and the rest. (Ba + Idakho or Isukha produces Bidakho and Bisukha.) One person is indicated by the prefix "mu" or "omu," as in Mukhayo or Omukhayo. Place is indicated by the prefix "bu," as in Busamia, and language by "lu," as in Luluyia or Lutiriki.

LOCATION

Abaluyia numbered around 3 million in 1999. Kenya's Western Province, the home area for most Abaluyia, is crossed by the Equator. It is bordered on the south by Lake Victoria, on the west by Uganda and the Sio (Suo) River, and on the east by the Kenya Highlands. The northern slopes of Mount Elgon (Masaba) define northern Luyialand.

Western Province is a land of steep hills, minor scarps, and undulating valleys cutting across the high plateaus of the downwarped Lake Victoria basin. Elevations range from about 1,100 m on the shores of Lake Victoria to about 4,300 m at Mount Elgon. Soils are of high to medium fertility and in most years rainfall is adequate for agriculture, though droughts are frequent and even in good growing years there may be a "hungry season" between harvests. Since temperatures are

equable year round, there are two growing seasons, one fed by the long rains of March to May, and the other by the short rains of August and September. Most people are peasant farmers, with high male participation in labor migration. With high population densities, marginal lands are cultivated, deforestation and erosion are growing problems, fuelwood and thatching grass are scarce, and, increasingly, farms are too small to be economically viable.

CULTURAL OVERVIEW

Bantu-speaking Abaluyia ancestors, migrating from what is now Uganda, entered the area roughly 500 years ago. Long-range and local migrations of Bantu and Nilotic (Kalenjin, Luo, Nandi, Teso) peoples continued well into the 19th century, making Luyia history a story of many migrations and numerous cross-cultural contacts and exchanges. Among Abaluyia there are uniformities and diversities, beginning with the Bantu dialects, some mutually intelligible only with difficulty, that unite the subgroups. There are widespread similarities (though not uniformity) regarding clans and kinship, ancestor spirits, religious beliefs, economic activities including labor migration, architecture and technology, land tenure, patriarchy and the subordinate position of women, gender roles, patrilocal residence, behavioral propriety, and child socialization—and marked differences in some areas such as male circumcision, tooth removal, and the age group system of the Tiriki. Along with many changes, there is much cultural persistence.

The precolonial Luyia economy was agropastoral, with intensive food crop cultivation and grazing of cattle and goats. People made everything they needed, from tools and weapons to houses. Goods and services were bartered or purchased with livestock, Samia-made hoes, and baskets of grain. It was a sustainable subsistence economy, integrated with the sociopolitical–religious–moral system in which it was embedded. Patrilineal exogamous clans (groups of persons descended from a common male ancestor) were the basic unit of social organization. Marriage outside one's own clan and the clans of one's mother for two generations up (clan exogamy) encouraged alliances across clans, with women residing patrilocally (in their husbands' homes) after marriage. The belief system of most Abaluyia included a creator god, Were or Wele, and spirits that inhabited rocks, trees, and other objects. In each homestead, shrines were constructed for ancestral spirits who could be approached for help with words and gifts (food and beer). There were no organized churches or priests.

Status differences among individuals were based on gender, age and seniority, kinship status, wealth (especially cattle), special abilities, and personal qualities. Land, held communally, was readily available for farming and collecting water, fuelwood, and wild foods. Elders allocated plots to men, who in turn allocated plots to their wives. Men were warriors, rulers in homes and clans, with superior access to resources (including women's labor) and therefore power. Women, though subordinate to men, had their own spheres of agency and decision-making. They controlled their farm plots and crops and the kitchen, that is, the preparation and distribution of food, and they had their own social hierarchy, with senior wives, mothers, and mothers-in-law at the top. Ritual and craft specialties enabled individuals to gain wealth and prestige. Only men could follow the most prestigious and lucrative specialties of ironworking, woodcarving, and rainmaking, but in many groups women were potters and also herbalists, tooth removers, healers and midwives, diviners, and spirit mediums.

In mid-19th-century Abaluyia took to fortifying their homesteads or living in small fortified villages because of cattle raids and land grabs by new Luyia immigrants and groups such as Baganda, Maasai, Nandi, and Teso. The walled villages constituted basic sociopolitical and defensive units, though with no centralized authority. At times some villages were united under the vigorous leadership of a particular man (*omwami*, in many Luyia dialects) who was likely to strengthen alliances through marriage (polygyny being common practice), but these affiliations were loose and shifting.

British explorers, missionaries, doctors, and soldiers arrived in the late 19th century. By about 1910 the British were firmly in control, appointing local men as chiefs in the colonial administrative system, introducing money and taxes, cash crops and wage labor, Christianity, formal education, and medical services. In western Kenya land was not alienated to Europeans, but Abaluyia were under great pressures to produce cash crops, work on colonial projects and in wage labor for colonists, and accept Christianity, Europeanized life-styles, and a standardized Luyia orthography. In response to such pressures, Abaluyia emerged as an ethnic and political identity in the 1930s. (Closely related Bantu speakers in Uganda, including many Abasamia, do not identify themselves as Luyia and are not included in this discussion.)

Many changes occurred in Kenya during the 20th century with transformations from a colonial to a modern independent state and from a kin-corporate mode of production promoting interdependence and reciprocity to a globally connected capitalist economy encouraging individual accumulation rather than collective well-being. Elementary education is now nearly universal, though more males than females continue beyond eighth grade. Many imported ideas and ideologies have become dominant—for example, most Abaluyia today are Christians. With the commodification of work and other aspects of life, the agropastoral subsistence economy has yielded to a dual system in which family survival depends on having members in the rural home raising food and cash crops (still using hoes and other hand tools) and other members away from home in wage employment, each supporting the other. Residence after marriage remains patrilocal—the wife goes to live in her husband's home. However, more and more women are going to other rural areas and to cities, accompanying husbands and themselves seeking employment. Land has been registered to individual owners, mostly to men, with no legal provisions for women's rights to land. Cattle retain their cultural significance as visible wealth, and indigenous views persist in other ways, for example, in explanations of events, the division of labor, the ways work defines the self and an individual's social status, and the complex ways in which gender is implicated in social and economic relationships across the life course. Overall, indigenous patriarchy melded with imposed British patriarchy, making women invisible and favoring men in access to productive resources, education, employment, and political power.

CULTURAL CONSTRUCTION OF GENDER

Gender differentiation is a strong characteristic of Abaluyia culture and society. Females and males are differentiated physically by attire, body ornament and posture, in work roles, in family and marital relationships—in almost every aspect of life.

Early European accounts described Abaluyia as "naked" because their clothing left large areas of skin exposed. To Abaluyia, clothing and ornaments signified sexual modesty and also social and ritual status. Babies and small children went naked. Older children wore genital coverings, men added a leather cloak, and older girls and women added a fringed "tail" of plant fibers that indicated their status as unmarried, married without children, with children, or postmenopausal, or widowed. From infancy, jewelry made of various materials was worn by both genders, mostly by females. Jewelry was a woman's personal possession and indicated her social status and her husband's wealth. Scarification of face and body, especially of females, was done for beauty, ritual protection, and men's sexual pleasure. Bodies were painted and hair was removed for esthetic and ritual purposes. For war and ceremonies, men wore elaborate headdresses. Male elders and political leaders wore clothing and ornaments indicating their high status.

Christian missionaries brought Victorian attitudes toward the body and clothes to cover it. Pressured by fines, taxes, and the requirements of missionaries and employers, Abaluyia abandoned most of their body arts and adopted European clothing by the 1930s. Now small children usually go naked, older boys wear T-shirts and shorts, and older girls and women wear dresses and sometimes earrings. School children wear uniforms: dresses for girls, shirt and shorts for boys. Footwear (if any) tends to be sandals. Men wear trousers, shirts, sometimes jackets and hats, and often a watch. Women often wrap a kanga (a cloth rectangle that originated on the Swahili coast in the 19th century) around their dresses; kangas are also used as baby slings, headwraps, and to sit on. In the 1980s girls and women sometimes wore trousers in Nairobi, but were subject to negative comments ("Does she think she's a man?") in rural Luyialand. By the mid-1990s wearing trousers in Buluyia had become more acceptable. Most people have short hair but since the 1970s some women plait their hair in elaborate patterns, an ancient African custom. For both genders, looking "smart" (well dressed and up to date) is considered attractive, and also being "fat," for fatness (especially of female breasts and buttocks) is associated with health, fertility, and prosperity. Physical strength is admired in men.

Posture is another marker of gender. Girls are expected to show deference (bowed head, lowered gaze, soft voice) to almost everyone, but postures of deference are also expected of women when in the presence of men. Conversely, men exhibit postures of domination. Domination and subordination are enacted in seating arrangements: men sit on chairs, and women (unless of high status) on the ground, legs straight out in front of them and crossed at the ankles—though in her own home a woman may sit on a chair in the presence of the men of her family.

GENDER OVER THE LIFE CYCLE

For Abaluyia, life moves from prebirth or birth through various stages to death and ancestorhood. Transitions between stages are not abrupt but take place through processes of gradual maturation and decline. Even in groups that have (or had) circumcision and initiation rites, full maturity did not arrive in the twinkling of a knife cut initiating boys into a warrior phase, but through a process of social advances involving marriage and having children. Many indigenous life cycle rituals for childbirth and naming, tooth removal, circumcision and initiation, marriage, death, and remembrance of ancestors have become attenuated or are no longer practiced, having been replaced by European and Christian practices.

Since different Luyia communities conceive of the life cycle in differing patterns, one group, Abasamia, are presented as an example. Samia conceptions of life stages vary, with a range of opinions about stages, ages, indicators, and transitions. For example, many Samia think that a fetus is a "thing" (esindu), not yet a person or human being (omundu), and that life begins at birth; others say that life begins at conception. For the first day of life, the infant is "just born" (omwana omwibulwe); for a few weeks it is "newborn" (omwana ori olwesi), physically dependent, and morally pure; thereafter it is a "small child" (omudoto). Omudoto develops physical skills, mental ability, and moral capacity, and is considered "to know reason" (okhumanya amakesi), to be able to think and know right from wrong, somewhere between ages 3 and 8. Such a child passes from childhood (obuyere) to youth (oburaga), and then to puberty, a state of being a "ripe" person (omwangafu), a person who is physically mature and ready for marriage. Marriage marks the beginning of adulthood (*obukhulundu*), a long period followed by old age (*obukofu*), and finally death and becoming an ancestor spirit (*omusambwa*).

Socialization of Boys and Girls

To be childless is a tragedy. Abaluyia value sons highly; men want sons to insure generational continuity of self and clan, and women want sons to insure support in their old age. However, girls are also valued for their labor and for the "wealth" (cattle and money) their bridewealth will bring to their family when they marry, which in turn makes it possible for their brothers to pay bridewealth so they can marry. Increasingly, daughters are also being seen as providers of support for elderly parents. Malnutrition, though fairly common, affects girls and boys about equally, seeming to be more the result of poverty and marital conflicts than gender discrimination. Until recently, people wanted a large family with many sons and many daughters. However, in the past decade Kenya's birth rate has dropped drastically (even in Maragoli, long known for its high fertility), suggesting a new ideal of smaller families in a context of some improvement in women's economic empowerment.

During infancy and early childhood, girls and boys are treated pretty much the same. Infants are breast-fed and held almost constantly, usually receiving much warmth and affectionate indulgence. When they are a few years old children begin helping their mothers with childcare and household tasks. Young girls and boys often play together with simple homemade toys and in games such as hide-and-seek and guessing riddles; they may also forage for snack foods such as grasshoppers and fruits. By age 8 or 9, play is more often in same-sex groups. Girls stay closer to home, working for their mothers, while boys are freer to roam around with brothers and friends, a pattern that continues through adulthood. All children learn—primarily by imitation and experience—work appropriate to their gender; all are trained to respect and obey anyone older than themselves, to practice emotional self-control, and to behave properly. Boys are encouraged to greater independence, while girls are expected to be modest and shy. Any child may be disciplined with harsh words and sometimes beatings, though girls are more likely to be beaten (as are wives).

A major change in children's socialization is school attendance. For much of the 20th century girls rarely and perhaps a quarter to a half of boys went to school, but today elementary education is nearly universal. Schoolchildren learn English and Swahili. They receive some instruction about indigenous cultures, but the emphasis is on knowledge different from the local knowledge of parents and grandparents. Schools encourage swiftness of thought and openness to innovation, in contrast to the indigenous emphasis on slow deliberate thought. This may indicate an emerging shift in cognitive style that is no doubt reinforced with television viewing. Thus in school and through television, children are exposed to new ideas about gender roles and, in the person of teachers and school heads, nontraditional role models.

Puberty and Adolescence

When youth (*oburaga*) shades into puberty, the Samia life course divides sharply along gender lines, with sharp distinctions in work activities and the social and spatial separation of females and males. A girl (*omukhana omuraga*) becomes a "ripe" or "mature" person (*omwangafu*) physically and socially when her body matures and she begins to menstruate. In indigenous society, she was ready to marry. However, a boy (*omusiani omuraga*) does not become *omwangafu* until he reaches full physical maturity and has the strength to do a man's work along with the ability to manage a home. Only then is he ready for marriage. In indigenous society girls married quite young, while male youth spent years as cattle herders and warriors before marrying. With the colonial suppression of warfare, male youth became migrant laborers. Today education has brought further changes in life patterns.

In the past about half the Luyia subgroups, including Bukusu, Idakho, Isukha, and Maragoli, had male circumcision and initiation ceremonies and named age-grades that served to reckon age or seniority among men (only Abatachoni circumcised females); a few communities still circumcise, though the ceremonies are much abbreviated to fit school schedules and are increasingly controversial. Tiriki, borrowing from Nilotic Terik neighbors, had male circumcision and initiation plus a formal age-group system that was the basis of Tiriki sociopolitical organization. Many Abaluyia, influenced by Nilotic peoples, removed one to six lower incisors of all children around age 6 or 7; for females, the resulting gap was regarded as a mark of beauty. In groups without circumcision, including Abasamia and Banyala, tooth removal marked the early stage of adulthood. All such practices were or are only the beginning of the long process of achieving adulthood.

Attainment of Adulthood

Adulthood (*obukhulundu*) is a time of meeting responsibilities to others. For girls it begins with marriage. A married Samia female is addressed as *omukhasi*, "wife" (also "woman"). However, a wife's early years of marriage are ruled by her mother-in-law; it is not until she has been married for several years and has two or three children that she gets her own kitchen and is considered to be truly adult (*omukhasi mudwasi*), able to manage her children and make her own decisions about food preparation and her work schedule. Some women today are refusing their mother-in-law's domination by setting up kitchens when they marry or going with their husband to live where he works away from home. When a man marries he is addressed as *omusacha*, "husband" (also "man"), but he too achieves full adult status through parenthood. Children make him *omusacha omukhulundu*, an elder of his family and clan. In the past, most women became fully adult in their twenties, men not until their thirties or even forties. Now, with earlier marriage for men and later marriage for women, this is changing. However, though women become socially adult, they remain jural minors and must be represented by male relatives in formal situations such as court cases.

Middle Age and Old Age

The transition from adulthood to old age (*obukofu*) is associated with the end of childbearing and decline in physical strength for everyone and, for women, the end of menstruation. There is little association with chronological age (many older people do not even know their chronological age). Most women in their fifties call themselves "old," while many men that age and even older say they are "mature" (*omwangafu*), not old. In old age, women and men become more alike, respected for their years and wisdom, able to carry out rituals and advise their juniors. Often these activities are referred to as "the work of old people," but this work has been diminished by the geographic dispersal of families under capitalism, literacy and its associated body of new knowledge, and other factors.

A very old person (*omukofu muno*), physically or mentally frail, can do little productive work and thus no longer meets the responsibilities of adulthood. This is a time of dependence on others for the essentials of life, a time of waiting to die. The very old are generally regarded as being close to the ancestors and therefore possessed of ritual powers; after their deaths, they join the ancestor spirits (*emisambwa*) and continue to play a role in family life. As *emisambwa* women finally achieve equality, for the spirits of women are as powerful as those of men.

PERSONALITY DIFFERENCES BY GENDER

Sociability is highly valued by Abaluyia, and both men and women are highly sociable, talkative among friends, and happy to welcome visitors in their homes. Most Abaluyia are soft-spoken and polite. Good manners are valued; speaking loudly and getting angry are not. However, boys and men are more independent and authoritative, more likely to be aggressive or express anger, while girls and young women are usually self-effacing and shy, very deferential to men, especially certain categories of men such as fathers-in-law, and to older higher-status females. Older women are likely to stand straight, look people in the eye, and speak firmly even to men—thus behaving like a man, a socially acceptable shift in behavior. For everyone, emotional restraint is characteristic, though women tend to be more emotionally expressive and far more nurturing than men.

GENDER-RELATED SOCIAL GROUPS

Gender-related social groups are common. For example, patrilineal descent groups tend to be localized, with fathers and sons, brothers and uncles concentrated in particular areas. Individuals belong to the clan of their father; at marriage women go to live with their husband and his kin but do not become members of their husbands' clans, remaining strangers in the home though they will be buried there. Though rare today, in the past adult men and old women (those "like a man") attended frequent communal beer drinks.

Work activities separate females and males during much of the day. Women spend most of their day with young children, older daughters, and other women.

Men spend much time with other men, working or relaxing and socializing. Some cooperative work groups and self-help groups are single sex, especially women's groups for revolving credit, income generating, and other purposes. Such groups help some women with their family responsibilities of providing food and clothing for their children and are also an important source of moral support. Church-based groups are likely to be mixed. Funerals (and there are many in this time of AIDS) bring together men and women of all ages.

GENDER ROLES IN ECONOMICS

Men's work includes clearing fields and other agricultural work, herding livestock, and building houses, granaries, and stock shelters. Abaluyia women (like many African women) work much harder and longer hours than men. They are the primary producers of both subsistence and cash crops, though they do not always control the products of their labor. Reproduction—the bearing and raising of children—and household maintenance activities are almost exclusively women's work. Women are also the major caregivers for sick, elderly, and disabled family members.

In the first half of the 20th century, missionary training in domesticity, including cleanliness, crop cultivation, and self-reliance, was aimed at "mission girls" and enabled a few educated women to fashion—with difficulty—new roles for themselves. Today in Buluyia some women are employed, mostly as nurses and teachers; some make and sell pots or other utilitarian items or practice indigenous healing arts or modern midwifery. Many men are labor migrants, thus withdrawing from the domestic economy for months or years, and then retiring in their forties or fifties to resume farming. Even if present in the homestead, few men will do women's work. Children's contributions to the family economy—mostly doing women's work—are substantially reduced by their school attendance. Women, expected to feed and clothe their families and provide school fees if the father fails in that duty, have little choice but to take up the work roles forgone by men and children, even if it means doing men's work. These factors, along with educational disadvantages and persisting patterns of patriarchal oppression (indigenous and colonial), have severely limited African women's roles in the formal economy, leading to heavy participation in the informal economy, especially as agricultural laborers and micro-entrepreneurs, and to a degree in craft production and ritual specialties.

Women are further disadvantaged by changes in land tenure from the precolonial communal control of land to the contemporary situation of individualized land tenure, with most land registered to men who inherited it from their fathers and will divide it among their sons. Women may "inherit" skills such as divining, but rarely inherit land or other material property. Lack of a land title deed makes it almost impossible for women to obtain loans to start income-generating projects. The many women managing farms in their husbands' absence, or because they are widowed, are less well served by agricultural extension services than are men who manage farms. Many Abaluyia women live on the edge, working long and hard under conditions of gender bias that severely limit their economic opportunities and threaten their health and the health and educational opportunities of their children.

PARENTAL AND OTHER CARETAKER ROLES

Mothers are responsible for childcare, but the actual care of small children is often provided by older siblings (girls and boys) or hired girls who are not in school because their families are unable to pay school fees. Mothers are usually warm and affectionate with children, and their punishments are likely to be verbal; mother–son and mother–daughter bonds are often very close. Fathers tend to be authoritarian and distant, are more likely to punish with beatings, and spend relatively little time with their children except for older boys, who usually eat the evening meal with their father if he is at home. Grandparents, especially grandmothers, tend to be indulgent with all their grandchildren, joke with them, teach them about sex, and give them treats. Many grandmothers are primary caretakers of children born to unmarried daughters or in situations where AIDS affects the parental generation; they, like younger women, struggle to make ends meet.

LEADERSHIP IN PUBLIC ARENAS

The public–private distinction was imposed on Abaluyia (and other Africans) through the processes of colonialism and capitalism and the "gospel of domesticity" of

Christian missionaries, resulting in greater male salience in many spheres, women's increased workloads, and loss of indigenous mechanisms to protect women's interests. In contemporary Buluyia, leadership in public arenas is almost entirely by men; most politicians, government administrators, and church and clan leaders are men. Women do have leadership roles as teachers, school heads, and community health workers, in church groups and religious orders, and in women's self-help and cooperative work groups. Women also have roles in their own clans (e.g., in funeral rituals) and participate in clan discussions about important matters such as marriage. While women, especially older women, are outspoken in their opinions, they are likely to let males make final decisions, thus maintaining a deferential attitude and saving face for men.

GENDER AND RELIGION

Women take leadership roles in many church activities, though almost none are priests. For example, women religious are heads of Roman Catholic girls' schools, offering to the girls a different model of womanhood from their cultural models. Among saved people (born-again Christians), many group leaders are women, and saved women sometimes succeed in rejecting customs such as widow inheritance with the help of other saved people including men. The Luyia high god, Were (Wele), is male, but ancestor spirits (emisambwa) are of both genders and equally powerful. Other gods and spirits are not gendered, except for the Christian God (Nyasaye), whose maleness is not questioned as it sometimes is by Euro-American feminists.

LEISURE, RECREATION, AND THE ARTS

Men of all ages have a fair amount of leisure time, but until women reach old age, most have little time to relax. Men spend much of their leisure time socializing with other men, discussing politics, listening to the radio, and drinking. Women socialize mostly with other women, often in a work context; their conversations revolve around their activities and the people in their lives. Older women, with fewer home duties, may use their leisure time for community-oriented activities such as serving on school committees, participating in prayer and dance

groups, and being community health workers. Children, often in mixed groups, enjoy storytelling, singing, and playing a great variety of games. Boys love to play soccer. Groups of youths, single-sex and mixed, stroll about, conversing; they also like to attend dances. Watching television (as people acquire television sets and run them off car batteries) is growing in popularity and opens a window on different worlds, including programs from England and the United States.

Luyia arts consist primarily of the making of utilitarian objects such as tools, baskets, clay pots, and four-legged stools. This is not art as self-expression, but functional art to produce familiar objects for practical, economic, symbolic, and ritual purposes. Traditional body decorations (jewelry and scarification) and modern-day plaited hair and women's jewelry, the occasional house wall painted with floral designs, and the use of flowers as house decorations are viewed as maridadi, esthetically pleasing or beautiful. Men and women have their own artisanal specialties, though their products must compete with imported goods such as aluminum cooking pots and plastic containers that have reduced the desirability of clay pots.

RELATIVE STATUS OF MEN AND WOMEN

Women are "only women"; they are strangers in the home and not to be trusted with family secrets, their political discussions are about "kitchen politics," and they need to be beaten from time to time to teach them proper behavior. Such is the opinion of many Luyia men about women. Yet those same men may honor and respect their mothers, and mothers may have considerable influence over sons. Most women do not have much authority, but they have a great deal of influence, often behind the scenes, especially as they grow older. Women (often older women) who are leaders of religious, self-help, and other groups speak their minds even when men are in the groups. Women know how to lead, how to make decisions—not surprising, because in their own female spheres of work and childcare, women make decisions independently of men. Educated women, women with jobs (often as nurses or teachers), are respected for their achievements. But in the end, most women come out a little—or much—lower than most men. Furthermore, patriarchal structures in land ownership and access to productive resources, education, and employment help keep women lower than men.

SEXUALITY

In indigenous Luyia society, sexuality was regarded as healthy and natural. Fathers' sisters (*senge*) and grandmothers instructed youth in sexual matters, which could not be discussed with parents. Premarital sex play (but not intercourse) was allowed. A bride was expected to be a virgin and her family was rewarded for her virginity, though there seems to have been no lasting stigma for a pregnant bride. Christian missionaries demanded the covering of bodies with voluminous clothing and condemned any sexual activity among unmarried youth, probably contributing to today's attitude that even holding hands or a brief kiss in public is tantamount to having intercourse. Today modesty demands that genitals be covered and also women's breasts (except when a mother is breastfeeding her baby), but not arms and legs (except for upper thighs). It is, in fact, a terrible curse for a woman to expose her genitals deliberately.

In the latter 20th century sexual controls loosened considerably, at least in part because of the erosion of the roles of grandmothers and fathers' sisters as instructors in sexual behavior and the increased vulnerability of schoolgirls, especially those in boarding schools who are away from family control for long periods. Premarital pregnancies are common, bringing problems to the girls (stigma, dismissal from school, family conflict) but not to the boys or men who impregnated them. Wives are expected to satisfy their husbands' sexual needs, but not vice versa. Women are also expected to be faithful to husbands, and many are, but men engage in much extramarital sex—no doubt a factor in the current AIDS epidemic. Clearly there is a "double standard" regarding sexuality. Asked about homosexuality, most people say nothing or insist that homosexuals are found "only in Mombasa."

COURTSHIP AND MARRIAGE

Formerly, parents (the father alone or in consultation with his wife) chose spouses for their children. For daughters they looked for a responsible strong man from a respected family; he could be an older man with other wives.

For sons they sought a girl of childbearing age who was hardworking and obedient. Negotiations were conducted between the families, bridewealth was paid (though perhaps only part of it to start with), and various ceremonies were carried out, culminating in a procession to convey the bride to her new home. Girls married young, sometimes even as small children, and often against their will, while men were likely to be in their twenties or even thirties at their first marriage. Often the bride and groom did not meet until the wedding. Once the protracted wedding ceremonies ended and the bride was left without her supportive bridesmaids in her new husband's home, it was a difficult and often lonely time for her as a stranger in her husband's home, socially inferior to almost everyone else, and expected to work hard for her mother-in-law.

Today young people are likely to choose their own partners, with sexual attraction and love playing a strong role and premarital sex likely. They may elope or the young woman may just move into her husband's house. If the family accepts her presence, the couple are considered to be married, though bridewealth is likely to be negotiated at some point and the birth of children makes the relationship stronger. With the traditional ceremonies no longer being performed, the couple may choose to have a church wedding or a civil wedding before a magistrate.

In the past marriage was universal, but today some women are choosing single parenthood over marriage. Women who are widowed (and most women are at least by the time they reach their sixties) would ordinarily be "inherited" by a male of the late husband's family. With younger women, such a marriage might become a "real" marriage; with women past childbearing it might involve little more than the purification rituals. Today, however, some widows are rejecting widow inheritance. Sometimes younger women choose their second husband themselves, and some older women (especially older women who are "saved," i.e., born-again Christians) are rejecting remarriage altogether and with it the possibility of domination by a new husband.

It is unusual to find a man, even a very old man, without a wife, since wives tend to be younger (sometimes much younger) than husbands and a polygamously married man will not be left without a wife even if one of them dies. In any case, a man (widowed or not) is free to marry when he wishes, constrained chiefly by his ability to pay bridewealth and (especially if he is old) attract a woman willing to marry him.

HUSBAND–WIFE RELATIONSHIP

The rule is simple: a husband rules his wife. If she is disobedient or behaves improperly (in his view), he may punish her. A man may beat his wife—though he should not seriously injure her—in order to teach her proper behavior. If he comes home late, he expects his wife to get up and cook him a meal and have sex with him, even if he is drunk and disgusting. He cannot cook his own meal, for it is shameful for a man to cook when a female (even a small girl) is present. Though women often do men's work, especially in a husband's absence, men rarely do women's work.

Marital relationships run the gamut from hostile and abusive to companionable and cooperative. The former may involve marital rape and frequent beatings; the latter may even see a husband going into the wife's kitchen (usually off-base for men) to discuss something with his wife or make a mutual decision.

Spouses usually sleep together, though a polygamist sleeps with each wife in turn if he is treating his wives fairly. He should also give equal presents to his wives, eat each wife's food, and pay school fees for the children of all his wives. The first wife a man marries is his senior wife; she is the manager of junior wives. Relationships among cowives may be congenial and cooperative, or antagonistic and hostile; whichever, their atmosphere pervades the homestead. Though the cultural myth is that cowives are always jealous and quarreling, in fact many get along well and cooperate with each other. Widowed cowives can be extremely supportive of each other. Sometimes cowives unite against the husband in a campaign to get him to do something they want, a situation men dislike intensely (no doubt because they do not feel in control).

Under customary law, divorce usually requires nothing more than for a wife to leave the homestead, though her family may try to persuade her—or even force her—to go back so they do not have to return bridewealth. In a sense a woman's first marriage is never dissolved, even if she marries someone else. When she dies, even many years later, the first husband or his heirs will be expected to bury her on his land. If it is the man who wants a wife to leave, and she is reluctant, he will pressure her to go, perhaps by ignoring her, or a hostile cowife can make life very unpleasant for her. Children belong to the father's clan; if very young, they may accompany their mother when she leaves, but will be returned to the father when

they are older. In any case, few men are willing to have another man's children in their home, so if a woman remarries, she is unlikely to find a welcome for her children. If the marriage occurred in a civil ceremony, a court case is necessary for divorce; if it is a church marriage, then church law applies.

OTHER CROSS-SEX RELATIONSHIPS

Respect is a fundamental value in Luyia cultures. Though the nature of particular relationships varies with the individuals involved, relationship styles can be categorized along a continuum ranging from hierarchical relationships of respect, formality, and restraint to relationships among equals marked by familiarity, informality, and joking. In the former, obedience and deference are expected. Only the latter may include discussion of sexual matters and lewd joking.

Respect relationships occur in hierarchical dyads, as between parents and children. Fathers are the most respected, especially by daughters, while relationships with mothers are more free and emotionally warm—though one must always respect one's mother. Disobedience to a parent is a failure of respect—a challenge to the status and authority of the senior person—and is quickly punished. Mother–son and mother–daughter bonds tend to be strong throughout life. Many women say they "fear" their fathers-in-law (husband's father and his brothers and male cousins) and avoid them by not shaking their hands (the usual greeting), sitting in their presence, eating with them, and so on. Sons-in-law are similarly respectful to mothers-in-law. The one person in the parental generation with whom junior females (and males too) may have a joking relationship is a father's sister (*senge*), who can be a confidant and sexual adviser.

In contrast, brothers and sisters—linked by the bridewealth that makes the marriages of each possible—enjoy a more free and open relationship. Sisters often go to their brothers when they have marital difficulties and other problems. A woman may be very free with her brothers-in-law, who are potential husbands if her husband dies and she is inherited by one of them. Even in these relatively egalitarian relationships, however, sex and age make males "more equal" than females, and older "more equal" than younger.

Grandparents and grandchildren are usually very free with each other. They make sexual jokes and, if of opposite sex, call each other "husband" and "wife." A grandfather and grandson call each other "brother," and grandmother and granddaughter call each other "cowife." Traditionally, children slept in their grandmother's house, listening to her stories and advices, and many still do. However, grandmothers' roles as educator and adviser have diminished greatly as schools, churches, and other institutions provide alternative ideas and practices that grandmothers (usually with no formal education or much experience outside their home areas) often know little about. Nevertheless, children enjoy being with grandparents, perhaps in part as a relief from sterner relationships.

CHANGE IN ATTITUDES, BELIEFS, AND PRACTICES REGARDING GENDER

Women in precolonial Luyia societies were far from equal to men, though as women grew older and moved up in kinship hierarchies, their status improved considerably over that of young girls and young wives. Colonial policies and practices imposed sweeping changes in all aspects of life including the household division of labor, gender roles, and childhood socialization. Colonial and capitalist processes swept men into wage employment and labor migration and greatly increased women's work burdens, diminished their access to productive resources and others' labor, and transformed gender relations. Today Abaluyia, with other Africans, are engaged in reevaluating and renegotiating their family systems of shared social support, their economic opportunities and other life chances, and gender roles and relationships in a contemporary political economy of scarcity, poverty, and powerlessness that affects men as well as women.

NOTE ON SOURCES

On Luyia history, see Sangree (1986), Wagner (1949), Wandibba (1985), and Were (1967). For gender issues, see Abwunza (1997), Cattell (1997, 2002), Kilbride and Kilbride (1990), Mutongi (2003), Thomas (2000), and Were (1990). Life cycle discussion is primarily from the author's research among Abasamia. For material culture, see Burt (1980). Weisner, Bradley, and Kilbride (1997) has chapters on many aspects of contemporary Luyia family life. Lijembe (1967) describes his growing up in an Idakho community in the 1930s and 1940s. Soper (1986) provides an overview of Abaluyia in Busia District.

BIBLIOGRAPHY

Abwunza, J. M. (1997). *Women's voices, women's power: Dialogues of resistance from East Africa.* Peterborough, Ontario, Canada: Broadview Press.

Burt, E. C. (1980). *Towards an art history of the Baluyia of western Kenya.* Unpublished doctoral dissertation, University of Washington, Seattle, WA.

Cattell, M. G. (1997). African widows, culture and social change: Case studies from Kenya. In J. Sokolovsky (Ed.), *The cultural context of aging: Worldwide perspectives* (2nd ed., pp. 71–98). Westport, CT: Bergin & Garvey.

Cattell, M. G. (2002). Holding up the sky: Gender, age and work among Abaluyia of Kenya. In S. Makoni & K. Stroeken (Eds.), *Ageing in Africa: Sociolinguistic and anthropological approaches* (pp. 157–177). Aldershot, U.K.: Ashgate.

Kilbride, P. L., & Kilbride, J. C. (1990). *Changing family life in East Africa: Women and children at risk.* University Park: Pennsylvania State University Press.

Lijembe, J. A. (1967). The valley between: A Muluyia's story. In L. K. Fox (Ed.), *East African childhood* (pp. 1–41). Nairobi: Oxford University Press.

Mutongi, K. B. (2003). *Widowhood, colonialism and gender.* Portsmouth, NH: Heinemann.

Sangree, W. H. (1986). Role flexibility and status continuity: Tiriki (Kenya) age groups today. *Journal of Cross-Cultural Gerontology, 1,* 117–138.

Soper, R. (Ed.). (1986). *Kenya socio-cultural profiles: Busia District.* Nairobi: Republic of Kenya, Ministry of Planning and Development, and Institute of African Studies, University of Nairobi.

Thomas, S. S. (2000). Transforming the gospel of domesticity: Luhya girls and the Friends Africa Mission, 1917–1926. *African Studies Review, 43*(2), 1–27.

Wagner, G. (1949). *The Bantu of North Kavirondo: Vol. 1.* London: Oxford University Press.

Wagner, G. (1956). *The Bantu of North Kavirondo: Vol. 2, Economic life,* L. P. Mair (Ed.). London: Oxford University Press.

Wandibba, S. (Ed.). (1985). *History and culture in western Kenya: The people of Bungoma District through time.* Nairobi: Were Press.

Weisner, T. S., Bradley C., & Kilbride, P. L. (Eds.). (1997). *African families and the crisis of social change.* Westport, CT: Bergin & Garvey.

Were, G. S. (1967). *A history of the Abaluyia of western Kenya, c. 1500–1930.* Nairobi: East African Publishing House.

Were, G. S. (Ed.). (1990). *Women and development in Kenya: Kakamega District.* Nairobi: Institute of African Studies, University of Nairobi.

Abelam

Richard Scaglion

ALTERNATIVE NAMES

Abelam are also known as Abulas, Ambelam, Ambelas, Ambulas, and various subgroup names including Kamukundi, Mamukundi, Manjekundi, Samukundi and Shamukundi.

LOCATION

The Abelam live on the grassy plains north of the middle Sepik River and in the foothills of the Prince Alexander Mountains in the East Sepik Province of Papua New Guinea.

CULTURAL OVERVIEW

Owing in part to ecological variation, there are some minor differences among Abelam subgroups. This article concentrates on the foothills-dwelling Samukundi (or Manjekundi) Abelam. The ethnographic present is the early 1970s.

The Samukundi are primarily swidden horticulturalists, growing yams, taro, and sweet potatoes as staples. Sago, coconuts, bananas, and breadfruit are other popular foodstuffs. Women do a large part of the gardening. Agricultural products are supplemented by keeping pigs and hunting, the latter activity being almost entirely the purview of men. Men net, spear, or shoot large game (pig, cassowary), while boys snare smaller game (small birds, wallabies, bandicoots, and opossums). Villages are self-sufficient in subsistence production.

Much of Samukundi Abelam life is structured by an elaborate ritual complex involving the growth and display of huge ceremonial yams (*Dioscorea alata*), which may attain lengths of 3 m or more. Ceremonial yams are grown only by men. The best tubers are given to ritual exchange partners in a competitive exchange process linking neighboring villages. To a large extent, male status, prestige, and power are dependent on the size and quality of the ceremonial yams grown. This yam-growing ritual complex, including its accompanying taboos during the growing season, acts to structure and synchronize many aspects of Abelam society, including the timing of births, the expression of conflict and violence, and the organization of trade, visiting, courtship, and marriage.

Village leaders are the well-known Melanesian "big men," who have no formal authority but achieve influence through ceremonial yam-growing and success in ritual activity, warfare, and oratory. Social organization is based on kinship and residence. Descent is nominally patrilineal and residence nominally patrilocal, but there is much variation. Extended families of about a dozen persons live in small hamlets. Nearby hamlets share a *kurambu* or spirit house, and together constitute a ceremonial group of about a hundred persons. Villages consist of loose confederations of ceremonial groups.

CULTURAL CONSTRUCTION OF GENDER

The culturally constructed categories of female and male are quite distinct and clearly marked socially. Traditionally, both sexes went nearly naked but wore gender-associated ornamentation. Until approximately the 1950s, Abelam women were scarified at puberty. Gender is strongly marked linguistically; it is virtually impossible to address a person without using gender identifiers (e.g., you [female] = *nyéné*; you [male] = *méné*). There were no other socially recognized gender categories apart from male and female. Division of labor by sex is very pronounced (see below), with many tasks considered appropriate only for men or women. Work and ritual activities frequently result in sex-segregated groups.

GENDER OVER THE LIFE CYCLE

Females come of age with a public ceremony marking the first menses. Afterwards, for a month or two, an adolescent girl is *naramtaakwa*, or "decorated woman," and wears particular shell ornaments, follows certain taboos, and refrains from work activities. Afterwards she is considered to be a woman (*taakwa*) and eligible for marriage. Males come of age more gradually in a series of elaborate initiation ceremonies that typically begin when they are only a few years old and end in their twenties. However, only in their forties, when they have acted as initiators of other males in another ritual cycle, are they considered truly mature men. Consonant with the gradual nature of the male maturation process, there is no clearly marked period of male adolescence. Males who have passed through various stages of the initiation process are entitled to wear particular ornaments and carry string bags adorned with decorations distinctive of their initiation grades. There are specific names for males who have completed each initiation stage. Generically, men are called *ndu*; young, unmarried men are called *kwinémbéndu* and recently married young men are *némbikarandu*.

Socialization of Boys and Girls

From the earliest age, females and males are encouraged to engage in gender-specific behaviors. Because small boys spend much of the time with their mothers, there are relatively few tasks for them to perform and most pass their days in play. Small girls, by contrast, are expected to help their mothers with food preparation, cooking, watching smaller children, etc. as soon as they are able. Thus girls continually learn gender-suitable behavior from their female relatives, whereas boys are introduced to gender-appropriate comportment through the male initiation process that begins when they are only a few years old. Initiation is divided into two broad stages, but the details of initiation and the names and particulars of various grades vary considerably from village to village (McGuigan, 1992; Schroeder, 1992). However, the initiations that all boys undergo involve seclusion, physical deprivation, beatings, and penis hazing. During the initiation process, boys are instructed in male-appropriate behavior and esoteric knowledge by initiated men.

All male initiation ceremonies include viewing and learning about sacred objects generically termed *mayéra*. In Neligum Village, in the first initiation grade called *Wulkétakwa* (bullroarer-woman), novices are introduced to certain sound-producing instruments (including the bullroarer) (Scaglion, 1998). In the secondly initiation grade, called *Kutakwa* (witch), which itself has several

parts, the initiates view certain wooden carvings. It is appropriate that the names *Wulkétakwa* and *Kutakwa* involve female imagery, because the rituals serve to separate boys from their mothers and other female relatives (from whom the rituals are kept secret) and to put them in the company of other males. Food taboos are in force during periods of seclusion and for roughly a year after a particular ceremony. Sexual taboos are reinforced by painful penis bleeding and penis hazing with stinging nettles and thorny leaves and vines.

Puberty and Adolescence

For girls, socialization continues gradually up to first menarche. Because preadolescent girls (*némbataakwa*) are in the company of older female relatives throughout the normal course of the day, continually assisting their mothers and other women in gender-related tasks, they receive instruction on a continuous basis. Preadolescent and adolescent boys, on the other hand, spend much time in the company of their age-mates (*naawi*) and undergoing the various grades of the secondly stage of initiation ceremonies, collectively called *Ngwalndu* (ancestral spirits). In Neligum Village, there are two grades of *Ngwalndu*, the abbreviated names for which are *Lu* (wooden carvings) and *Puti* ("discard" skin/be reborn). At the climax of the *Lu* ceremony, initiates are ushered into a chamber lined with *Lu* carvings in the center of the men's house. The culmination of the *Puti* ceremony involves the viewing of a very large seated figure. Both the *Lu* carvings and the *Puti* figure are representative of ancestral spirits. During the seclusion period for these rituals, which also involve various sorts of hazing, novices are instructed in and exhorted to think about men's activities like growing yams, engaging in ritual activity, obtaining pigs, etc.

Attainment of Adulthood

For males, puberty generally occurs at some time during the *Ngwalndu* stages of initiation, but is not marked in any particular way separately from the initiation ceremonies themselves. Thus boys come of age collectively, with their age-mates. For females, maturity is recognized individually. When a young woman has her first menstrual period, she enters the menstrual hut to begin a brief period of seclusion, and her mother or other female relative notifies the girl's father and mother's brother. After several days, a feast is prepared in the young woman's honor. Her paternal and maternal relatives all contribute yams, coconuts, and other foodstuffs. Yam soup containing shredded coconuts is the most common fare. Guests are given yams and other provisions to carry away with them when they leave. While in the menstrual hut, the young woman is instructed in women's affairs, and rites are conducted from which men are banned. Traditionally, the young woman would have been scarified. A female specialist would cut standardized patterns on her breasts, stomach, and upper arms. After several days, the young woman emerges from the menstrual hut and is ritually washed in public. Standing naked, she is struck with stinging nettles and washed with special water from the forest (*banguréngu*). The next day, she leaves the menstrual hut, is decorated, and becomes *naramtaakwa*. She is given a special bowl-like haircut in which the hair is shaved from her sideburns and the back of her neck. She wears wristlets of shell and other shell necklaces and decorations, and carries a special string bag with shell valuables. Traditionally, the young woman would follow a series for taboos for some months, gradually removing the shell decorations and resuming her normal diet, although a taboo against eating meat continued until she was married. Nowadays, she usually resumes her normal activities after just a few days. Traditionally, many women were married soon after becoming *naramtaakwa*.

Middle Age and Old Age

The prestige of both men and women generally increases with age so long as they remain physically fit and able to work. Once they become too frail for effective labor, and have to depend on the care of others, they may still be respected for their knowledge, but their prestige declines. However, the elderly are treated well and looked after by their families for as long as they live.

PERSONALITY DIFFERENCES BY GENDER

"Good" Abelam men and women are hardworking, kind, good-humored, and generous to relatives and to others. However, men cannot allow others to take advantage of them, particularly in political affairs. Thus men are also expected to be strong and forceful, exercising leadership as circumstances dictate. In contrast, "good" women are expected to be more collaborative than argumentative. As a result, women's groups seem to work out problems more efficiently and cooperatively than do men's groups, particularly men's groups containing political rivals. Boys and girls emulate the personality traits expected of their same-sex elders.

GENDER-RELATED SOCIAL GROUPS

Abelam are nominally patrilineal and patrilocal, but there is a great deal of flexibility in these arrangements. Members of patrilineal lineages (subclans) usually live in close proximity, often in the same hamlet. Clans are named exogamous totemic groups, with each clan having a bird totem (*njambu*). There is also a moiety system (*ara*) based on patrilineal descent. A woman remains a member of her clan of birth even though she moves upon marriage. This kinship idiom of social organization is essentially a social construct. Another construct is geographical–political, consisting of hamlets, ceremonial groups, and village segments that can be plotted on a map. Women normally marry close to home and in most cases remain closely affiliated with their natal clans, although they are also associated with the geographical–political units in which they reside. Accordingly, children grow up with ties to both father's and mother's groups. If resources are scarce in his father's group, a young man may choose to reside with his mother's group, or with his wife's group after marriage, becoming gradually associated with their residence group (although he remains a member of his natal clan). In practice, geographical–political residence groups are of considerably more importance in everyday work groups, politics, and ritual than are the kinship-based groups.

GENDER ROLES IN ECONOMICS

Division of labor is an organizing principle of Abelam society, and men's and women's roles are clearly defined. Women collect firewood and water and do the everyday cooking. Occasionally they may be assisted by males (especially by boys) in food preparation, such as in scraping coconuts, but the major responsibility belongs to the women. Women are also responsible for taking care of the children, although they may be assisted by men. Women sew and weave string bags, which are used for carrying most everything. They also care for the pigs, which are butchered and cooked by men. Men do the hunting, build the houses and fences, weave mats, and cut timber. They also do the majority of arts and craft work, including carving ritual wooden objects, painting with clays and ochers, making spears, adzes, and other tools, and decorating utilitarian objects.

Although division of labor is pronounced, men and women can be seen working together on many economic activities, each laboring at their own tasks. In gardening, for example, women and men often cooperate. Men clear the heavy brush and cut down trees, while women cut the smaller or secondary undergrowth. Men build trellises and make and repair fences. Women do the weeding as needed and harvest most of the crops. Certain cultivars are more associated with certain genders. Women plant and harvest taro (*mayé*) and, generally, greens, bananas and sugarcane. Men are solely responsible for the planting of the ceremonial yams (*waapi*) and, generally, for planting the shorter food yams (*njaambi*). Taro gardening and taros themselves are particularly rich in female imagery and symbolism, while the ceremonial yams personify maleness.

There is no explicit prohibition against one gender performing most of the labor assigned to the other, but it is thought to be inappropriate. People feel sorry for a person forced to perform the duties of the opposite gender, and make disparaging remarks about the laziness of opposite-sex relatives who make this necessary. Once, before I fully appreciated the "femaleness" of taro, I publicly remarked about planting some in my garden. Several of my adopted female relatives immediately offered to do it for me to spare me (and themselves) from embarrassment, and later chided me for offending them in public.

In the daily round, women and men are often separated. Wives and husbands, and less frequently brothers and sisters, often sit together in the mornings, discussing plans for the day as they eat a simple breakfast prepared by the women. During the day, women may garden and men may tend ceremonial yams, engage in ritual activities, or hunt. At times, families garden together. People normally return to the village in the evenings. Women usually gather around the cook houses as they prepare the evening meal, while men gather around rest houses or yam houses to gossip, smoke, and chew betel nut. In small groups, men and women may eat and chat together in the evenings, but larger groupings are usually sex segregated. A husband and wife may sleep together,

although the more common pattern is for women to sleep in a cook house with the small children and for men to sleep in yam houses or rest houses.

Occasionally, men will travel afar for extended periods for wage labor, trade, and exchange, or to attend ceremonies in other villages. It is less common for women to travel away from their own villages. Ritual activities involve gender cooperation, with each attending to its assigned tasks. Women generally prepare the food, which men distribute. The actual performance of the ritual is the obligation of the men.

PARENTAL AND OTHER CARETAKER ROLES

For the first few years of a child's life, the mother and other close female relatives are the primary caretakers. Fathers may be very loving with their small children and play with toddlers of both genders, but their time with them is limited. Abelam of both genders are generally very affectionate with their children and very indulgent of them. Disciplining small children with physical punishment is very unusual in Abelam society (Scaglion, 1999a). When discipline becomes necessary, scolding or withholding food are more common punishments, and, as the primary caregivers, females are usually the disciplinarians. After the first several years, men take a more active hand in parenting boys, while women continue their primary role in socializing girls. When young girls are of an age to be sexually active, men again take a strong interest in their socialization. Abelam believe that sexual activity may be harmful to yam growth (Scaglion, 1998), and fathers and brothers are accountable for controlling the sexuality of their daughters and unmarried sisters. Men also share with women concerns to assure good marital matches for younger female relatives.

LEADERSHIP IN PUBLIC ARENAS

Leadership in public political arenas is almost exclusively restricted to men. This is not to say that women do not have power and do not make decisions. Women have considerable influence over the timing of major festivals (which depend on produce which the women control), over reproduction and child-rearing, and over subsistence.

Often, women meet informally in gender-exclusive groups and discuss these matters. But women's deliberations and decisions, whether individual or collective, are not aired in public village meetings.

In contrast, almost all of men's political discussions are conducted publicly in full view of both genders. An exception involves the aforementioned men's initiation complex, which excludes women. But political meetings and litigation are public. When "trouble" (*paaw*) breaks out in the village, big men call together informal meetings of concerned parties for talk, or simply show up at the scene of a dispute. Soon a crowd gathers, and public discussions (moots, literally "talk" or *kundi*) are held. Although women are permitted to talk at these meetings, and sometimes do so when urged, men dominate.

Gender and Religion

If Abelam women are the primary custodians of children, men control ritual and religion. Women have secrets related to birth, but men have ritual secrets. Each gender is excluded from the specialized knowledge of the other. A supernatural life force called *ngwaal* (soul substance) is thought to animate nature. This force is personified in ancestral spirits called *ngwaalndu* (literally, "spirit-person" or "grandfather-person"), normally male. Initiates are introduced to the *ngwaalndu* in the tambaran cult, the series of male initiation stages described above, from which women are barred. Each clan has an important *ngwaalndu* associated with it. Other lesser supernatural beings, such as *waalé* (water spirits), are equally known to both genders. Sorcerers (*kwisndu*), male magicians who learn to control *ngwaal*, and *kutakwa*, female witches who harm others, often involuntarily, are also thought to exist. It is thought that, when the world began people lived in a hole in the ground near the Sepik River. They were starving, having nothing to eat but dirt, even though there was a garden of plenty growing above on the earth. A dog found its way to the surface. Later its (male) owner followed the dog, discovered the way out, and led the people to the surface of the earth.

Leisure, Recreation, and the Arts

While any judgment about leisure time is somewhat subjective, a formal time allocation analysis (Scaglion, 1986b) revealed that Abelam of both genders have a reasonable amount of spare time. Basic subsistence is accomplished without undue exertion. Collectively, Abelam average about 3 hr a day gardening and 1 hr hunting. They sleep an average of 9 hr 24 min per day. Males spend about 10.4% of their time idle, compared with 9.5% for females; women spend about 6.0% of their time visiting compared with 4.5% for men. Much leisure time is spent in the company of persons of the same gender because of gender segregation during the workday. Both genders like to gossip, chat, and tell stories. Men often discuss politics, yam growing, and ritual matters. Personal relationships are more frequently the topics of conversation for women. Much visiting and socializing takes place after dark, when possibilities for economic activities are more limited, and people come together in both mixed and same gender groupings. Abelam do not normally engage in "games" for recreation.

Relative Status of Men and Women

The overall relationship between Abelam women and men has been described as one of "duality," "balanced opposition," or "complementary opposition" (Losche, 1982; Scaglion, 1986a). Here, "opposition" should not necessarily be understood as adversarial or antagonistic, but rather as a dialectical process. In traditional Abelam society, reproduction and ritual are equally significant. Both are thought to be crucial for the continuance and well-being of humanity. One is the domain of women, and the other of men. Each gender has secrets relative to its own realm. Each is excluded from the other's area, but neither seems to feel unworthy because of it. Men are barred from menstrual (birthing) huts; women are excluded from spirit houses. For this reason, both women and men enjoy relatively high status in Abelam society.

Influenced by other literature, I have previously described certain relationships between the sexes, especially during the yam growing season, as potentially "polluting" (Scaglion, 1986a). More recently, I have come to understand these relationships somewhat differently, and I now use this term in a more limited sense. In general, nubile females are powerful and can upset the balance of certain male activities. Likewise, virile young men can upset female activities. For this reason, the genders are often segregated. "Pollution" has a denotation of uncleanliness that is not always appropriate for these situations. "Power" and "danger" might be more accurate renderings of the ideas involved. For instance, sexual intercourse is thought to be inimical to yam growth. Thus, to insure good ceremonial yams, it is better to keep males and females apart to avoid temptation. Consequently, women are kept out of ceremonial yam gardens. This taboo does not apply to all females, though. Adolescent girls and elderly women are permitted entry because their sexuality is not considered dangerous.

There are many areas of Abelam life in which the rights and privileges of men and women are equivalent. Both may inherit gender-specific property from their relatives, for example. Both have comparable rights in land, and both control the fruits of their labor. However, despite the overall principle of gender equality in Abelam society, there are some specific areas of inequality in which women are disadvantaged. One involves a sexual double standard. Since Abelam practice polygyny, it is not always considered wrong for a married man to have a sexual relationship with an unmarried woman who might be a potential marriage partner. On the other hand, it is always considered wrong for a married woman to have an affair. In this sense, a husband controls his wife's sexuality, but not the reverse. Furthermore, there is a facade of male superiority in which women, particularly young ones, are thought not to be able to control their own actions, and particularly their sexuality. Therefore it falls to male relatives to look after them for their own good. In "controlling" the unseemly behavior of their female relatives, it is sometimes considered culturally appropriate for husbands to "discipline" their wives and for brothers to "discipline" their sisters by employing physical punishment (Scaglion, 1999a). Therefore the greater proportion of Abelam family violence is directed against women. Also, in legal matters, women were traditionally considered to be "jural minors" and were normally represented by male relatives, whereas men routinely represented themselves. While these patterns are changing (Scaglion, 1990), women have not yet achieved equality in the legal realm.

SEXUALITY

Sexual relationships, while recognized as enjoyable, are thought by the Abelam to be potentially dangerous and harmful. Consequently, there are many occasions during which sexual activity is prohibited. The most important is throughout the yam growing season, a period of roughly 6 months, when there is in fact very little sexual activity, even between spouses. Apart from being detrimental to yam growth, sex distracts men from their important tasks and is therefore considered dangerous. It is also thought that sex robs men of their strength. Men who are physically small are thought to have engaged in sexual activity too early or too frequently, preventing them from growing properly. Some of the reasons for penis bleeding during certain male initiation rituals include eliminating "bad blood" resulting from sexual intercourse and limiting possibilities for intercourse for some time afterwards. Men's penises are routinely bled after their honeymoons because of increased sexual activity. It is thought that women can purge themselves regularly through menstruation; penis bleeding is the male functional equivalent.

Both genders are recognized as having sexual appetites, and both may make sexual overtures. However, because sex has more potential danger for men, it is thought that women often seduce men. Because any sort of sexual activity is equally prohibited during taboo periods, autoeroticism and homosexuality do not substitute for heterosexual activity during these times. Owing in part to the strict sexual division of labor, individuals of ambiguous gender are uncommon, but nonconformity is not socially censured.

COURTSHIP AND MARRIAGE

There are two forms of courtship and marriage, one formal and one informal. In the formal type, a male suitor makes his intentions known to the family of his intended during her *naramtaakwa* period. The suitor will cook a yam and send it to the girl and her family. If the family does not approve of the match, they will send it back. By accepting the yam, the family indicates consent for a marriage. If the young woman likes the suitor, she will eat the yam and the couple are formally engaged. If she refuses the yam, thereby rejecting the suitor, the family is shamed and they eat the yam themselves.

If an engagement results from formal courtship, the couple are married some months later. The man's family prepares a house to which the newlyweds retire. For a week they stay in the house, leaving only to relieve themselves. Food is brought to them. When they emerge, the man's penis is bled and he is washed; the woman's family washes her. Subsequently, the couple observe taboos against certain foods. They do not drink cold water or eat coconut, meat, and certain other foods. They plant a garden together, and when it is harvested, the taboos are lifted.

If no marriage is contracted in this formal way, many informal arrangements are possible. The young woman's parents may arrange a match for her and urge her to accept it. She may simply begin living with a man she likes and try to get her parents to accept it. A couple may elope. But regardless of how a couple comes together, when a child is born some sort of formal arrangements must be agreed upon with the woman's family in order to legitimize the child as a member of the man's kinship group. Abelam would call this brideprice, since they see it as formally recognizing the marriage, but it also acts as progeny price, legitimizing this and subsequent children. A typical brideprice might be six or seven shell rings (*yéwaa*), a sort of general-purpose currency. Sister exchanges are also common. If no agreement about brideprice can be reached after the birth of a child, the trial marriage usually breaks up, the woman returns home, and the child becomes a member of the mother's kinship group. There is no prohibition against premarital sex, and no shame attaches to a child who becomes a member of the mother's group in this way.

Unmarried people are allowed a great deal of sexual freedom so long as they pursue their courtships at culturally appropriate times and places. Both genders may make sexual overtures or indicate an interest in a potential partner. Marriages are thus a combination of arrangements between families and a couple's inclinations. Clan and moiety exogamy are observed in considering appropriate partners. Widows and widowers are free to remarry, and often do.

HUSBAND–WIFE RELATIONSHIP

The early years of many marriages, especially polygynous ones, are marked by sexual jealousies and strife (Scaglion, 1999a), since a new cowife represents a threat to her counterpart. New marriages of all types frequently fail. Either gender may decide to terminate an unsatisfactory relationship. If brideprice has not yet been paid (see above), the wife and any children return to her family. If brideprice has been paid, the children, especially if they are older, typically remain with their father. If a woman for whom brideprice has been paid

remarries, the new husband pays brideprice to the former husband. Women always have a place with their natal families, where they will be looked after by their father, uncles, and brothers. Similarly, single men will be looked after by their female relatives. But, marriage being a desirable state, few adults remain single.

Once a marriage becomes stable, it typically lasts until the death of one partner. A great deal of love, affection, and cooperation can be observed between many married couples. A wife and husband often sit together in the morning and evening, discussing the day's activities and making plans for the future. Men and women complement each other in many ways, and single adults are thought to be incomplete.

OTHER CROSS-SEX RELATIONSHIPS

Besides marriages, the most significant cross-sex relationships are between brothers and sisters. Sisters always have a home with their brothers. If their marriages break up, if their husbands are ill, or during whatever sorts of crises, women can count on the help and support of their brothers who will perform all the male tasks necessary for their welfare as needed. Similarly, brothers can count on sisters to feed them when their wives are away in menstrual huts and to perform whatever female tasks are necessary for their welfare as needed. This strong relationship provides a ready alternative to bad marriages, such that Abelam women and men do not have to tolerate domestic strife or abuse.

CHANGE IN ATTITUDES, BELIEFS, AND PRACTICES REGARDING GENDER

Many changes have occurred in Abelam society since the ethnographic baseline presented here. Increasing exposure to western culture and the continuing education of both genders has resulted in social change that has generally been in the direction of western patterns. Polygyny is much less common today, for instance. The sexual division of labor has become less marked. At the same time, family violence seems to be increasing. Young people's families have increasingly less say in whom they marry, and marriages appear to be less stable than before. Belief in the tambaran cult has declined, and male initiation has been abbreviated where it still exists. Many children attend school, and the long periods of seclusion during adolescence have been eliminated or greatly attenuated. Ceremonial yam growing is still important, but many taboos have been relaxed. As a result, sexual activities are more frequent and less carefully controlled, and the Abelam population has burgeoned. Wage labor has opened up new opportunities for women. The Constitution of the Independent State of Papua New Guinea and the National Goals and Directive Principles both explicitly recognize the rights of women in various realms, including political behavior. It will be interesting to see what changes in Abelam gender ideology result.

BIBLIOGRAPHY

Hauser-Schäublin, B. (1995). Puberty rites, women's *naven*, and initiation: Women's rituals of transition in Abelam and Iatmul culture. In N. C. Lutkehaus & P. B. Roscoe (Eds.), *Gender rituals: Female initiation in Melanesia* (pp. 33–53). New York: Routledge.

Huber-Greub, B. (1988). *Kokospalmenmenschen: Boden und Alltag und ihre Bedeutung im Selbstverständnis der Abelam von Kimbangwa (East Sepik Province, Papua New Guinea)*. Basel: Ethnologisches Seminar der Universität und Museum für Völkerkunde.

Kaberry, P. M. (1940–41). The Abelam tribe, Sepik District, New Guinea: A preliminary report. *Oceania, 11*, 233–258, 345–367.

Losche, D. B. (1982). Male and female in Abelam society: Opposition and complementarity (Doctoral dissertation, Columbia University, 1982). *University Microfilms International* 8307604.

McGuigan, N. D. (1992). *The social context of Abelam art: A comparison of art, religion and leadership in two Abelam communities.* Doctoral dissertation, University of Ulster, Northern Ireland.

Scaglion, R. (1976). Seasonal patterns in western Abelam conflict management practices: The ethnography of law in the Maprik Sub-district, East Sepik Province, Papua New Guinea (Doctoral dissertation, University of Pittsburgh). *University Microfilms International* 77-15,238.

Scaglion, R. (1981). Samukundi Abelam conflict management: Implications for legal planning in Papua New Guinea. *Oceania, 52*, 28–38.

Scaglion, R. (1986a). Sexual segregation and ritual pollution in Abelam society: implications for data collection. In T. L. Whitehead & M. E. Conaway (Eds.), *Self, sex and gender in cross-cultural fieldwork* (pp. 151–163). Urbana: University of Illinois Press.

Scaglion, R. (1986b). The importance of nighttime observations in time allocation studies. *American Ethnologist, 13*, 537–545.

Scaglion, R. (1990). Legal adaptation in a Papua New Guinea village court. *Ethnology, 29*, 17–33.

Scaglion, R. (1998). Abelam: giant yams and cycles of sex, warfare and ritual. In M. Ember, C. R. Ember, & D. Levinson (Eds.), *Portraits of culture: Ethnographic originals* (Vol. 4, pp. 277–300). Upper Saddle River, NJ: Prentice-Hall.

Scaglion, R. (1999a). Spare the rod and spoil the woman? Family violence in Abelam society. In D. A. Counts, J. K. Brown, & J. C. Campbell (Eds.), *To have and to hit: Cultural perspectives on wife beating* (2nd ed., pp. 137–152). Urbana: University of Illinois Press. (Adapted and reprinted from *Pacific Studies, 13*, 537–545.)

Scaglion, R. (1999b). Yam cycles and timeless time in Melanesia. *Ethnology, 38*, 211–225.

Schroeder, R. (1992) *Initiation and Religion: A case study from the Wosera of Papua New Guinea.* Fribourg, Switzerland: Studia Instituti Antropos.

Armenians

Armine Ishkanian

ALTERNATIVE NAMES

In Armenian, Armenia is called *Hayastan* and Armenians are known as *Hai*.

LOCATION

Armenia is a small (29,800 km^2) landlocked mountainous country (37.2% mountains) in Eurasia. The remainder of the land is a combination of pastures (29.8%), woodlands (12%), farmland (3.2%), and arid plains (17.8%). The highest peak is Mount Aragats, with an elevation of 4,090 m, and the largest body of water is Lake Sevan. The Arax, Akhurian, Medsamor, Razdan, Azat, Arpa, Vorotan, Debed, and Agstev are the primary rivers running through Armenia. Armenia shares a border with Georgia to the north, Azerbaijan to the east, Iran to the south, and Turkey to the west. Armenia has a population of approximately 3.8 million (3,754,100) and a territory of 11,490 square miles. The largest city in Armenia is the capital, Yerevan. The population is 96% Armenian and the other 4% is made up of various minorities: Russians, Kurds, Yezidis, Greeks, Jews, and Assyrians. Armenian (*Hayeren*) is the official language and the official state religion is the Armenian Apostolic Church (*Hayastaneayts Ekeghetsi*).

CULTURAL OVERVIEW

The 3,000 year history of Armenia has been filled with a continual cycle of wars, violence, and loss of independence, interspersed with brief periods of renewal, renaissance, and autonomy. When the last independent Armenian kingdom of Cilicia collapsed in 1375, Armenians became scattered around Anatolia, Persia, Transcaucasia, and other smaller communities across Europe and South Asia. Over the next five centuries Armenia would be successively ruled by the Mameluks of Egypt, Mongolian Tartars, the Ottoman Turks, Safavid Persians, and the Russians.

By the 19th century and in the first two decades of the 20th century most Armenians were peasants living in the Ottoman Empire, where they were identified as the *Ermeni Millet* (the Armenian Community, which was identified upon a religious basis), and in the Russian Empire under a system of *polozhenye* (statutes). In these scattered communities the Armenian Apostolic Church was the center of communal life and, along with the family, it was the only means by which a distinct Armenian ethnic and religious identity was maintained. Extended families (*gerdastan*) were patriarchal with patrilineal descent. The family was not only the source of identification and support for Armenians, but it also served as a protector during periods of famine, feud, and warfare. In villages, homes were built directly next to one another to provide greater security. Children were taught to honor and obey their elders and to develop a sense of duty, obligation, and loyalty to the family and other relations. Obligations and loyalty were first to family members, kinsmen, friends, neighbors, and lastly strangers (Hoogasian & Matossian, 1982).

Extended families were a part of exogamous clans and wives could be taken from different clans within the same village or from clans in other villages. Clans were led by the patriarchs of extended families, and within these families power and responsibilities were divided according to age, gender, and position within the family. Children and new wives (especially those who had not yet given birth to a son) had the lowest status. In some areas in Armenia a girl lost her individuality after marriage, and in some villages these new brides (*nor hars*) had to remain mute for several years after marriage as a sign of their modesty and respect for their elders. In many families, the young woman was never addressed by her Christian name, but was always referred to as "bride" (*hars*). These women could only communicate with their older children and husband if no one else was around. If they wished to convey a message to anyone else in the family, including their mother-in-law, they would tell the children who would then act as messengers. The release of the bride from her muteness was at the discretion of the mother-in-law who could do so as early as the birth of the first male grandchild or as late as 10 years after the marriage. This muteness reinforced the lower status of women both within the household and in the larger community. The symbolic subordination of girls began as early as birth when the umbilical cords of girls were buried in the front yard to insure that the girl would grow up to be a respected homemaker (*dahn deegeen*), whereas the umbilical cord of boys was buried outside the fence to insure his success in worldly affairs and that he would not grow up to become a homebody. At that time, it was also common for people to express condolences at the birth of a daughter. During this period, women's only path to power was if they lived long enough and had sons in whose homes, in old age, they would be regarded as powerful matriarchs (Hoogasian & Matossian, 1982).

Between the 15th and 19th centuries there were many unsuccessful attempts by individuals and organized groups to reestablish an independent Armenian state. These national aspirations eventually led to organized resistance and rebellion beginning in the late 19th century, when Western-educated Armenian intellectuals pursued an agenda for national independence, individual freedom, and political rights. However, beginning in 1915, the nationalist struggle evolved into a struggle for sheer survival as the Ottoman Turks began a systematic genocide that included mass killings and the deportation of over 1.5 million Armenians living in the Ottoman Empire. Those who survived fled east and settled in and around Yerevan. On May 24, 1918, Armenian troops were able to hold off the Turkish eastward advance at Sardarabad, a town 25 miles east of Yerevan, and 4 days later the Armenians declared their independence and established the Republic of Armenia. The new government attempted to establish a parliamentary democracy, but its efforts were complicated by the severe internal and external difficulties facing the nation after World War I. Independence came to an abrupt end in December 1920 when the Soviet Red Army marched into Yerevan, annexing Armenia to the Soviet Union (Hovannisian, 1967).

When Armenia became part of the USSR, the Soviet government, in an effort to consolidate its power, began to challenge the traditional values and "break the cake of custom" (Matossian, 1961). Breaking the cake of custom meant that Communist/Soviet culture was to supersede all ethnic cultural beliefs and traditions. Since the family was and continued to be the focus of conservative resistance against the new communist regime, the communists sought to "emancipate" women and develop loyalties outside the traditional patriarchal household. In the Soviet constitution the political equality of the sexes was mandated and women were given the same rights as men.

The Soviet period brought many changes: arranged marriages were banned, divorce became easier to obtain, the state provided free health care (including abortions), childcare, and even counseling for women. In the 1920s several women's organizations, including the Women's Division of the Communist Party (*Kinbazhin*) and the Commission for the Improvement of the Way of Life of Women (*Kanants Kentsaghe Barelavogh Hantznazhogove*), were established to encourage allegiance to the state and promote its communist projects.

Women were encouraged to enter public life, and by 1931 more changes had begun to take place to facilitate the entry of women into the work force. Many nurseries, kindergartens, and day-care centers were established to allow women to work. Consequently, in the 1930s women constituted a larger proportion of the work force than had previously been the case. Beginning in the 1930s girls were also entering technical and higher educational institutions in large numbers. The state attacks upon traditional families and gender roles only abated during and immediately after World War II, since the Soviet Union had suffered great human and material losses. To recoup these losses, the state encouraged couples to have many children (four or more) and rewarded them with subsidies such as free milk, living stipends, and better homes. Although women made gains in public life, attitudes about the family and women's role within the family continued in a traditional patriarchal pattern.

Following the collapse of the Soviet Union, women have suffered many setbacks in the political and economic realms. It is now apparent that gender equality in the Soviet Union was due to legislative quotas rather than to changes in beliefs about gender roles and relations. Although there has been a return to patriarchal beliefs, contemporary attitudes regarding gender roles are a mixture of Soviet and pre-Soviet beliefs, as women who enjoyed certain rights and privileges during the Soviet period have been reluctant to surrender them in the post-Soviet period.

Cultural Construction of Gender

In Armenia, men and women are believed to be physically and psychologically different. The culture recognizes both genders as equally important to the survival, preservation, and success of the nation and people (*azaga bahbanoom*). Although the Armenian homeland is referred to as the "Fatherland" (*Hayrenik*), the symbol of the nation is "Mother Armenia" (*Mayr Hayastan*).

As far back as the pre-Christian period, the family was considered to be the most sacred of all institutions and an individual's identity and social status depended on their belonging to a particular family and their role within that family (Zeitlian, 1992). Family is still perceived as being of the highest value in its capacity as an intermediary, located between the individual and the state. People in Armenia feel isolated, economically vulnerable, marginalized, and unable to advance socially, economically, or politically without strong family ties. Armenians explain the centrality of family in the culture as being due to the fact that Armenia was not independent for many centuries and that in this absence of statehood, the concept of "Nation-as-a-Family," a sui generis "familism," evolved in Armenian society (United Nations Development Program, 1998).

Within the family men are supposed to be strong, assertive, decisive, and firm in their convictions and opinions. The father, as the head of the household, is considered the "keeper of the household flame" (*dahn odjakhi tsooghuh bahoghuh*) because he goes out into the world and works and/or fights to protect his home and family. The mother, meanwhile, is considered to be the hearth (*odjakh*) of the home because she selflessly tends to the home built by and supported by her husband. The gender roles and stereotypes ascribed to men and women within the family apply in the public sphere as well, where men are the leaders and decision-makers in the political, economic, and military realms, while women are the self-sacrificing nurturers and supporters of the nation (i.e., the family writ large).

Attractive women are those who are slender, have clear unblemished skin and large eyes and lips, and are chaste, reserved, soft-spoken, and modest. Although many women in Armenia have careers and work outside the home, their primary concern should be their family. Women should refrain from being aggressive, overly ambitious, and assertive as these are "masculine" (*dkhamartkayin*) traits and mark a woman as being a "manly woman" (*dkhamart-geen*). Attractive men are those who are confident, self-sufficient, hard-working, and ambitious, and who are able to provide for their families and protect their honor.

Following Sovietization, Armenians adopted modern forms of dress and men wore pants and suits, while women wore dresses and skirts with hemlines below the knee. Until the mid-1990s, most women did not wear pants or shorts. In the post-Soviet period young women in Yerevan have adopted a more liberal style of dress, and they wear shorts, pants, miniskirts, and high- or platform-heel shoes. Rural women and women in provincial cities continue to abstain from wearing pants, shorts, and short skirts. Men in both rural and urban areas wear pants all year round and short- or long-sleeve shirts.

Gender over the Life Cycle

Childhood (*mangootyoon*) is supposed to be one of the happiest times in a person's life. Boys (*dghaner*) and girls (*aghchigner*) are both given a great deal of love and care. In both rural and urban areas children are cared for by their mothers, grandmothers, and less frequently their older sisters or aunts. Although most couples wish to have a boy as their first child, once born, girls are treated equally; they do not receive less food, love, or care than boys. In urban and rural areas girls and boys attend school until age 17 and are expected to learn to read and write. Since Armenia has a 98% rate of literacy, it is clear that the majority of children successfully acquire these skills. In urban areas a university degree is considered a part of a woman's dowry, and a university-educated woman is considered a more desirable spouse and mother because she will be able to educate and discipline her children better and assist her husband to advance politically. In rural areas the majority of men and women marry immediately after graduating from high school and very few villagers attend universities or technical schools.

The passage from childhood to adolescence (*badanegootyoon*) is not publicly marked, but following puberty boys and girls begin to act and to be treated by differently by their parents and others.

Socialization of Boys and Girls

Mothers and grandmothers are primarily responsible for early child-rearing. During infancy and early childhood, breast milk or food is not withheld from children of either sex. Depending on the socioeconomic and educational background of the family, girls are often given music and art lessons. Urban Armenian families strive to bring up their daughters to be cultured and courteous young woman who will one day become respected homemakers (*dahn deegeen*). Regardless of whether or not a woman has a career, and many urban women in Armenia have careers, a woman must also be a good homemaker and be able to keep an immaculate home, cook traditional meals, and bake exquisite pastries. In rural areas, where women do not pursue careers, girls are taught to cook, clean, grow vegetables, and tend to the farm animals; they are not given music and art lessons. In urban areas, boys are encouraged to play sports and chess, and to take music lessons. In rural areas, boys work as shepherds or help their fathers in the fields. Boys in urban and rural areas are discouraged from helping their mothers with household chores because parents believe that this will make them less masculine.

Parents and grandparents purchase most of the toys children play with. Girls are given dolls, teasets, paint sets, and craft sets, while boys are encouraged to play with building sets, cars, trucks, toy swords, and bows and arrows. From the age of 6, boys are allowed to play outside in the communal yards (*pag*) or public parks with other boys, but from a very young age girls are discouraged from spending too much time playing in the communal yard and often spend most of their time indoors. When girls are allowed to play in the yard and parks, they are supervised and only allowed to play games such as hopscotch or jump rope with other girls.

Children of both sexes are expected to behave and listen to their caretakers, but boys are expected to be more adventurous and to engage in more daring activities. When boys misbehave, parents explain their sons' misconduct by saying, "He is a boy and this is how he learns about life" (*dgahe, ayt bes e sovorom gyanki masin*). Although the type of disciplinary methods used varies among those families who believe in and practice corporal punishment (generally spanking) to those who prefer to discipline children verbally, girls are generally spared corporal punishment and instead are verbally reprimanded and "shamed" by their parents. Very often a girl who misbehaves or does something which is thought to be unseemly for an Armenian girl, she is told, "It is shameful" (*amot e*). By constantly emphasizing the importance of being proper and avoiding "shameful" behaviors, girls learn to censor their actions in order to avoid being reprimanded by their parents. Parents rarely use this strategy in disciplining boys, and there are very few behaviors that are considered "shameful" for boys.

Puberty and Adolescence

In adolescence (*badanegootyoon*) boys have more freedom than girls. A girl's freedom of movement, already limited in childhood, is further restricted in adolescence. Teenage girls are expected to come home directly after school and to keep their parents informed of their whereabouts at all times. If a girl has older brothers, she is expected to obey them as she obeys her parents and to respect their opinions. Meanwhile, a boy regardless of age, is expected to protect his sisters and to guard their honor, which often means fighting with other boys. During adolescence, boys begin to smoke cigarettes and drink alcohol. Since there is no enforced legal drinking age, boys spend a great deal of time drinking with friends in cafés and bars. Increasingly, girls are also beginning to spend time in cafés and bars either with their boyfriends or with a group of girlfriends. However, girls generally frequent bars and cafés where parents, neighbors, or relatives will not see them and, unlike boys, avoid smoking in outdoor cafés and abstain from drinking alcohol.

Adolescent girls are constantly warned about the dangers of being harassed by boys or men on the streets or of being kidnapped and forced into a marriage by an undesirable suitor. This leads many girls to travel in groups to avoid unwanted advances.

Attainment of Adulthood

Graduation from high school at age 17 marks the entry of adolescents into adulthood. Attainment of adulthood means that a young man or woman is able to marry and attend college, but it does not mean that he or she may move out of the parental home. Single men and women in both rural and urban areas rarely live independently of their parents; they only move out of the parental home after marriage. Therefore, while graduation from high school marks the end of adolescence, marriage marks the entry of women and men into independent adulthood. Men and women stay with their parents because of financial and cultural considerations (i.e., it is shameful to live alone). When living with their parents, adult children are not expected to contribute to the family budget, except when one or both parents is unemployed or deceased.

Middle Age and Old Age

Until recently many urban Armenian men and women looked forward to middle age because it meant that they could retire and spend more time with their families and on leisure activities. As pensions have dwindled and social services have disappeared in the post-Soviet period, women and men no longer look forward to retirement, because it has come to mean impoverishment and powerlessness. However, in rural areas, where patriarchal traditions are more prevalent and where pensions were never an integral part of one's retirement income, women still look forward to middle age because it brings a gain in stature. In old age, men and women become equal. Elders are respected in Armenian society and are referred to by family members and strangers as "father" (*hayrig*) or "mother" (*mayrig*).

PERSONALITY DIFFERENCES BY GENDER

Men are expected to be decisive, outspoken, clever, ambitious, and firm in their decisions and opinions. A weak man is one who bends to his wife's will and is unable to make his own decisions in life. Such men are ridiculed and not respected. Women, on the other hand, are supposed to be patient, kind, modest, sweet-tempered, and flexible. Although Armenian women are not assertive, they have developed strategies that allow them to pursue their objectives without appearing to be aggressive and confrontational. Armenian women often feign agreement in order to avoid an argument, and use subterfuge and subtle manipulation to achieve their objectives. Avoiding conflict is a priority for Armenian women, and from a very early age girls learn how to achieve their goals surreptitiously.

GENDER-RELATED SOCIAL GROUPS

The family is structured around and relies upon the presence and active participation of both parents. Divorce is taboo and discouraged in Armenia except in cases where there is an extremely abusive husband or when a wife is caught having an extramarital affair. Until recently, most married couples in urban areas lived with the parents of the groom. If there was more than one son

in a family, the eldest lived with the parents while the younger sons rented or bought their own homes. Since 1991, between 700,000 and a million people have emigrated from Armenia; departing families often sell their homes. Young married couples are beginning to take advantage of the better housing market to purchase their own homes, and few couples now live with the husband's parents, except in rural and more traditional urban families. It is still shameful for a man to move in with his wife's family. Such men are called "house groom" (*dahn pessa*) and are thought of as being weak.

Relations with both matrilineal and patrilineal kin groups are maintained, and the relationships individuals have with matrilineal and patrilineal kin varies from family to family. Generally the closest relationships are between same-sex cousins.

For most urban women, their nonkin gender-related social groups are comprised of their friends from high school and college. Until marriage, most young urban women maintain these relationships and consider their friends as confidantes and helpers. After marriage, young women have a difficult time maintaining their friendships because of the double burden of housework and work outside the home. After marriage, women develop friendships with their female neighbors. Female neighbors drink coffee together, smoke cigarettes, and trade gossip. Neighbors also often lend money to one another, baby-sit one another's children for short periods of time, and help each other in preparing feasts.

Nonkin gender-related social groups for men are comprised of their friends from high school and college, as well as their friends from their neighborhoods (*tagh*) and/or yards. Men are expected to maintain their closer friendships well beyond marriage because these friendships serve as the basis for political advancement and business networking.

In rural areas most women only associate with same-sex cousins and aunts until marriage, and with neighbors and their husband's female cousins after marriage. Rural men associate with their uncles, same-sex cousins, and neighbors both during and after marriage.

GENDER ROLES IN ECONOMICS

In rural areas there is a gendered division of labor among men and women. Women in the household do much of the work on the farm: they milk the cows, feed the chickens and pigs, bake the bread, make cheese, butter, and yogurt, and tend to the small household gardens. Although men work the large agricultural lands, build structures, and dig wells, the division of labor is uneven because women work throughout the year while men only work in the planting and harvest seasons.

In urban areas, there is also a gendered division of labor. Depending on a man's educational and socioeconomic background, he can choose from a variety of professions including law, medicine, academia, politics, government, engineering, law enforcement, trade, and service work. With the same socioeconomic and educational restrictions, women can choose from the following professions: law, medicine, education, academia, engineering, and the arts. In the home, women are responsible for all household chores, including cleaning, cooking, laundry, shopping, and making preserves. Men, however, are only responsible for maintaining the family's automobile.

With the transition to a market economy, many men and women have become involved in trading. Both men and women have become shuttle traders, traveling to foreign countries to bring back goods to sell in Armenia. Traditionally, men were the ones who were absent from home because of work, trade, and warfare. With the globalization of the economy, the number of women who leave Armenia to work abroad as labor migrants or shuttle traders is increasing. Both men and women can equally inherit land, money, and property.

PARENTAL AND OTHER CARETAKER ROLES

Women are the primary caretakers and motherhood is seen as being sacred (*soorp*). "Sacred" motherhood refers to the Armenian belief dating from Armenia's pre-Christian past when the primary deity in the pantheon was Anahit, the goddess of fertility, morality, and maternity (Zeitlian, 1992). The role of mothers in Armenia has traditionally been to transmit and perpetuate the Armenian culture, Christian faith, values, and traditions. As the hearth (*odjakh*), pillar (*syun*), and light-giving lamp (*jrak*) of the family, the Armenian mother is expected to love and nurture her children and to sacrifice her own needs and desires for those of her family. Women who are not mothers are pitied because they have not

attained the highest status a woman can achieve. Meanwhile mothers who do not sacrifice their own needs for the needs of their own children are looked down upon and criticized. The mother–child relationship is the closest relationship among Armenians, regardless of the gender of the child, and mothers act as confidantes to both their sons and daughters. They view their sons as their protectors (*bashban*) and their daughters as their helpers (*ogknagan*). In Armenia, the most common pledge is "*mors arev*" which means "upon my mother's life."

Fathers are mainly concerned with providing for their children, protecting them from strangers, and disciplining them. Fathers strive to set a positive example for their sons and endeavor to make them physically and mentally strong. They also assist their sons to advance politically and in their chosen careers. Fathers make every effort to protect their daughters and to provide them with a good education and cultural training. Children are supposed to love their mothers and to fear their fathers. While this is true in rural areas and in most patriarchal households, in most egalitarian families children love and respect both parents.

LEADERSHIP IN PUBLIC ARENAS

Men dominate in the realms of politics and government. There are very few women involved in over 50 political parties registered in Armenia and, following the 1997 parliamentary elections, there are only eight women in the National Assembly. Armenians believe that women are not supposed to be involved or interested in politics because politics is believed to be "men's work" and inherently corrupt. Therefore most women are less inclined toward an active involvement in politics and public life except for the nearly 3,000 nongovernmental organizations (NGOs) that have emerged in the post-Soviet period. Even though women are active in the NGO sector, where they lead two thirds of these organizations, they have not yet been able to advance in the realm of politics and in the Armenian government.

Although a number of Armenian women fought and defended their homes during the Turkish Genocide of the Armenians (1915–18) and the Nagorno Karabagh conflict (1988–94), men have traditionally been the warriors and military leaders in Armenian society. Currently, women do not serve in the Armenian army.

GENDER AND RELIGION

Until the adoption of Christianity as state religion in 301 CE, Armenians worshipped various deities. The primary deity in the Armenian pantheon was the goddess Anahit, a morally pure and virtuous goddess who nurtured her worshippers, provided them with guidance, and comforted them in their times of need. After Armenia adopted Christianity, Armenian society became more patriarchal and the beliefs related to Anahit were transferred to Mary (*Astvatazin*) (Zeitlian, 1992, p. viii). Today, Armenian women play a marginal role in the Armenian Church, and although there are male and female saints, Armenians do not have any monastic orders for women nor are there any female priests.

LEISURE, RECREATION, AND THE ARTS

In rural areas single and married men have more leisure time than women. They either spend this time with friends and male kin in family gardens, where they are served food and drink by the women of the household, or at the village social club playing chess, checkers, dominos, or backgammon. In rural areas women spend what little leisure time they have catching up on secondary chores (e.g., sewing, knitting) or, if they are relatively well off, watching television, drinking coffee, and gossiping with neighbors. In urban areas, men also have more leisure time than women because they do not have the double burden. Urban men, depending on their socioeconomic status, spend time at friends' homes, cafés, or restaurants eating, drinking, and networking. Older men, or men who cannot afford cafés or restaurants, spend their time in public parks reading newspapers, playing dominos or chess, or discussing politics. In the home, men spend their leisure time watching television (news or sports events) or playing cards, dominos, or backgammon with their sons and male neighbors or friends. Urban married and single women spend their leisure time drinking coffee and gossiping with female friends and neighbors in their homes. Increasingly, however, single women are beginning to spend their leisure time at cafés with their girlfriends. During weekends families spend time on country outings or visiting relatives. On weekends and weekday evenings married urban couples also visit each other and spend time playing cards, drinking wine, vodka, or cognac, and discussing politics, arts, and culture.

RELATIVE STATUS OF MEN AND WOMEN

Men have a higher status than women in the economic and political spheres. In the family, men are seen as the "head of household," and in rural areas or more traditional urban families men are the primary decision-makers. In urban educated middle-class families men and women participate equally in decision-making.

Although women are also able to voice their marriage choices and initiate divorce, men have more control over their sexuality and marriage choices. However, in educational matters men and women are equal, because their choices are heavily influenced by their parents who not only advise their children regarding career choices, but also assist them in getting accepted by a university.

SEXUALITY

Women are supposed to be virgins at marriage, but men are expected to have had some sexual experience prior to marriage. How they gain this experience varies from individual to individual; some boys have their first sexual experiences with prostitutes, others with their girlfriends. From puberty, children are taught that sex is a private act between two people, and that it is a dangerous act that is only sanctified by marriage. Sexual experimentation is forbidden and children are warned about the dangers of sex and masturbation. Because sex education courses are not taught in schools and parents are too ashamed to speak with their children about sex, girls and boys learn about sex from their friends and older siblings. Although premarital sex is still considered taboo, following independence more and more young Armenian couples are having sex before marriage.

Within marriage, sex is considered a marital duty (*amoosnagan bardaganootyoon*); men are obligated to satisfy their wives and women are obligated to have sex with their husbands whenever the husband wishes it. Armenians believe that if a man's sexual needs are not fulfilled, he may have physical problems and become seriously ill. Although extramarital affairs are not condoned for either gender, men are usually forgiven while women are punished, stigmatized, and, in extreme cases, murdered. If a man learns that his wife is having an extramarital affair, he must divorce her or risk losing his position and respect in society. Homosexuality, cross-dressing, and cross-sex identification are considered deviant behaviors.

COURTSHIP AND MARRIAGE

Armenians are monogamous and there are very few arranged marriages. Most couples in urban and rural areas marry for love. In rural and urban areas, most couples marry shortly after both families agree on the union; long engagements are rare. Men initiate courtship and marriage. Courtship leading to marriage begins when a young man, who is in love with a young woman, goes to her house and asks her father for his daughter's hand in marriage (*aghchig oozel*). If the father agrees, the young man and his relatives bring gifts, including jewelry, cognac, and flowers, to the bride-to-be and celebrate the couple's *khosgap* (tying of words). Following the *khosgap*, the couple date for a few weeks or months and either become engaged (*nshanvel*) or immediately marry (*amoosnanal*). Given the difficult socioeconomic conditions in Armenia, most couples no longer follow these steps and formalities in the courtship process. Instead, most couples nowadays marry shortly after receiving the bride's father's blessing. Couples can marry in a church or at the state office for marriages. Either partner can call off the engagement by returning or asking for the return of the engagement ring (*nshani madani*).

In rural areas, villagers maintain the "red apple" (*karmir khnzor*) tradition in which the groom's family must display the bloodied sheets from the marriage bed on the day after the wedding. However, urban residents do not maintain this tradition; they perceive it as backward (*hedamnatz*).

Many couples in Armenia begin to have children soon after marriage. If a couple fail to have a child during the first 2–3 years of marriage, families on both sides become concerned. In rural areas and in some urban families, a couple's infertility is blamed on the wife and it often leads to divorce. Women who are divorced because of infertility rarely remarry. They are pitied and looked down upon because they are unable to achieve the status of sacred motherhood. "Infertile" women in rural areas either leave their villages and move to cities, where they attempt to remarry, or they live quiet unassuming lives with their parents. In some cases, especially in urban areas, "infertile" women marry widowers and begin to care for their husband's children.

HUSBAND–WIFE RELATIONSHIP

In the Armenian Church marriage ceremony, the bride promises to be obedient (*hunazand*) to the husband and the groom promises to protect (*der gangnel*) his bride. Rural husband–wife relationships are more traditional and patriarchal, as the wife is expected to be submissive and obedient. While there is still a degree of inequality in most marriages, many urban marriages, particularly those among educated couples, are far more egalitarian than marriages in rural areas or in lower-working-class uneducated urban families. Married couples share a bed and they eat their meals and spend their leisure time together.

Divorce, except in cases of infertility or infidelity, is to be avoided at all costs for the sake of the children. If there is a divorce, children younger than 10 stay with mothers and those that are older than 10 may live with either their mother or their father. The court decides and grants custody of the children in divorce cases.

Women who are divorced or widowed describe themselves as *ander* (without a protector) and believe that they easy targets for the sexual advances of other men. Very few divorcées or widows remarry and in the few instances when they do, they tend to marry divorced men or widowers.

OTHER CROSS-SEX RELATIONSHIPS

The closest cross-sex relationship is between brothers and sisters. Brothers are considered their sisters' protectors, and sisters are the caretakers and nurturers of their brothers.

CHANGES IN ATTITUDES, BELIEFS, AND PRACTICES REGARDING GENDER

Although in the post-Soviet period there has been a partial return to patriarchal beliefs, contemporary attitudes regarding gender roles are a mixture of Soviet and pre-Soviet beliefs as men and women in Armenia attempt to redefine their roles with the family and in society in a constantly changing socioeconomic and political climate.

REFERENCES

Hoogasian, S. V., & Matossian, M. K. (1982). *Armenian village life before 1914*. Detroit, MI: Wayne State University Press.

Hovannisian, R. (1967). *Armenia on the road to independence*. Berkeley: University of California Press.

Matossian, M. (1961). *The impact of Soviet politics in Armenia*. Amsterdam: Leinden Press.

United Nations Development Program. (1998). *1998 Armenian Human Development Report: The Role of The State* (p. 17). Yerevan, Armenian: UNDP Press.

United Nations Development Program. (1999). *Armenia: Women Status Report—The Impact of Transition*. Yerevan, Armenia: UNDP Press.

Zeitlian, S. (1992). *The role of Armenian women in the Armenian revolutionary movement*. Los Angeles: Hraztan Sarkis Zeitlian.

Aymara

Winifred Mitchell

LOCATION

The Aymara live throughout the rugged altiplano (high plain), a series of semiarid basins surrounding Lake Titicaca, in southern Peru and northwestern Bolivia in South America. There are approximately 2 million speakers of the Aymara language in this region.

The altiplano lies between two massive ranges of the Andes and is described as one of the world's most difficult environments; its altitude ranges from 3,800 m above sea level at the lake shore to over 4,100 m near the foothills. The soil is loose and spongy, allowing moisture to disappear rapidly from the surface, but rainfall agriculture is possible due to adequate summer precipitation. Its tropical location at only 18° south of the equator moderates the climate and makes the growing season sufficient even at such high altitude. Lake Titicaca is the highest navigable body of water in the world, with an area of 8,290 km². Its shoreline of over 700 km is lined with Aymara villages. The people use the lake for various economic pursuits including fishing, collecting fodder for livestock, harvesting reeds for basketry, and commercial transport.

CULTURAL OVERVIEW

Economy and Settlement Patterns

Highland Aymara communities consist of scattered sod house compounds with tin or thatch roofs separated by tiny plots of agricultural and pasture land. On their landholdings of 5–20 ha, families coax a living using labor-intensive agriculture and careful animal husbandry. The most common household unit is the nuclear family, but the more traditional patrilineal extended family unit is also quite common. Many people raise most of what they need to eat, relying on the staple crops of potatoes, quinoa, and barley, and keeping a few pigs, chickens, and guinea pigs and small herds of sheep, cattle, and the native Andean species of llama and alpaca. Communities with access to some land at lower elevations (below 3,200 m) also produce corn. There is little surplus for sale in some regions, but others specialize in producing onions or other small cash crops or in fattening cattle for sale. Drought, flood, hail, and frost are all possible impediments to successful farming, so families and communities must be well organized and resourceful in managing production.

Centuries of adaptation have resulted in distinctive subsistence patterns, social organization, and ideology that enable the Aymara to survive in their harsh environment. Special subsistence patterns involve the use of multiple ecological zones (from lowland agricultural zones that produce such crops as corn, coffee [Collins, 1988] or coca to regions that are too high for agriculture and are used exclusively for herding llamas and alpacas). The people have developed labor-intensive agricultural techniques such as cultivating between rows of crops and building up planting areas to facilitate drainage and protect the plants. Their inheritance pattern, which divides the land among all heirs, results in each farmer's numerous tiny plots being dispersed through multiple micro-ecological zones to maximize chances of some successful harvest.

The Aymara have traditionally relied on the reciprocal labor assistance of the kindred for many agricultural tasks, but modern dependence on temporary wage labor to generate cash has reduced the extent of this ancient system (Brown, 1987; Collins, 1988). Fictive kin are also important sources of mutual help. *Compadrazgo* (literally, co-godparenthood) is established among adults for assistance with various ceremonies and special events, and the relationship, once entered into, remains important for life.

Social Organization

In pre-Spanish times (and through the colonial period in some regions) the Aymara were organized by *ayllu*, a local patrilineage that held land communally. The political and economic head of the ancient *ayllu* kept careful

274

account of usufruct landholdings and periodically redistributed land and produce when a family had more than its share.

The modern Bolivian and Peruvian republics have legislated bilateral inheritance, with all children inheriting. This inheritance pattern functions somewhat as a haphazard redistribution pattern. Landholdings are rearranged and consolidated somewhat by allocation of plots according to the marriage choices of the children. For example, a family may include a plot of land in a particular daughter's inheritance because she marries a man whose family has a contiguous or nearby plot.

Today's communities are the rough equivalent of the *ayllu* in the spatial arrangement of land and families. They are organized politically with a group of elected officials who lead periodic town meetings, settle minor disputes, and represent the community to the larger political units of districts, departments, and the nation.

The rural Aymara are a socioeconomic class occupying the bottom of a hierarchy rigidly controlled by the tiny minority of whites (mestizos) who live in the altiplano, and they are allowed only slight participation in the social and economic affairs of Peru and Bolivia. The land reform and revolutions of the 20th century have removed the legal statutes preventing the upward social mobility of the Aymara which were still operative in the 1930s. Today, the barriers are economic, cultural, and ethnic. People who speak little Spanish and read less and who wear indigenous dress are marked as country bumpkins. They are targets of discrimination, rudeness, and financial trickery by people from more sophisticated or powerful social classes.

Communities vary in their character, depending on their size and their proximity to the lake or the foothills, roads, market towns, or the cities of La Paz, Bolivia, or Puno, Peru. Rural villages may have fewer than 300 people, often descended from a few founding families (Brown, 1987; Mitchell, 1986), but can have as many as 800 or more people (Lewellen, 1978). Communities closer to roads and market centers are larger; for example, Compi, the community in Bolivia studied by Buechler and Buechler (1971), had a population of 1,230 during their study period. The people were involved in production of onions as a cash crop and in many market ventures in nearby La Paz. Since the 1980s, many lake-shore communities have become involved in (and prospered considerably from) the international smuggling of coca products between Bolivia and Peru.

CULTURAL CONSTRUCTION OF GENDER

Male and female are the basic gender categories for the Aymara, who see the two genders in an ideal balance referred to as the *chachawarmi*, the man–woman, a cooperative household unit that is the base of Aymara culture. The formation of a household by a same-gender pair is not evident in the countryside, and homosexuality is denied or not referred to directly. A woman who prefers not to marry a man might stay with her parents, or she might adopt children and form an independent household. A man who does not marry a woman would only have the option of remaining with his parents or leaving the village.

Gender identity is expressed by clothing and hairstyle throughout life. A baby's apparel may indicate gender by the shape of the cap if the family is wealthy enough to make such a distinction. Boys ideally wear the typical Andean *chullo*, a knitted cap with ear flaps, while a girl's knitted cap is more conical with a soft floppy edge and brighter colors. Other baby clothes are quite unisex, with swaddling rags and open diaper skirts for all toddlers. Beyond infancy, headgear always differs by gender, with feminine and masculine styles of brimmed hat added as the children become marriageable adolescents. (Men simply put their brimmed hats over their knitted caps.) Perhaps the best-known Aymara woman's hat is the bowler worn by the women of the Titicaca basin, but styles vary by region.

Boys and men wear trousers which may be homespun and short for daily work or purchased and tailored for a more formal or urban look. Ponchos or European-style coats may be worn. When men carry burden cloths, they are slung over one shoulder. Men's colors are mostly the muted earth tones of undyed wool or the gray or black of manufactured clothing. Boys sport very wild tangled mops until the first haircut, after which their hair is always kept short.

Girls and women wear the *pullera*, the distinctive full skirt of the Andean woman, and wool sweaters or blouses. An adult woman's costume is completed with a shawl and burden shawl tied around both shoulders for carrying everything from babies to potatoes. Everyday wear may be plain undyed natural wool, but dress-up clothes are bright and colorful. As soon as it is long enough, a little girl's hair is captured into the two braids that all traditional adult women wear. Adult women tie their waist length braids together across their backs with a wool tassel and are very proud of their long hair as a statement of their femininity. Except for girls' school uniforms, any deviation from the *pullera* and long braids indicates that a girl or woman is hoping to take on a less indigenous identity.

GENDER OVER THE LIFE CYCLE

All phases of Aymara life are explicitly gendered. A baby's gender is its first identity after birth. Even gestation is believed to be different, with boys requiring 8.5–10 months and girls only 7 or 8 months (Buechler & Buechler, 1971, p. 21). The word for baby, *wawa*, applies to both genders, but the new infant may be described as either a "little man" or "little woman." The child will not receive a formal name until its first haircut as a toddler when the soul is considered to be firmly established in the body. Until then, various gender-appropriate names may be tried out. Neither the soul nor the first haircut and naming ceremonies are differentiated by gender, however.

Beyond infancy, children are referred to by the terms *yokalla* (boy) and *imilla* (girl). La Barre (1948) collected a detailed list of other age-grade terms, but these are not in common use today. Puberty is not publicly marked by ritual, but true adulthood is ceremonially signaled by marriage.

Socialization of Boys and Girls

Children of both genders are welcomed at birth, but Aymara women say, "A girl is only born to suffer." Everyone agrees that a family with only daughters would be cursed, but that all sons would not be so bad. Demographic figures show better survival rates for boy infants than girls, suggesting that they may receive better care.

"As soon as they are able to run about steadily," (Tschopik, 1951, p. 164) both boys and girls are put to work. They fetch water, herd sheep, and care for younger siblings. Girls as young as 6 years are left to baby-sit alone in the house and may be expected to have meal preparations underway when adults return.

Children are assigned to help their same-sex parent more often as they get older. Men expect sons of age 10 or older to work beside them in the fields or travel with them for temporary wage labor, and girls of the same age are mastering the jobs of adult women such as cooking, knitting, spinning, and livestock care. A distinction that emphasizes the greater importance of boys is that they are referred to as "working" beside their fathers in the fields, but girls "help" their mothers. Punishment for slacking responsibilities is harsh, but children find some time for games and fun, especially while they are herding together in groups of boys and girls. Most women say that men should administer physical punishments, but adults tell stories of being beaten by either parent for not doing assigned chores.

Both boys and girls attend school, but girls are more likely to be kept at home intermittently to help their mothers and to drop out of school sooner. Thus boys become more fluent in Spanish, the language of education, politics, commerce, and city life.

Families may give away or loan a child to a relative or *compadre* who may take the child to work for them in another rural community or in town. "Extra" daughters are more likely than sons to be given away in this manner. Children are often harshly treated at the hands of their new guardians. They sometimes run away or may be eventually rescued by their parents.

Puberty and Adolescence

Transition to adolescence is not officially or ritually marked in Aymara communities, but there are new terms for the stage: *waynito* (teen boy) and *tawako* (teen girl). Children's work changes into adult gendered tasks with responsibility increasing by age until a person in the late teens is doing all the work of an adult. Adolescents drop the games of childhood and associate more with young people of their own genders. They also begin to attend fiestas splendidly dressed in adult-style clothing. Young people begin to look at each other from afar with laughter and flirtatious looks.

During adolescence, boys often accompany their fathers or other male relatives to seek temporary wage-labor jobs. They may be apprenticed in town to learn a trade such as baking, pottery-making, or bricklaying. Girls may also leave home with a female relative or fictive kin (but usually not their mothers who stay at home) to work or to be engaged as a maid with a family in town. These absences may become permanent out-migrations, but usually begin as temporary.

Attainment of Adulthood

To become fully adult in Aymara society, a *chacha* (man) or *warmi* (woman) must be married. In fact, Hardman (1976) observes that the Aymara word for marriage, *jaqichasiña*, translates literally as "to cause oneself to become a person." In the countryside, no one lives alone. Young men who are not married will live with their parents; widowers either quickly remarry or live with relatives who can help raise the children. A woman may become an independent householder (and hence a functional adult) without a husband if she has children to care for. These may be her own biological children, orphaned siblings, or adopted children. As a householder she is viewed with the same autonomy as other heads of household. Without this independent household status, young people may be well into their twenties and still be seen as not fully adult. For young men, military service is often also part of their transition to adulthood (Buechler & Buechler, 1971, p. 35).

Once married, young adults begin to develop some independence from their parents but, like marriage itself, this is a process. Newlyweds who live with the husband's parents (the most common pattern) are subject to the direction of the older adults; the bride is given all manner of domestic chores by her mother-in-law and is admonished not to be lazy and just sit around caring for her baby. Her husband and father-in-law may be encouraged to beat her to emphasize her inferior status and teach her to obey. The young man works with his father on the family lands or other economic pursuits.

After 2 or 3 years, the couple receive some or all of their inheritance from both parents and begin to construct a separate house compound. Ties with parents ideally remain close enough that family members frequently drop in unannounced for a meal or to borrow a tool. An increasingly popular alternative to this patrilocal postmarital residence is a neolocal option in which the young couple relocate (or elope) to an urban or coastal location where one or both already have contacts or employment.

Middle Age and Old Age

Middle age is a time when householders achieve their highest level of prosperity (although they are still quite poor by standards outside the countryside). Children are grown up enough to contribute real labor power to the family, so they can obtain the most production from their lands, livestock, or even wage-labor and market efforts. Their *ayni* (reciprocal labor relationships) are well established and maximally productive. Middle-aged men take on positions of responsibility in their communities and sponsorship of prestigious fiestas. Middle-aged women have informal reciprocal networks to call upon for help with cooking and hosting such events and other economic exchanges they may require. They can also expect to have new daughters-in-law who live with them and provide almost an indentured servant level of domestic service (Mitchell, 1998). Women who may have borne nearly a dozen children experience the relief of declining fertility.

The achievement and prestige of middle age slowly give way to the reduced responsibilities and lower prestige of old age. As children mature and marry, older adults begin to retire from their farming responsibilities and turn more land over to their children. A favorite child will marry but remain in the parents' household and eventually take responsibility for caring for the aging parents. Some older people of both genders continue to be active in managing small amounts of their land, caring for grandchildren, or serving the community as a *yatiri*, or shaman. When they relinquish these active roles, old women may help care for babies, tend the kitchen fire, gather brush for tinder, or sit quietly spinning or knitting. They seldom offer their opinions in family discussions and may be ignored if they do. Very old men, fewer in number, often complain that they are not receiving proper respect from their grown children, but their complaints seem to fall on the deaf ears of their busy middle-aged offspring.

PERSONALITY DIFFERENCES BY GENDER

Allowing, of course, for individual variation, Aymara men's and women's personalities reflect their different status and roles. Women in the countryside are usually very shy, quiet, and deferential to men and to outsiders. They are easily moved to tears as they speak in muted tones about the hardships of their lives. Men, on the other hand, are suitably respectful to people of the more powerful social classes, reflecting centuries of oppression, but they are more dominant and outspoken within the community and household. A virtuous woman is hardworking, and her hands are never idle. She may defer to her husband, but she can be quite sharp-tongued and impatient with her children and rough with her livestock without being criticized. Being completely nonneighborly and hostile to passers by is not condoned, however.

Men and women earn respect in very different ways. A man is considered successful if he prospers at his agricultural or other work efforts and is dependable, especially with regard to his *ayni* obligations. Women do not derive prestige from these economic spheres unless they are independent heads of household. A married woman is respected for her submissiveness to her husband and her resourcefulness in keeping her family together against all the challenges of rural poverty, including an abusive or drunken husband. An informal village hierarchy honors the most long-suffering women (Mitchell, 1993).

The manner of urban market women contrasts sharply with that of the country people. The market *chola* (someone of indigenous background who has become a town dweller and aspires to a higher social class) is all business. Her voice can be strong and argumentative and her body language likewise as she assertively pushes her way onto a bus or truck, elbowing people energetically to make room for herself and her bundles (Buechler & Buechler, 1996).

GENDER-RELATED SOCIAL GROUPS

Aymara kinship terminology is a modified Hawaiian type which gives equal importance to relatives on both sides of the family (Carter, 1964). The patrilineal heritage of preconquest times is evident in today's preference for virilocal postmarital residence, but children of both genders inherit land from their parents under modern law. Land is not strictly passed mother to daughter or father to son but is instead allocated to offspring according to parents' favoritism and considerations such as quantity and location of children and their spouses.

Cooperative relationships are very important for Aymara women and men, and most of these are with people of the same gender. Men maintain *ayni* (reciprocal labor relationships) with other men and keep careful track of labor and cash contributions from one another. A woman head of household may also have *ayni* relationships with male relatives who plow or harvest for her, but this labor would be repaid with the loan of a team, not with a woman's work, which is not considered equal to a man's. Women maintain many reciprocal exchanges for food and services, such as raising a cow for another woman or weaving for her or helping her cook at a fiesta, but these exchanges are not considered *ayni*, just mutual help. As such they are more flexible than the specific job equivalencies required in traditional male exchanges (Brown, 1978).

GENDER ROLES IN ECONOMICS

Division of labor by gender is the basic organizing principle of work in an Aymara community. Aymara women say, "The woman is the soul of the family; without her a hearth grows cold and husband and children scatter." She is responsible for the myriad domestic tasks of subsistence farm life. As in many cultures, a woman's tasks are more numerous than a man's. His work is defined by agriculture and other economic pursuits, while she does everything else including helping her husband with planting, weeding, cultivating, and harvesting. The man is considered to be doing the real work, with a wife or older sons assisting. A woman may delegate some work to children of both genders, but without their help, she must do everything from watching livestock and hauling water to cooking, caring for children, and maintaining the house, with any otherwise unoccupied moments filled with spinning, weaving, or knitting. It is interesting that a 16th century writer observed that Andean women were "so fond of spinning" that they carried their spindles everywhere and spun as they walked, just as they do today.

Some women learn to weave beautiful complex textiles, while others make only simple homespun or do not weave at all. A few men weave the long simple bolts of *bayeta*, homespun wool, which is then dyed and sewn (also by men) into various utilitarian articles of clothing.

During the agricultural off-season, many Aymara men migrate temporarily to the cities and lowland plantations for wage labor. The cash income from this work (often only U.S.$1000) supplements the farm family's subsistence living, enabling them to purchase supplies such as kerosene, sugar, flour, and some processed foods and manufactured items. Men who migrate may be heads of household or young unmarried males. Some unmarried women also go to cities to work, often as domestics, but married women with homes and farms in the countryside remain there. As in many parts of the developing world, this arrangement results in a heavy but undervalued workload for these women.

More women than men participate in marketing, another source of cash. They usually travel to a nearby weekly market and buy and resell goods, such as wool or fruit, and occasionally sell or barter farm products, livestock, or textiles. Women who only work in the markets 1 or 2 days a week earn much less money in a year than a man can bring home from a few months of wage labor, reinforcing the traditional notion that it takes a man to really bring wealth into the household. The market work of women who leave the countryside and make a career of marketing in the city is much more lucrative, however (Buechler & Buechler, 1996).

PARENTAL AND OTHER CARETAKER ROLES

Parenting is mostly a woman's job, but major physical discipline may be left to fathers. Children nurse through their toddler years, and women carry their children wherever they go. Both men and women are affectionately tolerant with children, their own or those of relatives, but will sharply correct their own children or grandchildren when they are not quiet or respectful. Neither gender cultivates an especially nurturing style with children.

LEADERSHIP IN PUBLIC ARENAS

Public leadership is a male domain in Aymara rural communities, but women are occasionally elected to a public office. Some jobs, like the Promoter of a Mother's Club, are designated for women by outside agencies. Traditionally, men were the sponsors of fiestas, with their wives helping with food and hosting, but today a woman who is a head of household may take on the host role for a day of festivities. One representative from each household speaks at community meetings, so these speakers are mostly, but not exclusively, men. Women tend to sit on the sidelines at community meetings and throw in short frequent comments, while men stand in the center and make longer speeches.

GENDER AND RELIGION

The Aymara cosmos is a world where balance must exist between the natural and supernatural, earth and sky,

men and women, and life and death. As the *chachawarmi*, the man–woman, a married couple complement each other's efforts and achieve a successful balance that will foster the success of their household. Indigenous and Catholic beliefs are intertwined, with some flourishing regions of Protestantism as well (Lewellen, 1978).

The Earth Mother, *Pachemama*, rules the land and its fertility and live-giving qualities. She is not automatically generous and nurturing but must be paid for her bounty. Ceremonies and offerings at harvest and during events that mark life transitions, such as the child's first haircut or the construction of a new house, include burying of offerings (e.g., the blood of sheep slaughtered for the harvest festival, or the child's shorn locks) to "pay the earth." Also, any drinking of alcohol is preceded by a libation to the Earth Mother. The Catholic Virgin Mary often serves as her syncretic symbol. For example, the grieving Mother of Christ who follows his coffin through the streets in Good Friday processions (which is during autumn in the Southern Hemisphere) is seen by the indigenous people as a symbol of the earth entering into its bereft winter period.

The male counterpart of the Earth Mother is the Christian God-the-Father who occupies the heavens and may mete out punishments for wrongdoings through Santiago, the Lightning Spirit (Mitchell, 1993) or other means. He too requires appeasing with ceremonies when his displeasure is expressed. This punishment seems to fit with the more prominent role in punishing children and women that men have, but the earth is also a stern taskmistress, not to be trifled with. The two deities do not seem to have much interaction, but complement each other with separate roles just as earthly men and women should do. It seems to this writer that the Earth Mother's role is more ubiquitous in country life than that of the male Father-God, a fitting parallel to the gendered division of human labor.

Place spirits and ghosts also have roles in Aymara culture and can be quite malign, stealing souls and causing sickness and death. Such spirits (*Tios*, which translates as "uncles") exhibit male characteristics like fighting with their victims.

An Aymara shaman, the *yatiri* or wise one, performs ceremonies to appease these various deities and spirits and to divine their reasons for causing trouble. Herbal curers (Spanish: *curanderos*) also treat illnesses that require less supernatural intervention. Most rural *yatiris* and curers are men, but a woman may (theoretically) also be called to this role by visions and dreams, just as a man would be. There are many women practitioners of magic and curing among the La Paz market women with Aymara roots (Buechler & Buechler, 1996). Pastoral workers trained by the Catholic or Protestant missionaries are men. The male bias in ceremonial roles, especially in the countryside, is clearly parallel with human politics.

LEISURE, RECREATION, AND THE ARTS

The yearly round of farming tasks occupies the time and energy of each household member and leaves little time for leisure or recreation, especially for the ideal *warmi k'apawa*, the hardworking woman. When people gather to relax and eat together, it is often as members of work parties. Some of these work groups, such as a threshing team, might be exclusively male, but other tasks such as harvesting or sorting potatoes could include both genders. Similarly, fiestas and the earth-paying that accompany them are attended by both genders. Both men and women dance at fiestas, but dancers are grouped together by gender more than they are arranged as individual dancing couples. Music-making is a male leisure pursuit that women rarely engage in except as singers. Festive occasions are a time to relax and talk, laugh, and eat together, but women are kept busier with cooking and have less real leisure than men.

RELATIVE STATUS OF MEN AND WOMEN

Male dominance pervades rural Aymara society. Men dominate in the economic, political, and religious spheres both within the household and in the community and its relations with the outside world. Rural men are more fluent in Spanish and better educated, averaging more than twice as many years in school as women. Even when inheritance for both genders and moderate premarital sexual freedom for both are taken into account, the balance of cultural custom still seems to favor men.

The force of male dominance is felt most strongly by married women. Women may express their opinions to their husbands about household economic matters, but ultimately defer to a man's choices. Wife-beating is nearly universal in rural areas, but varies in intensity depending on a couple's relationship. Women often say

that they were beaten more by their husbands as young wives "for not obeying" or for not having cooked food ready at whatever time he arrived home. They may say that their husbands rarely beat them, except when they have been drinking. The suffering ethic of Aymara women dictates that the best course a woman can take in an abusive marriage is to stick it out and keep her family together. The emotional and economic risks of running away, giving up their married status and (often) leaving their children, are so great that few women attempt it.

Early in the marriage process, a young woman may choose to leave an excessively abusive husband and return home to her parents without shame, even with a child. She may marry someone else or remain a single mother in a semi-independent relationship with her parents. Similarly, widows have the choice of whether to remarry, and very few choose to do so for fear of mistreatment of themselves or their children. They may be poor and subject to some sexual harassment, but they are free to function as heads of household more or less equally with their male peers.

SEXUALITY

Sexuality is not openly discussed. In describing an ideal marriage partner, both men and women mention personality rather than physical traits. Despite this apparent prudishness, sexual relations are a normal part of life and not shameful or polluting. Children engage in sex play and adolescents seek sexual opportunities, especially during fiestas when their parents are less vigilant. Adolescent and young adult women and men may exercise moderate sexual freedom without the dire consequences that a middle-class town dweller might face. A young woman is said to have "found her husband" when she is suspected by her friends of having a sexual encounter, but she is not required by society to marry this partner if their marriage process does not proceed successfully. The marriage ceremony is often an acknowledgment of the couple's already established relationship, rather than its beginning.

Rural people are very modest, never totally undressing, even when changing clothes or bathing. Modesty extends to bodily functions which are done at a distance from the house. However, personal modesty is not an issue when it comes to women's breasts. Women nurse their babies and toddlers on demand in a no-nonsense manner wherever they happen to be.

Courtship and Marriage

As the previous sections have indicated, marriage is the key to full adulthood in rural communities. The beginning of marriage may not be marked by ceremony because marrying is a process that takes approximately 3 years during which at least one child is born. Described in a classic article by Carter (1977), the marriage process begins with *sirvisiña*, living together. Young men and women have considerable independence in choosing a spouse and in deciding whether to break off an unsatisfactory relationship early in *sirvisiña*. If their families agree with the relationship, they acknowledge it by ceremonially locking the couple up together for the night in a vacant room. Couples can also be pushed into marriages that their parents desire by a surprise lock-up. Bride capture, practiced through at least the first half of the 20th century, involved the kidnapping and transport of a young woman (often with her relatives' assistance) to the lock-up site. While less common than mutual choice, this method of beginning marriages also resulted in long-term commitments.

Parents prefer that their children marry people from the same or nearby communities—people whose families are known or related, but not too closely. Young people are strongly discouraged from marrying while working out of the community, and many comply with their parents' desires. Marriage within one's own or a nearby community is the ideal among people who continue to reside in the countryside.

The newly married couple usually live with the young man's parents, but living with the bride's family or alternating between the two also occurs. Bride and groom frequently visit their birth families, even if in a nearby community, so brides are not forcibly isolated from their original homes. Isolation of new brides did occur formerly with bride capture. Increasingly, couples choose neolocal residence, especially if they are employed away from the community.

As previous sections indicate, remarriage is possible for both genders, but much more common for men. The informant's statement that a "woman is the soul of the family" accurately explains a widower's need to seek a new wife. Widows, on the other hand, have achieved the adult status of married woman and mother, and often choose to stay single.

Change in Attitudes, Beliefs, and Practices Regarding Gender

Increases in population, out-migration, communication, and transportation throughout the 20th century have drawn rural people into more relationships with the rest of the world. The Bolivian and Peruvian Aymara were as affected as their compatriots by the political and economic turmoil of the late 20th century. Terrorism in Peru, the growing, trading, and processing of coca and cocaine in the Bolivian lowlands and its trade through Peru, dizzying rates of inflation, and many changes in governments have affected many aspects of Aymara life including gender roles.

The increase in women's work with so many migrating family members is as noteworthy among the Aymara as elsewhere in the developing world. Economies that are based on seasonal wage labor would flounder without the unacknowledged work of the stay-at-home women who keep the work force provisioned. The balance of the *chachawarmi*, the man–woman dyad, must always be renegotiated to maintain the rural subsistence part of the national economy. Returning migrants may bring mestizo cultural notions of female frailty and worthlessness which conflict with the notion of cooperation between genders (Collins, 1985) and with the *warmi k'apawa* value—the hardworking woman who keeps her family together at all costs. While this arrangement is not an equal partnership between spouses, it is the basis for women's self-respect.

On the other hand, some ideas that transfer to the country from the city have a positive effect on women's status. Rural education campaigns are increasing women's literacy, Spanish fluency, and knowledge of their civil rights. Peruvian Aymara women believe that these campaigns have lowered the rate and severity of family violence in their communities. Girls who spend more years in school than their mothers did become interested in life outside the rural areas. They wear school uniforms instead of *pulleras* and sometimes decide to adopt town clothing styles and cut their long hair. Marketing also enables rural women to step out of their submissive roles and avoid what they consider the traps of male dominated *campo* life (Buechler & Buechler, 1996).

When the colonial chroniclers' accounts of indigenous customs are compared with those of 20th century ethnographers, the cultural persistence is striking. However, the key to Aymara cultural longevity may be its flexibility. The Aymara have never been isolated in their rural villages—the outside world has required their labor or produce since pre-Inca times. Gender roles can shift and readjust to the new demands of a global economy as they did in the past with changes in inheritance and fiesta sponsorship. The rapid changes of recent decades will take a while to reach a new equilibrium in *campo* households, but some new version of the *chachawarmi* balance is bound to emerge during the 21st century. How such changes may affect the relative status of men and women will indeed bear watching.

ACKNOWLEDGMENTS

The author gratefully acknowledges the hospitality of the Aymara villagers and the support of the Fulbright Commission and the InterAmerican Foundation for fieldwork in Peru.

REFERENCES

Brown, P. F. (1978). *Fuerza por fuerza: Ecology and culture change among the Aymara of southern Peru*. Unpublished doctoral dissertation, University of Colorado, Boulder.

Brown, P. F. (1987). Population growth and the disappearance of reciprocal labor in a highland Peruvian community. *Research in Economic Anthropology, 8,* 225–245.

Buechler, H. C., & Buechler, J.-M. (1971). *The Bolivian Aymara.* New York: Holt, Rinehart & Winston.

Buechler, H. C., & Buechler, J.-M. (1996). *The World of Sof'a Velasquez: The autobiography of a Bolivian market vendor.* New York: Columbia University Press.

Carter, W. E. (1964). *Aymara communities and the Bolivian agrarian reform* (University of Florida Monographs in the Social Sciences No. 24). Gainesville: University of Florida Press.

Carter, W. E. (1977). Trial marriage in the Andes? In R. Bolton & E. Mayer (Eds.), *Andean kinship and marriage* (Special Publication No. 7, pp. 177–216). Washington, DC: American Anthropological Association.

Collins, J. L. (1985). *Gender, labor markets, and peasant productions in Southern Peru.* Paper presented at the annual meeting of the American Anthropological Association, Washington, DC.

Collins, J. L. (1988). *Unseasonal migrations: The effects of rural labor scarcity in Peru.* Princeton, NJ: Princeton University Press.

Hardman, M. (1976). Andean women [film essay]. In *Faces of change: Bolivian series.* Hanover, NH: Wheelock Educational Resources.

La Barre, W. (1948). The Aymara Indians of the Lake Titicaca Plateau. *Memoirs of the American Anthropological Association, No. 68.*

Lewellen, T. C. (1978). *Peasants in transition: The changing economy of the Peruvian Aymara: A general systems approach.* Boulder, CO: Westview Press.

Mitchell, W. L. (1986). *Male and female counterpoint: Gender relations in an Andean community.* Unpublished doctoral dissertation, University of Colorado, Boulder.

Mitchell, W. L. (1993). Lightning sickness. *Natural History, 102*(11), 6–8.

Mitchell, W. L. (1998). Women's hierarchies of age and suffering in an Andean community. In J. Dickerson-Putman & J. K. Brown (Eds.), *Women among women: Anthropological perspectives on female age hierarchies.* Chicago: University of Illinois Press.

Tschopik, H. (1951). The Aymara of Chucuito, Peru. *Anthropological Papers of the American Museum of Natural History, 44.*

Bakairí

Debra Picchi

ALTERNATIVE NAMES

Alternative names are Bacaeri, Bacaery, Bacairi, Bacayri, Bakaeri, Bakaery, and Bakaire.

LOCATION

The Bakairí are located in the state of Mato Grosso, east of Rondonia, central Brazil, South America (see Figure 1).

CULTURAL OVERVIEW

The Bakairí economy is dependent on a combination of gardening using slash-and-burn horticulture, farming with modern technology, working for wages, and receiving government stipends. By far the most significant aspect of their livelihood are the household gardens that they make in the forests that lie along the rivers in the reservation. Harvests provide the Indians with such staples as manioc, as well as other important foods such as rice, corn, banana, squash, and beans.

Figure 1. Rondonia and Mato Grosso in relation to other Brazilian states.

Their traditional diet is augmented with rice grown using industrial agricultural techniques in the *cerrado*, the prairie-like part of the reservation. In 1980 FUNAI (the National Indian Foundation in Brazil) began a development project on the reservation (Picchi, 1991). They showed the Indians how to use tractors, fertilizers, and pesticides. The harvests are distributed to households in the reservation, and the surplus is sold in nearby towns for cash. Other sources of cash include nearby ranches where men work for wages and government social service stipends received by some families. The Bakairí also raise cattle herds. In the middle of the 20th century, FUNAI agents began cattle herding in the reservation, and in the 1980s FUNAI distributed these herds to indigenous families.

Traditionally, the Bakairí depended upon headmen to lead their communities. Headmen used to inherit their titles from their fathers, but during the era immediately following contact when large numbers of Bakairí died from diseases, such successors became more difficult,

and ultimately impossible, to find. Today, consensual leaders emerge from the ranks of the villagers as they are needed. Those men with large extended families are more likely to assume leadership roles. Headmen use a variety of techniques to lead their communities, but in general they are more persuasive than authoritarian.

In 1999 about 500 Indians inhabited seven villages in the reservation. The largest settlement is called Pakuera which is the name for the Paranatinga River on whose banks the village is located (Figure 2). The 20th century was marked by dramatic changes in the population size and in the number of settlements. In the first part of the century, the Bakairí migrated into the Paranatinga River area from the headwaters of the Xingú River. Epidemic diseases caused their population to decrease, a trend that was exacerbated by out-migration to towns in search of wage-paying jobs. During the second half of the century, better medical attention became available and the number of Indians increased. Simultaneously, as a result of a downturn in the regional economy in the

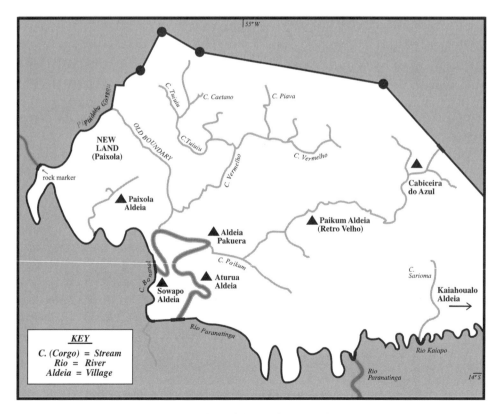

Figure 2. Bakairí villages in reservation.

1970s and 1980s, some Bakairí returned to the reservation to live. Between 1979 and 1989, the number of people in the reservation grew by 36.8%, from 288 to 394 individuals. Between 1989 and 1999 it increased by 26.9%, from 394 to 500. The growing number of people in Pakuera contributed to tension and conflict, and eventually to the division of this settlement in the 1980s and the formation of other villages (Picchi, 1995).

The Bakairí used to practice polygyny. However, FUNAI agents and missionaries actively discouraged this tradition, and the Indians now practice monogamy. Their marital unions tend to be village endogamous, but some marriages with Indians from other reservations and with non-Indians takes place. The Bakairí also prefer marriages to occur within extended families. When such a marriage occurs, it is between cross-cousins, defined as first cousins who are children of opposite-sexed siblings of parents. Immediately after marriage, couples live with the wife's family until the birth of their first child. Then the couple build their own house, usually near one or both of their parents' homes.

The Bakairí are in regular contact with Brazilians. They frequently leave the reservation to travel, work, and make purchases. Some Indians have family members living outside the reservation, with whom they visit. In 1999 the reservation was informed that the government of Mato Grosso planned to provide electricity to remote parts of the state, such as the region in which they lived. They reported looking forward to having televisions and to watching soccer programs.

The Bakairí practice animism—the belief in supernatural spirits who inhabit the world. These spirits can be contacted and even manipulated by shamans, who are village semispecialists capable of curing diseases and practicing sorcery. According to the Indians, guardian spirits of animals and fish exist. The Bakairí make huge oval and square masks to represent these guardian spirits, and men dance inside them during the dry season. Other village festivities celebrate such events as garden harvests.

Cultural Construction of Gender

The Bakairí recognize two genders: male and female. Since the 1930s, they have worn clothing, having adopted the typical regional Brazilian style of dress. Men wear shorts or slacks and shirts, and women wear skirts or dresses. Men's hair is cut short, and women let their hair grow long. Recently some younger women have started to wear make-up. Red and black body paints are used by both men and women during festivities. Adults used to file their front teeth into points, but they have discontinued this tradition (Petrullo, 1932). Scarification of the arms and legs of individuals takes place. When young women begin to menstruate and young men are in their teens, they undergo the procedure of scraping the legs or arms until blood is drawn with an instrument called a *paiko*, which is made of fish teeth. This tradition is continued into adulthood to strengthen the body. Although height–weight studies found no evidence of obesity in the reservation, the ideal body image of the Bakairí man or women tends to be more robust than the North American body image. Strength and endurance are admired in both men and women.

Gender over the Life Cycle

The Bakairí recognize infancy, childhood, coming of age, young adulthood, and oldness. The coming-of-age period is punctuated with a puberty ritual for both men and women. Young adulthood is publicly marked with a marriage ceremony in which the men of the village escort a young man to the home of bride and hang his hammock underneath hers. Most work is done by adult men and women; however, children and elderly people make important contributions to the household economy.

Socialization of Boys and Girls

There is no preference for either male or female children, and the sex ratio in the reservation is remarkably even. Indigenous informants point out the importance of having the same number of young men and women for marriage purposes, indicating that they have a general awareness of the significance of balanced sex ratios. Bakairí children are typically indulged, although corporal punishment of children occurs. Disciplinary action tends to be verbal, with public shaming, although physical punishment of adolescents in the form of scraping the body with fish teeth or hitting takes place. As is common in many societies, girls are encouraged to play a quieter and more demure role, while boys are allowed to be louder and more aggressive. Mothers care for infants, and both parents contribute to raising older children. Siblings, grandparents, and other extended family members participate in the process. Older women past the age of child bearing frequently adopt children of relations.

By the time a child is 4 or 5, it is considered toilet trained and is expected to excrete outside the house. It is at this juncture that children begin to learn what will be expected of them in life. Little boys begin by learning to clean the home—a skill that will later be transferred to the garden. They get milk from the stable where the cows are milked by older men, collect firewood, help their fathers hunt and fish, make their own bows and arrows with which they kill lizards and birds, and run errands. By the time they are 12 years of age, they can stay out nights and learn the mask songs. Girls help their mothers get water from the river, make fires, carry firewood from the garden, wash clothes, and prepare food. They learn early in life to process bitter manioc and to turn it into manioc flour. They also learn to spin cotton into twine, with which they make hammocks, and to thresh rice with huge wooden pestles. Some Bakairí households now have sewing machines that are powered by a foot pedal. Older girls learn to make shifts for themselves and other family members out of fabric purchased in town. Both boys and girls run errands for their parents. Children go to school in the morning for part of the year. They learn to read and write in Portuguese and to do some arithmetic. Prior to the 1980s, teachers were Brazilians who spoke no Bakairí, but since the 1980s all teachers in the reservation are young Bakairí men and women.

Puberty and Adolescence

During their teens a few of the better male students, who have families that are supportive of them leaving the reservation, are chosen to study in boarding schools in nearby towns. Women are rarely chosen for this. These young men study in the equivalent of North American high schools and sleep and eat in religious hostels where nuns and priests supervise them. They come home for holidays and for the summer months.

However, they are a minority. Between the ages of 16 and 17 most young men learn the ear-piercing songs in preparation for adulthood, prepare to take full responsibility for a garden, and go on multiple-day hunting trips with the men where they practice using guns. They play soccer with others their own age, perform mask dances, sit in the men's house listening to their elders, flirt with young women, and travel. Some men learn to ride horses

and work with the cattle herds, while others learn to drive the FUNAI truck and the villages' tractors. Young men in particular travel a great deal, using the truck to go to the city where they make purchases for their families, take messages to FUNAI offices, and visit relatives. Sometimes they have adventures which lead to problems. For example, some drink alcoholic beverages, have sex with women, contract sexually transmitted diseases, and are robbed.

Young women do not have these kinds of experiences because they travel less frequently outside the reservation and are discouraged from experimenting in this way. Women's adult routines are established earlier than men's, and by 15 or 16 they are married with their first child and managing their homes. However, the role of women in Bakairí society is changing. They currently have more choices, and young women in particular are considering the value of getting an education, working outside the reservation, and earning wages.

Attainment of Adulthood

Boys in their late teens and girls in their early teens pass through puberty rituals that mark their gradual transition to adulthood. Young men go through an ear-piercing ritual which lasts for 2 days. The ritual takes place in the *caduete* (the men's house) which is a ceremonial and political center for male activities. Men are required to observe food taboos during this time.

When the onset of menses occurs, young women are confined to their houses for a week where they are expected to remain silently in their hammocks. Their bodies are scraped with the *paiko*, the instrument made of fish teeth, and a hot cloth with oil on it is placed on the girl's stomach. During the first and subsequent menstruations, women abstain from eating fish. It is believed that if they do not abstain, their bodies will swell up and become distorted. They also are not allowed to have sexual relations. An early-morning purification bath ends this seclusion.

Full adulthood is typically realized when a man and woman have married, seen the birth of their first child, cleared their own gardens or partnered the clearing of a garden with a kinsmen, and built their own house close to or attached to a parent's house.

Men sometimes drink alcohol, but there is no evidence that women do so. Both men and women may from time to time perform violent acts, but men are more likely to do so. Men fight each other with fists, knives, and guns, and they sometimes hit their wives. Women also attack their husbands physically.

Middle Age and Old Age

As Bakairí men age, they may assume the roles of shaman, headman, political counselor, and/or extended family leader. Middle-aged women help with household organization and childcare. They tend to be more outspoken than younger women. Both old men and old women remain as economically productive as they are able. In old age, they live with or near their adult children, preferably their daughters. Elderly women especially do not feel comfortable living with their sons because of the tradition of restraint in relations with daughters-in-law. Women are not allowed to address their son's wife by name and call her by her kin name. Interactions between the two women are minimal.

PERSONALITY DIFFERENCES BY GENDER

Young people are expected to be reserved, quiet, and obedient. As they age, they become more assertive. More men than women speak Portuguese, and men are notably more assertive in interactions with non-Indians. Both men and women report being possessed by spirits, and shamans treat them. Sometimes this occurs when individuals have spent long periods of time outside of the reservation or when they have consumed alcoholic beverages, something that men experience more than women. However, possession can also take place in the reservation.

GENDER-RELATED SOCIAL GROUPS

The Bakairí recognize extended families that consist of two or more individuals related by blood and their spouses and children. In the past these families lived together in large elliptically shaped communal houses, but today the Indians reside in small square houses made of clay with tin or palm thatch roofs. Nuclear families, sometimes with an older relative, occupy these homes. Nonetheless, extended families remain important, and they are organized around the female side of the family.

Women, their married daughters, and granddaughters make up a tightly knit core of individuals who are loyal to each other. They tend to have homes located near each other, accompany each other to the river several times a day to bathe and wash clothes, work together in the gardens, and defend each other's interests in the community. Nuclear families, consisting of a married couple and their children, are important for reproduction, childrearing, and economic activities. Although embedded in the larger extended family, they operate in a semiautonomous fashion.

In Bakairí extended families, members distinguish two kinds of cousins: cross cousins and parallel cousins. Cross cousins are the children of opposite-sexed siblings of parents, (i.e., children of either mother's brother or father's sister), while parallel cousins are those of same-sexed siblings of parents (i.e., children of either mother's sister or father's brother). Parallel cousins tend to be lumped together with siblings, and marriage between them is forbidden on the basis of incest rules. Cross cousins, on the other hand, are encouraged to marry, a tradition that reinforces solidarity within the extended family. Although not all Bakairí marriages are between cross cousins, many are.

Bakairí women are not organized into nonkin groups; rather, their solidarity is based on kin connections, which are strengthened through a lifetime of cooperation and shared experiences in the domestic sphere. Men are organized into two different nonkin groups. Those who pass through the puberty rite of ear-piercing at the same time make up a loosely organized age-set. Although their responsibilities toward each other are not rigidly defined, they tend to fraternize, hunt, and assist each other in garden projects more frequently than with those in younger or older cohorts. They compose a type of political interest group in that they share common experiences, aims, and concerns that are different from other men's. They marry and have children at about the same time, and move simultaneously through other developmental stages such as the death of parents. Their demeanor towards each other is playful. This is quite different from the respectful way they must interact with the elders, and the instructive way they act toward those younger than they. Men in the same age-set may find their sense of solidarity temporarily affected by village disputes and rivalries, sexual jealousy, and personal animosity. Yet relationships between members remain strong and usually endure until death. On the other hand, they never eclipse, or even compete seriously with, those blood relationships that claim an individual's allegiance.

Bakairí men also belong to a men's association that plays a dominant role in the political and religious lives of the villagers. Following the ear-piercing ceremony, they are allowed to participate in the key activities that take place in the *caduete* (men's house) which is located in the center of the village. The *caduete* is shrouded in secrecy, and women are forbidden to enter it on penalty of rape. Inside the men store sacred and/or musical artifacts and ritual masks, and they perform rituals. Unlike age-related ceremonies that divide men into groups, the men's house unites them and places them in opposition to women.

GENDER ROLES IN ECONOMICS

Time-allocation studies showed that the Bakairí spend most of their time engaged in three major types of activities: (1) interacting with each other in some kind of social activity, (2) engaging in an economic activity, and (3) doing housework. About 47% of Bakairí time was spent on tasks that involve productive labor, which ensured the survival of the household, or reproductive labor, which allowed society to continue over generations. The former included activities such as gardening, hunting, wage labor, and fishing, while the latter involved childcare, cooking, and household construction. About 43% of the rest of Bakairí time was spent resting, socializing, and attending to personal needs (Picchi, 2000).

Men, in general, are three times as likely as women to be found doing garden work. One reason that women are not involved more in these activities is that most Bakairí gardens are located far from the village. Women, who are generally the primary caretakers of young children, find it difficult to travel such long distances regularly. If they did, they would either have to carry their children or leave them with others for long periods of time. In addition, only men leave the reservation to work for wages on nearby ranches. They tend to be gone from the village for about 2 weeks at a time.

Gender determines other kinds of economic contributions. Men are responsible for hunting, fishing, manufacturing certain goods such as baskets and bows, and dancing inside ritual masks. In addition to child-rearing, women plant, weed, and harvest crops, and they process

food, cook, wash clothes in the river, fish, manufacture goods such as hammocks, keep the house clean, and teach male mask dancers the songs of the masks.

A clear distinction exists between most work done by men and women, and there is little overlap in these cases. Women do not perform such activities as cutting down trees or hunting, and men do not cook or wash clothes in the river. There is also a distinction between work done by adult men and young men. Boys under the age of 15 are not involved in heavy farming work or ritual dancing. These activities are the sole purview of men—15 years and older.

The cycle of a day is organized differently for men and women. Bakairí days begin early by most American standards. People wake up at about 4 a.m., and by the gray light of dawn they are on their way to bathe and get water from the river. Women heat up coffee and food such as rice or manioc from the day before. By 7 a.m. the men have gathered at the men's house or are on their way to the gardens. They clear their fields of brush, weed, plant new crops of cotton, move manioc cuttings around, and harvest manioc tubers to take home with them. If they do not need to go to the garden to weed or harvest crops, then they go fishing or work on projects such as basket-making. Women do housework, sweeping a layer of dust from the hard dirt floors with palm fronds. They may go to the gardens with their husbands if there is weeding or harvesting to do. If not, they go down to the riverbank where they spend hours washing clothes, watching the children play, and visiting with their kin and friends. By noon, most people return to the village to eat something and then to rest during the hottest part of the afternoon. Women and men both work on projects such as hammock-making and bench-carving.

By about 3 p.m., it begins to cool off and the pace of the village noticeably quickens. Everyone goes down to the river to bathe before engaging in mask dancing, if they have ceremonial obligations, or in visiting friends and family. A light meal is usually eaten as twilight sets in. If it is a moonless and rainy night, people turn in early, sometimes at 7 p.m. right after it becomes dark. They rest, chatting and swinging in their hammocks. Elderly men and women tend to smoke a cigarette they have rolled themselves from tobacco they grow in their fields. They smoke only at night, using the substance as a soporific. If it is a bright moonlit night, people sit out in front of their houses and visit with each other. Young men gather in front of the men's house and sing, and children run around and play.

Land in the reservation is communally owned. However, during the last 20 years, FUNAI cattle herds have distributed to families and kin groups now own them. It is not clear how they will be passed down from generation to generation since there is no precedent for this type of situation.

PARENTAL AND OTHER CARETAKER ROLES

Both men and women play important roles in child-rearing. Women are the primary caregivers during the first 4 years of life while the child nurses on demand. After the child is weaned, men play an increasingly significant role with both male and female children. Grandparents and classificatory parents are important influences on children. All children are encouraged to be obedient, respectful, and quiet, and thus do not tend to be rambunctious. Parents and older kin model gender roles and economic tasks associated with each gender.

LEADERSHIP IN PUBLIC ARENAS

Leadership in the political arena is controlled by men and is dominated symbolically and practically by the *caduete*, the men's house located in the plaza in the center of the village. The literature from the late 19th and early 20th centuries, when the Bakairí were first contacted, indicates that older women in particular, but women in general, were important authorities in the village and that they openly participated in the public arena in ways that are not seen today (Petrullo, 1932; von den Steinen, 1886/1966). It is probable that contact with Brazilians during the 20th century affected the role of women, making it more subservient to the man's role. Today women influence public events through their husbands and sons.

Men and women control different parts of the village. Men control the central plaza, the *caduete*, and the soccer field. Women avoid these areas. Maintaining a low profile, they skirt public areas and use the back paths that connect the houses to the gardens and the river. If they inappropriately venture into the plaza, they are socially sanctioned by gossip. At times, when there are important ritual events in the plaza, the women ring its periphery, making sure not to move off the sidelines.

Women control the back areas of the village. Men avoid these back yards except to set up clandestine meetings with women, and if they are found there too often, they are teased.

The mobility of men distinguishes them from women. Men in general, but young men especially, have many opportunities to take trips outside the reservation. When they are young, they travel out of curiosity, and when they are older, they go to Cuiabá, the capital of the state of Mato Grosso, and even to Brasilia, the nation's capital, for political and financial reasons. They also go to ranches to earn wages. They remain there for days or even weeks before returning home. Talking about their experiences is frequently converted into status and prestige in the village. Women are discouraged from traveling outside the reservation. Child-rearing responsibilities, their inability to speak Portuguese as well as men, and their alleged shyness prevent them from leaving the reservation. Recently this has changed among the Bakairí. In the late 1980s and 1990s, women began to work for wages both inside and outside the reservation. Some work in Cuiabá in shops and at FUNAI headquarters as domestic helpers, and a smaller number have assumed more responsibility, working as teachers and medical attendants.

GENDER AND RELIGION

Men and women play complementary roles in religion although the public role of the male is more developed. The Bakairí are animistic in that they believe in the existence of a sacred realm that is inhabited by supernatural beings who live inside such things as animals and plants and who behave in much the same way as humans. People are able to see these beings, but they typically stay hidden. Spirits can sometimes be contacted and even manipulated by shamans who are religious semispecialists. Shamanism is the exclusive domain of men who learn to contact and direct spirits with whom they have special personal relationships. They learn to do this through long and arduous periods of training and through the use of tobacco which induces a trance. These supernatural beings intercede on behalf of shamans, enabling them to cure diseases and to perform sorcery against their enemies.

One of the enduring traditions of the Bakairí noted by many researchers who visited them in the last century concerns the way both men and women traditionally pass through rites of passage during which time they are in great spiritual danger (Altenfelder Silva, 1950; Oberg, 1953). These periods are at birth, puberty, and when someone close to them dies. To defend themselves individuals go into ritual seclusion, which is called *wanki*. Following seclusion and fasting, the individual rejoins the community. The end of the *wanki* period is marked with a festival called a *tadaunuto*.

Another aspect of their religion is mask dancing. Bakairí masks are 1 m long and a 0.5 m wide. *Kwamba* masks are oval, and *yakwigado* are rectangular. They are made of wood or tree bark and decorated with black, red, and white colors. The black is derived from crushed charcoal or *genipapo*, a berry, and the red is from another berry called *urucu*, which the Bakairí cultivate. The white is from chalk that the Indians scrape from deposits in the nearby river. The masks are attached to "hair" and "clothes" made from palm. Although the women are the owners of the masks, preserving them and handing them down from generation to generation through the female side of the families, the men make the masks and dance inside them. The women also prepare the palm costumes for the mask dancers to wear, choose the men who dance inside of their masks, and teach them the mask songs.

Men and women play complementary roles in mortuary practices. After a death, the husband of a daughter of the deceased does the actual burying unless he has small children or a pregnant wife. The spirit of the dead person is considered dangerous, and can cause illness or even death of those who are weak or small. The Bakairí traditionally buried the dead wrapped in a hammock marked with red paint inside the house, but FUNAI agents convinced them to bury them in wooden boxes in areas away from the village. These de facto cemeteries are not visited after the burial, nor are markers of any kind set up. Families go into a mourning period for several months after the burial. They cut their hair, remain secluded indoors, and observe food taboos. If a man has died, the men of the village gather and beat the inside walls of the house to chase the spirit away from the home, and if a woman has died, the women villagers do the same. Eventually a time to end mourning is set, and the villagers accompany the dead person's kin to the river where they take a special ritual purifying bath.

Some Bakairí claim to be Christian and make efforts to have their children baptized or to assume the role of godparent of Brazilian children in the area. Evidence of syncretism exists in that they traditionally believe in twin culture heroes who are identified with the sun and moon. According to some Indians, the Christian God is synonymous with the sun culture hero.

LEISURE, RECREATION, AND THE ARTS

Men and women have substantial amounts of leisure time during which they visit with each other, do crafts, and rest. Time-allocation studies indicate that about a third of their waking hours are spent in such activities. Some gender differences include the constant involvement of women in watching young children and processing food, and of men in political discussions with other men and playing soccer. Young women are also allowed to wrestle with each other in public. Kinds of gender segregation that exist include the two sexes using different bathing areas and only men being allowed to frequent the men's house and to dance inside the masks.

RELATIVE STATUS OF MEN AND WOMEN

Men and women share the responsibility of performing many tasks. The historic literature on the Bakairí suggest that this is not new. A marked egalitarianism and/or complementariness has long characterized most aspects of village life (Petrullo, 1932). Both men and women manufacture crafts, such as baskets and benches in the case of the men and hammocks in the case of women. They both fish, participate in gardening, play important roles in child-rearing, have a say in family and community decisions, and make recognized contributions to the religious dimension. They control their own sexuality in that they decide with whom to have sex, and although parents play an important role in choosing marriage partners, they are able to express their own wishes in affecting how the relationship works out. Both men and women can initiate divorce. However, only men hunt, become shamans, dance in masks, work in the men's house, and leave the reservation to work for wages. In contact situations with Brazilians, men are favored by the non-Indians and thus have assumed a more dominant role in such interactions.

SEXUALITY

Men and women view sex as a natural process. They frequently joke about it and tease each other about their lovers. Premarital sex is viewed as normal. Young men and women begin having sexual relations at an early age and are expected to have many sex partners before they marry. People are allowed to be involved sexually with more than one person at a time. Extramarital sex occurs frequently. Nonetheless, extramarital affairs can lead to quarrels, violence, conflict between families, and even divorce. Sexual taboos exist during pregnancy and after the birth of a child. Men and women are expected to abstain from sex for 2–3 years while the woman is nursing or the child may not learn to walk or talk. Sex occurs rapidly in hammocks in houses or in the gardens where there is more privacy. Both male and female orgasms are recognized. There is no evidence of oral and anal sex, and genital–genital sex with a variety of positions is practiced. Adult men and women tend to be modest and do not expose their genitals to the opposite sex. They bathe and excrete in separate areas. Women wear dresses and are careful to keep their legs together when sitting. There was no evidence of cross-sex identification or cross-dressing. Male homosexuality does not appear to exist, and a rumored lesbian relationship between two adolescent women was publicly denounced.

COURTSHIP AND MARRIAGE

Almost all Bakairí men and women are married or have been married. Single people tend to be widows or widowers, and they express the desire to remarry. One typical pattern of male–female courtship and marriage is young people having sex with each other and gradually becoming closer and ceasing sexual relations with others. They then marry. Another equally acceptable pattern is parents deciding on unions between two adolescents who have known each other all their lives. The Bakairí report that love is part of a marriage, but that the degree of relatedness and the industrious nature of the individual are also important considerations. Males and females consider that they have a choice in when and with whom they can marry. When a marriage occurs the men and kin of the groom accompany him to the house of his bride where he hangs his hammock below hers. The fathers of the two individuals loudly proclaim the union while the bride and groom look extremely embarrassed.

HUSBAND–WIFE RELATIONSHIP

The husband–wife relationship tends to be characterized by affection and companionability, although some couples are clearly in conflict. Husbands and wives sleep in the same house in separate hammocks unless the husband is traveling. They frequently go to the garden together and eat together when food is prepared. Although the man and woman perform complementary tasks, in some areas, such as hunting and clothes washing, there is a strict division of labor. If the marriage is not satisfactory, either the husband or the wife may initiate the divorce. Children up to the age of 4 go with their mothers, and older children are distributed between the father and other kin. Infidelity is not automatically grounds for divorce; however, if an affair goes on too long or if the woman becomes pregnant, then divorce may take place.

OTHER CROSS-SEX RELATIONSHIPS

Men–women friendships do not appear to exist. Those who are potentially sexual partners tend to have joking and teasing relationships. Grandparents play an important role in raising their grandchildren, and siblings defend each other in the community.

CHANGE IN ATTITUDES, BELIEFS, AND PRACTICES REGARDING GENDER

Contact with non-Indians, especially Brazilians, has affected the role of Bakairí women. When the Bakairí were first contacted in the late 19th century and later visited by ethnographers in the early part of the 20th century, women reportedly played a much more assertive and significant role in public village life (Petrullo, 1932; von den Steinen, 1886/1966). Today, they tend to influence village politics and decision-making through their male kin. On the other hand, women are being formally educated in schools on the reservation. Jobs as teachers and medical attendants are available to them. A small number of women have left the reservation to work for wages in towns.

Attitudes towards men have also changed as a result of contact with non-Indians. Traditionally, men are expected to be respectful of their elders, especially of older kin. Relationships between other men are characterized by a casual comradeship. However, the hierarchical nature of relations between Brazilians has introduced the concept of subordination versus dominance in personal relations that did not exist previously. This concept is strengthened by emerging differences in wealth between Bakairí families.

BIBLIOGRAPHY

Altenfelder Silva, F. (1950). O estado de wanki entre os Bakairí. *Sociologia, 12*(3), 259–271.

Brown, M. (1993). Facing the state, facing the world: Amazonia's native leaders and the new politics of identity. *L'Homme, 33*, 307–326.

de Souza, C. F. M. (1994). On Brazil and its Indians. In D. L. Van Cott (Ed.), *Indigenous peoples and democracy in Latin America* (pp. 213–233). New York: St. Martins Press.

Freidl, E. (1975). *Women and men: An anthropologist's view*. New York: Holt, Rinehart & Winston.

Levi-Strauss, C. (1948). The tribes of the Upper Xingú River. In J. Steward (Ed.), *Handbook of South American indians: Vol. 8 The Tropical Forest Tribes* (pp. 321–348). New York: Cooper Square.

McKee, L. (1997). Women's work in rural Ecuador: Multiple resource strategies and the gendered division of labor. In A. Miles & H. Buechler (Eds.), *Women and economic change: Andean perspective*. (Society for Latin American Publication Series, Vol. 14, pp. 13–30.) Washington, DC: Society for Latin American Studies/American Anthropological Association.

Morgen, S. (1989). Gender and anthropology: Introductory essay. In S. Morgen (Ed.), *Gender and anthropology—Critical reviews for research and teaching* (pp. 1–20). Washington, DC: American Anthropological Association.

Oberg, K. (1953). *Indian tribes of Northern Mato Grosso, Brazil* (Publication No. 15). Washington, DC: Smithsonian Institution.

Petrullo, V. (1932). Primitive peoples of Matto Grosso, Brazil. *Museum Journal* [Philadelphia, University Museum], *23*, 83–173.

Picchi, D. S. (1982). *Energetics modeling in development evaluation: The case of the Bakairí Indians of central Brazil* (Doctoral Dissertation, University of Florida). Ann Arbor, MI: University Microfilms.

Picchi, D. S. (1991). The impact of an industrial agricultural project on the Bakairí Indians of central Brazil. *Human Organization, 50*, 26–38.

Picchi, D. S. (1995). Village division in lowland South America: The case of the Bakairí Indians of central Brazil. *Human Ecology, 23*, 477–498.

Picchi, D. S. (2000). *The Bakairí Indians of Brazil: Politics, ecology, and change*. Prospect Heights, IL: Waveland Press.

Schmidt, M. (1947). Os Bakairí. *Revista do Museu Paulista* (NS), *1*, 11–58.

Sponsel, L. (Ed.). (1995). *Indigenous peoples and the future of Amazonia: An Ecological anthropology of an endangered world*. Tucson: University of Arizona Press.

von den Steinen, K. (1966). *Through central Brazil: Expedition for exploration of the Xingu in the year 1884* (F. Schütze Trans.). Leipzig: F. A. Brockhaus. (Original work published 1886.)

von den Steinen, K. (1966). *Among the primitive peoples of central Brazil: A travel account and the results of the second Xingu expedition*. (F. Schütze Trans.). Berlin: Reimer. (Original work published 1894.)

Bakkarwal

Aparna Rao

ALTERNATIVE NAMES

An alternative name used in government records and some scholarly literature is Gujar-Bakkarwal.

LOCATION

The Bakkarwal are located in Jammu and Kashmir (in the western Himalayas).

CULTURAL OVERVIEW

The Bakkarwal of Jammu and Kashmir are a patrilineal Sunni Muslim community of nomadic pastoralists consisting of 39 preferentially endogamous descent groups or "patrilineages" known as *zaat* or *khel* (Rao, 1988/1995). *Zaat* derives from the same Indo-Iranian root as the *jaati* of the Hindu *varna-jaati* system, while *khel* denotes units of social organization in areas of Pashtun influence. Although taxonomically different, Bakkarwal *zaat* and *khel* are organically and functionally indifferentiable, but they indicate different origins. Despite preferential endogamy and concepts of intergenerationally transmitted *zaat*- and *khel*-specific characteristics, these units cannot be glossed by the term "caste," since a formal ideology of social ranking is absent. Thirty-six *zaat* form one subdivision (that of the *Kunhaari*); the remaining *zaat* and two *khel* form a second subdivision (that of the *Allaiwaal*). These two subdivisions are named after the two valleys of Allai and Kunhar, in present day Pakistan, from where the ancestors of all Bakkarwal are said to have migrated into their present area (Rao, 1999).

The Bakkarwal herd mainly goats, but also sheep, and use horses and mules as pack animals. Some of the very wealthy also have cows, buffaloes, and land. There is increasing economic stratification within the community (Khatana, 1992; Rao, 1998a). Whereas the poorest must often supplement their income by working as hired shepherds (Rao, 1995) or manual laborers, the well-to-do have annual surplus budgets.

Positions of authority within the community are occupied by several wealthy men of influence who, by common consent, are the "most capable"; known as "big men," they have specific units of social organization linked to them (Casimir & Rao, 1995).

CULTURAL CONSTRUCTION OF GENDER

All creation is considered to belong to one of two sexes and genders (male and female), only God being conceived of as sexless and genderless. Among all mobile beings, be they animal, human, or superhuman (such as fairies), the fundamental process which takes place at conception is the mixing of male semen with female blood (Rao, 2000).

Major aspects of one's inherent nature and innate temper are determined at birth (at age 0 years) by one's sex. Females are considered imperfect from birth, and this inherent imperfection precludes every female attempt to reach certain social and moral standards. It restricts a woman's capacity and ability to be responsible and accountable and has lasting consequences for her access to information (Rao, 1998a). This, in turn, is largely why she is perceived by others (and ideally also by herself) as incompetent to choose and take decisions.

Gender markers vary over the life cycle and are indicated through dress, make-up, etc.

GENDER OVER THE LIFE CYCLE

The Bakkarwal divide the human life (cycle) into seven major phases (Rao, 1998a); terminological gender differentiation begins at about 4 years of age. In the first three phases girls and boys are referred to as *baalak* (child), and thereafter as *jawaan* until they themselves have a few children. After this no specific term of classification exists until one reaches old age.

Four phases are distinguished within childhood; the first four years of life are said to constitute roughly the first of these four subdivisions. Although passages from one stage to another are not publicly marked by specific ceremonies, there are subtle markers that are expressed through the body, body behavior, and apparel.

Socialization of Boys and Girls

Children are highly valued; great care is taken to protect them from all evil influences and infants are exposed as little as possible to the stares of strangers. For roughly the first 2 years of their lives, both male and female infants are nursed regularly on demand and then only very occasionally during the day. At night, every infant is given the breast as long as it does not have a younger sibling. There is no regular toilet training and infants of both sexes are carried around, either piggyback in a sling or in arms. A youngest child sleeps with its mother either until the birth of the next child, or until it is at least about 7 years old. If a younger sibling is born, the older child sleeps, if male, with its father, if female, with an older sister, or with its father's mother if she is a widow, or failing this, close to its own mother. As a baby girl or boy grows, notwithstanding the presence of a younger sibling of either sex, the physical and verbal expressions of affection toward it by its mother continue and are supplemented by those of grandparents, father, and older siblings.

Infant boys and girls are clad in long shirts reaching down to their ankles, but whereas from the age of about 2 years a girl must wear trousers to keep her private parts covered, little boys run around without trousers for much longer, sometimes until they are circumcised. Over their trousers, girls wear a shirt which stretches to a little below their knees. However cold it may be, girls wrap only a shawl around themselves, like their mothers and elder sisters, whereas men and little boys whose families can afford it keep themselves warm in woolen coats.

Being properly clad is part of being well mannered and well behaved, and really good manners are attributed only to the wealthy, especially to wealthy men. The learning of basic good manners begins in early childhood and goes on till after puberty. The basic elements relate to dress and body postures—notably the hair and head-covering—and are gender specific in their details. Covering the head can be an expression of social power; but it can equally underline the acceptance and

acknowledgement of reduced autonomy for women—a phenomenon which is closely linked to concepts that have often been glossed as "shame," "shyness," and modesty.

At 6 months, every infant receives its first haircut, an event celebrated by cooking a sweet dish for the entire camp. At this stage, the head is considered "pure" and this hair, which is also pure, is hidden away from evil creatures in a hole. There is no gender differentiation as yet, but a little girl's hair is never cut after she is about 2 years old, whereas boys and men are expected to have their heads shaved regularly.

Around a week after its birth, every infant receives a tiny cloth cap, with two earflaps, tapered at the back and embroidered colorfully. This type of cap is worn (in larger sizes) by the child until it is about 4 or 5 years old. After this, however, a gender-based difference marks the caps of boys and girls. Ideally, boys are shaved and given a flat white flapless cap, which resembles that of adult men and is embroidered like these with white needlework; on this a turban is ideally tied. Usually, however, boys wear either a cap or a turban, and sometimes neither; girls, on the other hand, are rarely seen with their heads uncovered. Unlike men's caps, all those worn by females after infancy are made of black cotton cloth and embroidered with colored silk thread.

While covering the head is more explicitly associated with community tradition and Islamic prescriptions, body postures are associated with secular social morals, summed up in a concept that encompasses a complex range of norms and values impinging on social responsibility, sexual control, modesty, the domestic space, and well-being. As they grow older, gender differentiation expressed in body postures and body movement prepares boys and girls for their future social roles.

Bakkarwal children are brought up with great indulgence. From their earliest years, children of both sexes are left to develop a certain physical autonomy. If food is available, children—especially boys—of all ages eat without waiting for others. Children below the age of 7 or 8 are never beaten or even severely scolded, since they are considered too young to undertake purposeful action and comprehend punishment. It is only from the age of about 7 onwards that increasing cultural competence is expected, and it is now that every little boy and girl is increasingly involved in the daily tasks of a herding household.

In early childhood work and play are intertwined. Toys are unknown, but when out herding, children weave grasses, construct toy tents, and play games individually and in twos, rather than in groups. Throughout the year Bakkarwal camps are small and scattered, and playgroups are very small. Children are not allowed to wander off on their own, for example, to other camps. A child's world consists primarily of its own camp members, and at this stage its access to social knowledge is still very reduced. In summer, young children accompany their mothers who collect fuel wood and wild vegetables; in winter they go with their siblings and neighbors to fetch fodder, tend animals, or wash clothes at the nearest stream. Whereas mixed groups of little boys and girls go gathering and collecting wood and fodder, fetching water is a purely female task, although a brother in arms may be taken along. Children start joining such work groups by the time they are about 3 years old, but are taken to steeper places only when they are about 5. Until they are about 8, most tend to play more than they work; this is especially true of boys, who are considered more immature than girls. But all children learn to recognize the right plants and trees, and practice how to handle the forests and negotiate the mountain slopes. Later in life, men forget much of this knowledge, especially that pertaining to medicinal plants.

Milking and churning are arduous but essential tasks; while the latter is done only by adult women, older children may milk if their mothers are sick, and younger children help their mothers. Herding is basically a male job, but in less wealthy families little girls herd near home from the age of 6 or 7 until they are about 10 years old; after this they may also graze animals during the day, but only if accompanied by their fathers or male siblings. Boys start herding when they are a little older, since as children they are considered less responsible than their sisters. Particularly fathers tend to praise their little daughters and de-emphasize the importance of their young sons' labor in herding. Mothers, on the other hand, often praise their sons and defend them when their fathers accuse them of laziness.

As they grow older, the mixed work and play groups split according to gender, with girls increasingly helping their mothers with domestic tasks and boys spending more time herding. Girls with younger siblings spend more time caring for them and practicing their future role as mothers. By the time a child is about 10 years old, the biological and social foundations are said to be laid for the capacity which develops to fend for him/herself and be responsible. There is now no need for elaborate care

and tending. From now until they reach puberty, a girl and a boy are termed *betki* and *laraa* respectively, and this change of terminology marks the entrance into the next phase of the life cycle.

A child younger than about 10 is still considered fairly vulnerable and delicate, but prepubertal boys and girls are thought of as basically sturdy, strength being one of the elements circumscribed by the term *jawaan*. Children in the phase in between are neither *baalak* nor *jawaan*. A *betki* and a *laraa* have crossed one set of dangers which threatened mainly their physical life; they will face a second set when they are around 16 or 17, and they must be prepared for this confrontation. These dangers are more social than physical, and must be manipulated through socialization. While this manipulation is required for both girls and boys, it is generally felt that girls are "less of a problem" than boys, if one is "a little careful." Girls are also said to "to grow up much more quickly" than boys. This is partly because—although by nature they end up with less capacity for reason than boys—in the early years they have more of it than do boys of their own age, and partly because they are not as easily exposed to bad influences from outside the family.

In this phase gender differentiation is often publicly marked by male circumcision, which usually takes place between the ages of 6 and 12; it may not take place after this, but also not before the child is at least 10 days old. This act finally confirms the boy as a Muslim, but it is also said to affect him physiologically and prepares him gradually for puberty, when his seminal level will greatly rise. The occasion is celebrated with food being cooked for the camp members.

Puberty and Adolescence

Bakkarwali language does not explicitly designate the period preceding sexual maturity or full adulthood, but conceptually this period is distinguished from other phases of life. Both girls and boys are deemed to become *jawaan* when they are between about 10 and 16 or 17 years of age and are also terminologically distinguished from those younger and older and are known as *gadri* and *gadro*, respectively. They are considered to develop and change physically, a process that intensifies after marriage. These changes are considered to be the outward manifestations of an internal psychological process, for now the levels of blood in a girl and semen in a boy start to rise—slowly in some and faster in others, all depending on their innate temper or inherent disposition. They rise to reach a certain plateau, the level of which, again, varies individually. The attainment of this plateau manifests itself in the phenomenon of menarche and ejaculation, but is not synonymous with the maximum, for the levels of blood and semen are said to spurt at regular intervals all through the adult phase. When these spurts take place regularly, one is considered a young adult. Girls who had reached menarche, but did not have regular menstrual cycles, were not thought to be fully *jawaan*, and hence, even if married, they were not considered ready for sexual intercourse.

To help his "strength ripen" a boy must now start accompanying the family's herds to the high pastures. In these expanses he can test his mettle and experience the beauty and hardship of a herder's life. And yet this phase is in many ways ambivalent, and this ambivalence is built into the term *jawaani* which is associated, exclusively in men, with what may be described as a carefree disposition. Romance and adventure are part of it, but so too are thoughtlessness and the lack of a sense of proportion. *Jawaani* in a young male who is physically *jawaan* is accepted as perfectly normal, but it is not considered befitting those who are much older. If the potentially negative aspects of *jawaani* are not curbed in time, they may lead to a man becoming too "hot" later in life.

"Heat" must always be regulated, since it has negative as well as positive effects. In the phase in which they gradually become *jawaan* every boy and girl tends to be humorally hotter than ever before, and to avoid problems in later life their intake of "heat" must be carefully tuned to their gender-specific requirements. The level of "heat" socially accepted in boys and men is considerably higher than that in girls and women, who are supposed to be "hotter by nature." Thus, while girls should avoid "hot" foods, such as raw onions, eggs, and too much salt or fat, there are no similar restrictions for boys. Excessive salt can dehydrate a girl and render her barren. But "hot" foodstuffs, and especially fat, also symbolize wealth and a good life. "Heat" thus conjures up luxury which, however, connotes self-indulgence and passion on the one hand and infertility on the other, and to abstain from "hot" foods is a metaphor for self-control. In keeping with this logic, the annual fast enjoined by Islam and first observed by girls at menarche and boys at around 15, is also said to help "cool them down." The general increase in heat in boys and girls leads to a rise in the levels of their body fluids, and this in turn to the levels of physical strength achieved in the years to follow. But this rise is also associated with the development of certain negative desires in them, and hence special care must be taken to achieve and maintain a highly sensitive equilibrium between "hot" and "cold." Excessive heat could make a girl sexually too demanding, and this in turn could make her ill and even barren; alternatively, later in life she could become so egocentric as to become a witch, turning others ill and barren. A boy with excessive heat is likely to become too power-loving and hence cruel. It is in this phase that character forms and beauty develops, and so, if a girl's parents are not careful enough, a pretty girl could grow so "hot" as to become too aware of her own beauty, and a sturdy boy overly conscious of his own strength.

With the onset of menarche, a girl attains a new social status and participates in new productive activities. Most women remembered their first menses because they also kept the first ritual fast following this. An adolescent girl is now expected to possess modesty and the sense of shame (*laaj*). If necessary, she may now milk and churn, except during her monthly periods, but until she herself marries and becomes a mother she may no longer go to the highest pastures, nor may she be present at the birth of a baby or at a burial (Casimir, in press; Casimir & Rao, in press), since she herself is no longer pure. With menarche, a girl may no longer be careless about wearing her cap, and indeed her mother now makes her a new cap. From now on it would be shameful for her to be seen bareheaded.

Attainment of Adulthood

There are no specific rites of passage marking the transition to adulthood, but generally boys and girls are married when they are considered adult. For girls this is at around 16 years and for boys at about 18 years of age (Rao, 1998a, 2000). Most girls are engaged shortly before their first menses. The formal engagement ceremony seals an agreement which may have been reached either shortly before or several years earlier between the respective (officially male) guardians of the girl and the boy. The social and public importance of engagement is symbolized for a girl by her outward appearance; for a boy there are no such symbolic status markers. An affianced girl applies collyrium to her eyes and henna to her hair. The combination of red (henna), black (collyrium), and white (considered to be the girl's own ideal skin color) serve an apotropaic purpose, but are also the colors of matrimony.

Ideally a girl's father, the latter's father and brothers, the girl's elder brother, and her mother's brother have the right to bestow her hand on whomsoever they consider most suitable. At least officially, the agency of the future bride and groom is entirely denied. Of paramount importance in the choice of prospective brides and grooms is social identity represented by *zaat/khel* and links of kinship. Partly from these follow two additional criteria, namely the reputation of the respective mothers in terms of character, and the economic status of the two families. In other words, women are considered as criteria in decision-making, even if they are not acknowledged as decision-makers.

In this phase, girls and their parents are anxious about the prospect of the bride's having to leave the natal home; this anxiety stems not only from the role changes that accompany the transition from unmarried daughter to married wife, but also from the often great physical distance between natal and marital homes. Bakkarwal children and youths are brought up in relative seclusion. It is only during migration that young girls have a chance to meet persons from beyond their nuclear or immediate extended family. Thus they are often not familiar with even close relatives. Therefore, leaving the natal home entails entering a whole new world and meeting one's parents and younger unmarried siblings only infrequently—often after the autumn migration, or at other slack periods of the pastoral work cycle.

In the early stages of her wedded life in her conjugal home, a woman tends to identify herself with her natal family; she is now identified by others also through her husband and his family. It is her duty to look after her husband and her "household," which may include his parents and siblings. If, for any reason, she fails to comply, her husband may even take another wife, and while this may not be appreciated, it is nevertheless considered "in a way natural for a man" in such circumstances. Outward markers of a married woman are a pair of special bracelets, eyes ringed with collyrium, and strands of henna in the hair. No such markers distinguish a married man, nor is he defined through his wife or affines—unless he is a live-in son-in-law, in which case his father-in-law acts as the defining person. Until he sets up his own "household," a married man is socially defined exclusively through his father, and even thereafter he is contextualized through his elder agnates.

Middle Age and Old Age

"By 40 one should be able to sit back and let the children and grandchildren do the work" is a wish commonly expressed by Bakkarwal women and men, and indeed by the time they are about 40 most do have sons and daughters who in their turn have become parents. Grandparents are entitled to greater respect within the family and, if they are wealthy, to greater control over resources. This also endows them with considerable status within the larger community, and many life histories collected among older men reflect this romantic and idealized phase of life.

Women and men, whether middle-aged or old, married or widowed, wear basically the same kind of clothes; there are no formal restrictions on color, but elderly women and men tend to wear less bright colors. Older men tend not to trim their beards, and while there is no formal age or statuswise restriction on wearing jewelry, older women generally wear less jewelry than young married women. In old age a woman is free to gift her jewelry to whomsoever she pleases; usually she distributes it among her daughters.

The entire process of life is conceived as a gradual increase and then decrease of bodily strength. This in turn is related to the gradual rise and fall of body substances which rise in youth to reach a certain plateau in maturity and fall slowly thereafter. Graying hair, pain in the joints, weak vision, loss of teeth, failing memory, general slowness, bad temper, etc. are all symptoms of this decrease. Menopause (there is no specific Bakkarwali term for this) is not considered a symptom of old age but rather its consequence, and a woman is considered old when she reaches this stage. It is explicitly connected to weakening vision and lack of strength, which themselves are the result of the decrease in the level of blood in the body. No chronological age is attached to climacterium, but it is believed that among men the level of blood (manifested in semen) sinks later than it does in women.

Ideally, at least one adult (young or middle-aged) woman is required in a household to take care of the elderly, and at no stage in the domestic cycle do old men or women live entirely alone. The Bakkarwal distinguish terminologically between being *budo/budi* (old, aged) and being *bujurg* (old, venerable, great), a distinction which appears to be closely related to gender and perceptions of power and well-being. Ideologically, one is considered *budo/budi* at the latest when one's eldest grandchildren have married and reproduced—that is, at around 60 years of age for both men and women. By this time a man must have long distributed his property among his inheritors; whether he still retains control over them symbolically or not depends on his social status— on whether he is considered *budo* or *bujurg*. A woman is never called *bujurg*, but whatever their biological age, wealthy old men in full possession of their mental and physical faculties are categorized as *bujurg*.

PERSONALITY DIFFERENCES BY GENDER

All social roles are subject to gender differentiation. Especially for boys from well-to-do families, these roles are imbued with sociopolitical meanings such as hospitality and control over one's large family. The more numerous a man's descendants, the larger his potential camp, and the greater his prestige. Physical control over humans (with their herds) coupled with social expansiveness, expressed in the generosity of a host and the kindness of an employer, are the hallmarks of good manners. For males, a certain expansiveness, coupled with the capacity to control, circumscribe the moral exercise of choice when shouldering responsibility for oneself and for others.

For girls and women, physical and social expansiveness are, on the contrary, considered undesirable as they contravene norms of shyness and modesty. Thus, not only are women expected to "crowd together," they should not laugh loudly or sit with outstretched legs in the presence of men. Women dropping in for a chat are not expected to be offered refreshments; men always are. At community feasts men are specially seated and served; women, even guests, sit wherever space is left.

GENDER-RELATED SOCIAL GROUPS

Throughout the year Bakkarwal settlements are small, varying from one to nine tents/dwellings and not consisting of more than three generations. Hence the size of a person's local social group is limited to campmates, most of whom are siblings or other close relatives. However, the children of a camp are of various ages, so that genuine peer groups hardly exist.

Larger social groups, all of which are kin based, are formed around rich and important men. The largest of these groups is a *tolaa*, which is a migrating unit at its maximum; the smallest is a *kumbaa*, a term denoting a collection of nuclear or extended families descended from one living man. Thus the term *kumbaa* denotes a specific type of descent group, headed by a man who has many living married progeny and male siblings, all of whom recognize his authority over themselves. If this last requirement is not met, the Bakkarwal speak of a man's *deraa* rather than his *kumbaa*. The principle of the Bakkarwal *kumbaa* is one of segmentation; while several *deraa* compose a *kumbaa*, these in turn make up a *tolaa*, which in turn generally consists of several *kumbaa*, represented by the units of humans and herds which actually move and camp very close together during the spring and autumn migrations. Like a *kumbaa*, a *tolaa* is usually explicitly linked to a living adult male, and also often named after him. No such larger social groups are formed around women.

GENDER ROLES IN ECONOMICS

Herding is basically a man's job, and only males go to the highest pastures. If there are no sons, shepherds are hired by the well-to-do; in less wealthy families little girls herd near home from the age of 6 or 7 until they are about 10; after this they may also go to graze during the day, but only if accompanied by their fathers or siblings. Adult men are also exclusively responsible for negotiating the sale of herd animals and the access to pasture in farmers' stubbles or fallows. However, the contribution of women to subsistence—through processing milk, gathering food, tending the ewes, lambs, and kids, etc.—is about as much as that of men (Casimir, 1991; Rao, 1998a).

Following Islamic norms, all children must inherit their share of all parental property, a daughter's share being half that of a son's (Rao, 1992, 2003). Intergenerationally transmittable parental property consists primarily of herd animals, access to pasture, cash, and, among the very rich, jewelry. Theoretically then, only the paternal herd size and the number of children are of importance. In practice, however, a herd is divided primarily among the sons, with each son's share depending on the size of the father's herd and the number of unmarried male siblings at the time of separation from the parental household. While men obtain herd animals through anticipatory inheritance, women get only a few through dowry (Rao, 1998b), the greater part of which consists of cash and jewelry. When the paternal herd is divided, so also are the rights to pasture. These are transmitted along the male line, since married daughters usually shift residence and move out of the paternal area. However, a daughter's son or an only daughter's husband can obtain pasture rights if he is adopted as heir.

The animals that a woman receives as dowry form the core of her theoretical herd and are legally considered her exclusive property, but in practice there is no separation between husband's and wife's property. However, the cash obtained from the sale of these animals is retained by the woman. She is also free to gift these animals and in case of a divorce they remain her property. On death a woman ideally leaves 40% of her animals to her sons and 60% to her daughters.

PARENTAL AND OTHER CARETAKER ROLES

Although the overall ideology is patrilineal, mothers are considered to be the exclusive transmitters of blood and crucial in the formation and development of children of both sexes. The father's semen, which acts only as a catalyst, bringing on conception, determines a baby's sex and hence also partly its inherent disposition or temperament. Sex and hence gender, it is said, tends to repeat itself along the paternal line. Thus semen, whose specific qualities are transmitted vertically from father to child (and especially to the son), is an important element in determining many basic characteristics of a community, and within this of a patrilineage.

Both mothers and fathers, and adults in general, spend a great deal of time with their infants of both sexes and also show their affection. But only mothers and other women and older siblings of both genders care for them physically—washing and dressing them, etc. In the mother's temporary absence, an aunt or even an old grandmother may put an infant to breast. Fathers, elder brothers, grandfathers, and uncles also participate in feeding toddlers and little children and putting them to sleep; they also play with them. However, as boys grow older, their fathers become less playful with them, while they continue to indulge their daughters.

LEADERSHIP IN PUBLIC ARENAS

There are several forms of semi-institutionalized leadership in the public arena, but women do not hold any of these positions. In this largely patron–client system only males are recognized as able to control and protect (Rao, 1995b). Leaders in this sphere are all men of influence, whose capabilities and authority are recognized at one or more levels of the patrilineage. Some positions of leadership are not necessarily hereditary, but if a leader's son is thought to have the proper personality, he is likely to be recognized as his father's successor when the latter dies or grows too old to fulfill his duties.

GENDER AND RELIGION

The Bakkarwal are Sunni Muslims, distinctly influenced by Islamic mystic traditions (Rao, 1990), and they conceive of God as sex/genderless. Muslim traditions are observed with regard to male circumcision, notions of modesty, concepts of inheritance, marriage and divorce rules, wedding and mortuary ceremonies, concepts and practice of sexuality, etc. However, Islamist influences are impacting on many traditional practices.

LEISURE, RECREATION, AND THE ARTS

Compared with winter, which is the lambing season, summer is a time of relative leisure for both women and men. There are no major differences in the ways females and males of all ages spend their leisure, nor is there any segregation of sexes. Husbands and wives spend much of their leisure time together and with other members of their family, chatting, singing, and telling stories. Young unmarried men and older boys occasionally wrestle with one another.

RELATIVE STATUS OF MEN AND WOMEN

The intrinsic imperfection of female nature limits drastically the degrees of freedom and autonomy to which she may even hope to aspire. These are further limited in practice by many patterns of social organization, such as residence which is generally patrilocal. Although women do take part in many decision-making processes, they are rarely acknowledged as decision-makers. This negation is also linked to notions and norms of shyness and modesty, which are far more rigid for women than for men. These notions also play a role in defining women through men, as is evident, for example, from the markers that distinguish women, though not men, who are engaged or married.

SEXUALITY

Religion regulates many attitudes towards sexuality, while the experience of daily pastoral life acts as a mirror in which to learn, understand, and interpret sexual practice. Male and female homosexuality and cross-sex identification find no expression.

Premarital sex for both girls and boys is considered extremely evil, and the vast majority of boys and all girls are virgins when they marry for the first time. Sexuality within marriage is considered natural and healthy for both men and women, provided that both partners are adults; intercourse with a girl who may look grown-up, but is not yet regularly menstruating, is considered sinful. Islamic injunctions are followed insofar as no intercourse takes place during menstruation and in the post-partum period.

Sex within marriage is considered normal, but extra-marital sex is frowned upon for both men and women, and provides grounds for divorce. This is especially so for women, for female sexuality is considered to be potentially dangerous and needs controlling. Hence young widows are looked upon with ambivalence, since there is no one to legitimately control their sexual "heat."

Rape within marriage is an alien concept, for rape is perceived of, not as a brutal imposition on the woman's wishes, but only as the illegitimate alienation of sexual resources. The humiliation and shame inevitably associated with rape stem from this illegitimacy and from her helplessness to prevent the alienation; these can, of course, never happen within a legally recognized marriage where the husband is considered the legitimate "owner" of these resources.

COURTSHIP AND MARRIAGE

Marriage is considered essential for all men and women, and indeed all women and almost all men are married at some point of time. All (first) marriages are arranged by the families of the bride and groom and wife-givers and wife-takers are considered of equal status. Theoretically, engagements can take place even at birth; suckling babies can be engaged and even married, and until divorce is declared these unions are valid. Invalidation can take many forms and have several reasons, but a man can repudiate his wife only after he has reached or completed the pubertal phase. In such early engagements the bridewealth is very low. Unlike a boy, a girl does not have the formal right to dissolve an engagement; if her family wants to annul an engagement, a community decision must be taken, and her father then has to pay the boy's family whatever amount they ask for as compensation. In practice, however, depending on how influential her family is and how resourceful the girl's mother is, engagements are annulled.

Proposals are always sent by the boy's family; it is for the girl's family to accept or reject. It is said that "it's the boy's side which goes asking," but it is also said that "a man takes a woman, and not the other way around." Once two families are genuinely interested in entering into a marriage alliance, they begin negotiations in earnest. These center around the financial transactions, which depend largely on the economic status of both families. This is the time to raise the question of the bridewealth and the compulsory Islamic *mahr* or dower. The latter is reserved for the bride in case of divorce and is related to the actual economic status of the groom's family. The amount of bridewealth is related to the intrinsic "worth" of the bride and her family. Thus a virgin "fetches" much more than a widow, a beautiful girl more than an ugly one, and generally a rich man's daughter more than a poor man's. In order to reach a compromise between financial ability and individual and family honor bargaining, both unofficial and official, can go on for months, but before the agreement is finally reached the amount of the bridewealth must be fixed. For the wedding to take place, it must be paid in cash or kind, or in the form of brideservice over a stipulated period of time.

A young widow may marry beyond the kin group of her former husband only if she has no young children by her deceased husband; if she does, junior levirate, though not compulsory, is preferred by his family. No similar restrictions or preferences are imposed on widowers.

HUSBAND–WIFE RELATIONSHIP

A woman is expected to fulfill the physical (sexual, nutritive) and psychological (caring) needs of her husband, as long as he fulfills her physical (material, sexual) needs. Although most forms of public demonstration of affection between husband and wife are frowned upon, such affection is very obvious in many cases and there are several subtle expressions of it which are approved of. Although in the public domain most decisions regarding both herds and households are projected as decisions taken by men, in practice husbands and wives take many such decisions together.

Depending on domestic and herding schedules, season, and household size, a couple may or may not eat together. Except when separated by herding schedules, husbands and wives sleep together. As they grow older, sexual desire is thought to decrease. Besides, it is thought improper to indulge in sex when one's own children have sexual relations. But the sleeping arrangements are not adjusted to meet such requirements. Monogamous couples continue to sleep in the same dwellings, which are rarely shared on a regular basis by other family members. Elderly women whose husbands are polygynous generally move out of the conjugal household to live with one of their sons. Of 285 unions, only 13.7% were found to be polygynous and men entering such unions came largely from wealthy families. Following Islamic practice, women cannot officially initiate divorce, but in practice they do so by deserting their husbands, who then grant them a divorce on the payment of monetary compensation.

OTHER CROSS-SEX RELATIONSHIPS

Numerous cross-sex relationships among kin are of importance. Cousin marriage, for example, is fairly frequent, and so are exchange marriages between sets of brothers and sisters. While a man may marry his deceased wife's sister, in keeping with Islamic norms, he may not marry two sisters in a polygynous relationship. Similarly, a man's widow may marry his younger brother in a levirate marriage, but she must always be deferential, and ideally even veil, before his elder brother and father. The relationship between grandparents and grandchildren is always affectionate, and if an elderly widow lives alone, she sometimes adopts a grandson as her heir and leaves him her property.

CHANGE IN ATTITUDES, BELIEFS, AND PRACTICES REGARDING GENDER

As in most countries, here too, rural communities are regarded as "backward," and their women specially so. As nomads, the Bakkarwal are considered to be even more backward than other rural communities in the area. The increasing exposure of the entire community to government programs and, through these, to the norms and values of middle-class sedentary urban society is leading to changes in many gender-related norms, attitudes, and practices. Traditional dresses and caps are being abandoned, and widow remarriage is on the decrease, for in the wider society in which the Bakkarwal live, those to be emulated (no longer) practice widow remarriage.

Greater formal schooling is also bringing about change. Bakkarwal children who had attended schools for longer periods spoke with contempt about their community, and notably about their mothers. Yet, most parents favor schooling, as they hope that at least their sons could then get government jobs. Fathers who wanted to send their daughters to school cited various reasons, all of which related to imbibing the culture of what they considered domesticity in the dominant culture; the mothers' arguments for schooling girls were economic. Those who did not favor schooling their daughters mentioned their fear of the child's learning evil ways.

The general upward social mobility is also leading to a certain Islamization. This is evident from the fact that wedding songs and brightly colored clothes were beginning to be frowned upon by some.

The ongoing armed violence in Jammu and Kashmir has affected Bakkarwal society over the last decade. Migration patterns have been impacted drastically, and several Bakkarwal families have been physically targeted by both terrorists from Pakistan and Indian military personnel—men, women, and children have been mutilated and killed, and there have been cases of rape. Further studies will be required to ascertain the impact of these events on gender relations.

REFERENCES

Casimir, M. J. (1991). *Flocks and food. A biocultural approach to the study of pastoral foodways*. Köln, Germany: Böhlau Verlag.

Casimir, M. J. (in press). Of liminal states and uncontested faith: Religious elements and mortuary practice in the Kashmir Valley. In T. N. Madan & A. Rao (Eds.), *The valley of Kashmir: The making and unmaking of a composite culture?* Oxford/New York: Berghahn Books. Delhi, India: Manohar.

Casimir, M. J., & Rao, A. (1995). Prestige, possessions and progeny: Cultural goals and reproductive success among the Bakkarwal. *Human Nature, 6*(3), 241–272.

Casimir, M. J., & Rao, A. (in press). The dog's gaze: Insights into the mortuary rites and conceptual transformations among the Gujar and Bakkarwal of the Kashmir Valley. In N. Balbir (Ed.), *Penser, dire et representer l'animal dans le monde indien*. Proceedings of an International Symposium, Paris; Editions du CNRS/Universit de Paris III – Sorbonne Nouvelle.

Khatana, R. P. (1992). *Tribal migration in Himalayan frontiers*. Gurgaon, India: Vintage Books.

Rao, A. (1990). Reflections on self and person in a pastoral community in Kashmir. *Social Analysis. Journal of Social and Cultural Practice* [special issue, Ed. P. Werbner], *28*, 11–25.

Rao, A. (1992). The constraints of nature or of culture? Pastoral resources and territorial behaviour in the western Himalayas. In M. J. Casimir & A. Rao (Eds.), *Mobility and territoriality: Social and spatial boundaries among foragers, fishers, pastoralists and peripatetics* (pp. 91–134). Oxford: Berg.

Rao, A. (1988). Levels and boundaries in native models: Social groupings among the Bakkarwal of the western Himalayas. In T. N. Madan (Ed.), *Muslim communities of South Asia. Culture, society, and power* (pp. 289–332). Delhi, India: Manohar. (Revised and reprinted from *Contributions to Indian Sociology, 22*(2), 195–227.)

Rao, A. (1995). From bondsmen to middlemen: Hired shepherds and pastoral politics. *Anthropos, 90*(1–3), 149–167.

Rao, A. (1998a). *Autonomy: Life cycle, gender, and status among Himalayan pastoralists*. Oxford: Berghahn.

Rao, A. (1998b). Prestations and progeny: The consolidation of well-being among the Bakkarwal of Jammu and Kashmir (western Himalayas). In T. Schweizer & D. White (Eds.), *Kinship, networks and exchange* (pp. 210–233). Cambridge, U.K.: Cambridge University Press.

Rao, A. (1999). The many sources of identity: An example of changing affiliations in rural Jammu and Kashmir. *Ethnic and Racial Studies, 22*(1), 56–91.

Rao, A. (2000). Blood, milk, and mountains: Marriage practice and concepts of predictability among the Bakkarwal of Jammu and Kashmir. In M. Böck & A. Rao (Eds.), *Culture, creation, and procreation: Concepts of kinship in South Asian practice* (pp. 101–134). Oxford: Berghahn.

Rao, A. (2003). Access to pasture: Concepts, constraints, and practice in the Kashmir Himalayas. In A. Rao & M. J. Casimir (Eds.), *Nomadism in South Asia* (Oxford in India: Readings in sociology and social and cultural anthropology series, pp. 174–212). Delhi, India: Oxford University Press.

Balinese

Lyn Parker

LOCATION

The Island of Bali is located in Indonesia.

CULTURAL OVERVIEW

Bali is famous for its rich, predominantly Hindu, culture. However, animist, Austronesian traditions prevailed in Bali until the beginning of the Christian era, when Indian and Chinese influences began to be felt, and the Balinese developed their own version of Hinduism. Wet-rice agriculture, organized around irrigation societies and with important royal ritual patronage, was practiced during the first millenium of the Christian era.

Precolonial Balinese society was stratified and organized in kingdoms based on wet-rice cultivation. Trade, especially in slaves and rice, has long been important, and Bali has never been as isolated as its tenure of Hinduism in the face of Islamization might suggest. There is a long history of culture contact, not only of Indianization and European colonization, but also of a strong Chinese presence in administration and trade, and Arabic and Indian influence. The literature has differentiated between the "lowland" mainstream society of courts and castes, and the "highland" Bali-Aga society, with tendencies towards gerontocracy, principles of precedence, and bilateral kinship organization, but recent research suggests a more complex situation.

Bali was finally pacified and colonized by the Netherlands from 1908. Following the Japanese interregnum and the revolutionary war for independence (1945–49), Bali was incorporated into the nation-state of the Republic of Indonesia. Internal administration has been in line with the homogeneous model implemented nationwide; the province has eight districts, each with subdistricts and administrative villages.

The careful cultivation of the "Bali as paradise" image by the Indonesian government and tourism industry has wrought an explosion in international tourism in Bali, with an associated process of export-oriented industrialization. There have been dramatic socio-economic transformations in Bali since 1970, involving a shift from a predominantly familial peasant mode of production to a wage-labor mode of production, urbanization, and incorporation into the global capitalist economy.

Population growth, caused mainly by declining mortality rates, has been dramatic. Bali's population increased from 800,000 in 1817 to 3.15 million in 2000 (BPS, 2000; Raffles, 1817/1978, Vol. 2, p. ccxxxii). However, there has been a recent sharp decline in fertility; the total fertility rate dropped from 5.96 in the period 1967–70 to 2.28 in the period 1986–89 (Hull & Jones, 1994, p. 135). The majority of the population still lives in the rural villages of the southern rice-bowl areas. Increasingly, prime farming land is giving way to roads, hotels, art shops, golf courses, and urban sprawl.

The affluence of Bali, compared with the poverty of other (especially more easterly) islands in Indonesia, and the attractions of the tourist industry have led to internal labor migration as well as urbanization; urban and periurban areas are increasingly heterogeneous, with mosques and churches now not unusual sights and a cosmopolitan life-style in the main tourist areas. The Balinese too have spread out across the archipelago, participating in processes of religious colonization, transmigration, and the bureaucratization of the nation-state.

Bali is often characterized as a caste society, divided into the four great Hindu divisions. The "high castes" comprise the priestly caste (*brahmana*), the royal rulers (*satria*), and traders/administrators (*wesia*), and are commonly known as the "three groups" (*triwangsa*) or "insiders" (*wong jero*). They are distinguished from the "outsiders" or commoners (*wong jaba*), who comprise perhaps 90% of the population. The *triwangsa* have their own descent groups and ideally marry endogamously. Caste differences are most obvious in levels of language used, personal names, respect behavior (e.g., seating positions), and in some social separation (e.g., in eating and some rituals). *Wong jaba* are optionally organized in descent groups, calculated from an apical ancestor.

Arguments over caste and status have dominated Balinese public discourse since the late 19th century, perhaps as a reaction to the Dutch "freezing" of what was once a more fluid and contestable social structure.

There is a patrilineal kinship system, a patrilocal residence pattern, and agnatic inheritance. Everyone in Bali must marry. Endogamy within a variety of groups (descent groups, caste/status groups, and villages) is desirable.

CULTURAL CONSTRUCTION OF GENDER

Only two recognized gender categories—male and female—are accorded full social acceptance. The genders are seen as complementary. Men are supposed to be active and dominant, rational, intelligent, virile, and physically strong. Women are ideally passive and subordinate, emotional, less intelligent, and less confident than men. The gender ideology is based upon the assumption of biological determinism, for example, that it is the *nature* of women to be docile and nurturing, that men are susceptible to unrestrained lust, and so on. These qualities translate into social roles. Men are seen as having the qualities that make them ideal as heads and masters of their families, responsible decision-makers, and public leaders. Men are supposed to play a strong role in community life, working in reciprocal labor arrangements and promoting village unity. Women are valued for their reproductive roles, their caregiving natures, and their contribution to custom, particularly through their intensive ritual (offering) labor. They are seen as the emotional heart of the family, the principal supports of their husbands, and as practical, efficient, flexible, and diligent. They are expected to be hardworking and good at coordinating activities.

There are alternatives to this dominant binary construct, especially for men, but such identities cause social marginalization. The most famous and accepted are the *banci*, an "indigenous" transgender category of feminized masculinity found not only in Bali but throughout the archipelago. The *waria*, an emerging national gay male identity, is usually associated with a modernized urban life-style. Some men participate in the gay tourism scene for money; simultaneously, they participate in mainstream village life.

GENDER OVER THE LIFE CYCLE

The life cycle is perceived as describing a downward arc of purity, with the beginning and end of life the times of highest purity, and the active middle period of life the most profane period. Perceptions of gender through the life cycle follow a similar arc. The new baby is an undifferentiated male–female entity, like a god, but created out of the union of differentiated male and female. At adolescence there is a redifferentiation of male and female, allowing for the creation of a new male–female being through sexual congress. Gender differences are most apparent at adulthood, when married couples are producing children, are most active economically, and lead more or less separate lives in public. With old age, men and women again become more androgynous as they approach the purifying transition of death.

Socialization of Boys and Girls

Although boy babies are generally more welcome than girl babies—for reasons of family- and kin-group maintenance, performance of death rituals, inheritance, and so on—there is no great difference in their treatment; babies of both sexes are treated "as gods" and are much loved. By the age of 6 or 7, however, there are quite perceptible gender differences, as expectations of the different future roles and responsibilities of men and women shape children's upbringing. Boys are generally free to play and they roam around the village and further afield with their friends. Girls are expected to help at home, minding younger siblings, doing domestic chores, and running small errands. Nowadays this difference is not quite so stark because almost all children aged 7–12 years attend school. Nevertheless, by the end of primary school, models of ideal femininity and masculinity have been absorbed: girls are usually modest, quiet, and shy, while boys tend to be bolder, noisier, and more "forward" in their socializing.

Puberty and Adolescence

With menstruation and the onset of puberty, girls are expected to become models of female decorum and beauty. "Woman" is the object of male desire, but is herself to be passionless. The principal goal of female adolescence is to land a good husband, so it behooves a young woman to keep her good reputation lest she materially damage her marriage prospects. Young women are supposed to be like flowers or dolls: beautiful, restrained, passionless, and passive. However, young men are likened to bees: attracted to spirited and flirtatious pretty young women. So it can be difficult for young women to balance the twin demands of keeping a good name and attracting the right partner.

There are different emphases according to caste/class: the feminine ideal of docility, stillness, and inactivity can really only be an upper-caste/class ideal; poorer girls are expected to be modest and restrained but also to grow into useful and hardworking young women. All young women are expected to put up a show of chastity; the loss of virginity and a sexual relationship prior to marriage are not uncommon, but should be the prelude to marriage, not the beginnings of promiscuity. In practice, if a girl becomes pregnant, she must marry.

Boys are supposed to be manly and brave, active, keen to project themselves in the world, passionate, and lustful. While there is a strong "macho" streak to Balinese masculinity, this is tempered by the ideals of politeness, restraint, and respect which are expected of all civilized human beings.

There is a ritual to mark menstruation but it is not often celebrated these days. It is often only a small private ritual. A more public, and more important, ceremony is the tooth-filing ceremony. Traditionally performed for boys between the ages of 6 and 18 and for girls after menstruation, nowadays, because of the high cost and the rationalization of ritual in Bali, tooth-filing often piggy-backs on other larger ceremonies which would happen anyway—especially weddings or death ceremonies. Tooth-filing is one of the ceremonies that every Balinese Hindu must perform in order to ensure the smooth transition of the soul from birth through death and reincarnation. It is a beautifying and humanizing rite.

Attainment of Adulthood

The Balinese consider that adulthood comes with marriage and parenthood. Marriage is virtually compulsory, not only for the perpetuation of the patrilineage and for attending to the deified ancestors, but also for the performance of social duties. Men begin to participate in the *banjar* 6 months after marriage—they attend monthly meetings, make financial contributions, and contribute their labor to communal working-bees. Upon marriage, women take up their responsibilities for making and presenting offerings at village rituals, fulfilling death ceremony obligations, and so on. The performance of public duties is triggered by marriage, and marks the arrival of adulthood and the acceptance of responsibility for community obligations.

Marriage is inextricably intertwined with parenthood—a childless marriage is usually blamed on the woman and is cause for taking a second wife. The purpose of marriage is the creation of children: lust and sex for procreation, fertility, reproduction, and sexuality are indistinguishable aspects of marriage.

Middle Age and Old Age

Middle age—the time from marriage until the marriage of children—is a time of maximum social obligation, involving work, family, and ritual responsibilities. The raising of a family is the principal task. Mature citizens are sensible hardworking members of a community, conscientious with ritual duties, and bearing the heaviest burdens in society. Gender roles are at their most differentiated.

Adults who have not married, particularly women, are suspect. Spinsters are highly anomalous—their sexuality is uncontrolled and their social usefulness limited. Spinsters are often accused of being witches. The only exceptions are very high-caste spinsters, who find it very difficult to find an appropriate husband in a small catchment population.

If a woman initiates divorce, she must leave home; if the man initiates it, the women will be evicted. Usually divorcees have to return to their natal home; there is stigma attached to their "used" status. Widows usually rely on the goodwill of their affines (preferably their sons or, failing that, their brothers-in-law) and try to stay in the marital house-yard.

Spinsters, divorcees, and young widows are problematic in ways that single men are not. Single men can remain in their father's house-yard, living out their days as productive bachelors or as divorced or widowered men. Single women, on the other hand, are entirely liminal. Their sexuality and reproductivity are not under the control of men, as is proper, and they do not have a proper ritual place in the community. Most famously, they are suspected of witchcraft, forever associated with Rangda, the fierce widow-witch of Balinese exorcistic drama.

Once sons are married, men "retire" from official duties in public life and gradually reduce their farming activities. Elderly women are typically engaged in helping with their grandchildren and are usually the offerings experts in the village. With old age comes economic dependence, decreasing community obligations, and a growing androgyny. Ideally, the elderly command respect by their quiet dignity. Death requires elaborate preparations and the mobilization of all human and material resources; sons and daughters scrimp and save and sell off land, and plan the long and elaborate death ceremonies that will purify and deify their parents.

PERSONALITY DIFFERENCES BY GENDER

"Personality" is quite a problematic concept to apply to Balinese ideas of personhood. While differences between individuals are perceived and commented upon, there is a very limited range of possible types and individualism is not encouraged. There is an idea of *karma*—that one's present position is the consequence of past actions and that present actions have implications for the future—but this is not an understanding akin to Western-style personality formation as a result of formative psychological experiences. The social ethos is one of group activity, social conformity, and cooperation to get things done. Further, the exigencies of life in very crowded living conditions, where virtually every activity takes place in public, and where the consequences of every action will rebound within one's moral community, are such that people downplay "personality" differences. That said, differences do attach to gender, as described above for ideal masculinity and femininity.

GENDER-RELATED SOCIAL GROUPS

Typically in village Bali, an extended family lives in a house-yard which is a subset of a patrilineal descent or ancestor group. The house-yard is usually allocated by the hamlet (*banjar*) or customary village (*desa adat*). Rights to residence entail ritual responsibilities related to community obligations for death ceremonies, upkeep of the village temples and respect for the ancestors, stewardship of the territory, public works, and obedience to the community's rules.

Residence rights require that a responsible married man occupies the house-yard. (This is an increasing problem as many younger men participate in the urban economy.) Such a family consists of a senior male with wife/wives and sons, each with wife and children living around their own kitchen. Daughters marry out. The basic social unit is a father–mother united in marriage.

The patrilocal residence pattern and agnatic inheritance tradition mean that women are marginal to the core structure of kin groups and residence units. Upon marriage, if it is exogamous, women take leave of their natal ancestors and adopt and honor their husbands' ancestors. Endogamy within a variety of groups (descent groups, caste/status groups, and villages) is desirable.

Social life outside the family is generally conducted in gender-segregated groups. Men are active in sports groups such as badminton, football, and snooker, and in neighborhood patrols. Women do not generally congregate for leisure, and have less leisure time than men. Both men and women often work cooperatively to make offerings and prepare for ceremonies, but always in gender-segregated groups with specific functions. Women rarely form corporate groups. However, both men and women participate in ephemeral purpose-specific groups known as *sekehe*—these are sometimes gender-specific (e.g., men go squirrel hunting) and sometimes open (e.g., men and women form a harvesting *sekehe* to raise money for an upcoming religious festival). Intergender social interaction is traditionally rare, to the extent that it is difficult for strangers to work out the families and married couples in a community. Increasingly, schools, work-places, shopping malls, and tourist venues provide sites for new types of social mixing; Western tourist behavior, television, and other global media provide new social models.

GENDER ROLES IN ECONOMICS

There is a very clear gendered division of labor in Bali, with economic and noneconomic roles allocated along principles of gender complementarity. The "conjugal economy" (Jennaway, 2002, p. 80) means that both men and women need to marry—there is no socially respectable alternative, and indeed no material alternative. Public life requires input from husband–wife couples. Subscriptions for temple maintenance and support of village priests are calculated on the basis of the husband–wife unit; public works are performed by gender-specific work teams with participation and contributions counted in terms of husband–wife units; obligations for village ritual cycles and certain life cycle rituals (notably death ceremonies) are calculated in terms of husband–wife units and performed according to gender (usually for weeks before ceremonies women prepare offerings individually at home, and men prepare meat offerings communally and eat communally). In the absence of a state welfare system, it is the family that supports the needy, sick, or aged. Sons are seen as the principal source of support for the aged, and the principle of male inheritance is justified in terms of the expectation that sons will sponsor the ceremonies that will eventually transform parents into deified ancestors. Hence procreation within marriage is the guarantee of security in old age and in the afterlife.

Some public roles have male and female counterparts; for example, the position of priests for village temples (*pemangku*) is occupied by a married couple. Much public and private work is divided along gender lines: women harvest, thresh, and carry the rice crop, and men plant, plough, irrigate, and weed; women raise pigs and chicken, and men raise cows, buffaloes and ducks; women carry sand, rocks, and bricks to serve the men building temples, houses, and public buildings; women spend an inordinate amount of time preparing incredibly ornate offerings from rice cakes, fruits, flowers, and leaves, while men spend much less time preparing offerings made of meat.

Some scholars have seen a high level of female autonomy in economic matters. Certainly, women enjoy personal sources of wealth—raising pigs for market, weaving or other handwork, the operation of food stalls—they dominate village markets, which are largely a female territory, and they control the household purse strings. This means that they are in charge of everyday family finances for food, clothes, amenities, schooling, and so on, but also it often means that they have to support their families. Since men control expenditure on large items (e.g., cars and motorbikes), kin-group rituals (especially cremations), and public buildings (e.g., village temples), inherit land and house-yards, administer the markets, dominate cash-crop markets, and are notorious for their lack of financial responsibility (being famous gamblers), women's economic "power" often does not translate into any significant control of resources. Further, women's economic work is ultimately the production of wealth for the patrilineage.

This is perhaps less obvious today as inherited land becomes less important as an economic resource. Now there is much investment in education for young people and in more ephemeral sources of income (minibuses, motorbikes, businesses). This can have the effect of shifting resources away from the patrilineage to nuclear families and individuals, though status competition between these larger groups remains a feature of Balinese social life, much in evidence at huge wedding receptions and internationally televised cremation rituals.

In the more modern and formal sectors of the economy, there is a gendered division of labor which bears much similarity to international patterns. In the government sector, women work primarily as nurses, teachers, and lower officials in the bureaucracy; men tend to work as doctors, teachers, engineers, managers, and higher officials. The national pattern of male domination of the higher ranks of the civil service obtains in Bali, and is partly the product of educational disparities. Educational levels in Bali have been low compared with national figures, with gender differences more pronounced than national averages indicate. It remains to be seen whether the dramatic improvements in literacy and schooling levels for girls will translate into more rewarding employment opportunities compared with those available to boys.

The growth in tourism and other tertiary industries has enhanced female labor force participation and income-earning, but men dominate control and ownership of businesses, decision-making, and more formal authority. Gendered divisions of labor are more apparent in the higher-class hotels and more specialized businesses such as diving and cruise charters, with women dominating housekeeping, restaurant, and accounting sections, and men taking up positions as guides, waiters, managers, drivers, guards, and maintenance and grounds staff. In the more informal sector of home-stays, handcraft businesses, and art shops, there are opportunities for women to be joint owners of family businesses with their husbands, and much expanded opportunities for mobility and income-earning, but these are often offset by heavier workloads, the reinforcement of existing gendered divisions of labor, and the persistence of male-dominated access to and control over decision-making and community management (Long & Kindon, 1997, p. 107).

PARENTAL AND OTHER CARETAKER ROLES

Motherhood and fatherhood are key social roles. "A Balinese [sic] feels that his most important duty is to marry as soon as he comes of age and to raise a family to perpetuate his line" (Covarrubias, 1937/1972, p. 122). Men have duties both "upwards" to their parents and ancestors and "downwards" to their children. Men who inherit the family land and house-yard in turn bear responsibility for supporting their parents in old age and for cremating their parents. They are also responsible for the upkeep of family temples and the "remembering" and honoring of the ancestral spirits. Fathers are regarded as the principal breadwinners, and are the moral authority in the family and the moral guardians of their children, particularly of their daughters. Fathers have the final word on all discipline and decision-making in the family, though in practice it is more usually mothers who allocate tasks, dispense resources, adjudicate on squabbles, discipline children on the rare occasions it is necessary, and otherwise deal with them on a day-to-day basis. Fathers are often very affectionate toward their children, and are often to be seen holding and playing with young children. They are usually regarded as a "soft touch" for extra pocket-money, lollies, and other favors, but as the children get older, during primary school, fathers become more distant and are gradually transformed into figures of authority who command a mix of fear and respect, especially from their sons.

Women value and are valued for their reproductive capacity, which is seen as a source of unique power. The ideal woman was primarily a mother, and secondarily a faithful wife and hard worker at home, in the fields, and in the performance of ritual offerings. Mothers are perceived to be the emotional heart of the family, and are held informally responsible for the health and happiness of the relationships therein. Their principal duties are domestic tasks associated with cooking, washing, and housework, childcare, including extended breast-feeding (up to 4 years), the provision of clothing and food, and moral teaching. Mothers usually find ways to combine income-producing work with mothering and domestic work, and bear a heavy burden of multiple roles (*peran ganda*—domestic, ritual, and productive work).

Women forfeit their children upon divorce, and perceive this as an extremely strong deterrent to divorce. Many women stay in unhappy marriages in order not to lose their children.

LEADERSHIP IN PUBLIC ARENAS

Men are the heads of families and represent their families in the public domain. The primary public institutions in

Bali are the hamlet (*banjar*) and customary village (*desa adat*). Married men attend the monthly meetings and often decide policies and implement regulations on issues, such as family planning or village water supply, that directly affect women. Men and women alike say that women are shy and reluctant to engage in public political debates; some women say that they reject participation in local decision-making because they are already too busy. This ideology of male leadership is very much in line with state gender ideology, which assumes male leadership and headship in public institutions, government departments, and organizations, and advocates a domestic role for women.

GENDER AND RELIGION

The cosmology of the Balinese links dual spheres: the heavenly sphere of the gods, the sun and the mountain, and the earthly sphere of the goddesses, the earth and crops. In esoteric contexts, maleness (*purusa*, penis) is associated with the spiritual dimension, with the heavens, the god Akasa, provider of water and symbol of the fertilizing element, and with essence. In contrast, femaleness is associated with the chthonian dimension, with the earth and the goddess of the earth, Ibu Pertiwi, provider of food and symbol of fertility, and with substance (*perdana*). The fecundity of women is associated with the fertility of soil and with agricultural fertility generally. It is the fusion of the two complementary sexual principles (*rua-bhinneda*, the two that are different: the *purusa* and the *perdana*) which ultimately creates and maintains the cosmos and animates all life.

Priests and healers are *sakti* (supernaturally powerful) because of their ability to mediate between the realms of the supernatural and the everyday. Both men and women can be *sakti*, but women are associated with dark chthonian powers and are thought to be more likely than men to practice black (or left, *pangiwa*) magic. Women's reproductivity is a double-edged sword; they are valued for their fertility, but considered both powerful and dangerous, and subject to transformative change—through menstruation, conception, parturition, and menopause. At these times women are rendered impure (*sebel*), and hence vulnerable to bewitchment and able to wield ambiguous power.

There are various types of priests, ranging from *pedanda*, who must be of *brahmana* birth and have undergone a long training, initiation, and baptism under the tutelage of a senior *pedanda*, to the more humble village temple caretaker priests, *pemangku*, who can be of any caste and are chosen and supported by the local temple congregation. A priest is generally perceived as a male person, but the position is held by a married couple, and the wife (*mangku isteri*, e.g.) can officiate at rites, sacralize holy water, etc.

Healing is traditionally dominated by men and includes a wide range of occupational specializations such as bone-setting, spirit possession, massage, midwifery, herbal treatments, exorcism, divination, dispensing of charms (especially for love magic), and textual knowledge.

LEISURE, RECREATION, AND THE ARTS

See above in "Gender-Related Social Groups." In the performing arts, the genders have for the most part been separated, with men dominating positions requiring leadership, knowledge, and authority. Men play the *gamelan* (percussion orchestra), perform as *dalang* (puppet-masters, narrating the epics and operating puppets), and participate in chanting groups (*papaosan*), an activity which requires knowledge of the epics and other arcane texts. Most dances and dramatic roles are identified as either male or female, and qualities of ideal masculinity and femininity are embodied in these dances and roles. Women's main participation in the arts is as dancers. Tourist patronage of the performing arts has radically changed genres, roles, ideas of sacred and profane, and patronage, as well as the practical organization such as length of time of performances, choice of libretto, costuming, venues, and costumes.

The most prominent female actors and, to a lesser extent, dancers, are usually the daughters of the grand masters. In everyday life, they often take on the male role as the breadwinner of their families and, these days, are highly mobile and often travel overseas. There are recent government-sponsored moves to break down some of the gender stereotyping in the arts, with competitions for female *gamelan* and, in schools, mixed competitions for oratory and chanting.

RELATIVE STATUS OF MEN AND WOMEN

In Bali, women are generally subordinate to men, and considered to be socially and culturally inferior to men.

Balinese society is strongly gendered: "The most important point is the complementariness of the sexes, male and female together making up an entity, complementing each other" (Belo, 1949, p. 14). However, gender complementarity does not mean equality; in community and family life men hold a superior and commanding position over women, and women are defined in relation to men. Men are the heads of households and families, and they occupy the apical position of patrilineages. Women should respect and honor men. Sons are more highly valued than daughters and to an extent receive preferential treatment and enhanced access to resources (education, inheritance, etc.).

Balinese gender ideology is in general reinforced by the state gender ideology, which also sees men as the heads of households and the heads of public institutions, female state president notwithstanding. The state gender ideology is based on the idea of the state as a family writ large. The apical position is taken by the father (*bapak*), who leads the family in furthering their common interest. Since the late 1960s, the common interests identified by the national government have been national unity, stability, and economic development. In this "family model," women's duties are to be, in order, producers of the nation's future generations, wife and faithful companion to her husband, mother and educator of her children, manager of the household, and, lastly, citizen.

Balinese women are often said to be good managers, to be financially astute and independent. However, as we have seen, their economic activity does not necessarily enable them to become economically powerful and it is not associated with high status; indeed, women's very "getting and spending" enables men to operate on a "higher" plane of existence. The image of the "fishwife" or market woman—bossy, brassy, loud, shrewd, even wealthy—has its counterpart in the image of the intimidated "henpecked" man, but ultimately the highest-status behavior is that which is restrained and refined. Men's distance from the grubby business of the market and women's need to be shrewd, practical, and careful in economic management justify men's higher status and women's lowlier status.

In the formal political arena of local politics, hamlet households are represented by married men; women are largely absent. However, the principle of *rua-bhinneda*, the two that are different, is often invoked as a principle of complementarity and equality, and some commentators have perceived the husband–wife relationship as a relationship of equality (Geertz & Geertz, 1975, p. 56).

The patrilineal basis of the kinship system means that men are central while women are marginal to the structure of social life. Of course, women are absolutely central to the operation of social life through their fertility, ritual and domestic work, and productive labour. Among the *triwangsa*, inheritance of the descent group's wealth is usually by primogeniture (i.e., the oldest son of the primary wife); among the *wong jaba* it is sometimes the youngest son who inherits, though this can be a bone of contention. The practice of nominating substitute heirs when a patriline cannot be otherwise continued is called *nyentana* and is reasonably common.

SEXUALITY

A heterosexual model is hegemonic. The Balinese acknowledge male homosexuality, but have a hard time imagining what lesbian sexuality might consist of. Male homosexuality is often regarded as a frivolous and passing whim, and is often associated with Westerners—Balinese partners often being regarded as just in it for the money. However, *banci* (effeminate males) have an anomalous identity which is accepted but never desired, for instance, by parents for their children, not least because of the probability that no marriage and therefore no children will be produced.

Sex is ideally initiated and controlled by men. Men talk of conquest in love; the usual expectation of young men is that women have to be pursued for some time until finally worn down by persistent flattery, cajoling, threats, etc. The model is of male activity, female passivity. There is almost no discussion of female sexual desire, orgasm, or of what women want in sex. For young women, passionlessness and chastity are ideals, though they talk extensively of their sweethearts and of love, and express erotic desires. Their great need is to find a marriage partner; hence there is a need to flirt and "shine," but this is dangerous as it might send the wrong message of sexual availability and spoil a reputation for modest marriageability. On the other hand, young women are afraid that if they say "no" the boy will leave for someone who will say "yes."

COURTSHIP AND MARRIAGE

Opportunities for courting are quite restricted because of the gender-segregated patterns of socializing described above. Boy–girl "dates" do not happen, and young people have to find covert opportunities to make contact. Traditionally this happened at night during or after performances, rituals, and festivals, or, more risky, in the *kebun* (gardens or crops). While boys have great freedom, and are really expected to be sexually experienced at marriage, girls should be secluded or accompanied at all times. This protocol encourages duplicity. Athough premarital sexual relationships are probably common, it is also the case that some claimed "boyfriend" and "girlfriend" relationships amount to no more than carrying a passport photo in a wallet. While fathers, especially, can act as puritanical guardians of their daughters' virtue, they tend to discourage daughters from marrying late, fearing the greater risks of premarital pregnancy the longer the wait.

Traditionally, marriages were arranged by families or conducted by elopement. The latter allowed young people to skirt parental and/or community disapproval, and also allowed persistent young men to prevail over unwilling brides-to-be. Nowadays probably most marriages are not arranged, but the conjugal alliance is still very much a partnership of families as well as a working partnership of individuals. Of course, *triwangsa* marriages were usually strategic alliances informed by considerations of interstate politics, economic relations, comparative status, and so on. Parental approval is still essential. Elopement remains fairly common, and fits well with contemporary Western and Indonesian notions of *cinta* (love).

Age at marriage seems to have been quite high by Indonesian standards and is rising. In 1964, women's age at marriage was 21.7 years; by 1985 it was 22.3 years (Hull & Jones, 1994, p. 137).

Endogamy is the desired pattern. The closest and most desirable marriage for a man is to marry the daughter of his father's brother; this keeps the patriline pure, the family strong and united, and minimizes problems of inheritance, house-yard division, and so on. However, there is also the idea that this can be a *tenget* (hot) marriage because of this very closeness. Failing this, marriage within the house-yard, or further patrilineage, is desired—the bride will not have to take leave of her ancestors and on leaving her natal house-yard she has relatives looking out for her. In some areas, the percentage of patrilineage–endogamous marriages can be up to 60%; certainly there are *banjar* which consist entirely of one patrilineage and high levels of endogamy in those cases are assured. However, among commoners, the endogamy ideal is not so frequent and most women marry out of their patrilineal descent group.

Polygyny is quite common among wealthy and especially high-caste (*triwangsa*) men, though the Indonesian state strongly encourages monogamy. One study found that 5% of marriages in North Bali were polygynous, but in socially conservative areas with a preponderance of higher castes, polygynous marriages can constitute a quarter of marriages. A polygynous marriage, even with an older man, is considered preferable to spinsterhood. Women may not have more than one husband.

Intercaste marriages are generally discouraged, and there is a strict prohibition upon high-caste women marrying "down" (i.e., to a lower-caste man). Such a marriage would upset the hierarchy of male : female, high : low. If plans for such a marriage were known about, the girl's family would take passionate, often violent, preemptive action to try to avert the catastrophe. A high-caste woman who makes a hypogamous marriage is cast out from her family (*makutang*) and is socially and ritually "dead" to them. In times past, the couple could be killed (Geertz & Geertz, 1975, p. 137).

Newly married women move into their husband's house-yard, coresiding with parents-in-law and brothers-in-law and their families. Until they produce a baby, especially a son, brides are in a rather weak and powerless position. The new wife is expected by her mother-in-law to take over the greater part of the housework, cooking, shopping, and laundry, so for many brides, marriage means work. Mothers-in-law often perform much of the ritual work of the house compound, especially the making of offerings. Thus there is considerable pressure on new brides to become pregnant quickly.

HUSBAND–WIFE RELATIONSHIP

Men are the heads of households, have authority over their families, and are responsible for the economic well-being of the family. Men seek to control their wives' sexuality and fertility. Women are generally subordinate to men, and wives are properly subordinate to husbands.

A sexual double standard operates by which sexual promiscuity is valorized for men, making them appear strong, potent, and attractive in the eyes of both men and women, but is never condoned for women. For women,

sexual activity must be confined to the marital relationship. Of course in practice this rule is disobeyed, but never publicly flaunted.

Women value and are valued for their reproductive capacity. The ideal woman was primarily a mother of sons and secondarily a faithful wife and hard worker at home, in the fields, and in the performance of ritual offerings. Indeed, women are perceived to be responsible for fertility, and an unreproductive marital relationship is blamed on the woman. This is an Indonesian-wide perception, enshrined in the Marriage Law of 1974: an infertile marriage provides legitimate grounds for a man to acquire a second wife, but a woman may not seek a second husband.

Polygyny is frequently viewed by men as a status marker—signifying not just sexual virility but also wealth—but it is also considered a tricky arrangement to manage. Separate households must be established, and wives and children kept apart—it is well known that cowives are bitter enemies, and that it is all but impossible to satisfy the requirement that a polygynous man treat his wives and respective children equally. Polygyny is sufficiently common that the possibility that a husband will seek another wife is a very "tangible threat undermining the matrimonial security of the currently married [woman]" (Jennaway, 2002, p. 80). Marriage as a cowife is a very real possibility for the young unmarried woman, especially if she becomes pregnant.

In many ways the marital relationship is a working partnership. The aim is the material and social well-being of the family, and ideally both husband and wife are united in working for this.

OTHER CROSS-SEX RELATIONSHIPS

There are no public signs of boyfriend–girlfriend relationships; it is difficult to work out husband–wife relationships from public behavior. By contrast, same-sex friendships and family relationships are marked by public signs of casual intimacy—holding hands, arms draped across shoulders—that are without sexual meaning.

Brother–sister relationships can be quite strong and affectionate, as can father–daughter and mother–son relationships. In contrast, older brother–younger brother relationships are often conflicted due to inheritance and status rivalry; father–son relationships are also often difficult and strained. Resident grandparents are respected and looked after; increasingly in villages, grandparents are in loco parentis as the primary mother–father are away working.

Outside the family, relationships between people of the opposite sex are rare except for strictly work-related purposes.

CHANGES IN ATTITUDES, BELIEFS, AND PRACTICES REGARDING GENDER

Balinese gender relations are in flux, as mass compulsory education, national state ideologies and development programmes, global popular culture and media, Western tourist culture, urbanization, and capitalist employment patterns all bring changing expectations and desires. The transformation of the economic base of Balinese society—the shift from a familial peasant mode of production to a wage-labor mode of production, with incorporation into the global capitalist system—has had gendered consequences. Declining infant mortality rates, improved educational opportunities and enhanced employment opportunities, higher ages at marriage, changing attitudes towards the value of children, state family-planning programmes, and the easy availability of contraceptives have combined to produce dramatically falling fertility rates.

Ideals of masculinity and femininity have shifted in tandem. The traditions of boys roaming the villages, having adventures, now find expression in older boys playing snooker, hanging out at shopping centers, playing arcade games, going to the beach to look at the topless tourist women, and mucking around with motorbikes. Young men are supposed to leave villages in search of employment, adventure, and experience. As men move out of agriculture, villages, and house-yards of extended patrilineal families, and into waged or salary work, cities, and rented suburban houses occupied by nuclear families, notions of the ideal man have shifted. Masculine ideals of physical strength and endurance, community participation, leadership, and responsibility are in decline; men are increasingly identified with, and measured by, the economic well-being of their nuclear family.

Young women, on the other hand, are still largely expected to be modest stay-at-homes, helping mother, being good girls, and waiting to get married. The persistent demands for sex by boyfriends, the strong pressure on them to find marriage partners, the boredom and

poverty of their humdrum village lives, and the exciting possibilities of leaving home can lead to compromising situations. New public issues are appearing: demands for sex education in schools and for easy contraception outside marriage (both argued as public health policy responses to the HIV/AIDS epidemic), for safe and legal abortions, and for public discussion of sexual harassment and domestic violence.

The ideal woman of the advertisements and of government is the beautiful, responsible, and consuming housewife—buying toothpaste, using contraception, sending children to university, getting her aging mother's eyes checked for glaucoma. Balinese women are no longer workers, sexual partners, and reproducers of their husbands' patrilineages; increasingly they have identities based on their nuclear families and new reproductive, sexual, and consuming duties. Once-fused notions of fecundity and sexuality are becoming separated, but ideas of women as independent workers and citizens, as leaders and decision-makers, are still largely absent.

Most recently, the resurgence of Islam nationwide and the rise of identity politics as part of the democratization process have triggered a new consciousness of Hindu identity. With this has come a new retreat into "authentic" Balinese *adat* and gender conservatism, as vigilante male youth gangs patrol streets and enforce a newly created tradition as the moral guardians of young women.

BIBLIOGRAPHY

Bateson, G., & Mead, M. (1942). *Balinese character: A photographic analysis*. New York: New York Academy of Sciences.

Belo, J. (1949). *Bali: Rangda and Barong* (American Ethnological Society, Monograph No. 16). Seattle: University of Washington Press.

Belo, J. (1970). A study of a Balinese family. In J. Belo (Ed.), *Traditional Balinese culture* (pp. 350–370). New York: Columbia University Press. (Original work published 1936.)

BPS (Biro Pusat Statistik). (2000). Retrieved from http://www.bps.go.id/sector/population/pop2000.htm

Connor, L. (1983). Healing as women's work in Bali. In L. Manderson (Ed.), *Women's work and women's roles: Economics and everyday life in Indonesia, Malaysia and Singapore* (pp. 53–72). Canberra, Australia: Development Studies Centre, Australian National University.

Covarrubias, M. (1972). *Island of Bali*. Oxford: Oxford University Press. (Original work published 1937.)

Eiseman, F. B., Jr. (1990a). *Bali: Sekala and Niskala. Vol. I: Essays on religion, ritual and art*. Periplus Editions.

Eiseman, F. B., Jr. (1990b). *Bali: Sekala and Niskala. Vol. II: Essays on society, tradition, and craft*. Hong Kong: Periplus Editions.

Geertz, H., & Geertz, C. (1975). *Kinship in Bali*. Chicago: University of Chicago Press.

Hull, T. H., & Jones, G. W. (1994). Fertility decline in the new order period: The evolution of population policy 1965–90. In H. Hill (Ed.), *Indonesia's new order: The dynamics of socio-economic transformation* (pp. 123–144). Sydney, Australia: Allen & Unwin.

Jennaway, M. (2002). Inflatable bodies and the breath of life: Courtship and desire among young women in rural north Bali. In L. Manderson & P. Liamputtong (Eds.), *Coming of age in South and Southeast Asia: Youth, courtship and sexuality*. (Nordic Institute of Asian Studies, Studies in Asian Topics Series No. 30, pp. 75–95.) Richmond, Surrey, UK: Curzon Press.

Long, V. H., & Kindon, S. L. (1997). Gender and tourism development in Balinese villages. In M. T. Sinclair (Ed.), *Gender, work and tourism* (pp. 91–119). London: Routledge.

Miller, D. B., & Branson, J. (1989). Pollution in paradise: Hinduism and the subordination of women in Bali. In P. Alexander (Ed.), *Creating Indonesian cultures* (pp. 91–112). Sydney, Australia: Oceania.

Parker, L. (1997). Engendering school children in Bali. *Journal of the Royal Anthropological Institute* [N.S. incorporating *Man*], *3*, 497–516.

Parker, L. (2001). Fecundity and the fertility decline in Bali. In M. Jolly & K. Ram (Eds.), *Borders of being: Citizenship, fertility and sexuality in Asia and the Pacific* (pp. 178–202). Ann Arbor: University of Michigan Press.

Parker, L. (2002). The power of letters and the female body: Female literacy in Bali. *Women's Studies International Forum*, *25*(1), 79–96.

Raffles, T. S. (1978). *History of Java* (Vols. 1 & 2, Oxford in Asia Reprints). Kuala Lumpur: Oxford University Press. (Original work published 1817.)

Bamiléké

Pamela Feldman-Savelsberg

ALTERNATIVE NAMES

Bamiléké is a collective term referring to the people of some 100 chiefdoms in the Western Province of Cameroon, and their descendants now living throughout the country and overseas. Bamiléké often use this collective term to refer to themselves, but also use the names of their specific chiefdoms. In these names, the prefix "ba" means "the people of." Scholarly literature often refers to the culture using the names of specific Bamiléké chiefdoms or locales. These include Aghem, Babadjou, Bafang, Bafou, Bafoussam, Bagam, Baloum, Bamaha, Bamendjina, Bamendjou, Bamenkoumbit, Bamenyam, Bana, Bandjou, Bangangté, Bangoua, Bangwa, Bangwa-Fontem, Bapi, Batcham, Batchingou, Bati, Batié, Dschang, Fe'e Fe'e, Fomopea, Fongondeng, Foto, Fotouni, and Mbouda.

LOCATION

The Bamiléké region encompasses most of the Western Province of the Republic of Cameroon, a country located on the hinge between West and Central Africa. More specifically, the 6,196 square kilometer Bamiléké region extends roughly from 5°N to 6°N and from 10°E to 11°E. Part of the Grassfields, a mountainous plateau spanning the Western and Northwestern Provinces of Cameroon, the Bamiléké region is bounded by the Bamboutos Mountains on the northwest and by the Noun River on the southeast. It is made up of five administrative divisions within the Western Province: Bamboutos, Haut-Nkam, Mifi, Menoua, and Ndé. At an average elevation of 1,400 m, the region is characterized by its irregular hilly relief, basalt and other volcanic outcroppings, and a striking mixture of high-altitude prairie and forest. Temperatures range from 13°C to 23°C, and rainfall tops 160 cm per year.

CULTURAL OVERVIEW

The name "Bamiléké" has been associated with a loose agglomeration of some 100 chiefdoms of what is now the Western Province of Cameroon since at least 1910, and possibly since the 1890s. The term derives from a colonial German mispronunciation of a Bali (western Grassfields) interpreter's designation, "Mba Lekeo," or "the people down there [in the valleys]." Since Cameroon's independence from French and British trusteeships in 1960, Bamiléké people identify themselves as Bamiléké when interacting with members of other ethnic groups, but refer to themselves as descendants of specific chiefdoms or villages when conversing with other Bamiléké. Starting in the 1990s, as ethnicity has become increasingly politicized, collective Bamiléké identity takes precedence over village and chiefdom identity in ever more contexts.

Bamiléké political organization is highly stratified, with a divine king (or sacred chief) and queen mother at the apex, followed by title-holding nobility, royal retainers, commoners, and (in the precolonial era) slaves. In the precolonial era, Bamiléké chiefs had power over the life and death of their subjects. They received counsel, as well as aid in the execution of orders, from the nobility, royal retainers, and members of secret societies (masked associations with particular religious–political jurisdiction). Chiefs currently have jurisdiction over civil court cases in rural areas, serve as justices of the peace, and are consulted and honored at many occasions. As in the past, Bamiléké chiefs and nobles practice active interchiefdom diplomacy, and visit the home-boy and home-girl associations of their urban-dwelling adherents. Increasingly, differences in wealth and power based upon commerce, education, religious affiliation, and participation in national party politics exist alongside the chiefdom-centered system of social stratification. There is no traditional overarching Bamiléké political organization. Bamiléké are active in several contemporary political parties, but are particularly associated with the major opposition party.

Rural Bamiléké are primarily farmers. Women grow maize (the preferred staple), beans, peanuts, cassava, tomatoes, onions, pumpkins, and condiments, tilling with iron hoes. Men grow plantains as well as coffee (the major cash crop) and some cocoa. The chief is the titular owner of all land, but through his quarter chiefs distributes usufruct rights to male heads of patrilineages, who in turn distribute plots of land to their wives, their noninheriting brothers, and their sisters. High population density (125 persons per square kilometer on average) and lack of land has contributed to high rates of rural to urban migration. A tradition of both male and female participation in trade, combined with a work and achievement ethic, has helped the Bamiléké gain a reputation as successful, even "aggressive," entrepreneurs.

Family and kinship provides the basis of ongoing rural–urban ties, the organization of labor, and childhood socialization. Bamiléké practice a system of dual descent, recognizing the importance of both patrilineages and matrilineages for each individual. Descendants seek to insure their good fortune by venerating the skulls of their ancestors and ancestresses. Marriage is lineage exogamous and virilocal; brides always come from another lineage than the groom, and relocate from their natal homes to the house or compound that the groom has prepared for his new bride. Polygyny is culturally valued, but it is increasingly beyond men's means to pay bridewealth and construct houses for more than one wife.

CULTURAL CONSTRUCTION OF GENDER

Bamiléké recognize two gender categories, male and female. Gender is conceptualized in a strictly binary fashion; there are no third genders in Bamiléké society, and no culturally recognized diversity of sexual orientation associated with multiple genders. In Bamiléké thought, male and female share their basic humanity, being made through the mystery of Nsi (divine creation) and through the mixing of male and female "waters" and/or "bloods" through sexual intercourse. Both have spirit (or "breath"), and after death both male and female skulls are exhumed, protected in clay pots or in tombs, and venerated. Both Bamiléké men and women consider themselves to be hardworking and shrewd.

Bamiléké believe that males and females differ in their anatomy and reproductive capacity, in their relative strength, and in their emotionality. In terms of reproduction, men contribute substance to the making of a new fetus (usually termed "water," the same word used for semen, but occasionally termed "blood"). If the child is born in wedlock, it is said to physically resemble its father. Women likewise contribute substance (usually identified as "blood" but occasionally as "water") to the new being, as well as actively forming the fetus through their transformational ("cooking") skills during gestation. Women further form the child through breast-feeding. Women are responsible, through both inheritance of traits and child-rearing practices, for the personality of the child. Women are considered to be physically less strong than men, but to have greater endurance. Bamiléké women are still expected to display considerable physical strength and fortitude, especially in their agricultural labors. According to Bamiléké cultural stereotypes, Bamiléké men are assumed to display self-control ("to hold their hearts"), while Bamiléké women are assumed to be emotionally volatile. In practice, Bamiléké men are emotionally forceful orators, and rage within marriage is considered normal and "within men's nature." Bamiléké women, by contrast, are highly suspicious of witchcraft attacks, and prudent in the information they share and the emotions they reveal. Postmenopausal women gain some of the privileges of manhood (e.g., right of way when walking on narrow forest or prairie paths) and are assumed to gain the emotional self-control characteristic of Bamiléké maleness.

Men and women distinguish themselves by dress and ornamentation. In the pre-colonial era, Bamiléké men wore loin cloths, while women wore a band of braided vines around the hips and a simple cloth or bark-cloth *cache-sexe*. Hats marked nobility for men, while circlets of cowrie shells marked royal parentage and, more frequently, royal marriage for women. Currently, men and women wear Western attire, or modern African fashion. Most men wear their hair close-cropped, while women display a creative variety of hairdos. Strength, proud bearing, and fashionable clothing are considered attractive in men, while hardworking endurance, humility, and fashionable dress are considered attractive in women. Despite these gender stereotypes, most Bamiléké women are relatively forceful and resolute rather than humble in their relations with men.

GENDER OVER THE LIFE CYCLE

While childhood is distinguished from adulthood, there are no cultural names for stages in the life cycle among the Bamiléké. There are also no organized age-grade societies for boys or girls. In the past *nja*, translated as "circumcision" but in reality referring to puberty rites, was practiced for both boys and girls as a prelude to marriage. Male circumcision was (and still is) universal. Families who could afford it would enclose their daughters in a fattening house or fattening room (*nda nja*) at puberty, followed by a public display of the now nubile girl. This female initiation rite did *not* involve genital surgery. Adulthood is attained gradually for both men and women, through building a house and the establishment of marriage for men, and through marriage and the birth of children for women. Marriage, parenthood, and heirship all bring with them increased rights and responsibilities for men and women.

Socialization of Boys and Girls

Bamiléké prefer and actively praise a balance of male and female children. Special rituals performed by the queen mother (the mother of the chief) aim to insure a balance of male and female children in the royal family. Boy and girl infants are treated equally, and traditional given names do not distinguish among male and female children (although praise names, *ndap*, do distinguish among the male and female descendants of a particular village). Infants are frequently bathed, held constantly, and passed from mother to visitor to sibling and, occasionally, to father. They are encouraged to sit and to walk, and to play give-and-take games with simple objects. Small rituals, associated with bathing, are performed by caretaking adults (especially mothers and grandmothers) to prevent convulsions, colic, and witchcraft attack. Once they reach toddlerhood, both boys and girls begin to practice the tasks of adulthood (carrying bowls of water and other objects on the head, learning to handle a hoe and machete). As childhood progresses, play and household work act as training for the gendered division of labor in adult life. Gender differentiation in work and play increases as children reach school age, and even more so for prepubescent children. Good behavior, especially polite and quiet hospitality, and prudence (not reporting what one has seen or heard) are expected of both male and female children. Mothers and older siblings,

especially but not exclusively sisters, are the most frequent caretakers of young children. Fostering of children over the age of 6 years is a common practice, considered to contribute to a well-rounded socialization and providing for some distribution of resources within broader kinship networks. Formal schooling is now the norm for both girls and boys, although more boys than girls continue on to secondary and university education. Formal education is now highly valued among Bamiléké, while in the past (especially during the colonial era) an early success in business was most valued.

Puberty and Adolescence

While Bamiléké do not identify puberty and adolescence with a specific term, they do recognize this period as an important stage in a child's transition toward adulthood. Socialization practices of childhood continue, but expectations of maturity and reflection and of contribution to the household economy increase. Girls are closely watched for signs of physical maturity. If a mother or grandmother fears that a girl is developing breasts prematurely, she will massage the child's breasts with grinding stones to "keep them from growing." Girls are also closely supervised to prevent precocious sexual activity. In the past, some pubescent girls were fattened by being enclosed in a special hut or room, fed rich foods, and prohibited from physical labor for up to 6 months. This participation in *nda nja* was considered a privilege that not all families could afford. There is no genital modification for girls. Boys, now circumcised soon after birth, were circumcised at puberty. No particular rites are associated with male circumcision. Male adolescents were organized into work and warrior societies called *manjo* during the precolonial and early colonial eras, but these associations now exist only in memory. More informal work parties, in which kin or neighbors work on each others' fields or help with house construction, may involve either adolescent girls or boys, depending upon the type of work involved.

Attainment of Adulthood

No specific rites are associated with the transition to adulthood for males and females. Education, but particularly marriage and child-bearing, mark a gradual transition into adulthood. The transition into manhood included expectations of building (or, in urban areas, buying) one's own house (a precondition for marriage). Men and particularly women are increasingly respected as adults if they bear many children, and even more so if they are parents of twins.

Middle Age and Old Age

Both parenthood and increasing age confer increasing respect on Bamiléké men and women. "Having seen a lot" because of one's age and experience is highly valued, and considered a precondition of sagacity. Middle-aged women, like their younger newlywed counterparts, are expected on the one hand to work hard and manage the household and farms independently, and on the other hand to demonstrate humility and submission to their husbands. Postmenopausal women are freed from some of these constraints of modesty. Postmenopausal members of the royal family may even counsel the paramount chief. Bamiléké men likewise gain more respect and power with increasing age. Cadets, or young, unmarried, and often noninheriting men, have little say, but they gain status as they establish households and families. In an impartible inheritance system, heirs gain status when they inherit the property, wives, and titles of their recently deceased ancestor (usually their father). Personal achievement, especially for men, is often marked through membership in title societies tied to the royal house, and through working one's way up through a system of ranked titles. New monied elites now "buy" neotraditional titles in some Bamiléké chiefdoms. Thus, age and rank combine to grant higher status, but are not equivalent.

PERSONALITY DIFFERENCES BY GENDER

In Bamiléké child-rearing practices, parents and other adults tolerate some wildness in boys, but expect more poised behavior from girls. These differences in expectations increase as the boys and girls approach puberty. For adults, women and especially men state that women are more emotionally volatile than men, and thus are not to be trusted at upsetting events such as public autopsies (now rare). This stereotype is belied by Bamiléké women's careful management of information and refusal to practice hearsay, based largely on fear of witchcraft. Both genders characterize Bamiléké as hardworking,

forward-seeing, and "prudent" when comparing their own ethnic group with others. The only strongly gendered culturally recognized mental illness is that of the *megni nsi*, or spirit mediums. *Megni nsi* are almost always women. Their initial spirit possession follows a set pattern of trembling, patting the ground, unintelligible speech, and running off into the bush. When properly treated through initiation into the role of spirit medium, the woman is not only "cured," but also highly respected as someone practicing a religious–medical calling. Lack of treatment/initiation is believed to lead to madness.

GENDER-RELATED SOCIAL GROUPS

Two main types of gender-related social groups exist in Bamiléké society: (1) kinship groups; (2) nonkin associations. Kinship relations organize religious duties of men and women, inheritance of property and titles, and access to land. Bamiléké practice a system of dual descent, recognizing each person's patrilineage and matrilineage and honoring ancestors from these two distinct lineages. At the center of each descent group are lines of heirs or heiresses who inherit the property, titles, and skull custodianship of their ascendants. Patrilineal descent determines village membership and the inheritance of titles, real estate, usufruct rights to land obtained from the paramount chief, and wives. Matrilineal descent determines the inheritance of titles, movable property, and moral and legal obligation to lineage members. Descendants' most profound religious duty is to venerate the skulls of their ancestors and ancestresses, offering food sacrifices, libations, and prayers to increase success, to ward off misfortune, and to seek relief from illness. Heirs and heiresses thus become conduits to sacrificing at ancestral skulls for their noninheriting relatives. Marriage is exogamous, preventing individuals from marrying members of the same matrilineage or patrilineage. Most marriages involve the exchange of bridewealth, which grants the groom reproductive, sexual, and domestic rights. In cases where no bridewealth is exchanged, the bride's father retains rights over the marriage and patrilineal identity of his granddaughters. Contemporary Bamiléké may also choose Christian (and occasionally Islamic) marriage, marriage by justice of the peace, elopement, or single parenthood. Traditional marriage is virilocal (the bride moves to the groom's residence), and men prefer to settle near their father if there is enough land. Population pressure on the land make this increasingly difficult for couples where the groom in noninheriting. Thus Bamiléké couples increasingly exhibit a neolocal postmarital residence pattern. Polygyny is a goal that fewer and fewer men can afford. In polygynous households, each wife has her own kitchen-house. Construction of this house is the groom's responsibility, and is a prerequisite for marriage. The term for marriage, *nâ nda* (to cook inside), condenses the symbolism of a married woman's confinement to her kitchen, cooking meals and producing children for her husband's lineage.

Nonkin associations include those associated with traditional Bamiléké royalty, and all the pomp and etiquette that entails, and those that are independent of royal control. Traditional title societies constitute the first type of nonkin association. While there are title societies for both men and women, most are for men, and all are gender segregated. These title societies mark both inheritance of rank (e.g., for heirs of nobility) and achievement. Rotating credit associations, dance societies, and churches form the most important nonroyal nonkin associations. The first two are almost always sex segregated. Bamiléké are famous throughout Cameroon for developing rotating credit associations into "an art," and organizing both modest farmers or merchants and elite professionals into mutual aid groups based on a combination of gender, ethnicity, and income or occupation. These rotating credit associations or *tontines* (also called *ncua*) exist both in the Bamiléké homeland and among Bamiléké migrants to cities and other commercial centers in Cameroon. For Bamiléké "exiles," these rotating credit groups form the core of home-boy and home-girl mutual aid and cultural associations in the urban setting.

GENDER ROLES IN ECONOMICS

Rural Bamiléké are primarily farmers, but also keep pygmy goats and sheep, and engage actively in commerce. Since precolonial times, women have been the major producers of food crops, including maize, beans, peanuts, and cassava. Men have been responsible for tree crops (plantains, and since the colonial era the cash crops coffee and cacao), clearing women's fields, and building fences. Hunting, small-animal husbandry, and war were also precolonial male pursuits. They have been replaced by cash-crop cultivation, shopkeeping, and taxi and truck driving. Women continue to grow food crops, and began

commercializing their food crop production as early as the 1920s (before men become involved in cash-crop production). Women and men are both involved in marketing; until recently, men were more often involved in longer-distance trade, while women sold foodstuffs (both raw and prepared) at local markets and roadside stands. In the current economic crisis, women are particularly involved in the informal economy, making ends meet by selling foodstuffs, soap, cooking oil, and other items at small roadside stands.

Women can inherit movable property and traditional titles from any matrilineal female relative as long as they are the designated heiress. Likewise, men can inherit real estate, wives, and titles from any patrilineal male relative, as long as they are the designated heir.

PARENTAL AND OTHER CARETAKER ROLES

Mothers and older siblings take care of babies (playing with them, encouraging development by propping them in a sitting position, frequently bathing infants to "fortify" them, and, of course, feeding them). When the child can talk, its father begins to correct its behavior and to discipline larger transgressions through shaming or corporal punishment. As they grow, children spend less and less time with their parents. They help in the fields and household, but otherwise spend most of their time with other children. Gender roles are already important in early child-rearing—parents indicate which games are important to their male and female children. In the rural area, these games often replicate the gendered division of labor. Among urban Bamiléké elites (the salaried middle and upper class), parents might help children with school work. Since these elite parents are often at work, they hire tutors and nannies for their children. Household help might watch out that children do not hurt themselves, while doing other duties; they are not expected to be engaged in children's games or schoolwork, reflecting the separation between the worlds of children and adults.

LEADERSHIP IN PUBLIC ARENAS

Bamiléké chiefdoms are highly stratified, with sacred chiefs and queen mothers at the apex, followed by various levels of title-holding nobility, royal retainers, and commoners. Although the queen mother and councils of title-holding women had some rights and responsibilities to counsel the (male) chief during the precolonial era, Bamiléké women have gradually lost their political rights and duties. Most title-holding nobility and royal retainers are men. The most important of these are the *nkam be'e*, or council of the nine highest nobles, who are responsible for the investiture of new chiefs. Men have more, and increasingly more, authority in the public arena than women. In the national context, Bamiléké men have easier and greater access to state bureaucracies, and thus to credit and markets, than women.

Gender and Religion

Traditional Bamiléké religious practice focuses on the care and reverence of ancestors and on etiquette surrounding the sacred chief. All Bamiléké share obligations to sacrifice to the skulls of their patrilineal and matrilineal ancestors. A complex calculation determines the extent (in terms of generations of antecedents) to which male heirs and nonheirs are responsible for sacrifices to patrilineal ancestors. All matrilineal ancestors can hold sway over their descendents, and thus require placation through sacrifice and prayer. Heirs and heiresses, as custodians of ancestral skulls, can sometimes wield considerable power over their noninheriting relations who need access to the skulls to perform sacrifices. The secret society *ba nda nsi*, or the people of the house of god, is a male title society associated with the ritual aspects of royalty and with maintaining the spiritual health of the entire chiefdom. Spirit mediums, by contrast, are usually women. Bamiléké women are very involved in a variety of Christian churches, with the great majority being either Protestant (Evangelical Church of Cameroon) or Roman Catholic. However, men hold the highest positions of authority within church hierarchies.

Leisure, Recreation, and the Arts

Children's play becomes increasingly sex segregated as they grow older. Adult men spend their leisure time socializing with friends and discussing chiefdom politics, particularly in the context of title societies. Male youth and adults are both enthusiastic soccer players or fans.

Bamiléké women engage in storytelling when they are preparing and eating meals with their children, evoking warm memories of the emotional as well as kinship ties among full siblings and their mother. Bamiléké women also discuss local affairs while walking to and from association or rotating credit meetings, when they meet at market, and while fixing each others' hair.

Relative Status of Men and Women

Both men and women hold formal positions in the public arena, including political offices and secret and title societies, and positions in church hierarchies, but men have considerably more opportunity than women to exhibit public leadership. The paramount chief (*mfen, mfo,* or *fon*), his council of nine nobles (*nkam be'e*), royal retainers, and most other title-holding nobility are all men. The duties of the queen mother (*ma mfen*) and title-holding women included advisory roles in statecraft in the past, but are increasingly limited to ceremonial and honorary roles. Over time, men in these public positions have gained more authority, while women's opportunities for formal participation in the public arena have diminished. Highly educated Bamiléké women, mostly migrants to the major cities, who are developing successful careers in the Cameroonian civil service and the liberal professions (medicine, law), are the exceptions to this trend. Women's position in church hierarchies is ambiguous; they are the most frequent and dedicated churchgoers in all denominations and practice considerable leadership there, but do not hold the highest positions within any of these churches. Within subsistence and the economy, men's and women's activities and budgets are quite separate, giving both considerable autonomy in many realms of economic decision-making. Among rural agricultural Bamiléké, men and women control the fruits of their labor, with men selling cash crops to parastatal coffee and cocoa cooperatives and women selling surplus food crops in local markets (occasionally in wider regional and national markets as well). However, owing to deeply felt responsibilities, Bamiléké women tend to invest in the immediate needs of their domestic group while men invest in longer-term business ventures or building a house. This leads to inequalities in men's and women's access to resources, as well as to authority within the household. Men have final authority within the household and kin group, and expect deference from their wives and daughters in particular, but also from junior men. Women, particularly wives in a polygynous household, do exercise some informal power through symbolic acts such as serving meals prepared without oil, cooking strikes, or refusing sex. Both men and women can initiate divorce, and there are no rules regarding child custody following divorce. However, there are strong societal pressures against divorce, and it is relatively rare among Bamiléké couples.

SEXUALITY

Sexuality among the Bamiléké was traditionally considered to be for procreation. Social mores insured that sexuality was exposed to others; sexual acts were kept very discrete. Daily life consisted of rather distant relations between men and women, including between sexual partners. Spouses did not share a bedroom; instead, the wife came to the husband's room only when he called. Sexuality between a husband and wife was rather hidden, and there were no public displays of intimacy. Currently, daily relations between men and women are less discrete; even older people now share a bedroom with their spouse, while before that was unthinkable. Women now have more (but not absolute) decision-making power in the household, including regarding their own sexuality. Kissing and hand-holding are now done in public (even if less demonstratively than currently in the United States). Urbanization contributes to this increasing daily proximity and intimacy between Bamiléké men and women. In rural areas, the division of labor still inhibits men and women from much daily contact.

The sex act is considered "hot" and full of transformative power. However, only menstruation is surrounded traditionally by clear restrictions ("taboos"): a menstruating woman cannot prepare food, cannot walk freely in public or stray far from home, and should have no sexual relations. Although Bamiléké do not practice menstrual seclusion (and are shocked by the suggestion that other peoples do!), a menstruating woman is expected to retreat somewhat from public life. Extramarital sex among those already married is considered polluting. A woman who has had sex with a man other than her husband is spiritually marked for life. She is not allowed to visit her husband if he should become sick, because her presence

has the potential to aggravate his illness or cause death. Women's infidelity has consequences for her own health as well, especially regarding difficult labor or a complicated pregnancy; she is only cured through rites of public confession to "open" the way. These consequences can last throughout a woman's lifetime. There are no parallel consequences for men's extramarital affairs, with two exceptions. If a man has an affair with a paramount chief's wife, he is sent away in exile (and in the precolonial era could have been buried alive with his paramour). All culturally defined incestuous relationships (including a man having sex with a relative of his wife) are polluting and cause illnesses such as edema, other swelling, and infertility.

In the past, premarital sexual relations were not accepted for girls, but tolerated for boys after circumcision (which was performed shortly after puberty, around the age of 17–18 years). In general, there was a much stronger control of sexuality of children. Boys and girls were often kept rather separate. Girls were subject to even more control than boys. The virgin marriage of a girl, announced through the display of a bloodstained sheet, was celebrated. In contrast, a non-virgin bride was called "oversalted," and her family received an oversalted meal from the groom's family. Premarital sex is now expected for boys, and even for girls (although virginity at marriage is still valued). It is now very rare that Bamiléké girls or boys enter into marriage without having experienced premarital sex. Among the Bamiléké, premarital pregnancies are still considered shameful, even though they prove fertility in a society that fears infertility. The main concern with premarital pregnancy is that it reflects badly on the family, and leads to conflicts between the parents of the pregnant girl. Children conceived outside marriage are often adopted by their maternal grandparents, and call their mothers *Tata* (auntie). Premarital pregnancy is one of the primary reasons for abortions, with grave secondary consequences for women's health. Bamiléké regard themselves as conservative with regard to premarital sex and child-bearing; perceptions appear to be changing faster in other parts of Cameroon.

Most Bamiléké assume that menopausal women do not have sex, even though the current reality is that elderly men and women do continue their sexual lives. Norms are that after a certain age, husband and wife will have separate rooms and end their sexual relations. Bamiléké women are subject to norms regarding social menopause, which state that a woman should not have sex or conceive after one of her children has had a child. However, elderly men often continue their sexual life either with younger wives or outside marriage, regardless of the existence of grandchildren.

In the past, modesty was considered part of the social protection of body, and these ideas were reinforced through early missionization and the introduction of clothing made of imported cloth. Nowadays the female body is much more exposed, especially among youth.

Although there is little expression in gesture or talk about sexuality among the Bamiléké, some festivals (such as royal enthronement and weddings) allow for the expression of sexuality, and even jokes about sexuality, through dance and song. These are specific situations where one can go against norms. Making jokes about sexuality outside these special occasions is frowned upon. Cross-dressing and same-sex sexual attraction is interpreted by most Bamiléké as an illness. Cross-sex identification is considered a kind of madness, or possession by a demon, and a person exhibiting such behaviors or tendencies is taken to a healer or diviner. Homosexuality, although it does exist, is not recognized in Bamiléké society. Currently, many consider homosexuality to be an urban phenomenon, an import from the West, or the result of grinding poverty (reflecting an association that many Bamiléké make among homosexuality, promiscuity, and prostitution).

COURTSHIP AND MARRIAGE

In the past, nearly all Bamiléké parents arranged the marriages of their children, although both the groom and bride had the right to refuse. Arranged marriage served two purposes: preventing unintentional incest (in the case of close lineage relations separated and masked by the passage of many generations), and the wish of the groom's family to be able to control their son's bride. After a period of covert investigation, the process of courtship was initiated by the groom approaching his future father-in-law with the expression, "I have no one to cook for me." As a prerequisite to marriage, the groom needed to build a house, including a kitchen, for his new bride. The Bamiléké term for marriage, *na nda*, means "to cook inside," symbolically referring to the containment of the wife's productive and reproductive labor "inside" the literal walls of the kitchen and metaphoric boundaries of the marriage contract. A series of prestations

(gift exchanges) would be made from both sides, culminating in a marriage ceremony that emphasized fidelity, fertility, and the alliance formed between two families. Bridewealth was paid by the groom and his family to the bride's father, his heir, or occasionally to her grandfather or *ta nkap* (if no bridewealth had been paid for her mother). The payment of bridewealth ensured that the children of the union would be members of their father's patrilineage. Bridewealth payments were often spread over long periods of time, and disputes over bridewealth and resulting ancestral wrath were interpreted as a major cause of reproductive illness. These customs persist to the present day, although youths currently choose their own spouses. Marriage is expected of everyone, and if youths wait too long, family members will choose spouses and exert considerable social pressure to marry. Bamiléké expect that the marriage will quickly result in a child; when pregnancy does not follow marriage within a few months, family members will start to suggest traditional medical practitioners and even hospital infertility treatment. Infertility is usually blamed on the woman, and leads to many problems with her affines (members of her husband's family).

HUSBAND–WIFE RELATIONSHIP

Except in economically and educationally elite or middle-class families, husband and wife eat separately. They spend little time together, and are discrete in their expression of intimacy. Even in monogamous marriages, extra-marital relations are rather common for men. Divorce is discouraged (see "Relative Status of Men and Women"), was rare in the past, and remains less frequent among Bamiléké than among the other major ethnic groups of Cameroon. Nonetheless, increasing numbers of Bamiléké couples get divorced. These divorces are rarely completed legally, but rather are considered like permanent separations. Most only seek out an official state divorce if they want to remarry. Because of the exchange of bridewealth, if a divorced or separated woman dies, she will still be buried in her husband's village. Bridewealth is not returned to the groom's family in cases of divorce unless the wife is infertile. Once a marriage is consumated, the bridewealth stays. In the case of a woman's remarriage, the bridewealth of her daughters by the secondly marriage still goes to first husband.

Other Cross-Sex Relationships

Outside marriage, the most important social relationships are with people of the same gender. For example, an uncle and his nephew may share names, creating material, moral, and affectual rights and responsibilities. Friendships and associational life also occur mostly in homosocial environments. Cross-sex relations are mostly discouraged.

Change in Attitudes, Beliefs, and Practices Regarding Gender

Changes over time in attitudes, beliefs, and practices have been discussed in previous sections. Taken as a whole, these changes paint an ambiguous picture regarding the relative values, rights, and privileges accorded to men and women within Bamiléké society. During the precolonial era, women practiced extreme deference toward men and were subject to capture in interchiefdom raiding. On the other hand, women had their own secret societies, were major actors in the local market economy, and held important titled positions within the royal hierarchy. Women's expected deference toward men currently is much milder than in the past, and they no longer need to fear capture. They enjoy expanded economic opportunities, and in some ways are more successful in the rural economy than are men. Nonetheless, they have considerably less access to the state bureaucracy for permits and credit, and attend secondary and higher education less frequently than men. Women in the rural areas often need to fulfill not only their own expected duties in the gendered division of labor, but also those of absentee husbands who have gone to urban areas in search of wage labor. Urban Bamiléké women must struggle due to their responsibility to feed their families during an extended period of economic recession. Inequalities within genders, for example between senior inheriting men and their junior noninheriting sons, nephews, and brothers, persist in present-day Bamiléké life. Old inequalities between genders and among Bamiléké of varying statuses in the traditional title system persist and

have been overlaid with new inequalities in economics, politics, and even sexual relations in the era of the AIDS pandemic.

Bibliography

Akam, E. (1990). *Infécondité et sous-fécondité: Evaluation et recherche des facteurs. Le cas du Cameroun.* Yaoundé, Cameroon: IFORD.

Ardener, S., & Burman, S. (Eds.). (1995). *Money-go-rounds: The importance of rotating savings and credit associations for women.* Oxford: Berg.

Dongmo, J.-L. (1981). *Le dynamisme Bamiléké (Cameroun).* Yaoundé, Cameroon: Université de Yaoundé.

Feldman-Savelsberg, P. (1994). Plundered kitchens, empty wombs: Fear of infertility in the Cameroonian Grassfields. *Social Science and Medicine, 39*(4), 463–474.

Feldman-Savelsberg, P. (1995a). Cooking inside: Kinship and gender in Bangangté metaphors of reproduction and marriage. *American Ethnologist, 22*(3), 483–501.

Feldman-Savelsberg, P. (1995b). Bamiléké. In J. Middleton & A. Rassam (Eds.), *Encyclopedia of world cultures: Vol. IX. Africa and the Middle East* (pp. 36–41). Boston: Hall.

Feldman-Savelsberg, P. (1999). *Plundered kitchens, empty wombs: Threatened reproduction and identity in the Cameroon Grassfields.* Ann Arbor: University of Michigan Press.

Feldman-Savelsberg, P., Ndonko, F. T., & Schmidt-Ehry, B. (2000). Sterilizing vaccines or the politics of the womb: Retrospective study of a rumor in Cameroon. *Medical Anthropology Quarterly, 14*(3), 159–179.

Fotso, M., Ndonou, R., Libité, P. R., Tsafack, M., Wakou, R., Ghapoutsa, A., et al. (1999). *Enquête démographique et de santé, Cameroun, 1998.* Yaoundé, Cameroon: Bureau Central des Recensements et des Études de Population, and Calvertan, MD: Macro International.

Goheen, M. (1996). *Men own the fields, women own the crops: Gender and power in the Cameroon Grassfields.* Madison: University of Wisconsin Press.

Hurrault, J. (1962). *La structure sociale des Bamiléké.* Paris: Mouton.

Ndonko, F. T., & Bignon-Makong, J. (2001). Sexualität und Fortpflanzungsverhalten bei Jugendlichen in Kamerun. *Zeitschrift für Sexualforschung, 14*(4), 285–307.

Nyamnjoh, F., & Rowlands, M. (1998). Elite associations and the politics of belonging in Cameroon. *Africa, 68*(3), 320–337.

Pradelles de Latour, C.-H. (1994). Marriage payments, debt, and fatherhood among the Bangoua: A Lacanian analysis of a kinship system. *Africa, 64,* 21–33.

Tardits, C. (1960). *Contribution à l'étude des populations Bamiléké de l'ouest de Cameroun.* Paris: Berger-Levrault.

Wakam, J. (1994). *De la pertinence de theories "Economistes" de fecondité dans le contexte socio-culturel Camerounais et Negro-Africain.* Yaoundé, Cameroon: IFORD.

Beng

Alma Gottlieb

ALTERNATIVE NAMES

The name "Beng" is the term by which Beng people refer to themselves. Akan-speaking people usually call them the "Ngan" or "Ngen," and Mande-speaking people tend to use the term "Gan."

LOCATION

There are about 12,000 Beng people, the vast majority living in the West African nation of Côte d'Ivoire. Most Beng live in villages on the northern edge of the rain forest; a smaller number of Beng live in towns, and some work as laborers on commercial plantations. Currently, only a tiny diaspora of Beng have left the country.

CULTURAL OVERVIEW

The Beng are one of the smallest ethnic groups in Côte d'Ivoire. The Beng language is part of the Mande language family. Most Beng are multilingual so as to communicate with their neighbors, whereas few non-Beng learn to speak the Beng language.

The majority of Beng practice a mixed economy of farming, hunting, and gathering. Since the 1980s, crop prices have dwindled precipitously, diminishing the cash base for smallholder farmers. Beng households consist typically of a man, his wife or wives, all their unmarried daughters, all their sons, and their married sons' wives and children. Until the 1960s, such families shared a large round house. The newly independent government required smaller square houses for all new constructions, but extended families still inhabit adjacent buildings surrounding an open courtyard. A two-layered system of clans ("dual descent") crosscuts the family structure, with each individual belonging to one clan traced in the female line and another traced in the male line. Neither men nor women change clan membership on marriage.

In theory, most villages are ruled by a male and female chief. Male chiefs hear cases of disputes that can be resolved at the local level. The villages are grouped into two regions, each of which is ruled jointly by a king and queen who, as with village chief pairs, are usually cousins belonging to the same matriclan and are classified as siblings (Gottlieb, 1989). The king hears legal cases that involve intervillage disputes or crises. Serious crimes such as grand theft or murder are referred to the national court system.

Until recently, nearly all Beng were adherents of their indigenous religion, which highlights the role of ancestors, partially independent bush spirits, and spirits affiliated with the earth, with all these entities seen as loosely subordinate to an overarching but distant sky god (*eci*) (Gottlieb, 1992/1996; Gottlieb & Graham, 1993/1994). Traditional religious practitioners communicate with these various spiritual entities on behalf of individuals or groups who seek protection from witchcraft, relief from sicknesses caused by spiritual disruptions, thanks for wishes granted or good luck experienced, or atonement for past sins.

In the past few decades, many Beng have embraced Islam and a smaller number have endorsed Christianity. However, some devotional practices of their traditional religion remain.

CULTURAL CONSTRUCTION OF GENDER

The Beng recognize two gender categories, *leŋ* (female) and *gɔŋ* (male). In the first few years, the only visual signs of gender difference are that girls nowadays (although not traditionally) have their ears pierced a few days after birth, and baby boys and girls may also wear different necklace and hair styles. Otherwise, all babies wear a variety of jewelry and face and body paints, undistinguished by gender, to prevent disease. Until approximately 5–7 years old, the gender of children is not significantly distinguished by clothes. Boys and girls enjoy playing with one another in mixed-gender groups throughout childhood (play-cooking, building play houses, dancing, playing a variety of physical games such as leapfrog). However, after they can walk confidently, young children begin spending progressively more time with the parent of their own gender (see "Socialization of Boys and Girls" below) and less time in play groups.

Flirtation begins during adolescence. Traditionally, some teenage girls elected to have cicatrices cut into their body for beautification, but this is rarely done today. Large beads wrapped in thick strands around a girl's or woman's waist, and worn underneath her long skirt to hold up her underwear, are sexually alluring to men. A young woman may attempt to refuse an arranged marriage if she judges that her intended has a "rotten face."

Married women typically wear scarves wrapped around their hair for events such as dances, weddings, and funerals. Women and, even more, men have adopted some Western fashions. Men often wear Western-style pants and T-shirts for working in their fields. Women still wear traditional wraparound *pagne*-style skirts exclusively, but the brightly colored patterns are now made of industrially produced light cotton. On special occasions, men now dress in colorful pants and matching shirts, or long-sleeved robes if they are Muslim; for festivals, women of the same village may organize among themselves to buy matching sets of colorful long *pagne* skirts and sewn blouses.

Some Beng cultural beliefs imply antagonism between the sexes. For example, elders say that when a sleeping infant boy laughs, he is dreaming of his mother's death and indifferent to the event, whereas if he cries, he is dreaming of his father's death and upset that he will not have his father to accompany to the fields, and conversely for a sleeping infant girl. Infant boys are said to breast-feed longer than infant girls, as boys are said to be unmoved by women's difficulties in breast-feeding whereas baby girls naturally sympathize with their mothers' labors. Nevertheless, such explicit statements of male–female antagonism are not the basis of a thorough-going world view; instead, they are frequently shrugged off as amusing beliefs that belie other more cooperative relations between the sexes.

GENDER OVER THE LIFE CYCLE

The early stages of life are undifferentiated by gender; later stages are differentiated as shown in Table 1. The duration of adolescence differs between the genders, reflecting that girls but not boys are initiated and that they marry at an earlier age.

Socialization of Boys and Girls

Adults generally say that they value boys and girls equally. Many couples desire an equal number of daughters and sons so that each parent later has sufficient help for their work tasks. However, women may value daughters more and fathers may value sons more.

All babies are cared for primarily by women—the mother as well as other females. Sometimes one girl or

---

Table 1. Named Stages of the Life Cycle

lɛŋ drɛ kro: fetus and young infant
lɛŋ yatrɔli: infant who can sit up
lɛŋ gbõlí: infant who can crawl
lɛŋ yalí: toddler; child who can walk, up to 3 years old
lɛŋ gbe gble gbe: middle childhood, approximately 3–11 years old

Girls	Boys
tonaŋ lɛŋ kákání kro: young girl, 11–13 years old	*zanaŋ gɔŋ kákání kro*: boy/young man, 11–20 years old
tonaŋ lɛŋ: young teenage girl, 13 years old to initiation (around 15)	*zanaŋ gɔŋ*: young man, 20 years old until he marries
lɛŋ da: married woman capable of giving birth, a mother	*gɔŋ dá*: man able to procreate
lɛŋ gbɔ kró: old woman, female elder, from when she gets white hair	*gɔŋ sia*: physically fit mature man
	gɔŋ gbɔ kró: old man, male elder, from when he gets white hair

woman (usually a relative) is designated as the official baby-sitter; this person carries the baby to and from the fields daily and/or cares for the baby in the village, and may develop a close relationship with the infant (Gottlieb, in press). Fathers and other male relatives enjoy playing with babies but rarely perform routine daily care.

By the time they are 2–3 years old, girls are expected to walk to the fields, while little boys often ride on the handlebars of their fathers' bicycles to their fathers' fields. In the fields, the youngest children nap, rest, and play around their parents, but they are soon encouraged to help in simple tasks.

In addition to agricultural work, girls learn domestic tasks. Between 1 and 2 years of age, girls begin by watching their mothers and other female relatives. What begins as play slowly transforms to helpful assistance. By 6, most girls can independently sweep, wash some dishes and laundry, carry light headloads, and do some food preparation tasks such as pounding corn in small mortars.

Boys and girls are not raised to become substantially different from one another. Children of both genders are taught to work hard, to share food, to value social ties with relatives and neighbors, to respect elders, ancestors, and (except for some Muslims and Christians) earth spirits, and to respect members of the other gender.

Puberty and Adolescence

Adolescence is a period during which boys and girls prepare actively for their adult roles as farmers. Nowadays, many teenagers are given their own fields to farm; even if they are not, as long as they are not attending school, they perform near-adult levels of work daily. Because of rural poverty, some teenage boys and girls now leave the villages to work for a contracted term, often a year or more, on a commercial plantation. They generally send home most or even all of their (usually meager) earnings to their parents, rarely returning with much cash for themselves. Beng teenagers have sometimes been compelled to work so hard by their bosses that they were given marijuana as a means of alleviating the mental and physical pains produced by the grueling schedule. Recent exposés of Ivoirian child labor practices in the Western media have put pressure on the Ivoirian government to reform such abuses (Greenhouse, 2002).

Toward the end of adolescence—usually between 15 and 18 years—girls of traditional (non-Christian) families in the villages are generally engaged by arrangement. Boys typically marry their first wives in their early to middle twenties.

Attainment of Adulthood

Boys do not undergo any gender-specific ritual passage into adulthood; for girls, the engagement ceremony mentioned above partly serves this purpose. In some ways, marriage inducts both genders into adulthood; parenthood continues this transformation. Expectations for adults include the following: adults should not run except in cases of emergency; adults should share resources with appropriate kin; adults should generally try to maintain their composure and practise self-restraint in the face of temptation.

Middle Age and Old Age

Elderhood is generally respected among the Beng. Children are taught from an early age to show deference to anyone older than they, and with the exception of joking behavior with grandparents (see below in "Other Cross-Sex Relationships"), this behavioral pattern continues through adulthood. Gender is generally irrelevant here; it is usually age that matters. Age may be the source not only of respect but also fear. Some old women who are widely feared by children because of ugly bodily features (e.g., chin hair, goiter, etc.) may be used to frighten young children if they are misbehaving. The mother or caretaker threatens to call over such an old woman to eat a misbehaving child; the child usually reforms his or her behavior immediately.

Despite the expectation that elders merit respect, the Beng recognize that the passage of age does not necessarily convey wisdom. When pressed, they may point out men and women who have become more foolish as they have aged. Nevertheless, no elders are ever completely abandoned—they are always fed and cared for by a relative who feels sorry for them.

There is no word for "menopause" in the Beng language. After they have stopped menstruating, the two changes that women may discuss are the cessation of the menstrual period itself, and an increase in energy levels and strength. Given the extremely active lifestyle of all healthy girls and women, osteoporosis and its debilitating effects seem to be unknown. According to the Beng, there are no emotional changes associated with menopause.

At death, funeral rituals vary by rank and age more than gender. Transformation into the state of respected (same-sex) ancestor occurs for all adults who die a normal death. Any ancestor may become reincarnated in a fetus of the same sex; they may or may not be related.

PERSONALITY DIFFERENCES BY GENDER

A few culturally attributed differences between the sexes are said to exist innately. For example, it is thought that girls and women naturally feel more shame than do boys and men. However, many intervening factors are also recognized in personality development, including birth order, twinship, and patriclan membership.

In some recent cases of mental illness, madness has taken the form of exaggerating gender differences. Several madmen suffer from delusions of grandeur, imagining themselves wealthy and powerful urban men, and uttering absurd commands to relatives and neighbors; some madwomen carry absurd head loads, mocking a central female work task.

GENDER-RELATED SOCIAL GROUPS

Daily social life is more segregated by gender for the Beng than it is in Western societies, but far less so than in societies that enforce a virtually complete separation of the sexes. After being married, couples typically live with the husband's family. However, men who work in distant cities may be unable to afford having their wives live with them, or their wives may prefer to remain in the village.

Matriclans and patriclans serve as organizing groups for both men and women. Male and female members of patriclans who are of the same generation see one another as siblings and may not marry. They tend to have an easygoing and comfortable relationship with one another. Men inherit yam fields from their fathers, whom they generally respect and sometimes fear. Male and female members of matriclans who are of the same generation also see one another as siblings, but they are not only

permitted to marry, they are often expected or even forced by relatives to do so. In such cases, the couple may already have been living near one another, and the bride's day-to-day life will barely be disrupted by moving in with her husband and his family, to whom she is already closely related. Men (and nowadays some women) inherit fields for cash-producing crops such as coffee, cocoa, palm, and kola trees from their elder brother (in the case of men) or from their mother's brother (in the case of men or women).

GENDER ROLES IN ECONOMICS

The Beng divide labor tasks to some extent by gender; however, many work tasks are somewhat flexible. In families with only boys, a mother who has failed to find a girl to adopt or foster-raise may train one or more of her sons to do women's work. Such a boy would never be teased by other children and in fact might be admired and praised by other women. As an adult, a man raised in such a household may be particularly helpful to his wife and/or sisters in domestic tasks. In any case, all boys learn to cook from their fathers while working in the fields—men often cook lunch for themselves and their sons while working if their wives are not available.

Many agricultural tasks are divided by gender, although not always rigidly so. For new fields, men and older boys clear the larger trees, and women burn the underbrush. Women and older girls sow, weed, and harvest most crops, such as corn, rice, tomatoes, eggplants, chili peppers, okra, and onions; they also collect wild foods such as mushrooms, berries, and edible tree leaves. Men and older boys may plant and harvest cash crops such as rice and peanuts. Men and boys exclusively build soil mounds in which to plant new yams, sometimes working in formally convened work parties for the task. In the villages, men make cords from the stripped bark of lianas; they use the cord to trail the growing shoots of new yam plants upward so as to catch the rays of sun through the gallery forest. Men do all gun hunting (notable success is said to require large amounts of both physical and spiritual strength), and boys and men do most trap hunting; women occasionally set traps as well. Adults and children of both genders may collect forest snails. Women and teenage girls fell small trees for firewood and chop them for hearth logs. Boys and girls between the ages of about 3 and 15 years join together for several weeks each year to protect ripening rice from marauding birds (a new problem since the colonial introduction of monocropping); all day, the children dance, sing, and play homemade instruments, and the boys use stones with slingshots, to scare away the birds. In polygynous marriages, cowives work side by side, since their fields are allotted next to one another as adjoining "slices" of a round "pie."

Traditionally, men owned all subsistence crop fields; nowadays, women may own some, generally given by their maternal uncles, though men still own the majority. Men also own the land on which cash-producing trees are planted (kola nut, palm, cocoa, coffee), and they plant all fruit trees. Although they do not own the land itself, women may own such trees, and they keep the profits from sale of their fruits or nuts. Out of modesty due to their skirts, they do not climb trees to harvest them.

Men and women engage in some gender-specific crafts. Men make bark cloth, build houses, and carve wood. Women make beaded jewelry for decoration or magical protection against diseases (Gottlieb, in press). Many men and women are petty traders in their spare time. Women sell firewood that they chop, crops that they grow and harvest (especially rice, corn, peanuts, fruits, and various vegetables), and cooked dishes. Men sell crops that they grow and harvest (especially yams, rice, corn, and peanuts), palm wine that they tap, a sugar-based alcohol that some men distill, and game meat. Much of this trade occurs in village markets that occur weekly in the larger Beng villages, although some Beng travel to nearby towns or cities when they have large quantities of goods to sell.

PARENTAL AND OTHER CARETAKER ROLES

For the first 2 years of a child's life, mothers carry out much of the work of childcare (Gottlieb, 2000a). They breast-feed their infants frequently, engage in a lengthy bathing routine twice daily, and carry their babies on their backs for many hours each day, though they are frequently helped by female relatives in this task (Gottlieb, in press). The occasional father who enjoys the basic caretaking tasks of feeding, carrying, bathing, and clothing babies is much appreciated by his wife, and no one would think of making fun of such a helpful husband.

As explained in the section on socialization, fathers become responsible for their sons. After the age of about 2 or 3 years, and by 5–7, most boys accompany their fathers to the fields nearly every day. Mothers bring their daughters to the fields with them, where the girls learn women's agricultural work tasks.

Both parents may serve as disciplinarians to their children; additionally, the mother's brother always looms large as a potential disciplinarian and may be feared even more than the father, although he may also be the source of much affection. Beyond this immediate circle, any adult may legitimately discipline a wayward child—the notion of collective responsibility for childcare is strong at the village level.

LEADERSHIP IN PUBLIC ARENAS

To a greater extent than in many societies, political power is divided fairly equally between the genders among the Beng. Ideally, each matriclan has a male and female chief, each village has a male and female chief, and each political region (savanna and forest) has a ruling king and queen. The two members of each pair are expected to rule cooperatively. It may happen that there is only one member of the pair ruling at a particular time because of unusual circumstances. During such periods, it is said that misfortunes may occur to the group at large—drought, childhood disease, and so on—that can only be rectified when a new officeholder is inaugurated.

Each king (but not queen) has a formal speaker, who must be male. Moreover, the king generally speaks during public occasions, holding trials and announcing decisions, whereas the queen (as with the female village chief) remains somewhat on the sidelines at such events, although she frequently advises the king privately. Beng explain the lack of a female speaker by claiming that women's "hearts are hot" or "heat up quickly," predisposing them to become angry and engage in disputes more quickly than men, making them poor leaders. Generalizing from this attributed quality, many adult men and women alike claim that women "can't rule in Bengland." Accordingly, during public meetings, men often sit at the center of a decision-making circle and women stand on the periphery. Nevertheless, women often make their ideas known about an issue at hand from the sidelines; their opinions may be decisive in some cases. Men acknowledge that although they appear to be in charge of political decision-making, they must always consult with the women involved in a case. Some men claim that, despite their imputed innate tendency toward disputatiousness, women naturally have more force (*lɛŋ drɛ kro*) than men. In general, a tendency toward male dominance of the political sphere is somewhat offset by a more gender-egalitarian model of power.

GENDER AND RELIGION

Some religious roles are open only to men while others are open to both genders. Masters of the Earth are virtually always male. These highly regarded specialists are regularly consulted by large numbers of Beng who adhere to the traditional religion, and occasionally by Christian and Muslim Beng as well. By contrast, diviners may be male or female, and both genders employ the same techniques to consult with spirits and convey their messages to human clients. Male and female diviners may be equally respected and renowned; some attract non-Beng clients from distant cities.

The sky god (*eci*) is gendered female but generally considered remote: people address prayers but not sacrifices to *eci*. The earth (*ba*) is gendered male, but spirits associated with the earth are assigned either a male or female gender. These spirits are said to lead lives parallel to those of humans. As with the classic Greek gods, they are said to marry, have children, argue, work, and eat. Both male and female ancestors may be propitiated.

Both men and women may be witches, although people tend to suspect women more than they suspect men. For either gender, the ability may be inherited from the mother's line or bought from other witches. Both genders may use the powers of witchcraft for good or evil. Village chiefs (male and female), as well as kings and queens, must all constantly use the powers of witchcraft to protect their constituencies (Gottlieb, 1989).

Many taboos (*sõ pɔ*) concern sexual matters (see "Sexuality" below). Some taboos that affect the genders differentially include menstrual taboos, which forbid menstruating girls and women to enter the forest to perform agricultural work. However, menstrual blood is a sign of a woman's fertility rather than a polluting substance (Gottlieb, 1988, 1990). Other taboos affect both genders equally. For example, adults are forbidden to brush their teeth after nightfall, otherwise their first spouse (whether or not they are still married) is at risk of

death. Additionally, all Beng observe food taboos that they inherit from their patriclans; these do not change at marriage, although wives also adopt their husbands' food taboos to protect their breast-feeding children.

In general, Beng religion includes some elements that favor men more than women. However, it also includes opportunities for spiritual practice by women, and in general is more gender-egalitarian than other religious traditions.

LEISURE, RECREATION, AND THE ARTS

All able-bodied adults work hard most of the year, though both men and women acknowledge that women tend to work harder due to their double work burden of being full-time farmers and carrying out the majority of child-rearing and domestic work. The original Beng calendar operates on a 6-day schedule, with one day designated a rest day, when work in the fields is forbidden. Many adults use the day to relax in the village or to perform craft or repair work (men strip vines to make string for yam plants, or repair thatched roofs; women replaster their house walls, repair broken jewelry, or tress one another's hair); others travel to nearby villages or towns to visit relatives or friends. Chiefs hold trials, and people consult with diviners and offer earth sacrifices via the Masters of the Earth.

Most evenings, there is an hour or two after dinner for relaxing around the courtyard. Villagers spend time with relatives, friends, or neighbors of their own or opposite sex—the groups are casual and evanescent, with much visiting back and forth between courtyards. The time may be passed recounting the day's events, gossiping, or telling stories, the latter always with children present.

RELATIVE STATUS OF MEN AND WOMEN

Since men own most subsistence and cash crops they tend to have higher incomes. Thus husbands generally buy presents and necessities for their wives rather than vice versa. Men sometimes claim that men "rule" women in general, and especially in the case of spouses. Thus wives cook and wash laundry for men—especially husbands but also, as circumstances dictate, fathers, brothers, and other male relatives. Certain arenas of daily social life require formal deference by women to men. For example, wives walk behind their husbands, and wives ask their husbands' permission to travel long distances. More Beng boys than girls now attend public schools at all levels of formal education.

However, age trumps gender in nearly all arenas of social life. Thus old women generally receive deference from younger men. In the family, women and men have some separate decision-making spheres. For example, each parent consults with her or his own family in arranging marriages for half the couple's daughters. In general, Beng society is nominally, and sometimes in fact, male dominated, but many spheres of social life also accord women privilege and status.

SEXUALITY

Sexuality is considered a powerful energy that may be used for good or for harm. For example, following the death of a pregnant woman, other pregnant women dance nude to propitiate angry spirits and protect their own pregnancies; a traditional ritual remedy for drought involved old women dancing nude at midnight. It is taboo for men to observe these dances, on pain of death.

The power of sexuality is hedged by numerous rules and taboos. Certain categories of relatives may not discuss sexual topics with one another, including parents with children, and nephews/nieces with their maternal uncles. Many rules specify when, where, and with whom sex may occur. A central rule is that no couple may have sex in the forest, including in the fields; violation of this rule results in a shaming ritual in which the couple are required to have sex in front of jeering and fire-wielding male elders. A permanently polluted state (*zozoa*) results for both the guilty parties. If they are single, it will be difficult for either to find a willing spouse. Sex may legitimately occur only in villages in which a kapok tree has been ritually planted by a Master of the Earth (Gottlieb, 1992/1996). For traditional adults, sex is at least in theory forbidden between approximately 11 p.m. and 3 a.m., when dangerous spirits are said to travel through the village; if conception were to occur at this time, the spirits might cause a monstrous infant to be born.

After developing breasts, most young girls feel modest about revealing their chests and generally wear shirts or at least brassières. However, once they begin breast-feeding their first baby, young women breast-feed readily in anyone's presence and may walk around with no shirt—the breast is no longer a sexual body part but a nutritional one.

All adults must bathe every morning in case they had sex the night before; anyone (male or female) who violates this rule is said to be polluting (*zozoa*) the next day and risks making sick any infant whom they contact that day. Another sign of the dangerous nature of sex for both men and women is that during sexual foreplay, both partners may only use their left hands to touch the other's genitals (Gottlieb, 1990).

In theory, girls should be virgins when they marry. Girls who have sex before they are engaged/initiated are said to be "dirty" and it is said that they may cause illness in infants they contact. It is a sin for a girl to become pregnant before she is engaged; traditionally, if she violated this rule, the newborn would have been killed, although the mother would not have been punished in any other way. This practice is no longer common. Moreover, there is no virginity check on the wedding night, and no punishment if a bride is discovered not to be a virgin.

Despite such rules and taboos, Beng openly discuss and even joke about sexuality with friends, and some categories of relatives, especially grandparents/grandchildren, and cross-cousins. There is a small repertoire of bawdy jokes (e.g., Gottlieb & Graham, 1993/1994, pp. 267–268) and a large repertoire of sexually oriented teasing insults (which, however, sometimes become more serious insults). Sex is considered a source of pleasure as long as rules and taboos are not violated in the pursuit of such pleasure. Old people may continue to be sexually active, although they may be teased if they make the fact known.

Rural Beng profess ignorance of homosexuality (both male and female). The only known instance of cross-dressing occurs during the funerals of some respected elders, when women may dress as men to the general hilarity of all present.

COURTSHIP AND MARRIAGE

All able-bodied and mentally competent people are expected to marry although a few, nearly always men, remain single. Some sculptors inspired by spirits may never marry; it may be said that they are actually married to an invisible spirit wife who jealously prevents them from marrying a human. Depending on the severity of their infirmity, those with significant physical or mental impairments, or who are alcoholics, may not marry.

Traditionally, virtually all first marriages of girls were arranged by their families; this is still the case for the majority of non-Christian girls. If it is an arranged marriage, the girl is expected to oppose her family's choice and must ritually wail her apparent displeasure, even if she happens secretly to approve the choice. A new couple may or may not begin their marriage with some degree of affection; in rare cases, they may not even know one another, although more frequently they are at least acquainted if not close relatives.

A couple's engagement is announced by male relatives in the prospective groom's patriclan in a highly ritualized series of formal speeches requiring an eloquent speaking style. The wedding itself is a large and joyous week-long event. Women from both families spend much time cooking and feeding villagers and visiting relatives. Treating her as a queen on the last day of the wedding, the bride's friends and young female relatives gaily wash all the bride's laundry from the previous week.

The existence of arranged marriage means that not only will some women be married against their will, but this is also the case for some men. In some cases, a plan for a second wife leaves both of the prospective cowives miserable, and the husband may be unhappy at the prospect of bitterly arguing cowives. Husbands are in theory allowed to reject a proposed wife; however, in deference to the authority of the family elders who have arranged the marriage, men normally accept the offer of an unhappy bride and hope for the best. A son receives from his father a new yam field during the first January following the wedding, when new fields are allotted for the slash-and-burn season.

Widowhood traditionally involved a long and elaborate series of rituals of mourning for both men and women. The levirate (a widow marrying her deceased husband's brother) and sororate (a widower marrying his deceased wife's sister) are both prohibited by Beng marriage rules. Many widows and widowers remarry new spouses of their own choosing. However, before they do so, at the end of the long period of mourning, non-Christians are ritually required to have sex with a stranger (Gottlieb, n.d., forthcoming).

HUSBAND–WIFE RELATIONSHIP

Whether or not a marriage begins with affection, having children is considered the catalyst for love to grow between husband and wife. If a Beng couple find themselves incompatible, only after they have had at least one child together, and ideally two or three children, is divorce readily agreed to by their families. A childless couple who are not getting along are generally advised to wait until they have had children—perhaps their relationship will improve because of their shared parenthood (Gottlieb & Graham, 1993/1994).

The lines of authority within a marriage are partly determined by the prior relationship between the spouses. Normatively, husbands have authority over wives. However, husband and wife must also normatively respect and exhibit shame toward one another, and each should fulfill expectations for proper conjugal behavior. A wife should plant and harvest corn, rice, and vegetable crops, cook for her husband daily, wash his laundry weekly, bring him bathwater twice daily, and find him medicines when he is sick; if she has enough cash, she may buy him clothes. A husband should grow and harvest yams, sow rice, clear old fields, kill snakes in the compound, buy his wife clothes, give her meat to cook after having given specified parts to certain relatives, find her medicines when she is sick, and carry her to the bathhouse to wash if she is too sick to walk.

In one form of cousin marriage—the union of a woman with her mother's brother's son—the wife has considerable authority over her husband insofar as she is considered a sociological replacement of sorts for her maternal uncle, who has authority over his son. Men often try to avoid such marriages to avoid being a "henpecked husband." Such marriages, while uncommon, do exist and may be quite amicable.

When a couple argue, despite the ideology that husbands normatively have authority over their wives, the husband should apologize to his wife. If the argument is serious, he must appoint a male spokesman (relative or friend) to apologize on his behalf to his wife. One reason concerns the Beng view of conjugal relations; the Beng say that men need wives more than women need husbands, and women will more readily leave an unhappy marriage because they are able to get along without a husband without much trouble, whereas men cannot do so. Specifically, women's cooking and hospitality roles are invoked; when visitors arrive, it is thought, only women can adequately welcome them with properly cooked food and pleasantly heated bathwater. By contrast, men say that a single man—whether bachelor, divorcé, or widower—is incapable of entertaining guests properly. The greater sense of shame that women are said to feel may lead them to divorce, if they are judged publicly in the wrong after a marital dispute; by contrast, men are said to bear public censure more easily. Men say that they will usually apologize after a marital argument even if they are convinced that their wife was at fault. If he does not apologize after having insulted his wife, the shame a husband feels may make him fall sick. If, during a marital dispute, one spouse throws a chicken at the other, the marriage is said to be ruined unequivocally. They may never sleep together again, and no apologies can be accepted. It is said that the couple's children, and later their grandchildren, will go mad.

Polygyny is accepted widely by men and variably by women. Men say that they endorse polygyny for one simple reason: after a woman bears a child, she must remain celibate until the child is weaned and can walk properly (Gottlieb, in press). During this long period of a wife's post-partum celibacy, men prefer a second wife so as not to have to look elsewhere for a sex partner.

As with many societies, the Beng observe a double sexual standard: married men are permitted to have affairs with unmarried women—in anticipation of a possible polygynous marriage—but unmarried women are not permitted extramarital liaisons. Husbands who know that their wives are conducting an adulterous affair enlist several male patriclanmates to beat up the lover, and then hold a male-only trial in which the lover apologizes and pays a fine in palm wine. Pregnant women who commit adultery are said to be at risk for miscarriage or a very difficult delivery—an excess of sperm is said to crowd out the fetus. If the infant does survive, the husband becomes the legal father. The natural father forfeits all rights and is said to suffer 7 years of bad luck if the child survives, and a lifetime of bad luck if the child dies. It is said that adultery by wives can produce impotence in their husbands; in such cases, a public trial may be held to judge the wife's guilt and the fine she must pay. Adultery by a politically important woman—a queen, female chief, or wife of a king or male chief—can produce a regional drought, which can only be alleviated by the lover being publicly judged and required to pay a hefty fine. In all cases, the adulterous women themselves may be beaten once by their husbands but are rarely further punished.

Some Beng women welcome, or at least accept, a cowife with little complaint or even gratitude—for the shared labor in domestic tasks such as cooking and childcare and/or the security of knowing that this second sex partner precludes her husband having affairs during her postpartum periods of celibacy. By contrast, other women rebel passionately against a husband's intention to take a second wife; in such cases, bitter disputes, often accompanied by accusations of witchcraft, may rule the household. Unless they are Muslim or Christian, the Beng do not observe any legal upper limit to the number of wives a man may marry; however, in practice, few polygynous men have more than two wives, and many Beng men are never married to more than one wife at a time.

In polygynous families, each wife cooks in a separate kitchen and sleeps in a separate bedroom. A strict rotation schedule for eating and sex is established; the husband visits each wife for a given period (usually 3 or 4 days) during which time she has sex with him and cooks his meals.

During the daytime, depending on the agricultural calendar, spouses may work separately. They may also travel separately and rarely dine together—instead, adults usually eat in same-sex groups with friends or relatives. In the evenings, however, husbands and wives may sit outside in their courtyard, often as part of a small gathering of relatives or friends, and chat quietly and even intimately. This is especially the case for couples who have been married happily for many years.

Reasons for divorce are multiple and, unlike in more patriarchal societies, do not discriminate significantly against women. Indeed, some men claim that only women and not men have the right to divorce in the case of arranged marriages. A husband who neglects his yam fields, who overly privileges another wife, who is an alcoholic, who beats a pregnant wife, who is a known thief, who bewitches the couple's children, or who is considered to have a "rotten character" is a legitimate candidate for his wife divorcing him, so long as at least one of her parents is agreed. For her part, a wife who neglects to cook or do laundry for her husband, does not work in his yam fields, or has an adulterous affair, may in theory have divorce proceedings instituted against her by her husband, although the husband must gain the consent of his patriclan members who usually try to convince him to remain married.

Following divorce, children typically remain with their mother; however, the father has the right to take any or all of them to live with him, or with his brother and sister-in-law, though the mother may visit the children whenever she wishes. A father who has substantially participated in raising a child will pass on his patriclan food taboos to the child, and he retains rights to arrange half his daughters' marriages, whereas a father who has not substantially participated in raising a child forfeits these rights. Certain Masters of the Earth are forbidden ever to divorce, no matter what the circumstances.

OTHER CROSS-SEX RELATIONSHIPS

The system of arranged marriage has a complex set of rules specifying who may, may not, or should marry whom. These rules color cross-gender relations significantly. Those who are considered legally eligible or even preferred spouses often maintain a sexual teasing relationship with one another even if there is a difference in age of several decades between them.

Brothers and sisters have an easygoing relationship and may be quite close. In the rare case of a dispute between brothers-in-law, a woman supports her brother rather than her husband.

Another especially significant cross-sex relationship is that between grandchild and grandparent. These individuals normatively have a joking relationship that is especially pronounced in the case of a cross-sex pair. The joking is frequently insulting and/or sexual, even for young children. In fact, babies sometimes learn their first words from their cross-sex grandparent who teaches the tot lewd insults that the baby is expected to repeat. "You black testicles," "You red vagina," and other such sexual insults are not infrequently a toddler's first mangled words, aimed with good effect at the opposite-sex grandparent, to the general delight of all present.

Due to the modified "Omaha" style set of terms used to refer to family members, certain kinds of cousins are classified as grandparents or grandchildren. This is the case for the children of one's "cross-cousins" (children of one's mother's brother or one's father's sister). Given that these relatives are addressed as "grandchildren," mock teasing defines their relationship as well. By contrast, "parallel cousins" (children of two sisters or two brothers) are considered siblings and treated in much the same way.

A mother's sisters are called "little mothers" or "big mothers" (depending on birth order) and have a similar relationship with their nephews and sons. A mother's brother is very close and may discipline his sister's misbehaving children.

Sons- and daughters-in-law should never discuss anything to do with sex in front of their parents-in-law, and a man should not eat in front of his mother-in-law; if he insults his mother-in-law, he would be publicly tried and fined a sheep or chicken, plus a bar of soap to wash off the insult. If a man's mother-in-law is also his father's sister, this is a particularly difficult relationship for him, as his mother-in-law has double authority over him (see "Husband–Wife Relationship" above). A man also feels shame toward and fear of his wife's sister, as he knows she will criticize him if he argues with his wife. For her part, a woman must never insult her husband's brothers, on pain of public trial. Her respect for her father-in-law usually leads to near-total avoidance.

Males and females among the Beng, especially if separated significantly by age, may count one another as friends in the Platonic sense.

CHANGE IN ATTITUDES, BELIEFS, AND PRACTICES REGARDING GENDER

Soon after the French conquered the region in the early 1890s, they forced Beng farmers to plant new crops (especially coffee, cocoa, and new varieties of rice and cotton) that were sold to the French in order to pay colonial taxes. The growth of a cash–based economy has resulted in more labor-intensive farming techniques based on monoculture; in turn, this has reduced the time available for hunting. The rising prices of bullets and trapping line have also reduced the amount of available animal protein.

Until recently, many Beng elders have consciously endeavored to maintain a certain independence from the West and its imports. For example, until about 15 years ago, many parents refused to send their children to government-run schools. Nowadays more and more young people are rejecting this conservatism of their elders, and an increasingly larger proportion of children are being sent to elementary school for at least a few years, although the dropout rate even at the elementary school level remains quite high. Many parents nowadays would like to send at least some of their children to school but are not able to afford all the expenses associated with the nominally free school system (including uniforms and school supplies). More Beng boys than girls attend schools, and more continue longer before dropping out. However, a small but growing number of Beng girls are continuing on to high school; the future may bring significant changes in village mores from the growing number of urban Beng, many of whom maintain close relations with their village-dwelling relatives.

ACKNOWLEDGMENTS

I am grateful for the financial support of the following agencies which has made possible my Beng research and writing over the years: Social Science Research Council, National Endowment for the Humanities, Wenner–Gren Foundation for Anthropological Research, American Association of University Women, Woodrow Wilson Foundation, U.S. Information Agency, John Simon Guggenheim Memorial Foundation, and several units at the University of Illinois (Center for African Studies, Center for Advanced Study, and the Center for the Study of Cultural Values and Ethics). For very helpful comments on this chapter, I am deeply grateful, as ever, to Philip Graham and Bertin Kouadio.

BIBLIOGRAPHY

Gottlieb, A. (1986). Cousin marriage, birth order and gender: Alliance models among the Beng of Ivory Coast. *Man, 21*(4), 697–722.

Gottlieb, A. (1988). Menstrual cosmology among the Beng of Ivory Coast. In T. Buckley & A. Gottlieb (Eds.), *Blood magic: The anthropology of menstruation* (pp. 55–74). Berkeley: University of California Press.

Gottlieb, A. (1989). Witches, kings, and the sacrifice of identity; Or, the power of paradox and the paradox of power among the Beng of Ivory Coast. In W. Arens & I. Karp (Eds.), *Creativity of power: Cosmology and action in African societies* (pp. 245–272). Washington, DC: Smithsonian Institution Press.

Gottlieb, A. (1990). Rethinking female pollution: The Beng case (Côte d'Ivoire). In P. R. Sanday & R. G. Goodenough (Eds.), *Beyond the second sex: New directions in the anthropology of gender* (pp. 113–138). Philadelphia: University of Pennsylvania Press.

Gottlieb, A. (1996). *Under the kapok tree: Identity and difference in Beng thought.* Chicago: University of Chicago Press. (Original work published 1992, Bloomington: Indiana University Press.)

Gottlieb, A. (1997, Summer). Fabrication d'un premier dictionnaire de la langue Beng: Quelques considérations éthiques [Construction of a first dictionary of the Beng language: Some ethical considerations]. *Journal des Anthropologues, 70*, 147–162.

Gottlieb, A. (1998). Do infants have religion? The spiritual lives of Beng babies. *American Anthropologist, 100*(1), 122–135.

Gottlieb, A. (2000a). Luring your child into this life: A Beng path for infant care (Côte d'Ivoire). In J. S. DeLoache & A. Gottlieb (Eds.), *A world of babies: Imagined childcare guides for seven societies* (pp. 55–89). New York: Cambridge University Press.

Gottlieb, A. (2000b). Secrets and society: The Beng of Côte d'Ivoire. *Mande Studies, 1*(2), 129–151.

Gottlieb, A. (in press). *The afterlife is where we come from: The culture of infancy in West Africa.* Chicago: University of Chicago Press.

Gottlieb, A. (n.d.). Stranger anxiety or stranger love? Sociable Beng babies (Côte d'Ivoire). In P. Frietzsche & M. Steinberg (Eds.), *The stranger, the strange, and estrangement.* unpublished manuscript (forthcoming).

Gottlieb, A., & Graham, P. (1994). Parallel worlds: An anthropologist and a writer encounter Africa. Chicago: University of Chicago Press. (Original work published 1993, New York: Crown Publishers.)

Gottlieb, A., Graham, P., & Gottlieb-Graham, N. (1998). Infants, ancestors and the afterlife: Fieldwork's family values. *Anthropology and Humanism, 23*(2), 121–126.

Gottlieb, A., Graham, P., & Gotilieb-Graham, N. (1999). Revising the text, revisioning the field: Reciprocity over the long term. *Anthropology and Humanism, 24*(2), 117–128.

Gottlieb, A., & Murphy, M. L. (1995). *Beng–English dictionary.* Bloomington: Indiana University Linguistics Club.

Greenhouse, S. (2002, May 31). World briefing. Africa: Ivory Coast: Cocoa exports questioned. *New York Times,* pp. A(1), 3.

Blackfoot

Alice Beck Kehoe

ALTERNATIVE NAMES

Alternative names for the Blackfoot are Blackfeet, Siksika, Kainai, Blood Indians, Pikuni, Piegan, and Peigan.

LOCATION

Blackfoot occupy the Northwestern Plains of North America (southern Alberta, Canada, and north-central Montana, U.S.A.). The region is short-grass prairie in the rain shadow of the Rocky Mountains, with conifer forests in the mountain foothills. Principal rivers include the North and South Saskatchewan Rivers with the latter's tributaries the Bow and Oldman Rivers, and the Milk River which flows into the Missouri River. Winters are cold, but relieved occasionally by warm chinook winds, and summers are short with some hot days.

CULTURAL OVERVIEW

The Blackfoot are an alliance of three principal nations: the Siksika or Blackfoot, the Kainai or Blood, both in Alberta, and the Pikuni or Piegan, which is divided into a northern branch in Alberta and a southern branch in Montana. The nations are composed of a number of independent bands, formerly nomadic but settled on reservations since the 1870s. Their language is classified in the Algonkian stock. Its syntax distinguishes animate from inanimate, but not "sex" (male, female, neuter).

Before the extermination of wild bison in the 1870s, Blackfoot depended on bison herds for subsistence and trade materials. The people lived in conical tipis sewn of bison hides, grouped in camps of about 100 persons, moving camp about 17 times each year. Large dogs bred to carry loads were used to help transport tipis and gear, either packed on the dogs' backs or on travois (pairs of poles with the upper ends fastened to the dog's shoulders and a hide or net across the lower portion to hold goods, and the lower ends dragged on the ground behind the

animal). After the middle of the 18th century, horses became available to the Blackfoot through trade from the Southwest where they had been introduced by Spanish colonists. Horses were then used for transport, for war raids and battles, and to hunt bison.

The traditional method of hunting bison was to drive a herd into a corral built against a bluff or at the end of a ravine. Corrals continued to be used until the extermination of wild bison in the 1870s, although pursuit from horseback was an alternative method for the final century of Blackfoot independence. Once the bison had been slaughtered in a corral, teams of six (men and women) butchered the kill. Hides were tanned for tipi covers, winter robes, and bedding. The meat was sliced thin and air-dried for preservation. Pounding dried meat with berries and rendered fat made pemmican, a highly nutritious compact food that could be stored in hide bags for months. Bison bones were made into cutting blades, scrapers, and tool handles. Bison wool could be spun and woven, although historically Blackfoot preferred to purchase woven bags from neighboring nations and cloth from European traders. Blackfoot made pottery before the European trade introduced more durable metal kettles.

Elk, deer, antelope, and smaller game were hunted, as well as bison. Blackfoot disdained fish but do eat trout. Berries, prairie turnips (an indigenous root vegetable), and camas bulbs (a lily) were significant carbohydrates in the diet, with a stew of meat. Women had the responsibility of collecting vegetable foods from carefully sustained fields, and of preparing family meals. They also tanned hides, cut and sewed clothing and tipis, made containers (mostly of hide), collected firewood, and packed and set up camps. Men had the responsibility of providing the animals to be processed, defending the nation, and learning and performing often lengthy rituals, assisted by their wives.

Blackfoot religion recognized an Almighty Power that manifests in a multitude of forms, from thunder and the sun to animals and rocks. Humans depend upon the benevolence of the Almighty, and beg its blessing through prayers; tobacco incense offered in pipes is pleasing to the Almighty. The principal annual ceremony is the Sun Dance or Medicine Lodge (Okan), held in the summer for all the community. This ceremony is led by a woman, assisted by other women and by men. Other rituals center on "medicine bundles," sets of objects that serve as icons for narratives linking ancient blessings to contemporary generations. Praying or dancing with the objects is expected to heal illness and misfortune, and the sets are kept inside bags rolled up in shawls or blankets, hence "medicine bundles." Individual Blackfoot own these bundles, but are obliged to hold their rituals upon petition from people in need, and to transfer ownership so that other families may have the privilege of caring for these holy shrines.

A number of associations carry out duties such as policing camps, organizing war raids (before the imposition of U.S. and Canadian rule in the 1870s), performing ceremonies, or holding secular dances. Most of the associations require members to be couples, normally husband and wife. Band membership was based on kin relationships, but individuals and families had the option of leaving to live in another band if they were dissatisfied. Sons-in-law were expected to provide meat for their wife's parents, an obligation implying that a young couple would live in the wife's family camp, but early reservation census records indicate that postmarital residence choices were quite varied. Certain families are considered to be of leadership status, bringing up their children to assume this responsibility; the position of band leader must be earned through good character, wisdom, and generosity. Respected leaders worked to bring prosperity to their bands, hosted visitors, and provided for band members unable to maintain themselves. Adult children assisted the elderly, and orphans would be adopted by relatives or family friends. In the 19th century, a period of heavy loss of fighting men in endemic frontier wars, polygyny was common, but whether this was so earlier is not known. Cowives ideally were sisters or cousins; foreign women captured on raids were kept as concubines and household help. A few persons did not marry heterosexually, instead feeling a vocation to live as the other gender. Men with this calling dressed and worked as women; women applied themselves to war and hunting. Each might share a tipi with someone of the same sex who fulfilled a spousal role, although women war leaders are said to have usually been celibate.

Blackfoot traded widely before Europeans entered their country in the 17th century (they were first contacted by a European, an employee of the Hudson Bay Company fur traders, in 1690). Some bison corral sites near river transport routes contain such large kills that archeologists infer that they were used to produce surplus meat to be traded to farming towns on the Missouri River and its tributaries in North Dakota. The entrance of European traders increased the market for pemmican, to which Blackfoot responded with vigilance over territorial rights. In 1801, a Blackfoot leader called Akai Mokti (Old Swan) visited the Hudson's Bay Company trader Peter Fidler in what is now southeastern Alberta, and at Fidler's request drew detailed maps of the country. Akai Mokti showed detailed familiarity with a vast territory from central Alberta to Wyoming, and from central North Dakota to Idaho; he knew the Snake River would lead to the Pacific coast, and drew that. Fidler sent a copy of Akai Mokti's maps to his superiors in London, who had them professionally redrawn and published. It was Akai Mokti's map that Thomas Jefferson gave to Lewis and Clark, with orders to follow it on their western exploration.

CULTURAL CONSTRUCTION OF GENDER

Blackfoot understanding of gender references a popular legend describing the initiation of marriage:

The women . . . made buffalo-corrals. Their lodges were fine. . . . They tanned the buffalo-hides, those were their robes. They would cut meat in slices. . . . Their lodges all were fine inside. And their things were just as fine. . . . Now, the men . . . were very poor. They made corrals. They had no lodges. They wore raw-hides . . . for robes. They wore the gamble-joint of the buffalo for moccasins. They did not know, how they should make lodges. They did not know, how they should tan the buffalo-hides. They did not know, too, how they should cut dried meat, how they should sew their clothes. The women's chief told them [the women]: Over there near the corral are the men sitting in sight. All these women were cutting meat. Their chief did not take off the clothes, she was [wearing] cutting the meat. They were told by her: I shall go up there first. I shall take my choice. When I come back, you will go up one by one. Now we will take husbands. Then she started up. Then she went up to all those men. She asked them: Which is your chief? the men said: This one here, Wolf-robe [Napi, Dawn-of-time or "Old" Man]. She told him: Now we will take you for husbands. And then she walked to that Wolf-robe. She caught him. Then she started to pull him up. Then he pulled back. Then she let him loose. He did not like her [work] clothes. (While the other women were picking out their husbands, the chief of the women put on her best costume. When she came out, she looked very fine, and, as soon as Old Man saw her, he thought, "Oh! there is the chief of the women. I wish to be her husband" [Wissler & Duvall, 1908, p. 22]). Wolf-robe was standing up alone. He was told by that chief-woman: Turn into a pine-tree, right there where you stand. He got angry. He commenced to knock down that buffalo-corral. And then he turned into a pine-tree (C.C. Uhlenbeck, 1912, pp. 167–169) . . . And he is mad yet, because he is always caving down the bank. (Wissler & Duvall, 1908, p. 22)

Women's innate reproductive capacity creates not only children, but also culture. Men lack this capacity so that, bereft of women, they are little more than beasts, incapable of creating homes, clothing, or properly prepared food. Women pity men and generously take them into their homes. In this, women are to men as Almighty Power manifestations are to humans, responding to pleas moving them to pity.

Gender over the Life Cycle

Socialization of Boys and Girls

Boys could go naked until the onset of adolescence, while little girls were given a simple tunic dress. David Duvall, half-Piegan collaborator of anthropologist Clark Wissler, wrote about 1910, "Girls are taught to be kind and helpful, to be always willing to lend a hand, to be virtuous and later, to respect their marriage vows" (Wissler, 1911, p. 29). Girls carried firewood and water for the home, took care of younger children, and assisted their mothers and grandmothers with household tasks, hide dressing, making clothing, and preparing food. Boys were hardened by daily morning baths in streams, even in winter; an elderly man would remind or take the boy. Boys learned weaponry and hunting tactics, and upon entering adolescence, accompanied war parties, serving the men in camp chores. These contrasts in child socialization described by Duvall (Wissler, 1911, pp. 29–30) were tempered by expecting girls as well as boys to snare small animals and to become familiar with weapons and hunting, historically riding out with male relatives to hunts and, as part of the entire band, cooperating in driving bison herds through marked drive lanes to corral entrances. Young married women not infrequently rode with their husbands to battle, participating in attacks and earning particular admiration through seizing enemy fighters' weapons.

Puberty and Adolescence

There were no puberty ceremonies as such. When adolescent boys joined a war party, they were given a nickname that they should erase by gaining respect through valor, receiving a new and more serious name in recognition. During a lifetime, men could receive a series of names signaling prestigious deeds or status achievements. Babies were ceremoniously given names by respected elders, more often men but sometimes women, who perpetuated illustrious deceased persons' names or referred to a notable event at the time of the child's birth, or a relative's accomplishment. Girls usually kept this name for life; no surnames were used. After the reservations were established, children were recorded with English Christian names followed by their father's name (e.g., Mountain Chief's son was recorded as Walter Mountain Chief) and married women recorded with their husbands' names as surnames. It should be noted that the English translations of Indian names were often inept to the point of disrespect; for example, the great Lakota leader Young-Man-They [enemies]-Are-Afraid-of-Even-His-Horses was officially recorded as Young-Man-Afraid-of-His-Horses.

Attainment of Adulthood

Adulthood, like adolescence, was achieved rather than formally bestowed. Girls seem to have been married soon after menarche, in their mid-teens, to young men a few years older selected by their parents. The couple would get their own tipi or, on the reservation, cabin and the young husband expected to work with his father-in-law in providing food for both generations, with the young wife continuing to work with her mothers (cowives in a polygynous marriage were jointly mothers to the children of the household). Later, a couple often moved to live with the husband's band. From early reservation period records, first marriages seem to have often ended after a few years, with the more mature spouses then selecting new partners. Either wife or husband could initiate divorce; the wife traditionally retained her tipi, furnishings, and household equipment. If a marriage had involved the groom's family giving bridewealth to the woman's parents, and the marriage had not lasted long or produced children, the husband could request his gifts of horses and goods returned. (Bridewealth was a sign of the groom's respect for his bride and her family.) People expected men and women to settle down, in their late twenties or thirties, with a spouse to whom they were committed to raise a family. Men could take additional wives and/or concubines if the senior wife/wives approved—sometimes demanded, to gain extra hands in family maintenance—while women properly had only one husband; however, a young woman married to an older man might have a lover, and there were cases where the elder husband openly gave his young wife to her lover if the younger man demonstrated ability and willingness to support her. Cuckolded husbands might punish and stigmatize offending wives by cutting off their noses.

Middle Age

Middle age, after about 40, was the period when one's children were young adults. No longer engaged primarily in childcare, middle-aged people might begin apprenticeship to spiritual leaders and healers. Apprenticeships could require the younger person to live with the mentor for weeks, assisting in preparations for rituals and memorizing plants, formulae prayers, and dances. Taking over custody of a medicine bundle involved a formal ceremony, but a bundle owner could request a qualified priest to carry out the bundle's ritual. Each "bundle opening" ceremony needed a woman to handle the bundle and its contents, unwrapping, presenting the icons to the officiating (male) priest, and rewrapping the bundle. In other words, women mediated between Power embodied in the bundle and men who invoked it; this seems to be part of women's innate reproductive power. Ritual sodalities recruiting mature (middle-aged) members, particularly the Horns for couples and Ma'toki for women, taught powerful religious knowledge and performed public ceremonies.

Old Age

Elders (grandparents) were privileged respite from daily labor, although elder women usually continued household work. The fact that a person had lived so many years that he or she had grandchildren proved that the person had been blessed with spiritual strength. Therefore elders were sought after to bless babies and people setting off on risky endeavors such as war. A postmenopausal woman ceremoniously helped a new mother put on fresh clothes and return to the household routine—an opportunity for the experienced woman to advise the young one. The greatest deference was, and is, given to "Old Ladies," senior matrons who have raised families and gained a reputation for skills and wisdom. Even more than elder men of repute, Old Ladies are respected and obeyed, in continuation of the superior position of women vis-à-vis men exemplified in the legend of the First Marriages.

PERSONALITY DIFFERENCES BY GENDER

Many stories are told about Napi, "Dawn-of-time Man" or "the Old Man." As in the legend of the First Marriages, Napi is impetuous, short-sighted, foolish, greedy, and lustful, but good-hearted. He is considered to personify men's innate nature. Women, again as in the First Marriages legend, are innately empowered to reproduce good homes, constantly working to process raw material into manufactures, including food. Boys, having Napi natures, roam around until able, in adolescence, to undertake responsibility. Girls have time to play but are expected to help with home tasks from about the age of 5 or 6. Groups of children play house, with the girls taking the role of homemaker and boys bringing them gophers to cook—although girls, too, snare small game. If girls are not playing with a group of boys, the boys will themselves skin and roast the gophers they catch. Each gender has an ideal and complementary role and personality, but pragmatically both men and women were capable of each others' tasks; before the reservations, parties of men were out at war for months, leaving camps of women to carry on provisioning themselves as well as processing raw materials. Settled on reservations, men might be away for days on ranching tasks.

Men talked about desiring docile modest wives, yet women were, and are, expected to be physically, mentally, and emotionally strong—partners with their husbands. A phrase, "manly-hearted" (translated also as "leader-hearted") applied to matrons known for strength of character and admirable accomplishments.

GENDER-RELATED SOCIAL GROUPS

Consonant with their strong respect for individual autonomy, Blackfoot did not construct formal unilineal kinship units. Related women and cowives formed task groups for women's work, as men formed war parties and the core of hunting parties. Men composed ad hoc police forces, commanded by band leaders, keeping order in multiband camps and hunts. As mentioned, at the multiband summer rendezvous where the Sun Dance was performed, a women's sodality, the Ma'toki or Women's Buffalo Society, carried out both secluded and public rituals to reinforce the community's intimate relationship with bison herds. Men auxiliaries assisted the Ma'toki. The so-called men's societies were actually for couples, with each man bringing his wife or, if not then married, a sister. Only the societies for adolescent boys omitted enrolling women. For the adult "men's societies," women helped with food and sang for the men dancing. Because the men in these societies were up front dancing and leading rituals, non-Indian observers overlooked women's importance, as they overlooked the critical role of women in mediating the opening and rewrapping of medicine bundles.

There was little enforced gender segregation, since it was the individual's choice in residence, work, recreation, and worship that was respected. Normally, women attended births, but male healers as well as the father, if he wished, were admitted. Both men and women participated in handgame teams (a favorite gambling game). Women played shinny (field hockey); apparently there were no men's ball games aboriginally, at least not described, but men did gamble on a game involving throwing lances at a rolling hoop and, historically, men raced horses. On the reservations, schools taught baseball to boys.

GENDER ROLES IN ECONOMICS

Following the model of the legendary First Marriages, women created and maintained the camp, which required working hides as well as all food preparation, making furnishings, containers, bedding, clothing, and making and setting up tipis. Men made their weapons and gear, and provided slaughtered big game; both men and women cooperated in butchering it. As the legend implies, women were fully capable of fulfilling all needs; men were considered dependent although useful. Historically, endemic wars related directly and indirectly to U.S. and British imperialism kept Blackfoot men on constant defensive alert; to what degree this distorted previous economic and social patterns cannot be discovered.

Western scholars gave much attention to the so-called *berdache*, a man who dressed and worked as a woman. The term, originally designating a North African boy prostitute, is distasteful to First Nations people and should not be used for American Indians. Observers of late-19th-century Blackfoot do not describe men living as women. There was one religious practitioner whose power came from the moon, gendered female in Blackfoot

cosmology, and who therefore wore a woman's dress when performing his ritual for young men seeking good fortune through him. This "medicine man" otherwise dressed and behaved as a man.

Trade was open to both men and women, with each person trading their own products. Thus men usually traded furs and women their manufactures. European and European American traders liked to select one leading man to bargain for his party, often naming him "captain" and presenting him with an officer's coat. Blackfoot recognized band leaders ("chiefs" in English), who hosted visitors to a camp if they did not have relatives in the band, but a band leader did not control economic enterprises. Because processed bison robes and bags of pemmican were the joint product of a household, the husband in a household traded these goods on behalf of the household. Women traded what they individually produced: ethnographer Clark Wissler remarked, "Even today [1910]. . . a man seldom speaks when his wife bargains away her own hand-work, bedding, and house furnishings" (Wissler, 1911, p. 27). Wissler noted:

In pre-reservation days a woman was judged by the number and quality of skins she had dressed, the baskets she had woven, or the pottery moulded; and her renown for such accomplishments might travel far. When by chance you met a woman who had distinguished herself, it was proper to address her in a manner to reveal your knowledge of her reputation, as: "Grandmother, we are happy to look upon one whose hands were always busy curing fine skins." (Wissler, 1938/1971, p. 290)

PARENTAL AND OTHER CARETAKER ROLES

Women were the primary caregivers for babies and young children—only they can nurse babies and, before the reservation was established, no other nourishment was available for infants. A memoir from the early reservation period mentions the innovation of canned milk brought from the trading post by a European American employee married to a Piegan woman. Fathers and everyone else enjoyed playing with babies and children. Striking or speaking harshly to a child was considered abhorrent and unnatural. Instead, children were encouraged to be quiet and observant of adults, ready to assist elders. Children might be teased; the appropriate response was to smile and remain calm.

Because the kinship system is "generational," extending the terms for brother and sister to what in

English are cousins, a Blackfoot child likely has several "mothers" and "fathers," "elder brothers" and "elder sisters," as well as grandparents. All of these are concerned for their relative's welfare. High mortality, from war, accidents, epidemics, and, after the bison herds disappeared, malnutrition, orphaned many children. If relatives did not take the child into their family, another family would do so. There are cases of an abandoned non-Indian baby taken by a Blackfoot family and raised as their own. During the first century of the reservation period, missionaries took children, often forcibly (backed by reservation police), to raise in boarding schools. Adoption of Indian children by non-Indians who removed them from their people was similarly encouraged, the principle being that a European American upbringing civilized the child.

Elderly Blackfoot expected to be supported by their children; one could call it "assisted living" as the elderly couple or widow remained in their own tipi or cabin, near the home of adult children. Legends describe "old women's tipis" where one or two elderly women lived alone. The hero of the tale is the old woman's grandson or adopted child, or a youth generously seeking to help a neglected elder. In real life, a granddaughter often went to live with the grandparent. Grandparents often cared for young children while the parents went on extended hunts or, after the bison were gone, for off-reservation jobs.

LEADERSHIP IN PUBLIC ARENAS

Men appeared to be band leaders and principal chiefs of band alliances. To what degree this can be attributed to European observers' expectations, traders' selection of spokesmen, and conquering governments' appointment of spokesmen at treaties and on reservations, cannot be evaluated. Wissler remarked that when a White man

stepped into the Indian's world . . . it was a red man who met him at the threshold because it was his habit to stand between his women and the stranger. Two or more centuries of experience had convinced him that the white man rarely looked upon an Indian woman disinterestedly and he had accordingly built up a set of rules and regulations which forbade his women to speak to a strange man. (Wissler, 1938/1971, p. 205)

In another passage, Wissler described an elder couple, both of them leaders:

Wolf Chief [the husband] had a methodical mind [and was] . . . a keen questioner . . . possessed of a superior mind . . . "Mother-of-all" was [his wife's] real name, and appropriate . . . the finest of women.

Her countenance was feminine, but with the stamp of leadership. Her carriage was graceful but always expressing dignity. . . . Though always dignified and high-minded had a sense of humor. . . . Wolf Chief also had a sense of humor . . . [He] was obviously proud of his wife, but like many a man married to a genius, was not always comfortable when she held the center of the stage . . . [At a feast for two girls of prominent families] Mother-of-all whose presence had been conspicuous during the proceedings of the morning . . . standing to one side upon a little eminence, leaning upon a long staff. She wore an elk-skin dress, decorated with elk teeth, the prized jewelry of her culture. . . . Apparently she was wrapped in meditation and about to begin a harangue . . . it was expected that some one, preferably an old woman, address the assembly at this time. . . . She began, speaking slowly and in well-formed sentences . . . on the level of oratory. (Wissler, 1938/1971, pp. 277–289)

It seems that the principle of respect for personal autonomy allowed both men and women of ability and self-confidence to act as leaders in appropriate situations. Demonstrated knowledge and skill, self-disciplined dignity, restraint, and generosity, and what Wissler termed a mind keen to grasp and analyze, were qualities of leaders, man or woman.

GENDER AND RELIGION

The religious arena reflected Blackfoot conceptions of male and female human nature. As mentioned above, women are superior to men as mediators between Power and human life. Because women are born with this capacity, they do not need to actively seek enhanced power. Men did, in adolescence going out alone to a secluded place to hold vigil, fasting, and praying until vouchsafed a vision experience of some manifestation of cosmic power promising to aid the youth in his endeavors. Historically, these visions tended to focus on success in war. It is important to note that in seeking blessing, people humbly made themselves pitiable by showing themselves alone, minimally clothed, hungry, thirsty, and pleading for benevolence.

Blackfoot Sun Dances require a respected woman to vow service as high priestess. She goes on retreat, fasting inside a tipi. In earlier times, the Holy Woman and her small entourage of women and men attendants moved camp four times (four is the ritual number, like three is for Indo-European cultures), ending in the place where the Sun Dance lodge would be constructed. When the lodge is ready and the congregation assembled, the Holy Woman walks from her tipi to the lodge. Weak from fasting, she is supported by her women. The Holy Woman wears an elkskin dress said to have been given to the priestess by the legendary Elk Woman, wrongfully accused by her husband of adultery and vindicated by displaying superior power. The Holy Woman wears a headdress with icons of Elk Woman and other legendary figures, and leans on a digging stick said to have been that used by Woman Who Married Morning Star. The costume and accoutrements form the Natoas (Sun) medicine bundle. An important ritual during the Sun Dance calls forth women of good character to come forward and slice meat to be given to elders; supposedly, a woman who had not lived honorably would be unsteady and mess up the cutting, revealing unworthiness.

During the Sun Dance encampment, several of the sodalities perform dance dramas. Today, that of the Crazy Dogs receives most attention and balances the Sun Dance itself; the Crazy Dogs are led by men (although women participate) and run like a pack of yelping dogs around the open ground surrounding the Sun Dance lodge, contrasting vividly with the solemn quiet inside the lodge. In the lodge, there is a portion of the ritual proceedings for war veterans to stand forward to recount their battle experiences, emphasizing that survival was due to the Almighty's benevolence. These veterans then dance; I have seen a woman dancing with them, who told me she was dancing in place of her two deceased husbands, both veterans. Kainai still perform, at the Sun Dance, the Women's Buffalo Society (Ma'toki) to invoke prosperity for the nation.

Medicine bundles and holy pipes can be owned by men and by women, and transferred through either inheritance or purchase (a person wishing to obtain blessing through caring for the holy icons gives gifts to the owner in honor of the bundle's power). Medicine bundles are hung on a wall in the home, high enough that they will not be jostled, or, if the family is living in a tipi, kept on a tripod frame. The woman of the household is responsible for keeping the bundle safe and handles it when moving or during rituals. Officiating priests at bundle rituals are men; the woman sits quietly and modestly behind the priest, although without her mediation the bundle should not be opened. Women prepare the feasts usually provided to celebrate rituals. They tend to sit in the outer circle of audience, but some ritual dances are performed by women. Men drum and play rattles; both men and women may sing, depending on the ritual.

Healers may specialize in herbs or in spiritual therapy. Women are more likely to be herbalists, in line with women's responsibilities for plant tending and gathering, but men may also train in herb knowledge. Upon collecting a medicinal plant, the herbalist prays and may leave a small offering, and the practitioner prays again in administering the herb (or herb mixture). Blackfoot belief that parents of young children are properly preoccupied with family care; leaving spiritual matters for the more mature middle-aged, who are free of such cares, means that women healers are likely to be past child-bearing years. Men, too, are likely to be older, in part because it takes years to complete apprenticeship to a ritualist. "Medicine men" are more often noticed, but the ethnographers Oscar and Ruth Lewis, with the Blackfoot in 1939, noted, "A woman could have more power than a m[e]d[icine] man," citing a narrative of a curse nullified by a Sun Dance Holy Woman (Lewis & Lewis, 1939, August 18).

LEISURE, RECREATION, AND THE ARTS

Both boys and girls were encouraged to race and play actively, with more stress placed on boys' endurance, strength, and speed as preparation for war. Historically, everyone rode and could care for horses. Everyone could swim—children enjoying frolicking in streams and adults bathing. Young boys roamed about in little groups; girls would play with each other closer to home. Boys and girls together played house, taking appropriate gender roles. Children had miniature tools and dolls, making their own little play figures with sticks or clay in addition to the sewn dolls that women made for girls.

A variety of gambling games are popular entertainments. Best loved is the handgame, accompanied with lively songs, a game of skill where two teams oppose one another to guess which hand of which person hides a marked stick. Bingo became popular in the late 20th century; men and women alike participate, with women predominating. Horse racing and rodeos are dominated by men and boys, except for rodeo barrel racing where girls ride. Aside from American games taught in schools, such as football, basketball, and baseball, Blackfoot had their own ballgames including shinny and catch. Women were more likely to play these games.

Social dancing, singing, and storytelling brought men, women, and children together. Powwows, the major secular celebration today, evolved during the 20th century from social dances combined with Independence Day (Fourth of July or Dominion Day) festivities encouraged by government Indian agents during the early reservation period. Powwow music is performed on European-style bass drums by groups of about half-a-dozen men sitting around the instrument, singing in unison and each pounding with a drumstick. Every year new powwow songs are added to the older repertoire. Women's "drums" (drum groups) are occasionally allowed in powwows—increasingly by the turn of the 21st century—against opposition by "traditionalists." Basically, drumming was considered a man's activity; women have always sung for ritual and social performances.

Visual arts include rock petroglyphs and pictographs, so far as is known done by men, painting on tipis and parfleches (large rawhide envelopes), and embroidery. Tipi covers and hide robes were properly painted by men in stylized realism, parfleches by women in geometric designs. Women assist men on tipi covers, which cannot be painted according to one's fancy but must either be icons of medicine bundles bestowed by a vision power, or exhibit a man's war record. Women decorated clothing, including horse ornamentation, embroidering with flattened dyed porcupine quills, native-made or trade-glass beads, shells, elk teeth, and colored threads. Clothing could also be painted and hung with strips of fur, fringes, tinkling dewclaws or metal cones, woven wicker ornaments, or whatever caught the sewer's or wearer's taste. Both men and women made necklaces, bracelets, and hair ornaments. Men and women were equally concerned with carefully groomed personal appearance, both genders devoting time to coiffures, clothing in good condition, and face and body painting (some painting for ritual rather than decorative purpose). Anecdotes about non-Indian portrait painters and photographers frequently tell of Blackfoot men or women stalking away from someone trying to take their picture when the Blackfoot person was wearing work clothes or had not been permitted to dress according to his or her own preference. Before the reservations, men wore tanned hide breechcloths, adding leggings, tunics, and fur robes in cold weather or for dress, and women wore long dresses, two tanned hides tied together at the shoulders or sewn, with or without sleeves. Both genders wore leather moccasins, and women wore wrapped leggings on the lower legs. Women were and are physically modest, averse to revealing their bodies, while men were accustomed to wearing little, facilitating body painting.

RELATIVE STATUS OF MEN AND WOMEN

Conceptually there were men's and women's domains, complementary rather than ranked. The First Marriages legend and innumerable foolish Napi stories imply higher status for women, as does women's vital, mediator role with medicine bundles and the Sun Dance. Perhaps one could say that Blackfoot women's status, based on innate reproductive capacity, was more secure, and men's status, based on accomplishments, was less so.

SEXUALITY

Sexuality, as distinguished from gossip about affairs, was not a proper topic for discussion among Blackfoot, except for joking with sisters' husbands/wives' sisters—potential spouses in polygyny. Parents' instructions to their children were minimal. On the other hand, living in tents in camps and caring for, hunting, and butchering animals exposed children to inadvertent observation of adults' and animals' sexuality. Men and women were expected to form marital relationships, for complementary household tasks as well as for sexual intimacy. Presumably some persons engaged in homosexual activities, but these are not discussed with outsiders. There does not seem to have been any explicit postpartum intercourse rule, but women felt "afraid of husband" for a month or 6 weeks after delivery, fearing another pregnancy too soon. Ten days after birth, a postmenopausal woman would dress the mother in new clothes and take away her old clothes and bedding; this ritual was supposed to prevent immediate pregnancy. For contraception, women seem to have been advised to use symbolic means such as not lending anyone else her shawl, not picking up young puppies, or wearing a copper bracelet with a hole in it around her neck, tied by a buckskin thong through the hole. Becoming pregnant while still nursing a child was considered a problem, because it was believed that the mother's milk would no longer be abundant enough to nourish the child.

Girls' parents discouraged premarital sexual intimacy, and an arranged marriage in the mid-teens, soon after menarche, was ideal. Youths were encouraged to sneak under a tipi cover into the bedding of a young woman, on a parallel with sneaking into an enemy's camp and stealing their horses. If the young woman did not wish the relationship, she could awaken her family sleeping around her. Rape was strongly disapproved, with gang-rape a possible punishment for an adulterous wife. Women captured in war raids, or traded as slaves, could be prostituted (leading some European travelers, failing to distinguish between these alien women and their hosts' families, to consider Indian women promiscuous).

COURTSHIP AND MARRIAGE

As noted, forming households through marriage was the norm. Parents selected adolescents' first spouses, allowing the young person to refuse if strongly upset by the choice but expecting obedience. The groom's family expressed honor to the bride and her family by presenting gifts; the bride's family outfitted her with a tipi (or, later, cabin) and household equipment. She herself was expected to have sewn and embroidered trousseau clothing and moccasins for her man.

Young men courted young women by waylaying them as they fetched water or firewood for their families, speaking to them on the margins of camp (later, near their family cabins) or at public gatherings, or daring to sneak under the tipi cover into the maiden's bed. Should the man be discovered in the tipi, the couple were considered married. A charming custom was for young men to ride around a camp singing love songs, taking the maidens of their choice up behind them on the horses as the circuits continued. Young women could court men by choosing to dance with them or in their honor if the man had performed an exploit to be celebrated. Propriety required the parents of the courting couple to meet formally to arrange a marriage.

HUSBAND–WIFE RELATIONSHIPS

Husbands and wives were expected to respect and support one another, socially and with complementary contributions to the household. Neither was permitted adultery, although men's extramarital sexual adventuring could be condoned and polygyny allowed men to keep more than one wife. Because polygyny ideally involved sisters married to one man, sisters- and brothers-in-law not only were permitted, but were expected, to joke lewdly with one another. Otherwise, propriety required avoidance of lewdness, even of telling obscene Napi stories, in the presence of in-laws. Men and their mothers-in-law showed extreme

respect by not speaking directly to one another or remaining together in a room or tipi. On this account, a widowed woman would not move into a married daughter's home but occupied a small tipi (or cabin) near it. Fathers-in-law were not obliged to avoid sons' wives but treated them respectfully, as fathers did their adult daughters.

According to early reservation ethnographers, divorce was frowned upon. Census records of the time reveal multiple serial marriages, some due to the high mortality of the time, but others apparently couples' more-or-less voluntary separations. One is told that "So-and-so stole" or "ran away with" X's wife. Men who abused their wives were ordered by her family to desist, or the woman returned to her family. The notorious 1870 massacre of a Piegan community by U.S. troops under Colonel Baker was precipitated by a woman's male relatives murdering a European American husband who persisted in abusing her, disregarding warnings by the Piegans.

OTHER CROSS-SEX RELATIONSHIPS

A person's comrade and confidante was expected to be of the same sex. Boys were encouraged to bond with a chum, sharing boys' activities and later adult employments, and girls with a sister or female cousin (English terminology). The only traditional cross-sex familiarity was between potential polygynous spouses, a man and his wife's sisters, between whom lewd joking was obligatory. A man's chum (there is a Blackfoot term for these comrades) might enjoy relaxed conversation with his chum's wife, but this extension of familiarity was not obligatory.

CHANGES IN ATTITUDES, BELIEFS, AND PRACTICES REGARDING GENDER

Imposition of European American/European Canadian rule after the 1870s abolished polygyny, although households of older people might continue with more than one "housewife," as politely termed. Boys and men were compelled to dress more fully than had been customary. Otherwise, there were relatively few changes regarding gender for Blackfoot. Missionaries perpetuated the homemaker role for girls and outside worker for boys. Women were less visible in leader roles; for example, few were elected to the Tribal Business Council. Unlike some reservations, the Blackfoot did not go through a period in the mid-20th century of predominantly women elected and appointed leaders, creating a backlash among men who felt disenfranchised.

In the last third of the 20th century, English rapidly replaced Blackfoot in daily use. This meant that Blackfoot were using Indo-European "sex" gender syntax (he–she–it), disregarding the animate–inanimate distinction used in Blackfoot speech. Whether this affected attitudes is difficult to evaluate, since much else changed—families moved from hamlets on the range to clustered housing in the agency town, a community college was created, network television came to homes, and an increasing proportion of the growing population is employed and living off-reservation.

Not a change, but indicative of continuing recognition of "leader-hearted women," the Montana Blackfeet reservation member Elouise Cobell achieved national recognition when she instituted a lawsuit in 1996 against the U.S. Department of the Interior, demanding accounting for the millions of dollars it held in trust for U.S. Indians. Mrs. Cobell had studied accounting in an off-reservation college, been appointed treasurer for the Tribe, and had taken over the defunct local bank, managing it to success. When her requests for documentation of Blackfeet trust funds were consistently ignored, she found an attorney to pursue the case. Mrs. Cobell's outstanding ability brought her a 1997 MacArthur Foundation "genius" award, which she used for legal fees. Contemporary with Elouise Cobell, revitalization of Blackfoot heritage on the Montana reservation is forwarded by men and women such as Darrell Robes Kipp, who holds a Harvard graduate degree, his colleague in language revival Dr. Dorothy Still Smoking, the native plant expert Wilbert Fish Sr., and faculty of Blackfeet Community College. On the Canadian side, men and women of Red Crow College in Alberta similarly carry on the Blackfoot heritage.

ACKNOWLEDGMENT

I am grateful to Ruth Lewis for providing excerpts from her field notebooks.

BIBLIOGRAPHY

Dietrich, S. S. (1939). *Field Notes, Blackfeet Indian Reservation, Montana*. (Typescript in Marquette University Archives, Milwaukee, WI.)

Dietrich, S. S. (1993, August 29). [Interview with A. B. Kehoe].

Ewers, J. C. (1955). *The horse in Blackfoot Indian culture* (Smithsonian Institution, Bureau of American Ethnology Bulletin 159). Washington, DC: U.S. Government Printing Office.

Ewers, J. C. (1958). *The Blackfeet: Raiders on the Northwestern Plains*. Norman: University of Oklahoma Press.

Farr, W. E. (1984). *The reservation Blackfeet, 1882–1945*. Seattle: University of Washington Press.

Goldfrank, E. S. (1945). *Changing configurations in the social organization of a Blackfoot tribe during the reserve period (the Blood of Alberta, Canada)* (Monograph 8, American Ethnological Society). Seattle: University of Washington Press.

Goldfrank, E. S. (1978). *Notes on an undirected life* (Publications in Anthropology No. 3). Flushing, NY: Queens College.

Grinnell, G. B. (1892). *Blackfoot lodge tales*. New York: Scribner's Sons.

Grinnell, G. B. (1896). *American Anthropologist* (Old Series), *9*, 286–287.

Grinnell, G. B. (1899). *American Anthropologist* (New Series), *1*, 194–196.

Grinnell, G. B. (1901). *American Anthropologist* (New Series), *3*, 650–668.

Grinnell, G. B. (1912). *Blackfeet Indian Stories*. New York, Scribner's Sons.

Grinnell, G. B. (1961). *Pawnee, Blackfoot and Cheyenne* (Selected by D. Brown). New York: Scribner's Sons.

Hanks, L. M., Jr., & Hanks, J. R. (1945). Observations on Northern Blackfoot kinship (Monograph 9, American Ethnological Society). Seattle: University of Washington Press.

Hanks, L. M., Jr., & Hanks, J. R. (1950). *Tribe under trust: A study of the Blackfoot reserve of Alberta*. Toronto: University of Toronto Press.

Hungry Wolf, B. [Little Bear]. (1984). *The ways of my grandmothers*. New York: Morrow.

Hungry-Wolf, B. [Little Bear]. (1996). *Daughters of the Buffalo Women*. Skookumchuck, BC: Canadian Caboose Press.

Kehoe, A. B. (1976). Old woman had great power, *Western Canadian Journal of Anthropology*, *6*, 68–76.

Kehoe, A. B. (1983). The shackles of tradition. In P. Albers & B. Medicine (Eds.), *The hidden half* (pp. 53–73). Washington, DC: University Press of America.

Kehoe, A. B. (1991). Contests of power in Blackfoot life and mythology. In A. Duff-Cooper (Ed.), *Contests* (pp. 115–124). Edinburgh: Edinburgh University Press.

Kehoe, A. B. (1992). Clot-of-Blood. In C. R. Farrer & R. A. Williamson (Eds.), *Earth and sky* (pp. 207–214). Albuquerque, NM: University of New Mexico Press.

Kehoe, A. B. (1995a). Introduction. In C. Wissler & D. C. Duvall *Mythology of the Blackfoot* (pp. v–xxxiii). Lincoln: University of Nebraska Press (Bison Book reprint).

Kehoe, A. B. (1995b). Blackfoot persons. In L. F. Klein & L. A. Ackerman (Eds.), *Women and power in Native America* (pp. 113–125). Norman: University of Oklahoma Press.

Kehoe, A. B. (1996). Transcribing Insima, a Blackfoot "Old Lady." In J. S. H. Brown & E. Vibert (Eds.), *Reading beyond words: Native history in context* (pp. 381–402). Peterborough Ont.: Broadview Press.

Lewis, O. (1941). Manly-hearted women among the North Piegan. *American Anthropologist*, *43*, 173–187.

Lewis, O. (1942). *The effects of white contact upon Blackfoot culture* (Monograph 6, *American Ethnological Society*). Seattle: University of Washington Press.

Lewis, O., & Lewis, R. M. (1939) [Field notebooks, Blackfoot].

McClintock, W. (1968). *The Old North Trail*. Lincoln: University of Nebraska Press (Bison Book reprint; original work published 1910).

Schultz, J. W. [Apikuni] (1907). *My life as an Indian*. New York: Forest and Stream.

Schultz, J. W. [Apikuni] (1962). In K. C. Seele (Ed.), *Blackfeet and buffalo*. Norman: University of Oklahoma Press.

Schultz, J. W. [Apikuni] (1974). In E. L. Silliman (Ed.), *Why gone those times? Blackfoot tales*. Norman: University of Oklahoma Press.

Uhlenbeck, C. C. (1911). Original Blackfoot texts. *Verhandelingen der Koninklijke Akademie van Wetenschappen te Amsterdam, Afdeeling Letterkunde, 12*(1). Amsterdam: Johannes Muller.

Uhlenbeck, C. C. (1912). A new series of Blackfoot texts. *Verhandelingen der Koninklijke Akademie van Wetenschappen te Amsterdam, Afdeeling Letterkunde, 13*(1). Amsterdam: Johannes Muller.

Uhlenbeck, W. (1911). *Blackfootreservation donderdag 8 Juni–Zondag 17 September, 1911*. MS. M8116, Glenbow Archives, Calgary. (Manuscript translated January 2002 by M. Eggermont-Molenaar.)

Wissler, C. (1911). The social life of the Blackfoot Indians. *Anthropological Papers, 7*(1), 1–64. New York: American Museum of Natural History.

Wissler, C. (1912). Ceremonial bundles of the Blackfoot Indians. *Anthropological Papers, 7*(2), 65–289. New York: American Museum of Natural History.

Wissler, C. (1971). *Red man reservations*. New York: Collier. (Original work published 1938 as *Indian Cavalcade or Life on the Old-Time Indian Reservations*.)

Wissler, C., & Duvall, D. C. (1908). Mythology of the Blackfoot Indians, *Anthropological Papers, 2*(1), 1–163. New York: American Museum of Natural History.

Canela

William H. Crocker

ALTERNATIVE NAMES

Alternative names are Canella, Kanela, Ramkókamekra, Rankokamekrá, Rancocamecra, Kapiekran, Mehim, but not Canelo (eastern Ecuador). The Apanyekra-Canela are neighbors.

LOCATION

The Canela are located in Brazil, 600 km southeast of the mouth of the Amazon River and 70 km south of the city of Barra do Corda in the center of the state of Maranhão.

CULTURAL OVERVIEW

The Canela Native Americans speak Gê, a subgroup of Macro-Carib. Gê speakers live in the central to eastern interior highlands, south of the Amazon River. The Canela are one of the Timbira nations that fought each other annually. These peoples lived in large circular villages accommodating 1,000–1,500 people, interacting almost every day with each other. They intermingled through participation in unusually extensive rituals, social activities, sports, and twice-daily meetings of the elders. Most of these tribes lived in savannah woodlands (*cerrados*), characterized by bushes and stunted trees rising no higher than 30 feet above poor sandy soils with grass cover. Only by the streams or small rivers, where forests enabled sufficient soil fertility, was their slash-and-burn horticulture marginally successful.

The Canela (i.e., the pre-pacification Kapiekran) surrendered to a Brazilian/Portuguese military garrison at Pastos Bons, Maranhão, in 1814. They had had devastating skirmishes with settlers for some 30 years. Decimated by smallpox during 1915, they hid in the hills of their former lands until about 1840, when the backland settlers of the area allowed them to live on about 5% (about 1,200 km²) of the territory they had controlled. Owing to their drastic loss of lands and their being primarily hunters and gatherers with very little horticulture, they had to adapt to far more intensive slash-and-burn agricultural methods using the settlers' axes and machetes. Even by 2001, they had not fully adapted to settled agriculture.

Thus, even in current times, the Canela do not produce enough on their farms to feed their families during the entire year. The values of the hunter, as formerly those of the warrior, are still highly prestigious, while the values of the farmer are merely respected. They put in about a 1 ha-size farm while the settler cultivates about 3 ha. In these farms, the Canela produce principally bitter manioc, rice, and beans.

Another vestige of their food-collecting past is the unusual extent to which the Canela relied on sharing to distribute the few products of their economy. Aboriginally, if you did not give freely and willingly when someone wanted a piece of your venison or a drink of water, you were considered stingy and evil. Currently, the unproductive person (disabled through illness, mourning, taboos, child-bearing, or by temperament) "begs" from the productive person. This general begging, and the compulsion to share, makes it difficult for any individual to raise sufficient foods. The production of a surplus to trade with other families or to sell on the open markets of surrounding communities or the city is infrequent and not economically significant. The backlanders surrounding the Canela reservation feel that since the Canela do not contribute to the common good of the area commercially, they do not deserve to retain their lands.

CULTURAL CONSTRUCTION OF GENDER

The Canela gender categories are just male and female. They distinguish males from females—besides through physical attributes—through clothing, body adornments, and roles in life. Men wear shorts or long pants while women use wraparound cloth to below the knees with no top. Away from their reservation, women cover their breasts with cloth or a blouse, and men put on shirts.

Aboriginally, both sexes went naked, but young girls wore belts securing leaves to cover their genitals during festival situations only.

Nouns, pronouns, adjectives, articles, and other parts of speech are not gender distinguished, but personal names are at least 95% distinguishable. A suffix (-khwèy) is sometimes added to a woman's name to indicate gender, but men do not have an equivalent designation. The sex of an animal, bird, or fish is indicated by the male suffix (-tsũm-re) or the female one (-kahãy).

The Canela are relatively dark-skinned, tall, and long-headed for Amazonian Indians. They prefer lighter shades of skin, straight long hair (not kinky), and relatively high speaking voices. These preferences are not differentiated for gender or age.

GENDER OVER THE LIFE CYCLE

The major stages, I call "life markers." The Canela distinguish them by the use of the suffix -tsà. They

are: birth, pèm-tsà (falling-occasion); puberty, ram ipinin-tsà (already sex-occasion); childbirth, pèm-tsà (falling-occasion); and death, tùk-tsà (death-occasion). The terms apply to both genders. Between these life markers are a number of minor stages that are either descriptions or social events. These stages are described through their translations in Table 1. The Canela apply most of these stage terms to both genders, but those between puberty and childbirth are gender differentiated. Two of these stages refer to male age-sets, when first formed (7) and when graduated (9), and so are gender specific. Stage 8 for men, which I gloss as "youths," pertains until these men are no longer raising "vulnerable" children (stage 10), while the same stage 8 for women pertains only up to childbirth (marker 3). Stage 9 for both men and women describes the free period of their lives—for men activities with their warriors' age-set (hakhrã-ntúwa) and for women their time of unrestricted sexual freedom (nkrekre-le).

The first three life markers are not publicly attended. They are family experiences. The fourth life marker,

Table 1. Canela Life Stages

Life marker 1: *pèm-tsà* (falling occasion) = birth		(+)
Stage 1: *tetet-le*	new and whitish	(+)
Stage 2: *kaprêk-le*	small, red, weak; drinks milk only, then later, solid foods	(+)
Stage 3: *ka?pôt-le*	they go on all fours	(+)
Stage 4: *kapôt-tèy-tu*	crawlers fully strong, get up but fall	(+)
Stage 5: *halíya ntúwa*	runs, but falters, falls	(+)
Stage 6: *a?khra-le*	children: viable young people who can talk, run, present, and understand well	(+)
Stage 7: *kô-ntúwa*	boys caught in the initiation festivals, including two girl associates	( )
Life marker 2: *ram ipinin tsà* = already having had sex		(+)
Stage 8: *ntúwayê*	youths (rarely women); through when children still "soft" (through Stage 10)	( )
Stage 8: *kuprè*	girls; from loss of virginity to childbirth, life marker 3	( )
Stage 9: *hakhrã-ntúwa*	men's graduated initiation age-class; warriors, now mature young men	( )
Stage 9: *to ?pre*	women now wear maturity belts	( )
nkrekre-le	women free, loose, having fun	( )
Life marker 3: *pèm-tsà* = childbirth		(+)
Stage 10: *khra-?tàm-túwa*	their children still raw and vulnerable to pollutants	(+)
Stage 11: *khra ?tèy tu*	all their children strong	(+)
Stage 12: *hĩĩtèy*	their condition firm/tough	(+)
Stage 13: *khà-le*	well hardened, mature, about 45	(+)
Stage 14: *khà*	well established, about 55, rarely applied to women	( )
Stage 15: *wey*	very old, about 70	(+)
Stage 16: *kêtyê*	does no work any more, over 80	(+)
Life marker 4: *tùk-tsà*	death	(+)

Adapted from Crocker, 1990, p. 181.

death and its funeral, is witnessed by the extended family of the deceased and by any others who chose to do so. The first three markers differ by gender, obviously, but funeral, burial, and mourning procedures are the same for either gender, though women are involved more extensively in mourning activities.

Puberty transforms boys into youths whom their uncles can sharply discipline. Her first sexual intromission, not puberty, transforms a girl into a married woman. First parenthood forces both genders from free living into serious responsibilities for the first time—the wife more completely than the husband.

Socialization of Boys and Girls

The Canela raise infants and babies of both sexes similarly, but by age 5 or 6 they treat boys quite differently from girls. They allow boys to go about quite freely, while they keep girls by their mothers and female relatives to carry out domestic chores. Boys roam the savannahs in groups, hunting and playing by the streams, and associating with their initiation-training age-set members.

The Canela value boys and girls equally; however, the genders have their own particular qualities, which are valued for themselves. The expectations are that boys will grow up to be good economic providers, especially of meat, and that girls will be good housekeepers and child raisers. Before pacification, they expected boys to avenge the death of an uncle by an enemy tribe. They raise boys to be obedient, respectful of elders, and generous. They especially valued the traits of hunters, such as agility, endurance, patience, and fast running. Girls should be gregarious and outgoing in personality, and they should quickly join in the merriment of groups, especially the sing-dance lines in the plaza.

While girls work continuously with their mothers and female relatives, helping on the farm and in the house, boys take more time for play and age-set activities, until their fathers involve them in farm work when they are approaching puberty.

You see both genders playing "house" together in the yards behind the houses until the boys are 5 or 6, when it becomes just girls playing house with miniature utensils and food. Fathers make toys for sons from the balsa-like stem of the buriti palm frond. Mothers made daughters dolls from the same material.

The early rites are similar for the genders, except for naming. A boy's uncle (his MB or M "B") ceremonially

shouts to announce his birth at sunrise, but a girl's birth is not called out. When a boy is 7 or 8 years old, his naming uncle brings him a small bow and arrow, while a girl's naming aunt brings her a small head-carried basket. Between 8 and 11 years of age, a boy has his earlobes pierced to inculcate obedience and the learning of customs, while a girl experiences no equivalent rite until her loss of virginity. Ear-piercing and defloration are seen as an opening up to society.

The Canela have no formal education except perhaps in festival singing for which the elders summon the boys of an age-set with their two girls. Each individual sings alone before them for daily criticism.

Shamans do not have apprentices; the young of either sex learn to be shamans on their own. The maraca sing-dance masters do not conduct serious apprentice training. The young men (no women) learn by listening and learning by heart what the masters are doing.

Puberty and Adolescence

The Canela do not speak of adolescence, but they mark the two first sex occasions emphatically with special events. I find that the terms, *kuprè* for the girl and *ntúwayê* for the boy (both stage 8), express the beginning of adolescence. They consider that a girl is a *kuprè* from loss of virginity up to childbirth. For the youth, the expression *ntúwayê* extends further than his first fatherhood. It goes through stage 10, until his last child is no longer "soft." By then he may be 45 or 50.

The boy experienced a sharp discontinuity in socialization at puberty. His uncle had been permissive and encouraging, but now, suddenly, he became tough, scolding, and demanding. When he heard that his nephew had had first sex, he ordered him to leave his maternal house to sleep in the plaza. There he had to avoid the women in their free period and commence his postpubertal restrictions against most foods and sex.

The adolescent girl experienced similar severity from the elders. Her aunts and uncles had been permissive and encouraging, but at puberty they became severe. The elders assigned her to a men's festival society as one of two girl associates. These men had sex with her sequentially several times. If she objected, she found no sympathy with even her female kin. This training served to make her generous with her body for most of the rest of her life.

Special rites for the girl were the following. Upon giving her virginity she had become married, so her family before or after this experience assembled to counsel her with her husband. They believed that sex brought on menstruation, so seclusion for her first menstrual period was her next rite, but one of little significance. Then her female kin secluded her for months to teach her the use of restrictions against certain foods and sex to enable her to grow up strong—a very important rite.

Special postpuberty rites for the youth are the following. Besides sending him to sleep in the plaza and hazing him before the elders, his disciplinary uncle ordered him to maintain restrictions against certain foods and sex for several years.

Attainment of Adulthood

They say that childbirth makes a young woman an adult, but she is still living in the same house with her mother and some of her close female relatives, who dominate her. Nevertheless, a Canela woman of this age and status must have her own farm. Thus she obligates her husband to prepare a field for her, which her female kin require their husbands to help establish.

A distinct move of independence comes to some Canela mothers when they leave their mothers' house and establish one of their own, next to or behind it. Older sisters with many children do this.

They say that a boy becomes a man when he fathers his first child. Formerly this occurred when he was 20–30 but now when he is 16–20. The other customary maturity indictor for becoming a man is his age-set's graduation from their final initiation festival, formerly when they were 17–27, but now when they are 12–22.

Middle Age and Old Age

Middle age for the Canela may be from about 50 to about 65. I suggest that their steps for entering middle age were menopause for women and retiring from racing with logs for men. Middle-aged women dominated their hearth groups, and middle-aged men entered the council of elders.

During old age for men, which begins at about 65, they continue their membership in the council of elders in the plaza, where they meet with the younger men in congenial conversation each day. Few men beyond 75 come to the plaza, but they may do so. Old women tend to lose their status in their extended families by 75. They do odd jobs as service to the younger women who are in charge.

Both genders continue to work in the fields until possibly their eighties. Such old men spend much time fishing, contributing in this way. Since the late 1970s, some older people receive government pensions as retired farm workers—women after 55 and men after 60. This minimum-wage income helps their relations with the younger members of their families.

PERSONALITY DIFFERENCES BY GENDER

Boys are clearly allowed to be more aggressive than girls. I have seen little boys act in ways that only could be called "fierce," while their adult female kin felt proud of such warrior tendencies. "Gleefulness" describes the frequent self-presentation of little boys, while little girls are likely to be coy but charming.

Women are allowed to be less generous or less quick in responding to requests for food. They can be more retentive. They can also be more expressive about complaints, especially against their husbands. In contrast, men are more likely to put up with their wives' complaints, bear up under trying duties, and say less that is negative.

The Canela allow women to be more emotional and individualistic. Their female kin may control them to some extent, while an age-set controls its male members more definitively. It is telling that social pressures almost always forced a man back to his wife, but that no pressures could force a woman to take back a husband she had come to dislike. Women can be more headstrong and stubborn.

Men tend to be more dominant and aggressive, while women are more nurturing and dependent. Nevertheless, women do not go around looking repressed and with subservient attitudes, nor do they lower their gaze for men. They can be straightforward and demanding should the situation call for it.

GENDER-RELATED SOCIAL GROUPS

The Canela sociocultural system involves male versus female oppositions. The male place is in the central plaza, while the female one is the ring of houses which line the outer side of the village's circular boulevard.

The Canela are not lineal; they reckon kinship bilaterally with a matrilateral emphasis, and they are matrilocal.

The principal social structure in the circle of houses is that of matrilines descending from a single female ancestor. An arc of houses on the village circle that is formed by such matrilines is called a longhouse. Longhouses have no names. In 1971, the village of Escalvado was composed of 13 longhouses ranging from 12 houses in length to one house. While brothers and mothers' brothers of the women of these houses visit them each day to govern certain activities, the women largely control most activities in their houses.

In contrast, the men dominate the activities that take place in the plaza. The elders, composed only of men, hold meetings there twice a day, led by the first chief of the tribe, a man. Decisions of many sorts emanate from the plaza. Judicial settlements of disputes between extended families take place there or in the house of the plaintiff or the defendant along the village circle of houses. In either location, men dominate the resolution of such problems. Thus the genders structure the principal social institutions to a very considerable extent.

Upon marriage, a young man moves in with his wife's family, with her mother and a number of her female kin and their spouses and children. Since divorce was almost impossible before 1975, the young man most likely stayed in this house past grandfatherhood until death.

The Canela are outstanding for their number of male societies. They maintain two daily active age-set moieties that are formed according to the age of their male members, not through their kinship. They also have three festival moieties that are formed through male name-transmission, the names passing from naming uncles to their named-nephews (from MBs to their ZSs). In addition, they maintain a high-honor society, which passes membership through male name-transmission, and a low-honor society, which acquires membership through its members' reputation for individualism and joking behavior.

Women do not form daily active societies or ceremonial societies that are occasionally active. They maintain female memberships—two young women—in almost all of the men's societies. The two men's societies that are of highest ceremonial honor have no women or only one female member.

GENDER ROLES IN ECONOMICS

The gender roles in economics are distinct, but women take on male roles when necessary, to the extent that they can, and men carry out female roles when circumstances require them to do so. Thus men tend babies and fetch water from the stream and firewood from the savannahs when their wives are ill, and women work at building houses and cutting down woods for a farm, when they cannot get men to do this heavy work for them.

The sons-in-law are especially responsible for earning the family living. They obtain meat for their nuclear families and their hearth-oriented extended families. The wives of the sons-in-law are more responsible for bringing grains and vegetables from the family fields and for processing these staples into meals for the nuclear families as well as for the extended family hearth groups. Thus, women spend a great deal of time processing bitter manioc, the basic staple, while men spend days away from home hunting or arranging to bring meat from backland communities.

Before pacification, men went away in groups to attack the enemy to reduce their numbers, preventing future attacks, while women stayed home. The men were probably not away for more than a month at a time. Until the 1960s, men went away to distant large cities of Brazil. They went for several months at a time to obtain goods to give away at home, as they had gone on trek for collecting foods before pacification. They seldom took women on these trips to cities.

Aboriginally, the Canela were involved in very little trade that took them outside their territorial boundaries. Groups of men went on trading trips without women, because such incursions into enemy territories were dangerous. Today, neither sex specializes in trading; both genders sell artifacts in the city. However, since men go to backland communities and cities more than women do, and since more men than women speak Portuguese, the men are the negotiators even when their women are with them.

Generally, women make most kinds of baskets while men make most kinds of mats, and women roll and make items out of tucum string, while men make items out of buriti cord. Men make their personal carrying pouches (*mõ?ko*) and bags (*paptu*), and they also carve staffs and ceremonial lances out of hard woods, while women do not carve.

Women own the houses and farms. Each gender owns the items they make. Women had few festival body adornments, while men had many, including the most colorful ones (*pàn-yapùù*, arara tail-feathers).

PARENTAL AND OTHER CARETAKER ROLES

The mother of a child is the one who gave birth to it, though a child calls his or her mother's sister "mother" as well as most of the latter person's sisters or classificatory sisters. Several of these many other "mothers" are actual part time caretakers, and one of them takes over the full care of a closely related orphan.

The same pattern potentially exists for fathers, but since these men's brothers, and their other classificatory fathers, live in other households, their care is seldom sought. The child's mother's husband is the primary father (MH = F), but the Canela also have "contributing fathers." They believe that semen introduced into a woman's womb after she has become pregnant becomes part of the fetus. Thus, the men who have contributed in this way become ethnobiological fathers to the fetus, sharing common blood, in addition to the mother's husband. Contributing fathers occasionally give their contributed-to children food, but they are not significant caretakers, and they do not assume the care of orphans related to them in this way.

The fathers who provide significant care and sustenance are the child's mother's husbands, whether presumed genitors or stepfathers. Such fathers live in the same house with the child's mother and spend considerable time taking care of their children, sometimes with great love and affection. Nevertheless, only the MH who is the presumed genitor can spank or hit his child, not its stepfather, because only shared "blood" (*kaprôô*) will give the hitter sufficient compassion to carry out the punishment constructively.

Besides the parental roles, the other significant caretaker roles are those of the father's sister and the mother's brother, immediate and classificatory. These uncles and aunts together handle the disciplinary matters of their nieces and nephews, since the children's parents are too soft on them, they believe. The parents handle daily matters, but if children get out of hand, they summon the uncles for both sexes and maybe the aunts for girls. The young people fear scoldings from their uncles and start obeying the moment their parents threaten to summon them.

The parents are ashamed to face the sexual matters of their children, so they leave such education to the uncles and aunts who have little sexual shame before their nieces and nephews. Uncles talked nephews out of sexual jealousies, and aunts coaxed nieces into sequential sex situations and private trysts.

If a youth was intransigent, his disciplining uncle saw to it that he was called before the female dance line in the late afternoon to be hazed cruelly by one of the toughest and most warlike elders. A girl who appeared to be menstruating before she had lost her virginity was accused of hiding the name of her lover. Sex brought on menstruation, they believe, so she must have had sex, but who was the young man? To find out, they summoned an aunt to examine her genitals, forcefully if necessary.

LEADERSHIP IN PUBLIC ARENAS

Public leadership among the Canela is primarily male. The first chief (only male) and the council of elders (all male) determine almost all political, social, ceremonial, and judicial matters—internal and external.

Female power lies in the houses, but does not extend even to an entire long[1] longhouse. Thus, while male power extends from the plaza to the whole tribe, individual female power does not extend far[1] beyond the hearth unit.

The Canela have one festival, the Festival of Oranges, during which they invert the gender roles. In it, two or three men accompany perhaps 100 women on their warlike expedition to obtain food from a backland community. The woman who assumes the full leadership, due to her own powers of persuasion and the respect the women have for her, holds this role only for the few days of the festival.

GENDER AND RELIGION

The original Canela human beings were Sun (Pùt) and Moon (Putwrè) who walked in the savannahs together. Sun found the ideal forms for living, while Moon changed them to create workable forms. One day Sun plunged into a stream's pond and came out with a file of beautiful young Canelas behind him, both men and women. He had made the genders together. Thus, Moon had to do the same thing, but he came out of the water with less than perfect men and women—the origin of physical differences.

Star Woman (Katsêê-ti-ʔkhwèy) came down from the sky and showed the Canela corn and other vegetables already growing in the woods. A Canela boy stole fire from a female jaguar. Awkhêê, a man, brought the concept of social hierarchy to the Canela. He offered the Canela the choice of the shotgun (the Brazilian world) or the bow and arrow (the Indian world), and when the Canela chose the latter, they had to remain subservient to the Brazilian, while the Brazilian had to support the Canela forever.

The Canela have several other culture heroes, all men, who visited the worlds of the skies, ghosts, fish, and alligators, and they came back with festival-pageants as models for the Canela to live by. While Star-Woman is the only female culture hero, they did not rate her stature as different from that of the men. However, Awkhêê has special status, because he is the only one whom they call upon today. He is their savior in the messianic movements and, as such, he has become synonymous with God and Jesus.

Canela shamans are largely men, though two women appear in Canela myths and I knew one female shaman during the 1970s. They said that women rarely had the strength to carry out extensive restrictions against certain foods and sex during their postpubertal years so that they seldom obtained sufficient purity of blood to attract ghosts who could make them shamans. Ghosts are recently dead Canela, so when ghosts come back to bother living Canela, their names are usually reported by living shamans. Thus, ghosts are of either sex.

These days, the Canela seem "addicted" to messianic movements to resolve their economic problems instead of relying on hard work in the fields to furnish sufficient staples. They had significant movements in 1963, 1980, 1984, and 1999, and about six lesser movements between 1984 and 1995. The prophet of by far the greatest movement, the one of 1963, was a woman, Maria Khêê-khwèy, but men led the other three significant movements.

LEISURE, RECREATION, AND THE ARTS

Visitors to the reservation are likely to comment that the Canela appear to be playing all the time. This is because they have a lot of leisure time and work in a playful manner, chatting and joking.

Men have more leisure time than women, because women's work is daily while men's work, like clearing fields, is more seasonal. Men hunt and fish during all months of the year, but such activities are sporadic.

Leisure time for men is spent at daily age-set gatherings or, when older, council of elders' meetings, where they talk about amusing experiences, rumors, scandals, and politics. Young men and women often dance three times a day—dawn, late afternoon, and evening. The Canela seldom work more than 5 hours in their fields (about 8 a.m. to 1 p.m.), and then, after sequential sex, the men race carrying heavy logs back from the fields to the village in the mid-afternoon. They hold track and sing-dancing events around the village circle in the late afternoon during the meetings of the elders and during the morning meetings of the elders as well.

It is hard to detect when women have leisure moments, because their family duties keep them occupied most of the time. However, during the afternoons, they may sing between naps while rocking their babies, and down by the stream they may have long enjoyable discussions with other women while washing clothes. None of their work seems hurried or pressured.

While the social singing and dancing in the plaza three times a day involves both genders, as do the personal trysts, the genders spend most leisure time apart, not because custom segregates them, but because of the nature of their activities.

Old men, but not old women, formerly gathered large groups of children and youths in the plaza during the late afternoon, while they told stories about the ancestors.

RELATIVE STATUS OF MEN AND WOMEN

Ceremonially, the Canela place high value on certain of their young of both sexes. They compare the ceremonially high girls (the *wè?tè*—aged 6 to 12) to beauty queens (*reinas*) in the Brazilian world. Similarly, the young male ceremonial chiefs (*mẽ hõ?pa?hi* and *tàmhàk*) receive deference, but command nothing. However, the mere arrival and presence of such honored persons of either sex before individuals or groups in conflict influenced them to stop their hostility and resolve their problems quickly out of respect.

The elders, men, award artifacts of honor to the best young festival performers of both sexes. They also assigned most girls, ages 12–14, to serve as girl associates to men's societies, involving them in sequential sex. Thus, older men controlled the development of the sexuality of young women to a considerable extent. Clearly, great status accrued in these ways to older men.

Economically, at the family hearth level, the man in the role of the senior father-in-law (*pàykêt*) is likely to dominate his sons-in-law (*mẽ ipiyõyê*) in determining what they do each day. The women of this hearth group, all close kin, clearly dominate their junior married-in husbands, (*mẽ iwawè*), but they may or may not dominate the senior male by the time he is a grandfather.

In kin-group matters, women dominate the domestic scene for food preparation and distribution and for simple childcare, but for questions affecting the kin group as a whole, the women's brothers, uncles, or great uncles determine most matters.

The Canela do not limit rights to important material resources to either gender. Economic commodities pass freely between the sexes. Fruits of the labor of either sex pass to the other one.

These days, the status of a young married man has risen because he can threaten to divorce his wife, and he does so increasingly.

SEXUALITY

Expressing sexuality was the great joy in Canela life, and the genders were equally involved. Sex for the Canela is natural, healthy, and a great pleasure, and to be undertaken for enjoyment and not just for procreation. It is only dangerous when it is "polluting." They believe that such pollutants come from rich meats and other "loaded" foods, and not the sexual fluids of either sex.

Premarital sex for girls does not exist, because her first act of intromission means that she has become married. Extramarital sex, both trysts and sequential sex, was compulsory for both sexes. Today, they hold the same belief about first marriage for a girl, but trysts and sequential sex are no longer compulsory for her. Extramarital trysts have become dangerous because they arouse the jealousy of husbands. Sequential sex has become rare, and may exist only for a group of men in a festival, when they pay for it. Thus, it has become more like prostitution.

Extramarital practices become less frequent over the lifetime of a woman, because after first childbirth, she found her domestic responsibilities too time consuming to have many trysts or sequential sex.

Such practices diminished over the lifetime of a man with the weakening of his sexual desires. Today, it is hard for a man to find sex partners outside of marriage without his having to compensate women considerably, even as a young bachelor. Women in general now have the sense that men must pay for sex, whereas formerly they gave sex as good women from a sense of sharing and generousity.

The cultural conception of male sexuality differs from the cultural conception of female sexuality, currently, in that men need sex more than women do and therefore they must take the initiative. Formerly, however, women took the initiative as much as men. Male informants say that, while having sex does not excite most women very much, having sex excites some women to an extreme extent. They may become far more excited than men do.

Nimuendajú reports that women were careful not to sit or stand so that they exposed their inner labia. A similar shame for men is for anyone, male or female, to see their glans penis.

The Canela used to allow young children of both genders to hear the sexual intercourse of older people at night. Young children also listened to the joking relationships taking place between somewhat distant classificatory uncles and nieces, and aunts and nephews. Also, aunts would say sex-loaded phrases for their little nieces of 4 years to repeat in the faces of their uncles. The same would happen between tiny nephews and their aunts. Nevertheless, they did not allow sexual experimentation between the sexes before a girl was 11 or a boy had reached puberty.

In earlier times, the elders limited the sexuality of both sexes during adolescence to infrequent sex with much older people, because they believed that frequent sex between young people was weakening due to the softness of youth. Building their own strength through the practice of food and sex restrictions was also a factor in limiting adolescent sex, more so for the man than the woman.

Limitations on adult sexuality were household duties for women and economic activities for men, especially work in the family fields. Nevertheless, during festivals and even during ordinary domestic life, joking between adults—aunts and nephews, uncles and nieces, or classificatory spouses—could result in mock acts of sexuality.

There were no stories or myths about earlier homosexual relationships among the Canela. However, I found three examples of this orientation during the 1950s and 1960s.

Two of the three homosexuals were born during the 1910s. They wore wraparound skirts like women, except that they did not cover their knees while the women always did. They gave up racing with logs and hunting, and they worked hard in the fields and in domestic work, preparing food along with the women. I was not aware that they took care of babies. Both married. One of them had children, but his wife made him leave. Occasionally, they met with the council of elders in the plaza, but were not active there. As individuals, they were tolerated and respected, but they were not cultural models.

The younger homosexual, who was born during the 1930s, sewed clothing at the Indian Protection Service's post and carried out duties more characteristic of women, but he did not wear a wraparound skirt. He married and had a baby in 1972, but others said that the child's contributing fathers had made it. However, since then the expression of such activities has been socioculturally suppressed, in keeping with encroaching backland Brazilian attitudes.

COURTSHIP AND MARRIAGE

Formerly, the Canela contracted marriages. The mothers of the potential couple got together because they wanted a connection between the two families. These contracted marriages were between a man aged 15–20 and a girl aged 5–7. However, most of these engagements, did not result in marriages.

More recently, the Canela had family hearings for a young couple to help them get together sexually, but currently they get together first and then have the family hearing after. All men marry and most women do. Only a few women choose to remain unmarried as a way of life (*mẽ mpíyapit*). A single woman lives with her sisters and helps support her extended family through contributions and the work she requires her lovers to do on her farm. A special role for a single woman was to go out on the community-work days to reward the workers with sex.

These days, marriage is the personal choice of both parties. Love is a primary factor, but women think of the hunting abilities of men and are concerned with their money-earning abilities.

The Canela have a number of marriage ceremonies, each securing the relationship more completely. They start with the interfamily hearings before and after virginity loss, which they call marriage. Later, the young wife's family "buys" the husband by carrying meat pies to his family's house. Still later, the wife takes her maturity belt to her female in-laws so they can paint it and her body red with urucu, in further acceptance of her.

The new wife had a brief "honeymoon" just after she gave her virginity to her husband, when she could be alone with him sexually. After 3–6 weeks, her classificatory husbands came asking her for sex, as this was their right. If she was too stingy, they arranged with her female kin for a special time and place when they could have sex with her in sequence to teach her the tribal lesson of generosity to all.

Both genders tend to remarry on the death of their spouses, but men do this more consistently than women do. When a woman dies, her family tries to retain her widower for their children by marrying him to one of them. The sororate is their preference. If a man dies, his widow undergoes a long period of mourning. The man who breaks her mourning has to stay with her, married, unless he pays a large fine.

HUSBAND–WIFE RELATIONSHIP

Most Canela couples have affection if not romantic love for each other, even though marriage is principally for raising children and family matters. Some young couples clearly have romantic love for each other. However, almost all Canela judicial hearings are about marital disputes. Considering that extramarital sex was extensive, we might expect that spouses were jealous of each other. At times they surely were, so that the uncles had to suppress their nephews' bad feelings. Nevertheless, I consider that the Canela cultural attitude of favoring fun, joy, and presenting oneself as a generous person has had a lot to do with keeping spousal relationships light-hearted and warm.

Spouses eat together with their children, apart from the rest of their hearth group. They also sleep together, though sometimes a baby or a child may be between them. Since the Canela way of life accentuates group living, amusements, sports, and festivities, couples are not together most of the time. However, they may bathe together, farm almost alone with each other for weeks, and occasionally take time for trysts in the savannahs. Spouses make certain decisions together, but the hearth-group leaders make some other decisions and the wife's brothers and uncles make still others. While there is a gender division of tasks, most tasks are interchangeable when necessary.

The Canela practice strict monogamy. In 1959, a married man who took the virginity of a young girl thereby became married twice. The other Canela teased him mercilessly, but he finally paid the girl's family almost everything he possessed to get out of his secondly marriage.

Until 1975, the elders and the chiefs of the tribe did not allow a man to leave his wife while they both had children growing up, except for very unusual reasons. Currently, young men leave their wives and children for simple matters—sex jealousy being the principal one. A woman may want her husband to leave because he drinks too much and becomes abusive while drunk, because he does not bring in enough meat, or because he does not treat her female kin respectfully. These days, either the husband or the wife can initiate divorce, but the wife rarely does this. After divorce, the children always remain with their mother, but she allows their father to visit them at any time.

OTHER CROSS-SEX RELATIONSHIPS

The aunt–nephew and uncle–niece relationships are the great joking institutions in Canela society, but this joking occurs only when the kinship is not immediate. Individuals related in this way feel that they have to joke sexually whenever they meet. Classificatory spouse relationships are similar unless the individuals happen to be living in the same house.

Informal friendship relationships involve lifelong camaraderie, but include playing practical jokes on each other as well as sexual humor. Women seldom became informal friends with men, and never with other women.

Primary formal friends carry out complete avoidance. They do not look each other in the eye and they scarcely speak to each other. They must come to each other's aid whenever necessary. They paint each other on ceremonial occasions and the survivor buries the other upon death. Women are involved in formal friendship relationships in the same way as men. These relationships are both same sex and cross sex.

The most serious consanguineal relationship is between uterine brothers and sisters. They respect each other and never joke, though they can carry out full communications. Classificatory opposite-sex siblings put names on one of each other's children of the same sex. This name-exchange relationship strengthens the tie between the classificatory siblings so that they are almost as close to each other as uterine siblings.

A naming uncle has a close relationship with his named-nephew. With the transferred set of names goes ceremonial membership in men's societies and rights to carry out certain ritual roles. While a naming aunt is equally close to her named-niece personally, she has little to pass on to her ceremonially.

CHANGE IN ATTITUDES, BELIEFS, AND PRACTICES REGARDING GENDER

I believe that in pre-pacification times, when a warrior's strength was vital, the Canela woman's position was considerably lower.

Nimuendajú writes only of men being made ceremonial chiefs. However, in 1966 I saw a husband and his wife made ceremonial chiefs together, and this has occurred regularly in later years.

The Festival of Oranges gives women a temporary leadership role. After the performance of one of these festivals during the mid-1990s, the first chief appointed the female leader to "permanent" status as a chief, but this position was not maintained by later chiefs.

These days the Canela even allow a talented female singer to chant around the village circle in the same style as men. I think that the elders would not have tolerated such behavior during the late 1950s.

The most conspicuous and significant general change over the decades is the loss of the control of the older generations over the younger ones. Thus the elders of today cannot, and do not, challenge the new initiatives of women, so women are succeeding in improving their status in relation to men.

NOTE

1. It would extend to an entire short longhouse, i.e., most cases today, and female power extends beyond most hearth units to the extended family in some situations, not all.

BIBLIOGRAPHY

Crocker, W. H. (1984). Canela marriage: factors in change. In K. Kensinger (Ed.), *Marriage practices in lowland South America* (pp. 63–98). Urbana: University of Illinois Press.

Crocker, W. H. (1985). Extramarital sexual practices of the Ramkokamekra-Canela Indians: An analysis of sociocultural factors. In P. Lyon (Ed.), *Native South Americans: Ethnology of the least known continent* (reissued ed., pp. 184–194). Prospect Heights, IL: Waveland Press.

Crocker, W. H. (1990). The Canela (Eastern Timbira), I: An ethnographic introduction. *Smithsonian Contributions to Anthropology, 33*. Washington, DC: Smithsonian Institution Press.

Crocker, W. H. (1994). Canela. In J. Wilbert (Ed.), *Encyclopedia of world cultures 7 (South America)* (pp. 94–98). New York: Hall.

Crocker, W. H. (2002). Canela "other fathers": Partible paternity and its changing practices. In S. Beckerman & P. Valentine (Eds.), *Cultures of multiple fathers: The theory and practice of partible paternity in lowland South America* (pp. 86–104). Gainesville, FL: University of Florida Press.

Crocker, W. H. & Crocker, J. G. (2004, forthcoming). *The Canela: Kinship* (Case Studies in Cultural Anthropology, G. Spindler Series Ed.) Belmont, CA: Wadsworth Thomson Learning.

Gregor, T. A. (1985). *Anxious pleasures: The sexual lives of an Amazonian people*. Chicago: University of Chicago Press.

Gregor, T. A., & Tuzin, D. (Eds.). (2001). *Gender in Amazonia and Melanesia: An exploration of the comparative method*. Berkeley: University of California Press.

Hemming, J. (1987). *Amazon Frontier: The defeat of the Brazilian Indians*. Cambridge, MA: Harvard University Press.

Mackay, J. (2000). *The Penguin atlas of human sexual behavior: Sexuality and sexual practices around the world*. Brighton, UK: Myriad.

Maybury-Lewis, D. (Ed.). (1979). *Dialectical societies: The Gê and Bororo of Central Brazil*. Cambridge, MA: Harvard University Press.

Nimuendajú, C. [Nimuendajú Ukel, Curt]. (1946). *The Eastern Timbira* (R. Lowie, Ed. & Trans.) (University of California Publications in American Archaeology and Ethnology, 41). Berkeley: University of California Press.

Schecter, S., & Crocker, W. H. (1999). *Mending ways: The Canela Indians of Brazil* [video]. Schecter Films/Smithsonian's Human Studies Film Archives. (Available from Films for the Humanities and Sciences, Princeton, NJ. Website: http://www.films.com/item.cfm?bin=9335.)

Suggs, D. N., & Miracle, A. (Eds.). (1999). Culture, biology, and sexuality. *Southern Anthropological Society Proceedings, 32*.

Cherokee

Mary Jo Tippeconnic Fox

ALTERNATIVE NAMES

The Cherokee are Iroquoian-speaking people and call themselves Ani-Yun'wiya, the principal people. Cherokee, the name, is most likely derived from the Choctaw word for them, Tsalagi, meaning people of the land of caves. The Delaware version of the name is Tallageni and the Creek version is Tsilki or Tciloki meaning people with different speech (Waldman, 1999).

LOCATION

The aboriginal homeland of the Cherokee is, today, the southern Appalachians of North America. Western North Carolina was the heart of their homeland, but the Cherokee also lived in South Carolina, northern Georgia, northeast Alabama, and eastern Tennessee. In 1838–39, the Cherokee were removed to Indian Territory (Oklahoma). The journey from their homelands to Indian Territory is referred to as the "Trail of Tears" (Perdue, 1989). Today, Cherokees live mainly in Oklahoma (Western Band) and North Carolina (Eastern Band).

CULTURAL OVERVIEW

The Cherokees were primarily farmers and hunters. They grew corn, beans, squash, pumpkins, sunflowers, and tobacco, and were skilled hunters of wild life such as deer, bear, rabbits, squirrels, and turkeys. Women were mainly responsible for the agriculture, and the men provided the meat. The society was matrilineal and matrilocal. The primary landholding unit was the household, and the crops produced from their fields went to the household. Households consisted of an extended family linked by women and usually included an elderly woman, her daughters and their children, the woman's husband, and unmarried sons. A husband and wife lived with the wife's family. The homesteads had several buildings including those for storage. Each household had a garden,

but most of the food came from large communal fields (Perdue, 1989).

The Cherokee lived in villages that often stretched for several miles along rivers and streams where they could farm and fish. Each village had a council house (town house) and plaza. The council house was a large circular building with walls constructed of interwoven saplings called wattle and covered with plaster substance of mud called daub. In the summer, the Cherokee lived in wooden shelters and in the winter in a conical house called *asi*, which had a hearth. Summer shelters were rectangular with peaked roofs, pole frameworks, cane and clay walls, and bark or thatch roofs. The *asi* or winter house was placed over a pit with a cone shaped roof of poles and earth. A wall of vertical logs for protection often surrounded the villages (Waldman, 1999).

CULTURAL CONSTRUCTION OF GENDER

The recognized gender categories were male and female. Kana'ti was the first man and Selu the first woman according to Cherokee tradition. Kana'ti provided meat for the family and Selu provided vegetables. The products from hunts were used for clothing and other household items. Cherokee women helped men dress skins and made them into clothing with bone needles. Traditional Cherokees wore little clothing with children wearing nothing at all. Men and women dressed similarly with short skirts and in the colder months added a skin cloak and moccasins. Both men and women wore jewelry of shells, bones, and copper. Capes from turkey and eagle feathers and bark were used for ceremonial purposes and feather headdresses. By the late 18th century, Cherokee women adopted the modest skirts, blouses, and shawls worn by Anglo-American women (Perdue, 1989).

Cherokee men and women had separate and distinct responsibilities. The tasks performed and the contributions of men and women were essential to the society and the integrity of the universe (Perdue, 1998). As Perdue (1998, p. 13) states:

Men did not dominate women, and women were not subservient to men. Men knew little about the world of women; they had no power over women and no control over women's activities. Women had their own arena of power, and any threat to its integrity jeopardized cosmic order. So it had been since the beginning of time.

Gender over the Life Cycle

Socialization of Boys and Girls

As soon as a child was born, the mother and other relatives took steps to form the child's personality and character. The mother's brothers and her other female relatives had the responsibility for the children. It was the family of the mother that controlled the lives of the children. A female child was considered the proper daughter of female relations. It was the maternal grandmothers or oldest female clan relative that named infant girls. Men assumed other responsibilities for clan children such as training and educating their sisters' sons. It was the uncles or mother's brothers who trained the boys to hunt and determined when they were old enough to go to war. The maternal uncles were the persons to whom the children owed their greatest respect. Each clan's specializations and customs moved through time and across generations in this way (Hill, 1997).

The relationship between parents and children was one of respect, which extended to aunts, uncles, nieces, and nephews. In kinship terms the relationships extended to all members of one's clan. If a child's parents died, clan members cared for the child. Mother was a social rather than a strictly biological role (Perdue, 1998).

Attainment of Adulthood

Once girls and boys learned the necessary skills to perform their roles in Cherokee society and they were of age, they became adults. Girls learned the necessary skills from their mothers and female clan members by helping in the fields and the household. Girls watched their female relatives and learned by example how to be mothers, sisters, daughter, storytellers and agriculturalists. Girls were taught the knowledge and skills needed to become a Cherokee women from the past, present, and for the future. They learned to make meals, baskets, clothing, pottery, and other household goods as well as gaining knowledge about plants, crops, seasons, and weather (Hill, 1997).

Some of the skills required of boys were to master the blowgun, bow and arrow, and fishnets to become hunters and warriors. Boys learned by example and observation. Traditionally, young men had to demonstrate martial skills and prove their valor to become a man though warfare or hunting.

Middle Age and Old Age

Middle-aged women cared for children, farmed, gathered firewood, carried water, and cooked food, as well as maintaining their households. Cherokees ate when hungry and did not have designated meals. Men of this age were hunters and warriors with clan uncles teaching sons of their sisters the skills needed to hunt and war. Older men were respected because of their valor in war or hunting and because of their age.

Postmenopausal women were held in high regard and performed tasks that required purity such as making the war ark that accompanied military expeditions, dancing–singing with the priests and warriors and delivering medicine to the ill during the Green Corn Ceremony. In addition, they brewed ceremonial medicine, nursed wounded warriors, and assisted with the purity rites of high priest. Elderly women, unable to perform heavy labor, helped in the fields by sitting on scaffolds and chasing away animals raiding the crops (Perdue, 1989). Both older women and men helped with the caring and education of children.

Gender-Related Social Groups

The basic kinship unit of the Cherokee was the clan, and lineage was traced through the woman (matrilineal). People belonged to the clan of their mother. Their relatives were those who could be traced through her, including siblings, maternal grandmother, maternal uncles, and maternal aunts. The children of maternal aunts were kin but those of maternal uncles were not. Children were not blood relatives of their father or grandfather. The total clan did not live together but the core members of a household belonged to the same clan.

Matters of kinship affected social interaction, demography, internal order, and foreign policy, which gave women status and power. The Cherokees of the 18th century had seven clans. The seven known clans were Anaiwahiya (Wolf), Anikawi (Deer), Anidjiskwa (Bird), Aniwodir (Paint), Anisahoni (Blue), Anigotigewi (Wild Potato), and Anigilohi (Twister) (Perdue, 1998). Most villages had members from each of the seven clans.

GENDER ROLES IN ECONOMICS

Men and women lived very separate lives. Women farmed, cared for children, cooked, made household goods, and performed other domestic chores. Men were hunters and warriors and helped the women occasionally with clearing fields, planting and harvesting. Women had status and economic power because corn was depended upon for subsistence, and it was the women who were the agriculturalists and owned the use of the fields. Access to land and crops came to men through the women. Also, Cherokee women coordinated the redistribution of produce for feasts and to aid those whose crops failed. In fact, during the 18th century Cherokee women held special dances to obtain crops for those in need.

The men were responsible for providing meat to the household, warfare, and foreign policy. Traditionally, Cherokee men hunted wild game such as deer, bear, and turkey. Hunting parties would often be gone for months. When not hunting, men spent much time playing games to improve coordination and to keep fit.

After contact with Europeans, economics came under control of warriors because deerskins and captives became trade items, and men were responsible for foreign policy. The 19th century brought the federal civilization policy which Cherokee women believed validated their role as farmers and expanded their responsibilities to animal husbandry, spinning, weaving, and sewing.

Many Cherokee men continued to hunt because it was one of the things that defined masculinity in their culture. As wildlife disappeared, Cherokee men restocked their hunting grounds with cattle and hogs. Horse stealing also became a substitute for war and a medium of exchange in the first decade of the 19th century (Perdue, 1995). In 1828, after 30 years of the civilization program, Cherokee men still had not fully adapted to farming. Throughout this time, men handled foreign policy and served as intermediaries between women and the federal government. Cherokee women and men adapted to new circumstances according to old definitions.

PARENTAL AND OTHER CARETAKER ROLES

The women tended to their children with the assistance of their extended families, which included mothers with children as well as older women. Child-rearing was a task shared with other Cherokee women. Cherokee children went to tend the fields with their mothers and if the child was old enough he or she helped with infants bound to cradleboards. Cherokees did not use physical punishment with disobedient children except a light scratching with thorns. Instead naughty children were shamed into good behavior by teasing (Perdue, 1989).

Civilization policies of the United States encouraged isolated nuclear families to replace extended kin groups and close-knit villages. The result was severed ties to the mother's brother and extended family that traditionally provided for divorced spouses and their children. Some of these children ended up in missionary schools.

LEADERSHIP IN PUBLIC ARENAS

In Cherokee society, the clan traditionally fulfilled the responsibilities of government through retribution and retaliation. Those of proven ability provided the leadership and men and women participated in decision-making.

Cherokee women held power within their families and within the village. In council, Cherokee women freely voiced their opinions as well as men. There was no shame attached to men who listened and severe public tongue-lashings to anyone who did not (Sattler, 1995). Issues were debated until a consensus was reached. A chief or national council did not rule the Cherokee until the 18th century. Men held these positions. At this time, each village had two chiefs, the White Chief or Most Beloved Man who helped make decisions concerning farming, lawmaking and disputes, and the Red Chief (who attained his rank through many victories) who gave advice about warfare (Waldman, 1999). It was a common language (three or four dialects), kinship system, and shared beliefs, not government, that unified the Cherokees of approximately 100 villages (Perdue, 1989).

One of the most serious issues a town council debated was whether or not to go to war. The reason for war was to avenge deaths of Cherokees who had been killed by an enemy, and the decision to participate in war was up to the individual. The council determined responsibility for fatalities and rallied support for a war party. War parties were made up of men, often with War Women to accompany them to cook and to carry water and firewood. Some of these War Women (Beloved Woman) distinguished themselves in battle and were responsible for captives. Children and female captives were often adopted, but warriors were usually killed (Perdue, 1989). It was importance to the Cherokee to seek vengeance for the death of a fellow tribal person to keep the world in balance. Families held the responsibilities associated with police and courts in today's society, and crime and punishment were understood in terms of kin and clan vengeance only. The matrilineal clan was the arbiter of justice (Perdue, 1998).

At the end of the 20th century, Cherokee women re-emerged onto the public stage. In 1985 Wilma Mankiller became the first Principal Chief of the Cherokee Nation in Oklahoma, and in 1995 Joyce Dugan became Principal Chief of the East Band of Cherokees in North Carolina. These women succeeded a series of men and were acclaimed for their service to community. They became chiefs because they embodied the values of generations for Cherokee women still honored and respected by men and women (Perdue, 1998).

GENDER AND RELIGION

Sustaining harmony was at the center of Cherokee religion. The Cherokee did not separate spiritual and physical realms, and they practiced their religion in private and public ceremonies. Purification rituals cured and prevented disease and prepare individuals for war, hunting, fishing, planting, childbirth and other activities. Most Cherokee dances honored spirits or commemorated important events while others were farcical. One of the most important ceremonies was the annual Green Corn Ceremony, which marked the social and spiritual regeneration of the community and redistribution of goods and produce. The role women played in this ceremony symbolized their role in Cherokee society. Selu was the first woman and the spirit of the corn. By honoring corn, respect was paid to Cherokee women. Villagers cleaned their houses and the council house, discarded any food and broken items from the preceding year, and extinguished old fires as gestures of renewal. Unhappy marriages were dissolved and all wrongs, except murder, were forgiven. Cherokee women presented new corn, prepared a feast,

and redistributed goods. The New Year began with order restored (Perdue, 1989). The ceremonies took place in the council houses or seven-sided temples (Waldman, 1999).

Cherokees believed that harmony and balance were necessary or disasters might occur such as droughts, storms, disease, or other disasters. It was their major purpose to keep everything in harmony and balance (Perdue, 1989). Traditional Cherokees did not have policemen or law courts, and it was up to the injured person or their clan to seek vengeance. Harmony also meant that nature was not to be exploited, which resulted in Cherokees never accumulating wealth.

Beliefs about purity and pollution explained Cherokee attitudes toward menstruation, childbirth, and menopause. They believed that the periodic contact with blood was powerful and dangerous. During menstruation blood was outside its appropriate place in the body and women had to take precautions such as retiring to menstruation huts, not participating in ceremonial activities, avoiding contact with the sick, or performing normal tasks. Cherokees believed that the power of blood would neutralize all the treatments of medicine people. Husbands also had regulations to observe, such as dancing behind others in ceremonial occasions and not having intercourse (Perdue, 1998).

When pregnant, a woman had to curtail many tasks such as not tending ceremonies, ball games, or visiting the sick. Cherokees did not eat foods prepared by pregnant women or walk on a path she traveled. In addition, foods eaten were restricted. There were also precautions for husbands such as not playing ball, dancing apart from other men in ceremonies, and not digging graves, loitering in doorways, or wearing hats with folds. Some evidence suggests that men did not hunt, fish, or fight during their wife's pregnancy (Perdue, 1998). These restrictions with ceremonies were to protect the baby and aid the mother's delivery.

Cherokee men went through rituals, which could last for days, that purified them before and after hunting or warfare. In war, the Cherokee believed that victory would happen only if they were spiritually pure. In hunting, the men apologized to the spirit of the animal for taking its life and never took more animals than needed. To do this could cause terrible things to happen such as disease (Perdue, 1989).

The distinct ways (menstruation, childbirth, hunting, and warfare) in which human blood was encountered helped to define women and men in Cherokee society.

Cherokees also believed in witchcraft. Witches were human beings with special powers used for evil purposes. Misfortune was attributed to witchcraft and conjurors (medicine people) were sought to counter the evil. Conjurors had a range of skills from naming a baby to resolving marital problems. The spiritual and physical realms were not separate and illnesses had spiritual causes and cures. Both men and women could be medicine people and conjure cures (Perdue, 1998).

In 1799, the Moravians sought permission to open a school both to civilize and to Christianize the Cherokees. Presbyterian, Baptist, and Methodist missionaries soon followed the Moravians. Many Cherokee accepted Christianity in the 18th century while others practiced traditional spirituality. Today, Cherokees continue to practice nonnative religions or traditional beliefs, and some do both.

LEISURE, RECREATION, AND THE ARTS

Women were the farmers, cooks, and manufacturers, and had little free time. What spare time they had was spent at the homestead with other women. Cherokee men were hunters and, when not hunting, they spent their time playing games to keep fit and improve their hunting skills. Some of these games were arrow-shooting contests, hurling sticks at a rolling stone, and stickball. Preparing to play stickball required the same rituals as going to war, which were fasting and scratching the skin. Villagers liked to watch these contests and often placed wagers on them (Perdue, 1989).

Crafts included plaited basketwork, stamped pottery, carved wood and gourds, masks (Booger masks represented evil spirits), and animal figure stone pipes (Waldman, 1999). The task of furnishing the house was the responsibility of women. Benches were crafted for sleeping and sitting from saplings, and baskets were made from river cane and strips of maple, oak, and honeysuckle. To decorate their baskets, the women created dyes from bloodroot, butternut, walnut, and other plants. Baskets had many uses and some had double layers to make them strong. Pottery was made from native clay and hardened in open fires, which darkened it (Perdue, 1989).

Men used bows and arrows, traps, blowguns, darts, hooks, and nets to hunt and fish. These had to be crafted by chipping flint, other stones, bone, and other materials.

RELATIVE STATUS OF MEN AND WOMEN

Kinship was traced solely through women and this gave them considerable prestige because kinship affected social interaction, demography, internal order, and foreign policy (Perdue, 1998). Kinship in Cherokee society was the clan. An entire clan did not live together but generally the households were quite large. A whole village could be made up near relatives. The only permanent members of the household were women, and husbands were considered outsiders. The brothers and sons of the female members had a permanent connection to the household. Occasionally, brothers challenged the domestic authority of their sisters, uncles, or nieces, but never their wives. Male presence in the household was irregular at best because husbands, brothers, and uncles belonged to different clans, which was awkward and caused conflict. Men made appearances at their homes and the houses of their wives but frequented communal sites (council house) in the company of other men. Besides, men were most likely hunting, at war, or in the council house (Perdue, 1998).

With Cherokees, relative age carried more weight than sex or gender in determining moral character. Maturity, reliability, and valued characteristics developed with seniority (Sattler, 1995). Demonstrated success in warfare, hunting, oratory, and similar activities contributed to prestige and personal power for men as well as age.

SEXUALITY

Within their clan system Cherokee women exercised considerable autonomy and sexual freedom. Some took partners for love and life, while others changed partners with ease and none suffered punishment for divorce or adultery. Both men and women enjoyed sexual freedom tempered by concern for the well-being of the society as a whole. Unmarried women controlled their sexuality as long as they observed the incest taboos and did not have intercourse with members of their own clan or those of their fathers. Married women also had sexual freedom. Husbands of unfaithful wives sometimes resorted to conjury, but most husbands ignored the infidelity or took another wife. Husbands that strayed caused considerable disharmony in the community (wife and her extended family) and were considered irreconcilable. Divorce and remarriage were the normal ways to resolve these sexual rivalries (Perdue, 1998).

Even though the construction of gender was rigid in Cherokee society, some men and women did cross the line by choice or circumstance. Both were anomalies, but only women acquired prestige by doing so. It is unclear, but men may have been ostracized or prompted jokes, which did not imply scorn but may have been used to recognize deviant behavior and incorporate it into the repertoire of acknowledged behavior (Perdue, 1998). In contrast, war parties often included women who carried water and prepared food, and in some cases became warriors (War Women or Beloved Women) if they distinguished themselves. They were exalted in political and ceremonial life, sat apart from other women and children at ceremonial events, and ate foods not normally given to women. Also, War Women decided the fate of captives, possessed extraordinary power through war and menstruation, and had male and female contact with blood.

COURTSHIP AND MARRIAGE

Embedded in the clan system was the regulation that clan members were forbidden to marry one another. To do otherwise was considered incestuous and carried a penalty of death. Marriages formed alliances among clans and guaranteed survival (Hill, 1997). It was the clans not the marriage that united Cherokees for life. Marriage was a family affair and a couple had to obtain consent from their relatives to marry. Relatives strongly encouraged marriage but never forced couples to marry against their will. Out of respect for their parents, children sometimes married someone they did not prefer.

If a couple wanted to marry, they would visit and make promises to each other. The couple's relatives would be notified of their commitment and, if there were no objections, the man cut cordings of wood to lie at the woman's door. If the young woman made a fire from the wood, it symbolized her acceptance and she would feed him. Publicly, the families reenacted the joining of the clans by building a fire from the wood provided and prepared a feast. This ritual signified the woman's willingness to be responsible for food and fire and the man's willingness to provide game (Hill, 1997).

In a Cherokee wedding, the couple step toward each other and meet in the middle of the council house. The groom presents venison, the bride presents corn, and their blankets are united. The ceremony symbolizes the centrality of tasks to the construction of gender (Perdue, 1998). In a society that is matrilocal and matrilineal, the couple live in the household of the mother, sisters, and her sister's husbands and children.

As a result of traders entering Cherokee country in the early 18th century, intermarriage occurred. The children from these unions were Cherokee as long the mother was Cherokee regardless of the race of the father. Yet, intermarriage upset the traditional Cherokee social organization because the woman lived in her husband's house; their children took the father's name and inherited the father's property, but affiliated with the mother's clan. In addition, the children often spoke English and Cherokee, received some education, and adopted the customs of Europeans (Perdue, 1998).

HUSBAND–WIFE RELATIONSHIP

Men and women lived very separate lives. Women farmed, cared for children, cooked, made household goods, and performed other domestic chores, while the men hunted and participated in warfare. Men at times helped in the fields but this was usually the responsibility of women. Since the society was matrilocal, the husband lived with his wife's extended family. The fields belonged to the matrilineage that used them, and they were inherited through maternal kin to succeeding generations of women.

Marriage of men to more than one woman (polygyny) of the same lineage, often sisters, was common and practical. In this case, the man did not have to divide his time between two households. Sororal polygyny was primarily practiced by Cherokees, which strengthen bonds among women and added to the status of women. No evidence of multiple husbands existed. If a marriage proved to be unsuccessful, the couple parted (divorced). This was preferred to not living in harmony. The man had no right to the property of his wife. If a spouse died, their partner had to observe a mourning period of no more than a year of seclusion before remarrying. Missionaries discouraged polygyny and the Cherokee National Council outlawed it in the 1800s (Perdue, 1998).

In Cherokee society, if a husband and wife divorced, the husband moved. The children always stayed with the mother because they were not related to their father. Yet, the children did know and respect their father. The man left his wife's house and returned to his mother's home. No stigma was attached to Cherokees who dissolved their marriages and later remarried.

OTHER CROSS-SEX RELATIONSHIPS

In Cherokee society, a special bond existed between sisters and brothers of the same clan. The brother had responsibility for his sister's children. In addition, all female clan members assisted with the raising of the children, and the uncle especially helped with the training of his sister's sons. Clan relations were extensive. Clan members always welcomed each other when traveling to other villages (Hill, 1997).

CHANGE IN ATTITUDES, BELIEFS, AND PRACTICES REGARDING GENDER

Europeans and their culture impinged upon the Cherokee in the 18th century when traders came into Cherokee country and eventually established year-round trading posts. Also, the crown and colonial governments called upon the Cherokee to form political alliances that became military alliances. Soon, Cherokees found themselves embroiled in wars. These developments impacted gender roles of the Cherokee, with trade and war elevating men above women. As hunters, the men provided the deerskins that become the currency of 18th-century Indian trade, and as warriors, they made the war alliances with Europeans. In addition, Europeans had their own construction of gender, which Cherokee women did not fit. They came to conduct men's business and expected women to remain on the periphery. This relationship between Cherokee men and the Europeans threatened to undermine the status of Cherokee women. As a result, Cherokee men became more central to life and livelihood, and women became more dependent on men for items wanted such as metal tools, pots, and fabrics. The focus was more on individual prowess than communal productivity. This shift in gender relationships grew out of the need to meet the challenges of European contact. Economic and political life moved toward individualism, hierarchy, and coercive power rooted in male culture. The status of Cherokee women was

jeopardized with the rise of warriors as a governing body delegating authority and power. Foreign policy was dominating Cherokee politics, and gender not kinship determined participation (Perdue, 1998).

By the end of the 18th century with a new government (United States) in place, the task was to civilize the Indians culturally into Anglo-Americans. The federal government led the effort to change Cherokee men into industrious republican farmers and women into chaste orderly housewives. It was the belief of the government that women in civilized societies belonged to men who headed the household and nation. This did not go well for Cherokee women as the remaining traditional divisions of labor were threatened. To civilize Cherokee men from hunters to farmers required the transformation of gender. Another motive for civilizing Cherokees was the notion that farming took less land, which would make land available for use by non-Cherokees. Some Cherokees believed that civilization was the best protection against removal. According to Perdue (1998), these Cherokees were the minority but they dominated Cherokee economics, political life, and history, with women mentioned incidentally.

In practice, the civilization program was adapted to the Cherokees' own expectations of men and women. The program was used to embellish the culture but it did not transform it. New crops such as cotton were added and new skills (spinning and weaving) learned. Yet, Cherokee women continued to farm, keep house, and tend children just as they always had. Hunting and warfare continued to be the basic ethic of men's culture. What the emerging civilized economy generated was native wealth, internal inequality, and problems never confronted before. As the 19th century ended, Cherokees were forced to face issues of individual ownership, state protection, legitimate enhancement, and inheritance (Perdue, 1998).

Some Cherokee men and women embraced change while others continued to adhere to traditional beliefs though they were impacted. Trade and war disrupted Cherokee lives in the 18th century, and the United States civilization programs restructured their lives in the 19th century.

Cherokees needed a more formal legal system in order to protect their holdings. Yet these laws of the new Cherokee Republic usurped the prerogatives of clans and undermined the principle of matrilineal kinship, especially those regarding property which replaced maternal blood ties with paternal material ties (leaving a husband's possessions to his wife). The Cherokee government also assumed responsibility for punishing murder and protecting a person's life by establishing a national police force. A sacred duty has passed from the matrilineal clan to a male council (Perdue, 1989).

A true national government was created which made the traditional town council obsolete. The town council was the venue for women's participation in government. These actions renounced blood vengeance. In 1827 the Cherokee wrote a constitution which provided for a General Council, a legislature, a National Council, and a National Committee. The Cherokee directly elected members of both houses but neither women nor descendants of African slaves could vote (Perdue, 1989).

The Cherokees established a national police force, reordered inheritance patterns, abolished clan vengeance, extended citizenship to descendants of intermarried white women, disenfranchised women, and made polygyny and infanticide illegal. Yet the evidence shows remarkable cultural persistence by some Cherokees, including women.

In 1838–39, the Cherokee were removed to Indian Territory in present-day Oklahoma. On the two journeys about 4,000 Cherokees died and others died upon arrival because of epidemics and a shortage of food. Other Cherokees hid in their homelands and were not removed. Women protested this removal as well as men. Allotment was forced on the Cherokee at the turn of the 20th century and Oklahoma became a state in 1907. Piece by piece, Indian lands were taken. In 1934, the policies of assimilation and allotment ended and tribes began to rediscover their cultural heritage. The 1950s brought termination, and Cherokees and other tribal peoples were encouraged to move to cities and join the economic mainstream. Since the 1960s, the federal government's policy has been self-determination which means Indian self-government and tribal identify (Waldman, 1999). All these federal policies have impacted the Cherokee and their gender identification.

Today, the Cherokee people are diverse, with some embracing traditions and language and others choosing a different path. The roles of men and women continue to be important for the survival of the Cherokee Nation.

REFERENCES

Hill, S. H. (1997). *Weaving new worlds: Southeastern Cherokee women and their basketry*. Chapel Hill: University of North Carolina Press.

Mankiller, W., & Wallis, M. (1993). *ManKiller: A chief and her people*. New York: St Martin Press.

Perdue, T. (1989). *The Cherokee*. New York: Chelsea House.

Perdue, T. (1995). Women, men and American Indian policy: The Cherokee response to "civilization." In N. Shoemaker (Ed.), *Negotiators of change: Historical perspectives on Native American women* (pp. 90–114). New York: Routledge.

Perdue, T. (1998). *Cherokee women: Gender and cultural change, 1700–1835*. Lincoln: University of Nebraska Press.

Sattler, R. (1995). Women's status among the Muskogee and Cherokee. In L. F. Klein & L. A. Ackerman (Eds.), *Women and power in Native North America* (pp. 214–229). Norman: University of Oklahoma Press.

Waldman, C. (1999). *Encyclopedia of Native American Tribes*. New York: Checkmark.

Chinese Americans

Xiaojian Zhao

LOCATION

Most early Chinese immigrants lived in Hawaii and California. In the early decades of the 20th century, the majority of Chinese Americans resided in segregated ethnic communities in urban areas, especially in the Chinatowns of San Francisco, Oakland, Los Angeles, and New York. After World War II most second-generation Chinese Americans moved out of Chinatown. Today, the state of California has the largest Chinese American population, followed by New York, Hawaii, Texas, New Jersey, Illinois, Washington, Florida, Virginia, and Massachusetts.

CULTURAL OVERVIEW

Chinese Americans, the largest Asian group in the United States since 1990, are Americans who or whose ancestors have come from China. Most of the early Chinese immigrants came directly from China. In recent decades, in addition to those from China, Hong Kong, and Taiwan, many immigrants of Chinese ancestry have also come from Southeast Asia and Latin America. There are many ethnic groups in China, but the immigrants in the United States are predominantly Han Chinese.

Chinese immigrants began to arrive in California shortly before the Gold Rush in 1849. By the time the United States enacted the Chinese Exclusion Act in 1882, about 125,000 Chinese lived in the United States; the majority of them resided on the West Coast. In addition, about 50,000 Chinese landed in Hawaii between 1852 and 1900. The Chinese who came to California during the Gold Rush were mostly independent laborers or entrepreneurs. After gold mining declined, they worked to construct the western half of the first transcontinental railroad. They also contributed to the early development of agriculture in the Pacific Northwest and light manufacturing industries in California. A significant number of Chinese specialized in laundry businesses, although washing clothes was not a traditional occupation for men in China.

More than 90% of the early Chinese immigrants were men who did not bring their wives and children with them. Before 1870, most female Chinese immigrants were young women who were imported to the United States and forced into prostitution. Chinese prostitutes were most visible in western cities and mining towns.

As the western population increased, the presence of Chinese laborers aroused great antagonism among European workers. Gradually Chinese workers were forced to leave their jobs in manufacturing industries. Harassment and mob violence also forced Chinese farm laborers to move to Chinatowns in San Francisco and other large cities.

In 1882 the Chinese Exclusion Act was enacted, which suspended Chinese immigration for 10 years (the law was extended twice in 1892 and 1902, and it was made permanent in 1904). During the exclusion, the only Chinese who could legally enter were members of the exempted classes: merchants, students, teachers, diplomats, and tourists. Later, Chinese who had left the country to visit their families in China were not allowed to reenter. Because there were few Chinese women in the United States and interracial marriage was illegal at the time, it was almost impossible for most of the Chinese immigrants to have families.

Largely isolated in segregated ethnic neighborhoods in urban America, Chinese Americans formed many associations based on kinship, native places, and economic and political interests. Two most important immigrant organizations are clan and district associations. These associations had a great impact on the day-to-day lives of the Chinese Americans before World War II. Hierarchically above the clan and district associations was the Chinese Consolidated Benevolent Association, which provided leadership for the entire community. Another important organization, the Chinese American Citizens Alliance (CACA), was organized by Chinese Americans who were born in the United States.

During World War II, a large number of Chinese American men and women served in the U.S. military or found employment in defense industries. For the first time in the 20th century, they had the opportunity to work outside Chinatowns. In 1943, all the Chinese exclusion acts were repealed. The repeal changed the status of alien Chinese from "inadmissible" to "admissible," although a quota of only 105 per year was allocated to Chinese.

Legislation after the war helped the growth of Chinese American families. The 1945 War Brides Act allowed the admission of alien dependents of World War II veterans without quota limits. This privilege was extended to fiancées and fiancés of war veterans in an Act of June 1946. The Chinese Alien Wives of American Citizens Act of August 1946 further granted admission outside the quota to Chinese wives of American citizens. As women constituted the majority of the new immigrants and many families were reunited, the sex ratio of the Chinese American population underwent a significant change. In 1940 there were 2.9 Chinese men for every Chinese woman in the United States. By 1960 this ratio was reduced to 1.35 to 1.

The 1965 Immigration Act established a new quota system and the principle of family unification. In the late 1960s and the 1970s, Chinese immigrants came largely from Taiwan and Hong Kong. After the United States recognized the People's Republic of China in 1979, China became a major source country of immigrants. In addition, immigrants of Chinese ancestry also entered the United States as refugees from Vietnam and other Southeast Asian countries. A very high percentage of Chinese American women worked outside the home in garment industries, restaurants, and domestic services.

CULTURAL CONSTRUCTION OF GENDER

Gender differences were specified in Confucian classics. Accordingly, men and women, like Heaven and Earth, should occupy their correct places. The *Book of Rites*, which sets rules of correct behaviors, stated that to be a woman meant to submit. Confucian ideology was the basis for gender-specific norms and expectations, which remained unchanged until the establishment of the People's Republic of China in 1949.

In traditional Chinese society, family was continued through male descendent lines. Only sons had the right to inherit family property, and the head of the house was always male. At marriage a woman would move from the house of her father to that of her husband. Her primary obligation was to bear sons, providing for the continuation of her husband's family. Patrilineal inheritance and patrilocal marriage were the foundation of a patriarchal society that subordinated women to men. Although the process of immigration led to changes in the family unit, traditional norms, customs, and practices had a great impact on the lives of Chinese Americans.

Chinese girls usually wore long loose dresses to avoid their body being seen in public. In the summer boys could be seen stripping down to their waist, but the girls had to remain fully clothed, with their body parts, except hands and heads, properly covered. It was improper for girls to wear short pants or dresses that would show off their legs or shoulders. The practice of footbinding, which applied to girls only, further differentiated men from women in their appearance. Small feet were associated with family status and beauty; it was an essential prerequisite for an advantageous marriage. Most immigrant women who came in the late 19th centuries had bound feet, but footbinding was not practiced by the immigrants in the United States. Footbinding was outlawed in China in 1911.

GENDER OVER THE LIFE CYCLE

According to the Chinese Classic for Girls (*Nü er Jing*), the ideal qualities of women over the life-cycle is the "three obediences and four virtues." The "three obediences" prescribe that a Chinese woman obeys the authority of her father when young, her husband when married, and her sons when widowed. The four virtues required her to behave in total compliance with the rules, speaking properly, knowing her place, and performing her domestic duties.

A girl learned at a very young age that she would eventually marry and move to another household. To a large extent she was raised to become the wife of a stranger and daughter-in-law of another family. Marriage was the most important event in a Chinese woman's life; it entailed the transformation of a young girl to a mature woman. A successful marriage would provide the woman with security and happiness.

If marriage marked a girl's passage to womanhood, it was also the beginning of the most difficult phase over her life cycle. In rural China parents usually arranged blind marriages for their children. It was common for a young woman to marry a man whom she had never met until the day of their wedding. The marriage arrangement usually included a payment from the groom's family to the bride's family. By paying a "bride price" the groom's family reimbursed her family for the expense of raising her. Through the marriage ceremony the bride left her own family, gave up all the protections and affectionate ties that she had been accustomed to, and entered the family of her husband. The woman was expected to assume obligations that include domestic labor, child-bearing, and child-rearing under the supervision of her mother-in-law.

It was not unusual for a Chinese man to take concubines and he could divorce his wife, but the movements of a married woman were closely watched by the husband's family. It was almost impossible for a woman to escape from an unhappy marriage. Even after the death of the husband, she would still be expected to remain faithful to him and his family. The traditional Chinese society honored faithful wives and encouraged the ideals of lifelong widowhood and widow suicide. If she remarried, a widow had no right over her children or her husband's property. Her deceased husband's family might even request a payment of "bride price" from her new husband's family.

A woman began to gain some status and respect in her husband's family after she gave birth to a son. As the mother she had some control of child-rearing and played an important role in making arrangements for her children's marriages. When she became a mother-in-law she had the power to supervise wives of her sons.

However, immigration broke the system of traditional family structure. Few Chinese American women shared the same roof with their parents-in-law. Since the immigrant man did not have affectionate ties with members of his family, the conjugal relationship between husband and wife strengthened. Working outside the home helped improve immigrant women's positions within the family. She was consulted on major family decisions, and she usually had the authority of supervising daily activities of the children.

Before World War II, most American-born Chinese women attended school. After the war, an increasing number of them received a college education and were economically independent. This new generation of Chinese American women challenged traditional norms and concepts, and most of them would not let their parents select marriage partners for them.

Socialization of Boys and Girls

The birth of a girl was less welcomed than that of a boy by families in traditional Chinese society, because the status of women was low in the patrilineal and patrilocal kinship system. In a traditional Chinese family, the sons had a permanent place in the house and could inherit family property, because they would carry on the family line. Daughters, who would eventually leave their own families at marriage, were not permanent members of their parents' house. Their place in the family was secondary compared with that of their brothers. Matrilocal marriage, in which the husband settled in the wife's family home on marriage, was negotiated under unusual circumstances, often in cases when the bride's family had no male offspring.

Chinese parents had different expectations for their daughters and sons. Only at a very young age could Chinese girls play with their brothers or other village boys. Like the boys, young girls would run in the fields, climb trees, or catch bugs. But as they got older, the girls were reminded that they were different from boys. While boys were praised for their physical strength, girls were discouraged for any boyish behaviors. Young girls were taught to walk slowly and speak softly. It was improper for them to run with their brothers and get muddy.

The practice of footbinding, which can be traced back to as early as the 10th century and was outlawed in the beginning of the 20th century, was widely practiced for a few hundred years among girls of all families except the poorest and certain ethnic groups. Parents would tightly wrap the feet of their young daughters with bandages to compress and restrict the growth to a few inches in length. Big feet were thought to be a sign of poor breeding.

Girls with bound feet had difficulties in playing with their brothers outside the house. They could not run or walk fast. While their brothers attended school or helped out in the fields with their fathers, the girls stayed at home under the supervision of their mothers.

A very small number of girls, mostly from gentry families, did learn to read, but until the late 19th century tutoring for girls was mostly accomplished at home. Not until the early 20th century did an increasing number of Chinese girls gain access to missionary schools or public schools for girls. As most of these schools were located in large cities, the majority of the girls in rural

China remained illiterate during the first half of the 20th century.

The early Chinese immigrants also favored sons over daughters. Though girls who grew up in the United States before World War II were taught proper behaviors according to Chinese tradition and were expected to perform domestic duties, few were confined to home. Footbinding was abolished in China in 1911 and was rarely practiced by the immigrants in the United States. Most Chinese American girls played games with their brothers at home and with classmates in school. Beginning in the early decades of the 20th century, traditional gender concepts were the subject of criticism within the Chinese American community. Even the most conservative immigrant parents found it impossible to confine their daughters to domesticity, and attempts at arranged marriages were often rejected. At school, church, and workplace, young Chinese American men and women had greater opportunities to socialize, and the majority of Chinese American men and women enjoyed the freedom of selecting their own marriage partners.

Puberty and Adolescence

In traditional Chinese society, young girls could be married off shortly after puberty. Once they reached adolescence, girls were usually confined to domesticity, while their brothers would join their fathers to work in the field. Farming and construction were jobs for men. Sewing, embroidering, washing, cooking, cleaning, or feeding family livestock were female-specific chores. Although washing was usually done in the river and occasionally adolescent girls were sent out to buy merchandise from peddlers, these activities took place near the home. Usually, adolescent girls would not have much contact with men outside the family. Socialization between adolescent boys and girls was disapproved. In Southern China, women sometimes worked in the rice fields during the busy transplanting and harvest seasons, but their work in agriculture was subsidiary, and their activities in the fields were supervised by male family members. Only after the Communist revolution in 1949 did large numbers of women join agricultural and industrial labor force.

Attainment of Adulthood

Marriage marked the passage to adulthood for both men and women. After the marriage ceremony a woman moved from the household of her father to the household of her husband. As a girl her hair was braided into one or two pigtails. Once married, a chignon replaced the pigtails. She was no longer under the protection of her parents. Supervised by her mother-in-law she was expected to do domestic work and give birth to heirs of her husband's family.

Upon marriage a boy entered manhood. No longer sharing rooms with his brothers, he and his young wife occupied a quarter of his parents' house. A married man was expected to take family responsibilities and provide for his wife and children. He would join his father and other adult male members of the family in business dealings and decision-making.

Before a young man's journey to America, his parents would usually find a wife for him. It was believed that a married man would be more responsible to his family. The new wife stayed in the village taking care of her children and parents-in-law. When the husband settled down in America, he wanted to send for his wife and children. However, after 1882 harsh laws were passed in the United States which made it extremely difficult for the Chinese women to immigrate. As a result, a large number of early Chinese immigrants had transnational families.

GENDER-RELATED SOCIAL GROUPS

Patrilineal inheritance and patrilocal residence were the foundation of patriarchy society. This social structure made women dependent on men. A married woman's subordination to her husband was reinforced through his kinship, which imposed various economic and social restrictions on her.

In the United States, a young man was away from his parents and free from the control of his kin. Instead of seeking advice from the elders of his family, the man consulted his wife on business and family matters. In a family-operated small business, the wife was the husband's indispensable partner. If the man worked as a laborer, his wife would most likely bring money home from her job in a garment shop. Their daughters and sons had equal rights as heirs according to the laws in the United States. The daughters went to school and gained independence economically; they stayed close to home after marriage. The aged immigrant couple helped care for grandchildren—children of their sons and daughters. The daughters assumed the same responsibility as the sons in taking care of their old parents.

GENDER ROLES IN ECONOMICS

One of the central features of the patriarchal Chinese society is the division of labor between men and women. In rural China, men primarily worked outside the home; they provided agricultural labor and brought food to the family. Women primarily worked inside the home. In addition to child-bearing and child-rearing, they cooked, washed, and tended livestock. Peasant women sometimes helped in the fields during the rice transplanting and harvest seasons, but their work was done under the supervision of male family members. The division of labor between men and women did not change until 1949.

Immigration changed the structure of the patriarchal family. Many women stayed in China for many years after their husbands left for America. In the absence of their husbands and other male members of the family, these women became heads of their families. In addition to domestic responsibilities, they delegated and supervised the work of the hired farmhands and made day-to-day decisions. Women in families that could not afford to hire farm laborers had to till the land themselves. When the Japanese military forces invaded China in the 1930s and 1940s, many peasant families went into hiding. Some women took their children to live with their own parents. They also looked for work outside the home. Some immigrants' wives engaged in trade and other business activities in China.

In rural China it was unusual for men to perform domestic tasks. Once in the United States, however, they had to avoid competition with European Americans and make a living in whatever trade was available. Some male Chinese immigrants took traditional women's jobs and operated laundry businesses, even though they had never washed their own clothes in China. In towns and cities in the American West, where women were few in the 1860s and 1870s, some Chinese men worked as domestic servants.

Wives who joined their husbands in America usually worked outside the home. Before World War II, most of them worked as seamstresses, shopkeepers, or domestics. Women's participation in the labor force helped improve their social status. When they became income providers, their importance within the household was elevated. Married women still had to work at home for most

child-rearing, cooking, and washing, but it became common for Chinese American men to share household responsibilities with their wives.

PARENTAL AND OTHER CARETAKER ROLES

As parents, the roles played by Chinese men and women were different. The job of a father was to bring food to his family. Because he worked outside the house, the time he spent with his children was limited. The mother was in charge of the activities inside the house; she took care all the needs of young children.

When sons were old enough, the father would teach them different types of agricultural skills. The father also made decisions regarding his children's education, although sometimes with input from his wife. Some men of gentry families tutored their children, including daughters, at home.

Except in the area of education, a father spent little time with his daughters. It was the mother's duty to teach a daughter proper behaviors and domestic tasks. She would set the rules for the daughter, making decisions on when and how to bind the girl's feet and how to limit her activities. To keep a daughter from public observation by confining her inside the house was an important means of securing her marriageability.

Parents believed that it would be shameful for unmarried boys and girls to think or talk about selecting marriage partners; they took it as their duty to make marriage arrangements for all their children.

Immigrant women often took jobs that could accommodate their household responsibilities, which allowed time to take care of the children. An immigrant mother would try to instill in her daughter traditional concepts about women's proper place, but confinement of the daughters became increasingly difficult. As the daughters entered high school or college, it became impossible for the mothers to watch their comings and goings.

LEADERSHIP IN PUBLIC ARENAS

The traditional Chinese society was a male-dominated society where men usually occupied leadership positions in the political arena. The immigrants carried this tradition to the United States. Before World War II, men dominated almost all major Chinese American community organizations. Most of the organizations did not accept female members.

Starting in the 1920s, an increasing number of Chinese American women became active in the public arena. They participated in community work, organized their own clubs, joined the labor movement, and involved in politics in both China and the United States. They made important contributions to the war effort in China against Japanese military invasion in the 1930s. Many Chinese American women joined the U.S. military and took jobs in defense industries during World War II. Beginning in the 1970s, a small number of Chinese American women also held important political posts.

RELATIVE STATUS OF MEN AND WOMEN

Because sons were favored over daughters, boys and girls had different status within the family. Before public schools became available in China, opportunities for education were mostly for boys. When a family or kin group decided to send a member overseas, the person selected was usually male. Except for the prostitutes and slave girls of the late 19th century, before 1950 most Chinese women immigrants came to the United States as dependents of their fathers or husbands. Only after 1965 did Chinese American women with U.S. citizenship gain the privilege of sponsoring their own partners, parents, and siblings.

Because few of them were gainfully employed outside the home before coming to the United States, the status of women within the family was low. A male head of the family was usually the decision-maker. However, a married woman did have some control over her children. She supervised the young children's daily activities, taught the daughters proper behaviors and domestic skills, and worked to arrange the children's marriages when they were older. Once she raised her son to maturity and found him a wife, she became the mother-in-law of the new wife and could exercise supervisory power over her.

The status of Chinese women greatly improved after they were able to work outside the home, in both China and the United States. As immigrants, women often had to work outside the home and contribute to the family income, which also helped improve their status within the family. Many immigrant women became business partners of their husbands; their labor and earnings were indispensable to their family.

The custom of patrilocal residence was no longer practical once the immigrants came to America; this helped improve the mother–daughter relationship. Mutual support between immigrant women and their daughters helped the younger generation of Chinese American women to have a career and family at the same time.

SEXUALITY

Confinement of young women was an important means for parents to regulate their daughters' sexuality in traditional Chinese society. Virginity was very much associated with a young woman's marriageability. Adolescent girls were strictly forbidden to mix with the opposite sex, but no such restriction was applied to adolescent men. While married women were also required to stay close to home, their husbands could enjoy greater freedom of movement. Concubinage was an accepted practice in China until 1950. However, to avoid disapproving gossip, a married woman would not want to form any friendship with men outside her own family.

Immigrant parents were concerned about protecting their daughters' virginity. However, maintaining control over their daughters' comings and goings was difficult in the United States. Strict parents were only confronted with stronger resistance from their daughters. Once in college, young Chinese Americans were free from parental supervision. Influenced by their peers and American culture, they rejected traditional moral standards on women's sexuality.

COURTSHIP AND MARRIAGE

In traditional Chinese society marriage was virtually universal for men and women. Chinese girls were usually married off shortly after puberty by arranged blind marriage. The brides and grooms often took no part in selecting their own partners. Negotiating the "bride price" and other financial transactions, setting a date for the wedding, and deciding how the marriage ceremony would be conducted were the jobs of the family elders.

The practice of blind marriage arrangement left no room for courtship. It was believed that love could only be created between husband and wife after their marriage. To have love before they were married was wrong. It was common for a couple not to meet each other until they wed.

In the early decades of the 20th century, better education for the young in China brought challenges to the custom of arranged marriage. In the United States, children of Chinese immigrants also rejected this traditional practice.

Husband–Wife Relationship

An old Chinese proverb says, "A woman married to a rooster has to follow the rooster, and a woman married to a pig has to follow the pig." Once married, a woman in traditional Chinese society was expected to obey her husband and remain faithful to him and his family. The husband and wife ate and slept together, but they had different responsibilities in the family. He labored outside the house with other male members of the family, while she worked inside the house under the supervision of her mother-in-law. They were not to show affection to each other in public. When the husband traveled, the wife usually stayed at home performing domestic duties.

Concubinage was accepted, especially if the wife failed to give birth to a son. The wife and the concubine might have lived in the same house in separate quarters. The concubine did not have the status as a wife and was sometimes treated as a servant. A concubine of a wealthy man might have lived in a separate house. Only after she gave birth to a son could a concubine gain some status in the family.

It was almost impossible for a woman to escape an unhappy marriage. Widows were encouraged not to remarry and to remain faithful to the families of their husbands.

As the 20th century progressed, marriage by free choice was advocated in China. Opportunities to attend school away from home helped young men and women escape blind marriage arrangements. The marriage law of 1950 in the People's Republic of China abolished the custom of arranged "buying and selling" marriage and prohibited concubinage and polygyny. It also gave women the right to sue for divorce and protected widows' rights to remarry.

Few early Chinese immigrants had the opportunities to select their own marriage partners, but in America the husband was away from his family and kin, making it possible for him and his wife to form close relationship. Most children of the immigrants denounced blind marriage arrangements and sought marital relationship based on love, affection, and companionship.

Change in Attitudes, Beliefs, and Practices Regarding Gender

The traditional patriarchal Chinese society made women inferior to men. Through the practice of footbinding and the customs of patrilineal inheritance and patrilocal residence, women were confined to domesticity and became dependents of men at different stages of their lives. Not until after the establishment of the People's Republic of China in 1949 did large numbers of Chinese women enter the public arena and join the labor force. They also gained rights to select their own marriage partners and to get a divorce.

Changes in attitudes toward women also occurred after immigrants came to the United States. Immigration changed the traditional family structure and allowed Chinese women a greater degree of freedom and independence. Away from the patriarchal kin, Chinese American couples were able to strengthen the relationship between them, and the opportunity to work outside the home helped improve women's status in the family. Children of Chinese immigrants challenged traditional gender concepts and made it difficult for traditional practices such as arranged marriage to continue. As more and more women demonstrated that they were no longer dependents of men, the relationship between mothers and daughters also underwent significant changes.

Bibliography

Croll, E. (1995). *Changing identities of Chinese women: Rhetoric, experience, and self-perception in the twentieth century.* Hong Kong: Hong Kong University Press.

Ono, K. (1989). *Chinese women in a century of revolution, 1850–1950.* Stanford, CA: Stanford University Press.

Yung, J. (1995). *Unbound feet: A social history of Chinese women in San Francisco.* Berkeley: University of California Press.

Zhao, X. (2002). *Remaking Chinese America: Immigration, family, and community, 1940–1965.* New Brunswick, NJ: Rutgers University Press.

Chipewyan

Robert Jarvenpa

ALTERNATIVE NAMES

In their own northern Athapaskan language the Chipewyan refer to themselves as *Dene* ("the people"). "Chipewyan" itself derives from the language of neighboring Cree Indians who used the term as a pejorative reference to the pointed tail-like caribou-skin ponchos worn by Dene men. In vernacular English, the abbreviation "Chip" has become a common expression of self-identity. Several major regional groups of Chipewyan have been known historically, including the *Etthen eldili dene* ("caribou eater people") along the forest–tundra transition west of Hudson Bay, the *T'atsanottine* ("copper people" or Yellowknives) in the forest–tundra zone east of Great Slave Lake and Great Bear Lake, the *Kkrest'ayle kke ottine* ("dwellers among the quaking aspens") in the full boreal forest between Great Slave Lake and Lake Athabasca, and the *Thilanottine* ("dwellers at the head of the lakes") in the full boreal forest near the headwaters of the Churchill River (J. G. E. Smith, 1975, 1981). Some persisting regional group or band identities derive from early fur trade associations, such as the *Kesyehot'ine* ("aspen house people"), those southern Chipewyan who began trading with Europeans at Ile à la Crosse (a fort built of aspen logs) in the late 18th century (Jarvenpa, 1980).

LOCATION

Geographically and demographically the Chipewyan are the largest of the northern Athapaskan groups with approximately 10,000 people of federally enrolled Treaty status, but there are many others of Chipewyan ancestry and cultural background who lack federal recognition. Most Chipewyan live in or near 16 major communities distributed between Hudson Bay to the east, Great Slave Lake and the Athabasca River to the west, and the Churchill River to the south. This region of subarctic boreal forest and tundra is roughly the size of Texas and embraces the northern sections of the provinces of Manitoba and Saskatchewan, northeastern Alberta, and adjacent portions of the Northwest Territories in north-central Canada.

CULTURAL OVERVIEW

Chipewyan culture is profoundly influenced by these peoples' historical experience as subarctic hunter–fishers. An adaptation to hunting herds of barren-ground caribou (*Rangifer tarandus groenlandicus*) which migrate long distances across the forest–tundra ecotone involves strategies of mobility, scheduling, and communication over immense territories. Those Chipewyan groups which moved southward with the expanding fur trade in the late 18th century retained aspects of this basic hunting economy while also learning to exploit moose (*Alces alces*), woodland caribou (*Rangifer tarandus caribou*), and other resources more common in the full boreal forest. The southern Chipewyan also developed complex interethnic relations, both positive and negative, with neighboring Western Woods Cree groups and with the "mixed-blood" or Métis peoples who occupied a niche as servants and laborers in the fur trade industry (Brumbach & Jarvenpa, 1989).

The prevailing social organization of the Chipewyan has been the *band*, that is, a geographically mobile community of closely related kin which is relatively egalitarian, politically autonomous and marked by short-term de facto leadership rather than formal centralized authority. Regional bands were rarely face-to-face communities except for short durations at summer fishing stations or, as became increasingly common in the 19th and early 20th centuries, at Hudson's Bay Company trade gatherings and at French Roman Catholic mission assemblages. For the bulk of the year between fall freeze-up and spring break-up Chipewyan were scattered in local bands, small clusters of five to ten interrelated families (about 20–50 people). These *eyana'de* or "winter staging communities" (also referred to as "hunting units" or "hunting groups") were distributed over vast territories and served as points for further dispersal into winter hunting teams. In the early 1900s, for example, the *Kesyehot'ine*, a regional band of about 150 people, ranged over 49,700 km^2, an area the size of West Virginia (Jarvenpa, 1998; Jarvenpa & Brumbach, 1988).

Bilateral kinship ties, that is, tracing descent from both father's and mother's relatives, were important in the formation of the winter staging communities. For example, the families were often linked to one another by sibling relationships (often brother–sister ties) and by parent–child relationships (often parent–daughter bonds) (Irimoto, 1981). At the same time, most people had some close relatives in their *silot'ine*, or "personal bilateral kindred," scattered across a number of *eyana'de* or winter communities in a region. Activating such ties was a means of gaining access and residency in these other communities, an important form of social insurance during times of food shortage, illness, and other stressful events.

Some Chipewyan have retained a remarkable degree of geographical mobility despite political–economic changes ushered in by federal treaty provisions in the early 20th century and a new era of settlement nucleation, service centralization, and wage labor emerging after World War II. In this context, the notion of a mobile "bush" life-style takes on added weight as a primordial characteristic of Chipewyan culture and identity. The seasonal exchange of trapping camp for fishing camp, long-distance travel by water routes and forest trails, and the eating of freshly procured caribou, moose, or whitefish are not simply mundane activities. These are among the most highly valued cultural experiences. Moreover, a delicate material–spiritual symbiosis between humans and food animals is a fundamental means of interpreting causality. For example, there is a tendency to interpret major historical changes in animal distribution or abundance as withdrawals or withholdings due to flagrant "disrespect" by hunters. One's ability to hunt, to cure illness, and to engage in sorcery is affected by the state of one's "supernatural" knowledge and power, or what the Chipewyan term *inkonze* (Jarvenpa, 1998; D. M. Smith, 1973).

CULTURAL CONSTRUCTION OF GENDER

Chipewyan gender ideology flows from the basic distinction between man (*deneyu*) and woman (*ts'ekwi*), or between male (*deyani*) and female (*ts'udai*). Traditional clothing was the most overt visual signal of gender roles. Men wore hoodless thigh-length caribou skin ponchos with distinctive points or "tails" in front and back over their leggings and moccasins. Women wore knee-length or ankle-length caribou skin dresses over their leggings and footgear (Oswalt & Neely, 1996; J. G. E. Smith, 1981). With the introduction of textiles and other trade goods, clothing became more westernized in the 19th and 20th centuries. In recent decades the apparel of Chipewyan men and women has resembled that of general rural and working-class Canadians. However, certain items of clothing are still made by Chipewyan women from locally procured furbearers and from the hides of moose and caribou. For special occasions, men may wear fancy beaded moosehide vests and coats. Footwear continues to serve as a visible gender marker, particularly for elderly Chipewyan. Women wear low-cut moosehide moccasins decorated with open beadwork designs, for example, while men wear high-cut moccasins with prominent ankle flaps and toepieces covered with solid beadwork panels of floral or geometric design. Moreover, unadorned moosehide work moccasins worn inside rubber boots are ubiquitous apparel for men working in the bush (Jarvenpa, 1980).

Oral lore and linguistic conventions continually draw a symbolic boundary between men and women. These include proverbs commonly recited in a jesting fashion by the opposite sex when observing others engaged in some strenuous activity. Thus a man butchering a moose or caribou who cannot remove a hindquarter or forequarter with one well-placed cut from his knife is judged "not ready for marriage." More ominously, a wife who pokes a hole in the thin-cut sheets when preparing smoke-dried meat is deemed fit to be "killed by her husband" (Jarvenpa, 1999).

Similar tensions and contradictions are expressed in more complex fashion in folklore. The battles of the magician Labidsas with an elderly Cree medicine woman and his eventual killing of her may be interpreted as a commentary on both Chipewyan–Cree and male–female conflict. Yet, the tale of Betsuneyenelshai ("his grandmother raised him"), a diminutive Chipewyan culture hero who proves his prowess to an old woman who adopts him, reveals the durability and resilience of women and underscores the complementarity of male and female roles as part of a comprehensive system of hunting. In their own origin myth, the Chipewyan people were borne of a union between a primeval woman and a dog-like creature. Also noteworthy as both a symbolic and literal commentary on the fortitude of Chipewyan women is the tale of Thanadelther, an early 18th century female Chipewyan captive among the Cree who helped Hudson's Bay Company traders negotiate a peace between Chipewyan and Cree groups competing for access to the fur trade at York Factory (Brumbach & Jarvenpa, 1989; Jarvenpa, 1998).

Gender differences are encloded in the physical landscape as well. In some Chipewyan settlements log smoking caches (*loretthe kwae*) are de facto women's spaces. Generally, each female head of a family household manages the smoke drying and storage of meat and fish in one of these detached structures. Located within 10–20 m of her family's dwelling, the same cache also serves as a center for safekeeping important pieces of a woman's personal processing gear such as pounding stones for pemmican, hide-making toolkit bundles, stretching racks, hatchets, knives, and babiche cordage (Jarvenpa & Brumbach, 1995).

By the same token, somewhat larger log storehouses or storage sheds (*t'asi thelakoe*) are implicitly men's spaces. Also located within 10–20 m of the family dwelling, each male head of a household generally maintains his own storehouse for protecting and occasionally repairing his personal hunting equipment— traps, snares, axes, rifles, outboard motors, and related gear. A key behavioral distinction is that men's spaces serve basically as storage for gear which is deployed or activated by men outside the village in distant, non-village, or bush settings. Women's spaces, by contrast, signal both storage and active use of gear by women for processing food animals in the village landscape (Jarvenpa & Brumbach, 1999).

GENDER OVER THE LIFE CYCLE

Socialization of Boys and Girls

Prior to adoption of European Canadian practices, the Chipewyan life cycle was unadorned by ritual observances. Families were limited to two or three children with births spaced several years apart. Young boys (*deneyuaze*) and girls (*ts'ekwaze*) alike became useful working members of the family and camp at an early age, fetching water and firewood, and helping carry supplies on trails and portages, among other chores. While girls

assumed a larger burden of the unremitting domestic work, tasks were not strongly differentiated by gender prior to adolescence. Children of both sexes were expected to help their parents by looking after their younger siblings, and play groups of younger children generally included both girls and boys. Despite some occurrences of female infanticide during the early historic period, Chipewyan infant girls and boys alike received considerable nurturance and attention from both their mothers and fathers. Young children were comparatively free to explore their immediate environment and handle a variety of adult tools and possessions, with subtle guidance or interventions by parents or older siblings to prevent harm.

Puberty and Adolescence

Between the ages of 13 and 16, Chipewyan adolescents received more intensive training in the economic skills they would need as adults. Young men (*cilikwi* or *denegodhe*) became partners and apprentices to older brothers, fathers, or uncles in various long-distance hunting, trapping, and fishing operations. While young women (*ts'kwiaze*) continued their mastery of a range of domestic and camp maintenance skills, they also began to learn hunting, trapping, and fishing skills from their mothers, grandmothers, and other older female relatives which could be conducted within modest distances from camps, as well as specialized butchering, food-processing, and storage techniques. Other than becoming an apprentice hunter, there was no ceremonial recognition of a boy's puberty. However, at first menstruation girls were briefly segregated from the camp and required to avoid men's equipment and game trails (Brumbach & Jarvenpa, 1997a; J. G. E. Smith, 1981; VanStone, 1965).

Attainment of Adulthood

Marriage (*hanits'udeli*) signaled the most visible transition to full adult status for a Chipewyan man (*deneyu*) and woman (*ts'ekwi*). Often marriages were arranged by the parents to build a network of useful affinal ties within and between winter staging communities. There has been a tendency toward short-term matrilocal residence. It was not uncommon for a newly married couple to reside with the wife's family for a year or two before moving elsewhere, and often this arrangement involved camping in adjoining tents or attaching a second room to the bride's parents' log dwelling. This may have represented a form of bride service, that is, compensation to the wife's family for the eventual loss of a productive daughter.

The weighting toward maternal relatives seen in residence behavior may also reflect differences in age and maturity between men and women at the time of marriage. Women in their teens often married men in their middle to late twenties or older. In part, the age gap is linked to the necessity for men to establish some economic independence from their natal families. Acquiring the skills, and particularly the capital and equipment, to operate one's own fishing and trapping ventures may take years beyond the apprenticeship period of adolescence. Women, on the other hand, are socially mature or marriageable when they have accumulated the child-raising and domestic skills, and hunting and food-processing knowledge needed for maintaining orderly homes and camps (Brumbach & Jarvenpa, 1989; Jarvenpa, 1980).

Middle Age and Old Age

During middle age, a married couple focused their energies upon raising their children into their apprenticeship years when the latter's assistance in providing a livelihood for the family became increasingly significant. Another major concern of middle-aged Chipewyan was finding good marriage partners for their young adult children from compatible families who would become sources of helpful in-laws during stressful times of need. As suggested previously, extending the network of one's personal bilateral kindred, or *silot'ine*, in this manner was an important form of social and economic insurance for an older Chipewyan man (*enekwi*) or woman (*ts'akwi*). Even so, old age was often an unenviable time when infirmity and the inability to contribute to the food quest or travel from one seasonal camp to the next could result in abandonment. In recent times, however, older Chipewyan women and men may become respected sources of moral authority, wisdom, and lore which they impart to growing numbers of grandchildren and great grandchildren. Even so, men who no longer remain physically active in bush livelihood may be regarded pitiably as "elderly," rather than merely old, a condition less likely for women who often display prowess in processing skills, such as hide manufacture and meat drying, well into their advanced years (Jarvenpa, 1999; Sharp, 1981a, pp. 106–109; VanStone, 1965).

PERSONALITY DIFFERENCES BY GENDER

An age gap of 6 years or more between marriage partners may be enough to produce different social–psychological conditions for men and women vis-à-vis their natal families. The new groom, who is beginning to test his status as an independent producer and provider in the community, may be somewhat less emotionally attached to his parents than his young bride, who has had less opportunity to develop a social identity and persona outside the environment of her natal family. As noted previously, the full transition to adulthood and married status for women is made less abrupt and less traumatic by bringing their new husbands into their parent's home for a short period (Jarvenpa, 1980).

GENDER-RELATED SOCIAL GROUPS

With the exception of a tendency toward short-term matrilocal residence, the general organization of Chipewyan society is based on flexible bilateral kinship with no strong weighting toward networks of male or female relatives. Moreover, there are no formal associations for males or females based on nonkin principles.

GENDER ROLES IN ECONOMICS

In the context of work, "partners" refer to one another as *sits'eni*, and when they derive from different family households, or when kinship connections are distant or obscure, the relationship may involve friendship and reciprocity far beyond the domain of work. All-male partnerships, especially in winter, hunt and trap in far-flung zones often dozens of kilometers and many weeks removed from family households in the winter staging communities of past decades or the centralized villages of recent times (Jarvenpa, 1980).

All-female teams hunt virtually year round, on a nearly daily basis, on short snare-lines radiating out a few kilometers from villages as well as via canoe paths within a day's or overnight trip's travel from staging communities or villages. Finally, mixed male–female teams occupy an intermediate position wherein husband–wife pairs and their children, especially during the summer and fall months, conduct moose-hunting forays of 2 days to 2 weeks duration in a radius of 10–45 km of staging communities and villages (Brumbach & Jarvenpa, 1997a).

Political–economic changes since World War II, including the emergence of permanent centralized settlements, have increasingly altered the patterns of livelihood noted above. While all-female teams continue to operate much as they have in the past, the mixed male–female teams have declined in importance over the past several decades as women and school-age children are tied increasingly to new services, schools, and other institutions in centralized settlements. Hunts for large game and commercial furbearers are now conducted increasingly by young and middle-aged males who, in many cases, travel longer distances and endure longer periods of separation from their family households than in any previous historical period. Chipewyan have adapted to the demands of the modern world by constructing gender roles that are increasingly divergent and specialized. Stated another way, men have become far-ranging logistically organized collectors, while women have become foragers who operate on a nearly daily basis from a central residence (Brumbach & Jarvenpa, 1997a).

Since the 1980s incursions of mining, commercial forestry, and road-building in Chipewyan territory have created new wage-labor opportunities, particularly for younger adults who commute to new mine sites and work on road crews for extended periods. While many of these jobs are occupied by men, some women are pursuing advanced schooling and employment as teachers, nurses, and constables away from their home communities. The historically familiar division of labor tied to subsistence hunting and commercial fur trapping and fishing is being transformed in subtle and unforeseen ways by this emerging industrial and service economy.

PARENTAL AND OTHER CARETAKER ROLES

As the primary food processors and tenders of camps and households, women have also assumed the major responsibility for nurturing and caring for young children. Women are assisted in this by older daughters and by their parents or husband's parents who frequently live nearby. Men begin taking a more active role in their children's everyday lives when the latter attain early

adolescence and can be socialized in hunting and other bush-living skills. Sometimes a father will train both sons and daughters in these matters.

It is not uncommon in Chipewyan society for aging grandparents to adopt one of their grandchildren either temporarily or on a permanent basis. Many Chipewyan women, in particular, have come of age learning vital bush-living skills from their grandmothers rather than their mothers.

LEADERSHIP IN PUBLIC ARENAS

Historically, formal authority took a back seat to highly flexible, short-term de facto leadership wielded by successful male hunters or other charismatic individuals (known variously as *dene gan kaltharae* or *gothare*) within the context of winter staging communities or hunting groups (D. M. Smith, 1982). Men who became outpost managers at seasonal trading posts, or who were otherwise prominent in the evolving fur trade economy, also had influence in local-level politics. With the rise of band governments ("First Nations" in current language) under federal Treaty provisions in the early 1900s, a formal authority structure of elected chiefs, councillors, and other community officials has emerged. Typically, these overt positions of power have been occupied by men, although some young educated Chipewyan women have been pushing for more active involvement in band or First Nations government. Moreover, elected officials are always subject to the "backstage" power of influential women, the competing interests of major families and kin alliances, and older notions of leadership based on individual competence, knowledge/power, and moral authority.

GENDER AND RELIGION

While all Chipewyan have access to (super)natural knowledge and power (*inkonze* or *inkoze*) there is some evidence that men and women may exhibit different means of acquiring and utilizing it (D. M. Smith, 1973, p. 8). For example, Sharp (1981b, 1988, 1991) argues that men obtain *inkonze* from spirit-animal beings in dreams and demonstrate the extent of their power in hunting success. The social divisiveness implicit in differential hunting prowess, in his view, is tempered within the hunting group by women, whose sharing activity binds the membership and occurs largely without direct reference to their men's *inkonze*. D. M. Smith (1982, p. 38) notes that women's *inkonze* was most often manifested in curing. However, these interpretations refer to northern Chipewyan groups where women appear to be less active in the direct harvest phases of hunting than among their southern relatives. It is true that southern Chipewyan men also acquire *inkonze* through dreaming, and they refer to the actual process of obtaining power from animals as *biu'aze* (Jarvenpa, 1998). While more research is needed in this area, preliminary information suggests that southern Chipewyan women's prowess in a variety of hunting, fishing, gathering, and processing contexts is, no less than men's, an overt manifestation of *inkonze*.

Since the mid-19th century Chipewyan magico-medicinal and religious knowledge has been in syncretic interaction with French Roman Catholicism and other Christian teachings and customs. However, involvement in church masses, choirs, pilgrimages, and related activity has not resulted in specialized men's and women's roles.

LEISURE, RECREATION, AND THE ARTS

It is generally accepted by both Chipewyan men and women that the latter have less leisure time. While men are involved in bursts of intense work during long-distance hunts and travel, women have an unremitting schedule of daily short-distance food procurement and processing plus the bulk of domestic and childcare duties. Casual visiting between households is often a male activity, with men seeking out their current work partners (*sits'eni*) for relaxed conversation. Women are more likely to incorporate visits with female friends into their work activities, whether making moosehide, cleaning fish, or caring for children.

Yet many leisure activities are not gender-segregated. Card-playing parties and bingo games are a favored activity of the middle-aged and elderly which invariably include both women and men. The same is true of the community dances popular among younger men and women. The short summer season often finds entire families or groups of families traveling together to various recreational festivals and pilgrimages in other communities.

RELATIVE STATUS OF MEN AND WOMEN

Much scholarship on northern Athapaskan societies, including the Chipewyan (Oswalt & Neely, 1996, p. 94), has noted the inferior or subordinate status of woman in traditional or historical circumstances. The vivid experiences of the Hudson's Bay Company explorer Samuel Hearne (1795), who traveled and lived with the Chipewyan extensively in the late 1760s and early 1770s, has become part of the received wisdom on female–male relations in that society. While certain behaviors, such as wife beating and female infanticide, might be taken at face value, others require judicious interpretation. Much of the discussion on "status" and "subordination" flows from an external European male perspective, with perhaps too little insight on gender differences, their meanings, and arenas of female and male influence from an insider's or Chipewyan view.

During the early historical period, some successful hunters or charismatic leaders, like Hearne's guide Matonabbee, had as many as seven wives. While this may be viewed as pronounced male dominance, stated another way, such individuals were *maintained* by as many as seven wives. Recent interpretations of Chipewyan gender relations have sought to temper harsh historical stereotypes with models of the *complementarity* of male and female behaviors in a comprehensive system of hunting (Jarvenpa & Brumbach, 1995) or as "asymmetric equals" in terms of power, influence and value within society (Sharp, 1995).

In recent history a patriarchal facet of Canadian federal Treaty law allowed a Treaty woman to lose her registered status simply by marrying a non-Treaty man or, conversely, for a non-Treaty woman to gain registered status by marrying a Treaty man. Treaty men kept their status regardless of marital history. Beginning in the 1980s this legal inequality has been rectified by Bill C-31 which permits any woman with prior Treaty status, who had become disenfranchised through marriage, to have her federal status restored.

SEXUALITY

With many people living in the confined quarters of tents, cabins, and other dwellings, children are exposed to sexual matters at an early age. Young men are expected to take the initiative in gaining sexual experience prior to marriage. Until recently, however, families were rather protective of their unmarried daughters. This creates a pattern of adventuring for some young men who seek sexual encounters when traveling to other communities, who acquire magical insurance such as Cree "love medicine," or who are accommodated by older women, often widows (Jarvenpa, 1998). Seeking privacy for premarital or extramarital affairs requires ingenuity in finding rendezvous spots in the bush or on the hidden sides of islands, or waiting for a lover's family or spouse to depart on a hunt or an errand (VanStone, 1965).

Pollution, at least historically, was a markedly negative aspect of women's sexuality. Without caution, it was thought that menstrual blood could contaminate dog harnesses, hunting equipment, and game trails, and thereby destroy a hunt or, at least, men's ability to hunt. The reverse side of this coin was that women's sexuality and fertility represented the power to reproduce Chipewyan society. While some Chipewyan women also took part in the direct harvest phases of hunting it is unclear how, if at all, their menstrual blood was thought to impact upon their own hunting activity.

COURTSHIP AND MARRIAGE

As noted previously, parents often play a significant role in arranging marriages which will create or reinforce useful ties between families and kindreds, such as hunting partnerships between brothers-in-law or between father-in-law and son-in-law. Often this involves encouragement or approval of a choice initiated by a son but eventually agreed upon by a prospective bride and her parents. In some cases, grandmothers or other older female relatives may have an influential role in encouraging and/or approving particular marriages. While there is variability among Chipewyan communities in these matters, marriage in the absence of parental approval has been unusual until recently (Sharp, 1979, pp. 52–53; VanStone, 1965, p. 63).

Preferential patrilateral cross-cousin marriage (i.e., a man marrying his father's sister's daughter, or a woman marrying her mother's brother's son) apparently was practiced by some eastern Chipewyan groups while avoided by those in the west. At the same time, southern Chipewyan groups have valued the sororate, the

preferential marriage of a man to his deceased wife's sister, viewing it as a way of maintaining previously established relationships between two linked families. Northern Chipewyan groups have resisted this practice (Jarvenpa, 1999; Oswalt & Neely, 1996; Sharp, 1979; J. G. E. Smith, 1981; VanStone, 1965).

Polygynous mariage was fairly common well into the 19th century when nearly 30% of married men in some communities had more than one wife. In the mid-19th century, however, Catholic missionaries began condemning first-cousin marriages and would sanctify only European-style monogamous unions. By the early 20th century monogamy was all but universal among the Chipewyan. This was a dramatic transition from a century before when skillful hunters or charismatic leaders, like Hudson's Bay Company explorer Samuel Hearne's Chipewyan guide Matonabbee, were maintained by as many as seven wives (Hearne, 1795).

In early historical times, there was no formal ceremony marking marriage and a union was regarded as somewhat provisional until the birth of the first child. There was also an institutionalized practice of wrestling to retain one's wife whenever challenged by another man, and a husband could lose his spouse to a stronger or more agile opponent (Hearne, 1795). As grim as this appears, women, perhaps, could better their own situations by influencing this system of challenges (Sharp, 1995, pp. 59–61). Since the introduction of Catholicism, formal wedding ceremonies (*haniyidihi*) have become part of the life cycle rites administered by church officials. In some communities, the conclusion of the wedding vows and mass may be punctuated by celebratory volleys of rifle shots. Shortly thereafter, dozens of kin and friends step forward to shake the hands of the newlyweds, and the rest of the day may involve much of the community in dancing, drinking, and feasting (Jarvenpa, 1999).

HUSBAND–WIFE RELATIONSHIP

While some notion of romantic love may be involved in courtship, this quickly gives way to a rather formal, if not austere, marriage relationship based upon the necessities of livelihood. That is, whether or not friendship and intimacy flourish, Chipewyan marriage is first and foremost a hunting enterprise requiring complementarity of work roles and performances to sustain the family unit. In some cases, adult cross-sex siblings may provide a reliable source of support and affection not easily attained between the marriage partners themselves. A further complication is that sexual jealousies can be ignited by patterns of community gossip which highlight infidelities, whether actual or imagined (Sharp, 1979, pp. 53–55).

OTHER CROSS-SEX RELATIONSHIPS

The importance of brother–sister ties has been discussed in the previous sections on "Cultural Overview" and "Husband–Wife Relationship." While more information is needed in this regard, some feelings of reserve and shyness between adult sisters and brothers, and between various in-laws of opposite sex, probably limit the frequency of contact and work between such individuals (D. M. Smith, 1982, pp. 20–25). On the other hand, avoidance behaviors, as between mother-in-law and son-in-law, appear to be neither as formalized nor as stringent as among some Athapaskan peoples of the Yukon and Alaska. Themes in Chipewyan folklore suggest that strong feelings of self-sufficiency and dependency create a fundamental tension in personality which applies to both men and women (Cohen & VanStone, 1963). Interethnic lore and imagery portray the Chipewyan as more reserved, but also more provident and enterprising, than their Cree neighbors, but again there is no apparent variability by gender (Brumbach & Jarvenpa, 1989).

CHANGE IN ATTITUDES, BELIEFS, AND PRACTICES REGARDING GENDER

Chipewyan family size increased concomitantly with expansion and intensification of the European fur trade economy in the 19th century, and there have been dramatic increases in the 20th century. For example, census data for southern Chipewyan communities reveal a significant historical increase in the number of children reared per adult woman. The statistic has increased from an average of 2.8 children with a range of 1–5 in 1838, to 3.1 children with a range of 1–8 in 1906, to 4.8 children with a range of 1–12 by 1974. A dramatic increase in the child-bearing and child-rearing responsibilities of Chipewyan women, particularly in the past 70 years,

may go a long way toward explaining the decreased participation of some contemporary women in hunting and other tasks that occur some distance from home. Such demographic trends also raise questions about models of work and gender based on synchronic ethnographies conducted in recent decades. Stated another way, prior to European contact and even quite late into the historical period, Chipewyan women bore fewer children, reared and cared for smaller families, and were more fully integrated into a comprehensive range of hunting activities (Brumbach & Jarvenpa, 1997b).

A pattern emerging in the 1980s and 1990s, and perhaps reflecting national Canadian trends, has been an increased number of out-of-wedlock children and a reluctance on the part of young Chipewyan couples either to formally marry or to form independent family households (Jarvenpa, 1999). While this is vexing for church officials and some older Chipewyan, children from such unions are often raised by one or the other set of grandparents. In some respects, this appears to perpetuate historically familiar forms of adoption in Chipewyan society (Sharp, 1979), but in the contemporary context it also contributes toward a socially isolative inward-looking stance. By not creating new family households, the network of *silot'ine*, or bilateral kindreds, collapses rather than spreading outward among a potential of opportunities and resources within and between communities across Chipewyan territory.

REFERENCES

Brumbach, H., & Jarvenpa, R. (1989). *Ethnoarchaeological and cultural frontiers: Athapaskan, Algonquian and European adaptations in the central subarctic.* New York: Peter Lang.

Brumbach, H., & Jarvenpa, R. (1997a). Ethnoarchaeology of subsistence space and gender: A subarctic Dene case. *American Antiquity, 62,* 414–436.

Brumbach, H., & Jarvenpa, R. (1997b). Woman the hunter: Ethnoarchaeological lessons from Chipewyan life cycle dynamics. In C. C. Claassen & R. A. Joyce (Eds.), *Women in prehistory: North America and Mesoamerica* (pp. 17–32). Philadelphia: University of Pennsylvania Press.

Cohen, R., & VanStone, J. W. (1963). *Dependency and self-sufficiency in Chipewan stories* (Bulletin No. 194, Contributions to Anthropology, 1961–62, pp. 29–55). Ottawa: National Museums of Canada.

Hearne, S. (1795). *A journey from Prince of Wales Fort in Hudson's Bay to the Northern Ocean in the years 1769, 1770, 1771 and 1772.* London: A. Strachan and T. Cadell.

Irimoto, T. (1981). *Chipewyan ecology: Group structure and caribou hunting systems* (Senri Ethnological Studies No. 8). Osaka, Japan: National Museum of Ethnology.

Jarvenpa, R. (1980). *The trappers of Patuanak: Toward a spatial ecology of modern hunters* (Mercury Series, Canadian Ethnology Service Paper No. 67). Ottawa: National Museum of Man.

Jarvenpa, R. (1998). *Northern passage: Ethnography and apprenticeship among the subarctic Dene.* Prospect Heights, IL: Waveland Press.

Jarvenpa, R. (1999). Surviving marriage and marriage as survival in Chipewyan society: Perspectives from northern hunters. In S. L. Browning & R. R. Miller (Eds.), *Till death do us part: A multicultural anthology on marriage* (pp. 105–122). Stamford, CT: JAI Press.

Jarvenpa, R., & Brumbach, H. (1988). Socio-spatial organization and decision making processes: Observations from the Chipewyan. *American Anthropologist, 90,* 598–618.

Jarvenpa, R., & Brumbach, H. (1995). Ethnoarchaeology and gender: Chipewyan women as hunters. *Research in Economic Anthropology, 16,* 39–82.

Jarvenpa, R., & Brumbach, H. (1999). The gendered nature of living and storage space in the Canadian subarctic. In B. Arnold & N. Wicker (Eds.), *From the ground up: Beyond gender theory in archaeology* (International Series 812, pp. 107–123). Oxford: BAR.

Oswalt, W. H., & Neely, S. (1996). The Chipewyan: Subarctic hunters. In W. H. Oswalt & S. Neely (Eds.), *This land was theirs: A study of North American Indians* (pp. 79–115). Mountain View, CA: Mayfield.

Sharp, H. S. (1979). *Chipewyan marriage* (Mercury Series, Canadian Ethnology Service Paper No. 58). Ottawa: National Museum of Man.

Sharp, H. S. (1981a). Old age among the Chipewyan. In P. T. Amoss & S. Harrall (Eds.), *Other ways of growing old: Anthropological perspectives* (pp. 99–109). Stanford, CA: Stanford University Press.

Sharp, H. S. (1981b). The null case: The Chipewyan. In F. Dahlberg (Ed.), *Woman the gatherer* (pp. 221–244). New Haven, CT: Yale University Press.

Sharp, H. S. (1988). *The transformation of bigfoot: Maleness, power and belief among the Chipewyan.* Washington, DC: Smithsonian Institution Press.

Sharp, H. S. (1991). Dry meat and gender: The absence of Chipewyan ritual for the regulation of hunting and animal numbers. In T. Ingold, D. Riches, & J. Woodburn (Eds.), *Hunters and gatherers: Property, power and ideology* (pp. 183–191). New York: Berg.

Sharp, H. S. (1995). Asymmetric equals: Women and men among the Chipewyan. In L. F. Klein & L. A. Ackerman (Eds.), *Women and power in native North America* (pp. 46–74). Norman: University of Oklahoma Press.

Smith, D. M. (1973). *Inkonze: Magico-religious beliefs of contact-traditional Chipewyan trading at Fort Resolution, NWT, Canada* (Mercury Series, Ethnology Division Paper No. 6). Ottawa: National Museum of Man.

Smith, D. M. (1982). *Moose-Deer Island House people: A history of the native people of Fort Resolution* (Mercury Series, Canadian Ethnology Service Paper No. 81). Ottawa: National Museum of Man.

Smith, J. G. E. (1975). The ecological basis of Chipewyan socio-territorial organization. In A. M. Clark (Ed.), *Proceedings: Northern Athapaskan conference, 1971* (Mercury Series, Canadian Ethnology Service Paper No. 27, pp. 389–461). Ottawa: National Museum of Man.

Smith, J. G. E. (1981). Chipewan. In J. Helm (Ed.), *Handbook of North American Indians: Vol. 6, Subarctic* (pp. 271–284). Washington, DC: Smithsonian Institution.

VanStone, J. W. (1965). *The changing culture of the Snowdrift Chipewyan* (Bulletin No. 209). Ottawa: National Museums of Canada.

Czechs

Timothy M. Hall

ALTERNATIVE NAMES

Bohemian, Moravian (Czech: Čech, Moravan).

LOCATION

The Czech Republic (formerly Czechoslovakia), is located in Central Europe, bordered by Austria, Germany, Poland, and Slovakia. Most of the borders are formed by hills or low mountain ranges, surrounding the rolling plains of Bohemia and Moravia (the western two thirds and eastern third of the country, respectively). The climate is relatively mild, with temperatures in the lowlands typically ranging from about 20°C in July to about −1°C in January.

CULTURAL OVERVIEW

According to the 2001 census, the Czech Republic has a population of approximately 10.2 million (4,982,071 men and 5,247,989 women), of whom some 93% are Czech or Moravian, 1.8% Slovak, and less than 1% each ethnic Poles, Germans, Ukrainians, or Vietnamese. Romani (Gypsies) are the most visible ethnic minority but make up less than 1% of the population. The predominant language is Czech, a West Slavic Indo-European language closely related to Slovak and Polish. Some 1 million ethnic Czechs also live abroad, mainly in Canada, the United States, Australia, and various parts of Central Europe.

The Czech lands have been inhabited since the 7th century CE by Slavic peoples. Christianity was introduced by saints Cyril and Methodius in the 9th century, and the Czech lands reached their political height in the 14th century when Prague became the capital of the Holy Roman Empire. Power later passed to the Austrian Habsburgs and the Czechs were subordinated to German-speaking Austria until the end of World War I. The Czechs and the closely related Slovaks were united in an independent Czechoslovakia in 1918 as the only stable democracy in Central Europe between the wars. This First Republic ended with the infamous Munich Agreement in 1938, when the Allies handed the Czechs over to Hitler as a protectorate and Slovakia became an autonomous fascist puppet state.

Czechoslovakia was reunited again in 1945 after liberation by Soviet troops, and a Soviet-backed Communist coup took power in 1948 under Klement Gottwald. A brief experiment with liberalization, the Prague Spring, was crushed by the invasion of Warsaw Pact troops in 1968, beginning a period of repressive "normalization." Communism finally fell with the Velvet Revolution in late 1989, and the Czech Republic and Slovakia peacefully separated with the so-called "velvet divorce" in 1993. The current government is a stable parliamentary democracy with several major parties ranging from reformist Communist to Christian Democrats.

Czech society is highly secularized, though with a visibly Roman Catholic past. Culturally, the Czech lands occupy a transitional space between Central and Western Europe. During the Communist period, Czech society became more "Eastern" under Russian influence; since the end of Communism in 1989, Czech society is once again approximating Western European patterns. Family structure is predominantly nuclear and of a Western European type.

From 1948 to 1989, Czechoslovakia had a "real socialist" economy with extremely effective income and wealth equalization and a strong emphasis on the development of mining (mostly brown coal, but also uranium and some metals) and heavy industry. Since the end of Communism and through an ongoing process of privatization, capital has turned back toward the more profitable light industry (glass, ceramics, leather, and textiles), and the service industries are growing. Social classes are re-emerging after the end of Communism, but are not yet highly differentiated. The economy is generally regarded as one of the strongest in post-Communist Central Europe, and the Czech Republic expects to join the European Union within the next few years.

CULTURAL CONSTRUCTION OF GENDER

The recognized gender categories are male and female. There is no culturally elaborated intersex category. Male and female heterosexuality, homosexuality, and bisexuality are recognized as orientations. The general cultural conception of gender categories is largely similar to traditional patterns in Northern and Western Europe. Men are expected to be strong, to be initiators of sex, to be the head of the family, and to be the main source of a family's income. Women are expected to devote themselves to their husband and children, to be more emotional then men, and to be sexually attractive, less assertive, and more interested in family than in politics or career. With the social changes of the last few decades and the high divorce rate, this ideal is often honored more in the breach, leading to widely voiced complaints that Czech father-breadwinners are absent and Czech women are too dominant in comparison with the cultural ideal.

Czechs dress similarly to their Western European counterparts. Men usually wear their hair fairly short (except among some teenagers and some subcultures). Under Communism, facial hair was associated with Russian/Communist identity and was avoided by non-Communist men; since the end of Communism, older men often now have short beards or goatees. Women tend to have longer hair than men.

Being slender and sexually attractive is important for Czechs of both sexes, at least through their twenties, and for women for some time thereafter as well. A slim athletic physique is preferred in men, and a slender figure in women. Dressing to be sexually attractive begins gradually during adolescence, and continues throughout young adulthood for men, and through to middle adulthood for many women.

Homosexual orientation is not as clearly marked by specific dress or hairstyles as in many Western countries. Jewelry such as hoop earrings and necklaces, and tattoos and piercings, are relatively common among young Czech men (as in contemporary Western Europe) and do not by themselves indicate sexual orientation.

GENDER OVER THE LIFE CYCLE

Childhood, adolescence, adulthood, and old age are all recognized as stages in the life cycle, but the transitions are usually gradual and are not typically marked by public ceremonies. Both males and females receive their citizenship card (*občanka*) at age 15, but this is not marked by any special ceremony and the rights and duties of legal adulthood are obtained gradually. The legal age of consent for sexual intercourse is 15 for both males and females, heterosexual and homosexual. At 18, one can vote and can legally purchase alcohol and tobacco. There are several transitions in schooling, from kindergarten to basic school, and then to gymnasium/college preparatory school or a technical/vocational school in the teenage years, but all of these are the same for both sexes, and differ more by class and one's ultimate profession than by gender. The military is almost exclusively male. Men are expected to serve several years of military service or substitute civilian service at some point in their late teens or twenties; many try to avoid it. Women can enter the armed forces, but it is not required and most do not. Compulsory military service is expected to be discontinued soon.

Socialization of Boys and Girls

Boys and girls are valued roughly equally, and the ideal Czech family is a married couple with two children, one boy and one girl. Parents do tend to identify more with the same-sex child in early childhood. Many mothers pay extra attention to their sons, continuing into adulthood. For instance, many adult bachelors regularly bring their clothes home to mother for washing and mending. This close relationship between mothers and sons can result in later competition between mothers and their sons' girlfriends or wives.

The mother is usually the primary caretaker. Paid maternity leave is now 28 weeks at 69% of the previous salary, but unpaid leave can last up to 4 years, during which the family continues to receive a small "parental subsidy" (*rodičovské přídavky*, previously *mateřské přídavky*). While either parent is entitled to take "parental leave," in the vast majority of cases it is taken only by women. Grandmothers, both maternal and paternal, also often provide a significant amount of additional childcare (Nash, 2003).

Socialization of children differs less now by gender than in the past, though there are differences. Children wear clothing similar to that worn by adults of the same sex, i.e., shirts and pants or shorts for boys, and shirts or blouses and skirts or shorts for girls. Boys' hair is usually cut very short, especially in summer, while girls usually wear their hair longer, often in braids or a ponytail. Girls' clothing tends to be of brighter colors and girls are more likely to wear flowery patterns. Boys' games often involve guns, cars, and pretending to be soldiers (highly romanticized during the Communist era as a role model for boys). Under Communism, a major experience for both boys and girls was the strongly encouraged participation in the Young Pioneers (*pionýři*), the Communist replacement for the Boy Scouts. Girls more often play with dolls or otherwise imitate maternal or domestic activities. Children are disciplined in approximately the same way for similar misbehaviors, though parents react more strongly to gender-atypical behavior in boys than in girls.

Puberty and Adolescence

Adolescence and puberty are named stages, but the words used for them suggest a relatively recent import of the concepts: *adolescence, puberta, teenager* (there also exists a calque of "teenaged"—*náctiletí*). Puberty is not specifically recognized by any special rites or dramatic changes of status; on the whole there is continuity in socialization from late childhood. The major change that occurs is the division of secondary school students into those preparing for university, who study in a *gymnázium*, and those preparing for some sort of trade, who study at one of a variety of technical and vocational schools. The decision to follow one path or the other is made sometime around the ages of 14 or 15, based on a combination of individual wishes, advice from the parents, and one's grades.

Sex education begins in the schools around the age of 12 or 13, and is usually preceded by some discussion of sexuality by one or both parents. Mothers seem to be more comfortable discussing sexuality with their children than do fathers. Fairly explicit depictions of sexuality are shown on television and substantial nudity is shown in advertising and magazines. Nude sunbathing and swimming are common at many lakes in the summer. Children around the ages of 7 or 8 often play "doctor," and there is some (largely speculative or hearsay) discussion of sex in the schoolyard in later childhood and early adolescence. Thus most children have some knowledge of adult anatomy and sexuality by puberty.

Homosexuality was illegal throughout most of the Communist period, and was not discussed in sex education texts. Teachers and other students joked about homosexuality and teased students, especially males, who exhibited gender-atypical or homosexual behavior. This has decreased somewhat since the end of Communism and the legalization of homosexuality. Contraception and sexually transmitted diseases are also discussed in the sex education texts.

Early adolescents, ages 13–14, begin having crushes and also talking about sex, though usually their claims of actual experience are exaggerated. Some 12% of adolescents have had sexual intercourse by age 15. The majority of adolescents begin sexual activity between 16 and 18 years of age; the numbers are similar for boys and girls (Weiss & Zvěřina, 2001). Around the age of 15–16, Czech adolescents begin actual dating, and also drinking and smoking. (Though the legal age for drinking alcohol and for smoking tobacco is 18, this is not strictly enforced and adolescents can easily obtain both.) During the period of dating, parents tend to be more protective of the opposite-sex child.

One of the few remaining rituals that clearly marks sexual differences takes place on Easter Monday, and for most Czechs is the highlight of the Easter festivities. Boys and young men in their teens and early twenties go around to the houses of girls and young women of roughly their own age group and switch them on the buttocks with a braided willow switch decorated with colored ribbons (*pomlázka*). Adolescent girls then give their persecutors colored eggs; these days older girls and young women often give out shots of liquor instead. This custom is not much observed in the cities, but every Czech who can returns to a village for the Easter Monday festivities. In former times, the more attractive and popular young women used to boast of how many boys had come to switch them. There was an associated practice in which young men would capture young women and throw them into tubs of water or into ponds or streams, or would splash them with buckets of cold water. This still occurs, but is less common than the *pomlázky*.

Attainment of Adulthood

Full legal adulthood comes at age 18, but recognition of social adulthood is more complex, as in Western societies, and comes through a combination of completing one's education, starting a career, and starting a family and an independent household. Under Communism, with artificial wage equalization and various pronatalist policies, there were few incentives to delay starting a family. During the 1970s and 1980s, Czechoslovakia had one of the youngest average ages of marriage in Europe, about 21 years for women and about 3 years older for men. With the increasing value of higher education, a decrease in economic benefits for having children (such as subsidies for children's clothing and preference in housing), increased personal freedom, and a general shortage of housing, the marriage age is rising rapidly and more young Czechs are delaying starting a family (Nash, 2003; Večerník & Matějů, 1999). This also means that a larger number of Czechs are living with their parents or in dormitories well into their twenties, and the sort of prolonged semidependent, semi-independent young adulthood seen in many Western countries is becoming more common in the Czech Republic. Even so, there has been a cultural lag, and many young Czech women in their middle or even early twenties express concern over their marriage prospects if they are not in a relationship with a reasonable chance of eventually leading to marriage.

Economic responsibilities for both boys and girls start in adolescence, as both look for part-time employment and summer jobs. Under Communism, there were few legal jobs for school-aged adolescents; with the advent of capitalism, many more opportunities are available and both boys and girls often begin working in part-time jobs at 16 or 17. Full employment starts around age 18 or 19 for those who have completed vocational or technical schooling. Parents expect both young men and young women to contribute financially to the household if they are still living at home and have completed their schooling.

Middle Age and Old Age

There are few substantial differences by gender in the aging process throughout adulthood. Older Czechs now feel out of touch with the changes since the end of Communism, and are faced with pensions and savings that are worth far less than they had expected. Consequently, they have neither the cultural nor the economic capital that they would have had in previous generations.

Younger Czechs of both sexes are expected to show a certain deference and consideration for older persons, especially older women and individuals who appear to be less physically able, for instance, opening doors and giving up seats on metros and trams. This is partly based on a realistic assessment of physical ability, and similar consideration is often given to pregnant women, parents with small children, or disabled individuals. Young men are expected to take the initiative in these acts of deference, but young women and older men also help.

PERSONALITY DIFFERENCES BY GENDER

Most Czechs see gender differences as rooted in biological differences between men and women (Holy, 1996, p. 175). Males in general are expected to be more assertive, less "emotional" (more level-headed, less likely to cry, more logical), firmer in their opinions, and more ready to assume leadership. (Strong assertiveness is not highly valued for either sex, and putting oneself forward or boasting is frowned upon in both men and women.) Open physical violence is much less common among Czechs than among their eastern or southern neighbors, but physical aggression is more common among men than women. Czechs of both sexes spend much time discussing and analyzing "feelings" or the emotional component of intimate relationships.

Women are expected to be more nurturing than men and are expected to defer to men. Many Czech males complain that Czech women are too dominant and aggressive; this is not immediately apparent to non-Czech observers.

GENDER-RELATED SOCIAL GROUPS

Men have historically been more active in the public sphere, and consequently dominated much of business, political life, and academia; however, this situation is changing as women increasingly enter economic and political life, and there are few single-sex institutions per se.

Marriage is ideally neolocal, with husband and wife setting up a new household separate from their parents. Many married couples live with one set of parents for a year or more while looking for housing. The location of the new household and connections with the husband's and wife's families depend mainly on personal idiosyncrasies and economic opportunities (e.g., if an aged parent moves in with a married child and his or her household, it will typically be to the household of the child to whom that parent is closest, or the child who can best afford it).

Historically, the basic unit of association was the nuclear or extended family, which existed within a village. There were no large kin-based or gender-based associations beyond these. Under Communism, concerns about privacy and safety from informants, as well as a general material scarcity and lack of funds for outside recreation, led most Czechs to associate mainly within the family or a close circle of relatives and friends. Today, the divorce rate is high, and young Czechs are marrying at a later age and are more geographically mobile than their parents' generation. Young Czechs still often socialize at least occasionally with their families, and a weekend at the family cottage (*chata* or *chalupa*) in the country is quite common, but many Czechs now comment on the erosion of the family associations which held under Communism.

As in most of Western Europe, kinship is recognized bilaterally, but surnames are typically patrilineal. Women bear a feminine form (ending in -ová or -á) of their father's surname until marriage. Czech law requires that women take the feminine form of their husband's name upon marriage; an exception was made in 2000 for Czech women who marry non-Czech men, and who now have the option of using their husband's surname without modification. The surnames of women foreign writers and celebrities are typically feminized (e.g., Danielle Steeleová, Hillary Clintonová), although this practice is slowly decreasing. Historically, Czechs typically had two or three given names, often taking the name of the same-sex godparent as a middle name. Most Czechs now have a single given name, except for some individuals from German or historically prominent families. Czechs do not have a Russian-style patronymic.

GENDER ROLES IN ECONOMICS

Men have traditionally played the role of breadwinner, and have also filled most of the more physically demanding jobs, as well as the more prestigious ones. Men and women have had equal rights since the abolition of the old Austrian legal code in 1948 (Nash, 2002), but the so-called "emancipation of women" by the Communists often meant in practice merely that women had to work outside the home in addition to continuing in their traditional roles as housewives and mothers. Generous maternity leave benefits and guaranteed jobs under Communism often acted to maintain this division of labor, as many women would stay home full time from the birth of their first child until their youngest child entered school. Economic pressures have now changed; with the loss of guaranteed jobs, many women now feel forced to choose between career advancement and having children (Nash, 2003). This is not a problem for men, who typically have minimal childcare responsibilities.

An effect of Communist wage equalization was that some professions typically dominated by men in Western countries were instead dominated by women, and were accorded less prestige. A majority of pediatricians, gynecologists, and other primary care physicians in Czechoslovakia were female, and a general physician is often assumed to be female. Nurses (*zdravotní sestry*) are almost exclusively female. The majority of teachers in elementary and secondary schools are female, while the majority of teachers at the university level are male.

Men and women have equal rights in inheriting property. Under Czech law, all children are entitled to a roughly equal inheritance. Both sexes participate in business and the professions, and the percentage of women in management positions is slowly approaching parity.

PARENTAL AND OTHER CARETAKER ROLES

Mothers are the primary caretakers for children, often assisted by both maternal and paternal grandmothers. Many Czech children now grow up in blended families, in which their biological mother provides most of the actual daily caring and disciplining, and a stepfather or mother's boyfriend is present but does not play a major role in the daily lives of the children. For Czechs who grow up in the more traditional nuclear family, the father is still not present in the home much of the time, being away at work during the day and sometimes socializing with his male friends or business associates after work. Discipline of the children may come from either father or mother, depending in part on the temperaments of the parents, though mothers seem less willing to punish sons. Children do not typically help much around the home, as the mother is expected to do most of the housework.

LEADERSHIP IN PUBLIC ARENAS

Women occupy some leadership roles in the political arena, and several prominent politicians are female. However, this is one domain in which men are clearly advantaged, and fewer than 10% of the Parliament since the end of Communism have been women (Holy, 1996).

GENDER AND RELIGION

Although survey numbers are rapidly changing and difficult to interpret, most Czechs are effectively atheists and highly secularized. The Czech lands were historically Roman Catholic, but the early reformer Jan Hus inspired a rebellion against clerical abuses in the 15th century. The Czechs were aggressively re-Catholicized when the Austrian Habsburgs regained control during the Thirty Years' War. All religious observances were discouraged under Communism. In the 2001 census, 27% of Czechs gave their religion as Roman Catholic, 2% belonged to the largest two Protestant churches together, and some 59% claimed no religion at all. As in most Catholic countries, few young people are now entering religious orders, and an increasing percentage of Catholic clergy and religious are coming from other countries, notably Poland. The general religious conception is thus post-Catholic: God is conceived as male, and the first humans were Adam and Eve. At present there is no strong cult of the Virgin Mary, though there was in historical times.

Czechs also have their own legends of pre-Christian times, in which Ur-father Čech led his tribe of Slavs into present-day Bohemia. Čech is a patriarchal figure clearly influenced in conception by the biblical Abraham. Čech was succeeded by his son, who died without male heirs and left the kingdom to his three daughters, each of whom possessed divine talents. The youngest daughter, Libuše, had the gift of prophecy and ruled over the Czechs until people began to complain that women made judgments more on the basis of emotion than justice. To make her people happy, she told them to go to a certain place where they would find a man hewing a threshold (*prah*); this man Přemysl would become her husband and king and legendary founder of the first Czech (Přemyslid) dynasty, and the place where they found him would be the foundation of Prague (*Praha*). Afterwards, a number of women complained at their loss of power and began to fight the men in the so-called "Maidens' War."

After several battles and much loss of life, the women were eventually subdued and were forbidden from ever again holding power in the Czech lands (Demetz, 1997).

LEISURE, RECREATION, AND THE ARTS

Women and men both have a fair amount of leisure time, though working women have slightly less because they still do most of the housework and childcare. Vacation time is generous (4–6 weeks a year for most people, not including frequent state holidays). Under Communism, restrictions on travel, scarcity of consumer goods, and a general retreat from public life into the safety of the family meant that much free time was spent with members of one's immediate family in activities that required only minimal financial resources: hiking, swimming, spending time at the family cottage, playing card games or board games, and drinking alcoholic beverages at home with friends and family or in a pub (beer and liquor prices were, and still are, artificially low in comparison with food prices). Both women and men enjoy singing songs, traditional Czech songs and more modern ones, while sitting around a campfire or during evenings at the cottage.

More men than women are found in the typical Czech pub, and groups of male friends or male business associates often gather there. Women also go to pubs, either alone or with a male partner or with other friends of either sex, but married women with children are more likely to stay at home. Young single women are more likely to go to dance clubs or bars, while older women will sometimes enjoy a beer at a neighborhood pub. Formal dancing, both traditional Czech dances such as the polka and classical ballroom dancing, is popular among young people of both sexes, and constitute major events during the social year for adolescents and young adults. In the villages, dances for people of all ages are still a major form of entertainment during festivals and holidays.

Certain games are associated more with one sex than the other. Men in pubs traditionally played a card game called *mariáš*, but the game is much less commonly played now. Women are more likely to play bridge. Boys usually play rougher games: soccer (*fótbal*), ice hockey, floorball, etc., while girls play sports such as badminton. Boys also played marbles (*marmany*) and collected various kinds of trading cards (*čéčka*), though these have now largely been displaced by video games.

RELATIVE STATUS OF MEN AND WOMEN

Czech women and men have equal rights under the law, with the major differences centering around the highly valorized role of women as mothers. Most women take advantage of maternity leave and are expected to devote much of their time and energy to their husbands and children. Women who succeed in the public arena are respected, but women in positions of authority are often regarded with ambivalence or resentment by men. Western-style feminism is often seen as alien and threatening to the family and to male–female relations, and is not well received by most Czechs (cf. Holy, 1996; Nash, 2002).

SEXUALITY

Overall, the Czech Republic is one of the more liberal societies in Europe in regard to sexual matters, though this varies by age, residence, and religiosity. (Older, nonurban, and actively Catholic or Protestant individuals are more likely to approve of sexuality primarily for reproductive purposes within a monogamous heterosexual marriage, and are more likely to have negative attitudes towards premarital, extramarital, or homosexual sex, as well as towards contraception and abortion.) Survey data (Weiss & Zvěřina, 2001) show the following attitudes of the general population: more than 50% of men and more than 60% of women believe that a woman has the right to decide whether to have an abortion, with only 3–4% absolutely opposed to abortion under any circumstances; more than 40% of men and about one quarter of women endorse the statement that "extramarital sex is natural and normal" and fewer than one in three individuals strongly condemn it; more than two thirds of men and more than 70% of women have favorable attitudes towards contraception, with only 4% of women and 5–7% of men strongly opposed; roughly two thirds of men and women consider masturbation to be natural and normal.

Younger Czechs are behaving in many ways more like Western Europeans with each generation, a trend that is increasing since the end of Communism. Age of first intercourse is decreasing, age difference between partners at first intercourse is decreasing, and use of condoms or other methods of contraception is increasing (Weiss & Zvěřina, 2001). In addition, an extended period of sexually active life before marriage is now common among young Czechs, and the age of marriage and first childbirth is rising. Among young Czechs, divorce and abortion are both considered undesirable in comparison with a happy marriage and a wanted child, but are considered better than the alternative of an unhappy marriage and an unwanted child (Fialová et al., 2000).

Women are expected to be more modest about showing their bodies than men, but sexual modesty is not emphasized to a great degree for either sex. Modesty about the body in single-sex situations, such as dormitories or changing rooms, or at home among family members, is almost nonexistent. Open displays of affection in public, such as kissing and petting, are common, especially among young adults in their late teens and twenties. Frank depictions of sexuality are common on television, and nudity (especially female nudity) is common in magazines and billboards. Nudity is common at beaches, though usually in a separate section from the nonnude bathing area, and children are sometimes taken to nude beaches with their parents.

Sexual harassment (*sexualní harašení*) is a concept recently imported from the West, and is still seen as a foreign word for a foreign concept. It is regarded with a certain amount of amusement by both men and women (cf. Holy, 1996, pp. 172–176). Women are expected to take care of their appearance and to be flattered by sexual attention from men. They are also free to say no, and are expected to be able to handle sexual situations without recourse to legal action.

Homosexuality was illegal under the Austrian criminal code and during most of the Communist period, but the situation became slightly more liberal in the 1980s, and there had been discreet gay establishments in the larger cities since at least the early 1900s (Fanel, 2000). Since 1989, Prague and some other cities have developed relatively large gay and lesbian communities, and same-sex registered partnership has been considered by the Parliament and narrowly defeated three times. Prague has also become a major destination for international gay tourists.

Czech society on the whole is quite tolerant of homosexuality, both male and female, though lesbians are far less visible than are gay men. Czechs living in the larger cities, and younger and more educated individuals, are particularly likely to have more favorable attitudes towards homosexuals, and more information about homosexuality (Janošová, 2000). Cross-sex behavior in one's children is a cause for concern, but most families other than those from strongly religious backgrounds accept homosexual adult children without much comment. Transvestite theater is relatively popular for heterosexual audiences in the cities.

Prostitution is outside the law and therefore effectively legal for both males and females over 18 years of age. Since the end of Communism, the Czech Republic has become a destination for sex tourists, both heterosexual and homosexual, especially from neighboring Germany and Austria. The Czech government has considered fully legalizing prostitution in order to tax and regulate it, but is prevented from doing so by European Union rules.

COURTSHIP AND MARRIAGE

Both males and females have a relatively free choice in whom they can marry, and widows or widowers and divorcées are free to remarry. The typical pattern under Communism was that a couple would date for some period of time, become pregnant, and set a date for the wedding (Fialová et al., 2000; Nash, 2003). Rates of marriage and birth both fell during and after the Communist takeover in 1948 and again after the Warsaw Pact invasion in 1968. In response, the Communist government promoted a strong pronatalist policy during the 1970s, under which nearly all men and women eventually married and more than 94% of women had at least one child (Večerník & Matějů, 1999, p. 110). Marriage was also desirable because married couples with children received preference in housing and larger families were eligible for larger apartments. Love was a major factor in choosing a spouse, because economic potential was roughly equal for everyone and class differences were minimal (Večerník & Matějů, 1999, pp. 99–101).

With increased opportunities for single individuals to work, travel, and study since the end of Communism, and with decreased government benefits for children, the age of first marriage and first conception are rapidly rising. Extended cohabitation has become more common, with the decision to marry often precipitated by pregnancy or the decision to have children (Fialová et al., 2000). In the 1980s, Czechs had some of the youngest brides in Europe, with an average age of 21 (with husbands about 3 years older); in the late 1990s the age had risen to 26.

Traditional weddings before Communism were large affairs, involving large extended families and an entire village, with a Catholic (or more rarely Evangelical) religious ceremony and a large wedding feast afterwards, in which the two families would be seated and symbolically joined around a U-shaped table. Under Communism and since, partly as a decline of extended community ties and partly through a decrease in material resources (and a disinclination to conspicuous consumption), urban weddings in particular tend to be smaller events, with immediate relatives and close friends at a reception following a civil ceremony.

HUSBAND–WIFE RELATIONSHIP

The husband–wife relationship is similar to the traditional Western model. Husbands and wives eat together and sleep together (though the sleeping arrangements are slightly separated; double beds are typically made of two single mattresses rather than one large mattress, and each person has their individual blanket and pillow). Cooking, cleaning, and other housework are typically done by women. Most Czech men do not contribute significantly to the housework.

The husband–wife relationship is ideally characterized by love, affection, and companionship; ideally also the husband is the primary breadwinner, has slightly more education than his wife, and is slightly older (typically, about 3 years older). Decision-making is shared to some degree, but men are expected to take some leadership in making decisions, especially decisions about money or other significant matters. Women, because of their presumed greater devotion to their families, often have a greater say than their husbands in regard to decisions about the welfare of the children or the household budget (Čermáková, 1995). Divorce is legal and common, and may be initiated by either partner. After divorce, children typically stay with their mother.

OTHER CROSS-SEX RELATIONSHIPS

Other cross-sex relationships are not highly elaborated culturally.

Change in Attitudes, Beliefs, and Practices Regarding Gender

The major historical periods for Czech society are (1) traditional village life, up until World War II and the Communist revolution of 1948, (2) Communism (1948–89), with collectivization of farms, a planned economy and pronatalist government policies, and active undermining of older Catholic/Christian or "bourgeois" attitudes and customs, and (3) the period of privatization, liberalization, and social differentiation since the fall of Communism in 1989.

See Salzmann and Scheufler (1974) for a description of social relations in a traditional Czech village and some of the changes that came with collectivization, Nash (2002) for a review of attitudes towards women and feminism in different periods, and Večerník and Matějů (1999) for an overview of changes in Czech society during the first decade after the end of Communism.

Bibliography

Čermáková, M. (1995). Women and Family. In M. Lobodzińska (Ed.), *Family, women, and employment in Central-Eastern Europe* (pp. 75–85). Westport, CT: Greenwood Press.

Čermáková, M., Hašková, H., Křížková, A., Linková, M., Maříková, H., & Musilová, M. (2002). *Relations and changes of gender differences in the Czech society in the 90s.* Prague: Czech Academy of Sciences, Sociology Institute.

Demetz, P. (1997). *Prague in black and Gold: The history of a city.* London: Penguin.

Fanel, J. (2000). *Gay historie.* Prague: Dauphin.

Fialová, L., Hamplová, D., Kučera, M., & Vymětalová, S. (2000). *Představy mladých lidí o manželství a rodičovství* [Ideas of young people about marriage and parenthood]. Prague: Sociologické nakladatelství.

Hajnal, J. (1965). European marriage patterns in perspective. In D. V. Glass & D. E. C. Eversley (Eds.), *Population in history: Essays in historical demography* (pp. 101–143). Chicago: Aldine.

Holeček, M., Rubín, J., Střída, M., & Götz, A. (1995). *The Czech Republic in brief.* Prague: Czech Geographical Society.

Holy, L. (1996). *The Little Czech and the Great Czech nation: National identity and the post-Communist social transformation.* Cambridge, U.K.: Cambridge University Press.

Hraba, J., Pechačová, Z., & Lorenz, F. (1999). *Deset rodin po 10 letech, 1989–1999* [Ten families after ten years, 1989–1999]. Prague: Academia.

Hupchick, D., & Cox, H. (1996). *A Concise historical atlas of Eastern Europe.* London: Macmillan.

Janošová, P. (2000). *Homosexualita v názorech současné společnosti* [Homosexuality in the opinion of contemporary society]. Prague: Nakladatelství Karolinum.

Možný, I. (2002). *Sociologie rodiny* [Sociology of the family] (2nd ed.). Prague: Sociologické nakladatelství.

Nash, R. (2002). Exhaustion from explanation: Reading Czech gender studies in the 1990s. *European Journal of Women's Studies, 9*(3), 291–309.

Nash, R. (2003). *Re-stating the family: Reforming welfare and kinship in the Czech Republic.* Unpublished doctoral dissertation, University of Virginia, Charlottesville, VA.

Salzmann, Z., & Scheufler, V. (1974). *Komárov: A Czech farming village.* Prospect Heights, IL: Waveland Press.

Sayer, D. (1998). *The coasts of Bohemia: A Czech history.* Princeton, NJ: Princeton University Press.

Večerník, J., & Matějů, P. (Eds.). (1999). *Ten years of rebuilding capitalism: Czech society after 1989.* Prague: Academia.

Weiss, P. & Zvěřina, J. (2001). *Sexuální chování v ČR—situace a trendy* [Sexual behavior in Czech Republic—situation and trends]. Prague: Portál.

Eastern Tukanoans

Janet M. Chernela

ALTERNATIVE NAMES

Alternative names are Tukano, Wanano, Desana, Bara, Barasana, Piratapuya, and Tapuya.

LOCATION

The Eastern Tukanoans are the Northwest Amazon, comprising the Uaupés River basin and adjacent areas in Brazil and Colombia.

CULTURAL OVERVIEW

A cluster of approximately 10 named tribes speaking Eastern Tukanoan languages is found in the region of the Uaupés River basin and adjacent areas in Brazil and Colombia. The area, referred to as the Northwest Amazon, is part of the Amazon river basin. The Uaupés River is an affluent of the Rio Negro, the Amazon river's largest tributary. The region is densely forested, yet the soils are poor, with the tree cover thinner than elsewhere in the basin.

Here, each named group possesses a distinct identifying language, yet no one group is autonomous. Rules of exogamy (out-marriage) require that one marry outside the "language group," so that the region is united through ties of intermarriage and may be said to share one common culture.

A language group consists of several villages arranged along the river edge. Generally speaking, villages are about 5 miles apart and contain up to 150 residents. According to preferences expressed by Eastern Tukanoan speakers, the villages of a language group should form a geographic unity. However, the more common pattern is one where villages of one language group are interspersed by villages of another language group. Villages are located on high ground at the river's edge, with paths leading to gardens deep inside the forest. The principal forms of livelihood are fishing, carried out by males, and root-crop horticulture, carried out by females. Males cut and burn new gardens, after which women plant, weed, and harvest several root crops, including manioc and sweet potato.

Because each group speaks a recognizable linguistic variant (a language or dialect within the Eastern Tukanaon family of languages), the groups have been called "tribes" (Sorensen, 1967) or "language groups" (Jackson, 1983) in the ethnographic literature. Members of a language group consider themselves to belong to one family, based upon an overriding principle of patrilineal descent from a single mythical ancestor. Each language group is in turn subdivided into patrilineal descent groups which have been called sibs (Goldman, 1963) or patriclans. See studies by Chernela (1993), C. Hugh-Jones (1979), H. Hugh-Jones (1979), and Jackson (1983) for groups that conform to the norms described here; see Goldman (1963), Århem (1981), and Chernela (1988a, 1989) for a discussion of departures from these norms.

On marriage, a bride from one language group must leave the village of her birth and reside among her husband's relatives, who are members of a different language group. Marrying inside her own language group would be considered incestuous. In this broad regional network, marital and kin ties unite some 14,000 speakers of diverse languages over an area of approximately 150,000 km^2.

In addition, Eastern Tukanoan descent groups are also ranked according to seniority, so that every patriclan and every individual within a language group has a distinct ranked relationship to every other.

The result is a uniquely coherent culture complex, with unilineal descent, rank orders, and cross-cousin marriage acting as major integrating structural principles.

The linguist Arthur Sorensen (1967) identified 13 languages as members of the Eastern Tukanoan language family: Tukano, Tuyuca, Yuruti, Paneroa, Eduria, Karapana, Tatuyo, Barasana, Piratapuyo, Wanano, Desano, Siriano, and Kubeo. He suggests that the member languages of the Eastern Tukanoan family are less closely interrelated than those of the Romance or Scandinavian groups.

CULTURAL CONSTRUCTION OF GENDER

All Eastern Tukanoans regard themselves as descended from ancestral brothers born of the body of a primordial anaconda. Each founding brother is the focal ancestor of a sib, whose members are spoken of as the "grandchildren of one man." One generation of brothers generates another through the name exchange. Men structure descent and generational time, linking descendant with ancestor, present and future with past. Although women participate in synchronic linkages, connecting different descent groups, they are absent from the descent model of reproduction.

A local village consists of a core of male relatives (called agnates by anthropologists), their in-marrying wives, and their unmarried daughters. The practice of patrilocality—when a bride takes up residence in the village of her husband—furthers the solidarity of a resident male brotherhood and exacerbates the political subordination of women.

The outsideness of women in the villages into which they marry is exacerbated by the combined practices of patrilineal exogamy and patrilocal postmarital residence. As a result, males inhabiting the same settlement are members of one language group, while in-marrying wives are speakers of other, "foreign," languages. In the Wanano village of Yapima, in which I conducted fieldwork, the eight in-marrying wives spoke five different languages. Conversation among wives is characteristically multilingual, while discourse among males and unmarried Wanano females is monolingual.

"Femaleness" and "maleness" are considered to be fundamentally different concepts. Moreover, a daily division in practical life between male and female activities still maintains a different, but concrete, separation between the genders.

Woman's anatomy is thought to be polluting and men feel they must protect themselves from female contamination. Males practice purging rituals and aspire to states of mental and physical control, including control of sexual impulses, thought to be outside the potentials of women. It is believed by men that women's bodies can endanger and defile the intellectual rigor and spiritual discipline practiced by men. In short, the dominant male ideology associates men with the head and the cerebral functions of speech, intellect, and leadership. It associates women with the body and the sensate (Chernela, 1988a).

Women began wearing cotton dresses in 1920, as a result of missionary influence. Yet there is no modesty regarding the upper body, and women occasionally go about in only skirts. Women smoke pipes, and maintain their hair long and straight. On ritual occasions women paint their bodies with fine geometric black designs, yet wear no colorful ornaments. In contrast, men's ornamentation in the same rituals involve colorful feather headdresses, body paint, and floral ornaments.

GENDER OVER THE LIFE CYCLE

Socialization of Boys and Girls

The birth of a boy or girl is marked by the parents by abstention from certain foods and activities. These practices and abstentions are both public and private; they culminate in a ritual bath for the parents, presided over by a shaman, who applies protective substances intended to bless the couple as well as the child. This ritual may be seen by all, as it takes place at the river edge. Until they are able to walk, infants remain in a body sling at mother's side; they sleep with mother in the same hammock. Toddlers stay close to mother, but young boys soon venture out to join the village horde of children. This group roams through the village without organized supervision; it contains children of all ages, with the oldest taking the responsibility for overseeing and protecting the youngest.

Language learning is an important vehicle for socialization. For speakers of Eastern Tukanoan languages, language is not only a matrix of symbols, it is itself a symbol, a marker of identity, and a primary definer of category. In the multilingual communities of the Northwest Amazon, speakers are competent in both mother's and father's languages but must supress mother's language as they mature.

In the processes of language acquisition a child must be socialized to perform but one language in a context of many. In the transfer of knowledge from one generation to the next, every attempt is made to avoid the mixing of languages, since it is considered essential that linguistic identities remain distinct and linguistic boundaries be kept stable.

A child is raised learning both mother's and father's languages but is socialized not to speak one of them. The situation is modeled for the child when people speak back and forth in two languages. Yet the child must learn to distinguish the two languages and discern which is appropriate for him to verbalize and which not. Overt instruction provides the child signals that mother's tongue has no social or public value.

For all children speaking competence, and for males rhetorical skill, are prized in father's language—the language of the speaker's descent group. Public demonstrations of mother's language, however, are strongly sanctioned. The result is a set of equivalences in which father-language is social and outside, and mother-language is private and inside (Chernela, 1997).

One part of this elaborate and socially embedded ideology of language is the belief that the well-developing child learns to speak his/her father's language with consistency, and will have the self-discipline to refrain from speaking mother's language, a language it is well understood that he or she knows. The well-bred and mature child speaks only father's language, and any deviation from this detracts from the child's respect among adults and peers.

Therefore language learning for the Tukanoan speaker is an early form of mother-separation. Apart from whatever emotional correlates may or may not attach to this process, the distinction between self and mother has social–structural implications and consequences. It distances and separates, at an early age, that which is mother from that which is self. As the alignment of like and unlike self is established in the course of Eastern Tukanoan language acquisition, mother becomes quintessential "other."

For Eastern Tukanoans, emotional alliances shift in the course of language acquisition and development. In effective linguistic socialization, a child learns to accept the differential values placed on mother's and father's languages and to fear the negative consequences of uttering mother's language.

The specific barrier to spoken bilingualism among the Tukanoan Wanano is the fear that if one speaks one's maternal language, one will be ostracized. Implied is the sense that a child who speaks mother's language is infantile. Furthermore, to speak mother's language is to be like mother, and therefore unlike one's peers. More explicitly, a child is threatened with open reproach if he or she utters mother's language or mixes it with father's language.

In addition, boys are socialized to speak openly and assertively. In general, women refrain from public speaking. Both sexes are hardworking, although boys, who do not participate in the strenuous work of garden cultivation

and food processing, have far more time for play. A girl who played to the same extent as boys could be admonished.

Girls and boys accompany the same-sex parent in economic activities from the time they are able to do so. From the time they can walk, girls, like their mothers, carry backpack-style baskets supported by strong tumplines running along the forehead. Girls assist their mothers in the arduous work of preparing, planting, weeding, and harvesting the gardens daily. The size of the harvest basket and the weight of material in it carried by a girl increases as she becomes older. When she is a young adult, she will, like her mother, carry about 40 lb of newly harvested manioc roots, firewood, and a small child from the gardens to the house. Girls and mothers work together to process the poisonous manioc roots. These tubers must be peeled, grated, and boiled until they are edible. Between morning garden work and afternoon preparations, girls and mothers work all day, every day.

Prepubescent boys, in contrast, have more free time to spend in play. They may set up a line of baited hooks at night and fetch their catch the next morning. Or, they may fish with hand line at dawn or dusk. But these activities are far less labor intensive than female tasks. Also, boys play no role in preparing the food they catch. They may pass the day among the clusters of young boys who run freely through the village and its surroundings, collecting edible fruits as snacks while they play.

Puberty and Adolescence

For both boys and girls the transition to puberty is marked by rites of passage. Although in some villages highly elaborate complex rituals are still carried out, in many other villages the ceremonies have become simplified (see S. Hugh-Jones [1979] for an in-depth discussion of male initiation rites). Where the full ceremony for boys is carried out, it is held in secret over several days. The simpler versions are shorter. Yet, no matter the length or level of fundamentalism, in all cases boys, guests, sponsors, and chanters are adorned in ritual paraphernalia. Long flutes, thought to carry the specialized powers of men, are played. (In the most traditional ceremonies sight of these flutes is tabooed to women, who either leave the premises or move to a secluded zone.) The sib ancestors are invoked by the flutes and by chants sung by specialized chanters. Formerly, boys were whipped with branches as part of the ceremony; I have not seen this in recent times. Sacred substances, including the hallucinogen ayahuasca, are imbibed and sacred tobacco smoke is blown on the young males as each receives his sib name. Through this process the boy becomes a social being, a member of his patri-line. The recipient of a sib name is thought to be endowed with the particular social status and identity of the ancestor whose name he bears. In a sense, the bearer of an ancestral name is the exchange (*kototaro*) for that ancestor—his incarnation or transformation in the present.

When a girl reaches puberty a ceremony of equal import is performed. Yet the purpose, emphasis, and participation in the ceremony differ from the male puberty ceremony. A girl's initiation occurs at the time of her first menses, and she experiences her own ritual as the only initiate. At this time she is considered to be in a vulnerable state and must be shielded behind an enclosure. Guests travel great distances to attend. The girl is painted with the red plant urucu and secluded behind a screen in the corner of a large dance house. While in seclusion she may eat only a few specially prepared substances. During the ceremony the girl is not visible to visitors. As in the boys' initiation ceremony, specialized chanters invoke protective spirits. However, while male initiations invoke the supernatural ancestors that emerged from the anaconda-canoe, Pamori Busoku, female initiations invoke a different supernatural creator spirit known as First Woman. First Woman, a powerful shaman, is said to have given birth and breath to herself at the Lake of Milk, origin of all Tukanoan-speaking peoples. From there she journeyed along the same path as the ancestral canoe; but whereas Pamori Busoku traveled below water, First Woman glides above ground, stopping at each village and sacred site to rid it of dangerous spirits. Her accomplishments are essential in protecting vulnerable menstruating girls and women. The chanter narrates in detail First Woman's voyage from Milk Lake to the girl's village, naming at each site her exploits and victories. These are the same challenges and dangers that might harm the menstruating girl, and by invoking them the young women is herself protected. Thus the female initiation ceremony stresses the powers of reproduction and the dangers associated with the powers, whereas the male ceremony emphasizes naming and place in the ancestral line.

Attainment of Adulthood

Once they have passed through the requisite puberty ceremonies, boys and girls are able to marry and have children. Boys are formally ready to parent, and, in doing so, to pass on clan identity.

Girls are by this time skilled horticulturalists, having worked for years alongside their mothers. Upon marriage a girl moves into the home of her husband and gardens alongside her mother-in-law. Eventually she will have a garden of her own, although she is likely to be adjacent to her mother-in-law, work with her in preparing meals, and eat together with her in-laws in a multigenerational unit.

This pressure on males to be good fishermen increases as they move into adulthood and marriage. If a wife does not believe that her husband is providing enough food she can publicly humiliate him (Chernela, 2002). When fishing is especially difficult, males sometimes go to fish in groups and remain away from the village for several days. Although most activities are divided by gender, fish poisoning is an activity in which everyone, including children, takes part.

Since the incest regulation forbids marriage with a member of one's own language group, and a woman moves to her husband's village upon marriage, women will live their adult lives in the villages of speakers of a different language group. Therefore women are marked by difference, even as they act as agents of articulation between groups.

Middle Age and Old Age

When a woman first arrives in a village she is relatively powerless. She may be a stranger to the other wives of the settlement, or even to her husband's family, with whom she lives. She has few manioc plants and must accrue these as she ages. At first she may share a garden with her mother-in-law.

Over time, as she comes to know her brothers-in-law and her cowives, and produces and raises children who "belong" to the village sib, she feels more secure in her position and gains more say in village life. A woman whose sons have married and brought new wives into the household may be quite powerful within that household.

Although males may be said to have a level of prestige not held by women, they do not abuse their privileges. Males do not harm women physically, and are generally not aggressive to women or to children.

The elderly may remain at home while their adult children carry out demanding chores. The elderly show signs of rheumatism, arthritis, and cataracts. An older woman who no longer wishes to work in the garden may stay in the house overseeing a toddler. Likewise, an elderly man who no longer wishes to fish may remain at home.

PERSONALITY DIFFERENCES BY GENDER

Men alone are privileged to speak formally and publicly. Tukanoans place extreme value on speaking skill and rhetorical abilities. Women neither have authority to speak for a group nor are they considered to have the capacity of producing "correct" and clear thought and speech. Men distinguish between the eloquent decorous speech of men and what they regard as the undisciplined chatter of women. Men are expected to engage in dominant and highly visible speech activities, while women are expected to remain quiet and to attend to the children. The greatest opportunities for women to express themselves are on the occasions of exchange ceremonies. Then, women chant spontaneous songs among themselves. In these songs they share personal details of their lives (Chernela, 1988a).

Eastern Tukanoan men view women as divisive and chaotic influences, especially through their uncontrolled critical gossip. Although in-marrying wives form bonds with each other, numerous factors limit their impact as a formal cohesive political power. For most women, input into village-level politics takes the form of gossip and other informal social criticism (Chernela, 1993, 1997).

When a child misbehaves, it is the mother who is assumed to be at fault. However, it may be another woman—the mother-in-law—who is the first to reprimand her son's wife. Both men and women enjoy joking and teasing. There is greater latitude in what women say as they become older.

Weeping, both spontaneously and performatively, is regarded as appropriate for women but inappropriate for men. The "Welcome of Tears," a departure ritual noted since earliest European visitors to the New World and involving texted weeping, is expected of women in the north of the Amazon basin. The same practice is performed by both sexes in the southern portion of the basin.

GENDER-RELATED SOCIAL GROUPS

Rules of incest and exogamy produce an overarching unity among diverse and sometimes distant language groups so that 14,000 Indians inhabiting some 150,000 km^2 are related by either kin (agnatic) or in-law (affinal) ties.

Eastern Tukanoan society provides one of the few known cases of strongly patrilineal societies in lowland South America. Members of a patrilineal clan speak a single signifying language and conceive of themselves as a group of agnates descended from ancestral brothers born of the body of an anaconda. Each of these founding brothers is the focal ancestor of a patriclan or sib, whose members are spoken of as the "grandchildren of one man."

This ideology of descent consitutes a unisexual model of social order and continuity. One generation of brothers generates another through the name exchange; men structure descent and generational time, linking descendant with ancestor, present and future with past. Although women participate in synchronic linkages, connecting different descent groups, they are absent from this descent model of reproduction.

Women are outsiders. Among Eastern Tukanoans, a local village consists of a core of male relatives, their in-marrying wives, and their unmarried daughters. (The few nonsib members found in most villages are relegated to visitor status, and are barred from local decisions.)

Although in-marrying wives form strong affective bonds with each other (often based on language commonality), numerous factors limit their impact as a formal cohesive political power. For most women, input into village-level politics takes the form of gossip and other informal social criticism. This "subversive" form of politicking undoubtedly has a substantial, though unmeasurable, impact. If a woman's comment is critical, yet made in a jesting satirical style, it is not considered provocative in the way that outright criticism would be.

With patrilocal residence, the rapport established between a wife and her in-laws is critical to her well-being. Ideal circumstances for both marital partners occur when the preferred practice of patrilateral cross-cousin exchange is followed. Then, a man marries his father's sister's daughter. In these marriages, a woman marries her mother's brother's son—a man who is a member of her mother's language group. In this home her father-in-law is a speaker of her mother's language. He calls her by an especially affectionate term and speaks to her in the cadences of her mother's tongue, although she responds in her father's, that is, her "own" language. In such marriages, a woman is said to be "marrying back" (Chernela, 1988a, 1993). Women who "marry back" are said to be "belongers" in the villages into which they marry, in contrast to wives whose husbands are not of the mother's group, and who are said to "mix" among "others" (Chernela, 1988a).

In the single case that I know of where a woman continued to live in her own village after her marriage, she was the last remaining descendant in the line of founding ancestors, known as the "Firsts." She was considered to be "First of the Firsts." By virtue of her location in the descent structure, she was recognized as having an authorized link to the ancestors. Her unique position within the social structure was manifest in her residence practice. Since she remained in the village of her birth, and her husband's family resided in the village, the case constituted a singular instance of regularized uxorilocal residence in the region. This woman was described to me as being "like a man" (Chernela, 1993, 1997).

GENDER ROLES IN ECONOMICS

Males are fishermen, while women are engaged in root crop production. Although men cut and burn new gardens, afterwards it is the work of women to plant, weed, and harvest the crop daily. Since manioc (*Manihot esculenta*) can be left in the ground and harvested as needed, women collect it on a daily basis. The poisonous manioc planted by Tukanoan women must be thoroughly detoxified by means of extensive cooking in which the soluble prussic acid is eliminated. Women prepare the manioc into a variety of dips, soups, beverages, breads, and flour. The last procedure is laborious but the flour is light and does not spoil; it is used in journeys and may also be traded or sold to passers-by. (See C. Hugh-Jones [1979] for a thorough discussion of food processing.)

Garden work begins just after breakfast at dawn and continues into early afternoon. Preparing the harvested roots, served as bread and drink at sundown, may take up most of a woman's afternoon. Before serving dinner at sundown, she always bathes herself and her children.

Since the Tukanoans are patrilocal, a new wife receives her garden and her first manioc seedlings from her mother-in-law and the cowives of the new village into which she marries. When she visits her own birth village, she finds other manioc cultivars, and brings them back to distribute or trade among cowives (Chernela, 1986).

Men specialize in making baskets and carved wood items for domestic use and for trade. These differences in gender specializations are strongly adhered to. Each language group specializes in a single craft product, made by the men of the group, that will be formally circulated throughout the basin (Chernela, 1992). Among these objects are shaman's benches, manioc graters, sieves, and baskets.

PARENTAL AND OTHER CARETAKER ROLES

Mothers hold infants in a simple shoulder sling or carry them on the hip until the child is ready to explore by crawling or walking short distances. A boy stays close to mother's side until he is mature enough to join the active band of village children. From early age, girls accompany mother at work in the fields or at home. Gardening is a daily task lasting 4–6 hr, and girls generally accompany their mothers far from their peers.

Fathers, by contrast, spend far less contact time with their children. Until adolescence, male work is not considered children's domain, even for young boys. Although Eastern Tukanoan men are affectionate and conscientious fathers, raising children is considered by household members—and by the husband and husband's mother in particular—to be the responsibility of the child's mother. A husband may reprimand his wife if he observes that his children are not behaving properly.

LEADERSHIP IN PUBLIC ARENAS

Leadership in the political arena is restricted to males. Women have no leadership roles (including social/political movements), nor do they have equal authority. For example, I know of no female shamans, despite the importance of First Woman as a powerful shamanic spirit.

Men alone are privileged to speak formally. Tukanoans place extreme value on speaking skill and discourse style. Women neither have authority to speak for a group nor are they considered to have the capacity of producing "correct" and clear thought and speech. Men distinguish between the eloquent decorous speech of men and what they regard as the undisciplined chatter of women. Men are expected to engage in dominant and highly visible speech activities, while women are expected to remain quiet and attend to the children.

Eastern Tukanoan men view women as divisive and chaotic influences, especially through their uncontrolled critical gossip. Although in-marrying wives form bonds with each other, numerous factors limit their impact as a formal cohesive political power. For most women, input into village-level politics takes the form of gossip and other informal social criticism.

Authority and certain types of knowledge are associated with the head. Authority is vested in the most senior man who is referred to as "our Head" (*dahpu*); the term refers not only to his leadership role, but also to the anatomical head which "leads," "organizes," and "speaks for" the body (Chernela, 1993). The term also refers to the head of the ancestral anaconda, from which the descendants of the first ancestors originated. Without a "head," a group cannot "speak" and is therefore mute or powerless.

Women are not prohibited from hearing stories, as they are prohibited from hearing ritual ancestral flutes. Yet, women may not tell stories. Women typically overhear the stories told by men, and although they may be attentive, that interest is not usually acknowledged. The body of oral literature that pertains to ancestral times has a distinctly male cast of performer–interpreters, resulting in a text shaped by a distinctly male gaze. Ancestral myth-telling is an activity that falls within men's roles. The exclusion of women either as ratified speakers or listeners reaffirms the male monopoly over ideology and ritual.

Occasionally a woman may "take the floor," creating, for a moment, a distinctly female space within the public sphere (Chernela, 1997). When this occurred once it was at the periphery, not the center of the dance house. The center is reserved for the rhetorical ceremonial speech of males.

GENDER AND RELIGION

Religious specialists, known by the anthropological label "shamans," are males. A powerful shaman is thought to be a transformation from a jaguar spirit. The power and reputation of a shaman among his own people rests upon his command of an extensive repertoire of songs, spells, incantations, and charms, many of which are in languages not understood by his clients. These sacred texts are accumulated in distant apprenticeships and are the secret specialized knowledge of shamans.

By spatial or imaginary passage, through dreams, smoke, hallucinations, and visions, through the mediations of animal spirits, images, and masks, the Tukanoan shaman physically bridges domains and attempts to restore violated integrities. As a mediator between social and supernatural worlds, between inside and outside, the body and those forces which govern the state and condition of the body, he is an advocate on behalf of his group, kinsmen, and clients against evil: enemy sorcerers, disease, malevolent spirits, and other threats to the well-being of those in his care (Chernela & Leed, 1996). His mediation is accomplished through his knowledge and skill in powerful foreign spells and drugs. A powerful shaman is capable of making his body a vehicle and a conduit of exchanges between domains.

The shaman carries out procedures that delineate a "world set apart"; he establishes the proper and rule-governed means by which it is entered, and its powers engaged and channeled. For example, the shaman masters the skills of separating, defining, protecting, and offsetting. He creates enclosures, shields, or other barriers that protect the vulnerable, whether persons or places. A shaman may encircle a threatened individual, house, or village with a protective wall of tobacco smoke, woven like a fish fence, and made more powerful by augmentation with power-generating incantations that function to block out invading spells and influences.

The shaman not only marks the boundaries that set apart and establish the integrity of a body, collective or personal, he also sets himself apart. A specialized compartment within the long house separates the shaman from the polluting influences of coresidents and visitors. This "separation" of the shaman from the group he serves renders him sacred, special, and powerful. He spends much of his daily life behind a screen that is intended to protect him from pollutants. He is brought mild foods by his wife or daughter and maintains a hearth apart from the rest of the household. This separation from the group is one of the precautions taken by shamans in the communal homes of the Tukanoans.

A Tukanoan shaman bridges domains through both thought travel—using a hallucinogen to experience travel—and active travel. Apprenticeship to a shaman of a different tribe or language group is one means by which the novice practitioner obtains foreign songs, spells, and incantations which are often considered more powerful and effective than those recited in comprehensible tongues.

It is clear that the shaman specializes in communicational actions—uttering words, "seeing" the normally unseen, defining, naming, explaining, singing, manipulating ritual objects, defending—and takes a moral responsibility for the physical condition of the patient. The wielder of the power of words and symbols appears to "cause" the change in condition of those who submit, physically, to his ministrations. And yet the "cause" of the cure is neither in the utterances of the shaman nor in the body of the patient, but in the union of the two, and in the relations the shaman embodies between worlds carefully kept separate.

Of extreme pollution and therefore danger to the shaman is the presence of menstruating women. For this reason men and women bathe in separate sections of the river, with the shaman farthest from the female bathing area. The level of threat brought about by menstrual blood is a measure of its power (albeit not benign) over men.

First Woman, invoked at the initiations of pubescent girls, is, by one set of interpretations, the most powerful of Eastern Tukanoan supernaturals. Yet she is not designated to a specific patriline and is not invoked in most clan rituals.

Myths recount the discovery of agriculture by women. A group of female farmers, painted red, are said to have been discovered by ancestral brothers while hunting. The subsequent union is attributed with the origins of agriculture, marriage, and family among the population of Eastern Tukanoans.

LEISURE, RECREATION, AND THE ARTS

Adults, whether men or women, have little leisure time. However, each does have greater and lesser periods of intensity in the work schedule. The most demanding work can provide an opportunity for "recreation." When women prepare flour, for example, many women work together for long hours. When gardens are cut the whole village works together and creates a festive occasion with drinking and joking. Fish poisoning, in the low-water season, is an occasion for festive communal work. On a daily basis, men who are not out fishing or setting traps may weave mats or baskets, play with young children, or converse with other villagers. Early evenings are generally times for relaxation. At these times, people gather in the cleared plaza at the center of the village, joking and

quietly talking. During these gatherings the sexes, ordinarily segregated in their work chores, are now brought together.

RELATIVE STATUS OF MEN AND WOMEN

Patrilineal descent reckoning and the practice of patrilocality assure the political subordination of women. Formal positions in the public arena are always assigned to men. This conforms well to the kinship composition of the residential unit since it is occupied by one or several patrilines. Decision-making and influence in subsistence and economy requires no authority, merely obedience to tradition. Collective work days, such as the cutting of a garden or the building of a house, may be called by the village chief who is always a man. However, his power is limited and if he encounters opposition he can be ignored. In family and community matters women have power by virtue of their obligation to tend to the upbringing of their children. It is they who are held responsible for the comportment and well-being of a child. This carries power, but not of the sort recognized as overtly political. It is important to recognize that there is no consolidation of power within one individual within a village.

Only men have rights to resources within their own villages by virtue of patrilineal descent. For example, men of the patriline may inherit certain fishing areas suitable to trap placement. Women may be said to own their own manioc plants. Males and females have similar access to plant resources as both depend upon the same rotating plots of land in which to plant their gardens. There is no ownership of these lands in the Western sense.

Women control or influence their choices of sexual partners and, along with their parents, marital partners. However, women are not the owners of their own children, who belong to the patriline of the husband. If a woman leaves her husband she may not take her children with her. If her husband dies and she chooses to remarry outside her husband's descent group, she may not bring her children with her.

SEXUALITY

Sexuality is considered natural and healthy under normal conditions. However, the bodily fluids of women may endanger or pollute a male's state of health. Premarital and extramarital sex are both widely practiced, yet they are always carried out with discretion and at a distance from the shared domestic areas (Chernela, 2002).

Some Tukanoan men may view women as divisive and chaotic influences, especially through their uncontrolled critical gossip. Tukanoans place extreme value on style of speech, and men distinguish between the eloquent decorous thought and speech of men and the undisciplined unthinking chatter of women. Lack of restraint, in the male view, extends to female sexuality: woman is the seductress, the seeker of sex, and, to use Murphy's phrase, "the reservoir of libidity."

Tukanoans appear to present an exception to the gender stereotype in which men are endowed with great, if not irrepressible, sexual appetites and, relatedly, are "natural sexual aggressors." Tukanoan models of sexuality are the opposite. Men view female sexuality as abundant and women as uncontrollably licentious. In contrast, they see themselves as rigorously protective of their own fragile chastity (Chernela, 1993, 1997, 2002).

Motives in myths suggest that woman's anatomy is seen by men as threatening. The ravenous female of an important myth devours a man's penis in her vagina. The literature on the Northwest Amazon mentions male purging rituals associated with cultural emphasis on strenuous mental and physical control, including control of sexual impulses. Woman's body endangers and defiles the intellectual rigor and spiritual discipline practiced by men. In short, the dominant male ideology associates men with the head and the cerebral functions of speech, intellect, and leadership. Women are associated with the body and the sensate.

Gender imagery is a subset of the larger ontological duality of self and other. Together, the two sexes constitute a totality, irreconcilably polarized by the fact that each confronts the other as object. There is therefore no single "conscious model" for gender; instead, men and women have different though complementary ways of representing gender.

Women do not see themselves as ravenous. As men claim to feel endangered by women, so women feel endangered by men. Women claim that the intelligence they once possessed was lost in ancestral times when a man disguised as a woman stole the powerful head ornaments (*siompuli*) from his mother-in-law, divesting women of their control over certain types of knowledge and authority. Women say that nowadays they do not "know" but that at one time they did (Chernela, 1997).

Complementing the male image of female as body is the female image of the male as expropriator of powers associated with the head. This opposition reflects the political relation of the sexes: males dominate descent—an ideology of reproduction—and fear loss of their reproductive powers. Females "speak too much"—exercise social sanctions through gossip—and fear loss of intellect and, ultimately, of political power. Each sex views the other as a dangerous usurper.

In fact, female sexuality is scarce to the extreme among Tukanoans. The extent of this scarcity rests on the simultaneous practices of linguistic exogamy and patrilocality, and on strongly restrictive, intensely enforced conditions for suitable marriage partners. For men, as we will see, the most proximate women are the wives of his uncles and sibmates. For an umarried woman, the most proximate males are sibmates with whom sexual relations are prohibited.

COURTSHIP AND MARRIAGE

Each sex is expected to give thought to marriage and begin, with their parents, planning a conjugal life. For boys this consists of finding a wife to move to his village. For girls it involves a move to the village of her husband, and entails careful consideration of the relatives among whom she will live. Girls are expected to be hardworking and, indeed, the attribute of hardworking is a principal criterion in considering a spouse. A girl who is strong and hardworking is considered a desirable and attractive spouse. Many marriages are arranged by parents whose families have exchanged daughters in marriage over generations.

Acquiring a wife can be problematic. Incest regulation forbids marriage with anyone in one's own language group and, conversely, requires that one marry into a different language or kin group. Furthermore, marriage practice is governed by two strongly felt preferences: marriage with a patrilateral cross-cousin, and sister exchange. Hence, a proper marriage requires that a man have a marriageable sister to exchange, and that his father (or father's brothers) have sisters with daughters of marriageable age.

The difficulty of finding such a mate is expressed in the lament of a bachelor who cannot find a marriageable *tanyo*—a female cross-cousin:

> Isn't it strange?
> I have no cousins;
> I am alone and I haven't any cousin.
> Fortunately for me,
> I have Fathers of my Fathers;
> But I have no cousin.

A Tukanoan male need not marry to find sexual partners. However, like rules of exogamy, Tukanoan incest prohibitions are restrictive, forbidding sexual relations with members of one's own language group. Occasional breaches of the far-reaching incest regulations might evoke intense criticism.

Thus, if the rule of patrilocality is strictly followed, as it most often is, all of one's age-mates in a village will be classificatory siblings and intercourse with them is forbidden. The only women not prohibited by the incest regulations are the in-marrying wives. These women are few in number, relative to the total population of the village, and highly sought after by their husband's sibmates. If we may speak of sexuality in terms of supply and demand, competition is acute for these few available women. Access to these married females is further obstructed by the threat of reprisals by jealous husbands or sorcery aimed at punishing paramours (Chernela, 2002).

A wife with lovers is expected to be discreet. However, women can and do commit indiscretions to humiliate and manipulate husbands. A dispute between a chief and his wife that occurred during my stay exemplified this practice. Females are given full responsibility for illegitimate relations; these confirm the belief that women are sexually ravenous.

The broad extension of incest rules creates a scarcity of nonincestuous sexual partners. As a result, the few sexual partners permissible to a man are the same ones as those permissible to his brother. And, the only nonincestous partners locally available to a bachelor are his brothers' wives. The bachelor in search of sex is faced with two problematic alternatives: adulterous nonincestuous relations, or nonadulterous incestuous relations. He is caught between two evils: incest, which is strongly prohibited, and adultery, which threatens solidarity among sib brothers.

To portray males as pursuers, then, would acknowledge competition among males. For the dominant ideology to proclaim this social reality would rupture male solidarity and in this way threaten social stability.

In this case, culture does indeed create an "artificial and untrue shortage of female sexuality." If we accept that women's value and related power derive from scarcity, we must conclude that the limited availability of female sexual partners, created by wide-ranging incest taboos, should place these women at a premium. The male view of woman as sexual pursuer denies scarcity by declaring female sexuality to be abundant. Whatever value would be expected to accrue to women from scarcity is effectively denied.

HUSBAND-WIFE RELATIONSHIP

The relationship between spouses is characterized by love, affection, respect, and companionship. I never saw hostility, antagonism, or aloofness. Husbands, wives, and children share a common hearth around which sleeping hammocks are arranged. With the exception of infants, who sleep with their mothers, each person sleeps alone in his or her hammock.

The strict division of tasks requires a strong interdependency among couples. Either husband or wife can initiate a separation if the marriage is not satisfactory, but this is extremely rare. However, if a woman leaves the village of her husband's sib she may not take her children, who belong to that sib, with her.

Extramarital relationships are not unusual. They are carried out with utmost discretion unless intended to openly provoke a spouse. Almost all sexual activity takes place in a woman's garden. The presence of visitors to a garden is usually indicated by the canoe that is left at the river-edge nearest the path to the garden.

OTHER CROSS-SEX RELATIONSHIPS

The relationship between an in-married woman and her brothers-in-law is expected to be characterized by generosity and harmony. As her own family is distant, the closest relations a woman has in her adult years are with her husband's family and the other in-marrying wives in her village. She retains ties to her own birth family and visits them whenever possible. When two families exchange daughters as wives over generations, a woman will find the comfort of having as her in-laws her own uncles and aunts.

CHANGE IN ATTITUDES, BELIEFS, AND PRACTICES REGARDING GENDER

All villages have elementary schools nearby. However, if boys or girls wish to continue their studies they must travel away from their home village and enter a mission school in a town. Some young women travel to large cities where they obtain employment as domestic servants or factory workers. Some of these women will return to the villages to marry and raise families. Others may marry in the city, and visit their rural relatives on occasion. Many of the women who remain in the city will never marry. Some take up residence together when they become elderly. In 1990 some elderly Tukanoan women had taken up residence together in the outskirts of the city to which they had migrated as girls. In 1982 Tukanoan urban migrant women formed an association known as the Associação de Mulheres do Alto Rio Negro (AMARN). It is the first indigenous women's association and the longest-running autonomous indigenous organization in Brazil.

BIBLIOGRAPHY

Århem, K. (1981). *Makuna social organization: A study in descent, alliance, and the formation of corporate groups in the North-Western Amazon* (Uppsala Studies in Cultural Anthropology 4). Stockholm: Almqvist & Wiksell.

Chernela, J. (1986). Os cultivares de mandioca (Tucano). In B. Ribeiro (Ed.), *SUMA: Etnológica Brasileira: Vol. 1, Etnobiologia* (pp. 151–158). Rio de Janeiro.

Chernela, J. (1988a). Gender, language and "placement" in Uanano songs and litanies. *Journal of Latin American Lore, 14*(2), 193–206.

Chernela, J. (1988b). Righting history in the Northwest Amazon. In J. Hill (Ed.), *Rethinking history and myth* (pp. 35–49). Urbana: University of Illinois Press.

Chernela, J. (1989). Marriage, language, and history among Eastern Tukanoan speaking peoples of the Northwest Amazon. *Latin American Anthropology Review, 1*(2), 36–42.

Chernela, J. (1992). Social meanings and material transaction: The Wanano–Tukano of Brazil and Colombia. *Journal of Anthropological Archaeology, 1*, 111–124.

Chernela, J. (1993). *The Wanano Indians of the Brazilian Amazon: A sense of space*. Austin, TX: University of Texas Press. (Paper back edition published in 1996.)

Chernela, J. (1994a). Tukanoan know-how: The importance of the forested river margin to neotropical fishing populations. *National Geographic Research & Exploration, 10*(4), 440–457.

Chernela, J. (1994b). What is a population?: Spouse import in the Northwest Amazon. In D. Price & K. Adams (Eds.), *The demography of small-scale societies: Case studies from lowland South America* (South American Indian Studies, 4, pp. 10–17). Bennington.

Chernela, J. (1997). Ideal speech moments: A woman's narrative performance in the Northwest Amazon. *Feminist Studies, 23*(1), 73–96.

Chernela, J. (2001). Piercing distinctions: Making and re-making the social contract in the Northwest Amazon. In N. Whitehead & L. Rival (Eds.), *Beyond the visible and the material: The Amerindianization of society in the work of Peter Riviere* (pp. 177–196). Oxford: Oxford University Press.

Chernela, J. (2002). Fathering in the Northwest Amazon of Brazil: Competition, monopoly, and partition. In S. Beckerman & P. Valentine (Eds.), *Cultures of multiple fathers: The theory and practice of partible paternity in lowland South America* (pp. 160–177). Gainesville: University of Florida Press.

Chernela, J., & Leed, E. (1996). Shamanic journeys and anthropological travels. *Anthropological Quarterly* [Special Edition], 69(3), 129–133.

Goldman, I. (1963). *The Cubeo*. Urbana: University of Illinois Press.

Hugh-Jones, C. (1979). *From the Milk River: Spatial and temporal process in Northwest Amazonia*. Cambridge, U.K.: Cambridge University Press.

Hugh-Jones, S. (1979). *The palm and the Pleiades: Initiation and cosmology in Northwest Amazonia*. Cambridge, U.K.: Cambridge University Press.

Jackson, J. (1983). *The Fish People: Linguistic exogamy and Tukanoan identity in Northwest Amazonia*. Cambridge, U.K.: Cambridge University Press.

Sorensen, A. (1967). Multilingualism in the Northwest Amazon. *American Anthropologist, 69*(6), 670–684.

Germans

Jakob M. Pastötter

ALTERNATIVE NAMES

The German name is "Deutsche" from Germanic *thiot* ("nation/people"). It does not go back to an ancient name or term but was developed following the line: *deutsche* (German) language—*Deutsche* (Germans)—*Deutschland* (Germany). The term was first coined as "theodiscus" in 768 under the rule of the Holy Roman Emperor Charles the Great, or Charlemagne, in the context of language to make a distinction from the Romance-speaking people. Thus, even today, *deutsch* strongly relies on culture and language, although the term *deutsche Kulturnation* (German Culture Nation), which is a phrase of the 18th and 19th century to describe the fact that German-speaking people share a common cultural heritage but do not live in a single state, is rarely used nowadays.

LOCATION

Today, Germans live in three states located in Central Europe: the Federal Republic of Germany (FRG), which embraces 357,021 km² following the reunification of West Germany and the former Communist East Germany in 1990, Austria with an area of 82,738 km², and Switzerland with an area of 41,293 km². There is also the small Dukedom of Liechtenstein between Switzerland and Austria with an area of 157 km². German minorities live in all adjoining countries, but few German settlements in Eastern Europe, some going back to medieval colonies, have survived the expulsions following World War II and 50 years of Communist and nationalist rule. Denmark and the Baltic Sea mark the borders in the north, The Netherlands, Belgium, Luxembourg, France, and French-speaking Switzerland in the west, Slovenia, Italy, and Italian-speaking Switzerland in the south, and Poland, the Czech Republic, Slovakia, and Hungary in the east. Germany's terrain includes lowlands in the north, uplands in the center, and the Bavarian Alps in the south. Austria includes the Austrian Alps and their foothills in the western and southern parts and

the Danube River basin in the north and east, while German-speaking Switzerland includes uplands in the north and the Swiss Alps in the south. The climate is temperate and marine. In 2001, Germany had an estimated population of 83,000,000, Austria of 8,000,000, and Swiss Germans accounted for 4,000,000 of the total Swiss population of 7,000,000.

CULTURAL OVERVIEW

Although there are many aspects affecting the individual habitus as the social, cultural, and economic fabric of the three German-speaking countries, it may be acceptable to neglect those in favor of a broader and more general picture, especially since the largest country, the Federal Republic of Germany, is in many cultural aspects heterogeneous. Differences between, for example, an East Berliner, who was socialized in the Communist German Democratic Republic, and a rural Catholic Bavarian are greater than those between a Bavarian and an Austrian (although they have lived in different states for many centuries). However, all Germans share a long history and tradition of paternalism and patriarchalism, which is still prevalent today. The main differences among the different regions are first based on a difference of the main denominations (or, of course, the absence of religion): Lutheran in Northern Germany; agnosticism in East Germany; Catholicism in South Germany and Austria; Reformed Protestantism and Catholicism in Southwest Germany and German Switzerland. Also, regional differences are rooted in the historical German "tribes" (Alemanni, Bavarians, Franks, Friesians, Saxons, and Thuringians), which refer to the migration era in late antiquity.

The most important historical and political developments in Germany are the unification of a dozen of medium-sized and small states when the German Empire was founded in 1870, followed by what one might call the "militarization" and bureaucratization of German society under Prussian predominance together with rapid and successful industrialization. With regard to Austria, her long history as the heartland of the Habsburg monarchy and the transition into a small state after World War I should be mentioned, and Switzerland has a long tradition as the oldest democracy with strong federal elements.

Today, all Germans live in democratic and industrialized states; farming exists only as heavily subsidized part of the economy. Environmentalist groups are strong; one of the reasons for this is that "nature" is highly valued by Germans, which shows that Romanticism as well as German Idealism left their marks. The majority of Germans live in cities or suburbs; in Germany the urban-to-rural distribution is 85% to 15%, with a higher balance in Austria and Switzerland. The literacy rate (those aged 15 and over who can read and write) is about 99%, with up to 100% attendance in 9 or 10 years of compulsory schooling. The per capita gross domestic product (purchasing power parity) is $23,400 in Germany, and even higher in Austria and Switzerland. The unemployment rate is highest in Germany at 9.9% and lowest in Switzerland at 2.6% (in 2002).

Although birthrates are well below the substitution rate with about 9% births but 10% deaths per 1,000 population, only Switzerland has an active immigration policy. Of the 7 million people in Switzerland, 2 million are immigrants, while the net migration rate in the other states is just 2.45 migrants per 1,000 population, also due to stressing the *ius sanguinis* over a more pragmatic approach. Immigrants are generally supposed to integrate or to live in their own areas, which has resulted in the development of a ghetto culture, especially in the largest group of immigrants in Germany, the Islamic Turkish (2.4% of the population). However, the "visibility" of immigrants is high, since ethnic restaurants (Chinese, Croatian, Greek, Indian, Italian, Vietnamese) can be found in even the smallest towns. The Turkish "döner" is the favorite fast food, more popular than the traditional sausages. "Salsa parties" in bars are a meeting point for German women and Arabic immigrants.

CULTURAL CONSTRUCTION OF GENDER

The recognized gender categories are male and female. The existence of intersex people plays no role in public, although awareness is slowly growing. Some transvestites have gained media fame, for example, Lilo Wanders as the moderator of the sex show *Wa(h)re Liebe* (True Love/Love as Consumer's Item) on Private TV. Cross-dressing is very popular during Carnival. In primary schoolbooks the men are pictured as earning the family income, whereas women stay at home, preparing hearty meals and caring for the children. This is surprising, since the laws have been much more progressive for decades, and offer the opportunity for both mothers and fathers to take paid leave of absence from work for childcare until the child's second birthday.

Apart from make-up and skirts, there are few differences between genders. Even same types of make-up and dyed hair can be seen in ultra-fashionable youths at techno music parties, like the millions of so-called "ravers" attracted to the "Love Parade" in Berlin or the "Street Parade" in Zurich. Shaving of the body hair has slowly become fashionable with women, and more slowly by men, though only a minority wear beards. Piercings and tattoos are in favor with both genders, if done at all. However, the more conservative and/or distinguished people have more traditional visual gender differences, such as short hair for men and long hair or permanent waves for women (regarded as feminine and sexually attractive). When it comes to certain hair colors and body shapes, opinion polls show that all types of hair color, breast sizes, and figures are accepted, with the exception of the obese. However, nearly half of German men would prefer a blonde women for sex, although there is no clear preference when it comes to a future wife. German women seem to prefer a dark complexion in men.

GENDER OVER THE LIFE CYCLE

The cultural names for stages in the life cycle are neutral: *Neugeborenes* (new born) up to the 10th day after birth, the neutral *Säugling* (baby) for children up to the 12th month of life, the neutral *Kleinkind* (toddler) or *Spielkind* (playing child) from age 2 to 5, the neutral *Schulkind* (schoolchild) or *Schulmädchen* (schoolgirl) and *Schuljunge* (schoolboy) from age 6 to 14, *Jugendliche* (female young person) and *Jugendlicher* (male young person) (also "Teenager") up to majority at 18, *Erwachsene* or *Frau* (female adult or woman) and *Erwachsener* or *Mann* (male adult or man), *Greisin* or *Seniorin* (very old woman), and *Greis* or *Senior* (very old man).

As in other Western postindustrial societies, there are only small traces of rites of passage left like baptism/name-giving, first day in school, confirmation/initiation (the latter is the agnostic ceremony in which 14-year-olds are given adult social status), driver's license, school degree, entering the job market, and retirement. If they are marked at all, it is only by the appropriate Christian ceremony and by gifts. As in all modern states there are certain legal rights and obligations connected with each age.

Socialization of Boys and Girls

In rural areas it is still common for friends and relatives to decorate the home of a newborn child with a wooden stork, baby clothes, and toys hanging on a line. While there is nothing special to announce the birth of a boy, if a girl has been delivered tins and a sign reading *Büchsenmacher* (tin-maker) referring to the father (*Büchsen* stands for the female genitals as well as the girl), are added to the line.

When surveyed, parents tend to state that they value girls and boys alike. However, when asked about the gender preference of their first (and often only) child, a change can be observed: no longer a son (as son and heir) but a daughter is preferred. One explanation is that, owing to welfare and social security systems, parents in Western societies do not depend on male heirs to support them financially when in old age but on daughters to do household and nursing tasks and to care for them emotionally. Also, the valuation of "masculine" aggressive behavior and "female" soft skills have changed. The first is regarded as more of a problem because boys attract attention as ruffians or trouble-makers with poor social skills as early as in kindergarten and elementary school (both domains of female teachers), while girls fit in better and do better in this environment because of their soft skills.

There are different emotional expectations of boys and girls, which also show in the color blue for boys and pink for girls in baby garments, as well as more technical toys and computer games for boys and dolls for girls. However, it is usually not regarded as a "problem" for girls to behave as tomboys or for boys to enjoy playing with dolls. At first glance, childhood seems to be a more or less "gender-free" phase, but nevertheless behavior judged as "natural" for boys or girls is either enhanced or discouraged. Girls must mind their manners, that is, be more disciplined and less noisy, but compassionate and generally "friendly". It can be observed, though, that some mothers are encouraging their daughters to be as aggressive as boys. Nevertheless girls are still supposed to help with household tasks, while only a minority of boys are expected to do cleaning, wash dishes, cook, and do the laundry. Such chores are considered to be girls' work; only taking the garbage outside is regularly done by boys. More than three quarters of men and women of the younger generation think that boys and girls should both help in the house.

Only few open differences in the upbringing and education of boys and girls exist, but there are still a number of smaller and less conscious signs which send clear signals in one direction or the other. Germans clearly tend to bring their children up and "educate" in an informal rather than a formal way about "proper" gender behavior.

Puberty and Adolescence

Owing to the earlier onset of puberty (compared with the parents' generation) many parents see their children still as "little ones" when in fact they are adolescents. The blurring of the differences in the behavior of young age groups under the influence of media is the most significant trend in German society. Peers are more important than the family when it comes to dealing with the specific changes of puberty. A remarkable development is that it has become more acceptable for girls to be more aggressive, while boys are expected to be less so. Although the so-called "girlie" (young woman behaving and dressing in a "self-assured" "girls just wanna have fun" manner) was a short fad, and positively judged as "postfeminist", at the end of the 20th century, self-assertive behavior has survived to a certain degree. Pubescent boys feel insecure and sometimes dominated by girls, partly because girls of their own age tend to prefer to date older boys. The gap between boy and girl becomes wider during "teenage" years (an English term also used in German). While girls do better in the social environment of school, boys develop an inferiority complex. A few rebel and revenge by developing a "macho" habitus (Nickel, 1992). Interestingly, some apparent "natural" sex differences disappeared over time in the German Democratic Republic. For example, while mathematics was despised by girls in the 1960s, over the next 20 years mathematics became their favorite subject, as it had been previously only for boys. This change also showed in the good achievements of girls in mathematics, as well as in other intelligence and creativity tests (Starke, 1992). At this age, both genders stress love as the reason for becoming sexually active; both share a view of relationship based on partnership. There is now little difference between the genders regarding the start of sexual activity or number of intimate partners; however, female university students seem to have rather more partners and earlier sexual activity than boys (Dekker, 1999). Only the Scandinavians among postindustrialized nations show a similar pattern.

Attainment of Adulthood

Attainment of adulthood varies with social and educational levels. For apprentices, adulthood is reached when the 3 years of apprenticeship training is finished (or at the earliest at the legal age of majority of 18). A student, possibly living at home and on a parental allowance, may be aged 25 or more before being considered an adult. Other "indicators" for adulthood are obtaining a driver's license, making a living, and renting one's own apartment; in other words, "standing on one's own feet". The *Kohabitarche*, i.e., the onset of sexual activity, is not an indicator of adulthood.

Middle Age and Old Age

Germans regard "youthful" behavior in middle-aged and old people as awkward and embarrassing. This is also true for sexual behavior. Men and women of a certain age are still widely thought of as asexual. Germans generally have difficulty in accepting that older people can fall in love and experience sexual arousal. The more the population ages, the more this attitude is likely to be discussed; so far, there is little discussion of these topics.

PERSONALITY DIFFERENCES BY GENDER

Many psychological problems are gender specific. While boys and men tend to suffer from aggression-related problems, women are more apt to experience depression. Substance abuse and alcoholism are also gender specific. While men form the majority of heavy drinkers and alcoholics, women form the majority of psychiatric drug abusers. While male alcoholics attract public attention because they usually behave noisily and aggressively,

female addicts are much less visible. Most bulimics and people with eating disorders are female, although males are slowly catching up. Obesity affects both genders equally, with increasing numbers of children affected. As in other Western societies most obese people are generally from lower social classes.

GENDER-RELATED SOCIAL GROUPS

There is one social group that seems to be self-explanatory at first glance—mothers. However, since the law gives fathers the opportunity to care for a baby at home, but experience the same kind of "exclusion" from this group as women of childbearing age with no children, it may be assumed that it is not just the fact of being a mother that is the reason for a certain exclusiveness of this group. There is little research on this matter yet, but the so-called *Müttergruppen* (mother groups) that the majority of German mothers form show that at certain periods in the life cycle groups can become a major factor even in highly individualistic societies. The activities of these mother groups vary: some just meet at one mother's house, discussing child-raising issues and giving each other advice while watching the children play; others organize short trips or even lectures on education. A high degree of social control can be observed in all of them.

Every third German is a member of some kind of society, association, or club, most of which are open to both genders. However, clubs attract more men and associations more women.

GENDER ROLES IN ECONOMICS

The constitutions of Germany, Austria, and Switzerland forbid any discrimination in the job market (including the armed forces in Germany since 2001) because of gender; however, differences still exist. In particular, qualified women experience an "invisible glass ceiling" at some time in their thirties or forties, and their career advancement stops. Because lower positions in the corporate hierarchy receive proportionately lower compensation, the "glass ceiling" means that women in West Germany earn about 78% of the gross salary per hour that men receive. In the former Communist East Germany, where many more women held full-time jobs and where they were paid equally before the Union, their salaries are now about 90% of those of men. The average income for women in all of Germany was 2297 Euro (about the same in US dollars) in April 2002, which is 21% less than that of their male counterparts. Although the proportion of female professors at German universities increased in the 1990s, they still constitute less than 10% of all professors. Only 5.9% of university professors of the highest and best-paid rank are women. Even if they work outside the home, most household tasks are still performed by women.

There are clear preferences in occupations that require training. Women prefer jobs that require mainly "soft" skills such as office administrator, retail sales-women, hairdresser, doctor's receptionist, dental nurse, and industrial manager. Men prefer jobs that require pre-dominantly manual skills like motor vehicle mechanic, painter, electrician, carpenter, cook, and metalworker. At university, women prefer humanities and social sciences, and men prefer natural sciences. Law, economics, and medical courses are gender equal.

Parental and Other Caretaker Roles

Mothers play the dominant role in child-rearing although more and more young fathers are unwilling to neglect their children in favor of a career. In divorce cases, fathers fight for their right to see their children; however, in most cases mothers obtain custody. There are only small differences regarding disciplining, education, physical care, affection, or how fathers and mothers spend time with their sons and daughters.

Leadership in Public Arenas

Although men and women enjoy the same rights in the public and political sphere, men are still predominant in leadership positions. Some of the reasons may be the lack of extensive female networks, the predominance of women in service jobs, the high degree of informal social "rules" that decide about a career in political parties (which cannot be taught or learnt because they favor and promote a certain social and communicative habitus that is predominantly male), and the high average age in traditional political parties. Women may also have some

physical disadvantages, such as their generally lower tolerance of alcohol. Alcohol consumption still seems to be a very important social "lubricant" in the traditional German political party and public administration net-works—a tradition that goes back at least to the early modern age. This makes it understandable that the pro-portion of women in politics is highest in the relatively new Green Party. This party had a high share of female membership from the very beginning and the average age of party members is low.

Gender and Religion

Traditionally, the majority of churchgoers are female, while the majority of priests are male. The example of female saints in Catholicism is that of a very traditional female life model: maternal and social qualities are favored. This also shows in male and female orders: the latter are predominantly engaged in teaching early grades, in hospitals, and in nursing homes. Informal religiousness, like the different forms of so-called "new age" religion, does not show much difference; women are presented as maternal, devote, patient, and passive. Here also the majority of followers are women.

Leisure, Recreation, and the Arts

Employees in the Federal Republic of Germany have the highest rate of leisure time of all Western countries; they spend just over 35 hours a week at work (4.5 days a week) and enjoy about 30 days of paid vacation. Nevertheless, Germans do not relax much; they are as busy in their leisure time as at work. Favorite pastimes are socializing at bars and visiting one of the numerous public festivals and funfairs. In the summer, sunbathing, water sports, and roller-blading are enjoyed, while in the winter, all kinds of winter sports are popular. In surveys of leisure-time activities, listening to music is often men-tioned, while reading is only occasionally mentioned. Germans spend an average of 3–4 hours a day watching television and playing computer games. The latter attract more boys than girls. Men prefer to watch sports and women prefer to visit art galleries and attend seminars. Also, more women than men are involved in charities.

RELATIVE STATUS OF MEN AND WOMEN

There are no legal differences between the value attached to men and women by the state or in authority, rights and privileges. Even informal differences are very difficult to pinpoint. Only the still very common "obsequious" behavior of girls and young women towards male leadership in organizational or technical matters may point in this direction, but it might also only be the result of a hierarchical gradient. Usually even these women who show a distinctive obsequious behavior deny, if asked, that they think that men in general are of higher value. However, in this context it is surprising that more female employees (6%) take the chance of a *Seitensprung* (a "bit on the side," (little) affair) at company parties than men (1%) according to a Forsa survey in 2000. Only the Catholic church is still a stronghold of formal male supremacy, although this might be changing because the German Catholic Church suffers a severe shortage of priests and so more and more tasks are taken on by female lay helpers. However, although they gain some informal influence because of these activities, they are not paid or distinguished with a hierarchical rank.

SEXUALITY

Together with the Benelux and the Scandinavian nations, Germans may have the most liberal attitude towards sexuality of all industrialized countries. Although many complain about what they see as the "typical German inhibition" and regard Asian or Latin American societies as more sexually fun loving, this view ignores the fact that actual knowledge about sexuality is very high, while social taboos connected with sexuality hardly exist at all. This is the case not only at the legal level but also in media and everyday lives. While a third of all men and a quarter of all women still have difficulties talking about sex, the majority have no inhibitions. The body, bodily functions, and sexuality are widely seen as "natural" and have positive connotations. However, 80% still say that they prefer to be alone in the bathroom. In contrast with many societies where others prohibit and proscribe sexual partners, there is a high degree of individual decision-making about with whom and when one would like to have sex. However, the main "reason" for having sex is the conviction that one has fallen in love. Differences between the concept of male and female sexuality are diminishing. Neither quality nor quantity are decisive, and only 37% of women say that they would not have sex on a first date, while 36% of them would neglect their conviction if they felt that the right moment had come already. This also shows that there is no longer a negative attitude towards premarital sex; the distinctive factor for sexual activity is falling in love. Nevertheless, fidelity is an important value, which leads to so-called "serial monogamy" or "chain marriage". The main reasons given for breaking up or divorcing are the lack of conversation topics and drifting apart.

Sexual expression during childhood, like touching and fondling the genitals, or so-called "doctor games" (where children discover each other's bodies and sometimes even pretend to have sex with each other), are widely accepted and regarded as "natural" at this early stage of life. Things change in prepubertal and adolescent years; parents seldom realize that children develop sexual interest in their early teenage years, which has resulted in a growing number of teenage pregnancies and abortions due to a lack of sex education by the parents. Parents rely on sex education taught in school. However, teachers have no formal training in sex education beyond the biological facts of life. In informing their children about sex, parents tend to be biased. Sons are usually less well informed than daughters. Morality standards are higher in Catholic regions and in the countryside, especially regarding girls. Adults are more or less free in their sexual activities as long as no sexual harassment takes place.

Only total nudity is still regarded a taboo in public, notwithstanding the fact that nude sunbathing is very popular and legal even in city parks. However, this takes place in special zones, designated for nudism or FKK (*Freie Körperkultur*—Free Body Culture), which are not regarded as being in the public sphere. Naked breasts are common at the Love Parade and other Techno festivals, as well as Christopher Street Day festivals. Cross-dressing is very popular at these festivities and during the long Carnival season from November 11 to Shrove Tuesday. The extent of expected modesty is gender equal.

Most Germans see themselves as tolerant towards homosexuals. More than 70% of Germans under the age of 40 accept homosexuality and, in a 1996 survey, 49% said they were in favor of a registry office marriage for homosexuals, 93% wanted homosexuals to have the same job opportunities, and two thirds suggested a law to protect homosexuals against discrimination. Austria and the German Federal State of Bavaria, which are the most Catholic regions, are also the most adverse to homosexuality. In 1994, Section 175 of the German Penal Code, which prohibited male homosexual activity (female homosexuality had never been prosecuted), was removed. Since 2001, homosexual couples can enter into a *Eingetragene Lebenspartnerschaft* (registered cohabitation). About half of all German homosexuals cohabit and, although not every such couple will decide for an *Eingetragene Lebenspartnerschaft*, the legal possibility is widely seen as a good thing. The argument is that all social commitments and responsibilities should be strengthened in a time of progressive social fragmentation. In the Swiss German speaking canton of Zurich a majority of 62% voted for a similar law in 2002; since 1999 the new federal constitution prohibits discrimination because of one's lifestyle. In Austria, homosexuality has not been punishable since 1975.

COURTSHIP AND MARRIAGE

Dating is informal in the German countries. There are no rules. Few women expect men to pay for restaurant bills or cinema tickets. However, the majority of women expect men to initiate the first step. Going steady and often cohabiting for some time is the main reason for a later marriage; men and women want to feel comfortable with each other, trust and fidelity are important, many men prefer a "buddy-like" wife, and hold caressing (62%) in much higher regard than sex (19%). Seventy-three percent of all Germans see marriage as a lifelong commitment—men and married couples even more so at 77% and 81%, respectively. Seventy-three percent think that marriage is a symbol of love, 59% say that it is important because of the children, 42% say that it serves the purpose of providing support, and 16% marry for a more regular sex life.

There is also a trend towards a new high regard of the family as an emotional home. Surveys show that 72% hope to find Mr./Ms. Right and 33% think that finding an ideal partner is the most important thing in life. Ninety-four percent of young people say that they believe in true love, 70% hope for a single lifelong relationship, and only 4% say that they are not interested in an intimate relationship.

Despite the ideal of the family as an emotional home, in 1999, only one in 25 Germans lived in a household with five or more individuals. Single households have quintupled since the beginning of the 20th century. In 1999, 36% of Germans were living alone. A third were living with one other person, 15% living with two others, 12% with three others, and only 4% in households of five or more. Most of the latter are located in small communities of less than 5,000 people; most of the former live in the big cities with more than 500,000 people. Nearly half of the 1.2 million Berliners between 25 and 45 are single. In the early 1990s, 20% of Germans between ages 25 and 35 lived in a single household; in 2000 this rose to 25%. It appears likely that by 2010 a third of this age group will be living alone. In 1998 17% of all children under age 27 lived with a single parent. One third of all Germans experience the single life-style as being forced on them.

Marriage ceremonies vary from a simple civil wedding with just two witnesses to a traditional farmer's marriage (although the couple do not have to be farmers) with hundreds of guests, beginning days before with a marriage messenger walking to each guest's house and inviting them with a poem. In the traditional marriage, the day of the wedding would start early in the morning with a wake-up call by a traditional brass band and a first opulent meal with all guests. All go to church together. After the ceremony the newlywed couple and the guests go to an inn where dinner is served. The expenses are shared evenly by the parents of bride and bridegroom. After dinner some traditional "games" are played, which aim at showing that the bridegroom has lost his freedom and the bride has to be a good housekeeper and mother. The texts are often sexually explicit, though not pornographic. In the afternoon, some male guests "kidnap" the bride and hide her. The bridegroom has to find her, assisted by the guests. After the search, people gather for wine and more games before the crowd goes back to the inn where another meal is prepared. Dancing, drinking, and eating can last until the early morning. Such a traditional marriage is followed by a honeymoon vacation of 1 or 2 weeks. There is no restriction regarding the remarriage of widows or widowers.

HUSBAND–WIFE RELATIONSHIP

Love is the main reason for getting married, and so couples consider love, affection, and companionship as being essential. For the majority, it is a sign of diminishing love if a couple do not share the same bed or spend their leisure time together. Many wives still depend on their husband for financial matters like insurance and retirement plans, but more and more young women have become responsible in these matters. When it comes to sharing household tasks, women still take on the greater workload, although they often have full-time jobs. A partnership model of equals is most in favor with East German girls and women with an academic education, and is least favored in Catholic rural regions.

Divorce can be filed by any gender, usually with reference to the principle of irretrievable breakdown. One in three marriages does not last; in the big cities it is one in two. The 1998 divorce rates were 85.7 per 10,000 marriages in West Germany and 105.7 per 10,000 marriages in East Germany. More than half of the divorces involved minor dependents, with the mother usually being granted custody. Four out of five divorced husbands had another partner within 10 months, while half of all women were still single after 3 years. Two thirds of all divorce petitions were filed by wives.

OTHER CROSS-SEX RELATIONSHIPS

No significant male–female relationships—brother–sister, grandparent–grandchild, uncle–niece, aunt–nephew, or others—seems to exist.

CHANGE IN ATTITUDES, BELIEFS, AND PRACTICES REGARDING GENDER

Although traditional German paternalistic and patriarchic persistence is strong in public as well as private life, many aspects point to a slow change towards female predominance: the communication style has become less authoritarian, a growing number of girls are better educated (more than half of all students today are female), "soft" skills are gaining importance in the job market, and women are less dependent on their husband to earn a

living. On the other hand, men have come to realize that there is no birthright for male dominance. Men also accept that aggression can be destructive, and that it is important to engage in discussion to solve problems.

BIBLIOGRAPHY

Bundeszentrale für gesundheitliche Aufklärung (BzgA), Abteilung Sexualaufklärung, Verhütung und Familienplanung (1995ff). *Forschung und Praxis der Sexualaufklärung und Familienplanung* [Research and praxis of sex education and family planning] (Vols 1–17). Köln, Germany: Editor.

Dekker, A. (1999). Veränderungen des Sexualverhaltens von Studentinnen und Studenten 1966–1981–1996. [Changes of sexual behavior of male and female students 1966–1981–1996.] In Bundeszentrale für gesundheitliche Aufklärung (BzgA) (Ed.), *Wissenschaftliche Grundlagen: Teil 2, Jugendliche* [Scientific fundamentals: Part 2, Adolescents] (pp. 141–155). Köln, Germany: Editor.

König, O. (1990). *Nacktheit. Soziale Normierung und Moral* [Nudity: Social standardization and morality]. Opladen, Germany: Westdeutscher Verlag.

Lautmann, R., & Starke, K. (1997). Germany. In R. T. Francoeur (Ed.), *The international encyclopedia of Sexuality* (Vol. 1, pp. 492–518). New York: Continuum International.

Mayer, K. U., & Baltes, P. B. (1996). *Die Berliner Altersstudie* [The Berlin study on aging]. Berlin: Akademie Verlag.

Nickel, H. M. (1992). Soziologische Aspekte männlicher und weiblicher Identität oder Rekonstruktion des Patriarchats durch Sozialisation [Sociological aspects of male and female identity, or reconstruction of patriarchy through socialization]. In K.-F. Wessel & H. A. G. Bosinski (Eds.), *Interdisziplinäre Aspekte der Geschlechterverhältnisse in einer sich wandelnden Zeit* [Interdisciplinarian aspects of gender relations in a changing time] (pp. 218–224). Bielefeld, Germany: Kleine Verlag.

Schmidt, G. (Ed.). (2000). *Kinder der sexuellen Revolution. Kontinuität und Wandel studentischer Sexualität 1966–1996* [Children of the sexual revolution: Continuity and change of student sexuality 1966–1996]. Giessen, Germany: Psychosozial-Verlag.

Starke, K. (1992). Unterschiede im Partner- und Sexualverhalten männlicher und weiblicher Jugendlicher [Differences in partnership and sexual behavior of male and female adolescents]. In K.-F. Wessel & H. A. G. Bosinski (Eds.), *Interdisziplinäre Aspekte der Geschlechterverhältnisse in einer sich wandelnden Zeit* [Interdisciplinary aspects of gender relations in a changing time] (pp. 225–240). Bielefeld, Germany: Kleine Verlag.

Glebo

Mary H. Moran

ALTERNATIVE NAMES

Alternative names are Grebo, Gedebo, Nyomowe, and Kuniwe.

LOCATION

Numbering under 10,000 people, the Glebo are one of many ethnolinguistic groups living in the Republic of Liberia on the west coast of Africa. They occupy a series of 13 towns along Liberia's southeastern coast, close to the international border with Côte d'Ivoire, and farm tracts of interior forest up to 30 miles inland from the shore.

CULTURAL OVERVIEW

Most Glebo are shifting rice farmers with a relatively egalitarian form of social organization in which the major status distinctions are age and gender. The Glebo language belongs to the Kwa or Kruan subfamily of the Niger–Congo group. Like the rest of Liberia's indigenous peoples, they reckon kinship through patrilineal descent, which means that children "belong" to their father's family in terms of the inheritance of rights to land and other privileges. Ideally, a woman moves to her husband's home town at marriage and farms land to which he has access. However, married women do not lose their affiliation with their own families of birth and can claim land for farming through their fathers and brothers. Despite a formal ideology of patriarchy, local-level political organization includes parallel public offices for men and women, and a series of checks and balances ensures that women have a voice in community-wide affairs. Although the coastal towns are important for social and political identity and are the sites of significant ritual events, they are fully occupied for only a few months of the year. Most people spend the majority of their time on their upland farms in a dispersed settlement pattern in which extended families farm adjacent land. The coast, with its sandy beaches and lagoons, is used for fishing and collecting shellfish.

Between the coast and the forest is about 10–15 miles of open grassy savannah, where cattle are pastured and cassava is grown. Rice, the primary crop, is grown in rain-fed fields in the high forest (mostly secondary growth) farther to the interior, where game animals are hunted and palm nuts, rubber, and other forest products are collected. The Glebo move constantly between these environmental zones as they carry out their subsistence activities.

Like other tropical forest-dwelling horticulturalists, the Glebo fall within what has come to be called "the female farming" belt of West and Central Africa. As the name implies, most of the work of subsistence agriculture is performed by women, and the status of family bread-winner is central to feminine identity. The most common occupation reported by women in my 1983 census of the Cape Palmas community was "farmer" (Moran, 1990). International development workers, conditioned to see men as farmers and women as "farmer's wives," have often introduced inappropriate and even damaging agricultural programs because of a failure to understand this basic division of labor. Men's occupations are often a combination of seasonal labor, cash cropping, hunting, and gathering forest products, but provisioning the household is not seen as a male responsibility. Where both spouses are involved in the cash sector, as with women who have gone into full-time market trading, the responsibility for providing food on a daily basis is still defined as female. Only among the "civilized," or educated, Western-oriented Glebo community is a married woman ideally to be supported by her husband, and even here, a woman will often have a small business selling baked goods or surplus produce in order to have her own income.

CULTURAL CONSTRUCTION OF GENDER

As mentioned above, gender categories are closely related to economic roles, with the provisioning of the household an essential aspect of femininity. If women are identified as "farmers," the male equivalent is "warrior," reflecting the long history of intergroup conflict in this region. Women are also said to be warriors in some contexts, such as childbirth, which demand courage and endurance. The funeral dances conducted for both men and women are referred to as war dances, although the men's version actually mimics the techniques of warfare while the women's focuses on complex steps and drum patterns. There are no culturally recognized third genders or cross-gendered persons, but transvestism is common in ritual contexts like the men's war dance and another funeral dance performed for women of child-bearing age. In the case of the men's war dance, transvestite elements signal the transcendence of the warrior over all normal social categories, including gender (Moran, 1996).

Liberia has been incorporated into the global economy for centuries through the trans-Saharan and Atlantic trade in salt, ivory, pepper, and slaves. Since the late 15th century, when European ships first made their way down the west coast of Africa, local communities have integrated Western items, including clothing, into their way of life. For everyday dress, men wear shirts and pants or shorts of foreign manufacture, usually purchased in second-hand clothing markets. When relaxing at home or in certain ritual contexts, men wear a length of cloth wrapped around the waist, sometimes with a second cloth draped over the shoulder. Women's attire is differentiated by status; uneducated farmers and market vendors wear the cloth wrapper, or *lappa*, with a blouse tailored from the same material or an imported T-shirt. Married women signal their status with two *lappas*, one of which is used to cover a baby that is tied to the mother's back. Educated or "civilized" women wear Western-style dresses in most public contexts, but may dress in *lappas* while doing housework at home. Local tailors produce elaborate "*lappa* suits" for urban professional women in which the wrapped cloth is replaced by a long skirt with a zipper.

Ideals of physical attractiveness include defined musculature and "smooth" (closely cut) hair for men, and smooth skin, beautifully arranged hair, and a full figure for women. Extreme slimness is taken as a sign of illness (translated into English as "looking dry") for both sexes. Both men and women are also admired for their ability to work hard, govern their emotions, and use discretion.

GENDER OVER THE LIFE CYCLE

Like many of their neighbors, the Glebo have an elaborate system of named age grades for men that functions as part of the local political structure. A set of age categories for women describe different aspects of the life cycle but do not have the same corporate or political functions as those of the men. Babies and toddlers are not distinguished by gender but are simply called *kyinibo* or *pede nyinibo* ("those who fail to look after their own excrement"). Young children who are fully mobile are collectively referred to as *wodo yudu* or "town children." Girls begin to have more household duties at this age, collecting wood and water and looking after younger siblings. Such tasks are not gender specific, however, since boys who have no sisters or who are simply available when the need arises will also be pressed into service.

Adolescent and young men who are not yet married constitute the *kinibo*, and in former times acted as a kind of police force, carrying out the judgments of older men. With marriage, a man enters the age group known as *sidibo* or "soldiers." This is a corporate age-based organization, with internal officers, shared ownership of ritual equipment and drums, and their own meeting house, the *tiba kae*. Based on the accounts of 19th century missionaries, historian Jane Martin (1968) has concluded that the internal politics of Glebo communities was dominated by an ongoing power struggle between the *sidibo* and the council of elders (the *gbudubo* or *takae*), made up of the oldest living male member of each resident *pano*, or patriclan, in a town. This council is not technically an age grade, since neither cohorts nor individuals are automatically promoted into it at a certain age or life stage; rather, some very elderly men remain "soldiers" all their lives due to the longevity of a slightly older kinsman (Moran, 1990, p. 30).

Women pass from the category of "town children" to "town women" (*wodo nyeno*) with marriage. Like men, they are recognized as "fully grown" about the age of 50; before that time they may be classified with adult men of similar age as *gofa*, or "youth." The women's council of elders, also known as *takae*, consists of a representative chosen by the women of each kin group in a town, either a resident daughter of the kin group or an in-marrying wife. The primary qualifications for election are demonstrated leadership and speaking abilities. All the women of the town choose one member of the council to hold the position of *blo nyene*, the "woman's president" (see below). The women's council meets jointly with the men's *takae* on community-wide affairs and separately on issues relating only to women. In general, both men and women gain in status and prestige as they age, although gender remains a significant means of stratification; a widely cited proverb holds that "men are always older than women."

Socialization of Boys and Girls

The birth of a girl seems as highly valued as that of a boy in Glebo society; since women are economically productive, bring bridewealth to their families at marriage, and remain members of their patrilineage for life, this is not surprising. Children of both sexes are given tasks to do as soon as they seem able, including sweeping the house and surrounding yard, fetching firewood and water, and minding younger siblings. Boys have more freedom of movement than girls and, unless there are no girls of appropriate age in the household, seem to be less burdened with household work than their female kin. Parents sometimes complain that it is not worth the trouble to find and compel young boys into work; girls are believed to be more compliant. Yet, domestic work is not strictly gender segregated and young unmarried men are expected to be able to cook for themselves and wash their own clothes if the need arises, skills which they undoubtedly learned as children.

Boys and girls usually play in gender-segregated groups. In coastal towns, soccer (football) is the preferred team sport for boys and almost any round object that can be kicked will be used as a ball. Girls may practice dance steps and chase each other in games of tag. Occasionally, a mixed-sex group of children will enact some adult activity, such as a development rally or witchcraft investigation. If family resources are limited, only the boys, or one boy, may be chosen to attend formal school. Parents fear that girls who are sent to school may become pregnant and leave before they acquire enough education for the wage sector. This common scenario is responsible for the very disparate numbers of boys and girls in the educational system. In general, boys are expected to be more active, aggressive, and mobile than girls. Although all young people are expected to behave with great respect towards their elders, girls are instructed to cast their eyes down and sit with their legs pressed closely together as a sign of modesty and deference.

Puberty and Adolescence

The Glebo have no formal initiation rites into adulthood, although one has been reported for men entering the warrior age grade among the neighboring Sabo

(McEvoy, 1971, p. 181). In contrast with the Mande-speaking peoples to their north, none of the Kwa-speaking groups practice genital cutting as a mark of initiation into adulthood. There is little formal emphasis on virginity for either males or females. A text contained in Innes's grammatical description of the Glebo language, contributed by an informant in London, describes the "sweetness" of youthful sexual experimentation: "love-making does not wait for maturity and old age, hence children make love, just as adults do" (Innes, 1966, p. 132).

Attainment of Adulthood

Marriage is an important means of attaining adulthood for both men and women, although there is little in the way of public ceremony to mark the event. Bridewealth negotiations and payments may be extended over many years, during which the couple live together and have children yet consider the marriage "not yet" completed. Men join the sidibo and begin to have community-wide responsibilities at this time, as women are recognized as members of the "town women" and are expected to contribute to funeral dancing and generally take an interest in community affairs. A long tradition of male wage-labor migration, going back to the 18th century, exists along the coast and many young men put off marriage until after a period of "seeing the world" and accumulating trade goods for bridewealth (Brooks, 1972).

Middle Age and Old Age

Fifty years of age is considered an important milestone among the Glebo, although it is not marked by a public celebration of any kind. At 50, a man or woman is considered "fully grown" and to have the wisdom and experience to advise others. Before this age, adults will continue to describe themselves as "small girls and small boys," particularly in relation to their older kin and teachers. "If the man who was my teacher is still alive, how can I consider myself his equal?" asked a 45-year-old Glebo Episcopal priest, commenting on the relative nature of who could be described as "old" or even adult. Adults who achieve and pass the age of 50 are honored at death with a "war dance" (*doklo* for men and *nana* for women), performed by all adult members of their gender in their own and related communities. Dances formerly existed to commemorate the deaths of younger adults; *boya* for a woman who died in her childbearing years and *kobo ta woda* for a young man (also performed for men leaving on periods of labor migration, in case they died while away), but these have rarely been performed since the 1970s. The most important rite of passage celebrated for any Glebo individual is that which marks the transition to the afterlife and the status of ancestor. Funerals are the largest, most expensive, and most elaborate ceremonies the Glebo practice.

PERSONALITY DIFFERENCES BY GENDER

Generally speaking, the Glebo believe that all people have the capacity for purposeful work, and hard-working practical qualities are looked for in both men and women. Women are expected to be most concerned with the welfare of children and of households in general, while men are more free to debate theoretical issues and argue the fine points of politics or witchcraft. Men are expected to be more articulate than women and to be masters of elliptical and indirect oratory, often using proverbs to avoid saying what they really mean. Women are sometimes disparaged for simply blurting out what they are thinking, or seen as lacking in refinement and discretion. Yet good speaking ability is highly valued in women and is one of the criteria for election to the female council and the position of *blo nyene*. Women will often show public deference to men, but quarrels between spouses are known to become heated and even physical on both sides. Adult women are recognized as physically strong and able to stand up for themselves.

Men and women spend much of their time in gender-segregated groups, and demonstration of affection between same-sex friends is common and implies no sexual intimacy. The sight of two men or two women holding hands or walking arm-in-arm is much more likely than that of two people of the opposite sex, which would be considered slightly scandalous, even for spouses. Yet men demonstrate much public affection for their babies and young children, often holding them on their laps and cuddling them in the evening.

GENDER-RELATED SOCIAL GROUPS

Patrilineal descent and patrilocal residence demand that a woman move to join her husband's family and that her labor and children will contribute to their overall wealth and prestige. Yet the proverb, "a woman does not perish in marriage" (Herzog & Blooah, 1936, p. 179) recognizes that she will maintain membership in her natal group and continue to fulfill responsibilities toward her own patrikin. In addition to the age-based associations mentioned above, men and women join a variety of other sex-specific groups including dance and masquerade societies, church groups, burial insurance societies, rotating credit associations, and sports clubs. Glebo who are living away from Cape Palmas in other Liberian towns or cities (or abroad) form development associations to raise funds for infrastructure projects "back home." These groups sponsor fund-raising events such as beauty contests, dance performances, and "rallies" to benefit their home communities. Although dedicated to a common cause, these urban-based associations usually have the parallel gendered structure of the rural town, with separate men's and women's officers and decision-making groups.

GENDER ROLES IN ECONOMICS

The division of agricultural labor in the production of rice, the staple subsistence crop, assigns the clearing of new fields and the burning of brush to men, while women are responsible for hoeing, planting, weeding, scaring away birds and small predators, and most of the harvesting. Since the period of their involvement with the major crop is quite limited, men are free to pursue other economic activities, such as growing cash crops (rubber, citrus, coffee, or sugar), hunting, and wage labor. Indeed, it is possible that the long history of male labor migration from this region is a consequence of the fact that women have a greater role in agriculture in the southeast than in other parts of Liberia (Moran, 1986). Women also grow cash crops, such as maize, peppers, eggplant, pumpkin, greens, and other vegetables, interplanted in rice fields. Very little domestically produced rice reaches the market (urban populations subsist on rice imported from abroad), but women sell other surplus crops and keep the profits for their own use.

Women dominate the wholesale and retail trade of locally produced foodstuffs in Liberia, while men may specialize in selling raw materials to foreign firms (particularly rubber and palm oil). Professional market women travel long distances on their own to bulk products from many small female producers and transport them to the urban centers along the coast. For many women, the transition from farming to marketing comes with divorce or widowhood; once freed from the obligations of a lineage wife, they can manage their own affairs, support their children, and maintain their own households. Often these women enter informal nonresidential relationships with "husbands" who have not paid bridewealth and so have no legal claim over them. As one woman put it to me, "If my husband sees money, he gives me a bag of rice. If not, the market feeds me" (Moran, 1990, p. 128).

However, "civilized" Glebo women are unable to sell in the public marketplace without jeopardy to their status. In fact, local gossip often circulates about women who "used to be civilized" but are now, due to economic adversity, selling in the market. The most visible sign of such a loss of prestige is when a woman exchanges Western-style dresses, which are never worn by market vendors, for the two wrapped cloths or *lappas*. Many civilized women contribute to and even support households with an almost clandestine marketing system of selling surplus produce from a small table by their back door. Others send their children to sell homemade cookies and similar treats in schoolyards or at major intersections (Moran, 1990). A few highly educated women occupy professional positions as nurses, clerks, or teachers in the cash sector.

Movable property can be inherited by both men and women, with personal items like cloth, household equipment, tools, and furniture transmitted from father to son and mother to daughter. Use rights to farmland and house plots are activated through membership in a patrilineal clan. Upon the death of a man, conflicts sometimes emerge between the claims of his wife and those of his patrilineal kin; in theory, the widow has no right to the house or the communal property of the marriage unless she can demonstrate that items were bought with her own earnings. At one time, a widow was "inherited" herself, coming under the protection of a male relative of her deceased husband, usually a younger brother, unless she preferred to refund part of the bridewealth and return to her own kin group. If the house and other property are inherited by an adult son, he is responsible for the support of his mother and any other cowives in their old age. Liberian women married under statutory law or in one of the Christian churches are entitled to inherit property from their husbands, but often their legal rights are not enforced by local officials. Various attempts have been made to pass national legislation regulating spousal rights, most recently in 2002.

PARENTAL AND OTHER CARETAKER ROLES

Maternal care of children is idealized in the notion of "feeding"; whatever else she may do for them, the primary role of a mother is to feed her children. This does not imply that she should spend all her time with them personally or even play a major part in their upbringing. Rather, it is through her economic activity that children are fed and nurtured. This pattern is similar across West Africa, where it has been noted that a woman who stays at home with her children all day instead of leaving them for the workplace is seen as a lazy and even unfit mother (see also Clark, 1994). Fathers are expected to be stern disciplinarians although, as noted above, they may be very affectionate with babies and young children. Both parents take part in "training" or preparing children for the rigors of the world, which is expected to involve some suffering and hard work. Fostering children out to other households is a common practice and is the primary route to Western education and "civilized" status for rural youngsters. Parents use bilateral kinship links to place children in households where they can attend school and acquire the behavioral traits of educated, civilized people. Sometimes these children are defined as servants (even if they are very young and not yet economically useful to the household), particularly if the placement is made on the basis of friendship or patronage rather than kinship. A servant is expected to "suffer," yet the host family is under strong obligation to see that their schooling continues and that they have at least a chance of attaining upward mobility. Prosperous families on the coast use this institution to enhance their domestic workforce and fill in gaps in their personnel; for example, one family took in a teenage girl as a servant when their only daughter died in childbirth, leaving them with four sons and an infant granddaughter (Moran, 1992).

LEADERSHIP IN PUBLIC ARENAS

Glebo political organization is a classic example of the "dual-sex" system described by Okonjo (1976) for

West Africa in general. Each town or cluster of related towns has a male official, the *wodo baa* or "town's name-sake" whose lineage is understood to have been among the founders of the community. Under the system of local administration imposed by the Liberian state, this office became the "town chief," with the power to collect taxes, hear civil court cases, and impose fines. The corresponding woman's position, the *blo nyene*, has no such official recognition. Neither the *wodo baa* nor the *blo nyene* hold executive power over decisions affecting the entire town; they depend on the *gbudubo*, or council of elders (both male and female, discussed above), for advice and attempt to reach consensus on anything of consequence. The *blo nyene* has veto power over any decision made by the men; in former times this was an important way in which women exercised control over men's ability to declare war on neighboring communities. Since a large proportion of the adult women in any town had married in from elsewhere, their support was crucial to any military campaign that might pit their husbands and sons against their fathers and brothers. Women are also known to use mass boycotts and labor strikes (leaving town en masse or refusing to cook or sleep with their husbands) to impose their will on male authorities (Moran, 1989). Other leadership roles include the officers of the *sidibo* age grade for men and of dancing and performance societies for women. Among "civilized" Glebo, leadership roles exist for men and women in numerous church-based and voluntary organizations. Leadership roles in the indigenous religious system are discussed below.

GENDER AND RELIGION

Missionaries from the Episcopal church of America established themselves among the Glebo as early as the 1830s and many people are at least nominally Christian. Although the Anglican church recognizes the ordination of women as priests, there have not been any female clerics among the Glebo to date. The indigenous religious positions, like so many other aspects of Glebo society, have parallel roles for men and women. The high priest (*bodio*) and his wife (*gyide*) have much in common with the "divine king" complex recorded elsewhere in Africa. Unlike the secular *wodo baa* and *blo nyene*, who are essentially farmers like everyone else, the *bodio* and *gyide* are true ritual specialists. They are supported by the agricultural efforts of the rest of the community, who give

them rice and other crops according to their needs. Their lives are tightly constrained by restrictions and taboos, for they must never leave the town for more than a few hours during daylight. They live in the cult house or shrine which houses the "medicines" on which the health and continuation of the town and its occupants depends. Their deaths cannot be acknowledged and they are buried secretly; in former times, they were probably ritually killed if they became seriously ill or infirm. They are highly respected for their willingness to sacrifice themselves for the good of the community and are assumed to control awesome spiritual powers. They are frequently called upon to settle disputes and to preside at witchcraft trials.

Within the Christian churches, the civilized–native dichotomy stratifies participation and leadership, particularly for women. The local Episcopal congregations set a higher tithe for civilized women than for "*lappa* women" and expect them to take the lead in the altar society, in women's prayer groups, and in organizing wakes, funerals, and other ceremonies. The other major source of spiritual power, witchcraft, is available to anyone whose "heart is strong," regardless of gender. Experienced elders are usually assumed to be powerful witches (otherwise, how could they have lived so long?) who can be both guardians of the community or a threat depending on how they are treated. Much of the respect and deference accorded to the elders stems from a fear that they will either actively harm young people who anger them or, at the very least, withdraw their spiritual protection. Women and young men are often accused of using witchcraft to harm others, an acknowledgement of both their subordinate status and their agency in resisting it.

LEISURE, RECREATION, AND THE ARTS

It is undeniable that men have more leisure time than women. In addition to their work of provisioning the household as farmers, market vendors or cash-sector employees, Glebo women are responsible for domestic tasks such as cooking, cleaning, supplying firewood and water, washing and ironing clothes, and supervising young children. These tasks are often done by children and teenagers of both sexes, but the ultimate responsibility lies with the female head of the household. The need for many hands to contribute to this work drives the system of child fosterage described above.

Men spend their leisure time in sex-segregated groups, talking local and national politics or listening to the radio, if available. Women spend what little free time they have in groups of other women, often braiding each other's hair and exchanging news. Younger people who are in school or otherwise considered civilized have more gender-mixed activities; church groups and school classes sponsor "disco dances" and video showings using a gas-powered generator to supply electricity. It is considered odd, and possibly indicative of witchcraft, for anyone to spend their leisure time alone.

RELATIVE STATUS OF MEN AND WOMEN

Men have formal authority over women in Glebo society. Women, through their role as producers and distributors of food, hold a great deal of informal power and can generally act effectively in their own interests. Women speak of "fighting with food," letting their husbands know they are displeased by giving them small portions of rice with little or no meat in the sauce. Women also withhold food, sometimes for weeks at a time, from adolescent or adult children who have offended them. A woman expects to be consulted in all major decisions affecting the family, including whether or not her husband should take an additional wife or wives. Because "a woman can make a rice farm without a man, but a man cannot make a rice farm without a woman" (Carter & Mends-Cole, 1982, p. 37), men have a strong incentive to keep their marriages intact. A woman who has divorced her husband can very easily get a new one, or support herself through market vending, but a man who has a poor reputation for satisfying his wife will find it difficult to marry again. The practice of polygyny also means that there are more men looking for spouses than women. Civilized Glebo women are in a much more difficult position since they cannot publicly participate in the market and are often literate but not educated enough for the wage sector. Such women may end up as secondary non-residential "wives" of prominent men.

SEXUALITY

All Glebo adults are assumed to be sexually active and celibacy for any extended period is believed to cause illness and "dryness" for both men and women. There is recognition that unrestrained sexuality can lead to conflicts and even violence or witchcraft; "woman palaver" refers to the competition between two men over the same woman. A 2-year postpartum taboo on sexual intercourse was common in former times; the milk of a nursing mother could be "spoiled" by the heat and exertion of sex and also by exposure to semen, endangering the child. Glebo men cited this belief as a justification for polygyny to disapproving missionaries in the 19th century.

Male-to-female transvestism is an element of masquerade, although I have never observed the reverse (i.e., women dressed as men). The men's funeral dance, or war dance, always includes some aspects of cross-dressing by one or two younger men, who add a bra or negligee to the warrior costume of raffia skirts and shredded animal skins. This warrior transvestism was common among rebels during the Liberian civil war of 1989–96 and was commented on at length by foreign reporters (Moran, 1996). Men also impersonate women in full costume at liminal moments like New Year's Day, or in the funeral dance performed for a young adult women. There is widespread denial that homosexuality exists at all, although public affection between people of the same sex is considered normal and natural.

COURTSHIP AND MARRIAGE

Although there are reports of the practice of child betrothal in earlier times, contemporary Glebo marriage requires the consent of both parties. A period of engagement, symbolized by the man placing a sliver of bamboo in his intended's hair, was followed by a trial period during which the couple lived together to "get to know each other's ways" (Innes, 1966). A series of gift exchanges, with specific payments to the brides' mother, constitute bridewealth and may continue for many years. Husbands and wives who have been together for decades may disagree publicly on whether or not they are "really married yet;" it is in the wife's interest to assert that all the payments are not complete. On the other hand, a wealthy man who makes a big show of bringing "two bulls" (or their cash equivalent) to his father-in-law can expect a lavish feast and high prestige for both his wife and himself. Civilized Christian Glebo aspire to a "white wedding" in a church with Western-style dresses, attendants, printed programs, and a cake-and-punch reception afterwards.

HUSBAND–WIFE RELATIONSHIP

In general, Glebo hold high romantic ideals for marriage, although they acknowledge that these are often not met. Managing a large harmonious household, especially a polygynous one, is recognized as requiring luck, wisdom, and a good sense of humor on the part of all. Family etiquette holds that a woman should serve her husband his portion in separate dishes at mealtimes; a loving relationship is signaled by his asking her to join her portion with his so that they can eat together. A couple make their relationship visible to the community by eating together outside the house in full view of passers-by. Women also cite a man's willingness to "show me the pay slip" if he is employed in the wage sector as a sign of his love and devotion. Men are expected to provide the physical structure of a house and to pay rent if necessary, but their other income is for use at their own discretion. Therefore divulging the full amount to a wife when they are not required to do so is an indication of trust.

Polygynous households are said to work best if each wife has her own separate kitchen and bedroom. They can then take turns cooking for the husband on different days of the week and he can "visit" them in privacy. Husbands are advised that they should avoid favoritism and treat multiple wives with absolute equality, especially when buying them gifts. A group of three women wearing suits of identical cloth was once pointed out to me as an example of an especially well-run household, in which the women signaled their solidarity by wearing their husbands' gift at the same time. Friendly relations among cowives can backfire on a man, however, if they "gang up" to sanction him by withholding food or sex.

OTHER CROSS-SEX RELATIONSHIPS

Brothers and sisters usually maintain close relations throughout their lives, although they may reside some distance from each other. Both have responsibilities to each other's children; the mother's brother is expected to be a friendly advisor, while the father's sister has a disciplinary and rather judgmental role in the lives of younger lineage members. Women continue to see themselves as in-laws to their husbands and children and feel close solidarity with patrikin. They expect to share in the inheritance of deceased kinsmen and loudly berate widows who try to claim "our property," even as they may try to make claims on conjugal resources when they become widows themselves.

CHANGE IN ATTITUDES, BELIEFS, AND PRACTICES REGARDING GENDER

Mission activity and colonization by American settlers in the 19th century certainly introduced new ideas into Glebo society, particularly surrounding civilized domesticity and the exclusive roles of male breadwinner and female homemaker that still finds expression in the economic restrictions on civilized women. However, it is important to realize that these were not the first changes introduced from abroad, and that the Glebo and other coastal peoples had been assimilating new practices, materials, and ideologies through centuries of trade, first with savannah societies to the north and later with European ships along the coast. In the 1990s, political unrest and civil war introduced new forms of militarization and hypermasculinity drawn from Western action films like the Rambo series (Moran, 1996). As men have been pulled into new forms of violence, women have suffered disproportionately as refugees and internally displaced persons (IDPs), unable to carry out their highly valued roles as providers for their children. With peace still elusive in Liberia, the future of sex and gender constructions among the Glebo remain to be determined.

BIBLIOGRAPHY

Brooks, G. E. (1972). *The Kru Mariner in the 19th Century: An historical compendium.* Newark, DE: Liberian Studies Association.

Carter, J., & Mends-Cole, J. (1982). *Liberian women: Their role in food production and their educational and legal status* (Profile of Liberian Women in Development Project). Monrovia, Liberia: U.S. AID/University of Liberia.

Clark, G. (1994). *Onions are my husband: Survival and accumulation by West African market women.* Chicago: University of Chicago Press.

Herzog, G., & Blooah, C. (1936). *Jabo proverbs from Liberia.* London: Oxford University Press.

Innes, G. (1966). *An introduction to Grebo.* London: School of Oriental and African Studies.

Johnson, S. J. (1957). Traditional history and folklore of the Glebo Tribe. Monrovia, Liberia: Bureau of Folkways.

Kurtz, R. J. (1985). *Ethnographic survey of southeastern Liberia: The Grebo-speaking peoples.* Philadelphia: Institute for Liberian Studies.

Martin, J. J. (1968). *The dual legacy: Government authority and mission influence among the Glebo of eastern Liberia, 1834–1910.* Unpublished Ph.D. dissertation, Boston University, Boston, MA.

McEvoy, F. D. (1971). *History, tradition, and kinship as factors in modern Sabo labor migration.* Unpublished Ph.D. dissertation, University of Oregon, Eugene, OR.

Moran, M. H. (1986). Taking up the slack: Female farming and the "Kru problem" in southeastern Liberia. *Liberian Studies Journal, 11,* 117–124.

Moran, M. H. (1989). Collective action and the "representation" of African women: A Liberian case study. *Feminist Studies, 15,* 443–460.

Moran, M. H. (1990). *Civilized women: Gender and prestige in southeastern Liberia.* Ithaca, NY: Cornell University Press.

Moran, M. H. (1992). Civilized servants: Child fosterage and training for status among the Glebo of Liberia. In K. T. Hansen (Ed.), *African encounters with domesticity* (pp. 98–115). New Brunswick, NJ: Rutgers University Press.

Moran, M. H. (1996). Warriors or soldiers? Masculinity and ritual transvestism in the Liberian civil war. In C. R. Sutton (Ed.), *Feminism, nationalism, and militarism* (pp. 73–88). Arlington, VA: American Anthropological Association and the Association for Feminist Anthropology.

Moran, M. H. (2000). Gender and aging: Are women "warriors" among the Glebo of Liberia? *Liberian Studies Journal, 25,* 25–41.

Okonjo, K. (1976). The dual-sex political system in operation: Igbo women and community politics in midwestern Nigeria. In N. J. Hafkin & E. G. Bay (Eds.), *Women in Africa: Studies in social and economic change.* Stanford, CA: Stanford University Press.

Greeks of Kalymnos

David E. Sutton

ALTERNATIVE NAMES

The alternative name is Kalymnian Islanders.

LOCATION

Kalymnos is part of the Dodecanese island chain, at the eastern edge of the Aegean Sea. The Dodecanese islands (which include Rhodes, Kos, and Patmos) were incorporated into the modern Greek State in 1948. Kalymnos lies about 3 miles off the coast of Turkey.

CULTURAL OVERVIEW

While Kalymnian Islanders are Greek by background and citizenship, and the vast majority are practicing Greek Orthodox Christians, certain aspects of their history and social structure make their gender system quite distinct from that which has been described for other parts of Greece. Kalymnians make the claim that "we used to have matriarchy on the island," referring to the perceived female power over key decision-making that sets the island off from a more patriarchal mainland Greek tradition. From an anthropological perspective, Kalymnos and a few of the other Dodecanese islands are extremely unusual in that they are not only matrilocal in their residence patterns, but they traditionally practiced a system of female primogeniture in inheritance, which I will examine further below.[1]

The Dodecanese islands have long been separated historically from the fortunes of the rest of Greece. From the 13th century, they were ruled successively by Venetian and Genoese merchants, by the Knights of Saint John, by the Ottoman Empire, and, for approximately 30 years prior to World War II, by the state of Italy as part of its attempt to develop a colonial empire. Foreign rule, however, was fairly light during most of this time, and islanders developed an elaborate system of local government known as the *Demogerontia* or council of elders, an annually elected body that administered the affairs of each island. It was during the Italian period (1913–42) that protest against foreign rule reached its zenith and took on the interesting gender dimensions discussed below.

Kalymnians, who number about 15,000 in local residence, refer to their home as "the barren island." It is 49 square miles of rock, of which less than a fifth is arable land. Thus, Kalymnians have a long tradition of seafaring, and have become known in the past century as "the island of sponge fishermen" (Bernard, 1976; Warn, 2000). Sponge fishing in the Mediterranean, which required male absence for 6–8 months of the year, has been an important factor in shaping the island's gender structure.

The sponge industry has been in decline since the 1970s, and the island economy has shifted to rely more on fishing, the merchant marine, tourism, and migrant remittances. Kalymnians practice seasonal and more permanent migration, and have established large migrant communities primarily in Darwin, Australia, and Tarpon Springs, Florida (U.S.A.). Tarpon Springs has been dubbed "little Kalymnos," and some Kalymnians continue sponge fishing off the coast of Florida. There are also over 100 non-Greek-born permanent residents of Kalymnos, many of whom are British, American, and Scandinavian women who are married to Kalymnian men (and more uncommonly, the reverse [Sutton, 1998a]).

CULTURAL CONSTRUCTIONS OF GENDER

Kalymnos is similar to the rest of Greece insofar as constructions of gender are heavily influenced by Greek Orthodox Christianity. Ideal gender images are closely tied to marital and reproductive roles. To be a complete man or woman you must be married with children. Older and married women tend to wear modest dress. Widowed men, and particularly widowed women, are traditionally expected to wear black for the rest of their lives. Until recently, sexual attractiveness was only a concern for unmarried women. Western influences and tourism have had some impact on dress styles, appearance, and make-up, especially among youth, and affect ongoing debates about proper/improper swimwear and beach decor. While dark hair is the norm, blond hair, because of its association with Western Europe, is often desired in both men and women. One woman described her newborn blonde granddaughter to me as having "specification from the European Union."

GENDER OVER THE LIFE CYCLE

Socialization of Boys and Girls

Before the 1970s, education beyond primary school tended to be a luxury of the well-off on Kalymnos. Now it is desired by all groups as a strategy for upward mobility. Education is highly valued for both boys and girls, and both are expected to achieve at school, although matrilocality means that mothers also hope that at least one of their daughters will not get a job, but rather share household duties with them. Parents are eager to find traits of intelligence and diligence in young children, and will reinforce them by calling attention to them on a regular basis, while upbraiding children for perceived laziness. The word "shame" (*dropi*) is used to enculturate modest dress and expression in young girls, and to discourage rambunctious behavior in boys. While parents and other caretakers commonly make threats of beatings, these are rarely carried out. Grandparents play a major role as caretakers (see below), and tend to seek personality traits (such as intelligence) which they can claim to have passed on to their grandchildren.

Puberty and Adolescence

This is a period where in the past boys enjoyed relative freedom in relation to girls. Girls, it is said "were locked up in their houses" in the old days on Kalymnos to protect their reputation. In the past a larger number of boys than girls attended school into adolescence, and those who did not attend school (boys and girls) were apprenticed to their mothers and fathers in various occupations (i.e., care of animals, running a store). Now almost all children attend school at least through 9th grade, and many strictures on girls' movements have been lifted, as unmarried

boys and girls go to Athens or further abroad to pursue their education. One 18-year-old who had moved to Athens on her own at age 16 to study at a beauty school told me that she had won out over her father's hesitations. Although her parents had heard comments from neighbors about allowing their daughter to go to Athens on her own, such things were occurring much more frequently now, so had none of the air of scandal that they might have in the past.

Attainment of Adulthood

There are no special rituals associated with the attainment of adulthood, apart from the marriage ceremony. However, given that many Kalymnians in the past, and in some cases still today, marry quite young (14 was not an uncommon age of marriage for females, slightly older for males), marriage did not mark a definitive transition to adulthood, which is a more fluid process involving other markers such as childbirth, work, etc.

Middle Age and Old Age

Grandparental status is very important on Kalymnos. Maternal grandmothers often are the de facto heads of matrilocal households, caring for children and organizing household tasks with their married daughter(s). Grandparents are congratulated on the birth of a child, especially if the child has been named after them (see below), since this means that their name has been carried on into the future, and this in some sense insures their immortality.

PERSONALITY DIFFERENCES BY GENDER

Such differences are not in evidence in Kalymnos to the same degree as reported for more patrilineal/patriarchal areas of Greece, where men are expected to be aggressive, to "perform their masculinity," and women are expected to be modest, reticent, and deferential (Campbell, 1964; du Boulay, 1974; Herzfeld, 1985, 1991). Women's words are not seen as a threat to the matrilocal group in the way that they would be in patrilocal situations, where women at marriage are outsiders who must prove their loyalty to the group (Hirschon, 1978). Thus women are voluble and "hold the floor" with men on a panoply of topics from sex to politics. Kalymnian women are considered to be "hard" like men, and are proud of their ability to perform hard labor and, in extraordinary circumstances, of their martial prowess (see below and Sutton, 1999).

GENDER-RELATED SOCIAL GROUPS

While there are no extended lineages on Kalymnos, and kinship is reckoned bilaterally, there are a number of aspects of Kalymnian practices that show a strong matrifocal bias. Matrilocality is the standard postmarital residence pattern, with the husband moving into a house owned by the wife, often attached to the residence of her natal family. This house is usually built through the labor of fathers and brothers, on matrilineal land, though increasingly women themselves contribute to the building. The house traditionally reverts to the wife's family in cases where the wife dies without offspring. Houses and land are transmitted matrilineally as well, associating women with the symbolic capital of family tradition. Thus, women are the stable elements in Kalymnian kinship, and men are "exchanged" between groups of women.

Perhaps the most noticeable feature of Kalymnian practice is the tradition of first-daughter inheritance, or female primogeniture. Under this system, the first daughter received the lion's share of the matrilineal inheritance. If the family owned 25 fields, the first daughter would get 20 and subsequent daughters would receive one each. If the father owned a boat, or less commonly a store, he would pass this on to one of his sons. But in terms of items associated with the home, sons would not inherit at all under this system, except under unusual circumstances. Ideally, the first daughter would have a dowry house built for her from the family income. However, if this was not possible, the first daughter often claimed the parental house upon her marriage, and the rest of the family was forced to rent a house. This system was tied to baptismal naming practices by which the first daughter received the Christian name of her maternal grandmother, and was thus linked to the ancestral inheritance of that grandmother (see Sutton [1998a] for a full discussion).

This system can be documented at least back to the 17th century (Sutton, 1998a). It was officially ended when Kalymnos was incorporated into the Greek state in 1948, with its laws of equal inheritance. It is still reflected today in the favoritism shown to daughters over sons in inheritance, and to first daughters over subsequent daughters, but retains few of the vast inequalities of the past.

GENDER ROLES IN ECONOMICS

Up until the 1980s, the majority of the male population was absent from the island for 6–8 months of the year on sponge expeditions. Some claim that it was this male absence, as well as the tendency of divers to "live it up" when they returned, that accounted for "women's rule" on the island. One woman, commenting on women's power over the "purse strings" and other critical family decisions, described it to me as follows: "The divers spent all their time at the coffee shops—music and retsina. And not home 'til the next morning. They said "we've been so long at sea, let's celebrate." And thus there was women's rule on the island" (Sutton, 1998a, p. 104). Thus women had control over household management, as well as involvement in informal small-scale animal husbandry and small-scale agriculture. Women *control* the kitchen, and often do not let their husbands enter kitchen spaces, claiming that they are incompetent at cooking, and would just mess things up.

The decline of the sponge industry has led men into other occupations, such as seasonal migration and the merchant marine, which continues their pattern of absence. Both men and women work in retail trade, and women are increasingly entering the professions on Kalymnos, as well as the increasing number of jobs provided by tourism. Women have an advantage here, as they own the houses that may be set up as "rooms" for the tourist trade (see Galani-Moutafi [1993] for other Greek islands). Women also dominate in the growth of tutorial schools, which supplement the local high-school system in areas such as foreign languages (Sutton, 1998a).

PARENTAL AND OTHER CARETAKER ROLES

Having done fieldwork accompanied by my wife and 6-month-old son, I was privileged to many discussions of the theory and practice of childcare on Kalymnos (Sutton, 1998b). I had initially assumed that my own participation in childcare might provoke negative comments in a "Mediterranean" culture. However, it coincided with a recent shift in values on Kalymnos toward fuller paternal participation. For the younger generation the ideal of sex-role equality was widely accepted. While the occupational structure which favored men still meant that women provided the majority of childcare, in cases in which wives worked and husbands, for various reasons, stayed home, it was seen as perfectly natural for them to care for and raise the children. Whether present or not, fathers are ideally seen as disciplinarians, and may be evoked as a threat ("wait till your daddy gets home ..."), though in fact mothers engage in everyday verbal and occasional physical reprimand of young children.

What seemed most distinctive about childcare from my "American" perspective was the way that responsibility was distributed over a three-generational family, and not vested exclusively in the parents. Thus, we would often receive advice from 15-year-old boys on how to care for our baby, reflecting the fact that older children are expected to look after their siblings on a regular basis. Furthermore, because of matrilocal residence, a woman often relies on her parents for advice and for regular day-to-day care. This was even more true in the past, when teenage marriage was common. But it also reflects the strong bond felt between grandparents and grandchildren, which is reinforced through the baptismal naming system (Sutton, 1998a). This means that a grandmother may have a particularly strong bond with the grandchild who bears her name (or a significant family name), and the same is true for grandfathers. Uncles and aunts often play an important caretaker role, and childless uncles and aunts who are well off financially can often adopt a child from their siblings. "Uncle" and "Aunt" are used by children as terms of respect to neighbors and other adults on Kalymnos.

LEADERSHIP IN PUBLIC ARENAS

Men have long controlled the official political structures of Kalymnos, as no woman has ever been elected mayor, vice-mayor, or regional governor, though women appear with increasing frequency on the town council. The church hierarchy is completely male as well, as is the case for Greek Orthodoxy at large. However, women often hold considerable influence, power, and leadership roles on Kalymnos through more unofficial channels. Never was this more the case than with Katerina Vouvali, the wife of one of Kalymnos' wealthy sponge merchants,

who outlived him by several decades and wielded her economic power to control the labor market on Kalymnos and to become, from the 1920s through the 1950s, the most powerful person on the island. Memories of "The Lady," as she was known, are mixed; some remembered her stinginess in relation to her workers. But both men and women also remember her for her intelligence in economic affairs, and employ the word for "legitimate intelligence" (*eksipsi*), rather than the word "cunning" (*poniri*), which is a trait often associated with women in Greece.

Vouvali is not the exception that proves the rule, as there are many other examples of women on Kalymnos in the past who have risen to prominence and influence economically, or in the fields of education, local scholarship, or religion, and whose names resonate in local memory (e.g., Vakina Soulounia, "The Teacher"). This continues to be the case today.

GENDER AND RELIGION

Many have noted a lack of fit between the official androcentric ideology of Greek Orthodoxy, which is similar to Western Christianity in its unequal treatment of males and females, and actual everyday religious practice (Dubisch, 1995; Hart, 1992; Hirschon, 1998). While men have strong anticlerical views, and do not generally attend church except on high holy days, women are active participants in church liturgies, in caring for chapels dedicated to different saints, in caring for gravestones and cemeteries (Kenna, 1976), and in taking religious excursions to various miracle-working sites, such as the Church of the Virgin Mary on Tinos (Dubisch, 1995). Women are responsible for the religious "health" of their husbands, children, extended family, and ancestors. They fulfill this duty through mundane acts such as bringing home communion bread for nonattendees or arranging for the proper memorial ceremonies and other significant ceremonies focused around the house and the extended family and ancestors, as well as through caring for saints' chapels in the belief that the saints will likewise take care of their family. Thus, women play a crucial role in this key domain of spiritual life on Kalymnos and in Greece more generally.

One event that encapsulates the significance of women's relationship to the church on Kalymnos is the famous Rock War of 1935. Over the course of 3 days, the women of Kalymnos, armed with rocks, fought the Italian occupying army to a standstill in a successful attempt to thwart Italian plans to transfer control of the church administration of the Dodecanese to the Pope. The Rock War was the largest and most successful protest during the 30 years of Italian rule over the Dodecanese islands. It became a point of reference in the consciousness of future generations, who for many years after would say, "He or she was born or died at the time of the Rock War" (Sutton, 1999). While local history provides different interpretations of men's absence from the protest, I would argue that it simply reflects the fact that Italians were laying claim to control over Kalymnian women's central domain of collective activity.

LEISURE, RECREATION, AND THE ARTS

If there is an area of life where men do exert control over women, it is that of movement outside the home and "free time." While men can spend their leisure time talking with friends (other men) at coffee shops, or on hunting or fishing expeditions, women tend to need to legitimate their activities away from the home. The restriction of women's movement is a phenomenon widely reported in the literature on Greece. When she leaves the house a woman opens herself up to comments by the community on her behavior: where is she going, how is she dressed, is she meeting a lover? (e.g., du Boulay, 1974; Seremetakis, 1991). Thus trips downtown for shopping or to the church on various religious duties are often a chance for married women to find time to socialize with friends, although they are often expected to give an account of their movements when they return home. However, this perspective has been contested and has shifted over the past 15 years, as young women move into new spaces such as the *Kafeteria* (a non-sex-segregated coffee shop; see Cowan [1991]). Going to the beach is one leisure activity that seems to be respectable and justifiable for women of all ages. Young women often go to the beach in groups unchaperoned by adults, while married women are often accompanied by their children if not their husbands as well. Beach excursions are, from all accounts, a long-standing Kalymnian tradition, although many people remember earlier times (before the 1960s) when men and women were expected to bathe at separate beaches.

RELATIVE STATUS OF MEN AND WOMEN

The issue of the relative status of men and women is a difficult one, given that Kalymnians themselves constantly debate "who's in charge," and whether they used to have "matriarchy" or "patriarchy" on the island. The fact that Kalymnos is part of Greece, a country with a largely androcentric dominant ideology, cuts against the grain of local practices of matrilocality and matrilineal inheritance. And Kalymnos's history of resistance to outside control—Ottoman, Italian, and in some cases the Greek state—make all claims to "authority" ring somewhat hollow. Thus sexuality is an area in which, at least in the past, men have had greater freedom than women. By contrast, women clearly predominate in economic and family decision-making, and they gain symbolic status given their more direct association with family continuity.

The vagaries of status and control are illustrated in the following joke, popular among Kalymnian men when I conducted fieldwork:

A study is being conducted of whether men or women run things. The researchers offer a horse to each household where the man is found to be in charge and a chicken to each household where the woman is found to be in charge. The researchers go through the entire village rewarding chickens, only chickens. Finally, they reach a house off on the mountainside where a large, heavily mustached man sits in traditional dress, sharpening his knife. When they ask him who runs his household, he responds with great offense that it should be perfectly clear that he is the boss—whatever he says, goes. The researchers tell him that he will be awarded a fine horse, would he like a white or a black one? He asks them to wait a minute, calls to his wife, and says "Wife, which horse shall we take, the white or the black one?"

SEXUALITY

Although men tend to be more sexually forward than women on Kalymnos, talk of sex is not taboo for either men or women, and I often heard ribald tales told by "respectable" married women. In part, this reflects the fact that sexuality (and other bodily pleasure) tends not to be stigmatized in Greek Orthodox tradition as long as it is channeled through proper kinship and marriage roles. Homosexuality is stigmatized largely insofar as it interferes with these demands. As in the rest of Greece, however, it is only the passive male partner who is labeled "homosexual" (*omofilofilos*, colloq. *poustis*). One can be an active male partner as an extension of male virility (Loizos, 1994). While there were several "known" homosexuals on Kalymnos, lesbianism is seen as an anomaly and as a foreign importation.

Control over sexuality has long been the source of tension *between* generations, and in particular between fathers and daughters. People still talk of "the old years" when fathers "kept their daughters locked up in their houses" in order to keep them from shaming the family honor through even the hint of premarital sexual behavior. Indeed, when people spoke of male power and control on Kalymnos, they generally did so in the context of the father–daughter relationship rather than the husband–wife relationship. This is also reflected at the level of island identity in claims that men on other neighboring islands "don't care if you sleep with their daughters." While other islanders "let their daughters" have relations with Italian men during the Italian Occupation, Kalymnians claim that their resistance to Italian rule was expressed in the fact that any Kalymnian women who had sexual relations with Italians were killed or exiled (see Doumanis [1997] for women's "counter-memories" on this topic).

COURTSHIP AND MARRIAGE

Traditionally, there were three types of courtship on Kalymnos: arranged marriages (*proksenio, synekesio*), marriages of "familiarity" (*tis gnorimias*), and "love marriages" (*tou erota*). Arranged marriages were controlled by parents, but occasionally involved intermediaries such as aunts or uncles. In these cases courtship could be quite short—only a period of several weeks. Marriages of familiarity could be initiated by the couple themselves, with their parents' approval, and often involved neighbor children who had grown up nearby and knew each other over a long period. These two types could blend into each other: neighborhood parents could arrange marriages between children who had grown up together, and courtships might be longer, extending until after the man had performed military service. One woman boasted of choosing the best of five sons that her neighbor had offered to marry to her daughter. Because of their long acquaintance, she knew which son was most honest and upright. The final type, the "love marriage," was initiated through sexual desire, and might involve the couple "stealing away" without the knowledge of one or both

parents to get married on a nearby island. Though parents still play a role in spousal selection, arranged marriages are growing increasingly uncommon on Kalymnos. With the advent of "dating" over the past 15 years, couples themselves have an increasingly larger role to play, and love becomes an important if not decisive factor in decisions.

Weddings often involve a day of celebrations before the actual ceremony. These celebrations include an opening of the couple's house to the guests of the family, firing of guns, or throwing of dynamite (Sutton, 1998a). The guests throw money on the nuptial bed as a gesture to symbolize the couple's future fertility. Often the wedding party walks in a procession through town to the church. The ceremony itself is conducted in the Greek Orthodox tradition (although political marriages were legalized by the socialist government of Andreas Papandreou in the early 1980s, they are uncommon). This involves the setting of crowns on the heads of the couple by a man and women chosen by the groom and bride respectively (the *koumbari*). The *koumbari* are close friends who often become godparents (*nonoi*) to the couple's children.

Until recently, divorce was highly stigmatized, and the prospects of remarriage were slim because both men and women would be stigmatized by gossip. While gossip still goes on, divorce and remarriage have become much more common. In cases where an affair leads to divorce, the partner having the affair (husband or wife) may leave the island to avoid criticism, leaving the remaining spouse to care for the children.

HUSBAND–WIFE RELATIONSHIP

While "companionate marriage" has become more common under Western influence, spouses still may retain primary allegiance to their natal kin, facilitated for women by matrilocality. The recent downplaying of dowry transmission at marriage reflects more "romantic" ideas about marriage. Young women feel that they do not want to be reduced to "something to be bought and sold" as the symbolism of dowry implies. By contrast, their mothers were among the most outspoken continuing advocates of the dowry during my fieldwork, as they see it as protecting wives from being financially dependent on their husbands. The control over everyday and significant decision-making is highly variable among couples.

However, there is a general tendency to give husbands the benefit of publicly seeming to be "in charge," while, in fact, wives are making key decisions "behind the scenes." This can be tied in part to male absence on sponge-diving expeditions. As one woman remembered, her mother sold their house while their father was gone and then found ways of sugarcoating the news to him when he returned.

OTHER CROSS-SEX RELATIONSHIPS

The importance of grandparents as caretakers and as providers of inheritance and names has been noted above. One result of this inheritance system, which led to favoritism toward eponymous children, and toward women more generally, has been that brothers and sisters may often come into conflict over the unevenness of property distribution. In former times, brothers were responsible for working for their sisters if their father could not provide a dowry house, and many dowries have provisions in which brothers promise to provide a certain sum of money for the new couple after a specified time. While this could lead to close bonds, it could also lead to cross-sibling resentment as well. In recent times, with equal inheritance becoming more the norm (although many still show favoritism toward daughters), there are increasing possibilities for property disputes. For example, a brother and sister were having a long-running disagreement over their mother's proposed distribution of her property. When the sister gave birth to her first daughter and named it after her mother, the brother angrily complained that the little baby had stolen his part of the property because now his mother would be more disposed to transfer the property to her eponymous grandchild through her daughter.

CHANGE IN ATTITUDES, BELIEFS, AND PRACTICES REGARDING GENDER

In the past the practice of female primogeniture meant that a class of women (first daughters) derived high status from both their economic preeminence and their symbolic association with the continuity of the family line, as expressed in houses, land, and baptismal names. As female primogeniture was replaced by equal inheritance, with marginal preference shown to first daughters

over subsequent daughters, and to daughters over sons, women have been able to retain an important source of status and power, but now must compete with men in an unequal job market for the money which buys access to consumer goods. At the same time, Western influences have led to increasingly greater freedom for young women to date and to travel unchaperoned by fathers, mothers, or brothers. Thus, the "double standard" in sexual behavior has eroded.

Clearly young women (and young men) have gained "freedom" in relationship to parental control, a phenomenon reported throughout Greece and Europe as parents no longer control the key resources and knowledge that children need for their adult life (e.g., Argyrou, 1996). However, the influence of Western ideals of romantic love and spousal companionship may increasingly separate women from their female kin who provided the day-to-day support to counter controlling or abusive husbands. As land and houses become less symbolically linked to family continuity, women potentially lose another key source of their previous status. The relationship between "freedom," "power," and "status" raises tricky analytical questions that are the subject of my ongoing research.

NOTE

1. Other islands which have been described by anthropologists in terms of their "matriarchal" practices include Karpathos (Vernier, 1984) and Fourni (Dimitriou-Kotsoni, 1993).

REFERENCES

Argyrou, V. (1996). Tradition and modernity in the Mediterranean: The wedding as symbolic struggle. Cambridge: Cambridge University Press.

Bernard, H. R. (1976). Kalymnos: The island of sponge fishermen. In M. Dimen & E. Friedl (Eds.), *Regional variation in modern Greece and Cyprus: Toward a perspective on the ethnography of modern Greece* (pp. 291–307). New York: Annals of the New York Academy of Sciences.

Campbell, J. K. (1964). *Honour, family and patronage: A study of institutions and moral values in a Greek mountain community.* Oxford: Clarendon Press.

Cowan, J. (1991). Going out for coffee? Contesting the grounds of gendered pleasures in everyday sociability. In P. Loizos & E. Papataxiarchis (Eds.), *Contested identities: Gender and kinship in modern Greece* (pp. 180–202). Princeton, NJ: Princeton University Press.

Dimitriou-Kotsoni, S. (1993). The Aegean cultural tradition. *Journal of Mediterranean Studies, 3,* 62–76.

Doumanis, N. (1997). *Myth and memory in the Mediterranean: Remembering fascism's empire*. London: MacMillan.

Dubisch, J. (1995). *In a different place: Pilgrimage, gender and politics at a Greek island shrine*. Princeton, NJ: Princeton University Press.

du Boulay, J. (1974). *Portrait of a Greek mountain village*. Oxford: Clarendon Press.

Galani-Moutafi, V. (1993). From agriculture to tourism: Property, labor, gender and kinship in a Greek island village (Part One). *Journal of Modern Greek Studies, 11*, 241–270.

Hart, L. (1992). *Time, religion and social experience in Rural Greece*. Lanham, MD: Rowman & Littlefield.

Herzfeld, M. (1985). *The poetics of manhood: Contest and identity in a Cretan mountain village*. Princeton, NJ: Princeton University Press.

Herzfeld, M. (1991). Silence, submission and subversion: Toward a poetics of womanhood. In P. Loizos & E. Papataxiarchis (Eds.), *Contested identities: Gender and kinship in modern Greece* (pp. 79–97). Princeton, NJ: Princeton University Press.

Hirschon, R. (1978). Open body, closed space: The transformation of female sexuality. In S. Ardener (Ed.), *Defining females: The nature of women in society* (pp. 66–88). London: Croom Helm.

Hirschon, R. (1998). *Heirs to the Greek catastrophe* (2nd ed.). Oxford: Berghan.

Kenna, M. (1976). Houses, fields and graves: Property and ritual obligation on a Greek island. *Ethnology, 15*, 21–34.

Loizos, P. (1994). A broken mirror: Masculine sexuality in Greek ethnography. In A. Cornwall & N. Lindisfarne (Eds.), *Dislocating masculinity: Comparative ethnographies* (pp. 66–96). London: Routledge.

Seremetakis, C. N. (1991). The last word: Women, death and divination in Innner Mani. Chicago: University of Chicago Press.

Sutton, D. (1998a). *Memories cast in stone: The relevance of the past in everyday life*. Oxford: Berg.

Sutton, D. (1998b). "He's too cold": Children and the limits of culture on a Greek island. *Anthropology and Humanism Quarterly, 23*, 127–138.

Sutton, D. (1999). Rescripting women's collective action: The cultural politics of gendered memory. *Identities, 5*, 469–500.

Vernier, B. (1984). Putting kin and kinship to good use: The circulation of goods, labour, and names on Karpathos (Greece). In H. Medick & D. W. Sabean (Eds.), *Interest and emotion: Essays on the study of family and kinship* (pp. 28–76). Cambridge, U.K.: Cambridge University Press.

Warn, F. (2000). Bitter Sea: The real story of Greek sponge diving. South Woodham Ferrers, Great Britain: Guardian Angel Press.

Hadza

Frank Marlowe

ALTERNATIVE NAMES

Alternative names are Hadzabe, Hadzapi, Hatsa, Tindiga, Watindiga, Wakindiga, and Kangeju.

LOCATION

The Hadza live around Lake Eyasi, North Tanzania, Africa, located at latitude 3°S, longitude 35°E.

CULTURAL OVERVIEW

The Hadza are nomadic hunter–gatherers who live in a savanna–woodland habitat around Lake Eyasi in northern Tanzania (Woodburn, 1968a). They number about 1,000 (Blurton Jones, O'Connell, Hawkes, Kamuzora, & Smith, 1992), of whom many are still full-time foragers, and the others are part-time foragers with virtually none practicing any kind of agriculture. Men collect honey and use bows and arrows to hunt mammals and birds. Women dig wild tubers and gather baobab fruit and berries. Camps usually have about 30 people and move about every month or so in response to the availability of water and berries and a variety of other reasons, such as a death.

The Hadza are very egalitarian and have no political structure, indeed they have no specialists of any sort (Woodburn, 1979). A slightly greater respect is afforded to older people, but it is not very marked compared with that in other East African societies. One manifestation of this respect is the fact that camps are usually referred to by the name of some senior man, usually in his fifties or sixties. The core of a camp, however, tends to be a group of sisters, one of whom the man has long been married to. There is no higher level of organization than the camp, and people move into and out of it with ease. Postmarital residence is best described as multilocal. Of those marriages where one spouse had parents living in the same camp, in about 60% it was the wife, 40% the husband (Woodburn, 1968b).

There are no clans, or unilineal kin groups of any kind. Descent is traced bilaterally with overlapping kin ties, so that any Hadza can usually decipher some kin connection to any other. Generation and gender are distinguished. For example, gender is distinguished among grandparents but matrilineal and patrilineal grandparents are not distinguished (though a suffix can be added to distinguish them). Cousins are distinguished by gender but matrilineal and patrilineal are not distinguished, nor are parallel cousins distinguished from cross cousins. The term for a female cousin is the same as for sister and male cousin the same as for brother, though in both cases they can be distinguished from siblings with a prefix. A distinction is made between maternal and paternal aunts and uncles. Father's brother is called by the same term as father, which may be related to the fairly often practiced levirate in which a man marries his dead brother's widow. Mother's brother is called by a different term than father. Maternal and paternal aunts, on the other hand, are both called by the same term as mother. When personal names are used, there is only a given name (and this is often changed). However, in recent times, when government officials, missionaries, or researchers ask for a surname, Hadza use the first name of the father as the child's second name.

The Hadza language, Hadzane, has clicks, and for that reason has often been classified with the San languages of southern Africa, but it may be only very distantly related (Sands, 1995). There are several different neighboring tribes of farmers and herders, the Nilotic-speaking Datoga and Maasai, the Cushitic-speaking Iraqw, and the Bantu-speaking Isanzu, Iramba, and Sukuma. Since Hadzane is in a completely separate linguistic phylum, this means there are four different language phyla represented, which is a high degree of linguistic diversity for such a small area. Some of these neighboring tribes have been in the area for a long time, the longest being the Iraqw, who moved down from Ethiopia 2,000–3,000 years ago (Ochieng, 1975). Relations between the Hadza and their neighbors are somewhat hostile but do involve some trading. For example, the Hadza give the Datoga honey which is made into beer and the Hadza in return get some beer or meat. The Hadza also trade meat and snakebite medicine for iron, cloth, and food. The Hadza resent the encroachment of the pastoralists, especially during the dry season when their herds can drink up all the water and eat up the plants needed to support the wildlife that the Hadza hunt. In days past, Hadza would occasionally hunt a cow belonging to the pastoralists but, if caught, would be hunted down and killed by a posse of pastoralists. When the first European explorers traveled in Hadza country, the Hadza would hide, which was probably their response to many outsiders (Marlowe, 2002).

CULTURAL CONSTRUCTION OF GENDER

Two genders, male and female, are recognized and homosexuality is apparently absent, except perhaps for the sex play of youngsters according to informants. The language, Hadzane, does not have a different way of speaking for males and females but different nouns do take two different genders and different suffixes.

Men and women wear skirts made of skins, though nowadays most wear factory-made used clothes they receive as gifts from researchers or missionaries. Men usually wear short pants and no shirt, while women wear *shukas* (a small sheet) or *kangas*, a piece of cloth worn by women in East Africa. Women usually cover their breasts. Both sexes will often wear bead necklaces they make from organic materials, though they prefer glass beads they get in trade. They will also wear bead headbands. Both sexes have scars, small vertical or horizontal slits, on their cheeks which they get when they are around 2–3 years of age. These are done by the mother, uncle, or grandfather, as a way to mark them as Hadza. Both cut their hair very short. Females also sometimes cut off their eyelashes.

The trait most often cited by women as important in a potential mate is "good hunter," followed by "character." The trait most often cited by men as important in a woman is "character," followed by "good looks" (Marlowe, n.d.). When asked what good looking is, the answer is often "a woman who looks like she can have lots of babies." The frequent mention of good hunter is interesting, given the fact that meat is so widely shared without an equal amount being paid back to the good hunter (Hawkes, O'Connell, & Blurton Jones, 2001a). Therefore it is not obvious what the benefit is to a woman who marries a good hunter.

Men feel some pressure to keep supplying meat to their wives and mothers-in-law to keep the mother-in-law from counseling her daughter to look for someone better. This pressure manifests itself in the storytelling tradition. Only men tell these stories and they often contain a motif of menacing mothers-in-law, for example, turning into monsters and chasing a man, biting off chunks of his flesh.

GENDER OVER THE LIFE CYCLE

Though there are no formal age-sets as such, there are terms for the various stages in life. *Ola-pe* is the term for children from birth to about 4 or 5 years old. *Tsetseya-pe* refers to those from about age 6 to 12 or 13. *Elati-nakwete* refers to boys during their teens and up till they get married at about 18–20. *Tlakwenakweko* is the term for girls in their teens up until they marry at about 17. *Elati* is the term for adults of both sexes, *elati-ka-eh* is the term for someone who has already had two or three children, *pa-nekwete* is the term for a person about 45–60 years old, *pa-nekwete-ka-eh* refers to someone in their seventies, and *balambala* is someone who is really old and becoming frail.

Girls undergo a puberty ritual. To become men (*epeme* men), males should kill a large game animal. There is no noticeable generation gap. Teenagers get along with older men and women. The absence of tension between younger and older men is less than in many other cultures because polygyny is rare and so competition between them for women is less intense. In addition, since there is no wealth, there is no threat of disinheritance that older men can hold over their sons to control their behavior. However, there is some tendency recently for males in their late teens and early twenties, especially in larger camps, to try to act tough, for example, in negotiations with outsiders, to cultivate a reputation and gain status as an alternative to being a good hunter. This can lead to disagreements with the elders who are less confrontational.

Socialization of Boys and Girls

Adults express no gender preference but welcome a male or female equally. Although men spend more time with boys, women spend slightly more time with girls, so that overall there is not a significant difference in how much care young children get (Marlowe, 2002a). Both boys and girls are reared with very little discipline. During the "terrible two's" children throwing tantrums will pick up sticks and beat adults with impunity. The adults will simply fend off the blows and laugh or, at most, make some noise of disapproval rather than take away the stick. However, when the 2-year-olds hit slightly older children, those children do take revenge. Once children have reached 4 or 5 years of age, they are in play groups with similar aged and older children and it is probably those older children who teach the younger ones that they cannot get away with spoiled behavior. By age 5, all children are well behaved and wait on adults without even being asked; for example, when seeing a man getting out his pipe and tobacco, a child will grab an ember from the fire and take it to the man to light the pipe.

Boys usually go naked until the age of 4 or 5 but girls are given a pubic apron or skirt around 3 years of age. They may also be taught modesty, for example, to cross their legs so others cannot see beneath their skirt. Otherwise, there is not much difference in the ways boys and girls are treated by adults, but differences in their behavior begin to emerge nonetheless. For example, while 3 or 4 years old, boys and girls often play together. By age 6 or 7 they more often play in same-sex groups. By age 8–10, boys go foraging or playing with other boys, while girls begin to go foraging with their mothers. Young girls do more work, such as food processing and tending younger siblings.

Puberty and Adolescence

At about age 16, females reach menarche and undergo a puberty ritual, which coincides with the ripening of the main species of berry. Girls are normally *tlakwenakweko* when this occurs, though they may be much younger (11 or 12), if there are few girls of appropriate age nearby and a larger group is needed. During this ritual, called *Mai-to-ko*, girls wear few clothes and are smeared with animal fat and adorned with many beads from head to toe. They may chase boys and try to hit them with a fertility stick, a 3-foot-long stick carved by males and thought to enhance a woman's fertility if she carries it around. They also undergo clitorectomy, with about half of the clitoris cut off with a knife. This is performed by the only real specialists that exists among the Hadza, a few old women who know how to do this. Males are not allowed to observe, but all women nearby attend. If men were to

watch, it is said they may die. Men say the reason why women are clitorectomized is that babies would otherwise have difficulty during delivery since the clitoris would protrude and obstruct the birth canal. However, at least one Hadza man also says that, without cutting off the clitoris, a woman will move around too much and make too much noise during sex.

Males are not circumcised and there is no ritual for male puberty. When a male is in his early twenties and kills a big game animal, he becomes an *epeme*, or adult man. Certain parts of the larger game animals can only be eaten by men. Females and subadult males cannot even see the men eat this meat or they could die.

Attainment of Adulthood

Occasionally, a boy may kill a big animal, such as a giraffe or buffalo or kudu when only 18 or so, and in this case he may join the *epeme* men early. However, it is usually not until about 20 years old that boys become *epeme* men. All men over the age of about 25–30 are considered *epeme* men, however, whether they have killed a big animal or not. Once they have reached this age, they join the other men in eating the *epeme* meat.

After a girl has had her *Mai-to-ko*, she is in the mating market but usually does not marry for another year or two. Girls in the late teens appear to shop around a bit before they get married. This is the cause of most violent disputes and murders, which are usually due to males competing for one of these single young females.

Middle Age and Old Age

As is the case generally throughout East Africa, respect is shown to elders, both men and women, but especially men. By comparison, the amount of respect shown among the Hadza is not as marked, but is still noticeable. One way that this is noticeable is that camps are referred to as the camp of one of these older men. He is usually in his fifties or sixties. By the time men are in their late seventies their status has dropped and camps are rarely called by their names. The man whose camp it is said to be is usually someone who has long been married to one of the women who belongs to a group of sisters that actually forms the core of a camp. When one looks at the relationship between people in a camp, most are related to one of these women and her parents or children.

Many postmenopausal women are single, either widowed or left by their husbands some time after menopause. They remain important in caring for and feeding young children. These older women usually remain hardy up until their seventies and bring in more daily calories of food than any other age–sex category. Hardworking Hadza grandmothers have received attention, especially in connection with the evolution of long life-span (Blurton Jones, Hawkes, & O'Connell, 2002; Hawkes, O'Connell, & Blurton Jones, 1997).

PERSONALITY DIFFERENCES BY GENDER

Both sexes have excellent abilities to navigate their way on forays, but males are clearly better at this. Women are very hardworking and hardy. "Hardworking" was the third most often cited trait that men said is important in a wife. Hadza women speak their mind and often have long loud bouts of bickering with other women in camp. Compared with men, they are modest when it comes to sexual matters. Women are very nurturing with their children, but they are also quite willing to pass them off to anyone who will hold them. Men are affectionate to children, and play with them more than women do. Men seem to be slow to anger but when they do become angry, they can quickly kill with poisoned arrow. All murders I am aware of were committed by men, and all were apparently disputes over women.

GENDER-RELATED SOCIAL GROUPS

In small camps, there is usually no segregation by gender; everyone sits and talks together. Men still hunt alone or with one other man, and women still go foraging with other women, but in camp all socialize together. A couple will spend much time together as well, especially in the early morning and once it starts to get dark. In larger camps, couples also spend those hours together, but during the rest of the day, the sexes are often segregated not just while foraging but in camp. Men will sit together at the men's place, usually the best shade tree, sharing a pipe of tobacco and working on arrows, while women sit together under another tree sewing, or grooming children and one another, and chewing tobacco. Much of the time in camp women are alone or with other women pounding baobab on large rocks.

GENDER ROLES IN ECONOMICS

Women go foraging everyday for an average of 4 hrs, usually in groups of about three to eight but never alone. Both sexes gather baobab and berries, but women take more of these back to camp than men or children do. Men spend an average of 6 hours foraging every day, usually alone, though sometimes in pairs, especially in the dry season when they hunt at night waiting to ambush animals that come to drink (Marlowe, 2003). Men always carry their bow and arrows and so are always ready to hunt, even when they are specifically going out for honey. They will climb tall baobab trees to get honey and sometimes fall to their death.

Husband and wife will often go foraging together once they get older, in their sixties. Even younger couples will forage together some during the honey season. The husband will look for honey while his wife is digging or gathering baobab nearby. The wife will take an infant with her, and sometimes even older children will accompany their parents. Toddlers are almost always left in camp because they are too young to walk far and too big to carry.

In camp, women do the food processing and cooking for the most part. However, men butcher large animals and will then sometimes put the meat on a fire to roast it. On rare occasions women kill some small animals, and they often butcher smaller animals and roast or boil the meat. Women (and children) fetch water and firewood every day. They usually tend the hearth, and it is interesting that they say they do not know how to make a fire with a fire-drill like men, but rather need to carry embers if no matches are available. Women do the sewing and also build the grass huts.

Females of all ages provide 55% of daily kilocalories brought into camp and males 45%. However, among married couples with children under 3 years of age, men provide 58% of the daily kilocalories brought into camp (Marlowe, 2003). The foods men bring into camp, especially large game, but also honey, is shared more widely outside the household than the foods women bring home, and therefore it is not clear how much men's food represents household provisioning (Hawkes, O'Connell, & Blurton Jones, 2001b). When a child's mother dies it is more likely to die, but it is not more likely to die if its father is not living with it (Blurton Jones, Marlowe, Hawkes, & O'Connell, 2000).

PARENTAL AND OTHER CARETAKER ROLES

In the first year of life children are held by their mothers 50% of the time, and 2.9% of the time during daylight hours by their biological fathers, which is 5.4% of the time their fathers are in camp (Marlowe, 1999). The rest of the holding is done by a variety of others such as grandmothers, siblings, and other female kin and friends. Nursing is on demand, with infants carried in a skin or cloth on the mother's back. There is no noticeable difference in the way male and female children are treated by men and women. Men spend more time with male children than they do with female children, but since women spend slightly more with female children, overall the two sexes appear to get about the same amount of care, though males do nurse more frequently (Marlowe, in press). Men provide more care to their own children than they do to stepchildren (Marlowe, 1999).

LEADERSHIP IN PUBLIC ARENAS

There are no formal leadership roles among the Hadza; egalitarian is the only way to describe them (Woodburn, 1979). The elderly are dominant over the young and men over women, but even these differences are slight. This does not mean that individuals never try to boss others around. This does occasionally happen when someone has some link to outsiders, such as missionaries or government officials, that gives them some leverage. Others tend to simply ignore them once the outsider who leaves.

While men may talk about moving camp, it is usually not until the women are ready to move that a move occurs. Moves often occur because women are forced to go too far to get tubers, or because berries have just ripened elsewhere. Old people who are not senile are often called upon to make decisions and settle disputes. Men do most of the public oratory and decision-making, but women voice their opinion, sometimes in public and plenty at home, often loudly.

GENDER AND RELIGION

There is no organized religion and no belief in an afterlife. There is a creation myth that explains how people came to be, and how there came to be different tribes. The sun (Ishoko) is female while the moon (Seta) is male. The stars are their children. The Hadza have a rich storytelling tradition. Stories are always told by men. There is a story about a woman long ago who was an expert hunter with bow and arrow. The men were getting none of the meat so they decided to sneak up and watch her and saw that she was eating meat. She saw them and gave them the *epeme* meat, certain special parts (heart, kidneys, genitals) of larger animals, so that they would go away. From then on, the *epeme* meat is only for men to eat.

There is a ritual *epeme* dance performed at night. It must be pitch black, with no moonlight or firelight. Men perform one at a time, stomping and singing and whistling to the women who sit and return their calls. The man attempts to rouse the women into getting up and twirling around him. The women try to guess who the man is through the call and shout, and his anonymity allows them to interact with him in a way they would not do otherwise, suggesting sexual overtones.

LEISURE, RECREATION, AND THE ARTS

Hadza men sometimes play a gambling game called *lukuchuko*, in which they toss pieces of bark against a tree and determine winners based on how they land, using arrows as the stakes. Girls (and to a lesser extent boys) sometimes play a game like jax using small rocks. Young girls play with dolls made out of old cloth or clay. Young boys often play with a tin lid found thrown away which is attached to a stick so they can roll it along on the ground like a wheel.

The main form of art is body adornment. Women make bead necklaces out of organic pods, bones, shells, and little sticks. They also sew skins into skirts which are also sometimes adorned with beads. For many years the Hadza have been getting glass beads from their neighbors such as the Maasai. They will use these to make headbands, which they were doing as long ago as the earliest photographs in the 1930s. Men will carve various items such as a fertility stick or arrow, or will sometimes carve geometric designs in a gourd used to carry water or honey. Another form of art is singing and dancing, which the Hadza do often. The only musical instrument is the voice. A few men occasionally play a *zeze*, a stringed instrument made with a gourd, or an *mbira*, a finger piano made from wood and metal, both of which have been adopted from their Bantu neighbors.

Men will sit making arrows and talking for hours while in camp. Women will sit together talking, sewing, and processing food, for example, pounding baobab seeds, or grooming each other and children. They will pick lice out of other's hair and eat them. They will also cut each others' hair and eyelashes. Men do not groom or get groomed as much, but sometimes a wife will groom her husband and men will groom a child.

RELATIVE STATUS OF MEN AND WOMEN

Men are only slightly dominant over women. A man may occasionally hit his wife, though others may disapprove and her kin may intervene. Wife-beating appears to be rare, but increases whenever men drink alcohol which they sometimes get from their agro-pastoralist neighbors. They make no alcohol themselves. Hadza women speak their mind, especially at home. They are quite independent and capable of feeding themselves and children, especially since they usually live with their kin.

SEXUALITY

Sex is considered natural. Women are modest and do not talk openly about sex, though some will answer questions about sex in private. Men are less private but still do not talk about sex publicly very much. There is usually premarital sex before a man and woman start living together. In fact, sex play occurs from an early age and by 10–12, males and females may actually copulate. Certainly in their early to mid teens some are having sex. This continues until a girl becomes pregnant or gets married. Very often, girls become pregnant before they get married and there is no disapproval of this.

All murders of Hadza by Hadza (prior to frequent alcohol consumption) appear to be related to male

jealousy. This may be when a man discovers that his wife has had an affair, in which case he may kill the other man and beat his wife, or kill both of them. More often, however, it is when two men are competing for the same single woman. Since marital infidelity is dangerous for females, and they never leave camp alone, it is probably fairly rare. Men, according to Hadza opinion and practice, are more likely than women to philander.

COURTSHIP AND MARRIAGE

During their teens, girls and boys begin courting. This often begins with a boy sending a go-between, such as his sister, to let the girl know he likes her. If he receives a positive response, they will sneak off at night for a sexual rendezvous. If they like each other enough, they begin living together and are then considered married. Sometimes the young man will need to talk to the young woman's parents and both males and females seek parental approval. Parents rarely object strongly and a couple can ignore their parents' wishes if they choose to. Good hunters find it easy to get married because women's parents want them as sons-in-law and encourage them to move to their camp and marry their daughter. Occasionally, parents will object to their daughter marrying a man if he has a reputation as a bad hunter and honey forager and if he sleeps around too much.

Age at first marriage is 17 or 18 for females and 19 or 20 for males. Median age at first reproduction is 19 (N. Blurton Jones, personal communication). Women experience far fewer menses than American women since they are usually pregnant or nursing an infant and thus less likely to be ovulating. One is not supposed to marry anyone who shares 12.5% or more of one's genes (parent, child, sibling, grandparent, grandchild, uncle, aunt, nephew, niece, half-sibs, first cousins). However, as with the few other rules the Hadza have, this is sometimes ignored and one man married his granddaughter with no repercussions. The practice of the levirate is common. When a man dies, his brother, especially if unmarried, often marries his widow and takes on his children.

There is no overt polyandry, and in fact, when some young woman has two male suitors at the same time, it is seen as a problem that affects everyone. A meeting may be called to tell the woman to choose one because there is a danger that one man may kill the other. Many women say that polygyny is acceptable, even if their husband wants a second wife; however, when women catch their husbands pursuing another woman they get mad and yell and throw things at them. Only about 4% of marriages are polygynous and these usually last only a year or two. Divorce is fairly common, especially in the first few years (Blurton Jones et al., 2000), and serial monogamy is the rule.

About 5% of women marry non-Hadza men. However, many of these return to live in a Hadza camp and bring any children from that marriage with them. They appear to experience little if any stigma. The reason they return, and perhaps why there is not more female exogamy, may be because Hadza women cannot put up with the sort of treatment they get from non-Hadza men, where they are forced to work long hours and may be beaten, and not just on the rare occasion when their husband is drunk, as with Hadza men.

HUSBAND–WIFE RELATIONSHIP

Husbands and wives sleep together on a skin on the ground close to a hearth with their young children. Once a child is about 12, he or she may begin sleeping with other similar-aged same-sex groups. Husbands and wives show no outward signs of affection, no hugging or kissing, but they say that they feel love for each other. When they sit together they often talk at length.

Women never go anywhere out of camp alone, except to relieve themselves. They are either with other women, or with a brother, father, or husband. This is probably less because there is any danger of being raped by a Hadza than being raped by a non-Hadza, or even captured and taken off. It may also be partly simply because without bows and arrows, women would be vulnerable to predators. At least when they are in a group and have their digging sticks, they can cooperate to defend themselves.

Women often do not know exactly when they have reached menopause since they are nursing their last child and so would not be menstruating anyway. After a woman is a few years beyond menopause, her husband may leave her for a younger woman. A very low percentage of women over 60 have husbands and some of them express bitterness that their husbands have left them. However, most postmenopausal women appear to embrace wholeheartedly their role as an important provider of food and care to their grandchildren.

OTHER CROSS-SEX RELATIONSHIPS

A man usually wants to impress his mother-in-law. If she thinks that he is not bringing in enough meat, for example, she may advise her daughter to look for someone else. The pressure men feel shows up in the stories they tell. Several stories feature mothers-in-law who transform into monstrous beasts, chasing them and biting hunks of flesh from them as they flee up a tree. A woman tends to talk little to her father-in-law.

CHANGE IN ATTITUDES, BELIEFS, AND PRACTICES REGARDING GENDER

These days, especially near the one large village in Hadza country, women are becoming much more promiscuous. They sometimes become quasi-prostitutes, sleeping with non-Hadza men in exchange for money or gifts. Near the village, men are drinking alcohol more and more. This results in more wife-beating, even wife-killing occasionally. Some men go into the village with their wives and let them sleep with village men in exchange for free alcohol. This promiscuity is bound to result in increasing rates of sexually transmitted diseases and death from AIDS.

REFERENCES

Blurton Jones, N., Hawkes, K., & O'Connell, J. (2002). Antiquity of postreproductive life: Are there modern impacts on hunter–gatherer postreproductive life spans? *American Journal of Human Biology, 14*(2), 184–205.

Blurton Jones, N., Marlowe, F., Hawkes, K., & O'Connell, J. (2000). Paternal investment and hunter–gatherer divorce rates. In L. Cronk, N. Chagnon, & W. Irons (Eds.), *Adaptation and human behavior: An anthropological perspective* (pp. 69–90). New York: Elsevier.

Blurton Jones, N., O'Connell, J., Hawkes, K., Kamuzora, C. L., & Smith, L. C. (1992). Demography of the Hadza, an increasing and high density population of savanna foragers. *American Journal of Physical Anthropology, 89*, 159–181.

Hawkes, K., O'Connell, J. F., & Blurton Jones, N. G. (1997). Hadza women's time allocation, offspring provisioning, and the evolution of long postmenopausal life spans. *Current Anthropology, 38*(4), 551–577.

Hawkes, K., O'Connell, J., & Blurton Jones, N. G. (2001a). Hadza meat sharing. *Evolution and Human Behavior, 22*, 113–142.

Hawkes, K., O'Connell, J., & Blurton Jones, N. G. (2001b). Hunting and nuclear families: Some lessons from the Hadza about men's work. *Current Anthropology, 42*, 681–709.

Marlowe, F. (1999). Showoffs or providers?: The parenting effort of Hadza men. *Evolution and Human Behavior, 20,* 391–404.

Marlowe, F. (2002). Why the Hadza are still hunter–gatherers. In S. Kent (Ed.), *Ethnicity, hunter-gatherers, and the "other": Association or assimilation* (pp. 247–275). Washington, DC: Smithsonian University Press.

Marlowe, F. W. (2003). A critical period for provisioning by Hadza men: Implications for pair bonding. *Evolution and Human Behavior, 24*(3), 217–229.

Marlowe, F. W. (in press). Who tends Hadza children? In B. Hewlett & M. Lamb (Eds.), *Culture and ecology of hunter-gatherer children.* New York: Aldine.

Marlowe, F. W. (n.d.). *Mate preferences among Hadza hunter-gatherers.* Unpublished manuscript.

Ochieng, W. R. (1975). *An outline history of the Rift Valley of Kenya up to AD 1900.* Kampala, Nairobi, Dar es Salaam: East African Literature Bureau.

Sands, B. (1995). *Evaluating claims of distant linguistic relationships: The case of Khoisan.* Unpublished Ph.D. thesis, University of California, Los Angeles.

Woodburn, J. (1968a). An introduction to Hadza ecology. In R. B. Lee & I. DeVore (Eds.), *Man the hunter* (pp. 49–55). Chicago: Aldine.

Woodburn, J. (1968b). Stability and flexibility in Hadza residential groupings. In R. B. Lee & I. DeVore (Eds.), *Man the hunter* (pp. 103–110). Chicago: Aldine.

Woodburn, J. (1979). Minimal politics: The political organization of the Hadza of north Tanzania. In W. A. Shack & P. S. Cohen (Eds.), *Politics in leadership* (pp. 244–266). Oxford: Clarendon Press.

Han Chinese

William R. Jankowiak

ALTERNATIVE NAMES

The alternative name is Han.

LOCATION

China is located in East Asia and with a land area that is larger than the United States. There are geographical differences between eastern and western China. Eastern China borders the Pacific Ocean. It is sometimes referred to as China Proper due to the high concentration of Han people (who make up 94% of contemporary Chinese ethnic population). The western region has been historically less populated and it is the home of some of China's largest ethnic groups (e.g., Tibetians, Mongols, and Uygurs). Since the 1950s China has sought to "fill up" this region through encouraging internal Han migration. The policy has been successful. Today, the Han outnumber local minority populations in every autonomous region.

There are 22 provinces and five autonomous regions (e.g., Inner Mongolia, Xinjiang, Tibet, Zhuang, and Ningxia). The capital is Beijing, located in northern China. Shanghai, located in the lower Yangtze region, is the largest and most developed city in China.

China's climates are seasonal. In the north the winters are long and are characterized by extreme cold, while in the south (all land south of the Yangtze River) the climate varies from a persistent damp chill in the high and low desert environments to mild and frost free along the southern coast. The Pearl River plain around Guangzhou (Canton) is the most important as well as the most densely populated in the region. With over 1.4 billion people, China's population is the largest in world.

CULTURAL OVERVIEW

China is an agrarian civilization in the process of becoming a urbanized society. Its image of the ideal family is intertwined with a rural heritage organized around the principles of patrilineal descent and patrilocal residence. In many parts of China, there were surname organizations, based on descent from a common ancestor that was reckoned exclusively through males, with memberships ranging from several hundred to over ten thousand. These associations provided the foundation of community organization (Johnson, 1983, p. 8). On the maternal side, kinship ties had significance primarily among the very rich (who use marriage to foster political and economic alliance) and the very poor (who needed mutual cooperation networks to survive) (Johnson, 1983, p. 8).

In practice, family structures varied geographically and with social class. Nevertheless, there were a few commonalities that are pan-Chinese. Women who left their natal family at marriage were viewed by the male's family as outsiders. It was not until the birth of a male child that a woman's status became more secure. Even then, she embraced her children as the primary source of emotional comfort and future security. Men, on the other hand, were linked to their father's patrilineage while remaining emotionally bonded to their mothers. Many Chinese mothers were perpetually anxious about being emotionally replaced by their daughters-in-law.

The urban Chinese family is organized primarily into two different forms: nuclear and stem. While the nuclear family is the preferred form of family arrangement, most Chinese, at one time or another, will enter into some form of stem family arrangement (i.e., a family with a married couple, children, and another relative, usually a parent). In urban China the family is organized around notions of bilateral descent and neolocal residence practices. The conjugal bond is embraced over the extended family.

CULTURAL CONSTRUCTION OF GENDER

Contemporary China is striking in its emphasis on gender. Masculinity and femininity are clearly defined social categories. In fact, people assume that the traits associated with a particular sex are innate qualities of a particular gender. This is a recent phenomenon. Historically, gender was one principle among many (e.g., kinship, generation, age, and class) that determined a person's position in the family and in society.

In traditional cosmology men and women were assigned values referred to as yin (female) and yang (male) which were regarded as opposite through not necessarily in opposition to one another. Together they form an integrated whole. Although the yin–yang construction is linked to a particular gender, it is not absolute. Women as mothers were seen as having more yang essence in relationship to her children, while a greater yin essence in relationship to their husband. In this way yin–yang construction is more about hierarchy than it is about an immutable gender essence. This cosmological assumption did not mean that the Chinese were incapable of perceiving sex differences. They did. It only means that they did not, as today, make a linguistic distinction between masculinity and femininity.

Every culture makes tacit, if not explicit, assumptions about the relations between genitalia and behavior. The Chinese recognize that there is sexual dimorphism, that females reach sexual maturity earlier and that males may have a longer reproductive career, and tend to have a higher preferred rate of copulation.

In Imperial China, femininity was intertwined with notions of virtue. A husband's sexual prerogative as head of a patriarchal family was closely linked with a moral interpretation that defined women's behavior as based in obedience (Mann, 2002, p. 53). In this milieu, women were expected to be chaste and obedient. The state did its part in upholding this ideal. For example, the Qing dynasty (1644–1911) promoted a cult of female chastity through giving honorific plaques and money to women who did not remarry (Mann, 2002, p. 47). The state also constructed ceremonial arches and shrines for widows who refused to remarry or committed suicide upon the deaths of their husbands.

Today, there are clear gender categories that are organized around promoting sexual difference. It is appropriate to acknowledge sexual attractiveness. Nubile women with symmetrical faces and a pale complexion are considered physically attractive. It is fashionable for women at any age to wear their hair long or short (in the 1980s young women wore braided hair and married women wore short cropped hair); short skirts, dresses, and pants are also deemed appropriate. These images of contemporary femininity are readily found on billboards and in magazine and television advertisements. For women, a man's relative age is not a primary factor in accessing his relative physical attractivess. Women appear to use a more complicated calculus that includes facial symmetry, relative age, and social position in assessing a man's overall physical appearance.

Masculinity is organized around a notion of wen–wu. Wen is based on the ideal of cultural attainment or gentility, whereas wu is anchored in the qualities of martial valor. Historically wu qualities were favored over wen. However, the advent of Confucianism contributed to promoting wen attributes which were embraced by the scholarly educated government officials. During the 1960s, the wu ideal which favored the worker and peasant over the scholar was promoted. Contemporary actors such as Bruce Lee, Jet Li, and Jackie Chan are representative of non-scholarly wu tradition. It is the dynamic tension between wen and wu that allows for numerous forms of masculinity to be expressed in Chinese society (Louie, 2002, p. 20).

GENDER OVER THE LIFE CYCLE

Women and men move through various stages in life from the youngest to teenagers to youth to married and old age. People in the countryside readily acknowledge that girls mature faster than boys but that in the end boys surpass girls in talent and accomplishments. In China's larger cities this distinction, especially among young people, is no longer firmly held. Most young men believe that women are equal to men in most things. For males and females, marriage and motherhood are the primary markers signifying the transition from youth to adulthood. In the past, marriage was central to defining adulthood so that women in their late twenties were referred to as old maids, while unmarried males were not teased until their mid-thirties. However, both sexes were expected to marry and have a child. In old age women tend to have greater authority due to the emotional bonds they have developed and maintained with their children. On the other hand, once they retire, men tend to have less authority within the family. During ritual occasions they are treated with respect, and then all but ignored.

In the Chinese family the status of women varies with the different phases of their lives. For rural women, there are two phases that are most critical. The first is marriage and subsequent entrance into her husband's family. The next phase occurs during middle age when her son takes a wife. In both phases women, first as brides and then as mothers-in-law, perceive a loss of control over their lives. The fragility of these transitional periods is reflected in the high suicide rates for women in their early twenties and mid-forties.

Because a woman is an outsider and only gains status through bearing a son, there is a strong incentive for her to form a kind of "uterine family" (Wolf, 1972) that is organized around an intense emotional bond between mother and child. It serves as a kind of a private shelter from the structural restraints imposed by patriarchal ideology.

Men's change in status is more gradual. Marriage is an important identity marker as in obtaining a good job in the city. A man's responsibilities gradually increase as he gets older. The measure of a man is often determined by how well he fulfills his numerous family duties.

Socialization of Boys and Girls

Throughout the history of Imperial China males were preferred over females. Female infants suffered infanticide at a higher rate than males. Today, female infanticide remains high in the countryside but not in the city. When a girl is born, people will call the event "small happiness," but when it is a male the event is called "big happiness." In China's largest cities this distinction is less apparent. Given the realities of the one-child policy combined with new residence and descent practices, urban girls are highly valued.

A "long life celebration" ritual for 100-day-old infants, regardless of gender, is practiced in the countryside. In this ritual close female kin gather together for food and conversation that ends with them lifting the infant through a large circular loaf of bread (*mantou*) calling out as they do so: "Have a long life." In northern China, some mothers might prepare an ordinary dish of noodles in which an extra long noodle is placed to signify "have a long life." This event is private and only the mother and father are present. Today individual birthdays, especially in the urban areas, are increasingly celebrated in the home or in upmarket public restaurants. In place of kin there are now classmates, and family friends are the primary people invited to attend the event.

Boys are given greater freedom and are not controlled in the same way as girls. Obedience is emphasized in rural China and, after the age of 5, corporal punishment, especially for boys, is pervasive. In larger urban settings there is less use of corporal punishment. Parents emphasize guidance over obedience in child-rearing practices. Daycare/preschool starts for most urban children when they reach 30 months of age. Teachers acknowledge that they discipline boys more than girls because boys misbehave more than girls. In the late 1990s teachers started to acknowledge that girls were becoming as mischievous as boys.

Puberty and Adolescence

Adolescence (*nianqing*) is regarded as a youth stage. This stage is between early teen years and extends to the mid-twenties. There are three paths of socialization into adulthood. In the countryside the most common is learning how to farm (Chau, n.d.). Some young women might be able to marry into a wealthier home. If not they marry locally and prepare for a life of farming. The second path is to receive schooling and then obtain a state-assigned job. Girls and boys are sent to primary school in equal numbers, but middle school, which is more expensive, usually finds parents investing more in their son's education. In addition, education investment seldom pays. It is more difficult for rural residents to obtain nonfarm employment. The third path is to run a business or to seek employment in the service sector (Chau, n.d.). For rural residents this means leaving the village to work in small township or moving a great distance to nearby cities.

For urbanites there are only two paths. Most prefer to attend primary and middle school and then be assigned to a state enterprise corporation. The college educated prefer to obtain employment as a manager in an international firm.

Attainment of Adulthood

The most notable shift to adulthood is marriage, which begins in countryside when a girl turns 21 and a boy is 23 years old. In more remote regions, girls often marry at 16 or 17. In this way, girls reach adulthood earlier than boys. In the cities obtaining a job and a separate apartment away from one's parents marks adulthood. However, complete adulthood is not truly gained until the urbanite marries and has a child.

Middle Age and Old Age

Except for major political leaders, retirement comes relatively early in China. Women retire at the age of 55 and men at the age of 60. Old age is celebrated symbolically with the eldest person being placed in the center of picture. In the countryside, once an elderly person can no longer function, he is relegated to the level of symbolic status with the day-to-day affairs being managed by his son.

Unlike their rural counterparts, urban married couples, in setting up a household, start by forming a nuclear family. Later, upon the death of one of their parents, the family structure changes to incorporate the living parent. However, this reincorporation does not lead to the elderly parent becoming the head of the family. While an elderly parent is referred to as the head of the family on ceremonial occasions, and given the seat of honor whenever a photograph is taken or a special dinner is cooked, the fact is that he or she is perceived to be an important but, sometimes, burdensome duty.

Elderly persons often lament that, although their physical needs are taken care of, they still do not receive the respect they desire or feel they deserve. Some elderly even talk as if their children have abandoned them. Significantly, fathers complain more often than mothers about the loss of their children's active attention and freely given respect. Observations of elderly parent–offspring interaction found that mothers were, in fact, treated with greater tenderness, attention, and respect than fathers. Obviously, mothers, and not fathers, are able to draw upon the strong intimate child–parent bonds which they established and maintained throughout their life span. Without property and other "resources of power," fathers who took little or no interest in their children's development are unable to command their children and therefore receive only a ritualistic admission of deference and a nominal articulation of love. The new emphasis on the market economy and the value of money will enable some elderly to command respect from their family and strangers.

PERSONALITY DIFFERENCES BY GENDER

The Chinese believe that the difference between men and women is a byproduct of biological and cultural forces. Masculine attributes are rough (*culu*), crude language (*maren hua*), "absent mindness" (*madaha*), self-confident (*zixin*), serious (*yansu*), adventurous (*furou jishen*), clever (*congming*), easy-going (*madaha*), quiet (*anjing*), aggressive (*haoshun xinsheng*), hide emotion (*han shu*), strong

(*shang zhuang*), and ambitious (for a promotion) (*you ye xinde*).

Feminine attributes are pretty (*piaoliang*), soft voice (*rou sheng*), not very strong (*rou wo*), gossip (*chuan xian hua*), dress well (*daban*), timid (*paixu*), use polite language (*limaohua*), gentle (*wen rou*), anxious (*danshide*), sentimental (*you yu*), slim figure (*miaotiao*), incline to make a fuss out of nothing (*cheng suifu*), and cannot do hard work (*taizhaoqi*).

The sum of women's images for an ideal husband (*hao zhangfu*) were as follows: a man who is tall (over 1.6 m), healthy, handsome, strong, intelligent, brave, well-mannered, and kind; a man who has status and could provide for a family. In the late 1990s, more in response to the forces of globalization, another trait was added: the absence of a double eyelid fold. The sum of men's images for an ideal wife (*hao qizi*) were as follows: a woman who is beautiful, tall, healthy, soft, kind, well-mannered, loyal, and virtuous; a woman who is skilled in domestic crafts (e.g., sewing, cooking, etc.) and can take care of children.

Whenever men and women engage in casual flirtations the gender traits are dramatized and exaggerated, and they strive to present an image that the opposite sex finds most attractive. Outside the sexual context (in their interactions with siblings, parents, classmates, and the public at large), men and women are more prone to assert non-gender-relevant traits. It is in these contexts that women do not, nor are they expected to, act timid, passive, mild, or coy; likewise, men are not expected always to appear confident, ambitious, and work-oriented. The central difficulty for individuals, of course, is living in social settings that are devoid of the other gender's participation.

An enjoyable activity for young Chinese men is to rank a woman's relative physical beauty. The sexual delight that men take in being aroused visually often leads them to buy pornography or, sometimes, make their own. The male's ability to become sexually aroused by visual stimuli can often result in extremely inappropriate social behavior. The male preference for beauty also affects the pace and growth of their involvement. Chinese men, like American men, fall in love quicker than women.

GENDER-RELATED SOCIAL GROUPS

For much of Chinese history, the social landscape was gendered. The villages were organized around families that were often organized into lineages that extended into clans. In every way this was a patriarchal-based society. Women exerted indirect influence only within the family. There was, and continues to be, a pronounced sexual division of labor.

Unlike their rural married counterparts who usually live their entire lives in the same village with or near the husband's parents, urbanites tend to live scattered through various neighborhoods. The neolocal (new) and not patrilocal (father's) residence norm is the most common. Because housing units are packed so closely together, living space cannot always be expanded to embrace a new nuclear unit. When there is a shortage of available housing, any apartment is better than no apartment. This pragmatic concern contributed to the Chinese rejecting the traditional patrilocal resident rule in favor of the more flexible neolocal norm.

GENDER ROLES IN ECONOMICS

There is a clear-cut sexual division of labor that is organized around a notion of complementary. In rural China women were and are busy all day—cooking food, drawing water, pounding rice, minding the farm, serving their mother-in law, suckling babies (Mann, 2002, p. 109). In the north, there is seasonal work. In the summer women sell produce in the local markets, while the men harvest the crop. In the winter most of the sellers in the produce market are men. In south China, which has three growing seasons a year, women work in the rice paddies as well as in the produce markets, small clothing shops, or restaurants. Most long-distance traders are men, though there are unmarried groups of females who sell various products. If married women participate, it is usually with their husbands who will be staying in a particular location for a considerable length of time.

Recently, many rural young women who want to increase their autonomy have migrated to other regions. Most of the young factory workers (commonly referred to as maiden workers) in south China are women (Lee, 1998). Throughout China the majority of shop assistants, waiters and waitresses, and hotel employees are rural migrants. Urban women and men generally refuse to take what they considered demeaning jobs. Instead, they hope to obtain a position in a state-run enterprise or work in an upmarket business.

PARENTAL AND OTHER CARETAKER ROLES

For much of Chinese history, the family was organized around an ideology of filial piety that encouraged total obedience, respect, and loyalty toward the father. By controlling the distribution of the family inheritance, a father could affect a special, if not psychological, dependency on the part of the child. On the other hand, a mother's parenting style was seen as much a result of being considered an "outsider" as it was of a "natural" attachment fostered through childbirth and early childcare. Given her lower status in her husband's family, the mother needed a friend, an ally, and what better one than her own child. In this way, the different access to and use of economic and psychological "resources" contributed to the elaboration of the two complementary parenting styles: the father as an aloof spouse and disciplinary provider, and the mother as an equally aloof spouse but, toward her children, an intimate nurturer.

Chinese have a clear sense of gender-specific duties. This sense is patterned by the setting, timing, and manner of parental interaction with the child. A child's age and sex affected the frequency and style of parental interaction. There are several developmental stages of parent–child interaction: early infancy, late infancy (*yinger*), and early childhood (*ertong*). During the infant stage the mother is the more involved parent, whereas the father's involvement increases when the child reaches the childhood stage (3–6 years old). This is especially so if the father is highly educated.

There are gender differences in parent–child caretaking styles. For example, women typically hold a child close to their body, while men hold the child away from their body. Mothers and fathers also differed in their degree of patience toward a stubborn child who refuses to move. Mothers waited twice as long before picking up a recalcitrant child. Men and women also differ in their style of walking with their child. Women rarely walked ahead of the child, while men did. The style of conversation also differs between mothers and fathers. If a mother holds the child she rarely talks to it, but as soon as she starts walking, she breaks into a continuous mode of verbal coaching and patter (this pattern is less common in southwest China). The mother cares for a sick child, dresses the child for school, and scolds the child when he or she misbehaves. The father remains somewhat aloof and only enters into the disciplinary role when something serious occurs. As a child enters late childhood parents are sensitive about touching him or her in public. This is especially so for father–daughter relations but not for mother–son interaction.

LEADERSHIP IN PUBLIC ARENAS

Within the village the major leadership positions are male. In the cities it varies. At national, regional, and local levels the top political leaders are male. Within various governmental departments there are some mature women officials who occupy an intermediate position of leadership. There is also a Women's Federation that is designed to transmit Communist Party doctrine to women. It is run by and for women. It has several administrative tiers and can be found at all levels of society (e.g., village, neighborhood, county, province, and national). Its ability to counter policy instituted by other branches of the government is minimal.

GENDER AND RELIGION

The Chinese folk cosmology reflects ordinary society. With the exception of the goddess of mercy or health (*guanyin*) and the mother ancestor (*masu*), the most significant deities are male (e.g., the war god (*guan gong*), the god of wealth (*caitse*), the earth god (*tudi gong*), the kitchen god (*jiao yangye*), and the laughing Buddha). The fox spirit is a mischievous female deity that assumed the shape of a pretty female in order to seduce men, killing them only after they had fallen in love with her.

At the community level, rural residents continue to practice ancestor worship (or reverence) that may or may not be linked to a lineage or ancestor association. Ancestor worship is based on the notion that there is an ongoing reciprocity between the living and the dead. At the level of the lineage, membership is determined by land and/or monetary contributions that are used to upkeep the ancestor hall. In this setting, only men occupy positions of leadership. In the family, ancestor reverence focuses only on immediate deceased kin or ancestors (i.e., those who have died in the last five generations). It is overseen entirely by women who are responsible for the upkeep of the family altars.

LEISURE, RECREATION, AND THE ARTS

In the city, men's and women's activities tend to overlap so that there are few exclusive all-male or all-female activities. There are activities that one gender tends to favor or the other. For men, it is basketball, soccer, and video games, while for women it is window shopping. Both genders prefer to hang out either as a couple or in a unisexual group at a restaurant, play cards and mahjong, go to the movies, play pingpong, and, in rural areas, attend temple fairs. Some of the more solitary activities favored by men and women are talking on the cell phone, window shopping, watching television, browsing the web in an internet café, reading, and going to a dance hall. In northern China, both genders enjoy singing and story telling.

RELATIVE STATUS OF MEN AND WOMEN

Men formally occupy a higher social position in rural China. In the cities, men informally occupy more leadership positions (e.g., government and business corporations) than women. Within the domestic sphere there is an enormous difference between rural and urban women's ability to command influence. Prior to and after marriage, a rural woman is instructed to obey her mother-in-law and husband. The emphasis is on obedience and deference. A newly married woman is reminded that, in time, she will become a mother-in-law and thus gain authority and independence over the incoming wife. Before this time, a woman must rely on deception and guile, whereas men, secure within their natal family, do not hesitate in openly expressing their opinions and demands. In effect, the prevailing view in the countryside is that women can only gradually, over the course of a lifetime, expand their authority in the family.

In urban China the theme of a powerful woman and the henpecked husband is a source of much joking. Chinese men believe that, in the past, husbands had an easier time controlling their wives than they do today. One man remarked that, "In the past the mother-in-law was fearsome, now the wife is fearsome". The frequency with which this expression is invoked suggests that males are more ambivalent and less secure than in the past with their position within the family and society.

The idea that relations between spouses should be based on equality and parity is increasing among rural and urban youths. However, marriage still places greater restrictions on women's behavior. On the other hand, men also regard marriage as restrictive. Whenever a man leaves or enters his home, for example, his wife will customarily ask him where he is going or has come from. This is not, by any means, a polite ritualistic expression but is motivated by an unspoken but palpable concern that their husband might be seeing someone else.

Because women are saddled with the double burden of working and handling domestic chores and childcare, they often feel overworked, exhausted, and numbed by their duties. Men, on the other hand, believe that it is more their responsibility, and not that of their wives, to gain promotion, increase household income, and expand personal connections. It is a responsibility, an expectation, that they find demanding and take seriously. Failure to perform satisfactorily often results in their wives complaining that their husbands "let the family down." It is a complaint that men do not want to hear because it is perceived as a stigma attacking the core of their gender identity.

SEXUALITY

Sexuality was traditionally regarded as a natural, dangerous, and potentially polluting act. From a naturalistic perspective, sex was conceptualized as an exchange of body fluids necessary to restore health as well as to reproduce. An orgasm was viewed as potentially harmful in that it resulted, especially for the male, in the loss of bodily fluids and thus the depletion of yang. However, if a man could prolong an orgasm or not have one at all, he would obtain valuable yin essence while not giving up any yang essence. It was also deemed dangerous as the loss of too much yang essence (or semen) could result in a weakened body, making it vulnerable to illness. This cosmology gradually gave way to a more scientific or Western-based interpretation of the sex act that saw it as a healthy and important activity. The transformation was gradual. For example, it was only in the 1990s that masturbation was no longer considered harmful; now, like all things sexual, it is deemed immensely healthy.

Until the 1990s virginity was an ideal state that applied equally to females and males in rural and urban China. In the 1980s sexual intercourse took place only after a couple had agreed to marry. A nationwide sex survey, conducted in 1987, found that 62% of all married couples had their first sexual intercourse on their wedding night (Liu, Ngg, Zhou, & Haeberle, 1997, p. 243). By the late 1990s this percentage was significantly lower due to the increased tolerance of premarital sex. Unlike early generations, where premarital sex was usually with one's fiance, the single-child generation (born after 1979) changed the moral code. Sexuality is no longer regarded as a tacit agreement to marry, but instead is perceived to be simply a pleasurable experience that may or may not result in marriage.

Chinese society, though not necessarily the betrayed spouse, has historically been more tolerant of extramarital sex for men. Many men have had concubines, mistresses, and girlfriends and have visited prostitutes. Women have been under tighter community control and thus the opportunities have been less. Today, sexual pleasure is regarded as a fundamental aspect of married life. In China's largest cities, it is easier for women to engage in extramarital sex than at any time in history. This corresponds to increased reports of sexual disharmony among married couples.

The sexual behavior survey in 1987 (Liu et al., 1997) found a pronounced difference in men's and women's response to sexual arousal.

1. Male students reported being more aroused through live visual stimulation, whereas females found sexual situations depicted in movies more stimulating.
2. Educational level and not occupation is the more critical predictor of attitudes toward sexuality (e.g., people with more education change sexual positions more often).
3. Marital satisfaction appears to be similar among farmers and urban couples. However, city women appear to be more disappointed than village women, suggesting that they have higher expectations.
4. Village couples had a higher frequency of sexual intercourse (5.43 vs. 4.66 times a month, or a little more than once a week).
5. There was a relationship between changing sexual position and sexual enjoyment.

Throughout China's history there has been an enormous variation in the attitudes held toward homosexuality. In Imperial China it was not unusual for an emperor to have male and female concubines. However, during the Qing dynasty (1644–1911) this attitude was replaced with a more puritanical view that regarded all forms of extramarital sex as unacceptable. Male homosexuality was regarded as a threat to patriarchal authority, while female homosexuality was not (Brownell & Wasserstrom, 2002).

This attitude continued through much of the 20th century. By the 1990s, homosexuality became tacitly tolerated, albeit with misgivings. There are known homosexual (gay and lesbian) bars in China's largest cities.

As in Mediterranean cultures, homosexuality has clearly defined roles of passive and active sexual roles. The active partner engaged in penile penetration of the passive partner. Unlike in the United States, where older men yield to the wishes of the younger partner, in traditional China, where principles of social stratification shaped people's relation to one another, the younger partner yields to the wishes of the senior partner (Hinsch, 1990, p. 12) .

COURTSHIP AND MARRIAGE

In the early decades of China's post-revolutionary period, marriage required parental approval. However, by the 1980s that was changing. In China's largest cities, a new generation had come of dating age and, through their ideas and actions, had expanded the customary notions of courtship, generating new expectations and demands for emotional satisfaction within marriage. Part of this thinking suggested that if dating could provide some emotional excitement and satisfaction, marriage could do the same. In this way marriage is no longer seen as primarily a vehicle for procreation, but rather it is regarded as the primary institution for achieving happiness, contentment, and emotional security.

The folk notion that love and romance could be combined within marriage is not a recent phenomenon. The two were not perceived as antagonistic or mutually exclusive, barring unfavorable circumstances. What is new is the state's legal endorsement of free choice, and thus love, as a basis for marriage and, more importantly, the eagerness with which that endorsement is being embraced by the younger generation who demand that love and marriage be synonymous or, at least, possible bedfellows.

In the early 1980s dating existed in urban but not rural China. It was organized around two different dating styles involving different conventions which can be called formal and informal and are complementary. Both were entered into with the intention of realizing an immediate practical gain, enjoyment, or marriage. Formal dating (or courtship) differs from informal dating in its emphasis on normative rules, social judgment, and conventional standards for articulating romantic involvement. It is conducted according to rules that organize dating into a semiritualistic sequence of private and semipublic meetings, characterized by incremental increases in the public expression of commitment, usually resulting in marriage.

Informal dating, however, is pursued according to very practical rules, based on shrewd common sense and situational standards. These rules are sometimes provisionally formed by the parties to avoid the pressure of social expectations or the disapproval of one's community. Informal dating may or may not culminate in marriage. Informal dating begins in secrecy, appears to be ad hoc or accidental, and is characterized by public denial of any intimate involvement. In general, informal dating is conducted by individuals who truly love one another but are restricted by prior obligations (e.g., already married, parental or work-unit disapproval, etc.) from publicly acknowledging or expressing their involvement. Within the formal style there can be what we call courtship (a relationship oriented toward marriage) or just plain going out with no stated intent to marry. Although in the case of formal dating an individual may use the services of an introduction agency or friendship networks to find a suitable mate, it should not be construed that this style is devoid of romantic excitement or aspirations.

Once a person decides that a particular individual fits their "ideal," or comes close to most of their criteria, there is a pronounced tendency to fantasize about the other, which can often result in one becoming overwhelmed with romantic anticipation. It was common for individuals who entered into a more formal courtship to become infatuated after a marital agreement had been reached. Romantic infatuation may arise in either form of courtship and is characterized by emotional intensity, a kind of anxiety, expressions of romantic endearment, and the idealization of the other. The two styles differ only in the domain of public expression but not necessarily the intensity of involvement. In the countryside, the two forms of dating continue.

By the 1990s, in China's large and mid-size cities, informal dating had moved away from secrecy to a new ethos of openness. Dating is now regarded as a public declaration of one's independence. It is not usual to see young couples openly hugging and kissing in public. In many ways, the adolescence or youth stage has been pushed back. People no longer marry as easily as they once did. And if they do, they delay starting a family. Today, urban youth regard dating as an opportunity to play, to seek pleasure, and to delay assuming the responsibilities of marriage.

HUSBAND–WIFE RELATIONSHIP

There are a range of responses to the meaning of marriage and family life. This was not always so. In Imperial China marriage was regarded as an alliance between families with the junior generation serving the senior generation. Thus, children continued to defer to their parents. By the early 20th century this ideal had been modified in the largest Chinese cities. In rural China it was not till the 1990s that marriage and family life was redefined to emphasize conjugal unity over the ideal of the larger extended family. Today, young couples in rural and urban settings share many similar values and life orientations.

In an urban arena there are a wide ranges of response to the meaning of marriage and family life. As a rule, if a couple love one another, they repeatedly strive to maintain mutual consideration. Thus marriage, is seen as "a bond between equals who do not keep secrets and who enjoy each other's company and should prefer to do everything together." Consideration and mutual respect are values used by spouses and outsiders to evaluate the quality and success of a marriage. They are not gender-specific traits. Sacrifice and compromise are not constitutionally foreign to either spouse.

The majority of Chinese assume that the loss of romantic intensity is an inevitable aspect of marriage. Typically, the intensity lessens following the birth of a child, which results in the couple's redefining their roles from lovers to parents. Other Chinese, especially young intellectuals, do not believe that romance has to wane, and tend to resent its waning deeply.

Those couples who enjoy one another's company and accommodate, if not actually enjoy, their spouse's personality style and individual quirks seem to have the more couples in satisfactory marriages. In addition to acceptance of a spouse's personality, couples in satisfactory marriages communicated their anxiety, especially fears of losing the other's love.

CROSS-SEX RELATIONSHIPS

In rural China, the kinship idiom continues to be a primary means by which individuals organize their daily lives. Relationships between cousins, uncles, and aunts are deemed important. In contrast, in urban areas, kinship is clearly regarded as much as a potential burden as a potential benefit or a familial necessity. Upwardly mobile kin often deliberately cut of blood ties which bind them to their more economically humble relatives. Parents, children, siblings, and other kin tend to work at different kinds of jobs, developing individual skills and thus unconnected networks of job-related friends. As a result, the dependence upon one's kin is greatly reduced in favor of increasing reliance on friends in the workplace. This change requires that Chinese pursue a broad-based strategy of social interaction that includes both kin and nonkin. One insightful informant, when asked to make a distinction between kin and friends, acknowledged that "friends are for mundane matters, family is for ritual affairs."

The rural ideal of the joint or "big family" as the preferred family organization no longer exists in urban China or, if it does, only in small numbers. Within the nuclear family, relations are ideally warm and supportive and, in truth, this ideal is more often honored than breached. In contrast to brothers, who display a great deal of sibling rivalry, brothers and sisters cooperate more than compete, with the closest ties being between an older sister and younger brother. For these ties it appears that a wide age gap is conducive to promoting a type of mentor–apprentice relationship which continues throughout an individual's life.

CHANGE IN ATTITUDES, BELIEFS, AND PRACTICES REGARDING GENDER

In urban China the *gradual* expansion of women's influence within the home has enabled contemporary women to achieve a sphere of power and domestic independence faster than had been the case in their mother's generation.

In the countryside the increasing value of female labor combined with a shortage of female marriage partners (due to the preference for male children) has led to rapid inflation in marriage-related expenditure by the groom's family but not by the bride's family. Before 1949, wife-givers incurred the major expense involved in marriage and families with more daughters than sons tended to become poorer. Now families fall into debt if they have more sons than daughters (Min Han, 2001, pp. 147–167).

There is a pronounced expansion of women's rights and overall respect that is as much due to the government one-child policy as it is to the expansion of economic consumerism and with it a greater emphasis on individuality.

BIBLIOGRAPHY

Brownell, S., & Wasserstrom, J. *Chinese femininities/Chinese masculinities*. Berkeley: University California Press.

Brownell, S. (2000). Gender and nationalism in China at the turn of the millennium. In T. White & M. E. Sharpe (Eds.), *China briefing 2000: The continuing transformation* (pp. 195–232). Armonk, NY: M.E. Sharpe.

Chau, A. (n.d.) Youth and youth cultural production in rural china. In W. Jankowiak & R. Moore (Eds.), *China youth* (Forthcoming).

Dikotter, F. (1995). *Sex, culture, and modernity in China: Medical science and the construction of sexual identities in the early republican period*. Honolulu: University of Hawaii Press.

Farrer, J. (2002). *Opening up: Youth sex culture and market reform*. Chicago: University Chicago Press.

Hinsch, B. (1990). *Passions of the cut sleeve: The male homosexual tradition in China*. Berkeley: University of California Press.

Jankowiak W. (1993). *Sex, death and hierarchy in a Chinese city*. New York: Columbia University Press.

Jankowiak, W. (1999). Review essay on gender, sexuality and Chinese studies. *Bulletin of Concerned Asian Scholars, 31*(1), 31–47.

Johnson, K. A. (1983). *Women, the family and peasant revolution in China*. Chicago: University of Chicago Press.

Lee, C. K. (1998). *Gender and the South China miracle*. Berkeley: University California Press.

Liu, D., Ngg, M. L., Zhou, L. P., & Haeberle, E. (1997). *Sexual behavior in modern China*. New York: Continuum.

Louie, K. (2002). *Theorising Chinese masculinity*. Cambridge, U.K.: Cambridge University Press.

Mann, S. (1987). Widows in the kinship class and community structures of Qing Dynasty China. *Journal of Asian Studies, 46*(1), 37–56.

Min Han. (2001). *Social change and continuity in a village in northern Anhui, China: A response to revolution and reform* (Senri Ethnological Studies No. 58). Osaka, Japan: National Museum of Ethnology.

Watson, R., & Ebrey, P. (Eds.). (1994). *Marriage and inequality in China*. Berkeley: University of California Press.

Wolf, M. (1972). *Women and the family in rural Taiwan*. Stanford, CA: Stanford University Press.

Hma' Btsisi'

Barbara S. Nowak

ALTERNATIVE NAMES

Btsisi' are also known as Ma' Betisék and Mah Meri.

LOCATION

Btsisi' live along the coast in the districts of Kuala Langat and Kelang in the State of Selangor, Peninsular Malaysia.

CULTURAL OVERVIEW

Btsisi' are an *Orang Asli* (Malay, "original people") tribe, who speak Btsisi' or Hma' Heh ("we people"), a South Asiian language belonging to the Mon-Khmer family of Austro-Asiatic languages. Traditionally, moving in and out of various ecosystems including the inland rain forests, mangroves, and the littoral, Btsisi' carried out opportunistic foraging in these environments. In the rain forests Btsisi' hunted and gathered; they would also cultivate small patches of cleared forest with hill rice and other food crops. In the mangroves, Btsisi' fished using nets, hook and line, and poison tubers. They also crabbed using a variety of techniques depending upon the tide. The mangrove forests also provided wood for houses and firewood. Along the strand, Btsisi' gathered clams, cockles, and other bivalves, and fished using long stationary barrier nets raised and lowered with the incoming and outgoing tides. In the Straits of Malacca, Btsisi' fished with long lines and palisade traps. Many of the traditional subsistence activities are no longer practiced, as a result of deforestation and mangrove clearing by commercial agricultural plantations, and commercial overfishing. While Btsisi' still fish and collect mangrove fauna, it is less productive and results in smaller catches. Modern Btsisi' work as wage laborers harvesting oil palm for plantations, while others work at the new international airport and nearby resorts as cleaners and baggage handlers. Cash cropping is now a major economic activity with oil palm, coffee, and fruit as the major crops.

One village has a well-established wood-carving cottage industry marketed to tourists.

Traditionally, Btsisi' lived along the upper reaches of mangrove rivers which gave them easy access to the various ecosystems they exploited. People built stilt houses along the tidal banks and others resided on small boats wandering in the mangroves. Today, a few Btsisi' still live in the mangrove, but most have opted to live inland and travel to the mangroves. With increasing integration into the cash economy, wealthier Btsisi' are beginning to build their houses with cinder blocks on cement floors. Poorer Btsisi' continue to build their houses on stilts using materials from the mangrove; however, building materials are becoming scarce due to the commercial oil palm plantation draining the mangroves.

Villages vary in size but most are no more than 60 households. There are seven island communities, and four mainland villages situated near the coast. There are also a scattering of Btsisi' who still opt to reside in the mangroves in small clusters of two to three houses. The Malaysian government census places the Btsisi' population at around 1,300 people.

Most decisions are reached at the household and kin group level. When a village meeting is called, everyone knows the issue or problem, thus allowing time and opportunity for extensive informal discussions before the formal meeting. People reach their opinions prior to the meeting; a married couple usually reach a joint opinion which the husband presents. Women rarely participate since they do not speak with appropriate decorum. There is no proscription on women learning proper behavior and speech, but they leave this to the men. Women attend meetings sitting amongst themselves, listening to the men. Meetings always end in consensus, highlighting the unity of the community.

CULTURAL CONSTRUCTION OF GENDER

Btsisi' recognize two gender categories: *hma' kdoh* (woman) and *hma' lmol* (man). Humorally, Btsisi' categorize females as "cool" while men are "hot." This makes females healthier than males. The biological role in reproduction requires females to have more strength than men. Since females have different needs than males, they are born with more ribs; they have more *nabi* ("prophets") to assist them and give them strength. Females are therefore born "cooler" or "healthier" than males, giving them more strength. A consequence of this is that females are also perceived of as being "more intelligent" (*akal*) than men. This belief does not translate in any obvious way in daily praxis.

Modern Btsisi' dress similarly to rural Malays. Women wear a sarong and blouse when working around the house or travelling into town. In the mangroves or when sea-fishing women wear a sarong or homemade pants and a blouse. Men wear running shorts and T-shirts during the day and sleep in shirts and sarongs. Traditionally, women went bare breasted, but when outsiders began coming into their communities, they became timid and embarrassed, and began covering themselves. Men keep their hair relatively short, although some younger men are now wearing long hair. Most women wear their hair long, preferring to put it in a single braid or tied up in a clip. Older women can often be seen wearing their hair in a bun at the back of their head.

GENDER OVER THE LIFE CYCLE

Babies and children are called *budek*; if qualification is necessary, people say *budek kdoh* ("female child") or *budek lmol* ("male child"). Adults are known simply as *kdoh* and *lmol* ("female" and "male"), while elders are *manggew* and, if qualification is necessary, the male or female describer is added.

During a person's life cycle, birth, marriage, and death are the only stages publicly or privately marked. Seven days after a newborn's birth, family and friends come together to celebrate. The ritual to purify the newborn, its parents, and midwives is followed by the bestowal of a name and payment to the midwives. The ceremony is no different for a male or female newborn.

Marriage (*nikah*) is the point a person enters adulthood. Slowly, over time a young, newlywed couple begin to accrue the rights and responsibilities of adults. The couple's parents will initially guide them, making sure they learn their new roles. Once they begin separating their household finances out from their parent's or when

they begin residing in their own domicile, the couple are considered an independent household with all rights, responsibilities, and power that accompany the adult status. The final life cycle stage Btsisi' mark is death (*kəbuis*). Death and mourning rituals are marked the same way for males and females.

Socialization of Boys and Girls

Btsisi' value all children and feel great joy when a child, boy or girl, is born. There is no feeling of failure if a family has only boys or only girls. However, there is a cultural preference for a girl to be the firstborn. Girls are born "cool," and hence stronger and more likely to survive. Boys at birth are deficient in strength; humorally, they are "hot" and thus weaker and less likely to survive. A "hot" person is in supernatural danger. A girl's coolness will help her survive being born, whereas a boy's natural heat makes his entry into the world precarious and dangerous. A firstborn male child is "lucky" to survive because he was probably a "sickly" child.

Early in a child's life there is little difference in parental care, but once a child begins walking and gains some independence, slight differences in parental responses to boys and girls begin. Parents ask girls to do little tasks around the house, while boys are given more freedom to do what they want. This difference becomes more obvious as children become older. Girls begin to take responsibility in the house—cooking and cleaning. Boys may also be required to take responsibility for younger brothers and sisters, especially if no girls are available to help. It is not unusual to see boys carrying a younger brother or sister on their backs when their parents are busy.

As children reach 10 or 11 years of age they begin to play more consistently in same-sex groups. Boys go wandering around and beyond the village. They build little boats to float in the village drainage ditches and catch small fish in the larger ditches outside the village bounds. Boys begin playing with the older teenaged boys, learning soccer and baseball. Girls, when they can get away from household duties, sit and talk in or around the village community house or at one of their homes. Girls frequently look at magazines and talk about all the images they see.

Puberty and Adolescence

Puberty goes unmarked for boys or girls. Even the commencement of menses occurs without note.

The absence of circumcision for a boy and girl distinguishes Btsisi' from their Muslim Malay neighbors. Btsisi' highlight this as a critical difference between themselves and the Malay community.

Both boys and girls go to local state schools. Parents do not restrict girls from going to school, and strive to find the money to send girls to secondary school where they live in a dormitory setting.

Attainment of Adulthood

Adulthood is reached upon marriage. It is one of the few life stages ritually marked. A tooth-filing ritual performed in the early stages of a wedding ceremony marks the transition into adulthood. The tooth filing occurs for boys and girls who have never been married, marking their transition into the world of adults.

If, by chance, a boy or girl marries before his or her elder sibling, the elder sibling must first have his or her teeth filed since it would be presumptuous for a younger sibling to enter adulthood first. Even though the older sibling's teeth are filed and he or she is technically an adult, the person's behavior, roles, and responsibilities do not alter. Thus, while the tooth-filing ceremony symbolically marks entry into adulthood, the real entry into adulthood is marriage when the youth's roles and responsibilities change.

Middle Age and Old Age

As a person grows older they command more respect from those younger than them. It is *tolah* (a "curse") to be disrespectful to elders; thus the older a person is, the more respect they garner. At community festivals, Btsisi' give men, and especially older men, a position of respect. Men, in general, and older men in particular, are always served food first. As there are usually more plates than people, older women will also eat in the first sitting of a meal, indicating their respected position in the community as well.

PERSONALITY DIFFERENCES BY GENDER

Btsisi' believe that all people should be kind, gentle, and nonaggressive. Fear of outsiders is instilled in both young male and female infants, but with time boys overcome their fear while girls' reticence increases. As girls pass through puberty they begin to fear sexual advances and sexual assaults by men from other ethnic communities. Btsisi' women talk in front of their daughters about "outside" men, passing on their fears and anxieties.

Btsisi' women have always been more apprehensive of leaving the village. Traditionally, men are characterized as being involved in activities that take them outside the village, while women's center of activity was inside the village. When women left the village on gathering expeditions, they went in large noisy groups to scare away the dangerous animals such as tigers. Btsisi' culture has numerous metaphors highlighting a male–female/outside–inside dichotomy.

As discussed in the section on leadership, women today do not play a central role in community meetings. They remain quiet and listen to the proceedings and rarely, if ever, contribute in an open public forum. Women do not know how to speak in public. They do not speak *halus* ("refined"). This is not perceived as an inherent biological difference but rather a value orientation. Women do not speak *halus* because they do not care to learn how to speak *halus*. If a woman wanted to learn to speak properly and learn appropriate protocol, she could. But women do not care to learn and become a titled elder. They do not desire to speak in public. They leave this to men.

While there are people suffering from mental illness, data suggest that it is not gender specific, although quantitatively more women than men seem to suffer. Alcoholism is an extensive problem for both men and women. Impressions are that more men than women struggle with alcohol abuse, although alcoholism among women is increasing.

GENDER-RELATED SOCIAL GROUPS

When a young couple first marry, they reside ambilocally. After shifting back and forth for a few months, the couple settle in the bride's parent's house. If there is insufficient room they will opt to reside with the groom's family. The couple remain under the watchful eyes of their parents, learning their new roles as husband and wife. They may join the parental household or form their own household, keeping their finances and resources separate. Following the birth of one or two children, the family establishes its own residence. Traditionally, village exogamy prevailed, but today nearly 80% of all marriages are endogamous; hence, neither bride nor groom is very far from their parents and kin.

Modern preference is for children not only to marry within the village but also within the *opoh* ("family"), the filiative cognatic descent group. Membership in an *opoh* is based on parallel filiation; technically, therefore, brothers and sisters belong to different *opoh* ("family"). Girls belong to their mother's cognatic descent group and boy's to their father's. Preference is for boys to marry their fathers' younger sister's daughter. By doing this, a boy is marrying into his father's *opoh* and a girl into her mother's; therefore they are both marrying kin and reuniting their grandparents' *opoh*.

GENDER ROLES IN ECONOMICS

Btsisi' division of labor is prescriptive rather than proscriptive. An ideology of cooperation between husband and wife means that women and men do whatever is necessary for the smooth productive functioning of the household. While ideally women are responsible for household maintenance and men for the provisioning of the household, in reality both men and women work jointly, as a team, cooperating for the household's success.

Women traditionally performed activities occurring within the village area while men took responsibility for those activities outside the village. This meant that women, besides doing the household and childcare activities, were also responsible for taking care of the swiddens and harvesting the fruit from village trees. Men, in contrast, hunted and did wage labor. The inside–outside dichotomy means, for example, that women sell fruit within the village. However, if the same fruit is sold to a middleman outside the village, it is the men who are responsible. Cash from the fruit belongs to whoever, man or woman, owns the trees, but in reality the cash, as all income, is controlled by the women of the household.

While there is a normative gendered division of labor, with men and women assigned different activities, in reality husbands and wives work together as a team. While women do not go gill- and seine-net fishing by themselves or in partnership with other women, they do go with their husbands. Similarly, men go bivalve collecting and hook-and-line fishing with their wives, even though they typically do not go on their own. No one

wants to do things by themselves without a friend, and who is your best friend but your spouse!

In their free time, women may weave sleeping mats and baskets. Preparation of the material is time consuming but, once done, the weaving occurs at a leisurely pace. While weaving is categorized as "women's work," a few men, in the privacy of their own homes, might do some weaving on their wife's mat. Wood carving is an important handicraft both traditionally and today as an income-generating cottage industry. It is an activity only men perform.

Traditionally, Btsisi' did not "own" land. There was a notion of usufruct, but people shifted their swiddens and with sufficient land no one was concerned about inheritance. Today, this is not the case. Land scarcity is severe. Most land traditionally used for hunting, gathering, and swiddening is no longer available as it is owned by a large multinational oil palm plantation. Land on the mainland is under pressure from national and state development projects like the new international airport. Land values are skyrocketing and village land is now under threat of state government revocation.

Village exogamy with uxorilocality (matrilocality) is no longer the norm. In the past men were not concerned about next year's swidden land, but today land is planted with cash crops and houses are permanent. Upon the termination of a marriage, men no longer want to return to their natal villages, abandoning their fields planted with cash crops. Village exogamy has been replaced with endogamy; therefore, even with marital dissolution, a man maintains control over land he or his father planted and cleared. Women and men can both own and control land; there is no difference, although fewer women seem to own oil palm trees.

Oil palm harvesting has become an important economic activity. Harvesters, using long bamboo poles with sharp sickle-shaped knives lashed to one end, cut down the fruit bunches which can be as high as 15 ft. Palm fronds are also cut from the trees. Harvesting oil palm is not an activity performed by one person. Typically, it is the work of whole families. While men cut the fruit down, women and children collect the 40 kg bunches into a pile and pick up the small individual fruits which have fallen away from the bunch. While whole families work at this activity, if employed by the commercial agricultural plantation, the employment rosters typically only note the men. Women and children do not receive any separate income for their work.

Parental and Other Caretaker Roles

Btsisi' recognize the nurturing role of mothers. Mothers carry a fetus for 9 months and 9 days, and then bring a child into the world with great effort. Mothers feed and carry the newborn almost single-handedly. Unlike single mothers, single fathers will foster their children out to relatives. However, if a widowed man wishes to keep his children, it is his right. But, unless they are sufficiently old and relatively independent, men find caring for children difficult. Upon remarriage following divorce, men only infrequently take their children with them because their new wives are guardedly jealous of their own children's position in the household. Women are pleased and proud if their stepchildren consider them to be "good" mothers.

While people should respect their fathers and grandfathers, Btsisi' do not believe that children must take care of them in old age or sickness, as they believe they must do for their mothers and grandmothers. Fathers do not nurture children as do mothers; consequently, no supernatural punishment occurs for "forgetting" them.

Yet, men are very loving and nurturing of their children. Fathers' child-tending supplements their wives' childcare activities. Time studies found men average approximately 15% of their day performing childcare activities compared with women's 62%. Men's participation in childcare varies according to the developmental cycle of the household. Where there are only young children, men's contribution is greatest. Toddlers whose mothers have younger siblings to care for will spend extensive periods under their fathers' care.

While a father plays an active role in finding his sons a spouse, he must demonstrate caution when organizing his daughters' marriages. It cannot be said that a father "sold" his daughter into marriage; thus a man must show care this does not happen. A man typically leaves his daughter's marital arrangements to her mother's cognatic descent group.

Leadership in Public Arenas

As mothers nurture their children and sisters nurture their sibling group, the *Batin* (village leader) nurtures the local group. Traditionally, with uxorilocality (matrilocality) and village endogamy, women formed the central core of the local community. The centrality of women in the local village is expressed in women's traditional role as holder of the political office of *Batin*. As a direct matrilineal descendant of the local group's founding ancestor *Batins* symbolize the local descent group. Btsisi' elders remember the last two women *Batin*, both of whom died without heirs. Thus their line was lost and there are no longer any women in the position. But elder women still have an important unofficial role in maintaining community peace and unity. Women will informally come together under the informal leadership of a female elder in the community to discuss issues that directly affect the women of the community.

While women's role was to maintain village life, men maintained external relations. Traditionally, men married into a community. Being "outsiders" they performed activities which took them beyond the village. This outward-looking view was reinforced by men holding the leadership position of *penghulu*', whose job was to maintain relationships with other Btsisi' communities and the wider outside world.

Today, all titled positions are held by men, inherited through the patrilineal line. However, if the elders consider a man unsuitable for the position, such as being too concerned about his and his family's welfare to the detriment of the community or drinking too much, his consanguineal relative, such as a brother or patrilineal cousin, will fill the position.

Gender and Religion

Btsisi' place great emphasis on the couple as the most important relationship in Btsisi' society. This notion is followed through in the belief system with God being both female or male. "How could it be anything other than this?," Btsisi' say. Ancestors (*Moyang*), who can be male or female, also have spouses. Two of the most prominent *Moyang*, Moyang Mlur and Moyang Lunyot, are husband and wife. This couple is responsible for providing Btsisi' with the rules of humanity (*adat*), which prescribed who people can and cannot marry. The emphasis on couples persists in the ideology of the shaman's spirit familiar. Most often, the spirit familiar is of the opposite sex of the shaman and has a metaphorical marital relationship with the shaman.

Btsisi' *trimbow* ("sacred origin stories") relate the creation of the world and humanity. The *trimbow* begins by describing the creation of humanity when God and God's assistant, a *jin* (genie) were alone in the world. The *jin* molded "heavenly earth" into a figure which God gifted with "life's breath." The *jin* then made a second figure to be a "companion" to the first. Both figures were molded from the same substance even though they were created separately. The story is unclear as to whether the male or female figure was made first. These figures were the parents of Pagar Buyok and her younger brother Busuh, the "original siblings" whose descendants populated the world.

Following a great deluge, the original sibling pair circled a mountain, the last remaining dry land, in search of mates. They discovered that they were the only remaining people in the world, so God allowed them to marry. Btsisi' celebrate the sibling couple by singing and dancing the *main jo'oh*. People dance around a *busut* ("mound") symbolizing the center of the world, the mountain the siblings circled around. Women dance in an inner circle around the mound with men in a circle outside the women's. Women in the inner circle are closer to the *busut*, suggesting that they are closer to the cosmic center than men. Women and men dance around the mountain in the same direction to avoid the possibility of brother and sister symbolically meeting.

Shamans are essential to rituals such as weddings and curing ceremonies. Women do not desire to become a shaman. Anecdotal evidence suggests that this is because women have another more direct route to the spirit world through their menstrual blood. Menstruating women do not bathe in rivers. Their blood opens a path directly to the spirit world. Thus women have an innate ability to communicate with the ancestors. Women do become midwives although, as is the case for shamans, fewer and fewer desire to learn the body of knowledge.

LEISURE, RECREATION, AND THE ARTS

Women and men both work very hard. Time spent in subsistence and income-generating activities changes seasonally and monthly with the tides and weather. Btsisi' who fish and collect animals in the mangrove and on the strand schedule their activity to the tides, leaving in their boats before the tide ebbs and returning with its rise. This might require a 3 a.m. departure.

Leisure time varies depending upon the developmental cycle of the household and people's livelihoods. Women with young children have substantially less leisure time than their husbands, but if women have the help of older children, especially daughters, they have more time to spend working or socializing and resting. Evidence indicates people who work as oil palm harvesters rather than fishing, have more leisure time. However, people who fish have greater flexibility to take a day off if tired.

When men socialize they are more likely to go off to the local toddy house and have a few drinks with their friends. Women also go, but usually not without their husbands. When women go to the shop on their own, they typically buy what they need and then return home, whereas when men go to the store they will linger, talking with friends and relatives.

RELATIVE STATUS OF MEN AND WOMEN

Even though there are titled elders, all of whom are men, Btsisi' should be viewed as an egalitarian society in which women and men are both considered valued, important, and equal members of the community. Women and men who are knowledgeable about maintaining the health and well-being of people are respected for their knowledge and recognized as valuable community members; however, they do not receive any special rights or privileges as a result of their roles.

Women and men jointly reach decisions that affect their lives. What wage and subsistence activities people do are determined mutually by those involved. Control over resources is shared among owners. If a brother and sister jointly own land, they will jointly determine what the land will be used for. In terms of marriage choices, both young men and young women have a similar ability to control the selection of their partner. The influence a person has is dependent not on whether they are male or female, but on their personality.

While there is officially no "head of household," people say that, if there is one, the woman of the household is the leader. Women are the household financial controllers. Men hand their income to their wives who in turn give their husbands "pocket money." Decisions on household purchases should be reached after discussion between a husband and wife, and a mutually agreeable solution is reached.

SEXUALITY

The topic of sex rarely comes up in everyday conversation with people of the opposite sex, except when people are drinking. While people do not approve of blatant bawdy behaviour, they do not express disapproval of sex or conversations about sex. Btsisi' myths of the origins of sex highlight the fact that sex is fun, and divine intervention was involved in making it easier. Btsisi' do not view sex as debilitating, nor do they perceive women's sexuality as threatening to men. Women seem to dislike sexual activity more than men, but this is because they fear pregnancy. While some women use birth control, not all do. Women who do use contraception say that they enjoy sex. Sexual activity among married couples is limited to no more than once a night otherwise, couples say, "they would be too tired in the morning." Both men and women remain fully clothed during sexual activity.

Extramarital activity occurs often. Men and women are both equally involved in extramarital activity. Men are the primary initiators of sexual activity, verbally alluding to or suggesting a liaison. If women are interested in a man they will attempt eye contact through winking or using other suggestive facial poses. Extramarital relationships do result in conception, which sooner or later becomes public knowledge, even if it is 20 years later. To accuse a spouse of adultery requires "catching" him or her in the act. Hearsay is unacceptable. If caught, the offending parties do not deny the act and give the wronged spouse "evidence" of the wrongdoing. The affronted spouse, whether the husband or wife, has the same rights. The accused lovers have the same rights and obligations. Adultery is insufficient cause for initiating a divorce unless the offending spouse is "caught" at least three times. The wronged spouse can then receive a divorce without being fined; if the injured spouse wishes to leave the marriage without catching his/her spouse three times, he/she will have to pay a fine to the elders.

Notions of modesty have changed with the encroachment of the outside world, especially with Malay morality. Traditionally, Btsisi' women did not wear clothing on their upper body. Today they do. During daylight hours, women no longer walk around their homes wearing just brassieres and sarongs. With more outsiders coming and going in villages, women have altered what they consider modest. Women will no longer even breast-feed outside the village, believing that the Malays will consider this immoral.

Little information is available concerning Btsisi' views on homosexuality; there are no ethnographic examples in the literature. While people seem willing to talk about children born out of wedlock and adulterous relationships, Btsisi' never speak of homosexuality. Cross-dressing is also a topic that is not discussed.

COURTSHIP AND MARRIAGE

Btsisi' youth have ample opportunity to get to know each other. At school, around the village, at the store, on the road, and at festivals youths mingle. Weddings, which are all-night activities, provide young couples great leeway to go off together and get to know each other. Today, youths own motorcycles, giving them the freedom of mobility to visit other villages.

Btsisi' women say that both they and men are attracted to light-skinned people. Fair skin is a sign of beauty. When preparing for a celebration, young women take great care in presenting themselves in an attractive way. They will powder their faces to lighten their complexion, put on red lipstick, oil and scent their hair, and put on their finest clothes. Women say that what most attracts them to a man is his heart, if it is good and kind. Women as well as men say a person's physical appearance is only of minor significance.

There is an expectation that all youths will marry. Extensive census collecting found only one middle-aged man who never married. His rationale for this was that he did not want to provide for a woman's superfluous and expensive desires. This man was never ostracized and he was never considered particularly strange. However, it is atypical.

Over half of all primary marriages are arranged by the couple's parents or grandparents. Girls have as much or as little to say over arrangements as boys. The ability to refuse an arrangement depends upon the child–elder relationship, but if a marriage has been arranged, in most cases it is a fait accompli. Youths rarely say no to their elders' arrangements. Primary weddings are expensive and youths (and parents) need the financial assistance of their families. Refusing the choice of an arranged marital partner will negate the possibility of financial assistance when the youth wishes to marry later.

Most marriages are arranged between kin. Families arrange for boys to marry into their father's *opoh* (cognatic kin group) and girls into their mother's.

Thus, a boy ideally marries his patrilateral cross cousin. Village endogamy is also a common occurrence in over 80% of all marriages.

Marriage ceremonies between *dara* ("never married") are very elaborate, something unique among *Orang Asli*. Ceremonies begin on a Friday night of a full moon. Gifts (*minang*) pass from the groom's family to the bride and her family. The *minang* includes a token amount of money, a small woven basket of cigarettes, and betel nut quid makings which go to the bride's family; clothes and other items that the bride will need to beautify herself for the following days' ceremonies go to the bride. On the following morning, both the bride and groom's teeth are filed, indicating their entry into adulthood. They are then separately sequestered until the night, when an elaborate ceremony takes place to ritually cool the couple, thus ensuring good luck and good health. Celebrants dance and sing through the night. On Sunday morning the groom and his kin, using martial arts, symbolically break through a line of bride's male kin protectors. The groom then "captures" his bride. The couple are then greeted by their parents who wash the feet of their new child-in-law. The couple then learn through action and lecturing what it means to be a wife and husband. They learn what their roles are and how they need to work together as a team. The couple then receive a new married name (*glaw odo'*) which they use to address and refer to each other; the same name is also used by the community. This highlights the cooperative joint status of a conjugal couple.

Widowed and divorced people (*janda'*) remarry. This is particularly the case for widowed men. Older widowed or divorced women will normally wait longer than men before remarrying. Men need the help of a wife more than women seem to need the assistance of a husband. People are free to establish their own secondary marriages. Elders cannot control widows or divorcees as they can young couples. "Customary law" only requires providing a meal to kin and villagers for secondary marriages. But many do not even bother with this.

Btsisi' have a marriage institution called *tukah kdoh* ("wife swapping"). This is when two married couples exchange partners for either a predetermined period of time or permanently. This arrangement is typically the result of an extramarital relationship which a couple wishes to make public, thus ending the worry of "being caught." In permanent swaps, the offended man and woman agree to the swap to avoid the divorce fines they would both otherwise have to pay.

HUSBAND–WIFE RELATIONSHIP

Ceremonies on the third day of a wedding focus on teaching the couple to work together in unison and to share the products of their labor. They are no longer two separate individuals but rather one unit with a shared identity and a shared purpose. They are an *odo'*, a couple, who have a cooperative relationship with shared goals. The relationship between husband and wife is a major venue of male–female relations, shaping the lives of both women and men. Ideally, a married couple should not argue. Life should be harmonious, with spouses helping each other, working together as best friends. A husband and wife must be companions collaborating for success. The traditional Btsisi' word for marriage, *kuyn-hodong*, is the compound of the words *kuyn* ("husband/man") and *hodong* ("wife/woman"). There are many metaphors symbolizing the joint cooperative relationship necessary between husband and wife.

While there is a conceptual scheme dividing men's and women's work into a complementary division of labor, flexibility characterizes the sexual division of labor. Few, if any, restrictions prohibit a person from performing tasks assigned to the opposite sex. Many of the activities Btsisi' perform require a partner. People prefer this partner to be their spouse. In this way resources remain within the household rather than being divided. Even if an activity can be performed individually, who would want to be alone? People want to do things with a friend, and their spouse is their best friend. If he/she is not, then why stay in the marriage? The lack of a rigid sexual division of labor and the need to have a partner reinforces interdependence and cooperation between husband and wife. A Btsisi' man said: "There is no difference in the work women and men do. We all do the same thing and we work together. This way it gets done faster." Working together means that women and men have mutual areas of discourse.

A good wife cares for her children and house, works with her husband in the fields and at sea, and she loves her husband and remains faithful to him. In turn, a good husband should not be lazy, he should be a good provider, and he should love his wife and remain faithful to her.

Polygyny is infrequently practiced. Women do not like their husbands to take a second wife and in most instances the man's first marriage will fail. Cowives do not get along and most often the wives will reside in different villages. Sororal polygyny is the only type of polygyny which is truly successful. Who can be angry with her sister? Polyandry is prohibited. If caught in such a relationship, the punishment is for the three people to be tied to a stake in the sea and drown with the rising tide.

Divorce is possible for both men and women. Reasons why women and men divorce do not differ nor do the fines for initiating a divorce. It is easier for men to initiate a divorce because they are more likely to have access to the funds needed to pay the fines, but this does not seem to inhibit women, who receive financial support from their families. If old enough, children decide with whom they want to reside. Usually they spend time with both parents, since village endogamy prevails. But fearing stepmothers, children prefer living with their mothers.

OTHER CROSS-SEX RELATIONSHIPS

Sibling bonds, especially the brother–sister bond, are central to Btsisi' culture. The original married couple in Btsisi' *trimbow* ("sacred origin story") were older sister and younger brother. Customary law does not allow brother and sister to marry as the original siblings did.

While the relationship between all siblings is very close, same-sex sibling relationships are generally closer. With parallel filiation, sisters and brothers are not "kin"; they do belong to the same *opoh* ("kin group"). By arranging their children's marriage, especially when it entails a boy marrying his patrilateral cross cousin, the brother–sister pair ensures that their grandchildren will be siblings as they are.

CHANGE IN ATTITUDES, BELIEFS, AND PRACTICES REGARDING GENDER

Although Btsisi' culture is undergoing dramatic changes with land loss, resource depletion, and wage labor, the relationship between women and men remains constant. Women and men remain true partners sharing in their

work and sharing in their play. This is atypical, but Btsisi' culture has buffered the most common negative impacts of colonialism and development on women's relationship with men. However, there is slight linguistic evidence suggesting that changes are beginning to occur in the cultural construct of the gender balance in Btsisi' society. In the past, terms of reference and address for affinal kin were the same regardless of the sex of the person speaking or the person being addressed. In 2002, the terms of address and reference for men and women are no longer the same; the terms of address and reference for females have altered. Whether this linguistic change foreshadows behavioral changes is not yet known.

BIBLIOGRAPHY

Karim, W.-J. (1981). *Ma' Betisek concepts of living things.* New Jersey: Humanities Press.

Karim, W.-J. (1993). With Moyang Melur in Carey Island: More endangered, more engendered. In D. Bell, P. Caplan, & W.-J. Karim (Eds.), *Gendered fields: Women, men and ethnography* (pp. 78–92). London: Routledge.

Mathur, S. (1982). The Besisi and their religion: An introduction to the people, the beliefs and the ritual practices of an aboriginal community of coastal Selangor, Malaysia. *Contributions to Southeast Asian Ethnography, 5,* 137–181.

Nowak, B. S. (1985). Can the partnership last? Btsisi' marital partners and development. *Cultural Survival, 8*(2), 9–12.

Nowak, B. S. (1987). *Marriage and household: Btsisi' response to a changing world.* Unpublished doctoral dissertation, State University of New York, Buffalo.

Nowak, B. S. (1988). The cooperative nature of women's and men's roles in Btsisi' marine extracting activities. In J. Nadel-Klein & D. Davis (Ed.), *To work and to weep: Women in fishing economies* (pp. 51–72). St. Johns: Institute of Social and Economic Research, Memorial University of Newfoundland, Canada.

Nowak, B. S. (2000). Dancing the *main jo'oh*: Hma' Btsisi' celebrate their humanity and religious identity in a Malaysian world. *Australian Journal of Anthropology, 11*(3), 345–557.

Nowak, B. S. (under review). Religion and the paradigm of domestic relations: The Btsisi' Odo'. In P. Martinez (Ed.), *Gender, culture and religion: Equal before God, unequal before man.* Kuala Lumpur, Singapore: Institute of Southeast Asian Studies (ISEAS).

Shanthi, T. (1999). *Orang Asli* women and men in transition. In K. S. Jomo (Ed.), *Rethinking Malaysia* (pp. 267–292). Kuala Lumpur, Malaysia: Malaysian Social Science Association.

Hmong of Laos and the United States

Dia Cha and Timothy Dunnigan

ALTERNATIVE NAMES

Alternative names are Hmoob, Mong, Moob, Miao, and Meo (derogatory).

LOCATION

In the 19th century, groups of Hmong engaged in large-scale migrations into Southeast Asia from the region of southern China, settling largely in the highlands of northeastern Laos. Thereafter, many Hmong fled Laos as the Pathet Lao assumed control of Laos in 1975. After living for a time in refugee camps in Thailand, these Hmong resettled in France, French Guiana, Australia, Canada, and the United States. This article focuses on the Hmong who immigrated to the United States from Laos after the Vietnam War, becoming Hmong Americans. These Hmong were born and/or raised either in the refugee camps of Thailand or in the United States.

CULTURAL OVERVIEW

Linguistic and Cultural Identifiers

Speakers of *Hmoob Dawb* or White Hmong call themselves *Hmoob*, whereas those who speak *Moob Leeg* (no English translation) refer to themselves as *Moob*. The presence versus the absence of preaspirated nasals is only one of the many differences, phonological, syntactic, and lexical, that distinguish these two major and, for the most part, mutually intelligible varieties of Hmong spoken in Laos and North America. Common ethnonyms used by outsiders for Hmong are Meo (in Laos, Thailand, and Vietnam) and Miao (in China).[1] The latter term is a general "nationality" label that applies to a number of groups with distinct languages and cultures (Schein, 2000). Western reporters who covered Laos during the Vietnam War followed the lead of Lao sources in using the denigrating term Meo when writing about the seemingly exotic Hmong or Mong.

Historical Overview

Hmong began moving into Southeast Asia during the 19th century to escape political instability and conflict in southern China. They established villages in mountainous northeastern Laos where they had to deal with Lao and French demands for tribute and labor. In reaction to these oppressive demands, a Hmong man instigated a rebellion that lasted from 1918 to 1922 by prophesying the return of the ancestors and the miraculous expulsion of the French from Indochina. Although French colonial authorities suppressed the uprising and executed its main leaders, they granted the Hmong a greater degree of self-governance. Becoming part of the official government created new problems for the Laotian Hmong when influential individuals and their followers took opposite sides in the political struggles that followed (see Quincy [1995] for more extensive history).

In the 1930s, two powerful Hmong families competed for French recognition near a key Laotian trading center situated near the border with Vietnam. The rivalry led to the formation of pro- and anti-French factions. The former transferred their allegiance to the Western-supported constitutional monarchy when it was established in 1949, and fought in defense of the Royal Laotian Government with extensive help from the Central Intelligence Agency of the United States (C.I.A.) beginning in 1961. The smaller anti-French faction joined with the Lao Issara (Free Lao movement) after World War II in agitating for complete political independence from the West. They subsequently became part of the communist Pathet Lao movement at the time of the Vietnam War when the Laotian military and the C.I.A.-assisted Special Guerilla Units, which were predominantly Hmong, opposed the Pathet Lao and the North Vietnamese Army. Other Hmong tried to encourage the formation of a coalition government, but compromise proved impossible. Almost 15 years of warfare, which was conducted primarily in northeastern Laos, devastated the Hmong population. After the Pathet Lao assumed control of Laos in 1975, a great many Hmong fled to Thailand where they were placed in camps and forced to live under harsh conditions. Most of these refugees were eventually resettled in Germany, France, French Guiana, Australia, Canada, or the United States (Cha & Livo, 2000; Hamilton-Merrit, 1993; Pfaff, 1995).

Economy and Politics

The Hmong who first migrated to Laos were swidden farmers. They created small tillable plots in the highlands by cutting down and burning the forest vegetation. The principal food crop was originally maize, but dry-land rice became increasingly important over time. Wet (paddy) rice farming was practicable in only a few areas accessible to the Hmong. They grew a variety of vegetables in house gardens, and kept chickens and pigs. Farmers with sufficient land raised horses and cattle. The Hmong planted poppies to obtain raw opium that could be bartered for salt, silver, and a variety of manufactured goods. The production and trading of opium carried no stigma or threat of legal sanctions. It was used domestically as a medicine and an analgesic. Addiction to smoking opium occurred, but was not very common except among ailing elders (Cooper, 1984; Cooper, Tapp, Lee, & Schworer-Kohl, 1996).

Hmong villages tended to be fairly small and temporary. When soil fertility declined and the fields ceased producing good crops, entire villages moved to new areas of virgin or regenerated forest. Where Hmong managed to establish more permanent settlements closer to urban centers, the boys could commute weekly to the city and live together while attending school. Catholic missionaries established an academy that trained several generations of Hmong boys. In order to garner greater political support in rural areas during the period of the Pathet Lao insurgency, which coincided with the Vietnam War, the government provided the Hmong and other non-Lao minorities with more educational opportunities. Hmong boys were encouraged to attend rural schools for at least 3 years, and a few progressed through the system until they received graduate degrees from foreign universities. Hmong girls were much less likely to be sent to school, although women from politically prominent families did graduate from high school in the capital of Vientiane (Yang & Blake, 1993).

The fighting that occurred in Laos between 1961 and 1975 created a large number of internal refugees. A majority of Hmong retreated to more secure areas near military bases. Loyalist Hmong families who stayed in embattled areas came to depend upon food dropped from C.I.A. planes (Garnett, 1974). A great many fathers and sons left their families to serve as soldiers. They learned how to operate modern military equipment, and a select few were given English lessons so that they could communicate with American support personnel.[2] Educated Hmong males were hired by the Laotian government and by international agencies to help carry out economic and social development programs. Comparatively high pay and other perquisites of power were available to men who ascended through the military or administrative ranks.

The U.S. government tried to minimize the impact of refugee resettlement by scattering Southeast Asians across the country. Refugees were pressured to find employment and attain economic self-sufficiency as soon as possible. Rather than staying put, Hmong migrated to mostly urban areas where they could reestablish extended kinship networks, find jobs, and get an education.

Former military officers, government officials, and staff members of international programs were among the first to find employment, often with resettlement agencies. The vast majority of Hmong lacked the language and work skills required for jobs that provided a living wage with adequate benefits. The men engaged in a national Hmong debate about the wisdom of undergoing training in the present in order to qualify for a good job in the future. Some chose vocational training over immediate employment, and became more dependent on the incomes earned by wives for performing unskilled work. Despite efforts to find jobs for Hmong men and women, and the willingness of husbands and wives, including those with small children, to work in shifts at full-time jobs, welfare dependence remained high for many years (Cha, 2000; Lo, 2001; Yang & Murphy, 1994).

Being educated largely or entirely in the United States has not insured economic success for the younger Hmong, but many are fulfilling the aspirations of parents by earning advanced degrees and embarking upon high-status careers. During the early years of resettlement, Hmong parents tended to encourage sons more than daughters to acquire a post-secondary education. This bias appears to be lessening as the economic value and prestige of academically successful daughters is increasing as they assume leadership roles in the community.

Drawing upon their experiences in Laos and Thailand, Hmong have started a variety of businesses in the United States, often by pooling the financial resources of related families. The possibility of owning a profitable business holds great appeal for Hmong, especially those who have little hope of ever earning high salaries in the corporate world. By contributing their business acumen and labor to these ventures, sometimes as the principal owners, a small number of women have become a force within the Hmong business community.

CULTURAL CONSTRUCTION OF GENDER

In Hmong society, only two genders are recognized, male and female. Hmong men are most admired for being tough, intelligent, wise, generous, and commanding. Above all, they must materially support, morally guide, and resolutely defend the family and sublineage. In order to achieve these ends, they also have to negotiate and maintain reciprocities with other kin groups. In this strategy lies a paradox for would-be civic leaders and politicians. They must be perceived as loyal family members who will not use their positions in the community to favor relatives. The appearance of kinship bias in the performance of public duties can seriously undermine a leader's support.

The ideal Hmong woman of one or two generations ago was nurturing, patient, forbearing, industrious, mature, quiet, and not given to gossip. She modestly avoided joking, or even talking, about sex. When faced with a serious tragedy, such as the death of loved ones, she displayed great emotion, but muted her feelings when dealing with the aggravating problems of everyday life. Rather than being assertive, she tended to withhold opinions that might contradict the views of others, particularly those of male leaders. Most of these qualities continue to be valued by Hmong in the United States, but the ascent of women into public positions of authority reflects a trend toward greater gender equality with respect to opinion sharing and problem solving (see Donnelly, 1994; Rice, 2000; Symonds, 1991).

GENDER OVER THE LIFE CYCLE

Socialization of Boys and Girls

Guided by the concept of *hlub*, "concerned love of others," Hmong parents are permissive and tolerant toward children younger than 7. Once they demonstrate

that they can start assuming productive roles within the family, children receive explicit guidance, and are subject to corporal punishment for serious misbehaviors.[3] More responsibility and discipline are imposed as children mature, and they are expected to be very well mannered by the time they reach adolescence.

In the poetics of Hmong ritual language, the placenta is referred to as the "silver and gold jacket" or the "silk shirt" that a baby sheds at birth and a deceased person puts on again before traveling back to the village of the ancestors. When they lived in dirt-floored houses in Laos, the Hmong buried the placenta of a male child around the base of the central house post, the *tus ncej tas* ("the post of all ancestral relatives"); many rituals were conducted near that post. His early physical association with the main support of the house indicated that he would help continue the descent line, maintain clan and lineage rituals, guide household members, and represent them in dealings with the larger community. The placenta of a female child was buried at a bedpost or under the bed to symbolize her future role in domestic affairs, particularly reproduction. Of course, these symbolic practices have been discontinued in the United States. What has not changed is the fact that Hmong females learn very early that they will leave their natal families and become "other people's daughters" when they marry.

Hmong children in Laos were encouraged to participate in activities appropriate to their sex. Boys began imitating their fathers and older male relatives by playing with miniature agricultural and hunting implements. By the time they were 8 or 9 they had regular farm chores to perform, and sometimes accompanied the men on hunting forays. The adolescent sons of farmers labored in the fields, and learned the wood- and metal-working skills needed to maintain the family operation. Businessmen, typically itinerant traders, kept their sons in school until their mathematical and literacy skills became a business asset. Late adolescence was a time when the importance of learning how to perform family rituals was impressed upon boys. Those who showed musical talent were encouraged to take up instruments like the ceremonially important multipiped *qeej*. Ancestor spirits sometimes brought illness upon a youth as a means of calling him to a type of curing known as *ua neeb*, "working with spirit familiars." He usually waited until adulthood before apprenticing with a *txiv neeb*.

Very young girls began their roles as caretakers and teachers of domestic skills by playing with *nkauj nyab*, handmade "daughter-in-law" dolls. At 6, or even 5 years of age they started sweeping the house floor and feeding the chickens. Before reaching adolescence, girls know the rudimentary aspects of cooking, keeping house, taking care of young children, maintaining the garden, and tending the smaller animals. Among their female peers, they sometimes spoke *lus rov*, a kind of reversed language that males did not know or bother to learn. This created a gender-exclusive social space that girls maintained until suitors began to show an interest in them. In the company of their mothers, grandmothers, and aunts, they sewed, wove textiles, and plaited baskets. A vast knowledge of domestic medicine was passed down within families from older to younger females. Such information was extremely valuable because a woman who is recognized as a *kws tshuaj*, or "expert in medicine," could command high prices for a variety of treatments, the most important being to increase a woman's fertility. A comparatively small number of women learned the arts of the *txiv neeb*.

Puberty and Adolescence

Late in childhood, brothers and sisters begin to sleep apart. The advent of puberty makes sexual privacy very important. Hmong in the United States, like their parents before them, try to monitor the activities and peer choices of their adolescent children. The prevailing attitude is that girls need close supervision, whereas boys can be permitted greater freedom of movement. Boys are expected to initiate flirting and take the lead in serious courting, but Hmong girls in the United States are becoming considerably less passive in these relationships (see Courtship and Marriage).

Attainment of Adulthood

There is no specific marker or rite of passage to attain adulthood in Hmong society. However, Hmong generally consider a married person, no matter how young he or she may be, as *laus* or old. In other words, marriage seems to mark adulthood or maturity.

Middle Age and Old Age

A woman enters marriage knowing that she must be compliant before her new parents and accommodating to all the *kwv tij* of her husband. (Given the pressures of adapting to, and winning the acceptance of, a new set of kin, it is not surprising that Hmong American women prefer to establish their own independent nuclear families as soon as possible after marriage.) She will be expected to bear at least one son, and preferably two or three. Her status increases as the family grows, and she comes to be regarded as nurturing mother and loyal wife. When a man has shown that he is a reliable family provider, kind father, and considerate husband, the *neej tsa* had a special ceremony to confer upon him a *npe laus*, an elder name, which he afterwards proudly used in conjunction with his given name.

Upon reaching 50 years of age or so in Laos, a couple looked to the youngest son and his wife to take over most of the duties of running the household. The institutionalization of elder care in the United States has caused Hmong to worry a great deal about the depressing prospect of being forced to live with strangers during their declining years. Rather than placing all of the responsibility on the family of the youngest son, infirm parents live, sometimes serially, with daughters as well as older sons. This has increased the value of daughters inasmuch as they and their families might become a major source of support in the future. When parents must be sent to a facility for specialized medical treatment or hospice care, members of the extended kin network, including the *neejtsa* as well as the *kwv tij*, arrange their schedules to be with them as often as possible.

GENDER-RELATED SOCIAL GROUPS

Every Hmong identifies with the *xeem*, exogamous patrilineal clan, of his or her father. (The French colonial administration used *xeem* names as surnames.) A *xeem* is a large descent category rather than a social group. The number of *xeem* distinctions has varied over time, but at least 18 are recognized in the United States. Hmong who are related through males to a common historical ancestor or who practice the same rituals as part of their patrimony consider themselves *ib caj ces*, that is, of "one root and trunk." A *caj ces* could be technically called a lineage. Families headed by males of the same *caj ces* frequently form a durable alliance and refer to themselves simply as a *pawg/pab neeg* or "group." They constitute a localized sublineage. The most influential members tend to be males belonging to a *tsev neeg*, a family or "household," headed by a particularly capable leader. This male elder functions as the primary spokesperson for the entire group and mediates disputes. He is "one who guides" or "one who puts out fires." Non-Hmong Americans often refer to all of these kinship structures, from *xeem* to *tsev neeg*, as "clans," and mistakenly assume that the *pawg neeg* leader exerts authoritarian control over all members. Patrilineal relatives refer to themselves collectively as *kwv tij*, "younger/older brothers." When a woman marries, she retains her *xeem* identity while following the cultural norms and practices of her husband's family. Her children are of the father's *xeem* and belong to his *kwv tij* (see Dunnigan [1982] and Leepreecha [2001] for more on Hmong kinship).

GENDER ROLES IN ECONOMICS

Before war disrupted the Hmong economy in the 1960s, women managed the house and garden, cared for the chickens and pigs, and worked in the fields. Men cleared land, built houses, manufactured tools, helped with cultivation and harvesting, tended the larger animals, and hunted wild game. If traders did not come to their villages, men took their horses, cattle, and opium to distant markets. Because they were in contact with outsiders, Hmong men had many opportunities to learn other languages, particularly Lao (Cha & Chagnon, 1993).

During wartime, the wives of soldiers and war widows functioned as family heads and were very resourceful in supplementing the family income. They became entrepreneurs who ran small restaurants or clothing stores. Others took over commodity trading from their husbands, and even expanded operations.

The period of internment in Thailand further reduced differences in the economic and educational statuses of Hmong men and women. Both attended language and literacy classes in order to prepare for the time when their families would be permanently resettled in another country. Since economic activity was restricted to the boundaries of the refugee camps, there was limited opportunity for agricultural activity. Everyone became dependent upon food and other basic necessities distributed under auspices of the United Nations High Commissioner for Refugees, but there were ways for camp residents to earn money (Cha & Chagnon, 1993; Cha & Small, 1994; Long, 1993).

Already adept at needlework, women started up full-time commercial sewing ventures that generated much needed income. The value of their work persuaded husbands to assume more cooking and childcare responsibilities. Some men took up sewing, and worked alongside the women. Both men and women set up candy, clothing, produce, prepared food, and tailor shops. Blacksmiths made money by forging knives and other tools from the leaf springs of junked military vehicles. Silversmiths fashioned jewelry, mostly necklaces and rings, from silver bars brought from Laos or purchased from Thai merchants. When silver became scarce, they learned how to work aluminum into the same forms of jewelry.

Older men who once held prestigious jobs in the Laotian military, civil service, or private commercial sector had the hardest time adjusting to the new economic realities of camp life. They could not wield as much of influence or demand the same degree of respect as they had in Laos. Their leadership skills, while still useful, no longer guaranteed the security of their families. Younger men, those with a command of English, had a much better chance of being employed by United Nations and private relief organizations that ran clinics and schools in the refugee camps. They were also in a position to sell their services as language and literacy tutors to Hmong preparing for relocation to the United States.

PARENTAL AND OTHER CARETAKER ROLES

In Hmong society prior to the resettlement in the United States, young girls are socialized at an early age to engage in *poj niam hauj lwm*, or "women's work." This includes cooking, cleaning, sewing, and caring for younger siblings. The Hmong female spends most of her time in such child-rearing activities as feeding, holding, carrying, supervising, furnishing love and encouragement, clothing, and giving shelter to children. The Hmong mother is also responsible for the welfare of any orphans left by her husband's brothers or male relatives, the care of elderly parents, especially in-laws, the care of her husband, both when well and when ill, the care of sick family members, and the care of any and all guests. Mothers and other female relatives are also expected to instill in their daughters a sense of discipline suitable to their future role, and to teach their daughters the sort of behavior appropriate to their gender. The Hmong female may also be called upon to assume responsibility for the care of all domestic affairs of those related through blood and marriage.

Such activities, while crucial to the child's survival and to the continuity of Hmong society, are "only women's work," and, in a male-dominated society, a man's tasks are ipso facto more important than those of a woman. These tasks are solving family and clan disputes, hunting, and performing rituals. The Hmong father, by his example and the force of his personal authority, engenders for the family a model of respect, prestige, and recognition, all essential to the community status of the family and thus the welfare of the children. Hmong males look after public affairs, devoting themselves to meetings, the purpose of which is the general welfare of the Hmong: *hlub kwv tij neej tsa.*

The young Hmong male without older siblings may occasionally find himself helping parents with child-rearing and household activities, but should he have any siblings who are female, he will be given a wider latitude for play than the girls. To the Hmong father, a son is more valuable than a daughter, and therefore he will not treat a daughter with the respect and high hopes accorded to a boy.

In the United States, these roles are changing as the Hmong confront and come to terms with the social pressures generated by American society, and it is possible to find daughters whose lives are every bit as respected, and even privileged, as those of sons, while there are sons who are accorded neither the variety of privileges nor the latitude of behavior enjoyed by their counterparts in Laos.

LEADERSHIP IN PUBLIC ARENAS

During their early years in the United States, from 1976 to 1980, Hmong utilized the services offered by various volunteer resettlement agencies (Volags). They also competed with them by establishing nonprofit mutual assistance associations (MAAs) that provided some of the same kinds of help directly to refugees. The officers and board members were initially exclusively male. Hmong females educated in Laos formed affiliated organizations that focused on the needs of women. Cooperation between the male- and female-run organizations was sometimes tense. New female leaders began to emerge from a widening base as more women acquired the requisite education and experience in the United States.

Governmental agencies and private foundations pressured their Hmong grantees to give important roles to women. Hmong MAAs responded by recruiting female board members and upper-level staff. Women now exercise considerably more authority within these organizations, but men continue to hold most of the top leadership positions.

Males functioned as the heads of Hmong villages. They also received appointments to district, provincial, and national offices from a government that needed Hmong political and military support after 1961. Several Hmong, including one woman, were elected seats to the National Assembly in Laos. The bureaucratic and legal structures that Hmong instituted at their military bases in Laos and later in Thailand refugee camps were male dominated. Hmong in the United States are just beginning to run for political office outside their local communities, and women are leading the way. A Hmong woman was elected to the St Paul, Minnesota, Board of Education in 1992, and was succeeded by a Hmong man 3 years later. A Hmong female attorney, who is also a wife and mother, became a Minnesota State Senator in 2002.

GENDER AND RELIGION

Hmong ideas about the supernatural represent the confluence of many religious traditions. Some individuals and families claim to practice just one religion, while others conduct ceremonies to solicit help from ancestral and domestic spirits (*ua coj dab*), participate in Buddhist rituals, and worship as Christians depending upon the circumstances. A woman is generally expected to follow the religious practices of her husband's family and lineage. However, men have given up *ua coj dab* and joined the Christian churches of their in-laws.

Hmong who *ua coj dab* divide reality into *yaj ceeb*, the normally visible and material domain, and *yeeb ceeb*, the spirit realm. The latter is also called *dab teb*, a world where tame spirits (*dab nyeg*) protect the house and garden, while dangerous wild spirits (*dab qus*) menace from beyond the pale of human settlement. Hmong also recognize a supremely powerful spirit for whom they have several names. All entities, both human and nonhuman, have spirits called *ntsuj plig*. After a person dies, his or her *ntsuj plig* is said to travel back to the village of the ancestors. Hmong also talk about a deceased's spirit being reincarnated and remaining at the place of interment, but this does not ordinarily occur within the same discourse.

Hmong say that the span of life is "inscribed" before birth, but do not see it as absolutely fixed. Life can sometimes be extended with the help of *txiv neeb*, who are mostly males (*txiv*) who work with spirit familiars (*neeb*) to keep *ntuj plig* from leaving the bodies of ailing clients. *Txiv neeb* also treat individuals when the *ntuj plig* either flees the body due to a traumatic experience or is captured by wild spirits, the *dab qus* (see Lee [1995] and Lemoine [1996] on Hmong spiritual beliefs and practices).

The cosmology of those who *ua coj dab* reflects the patrilineal descent system and family-oriented structure of Hmong society. Like Hmong Christians, they refer to the greatest supernatural being as a male, but one who has a wife. They are the Guardian Couple, *Nkauj Niam Txiv Kab Yeeb*, who bring children to their earthly parents and protect them throughout their lives. *Ntxwg Nyug* is an imposing and frightening male spirit who, from the highest mountain top in the spirit world, sends illness and death to the living when their allotted time has expired. With the help of *Nyuj Vag Tuav Teem*, his assistant, *Ntxwg Nyug* examines how each dead person treated others during his or her earthly existence, and determines what material form the *ntsuj plig* will join in the next life, and for how long. Several ranks down from these top male spirits is the female *Njauj Iab* who, before allowing the dead to pass into the spirit world so that they can be reincarnated, cleanses them of all memories with pure water. The rarity of important female spirits is paralleled by absence of woman from the performance of *dab qhuas*, rituals that express the unique identities of patrilineal kin groups. Women are rarely *txiv neeb*, and only a small number have become marriage negotiators (*mej koob*). Similarly for Christian Hmong, relatively few women are pastors, choir members, or church soloists.

LEISURE, RECREATION, AND THE ARTS

Hmong needlework is becoming more of a specialty in the United States as fewer females grow up knowing how to produce the ornately paneled clothes that they are expected to wear at weddings and public celebrations. Interest in male crafts and ceremonial roles is also declining. Alarmed by these trends, Hmong MAAs and cultural centers are recruiting recognized experts to instruct youths, both males and females, in a broad range of heritage practices. Although cultural maintenance is the stated goal, new forms of art and entertainment are emerging from a mix of programs that reflect a long and complex history of acculturative experiences.

Hmong boys were introduced to the game of soccer in Laos, and it is probably their most popular organized sport in the United States. Major tournaments are held throughout the country during the summer. Teams also continue to play *kab taub*, a game with both volleyball- and soccer-like elements. A wicker ball is volleyed over a net with head and foot strikes. Measured in terms of total participation, volleyball is eclipsing *kab taub* in popularity. Boys compete at spinning tops less often now than was the case in Laos. Possibly the most dramatic change in Hmong sports activity in the United States is the participation of girls. Unlike in Laos, it is considered normal, even desirable, for girls to spend time playing games like volleyball and badminton, and they have excelled at these sports at interscholastic competitions.

Music associated with courtship is discussed in the section on Courtship and Marriage.

RELATIVE STATUS OF MEN AND WOMEN

Although the construction of gender in Hmong society varies regionally, as well as over time, the privileged status of males within the family appears to be a constant. Because they perpetuate the descent line and remain closer to the parents, sons were, and still are, considered more valuable than daughters. When a boy was born in village Laos, the parents announced that he would be "the little one to shoulder fire wood," that is, he would remain with the parents and carry on the family traditions. A female newborn was called "the one to pluck greens for the pig" and "the other people's daughter." Said more directly, she would help the family until old enough to marry and move out. Patrilocal residence tended to keep male siblings and their male offspring closer together, whereas married females usually resided with their husband's kin group. Ideally, the families of close male patrikin formed *pawg neeg* (see above) in order to share resources and to help one another solve problems. According to one Hmong proverb, "Nine fireplaces are not as warm as the sun; nine daughters do not equal one son" (Vang & Lewis, 1984, p. 71). Metaphors that downplay the value of daughters are heard less often in the United States, but sons are still considered essential to the completion of a family.

In Laos, men performed the clan- and lineage-specific rituals while women functioned in supporting roles. The handling of a family's most prestigious goods in public was the prerogative of males. For instance, at large feasts associated with funerals and New Year celebrations, women were restricted to preparing common staples like rice and vegetables, even though they prepared all types of food at home. Men assumed the more important task of cooking the meat dishes, which symbolized family wealth and success.

Hmong family celebrations in the United States are becoming smaller as kin, affines, and friends find it increasingly difficult to coordinate their busy schedules. At these increasingly intimate affairs, the women usually prepare the food while the men socialize with guests. This role shift may reflect the fact that the provisioning and preparing of meat has lost some of its symbolic value inasmuch as it is no longer difficult to obtain nor particularly expensive. Hmong men may also be responding to what they see as a prevalent cultural pattern in the United States, that men do not cook inside the home. Some kin groups continue to have male cooks prepare the meat dishes at large celebrations.

COURTSHIP AND MARRIAGE

Courtship

Daily life in Laos presented limited opportunities for romantic contacts between single Hmong males and females. When a young man developed a fondness for a particular girl he tried to work near her in the field and assist her in performing chores such as collecting firewood, fetching water, and gathering pig fodder. Doing these tasks together, usually in the presence of a female relative of the girl, allowed them to gradually learn about each other before making any definite commitment. By helping the girl in an energetic way, the boy demonstrated his industriousness to the girl's parents.

At night, single males circulated through the village trying to engage girls in conversations whispered through the bamboo or loose board walls of the girls' bedrooms. Visits by a boy to a particular girl could become frequent and gradually more intimate. The boy might try to

persuade the girl to meet him elsewhere for a tryst, but success was unlikely. If the relationship developed into a strong romantic attachment, the boy asked his father and other close males relatives to visit the girl's family formally to propose marriage. Boys tried to act out their sexual desires, while girls were expected to resist and remain virgins until married. If caught in an apparent tryst, and even if sexual intercourse has not occurred, a couple will often be pressured by their respective families to marry in order to prevent scandal. As an alternative, a compensation payment may be demanded by the girl's side for damages caused to the reputation of the girl and her family.

The arts of courtship in Laos included flute playing, serenading as well as antiphonal singing between all-boy and all-girl groups, using a mouth harp or leaf reed to hum intimacies, competitive riddling, and various forms of stylized teasing. These genres are rarely practiced in the United States, but older Hmong occasionally demonstrate some of them at community celebrations. The get-acquainted game brought from Laos and performed in connection with New Year festivities involves the tossing of a stuffed sack or ball between opposite-sexed partners. Volleyball games between mixed teams at kin group picnics do more in the United States to facilitate intersex bonding.

Hmong boys in the United States still go out at night in groups in order to visit girls, but the encounters must take place in living rooms where there is less privacy. Under these circumstances, the exchanges must be more circumspect, and it is often unclear to the parents which boy is interested in their daughter. Youths, particularly boys, are less inclined to dress in distinctive Hmong clothing and jewelry while participating in the ball-tossing game at New Year celebrations. They see little value in singing Hmong folksongs or playing Hmong musical instruments. When elders speak about the beauty and utility of such accomplishment, young Hmong respond with indifference, and even bewilderment. They prefer listening to popular American music emanating from portable radios, CD players, and computers. Rather than improvising rhyming couplets to fit standard folk melodies, a talent highly valued in Laos, they are more comfortable singing the lyrics and tunes provided by karaoke machines.[4]

Up until the mid-1990s, Hmong males took the initiative in telephoning, writing, and visiting their usually younger love interests. If a Hmong female agreed to attend a public event with a suitor, she was chaperoned by a family member. It was the male's prerogative to propose marriage, and his fiancée had little to say in the planning of the wedding. Hmong females are now much less hesitant to call boyfriends, and they see nothing wrong in encouraging the attentions of same-aged or younger males. An increasing number are neither abashed nor restricted from going out unescorted with boyfriends. They are more assertive about whom they wish to date and marry, and about how their weddings should be celebrated.

Hmong Americans who have come of age in recent years tend to see marriage not as a joining of families embedded in larger kinship networks, but as a union of two individuals who share a romantic love. Parents and grandparents wonder whether "a house built on two supporting poles can be as strong a one built on four or six supporting poles."

Marriage

Hmong do not want their children to "remain in the garden too long" (like ripening fruits and vegetables) before marrying. Single females risk being viewed by the first generation of Hmong immigrants as *nkauj laug* (old maids) after the age of 18, whereas single males do not start to be considered *nraug laus* (old bachelors) until they reach 30 or so. It is becoming more acceptable for Hmong females to marry in their early twenties as an increasing number see the advantages of first finishing college and starting a career.

Whether they honor the spirits or practice a form of Christianity, Hmong want the marriages of their daughters to be respectfully arranged in their homes. A suitor asks his father and other close male relatives to present a proposal of marriage to the family of his intended bride. This is done through a *mej koob* who advocates on behalf of the suitor's family. The family receiving the proposal enlists their own *mej koob*. If the two sides, including the couple, agree that marriage is a good idea, the *mej koob* negotiate the *nqis tshoob*, a marriage payment that the suitor's relatives make to those of the intended bride. It is in the house (*tsev*) of the bride that marriage is discussed (*hais*). Thus, the phrase *nqis tsev hais* describes the manner in which most Hmong enter into marriage.[5]

Betrothals can be formalized before youths are old enough, or are otherwise prepared, to marry. If opposite-sexed relatives, affines, or close friends want their children to marry in the future, the boy's side makes a down payment on the *nqis tshoob*. Marriage between first cross cousins is considered by Hmong to be advantageous because it further strengthens relationships between already close kin groups.

Either side may later ask to be released from the agreement (*qhaib*). If just the girl's side is reluctant to go forward, the amount already given must be returned with interest. The family of a replacement suitor usually pays. If the boy's side wants to abrogate the *qhaib*, they forfeit their investment and are charged a fine.

When a young woman wants to get married against the wishes of her family, she elopes or "goes quietly" (*mus ntsiag to*) with her lover to his *kwv tij* (patrilineal relatives). Two male emissaries are sent by the *kwv tij* to the woman's parents requesting a future marriage negotiation. They may refuse but, when their disappointment and anger subsides, the woman's birth parents are likely to accept their new status as *neej tsa*, the family who provided a wife to others, and indicate that they are open to a payment of *nqis*. It is difficult for a young man to defy his parents when choosing a mate if he expects to reside patrilocally after marriage, and to pay a respectable *nqis tshoob* to the *neej tsa*. When faced with parental resistance, he can ask other relatives to help argue his case.

The expression *zij poj niam*, which literally translates into English as "seizing a woman," had a much more restricted meaning before the 1961–75 war in Laos. It applied to instances where a man intercepted a single woman outside her home and held her by the arm at the location of the encounter until her father and other male relatives could be summoned. The intention of the man was to extract a promise that he would at least be allowed to begin the process of *nqis tsev hais*, although his proposal might later be rejected. When a man forcibly carried away a woman whom he wanted to marry, the act was called *nyiag (zij) poj niam*, or "secretly stealing a woman." The old and less violent stratagem of *zij poj niam* is no longer practiced, but many Hmong continue to use the expression as a synonym for *nyiag (zij) poj niam*.

What happens after a woman is taken against her will depends upon whether the captor sends word right away to the woman's parents about what has happened and where their daughter is being held. If the parents are so informed, they have the choice of doing nothing, or going directly to their daughter and bringing her back if she does not want to stay with her captor. Another option is to hold the woman incommunicado for 3 days or longer in order to convince her parents that the marriage has been consummated and must be accepted. Some women "stolen" into marriage have learned to accept their fate and develop loving relationships with their husbands. Others have endured miserable lives or committed suicide.

It is difficult to say how often *nyiag (zij) poj niam* has occurred in recent times. Although relatively rare, anecdotal evidence suggests that it happened with greater frequency during the 1961–75 Laotian War when men had more opportunities to assert power over others and intimidate the parents of women they desired. A number of "bride captures" were reported in the newspapers during the early years of Hmong resettlement in America. Some of these turned out to be elopements where runaway brides regretted their rash acts and sided with vengeful parents when they complained to the police. In other cases, women held by suitors against their will were not physically violated before being allowed to return home. Actual cases of Hmong men taking young single women by force and having sex with them did occur, but media stories gave the impression that Hmong generally accept such behaviors. In fact, the vast majority regard them as deplorable acts most often perpetrated against vulnerable women whose relatives are too few and weak to retaliate.

In the late 1980s, school authorities in the United States became alarmed over what they assumed to be a "traditional" Hmong practice—adolescent marriage. Compared with other ethnic groups, a surprising number of Hmong high-school students, mostly girls and some younger than 16, were living in marriage-like relationships. Hmong attending U.S. high schools have been pressured into marriage after being discovered in a real or apparent romantic relationship by their parents. Youths may also see marriage as a means of leaving troubled childhoods and assuming positions within the family and kin groups that confer respect and a measure of independence.

Older immigrants have tried to persuade their young people to wait until they finished high school or even college before becoming involved in a permanent relationship. Young people, especially girls, actually receive mixed messages. Besides being advised to wait and get a good education, they also hear that (1) it is a mistake to be single too long because it embarrasses parents to have apparently unmarriageable children, and (2) older and more educated women can expect to have difficulty in finding suitable mates. They are also aware that elders sometimes resent unmarried professionals for being viewed as role models by younger Hmong. Fortunately, the so-called "early marriage problem" seems to be fading as youths realize the advantages of waiting longer before attaining full adulthood, and Hmong parents become somewhat more comfortable with the American concept of unsupervised dating.

When the head of a family died in Laos, it was considered proper for one of his younger brothers or younger paternal parallel cousins (called brothers) to marry the widow and raise the deceased's children. Technically known as the junior levirate, the practice kept important affinal linkages intact and insured the continuation of the descent line. The sons and daughters of immigrants are reluctant to continue this custom, but elders still look within the sublineage to find replacement husbands for young widows with children.

Men able to afford multiple marriage payments and support several households have sometimes added a second or third wife to their families. These can be compatible unions, but conflict-ridden marriages involving multiple wives have resulted in long-lasting enmities between kin groups. When tried in the United States, polygyny has seldom resulted in stable marriages or cooperative joint households. Men have come to see such arrangements as causing more problems for the *kwv tij* than they return in benefits, and women generally regard them as oppressive.

Divorce

Senior male members of the husband's *kwv tij* are expected to intervene when a couple are having serious marital problems. The wife's birth family, the *neej tsa*, becomes involved, short of a divorce action, only when the husband's side either invites their help or ignores the problem entirely. If a marriage cannot be repaired, elders representing both sides must determine fault, decide the disposition of the marriage payment, and levy additional penalties if warranted. Every attempt is made to avoid divorce because of the threat it poses for relationships between the *kwv tij* and *neej tsa*. In Laos, a woman risked losing everything, including her children, if she insisted on divorcing despite efforts at appeasement made by the husband and his *kwv tij*. Access to the courts in the United States has given Hmong women more rights with respect to child custody and support (Thao, 1986).

Infertility or the lack of a male heir has been used by some husbands as justification for divorce or taking a second wife.

In Laos, a Hmong family erected a small house in preparation for the return of a divorced daughter who no longer had any ties to her ex-husband's *kwv tij*. At marriage, her spirit had been placed under the protection of the *caj ces* (lineage) spirits of the husband. If she became ill or gave birth after divorcing, she could not be properly treated within the house of her parents, nor could spirit rituals be performed on her behalf without the involvement of her ex-husband's male relatives. So long as she remained divorced, a woman was considered *tu caj tu ces*, cut off from lineage rituals. If she died in this state, no kin group could give her a proper funeral. Hmong parents in the United States are still uncomfortable taking divorced daughters back into their homes, although it is done.

A woman of good character is often encouraged to remain with the *kwv tij* after separating from her husband, especially if she has a grown son who can provide her a home. This arrangement protects an ex-wife from the stigma of spurning the *kwv tij* and living without spiritual protection. In Laos, the *kwv tij* could claim the right to raise the offspring of women who wanted to leave them. However, a divorced woman who returned to the *neej tsa* was sometimes allowed to keep young children, even boys. In the event that the ex-husband's relatives gave up all claims to the children and the women remarried, the *kwv tij* of the new husband could adopt the children into their *xeem* (clan).

More Hmong are divorcing in the United States than was the case in Laos. It has been difficult for older men to share decision-making responsibilities with their wives, although younger couples are finding a better balance. Wives are now less tolerant, or more openly critical, of male infidelity, while some husbands tend to be uneasy about the kinds of contacts that their wives unavoidably have with other males in the course of their daily activities. The process of marriage dissolution still begins with the involved relatives, and stays there even when a parallel civil action is progressing to a conclusion in the courts. Hmong women are still expected to endure marriages that are loveless and even abusive. Those who resort to divorce can be called a *tus siab phem*, an "evil/wicked liver."

Hmong Americans are trying to deal with cases of domestic abuse by participating in innovative community circle and restorative justice projects where men and women contribute equally. Hmong mutual assistance associations are experimenting with "clan councils" like those established in the refugee camps of Laos and Thailand for the purpose of resolving interfamily disputes. Complaints voiced by Hmong women about the all-male character of these tribunals have prompted funding agencies and non-Hmong advisors to insist on female representation. Although there is still some resistance to this idea, women have been recruited to fill key administrative posts.

CHANGE IN ATTITUDES, BELIEFS, AND PRACTICES REGARDING GENDER

Hmong gender relationships began to be profoundly altered 40 years ago as Laos became embroiled in a civil war that was fed by superpower politics. We briefly covered this and earlier periods for two reasons. We felt it important to delineate the origins of important changes that are today strikingly evident in the United States. We also wanted to counter the common presumption that the Hmong exchanged a static custom-bound, traditional existence in Laos for a dynamic life in the United States, requiring adjustments that were totally novel to refugee families. Space limitations prevent us from saying more about the ways in which Hmong culture was affected by global trends before the great migration to the West. Instead, we will simply refer to remarks made by Dr. Yang Dao, who earned a Ph.D. from the Sorbonne and served as a Hmong representative to the short-lived Laotian coalition government before the communist Pathet Lao victory in 1975. On a number of occasions he has told a story about Thai government officials being greatly surprised that Hmong refugees from Laos not only knew about rock and roll, but they also performed it! During an episode of the U.S. television drama *The Trials of Rosie O'Neill*, which aired on November 22, 1991, the leading character claimed that the Hmong did not know about incandescent light and other electrical appliances before coming to the United States.

We have eschewed certain English terms, such as tribal, traditional, animism, ancestor worship, etc., to avoid applying culture-bound and inappropriate concepts to the Hmong. Expressions like these are frequently used to describe Southeast Asian immigrant groups who were cultural minorities in their homelands. Unfortunately, they project American folk theories on cultural others. We thought a better approach would be to impose on the patience of readers by using Hmong labels for key concepts and providing brief explanations of these terms. Better ways of interpreting Hmong culture in English are still in development.[6]

NOTES

1. In the following description of Hmong culture, White Hmong terms are provided for key concepts whenever English glosses might, if used alone, obscure important meanings or connote ideas not intended. We will employ the most widely used system for spelling Hmong, the Romanized Popular Alphabet (RPA) devised by Christian missionaries in the 1950s for White Hmong (see Heimbach, 1979). In RPA, word final *b, j, v, d, s, m,* and *g* represent, from highest to lowest, seven of eight distinctive tones. Words ending in any other letter are pronounced with a mid-tone. Double vowels indicate a vowel plus an angma or –ng. Thus, the spellings Hmong and Mong fairly well represent how *Hmoob* and *Moob* are pronounced, except for the high *b* tone. Inasmuch as the American public is familiar with the term Hmong, we will use it as the general cover term.

2. Hmong who attended school beyond the third grade before the middle 1960s acquired some knowledge of French, but English became a more popular subject as American military and economic aid to the country increased.

3. In the United States, allegations of excessive and inappropriate corporal punishment have caused legal difficulties for many Hmong parents and other responsible elders who have struck adolescents and young adults for persistent misbehavior, such as "dating" a clanmate. The seriousness of transgressions like intraclan sexual relations is often difficult for non-Hmong to appreciate.

4. Reliance on high tech forms of communication has helped, as well as frustrated, preserve Hmong culture. Families began keeping photographic and documentary records before leaving Laos, and cassette tape recorders were used in the refugee camps of Thailand to make copies of oral histories for family members in case they became separated during final relocation to other countries. Dispersed kin have continued to function as transnational groups via the telephone, mail, and the internet. Video and digital cameras give localized family groups additional ways of documenting their life in the United States. Young Hmong are employing contemporary materials, techniques, and machines to create new literary, oral, and visual art forms that celebrate and further develop their esthetic heritage. Additional information about the unique uses of technology by Hmong can be obtained from websites maintained by the Hmong Cultural Center (www.hmongcenter.org), the Hmong home page (www.hmongnet.org), and the Center for Hmong Arts and Talent (www.aboutchat.org).

5. Minnesota State legislators have been unsuccessful in trying to draft a law that allows Hmong to marry legally without the involvement of clergy, court officers, or other traditional representatives of the state. The plan has been to give *mej koob* the authority to "perform" marriages and the responsibility of making sure that all relevant

statutes were being obeyed. Persons who act as *mej koob* see their proper role as one of merely facilitating the process by which the involved families agree to various conditions, such as the amount of the *nqis tshoob,* or "marriage payment." These negotiators do not want to monitor the actions of parents on behalf of the state, and Hmong advocates for women's rights question the fairness of a law that privileges a status role occupied almost exclusively by men.

6. Additional information about Hmong history, culture, and social organization can be found in Hutchinson (1997) and Keown-Bomar and Dunnigan (2002). Koltyk's (1998) short ethnography describes the acculturative experiences of Hmong refugees in a U.S. midwestern city, while Donnelly (1994) focuses on the lives of Hmong women who migrated to Seattle. The intersection gender and generation in Hmong society is the subject of a master's thesis by Hagemeister (1994).

REFERENCES

Cha, D. (2000). *Hmong American concepts of health, healing and illness and their experience with conventional medicine.* Unpublished Ph.D. dissertation, University of Colorado at Boulder.

Cha, D., & Chagnon, J. (1993). *Farmer, war-wife, refugee, repatriate: A needs assessment of women repatriating to Laos.* Washington, DC: Asia Resource Center.

Cha, D., & Livo, N. J. (2000). *Teaching with folk stories of the Hmong: An activity book.* Englewood, CO: Libraries Unlimited.

Cha, D., & Small, C. A. (1994). Policy lessons from Lao and Hmong women in Thai refugee camps. *World Development, 22*(7), 1045–1059.

Cooper, R. (1984). *Resource scarcity and the Hmong response: Patterns of settlement and economy in transition.* Singapore: Singapore University Press.

Cooper, R., Tapp, N., Lee, G. Y., & Schwerer-Kohl, G. (1996). *The Hmong.* Bangkok, Thailand: Artasia Press.

Donnelly, N. D. (1994). *Changing lives of refugee Hmong women.* Seattle: University of Washington Press.

Dunnigan, T. (1982). Segmentary kinship in an urban society: The Hmong of St Paul–Minneapolis. *Anthropological Quarterly, 55*(3), 126–134.

Dunnigan, T., & Vang, T. F. (1980). Negotiating marriage in Hmong society: An example of the effect of social ritual on language maintenance. *Minnesota Papers in Linguistics and Philosophy of Language, 6,* 28–47.

Garrett, W. E. (1974). No place to run: The Hmong of Laos. *National Geographic, 145*(1).

Hagemeister, A. K. (1994). *Gender in Hmong families: Voices from two generations.* Unpublished master's thesis, University of Minnesota.

Hamilton-Merritt, J. (1993). *Tragic mountains: The Hmong, the Americans and the secret wars for Laos, 1942–1992.* Bloomington: Indiana University Press.

Heimbach, E. E. (1979). *White Hmong English dictionary* (Rev. ed.) (Southeast Asia Program Data Paper No. 75). Ithaca, NY: Cornell University.

Hutchinson, R. (1997). Hmong. In D. Levinson & M. Ember (Eds.), *American immigrant cultures: Builders of a nation* (pp. 384–394). New York: Macmillan Reference USA.

Keown-Bomar, J. & Dunnigan, T. (2002). North American Hmong. In M. Ember, C. R. Ember, & I. Skoggard (Eds.), *Encyclopedia of world cultures—Supplement* (pp. 231–234). New York: Macmillan Reference USA.

Koltyk, J. A. (1998). *New pioneers in the heartland: Hmong life in Wisconsin*. Boston: Allyn & Bacon.

Lee, G. Y. (1995). The religious presentation of social relationships: Hmong world view and social structure. *Lao Studies Review, 2,* 44–60.

Leepreecha, P. (2001). *Kinship and identity among Hmong in Thailand*. Unpublished Ph.D. dissertation, University of Washington, Seattle.

Lemoine, J. (1996). The constitution of a Hmong shaman's powers of healing and folk culture, vol. 4, nos. 1–2. National Centre of Scientific Research: Paris, France.

Lo, F. T. (2001). *The promised land: Socioeconomic reality of the Hmong people in urban America (1976–2000)*. Lima: Wyndham Hall Press.

Long, L. D. (1993). *Ban Vinai: The refugee camp*. New York: Columbia University Press.

Pfaff, T. (1995). *Hmong in America: Journey from a secret war*. Eau Claire, WI: Chippewa Valley Museum Press.

Quincy, K. (1995). *Hmong: History of a people*. Cheney, WA: Washington University Press.

Rice, P. L. (2000). *The Hmong way: Hmong women and reproduction*. Westport, CT: Bergin & Carvey.

Schein, L. (2000). *Minority rules: The Miao and the feminine in China's culture politics*. Durham, NC: Duke University Press.

Smalley, W. A., Vang, C. K., & Yang, G. Y. (1990). *Mother of writing: The origin and development of a Hmong messianic script*. Chicago: University of Chicago Press.

Symonds, P. V. (1991). *Cosmology and the cycle of life: Hmong view of birth, death, and gender in a mountain village in northern Thailand*. Unpublished Ph.D. dissertation, Brown University, Providence, RI.

Thao, C. T. (1986). Hmong customs on marriage, divorce and the rights of married women. In B. Johns & D. Strecker (Eds.), *The Hmong world*. New Haven, CT: Yale Southeast Asia Studies.

Vang, L., & Lewis, J. (1984). *Grandmother's path, grandfather's way*. San Francisco: Zellerbach Family Fund.

Yang, D. (1993). *Hmong at the turning point*. Minneapolis, MN: Yang Dao/WorldBridge Associates.

Yang, P., & Murphy, N. (1994). *Hmong in the '90s: Stepping towards the future*. St Paul, MN: Hmong American Partnership.

Hopi

Alice Schlegel

ALTERNATIVE NAME

The name Moqui is used in very old literature.

LOCATION

The Hopi are located in northeastern Arizona, U.S.A.

CULTURAL OVERVIEW

The time period under consideration spans from the last two decades of the 19th century to about 1950, although some of the cultural features of that period were present when I did my major field work in the 1970s. Following this cultural overview, I shall use the present tense in describing facets of Hopi culture.

The Hopi inhabited dry plateau country, where rain was scanty and farming relied on trapping run-off and tapping groundwater. Their major crop was corn, supplemented by beans, squash, and a few fruits and vegetables that the Spanish had brought into the Southwest in the 17th century. Men still hunted game, but by the 18th century mutton, from sheep the Spanish introduced, was a major source of meat. Wild plants provided additional food and were used medicinally. In addition to food crops, the Hopi grew a form of cotton that they used for textile production, both for home consumption and for trade with other Indian peoples.

By the 1890s, manufactured clothing was worn by some, paid for by wage labor both close to home, as the U.S. government began the economic development of the Southwest, and away from home in the towns springing up along the recently built Santa Fe Railroad. A few individuals began small-scale trading and carting enterprises, and some made pottery and other craft items to sell to tourists at the Santa Fe train stops. After the Moqui (Hopi) Agency was established in 1887, Hopis were employed at the schools and other government establishments. When government-licensed trading posts opened up, some Hopis sold farm commodities, mostly corn for animal feed, and some craft items.

The Hopi, population about 6,000 in the early 20th century, lived in villages on three mesas, finger-like plateaus extending out from the high tableland of Black Mesa. Village size ranged from about 300 to 2,000. The houses, two or three stories high, were clustered around one or two village plazas, where ceremonies were held, and along the lanes leading out from them. Built of native stone, they seemed to grow out of the rock that supported them. A house consisted of one or two rooms for living plus storage rooms where dried corn and meat and other goods were kept.

With a few exceptions, the villages were politically autonomous. Each village was composed of a number of clans accorded different ranks, and the leading ceremonial and governmental officers came from the high-ranking clans. The government consisted of a village chief and his council, all of whom held ceremonial offices as well. Additional ceremonial officers had no official role in village decision-making, but their influence was very strong as they had the support of both their clans and the sodalities (see below) in which they held office.

A Hopi village could be thought of as a federation of clans. These clans were matrilineal. Each was led by a woman (Clan Mother) and a man (Clan [maternal] Uncle) who were usually actual sister and brother, although all clan members of the same generation called each other "sister" or "brother." The Clan Mother trained one of her daughters, often the oldest, to be her replacement, and one of her sons was usually chosen by the Clan Uncle as his heir to the office.

Clan unity was expressed in several ways. Clans owned the best farmland, the quality of the land roughly corresponding to the rank of its owning clan. This land was distributed to individual clan households for their use. Houses were owned by women, and men left their mothers' homes at marriage and joined the households of their wives. They divided their time between the house of the wife and the house of the mother or sister, where they had considerable authority over the sons of their sisters.

Clans also controlled ceremonial offices, and some of the highest-ranking clans controlled the sodalities (ceremonial societies) that put on the major ceremonies of the ceremonial calendar. While anyone could join any sodality, and all Hopis belonged to at least one and sometimes several, only members of the controlling clan could take on leadership roles within a sodality.

Clans often competed for political power and for land, but the village united in producing the ceremonial calendar. They also united in warfare. During this time period there was no intervillage warfare, but there were enemies from other tribes, primarily Navajo, who raided fields and stole animals.

CULTURAL CONSTRUCTION OF GENDER

Like other Pueblo Indian peoples, the Hopi view their world as oppositions in balance: night and day, summer and winter, etc. Linked to all of these is gender: females are associated with earth, summer, life (e.g., plants and fertility), south and west, and soft substances; males are associated with sky, winter, death (e.g., hunting and war), north and east, and hard substances. These forces are in balance. Female force, inherent in the earth and women, contains life, but it has to be activated by male force. This principle is dramatically expressed in Hopi understanding of plant fertility. Crops are planted in the (female) earth, but they do not grow unless they are energized by the (male) celestial forces of sun and rain. These forces are potentially dangerous, however, because the sun can burn the crops and rain can wash them away, if not controlled. Lightning, the most concentrated form of male energy, kills, but the field it strikes will be very fertile.

Like the cosmic principles of maleness and femaleness, men and women have different natures. Women have a single nature, a maternal life-giving one. This does not mean that they are passive, for like mother animals they can be fierce in protecting their children and home, and a favorite mythical figure is the warrior woman who saved the village by rousing the women to defend it when the men were away in battle. Men have a dual nature, being both fathers, that is, providers and protectors, and potential killers. Since life has the highest value, killing of enemies is a necessary evil and its effects are neutralized through ritual. Even the killing of game animals is

accompanied by small rituals. While prowess in warfare was respected, the most honored positions for men were the ceremonial ones that had nothing to do with war.

Women and men are respected when they fulfill their duties earnestly and patiently. Women's important role is as mothers, to their own children and to all the people, through care and feeding. Men's role is to provide for their families, and to a lesser degree their matrilineal kin, and to protect the village. Both genders have important spiritual duties that must be performed so that they, their families, and the community will prosper.

GENDER OVER THE LIFE CYCLE

Two stages in the life cycle have gender-specific terms. For women, these are *mano* (girl) and *wuhti* (woman). For boys, these are *tiyo* (boy) and *taka* (man). A girl becomes a woman when she marries, at about age 16–18. A boy becomes a man when he goes through an initiation into one of the four ceremonial fraternities at about age 18–20.

Socialization of Boys and Girls

Before children are able to walk, there is little or no difference in the treatment of boys and girls. Infant girls are given miniature *kachina* dolls, representations of the *kachinas*, or deities, whom the men portray in the public *kachina* dances. The *kachinas* are believed to bring rain and an abundance of all good things like food and fertility. The presentation of the doll to the girl infant and child represents a wish or prayer for her future health and fertility. However, the dolls are not sacred. Little girls play with them as with any baby doll. Infant boys are given miniature bows and arrows, an indication of their future role as hunter and defender.

Mothers make little fuss over toilet training, encouraging toddlers to go outside in the lane to eliminate, and cleaning up any mess the children make in the house. Training in table manners begins by age 2 or 3. Children are instructed to dip their fingers into the communal bowl of stew only to the first knuckle, for to dig in deeper shows greed. Little children are also sent to take a bit of the food and put it outside the door before the family eats, so the spirit beings can consume the essence of the food while humans are eating the substance. Both genders and all ages eat together.

Girls are favored over boys, for several reasons. Ideologically, women are the repositories of life, whereas males are more expendable. It is men's duty to protect and provide for women so that life can continue. In more practical terms, men and women want the women of the clan to be fertile so that the clan will grow and prosper; thus men are interested in the fertility of their "sisters," that is, female clanmates of the same generation, and these women's daughters. Women and men want daughters for personal security, for elderly parents are cared for by the daughters and their husbands who remain in or near the family house. By the time little boys are 7 or 8, they realize that their sisters are more favored than they are, and that they are expected to look after the welfare of these girls. The preference is obvious when a baby is born. Even though Hopis insist that they want children of both sexes, baby girls are greeted with much more rejoicing than baby boys.

Girls and boys differ somewhat in their play pattern. Groups of little girls, sometimes with toddler brothers in tow, play house, using stones to demarcate houses and sheep corrals, and animal bones of different sizes to represent humans and animals. The dusty lanes between the family houses become their playground. As soon as boys are fairly mobile, they join other groups of boys in rough-and-tumble play or competitive games. Older girls also play competitive games together. Girls stay closer to home than boys do, although they are free to go anywhere in the village.

Children are put to work quite early in life. As young as age 4, a boy might be sent to the cornfield to make sure that the donkey does not get into it and eat the corn. One elderly Hopi man told me how, as a child of 4, he was in the cornfield watching the donkey when his attention was attracted by some beetles. He played with them, neglecting the donkey who got into a neighbor's field and ate quite a lot of corn before the boy discovered what was happening and retrieved him. He remembered that his father did not punish him, in fact did not even reprimand him, but loaded up the donkey with dried corn from the family storehouse to replace the corn that was eaten. This man remembered into old age how guilty he felt for his negligence, which meant that his family had less corn against the coming winter.

At about the same age, girls begin to baby-sit infant siblings and help their mothers with various tasks. A couple of years later, her father makes her a small grinding stone and she begins to grind corn alongside her mother. The early results are usually rather unsatisfactory and are fed to the chickens. Also at about age 6 she learns how to make *piki*, a wafer bread, like large rolled sheets of tissue paper, made from a thin batter of corn meal, water, and sometimes additional flavorings. This requires spreading a sheet of batter on a hot stone to cook. Little girls go around with sore burnt fingers until they develop calluses.

Girls spend most of their time at home with their mothers and other female relatives or playing with other girls, in the lanes or in their houses. From about age 6 or 8, Hopi boys start to spend some time in the kivas when they are in use as men's clubhouses. Usually the men, who have gone through their initiation into a ceremonial fraternity, sit in the center of the kiva, and the uninitiated boys sit off to the back. From time to time an elder will recite a legend or cautionary tale, raising his voice so that the youngsters will be quiet and learn. Boys talk among themselves, but if they get loud or rowdy the men will reprimand them.

Children begin to wear gender-specific clothing as soon as they are walking, although little boys may go about naked until age 6 or so if the weather is very hot. Fathers make the clothing for the family, and the gift of a woven dress from her father makes a little girl happy. Both sexes wear their hair short.

All girls and boys go through a ceremonial initiation when they are about age 6–8. Previous to this, they believe that the *kachina* dancers, masked dancers who impersonate the spirit beings called *kachinas*, are the real *kachinas* performing in the kivas and plazas. In this initiation into Hopi ceremonial life, they go through various rituals to impress on them the importance of their future religious duties. The most dramatic part of the initiation process for children comes when they all sit together in a kiva and the *kachina* dancers take off their masks, exposing themselves as the everyday men the children know. Some children already suspected this, finding it odd that a *kachina* had a scar or birthmark just like father's. To many, however, it is a great disillusionment, and some children become quite depressed for a time at what they feel is adult duplicity. After this initiation children begin to take a minor part in the village *kachina* ceremonies, and little boys can begin wearing the masks and dancing in the public performances as soon as they are strong enough.

Puberty and Adolescence

While there are no specific terms for adolescence as a life stage, it is recognized in other ways for girls. Some time after menarche a girl goes through a small private initiation ceremony. She grinds corn for 3 days, after which a kinswoman puts her hair into a distinctive style of two large coils, one on either side of her head. This indicates that she is now an adolescent and ready to think about marriage and courtship. At this time her life becomes much more restricted. Her mother keeps her at home doing domestic tasks, although girl friends sometimes have corn-grinding parties in one of their homes. She is warned about being alone with an adolescent boy or man, and that she should not run about the village as she did earlier. At the same time, she is supposed to attract a suitable boy for her future husband. This presents a dilemma. The girl's movements are restricted just when her parents and fellow clan members expect her to find a suitor, and relations between mother and daughter often become rather tense.

Boys, on the other hand, experience greater freedom in adolescence than they do at any other time of life. They are required to help their fathers and maternal uncles in farming and herding, but they can do what they like at other times. Groups of boys usually go about together, playing games or just relaxing. After puberty it is quite common for groups of boys to sleep in the kiva when the weather is cold, along with unmarried young men and widowers, and when it is warm, they spend the night sleeping on a house roof.

Although parents are supposed to train adolescent boys to be hardworking, they often indulge their sons, rationalizing that these boys will soon be put to work under the strict supervision of their fathers-in-law. At the same time that adolescence is a time of restriction and tension for girls, for boys it is a time of freedom and male companionship.

Attainment of Adulthood

Girls become women when they marry. Boys become men when they have gone through their initiation into one of the fraternities. For girls, marriage results in a relaxation of the tension brought about by the pressures on her to bring a husband into the house. She hopes to become pregnant soon, thus contributing to the continuity of the household and clan. Her early years of marriage are regarded as a happy time for most women, since she has met her goal and relations with her mother once again become warm and close.

Once a boy is initiated, he is expected to become more responsible and to look for a wife. Marriage itself represents a restriction on his freedom. He lives in a house owned by his mother-in-law and is expected to help his father-in-law diligently and without complaints. He can see his friends in the kiva during leisure hours, but to run about with them would be unseemly.

Middle Age and Old Age

Once adult, there are no terms marking different stages of life. People age gradually, giving over responsibilities to young people when they feel that they can no longer carry them out. This is a slow transition and seems to come to the elderly as a relief rather than a loss of status. However, chronic illness or other forms of incapacity are feared, for one loses status if one cannot contribute. I have seen an old man, so crippled with arthritis that he had to use a walker, hobbling from one corn plant to another as he hoed his corn field. Old people without children will be given some food by fellow clan members, but no one is specifically responsible for this. Parents and grandparents may be loved and cared for, but the elderly do not receive any particular honor or recognition. Old women may fare somewhat better than old men, since women in general are supposed to be provided for more than men are. There are no significant gender differences in the treatment and burial of the dead.

PERSONALITY DIFFERENCES BY GENDER

Hopis of both genders are supposed to be even tempered, hospitable, and good-natured, for "bad thoughts"—sorrow, anger, jealousy, despondency, greed—put one's inner being out of balance and can shorten life. High value is placed on humility, and Hopis are not being disingenuous when they claim that they are only humble persons when they are clearly people of note in the community. Competitiveness is only approved in certain situations, such as when groups of *kachina* dancers compete to put on the best performance.

Even though women and men are expected to behave in more or less the same way, I was often struck by how direct and politely assertive many Hopi women were and how mild and unassuming many Hopi men were. Men sometimes complain that women always get their way, and women are certainly not deferential to men. Women seem to be well aware of their centrality in the home and clan.

GENDER-RELATED SOCIAL GROUPS

Gender is a critical feature of Hopi social organization. As already indicated, the village is made up of matrilineal clans. Households are matrilocal. Kivas, when not used for ceremonies, function as clubhouses where men spend much of their leisure time. Thus, the genders are socially located in two different kinds of structures, household and kiva.

The household is the domain of women, who remain in or attached to the house in which they were born. Men have dual residence, the house of their mother, or after her death their sister, and the house of their wife. This ambiguity becomes clear on days when public ceremonies are held. It is proper for a man to invite guests to eat at his home; it is the mother's or sister's house that receives a man's visitors, not his wife's and her mother's.

As owner of the house, the woman is its head. Her house receives some or all of its farmland through her clan. When her husband brings the first of the harvest into the house, he presents it to his wife and she thanks him formally. It is hers, even though it is the fruit of his labor. If she wishes to barter some corn for a shawl or other item, he has no control over her decision. If the couple separates, he leaves and returns to his mother's or sister's house.

Kivas are the domains of men when they are not eating, sleeping, or doing necessary work in the fields or at home. They are where men go to relax, taking their handicrafts to work on while they chat and joke. Kivas draw their members from all clans. A boy usually starts attending the kiva his father belongs to. It is possible to switch membership, although that rarely happens unless a new kiva is built and recruits its members from existing ones. It is the kiva groups that put on the *kachina* dances. In the winter dances, each kiva selects the *kachina* it will portray. Kiva groups vie with one another for the best songs and the most polished performances. When the men return to their home kiva after the performances, they tell each other "we really killed them" if they excelled, or ruefully admit that "they killed us" if their performance fell short.

Women and men meet as equal partners within the clan. The Clan Mother is responsible for internal clan matters and prays and conducts rituals for the well-being of its members. Important clan-related ritual paraphernalia is kept in her house. The Clan Uncle represents the clan to the village and negotiates with other Clan Uncles if there are disputes over land boundaries or other matters. One of the Clan Mother's important prerogatives is her final authority over clan land. The men of the clan allocate land to individual households, for as farmers they know the plots and try to divide land fairly. However, if any woman is dissatisfied, she appeals to the Clan Mother. If the Clan Mother agrees with her, the men are obliged to reallocate land to satisfy the needs of the complainant.

Ceremonial societies are to some degree gender based. I shall discuss this below.

GENDER ROLES IN ECONOMICS

The Hopi were a society without private property until the Spanish introduced sheep. Even then, their herding was on a very small scale, for subsistence rather than commerce, until they began commercial cattle raising in the early 20th century. Land is owned by the clans, and land unclaimed by clans belongs to the entire village for the chief to allocate to those who appeal to him for use of it.

Men's subsistence tasks are farming and herding, along with some hunting of small and large game. They provide the food for their wives and children, and from the cotton they grew they weave the family's clothing. Women do some gardening on plots close to the village, cultivating plants introduced by the Spanish and later the Americans. They also gather wild plants for food, basketry, and other uses.

Men's crafts are principally weaving, wood carving, and leather work. Before a commercial market opened up for carved *kachina* dolls, their trade was mainly in textiles to eastern Pueblos and other Indian peoples. Women make pottery for home use and some local trade, and it has become a commercial item to tourists. Basketry is an important female craft, for large quantities of baskets figure in the exchange of goods at marriage. Mothers collect baskets at the time of their daughters' weddings, and then spend months or years weaving baskets to pay back the lenders. Women sometimes set up small informal stands in front of their houses, trading a few baskets of peaches or other items for something they wanted. When Navajos enter the village with meat or pinyon nuts, women barter dried corn and other goods for these products.

Women rarely leave the village. However, men sometimes walk long distances to trade. They make occasional expeditions to the Gulf of California to gather salt.

The only kind of private property of any value consists of sheep. These animals belong to individual men. Fathers and sons often herd together, and sons usually inherit their fathers' flocks.

PARENTAL AND OTHER CARETAKER ROLES

Children are believed to be the products of both parents' bodies, the father's semen and the mother's uterine blood. It is not unusual for a father to help his wife deliver the baby. While mothers take more responsibility for childcare, fathers often mind infants and toddlers, especially when the mother is busy, holding them and singing lullabies and *kachina* dance songs to them. As in many matrilineal societies, the mother's brother is more of an authority figure than the father, especially to boys as they grow older. The father is seen primarily as a protector, provider, and nurturer. Relations between fathers and children are often close and tender, and the word "father" connotes loving protection rather than authority or distance.

The closest relationship for both boys and girls, however, is likely to be with the mother. She is all-loving and all-giving, at least in theory. The maternal grandmother shares some of these features.

Parents begin treating girls and boys differently when they are about 4 or 5. Girls are discouraged from wandering too far from home, while boys are expected to be away much of the time. Mothers train their daughters in domestic tasks, as fathers and maternal uncles train the boys in farming and herding. As indicated above, training for girls becomes more systematic when they reach adolescence. Both parents are somewhat likely to indulge adolescent boys, rationalizing that they have only a few years of freedom. The maternal uncles are expected to do any necessary disciplining.

Parents seem to expect children to pick up what they need to know, rather than giving them a lot of detailed instruction. When children misbehave, they are reprimanded but rarely punished physically except in one way. A parent or other adult might throw a dipper full of water in the small child's face, a startling and unpleasant experience. After a time the adult has only to move toward the water barrel for the child to stop its misbehavior. This punishment is symbolic as well as real, for water is a purifying agent and will help cleanse the child of any antisocial tendencies.

A much harsher punishment, generally reserved for boys, is to smoke the child. Smoke is also a purifying agent. The truly misbehaving boy is held over a smoking (but not hot) fire, gagging and coughing, until his punishers feel that he has had enough. This kind of punishment is generally administered by maternal uncles, not fathers.

Another treatment reserved for boys is something of a punishment but more of a healing ritual. A boy who consistently wets the bed is carried from house to house on the back of a maternal uncle so that people can pour small amounts of water on him. Either girls do not wet the bed often or, if they do, no fuss is made about it.

LEADERSHIP IN PUBLIC ARENAS

Men and women both have leadership roles in the clan as Clan Uncle and Clan Mother. They are expected to make decisions jointly, and one cannot supersede the other in decision-making.

The principal public arenas are political and ceremonial. The chief and his council members are men. These men, in consultation with other important male clan leaders, make the major political decisions for the village, which consist primarily of adjudicating disputes over land. Punishment of miscreants is mainly left to individuals to settle, there being no police force.

While political decision-making may appear to rest in the hands of a few, it is actually quite inclusive. All men belong to kiva groups, and it is there, in the general discussions, that the leaders get a reading of public opinion. Furthermore, men bring to their discussions the opinions of their wives and female clanmates. No man would be so foolish as to make a public pronouncement that his wife and her family disapproved of if he wanted any peace at home, and he certainly would not go against the perceived best interests of his female clan members. Women have considerable political power behind the scenes, although their men speak for them in public.

Both men and women take leadership of religious sodalities. Most of these sodalities are led by the male leaders of the clans that control them, but three are women's societies and have female leaders. Even those with male leaders have female members, as the women's societies have a few male members whose participation is necessary for the ceremony to be conducted.

GENDER AND RELIGION

I have already discussed the ideology of a balance of oppositions, two of these being male and female. In this respect there is no distinction in value placed on the genders: they are equal and equally necessary to the whole. However, in one respect females have greater spiritual value than males. This will be discussed below under witchcraft. In the pantheon of deities, female deities are as central and powerful as male deities.

In Hopi eyes, all sodalities and their ceremonies are important and necessary for the ceremonial year to be complete. However, some ceremonies are more symbolically loaded than others. Probably the single most important ceremony is Wuwucim, held in November, which opens the ceremonial year. It celebrates the emergence of the Hopi from the Underworld and their establishment as a people on earth. It is during this ceremony that every boy is initiated into one of the four fraternities, each of these symbolically dedicated to one important aspect of Hopi life. Soyal, held in January, is when the chief and his council meet to plan the remainder of the ceremonial year. It is at this time that the first *kachinas* reappear in the villages; after this ceremony, public *kachina* dances take place in the kivas and later in the plaza. Powamuya, held in February, is a celebration of the planting season to come, and it is the time when young children undergo their initiation into Hopi religious life. Niman, in June, is also called the Home Dance, because it celebrates the leave-taking of the *kachinas* until the following year. These ceremonies are organized by male-centered sodalities, as are the Snake and Flute ceremonies held in August.

The three women's sodalities are Marau, Lakon, and Oaqul. Marau is considered to be the women's Wuwucim, and indeed it contains parallels to all of the ritual acts and paraphernalia of Wuwucim. Hopis say that, in earlier times, all females were initiated into it. Lakon and Oaqul are sodalities that put on so-called basket dances, because the female performers dance holding elaborate woven baskets. These dances are held in October and contain

symbolism of warfare and hunting, activities that are carried on at this time. It is possible that Lakon and Oaqul originated as women's basketry guilds, both controlling the production of women's wealth and exerting moral control over their members as craft guilds have done in many parts of the world.

Parallel to the sodality ceremonies, and intersecting with them at some points, are the *kachina* celebrations. *Kachinas* are spirit beings somewhat analogous to angels, and they bring abundance of all kinds (although there are some whipper *kachinas* as well, a reminder that bad thoughts and acts are punished by illness and shortness of life). The *kachina* dances, held from Soyal to Niman, are planned and performed by the kiva groups and thus are male-centered, men portraying both male and female *kachinas*.

The fact that men take more roles in ceremonial life than women do does not mean that men have greater or higher spirituality. It is part of their duty as protectors of life, which is inherent in women and the female principle. Through ritual, men give spiritual protection and they propitiate the deities to grant fertility and the abundance of all good things, not only material goods but also social peace, harmony, and well-being.

Witchcraft beliefs indicate the spiritual value of females. A witch is a person, it is believed, who has bartered his or her heart (life force) to some supernatural forces or beings—here Hopi explanations are not very clear—in order to gain temporal power of some sort. This could be used for personal enrichment, for political power, or even to bring rain during a drought, with the result that anyone above average is potentially suspected of being a witch. Having lost his heart, the witch has to steal the heart of another person in order to stay alive. It is said that a child's heart is preferred, since children have a stronger heart, that is, they have a longer life, than an older person. It is also believed that the heart of a girl will give the witch twice as long to live as the heart of a boy. This reflects the value put on females and the life they contain.

LEISURE, RECREATION, AND THE ARTS

Hopis rarely relax without busying their hands with some handicraft or small repair task. Most leisure time, in fact most time when not eating, sleeping, or doing some other home-based activity, is spent with members of one's own sex. Women, usually relatives and neighbors, gather in someone's home, while men go to their kiva for companionship. Women's closest friends tend to be sisters and other relatives, while men's friends are more likely to include unrelated men whom they know from their adolescence and meet in the kiva. These times with companions, for both sexes, are opportunities to gossip and to discuss village matters. Men acknowledge that there is a lot of joking and teasing in the kivas, particularly about sexual matters ("private wives," "hunting for two-legged deer," etc.). This joking is a kind of verbal horseplay, each trying to outdo the other with veiled allusions to transgressions of the other or the other's female relatives. No one takes this seriously, including the women who have been so accused, and this joking competitiveness enlivens the time in the kiva and provides a respite from the obligations that the Hopis bear.

RELATIVE STATUS OF MEN AND WOMEN

This is a sexually egalitarian culture. Women are more highly valued than men—ideologically as the source of life, and practically for their centrality in the clan and household (see above). Men are responsible for conducting most of the ceremonies, which they view as protecting the village, primarily the women and children. Men also take responsibility for political decisions, but, as we have seen, women are a major power behind the scenes. Nevertheless, women depend on men to fulfill these responsibilities. They also depend on men in a more immediate sense, to farm and provide clothing and other goods for them. Just as men's power is checked by their reliance on wives and sisters, so is women's power checked by their reliance on husbands and brothers. A favorite Hopi expression is *pi um'i*, meaning "it's up to you." No one should try to control another person, and this applies to relations between women and men as well.

SEXUALITY

Sex is good, mainly because it results in children but also because it brings pleasure. It should not be misused in adultery or rape; nor should children be born out of wedlock, for then they do not have the fathers and fathers'

relatives that are so important in Hopi life. However, there is no particular value on virginity, and the ideal feminine beauty is the young mother, not the virgin.

The general attitude toward sexuality is relaxed. No one ever mentioned masturbation to me as a problem in child-rearing, nor did anyone ever remark on adolescent homoerotic play. Women are expected to cover their bodies more than men, but there is no reluctance to breast-feed in public. Men speak rather lasciviously about the Marau dancers, who wear knee-length skirts and thus expose their legs, and sometimes young women are shy about participating because of this.

Homosexuality is regarded as odd and somewhat ridiculous, but not in itself evil or disturbing. The few individuals who have made attempts at cross-dressing are socially accepted but privately laughed at.

For all the gossip and joking about sex that both women and men relish, Hopi life gives little opportunity for much privacy in which to enjoy it. Families sleep together in one room, and couples wait until they think that everyone is asleep before they make love quietly. Suspicions are aroused if any man and woman who are not spouses or close relatives are alone together, and there is little opportunity for this to occur. Nevertheless, there is gossip about men visiting women after dark when husbands are believed to be in the sheep camp or otherwise away from home. (How they eluded others in the household was never explained to me.)

COURTSHIP AND MARRIAGE

In theory, people marry for love and have freedom of choice. In actuality, the girl's family has to approve of the boy she is bringing into the household and who will father children for her clan. A stubborn girl might insist on marrying a boy she loves, but if her family really did not approve they would make life so miserable for him that he would leave. A girl might force an unwelcome marriage on her family, because girls do the proposing since they are inviting the boy to come to them.

Girls propose by presenting the favored boy with a special small corn cake. This is a token that unmarried girls give to any boy or man they like, and men are extremely pleased when a favorite niece or granddaughter presents them with one. It can be viewed as a token of friendship as well as love, rather like a valentine. The boy who receives it must accept, but he can choose to interpret it as friendship and do nothing further. Even if he loves the girl, self-respect demands that he not jump too quickly. Meanwhile, the girl is tense with anticipation. If he has not accepted the proposal within a couple of weeks, she knows that she has been rejected. If he accepts, the families begin the wedding preparations. There is a feast and an elaborate exchange of gifts between the families, the bride's giving more to the groom's in a kind of groomwealth. I have heard Hopi women remark "we paid for him" about a young male in-law.

Even if the couple are in love, the early days of marriage are hard for young men as they adjust from life with rather indulgent parents to the authority of parents-in-law and the need to prove themselves worthy. It is not unusual for young grooms to return home for several extended visits before they settle in.

Hopis only formally marry once, and the spouse in this life will be the spouse in the afterlife, in the village of the dead. However, informal remarriage is possible for widowed and "divorced," (i.e., permanently separated) people.

HUSBAND–WIFE RELATIONSHIP

The husband–wife relationship is probably at its best in old age after long years of cooperation. It is only then that spouses gently tease one another and openly show affection. Earlier years are burdened with responsibilities, and men can be torn between obligations to their wives and in-laws and to their sisters and sisters' children. The dependence that women have on men to provide for them makes them vulnerable to being left, just as women's control of the home makes men vulnerable to being replaced. If men leave voluntarily or under pressure, they lose close contact with their children. They may see their sons in the kiva, but they may not often have much time with their daughters.

Nevertheless, the relation between spouses is expected to be loving and close, and it often is. They sleep and eat together and are expected to support one another in their political and religious duties.

OTHER CROSS-SEX RELATIONSHIPS

The primary cross-sex relationship outside of marriage is the sister–brother one. This is at the core of the clan.

While discord between spouses is deplored, that between cross-sex siblings is scandalous. The depth of feeling is indicated by witchcraft beliefs, which hold that, since the most precious life for a man is his sister's daughter, she is the preferred victim of his heart stealing.

Mothers' brothers are gentler in exerting authority over their sisters' daughters than their sisters' sons. Fathers' sisters (women of the father's clan) are often close to their brothers' daughters and may be their confidantes, but they have a special relationship to their sisters' sons. This involves the pretense of sexual interest and romantic feelings. There are many jokes and much teasing about a man's "aunts," the English word used for these kinswomen. He is expected to flatter them and make them feel loved and attractive.

CHANGES IN ATTITUDES, BELIEFS, AND PRACTICES REGARDING GENDER

The period postdating this ethnographic sketch has seen major changes in Hopi life. The major ones regarding gender have been the reduction in importance of the clan and the transition to nuclear-family households, with increasing responsibilities for husbands and fathers and decreasing responsibilities for mothers' brothers and brothers. The husband–wife bond has become more central to people's lives over the past 60 years or so, and men spend more time at home with their wives and families.

Some women entered wage labor in the early 20th century, and now it is commonplace. Women also participate in modern political life. Some of the ceremonies have died out, but the three women's ceremonies are still held. While gender roles have undergone considerable change in the last 50 years or so, Hopi remains a sexually egalitarian culture.

BIBLIOGRAPHY

Schlegel, A. (1973). The adolescent socialization of the Hopi girl. *Ethnology, 12*, 449–462.

Schlegel, A. (1977). Male and female in Hopi thought and action. In A. Schlegel (Ed.), *Sexual stratification: A cross-cultural view* (pp. 245–269). New York: Columbia University Press.

Schlegel, A. (1979). Sexual antagonism among the sexually egalitarian Hopi. *Ethos, 7*, 124–141.

Schlegel, A. (1984). Hopi gender ideology of female superiority. *Quarterly Journal of Ideology, 8*, 44–52.

Schlegel, A. (1988). Hopi widowhood. In A. Scadron (Ed.), *On their own: Widows and widowhood in the American Southwest, 1848–1939* (pp. 42–64). Urbana: University of Illinois Press.

Schlegel, A. (1989). Fathers, daughters, and *kachina* dolls. *European Review of Native American Studies, 3*, 7–10.

Schlegel, A. (1990). Gender meanings: General and specific. In P. Sanday & R. Goodenough (Eds.), *Beyond the second sex: Essays in the anthropology of gender* (pp. 21–42). Philadelphia: University of Pennsylvania Press.

Schlegel, A. (1992). African models in the American Southwest: Hopi as an internal frontier society. *American Anthropologist, 94*, 376–397. [Background reading.]

Schlegel, A. (1999). The two aspects of Hopi grandmotherhood. In M. Schweitzer (Ed.), *Bridging generations: American Indian grandmothers, traditions and transitions* (pp. 145–158). Albuquerque: University of New Mexico Press.

Simmons, L. W. (Ed.). (1942). *Sun chief: The autobiography of a Hopi Indian*. New Haven, CT: Yale University Press. [Biography of a Hopi man.]

Spicer, E. H. (1962). Western Pueblos. *Cycles of conquest* (ch. 7, pp. 187–209). Tucson: University of Arizona Press. [Historical background reading.]

Udall, L. (1969). *Me and mine: The life story of Helen Sekaquaptewa*. Tucson: University of Arizona Press. [Biography of a Hopi woman.]

Hungarians

Barbara A. West and Irén Annus

ALTERNATIVE NAMES

Hungarians are also known as Magyars.

LOCATION

The Republic of Hungary is located in the center of Europe, between Austria to the west, Slovakia and Ukraine to the north, Romania to the east, and Serbia and Montenegro, Croatia, and Slovenia to the south.

CULTURAL OVERVIEW

The Hungarian people have had a tumultuous history since arriving in their present location in 896 CE. They were invaded by the Mongols, Turks, Habsburgs, and Soviets, they had two major failed revolutions, in 1848 and 1956, and they were on the losing side of two world wars. Yet each time the Hungarians emerged as a people both cognizant of their differences from their neighbors and willing to fight to maintain them. One of the most important of these differences is linguistic. The Hungarian language, Magyar, is a member of the Finno-Ugric language family and thus completely unrelated to the German, Romanian, and Slavic languages spoken by Hungary's neighbors. Hungarians are also predominantly Roman Catholic or Calvinist, and so consider themselves very different from their Orthodox neighbors to the east and south.

The two most significant historical events shaping contemporary Hungary are the loss after World War I of two-thirds of the territory claimed by Hungarians and the 45 years of Soviet domination following Hungary's defeat in World War II. The first event, while it left many ethnic Hungarians living in Hungary's neighboring countries, has also resulted in Hungary being one of the most ethnically homogeneous countries in contemporary Europe. Currently, the population of Hungary is about 95% Magyar.

The creation of a Soviet-style one-party state after World War II provided the context for most of the political, economic, social, and cultural features of contemporary Hungary. Politically, Hungary has had four rounds of free elections since the end of the socialist era in 1990, but no government has been reelected and no political ideology has been able to dominate national discourse for long. Two exceptions to this may be a push for "traditional" Hungarian gender and family roles and the desire to "join Europe." Economically, Hungary was transformed during the second half of the 20th century from a largely agrarian country to an urbanized industrial one. Today, 65% of Hungarians live in cities or towns. Unfortunately, since 1990, both the urban and rural work forces have suffered under high rates of inflation, unemployment, and a restructuring of the social service benefits they had grown accustomed to during the socialist era. Some of the most significant of these are education funding, childcare and maternity benefits, childcare centers, pensions, and healthcare. Socially, many Hungarians have experienced a diminution in the number and depth of friendships since 1989. Culturally, Hungary has been transformed by films, television programs, magazines, advertising, pornography, and other consumer items from the West, as well as by legal and illegal workers, shoppers, and immigrants from the other former socialist countries.

In addition, Hungarians are now unsure about their gender roles. While women were technically "emancipated" by the socialist state, the benefits they received were experienced by many women as hardships (Bollobás, 1993). While the guarantee of paid employment sounds wonderful to Western ears, to Hungarian women it meant a tremendous burden of full-time paid employment and full-time housework without the benefits of most of the machines and products that ease the workload of most Western women. In addition, public discourse critical of women, depicting them as deleterious to men, children, and society, has left many women feeling betrayed, exhausted, and confused about their place in contemporary society (Goven, 1993). Like women, many Hungarian men are also struggling to reconcile cultural ideals, which depict them as breadwinners, with economic realities that have left many of them unemployed.

CULTURAL CONSTRUCTION OF GENDER

The two recognized gender categories in Hungary are woman or girl and man or boy, depending on a person's age. These categories are assumed by most people to be distinct and, despite 45 years of de jure gender equality during the socialist era, also hierarchical. Within the parameters of class, educational, and even regional differences, in Hungary men and boys generally have a distinct advantage. For example, women who are well into their twenties and even early thirties are often referred to as *kis lany*, "little girl" (West, 2002) by older people and the generic word for person, *ember*, is often used to refer to men only. Furthermore, in the past, and even today in some elderly households in rural communities, men's hierarchical position is reflected in women using the formal pronoun and verb endings to refer to their husbands while men use the informal with their wives.

While just a very few Hungarian women continue this practice, many other gender differences continue to be evident throughout Hungarian society. Hungarian boys are freer to join clubs and sports teams while girls are expected to participate in household labor to a greater extent. In adulthood, women's primary responsibilities are to raise at least one child and take care of the home. Most women also expect to work, but in both their own estimation and that of society at large, their economic role outside the home is secondary to their domestic role within it. Even during most of the socialist era, which saw the emancipation of women based on their "right" to work, women were seen primarily as mothers rather than as wives or women (Haney, 1994). Men, on the other hand, are expected to be the main economic providers for their families. Unfortunately, the change in the Hungarian economy has not made this cultural ideal possible for most men, but this fact has not mitigated its social force.

GENDER OVER THE LIFE CYCLE

The most important rites of passage that mark the life course of both females and males in Hungary are marriage and having the first child, although graduating from elementary school, leaving school entirely, and retirement are also fairly important. All Hungarian men are also required to spend 6 months serving in the military. Some religious Hungarians also mark baptism, first communion, and confirmation, bar mitzvah, or other similar rituals, but none is as important as marriage and having children.

In addition to the differences in life course due to men's military service and gendered expectations for education, work, and household participation, the life course of Hungarian women and men also differs because women generally have a much longer elderly phase of life. While the average life expectancy of Hungarian women is 75.2 years, for men it is only 66.1 (Pongrácz & Tóth, 1999).

Socialization of Boys and Girls

Much of the socialization that takes place in the home, childcare centers, and elementary schools in Hungary is a process of exposing children to somewhat traditional gender and family roles. For example, although 90% of all children between ages 3 and 6 attend kindergartens (Vajda, 1998) and education is compulsory for all up until age 16 (it will be 18 for children who were 6 or younger in 2002), boys' and girls' experiences are not the same. Elementary school texts highlight the activities of men and present no alternative to the nuclear family with its gender-segregated roles; elementary schools also require students to read no novels written by women (International Helsinki Federation for Human Rights, 2000). This early socialization is very important in Hungary because the kind of high school a student enters, whether academic or vocation specific, depends on choices made when children are very young. Therefore, in a variety of ways, parents and teachers continue to channel students into a somewhat segregated work force (Lobodzinska, 1995), even if this segregation is not as great as it was in the past.

Puberty and Adolescence

For the most part, the path set down for female and male children is merely continued into adolescence, although rural children who want to attend high school must move to a nearby city and live in a dormitory in order to do so. Nonetheless, adolescent girls continue to feel more pressure from their families to conform to their family's and society's constraints upon them, while boys are given more freedom to explore the world on their own. Mothers, particularly older ones and those in rural areas, continue to want their daughters to entertain boys at home rather than to go out with them (Vajda, 1998), although most girls prefer to go out on dates. Girls generally also experience heavier family sanctions against alcohol use and as a result experience drunkenness less than their male counterparts. Nonetheless, both adolescent girls and boys do drink alcohol, so much so that by 11th grade fully 100% of the boys and 94.9% of the girls in a recent study had tried alcohol (Swaim, Nemeth, & Oetting, 1995).

Another aspect of adolescents' lives that is a continuation from childhood is the emphasis on different kinds of education. Interestingly, this difference has contributed to a positive outcome for more Hungarian women than men during the change from an industrial to a service economy in the 1990s. In Hungary, girls and young women complete academic secondary school and both 3- and 4-year colleges more than boys and young men (Hrubos, 1994). Training in such fields as accounting, clerical work, and languages were predominantly seen as female, while boys were directed via vocational high schools into the industrial work force, with its opportunities for hands-on training and high industrial wages (Koncz, 1995). In addition, currently, more women are entering into formerly male-dominated fields such as economics and computer science (Hrubos, 1994). As a result, younger women make up a greater proportion of the well-educated Hungarian population and tend to have greater educational qualifications than men of the same age (Lobodzinska, 1995).

Attainment of Adulthood

While young men's military service is an important part of the phase between adolescence and adulthood, for both women and men the first phase in the passage to adulthood is their 18th birthday, as that is the age of legal adulthood in Hungary. The most important social marker of adulthood is the *eljegyzés*, engagement. The engagement process in Hungary generally begins with a verbal proposal by the man and the woman's acceptance. Following this proposal, the couple shops together for their wedding rings. These are first exchanged at the *eljegyzés*, which is usually a lunch attended by the couple, their parents, and sometimes their godparents.

At this event, the man formally asks the woman to marry him and seeks the approval of her parents. At this point, both the man and woman wear their wedding ring on their left hand, to indicate that they are engaged. At the wedding, they will exchange these same rings and switch them to their right hands. The woman may also receive an accompanying ring, another piece of jewelry such as a necklace or bracelet, or nothing at all.

After the engagement and wedding, the next most important marker of adulthood is having a child. In a recent Hungarian survey, which has been echoed in the works of many Hungarian sociologists, researchers discovered that 80% of Hungarians believe that not having a child leaves one incomplete (Wolf, 2000). While women more than men think that raising children is their most important function, Hungarians of both genders feel the significant social stigma of not having at least one child (Tóth, 1999b). Indeed, the word for family (*család*) is often used to refer to children, so that a married couple generally do not acquire family status until the birth of their first child.

Middle Age and Old Age

In terms of career development, older age begins in Hungary for both women and men by the time they have reached their mid-30s. At this time, most people find it extremely difficult to change career paths because of discriminatory hiring practices. At the same time, in her delineation of the Hungarian woman's life course, Tóth (1994a) considers the period of child-rearing, late twenties through forties, as middle age. For most Hungarian women, this is also the most difficult time of their lives. Most are attempting to combine raising children, taking care of their home, working outside of the home, and possibly caring for older relatives (Tóth, 1994a).

Retirement and/or having grown children mark old age in Hungary. As of the late 1990s, 19% of the Hungarian population was over 60 years of age (15.8% of the total male population and 21.8% of the total female population) (Földesi, 1998). While there are many reasons for the difference between men and women, a few contributing factors are that many more men than women in this age group smoke cigarettes, drink alcohol regularly, and remain unwilling to change their traditional diet for a healthier one. At the same time, only 1% more of the men in this age group (5% vs. 4% of women) have remained physically active into their old age, which might have helped offset a lifetime of poor nutrition and bad habits (Földesi, 1998). However, despite the fact that women live significantly longer than men, they are not necessarily healthier or happier. Hungary's suicide and depression rates for people of this age are both amongst the highest in the world and relatively comparable for women and men (women's are slightly higher) (Elekes, 1999).

In addition, a large number of elderly Hungarian women feel that they are the losers in the recent political, economic, and social changes because the system they worked all their lives to support, and which in turn promised to care for them in their old age, has failed them (Földesi, 1998). For example, women receive 23% less pension on average than men (Széman, 1999). Other contributing factors to elderly women's discontent may be that they are alone because they live longer than men by 9 years, they are more likely to live in single-person households, and they face a lack of wide social relations and activities (Széman, 1999). Far more older women (32.2%) than men (13.2%) are also unmarried (Földesi, 1998), because of their greater numbers and men's greater desire to remarry, particularly younger women.

While some elderly Hungarian women are experiencing loneliness and inactivity, many others continue to contribute substantially to their adult children's households. Many older women find themselves retiring, or even timing their own retirement, to coincide with the birth of their grandchildren so that they can provide much-needed childcare (Vajda, 1998). Indeed, most older women take on the role of active grandmother, either taking their grandchildren into their own home or flat and providing meals when the children's mother is at work, or living with their son's or daughter's family to provide constant domestic support. Some women who were mothers in the 1950s feel that they missed out on spending significant amounts of time with their own children and use this active-grandmother phase of life to make up for that earlier loss (Tóth, 1993).

PERSONALITY DIFFERENCES BY GENDER

On the whole, women in Hungary tend to express their feelings more than men do. This is true of both positive feelings such as affection and tenderness and negative feelings such as anger and frustration. According to a survey in the late 1980s, many Hungarian men would prefer to be more open about their positive personal feelings with other men, but are not sure how to do that. Hungarian women want to be less quick to show anger (Reisman, 1990).

A second area of difference concerns the guilty feelings that Hungarian gender ideologies and society more generally have produced in women (S. Molnár, 1999). Women are often depicted as the cause of Hungary's negative birth rate. They are also held responsible for any problems their children have in school or elsewhere. The greatest area of concern, both for many women and for society more generally, is the balancing act that women must engage in with regard to work and home. Since women's wages are socially seen as supplementary to men's, regardless of economic reality, if they continue to work and family problems arise they tend to feel that they are to blame (Tóth, 1997).

A third area of difference, one that seems somewhat anomalous given the guilt that most Hungarian women feel, is the connection many women feel to their work. In a survey in the early 1990s, 25.1% of Hungarian women said that they enjoy working and would continue to do so even if they did not need to; the figure for men was only 19.3% (Tóth, 1994b). In a related survey in 1997, more men accepted the view that work is for money rather than for personal well-being; this difference was true for all educational groups (Pongrácz & Tóth, 1999). In addition, women are also a bit more optimistic about the future of their jobs than are men (Tóth, 1994b).

Finally, as might be expected in a society that tells women that their work is less significant than men's, women tend to diminish the value of their work and to explain their own successes in terms of luck or outside factors rather than their own abilities or performance (Nagy, 1997). Hungarian men are generally more confident and willing to take credit for valuable work and a job well done.

GENDER-RELATED SOCIAL GROUPS

The single most important social group in Hungary is the family, which refers to members of one's household who share ties of descent or alliance. Fully 85% of the population reside in families (Hungarian College of Catholic Bishops, 1999). Those who do not reside in the same household, whatever their biological relationship, are often referred to as relatives rather than family

(West, 2002). Hungarians do not recognize lineal or other forms of institutionalized extended kin groups. Nonetheless, much of the literature on Hungary from sociology, anthropology, and psychology refers to this society as both child centered and family centered. This is the result of a number of factors, from the traditional value on children to the recent economic downturn that has caused many domestic units to turn inward for respite against the vagaries of unemployment, inflation, and diminished social services (West, 2002). Although this has changed quite a bit since even the early 1990s, many households, or families, in Hungary in the recent past were multigenerational (Buss, Beres, Hofstetter, & Pomidor, 1994). Even in the early 1990s, 75% of young married couples lived with either the bride's or groom's parents or grandparents (Tóth, 1993); this figure is somewhat lower today with the advent of low-interest housing loans.

Other groups that are important in the lives of some Hungarian men are drinking groups, work circles, and peer groups developed during childhood and early adolescence. Hungarian women participate in fitness groups more than men, but less than men in work circles. Fewer women also maintain friendships across the entire life cycle (Reisman, 1990). As in most areas of gender difference, class, education, age, and region are very important in determining an individual's participation in these groups. For example, it is largely young urban women who take fitness classes.

GENDER ROLES IN ECONOMICS

In some ways the economic position of women in Hungary today is stronger than that of Hungarian men (Frey, 1996; Koncz, 1995) and than that of women in most of post-socialist Eastern and Central Europe (van der Lippe & Fodor, 1998). In 1998, unemployment was 7% for Hungarian women and 8.5% for men (Pongrácz & Tóth, 1999). There are many reasons for this difference. First, because of their dominance in the fields of heavy industry during the socialist era, men more than women have lost their jobs due to factory closures. Second, because their earnings have always been seen as secondary, women have been much more willing than men to take advantage of the part-time, temporary, and home-based work opportunities that have opened up since 1990 (Szalai, 1998). Third, traditional gender roles in Hungary have also allowed far more women than men to exit the labor force and yet remain economically active as the recipients of childcare and maternity benefits, "nursing fees" to care for elderly parents and in-laws, and early retirement (Szalai, 1998). Fourth, women in Hungary have been more willing to take advantage of retraining programs (Szalai, 1999). Fifth, Hungarian women began more than 40% of the small private businesses started in Hungary between 1990 and 1998 (Frey, 1999). Finally, many women have been able to combine one or more of these kinds of "supplementary" incomes to support their entire families (Szalai, 1998); 44% of women and 41% of men have other sources of income besides their primary employment (Nagy, 1995). The result of all these factors is that women generally are more likely than their male counterparts to retain the occupational class attained by their fathers (Pongrácz & Tóth, 1999).

At the same time, despite 45 years of de jure gender equality, Hungarian women earn only around 80% of the salaries of men (Pongrácz & Tóth, 1999), leaving women more vulnerable if they divorce (Utasi, 1997) or, as only rarely happens, they remain single. Younger women and women with children suffer much more discrimination with regard to their access to well-paying jobs and prestige (International Helsinki Federation for Human Rights, 2000). During the socialist era, women had much less access to private economy work opportunities, usually because of their responsibilities at home, leaving them with fewer skills and less access to private work today. As a result, women constitute nearly three quarters of the state sector and only one third of the much more lucrative private sector (Koncz, 1994). Women are also less likely than men to move in order to take a higher-paying job (Wong, 1995). Finally, women managers have much less access to top positions. While almost all successful male managers have wives at home to support their efforts, women who are able to engage in the work activities necessary to rise to that level are often divorced or single. In addition, since nearly all Hungarian women want at least one child, they must rely upon mothers and day-care providers for childcare (Nagy, 1997).

PARENTAL AND OTHER CARETAKER ROLES

Since Hungarian marriages have begun to occur at later ages, the age at which women are having their first child has also increased recently, from 23.1 in 1990 to 25.4 in 1999 (Kamarás, 2000). The primary reasons for these increases are financial instability and increased opportunities for female education and career development.

For both men and women in Hungary, the birth of a first child is the final step in the attainment of full personhood. In recognition of this most important of roles, the Hungarian state allows parents (or even grandparents) with permanent jobs to take 2 years of maternity and childcare leave at 70% of their salary and a third year with a flat amount of 20,000 forints per month. While these kinds of benefits were initially provided in the 1970s to boost Hungary's falling birthrate, they have been maintained despite their failure to affect the birthrate significantly (Lobodzinska, 1995). Today, almost all Hungarian women take at least 6 months of paid leave after the birth of a child in order to breast-feed their infants. Unfortunately, the guarantee that a parent's job will remain after their leave has been eliminated. Therefore, generally the only parents (primarily, but not solely, women) who take advantage of the 2-year leave are those who are fairly certain that their jobs will be eliminated anyway (Jakus, 1993), those who are well to do, or those who have received a guarantee that their jobs will remain available to them.

Since 1989, childcare centers have also been cut way back, forcing more women to rely upon their parents or in-laws for childcare (Lobodzinska, 1995). Because some Hungarians live in extended families anyway, due to housing shortages and a significant lack of nursing homes (Buss et al., 1994), this is not always difficult. However, the contributions of active grandmothers in the household may also encourage the lack of participation of many Hungarian fathers in childcare, particularly with very young children (Vajda, 1998). The presence of multigenerational households may also add to women's workload, since older family members may need a significant amount of care.

Although more fathers today, particularly those with more education, are participating in child-rearing activities than in the past, motherhood and fatherhood continue to be two very different social roles in Hungary. Mothers have historically been seen, and continue to be seen, as central figures not only in households but also in the nation as a whole (Huseby-Darvas, 1996). In addition to providing most of the household labor and childcare, Hungarian mothers also largely determine the cultural level of their children by exposing them (or not) to museums, art, literature, music, etc., while Hungarian fathers largely determine their economic level (Tóth, 1993). Mothers also tend to determine their children's religious affiliation and activity (Tomka, 2000).

LEADERSHIP IN PUBLIC ARENAS

During the socialist era, when the Party held all true leadership and representation was largely for show, women were represented at all levels of national and local governance. In 1987, women made up 21% of Hungary's parliament (LaFont, 2001). With the transition, when political power became real and representation vitally important, women have become less and less visible in formal governing processes. Party politics quickly became male dominated; by 1993 women held only 6.7% of parliamentary seats (8.5% in 1998; Lévai & Kiss, 1999) and masculine issues dominated the agenda (Koncz, 1995). In part because of the history of the socialist state's concern with women and gender equality, since 1990 men and women alike have been reluctant to raise these as political issues. In addition, the few feminist or womanist organizations that developed in Hungary after 1990 have changed their focus or disappeared in the past decade (Szalai, 1998).

Nonetheless, women have not disappeared entirely from the political process in Hungary. First, while the more conservative political circles and parties tend to favor and lobby for traditional gender and family roles, others have run women candidates and appointed women to key positions. For example, in 2002 the Hungarian Socialist Party named a woman as Minister of the Interior, the second most powerful person in the government. Second, women and men have voted in equal numbers in all local and national elections since 1990 (Szalai, 1998). Third, women participate heavily in the professional administration of local governments. They make up 34% of the non-elected members of local social policy commissions (Szalai, 1998) and in that capacity were instrumental in the national parliament's decision in 1993 to pass the most liberal abortion act ever seen in Hungary. Finally, women tend to occupy leadership positions in areas where their subordinates are also women, and thus remain invisible in the national (and international) sphere (Koncz, 1994; Nagy, 1997).

GENDER AND RELIGION

A large proportion of the Hungarian population has been baptized into the Roman Catholic church (almost 7 million members in 1998), the Hungarian Reformed church (just over 2 million members in 1998), or some other Christian denomination (Tomka & Révay, 1998). Yet, aside from some elderly women, many of these people have not had much continued relationship with a church community. During the socialist era, the Party State apparatus actively discouraged religious affiliation and most monasteries and church-run schools were closed. Since 1990, most of these institutions have reopened and religious participation has increased somewhat, particularly at such ritual times as Christmas, Easter, and weddings. In 1997, there were 998 monks and 2311 nuns serving in 91 monasteries and convents in Hungary (Tomka & Révay, 1998).

Churches in general in Hungary tend to favor traditional gender and family roles; however, in 1999 Catholic bishops in Hungary issued a statement calling for happier families. One of their suggestions was for Hungarians to recognize the double-income family as appropriate for the 21st century. They also stated that women have a rightful need to study and work (Hungarian College of Catholic Bishops, 1999).

LEISURE, RECREATION, AND THE ARTS

As is the case elsewhere, Hungarian women have less leisure time per day than men, an hour less on average (Tóth, 1997). Women also have fewer friends than men, are members of fewer organizations that would allow for socializing outside of the home, and sleep less than men (Lobodzinska, 1995). They spend less time on cultural activities and have more home-based leisure activities, such as hobby cooking, gardening, reading, needlecraft, or listening to the radio (Wolf, 2000). However, some younger women in urban areas do participate in aerobics and other fitness classes. The most significant leisure activity for Hungarian women generally, but particularly working women, is watching television (Tóth, 1993). Nonetheless, in 1993, men watched more television per day (159 minutes) than women (139 minutes) (Pongrácz & Tóth, 1999).

Both adult men's and women's friendships are largely instrumental rather than emotional in Hungary (Tóth, 1993), men's even more than women's (Albert & David, 1998). Hungarian men also spend more time in the company of friends and colleagues than women do and they go out more often (Albert & David, 1998). Male leisure activities include home crafts and building, attending sporting events, watching television, and listening to music, and for some younger men, surfing the internet and other computer activities (Wolf, 2000). In addition, heavy drinking is also considered a socially acceptable male activity. Nearly 22% of men in the late 1990s drank alcohol every day; the figure for women was only 2.9% (Pongrácz & Tóth, 1999).

Since the beginning of the transition, Hungarian leisure time has changed fairly significantly. Hungarians had one of the longest work days in Europe in the 1980s (13.4 hr per day at their main jobs), but the economic downturn of the transition has decreased that substantially so that Hungarians now spend only 11.8 hr per day at their main job (Bod, 2000). However, for most people, this has not meant more time for most leisure activities but rather more time searching for work, upgrading their education and skills, and/or working in a garden or at some supplementary job. In addition, more households have turned inward against the economic difficulties of the transition, leaving both women and men with fewer affective bonds outside their families (West, 2002). Like their parents (Vukovich & Harcsa, 1998), children are also now participating at far lower rates in sports activities and other extracurricular activities and watching far more television. This increased viewing has resulted in a broadening of children's horizons beyond Hungary's borders, but has also had a negative effect on both their desire and ability to read (Somlai, 1998).

RELATIVE STATUS OF MEN AND WOMEN

Although women and men have enjoyed equal status under the law since the late 1940s, in real-life situations men usually have a distinct advantage. They make more money than women do, they hold the top positions in government, business, education, and almost all other public arenas, and they are the authority figures in most households. As Hungary is a predominately Catholic country, men make up the entire leadership in religious circles, although a minority in most congregations.

Society and the law also tend to ignore male violence against women, whether in marriage or not, and whether it includes rape, battery, and/or psychological violence. According to one Hungarian study, most Hungarian women and girls have experienced sexual harassment or humiliation, rape, or some other kind of mental or physical abuse at the hands of one or more men. This occurs in the home, at school, at work, and on the streets, so that there are few places in which many Hungarian women generally feel safe (Bollobás, 1993). In addition, threats and violence against women are largely supported by Hungarian gender ideologies. According to Tóth (1999a), 25% of women in Hungary believe that women are responsible for rape, 45% do not know that rape can occur in marriage, 41% of women with less than an eighth-grade education believe that wife-beating should not be punished, and 65% of women who have been raped or the victim of some other violence are so ashamed that they never report it.

One of the few areas in which women do have an advantage over men is in retaining custody of children and holding onto apartments when a couple divorces. Because women are seen by Hungarian society largely in terms of motherhood, mothers rarely lose custody of their children, even if their ex-husbands could provide equal or better child-rearing. In addition, because they retain custody of children, women are also better situated for holding onto a couple's house or flat upon divorce. In 1996, only 10% of all homeless people in Hungary were women (Pongrácz & Tóth, 1999). A second area in which women are currently better situated than men is their ability to remain economically active. While men who are working tend to make more money than similarly situated women, fewer women are unemployed (Szalai, 1998).

SEXUALITY

Sexuality is a difficult subject for most Hungarians to discuss openly due to a number of historical factors: conservative cultural traditions, Catholicism, and socialist morality. While sex education has been presented in schools since the 1970s, it includes only the most rudimentary factual information. As a result, knowledge about sexual relationships, contraception, sexually transmitted diseases, and even sexuality more generally is fairly limited (Hochberg, 1997). But Hungarian women have access to a range of choices for contraception and these are available at relatively low cost. As a result, about 75% of Hungarian women between 19 and 41 use birth control (Jozan, 1999). Abortion is also quite common (Kamarás, 1999), especially for teens and women over 40 (Pongrácz & Tóth, 1999). Since 1993, abortion has been available up to the 12th week of pregnancy almost without restriction. Prior to this time, it was legal, available, and common, but a woman was subject to a waiting period and invasive questioning by her doctor (Jakus, 1993).

Sexuality is an area that has changed significantly over the past two or three decades. While many older women in Hungary continue to live by the double standards with which they grew up, which valued women's virginity, women's sexuality only in the context of marriage, and other conservative norms, younger women tend to see sexuality as a natural part of their relationships with men (Kende & Neményi, 1999). Today, a majority of young people have their first sexual experience by age 18.2 (Kamarás, 1999).

One of the most incongruous aspects of contemporary Hungary is the social and political position of homosexuality. On the one hand, homosexuality has been legal since 1961 and, outside of Scandinavia and The Netherlands, Hungary has one of the most liberal domestic partner laws in the world (Long, 1999). Same-sex couples have most of the same rights as married couples (Farkas, 2000), and in Budapest and a few other large cities gays and lesbians have formed a number of activist and social groups. Yet, at the same time, there is no real national organization, lobbying group, or even lasting local organizing group for gays, lesbians, bisexuals, or transgendered people (Long, 1999). Several organizations have also been prevented from forming because they refused to bar membership to those below 18, the legal age of consent for homosexual sex (it is 14 for heterosexuals) (Long, 1999). Until very recently, there was no real gay and lesbian community in Hungary, in part because of the refusal of gay men to work with lesbians or feminists, in part because there was no consensus on what the community should be or do, and in part because of the relative silence about sexuality more generally (Long, 1999). Despite the increasing visibility of groups for sexual minorities, silence and loneliness continue to be the two most devastating facts of life for gays and lesbians in Hungary (Birtalan, 2000; Sándor, 2000).

COURTSHIP AND MARRIAGE

Marriage patterns in Hungary have slowly changed over the past few decades so that few couples marry before age 20, more couples live together prior to marriage or without any expectation of marrying, and more couples have their first child before marriage. Up until the 1980s, the average age for women to become engaged was 17 or 18; for men it was their early twenties. By the mid-1990s, only 18–20% of Hungarian women married before age 20, primarily due to the expansion of educational opportunities for women (Tóth, 1999b). In 1998, the average marriage age for women was 26.7, while for men it was 29.7 (Pongrácz & Tóth, 1999). Despite waiting longer, most Hungarians marry at least once during their lifetime and remarriage after divorce or the death of a spouse is not uncommon, although less frequent today than a few decades ago (Tóth, 1999b).

In addition, although marriage itself may be modernizing in Hungary, the phrases used in Hungarian to talk about getting married continue to emphasize its hierarchical nature. When a woman marries, the verb used is *ferjhez megy*, to go to a husband, while men either *elvesz*, buy a woman, or *elnõsül*, get "womaned."

HUSBAND–WIFE RELATIONSHIPS

Since 1989, an important advantage of marriage, especially for those with the least education, has been relative financial security. Most women also value it for providing legitimacy for their children (Tóth, 1999b). Men should also value it for improving their morbidity and mortality rates since married men live longer and healthier lives than men of any other marital status. Perhaps as a result, 71% of married men in a recent survey stated that married people are happier than other people; only 58% of married women agreed (Tóth, 1999b). This lower figure for women may be caused by the double burden women experience, the increasing financial opportunities for women without family responsibilities, or the widespread belief that fighting is common between spouses (80% of the time, fights are over money) (Tóth, 1999a). Hungarian husbands spend very little time on such housekeeping chores as cleaning, shopping, and caring for children (Lobodzinska, 1995), although more Hungarian men have become participants in household chores recently. In 30% of households, it is

even the wife's task to manage the family finances, while in 60% the husband and wife manage them together (Nagy, 1999).

Another reason women are less happy in marriage than men may be the traditional acceptance of domestic violence. One third of married women in the late 1990s had been beaten or threatened and only 19% of these women had sought police help, usually in vain since only 5% of that number actually received any assistance (Tóth, 1999a). The Hungarian proverb, "Money is best when counted, a woman is best when beaten," continues to be many people's reaction to evidence of domestic violence and even marital rape (Hochberg, 1997; International Helsinki Federation for Human Rights, 2000).

OTHER CROSS-SEX RELATIONSHIPS

Perhaps the only fairly significant cross-sex relationship outside marriage and parenting for some Hungarians is that between a godparent and his or her godchild. This institution only exists for Catholics and members of the Hungarian Reformed Church, although it is much more a cultural practice than an indication of church membership. The two most significant events at which the institution is visible and important are the child's baptism or christening, when the godparent promises to act as a lifetime moral religious guardian, and the child's wedding, when the godparents often serve as the witnesses.

CHANGE IN ATTITUDES, BELIEFS, AND PRACTICES REGARDING GENDER

Since the end of the socialist era in 1990, the most important changes in Hungary with regard to sex and gender have been the almost complete erasure of women's issues from the political scene, an emphasis on women's primary role as homemaker and mother, high male unemployment, and the development of a consumer culture.

The first two of these changes are the result of the degree to which the socialist state made women's employment (as the only path toward emancipation) a political, ideological, and moral imperative. In the anti-communist backlash of the 1990s and beyond, any political voice raising women's issues has been labeled reactionary, ideological, or anti-Hungarian. As a result, women are as likely as men now to agree that women should not work full time when they have small children (in 1988, far more men than women felt this way) (Tóth, 1997). Some younger women have reacted to this change with pleasure, since they had watched their own mothers struggle with juggling full-time work and full-time housework and do not want to live that life themselves (Kende & Neményi, 1999). Yet, many other women, and some men as well, have reacted with disgust to what is essentially the repoliticization of women's lives under the guise of tradition, family, or choice.

The third change, high male unemployment, is important because of the cultural context that constructs men primarily as breadwinners. Like many women, who are struggling to reconcile their early socialization that directed them into the work force with cultural norms about their roles as mothers and homemakers, men too are struggling to reconcile economic reality with cultural expectations. This struggle may be a factor in the high rates of male alcoholism, suicide, and depression, although women have slightly higher suicide and depression rates than men (Elekes, 1999).

Finally, consumerism has changed most areas of Hungarian life, including gender. Mothers are now under pressure from advertisements that use the voice of male doctors or other "experts" to direct them to purchase disposable diapers, children's vitamins and other supplements, and baby toiletries (Vajda, 1998). The formerly state-run magazine *Nők Lapja*, which had been filled with articles on work and politics, is now equivalent to any Western women's magazine, including many articles on dieting, fashion, and gossip (Haney, 1994; Tóth, 2001; West, 2000). While women are the primary targets of such consumer propaganda, younger, especially well-educated, Hungarian men in certain types of jobs are now also concerned that they smoke the right cigarettes, drink the right alcohol, wear the right clothes, and drive the right car. Just as women are being told that beauty, femininity, health, and popularity are available at a price, men too are confronting a world in which masculinity is only available to the man who can afford to buy the right accessories.

REFERENCES

Albert, F., & David, B. (1998). A barátokról [About friends]. In T. Kolosi, I. Tóth, & Gy. Vukovich (Eds.), *Társadalmi riport 1998* [*Report on society 1998*] (pp. 257–276). Budapest: TÁRKI.

Birtalan, B. (2000). A homoszexuálisok helyzete az egyházban és a társadalomban [The status of homosexuals in the church and in society]. In Háttér Baráti Társaság a Melegekért (Ed.), *Amszterdam után: A szexuális orientáció az Európai Unióban és Magyarországon* [*After Amsterdam: Sexual orientation in the European Union and Hungary*] (pp. 129–133). Budapest: Editor.

Bod, P. A. (2000). Magyarország gazdasági, pénzügyi és szociális állapota [The economic, financial, and social state of Hungary]. *Távlatok, 49,* 348–356.

Bollobás, E. (1993). "Totalitarian lib": The legacy of communism for Hungarian women. In N. Funk & M. Mueller (Eds.), *Gender politics and post-communism* (pp. 201–206). New York: Routledge.

Buss, T., Beres, Cs., Hofstetter, C. R., & Pomidor, A. (1994). Health status among elderly Hungarians and Americans. *Journal of Cross-Cultural Gerontology, 9,* 301–322.

Elekes, Zs. (1999). Devianciák, mentális betégségek [Forms of deviance and mental illness]. In T. Pongrácz & I. Gy. Tóth (Eds.), *Szerepváltozások: Jelentés a nők és a férfiak helyzetéről 1999* [*Changing roles: Report on the status of women and men 1999*] (pp. 125–142). Budapest: TÁRKI.

Farkas, L. (2000). Szép szavak: A melegek jogai és a III. Köztársaság [Nice talk: Gay rights and the Third Republic]. In Háttér Baráti Társaság a Melegekért (Ed.), *Amszterdam után: A szexuális orientáció az Európai Unióban és Magyarországon* [*After Amsterdam: Sexual orientation in the European Union and Hungary*] (pp. 86–95). Budapest: Editor.

Földesi, Gy. Sz. (1998). Life-styles and aging: The Hungarian case. *Women in Sport and Physical Activity Journal, 7,* 171–190.

Frey, M. (1996). A nők munkaerőpiaci esélyegyenlőtlenségéről [The inequality in chances for women in the labor market]. *Társadalmi Szemle, 5,* 55–61.

Frey, M. (1999). Nők a munkaerőpiacon [Women in the labor market]. In T. Pongrácz & I. Gy. Tóth (Eds.), *Szerepváltozások: Jelentés a nők és a férfiak helyzetéről 1999* [*Changing roles: Report on the status of women and men 1999*] (pp. 17–29). Budapest: TÁRKI.

Goven, J. (1993). Gender politics in Hungary: Autonomy and antifeminism. In N. Funk & M. Mueller (Eds.), *Gender politics and post-communism* (pp. 224–240). New York: Routledge.

Haney, L. (1994). From proud worker to good mother: Women, the state, and regime change in Hungary. *Frontiers: A Journal of Women Studies, 14,* 113–150.

Hochberg, A. (1997). The feminist network: A history. In T. Renne (Ed.), *Ana's land: Sisterhood in Eastern Europe* (pp. 107–112). Boulder, CO: Westview.

Hrubos, I. (1994). A férfiak és a nők iskolai végzettsége és szakképzettsége [Level of education and skills among men and women]. In M. Hadas (Ed.), *Férfiuralom: Írások nőkről, férfiakról, feminizmusról* [*Male dominance: Writings on women, men, and feminism*] (pp. 196–208). Budapest: Replika.

Hungarian College of Catholic Bishops. (1999). *A boldogabb családokért! A Magyar Katolikus Püspöki Kar körlevele a hívekhez és minden jóakaratú emberhez a házasságról és a családról Magyarországon* [*Happier families! A letter from the Hungarian College of Catholic Bishops to the faithful and all people of good will on marriage and the family in Hungary*]. Budapest: Hungarian College of Catholic Bishops.

Huseby-Darvas, É. V. (1996). "Feminism, the murderer of mothers": The rise and fall of neo-nationalism reconstruction of gender in Hungary. In B. F. Williams (Ed.), *Women out of place: The gender of agency and the race of nationality* (pp. 161–185). New York: Routledge.

International Helsinki Federation for Human Rights. (2000). *Women 2000: An investigation into the status of women's rights in Central and South-Eastern Europe and the Newly Independent States.* Vienna: International Helsinki Federation for Human Rights.

Jakus, I. (1993). The new abortion act. *Hungarian Quarterly, 34,* 83–86.

Jozan, P. (1999). A nők egészségi állapotának néhány jellemzője [Some characteristics of women's state of health]. In T. Pongrácz & I. Gy. Tóth (Eds.), *Szerepváltozások: Jelentés a nők és a férfiak helyzetéről 1999 [Changing roles: Report on the status of women and men 1999]* (pp. 101–115). Budapest: TÁRKI.

Kamarás, F. (1999). Terhességmegszakítások Magyarországon [Abortions in Hungary]. In T. Pongrácz & I. Gy. Tóth (Eds.), *Szerepváltozások: Jelentés a nők és a férfiak helyzetéről 1999 [Changing roles: Report on the status of women and men 1999]* (pp. 190–216). Budapest: TÁRKI.

Kamarás, F. (2000). Termékenység, népesség, reprodukció [Fertility, population, reproduction]. In T. Kolosi, I. G. Toth, & G. Vukovich (Eds.), *Társadalmi riport* [Social report] (pp. 409–432). Budapest: TÁRKI.

Kende, A., & Neményi, M. (1999). Two generations' perceptions of femininity in post-socialist Hungary. In A. Pető & B. Rásky (Eds.), *Construction, reconstruction: Women, family and politics in Central Europe, 1945–1998* (pp. 147–185). Budapest: Central European University Press.

Koncz, K. (1994). Nők a rendszerváltás folyamatában [Women in the process of the regime change]. In M. Hadas (Ed.), *Férfiuralom: Irások nőkről, férfiakról, feminizmusról [Male dominance: Writings on women, men, and feminism]* (pp. 209–222). Budapest: Replika.

Koncz, K. (1995). The position of Hungarian women in the process of regime change. In B. Lobodzinska (Ed.), *Family, women, and employment in Central–Eastern Europe* (pp. 139–148). Westport, CT: Greenwood.

LaFont, S. (2001). One step forward, two steps back: Women in the post-communist states. *Communist and Post-Communist Studies, 34,* 203–220.

Lévai, K., & Kiss, R. (1999). Nők a közéletben: Parlamenti és önkormányzati választások, 1998 [Women in public life: Parliamentary and local elections, 1998]. In T. Pongrácz & I. Gy. Tóth (Eds.), *Szerepváltozások: Jelentés a nők és a férfiak helyzetéről 1999 [Changing roles: Report on the status of women and men 1999]* (pp. 40–50). Budapest: TÁRKI.

Lobodzinska, B. (1995). Hungary. In B. Lobodzinska (Ed.), *Family, women, and employment in Central–Eastern Europe* (pp. 131–137). Westport, CT: Greenwood.

Long, S. (1999). Gay and lesbian movements in Eastern Europe. In B. D. Adam, J. W. Duyvendak, & A. Krouwel (Eds.), *The global emergence of gay and lesbian politics* (pp. 242–265). Philadelphia: Temple University Press.

Nagy, B. (1995). Üzletassonyok és üzletemberek: Női és férfi vállalkozok az 1990-es évek elején [Businesswomen and businessmen: Female and male entrepreneurs at the beginning of the 1990s]. *Szociológiai Szemle, 4,* 147–164.

Nagy, B. (1997). Karrier női módra [Careers a la Woman]. In K. Lévai & I. Tóth (Eds.), *Szerepváltozások: Jelentés a nők helyzetéről [Changing roles: A report on the state of women]* (pp. 35–51). Budapest: TÁRKI.

Nagy, I. (1999). Családok pénzkezelési szokásai a kilencvenes években [Practices in family finances in the 1990s]. In T. Pongrácz & I. Gy. Tóth (Eds.), *Szerepváltozások: Jelentés a nők és a férfiak helyzetéről 1999 [Changing roles: Report on the status of women and men 1999]* (pp. 74–97). Budapest: TÁRKI.

Pongrácz, T., & Tóth, I. Gy. (Eds.). (1999). *Szerepváltozások: Jelentés a nők és a férfiak helyzetéről 1999 [Changing roles: Report on the status of women and men 1999].* Budapest: TÁRKI.

Reisman, J. M. (1990). Intimacy in same-sex friendships. *Sex Roles, 1/2,* 65–82.

S. Molnár, E. (1999). A gymermekvállalás konfliktusai [Conflicts in choosing to have children]. In T. Pongrácz & I. Gy. Tóth (Eds.), *Szerepváltozások: Jelentés a nők és a férfiak helyzetéről 1999 [Changing roles: Report on the status of women and men 1999]* (pp. 151–172). Budapest: TÁRKI.

Sándor, B. (2000). A melegek és leszbikusok társadalmi helyzete Magyarországon [The social status of gays and lesbians in Hungary]. In Háttér Baráti Társaság a Melegekért (Ed.), *Amszterdam után: A szexuális orientáció az Európai Unióban és Magyarországon [After Amsterdam: Sexual orientation in the European Union and Hungary]* (pp. 96–99). Budapest: Editor.

Somlai, P. (1998). Children of the changeover. *Hungarian Quarterly, 39,* 90–100.

Swaim, R. C., Nemeth, J., & Oetting, E. R. (1995). Alcohol use and socialization characteristics among Hungarian adolescents: Path models. *Drugs and Society, 8,* 47–63.

Szalai, J. (1998). Women and democratization: Some notes on recent changes in Hungary. In A. Pető & B. Rásky (Eds.), *Construction, reconstruction: Women, family and politics in Central Europe, 1945–1998* (pp. 103–125). Budapest: Central European University Press.

Szalai, J. (1999). Közös csapda. A nők és a szegények [Shared trap: Women and poverty]. In K. Lévai, R. Kiss, & T. Gyulavári (Eds.), *Vegyes váltó. Pillanat-képek nőkről, férfiakról [Relay-race. Snapshots of women and men]* (pp. 44–56). Budapest: Egyenlő Esélyek Alapítvány.

Széman, Zs. (1999). Az idősködő nők problémái—szerepük a magyar társadalomban [The problem of elderly women—their role in Hungarian society]. In K. Lévai, R. Kiss, & T. Gyulavári (Eds.), *Vegyes váltó. Pillanat-képek nőkről, férfiakról [Relay-race. Snapshots of women and men]* (pp. 153–165). Budapest: Egyenlő Esélyek Alapítvány.

Tomka, M. (2000). Gondolatok a gyermekimáról [Thoughts on children's prayers]. *Távlatok, 48,* 230–239.

Tomka, M., & Révay, E. (1998). Papok, férfi szerzetesek, apacák [Clergy, monks, nuns]. In T. Kolosi, I. Gy. Tóth, & Gy. Vukovich (Eds.) *Társadalmi riport 1998* [Social report 1998] (pp. 216–234). Budapest: TÁRKI.

Tóth, O. (1993). No envy, no pity. In N. Funk & M. Mueller (Eds.), *Gender politics and post-communism* (pp. 213–223). New York: Routledge.

Tóth, O. (1994a). A női életút Magyarországon: Extrem modon hosszú és rövid életperiodusok [Women's life course in Hungary: extremely long and short periods]. In M. Hadas (Ed.), *Férfiuralom: Irások nőkről, férfiakról, feminizmusról* [Male dominance: Writings on women, men, and feminism] (pp. 223–234). Budapest: Replika.

Tóth, O. (1994b). Family affairs. *Hungarian Observer*, *7*, 31–32.

Tóth, O. (1997). Working women: Changing roles, changing attitudes. *Hungarian Quarterly*, *38*, 69–77.

Tóth, O. (1999a). Erőszak a családban [Violence in the family]. In K. Lévai & R. Kiss (Eds.), *Vegyesváltó: Pillanat képek nőkről, férfiakról* [Relay race: Snapshots of women and men] (pp. 178–201). Budapest: Egyenlő Eselyek Alapítvány.

Tóth, O. (1999b). Marriage, divorce and fertility in Hungary today: Tensions between facts and attitudes. In A. Petö & B. Rásky (Eds.), *Construction, reconstruction: Women, family and politics in Central Europe, 1945–1998* (pp. 127–145). Budapest: Central European University Press.

Tóth, O. (2001). Az állami díjas szövőnőktől a tenyérjóslásig: A Nők Lapja 1989-től 1999-ig [From state award winning female weavers to palm reading: Nők Lapja from 1989 to 1999]. *Szocioiógiai Szemle*, *1*, 3–21.

Utasi, A. (1997). A válás és együttélés rétegkülönbségei [Differences in divorce and cohabitation without various layers of society]. *Társadalmi Szemle*, *7*, 56–66.

Vajda, Zs. (1998). Childhood and how children live now. *Hungarian Quarterly*, *39*, 80–89.

van der Lippe, T., & Fodor, É. (1998). Changes in gender inequality in six Eastern European countries. *Acta Sociologica*, *41*, 131–149.

Vukovich, Gy., & Harcsa, I. (1998). A Magyar társadalom a jelzőszámok tükrében [Hungarian society in the index numbers' mirror]. In T. Kolosi, I. Tóth, & Gy. Vukovich (Eds.), *Társadalmi riport 1998* [*Report on society 1998*] (pp. 21–31). Budapest: TÁRKI.

West, B. A. (2000). Personhood on a plate: Gender and food in the construction of proper Hungarian women. *Anthropology of East Europe Review*, *18*, 117–123.

West, B. A. (2002). *The danger is everywhere! The insecurity of transition in postsocialist Hungary*. Prospect Heights, IL: Waveland Press.

Wolf, G. (2000). How the young live now. *Hungarian Quarterly*, *41*, 60–76.

Wong, R. S.-K. (1995). Socialist stratification and mobility: Cross-national and gender differences in Czechoslovakia, Hungary, and Poland. *Social Science Research*, *24*, 302–328.

Iatmul

ALTERNATIVE NAMES

The Iatmul are also known as the Iatmoi.

LOCATION

The Iatmul are located on the middle Sepik River, Papua New Guinea.

CULTURAL OVERVIEW

Some 25 Iatmul-speaking villages line the middle Sepik River. For Melanesia, these villages are large—upwards of 1,200 people. They are also prosperous, with fertile gardens, access to jungle and grasslands, and a continuous source of water for drinking, bathing, and food.[1] The river, which recedes and floods in an annual rain cycle, provides fish, prawns, and mayflies. Extended families tend small horticultural gardens of taro, yam, sweet potato, and fruit trees (e.g., coconut, banana).

Colonial administrations, beginning in the 1880s, introduced beans, cucumber, pineapple, watermelon, and other crops. Iatmul may also eat chicken, wild bird, turtle, crocodile, snake, frog, sago grubs, lotus seeds, bandicoot, cassowary, and, during ritual, pig, and sometimes dog. Iatmul attribute bodily strength and cultural vitality to sago, a starch produced from the *Metroxylum sagu* palm, which is associated with maternal nurture and, say some men, breast-milk.

Today, trade stores stock rice, canned fish and meat, biscuits, flour, beer, cooking oil, tea, coffee, powdered milk, cookies, and biscuits. Additionally, Iatmul—mainly women—regularly schedule markets with bush-dwelling Sawos-speaking hamlets to obtain sago and sometimes meat (Hauser-Schäublin, 1977). Formerly, Iatmul exchanged fish; now, they mainly pay cash.

Iatmul villages are organized into a nested hierarchy of patrilineal descent groups, sometimes forming totemic moieties. Each patrilineal group justifies its existence on the basis of an exclusive corpus of totemic names that refer to mythic-historic migrations. Men tend to have custodianship over these names.

Yet matrifiliation and maternal sentiment are profound and, in some contexts such as disputes, eclipse the androcentric social structure. Villages are acephalous. Political leadership is male and extends only to the limits of the descent group. Residence is normally patrilocal; marriage generally takes place within the village. Warfare, once endemic, is extinct. But men and women still manifest an assertive, often aggressive, ethos that nonetheless coexists with the high moral value of mothering.

CULTURAL CONSTRUCTION OF GENDER

Gender influences all aspects of Iatmul culture and social life. A major theme of the culture is the clarification of the relationship between male and female as they are defined in terms of a pervasive maternal schema.

Iatmul recognize two genders: male (*ndu*) and female (*tagwa*). From one angle, these genders are exclusive, distinct, and complementary (Weiss, 1994). Men fish with spears, women set traps; men stand in canoes, women sit; men carve, women weave; etc. This omnipresent dichotomy is also natural and biological: men have penises and testicles, women have vaginas and wombs. The traditional and modern person is unambiguously gendered through clothing, personal adornment, treatment of the body, and even gait and verbal intonation. Today, men wear pants and often go shirtless, while women don skirts and, unless elderly, mission-derived floral blouses. Little boys run naked; girls never do. Many men are scarified, as I discuss below, while women may tattoo themselves with soot. During rituals too, men and women are differentiated by ornamentation such as body paint. Even when men and women ritually switch their stereotypical garb, as in the famous *naven* rite that celebrates first-time cultural achievements for everybody (Bateson, 1936/1958), differentiation is preserved.

<figure>487</figure>

Yet the symbolism of Iatmul gender, especially in religious contexts (e.g., ritual, myth, art), expands beyond a dichotomy to a "common pool" of dispositions and values. From this angle, both men and women define themselves through competing claims to fecundity, reproductive primacy, and nurture—that is, to the cultural idea and ideal of motherhood (Silverman, 2001). Therefore Iatmul gender is dual and unitary, a matter of difference and emphasis. Men's ritual prerogatives signal their difference from, and superiority over, women. Yet the symbolism of ritual is thoroughly infused with uterine themes (see below). Women, by contrast, never aspire to the culturally perceived bodily capacities and qualities of fatherhood. True, women may desire male privileges. But the symbolism of womanhood does not disclose a wish to become fathers in the same way that the symbolism of manhood discloses the wish to become mothers.

For the Iatmul, dichotomous gender is pervasive and natural. At the same time, Iatmul culture often appears to be a grand irreducible dialogue of ambiguity and ambivalence, voiced in a maternal idiom, concerning the relationship between male and female. For men, maintaining a divided world by excluding women is vital. Women are far less compelled to maintain this gendered dichotomy and often, argues Hauser-Schäublin (1977, p. 260), strive for synthesis and unity.

Attractiveness for both men and women is largely visual: pronounced nose, clear and shiny skin, and bodily cleanliness. Men desire women with firm breasts, while women desire strong muscular men.

GENDER OVER THE LIFE CYCLE

The cultural stages of the Iatmul life cycle are relatively congruent for men and women, with one exception. Men traditionally underwent a male initiation ceremony, which I discuss below. This was the only significant regularly performed rite of passage for either men or women.

There is a tacit sense that postmenopausal women shift somewhat into an unnamed category that is less of a threat to men. The female body, especially her genital secretions, are polluting to men and male ritual—she "cools" the magical "heat" associated with masculine aggressiveness and potency, and the efficacy of spirits. As Iatmul men and women move through the life cycle, they tend to acquire increased politico-ritual rights as well as

responsibilities for overseeing a kin group and its residential ward and resources. With age, too, men and women gain prestige and authority, especially in matters of ritual, magic, and, at least today, knowledge of "tradition" or "custom."

Socialization of Boys and Girls

Infant boys and girls tend to be socialized similarly. Both boys and girls interact with the same expansive kin group although grandfathers and mothers' brothers tend to be more interested in boys. The major caretakers and socializers of children are mothers, older siblings (typically female), and matrikin. Infancy and childhood entail no distinct rites for boys and girls, and there are no major gendered expectations.

Boys are valued over girls in regard to the inheritance of totemic names and the reproduction of the patrilineage. Yet girls are prized, since married daughters, more so than sons who are said to be busy with brideservice obligations, care for elderly parents. Furthermore, a son-in-law performs labor for his wife's parents: hews canoes, clears gardens, etc. By contrast, a daughter-in-law is said to be greedy.

Below the age of about 7, there is little gendered differentiation in the tasks of boys and girls (Weiss, 1990, p. 339). But since women are the primary adult caretakers, boys tend to assist their mothers and women more than their fathers and men. Additionally, Mead (1949, p. 112) reported, Iatmul boys were somewhat feminine; their play often recalled the events of childhood rather than their future participation in the "splendor" of male life. At the same time, boys seem slightly masculine when they perform female tasks.

The play of young children tends to exhibit little significant gender distinction. Children form autonomous groups, roaming the village and foraging for snacks. However, older prepubescent boys and girls do often enact the gender-specific roles of adults. But this distinction is largely informal; boys and girls do not fully segregate their peer groups until puberty. The possessions of older prepubescent children do somewhat reflect gender (Weiss, 1997). Thus, boys have stools while girls, like adult women, sit on the ground. Boys are more aggressive in their play (e.g, athletics and shooting slingshots). Boys and girls may stage a "ritual" for themselves (Weiss, 1983). Mirroring adults, the boys parade in masked costumes while the girls dance in celebration.

But these youthful outings are less segregated than their grown-up counterparts.

Prior to puberty, there is little formal education or apprenticeship, gendered or otherwise. Caretakers tend to educate, instruct, and discipline boys and girls similarly. Boys seem to be hit more often than girls, and girls seem to get into trouble more often than boys, perhaps because they have greater responsibilities.

Both boys and girls run errands—ferrying messages, fetching things—for adult men and women (Weiss, 1981). But girls have greater responsibility than boys for household chores and supervising younger kin. (I have two enduring images of prepubescents: boys wrestling, and girls holding younger siblings.) Weiss (1990) emphasizes that Iatmul mothers can only perform all their daily tasks (fishing, gardening) if children look after the younger ones. Men are far less dependent on children.

Puberty and Adolescence

Older children, to repeat, begin to manifest gendered patterns of play, games, and leisure. They increasingly model their behavior after adults. At puberty, boys and girls form sex-segregated groups. Today, these groups freely roam the village, often to the annoyance of adults who complain about the erosion of traditional authority and public behavior. These complaints typically mention the sexual licentiousness of young men and women.

Gendered socialization becomes increasingly important with age, especially for boys who, as children, spend most of their time with other youths and women. Adolescents are more self-conscious in their gender identification. Girls continue to assume regular household chores and obligations. Boys, too, begin to participate in the affairs of adult men, especially in regard to ritual. But while girls in their early teens are capable of performing nearly all female tasks, boys do not become fully competent males until their late teens (Weiss, 1990, p. 339).

With the exception of male initiation, which I discuss in the next section, there is general continuity in socialization around puberty.

Attainment of Adulthood

For both men and women, adult personhood is attained mainly on the basis of marriage and the subsequent birth of children. Traditionally, Iatmul men were initiated into adult manhood and the male cult. The bloody painful ordeals of initiation allowed men to emulate the fortitude of women during childbirth, and to "grow" boys into adult males. Although men never attend birth, since they deem it polluting, male initiation is permeated by symbols of parturition and maternal nurture. This way, men effectively supplant the culturally lauded role of motherhood. Cicatrization purges neophytes' bodies of maternal blood, which inhibits the development of a masculine physique. But the resulting scars, which are visible emblems of manhood, are said by men to resemble the breasts and genitals of woman and female crocodile spirits. The rite forges exclusive masculine identity by aggressively exaggerating birth, maternal feeding, and moral mothering. At the same time, male initiation associates the female body with danger, pollution, castration, and somatic atrophy. Initiation thus constructs Iatmul manhood as an identity that opposes yet emulates motherhood.

Women were once initiated if men judged them to be excessively aggressive, if they espied male cult secrets, or if a sonless father wanted a daughter to inherit his totemic esoterica and magic (see also Hauser-Schäublin, 1977, p. 178; 1995). But this practice was rare; it remains poorly understood today by either ethnographers or Iatmul.

Initiation offered novices only a little guidance about adult behavior. However, they were admonished to avoid adultery and practice birth spacing. Upon the attainment of adulthood, men and women are expected to be busy with adult activities, which are almost always gender segregated. Men tend to gather in cult houses and related ritual spaces unless otherwise engaged in occasional subsistence and work activities. Women are responsible for daily fishing, preparing meals, and maintenance of the household.

Middle Age and Old Age

Middle age offers few real changes to men and women. However, old age confers increased respect and prestige. Older men are the custodians of totemic knowledge, myth, kinship, ritual rules, and overall cultural lore. They also tend to supervise major communal labors and ceremonies. Elderly women are also viewed with respect for their lore, magic, knowledge about childbirth and healing, and general cultural erudition. At the same time, elders ponder the inevitability of death and their waning authority as younger adults assume roles of leadership.

PERSONALITY DIFFERENCES BY GENDER

Bateson (1936/1958) summarized the ethos of Iatmul men as histrionic, aggressive, competitive, and flamboyant. Women were more demur, nurturing, cooperative, and practical. Male personhood is expansive and public; women are more domestic and personal. Women, too, take pride in male kin who uphold the showy self-important swagger of manhood (Hauser-Schäublin, 1977, p. 130). But since men tend to restrict their politico-ritual voice to the cult house, one hears in the village mainly women as they loudly talk, laugh, yell, and fight. The ethos of masculinity notwithstanding, women are far more likely to scuffle than men. In fact, men often attribute social tensions between groups to women, especially female sexuality, which men regard as divisive.

When normal coping mechanisms fail, men may try to kill the source of their frustration. Women may commit suicide (Hauser-Schäublin, 1977, pp. 128–139).

Iatmul women tend to laugh more than men. They also seem to have greater freedom for informal sociability and emotional expression since they are less beholden than men to the strict rules of decorum that govern the male cult. Both men and women are ashamed by dependency. Men, more than women, are driven by dominance. Both genders are shy, or reticent, when making requests, which signals child-like dependence. Men are apt to be more suspicious and guarded, especially in matters of totemic and mythic knowledge. Yet, as elsewhere in Melanesia, men and women habitually refuse to speculate on other peoples' unstated motivations. Men are particularly prone to prideful insults. However much they attribute conflict to women, men are the ones who constantly require conciliatory gestures.

Men are more likely than women to think about the world in terms of dualities and distinctions (Hauser-Schäublin, 1977, pp. 243–245). They tend, for example, to divide social groups and gender. Cognitively, women strive for unity. Men are greatly concerned with maintaining social and gendered boundaries. They fear the possibility that women might intrude on their all-male spaces. Women exhibit little comparable concern. While women often desire the exclusion of men, it is not because a male presence would threaten the definition of Iatmul femininity. (Women, I sense, simply want time away from male swagger!) Men, however, exclude women from male rituals precisely because a female presence would call into question the procreative, uterine dimensions of Iatmul masculinity.

Iatmul men frequently conceptualize kinship as an abstract system of rules. Women tend to think about kinship in terms of specific relationships and actual persons (Hauser-Schäublin, 1977, p. 152).

GENDER-RELATED SOCIAL GROUPS

All significant social institutions in Iatmul society are structured around males or females. When men and women form a single group, gender defines their respective social roles.

Village residence wards correspond to patrilineal groups, which are largely exogamous. Residence is typically patrilocal. Since Iatmul villages are endogamous, the proximity of natal kin reduces a bride's psychological distress when she relocates to her husband's residence ward. (Some men view the idea of living with affines to be shameful.) Generally, an extended patrilineal family inhabits the house. Men sleep near the central areas and entrances of the dwelling, while women (wives and unmarried daughters) reside along the periphery. This way, the Iatmul house, like the internal spaces of canoes, reflects the gendered spatial organization of the society.

Iatmul gender is also shaped by an opposition between what Bateson (1936/1958) called "patrilineal structure" and "maternal sentiment." Although descent is patrilineal, kinship is more fluid, with men and women using both male and female links to determine relationships. Larger kin groups and ritual moieties tend to be patrilineal. But people do follow matrilateral "paths" when defining group affiliation for some ceremonies and prohibitions. There are no important, or formal, nonkin associations for either males or females.

GENDER ROLES IN ECONOMICS

Married women tend to remain and work within their husband's residence ward, gardens, and riverbank. Women, as noted earlier, are responsible for daily subsistence. They fish by canoe with traps and nets, tend gardens, catch prawns, and cook all meals. Because women are associated with the warmth of houses, they also care for the small hearths that smoulder underneath dwellings.

Men, too, work in gardens, but this labor, like other male tasks—felling trees, hewing canoes, building houses, clearing gardens—is intermittent. (I have heard some women complain that men, for all the work they do, are like children!) Men's work is often collaborative, involving different descent groups. Women mainly work individually. When they labor collectively, women generally perform parallel tasks within their natal or husband's group.

Men and women work together, albeit in well-defined roles, when gardening and producing sago. The latter activity is a cultural symbol of gender complementarity. Men chop the pith, which women knead and process through an apparatus of troughs and filters. Women fry or boil the sago—as men say, only women can properly cook it.

Women, reported Mead (1949, pp. 180–181), work more willingly than men, who labor begrudgingly. Economic independence is highly valued in women, especially by men (Hauser-Schäublin, 1977, p. 148).

Traditionally, both men and women participated in prestige exchanges. Women pleated baskets and sleeping mats, cultivated tobacco and tubers, harvested fish, raised pigs, and fed visitors. Husbands exchanged female products for shell valuables and prestige, which also enhanced the status of their wives. However, men do consult with female kin before transactions.

Today, men and women derive intermittent cash income from the sale of tobacco, betel nut, fruit, fish, chicken, pig, crocodile skins, and cocoa. Villages contain small trade stores. They are largely, but not exclusively, owned and managed by men. Many Iatmul men and women migrate to towns and cities for employment as teachers, soldiers, lawyers, mine workers, civil servants, hotel staff, policemen, store clerks, and so forth. They may periodically return and send remittances. My sense is that more men are employed in these capacities than women (in Tambunum, one third more adult women than men reside in the village). But this may reflect more on a capitalist division of labor than Iatmul culture.

Traditionally, neither men nor women labored outside the village environs. Today, Iatmul who relocate for jobs are commonly accompanied by spouses and children. Employed women still remain responsible for female-coded domestic tasks such as cooking (Stanek & Weiss, 1998, pp. 320–321). Because women produce most food in the village, Stanek and Weiss continue, unemployed women who live in town find themselves in a new position of total economic dependence on their husbands.

Tourism is the primary source of income today in the village. Men carve wooden objects such as masks, tables, animals, and ornamented stools, while women create netbags, baskets, and small rattan animals (Silverman, 2000). Often, wives and female kin decorate a man's woodcarvings.[2] Proceeds are dispersed to those who contributed materials and labor, regardless of gender. In the town of Wewak, women rent stalls at outdoor markets to peddle baskets and occasionally woodcarvings. (Travel by truck on the dirt roads to Wewak lasts anywhere from 4 to 15 hours.) Women, too, sometimes with men, vend objects outside a Wewak hotel. A tourist guesthouse in one Iatmul village (Tambunum) employs men and women as security staff, grass cutters, maintenance staff, housecleaners, and cooks. Tourists, too, occasionally pay men as canoe drivers and guides.

Both men and women within the patriline inherit property, which is often gender specific: houses, canoes, outboard motors, fishing nets, cooking implements, storage jars, kerosene lanterns, and sometimes a little cash. Men, not women, tend to inherit totemic names, magic, and ritual prerogatives. A widow remains in her husband's house and continues to have full access to his gardens, property, and so forth. I am unaware of either major disputes between men and women over the inheritance of material property or any eviction after a spouse's death.

PARENTAL AND OTHER CARETAKER ROLES

Caretaking and custodial roles in Iatmul culture are envisioned as forms of mothering. Mothers are associated with food, feeding, cooking, warmth, house-cleaning, flower gardens, dishwashing, laundering, and the like. Mothers breast-feed infants, soothe tears, teach toddlers to walk, bathe children, cleanse their urine and feces, and carry them throughout the village. When men assume these roles (e.g., the socializing mother's brother), they also act maternally. Motherhood is clearly idealized. Yet mothers and not fathers are primarily responsible for punishment, which can be brusque and rough.

In ideology, the father–son relationship is tense and oedipal. Thus it differs dramatically from the mother–child bond. Sons are said to replace their father in the political–jural order of society. Moreover, sons inherit from fathers a large domestic house—a house that was not only built at considerable expense and labor by the father, but which also symbolizes a mother. Often, sons physically displace their father from his house-mother, consigning him to live out his days in a small shack. Why, then, do fathers build houses only to cede them to their sons? Because fathers fear ridicule, especially from their daughters-in-law.

Men and fathers, far more than women and mothers, tend to shoo children from their activities, especially at the cult house. They encourage children to return to their mothers. I myself was once chastised by a father to "Go walk with your mother! You don't walk with your father!"

Mothers abide by less numerous and restrictive avoidance taboos than fathers in regard to children. Mothers dominate early childhood in terms of education, physical proximity, care, time, supervision, and affection. Fathers have little normative role in formal child-raising other than bestowing magic and totemic names onto sons, arranging (and funding) children's marriages, and ensuring that sons are initiated or otherwise integrated into the male cult. The father is not a primary male socializer. This role belongs to the mother's brother, as a "male mother," and other men from the father's age grade.

Iatmul describe fathers as distant, tense, and unloving. But fathers can be, and often are, quite tender and nurturing. For both mothers and fathers, then, the ideology of parenting often clashes with actuality (see also Bateson, 1936/1958, p. 76; Mead, 1949, p. 114).

Iatmul children and adults highly value individual autonomy and initiative. Children may view daily school attendance as an unjust constraint. If Iatmul parents want their children to attend school regularly, which mainly occurs in urban settings, they may experience shifts in normative parenting. A father may become more active in the everyday affairs of his children. But since childcare is a female role, it is the mother who must discipline the children and restrain their autonomy. Thus she, not the father, clashes in a negative way with Iatmul norms for the parent–child relationship (Stanek & Weiss, 1998, pp. 322–323).

LEADERSHIP IN PUBLIC ARENAS

Most village leaders are men since women are banned from the male cult house, the center of political debate and ritual preparation. Leadership largely arises from totemic erudition, which is mainly restricted to men. Formerly, leaders were also noted sorcerers and warriors, two social roles denied to women. While there are female leaders among women, their prestige and authority is less expansive than male leadership, confined to the domestic organization of a residential ward and household. Women leaders have no public arena on par with the men's house from which to mobilize resources and labor. In short, female leadership lacks equal authority.

GENDER AND RELIGION

The central feature of Iatmul religion is the male cult, which by definition excludes women. However, the Iatmul pantheon is dominated by neither male nor female spirits. The spirits mete out magical punishment to those who transgress social and ritual norms. More broadly, they are responsible for creating and sustaining the cosmos. But the spirits communicate only through men since men alone are the current custodians of magic, flutes, ceremonies, and other sancta. Men, not women, recollect cosmogonic events by chanting totemic names during ritual. Men alone impersonate spirits during religious rites in the guise of bamboo flutes and other sound-producing objects, masked costumes, and various artistic displays. Female religious practices, such as keening before effigies during annual funerary rites, are said to be subordinate to rituals enacted by men.

Virtually all forms of male-enacted ritual are intended to awe (and sometimes seduce) women with beautiful melodies, frightening sounds, and dazzling spirit displays. Women are not supposed to know that spirit expressions are male impersonations. A major concern of men is to prevent women from achieving this revelation.

But men did not always maintain exclusive custodianship over religious rites, sacra, and spirits, at least according to myth. Originally, women blew the flutes— and gave birth. One day, men frightened away the ancestresses with the sound of bullroarers and stole the flutes and ritual paraphernalia. Ever since, men have blown the flutes—although never with the beauty of the original ancestresses. Today, women hear the flutes during ritual—but they must never glimpse them. Otherwise, men say, women might steal them back! Major Iatmul rituals are thus dangerous to men since women might reclaim their dominance over cosmic forces by unveiling the spirits as men and stealing back their sacra. Ritual, too, is dangerous to women. Their reproductive potential is imperiled if they glimpse the flutes or view "too carefully" the sacred art. In sum, Iatmul religion expresses yet denies male desire for female fertility (see also Hauser-Schäublin, 1977, p. 147; Mead, 1949, ch. 4). While men purloined the flutes from ancestresses, primal women stole nothing from men. The ability to birth children is a considerable source of pride for women (Weiss, 1987, p. 163). I suggest that, through their rituals, men aspire to the same form of self-respect.

In Tambunum village, an elderly woman must always know the "truth" about the flutes and sacra—that men stole them from women. In another village, all women are knowledgeable about the primal theft and, indeed, they are proud of this former privilege (Hauser-Schäublin, 1977, p. 165). There, too, some female rites mock male ritual. Hence, Hauser-Schäublin (1977, p. 146) describes the flutes as "secretive," not "secret." Yet these women do not view this myth as a model for an egalitarian society. Rather, suggests Hauser-Schäublin (1977, p. 66), the primal theft expresses the cultural value of motherhood, the dominant maternal role in child-raising, and early male cross-sex identity through the close mother–child bond.

The mythic origin of the cosmos—and its possible demise—was aquatic. Water, especially the river, is feminine. Trees, land, and villages, which were created by male culture heroes in mythic history, are masculine. The yearly cycle of rain, flooding, and dryness thus corresponds to a cosmological tension between female watery erosion, which is also linked to death, and masculine stability. Mythic time is also gendered: male time moves forward, while female time moves backwards (Silverman, 1997). Aesthetic idioms of watery fluidity and terrestrial permanence, which evoke notions of female and male, pervade the religious system.

Witchcraft, now largely extinct, was attributed to both men and women. Yet most witches were female. Witchcraft was often transmitted from mother to daughter, and menstruating women were particularly prone to this nefarious craft (Hauser-Schäublin, 1977, pp. 139–140). Conversely, only men were sorcerers. Both men and women know myth, but male tales contain totemic names and are thus more "truthful." Still, some men ironically rely on their wives for mythic knowledge. This way, male prestige is supported by female erudition (Hauser-Schäublin, 1977, p. 169). Both men and women can employ magic, but male spells are more potent. Women may call upon male magicians to assist pregnancy and birth.

Today, men and women adhere in varying degrees to Christianity as well as to the traditional religious system. But this new religion tends to empower women by extolling the virtues of cooperation, passivity, and temperance. Still, Iatmul women do not harness Christianity to any sustained critique of the male cult and its religious conceptions.

LEISURE, RECREATION, AND THE ARTS

If, by leisure time, we refer to activities that do not result in material products such as food, then men have considerably more leisure than women. Men often congregate in the men's house, sometimes just to laze in the shade and nap, or to chat about the day's events. Men, too, much more than women, discuss politics, recount myths, plan ritual, and so forth, typically in the men's house. In this respect, adult leisure is gendered.

Still, neither men nor women, in my assessment, are so burdened with daily toil that they are unable to enjoy at least some daily leisure. Both men and women socialize with friends—who, in this society, are kin. Men often socialize during collective work efforts—say, hewing a large canoe. Women do likewise while engaged in productive activity. Hence, a group of women might individually prepare reeds for basketry while chatting about village events.

Women may sing during the day, sometimes dirges to deceased kin. Men may blow flutes during communal labor. In the main, though, music and dancing is confined to ritual, both traditional and Christian. Both men and women sing during "prayer meetings," but men alone play musical instruments.

There is another gendered dimension to art. Ritual carvings and masks, when decorated for display, are wooden "bone," which directly recalls the paternal contribution to conception. The floral ornamentation is female "skin," which derives from the mother's blood. Paint colors are also gendered. Black evokes masculine power. White symbolizes semen. Red recalls menstrual blood or blood shed during warfare, which is masculine. Yellow is the color of birds and femininity.

Tobacco and betel nut are currently used by both men and women. Traditionally, some say, these substances were utilized mainly by men. Beverage alcohol is consumed by men with very few exceptions, and then typically during the honorific *naven* celebration when women assume the demeanor of men.

RELATIVE STATUS OF MEN AND WOMEN

To repeat, the fundamental structures of Iatmul villages are patrilineal: clans, lineages, and sublineage "branches," as well as ritual and sometimes totemic moieties. Inheritance is also agnatic. Leadership is mainly male. It is determined by primogeniture, and reinforced through prestige activities such as totemic erudition, ritual prominence, magical renown, and, formerly, warfare and sorcery. Men have greater access to spirits as well as traditional and modern technology. Some women own sewing machines, but only men use guns, outboard motors, bicycles, and large canoes. Men, not women, regularly gather at an exclusive shelter (the cult house). The male village "path," unlike the female "passageway," is privileged to run through the center of the village or next to the river. Women exercise considerable influence over the economic and social activities of kin groups. But men have greater access to public decision-making processes that affect the entire community and its relationship to other villages. All told, Iatmul men enjoy greater rights, privileges, and authority than women.

Women have considerable autonomy in regard to their sexuality, modern education, marriage, and divorce—but so do men. While elder women, too, accord respect, senior men elicit greater deference due to their ritual, magic, and totemic knowledge.

But the gender hierarchy that is so apparent in Iatmul culture is called into question by the ideology of manhood and mothering. One symbol of male leadership is the wooden "stool." But the real stools, men say, are mothers since only mothers bear and feed children. Likewise, the superstructure of the male cult is female; the roof of the cult house is literally supported by a carved ancestress. In this sense, the relative status of men and women is less clear than it first appears. From one angle, men dominate. From another angle, male superiority is compensation for men's lack of uterine maternal powers.

SEXUALITY

Iatmul sexuality is aggressive (Bateson, 1941, p. 52; Hauser-Schäublin, 1977, p. 135; Mead, 1949, p. 208; Silverman, 2001). For men, erotic passivity contravenes the martial ethos of manhood. Men may even compete with female partners to see who can first induce the other to orgasm. (Likewise, mourning women may "compete" with men during funerary ritual to see whose sounds, keening or flute music, are loudest.) A child's sex is determined by the parent with the "strongest" procreative substance.

Linguistically and culturally, men are sexually active while women are passive. Grammatically, Iatmul can only say: "He (active subject) has sex with her (passive object)." In practice, though, both men and women initiate lovemaking. Yet while women often refuse sexual advances, a man would be ashamed to do likewise since a woman's flirtations challenge his masculinity (see Bateson, 1936/1958, p. 149). Iatmul women often directly approach potential partners. Men are more reticent. They rely on intermediaries and the psychological support of love magic (Hauser-Schäublin, 1977, p. 75). Women also tend to be more bawdy than men in joking relationships (Hauser-Schäublin, 1977, p. 74). Men associate women with uncontrolled sexuality, and themselves with self-restraint (Hauser-Schäublin, 1977, p. 75). But a "bad" woman, Hauser-Schäublin continues, is not promiscuous; she is a neglectful mother.

Men and women view sexuality to be natural and pleasurable. Carnality is neither shameful nor solely reproductive. Sexuality is not, as in some Melanesian cultures, banned from the cultural spaces of the village. Yet men view any sexual contact with women to be potentially depleting and harmful through the loss of semen and, more seriously, contact with polluting vaginal fluids. (Cunnilingus is anathema to men.) Menstrual taboos, men say, protect them from female defilement. However, women view menstruation as purifying, not polluting (Hauser-Schäublin, 1977, p. 137).

Little honor is accorded to female or male virginity. There are no expressed norms against premarital sexuality, and little attempts to censure children's erotic play. Hauser-Schäublin (1977, p. 135) remarks that Iatmul men did not traditionally view women as sexual objects.

Affectionate touching in public occurs solely between the same gender. Men and women deny the occurrence of ritualized or everyday same-gender sexual relations.[3] Little boys who once exhibited homoerotic interaction were made to fight (Bateson, 1936/1958, p. 291). For men, receptive homosexuality bespeaks an unacceptable feminine identity. What many men find particularly shameful about homoerotism is the possibility of discovery in flagrante delicto by women.[4]

Still, men privately mention the homoerotic activity of their peers. Innuendo is common, especially as insult. Yet same-gender liaisons do occur among men, albeit clandestinely. Male initiation lacks ritualized homosexuality but is replete with homoerotic themes and gestures. These antics, if seen by women, would be highly shameful to men. In the male cult, though, they are shielded from women and lent a cosmological inflection.

Today, both Iatmul men and Iatmul women fear rape by youth gangs that prowl highways and towns (see also Mead, 1949, p. 113). Iatmul women did not engage in prostitution as a means to material benefit (Hauser-Schäublin, 1977, p. 135). Men use sex as a form of violence to manipulate persons, while women use sex as a means to emotional security or love.

Despite the maternal ideology of manhood and cross-sex identification by men, Iatmul society permits no mundane cross-dressing or transvestism. Only during major cosmogonic ritual and the common famous *naven* rite can men and women assume the demeanor of the other gender. A *naven* celebration may climax when a maternal uncle slides his buttocks down his nephew's leg (Bateson, 1936/1958; Silverman, 2001). This gesture flirts with the feminine and homoerotic dimensions of masculinity that are otherwise muted by the ideology of manhood.

COURTSHIP AND MARRIAGE

All Iatmul are expected to marry. Nearly everyone does so except people with physical deformities or cognitive impairments. However, it is particularly important for a man to have a spouse. Hence, there are more single women than single men (Weiss, 1995). Men depend on women for daily meals. Women need male labor only intermittently (Weiss, 1990, p. 338). Unmarried adults are not formally barred from politico-ritual authority. Yet, unless they are elderly widows and widowers, they tend to be marginal.

Iatmul practice several marriage patterns: sister exchange, second-generation cross-cousin marriage (a man weds his father's mother's brother's son's daughter [FMBSD], a woman called *iai*), and elective marriage. Only the latter formally admits love prior to the union. The other forms of marriage are usually arranged by the spouses' kin. They forge alliances and, most importantly, instance maternal sentiment since, when a man weds his FMBSD, he marries a woman his father calls "mother" (Silverman, 2001). The cultural sentiment underlying *iai* marriage—that a man (the father) should "get his mother back" (his son's bride)—is equally strong for men and women. No marriage can occur unless both spouses consent. Men and women can, and do, refuse betrothals. Today, romantic love and companionship are increasingly important ideals in marriage, especially among the young. This change is part of a wider assimilation of "modern" personhood that includes individualism, the importance of personal choice in a capitalist consumer economy, and the rise of coeducational settings such as schools, urban areas, and disco dances.

Many men wed polygynously—usually two wives, but sometimes upwards of four or five. This way, the husband can draw on a broad economic base of female labor. Today, male prestige is largely detached from the ceremonial exchange of female labor products such as baskets. Therefore it is less clear, even to Iatmul themselves, why some men still desire multiple spouses.

Divorce is acceptable and relatively common. It entails mainly the return of brideprice. The typical divorce occurs while the spouses are young, and the husband weds a second wife. Divorcees tend to remarry. Sometimes, a woman's first husband receives compensation for his brideprice from her second spouse. Widows and widowers can remarry, but surviving spouses who are elderly tend to remain single.

Both genders desire hardworking spouses and complain loudly about laziness. Some Iatmul court to raise their prestige or access to magical and/or material resources.

There is no formal wedding. Typically, the bride publicly spends the night with the groom in his house or garden shelter. Later, her brothers may march to the groom's house to demand a preliminary token of brideprice, which is negotiated by the spouses' kin. Husbands also perform groomservice. Ideally, *iai* marriage entails long-term balanced reciprocity between affines.

Traditionally, there was little premarital sex. Men were initiated into the cult prior to intercourse, and they were admonished to marry before sexual activity.

The brief period after marriage is awkward for both spouses, who must adjust to new relationships, new obligations, and, for one spouse at least, a new residence. There is nothing on par with a Western honeymoon, or even much public interaction between newlyweds.

HUSBAND–WIFE RELATIONSHIP

To the extent permissible in a culture that so consistently segregates the genders and encourages an ethos of aggression, the husband–wife relationship is marked by affection and companionship. But matrimonial gestures of tenderness are often muted—say, when spouses smile while quietly uttering a few words on a village path, or when a husband gently tosses his wife a few betel nuts. Public tenderness is confined to same-gender relationships. Aloofness is common; cooperation is always tenuous and, at least for men, reluctant. Hence, the husband–wife relationship is unable truly to develop into empathetic intimacy and companionship. Traditional Iatmul marriages effected a kind of balance sustained by fear. A wife's behavior influenced her husband's success in warfare. If she acted immorally, he might be killed. Conversely, the husband's behavior influenced his wife's pregnancy. If he erred, she might miscarry. Perhaps it would be best to characterize Iatmul marriage as brief moments of loving affection in a relationship of tolerated, even relished, antagonism.

Husbands and wives almost never eat together. Iatmul households do not value communal dining. When a woman prepares a meal, she offers some food to those who are present. The rest is wrapped in banana leaves or left in the pot for absent kin to partake later. Since women cook, children frequently dine with their mothers. Even then, there is a sense that each person eats alone.

Spouses do not traditionally sleep together under the same mosquito net. Most men spend little time with their wives since they relax, nap, and socialize at the men's house. Yet men and women do make joint decisions, especially about gardening, economic matters, and those major efforts such as ritual and house-building that require the husband to feed other men.

A wife focuses on maintaining household harmony while her husband is more focused on communal affairs such as ritual (Hauser-Schäublin, 1977, p. 134). Matrimonial conflict over sexuality is common, especially when women adhere to postpartum taboos (Hauser-Schäublin, 1977, p. 127). Husbands and wives may also fight over food.

Either spouse can initiate divorce. (Sometimes a disgruntled cowife will simply relocate to another residence, usually with agnates, but the marriage remains intact.) Custody is fluid. Young children tend to remain with their mother. If a wife leaves her husband, she may forfeit custody. Unless there is an explicit agreement of adoption, the children of divorcees retain membership in their father's patriline and share the inheritance.

The cowife relationship is tense. It often erupts into physical assault and fighting, usually over perceived imbalances in sex, work, and food. When cowives are hostile, suggests Hauser-Schäublin (1977, p. 132), their husband's role in the household becomes more secure. Cowife hostility, too, actually reduces domestic violence since neither woman wants to alienate her husband. Some Iatmul contend that a man's first wife is dominant; others deny the presence of any such rule, or assign this role only to an *iai* wife.

OTHER CROSS-SEX RELATIONSHIPS

There are two other significant male–female relationships. First, as mentioned above, the mother's brother is a key figure in the life of his sister's children, male and female. He constantly interacts with them in a mode of tenderness and affection that is modeled after the ideal of motherhood. However, the mother's brother forges a closer relationship with nephews than with nieces. Generally, the father's sister has no close relationship to either her brother's son or daughter. The brother–sister relationship is also important. The sister often acts a mother-figure to her brothers, who in turn look after their sisters' welfare. The village is endogamous, some men say, because brothers do not want their sisters to leave the community.

CHANGE IN ATTITUDES, BELIEFS, AND PRACTICES REGARDING GENDER

Throughout this entry, I have mentioned the many important changes that have altered gender roles and relations. Despite the introduction of capitalism, modernity, Christianity, citizenship, tourists, etc., men and women remain opposed, complementary, and antagonistic. Pollution beliefs regarding women, and male initiation, have waned. New economic, educational, and religious opportunities now exist for women. But the essential differentiation remains mostly intact. Likewise, men continue to define themselves in opposition to, yet as a type of, mother.

NOTES

1. Despite sociocultural variation across the Iatmul language group, I generalize, often from my own ethnographic focus which is the Eastern Iatmul village of Tambunum.
2. One young woman in Tambunum village assumed the clothing and habits of men, and was rumored to engage in same-gender sexuality. Like a man, she wore trousers, stood in canoes, and carved wooden objects.
3. Some men report that homosexuality was introduced into the Sepik by colonial Europeans (see also Mead, 1949, p. 113).
4. In ritual, men dramatize a fantasy of an anal clitoris (Silverman, 2001, p. 169).

REFERENCES

Bateson, G. (1941). The frustration–aggression hypothesis and culture. *Psychological Review, 48*, 350–355.

Bateson, G. (1958). *Naven: A survey of the problems suggested by a composite picture of the culture of a New Guinea tribe drawn from three points of view* (2nd Rev. ed., with new epilogue). Stanford, CA: Stanford University Press. (Original work published 1936.)

Hauser-Schäublin, B. (1977). Frauen in Kararau: Zur Rolle der Frau bei den Iatmul am Mittelsepik, Papua New Guinea [Monograph]. *Basler Beiträge aur Ethnologie, 18*.

Hauser-Schäublin, B. (1995). Puberty rites, women's *naven*, and initiation: Women's rituals of transition in Abelam and Iatmul Culture. In N. C. Lutkehaus & P. B. Roscoe (Eds.), *Gender rituals: Female initiation in Melanesia* (pp. 33–53). New York: Routledge.

Mead, M. (1949). *Male and female: A study of the sexes in a changing world*. New York: Dell.

Silverman, E. K. (1997). Politics, gender, and time in Melanesia and aboriginal Australia. *Ethnology, 36*, 101–121.

Silverman, E. K. (2000). Tourism in the Sepik River of Papua New Guinea: Favoring the local over the global. *Pacific Tourism Review, 4*, 105–119.

Silverman, E. K. (2001). *Masculinity, motherhood, and mockery: Psychoanalyzing culture and the Iatmul naven rite in New Guinea*. Ann Arbor: The University of Michigan Press.

Stanek, M., & F. Weiss. (1998). "Big Man" and "Big Woman"—The village elite in the town. The Iatmul, Papua New Guinea. In V. Keck (Ed.), *Common worlds and single lives: Constituting knowledge in Pacific societies* (pp. 309–327). Oxford: Berg.

Weiss, F. (1981). Kinder Schildern ihren Alltag: Die Stellung des Kindes im ökonomischen System einer Dorfgemeinschaft in Papua New Guinea (Palimbei, Iatmul, Mittelsepik) [Monograph]. *Basler Beiträge zur Ethnologie, 21*.

Weiss, F. (1983). Une fête d'enfants masqués [A festival of masked children]. In F. Lupu (Ed.), *Océanie le masque au long cours* (pp. 187–193). Rennes, France: Ouest France.

Weiss, F. (1987). Magendua. In F. Morgenthaler, F. Weiss, & M. Morgenthaler (Eds), Conversations au Bord du Flueve Mourant: Ethnopsychanalyse chez Les Iatmouls de Papouasie/Nouvelle-Guinée. Geneve: Editions Zoe.

Weiss, F. (1990). The child's role in the economy of Palimbei. In N. Lutkehaus, C. Kaufmann, W. E. Mitchell, D. Newton, L. Osmundsen, and M. Schuster (Eds.), *Sepik heritage: Tradition and change in Papua New Guinea* (pp. 337–342). Durham, NC: Carolina Academic Press.

Weiss, F. (1994). Rapports sociaux de sex et structures socio-economiques dans la société Iatmul. In F. Weiss & C. Calame (Eds.), *Rapports sociaux de sexe et cérémonie du naven chez les Iatmul de Nouvelle Guinée*. Lausanne, Switzerland: Institut d'Anthropologie et de Sociologie.

Weiss, F. (1995). Zur Kulturspezifik der Geschlechterdifferenz und des Geschlechterverhäältnisses: Die Iatmul in Papua Neuguinea. In R. Becker-Schmidt & G.-A. Knapp (Eds.), *Das Geschlechterverhältnis als Gegenstand der Sozialwissenschaften*. Frankfurt—Main, Germany: Campus Verlag.

Weiss, F. (1997). People, not furniture: The Iatmul of Papua New Guinea. In A. von Vegesack & L. Bullivant (Eds.), *Kid size: The material world of childhood* (pp. 129–139). Milan, Italy: Skira.

Ifugao

Lynn M. Kwiatkowski

ALTERNATIVE NAMES

"Ifugao," translated as "hill (or mountain) people" (Barton, 1930/1978) is the term used to denote the ethnolinguistic group of people whose ancestors are from the area that, since 1966, has been designated as the national political unit of Ifugao Province. Ifugao additionally refers to the set of languages spoken by Ifugao people, of which there are three major dialect clusters (Conklin, 1980). Ifugao languages are part of the Austronesian/Malayo-Polynesian language group, and they are not written languages. Prior to and during the Spanish colonization of Ifugao, people living in the area now designated as Ifugao territory did not conceive of themselves as belonging to one cohesive ethnolinguistic group. Instead, district or village names, such as Alimit, Kiangan, Mayoyao, and Banaue, served as the markers of identity and territory, which are still recognized today (Dumia, 1979). The name Ifugao was a term borrowed by the Spanish from lowland Gaddang and Ibanag groups (Conklin, 1980). *Pugao* is another term that was historically used to refer to "Ifugaoland," and other variations of the word Ifugao currently in use are Ifugaw and Ipugaw (Barton, 1930/1978; Conklin, 1980). Spanish colonizers generically labeled all Cordilleran mountaineers, who were generally uncolonized by the Spanish (including Ifugaos), as *Igorots*, meaning "mountain people," though Ifugao people have not fully identified with this name (Barton, 1930/1978; Conklin, 1980; Dumia, 1979).

LOCATION

The Ifugao are one among approximately eight major ethnolinguistic groups living in the Gran Cordillera Central mountain range of northern Luzon Island of the Philippines. The Cordillera mountains lie on the western central portion of Luzon Island, with Ifugao being located on the eastern side of the mountain range (Conklin, 1980). According to the Philippine government census in 2000, 161,623 people live in Ifugao Province, the great majority of whom are of Ifugao ancestry. Ifugao shares a border with the upland provinces of Benguet and Mountain Province, and the lowland provinces of Isabella and Nueva Vizcaya, allowing for easy access to lowland communities and cultures. Ifugao is considered a remote province, as most areas of the province are only accessible by footpath.

CULTURAL OVERVIEW

Ifugao culture has developed historically in relation to the ecological setting of the Ifugao mountainous landscape. Swidden agriculture and wet-rice cultivation on terraced mountainsides are the two main economic activities of Ifugao people, with approximately 75% laboring as farmers. Ifugao is known internationally for its grand rice terraces, which grace the steep mountainsides. The main staple crops produced are rice and root crops, usually sweet potato tubers. Vegetables are also cultivated on the swidden fields, in and around the wet-rice fields, and, more recently, in Western-style home gardens. Farmers also raise fruit trees and plants, and gather wild fruit, vegetables, and insects in the forests for consumption. Agricultural labor is carried out by family groups, except during labor-intensive planting and harvesting periods when community-wide cooperative labor is reciprocated, or paid in kind with bundles of rice or cash. Historically, animals were hunted in the forests, though hunting is no longer viable as a significant source of food and income. Small-animal husbandry is an important source of protein. Ifugao farmers also manage family-owned forests. Other significant economic activities in the contemporary period are marketing, tourism-related employment, craft production, wage labor, and government employment. Many Ifugao people have migrated to areas outside the province and country to acquire land or gain more profitable employment.

Trade with upland, lowland, and coastal ethnolinguistic groups, as well as with Chinese and Japanese traders, has influenced Ifugao culture for several centuries. Ifugao relationships with upland and lowland groups also included periodic raids, involving headhunting and slave capturing expeditions—activities that were curtailed during the 20th century. The Ifugao area was contacted by the Spanish at least as early as the 18th century, and was visited more frequently by Spanish colonizers and missionaries beginning in the early 19th century. Historically, while the Spanish had tried to penetrate and control Ifugao, as well as other upland territories in the Cordillera Mountain region, they were not highly successful (Conklin, 1980). This allowed for the Ifugao people's greater retention of indigenous beliefs, practices, and forms of social organization by the 20th century. American colonizers administered Ifugao for almost 40 years, beginning in 1903, and had an important impact on Ifugao culture, especially economics, political organization, religion, and education. Japanese soldiers occupied Ifugao during World War II. With national independence in 1946, Ifugao was integrated into the national economy and political culture.

Kinship in Ifugao is bilateral, and kinship relationships created out of consanguineal ties form the most important social bonds for Ifugao people. Other important social bonds are derived from friendship ties based on propinquity, patron–client relationships, and other debt relationships (Conklin, 1980). The nuclear family was historically the most basic and smallest social unit, averaging about six to eight members.

Further social organization was traditionally based on hamlets, which are clusters of homes located near agricultural fields. Irrigation groups managing irrigation systems within the hamlets are also important social groups in local communities. The largest recognized form of traditional social organization are agricultural districts, which are composed of several hamlets that center around the first rice field to have been cultivated in the district, usually owned by a traditionally wealthy person and leader, the *tomona* (Conklin, 1980). Today the Ifugao are also incorporated into the national system of political administration. A group of *barangay*s are organized into municipalities. Ifugao Province, composed of 11 municipalities, is part of the Cordillera Autonomous Region, which administers Ifugao Province along with the national government.

Ifugao traditionally had no system of government, yet they developed an extensive set of laws that were based on taboo and custom and linked to the Ifugao religion. Legal procedures were carried out by and between families, usually with the assistance of a mediator, the *monkalun* (Barton, 1919/1969). The *tomona* continues to serve as a district agricultural leader. Historically, traditionally wealthy owners of wet-rice fields, or *kadangyan*, were considered to be community political and social leaders, who acquired their position through birthright, possession of property, and the performance of specified rituals (Scott, 1982; Brosius, 1988). *Barangay* captains, municipal mayors and councillors, and a provincial governor and board members make up the contemporary official leadership of the province. Today, the Ifugao are also subject to national and local government laws and judicial system.

Ifugao religion, *baki*, combines polytheism, mythology, magic, and animism. Religious beliefs and ritual are integrated into important aspects of everyday life. Ancestor worship is an integral part of the Ifugao religion, playing a central role in Ifugao religious ritual. Catholicism and Protestant religions have had a tremendous impact on Ifugao religious practice and beliefs, with 80% of Ifugaos identifying as Christian by the 1990s. However, most Christians still participate in Ifugao religious rituals.

CULTURAL CONSTRUCTION OF GENDER

Ifugao men (*lala-ee*) and women (*bfwabfwa-ee*) are culturally viewed as distinct from and complementary to each other. Traditional modes of dress specific to each are made from fabric woven by Ifugao women with yarn. Women wear skirts that reach from their waists to their knees (*torkay* or *tapis*), and men wear loincloths (*wanoh*) (Barton, 1919/1969). The woven designs of the clothing are gender specific, as well as evocative of Ifugaos' village and social class identities. Men historically carried a spear with them whenever they traveled from their homes. Male farmers typically wear a machete, or *bolo*, on their belt. Both men and women traditionally adorned themselves with gold neck ornaments and earrings, bead necklaces and hair ties, especially amber-colored glass beads, mother of pearl, brass ornaments, and feathers. Historically, some wore tattoos and filed and/or blackened their teeth as a mark of beauty. *Kadangyan* men and women wore special clothing and ornamentation, indicating their higher status. Men's hair was traditionally styled in a rounded cut above their ears, and women's hair was grown long, but pulled up and tied on top of their heads with strings of beads or a piece of cloth. Historically, some men wore headdresses at ritual events (Barton, 1930/1978). With modernization processes and the introduction of Christianity during the 20th century, many Ifugao men and women wear Western clothes specific to each gender, with women dressing in a conservative manner. Most young women wear a Western shirt above their *torkay*. Shorts and pants have replaced the *wanoh* for many men. Hairstyles also conform more to currently fashionable Western styles for men and women of different age groups. However, many farmers over 40 years retain the traditional style of dress.

The significance of men and women relating to each other as husband and wife, and the importance of reproduction through their relationship, is given expression in the popular Ifugao oral history about the first Ifugao who populated the Ifugao territory following a massive flood. An Ifugao woman, *Bugan*, and her brother, *Wigan* (or other names), were the sole survivors of the flood. While sexual relations between siblings are forbidden in contemporary society, *Bugan* and *Wigan* conceived a number of children, who later conceived more children who populated Ifugao.

Today, what could be conceived of as new third-gender categories are recognized to some degree among Ifugao people. Men who behave in a feminine manner, engage in both male and female activities, but still dress as males, and, in some cases, are assumed to have a same-sex sexual orientation are referred to as *bakla*, a Tagalog term for a male transvestite. Women who behave in a masculine manner, engage in both female and male activities, sometimes dress in Western male clothing, and, in some cases, are also assumed to have a same-sex sexual orientation, are referred to as "tomboys," derived from the English term.

While physical beauty is an admired attribute, it is not one demanded of Ifugao women. A female marriage partner is most valued for her ability to work hard, particularly in agricultural labor for farmers.

GENDER OVER THE LIFE CYCLE

Socialization of Boys and Girls

Ifugao boys and girls are reared similarly through infancy and childhood. Markers of gender difference are typically hairstyles, cutting boys' hair short and leaving girls' hair

long, and dress, with boys wearing shorts and shirts, and girls wearing dresses as well as shorts and shirts. Both infant boys and girls are provided with a *baki* ritual named *bagor* soon after birth, to introduce them to the spiritual beings. Christian Ifugao may also, or only, have their infant children baptized in a Catholic church or participate in a Protestant dedication ritual. Ifugao conduct a *baki* ritual when naming their children. One early rite of passage in which only boys participate is the first cutting of their hair, which includes a *baki* religious ritual and feast (Barton, 1911).

Ifugao "native" houses are one-room wooden structures, with a loft for storage of domestic goods and rice, built on four stilts. Traditionally, beginning at the age of 3 or 4, children slept in a dormitory, located in the houses of widowed women or in empty houses. Boys and girls could sleep together in the girls' dormitory, as long as they avoided their relatives of the opposite sex. The boys' dormitory was limited to boys and young bachelors (Barton, 1930/1978, 1938/1979). Today, dormitories still house children, and an older chaperone usually sleeps with them.

Young boys and girls play together within the area near their homes, with toys fashioned from local materials. Boys practice playing gongs, an important musical instrument played by men during ritual and secular feasts, at a young age.

Young boys and girls are expected to care for younger siblings while their parents work, sometimes as early as age 5. They are also taught to carry out simple tasks at a young age, such as fetching water and carrying small amounts of firewood. As they grow older, boys tend to have more freedom than girls to roam the *barangay*, visiting relatives and friends, and exploring the forest. Since girls begin to learn domestic labor at an early age, such as cooking, hand-washing clothes, and pounding the husks off rice kernels, they are more restricted to the household than boys. As boys grow older, approximately 7–10 years old, they begin to spend more time with their fathers, learning about the labor of men in their community, such as preparing rice fields, plowing, fishing, etc., though boys also learn to perform some domestic chores such as pounding rice and cooking. As girls grow older, also approximately 7–10 years old, they begin to learn some of their mother's tasks in agricultural fields.

Both girls and boys are equally valued as children, as each perform different roles that are helpful to parents. Parents value initiative, particularly in labor, in both boys and girls, but they expect girls to be more reserved and remain closer to home, and boys to be more assertive and explore their larger community. Most boys and girls acquire some formal education.

Puberty and Adolescence

The onset of puberty is marked mainly by physiological changes that the boys and girls undergo, including their emerging sexuality, and by new labor responsibilities for their families. During puberty, most children decide whether to terminate their formal education during elementary school, or to continue their education through secondary school. Many poor Ifugao children become full-time laborers at this time, working with their natal families. Most who choose to attend secondary school must usually move from their family's home to attend one of the few distant high schools within each municipality. The students live either in school dormitories, or with relatives or other family friends, often while working as domestic laborers for them. Through formal education, young men and women learn modern Filipino and Western ways of thinking and behaving, providing socialization beyond that offered by their parents and relatives. While in the past century more young men attended secondary school than young women, the rates of the latter attending secondary school have increased.

With puberty, young women and men emerge into a period of sexual development and interest. Both tend to become more interested in beautifying themselves, wearing stylish jewelry, clothing, and haircuts.

Labor expectations for young women and men are greatly increased with adolescence. Young girls are expected to be proficient and industrious at domestic labor, including cooking, pounding rice, cleaning, weaving, and hand-washing clothes. Young women also participate in agricultural labor, either full time or part time if they are attending school. The workload for young men is less demanding on a daily basis, though they are expected to gather and carry firewood, fish, feed domestic animals, and carry out agricultural labor and, for some, craft production. Sibling relationships are very significant, as elder adolescent siblings must care for their younger siblings.

Attainment of Adulthood

Transition to adulthood usually entails becoming engaged and marrying, between the ages of about sixteen to the early twenties. With adulthood, both men and women are expected to be serious and responsible in their full-time work inside and outside their homes, to provide well for their families, to move into their own home, and to begin to sponsor rituals expected of families, either *baki* or Christian. Having children confers greater responsibilities for men and women, as well as more social esteem and recognition as adults. Adult elder siblings are responsible for providing emotional and financial support to their younger siblings. Attending college as a single person can also confer adulthood, since college students are viewed as being engaged in a serious professional pursuit as well as living on their own. A person who does not marry but takes on adult work responsibilities, and, for some women, has a child, is also recognized as an adult. While Ifugao adults typically establish their own families, they are expected to request and usually follow the advice of their parents throughout their adult lives.

Middle Age and Old Age

Age ranking is an important feature of Ifugao culture. Therefore, with middle age comes increased respect and responsibility for both men and women. Men, more than women, are expected to contribute to community leadership, though women contribute to this as well.

Middle-aged adults must care for their elderly parents. Many older women and men must work, or choose to work, as long as they are physically capable of doing so, regardless of their social class position. Many elderly women suffer from severe osteoporosis, which results in their being bent almost horizontally. Yet, even many of these women continue to engage in agricultural labor (Hewner, 2001). Older women, more so than older men, care for their grandchildren while the children's parents are working. For poor widows, middle and old age can entail greater respect, but also a period of increased poverty, since women generally earn lower wages than men.

PERSONALITY DIFFERENCES BY GENDER

Generally, boys are culturally expected to be more active and aggressive than girls. Men are expected to be more proficient at oration than women, and therefore generally appear to be more expressive in leadership roles at social gatherings than women. Women are expected to repress their anger, and instead cooperate with other family and community members, although in practice some women do express their anger. Women and men are expected to rely on each other, particularly because of their complementary labor, but not to be dependent on one other.

GENDER-RELATED SOCIAL GROUPS

Historically, men participated in a separate group or club, where men would socialize, though men's clubs are no longer formed (Barton, 1930/1978). Peer groups, referred to as *barkadas*, are often sex specific. Residence for married couples is usually ambilocal, with a couple living in the community of either the husband's or the wife's family. Recently increasing rates of out-migration due to population growth and limited employment opportunities has altered this pattern of residence. Most agricultural work is carried out in sex-specific groups, as are some other types of work (i.e., drivers and mechanics are male, and midwives are female). Some Christian religious groups are sex specific. Most other aspects of Ifugao social structure are not male or female oriented.

GENDER ROLES IN ECONOMICS

Ifugao farmers are almost equally male and female. Male farmers traditionally construct and maintain rice fields, plow rice fields (except in the Kiangan area), carry loads of harvested rice from fields to homes, raise and catch fish, hunt, trap, engage in carpentry work and forestry, care for domestic animals, and collect and chop wood. Some men carve wood to make crafts, and smith iron. Historically, men also engaged in pot-making, warfare, headhunting, revenge murder, and capturing and selling slaves. Men also serve as mediators, or "go-betweens" to aid in dispute settlements or transactions between families. Female farmers prepare rice seedlings, weed rice fields, plant and harvest rice, carry harvested rice to homes from fields, raise vegetables, sell food they have cultivated, collect fire wood, and weave. Women's agricultural work involves extensive stooping, probably playing a role in the severe bending of their spines with osteoporosis. Women also engage in weaving, sanding and, less, carving of wood, and other forms of handicraft production. Both men and women perform domestic labor, with women taking on the majority, especially managing finances, cooking, washing clothes, and pounding rice. These gender divisions of labor are typically adhered to, except in special cases that are well accepted, such as widowhood, illness of a spouse, divorce, single-parenthood, single adult status, or migration of a spouse.

Both men and women obtain property, including rice fields, parents' houses, heirlooms, and personal property from their parents, with no distinction being made because of their gender. Property is obtained through assignment while the parents are alive and by inheritance (Barton, 1919/1969). Sibling relationships are based on a system of primogeniture, which also influences patterns of property assignment and inheritance (Barton, 1919/1969; Conklin, 1980). With primogeniture, the largest proportion of property is assigned to the eldest child, and the remaining property assigned proportionally by age rank to younger children. Only wealthy families can provide rice fields to all of their children (Barton, 1919/1969). When children marry and establish a new home, they receive the assigned property from their parents. Married men and women each retain ownership of their own agricultural land and other heirlooms, but jointly own property purchased after marriage. Property is provided from both, or either, father or mother.

Both men and women create and work in swidden fields, raise vegetables in a garden, feed domesticated animals, make baskets, gather wild food, and fetch water. Both have traditionally worked as short- and long-term migrant laborers, either within the Philippines or internationally, due to differential planting and harvesting times in various Philippine provinces, low wage rates, and high levels of unemployment. But more men than women work as short-term migrant laborers, usually during periods of low agricultural labor in their home regions, ranging from a few weeks or months, leaving women to manage their households during these periods. Some men are military soldiers or work on international ships, leaving wives for long periods of time. Married women also work abroad for periods of 2–10 years, usually those with school-age or adult children. Mainly men work as short-term manual laborers on government projects, though some women also do; both make handicrafts; and women wash clothes for other families. Women have traditionally dominated in marketing, working as traders, and as business owners (Barton, 1919/1969; Milgram, 2000, 2001a,b). Women also dominate the professions, yet most women are low-salaried teachers and nurses. Positions of power, such as government officials, executives, managers, managing proprietors, and supervisors, are predominantly held by men.

PARENTAL AND OTHER CARETAKER ROLES

Children's major caretakers are their parents, and older siblings care for children as well. While both men and women are nurturing toward their children, women are viewed as naturally nurturing, and men are often criticized for being less attentive to their children's needs. Mothers are the primary childcare providers. This is viewed as a natural role for women due to their ability to breastfeed children, their greater patience with and attentiveness to children, a higher value being placed on men's labor outside of the home, and the idea that children naturally feel closer to their mother. Still, fathers play an important role in childcare, particularly when they do not have work demands and their wife is working. While parents raise all of their children, they each emphasize socializing and educating those of their own sex to fulfill their appropriate gender role. Mothers spend a greater amount of time with young children than fathers.

Both mothers and fathers easily publicly display physical affection and love toward their young children. However, physical expressions of love are uncommon between parents and their adolescent and adult children. Grandmothers, aunts, and female neighbors also sometimes care for young children while their parents are working.

LEADERSHIP IN PUBLIC ARENAS

Leadership in the wider community historically and today has been dominated by men, although leadership has never been strictly restricted to men, except in warfare. The traditional community leaders, the *tomona* and a number of wealthy and powerful *kadangyan*, were a group of persons who had influence but no actual authority or power over other Ifugao people. Women historically participated in militarily defending their communities, but did not travel to engage in warfare or headhunting. Headhunting success, to which women did not have access, accorded power and leadership to an

individual. This has changed today, with some Ifugao women participating as soldiers in the military wing of the communist New People's Army. Female official political leadership is increasing today, with women having equal authority with men in the same positions, but the great majority of *barangay*, municipal, provincial, and national political leaders are men. Men are perceived to have naturally superior oratory skills, believed to be necessary for successful leadership. Women typically exert leadership in the areas of business, healthcare, education, and social work. Religious leadership involves both men and women, with male leaders having a higher status in the *baki* and Catholic religions, and male and female leaders having generally equal status in Protestant religions.

GENDER AND RELIGION

Historically, all men became *baki* priests, or *mumbaki*, but only certain men do so today, likely due to the influence of modern ideologies and Christianity (Barton, 1940). *Mumbaki* lead *baki* ritual ceremonies, reciting the names of gods, other spiritual beings, and ancestral spirits, reciting myths, becoming possessed by the spiritual beings, and making offerings to them. *Mumbaki* also perform divination rituals. The rituals are performed for most significant life events and practices.

Mama-o, or *baki* female priestesses, play important roles in ritual practice, particularly that of diviners and spirit mediums. They also pray during some *baki* rituals, sometimes in a separate location from the *mumbaki*. While the *mama-o*'s role is complementary to the *mumbaki*'s, women's role in the *baki* religion is more limited than men's. *Mama-o* are highly respected as religious leaders, but a higher status is usually accorded to the *mumbaki*. Boys and girls learn to become *baki* leaders by observation during ritual ceremonies and through apprenticeship, often from their father or mother. If a *mumbaki* has no sons, in some cases he may teach his daughter to become a *mumbaki*. Almost equal numbers of men and women attend *baki* rituals. Exceptions are during the harvest feast, at which men are the primary participants since most women are in the fields harvesting rice, and when women are caring for small children. Male and female participants have different roles to play during *baki*, specific to the type of ritual being performed.

Catholic doctrine allows only men to become priests and only women to become nuns. Protestant religious leaders are male and female, though fewer are female in Ifugao. Men and women participate in Christian religious services, prayer sessions, and rituals, some of which take on aspects of the structural form of the *baki* ritual.

The pantheon of the *baki* religion consists of more than a thousand male and female gods, other male and female spiritual beings, and ancestor spirits (Barton, 1940; Lambrecht, 1962). The creator god is male and is accorded the greatest importance and status. The primary mediators between the greater god and human beings are a set of male gods, who have wives. Male and female ancestors of both husband and wife sponsoring a *baki* ritual are prayed to, and each are considered equally important, a reflection of the bilateral kinship system.

LEISURE, RECREATION, AND THE ARTS

Men tend to have more leisure time than women, in part due to women's extensive responsibilities in both the home and work place outside the home. Leisure time is spent with one's *barkada*, family members, or friends of both sexes. Sex segregation during leisure time is voluntary. Men tend to spend more money than women on leisure activities, including drinking alcohol, buying alcoholic beverages for their friends, and gambling. Fewer women than men drink beer or gin and become drunk, though women do drink rice wine at rituals and secular feasts. People commonly meet friends of the same sex at a *sari sari*, or small store, to socialize, snack, and drink soft drinks, or beer for men. While males and females listen to music broadcast on radios, adolescent girls especially enjoy radio soap operas. Women occasionally cook special sweet treats during their leisure time that they share with other family and community members.

RELATIVE STATUS OF MEN AND WOMEN

Traditionally, no Ifugao person had authority over another (Barton, 1919/1969). Yet, in everyday social relations, people are ranked according to relative status levels associated with wealth, age, kinship group, religious affiliation, occupation, educational level, and,

historically, warfare and headhunting prowess. Power and prestige is most strongly determined by wealth, particularly, traditionally, ownership of rice fields and the ability to eat rice throughout the year, and, more recently, accumulation of money and other forms of capital (Brosius, 1988). Gender status relations are also constructed in relation to these status categories. Ifugao women's and men's status is situationally variable, depending on the men and women involved, the social position of each, and the kind of status being considered. But in some very important social arenas, especially economic, political, and domestic, the majority of women experience lesser power in gender relations.

For example, Ifugao women maintain autonomy in their work, as they are viewed as holding special knowledge and skills required for their labor. Yet, women's labor in a number of areas, including agriculture, wage labor, and some professional labor, is paid less than men's. Men are viewed as performing more difficult and demanding work than women, resulting in what is also perceived to be a traditional differential pay rate. There are exceptions, as some women are very successful businesswomen, or professionals whose wages are higher than that of many men, or are members of wealthy families (Milgram, 2001a).

There are situations in which women's status can surpass that of particular men. For example, since children acquire property from their parents through a system of primogeniture, the eldest sibling, male or female, who acquires the greatest amount of property and wealth is usually considered to be the family leader, counsellor, and advocate (Barton, 1919/1969). Upper-class women's status position is higher than that of lower-class men's, and older women are highly respected by younger men. Male and female *kadangyan* and *tomona* are regularly consulted, and the *tomona*'s agricultural decision-making for the village is usually unquestioned.

Men generally turn most of their earnings over to their wives, who manage the family's finances, but spouses do not spend the other's earnings freely. The majority of husbands and wives share decision-making in family matters, and each participate in the decisions of their own kin group. Many women feel pressured by their husbands to refrain from using contraception and to have intercourse when they would prefer not to. Women and men participate in religious practices and become educated to the extent that they each choose to.

SEXUALITY

Ifugao men and women perceive sexuality to be a natural aspect of married life, one that brings pleasure to both men and women, as well as the ability to reproduce and generate a family. Traditionally, children were sexually free. Sexuality was accepted among young, unmarried women and men, with couples sometimes sleeping together in the dormitories for the unmarried. Yet young women had to show a good amount of modesty and indifference prior to acceding to a suitor's advances (Barton, 1930/1978). This ideology has generally continued today. Women conceiving children out of wedlock is not uncommon, with a resolution being marriage if the couple agrees. Single mothers are well accepted and integrated into the community, though they often experience economic hardship. Traditionally, children were regularly conceived during a long engagement period, while a couple were living together, sometimes with their in-laws or parents, and collecting the resources needed to finance the marriage ceremonies.

Men are generally viewed as having a greater interest in sexual relations than women, and are accorded greater license to engage in sexual activity prior to and during marriage. However, adultery is not well accepted or widespread. Historically, a person could be killed for committing adultery by the offended spouse. More often a fine was required, and divorce would often occur, particularly if the offended spouse was the man because of his jealously and lesser attachment to his wife. Women usually did not want to learn of their adulterous husband's affairs, in order to be exempt from grieving the adultery. Rape, involving spouses, acquaintances, and strangers, is uncommon in Ifugao, along with incest, although incidences of each have occurred there, historically and in recent years (Barton, 1919/1969). Gang rape of a captured enemy woman was sometimes a part of warfare, believed to bring about a good harvest and fertility of domestic animals (Barton, 1930/1978). A small number of Ifugao women work as prostitutes, the practice having begun during the Spanish colonial period, but most commonly work outside Ifugao in nearby urban areas or Manila (Barton, 1930/1978). A small proportion of Ifugao men hire prostitutes.

Both Ifugao men and women are modest in terms of their bodies, according to Ifugao cultural conceptions of traditional or modern conceptions of modesty, both of which include covering the genitals. Only youths who have lived in urban areas express physical affection toward the opposite sex in public, although this is very common among persons of the same sex. A married woman must be very modest around men other than her husband, lest other people suspect an adulterous relationship.

There is general acceptance of persons having alternative genders (*bakla* and "tomboys") and same-sex sexual orientations, although there is no tradition of these forms of gender and sexuality in Ifugao. Cross-dressing in a Western style is more typical of women than men within Ifugao, as women wearing pants and a male-style shirt are more readily accepted than men wearing a skirt or dress.

COURTSHIP AND MARRIAGE

Marriage is anticipated for all Ifugao people, and the great majority do marry, although marriage is not necessarily expected of *baklas* and "tomboys" today. The duration of a marriage union is undefined, except for Christian marriages which are expected to be lifelong. Polygyny and concubinage were practiced historically in Ifugao, but only among the very wealthy men, the *kadangyan*. The first wife held a higher status than the succeeding wives (Barton, 1919/1969). Monogamy was the norm among other men and women. Polygyny is only practiced informally by a small number of men today, who legally marry one woman and have relationships with one or more other partners. In these modern cases, the women have an antagonistic relationship with each other. This form of marriage and partnership is not highly accepted, as monogamy is the legal and cultural norm today.

Children of the *kadangyan* were historically married at a very early preadolescent age, or even engaged while *in utero*, to a child of another *kadangyan* family through an arrangement made by their parents, with property assignment having been made at that time. This avoided what would be deemed an inappropriate marriage in the future, and created alliances with other wealthy kin groups. For less wealthy families and the younger children of more wealthy families, romance, courtship and premarital sex more commonly led to their deciding independently to marry, at any age. The consent of parents was not required. Today, couples freely choose their spouses. Marriage between siblings and first cousins is tabooed, and historically the marriage of cousins within the third degree was tabooed, but could be overcome (Barton, 1919/1969).

Courtship historically involved visitations to the dormitories by adolescent boys and young men, who played a "lover's harp" and chanted spontaneous romantic phrases, which were similarly responded to by girls or young women (Barton, 1930/1978). Sexual relations often followed a long courtship. Adolescent girls and young women could accept or reject the advances of the suitor, but only accept one suitor at a time. This restriction was looser for young men. Today, young men and women usually socialize and "date" together within a group of peers, and they occasionally meet alone. Courtship sometimes still involves singing modern songs to one's love interest.

There is no traditional religious consecration of the marriage; instead marriages were seen to be civil unions, as well as trial marriages. But *baki* rituals were celebrated throughout the marriage process to ensure prosperity and children for the couple. To initiate the marriage and establish the engagement, a distant relative or friend of the man brought betel nut to the woman's parents to ask for permission to marry her. Four *baki* ceremonies and gifts from the groom's family to the bride's kin were required to fulfill a marriage process. In some Ifugao areas, these involved the groom's family sending one pig for each ceremony to the girl's family, who performed a *baki* ritual and read the bile of a pig to uncover a good or bad omen. The girl's family usually returned smaller gifts to the boy's family (Barton, 1919/1969). These practices varied by economic group and village, and continue to be practiced by some Ifugao people today. For Christian couples today, a Christian ceremony is performed to religiously consecrate a marriage, followed by a secular feast, traditional or modern music, dancing, and gift giving. Ultimately, marriage is viewed primarily as an alliance, wherein spouses' ties to their own kin group remain stronger than their marital ties (Barton, 1919/1969).

Widows and widowers can remarry any nonkin person. But they should wait for a period of a year from the death of the spouse, and they or their future spouse must make a payment to their dead spouse's family to officially terminate the marriage (Barton, 1919/1969).

HUSBAND–WIFE RELATIONSHIP

Husbands and wives generally have respectful, warm, and loving relationships, and they relate to each other as companions. Spouses rarely show affection or touch each other in public. Husbands and wives usually eat their morning and evening meals together, but often eat their lunch apart from each other owing to their busy work schedules. They sleep together, with their infant children in the same one-room house, unless they live in a larger "modern house" and sleep with all their children in the home. Generally, men are expected to perform a dominant role in the household, as the "head of the household." In practice, though, many couples participate equally in domestic decision-making. Men and women can each perform all domestic tasks, yet most of the burden of domestic labor rests with women. Wife-battering and marital rape are rare in Ifugao, although there have been cases of each. Historically, if a couple wished to divorce, either a man or a woman could initiate the divorce, and a *baki* ritual would be performed for this event (Barton, 1919/1969). Divorces were common and easy, and a divorced couple could remarry, but not marry their original spouse (Barton, 1919/1969). With the domination of Catholicism in much of Philippine national law, divorce is currently illegal, restricting Ifugao spouses from legally divorcing. Instead, given the historical acceptance of divorce, a couple may separate, initiated by either the husband or wife, and enter a new committed relationship that resembles a marital relationship. A couple is not required to meet specific standards of reasons for separation today, but historically there were approximately 22 justifications for divorce (Barton, 1930/1978). Children usually remain with their mother upon a couple's separation, although this is not a strict rule. Historically, women had the right to keep the couple's children after divorce, though the husband could raise one or more of their children through a special agreement (Barton, 1919/1969).

CHANGE IN ATTITUDES, BELIEFS, AND PRACTICES REGARDING GENDER

As discussed above, traditional Ifugao attitudes, beliefs, and practices are changing, including those associated with gender, as Ifugao people become more solidly integrated into the global capitalist market, experience increased international and national development, and migrate outside Ifugao. The Philippine women's movement entered Ifugao in the 1980s, and has had some, albeit minor, impact on women's gender ideologies. For example, some women have begun contesting the unequal pay rates in Ifugao agricultural and other types of labor. However, fundamentalist Christian ideologies are also increasingly permeating Ifugao culture, offsetting ideas of gender equality promoted by the women's movement. International development projects have often effected the reinforcement or decrease of women's already lower gender status in economic, political, and domestic arenas (Kwiatkowski, 1998; McKay, 1995). Likely, there will be greater variability in gender conceptions among Ifugao people in the future as a result of these outside influences.

REFERENCES

Barton, R. F. (1911). The harvest feast of the Kiangan Ifugao. *Philippine Journal of Science, 6*, 81–103.

Barton, R. F. (1940). Myths and their magic use in Ifugao. *Philippine Magazine, 37*, 348, 351.

Barton, R. F. (1969). *Ifugao law*. Berkeley: University of California Press. (Original work published 1919.)

Barton, R. F. (1978). *The half-way sun*. New York: Brewer & Warren. (Original work published 1930.)

Barton, R. F. (1979). *Philippine pagans: The autobiographies of three Ifugaos*. London: George Routledge. (Original work published 1938.)

Brosius, J. P. (1988). Significance and social being in Ifugao agricultural production. *Ethnology, 27*(1), 97–110.

Conklin, H. C. (1980). *Ethnographic atlas of Ifugao: A study of environment, culture, and society in northern Luzon*. New Haven, CT: Yale University Press.

Dumia, M. A. (1979). *The Ifugao world*. Quezon City, Philippines: New Day.

Hewner, S. J. (2001). Postmenopausal function in context: Biocultural observations on Amish, neighboring non-Amish, and Ifugao household health. *American Journal of Human Biology, 13*, 521–530.

Kwiatkowski, L. (1998). *Struggling with development: The politics of hunger and gender in the Philippines*. Boulder, CO: Westview Press.

Lambrecht, F. (1962). The religion of the Ifugao. *Philippine Sociological Review, 10*(1–2), 33–40.

McKay, D. (1995). Gender, trees, and tenure: Land-use priorities in an indigenous upland community—Ifugao, Philippines. *Journal of Business Administration, 22–23*, 143–156.

Milgram, B. L. (2000). Reorganizing textile production for the global market: Women's craft cooperatives in Ifugao, upland Philippines. In K. M. Grimes & B. L. Milgram (Eds.), *Artisans and cooperatives: Developing alternative trade for the global economy* (pp. 107–127). Tucson: University of Arizona Press.

Milgram, B. L. (2001a). Situating handicraft market women in Ifugao, upland Philippines: A case study for multiplicity. In L. J. Seligman (Ed.), *Women traders in cross-cultural perspective: Mediating identities, marketing wares* (pp. 128–159). Stanford, CA: Stanford University Press.

Milgram, B. L. (2001b). Operationalizing microfinance: Women and craftwork in Ifugao, upland Philippines. *Human Organization, 60*(3), 212–224.

Scott, W. H. (1982). *Cracks in the parchment curtain and other essays in Philippine history*. Quezon City, Philippines: New Day.

Igbo

Daniel Jordan Smith

ALTERNATIVE NAME

The Igbo are also known as Ibo.

LOCATION

In contemporary Nigeria, five states (Abia, Anambra, Ebonyi, Enugu, and Imo) are almost entirely Igbo speaking, and these, along with smaller parts of several neighboring states, constitute the geographic area colloquially known as Igboland. Located in southeastern Nigeria, Igboland is characterized by a tropical climate, with regular rainfall between the months of May and October and mostly dry weather between November and April. Igboland was once covered with thick forest (especially in the southern areas), but high population densities have resulted in extensive deforestation and increasing soil erosion. With one of the highest population densities in sub-Saharan Africa, Igboland is most striking in the degree to which human activities have extended to and had significant effects in all parts of the region. Gradually, the distinction between village and small town is dissolving.

CULTURAL OVERVIEW

Igbo-speaking people are the third-largest ethnic group in Nigeria, numbering approximately 20 million. Perhaps not surprising given the large population, forms of social organization and cultural patterns vary widely across Igbo communities. Inevitably, any attempt to sketch an overview will oversimplify this variation and may appear, from the perspective of particular sections of Igboland, to be inaccurate. With this qualification, a number of cultural features are common and very significant across much of Igbo society.

Prior to British colonization, Igboland was characterized primarily by a large number of self-governing village groups. Though some of these village groups were loosely tied through trade, marriage, and alliance in warfare, in precolonial times Igboland was largely decentralized and each Igbo village group was an independent political entity. Indeed, consensus in the historical literature is that the notion of a pan-Igbo identity emerged only in the context of colonialism (Isichei, 1976). The sense of Igbos as one people was further solidified shortly after independence by the Biafran War (1967–70), during which the predominately Igbo-speaking southeast sought unsuccessfully to secede from Nigeria. A number of scholars have argued that women's political role was greater in precolonial times and that the legacy of the colonial system has continued to have negative consequences for women's status in post-independence Nigeria (Amadiume, 1987; van Allen, 1976).

In the wider Nigerian collective imagination and in scholarly literature, Igbos are perceived to be economically resourceful and successful and highly entrepreneurial (Green, 1947; Isichei, 1976). Much has been written about the Igbos' entrepreneurial spirit, their economic acumen, and their domination of certain sectors of the marketplace across Nigeria. The idea that Igbo culture is "individualistic" and achievement oriented pervades discourse among other groups in Nigeria, and is reproduced and explored in anthropology (Henderson, 1972; Ottenberg, 1971). Individual achievement is certainly highly rewarded in Igbo culture, but characterizing the society as "individualistic" misrepresents the degree to which personal success is valued most as a fulfillment of group expectations that wealth should be shared, with extended family and community of origin being the most important groups for most Igbo people.

Involvement in trade, ranging from large-scale importation of industrial commodities to the sale of goods in informal petty businesses, has contributed to a huge volume of rural–urban migration in Igbo society. At present, most Igbo communities, indeed the vast majority of Igbo households, have members who have migrated to cities and towns across Nigeria. But one of the most significant features of Igbo migration and of social organization in rural Igbo villages is the continuing tie of migrants to their communities of origin and their kinship groups (Smith, 2001a). Rural and urban Igbo communities are interdependent, with migrants and those who reside in rural villages connected to each other politically, economically, socially, and culturally. Most rural households rely on a combination of subsistence agricultural, small-scale trade, and often some wage labor and employment. In addition, many households depend on their migrant members for remittances, but also for social connections that facilitate access to resources such as education, jobs, business contracts, and government services (Smith, 2001a). Kinship in most of Igboland is reckoned patrilineally, though Igbo groups that are matrilineal and that practice double descent are well documented in the literature (Nseugbe, 1974). Even among patrilineal groups, the importance of women as daughters, wives, and mothers, and the strong ties to lineages other than an individual's own patrilineage are central to understanding the cultural construction of sex and gender in traditional Igbo society and in the present.

The proliferation of formal education, the almost universal conversion of Igbos to Christianity, and the increasing urban influence on people's lives in both rural and urban areas have had significant effects on the organization and meaning of sex and gender. Yet, perhaps obviously, contemporary trajectories of ideas and practices are very much shaped and informed by the past. The Igbo sex/gender system is complex, with gender roles often being more flexible than they appear (Amadiume, 1987), with the statuses of daughter, mother, and wife, for example, entailing quite different meanings for the same gender, and with continuous social change reorganizing the context in which beliefs and behaviors occur and are transformed.

CULTURAL CONSTRUCTION OF GENDER

Strictly speaking, Igbos recognize only two gender categories: male and female. Not only are the categories of male and female sharply distinguished, but these distinctions are manifest in a mostly sex-segregated social system (Green, 1947; Miller, 1982). The structure and character, as well as some of the contradictions, of this system are elaborated in greater detail below. However, it is important to note from the outset that conceptually strict gender categories and the largely sex-segregated social system are, in fact, more fluid in practice than they appear in ideology, particularly when gender is considered in the context of social action rather than essentialized categories. In Igbo society, for example, it is possible for women to marry wives, and daughters can undertake many of the social roles of sons, reversing the typical associations between gender categories and social position (Amadiume, 1987). However, even in cases of these social role inversions, Igbos retain durable and strict ideas about the differences between male and female. "Male daughters" and "female husbands" do not look or, in most respects, behave like men.

Though it is difficult to summarize briefly how Igbos conceptualize male and female gender, perhaps the most useful starting point is to note that the cultural construction of gender is most significantly manifest in the categories and roles of son/husband/father for men and daughter/wife/mother for women. Though certain characteristics of male and female gender connect each of these life-course stages (with men conceived of as more aggressive, independent, and publicly oriented, and women seen as more nurturing, dependent, and domestically oriented), the invocation of a life-course perspective highlights the extent to which gender is significantly tied to social context.

Dress and hairstyle are probably the most obvious culturally inscribed bodily markers of gender. Women generally grow long hair that is braided or styled and men keep short hair. Dress is more variable, but in contemporary Igboland men typically wear trousers in both traditional and Western garb and women are most likely to wear wrappers, dresses, or skirts. Women almost always pierce their ears; men do not. Features that make men and women attractive are extremely variable based on individual taste, and tastes seem to be shifting rapidly with changing fashions, but it is probably fair to say that markers of wealth, such as fine clothing and educated language, are most important.

GENDER OVER THE LIFE CYCLE

Puberty initiation rituals that used to mark the transition from childhood to adulthood for both men and women (Ottenberg, 1989) are no longer practiced in most Igbo communities. The introduction of formal education, now available to and desired for both boys and girls, has meant that school stages have become among the most important markers of life stage for children and adolescents. Most Igbo families now consider that young persons who have finished secondary school have achieved adulthood. However, traditional categories and roles of son/husband/father and daughter/wife/mother remain extremely important, and it is fair to say that, even now, marriage and parenthood mark the full attainment of personhood for both men and women. Both marriage and childbirth are celebrated with important social rituals, and though marriage ceremonies and child-naming rites are not explicitly about creating and defining gender roles, they certainly serve that function. For both men and women, the transition to elder status (not marked by any specific ritual, but usually closely associated with the achievement of grandparenthood) brings greater respect. In addition, in some ways, elder status mitigates more polarized expectations of gender roles that apply to younger people (e.g., older women are typically outspoken and older men are judicious and patient).

Socialization of Boys and Girls

Igbo people recognize that the birth of a son is extremely important for the purpose of reproducing and maintaining the patrilineage. For women, the birth of a son solidifies her place in her husband's family. Thus, in some respects, the birth of a son (especially the first son) is more eagerly anticipated than the birth of a daughter. Nonetheless, the birth a child of either sex is extremely joyful, and though boys and girls are eventually socialized quite differently, there is little sense in Igbo society that one sex is ultimately preferred over the other. In the first few years of life, socialization of boys and girls is not markedly different, with both sexes closely attached to the mother (Ottenberg, 1989). By and large, both boys and girls assist their mothers with (mostly "female") domestic tasks until at least the age of 10 or 12. However, by school age it is apparent that adults treat boys and girls quite differently and have different expectations regarding their behavior. By the time children go to school (even preschool) gendered dress is common and the use of gendered kin terms (and even playful "sexual" banter) is clearly observable. In general, boys are granted more liberties than girls, especially with regard to venturing and playing outside the domestic compound, though, as children, boys also remain very much under the strict supervision of adults.

In contemporary Igbo society, much of the way gender is socialized clearly takes place at school. Unfortunately, this aspect of gendered socialization in Igboland has not been adequately studied. It is clear, however, that school curricula and social organization are extremely gendered in Nigeria. Though both sexes attend primary school in equal proportions and girls are almost as likely as boys to go on to secondary school, the expectations of what each sex will do with his or her education are quite different.

Puberty and Adolescence

As indicated above, in most parts of Igboland initiation rituals that marked the transition from child to adult (usually occurring at or shortly after puberty) have been abandoned in the wake of formal education and conversion to Christianity. Related to the growing duration of time between puberty and marriage, the concept of adolescence seems to be of recent origin in Igboland (Ottenberg, 1989). Though gendered differences in appearance and behavior are apparent in childhood, they are more significantly marked after puberty. As young people's bodies develop and become more sexually dimorphic, cultural inscriptions of gender difference are also made more elaborate. In adolescence, relations between males and females become obviously stylized in terms of sexuality, and this emphasis on sexuality seems to be part of a process that fixes gender more rigidly. Interestingly, in many secondary schools sexual maturation is marked by relaxed rules of dress and hairstyle. For example, as they reach senior secondary school (usually around age 16), boys are allowed to wear long trousers (instead of short trousers) and girls are allowed to grow their hair.

Attainment of Adulthood

Because marriage and parenthood are the ultimate indicators of full adult status, one could argue that adulthood is being postponed to later and later ages in Igboland. Indeed, many contemporary problems of youth in Nigeria can be related to the erosion of socially sanctioned passages to adulthood, such that many young people spend up to 10 years in a kind of liminal life stage where they have the material ambitions of adults but few of the obligations and responsibilities and little of the recognition that come with marriage and parenthood.

Middle Age and Old Age

There are no universal rites marking passage to elderhood for men and women in Igboland, though many kinds of social ceremonies are related to aging. Generally, only senior men are given chiefly titles, for example, and in Igbo societies that have male age sets, the transition in age sets is a kind of marker of seniority. As mentioned above, aging seems to mitigate and even reverse some of the most dramatic differences in behavior associated with gender—such that, for example, older women become more like men in their outspokenness and irreverence, and older men become more like women in their capacity to mediate and act empathetically. Perhaps most important with regard to aging and gender is that both men and women gain increasing respect in a society that honors seniority. Yet in contemporary Igboland, where young people often question, challenge, and resist tradition, the exalted place of the elderly seems to be eroding.

PERSONALITY DIFFERENCES BY GENDER

From the perspective of non-Igbos, Igbo people, both men and women, have outgoing, even boisterous, personalities. Compared with many other ethnic groups in Nigeria, Igbos appear to be aggressive and outspoken, but also welcoming and gregarious. To a first-time observer, Igbo conversations often sound like arguments, and both men and women are quick to defend themselves against perceived slights. While it is certainly the case that children are supposed to be deferential to adults, and juniors respectful to elders throughout the life-course (regardless of gender), Igbo adults of any age are usually prepared to do verbal battle with someone they believe has failed to accord them appropriate respect or recognition. Within Igbo society, women are expected to be more deferential to men than vice versa, but the extent of this deference is variable and often minimal. It is not uncommon for Igbo women to verbally chastise Igbo men, and men often joke about what a mistake it is to vex women. Perhaps the most striking personality differences by gender are related to the importance of motherhood as the primary locus of family nurturance and affection. Though great variation characterizes men's and women's personalities, it is probably fair to say that women are generally more nurturing and affectionate, especially in relations with children.

GENDER-RELATED SOCIAL GROUPS

Numerous scholars have noted the sex-segregated nature of Igbo social organization (Green, 1947; Miller, 1982). Many social institutions are structured by gender, with men and women often participating in parallel but separate spheres. Because descent is generally reckoned patrilineally and postmarital residence is traditionally patrilocal, women's structural position vis-à-vis kinship groups changes more fundamentally than men's over the life cycle. While both men and women experience significant changes in status as they pass from son/daughter to husband/wife to father/mother to grandparent/elder, for women marriage marks a radical change that can be both empowering and problematic (Smith, 2001b). Because a woman typically moves at marriage from her own patrilineal compound/village to her husband's, she becomes, in a sense, an outsider in her married home. This is particularly the case until she gives birth to a son, and the Igbo language is replete with proverbs about a woman's precarious status as wife and the importance of parenthood in securing her position. While the status of wife is, in part, one of "stranger," the status of mother is perhaps the most valued and emotionally exalted kin position.

In precolonial patrilineal Igbo communities, men of the same lineage group constituted one of the principal structures of local political organization. Other more horizontal forms of male social organization, such as secret societies, age grades, and title societies, cut across lineages, facilitating cooperation at village and village group levels (Ottenberg, 1971). Each of these institutions was characterized by exclusive male membership, and notions of secrecy were related to the perceived power of these groups in regulating community activities—and particularly in controlling women (Ottenberg, 1989). The importance of all-male societies has waned in the postcolonial period, as forms of state authority have usurped many of their original functions, but lineage groups and village development unions remain strong institutions in most Igbo communities, with one of their chief functions now being the management of relations between village residents and their many migrant relatives (Uchendu, 1965a).

For almost every male social group there is a parallel women's group. Though women move away from their lineages at marriage, they maintain lifelong ties to their patrilineages as daughters and this relationship is formalized through daughters' associations. Contrary to what seems to be implied in some of the literature, and in contrast to implicit ideas in some Igbo (mostly men's) rhetoric about women, as daughters, most Igbo women remain vital members of their patrilineages throughout their lives and their importance is ritually marked at marriage and burial ceremonies (Amadiume, 1987). Women also belong to associations of wives in the place they marry, to women's branches of the village development unions (often in both their natal community and their postmarital place of residence), to groups of women who have married in one community but originate from the same natal community, and to savings–loan unions that can be constituted along any number of lines. The sheer number of sex-segregated social groups and the fact that men and women maintain parallel associations at almost every level is one of the most striking features of gender-related social organization in Igbo society.

GENDER ROLES IN ECONOMICS

Perhaps the most striking aspect of gender roles in economics among the Igbo is the heavy involvement of both men and women in trade. As mentioned previously, Igbos are renowned in Nigeria for being entrepreneurs—traders who dominate major sectors of the marketplace. If anything, women have a longer tradition of managing the marketplace in Igbo society, as they historically dominated trade in foodstuffs (Amadiume, 1987). While men played a role in trade even in precolonial times, it was the growth of international trade and large-scale introduction of nonagricultural (mostly imported) commodities that contributed to men's intensifying participation in trade—a change that some have argued has contributed to a decline in women's economic status (Amadiume, 1987; van Allen, 1976). However, in contemporary Nigeria, both men and women remain heavily involved in trade, and though women are still more involved in agricultural trade and men remain dominant in nonagricultural trade, huge numbers of men and women participate in every form of commerce. The degree to which the proceeds of trade are kept and managed by individual men and women, rather than pooled or handed over to a spouse, is an interesting question with no clear answer. While each sex traditionally managed the proceeds of trade independent of a

spouse, in contemporary society, with the diminution of polygyny and the emergence of more conjugal marriages, household budgets are more likely to be shared and more couples embark on joint business ventures.

Though trade is an important component of the Igbo economy even in rural communities, almost all rural households rely significantly on subsistence agriculture. Generally, men are responsible for clearing land in preparation for planting, but women undertake the bulk of agricultural labor. The rise of cassava, generally considered a woman's crop, as the staple in Igboland, replacing yam, which is clearly considered a man's crop, contributed significantly to women's increasing responsibility for agricultural subsistence. Because only men inherit land in patrilineal Igbo communities, women have access to land through their husbands, though their rights of usufruct are well established. The rights of women to land (as well as to other community entitlements) are further secured through the birth of sons, because it is through having a son that a woman can be assured that her "kitchen" inherits its share of the patrimony. The domestic division of labor is strongly gendered in Igbo households, with women (and children) being almost exclusively responsible for tasks such as food preparation, sweeping the compound, and washing clothes.

As Nigeria's economy modernizes and the division of labor becomes more specialized, modern occupations are also gendered. For example, men dominate occupations such as drivers, carpenters, and mechanics, while women fill roles such as nurses, hairdressers, and receptionists. Much of this modern gendered division of labor reflects similar patterns in industrialized societies. Extremely high levels of rural–urban migration sometimes result in women and children being left "at home" in the village while men pursue employment or business in cities. However, a more typical pattern is for husbands, wives, and children to migrate as a unit. The phenomenon of men in the city and women and children in the village is much less frequent in Igboland than has been described in other sub-Saharan African societies.

PARENTAL AND OTHER CARETAKER ROLES

Gender differences in parental roles are large and profound. In Igbo society almost all primary child-rearing responsibilities are undertaken by the mother, or by another women who acts as a social mother. The maternal role is especially pronounced during the first 4 or 5 years of a child's life, when her/his principal bond is with the mother (Ottenberg, 1989). Fathers are generally more distant figures in children's lives and are often viewed as enforcing discipline. They typically spend much less time than mothers do with children. Recently, with the rise of more conjugal marriages and somewhat more nuclear household structures (especially in cities), many younger fathers are taking a more active and overtly affectionate role in the rearing of children, but the idea that child-rearing is principally a woman's responsibility remains pervasive and influences behavior in even the most modern households. Generally boys and girls are treated quite similarly during the first few years of life, with no obvious preference by gender. Despite the widespread idea that having a male child is essential for the reproduction of the patrilineage, and for the rights and recognition that come with it, in practice girls seem to be equally welcome and valued as boys. However, beginning around the age that children go to school, there are marked differences in the way parents treat boys and girls, with girls increasingly required to carry out more domestic tasks and boys encouraged to undertake more public activities.

LEADERSHIP IN PUBLIC ARENAS

At all levels of Igbo society men dominate leadership in public arenas. Igbo men far outnumber Igbo women in positions and influence in Nigerian federal and state government institutions. While some women are elected or appointed to political office, there have been no female Igbo governors, relatively few female ministers, senators, and representatives at the federal level, and few female commissioners and other political appointees compared with males at the state level. In addition, men clearly dominate the civil service, though less dramatically than political offices. Given Nigeria's postindependence political history, it is important to note that the top posts in military are, and have always been, entirely male.

In local government, women are represented in larger numbers, as local government chairpersons and councilors. But even at the local government level, men dominate. Significantly, at the nexus between traditional community authority and the Nigerian state, where the office of *eze* (chief/king) is a legacy of the British colonial

imposition of a warrant chief system, men are in charge almost entirely. Almost every community in Igboland is ruled by a male *eze*, and most *eze*'s cabinets (the body of local influential leaders who advise him) are almost exclusively male. Typically, an *eze*'s cabinet has one woman's representative and a dozen or so men. Even at the most grassroots level, public leadership is primarily in male hands, so that village and hamlet (the smallest unit above the family/compound) headships are almost universally male in Igboland.

This male dominance of leadership in public arenas obscures two important points. First, both historical and anthropological research suggests that male dominance in the public arena may not have been as prevalent in the precolonial period (Amadiume, 1987). Some evidence suggests that the importance of female deities in traditional Igbo religion and the powerful role of women who held traditional titles associated with these deities placed women in strong positions of public leadership. Further, women's relative domination of the marketplace in the precolonial period may have afforded them more significant public roles. Second, men's monopoly of public leadership positions conceals the extent to which women influence decision-making. Particularly at local levels, through the parallel women's associations and the fact that Igbo men openly acknowledge that women must consent to any decision that is to have significant effect, women have a much greater say in the conduct of Igbo affairs than their lack of prominence in public leadership reveals. Indeed, the historical literature on the Igbo is well known for incidents where women's political action proved effective (Mba, 1982; van Allen, 1976), and anyone who has worked in Igbo communities in contemporary Nigeria has been told by male public leaders how important it is to gain women's collective cooperation. How all this must be weighed in assessing the relative status of men and women is considered further below.

GENDER AND RELIGION

More than 90% of Igbos now identify their religion as Christianity. Though men and women are Christian in almost equal proportions, women's church groups are particularly active and in many, if not most, churches women appear to dominate the everyday activities of the lay congregation. However, men control the official hierarchy of almost every (if not every) denomination.

The impact of Christianity on gender and on the relative status of men and women is a matter of considerable interest and debate. On the one hand, in traditional Igbo religion a number of important deities were considered "female", and women titleholders and priestesses sometimes wielded substantial power. The traditional conception of gods as both female and male contrasts sharply with the Christian belief in a single male god. Some scholars have argued that Christianity, in combination with colonial policies, had the effect of lowering women's status. However, Christianity's role in curtailing polygyny and in promoting more companionate models of marriage may also, arguably, have provided women with new leverage in negotiating relationships with men (Smith, 2001b). Few of the vast majority of Igbo women who are Christian would assert (or accept) that Christianity is to blame for whatever discontents they may have with their social role as women. Indeed, most Igbo women seem to view Christianity and church as a refuge from whatever else might be wrong about the world.

LEISURE, RECREATION, AND THE ARTS

As Igbo people's mode of subsistence becomes increasingly enmeshed in the larger regional and world economy, people seem to have less and less free time. Balancing the continuing demands of subsistence agriculture with involvement in trade and other demands of more urbanized or urban-like work lives means that both men and women spend a lot of time earning a living. Compared with many other parts of sub-Saharan Africa, Igboland strikes the observer as a very busy, sometimes almost frantically paced, place, though much more so in cities and towns than in rural village communities. Nonetheless, leisure and recreation, particularly time spent socializing with friends and family are important aspects of everyday life.

In rural communities men appear to have more leisure time than women because women must combine extradomestic economic work (which is often at least as intensive as men's) with the primary household duties of childcare, food preparation, sweeping, and washing clothes. Women receive significant assistance in these activities from children of both sexes, and the degree to which women manage to combine domestic chores with "leisure" activities such as socializing, singing, and

storytelling is significant. But, overall, women clearly have less pure leisure time than men. Igbo men are wont to say that women spend an inordinate amount of time gossiping, but the truth is that both sexes spend a considerable amount of leisure time talking about other people. Men are more likely to spend leisure time playing games. The board game "draughts" (checkers) is popular and men often play it in the early evening. Boys and younger men frequently play soccer. At very young ages, girls sometimes also play, but by the time children reach adolescence the games are almost always all male. Men are much more likely than women to drink beer at local bars or frequent village palm wine sellers, though not all men drink and a significant portion of Igbos who are "born-again" Christians view drinking negatively. Many women also enjoy alcohol, but women's drinking is less frequent and usually not done in public settings such as bars, though this is changing in urban settings. Like other arenas of Igbo cultural life, leisure activities tend to be sex segregated, with the exception of events like "disco" dances or public cultural performances that are enjoyed by men and women together.

RELATIVE STATUS OF MEN AND WOMEN

Considerable consensus exists in the characterization of Igbo society as largely sex segregated in terms of economic, political, and social organization, with men and women often engaging in parallel activities and associations rather than cooperating or competing in the same arenas. However, whether the Igbo sex/gender system values men and women relatively equally in their own terms, or whether this system specifically favors men, has been the subject of debate. Several scholars have argued that colonial policy and Christian missionizing had the effect of reducing women's economic and political decision-making powers by abolishing female titles associated with traditional deities, appointing all male chiefs, and moving men into the previously female-dominated marketplace (Amadiume, 1987; van Allen, 1976). In contemporary Nigeria, men clearly dominate public political decision-making and, through their control of land and ascendancy in the nonagricultural marketplace, they are in command of key economic resources. But women are by no means powerless in Igbo society. In addition to the fact that Igbos strongly value women precisely in their roles as daughters/wives/mothers—roles that are culturally celebrated rather than denigrated—the fact that Igbo women are organized collectively in associations that parallel men's organizations means that women can wield considerable collective power and often do so when they feel their interests have been compromised.

SEXUALITY

Generalizing about Igbo attitudes toward sexuality is extremely difficult because so much variation exists based on axes of diversity such as age/generation, education, socioeconomic status, religious affiliation, and degree of urban experience, but also because attitudes to sexuality are often contradictory. Broadly, Igbo attitudes about sexuality are much more restrictive for women than for men, particularly with regard to premarital and extramarital relations. With rises in the average age at first marriage over the past several decades, the length of time between sexual maturity and nuptuality has increased dramatically. Though many elders maintain an ideal that sexual intercourse should occur only after marriage (especially for women), and though the association between ideas about sexuality and beliefs about procreation/reproduction are very strong in Igbo society, for many young people premarital sexuality is linked to the construction of a modern identity (Smith, 2000). Most young Igbos, both male and female, engage in sexual relationships before marriage. Though young women's sexuality is more closely scrutinized than young men's, as long as a girl does not have a child before marriage, having had premarital sex is usually no obstacle to marriage. Within marriage, Igbos generally view regular sexual relations as healthy, and the idea that both men and women experience and are entitled to sexual pleasure is widely accepted. The gender disparity in attitudes about sexuality is most profound with regard to extramarital sexuality (Smith, 2001b). Male extramarital sexual relations are common and carry little stigma. In fact, male extramarital sexuality is often symbolically rewarded in male peer groups, particularly in urban and elite contexts. For women, extramarital sexual relations are extremely risky and heavily stigmatized. Once a woman is married, it is expected that she will remain sexually faithful to her husband.

Igbo conceptions of male and female sexuality are in many ways contradictory, especially in male discourse. Men are viewed as needing sex more than women and are supposed to be the initiators or aggressors in sexual relationships. Women are supposed to be more passive, yet the idea that women are sexually dangerous and that men can be manipulated by women's sexual power is also prevalent (Smith, 2001b). Sexual banter between men and women is relatively common, but physical modesty is expected for both men and women. The increasingly immodest dress that is becoming more popular in urban areas is viewed somewhat scandalously by elders and in village communities generally. Some scholarship suggests that precolonial Igbo society was sexually more liberal than during the colonial and early postindependence period, with children and adolescents provided socially accepted avenues for sexual experimentation and both men and women freer to take extramarital lovers (Uchendu, 1965b). In contemporary Igboland the relative taboo of open discussion of sexuality contrasts with the prevalence of nonmarital sexual relations.

Igbo society is quite striking for its lack of any overt cross-sex identification and an almost complete denial of any form of male or female homosexuality. A study of homosexuality in this strongly dual (hetero) sex society is badly needed, though it would be very difficult to undertake.

COURTSHIP AND MARRIAGE

Changes in courtship and marriage are among the most significant ongoing transformations with regard to sex and gender in Igbo society. Whereas men and women traditionally married very young and marriages were mostly arranged by the extended families of the husband and wife, in contemporary Igboland, men and women increasingly choose their own marriage partners (Smith, 2001b). Modern courtship often involves notions of love, and most young Igbos marry with the intention of remaining monogamous. In these romantically cast premarital relationships, gender dynamics are relatively egalitarian because men and women are viewed as equal partners in an individualistic (or at least dyadic) project, and the terms of the relationship are negotiated based on ideas of love, trust, and emotional intimacy. While couples themselves now frequently initiate the process that leads to marriage, once initiated, families and communities become heavily involved in both the wedding ceremonies and the marriage itself. Though polygyny was once common, relatively few people practice it today. Among young people, polygyny is almost universally rejected and fewer and fewer Igbo marriages are likely to become polygynous.

Despite these changes in patterns of courtship and in the criteria for marriage, three elements remain paramount: the social expectation that everyone must marry, the importance of marriage as an alliance between two kin groups, and the centrality of parenthood as the foundation for a successful marriage. Traditional marriage ceremonies, in which the extended families and communities of origin of both the husband and the wife participate, continue to constitute the principal rite of passage marking marriage. Though many couples now choose to be married in their Christian churches, as well as in the traditional ceremony, the traditional ceremony is obligatory, while the Christian ceremony is optional (though, for many, highly desirable). The years after marriage are characterized by great anticipation of pregnancy and childbirth, and nothing is more important in establishing the stability of a marriage than parenthood. The transformation of a couple's relationship from courtship to marriage, where the roles of mother/father and husband/wife become primary, and where many more people are socially invested in the relationship, has significant consequences for the dynamics of gender (Smith, 2001b), tying women to their roles as mothers. In general, the importance of the quality of a couple's personal/emotional relationship recedes after marriage, especially after the birth of children. In the case of the death of a spouse, the likelihood of remarriage is greatly dependent on age and whether the surviving spouse has children. Traditional practices of levirate are now mostly abandoned, and many women whose husbands die remain unmarried if they already have several children.

HUSBAND–WIFE RELATIONSHIP

The degree to which marriage relationships are characterized by love, affection, and/or companionship is highly variable, though, generally, younger couples are much more likely to emphasize these aspects of the conjugal relationship than their elders. In more traditional marriages, affection and companionship are often quite important and can become very deep over time. However, for older Igbos, the idea that a marriage relationship should be the primary locus of intimacy is much less common than among younger couples. Even in more modern marriages men and women spend a significant amount of time and find a large part of their social satisfaction in same-sex peer relationships and in interactions with a wide range of kin.

Traditionally, Igbo husbands and wives did not eat together, they had separate sleeping rooms, and most social activities were sex segregated. While this is changing in the context of more conjugal marriages (many monogamous couples, e.g, now share the same bedroom), even in relatively modern marriages, a man is more likely to eat separately from his wife and children than with them. In addition, gender roles in the household remain quite polarized, with women almost exclusively responsible for food preparation and childcare.

Bridewealth in Igboland is perhaps the highest of any ethnic group in Nigeria, and once a couple has children, there are few socially acceptable reasons to divorce. If a couple does divorce, the children of the union are generally considered to belong to the husband and his lineage. A man may legitimately seek to dissolve a marriage if his wife has been sexually unfaithful, but a woman will be on much firmer ground seeking divorce if she can show that her husband has failed to provide for her and the children. She will receive relatively little social support if she cites problems in their personal relationship or the man's infidelity. Though divorce is heavily frowned on, in urban areas it is more common now than in any recent time.

OTHER CROSS-SEX RELATIONSHIPS

Cross-sex relationships within kin groups are common and often highly affectionate. These relationships are not (or are at least rarely) sexual, but warm relationships between opposite-sex relatives of various sorts are extremely pervasive. While opposite-sex sibling relationships are sometimes competitive, by and large brothers and sisters (especially of the same mother) are close, and these relationships endure over a lifetime. As adults, siblings remain interested in and protective of each other and each other's children. In addition, cross-sex relationships between various assortments of cousins, uncles/nieces, and aunts/nephews can be extremely affectionate and are frequently characterized by some degree of sexual allusion or joking (most often on the part of the older member of the cross-sex pair and in contexts where actual sexual relations are least likely—e.g., between adult and child). The warmth that characterizes these intrakin cross-sex relationships is clearly a source of great joy and accounts, in part, for the affective attachment that Igbos feel for their kinship networks.

REFERENCES

Amadiume, I. (1987). *Male daughters, female husbands*. London: Zed Books.

Green, M. M. (1947). *Ibo village affairs*. New York: Praeger.

Henderson, R. (1972). *The king in every man: Evolutionary trends in Onitsha Ibo society and culture*. New Haven, CT: Yale University Press.

Isichei, E. (1976). *A history of the Igbo people*. New York: St. Martin's Press.

Mba, N. (1982). *Nigeria women mobilized: Women's political activity in southern Nigeria, 1900–1965*. Berkeley: Institute of International Studies, University of California.

Miller, P. (1982). Sex polarity among the Afikpo Igbo. In S. Ottenberg (Ed.), *African religious groups and beliefs: Papers in honor of William R. Bascom* (pp.79–94). Meerut, India, and Berkeley, CA: Archana and Folklore Institute.

Nseugbe, P. (1974). *Ohaffia: A matrilineal Igbo people*. Oxford: Clarendon Press.

Ottenberg, S. (1971). *Leadership and authority in an African society: The Afikpo village-group* (American Ethnological Society Monograph Series, No. 47). Seattle: University of Washington Press.

Ottenberg, S. (1989). *Boyhood rituals in an African society*. Seattle: University of Washington Press.

Smith, D. J. (2000). "These girls today *na war-o*": Premarital sexuality and modern identity in southeastern Nigeria. *Africa Today*, *47*(3–4), 98–120.

Smith, D. J. (2001a). Kinship and corruption in contemporary Nigeria. *Ethnos*, *66*(3), 344–364.

Smith, D. J. (2001b). Romance, parenthood and gender in a modern African society. *Ethnology*, *40*(2), 129–151.

Uchendu, V. (1965a). *The Igbo of southeast Nigeria*. Fort Worth, TX: Holt, Reinhart & Winston.

Uchendu, V. (1965b). Concubinage among the Ngwa Igbo of southern Nigeria. *Africa*, *35*(2), 187–197.

van Allen, J. (1976). "Aba riots" or "Igbo women's war"? Ideology, stratification, and the invisibility of women. In N. J. Hafkin & E. G. Bay (Eds.), *Women in Africa: Studies in social and economic change*. Stanford, CA: Stanford University Press.

Iranians

Mary Elaine Hegland

ALTERNATIVE NAMES

Iranians are also known as Persians.

LOCATION

A Middle Eastern and Muslim nation located in western Asia, Iran shares borders with a number of different countries. Starting with the Persian Gulf to the south and going clockwise, Iraq and Turkey lie to the west, Azerbaijan, the Caspian Sea, and Turkmenistan to the north, and Afghanistan and Pakistan to the east.

CULTURAL OVERVIEW

Only a few decades ago, Iranians engaged primarily in agriculture, trade, herding, and crafts. Local and regional political groups organized around control over land, trade wealth and opportunities, and family and kinship connections. Such connections could be through patrilateral or matrilateral lines, created partnerships, and patron–client type relations for political protection and access to means of production. Middle- and upper-class extended families typically lived in large homes with rooms arranged around a central courtyard. Members of wealthier families might have homes located near each other, and peasant and lower-class urbanites might well live with the husband's family at least for a period after marriage. Generally, wives continue to maintain close ties with their natal families. Typically, females socialized with each other, while males went off to work in fields, trade and craft shops, and to herd animals. Outside the family, the genders segregated for weddings, mourning gatherings, outings, religious rituals, and political and economic interaction.

Intent on modernizing Iran, the two Pahlavi shahs attempted to demonstrate Iranian progress and modernity through deveiling women, educating them, and bringing them into the public work force. To centralize political power, the Pahlavis squelched other power centers, such as tribes, religious leaders and organizations, and regional leaders and large landlords. In the 1960s, and even more in the 1970s, the oil boom brought urbanization, industrialization, construction, education, health services, bureaucracy, and westernization. However, the Pahlavis did not institute political liberalization and democracy. Unhappy with the pervasive influence of Western culture and what they saw as modern vulgarity, religious figures with financial support from successful merchants and business people organized to try to regain some lost power. Students and professionals, empowered by education, joined middle- and lower-class people who were influenced by the clergy and unhappy with repression and increasing extremes in wealth to bring about the Iranian Revolution of 1978 and 1979. Under the leadership of Ayatollah Khomeini and then the Islamic Republic of Iran, formed in 1979, governmental and societal gender policies changed radically. Whereas the Pahlavis had attempted to educate women and bring them into the public work world, even making veiling illegal during one period, the Shi'a clerics attempted to reverse these developments. Relying on Shar'ia (Islamic law), the Hadith (traditions of the Prophet Mohammed, provided by his followers and passed on through chains of authority), and cultural traditions, Islamic Republic officials have declared women and men to be different by nature. Men are fit for the rough and tumble of politics and economics. Women, because of their more gentle, emotional, and nurturing characters, should devote themselves to household, husband and children. In return for obedience and service, women are entitled to financial support from men. Islamic Republic clerics reversed family laws beneficial to women and enforced gender segregation and female veiling. However, the war with Iraq (1980–88), gender-segregation policies, and women's political voice forced government officials to recognize the need for a female labor force. Since 1979, in the political competition among Islamists, secularists, and modernists, women and gender have been a focus of contention.

CULTURAL CONSTRUCTION OF GENDER

In Iran, the two gender categories of male and female are recognized. The term *hamjens parast*, or those who are sexually involved with the same sex, refers to homosexuals, but they are nevertheless seen as males and females. Eunuchs likewise were seen as males, but as males unable to procreate. In Iranian Muslim culture, males are seen as stronger, intelligent, wiser, virile, able to control their emotions, just and moral, and fit to handle political and economic affairs. Women are seen as weaker, emotional, susceptible to the pull of personal ties, nurturing, and unable to control their sexuality. Males used the perception of women as weak and foolish as a rationale to forbid them to gain literacy, education, and employment. Men often see women as a whole as manipulative, conniving, and unreliable. However, many men think very highly of their mothers, feel great affection for their sisters, and rely upon their wives. Women often see men as aloof, unable to control their anger, sexually promiscuous, and socially less competent. Because women are viewed as strongly sexed and unable to contain themselves sexually, they are required to veil in order to avoid arousing men sexually, thus leading to family and societal instability.

Iranian men wore a form of trousers, and women wore long skirts over loose trousers and a scarf, although men often also wore ethnic or regional hats. Affluent men could afford to veil and seclude their womenfolk at home, thus demonstrating their status. However, hardworking tribal and peasant women did not wear veils. Reza Shah Pahlavi forcibly removed women's veils—policemen tore off their scarves and veils—to symbolize Iranian modernity and westernization. He encouraged Western dress. Men took on Western clothing: trousers, suit jackets, ties, and hats. Women more often retained ethnic, tribal, or regional dress. Men wear their hair shorter and might have beards and mustaches. As infants and toddlers, mothers dressed girls and boys similarly in homemade shirts and pants, and only began to put dresses or skirted pullovers on girls, rather than boys' shorter pullovers, after the age of 2 or 3. People believe that girls should cover their hair by the age of 7, although girls might beg for a scarf or veil before then. At an early age, girls are expected to stay at home and not roam around the neighborhood with friends, as boys do. Use of make-up visibly marked the transformation of a girl to a married woman. Particularly during the time of Mohammad Reza Shah,

middle- and upper-class urban women took to Western fashions, make-up, nail polish, and beauty shop hair care. In the 1960s and 1970s, girls wore uniforms to school, and generally teachers did not wear veils. Upper- and middle-class women, especially professionals, often did not wear veils except when attending religious gatherings.

All of this distressed Shi'a Muslim clerics. Soon after the 1979 Revolution, Ayatollah Khomeini began to restrict clothing, social integration, and behavior of women. It became illegal to go without veiling or to wear make-up (Moghissi, 1999; Tabari & Yeganeh, 1982). Women were required to wear a veil or a scarf covering all their hair and a long raincoat-like outer garment. Men should wear long sleeves and long, rather loose pants, and to demonstrate that they were "Islami" wear a beard or stubble and avoid the Western tie. Currently, women can show hair under their scarves, and wear make-up and nail polish. Covering tunics are becoming briefer. Particularly for younger females from less conservative families, they may be tailored to fit the form snugly, fall just to cover the hips, and button only to above the waist, allowing the front to swing open and reveal tight pants underneath.

Standards of female beauty have changed drastically over time. Not many decades ago, females were to be plump, with long thick black hair. Now females want to be slender. Middle- and upper-class women may go to the gymnasium and aerobics classes to attain a toned slim body. Many women dye their dark hair lighter colors. Many females have plastic surgery to have a smaller nose, and some even restructure other parts of their faces and bodies.

GENDER OVER THE LIFE CYCLE

Infants may be called by a gender-neutral term, such as *neenee, nozad*, or *baqeli*, and then a bit later called a *bacheh* or "child," although sometimes this term has a male connotation. From birth until marriage, males are called "boys" or *pisar* and females are called girls or *dokhtar*. Circumcision and marriage defined the main stages of life for males. Circumcision, performed before going to school, marks boys as cleaner and better Muslims, and as moving toward manhood. Families celebrate the occasion, and boys receive praise, gifts, visitors, and special food. Boys do not show embarrassment at the attention focused on their penises. Under Islamic Republic laws, the legal marriage age for girls was lowered to 9 and that for boys to 16. Upon marriage, and thus initiation into sexual activity, females are called "women" or *zan* and males "men" or *mard*. Upon consummation of the marriage, the status of the two changed to that of *arus*, bride or daughter-in-law, and *damad*, groom or son-in-law. In the past, the daughter-in-law became subordinate to the mother-in-law and her competitor for the affections of her son. With the arrival of a child, particularly a boy, the young woman gained some status. The young couple then became *bachehdar*, those who have children, or parents. The parents, and more often the mother, might then be called by the name of her son: Naneh-ye Mohammad or Mama-ne Mohammad—Mohammad's Mother. Generally, the bride's mother provided the first set of clothing for the child. Relatives, especially women, came to congratulate the mother, bringing gifts if possible. As the couple had more children and then married them off and became grandparents, they gained status. In their older years, depending on their vitality and leadership, men could be called *reesh sefid*, white beard, and women, less commonly and with less power connotations, *sar sefid*, white head. Finally, the elderly were called *pir zan*, old woman, and *pir mard*, old man. Although younger people still demonstrated deference to them, they generally lost power and authority.

Socialization of Boys and Girls

Not long ago, families favored boys over girls. A young bride wanted to produce a boy which would increase her own status. A friend told me how her mother had turned her face away, wept, and refused to nurse her first-born daughter in shame that she had not produced a son for her husband, until her aunts and other female relatives urged her to do so. When asked how many *bacheh* (child, although sometimes taken to mean boy) he has, a father may count only the boys. In my experience, when men recited the list of their ancestors and their lineage, they gave the names of males only. Females asked if I wanted them to list the women too, or just the men. Traditionally, mothers and others tended to male infants more than to female infants, breast-feeding them longer, and responding to their crying. Parents generally provided boys with more food, clothing, medical care, and education than

girls (Friedl, 1997). Educated modern couples tend to expend as much care on daughters as sons.

Mothers are the main caretakers of babies, although fathers interact with boys later on. Anthropologist Erika Friedl (1997) found that parents and others in a Lurish village expected girls to be quiet, obedient, helpful, clean, and homebound. From very early on, girls' genital areas are always covered, while little boys may be naked. Mothers taught girls to acquiesce to male domination. Although mothers complained about their sons' devilishness, wildness, and destructiveness, they also saw this behavior as masculine assertiveness.

Puberty and Adolescence

Many urban middle-class Iranian young people now enjoy music, getting together with other young people, and talking with, even dating, the opposite sex. Only a few decades ago, Iranians did not separate out or name an adolescent period, especially for girls, nor did they expect teenagers to display awkwardness, touchiness, or rebelliousness. People might refer to teenage boys as *javanan* or youths and expect them to go out of the house. Girls' menarche, rather than celebrated, is private and polluting. Menstruation makes girls ritually impure, unable to pray or touch the Qur'an.

Attainment of Adulthood

A boy (*pisar*) becomes a man (*mard*) through marriage and initiation into sexuality. In order to marry, he must be old enough to be earning money to support a family. He or his family must have gathered the money to provide gifts to the intended wife and her family as well as to give the bride's father a *mehriyeh* or brideprice. Likewise, a girl (*dokhtar*) becomes a woman (*zan*) through marriage and initiation into sexual activity. In order to be eligible for marriage, or at least before consummation of marriage, a girl must have gone through menarche and thus be able to produce offspring. Part of the preparation of a bride included removal of her body hair, marking her transition from a girl to a sexually active woman. Although customs differ greatly among ethnic, tribal, and religious groups, class, settlement size, and age groups, changes in hair style sometimes mark married women. For example, Kurdish women cut some hair on both sides to frame the face after marriage. In Iran, women have long worn eye make-up (kohl), and with westernization, began to use other types of make-up, particularly for brides. After marriage, a man is expected to act responsibly and support his wife and children. Men should make sure that their wives and children are respectful to them and careful about family reputation. Married females should industriously clean house, cook, and wait on their husbands and husbands' parents, particularly if they live with them. Until several decades ago, males interacted with males and females with females. People did not expect marriages necessarily to be companionate, but rather a household and children-producing team. Now, even females may find careers, postponing marriage, and receive respect from others.

Middle Age and Old Age

With several children, men and women gain status and respect. As a householder, with a wife and growing children, a man may be called upon for religious or community leadership. Mature men and women who controlled economic, political, religious, and social resources enjoyed the most power and influence. More recently, when younger adults can gain influential and rewarding positions through education, independent jobs, modern expertise, or religious dedication, they may threaten older people's authority. As time goes on, and men begin to lose their strength and abilities, their wives may gain power. When their husbands become frail, wives who are most often some years younger may still be at the height of their powers, managing family and community events and relationships. In the past, elderly parents lived with children and grandchildren who ideally placed them at the center of the family and cared for them with love and compassion. Now, young couples want their independent lives and do not appreciate interference from parents. Old men tend to become relatively marginal and dependent upon others to care for them. Older women are often more resourceful, remaining active in cooking and household work as well as in family, kin, and neighborhood affairs. Now more and more elderly live by themselves in their own homes rather than with children. There are also old people's homes for those elderly whose children cannot or do not wish to care for them. Because divorced or widowed men, more than women, tend to remarry, old men can usually count on wives to nurse them at home. Far more women than men reside in homes for the elderly.

PERSONALITY DIFFERENCES BY GENDER

Shi'a Islam, religious leaders, myths, and rituals all teach men to be brave, to be able to support and defend women, children, and dependants, to be wise, just, combative, and devoted to God and religion, to be able to control themselves, and to participate in the public world of religion, politics, and economics. Women, in contrast, are supposedly weak, delicate, emotional, nuturing, unable to be objective and thus to be just, unable to control themselves and resist sexual temptation, and suited by nature to home, household, and ministering to men and children. In actuality, it is often women who hold the household together and manage interpersonal relations.

Little girls usually are more docile, obedient, and shy. Little boys can behave in a more unruly fashion and hit and act aggressively toward others. Little girls stay at home, whereas boys can more easily escape the house and their mothers' control over them. As they grow older girls should become increasingly deferential to males, work hard for their mothers, behave modestly, cast their eyes downward, keep well covered, and keep any needs and wants to themselves (Friedl, 1997). A boy can order mother, sisters, and younger brothers around and be more assertive about his wishes, although required to demonstrate respect to his father and other older family males.

GENDER-RELATED SOCIAL GROUPS

Male–female separation characterizes much of Iranian social life. Females spend much of their time in the company of other females. Before the employment of many women in the public sector during the 1960s and afterward, females (except the poor) generally stayed at home with female family and relatives, running the household, and interacting with kin and neighbors. Upon marriage, a young couple typically lived with the groom's family, at least for a time. However, the Iranian kinship system is basically bilateral, and wives maintained close connections with their own families and relatives. Male relatives, such as a father and his sons and perhaps uncles and cousins, might well form the basis for political groupings, particularly in tribal and rural areas, and economic endeavors. However, kinship groups in Iran exhibit a network character of changing alliances rather than a corporate nature. People could also utilize connections through women and partnerships with unrelated persons to form interest groups. During kinship, neighborhood, religious, and political gatherings, wedding celebrations and mourning ceremonies, and religious rituals, men and women gathered in separate buildings, rooms, or spaces. During ad hoc political meetings and economic consultations of men, women might find opportunities to listen discreetly while serving tea and other refreshments. Urban middle-class men often joined one or more *dorehs* or circles, meeting regularly with a fixed membership, although more recently often both husbands and wives attend such gatherings. Segregation along gender lines continues to organize social life. Since the formation of the Islamic Republic, government officials have required the segregation of unrelated women and men.

GENDER ROLES IN ECONOMICS

In nomadic tribal groups, men herded the animals. Women milked animals and processed animal products, such as dairy products and wool, making cheese, yogurt, dried yogurt, and various woven products such as tents, saddlebags, rugs, and other textiles. Now, nomadic migrations are virtually a thing of the past. Families do not follow migrating herds, and men handle any animal movement with vehicles.

In agriculture, men generally prepared land, planted, and harvested, although in some areas, such as in rice- and tea-raising areas along the Caspian Sea, and harvesting nuts, women work in the fields. Otherwise, village women cared for children and home, processed and prepared food, and cared for and milked any animals. Generally men worked as traders or in shops. A few rural women, usually widows, did some buying and selling, minor moneylending, and perhaps sewing to earn a little money. Commonly, middle-class homes employed poorer girls and women as maids, often bringing them from villages. Girls and women knotted Persian carpets, although men usually arranged the marketing and managed carpet workshops. Other than knotted, woven, and knitted wool products, men monopolized arts and crafts such as metal and woodwork, silver work and jewelry, tiles, hand-printed cloth, tailoring, and handmade shoes. Now, villagers are less self-sufficent.

Rural people have migrated to urban areas, and those men who maintain their homes in villages frequently commute to work. Village women have fewer animal-tending and food-processing responsibilities. Factory-produced goods have replaced handicrafts. Men dominated the arts as well, writing the poetry so central to Iranian culture, painting Persian miniatures, and working as professional musicians. Since the 1960s, when women gained educational opportunities, they have begun to publish, paint, create, and perform, although less than men. The much-loved female poet, Forugh Farrokhzad, began publishing her poems in the 1950s. The first female novelist, Simin Daneshvar, wife of the outstanding author, Jalal Al-e Ahmad, published her book *Savushshun*, or *The Mourners of Siyavush*, in 1969 (Milani, 1992). Women have become teachers, work in government offices, and serve in medical capacities. Now women work in virtually every type of field and position, although as a minority in non-nurturing areas. Men generally hold the more powerful positions.

PARENTAL AND OTHER CARETAKER ROLES

According to Islamic dictates, husbands and fathers must maintain their families, providing home, food, and other needs. Fathers procreate and their wives and children respect and obey them. Mothers do the day-to-day care for children, and develop more intimate and informal relationship with their offspring (Fathi, 1985). Generally, mothers call upon fathers' authority for disciplinary purposes. Mothers spend far more time in the company of their children and are usually more openly affectionate with them. When women had little power in a family because of their lack of control over economic resources and cultural expectations, women might cultivate the affection and goodwill of children, particularly sons, to develop some leverage. Fathers may be attached to their daughters but have formal, distant, and uncomfortable relationships with sons. In recent years, as children become educated, gain employment away from the control of fathers and relatives, and wish for more independence, conflicts may develop between fathers and children over whether or not children should accept their fathers' control. Many urban middle- and upper-class young people are finding ways to evade parental control and sometimes associate with other young people.

LEADERSHIP IN PUBLIC ARENAS

Males have generally held leadership positions in Iran, as shahs, provincial and tribal heads, parliamentary and government officials, kinship and extended family heads, and religious figures. Although women work behind the scenes and attempt to influence male relatives, males led the Constitutional Revolution of 1905 and 1906, the nationalization of oil in 1951 and subsequent conflict between Prime Minister Mosaddeq and the Shah who was backed by the United States and the Central Intelligence Agency (C.I.A.), and the Iranian Revolution of 1978–79. In all of these efforts, women played significant roles (Sanasarian, 1982; Paidar, 1995). For example, women formed some half of the people in street demonstrations and marches, the most crucial revolutionary activity, during the 1978–79 Iranian Revolution (Nashat, 1983). However, the roles played by women have usually been supportive rather than pivotal. Even the leftist movements used women as supporters and silenced feminist interests (Moghissi, 1994). During the Reza Shah Pahlavi period, a woman, Farokhroo Parsa, served as Minister of Education. (She was executed in 1979 by the Islamic Republic of Iran.) Since the formation of the Islamic Republic of Iran, women have served as members of parliament, and held several less significant executive positions. Maryam Rajavi, female leader of the Mojahedin anti-regime group is the exception to the general absence of women in leadership positions, but she took the position after the death of her husband, the former head. Women and youth generally voted for the more moderate cleric, President Khatemi, in the 1997 presidential election.

GENDER AND RELIGION

Since the time of the Prophet Mohammad and his 12 successors, male imams have assumed the leadership roles in Shi'a Islam. However, when Imam Husein, grandson of the Prophet, and other males were martyred at Karbala, his sister Zaynab led the womenfolk of the group as they were taken captive to Damascus. Her mourning and speaking kept the memory of Imam Husein and his martyrdom alive as the central Shi'a myth. The highest religious leaders, the ayatollahs, take charge of guiding Shi'a Muslim believers. Very few women have qualified to be ayatollahs, and men are the clerics and preachers or *mullahs*. However, women may lead women's home rituals of Qur'an study, mourning commemorations for the Karbala martyrs, or gatherings featuring food provided in honor of the martyrs or saints. Women make pilgrimages to local shrines and make contracts with the saints in the interests of family members. Older women, especially, may make government-run religious pilgrimages even to Damascus, although men still predominate in making the *haj*, the pilgrimage to Mecca required of Muslims who can afford it. Since the institution of the Islamic Republic in 1979, women have increasingly entered into public religious activities. Now they teach and study religion and some even attend seminaries, formerly a male prerogative. Women sometimes speak in mosques and mixed gatherings and lead neighborhood women's gatherings to discuss the Qur'an and religious issues (Kamalkhani, 1997). Despite these advances, males control the Islamic Republic, its executive positions, and policy formation. Men sit on the Council of Experts who rule on who may become candidates in elections and on other proposed political moves. But many women are now studying religious sources themselves and questioning male interpretations of Islam.

LEISURE, RECREATION, AND THE ARTS

Men have generally enjoyed more leisure time than females, as women are responsible for endless household tasks, childcare, and hospitality. Several decades ago, very few women had opportunities for leisure and recreation outside of socializing with family, relatives, and neighbors. Women interacted with other women at family and life-cycle gatherings or as individuals. Sometimes women sang and danced together, especially at wedding celebrations. Some women might excel at singing or drumming to entertain family and friends. Men often sought out the company of other males, sitting and chatting in sunny spots or teahouses, and perhaps hiking and picnicking outside of settlements. Since the 1960s, some females participated in performances and sports, and might even attend scout camps. With modernization during Mohammad Reza Shah's rule, some females began to attend movies, travel with families to hotels along the Caspian Sea or other tourist areas, travel abroad for education and enjoyment, and participate in the arts and a wider selection of sports. Now, Islamic Republic officials require strict sex segregation during sports and outings, except for family members. Males are not allowed to watch female sports, nor do females attend male sports competitions. However, women have forced their way into the stadium during an international male soccer match. Women have struggled for equal access to sports facilities, and have obtained women's hours at government-run gymnasiums. Many Iranian women have become sports enthusiasts. Women are coaching, teaching, and serving as referees in women's sports. Women hike, ski, and ride bikes, although in smaller numbers than men.

In general, girls and women tend to spend more time in domestic settings, whereas boys and men are freer to move out of the house for company and entertainment. Even in old age, women busy themselves with household tasks, while old men are at leisure. Outside activities, other than family outings, must be sex segregated. However, urban middle- and upper-class people may host integrated parties behind closed doors. People read novels, magazines, and newspapers, listen to tapes and CDs, watch television and smuggled film videos, log on the internet, and talk on the phone within Iran and to friends and relatives living abroad.

RELATIVE STATUS OF MEN AND WOMEN

Compared with Iranian women, Iranian men have enjoyed much higher status and access to authority, rights, and privileges. Men took public leadership and decision-making positions and control of group and family, and females were supposed to be out of sight and uninvolved. Even when girls and women worked or produced carpets, their male relatives generally controlled their earnings. Usually men owned and controlled land, animals, and businesses. According to Islamic law, women should inherit half the share of male children. However, most often women turned their shares over to brothers, wishing to avoid censure and hoping for their brothers' support. Widows also did not gain access to much inheritance, and usually had to rely on assistance from grown children.

From an early age, girls were taught to control their dress, postures, and interaction with males by the implicit threat of shaming self and family, or worse. Men controlled sexuality and could marry daughters off at age 9 or even younger, although consummation should not take place before the onset of menstruation. Fathers and other family males controlled marriage choices, although sons might inform parents about preferences. Ideally, Muslim law allows girls the chance to refuse chosen mates, but this did not happen often.

Men largely monopolized divorce decisions, but unhappy wives might obtain a divorce in exchange for dropping demands for their marriage settlements. Even if extremely unhappy, most women avoided divorce because it would humiliate them, they often had no alternative support, and they would lose their children. Supposedly, boys could remain with mothers until the age of 2 and girls until 7, although often husbands and their families did not follow these rules.

Fathers decided the level to which boys and girls could go to school, and, for those relatively few who went to university, their majors. From an early age, a boy could lord it over his sisters, younger brothers, and even mother. He was expected to treat his father with the utmost respect and deference, even into middle age. Respect and deference for women might increase somewhat over their life cycle. As competent housewives, loyal wives and mothers, and kinship connection managers, they might gain husbands' trust and children's and other relatives' respect (Friedl, 1989). After modernization in the 1960s, more women gained an education and employment in the public sector, but this did not always translate into more power and authority with husbands.

Since formation of the Islamic Republic of Iran, government policy has attempted to control women's dress, activities, and mobility, insisting that proper Muslim women must be modest and avoid attracting the attention of unrelated men. Islamic Republic leaders overturned laws that had improved women's position and influence in marriage, family, and employment. Women have struggled to work for women's rights and have been able to achieve minor changes. With so many women gaining education and employment, extended family dynamics have changed. Now daughters-in-law are not willing to live with their husbands' families or tolerate much interference from them. Educated sons and daughters do not depend on families for access to economic resources. The ability of parents to run their children's lives has declined.

SEXUALITY

Muslims view sexuality as healthy and good, a necessary part of the human experience, and the means to produce offspring and maintain family continuity. Muslims do not admire abstinence or consider it a way to serve God and attain greater spirituality. Initiation into sexual activity is viewed as so integral to life, especially to males, that parents whose sons have died before marriage may construct replicas of bridal bowers as part of their mourning activities. People relate sexuality and marriage to having children. In-laws expected brides to become pregnant almost immediately, and if they did not, in-laws and husband might insult them and dissolve the marriage. Recently, however, couples often put off having children and limit their number. Fertility rates have dropped dramatically. Sexual contact pollutes, and people, especially women, must go through religious purification through washing (*qosl*) afterwards. Female sexuality is traditionally viewed as a threat to society. A woman's unfettered sexuality could ruin the honor of her family, relatives, community, religion, and nation (Najmabadi, 1998). To protect men from temptation and society from corruption, as well as to maintain the family's reputation, males needed to control female sexuality (Azari, 1983). Mothers strictly monitored girls' dress, mobility, and interaction with males. Brothers might assist in the overseeing of sisters. Fathers were anxious to marry girls off as soon as possible in order to avoid any potential gossip or scandal. People suspected widows and divorced women, for they had been sexually active but now had lost the male responsible for managing their sexuality. Females could not engage in premarital sex, or even be seen talking with a boy on the street. During the first few decades of the 20th century, people believed girls should not learn to write, as they might use this skill to communicate with boys. After marriage, women should be totally faithful to their husbands. Boys and men enjoyed greater sexual freedom. People generally did not condemn male premarital sexual activity. Males could seek out temporary wives, prostitutes, or loose women. Maids, often young girls from a village, faced the danger of sexual predation from sons of their employing families and even married men. Although parents and others might affectionately touch or refer to little boys' genitals, little girls must cover up. Parents required girls to refrain from notice of their own bodies, except to shame nakedness. Girls could not express sexuality in any way and were supposed to be ignorant about sexuality. Mothers generally did not make any attempts to provide sexual information before marriage. Expected to be a totally asexual creature and prevented from contact with marriageable males, even to the extent sometimes of not seeing husbands-to-be before the marriage night, young women found consummation of marriage on the wedding night to be extremely traumatic. Often this abrupt and forced initiation to sexuality colored their attitudes toward sex and their husbands for some time. People expected married women to be sexually active with their husbands and to enjoy it. However, men dominated the sexual relationship, and women were not supposed to initiate sex openly or to express their wishes. Even married couples should not display affection to each other or otherwise acknowledge their sexual relationship in front of others. People assumed older people to be less sexually active. If a mother with almost adult or adult children became pregnant again, she would feel embarrassed about this evidence of ongoing sexual activity.

Parents and others reprimanded children who behaved like or engaged in activities characteristic of the opposite sex. People rigidly defined gender-appropriate behavior and activities and disapproved of transgression. But females might dress as males to play male parts and sing, for example, to female audiences at segregated wedding celebrations, or in school performances. Males took the part of female members of Imam Husein's band being marched into slavery at Damascus in commemoration of the Karbala martyrdoms. Otherwise, Iranian culture does not include traditions of cross-dressing, as far as I am aware.

Given sexual segregation and close companionship among same-sex individuals, sometimes male adolescents engaged in same-sex activity. In Iranian tradition, especially among the upper-middle and upper classes, some men valued male adolescent beauty and engaged in sexual activity with male youth. Although generally not publicly discussed, same-sex relations did not bring shame, except to the recipient if he was past youth. If young men did engage in same-sex relations, it was viewed as a stage in life that would end upon marriage. In general, very little research about sexuality has been conducted in Iran. This lack extends to homosexuality, particularly to female homosexual relations. Under the Islamic Republic, homosexuality is illegal and carries the death penalty. The problem of AIDS does not receive adequate attention.

In the last few decades, many aspects of sexual attitudes and activities have changed. During the Pahlavi modernization period through 1978, some young men and women attended coeducational universities and might find their own mates. Especially among urban middle- and upper-middle classes, young people might date. People still expected girls to remain virgins until marriage, but restrictions on opposite-sex interaction declined, especially for upper-middle- and upper-class youth. With study abroad and the import of foreign ideas, some married couples became more open with each other about sexual expression and wishes, and some wives became more equal sexual partners. Virginity tests that produced a blood-stained white cloth after consummation of marriage became less common, but marriage license offices continued to offer virginity examinations as a free service.

After the formation of the Islamic Republic, lowering the legal marriage for girls, and enforcing modesty and seclusion for women, some of the relaxation of attitudes and practices about sexuality has reversed. Clerics have encouraged temporary marriage as a way to support war widows and prevent the corruption of youth, as they say has happened in the West. Many clerics and more conservative men take advantage of the Shi'a institution of temporary marriage to attain a full sex life. However, for a female, status as a temporary wife is demeaning and will ruin her chances of a good marriage. Poorer women, divorcees, or widows who lack other alternatives may engage in temporary marriage to secure financial support.

More recently, some young people are finding ways to go out together. Despite the clerical rule, sexual mores are easing for some Iranians. Because prostitution has increased, some clerics wish to establish government-run prostitution or "temporary marriage" centers.

COURTSHIP AND MARRIAGE

Several decades ago, when males finished education or apprenticeship, and entered into income-generating activities, their mothers and other female relatives looked for suitable mates, although fathers held formal control over offspring's marriages. After discrete inquiries of the other family as to the response, the groom's family's made a formal visit to the bride's family. Traditionally, the perspective bride came into the room to serve tea. The groom's family acceptance of offered refreshment would indicate their inclinations. Some families might make marriage arrangements and not tell the girl until the marriage date grew close. Generally fathers negotiated about the *mehr*, the financial arrangements for the marriage. Depending on class, the fathers and perhaps other male relatives would attempt to come to an agreement about the money and property which the groom and his family would give to the bride's father. If a large *mehr*

was demanded by brides' families, grooms often had to wait much longer than they wished for the marriage. Families gathered information about the health of the potential spouses and their family standing. Grooms' families wish for pretty, obedient, and modest brides, and brides' families want financially well-off grooms who can provide comfortable lives for their wives. In the past, families almost always arranged marriages. Although, according to Islamic law, girls are supposed to have the right to refuse, this was not always the case. Boys might have more say in the choice of marriage partner.

Marriage ceremonies consist of two main parts. The first is the signing of the marriage contract or *aqd* conducted by a Muslim cleric. If the bride was present, the cleric asked her if she consented to the marriage. An affirmative answer, generally in a low modest voice, or silence meant consent. Alternatively, the girl's guardian or representative came in her stead. The second part, the wedding celebration or *arusi*, might take place shortly after the *aqd* ceremony or some time later. Although families generally kept the *aqd* ceremony small, they wished to have a wedding celebration that was as extravagant as possible. Some decades ago, well-off families might even have had a 7-day celebration. Brides' and grooms' families held separate wedding parties, where males and females sat in separate rooms or separate buildings. People served tea, refreshments, and meals, laying out tablecloths on the floor and setting out dishes of rice and stews and other foods at intervals for people to help themselves. Families hired musicians so people could do circle dances in alley ways or courtyards. Males and females danced in separate lines, but young people could covertly watch each other celebrating. The bride was not supposed to be part of the celebrating crowd, but sat immobile, face downturned. Ideally, she should not eat or drink or move away from her position.

On the afternoon or evening of the *arusi*, the groom's family went to the bride's home, singing and making noise. They brought the bride, traditionally dressed in green, head covered with a pretty cloth, back to the groom's home. Particularly in tribal and rural settings, male relatives shot rifles into the air to celebrate the taking of the bride. The bride and groom might be seated together on chairs for a while in both the male and female sections. Finally, with singing and noise making, the crowd led the couple to the bridal bower or *hejleh*, decorated by the groom's young male relatives with colorful cloth hangings. The groom was then expected to consummate the marriage. He felt pressured to demonstrate his virility, and the bride was expected to show her modesty and lack of sexual knowledge. The latter was usually not a problem, as girls did not receive any sex education. Indeed, girls' parents ideally would meticulously keep them from any contact whatsoever with unrelated males. A white cloth bloodied with evidence of virginity and penetration might be brought out afterwards to show to guests. In the morning, overnight guests congratulated the groom upon his exit from the bridal room. Ideally, the bride remained in the *hejleh*, and for several days female relatives visited her there. On the morning after the marriage, the bride's mother and other female relatives came to see her, and might bring special foods to strengthen her or even penicillin to guard against weakness or infection caused by sexual initiation. Some time after the marriage, the bride's male relatives traditionally came to escort her to her parents' home, where they would be served a meal by the groom's family. The bride stayed with her family for several days, and then the groom's family came to fetch her.

Parents saw finding suitable mates for children as a main duty in life. Very few people failed to marry, although the disabled faced challenges in finding a mate. The rare single female generally remained in her parents' home.

Husbands could divorce at will, just by declaring three times, "I divorce you, I divorce you, I divorce you." Further, a husband could take as many as four wives, without the permission of any of them, and he could take as many temporary wives (*sigheh* or *muta'a;* Haeri, 1989), as finances allowed, making an agreement for the length of time and the money to change hands. Divorced or widowed men generally remarried within a short period of time. Men did not like to marry divorced or widowed, and thus non-virgin, females. Females did not remarry as often, and remained dependents of fathers, brothers, or sons.

The last few decades have seen radical transformations in courtship and marriage. As the Pahlavi regime developed state education, females left the house. Although educational officials generally tried to schedule classes so that boys and girls were let out of school at different times, the greater mobility of girls sometimes allowed young people to catch sight of each other. Males and females attended university courses together. In particular, those upper-middle-class young people who attended university and then worked in government positions, businesses, or services might chose their own mates. The young people, especially the females, generally had to obtain parents' assent for such marriages.

Even since the formation of the Islamic Republic, when government clerics attempted to reinforce sexual segregation and patriarchy, they have not been able to recreate the social control over male–female interaction that used to be associated with arranged marriages. Depending on class, boys and girls might be able to talk on the telephone or see each other. Middle- and upper-class males and females are sometimes able to co-mingle at wedding celebrations and parties behind closed doors.

HUSBAND–WIFE RELATIONSHIP

Generally brides were one or even several decades younger than grooms. The sexual initiation on the marriage night often left brides shocked and traumatized. Subsequent sexual initiatives by their husbands were distressing. Unless the two were close relatives, they did not really know each other, and might well never have seen each other before marriage. The bridal couple, and married couples in general, did not show affection for each other in front of other people and in fact could hardly talk together in the company of others. Most contact took place during the night hours while others were sleeping. Given the fact that they barely knew each other and yet were abruptly thrown into physical intimacy, both partners, particularly the bride, felt awkward and uncomfortable. Many couples lived with the groom's family for at least a while after marriage. A bride spent much more time with her mother-in-law and other female family members and relatives of the groom than with the groom. Generally, after a few days, if not sooner, he returned to his work. A bride frequently felt alone among watchful strangers waiting to find fault with her. She had to learn to work with her mother-in-law. Conflicts often arose between bride and mother-in-law as they jockeyed over loyalty and support from the groom. Husbands wanted others to realize that they kept their wives under control and that their wives were obedient, hardworking, and competent. The husband's own reputation and that of his family rested on his ability to maintain authority over his wife and children; he needed to exact deference from them.

Producing children, especially sons, gaining household competence, and showing loyalty made her in-laws think better of a young wife. Sometimes affection and respect might develop between the couple. People viewed marriage not as an institution to give companionship and intimacy, but rather for the formation of a household and child-rearing team in order to continue the family line. People favored marriage between cousins so that they could feel more knowledgeable about the potential spouse and family, and the bride more comfortable in her new home. The groom's family had to give a stipulated amount of the *mehr* upon marriage. In theory, the bride could demand the remaining part of the *mehr* whenever she wished. If the groom decided to divorce his wife, he was supposed to give her the remaining part of the marriage settlement. However, brides often did not receive the *mehr* upon divorce (Mir-Hosseini, 2000). A husband who wished to divorce a wife might make her life so miserable that she finally consented to divorce without receiving the *mehr*. A wife found it humiliating when her husband married a second wife, forcing her to share her husband and his resources with a second younger wife and their children. Wives were afraid of divorce because of the shame and because the *mehr*, even when they obtained it, did not support them for long. An unfavorable marriage was sometimes the only defense against poverty. Upon divorce, the father retained custody of the children; often women stayed in unhappy marriages partly because they did not wish to leave their children. When wives divorced, they frequently cited difficulties with mothers-in-law as a main reason. Husbands or in-laws frequently abused wives physically or emotionally. The Qur'an allows husbands to chastise disobedient wives physically. However, somewhat reminiscent of the English "rule of thumb," the physical chastisement of wives should not be so severe that it leaves a mark on their bodies.

When marriages survived into middle age, they sometimes became partnerships of two people concerned about their children and family interests. As men aged, they often became more dependent on their younger and more socially engaged wives. Therefore women might gain de facto power in the marriage. Even if the husbands had been domineering and self-centered, wives typically nursed their husbands in sickness and old age.

The thought of their husband taking another wife or a *sigheh* (temporary wife) frightened women dreadfully. Women might threaten or even attempt suicide. After Mohammad Reza Shah Pahlavi's Family Protection Act, men were required to obtain their first wife's permission to marry a second wife, although not to take a *sigheh*. Men might find ways of evading this requirement. Especially with *sighehs*, wives might not be aware of the other woman. Generally, cowives felt angry and suspicious of each other, resenting attention and

resources which the man gave to the other wife and her children. Wealthier men might provide different houses for each wife and her children and so keep more of a distance between them. If they lived in the same home, each wife usually had her own room.

The average age of first marriage for females has increased to 27, and the age disparity between bride and groom has decreased. Because young couples are now much more likely to live on their own, the nuclear family has become a more significant unit. For many Iranian wives, these changes translate into a more equal relationship with husbands. However, in other cases, couples left to their own devices feel their dissatisfaction more. Divorce rates have risen.

OTHER CROSS-SEX RELATIONSHIPS

Iranian males often have close relationships with their mothers, who usually had invested time and energy in building their sons' love and attachment. Given the importance of family and relatives and separation between unrelated boys and girls, brothers and sisters frequently became close companions. Parents generally expected their sons to protect their sisters and defend them and thus the family against any potential loss of reputation. Therefore, brothers often oversaw sisters' behavior, dress, and contact with others, and might treat sisters harshly if they suspected any wrongdoing. Usually girls and women felt the need to obey and please brothers because of their dependence on them for assistance. Although daughters should receive half the inheritance of sons, most often sisters handed property over to their brothers, fearing conflict and loss of family reputation if they demanded their rights. Lacking other alternatives, they also hoped for a possible refuge in the case of marital difficulty. Male and female cousins often became friends. They might even live in the same home or complex. As cousins can marry and cousin marriage is favored, parents generally restricted their interaction when they approached puberty.

CHANGE IN ATTITUDES, BELIEFS, AND PRACTICES REGARDING GENDER

The last few decades have seen drastic changes in gender in Iran, as previous sections have indicated. Mohammad

Reza Shah Pahlavi wanted to educate women and bring them into the public sphere as a significant symbol of Iranian modernization and westernization. His father even outlawed women's veils and scarfs for a time, forcing most women to stay at home rather than expose themselves. Until the Iranian Revolution of February 11, 1979, Iranian women, especially of the middle and upper classes, were gaining literacy, education, and jobs in the modern public sector, and even traveling abroad for education. Many women, especially in middle- and upper-class urban areas, wore chic Western fashions rather than veils or even scarves. Courtship, marriage, nuclear family organization, level of control of parents, status and power of women, gender and family laws, and women's public roles were all being transformed. Then, with the formation of the Islamic Republic of Iran, conservative clerics attempted to reverse the changes in gender and sexuality, reestablishing sex segregation, females' family roles, and male control over females, sexuality, family, and public space. Females caught wearing lipstick or nail polish or showing a strand of hair or glimpse of skin under their veils or *rupushes* (raincoat-like covering) faced imprisonment and harassment. Family laws did away with the rights women had gained during the Shah's regime. The legal age of marriage for females went down from 16 to 9 again. Recently, more females have been attaining an education, and the majority of university students are now female (Afkhami & Friedl, 1994). Women have found many ways of resisting the new stricter restrictions and to press for changes beneficial to women. With increased access to literacy and Islamic scholarship, some women are questioning male misogynist interpretations of Islamic sources. The legal age of marriage for females has risen to 15, and men are now supposed to pay a *mehr* adjusted for inflation when divorcing a wife.

Women and sympathetic males face great obstacles in trying to modify gender constructions. Clerics point to Iranian females' dress, modesty, and devotion to family and religion as the main markers differentiating Islamic Iranian society from what they view as the corrupt and morally bankrupt West, where women go "naked," sexuality is unfettered, and the family has dissolved. Gender and sexuality lie at the center of reformers' and conservatives' struggle to influence the present and future of Iran (Mir-Hosseini, 1999).

ACKNOWLEDGMENTS

Much of the information presented draws on my years of living and conducting research in Iran (1966–68, summer of 1970, 1971–72, summer of 1977, and 1978–79) and extensive interviewing and participant observation among Iranians and Iranian Americans in the United States from 1969 on. I am most grateful to all these Iranians and to the Social Science Research Council and American Council of Learned Societies.

REFERENCES

Afkhami, M., & Friedl, E. (Eds.). (1994). *In the eye of the storm: Women in post-revolutionary Iran.* Syracuse, NY: Syracuse University Press.

Azari, F. (Ed.). (1983). *Women of Iran: The conflict with fundamentalist Islam.* London: Ithaca Press.

Fathi, A. (Ed.). (1985). *Women and the family in Iran.* Leiden, The Netherlands: E. J. Brill.

Friedl, E. (1989). *Women of Deh Koh: Lives in an Iranian village.* New York: Penguin.

Friedl, E. (1997). *Children of Deh Koh: Young life in an Iranian village.* Syracuse, NY: Syracuse University Press.

Haeri, S. (1989). *Law of desire: Temporary marriage in Shi'i Iran.* Syracuse, NY: Syracuse University Press.

Kamalkhani, Z. (1997). *Women's Islam: Religious practice among women in today's Iran.* London: Kegan Paul.

Milani, F. (1992). *Veils and words: The emerging voices of Iranian women writers.* Syracuse, NY: Syracuse University Press.

Mir-Hosseini, Z. (1999). *Islam and gender: The religious debate in contemporary Iran.* Princeton, NJ: Princeton University Press.

Mir-Hosseini, Z. (2000). *Marriage on trial: A study of Islamic family law in Iran and Morocco.* London, New York: I. B. Tauris.

Moghissi, H. (1994). *Populism and feminism in Iran: Women's struggle in a male-defined revolutionary movement.* New York: St Martin's Press.

Moghissi, H. (1999). *Feminism and Islamic fundamentalism: The limits of postmodern analysis.* London: Zed Books.

Najmabadi, A. (1998). *The story of the daughters of Quchan: Gender and national memory in Iranian history.* Syracuse, NY: Syracuse University Press.

Nashat, G. (Ed.). (1983) *Women and revolution in Iran.* Boulder, CO: Westview Press.

Paidar, P. (1995). *Women and the political process in twentieth-century Iran.* Cambridge, U.K.: Cambridge University Press.

Sanasarian, E. (1982). *The women's rights movement in Iran: Mutiny, appeasement, and repression from 1900 to Khomeini.* New York: Praeger.

Tabari, A., & Yeganeh, N. (Eds.). (1982). *In the shadow of Islam: The women's movement in Iran.* London: Zed Books.

Israelis

Marilyn P. Safir and Amir Rosenmann

ALTERNATIVE NAMES

Israelis are also known as Yisra'elim.

LOCATION

Israel is situated in the Middle East. It is a crossroad between Asia, Africa, and Europe. The Mediterranean forms Israel's western border. It shares its northern border with Lebanon. To the east, it borders with Syria and Jordan, a border that ends at the Red Sea where both Israel and Jordan have outlets. Israel shares a border with Egypt in the south.

CULTURAL OVERVIEW

In 1947 the United Nations passed a resolution to divide Palestine into two separate national entities: a Jewish Israel, and an Arab Palestine. Following this resolution, Israel declared its independence (1948), declaring itself as the homeland of the Jewish people. A war between Israel and the neighboring Arab countries resulted from their rejection of these developments. Although peace treaties were signed with Egypt and Jordan in the 1980s and 1990s, hostilities between Israel and the surrounding Arab states, as well as with Palestinians living in territories Israel occupied following the 1967 war, have been continuous. These hostilities have insured that the Israeli army maintains a pivotal role in Israeli society. Hence, all 18-year-old Jewish men and women are required, de jure, to complete mandatory military service.

The first wave of Jewish settlers fled Eastern Europe to Palestine to escape anti-Semitism by establishing a Jewish homeland in *Zion* (and hence—*Zionism*) in the latter part of the 19th century. The second wave of settlers, who were largely responsible for the egalitarian image of Israeli society, sought personal redemption through a commitment to both Zionist and Socialist values. They believed that physical labor, reclamation of the land, and the establishment of communal settlements in a Jewish homeland would produce a society with social equality. This utopian vision regarding a common good meant sacrificing the rights of individuals and nonhegemonic groups (Swirski & Safir, 1993). This Zionist–Socialist way of life came to fruition with the advent of the "kibbutz", a communal settlement in which inhabitants theoretically share all responsibilities and prerogatives. With the gradual move towards a more capitalistic economy following the Six-Day War and the strengthening of politics and cultural ties with the United States, Socialist Zionism lost its hegemonic status, and other, hitherto disenfranchised, groups started asserting their agendas.

Israel is a land of immigration. Following World War II, Israel's population more than tripled by an influx of Jewish refugees. The trauma of the Holocaust in Europe and the expulsion of Jews from Islamic countries could not but leave a distinctive mark on the new society. The latest major wave of Jewish immigrants has been from the former Soviet Union, primarily in the 1990s. During this period, there was a 25% increase in the Jewish Israeli population.

In addition to these waves of diverse Jewish immigrants, a fifth of contemporary Israel's citizens are Arabs. Within this national minority population, there are distinct religious/cultural groups, the majority of whom (16%) are Muslim, with about 70% living in small villages, Christians (1.9%), who live primarily in cities, Druze (0.9%), members of a secretive religion living in relatively closed communities, and other even smaller groups. These minorities have been increasingly torn between their identification with the Palestinian people and their identification as citizens of Israel (Suleiman & Beit-Hallahmi, 1997).

Following the creation of the State of Israel, Jewish religious law was integrated into state law. As a result, rabbinical courts were granted jurisdiction over personal status. For Muslims, Christians, and Druze too, matters of personal status were left to the jurisdiction of the respective religious courts. While religious law is incorporated into Israeli state law, most Israelis do not define themselves as religious (Levi, Levinsohn, & Katz, 2000). These are but a few of the factors that combine to make contemporary Israel a bizarre amalgam of a socialist welfare state with egalitarian ideology, a capitalist economy, and strong religious/traditional influences and institutions.

CULTURAL CONSTRUCTION OF GENDER

Israel is perceived by Westerners, as well as most Israelis, as being a part of the contemporary Western world, thus sharing its binary view of gender. Despite this Western orientation, even secular Jewish society is relatively traditional, resulting in a more conservative definition of gender then found elsewhere in the West. In a comparative study of American and Israeli subjects, researchers found Israeli participants to be significantly more conservative, maintaining stronger stereotypes about homosexuality, femininity, and masculinity, and a greater gender role gap (Leiblich & Friedman, 1985). This conservative gender value system is rooted in Jewish traditions and religious beliefs that impact every facet of life in Israel, and is compounded by the centrality of the army in Israeli life (Azmon & Izraeli, 1993).

Israeli society puts greater emphasis on the centrality of the family, family values, and the mothering role of women in comparison with most other Western societies (Azmon & Izraeli, 1993; Safir, 1993a). This can easily be deduced from the average number of children per Jewish mother, which was 2.66 in 2000 (Israel Central Bureau of Statistics, 2001), compared with only 1.87 for the average American woman in the same year (U.S. Census Bureau, 2001). Current social values encourage women to structure their identity within the context of the family so that they willingly put their careers in second place (Leiblich, 1993). Today women comprise over 54% of the labor force, but women's paid work is considered secondary to their husband's work (Fogel-Bijawi, 1999). The prototypical Israeli family generally operates well within the framework of traditional gender roles that are supported by social and state institutions. Whilst husbands may share some of the burden of housework and childcare, these areas are clearly regarded as women's responsibility by both women and men (Safir, 1993a).

The centrality of the traditional family is also evident linguistically. The Hebrew word for "family" (*mishpacha*) is usually applied only to the prototypical

family of mother, father, and children (excluding couples with no children, single-parent households, and same-sex partnerships). Another example is the Hebrew word for "orphan" (*yatom*), which is applied even to a person who lost only one parent. The death of a parent entails a break in the prototypical family, and appears more socially significant in Israel then elsewhere.

Given this preoccupation with traditional family structure, infertility is considered a major tragedy. Every Israeli woman, without regard to an upper age limit, religion, or marital status, is eligible to request unlimited attempts at in vitro fertilization. Complete payments for these treatments are covered by her health insurance, until she has two children. The number of infertility clinics in Israel, per capita, is the highest in the world, with 24 units available to 5.5 million Israelis in the mid-1990s (Kahn, 2000). On the other hand, birth control is not covered by health insurance. Israel also grants special "birth allowances"; large families receive massive monetary incentives from the state (Safir, 1993a).

The Jewish religion, and its traditions detailed in a later section, is one of the major influences that result in great emphasis on family values. Orthodox Jewish patriarchal representatives hold immense political power (Gerabi, 1996), as well as directly influencing Israeli society and values (Safir, 1986).

An additional patriarchal epicenter in Israeli society is the army. As Israel has been in an almost continuous state of war since its establishment, the Israeli Defense Force (I.D.F.) is a primary influence on Israeli society as a whole (Gerabi, 1996). The army also overvalues narrowly defined masculine gender roles. Research describes this militaristic manhood as an antithesis to the stereotypical Jew from the European diaspora, who was viewed as feminine, weak, subservient, and helpless. Many of the early leaders of the Zionist movement strived to "restore manhood" to Jewish men by restructuring it to follow idealized images of European men, healthy in mind and body and willing to fight and die for the nation (Gluzman, 1997). This new "Israeli" manhood, replacing the old "Jewish" manhood, was embodied in two related images—the pioneer, enduring great hardships to reinstate the national home, and the warrior, defending the nation and commanding respect. In contemporary Israel, these ideals of self-reliance, national pride, and self-sacrifice are personified in the combat soldier, whose image constitutes this hegemonic standard of manhood (Lomski-Feder & Rapoport, 2000).

However, in recent years, there have been more opportunities for women to enter previously exclusive masculine roles in the army (Dimitrovsky, Singer, & Yinon, 1989), a trend that has now sparked off a political struggle between liberal and religious parties in Israel. Religious men have refused to serve in units in which women soldiers serve. Regardless of this public debate, ethnographic research demonstrates that greater integration of women in the armed forces is contingent on their assimilation into an all-masculine value system, while devaluating feminine gender roles to the point of subjectively breaking away from female identity (Sasson-Levi, 1997).

In this prototypical masculine world, women are viewed as contributing their part as long as they assist and support the (male) soldier (Bloom, 1993). In this militaristic sphere, women are given voice through their relationships with men who shoulder the strain of battle, via their positions as mothers and wives of warriors (Gillath, 1993). Thus women's protests had been viewed as illegitimate nor had women been perceived as entitled to any form of direct power or influence (Helman & Rapoport, 1997).

Zionist ethos also sustains the myth that in the early days of Israel's statehood, and in pre-state Israel, women and men were truly equal—an equality that meant sharing "male" activities. They are portrayed as pioneers: building settlements, paving roads, farming, and serving in the army (Swirski & Safir, 1993). However, women's integration in these activities was only partial; often they were rejected because they were women. Moreover, the majority of unmarried women worked as maids in the houses of the more affluent Jewish families during this pre-state period (Bernstein, 1987). The overall picture emerging here is characterized by strong pressure toward gender conformity, interlaced with a greater value placed on masculine gender roles (Singer, 1997).

Traditional values are even more central within the Arab minorities. A majority of the Arab population live in traditional cultural and social settings, a setting in which Western ideas about gender equality are frequently irrelevant (Lobel, Mashraki-Pedhatzur, Mantzur, & Libby, 2000). This is especially true for 70% of the Muslim population, who live largely in rural areas and have relatively little interaction with the Jewish majority (Al-Haj, 1995).

The Arab minorities are torn between two cultural vectors. On the one hand, they are linked, with varying degrees of intensity (Abu-Baker, 1985), to Jewish Israeli society, with its "modern" and "Western" aspirations.

On the other hand, they are allied with the traditional Arab world, which often opposes and resists the values of the contemporary West (Al-Haj, 1995). According to Al-Haj, Arab society is a developing society coping with changes associated with modernization and at the same time the constraints stemming from being a nonassimilating national minority in a Jewish state.

One result of these contradictory forces can be seen in the cleft between the conspicuous process of individual modernization within the Arab communities, and the persistence of conservative social values and reverential adherence to age-old traditions. While individual modernization is reflected in different fields (the rise of level of education, improvements in standard of living, wide exposure to mass media, and the development of a nationwide leadership), many traditional values persist on the community level (Al-Haj, 1995). The patriarchal/traditional nature of this society is intensified by the subjection of this minority to national, political, social, and cultural oppression (Hassan, 1993).

In this cultural tug-of-war, gender issues are often viewed as an important bastion of authentic Arab tradition, a cornerstone of Arab culture (Soliman, 1985). Those who oppose the pull of Israeli Western-like values may be adamant in their rejection of any liberal or feminist notions. This complete rejection of Western gender-related values can be seen in its most extreme form in the murder of women in the name of "family honor". Although infrequent, such cases surface from time to time in Muslim Arab communities in Israel (Hassan, 1993, 1999). These killings are anathema to liberal values of women's (or indeed human) rights, but are still seen by some as an appropriate reaction to rumors, gossip, and knowledge of sexual misconduct that become part of the public sphere (Glazer & Abu Ras, 1994).

Tradition is also important in governing other less extreme behaviors regarding gender. Many Arab women are expected to devote their lives completely to their roles as homemakers in their extended family or clan (*Hamula*) (El-Mehairy, 1985; Lobel et al., 2000). In this cultural system, strict adherence to such social roles is usually expected of all individuals. In fact, poorer and less educated Arab women may perceive mothering as the only future role open for them (Shtarkshall, 1987).

In sum, Israeli Arab society is highly patriarchal and traditional (Hassan, 1999). Women are largely devalued by this social system, as is evident elsewhere in the Arab world (Crawford & Unger, 2000; El-Saadawi, 1980).

This is most true for the majority of Arab women, living in villages and Arab cities, who rarely have the opportunity to assert themselves in a more liberal context. Women who attain higher education, or live in mixed cities (where there is abundant contact with less traditional Jewish values), seem to be less willing to accept traditional roles ascribed for them by their patriarchal culture (Abu-Baker, 1985; Seginer, Karayanni, & Mar'i, 1990).

GENDER OVER THE LIFE CYCLE

Socialization of Boys and Girls

Israeli society, with its strong connections with Jewish patriarchal traditions, bestows higher status on boys from infancy. The Brit-Mila, or circumcision ceremony, held when the infant is 8 days old, becomes a celebration of the birth of a baby boy. This status is reconfirmed at age 13 when the vast majority of boys participate in a Bar Mitzva (coming of age) ceremony (described in more detail below).

School attendance in Israel is compulsory for both sexes from the ages of 6 to 16 and public school education is free. However, higher cultural regard for boys is evident in teachers' unconscious, but pronounced, preference for boys over girls (Ben Tsvi-Meyer, Hertz-Lazarovitz, & Safir, 1989). This preference impacts on the pupils' evaluation of boys and girls in the earliest years of grade school, so that girls also view boys as more outstanding when evaluating classmates (Safir, Ben Tzvi-Meyer, Hertz-Lazarovitz, & Kuppermintz, 1992). These authors have suggested that the unusual findings indicating boys' superiority on tests of *both* verbal and performance abilities (Safir, 1986), as opposed to girls' superiority in grade-point average throughout all levels of schooling, may be attributed to girls' insecurity in taking ability tests, resulting from this continuous cultural preference of boys.

In contrast to these unusual differences between Israeli boys and girls, the social experiences of children of both genders are generally similar. Unlike other Western countries, Jewish children of both sexes are encouraged, from a very early age, to play in outdoor settings. This early gregarious behavior, in combination with the mild to hot Israeli climate, makes playing outdoors a preferred activity for many girls, as well as boys. Such outdoor games are usually physical and lively, quite the opposite

of what is expected of "girls" elsewhere in the West (Safir, Rosenmann, & Kloner, 2003).

Social interaction between the sexes also begins at an earlier age then in other Western countries, because of socialist norms, encouraging women to work outside of their homes (Lavee & Katz, 2003). As a result, day-care facilities are provided throughout Israel for children from age 6 months. For example, in 1988, 67% of 2-year-olds, 92% of 3-year-olds, and 99% of 4-year-olds were in some preschool setting (Izraeli & Safir, 1993).

Additional factors that mitigate behavioral differences between Israeli girls and boys are the "Israeli ethos" and the hegemonic Israeli narrative, which emphasized the importance of enduring hardship for the sake of the common national good. In addition, hiking throughout the country to experience it "hands on" is socially approved, often occurring under the auspices of one of Israel's many scout youth movements, where boys and girls take part in the same activities and are taught the same national values.

These activities, in which young Israeli girls participate, could easily be classified as "tomboyish" in the United States, but are simply the norm in Israel (Safir et al., 2003). Unfortunately, it appears that the ever-increasing cultural impact of American values on Israeli society is changing these gender-blind behavioral patterns. A recent study provides alarming evidence of one such possible negative cultural impact on Israeli children. This study reported an increasing spread of dissatisfaction with body image, as early as elementary school, in both girls and boys (Flaisher-Kellner, 2002).

Puberty and Adolescence

While most Jewish Israelis do not self-identify as religious, the majority participate in some religious ceremonies and traditions (Levi et al., 2000). The most notable example of such ceremony is the *Bar-Mitzva*, which is a religious rite signifying the transition from boyhood to manhood. Following his Bar-Mitzva, a boy is considered an adult man for all religious purposes. It is customary to hold a Bar-Mitzva celebration, to which hundreds of guests are invited for a six-course meal served in special reception halls. In especially lavish celebrations, one often hears the comment "the only thing missing was the bride." While the Bar-Mitzva is a grand milestone on the road from boyhood to manhood, girls' transition usually goes publicly unnoticed (Izraeli & Safir, 1993).

Another factor that maintains the spotlight on boys is the centrality of army in Israeli life, and in its definition of manhood. For teenaged boys, the army has a pivotal role in their transition into manhood and inauguration into the Israeli collective (Lomski-Feder & Rapoport, 2000). In light of looming military service, research has revealed that Jewish Israeli adolescent boys, unlike their Arab Israeli and American counterparts, see their future as inextricably intertwined with the future of their respective national collective (Magen, 1983).

In the Arab community, most teenagers do not serve in the army (Druze and Bedouin are exceptions). However, Arab culture is highly collectivistic because of the intense nature of family ties within this society (Lobel et al., 2000). This produces even greater demands for gender role conformity (Lavee & Katz, 2003). In fact, gender conformity is sufficiently strong in Arab adolescents to bias dramatically their judgment of a highly qualified, albeit feminine, male candidate. Research participants judged this candidate less favorably than an inferior masculine candidate. Judgment bias, based on normative gender roles, was much more pronounced in Arab participants than in Jewish participants (Lobel et al., 2000).

For teenaged Arab girls, this highly gendered culture demands their strict adherence to roles of sexual purity, which becomes central with the start of menstruation. Social supervision of these girls is meticulous, and their behavior is constantly scrutinized (Hassan, 1993).

Attainment of Adulthood

As was previously mentioned, mandatory army service has a pivotal role in defining the Israeli adult, and in particular the Israeli man. Army service, usually commencing immediately following completion of high school, replaces the American experience of "going off to college." For most Israeli boys, army service is the first time they have to fend for themselves away from their families and homes. Girls are usually stationed near to, and continue to reside in, their family homes.

In a more substantial sense, once in the army, young men are expected to make life-and-death decisions. While men are assigned to combat units, women have recently been "awarded" the privilege of volunteering for combat units. A minimal number of women currently serve in these units. This type of service places a great deal of responsibility on the shoulders of the young individual, and is a distinct break from the years of schooling. Because boys and girls are drafted into the army at age 18, they are considered to be full-fledged adults at this age and are eligible to vote, purchase tobacco, and drink alcohol.

The army is an institution that overvalues masculine traits, and is especially relevant to the construction of the hegemonic Israeli man (Lomski-Feder & Rapoport, 2000). Men who serve in combat positions are viewed as the epiphany of masculinity, maturity, and character. These attributes supposedly make them romantically and sexually appealing to women, and indeed, a few years ago *Shakel* was a slang term widely used to denote a man's man, especially in a sexually context. (This slang term is an abbreviation of "fighting combative bull" in Hebrew.)

On the other hand, men who do not serve in the army are often ostracized by mainstream Israeli society, and are reinstituted as the "other" (Lomski-Feder & Rapoport, 2000). Numerous job offers require completion of army service, thus signaling clearly the line between the normative and the "other": the Arab, the dropout, the inadequate, the outsider.

Middle Age and Old Age

Israeli society's emphasis on familial ties affects the way that elderly people are viewed and treated. The majority of older adults live in close proximity to their offspring, and remain involved in their children's life as long as their health permits. Older parents are frequently consulted by their adult children. They also often take a role of secondary caretakers to their grandchildren, thus easing the load from the parents (Lavee & Katz, 2003). As parents become elderly, they often move in with their children's families. As a result, more then 95% of the elderly who are in good physical shape, and 76% of the disabled, live with their children (Brodsky, 1998; cited in Lavee & Katz, 2003). This appears to be especially true in the more traditional sectors of both Arab and Jewish society.

PERSONALITY DIFFERENCES BY GENDER

In its construction of gender, each society assigns different attributes for each gender, clarifying the role each should adopt. Several studies indicate that Israeli construction of gender-related personality attributes is different to that found elsewhere in the West (Lobel, Rothman, Abramovizt & Maayan, 1999; Safir et al., 2003; Safir, Peres, Lichtenstien, Hoch, & Shepher, 1982). These studies utilizing gender trait inventories find that the range/number of gender relevant traits is more limited in Israel. It appears to us that, while the range of behavioral traits perceived as overlapping for both genders is greater in Israel than elsewhere, gender-specific behavior is very narrowly defined. Thus, while many traits and behaviors are typical for both women and men, each gender is expected to conform to a very narrow range of stereotyped behavior patterns (Safir et al., 1982). In these studies, the list of masculine and feminine items was similar to those found in the United States, but halved in number. As the range is more limited, deviation is more easily discernible, enabling greater social pressure to conform. This is evident in gender role identity as well: For instance, many more Israeli women, in comparison with American women, self-identified as feminine and fewer self-identified as androgynous (Safir et al., 2003).

GENDER ROLES IN ECONOMICS

In 2000, 77.5% of Jewish women and 29.7% of Arab women were in the civilian Israeli labor force (Adva Center, 2002). In contrast, 85% of Jewish men and 79.5% of Arab men participate in the work force. Even with high level of participation by Jewish women, their salaries are 62% of men's wages. However, since women work 35 hours a week, on average, and men 42 hours a week, an hourly comparison reduced the gap to 82% (Adva Center, 2002). This occurs despite the fact that, as early as 1965, laws were passed, for equal pay for equal work (Raday, 1993b).

Efroni (1988), in the most extensive survey of salary differences between male and female civil servants, reported that women earned 78% of what men with similar qualifications earned. She reported that if women were paid on the basis of their qualifications, they should have been paid 102% of men's salaries. Efroni's report was widely read and sparked a public outcry. As a result committees were created throughout all governmental agencies to improve the status of women. Efroni (personal communication, November 14, 2002) informed us that a recent internal examination by the Treasury found that the relative differences in men and women's salaries in civil service (20–30%) remain unchanged today.

In addition to gender differences in earnings, women and men also tend to work in different sectors, with more than half of Jewish women employed as clerical and service workers (Adva Center, 2002), as opposed to only 24.6% of Jewish men. About 35% of both genders are employed in professional, academic, and managerial sectors, but, as elsewhere, men tend to occupy the top positions (Efroni, 1988).

The socialist ideology of the kibbutz viewed the traditional patriarchal family as the cornerstone of capitalist oppression. As a result, men and women were accepted as equal members, and tasks which were typically performed by women in the traditional family became communal responsibility. However, the implicit belief that women are "naturally" better suited to nurturing tasks meant that women were assigned to childcare and teaching, which became long-term jobs. The less fortunate women were rotated through nonprofessional work duties such as laundry, kitchen, and light agriculture work. Although this resulted in a status hierarchy, each person received the same stipend (Safir, 1993b).

PARENTAL AND OTHER CARETAKER ROLES

As in other Mediterranean countries, lunchtime is the major meal of the day, with businesses closing between 2 p.m. and 4 p.m. Although this practice of closing businesses disappeared in the 1960s, dinner remains a light meal. The short school day reinforces the status of lunch as the main meal, seriously curtailing mothers' ability to take on full-time jobs (Izraeli & Safir, 1993). However, Lieblich (1993) found that Israeli career women were not resentful of their husbands' lack of participation in childcare and housework when compared with a matching American group. As a result, Israeli women experienced less role conflict. These women reported that their careers take second place to their family roles as mothers, wives, and caretakers, roles that are seen as more central to their sense of identity. Mothers often experience increases in their caretaker/nurturing roles when their children serve in the army—especially those with sons in combat units (Azmon & Izraeli, 1993). For example, the army does not provide laundry service, and soldiers' uniforms must be washed and ironed at home over the short weekend. In addition to doing the laundry, mothers are expected to "spoil" their children by preparing special meals and treats that can be taken back to the army.

LEADERSHIP IN PUBLIC ARENAS

In a nation that perceives itself as being under constant threat of extinction, the major focus of Israeli politics is on security issues (Gerabi, 1996). The discourse of national security remains an almost exclusively masculine arena (Gillath, 1993), dominated by men who came to the forefront of national politics following an illustrious military carrier. Since being a general, if not Chief of Staff, appears to be a prerequisite for most high-level political positions in government, women are effectively excluded from the national decision-making processes. In fact, in the 29th Knesset (which has the largest number of women members of Knesset (MKs) ever—16 out of 120), Prime Minister Ariel Sharon, only appointed three women ministers out of 24 available ministerial positions (Knesset Site, 2002).

This republican view of citizenship, which conjoins combat army service and entrance into the political sphere, also denies women's grass-roots social movements their legitimacy (Helman & Rapoport, 1997). When women entered the national debate and dared to voice unpopular antiwar views, they were seen as transgressing against their republican duty to support the fighting men. They were perceived as almost guilty of treason, failing in their duties towards their men and their nation (Herzog, 1996).

The all-encompassing importance of national security issues in Israeli politics was also detrimental to efforts to raise a feminist or women's rights political agenda. These issues were seen as trivial in comparison to the life-and-death questions of security, in particular as they were viewed as apolitical, domestic, and private matters, not pertinent to "serious" politics (Herzog, 1996).

Once introduced into the public sphere, women's agendas usually collide with those of the ultra-orthodox sectors in Israeli society. These sectors wield a great deal of political power because no major political party has managed to obtain a majority in the Knesset without incorporating them into a coalition.

GENDER AND RELIGION

As was previously noted, Israel defines itself as a "Jewish State," referring to both the national and the religious facets of Jewish identity. The fact that Jewish law is incorporated into state law lends great influence to the views of the rabbinical apparatus, which controls all personal legal status—from birth to death. In Jewish religious courts, children, retarded individuals, and women are not considered competent witnesses. It is worth noting that the elaborate state rabbinical system, and the Minister of Religious Affairs, and political appointments in the Ministry of Religious Affairs have been manned solely by men (Swirski & Safir, 1993).

In fact, the religious establishment's rejection of the concept of gender equality is one of the major reasons why Israel does not, to this day, have a constitution. Maintaining the status quo between the religious and secular segments of Israeli society has been deemed more important then signing a binding constitution declaring that women are men's equals in every sense (Raday, 1993a).

This interaction between contemporary ideas and age-old traditions is also evident in the lives of the vast majority of Israelis, who do not define themselves as religious (Levi et al., 2000). Even in the relatively secular portion of society it is the norm, during the High Holidays, to attend prayer services at Orthodox synagogues (which receive state funding, unlike the small number of Reform and Conservative synagogues in Israel). Only men can actively participate in these prayer services as well as perform the Kadish prayer for the dead. In addition, men's daily morning prayer includes the Hebrew phrase *Barukh shelo assani isha* ("Blessed is God for not creating me a woman"). In these Orthodox synagogues, women are hidden from men's sight and are excluded from praying aloud, so that they do not distract the men. Even in the traditional Orthodox wedding ceremony, the woman is not an active but a silent participant.

RELATIVE STATUS OF MEN AND WOMEN

Since Israel is a traditional gender-conservative society, women are disadvantaged in many public arenas. On the other hand, the Israeli woman is glorified as the mother of the nation and, in a family-oriented society like Israel, such a position may provide certain privileges.

SEXUALITY

Aspects of sexuality vary drastically between different segments of Israeli society. For example, while cohabitation is acceptable for secular Israelis, virginity is required of brides in the religious Jewish and Moslem sectors (Lavee & Katz, 2003), and gynecologists have developed a specialization in the reconstruction of the hymen.

When seeking help with sexual problems, Israelis generally emphasize issues pertaining to fertility and not feelings of individual dissatisfaction (Safir, 1999). Despite this, men's potency is a major element in the masculine ideal. A private clinic that treats (im)potence, with branches nationwide, advertises its service on the radio and in daily newspapers. An advertisement direct at middle-aged men has recently been appearing on television indicating that men can be helped to regain their masculinity by asking their doctor to prescribe Viagra.

COURTSHIP AND MARRIAGE

In the Jewish secular sector of Israel, grammar school children use the term "boyfriend" or "girlfriend" to designate special friends of the other sex. However, such relationships are usually kept within the peer group, and the early "couple" will not usually meet outside their peer group. Later, usually in early to middle adolescence, more romantically oriented pairs will form and dating will commence. Casual dating is not encouraged, and usually a couple will date for at least a few months. These young couples sometimes stay together for long periods of time, and eventually marry. Early sexual experiences may be a part of these committed relationships, even at a relatively early age. Many more couples form later, during or following mandatory military service (Lavee & Katz, 2003).

The median age of first marriage has been rising (Table 1). The only exception to this pattern is found for Muslim women (as well as ultra-orthodox Jewish women) whose age of first marriage has remained virtually constant. This finding also indicates the ever-deepening cultural cleavage between secular Western-oriented Israeli sectors, and the more traditional segments of Arab and Jewish societies.

Table 1. Median Age of First Marriage, by Sex and Religion, in Three Time Periods

		Jew	Muslim	Christian
1970	Women	21.5	19.3	21
	Men	24.1	23.4	27
1985	Women	22.7	19.8	22.4
	Men	25.7	23.7	27.3
2000	Women	24.4	20.3	23.1
	Men	26.7	25	28.3

In ultra-orthodox Jewish and Muslim communities the family is heavily involved in matchmaking. The young woman has veto power over the husband candidate. If she accepts him, the marriage is quickly arranged. In these communities, special permission is often sought to enable the young woman to marry at 17. In fact, the minimum age of marriage was set by law at age 18 in order to prevent these communities from arranging marriages for girls aged 15–16, or even younger girls (Hassan, 1993; Lavee & Katz, 2003).

Upon marriage, the wife moves to and becomes part of her husband's family in traditional Arab sectors. As a result, investing in a daughter's education was not seen as relevant, as her family would not benefit from this investment. This attitude is changing in the more socially affluent sectors of Arab society (Mar'i & Mar'i, 1985).

HUSBAND–WIFE RELATIONSHIP

The emphasis on family life is clearly evident, and the vast majority of Israelis of all walks of life do, in fact, choose to marry. The family centeredness of Israeli society also affects couples' priorities in marriage, and many Israelis feel that joint children are a sufficient reason to maintain an otherwise unfulfilling marriage (Lavee & Katz, 2003).

Since religious law governs all personal matters, divorce is not a judicial act, and only men can grant divorce. If the husband does not agree to divorce his wife—she cannot remarry. If she divorces in civil courts outside Israel and remarries, any children born from this new relationship would be considered *mamzerim* (bastards—a child born to an adulteress). Under Israeli Jewish law, these children and their offspring cannot marry for 10 generations. If a married man has a relationship with an unmarried woman, these children have the same rights and standing as his children from his marriage. There are even provisions for a man to marry a secondly wife, if his first wife will not agree to the divorce (Raday, 1993a). The only situation in which a divorce might be granted to a woman without her husband's consent would be if she could prove that her husband is infertile. The fact that the husband can refuse to allow his wife a divorce, thereby placing her in limbo should she wish to have a family with another man, gives the husband great power. It should be noted, however, that if both partners want a divorce, it is very easy to obtain.

CHANGE IN ATTITUDES, BELIEFS, AND PRACTICES REGARDING GENDER

Israeli society is becoming increasing open to liberal ideas about gender equality. This may be attributed to the fact that the early socialist pressure to conform to the collective's needs and values is decreasing. Western, and specifically American, emphasis on civil rights and individualism are reflected in the national discourse regarding social and economic disparities between men and women, and other minority groups (Efroni, 1988). We have also noted that more women are moving into nontraditional positions in the army, and into other male-dominated professions. It appears to us that, unfortunately, these changes are often only "skin-deep." In the case of previously male-dominated professions, such as law and medicine, women are concentrated in the public sector where the work structure is more compatible with their roles as wives and mothers, while men work in the private sector with all the benefits that this entails (Izraeli, 1993).

As noted previously, some minor changes are also occurring in the structure of the Israeli family, with the rising age of first marriage and the increase of divorce rates (Lavee & Katz, 2003). These changes notwithstanding, the family-oriented nature of Israeli society is not presently threatened.

Perhaps the most outstanding changes have occurred in the public sphere, with regard to both mainstream and radical women's movements actively and publicly demanding changes to "right the wrongs." Even the right-wing National Religious Party has guaranteed to hold the fifth seat on its list for a woman in the national elections of January 28, 2003.

As a result of the breakdown of the national consensus following the Lebanon War in 1982, women's antiwar movements have begun to influence issues of national security. Employing their legitimate, almost sacred, status as mothers, several nationwide grassroots women's movements have affected the national discourse on matters of security and international relations (Gillath, 1993). These women evoked their powers as mothers, thus gaining access to mainstream politics. However, they did not contest the basic tenets of the family-oriented Israeli society.

REFERENCES

Abu-Baker, K. (1985). The impact of cross-cultural contact on the status of Arab women in Israel. In M. P. Safir, M. Mednik, D. Izraeli, & J. Bernard (Eds.), Women's worlds: From the new scholarship (pp. 246–250). New York: Praeger Publications.

Adva Center. (2002). Information on equality and social justice in Israel. Retrieved from http://www.adva.org/pearim.htm

Al-Haj, M. (1995). Kinship and modernization in developing societies: The emergence in instrumentalized kinship. Journal of Comparative Family Studies, 26(3), 311–328.

Azmon, Y., & Izraeli, D. N. (1993). Introduction. Women in Israel—A sociological overview. In Y. Azmon & D. N. Izraeli (Eds.), Women in Israel. Studies of Israeli society, Vol. VI (pp. 1–24). New Brunswick, NJ: Transaction Publishers.

Ben Tsvi-Meyer, S., Hertz-Lazarovitz, R., & Safir, M. P. (1989). Teachers' selections of boys or girls as prominent pupils. Sex Roles, 21, 231–247.

Bernstein, D. (1987). The struggle for equality: Urban women workers in pre-state Israel. New York: Praeger.

Bloom, A. R. (1993). Women in the defense forces. In B. Swirski & M. P. Safir (Eds.), Calling the equality bluff: Women in Israel (pp. 128–138). New York: Teachers College Press.

Crawford, M., & Unger, R. K. (2000). Women and gender: A feminist psychology (3rd ed.). Boston: McGraw-Hill.

Dimitrovsky, L., Singer, J., & Yinon, Y. (1989). Masculine and feminine traits: Their relation to suitedness for and success in training for traditionally masculine and feminine army functions. Journal of Personality and Social Psychology, 57 (5), 839–847.

Efroni, L. (1988). Nashiim basherot hamemshalti: nitu'akh hashva'ati, shnat 1978 le'umat 1988 [Women in governmental services: Comparative analysis of year 1978 and 1988]. ma'amad ha'isha, 21. Israel Prime Minister Bureau, 171–180.

El-Mehairy, T. (1985). The status and education of women: A perspective on Egypt. In M. P. Safir, M. Mednik, D. Izraeli, & J. Bernard (Eds.), Women's worlds: From the new scholarship (pp. 239–245). New York: Praeger Publications.

El-Saadawi, N. (1980). The hidden face of Eve: Women in the Arab world. London: Zed Press.

Flaisher-Kellner, S. (2002). svi'ut haratzon shal yaldey beyt hassefer hayessodi migufam: hashpa'at hahorim u'bney hagil vehakesher leha'arakha atzmit [Body image satisfaction in grammar school children: The influence of parents, peer group and the connection with self-esteem]. Unpublished MA Thesis, University of Haifa, Israel.

Fogel-Bijawi, S. (1999). Mishpakhot beyisra'el: ben mishpakhtiyut lepost-moderniyut [Israeli families: Between family values and post-modernism]. In D. Izraeli, A. Freedman, H. Dahan-Kaleb, S. Fogel-Bijawi, K. Hertzog, M. Hassan, & K. Nave (Eds.), Min, migdar vepolitika. Tel-Aviv: Hakibutz Hame'ukhad.

Gerabi, A. (1996). Hamekhir hakaful: ma'amad ha'isha bakhevra hayisra'elit veshirut nashim betzahal [The doubled cost: Women's positions in Israeli society and women's service in the IDF]. Tel-Aviv: Ramot Publishing, Tel-Aviv University.

Gillath, N. (1993). Women against war: "Parents against silence". In B. Swirski & M. P. Safir (Eds.), Calling the equality bluff: Women in Israel (pp. 142–146). New York: Teachers College Press.

Glazer, I. M., & Abu Ras, W. (1994). On aggression, human rights, and hegemonic discourse: The case of a murder for family honor in Israel. *Sex Roles, 30*(3–4), 269–288.

Gluzman, M. (1997). hakmiha lehetrosexu'aliyut: Tziyonuy veminiyut be'altnoiland [Longing for heterosexuality: Zionism and sexuality in Altneuland]. *ti'orya vebikoret, 11*, 145–162.

Hassan, M. (1999). hapolitica shel hakavod: hapatri'arkhiya, hamedina veretzakh nashim beshem "kvod hamishpakha" [The politics of honor: The patriarchy, the state and the murdering of women in the name of "family honor"]. In D. Izraeli, A. Freedman, H. Dahan-Kaleb, S. Fogel-Bijawi, K. Hertzog, M. Hassan, & K. Nave (Eds.), *Min, migdar vepolitika* (pp. 267–306). Tel-Aviv: Hakibutz Hame'ukhad.

Hassan, M. (1993). Growing up female and Palestinian in Israel. In B. Swirski & M. P. Safir (Eds.), *Calling the equality bluff: Women in Israel* (pp. 66–75). New York: Teachers College Press.

Helman, S., & Rapoport, T. (1997). Women in black: Challenging Israel's gender and socio-political orders. *British Journal of Sociology, 48*(4), 681–700.

Herzog, H. (1996). Why so few? The political culture of gender in Israel. *International Review of Women and Leadership, 2*(1), 11–17.

Israel Central Bureau of Statistics. (2001). Retrieved from http://www.cbs.gov.il/engindex.htm

Izraeli, D. (1993). Women and work: From collective to career. In B. Swirski & M. P. Safir (Eds.), *Calling the equality bluff: Women in Israel* (pp. 165–177). New York: Teachers College Press.

Izraeli, D. & Safir, M. P. (1993). Developmental aspects of male/female gender roles in Israel (1992). In L. L. Adler (Ed.), *International Handbook of Gender Roles* (pp. 144–158). New York: Praeger/Greenwood.

Kahn, S. M. (2000). *Reproducing Jews: A cultural account of assisted conception in Israel.* Durham, NC: Duke University Press.

Knesset Site. (2002). Retrieved from http://knesset.gov.il/govt/heb/membyparameter.asp?par=1

Lavee, Y., & Katz, R. (2003, in press). The family in Israel: Between tradition and modernity. *Marriage and Family Review, 35*(1–2).

Levi, S., Levinsohn, H., & Katz, E. (2000). *A portrait of Israeli Jewry: Highlights from an in-depth study.* Jerusalem: Guttman Center of the Israel Democracy Institution.

Lieblich, A. (1993). Comparison of Israeli and American successful career women at midlife. In B. Swirski & M. P. Safir (Eds.), *Calling the equality bluff: Women in Israel* (pp. 90–98). New York: Teachers College Press.

Lieblich, A., & Friedman, G. (1985). Attitudes toward male and female homosexuality and sex-role stereotypes in Israeli and American students. *Sex Roles, 12*, 561–570.

Lobel, T. E., Mashraki-Pedhatzur, S., Mantzur, A., & Libby, S. (2000). Gender discrimination as a function of stereotypic and counterstereotypic behavior: A cross-cultural study. *Sex Roles, 43*(5–6), 395–406.

Lobel, T. E., Rothman, G., Abramovizt, E., & Maayan, Z. (1999). Self-perception and deceptive behavior: The uniqueness of feminine males. *Sex Roles, 41*(7–8), 577–587.

Lomski-Feder, E., & Rapoport, T. (2000). Meskhakim bemodelim shel gavriyut: mehagrim yehudim russim batzava hayisra'eli [Playing with models of masculinity: Russian Jewish immigrants in the Israeli army]. *sotzyologia yisra'elit, 3*(1): 31–51.

Magen, Z. (1983). Re-formatting the boundaries: A trans-cultural comparison of positive experiences among adolescent males and females. *Adolescence, 72*, 851–858.

Mar'i, M., & Mar'i, S. (1985). The role of women as change agents in Arab society in Israel. In M. P. Safir, M. Mednik, D. Izraeli, & J. Bernard (Eds.), *Women's worlds: From the new scholarship* (pp. 251–259). New York: Praeger Publications.

Raday, F. (1993a). The concept of gender equality in a Jewish state. In B. Swirski & M. P. Safir (Eds.), *Calling the equality bluff: Women in Israel* (pp. 18–28). New York: Teachers College Press.

Raday, F. (1993b). Women, work and the law. In B. Swirski & M. P. Safir (Eds.), *Calling the equality bluff: Women in Israel* (pp. 178–186). New York: Teachers College Press.

Safir, M. P. (1986). The effects of nature or of nurture on sex differences in intellectual functioning: Israeli findings. *Sex Roles, 14*, 581–590.

Safir, M. P. (1999). hityakhassut lereka tarbuti velehevdelim bein hamigdarim betipul mini beyisrael [Referring to cultural background and differences between the genders in sex therapy in Israel]. In C. Rabin (Ed.), *lihiyot shone beyisrael* (pp. 315–325). Tel-Aviv: Ramot.

Safir, M. P. (1993a). Religion, tradition and public policy give family first priority. In B. Swirski & M. P. Safir (Eds.), *Calling the equality bluff: Women in Israel* (pp. 57–65). New York: Teachers College Press.

Safir, M. P. (1993b). Was the Kibbutz an experiment in social and sex equality? In B. Swirski & M. P. Safir (Eds.), *Calling the equality bluff: Women in Israel* (pp. 251–260). New York: Teachers College Press.

Safir, M. P., Ben Tsvi-Meyer, S., Hertz-Lazarovitz, R., & Kuppermintz, H. (1992). Prominence of girls and boys in the classroom: School childrens' perception. *Sex Roles, 27*, 439–453.

Safir, M. P., Peres, Y., Lichtenstien, M., Hoch, Z., & Shepher, J. (1982). Psychological androgyny and sexual adequacy. *Journal of Sex and Marital Therapy, 8*(3), 228–239.

Safir, M. P., Rosenmann, A., & Kloner, O. (2003). Tomboyism, sexual orientation and adult gender roles among Israeli women. *Sex Roles, 48*, 401–410.

Sasson-Levi, O. (1997). hen holkhot zkufot vege'ot [They walk proud and straight]. *Noga, 32*, 21–30.

Seginer, R., Karayanni, M., & Mar'i, M. M. (1990). Adolescents' attitudes toward women's roles: A comparison between Israeli Jews and Arabs. *Psychology of Women Quarterly, 14*(1), 119–133.

Shtarkshall, R. A. (1987). Motherhood as dominant feature in the self-image of female adolescents of low socio-economic status. *Adolescence, 87*, 565–570.

Singer, Y. (1997). *hakesher beyn tkhunot nashiyot vegavriyot leveyn midat hat'amatam vehatzlakhatam shel khayalim vekhayalot bakurssim hashonim betzahal* [The connection between masculine and feminine traits and the degree of adjustment and success of male and female soldiers in various IDF courses]. Unpublished MA Thesis, Bar-Ilan University, Ramat-Gan, Israel.

Soliman, A. (1985). The socialization of the Arab woman. *Arab Journal of Social Science, 2*(2), 235–255.

Suleiman, R., & Beit-Hallahmi, B. (1997). National and civil identities of Palestinians in Israel. *Journal of Social Psychology, 132*(20), 219–228.

Swirski, B., & Safir, M. P. (1993). Living in a Jewish State. In B. Swirski & M. P. Safir (Eds.), *Calling the equality bluff: Women in Israel* (pp. 7–17). New York: Teacher's College Press.

U.S. Census Bureau. (2001). Retrieved from http://www.census.gov/population/socdemo/hh-fam/tabFM-3.xls

Italians

Victoria A. Goddard

ALTERNATIVE NAME

Italians are also known as Italiani.

LOCATION

Italy consists of a peninsular mainland, the two large islands of Sicily and Sardinia, and a number of smaller islands. The physical environment of Italy is very varied, ranging from the Alps in the north, to the fertile plain of the Po river in the northeast, to the rugged coastline of the Mediterranean. Rome, Italy's capital city, is also the location of the Vatican City, the center of the Roman Catholic Church.

Naples, which is the focus of this chapter, is Italy's third city, with a population of 1.2 million. The city is located in the region of Campania and is the major urban center of the south. Founded by the Greeks, the city came under the domination of many outside forces throughout its history but it also played the role of a political and cultural center to a number of different polities. For example, Naples was the capital of the Bourbon Kingdom until the unification of Italy in 1860. With its spectacular bay, Naples has been a major tourist center since the 19th century. But the city's grand architecture and beautiful natural location have been contrasted with the conditions of life of much of its population, who have gained a reputation for resourcefulness in the face of long-term poverty and underemployment.

CULTURAL OVERVIEW

In much of the anthropological literature, Italy would be included within the Mediterranean ethnographic region, which has been frequently characterized in terms of a cultural system based on "honor and shame." These values are embedded in gender relations and local discourses of sexuality, usually entailing a strong emphasis on male reputation and on the control of

women's sexuality (Gilmore, 1987). But although the codes of honor and shame have generated an extensive and interesting literature on gender and sexuality in the area, they are of limited use in the Italian context (Goddard, 1994). Indeed, any convenient characterization of gender ideals and relations is problematic, as Italy is highly diversified in terms of physical, cultural, and social characteristics.

Throughout the modern period the Italian peninsula consisted of numerous political entities, ranging from large kingdoms to small city-states, until the *Risorgimento* movement promoted and supported the unification of Italy under the leadership of Piedmont and the House of Savoy. Unification was accomplished in 1860, bringing together very different kinds of economic, political, and social structures. The incorporation of a semi-feudal south into the new Italian nation-state did little to accelerate the development of the area. On the contrary, the differences between the north and the south have endured and have long been the subject of debate and policy. Today, the standard of living of the southern population has improved dramatically compared with the poverty that prevailed after World War II. But the south remains different from the rest of the country. In a country with amongst the highest rates of unemployment in Europe, the south displays higher levels of unemployment and poverty. Here there are also higher levels of fertility than the rest of the country, more marriages, and larger families.

But despite the continuing significance of the differences between southern and northern regions, a simple north–south dichotomy fails to account for the complexities of Italy. Bagnasco (1977) has made a convincing case for the specificities of the central and northeastern regions, suggesting that there are in fact "three Italies" rather than simply two, each with their distinct history, culture, and economy. These regional differences are also evident at the level of the private domestic arena, there being important differences in family types and in patterns of gender relations between these regions.

Despite drives to create a coherent national whole since the Unification, most notably under the fascist regime, regional and local variations remain strong. There have been a number of centrifugal forces at work. Observers have pointed to the phenomenon of *campanilismo*, a term derived from *campanile*, the church bell tower, to suggest the importance of loyalties attaching to the vicinity of the local church. A number of political and anthropological works have pointed to the strength of attachment to the locality and of suspiciousness toward outsiders, including representatives of the state (e.g., Silverman, 1975b). Since the 1980s, the decentralization of government to the regions has enhanced regional differences and resulted in significant variations in local policy and the provision of welfare services and support (Bimbi, 2000).

On the other hand, there have also been powerful unifying forces. The Catholic Church and different strands of Catholic ideology have been widely influential and have shaped national policy, particularly with regard to the family, sexuality, and reproduction. The Church has upheld the centrality of the family and has exerted a strong influence on the kind of family and the associated gender roles that are supported by government. The influence of the Church has meant that, in fact, state welfare policy has never seriously challenged the "family paradigm" whereby the family is the principal provider of care, support, and welfare (Bimbi, 2000; Saraceno, 1994).

The term "familism" has often been used in connection with Italian society to refer to the importance of ideologies and practices that place the family unit firmly at the center of individual and social reproductive strategies and ideologies. Some authors have stressed the negative effects of what they have seen as the isolationist effects of familism (Banfield, 1958). Banfield's analysis of a poor rural center in the south of Italy in the 1950s argued that "amoral familism" prevented wider cooperation and was responsible for the backward conditions of the village. Others have focused on the relations of cooperation, pooling, and solidarity that familism is able to sustain and legitimize (Ginsborg, 1990; Goddard, 1996; Saraceno, 1994). Ginsborg uses the term "moral familism" to describe forms of collective action, such as those initiated by the families of the 110 victims of a terrorist attack at Bologna station in 1980 or the organization of a group of mothers to combat the sale of hard drugs to children.

Despite declining birth rates, and Italy has one of the lowest fertility rates in the world, the family continues to be a strong and important institution (Ruspini, 2000). In central Italy the family has been identified as the keystone of a specifically Italian version of capitalism based on small firms and strong family-based solidarity (see Yanagisako, 2002). In the south, the family constitutes a refuge and a safety net in the face of unemployment and poverty (Goddard, 1996; Ruspini, 2000). In either case, the prevalence of the family and the influence of the Catholic Church on the ways in which the family is conceptualized and upheld have important implications for the opportunities open to men and women in Italian society.

CULTURAL CONSTRUCTION OF GENDER

Alongside the regional variations that characterize Italy, there are striking differences with regard to gender roles and ideals, depending on region, class, and generation. But it is possible to make some generalizations, particularly where the connections between the family and gender constructs are concerned. Given the centrality of the family, it is perhaps not surprising that the qualities associated with parenting, and especially with motherhood, shape and inspire ideal gender identities.

Men and women are expected to be different, in terms of physical, cultural, and emotional characteristics. So where men might be expected to be strong and assertive, women should ideally be gentle, sympathetic, and nurturing. But beyond these very general expectations, men and women display a wide range of characteristics and forms of behavior. In Naples, although women may defer to the opinions of men on some subjects, or assume a subdued attitude in the presence of their husbands or other men, in other circumstances they will quite appropriately express their opinions assertively and interact freely with both men and women.

Throughout Italy there are different, or indeed competing, ideals of masculinity and femininity. For example, research in the city of Florence illustrates the ways in which working-class men elaborate alternative measures of masculinity. These enable them (or some of them) to achieve a successful masculine identity in the absence of the means to achieve the ideals dictated by middle-class values and expectations and which are largely promoted by the media (de Bromhead, 1999). Similarly, there are women who occupy influential positions in the public sphere (see "Leadership in Public Arenas"), and work and career are increasingly important sources of fulfillment and pride for women. However, despite these variations and changes, it is still the case that the family provides a crucial context for evaluating gender performance across the divides of class and region. In particular, ideals regarding women and womanhood are still largely embedded in the family.

GENDER OVER THE LIFE CYCLE

Sydel Silverman's research, conducted in the 1960s in a community in the province of Perugia in central Italy, suggests that the life cycles of women are likely to differ significantly from those of men, being marked more strongly by and in a closer relationship with reproduction (Silverman, 1975a, 1975b). But in Colleverde, where her research was carried out, there were also significant differences amongst women, particularly regarding the points at which life crises occur and the intensity of such crises.

Silverman notes that in general there was little concern over the changes associated with puberty or with menopause. Instead, the critical period in a woman's life was the period of courtship. Courtship initiated a crisis and a state of insecurity that was only partially resolved at marriage and fully resolved only at the birth of the first child. Silverman (1975b) points to a parallel between her findings in this rural area of central Italy, and those of Anne Parsons who was working in Naples at the time. Parsons (1967) also indicated that the years of courtship were the most distressing in a woman's life. The stress and anxiety related to the numerous pressures that the girl was subject to once she was engaged to be married, not least those provoked by the turmoil of the relationship itself. Young fiancées were also vulnerable to gossip. But Silverman shows that in the central Italian area where she carried out research, the intensity of the crisis varied significantly, especially between girls in the villages, for whom a good reputation is an important asset, and the girls belonging to *mezzadri* farming families. The *mezzadria* is a form of sharecropping, in which family labor is a major resource. This meant that the girls living on the farms were valued for their contribution as workers, and their reproductive capacity was a clear asset so that they were less vulnerable to gossip regarding their sexual conduct. For example, in such families a premarital pregnancy might be welcomed rather than be seen as shameful (Silverman, 1975b).

Socialization of Boys and Girls

The socialization of boys and girls needs to be contextualized within the family and the organization of the household. Whereas girls are likely to assist in household chores, this would not usually be expected of boys. In Naples even young girls might take on quite heavy responsibilities in the home, especially when their mothers were at work. However, this situation was reversed in rural areas. Although girls continued to help in the household, boys had a heavier burden of work, helping with the agricultural tasks (Davis, 1973). In either case, the division of labor in the household clearly endorses the sense that boys and girls are different and can expect to have different life experiences and rewards.

Children are highly valued in Italian families. In Naples, babies and toddlers are treated with a great deal of affection and indulgence. Physical affection is shown openly and effusively. It is not unusual for a baby to be passed around a gathering, each person in turn bestowing some form of caress or appreciation on the child. Differences between boy and girl babies are recognized and elaborated. Boys and girls are dressed differently, they are associated with different colors, and given different toys. Boy babies and toddlers in particular elicit a lot of attention. Playful reference to a boy's penis is considered quite appropriate, and a female carer such as the mother, aunt, or older sister might play with a baby's penis while changing and cleaning him, or while playing. Slightly older boys will be teased and tested for what many considered to be desirable masculine traits, such as bravery and defiance and willingness to stand up for themselves and their family. One 5-year-old boy provoked both pride and hilarity when he responded defiantly and courageously to a mock attack on his father, undeterred by the size and age of his opponent. Davis (1973) recounts a similar situation that he witnessed in Pisticci, in the south of Italy, in the 1960s, when a boy was tested through verbal provocation. Other accounts and observations suggest that teasing is used quite widely as a socialization strategy to elicit the appropriate response from a child who is then rewarded when a suitable reaction is forthcoming.

Little girls would not be engaged in the same kind of play as boys. Instead, jokes and comments would focus on what are considered to be a girl's feminine qualities. A little girl is likely to be praised because of her prettiness or her charm, although the qualities of cleverness and mental and verbal agility are desirable and encouraged in both girls and boys. So, although all children are treated with great affection and receive a lot of attention, the ways in which they are approached and the expectations expressed toward them differ so that in a number of ways boys and girls are encouraged to develop different strengths and qualities.

Puberty and Adolescence

For families who adhere to Catholicism, and even for many who do not, a child's first communion is an important ritual occasion. In theory it marks the transition from childhood into a process leading to adulthood. But first communion takes place when a child is young and it is only loosely and implicitly associated with puberty. In fact, the onset of puberty itself is somewhat unmarked and unremarkable.

The experience of adolescents varies, not least as a result of their family's economic status. It was not unusual for men and women of the poorer districts of Naples born prior to the 1970s to have started working for wages in some form at a very early age, some as young as 8 or 10, many more starting paid employment around the age of 14. Although such children would still live at home and would be expected to show respect for their parents, the work experience could foment a greater sense of responsibility and maturity in them.

Men and women with children in the 1970s and 1980s showed a strong commitment to the education of their children, and rates of completion of schooling have been improving steadily. This means that adolescents spend more time at school and remain dependent for longer, although many will contribute in some way or other. As mentioned, girls are more likely than boys to make a direct contribution to the household by performing household chores and caring for younger siblings or even nephews or nieces. At the same time, throughout Italy girls have entered education and succeeded to the extent that they are surpassing the achievements of boys.

Adolescence is a time when boys and girls may initiate relationships with the opposite sex. Girls, in particular, may become seriously involved in a stable relationship by the age of 16 or 17. If this is the case, the girl's social life will change significantly, as it will tend to revolve more around her fiancé and the families of the young couple than her peer group.

Attainment of Adulthood

The attainment of adulthood is a gradual process and several events can be seen as steps toward adulthood. Earning an income is one such step, although many Neapolitans start their work careers whilst very young and still very much under the authority of their families. For many others work is an erratic and unreliable basis for building a sense of identity. A clearer marker of entry into adulthood is marriage and in particular having a child. With adulthood and parenthood come heavy responsibilities, and the expectations regarding both men and women will change. Although the situation has been changing over the last decade or so and careers are important for women as well as men, having a family of one's own, and in particular having children, is highly desirable and indeed remains a priority. This is evident in the figures that show that many women leave work after marriage and especially after the birth of their first child. So, despite changes in education and the labor market, motherhood and, to a lesser extent, marriage still represent an obstacle to the open and full employment of women (Bettio & Villa, 2000).

For many women in particular, establishing a household of their own is a means of becoming autonomous and exercising some control over their time and space. Even those who were content to live in the parental home generally aspired to having a family at some time in the future. On the other hand, housing shortages in much of Italy mean that many children are forced to remain in the family home well into adulthood.

Middle Age and Old Age

Men and women whose children have grown up, and perhaps had children of their own, continue to play an important role in the life of their families. As mentioned, there are several obstacles to establishing an independent household and adult children may well remain in the parental home for many years. During this time they are likely to expect, and probably receive, care from their parents, especially their mothers.

For many families, especially those that require both partners' involvement in wage work, having access to their children's grandparents can be crucial. In many households in the poorer districts of Naples, grandparents, and especially grandmothers, would take on a great deal of responsibility for their grandchildren. In some instances meals might be shared by a group of kin to help those who are short of income, or children might eat or even sleep in their grandparents' homes if their own homes were small or inadequate.

So families continue to be an important focus for the individual and, where physical proximity allows it, family and kin will interact on a daily basis. Peer-group socializing is also important for many people. Women will tend to visit friends and family and socialize in each other's homes. Men are more likely to meet outside the home, in coffee bars or in one of the local social clubs associated with political, civic, or religious organizations, where they might play cards and chat. In the older age group there appears to be a greater emphasis on single-sex groups, and socializing as couples appeared to be far less frequent.

PERSONALITY DIFFERENCES BY GENDER

It is important to recognize that in Italy there are currently a number of alternative views of masculinity and femininity, not least those promoted by the media, so that a number of different personality traits are quite acceptable in men and women. However, a fairly "hegemonic" form of masculinity (Cornwall & Lindisfarne, 1994) would usually entail some quite specific characteristics, such as assertiveness and self-confidence, virility, and the ability to support one's family. Depending on the context, this might also entail a certain verbal competence, or the ability to drink without losing control, or to display physical prowess in some field. The counterpart to such a "hegemonic" masculinity would be a gentle, submissive, and attentive woman, a good mother to her children, and a caring partner to her husband. The demands of such a model of masculinity can result in a dichotomous view of women, whereby the "good" and virtuous woman, ideally suited for motherhood, is contrasted with the "bad" sexually and morally loose woman whose behavior is in direct contrast with that of the virtuous wife.

Although these various stereotypes would be recognized in Naples, the differences between "hegemonic" and alternative masculinities on the one hand, and good and bad women on the other were actually blurred and contradictory. A quiet gentle man might be respected as much as, or more than, a confident extrovert. And although many women, wives in particular, might be

quietly submissive in the presence of their husbands or fathers, they may equally be talkative, assertive and humorous, and quite ribald without eliciting criticism. In fact, both men and women are expected to participate in, and contribute to, a social gathering. Humor, wit, and self-confidence are qualities that are appreciated in both women and men.

GENDER-RELATED SOCIAL GROUPS

In Italy, personal relations associated with the family and with kinship are important resources for cooperation and social solidarity. This was very clearly the case in Naples, where kinship and neighborhood networks were extremely important sources of support and cooperation, especially for women. Neighbors might help each other in a number of ways—with childcare, lending some crucial ingredient for the preparation of the midday meal, sometimes assisting with work, or providing companionship and support when this was needed.

The relationship between a mother and her children was considered to be especially strong and enduring. Mother–daughter relations were especially important in the everyday life of women, especially in the old quarters of the city where families might live in close proximity. However, a shortage of affordable housing means that many young couples are unable to find accommodation close to their families and are forced to find alternative (and usually better) accommodation on the outskirts of the city, making such intensive contacts extremely difficult.

GENDER ROLES IN ECONOMICS

It is now widely accepted throughout Italy that women have a role to play in the labor market (Bimbi, 1993). However, the opportunities for paid employment are unevenly distributed and in many regions there is an acute shortage of jobs, so that women's aspirations remain unfulfilled. In Naples, a combination of limited work opportunities and the constraints of parenting and domestic duties encouraged many women to become outworkers (Goddard, 1996). In Baunei, a village in north Sardinia, women did aspire to working outside the home but the lack of opportunities meant that only a few managed to live up to this ideal. At the same time, the content of housework has changed. The growth of a consumer culture has radically altered the technology of domestic work and shaped the aspirations of men and women. These various changes mean that now women who are at home feel frustrated because "to be a housewife with few cash resources of one's own in a consumer society is very different from the role played by the self-respected female heads of household in a subsistence economy" (Assmuth, 1997, p. 17).

As in other parts of Europe, the Italian labor market is markedly gendered. Women tend to fill certain niches and to be concentrated in certain trades such as textiles, garments, and services. But women have played a crucial role in another important dimension of the Italian economy: during the 1980s Italy became known as the exponent of a new version of capitalism, frequently described as "flexible accumulation" (Piore & Sabel, 1984). The principal characteristic of this form of production was its reliance on the family as a basis for entrepreneurial activities. In the north and center of the country the family provided the resources for a successful strategy of accumulation. Although families were also important in the south, for pooling labor and resources, the different conditions in the region tended to act as a brake on the consolidation of successful family enterprises.

The leather trade of Naples was a particularly important source of work for women, whether as workers in the factories or as outworkers working in their own homes. Although the ideal of a male breadwinner was shared by the majority of Neapolitans, the reality of unemployment and insecure employment meant that it was extremely hard to rely on a single income and wives were frequently involved in some kind of income-generating activity (Goddard, 1996). Because the family, and in particular parenting, remained the most valued activity, home-based work was seen as a solution to the conflicting needs of the household, for money on the one hand and attention, and services on the other. Another solution was provided by the assistance of older children (daughters), mothers, mothers-in-law, sisters, and other relatives, who could free up the time of female relatives to enable them to engage in wage work.

PARENTAL AND OTHER CARETAKER ROLES

Parenting is an important and fulfilling task for both men and women. A characteristic of most Neapolitan families was the pleasure openly taken in children, who were always treated with great affection. This attention was not restricted to the child's parents. Other kin, such as grandparents, aunts, and uncles, were likely to be involved in some way in the care and entertainment of children.

Motherhood has had a privileged position within Italian cultural representations. Neapolitans often stated that a person's mother is his or her most trustworthy ally and support. This claim was sustained even by those who had experienced serious conflicts with their mother and their families. Despite the possible shortcomings of specific individuals, mothers were to be respected and loved: "*la mamma è sempre la mamma*" ("the mother is always the mother") was often the concluding remark, even in a tale of family woe.

However, research indicates that some significant changes are afoot in parenting practices, particularly where men are concerned. Bimbi's research in three different regions of the country indicates that ideas about fatherhood have changed (Bimbi, 1993). The figure of the authoritarian father associated with prewar society has given way to a more caring and engaged paternal involvement. Her research also shows that the domestic space is no longer identified as closely with women as in the past and that, just as both parents now play an active role in the care of children, women as well as men are involved in work outside the home.

Changes in parental practice reflect changes in the content of parent–child relations and the aspirations of parents where their children are concerned. Younger couples in Naples frequently expressed the intention to limit family size so as to be able to invest more effectively in their children's education. Parents wanted their children to surpass them in terms of socioeconomic status and achievements.

LEADERSHIP IN PUBLIC ARENAS

During the fascist period Italian women were defined primarily in terms of reproduction, and their activities in the public arena were radically curtailed. A slogan from the period sums up the fascist regime's polarizing view of gender relations: "Maternity is to women what war is to men." However, the experience of authoritarianism and war prompted many women to become involved in the anti-fascist resistance. With the fall of fascism and the establishment of the Republic, many of these defiant women found a respected place in the world of politics. It was also in the postwar period that the Unione Donne Italiane (the Italian Union of Women) was founded. This organization has played a crucial role in shaping policy regarding women's rights and legislation concerning the family. Then, in the late 1960s, feminism became a small but vocal and influential force and to this day continues to provide an alternative view on all aspects of Italian politics and culture (Bono & Kemp, 1991).

Currently, men occupy the majority of public roles but there are a number of prominent women in parliament and several women hold or have held ministerial positions or other important public positions, such as in Naples where the position of mayor is currently held by a woman.

Interestingly, Silvio Berlusconi, the current head of government, displays many of the qualities associated with hegemonic masculinity: he is successful, supremely confident, his beautiful wife testifies to a successful virility, and, although not a famous sportsman himself, he is the owner of what many consider to be Italy's most famous football club, AC Milan. There are also some parallel flamboyant displays of feminine success in the political arena. Alessandra Mussolini, Benito Mussolini's granddaughter, is a graduate from medical school as well as an actress whose good looks have been widely publicized in the media. She is currently a councillor in the local government of Naples, representing a right-wing party. Like Berlusconi she exudes self-confidence and has a somewhat brash manner not immediately associated with femininity, while maintaining an aura of glamor and feminine attractiveness.[1]

Other women politicians rely on their distinguished career rather than a glamorous profile, as in the case of Emma Bonnino, a Radical who entered the world of politics through her involvement in the campaigns for the legalization of abortion and divorce. Similarly, Tina Anselmi was a prominent member of a number of Christian Democrat governments. As Minister of Employment and, before that, as head of the National Equal Opportunities Commission, she exerted a great deal of influence, undoubtedly facilitating the approval of legislation promoting gender equality in employment.

GENDER AND RELIGION

Italy is predominantly Roman Catholic and has historically strong ties with the Vatican, not least because of the presence of the Papal State within Italian territory. It is undeniable that Catholicism has exercised a strong influence on Italian culture and values. In particular, the Lateran Pacts conceded a great deal of control to the Church, especially in relation to education. The Christian Democrat party, which governed Italy for four decades after World War II, did much to consolidate the interests and values of the Catholic Church by translating them into policies.

The social philosophy of Italian Catholicism placed the family at the center of society and defined the attributes and roles of men and women in relation to the harmonious functioning of the family. Christian Democrat governments embraced this philosophy with varying degrees of conviction, promoting familial roles and values through specific institutional arrangements and policies. However, the capacity of the Italian Catholic Church to have a direct influence on public opinion has waned. An indication of this is the general decline in church attendance. According to Nanetti (1988, p. 66), 80% of women and 57% of men claimed that they attended church almost every Sunday in the mid-1950s. By 1985, the figure had dropped to 19% of men and 38% of women. Other indicators of the limits to church influence and the changing attitudes of the Italian public is the overwhelming approval given by the public in the referendum on the divorce law.[2]

In Naples there was an apparent contradiction between the declared religiosity of people and their equally open distrust of representatives of the Church. Few men attended mass and even many women only attended erratically. Men were quite openly skeptical about the benefits of churchgoing, but women were more concerned about their poor track record. Lack of time was a factor in this and many preferred to fit in their worship around their tasks. For example, they might visit a church briefly while out doing the shopping. Or they might limit themselves to worshipping in private, in their own homes. In fact, it was quite usual for homes in the old city to have small altars where sacred figures were displayed.

The devotion of the inhabitants of the poorer areas of the city is evident in the care bestowed on the shrines that dot the streets and alleys. It was usually women who took it upon themselves to ensure that the shrines were clean, the flowers were fresh, and bills were paid so that the lights would always illuminate the images they encircled. Many shrines are dedicated to various manifestations of the Madonna, reflecting the importance of the

Catholic cult of the Virgin Mary. The Virgin Mary was an extremely appropriate icon for the poor women of the city, and many said that they found inspiration in the compassion and devotion of the Virgin as mother of Christ. Women who were outworkers and largely confined to their homes were prepared to spend part of their meager earnings to support the shrines, finding solace and inspiration in the presence of their Madonnas. The Madonna, they felt, watched over them and their families.

LEISURE, RECREATION, AND THE ARTS

Hospitality is a key quality throughout Italy. In Naples the practice of hospitality is clearly gendered. Men tend to offer hospitality in public spaces such as cafés or bars, while women are responsible for hospitality offered in the home. This could take a number of different forms, ranging from offers of coffee or liqueurs to extensive offerings of food. A special invitation required elaborate and lengthy meals, consisting of a number of different carefully prepared courses that testified to the hostess's generosity and culinary skills. Food is a key component of social interaction, especially among kin, and between mothers and their dependants. Carefully prepared homemade food was also important as the highest form of hospitality.

Television is an important source of recreation and is often at the center of family meals and reunions. Italian cinema has also flourished and has produced many very popular films focused on questions of gender and sexuality. These same themes, with a stronger emphasis on questions of reputation, betrayal, and revenge are common threads in the plots of the Neapolitan *sceneggiata*. This is a traditional form of theater in which the audience is presented with a moral dilemma within a highly charged emotional situation. The audience is expected to express their opinion as to the appropriate outcome of the play: Should the betrayed lover forgive his fiancée? Should he repudiate her? Should he seek revenge?

Some recent cultural products challenge the very premise on which the *sceneggiata* is based, that is, the clarity of domestic roles and the sanctity of the family unit and especially of the mother–child relationship. *L'amore molesto* (Martone, 1995) is set in Naples and deals with the relationship between mother and daughter—so often the basis of moral and material support among the Neapolitan population. In contrast with the jovial and life-affirming approach to sexuality of earlier generations of Italian cinema (pace Pier Paolo Pasolini), *L'amore molesto* unsettles comfortable certainties and subverts expectations of a natural order of gender, kinship, and sexuality.

RELATIVE STATUS OF MEN AND WOMEN

Few people in Italy would assert that women are inferior. On the other hand, a discourse of difference may find acceptance among both men and women. The identity of the sexes is considered quite undesirable, and the differences between men and women and the complementarity of their qualities and their specific contributions are upheld and celebrated. This difference can translate into disparate and lopsided patterns of participation in different activities and social spaces. It also allows scope for double standards, particularly in the field of sexuality.

SEXUALITY

Sexuality is considered to be an integral and important part of the identity of men and women. Sexual fulfillment is considered an important ingredient of personal happiness. In Naples this fulfillment would ideally be realized within established and recognized relationships, preferably within a marriage. This view clearly privileges heterosexual relations above others, and indeed homosexual relations between men were the cause of some hilarity rather than hostility. But circumstances—and attitudes—varied considerably. Attitudes to those who deviated from the heterosexual norm were difficult to predict. On one occasion, during a pilgrimage to a site considered to be holy and miraculous by many Neapolitans (though not by the Catholic Church), I shared the queue with a group of middle-aged women. They spent much of the long time in the queue comforting and encouraging another similarly dressed person who was in fact a transvestite who felt that his presence in a holy site was inappropriate. Instead, the women stood firmly by him, in the certainty that, as they claimed, everyone is welcome in the sight of God.

Although both men and women were considered to have sexual needs, the needs of men were often seen as being more immediate and less mediated by conventions and rules. Thus, for some, it was acceptable that married men should indulge in extramarital relations, whereas it was far less acceptable for a woman to do so. The explanation for the double standard was once expressed—albeit as a joke—in the saying that "the man is a hunter" and women were limited to being the prey.

Early research in rural areas (Davis, 1973; Silverman, 1975b) suggests that sex before marriage was frequent, and even accepted or encouraged as a guarantee of successful reproductive union. In Naples too there were many instances of jokes, rumors, and open acceptance of pregnant brides. But it was usual and extremely important that, where a premarital pregnancy took place, marriage would follow as quickly as possible. Interestingly, Italy has the lowest rate of single mothers in Europe (Ruspini, 2000).

COURTSHIP AND MARRIAGE

Marriage is a highly desirable state for men and women and most expect and want to marry and set up a family of their own. The aspiration is that a successful relationship will be consolidated through marriage.

In Naples many people recognized two forms of engagement. Engagement "outside the home" referred to relationships that might still be on trial, or more casual, and that did not involve the couple's families. Engagement "in the house" referred to an official and recognized relationship. This was achieved through fairly formal visits to each other's homes and meetings between the families. It was expected that the relationship would result in marriage. Once formally engaged, a young woman's social life changes considerably and she is expected to behave with decorum. Parsons' research in the 1950s suggested that the period of courtship was extremely stressful for young women as they are vulnerable both to gossip and to the volatile nature of the courtship relationship (see "Gender over the Life Cycle").

Ideally, married couples will live neolocally, but the shortage of housing and secure jobs poses problems for many young people and courtship can last many years. During the courtship years the couple will prepare for the future. The girl might well have started to put together her *corredo*[3] or dowry even before courtship. But once engaged, the process of accumulating items for the home will be accelerated. An ideal wedding is a white wedding, held in church, although many couples opt for a civil wedding particularly if they are not practicing Catholics.

HUSBAND–WIFE RELATIONSHIPS

Parsons' work in the 1960s combined anthropological and psychological approaches to the study of family structures of the poor neighborhoods of Naples. She suggested that, here, economic conditions undermined the authority of adult men as heads of a family. Families were thus strongly matrifocal and the mother's influence had quite specific consequences for the kind of gender identities that were learnt in the context of family life. One of the most significant consequences was the enduring bond between parents and children, especially mother and son, which lasted well into adulthood. The strong attachment of adults to their family of origin made the creation of a new family unit extremely difficult. Characteristically, conflict between husband and wife would maintain a distance between them and reinforce the tendency to invest emotionally in the children rather than the spouse (Parsons, 1967). Thirty years on from Parsons' research, many couples interviewed in Naples claimed that the most important focus of their emotional lives was their children. A number of the men interviewed stated that their love for their children surpassed their love for their partner. Many women would agree with this view, although the comparison might not be made so bluntly.

However, the quality of relations between husband and wife varied considerably, depending on the background and life experience of each of the partners. In a number of married couples the wife would defer to her husband on matters of politics or other "public" issues. However, they retained full confidence in their superiority in the domestic sphere and could derive considerable delight from their husband's shortcomings in this field. In couples where both partners had experience in the field of work or politics, the emphasis was on equality of participation and opinions.

In Italy as a whole, important changes have taken place in the expectations of couples. An egalitarian ideology now informs the lives of married couples, and the expectation is that husband and wife will share in household chores and responsibilities. In fact, men assume little of the burden of housework, so that women still carry most of the responsibility for it, and the input of husbands is most evident in relation to childcare (Bimbi, 1993).

OTHER CROSS-SEX RELATIONSHIPS

According to Parsons (1967), cross-sex relations in the Neapolitan family are more significant than same-sex relations. She was referring specifically to the mother–son and the father–daughter relations that she considered to be enduring and influential. However, my own research indicated that mother–daughter and sister relations were strong and played a crucial role in the lives of many women and their families. And these relationships were not only important from a pragmatic point of view, they were also emotionally significant. Brother–sister ties may also be strong. Traditionally, brothers were held somewhat responsible for the reputations and safety of their sisters, especially if they were unmarried. Nowadays this is much more subject to personality or specific circumstances.

CHANGE IN ATTITUDES, BELIEFS, AND PRACTICES REGARDING GENDER

Bimbi (1993) suggests that women born after World War II have embraced a different model of female identity than that of their mothers or grandmothers. The youngest group of women in her research felt that having children or obtaining educational qualifications were rights rather than duties or privileges. In general, attitudes to the roles of men and women in the family and to sexuality have changed very significantly and show clear departures from the position of the Catholic Church. This was evident in the public support for legislation facilitating divorce and abortion in the 1970s and for the changes in family law that have taken place since then. Responding to changes in the attitudes of the public and to organized public pressure, government has granted men and women greater equality not only in public life but in the private domain as well. Changes have taken place not only in legislation but in everyday practice. There have been shifts in parenting patterns, and the value placed on the education of girls has been increasingly placed on a par with the education of boys. However, limited work opportunities in many regions of Italy remain an obstacle for young people despite their impressive educational qualifications.

Changes in gender relations and in the experience and conduct of sexuality are also evident in trends regarding marriage and family size. Marriage rates and family size have declined, and Italy as a whole has registered zero population growth. However, there are important regional differences. Naples and the region of Campania have the highest rate of marriage, the highest average family size in the country, and the smallest increase in the number of illegitimate births.[4] Whilst it remains important and valued, the family is changing in Naples and in Italy as a whole, and, with thus change, the contents of gender roles and the opportunities for men and women are shifting too (Calabretta, 2001).

NOTES

1. It is interesting that Italy is one of the few—or the only—countries where a porn star, Cicciolina, became a political figure. This seems to suggest that the public political domain is currently a form of display or performance—rendered increasingly feasible and desirable with the growth of the media—in which contradictory signifiers of gender and morality have been mobilized in ways that suggest that, although it is difficult to talk about distinct gender and sexual identities, these are nevertheless important in the perception of public life as well as in the experience of private life.
2. In 1974 a referendum was held to measure public feeling about the 1970 bill that legalized divorce, against the position of the Vatican on this issue. A similar situation arose a few years later with the law that legalized abortion in 1977. A referendum in 1981 ratified the law, again against the recommendations of the church to its faithful.
3. There has been an interesting evolution in the *corredo*. Up until the 1970s women in many areas, especially in rural areas, put together a *corredo* that consisted primarily of linens and other household items. In many parts of the country women were expected to produce much of their *corredo* themselves, for example, by crocheting doilies, embroidering pillow cases, and so on. In the cities and as young women gained greater opportunities of paid employment, there was a shift toward buying these items, although an embroiderer might be employed to add some design or initials to customize the factory-produced items. In the 1970s in the urban centers there was also a marked shift away from linens toward domestic appliances, ranging from television sets to kitchen appliances and the like. In other words, there has been a gradual commodification of *corredo* items and a decline in the value of the young women's labor as embodied in these items.
4. The family has declined from an average of 3.3 members in 1971 to 3.0 in 1981. Campania shows the highest average family size in the country with 3.5 members in 1981. Marriage rates have declined in Italy but Campania still has the highest rate in the country. The number of illegitimate children has also risen from 22 per 1000 in 1970 to 48 per 1000 in 1983, but in Campania the increase is from 21 to 35 per 1000 for the same period.

REFERENCES

Assmuth, L. (1997). Women's work, women's worth [Monograph]. *Transactions of the Finnish Anthropological Society, 39*.

Bagnasco, A. (1977). *Tre Italie. La problematica territoriale dello sviluppo Italiano*. Bologna: Il Mulino.

Banfield, E. (1958). *The moral basis of a backward society*. New York: Free Press.

Bettio, F., & Villa, P. (2000). To what extent does it pay to be better educated? Education and the work market for women in Italy. In M. J. González, T. Jurado, & M. Naldini (Eds.), *Gender inequalities in southern Europe. Women, work and welfare in the 1990s* (pp. 150–170). London: Cass.

Bimbi, F. (1993). Three generations of women. Transformations of female identity models in Italy. In M. Cicioni & N. Prunster (Eds.), *Visions and revisions. Women in Italian culture* (pp. 148–163). Oxford: Berg.

Bimbi, F. (2000). The family paradigm in the Italian welfare state (1947–1996). In M. J. González, T. Jurado, & M. Naldini (Eds.), *Gender inequalities in southern Europe. Women, work and welfare in the 1990s* (pp. 72–88). London: Frank Cass.

Bono, F., & Kemp, S. (Eds.). (1991). *Italian feminist thought*. Oxford: Blackwell.

Calabretta, M. (2001). *Mutamento e conflitto nell'antropologia Napoletana*. Unpublished thesis, Università degli Studi di Siena, Italy.

Cornwall, A., & Lindisfarne, N. (Eds.). (1994). *Dislocating masculinity—Comparative ethnographies*. London: Routledge.

Davis, J. (1973). *Land and family in Pisticci*. London: Athlone Press, New York: Humanities Press.

de Bromhead, A. (1999). *Masculinity and sexual identity amongst a small group of petty criminals in a Florentine street*. Unpublished doctoral thesis, University of London.

Goddard, V. (1994). From the Mediterranean to Europe: Honour, kinship and gender. In V. Goddard, J. Llobera, & C. Shore (Eds.), *The anthropology of Europe. Identity and boundaries in conflict* (pp. 57–92). Oxford: Berg.

Goddard, V. (1996). *Gender, family and work in Naples*. Oxford: Berg.

Gilmore, D. (Ed.). (1987). *Honor and shame and the unity of the Mediterranean* (Special ed. No. 22). Washington, DC: American Anthropological Association.

Ginsborg, P. (1990). *A history of contemporary Italy. Society and politics 1943–1988*. London: Penguin.

Martone, M. (1995). *L'Amore Molesto*, Lucky Real Teatri Rivniti.

Nanetti, R.Y. (1988). *Growth and territorial policies: The Italian model of social capitalism*. London: Pinter.

Parsons, A. (1967). Is the Oedipus complex universal? A South Italian "nuclear complex." In R. Hunt (Ed.), *Personalities and culture* (pp. 352–399). Garden City, NY: Natural History Press.

Piore, M., & Sabel, C. (1984). *The second industrial divide*. New York: Basic Books.

Ruspini, E. (2000). Social rights of women with children: Lone mothers and Poverty in Italy, Germany and Great Britain. In M. J. González, T. Jurado, & M. Naldini (Eds.), *Gender inequalities in southern Europe. Women, work and welfare in the 1990s* (pp. 89–121) London: Frank Cass.

Saraceno, C. (1994). The ambivalent familism of the Italian welfare state. *Social Politics, 1*, 60–82.

Silverman, S. F. (1975a). *Three bells of civilisation. The life of an Italian hill town*. New York: Columbia University Press.

Silverman, S. F. (1975b). The life crisis as a clue to social function: The case of Italy. In R. Reiter (Ed.), *Toward an anthropology of women* (pp. 309–321). New York: Monthly Review Press.

Yanagisako, S. J. (2002). *Producing culture and capital. Family firms in Italy*. Princeton & Oxford: Princeton University Press.

Jamaica

William Wedenoja and Diana Fox

ALTERNATIVE NAMES

The original inhabitants of Jamaica, referred to as Arawak and Taino, are said to have called their island *Xaymaca*, which supposedly meant "land of wood and water."

LOCATION

Jamaica is a famously beautiful island, 82 km wide and 235 km long, located in the Caribbean Sea. It is the third largest island in the West Indies, after Cuba 145 km to the north and Hispaniola (where Haiti and the Dominican Republic are located) 161 km to the east. Most of the island is hilly, mountainous, and verdant, with many rivers, deep valleys, and a narrow coastal plain. The tropical climate is hot and humid year round, with a mean annual temperature of 27 °C and a mean annual rainfall of 198 cm.

CULTURAL OVERVIEW

Jamaica was originally settled by a Native American group known as Tainos about 1000 CE. Christopher Columbus landed in Jamaica on May 4, 1494, on his second voyage to the "New World." The estimated 60,000 native inhabitants perished during the Spanish occupation, which ended in 1655 with an invasion by Great Britain. Jamaica was a British colony until 1962, when it gained independence. Plantations were established in the late 17th century, and about 750,000 slaves were brought in from West Africa to work them. The slave trade was abolished in 1807 and the slaves were freed in 1838.

The main industry during slavery was sugar cane. After Abolition sugar fell into permanent decline but is still a significant export today. A strong domestic agriculture system or peasantry, along with an internal marketing system, rapidly took shape after Emancipation and is still very important. Bananas were first exported in 1866, and Jamaica rapidly became the largest producer in the world, but the industry peaked in 1937.

Manufacturing grew rapidly in the 1950s and 1960s, but has struggled since then. The most valuable export over the past five decades has been bauxite ore and its refined derivative alumina, the basis for aluminum. Jamaica became a major supplier of marijuana to North America in the 1970s, as well as a trans-shipment point for cocaine from South America in the 1980s. Tourism, which began with banana boats over 100 years ago, reached 1.2 million visitors in 1998.

The population of Jamaica was estimated to be 2,665,636 in July 2001. The birth rate of 40 per 1,000 in the 1960s fell dramatically to 18 per 1,000 in 2001, with a growth rate of only 0.51% and a total fertility rate of 2.08 children per woman. Many Jamaicans have emigrated over the years in search of greater opportunity, and the Jamaican "diaspora" includes 1–2 million Jamaicans and their descendants now living in Panama, Costa Rica, Canada, the United Kingdom, and the United States.

According to the 1991 census, the population is 90.5% black, 7.5% mixed, 1.3% East Indian, 0.2% white, 0.2% Chinese, 0.1% Syrian (Lebanese), 0.1% other, and 0.1% not stated. Black Jamaicans are descendants of African slaves and mixed Jamaicans are mulatto offspring of white colonials. Indentured servants were brought in from India and China in the mid-19th century to replace freedmen on the plantations. Lebanese emigrated to Jamaica in the early 20th century. The white British population has dwindled as the white American population has grown. The only other significant minority are Jews, who settled in Jamaica after their expulsion from Spain and Portugal in the 17th century.

Slave society was stratified into free whites, mulattoes or free people of colour, and black slaves. After Emancipation, this caste system was transformed into a "colour-class system" wherein white became synonymous with a small elite upper class, mulatto or brown with a small middle class, and black with a vast working-class majority. The Chinese and Syrians attained the status of "honorary whites" after gaining wealth through business enterprises. Since Independence, Jamaica has struggled to eliminate white colonial bias and privilege and live up to the national motto, "Out of Many, One People," but color and ethnicity are still important symbols of status.

Jamaica enjoyed one of the highest rates of economic growth in the world in the 1960s, when it also had one of the highest degrees of inequality. However, the economy has seen little real growth over the past three decades. During this period life in rural areas basically stagnated, while urban areas became increasingly divided into rich and poor, and the inner city turned violent. Guns, gangs, and drugs have led to what is now the fourth highest murder rate in the world. The violence is generally blamed on poverty and inequality; however, the rate of poverty fell from 30.5% in 1989 to 17% in 1999, and the GINI index, a measure of inequality, is only 36.4, equal to that of the United Kingdom. The gross domestic product per capita in 1999 was $3,561 (U.S. dollars), 78th in the world, on a par with China and Egypt.

CULTURAL CONSTRUCTION OF GENDER

Gender is largely constructed through an understanding of the binary opposition of male and female—notions of masculinity and femininity that revolve around rigid norms of heterosexuality. There is no room for sexual ambiguity: a "man" is masculine and a "woman" feminine only if he or she has sexual relations with the opposite sex. A "chi-chi man" or "batty boy" is a homosexual male, a highly despised category. The attributes of men and women are regarded as both distinct and interdependent.

Men and women enhance sexual dimorphism mainly through dress, hairstyles, and bodily comportment. Differentiation in dress begins early and is distinguished particularly through school uniforms. Schoolboys from "infants" through high school wear khaki uniforms, while schoolgirls wear variously colored jumpers (depending on district and age). In adolescence, girls are encouraged to hold themselves as ladies by walking erect and maintaining restricted bodily movements that express sexual modesty. On Sundays, both men and women dress up; church ladies, young women, and girls put on frilly frocks and wide flowery hats, while men wear suits. Young women spend a lot of time and resources on elaborate hairstyles.

Sexual attractiveness varies by class and subculture. Generally, young men who are part of the reggae/

dance-hall culture are drawn to women who do not hide their voluptuousness and who demonstrate sexual availability. Working- and middle-class men seek out women who are neat and well groomed. Upper-class men seek "ladies" who aspire to a North American ideal: well coiffed, thin, petite, and "white." Even working- and middle-class men prefer women with lighter complexions, as do women who tend to refer to "black, black" men as "ugly." Rastafarians, by contrast, praise "black" women in the spirit of racial pride and "black is beautiful."

GENDER OVER THE LIFE CYCLE

Socialization of Boys and Girls

Having children is considered to be a normal, natural, and essential part of life in Jamaica, where children are generally welcome regardless of one's situation. Indeed, a childless woman is referred to derisively as a "mule." Working-class children grow up in multifamily "yards" in the cities and towns or extended family households in the countryside. Children are cared for not only by their parents, but also by older siblings and adults, kin or nonkin.

According to Sargent and Harris (1992), there is a strong preference for daughters, at least among women in the inner city. Boys are said to be harder to control and more likely to get into drugs, gangs, and crime. Girls generally help more around the house, do better in school, and are thought to be less likely to abandon their parents in old age.

The yard or home is the domain of women, and men avoid spending much time there. Their place is beyond the home, in the fields, the streets in the city, the square in the country, bars, and the work place. The yard is considered to be a place of safety and nurturance while the world beyond is seen as dangerous, especially in the inner city. Young children are closely watched and confined to the home until they are old enough to go to school.

There is little difference in the socialization of boys and girls until they begin "basic school" at the age of 4 or 5. From then on, however, they live in increasingly sexually segregated worlds. Mothers are strict with daughters and burden them with household chores such as cooking, cleaning, and looking after younger siblings. Consequently, girls learn hard work and responsibility at an early age. Girls take pride in their household responsibilities but may resent the privileged position of boys.

Mothers give their sons some household chores, so they can learn to take care of themselves, but not to the same extent as girls. If a chore requires leaving the yard, or if it is "rough work," then it will be given to a boy.

Children are generally believed to be "rude," and are subjected to harsh discipline to teach "manners." Discipline takes the form of verbal threats, "bad words," and "floggings" by the mother or father and other adults in the household. Mothers are generally responsible for the discipline of young children and girls. Older boys are believed to be particularly "rough" and therefore in need of a father's discipline. Although a boy may have little contact with his father, who may not live with or near him, boys receive significantly more punishment than girls and physical abuse is a problem, particularly with stepfathers (Bailey, Branche, McGarrity, & Stuart, 1998).

Puberty and Adolescence

The socialization of boys and girls diverges more sharply in adolescence. Parents try to confine girls to the home to avoid pregnancy, which would bring shame on the girl and her family and interfere with her education and future employment prospects. Boys, on the other hand, are now hanging out on the street, the domain of men, and becoming independent. Mothers know that they should not be too "soft" on boys. If a boy stays at home and does household chores, he risks being labeled a "mamma-boy." Men are expected to be strong, tough, dominant, and providers. Boys need to move to the streets to develop these characteristics.

Girls attend school more often than boys, generally do better in school, and receive more education, mainly because school is essentially a feminine institution. The adolescent boy is learning that a man should be making money to support women, a household, and perhaps a flashy lifestyle. Consequently, boys tend to leave school earlier than girls. However, there are few economic opportunities for adolescent boys who drop out of school, at least in the formal sector. They gather in peer groups, on street corners or at "rum shops," talking, joking, drinking, dancing, gambling, playing dominoes or sports, and making advances to passing girls. Assuming they have money, adolescent males will dress up in flamboyant fashions and sport at dance clubs and bars in the evening. The lack of jobs and pressure to have money lead many in the inner city into drug dealing, gangs, hustling, and theft at a surprisingly young age.

The most pressing concern of adolescence is becoming sexually active. Parents rarely discuss sex with their children, who learn from older peers. While protecting their daughters, parents ignore or at least tolerate the sexual activity of their sons. Male sexual prowess is idealized in the culture. In order to be a man, a boy must become sexually active, preferably with several girls, and is under pressure from his peers to do so. He must also prove his heterosexuality, because men are homophobic. Boys generally become sexually active between the ages of 14 and 15, and girls between 16 and 17.

Attainment of Adulthood

A boy becomes a man when he is able to defend himself, dominate women, and is sexually active. He can then enter into a regular sexual relationship publicly. He becomes an adult when he earns enough money to establish a household and support himself, a woman, and his children. This is particularly difficult for working-class men, owing to a lack of good jobs. Consequently, for many men adolescence is prolonged well into their twenties, during which time they may continue to live with their parents.

A girl starts to become a woman with her first menses. In order to be an adult, she must break free of the generally severe restrictions of her parents. In the middle class, this is often accomplished through marriage. However, in the working-class majority, it is typically achieved through pregnancy, which could be seen as an act of rebellion or defiance. In 1996, 47% of women having their first child were under the age of 20. The first pregnancy for a teenager living with her parents assumes a ritualized process akin to a rite of passage. The pregnancy is first met with strong disapproval by her parents, causing the girl to seek refuge with kin or friends who intercede with her parents on her behalf so that she can return home. After the birth of the child, the girl's mother assumes full control over it, but it is understood that the daughter will be responsible for the care of subsequent children (Chevannes, 1993).

Subsequently, a young woman is freer to enter into the world of the street and adult life and form relationships with men, both casual and long-term, including co-residential unions. Typically, a working-class woman will have several "visiting" relationships in her late teens and twenties, resulting in children from several fathers. Pregnancy sometimes seems to be an attempt to "cement" a relationship (Brody, 1974). The illegitimacy rate is very high—87% in 1995. Of those born out of wedlock, the father was legally registered in only 41% in 1995, although a majority will acknowledge paternity informally and offer some support.

Middle Age and Old Age

Marriage is an exalted state of union in Jamaica, a special and relatively rare relationship, carrying high prestige. Slaves were not permitted to marry, but missionaries made marriage a priority following Emancipation, and marriage is still a major issue in Christian churches today. In the working class, marriage is the ultimate culmination of a relationship, not the beginning, and so it occurs late, if at all. In fact, marriage tends to occur near the end of, rather than before or during, child-bearing. Eighty percent of the total population is legally single, including 69% of those over the age of 16. On the other hand, many adults are involved in relatively long-term, often stable, co-residential "common-law" unions. The marriage rate has been increasing of late, rising from 4.7 marriages per 1,000 people in 1989 to 10.3 in 1999. The average age at first marriage is 33. According to a recent report in the *Jamaica Weekly Gleaner* (December 20–26, 2001), Jamaica has the latest age of first marriage for women and the second-latest age for men in the world. Marriage is more common, and occurs earlier, in the middle and upper classes, than in the working-class majority. One important reason for the low rate of marriage, and the late age of marriage, is lack of economic stability for men in young adulthood.

Marriage is a sign of conjugal and economic stability, and it garners respect in the community, signified by the use of the honorific titles "Mister" and "Mistress." It is perhaps a prerequisite for active involvement in church and community organizations and affairs.

Older adults often become parents again, in that a great deal of child-shifting goes on. The most common form is for a young working women, in a city or abroad, to send some of her children home to the country to be minded by her aging mother or parents.

PERSONALITY DIFFERENCES BY GENDER

The personality traits of men and women are strongly influenced by sexually segregated parental roles, the socialization of children into those roles, and widely accepted beliefs about male and female "nature." Color, ethnicity, class, and residence shape children's experiences by influencing household composition and children's relationships to kin and nonkin.

In working-class families, both boys and girls stay in their yards where they receive intensive contact with their mothers and female kin. Mothers identify strongly with their daughters. Boys acquire a gender-appropriate identity through separation from their caretakers and active association with older boys and men. When coeducation begins, boys are encouraged to run errands, congregate with other boys, and, in adolescence, acquire sexually aggressive norms of behavior. Girls play with other girls, continue to identify with their mothers and other female kin, take on greater household responsibilities, and assume the traits of a lady.

Men are expected to display dominance in the household, independence, male camaraderie, and sexual promiscuity. Upper-class men may be sexually promiscuous, but are predominantly viewed as caring and faithful family leaders (Douglass, 1992). Women are taught to keep social distance from men, although comfortable joking and banter occurs. Jamaicans distinguish between "women" and "ladies." A lady is the ultimate expression of femininity achieved through education, refinement, attention to a well-groomed appearance, and unobtrusiveness. Hypothetically, a lady can be "white," "black," or "brown," but the lighter the female, the more likely she will be considered a lady (Douglass, 1992).

GENDER-RELATED SOCIAL GROUPS

Caribbean society is often incorrectly characterized as matriarchal. The social institutions of Jamaica—the family, education, medicine, politics, religion, etc.—are generally based on strong female participation, segregation by gender, and male dominance. The family, for example, is often referred to as "matrifocal" or mother centered, because the mother assumes virtually the entire responsibility for the household and childcare, but the man of the house has ultimate authority, even though he spends little time there.

Over 70% of Jamaican women eventually give birth, and the average mother now has three children. In many cases, a woman will have children by more than one man, and maintain relations not only with those men but also with their parents and families, particularly the "babyfather's" mother, creating an extensive kinship network, although people generally are closest to their mother's kin.

Adolescent boys and young men typically form into same-sex same-age groups and spend a great deal of time together, simply "idling" on the streets, gambling, playing dominoes, cricket, basketball, or football. In the inner city, they are quite likely to become involved in the infamous and violent gang underworld. Girls are less likely to spend time in peer groups, mainly because they are usually restricted to the home and have chores to perform.

There are many voluntary associations in Jamaican society, particularly in the middle-class and urban areas, including football clubs, library associations, professional organizations, trade unions, and political parties. Some are male, some female, and some mixed, and in the latter case the leadership is primarily male even where the membership is predominantly female. This pattern prevails in the church, one of the most important social institutions. A large majority of churchgoers are women, and women are more actively involved in church activities than men; nevertheless, men hold most of the leadership positions.

Education is perhaps the most female-dominated institution in Jamaican society. Sixty-four percent of principals and 92% of teachers in primary and all-age schools are women. The average academic performance of girls is much better than that of boys, and the dropout rate is higher for boys; therefore girls generally advance farther in the system. At the University of the West Indies in Kingston, for example, men made up only 26% of the graduating class of 1998. Errol Miller, Professor of Education at the University of the West Indies, warns that this educational trend is leading to a "marginalization of the black male" in society.

GENDER ROLES IN ECONOMICS

According to the International Labor Organization, 10.3% of men and 22.3% of women were unemployed or without paid work in 1999, and 73% of men and 55% of women were economically active. Women predominate in the informal sector as market women or *higglers* selling farmers' produce which they have purchased, or homemade sweets, clothing, household goods, or school supplies at small stands outside school buildings. Some men are higglers as well, but it is regarded as women's work. Higglers play a central role in Jamaican folk culture as strong independent women, but are nonetheless of low status, along with other female-linked informal sector positions such as domestic workers and prostitutes.

Poor women and some men engage in informal savings institutions known as *pardner*, pooling their money in a common fund and taking turns drawing from it to pay for major expenses such as a car, school fees, or the creation of a microenterprise. Another key strategy for getting out of poverty is migration for both men and women. In 1999, 47% of migrants traveling to Canada and 49% traveling to the United States were male. Female migrants take positions as domestics, nannies, and cooks. Increasing numbers of Jamaicans migrate to work in tourist communities along the north coast. Women work as souvenir and craft vendors and as maids. They may manage small resorts for their husbands and sons, but men are the main beneficiaries of the big money in tourism derived from land speculation and enterprise, as well as drugs. Men also produce and sell woodcarvings and jewelry (McKay, 1993).

The growth of the electronics and textile manufacturing sectors in the 1960s and 1970s led large numbers of young women to relocate to urban areas to work in factories with low wages, few benefits, cramped working conditions, and long hours in insecure jobs. Women continue to work on the factory floor in free-trade zones. They have not been encouraged to join labor unions, even though they are the most exploited workers, receiving the lowest wages and the least opportunities to increase their skills. Both men and women work long hours with little pay on agricultural plantations (e.g., banana, cane, coffee). Throughout the economy, men predominate in managerial and executive positions, and in labor unions.

PARENTAL AND OTHER CARETAKER ROLES

Women are largely responsible for the care of children and they acquire significant status through mothering activities. Many working- and middle-class women without children take in others' children, caring for them as their own. Motherwork, which extends to aunts and grandmothers, includes nurturing and affectionate behavior, mild scolding, and instruction in sex-linked household chores.

Girls learn feminine tasks, such as cooking, clothes washing, sweeping, and sewing, from their mothers.

In rural areas boys help their fathers with farm activities, hauling water, caring for livestock, and collecting wood. In practice, sex role training is fluid in that boys and men will help with household chores and girls also work with their fathers in productive activities outside the home (Fox, 1999).

Fathers are defined predominantly as breadwinners and disciplinarians of children across class lines. Mothers flog their daughters, but fathers protect children, especially sons, from becoming "bad" with the threat and occasional administration of "wicked" floggings (Chevannes, 2001). Although households are mother centered, fathers maintain social dominance even in absentia. Fathers are more likely to be stable members of households in middle- and upper-class families, but their activities also take them away from the household and they are rarely available as emotional resources for boys. In Rastafarian households and communities, fathers try to take on more nurturing and affectionate roles; however, here too they are disciplinarians and women are nurturers.

LEADERSHIP IN PUBLIC ARENAS

Politics is generally considered to be a man's world in the Caribbean, where it is viewed as unfeminine (Senior, 1991). Women, particularly from the working class, are overburdened with domestic responsibilities, leaving them with little or no time for politics. Men, on the other hand, being largely free of domestic responsibilities, can dominate the political arena. Middle-class women are active in political parties, especially in campaigns, but serve mainly in supportive roles, at the lowest levels, as in other spheres of Jamaican life. However, women are beginning to gain greater influence in politics and other public arenas. One reason is that feminism became an active force in the region in the 1970s, generating much research, raising issues of special relevance to women, and spawning a number of organizations for the advancement of women. In addition, women are advancing into middle- and upper-level managerial and professional roles.

GENDER AND RELIGION

Jamaica is an exceptionally religious society. Religious beliefs permeate every aspect of daily life, and the church is often as important to an individual as work and family. Although the leaders of most churches are men, women are in the majority, in attendance and membership, and are much more involved in church activities. As in other areas of Jamaican life, men perform public roles that are typically expressive, conspicuous, performative, and status bearing, such as preaching, while women are responsible for more inconspicuous, typically domestic, tasks. Women are believed to be more "spiritual" than men, that is, more often ecstatic in services, although statistics collected by Wedenoja do not bear this out.

There are four significant forms of religion in Jamaica today. The orthodox Christian churches, including the Anglicans, Baptists, Methodists, and Presbyterians, were established in the early 19th century and hold the allegiance of 25% of the population, according to the 1991 census. Their membership has declined drastically during the 20th century. Revival, an indigenous, folk, or Creole religion (also known as Zion and Pocomania) that developed in the mid-19th century, is not recorded in the census. The Pentecostal Christian churches, which date from at least 1918, have grown steadily and are now the most popular, at 29%. Finally, the famous messianic millenarian Rastafarian movement, which originated in Jamaica in the 1930s, has had a dramatic impact on Jamaican culture even though it accounts for less than 1% of the population.

Orthodox Christianity brought European morality to Jamaica where it became the bastion of middle-class respectability, centering on the sanctity of marriage, the nuclear family, the patriarchal role of the husband as provider and head of the family, and the wife as homemaker and mother. The working-class was thereby excluded, and developed Revival as an alternative. However, when a working class woman gets married, she often joins an orthodox church as a sign of her new status. The orthodox churches are always led by men, and about 45% of their members are male. About half of all Revival churches, on the other hand, are led by women, and men made up only 37% of a large congregation studied by Wedenoja.

Pentecostalism and Rastafarianism both developed in the early 20th century and are markedly gendered (Austin-Broos, 1987). According to the 1991 census, 57% of Pentecostals are women, although the percentage of women at services is generally much greater. In contrast, 81% of Rastafarians are male.

Pentecostal churches attract young single working-class mothers in particular. Although Pentecostal congregations are led largely by men, women can attain positions of leadership, including that of pastor. The ideology of these churches is essentially a protest against male domination and exploitation of women, particularly male "promiscuity" and "irresponsibility." Women follow strict rules of dress and demeanor associated with modesty. Pentecostalism promises to "cleanse" women from "fornication" and make them "brides of Christ" with the support and protection of the congregation. Jesus is depicted as the faithful dependable husband, apparently lacking in "the world", as well as an alternative role model for male converts who have been "saved" from the "world of sin" on the streets.

The Rastafarian movement seeks to liberate black people from white oppression; ironically, it also promotes male domination and female subordination (Lake, 1994). Men are the designated spiritual leaders of the movement, the heads of households, and the rulers of women. They are to "spread their seed" without regard to their marital status, while their wives must remain faithful. At the same time, however, men should be sensitive to the needs of their wives and develop a close relationship with their children. A woman becomes a Rasta through her man. She should wear a long dress and cover her head. She should not speak in church or talk directly to God, and is subject to menstrual taboos when she is "unclean." One of the main aims of the Rastafari is to reassert the dominance of poor and working-class men, perhaps in response to a matrifocal upbringing. It also offers a new male identity, based on Haile Selassie, the black messiah, possibly as a substitute for the absent father.

Many revivalists practice a popular form of healing known as *balm*, which is usually performed by an older woman referred to as a "Mother," who offers divinations, baths, herbs, candles, incense, and prayers to cure spiritual afflictions. Therefore healing is associated with women, and the healing relationship is modeled on the mother–child relationship. In contrast, *obeah*, the practice of sorcery, is always practiced by men, as is Science, the use of magic for good fortune (Wedenoja, 1989).

LEISURE, RECREATION, AND THE ARTS

Leisure activities are structured according to class and gender. Boys have fewer chores than girls, and learn early on that public space is a domain for male leisure and recreation. In late afternoons after school, adolescent boys can be seen playing football or basketball in schoolyards, while girls play netball.

Men seek leisure outside the home—including sexual satisfaction. Men also engage in drinking, gambling, joke telling, boasting, and story telling. Working-class adolescent boys and men gather in groups known as "crews" or "loafing groups" on street corners and in rum bars, or play dominoes in shops. Upper-class men meet in yacht club bars and engage in bird shooting, sailing, and fishing tournaments. Upper-class "ladies" devote significant time to beautifying practices such as exercising, shopping for clothing and make-up, frequenting spas, and going to the beauty parlor. Middle-class women devote significant leisure time to voluntary social groups.

On weekends, young women socialize on the street as well, since this is the time when "sound systems" are brought out, "DJ" parties take place in town squares or city neighborhoods, and "jerk" stations are set up. Outdoor DJ parties draw large crowds, and usually begin late and last till early morning hours. Many communities also have dance halls, which are frequented predominantly by working-class men and women. Some also house bars and strip joints, which are patronized by men and a few women of low respectability. Many communities host weekend bingo tournaments, which draw large crowds of working- and middle-class men and women.

Marijuana or *ganja* smoking is an important leisure activity in the working class. Men enjoy smoking during breaks at their work sites, in groups away from work, or as a solitary experience in the mornings and late at night in their yards. Rastafarian men engage in "reasoning" sessions where they ritually smoke ganja, philosophize, and reinforce male bonds. Women's smoking is infrequent and generally prior to sexual activity.

RELATIVE STATUS OF MEN AND WOMEN

Women are better educated, have a higher rate of literacy, and a greater life expectancy than men, but in every other respect are marginalized. Men are the heads of households, the leaders in government, politics, and churches, and the managers of businesses and industries. Men control the major institutions of society, including the economic and political systems and the media. Women, regardless of class, are subordinate to men in almost every sphere of life. The main areas in which women have influence are the home, child-rearing, education, churches, higglering, healing, and nursing.

Male dominance is particularly clear in relationships between the sexes, which have been characterized as "adversarial" and lacking in trust (Bailey et al., 1998). Women are expected to cater to the needs of men. The double standard prevails, in that men but not women can have multiple relationships without sanction. Men also feel free to coerce women physically, and are thought to be "soft" if they do not, although women are not supposed to strike men (Chevannes, 2001). Women suffer a high rate of violence from men, including rape, with little recourse.

Women are free to choose their mates and decide whom they will live with and marry. The home or yard is considered to be women's space and, indeed, women often hold title to the house they live in. Men feel little obligation to help with household chores, which they consider to be demeaning if not polluting. Spouses generally control their own incomes and assets, and keep them separate, at least in the working class. Women typically use their assets for the well-being of their children—to clothe, educate, and provide medical care for them. Women are most highly valued as mothers; indeed, this is a near saintly status.

SEXUALITY

Jamaica is a profoundly heterosexist society in which homophobia is widespread. Discrimination and violence against gays and the absence of a gay rights movement characterize dominant Jamaican attitudes toward same-sex relations. While lesbianism is decried as well, gay men receive the brunt of virulent homophobic sentiment. While there is somewhat more tolerance among the elite, antihomosexuality is a key aspect of the ideology of heterosexual relations in the drawing of distinct boundaries around acceptable definitions of heterosexual masculinity and femininity.

Children are guided toward gender-appropriate sexuality early on. Adult sexuality is familiar to children, many of whom, particularly in rural and poor urban areas, live in close quarters with adults, sharing the same room or bed where they are exposed to sexual behavior. Parental control over boys' sexuality decreases in adolescence when they are encouraged to seek sexual experiences. By contrast, pubescent girls are guided toward

modesty, and control over their sexuality tightens. They are warned about the constant sexual desires of men and the pressure they will receive from them to engage in intercourse. Significant numbers of girls are introduced to sex through rape, which is feared by girls and women.

Children grow up in a sexually paradoxical world, where double standards abound. The church and middle-class morality constrain the sexual expression of women, while sexually explicit lyrics permeate reggae, hip-hop and dance-hall music, referring particularly to women's vaginas as the proper locus of male attention and to chi-chi men as societal scourges. Soft pornographic girly pictures are also rampant in advertising and public spaces. Dance-hall culture, centering on the sexually explicit hip movements of young women, has been adopted by some working-class women as a form of resistance to the constraining respectability of middle- and upper-class values of feminine sexuality. Others view dance-hall as explicitly misogynist (Cooper, 1995).

COURTSHIP AND MARRIAGE

Since 1887, when civil registration for marriage was first institutionalized, marriage rates have remained low among Jamaica's working-class majority. In 1988, the rate was 4.4 per 1,000. Three forms of partnering prevail, including legal marriage, common-law marriage and visiting arrangements. Multiple partnering is also common. It is culturally acceptable for a man to have more than one woman since men are expected to be promiscuous by nature. Women also seek multiple partners as sources of economic support.

The working class tend to marry later in life, typically when men and women are in their forties, can pay for the ceremony and a separate household, and have already produced offspring from previous nonlegal unions. Among the upper classes, marriage is hypergamous and occurs earlier in life, with women in their early twenties and men in their late twenties (Douglass, 1992).

Christian, working-class, and middle-class marriage ceremonies take place in churches with receptions often occurring outdoors at a relative's home. Amidst music arranged by a DJ, toasts are made and "box lunches" of fried chicken or curried goat are served, along with "mannish water" (goat soup). Among the upper classes, church weddings are followed by lavish receptions on the estates of the bride's parents, where extravagant meals of traditional Jamaican fare are served and men make toasts in honor of their wives.

When working-class women marry they do not expect romantic love, although it does exist. Instead, they "look money" and status, while men "look sex" (Sobo, 1993). Many men and women avoid marriage because of lack of trust, poor communication, and economic wariness. Women believe men will avoid financial responsibility and men fear women's control over them. Common-law arrangements indicate a common household without legal sanction, while visiting relations involve neither legal sanction nor a common household. Common-law is by far the most popular conjugal bond of the working class. Working-class women first enter into visiting relationships in their twenties, but tend to move into common-law arrangements after they have their first child. Visiting relations are a form of extended courtship with a sexual component, involving frequent meetings when couples reside close by. Men are expected to help financially with a woman's children, particularly if the man is her "babyfather." During visiting meetings couples go on outings together to clubs, parties, sports events, the beach, and church (Roberts & Sinclair, 1978).

Children learn by early adolescence that men initiate courtship through the use of their bodies and that women who do so are considered "bad" women, without sexual control. Women are subject to sexual comments by men who "lyrics them," accepting advances by permitting men to hold their hands (Chevannes, 2001).

HUSBAND–WIFE RELATIONSHIP

Although mistrust characterizes many working- and middle-class male–female relationships prior to marriage, affection between men and women grows, especially with age, as reproductive roles become less significant and trust increases (Fox, 1999). Still, a man's influence extends over his family and wives are supposed to listen to husbands. Both legal and common-law marriage are regarded as economic arrangements to share sexually divided work, although this ideal is not as rigidly adhered to as it is described, and husbands and wives often assist one another. Because marriage is a symbol of respectability, legally married couples in particular work to maintain an image of stability, legitimacy, and propriety in the eyes of the community by participating in community life. Love and status are important motivations for marriage

for the upper classes. Middle-class families strive to emulate husband–wife relationships in elite families.

Jamaica ranks tenth on the list of lowest divorce rates in the world. In 1999, there were 4.4 divorces per 10,000. Women instigate divorce more often than men. Divorce remains a stigma for women, many of whom move abroad or away from the community to avoid social isolation (Douglass, 1992). There is a "cultural promiscuity of violence" perpetuated by men who view wife-beating as an expected form of husbandly chastisement for what they regard as insufficient domestic or sexual services, or lack of respect. Men also identify women with children, using violence as a form of punishment for disobedience (Bailey et al., 1998).

CHANGE IN ATTITUDES, BELIEFS, AND PRACTICES REGARDING GENDER

Caribbean feminism began to permeate public consciousness through activist groups in the 1970s. The well-known Sistren Collective is an independent women's cooperative and theater group. Initiated by working-class women, Sistren organizes workshops and presentations around women's work, violence against women, and women's history. Rising feminist consciousness and greater education have led more women to express a desire for economic independence and the greater freedom it affords, including the ability to move out of abusive relationships. Organizations such as the Women's Bureau provide women with links to services such as medical care, agricultural extension, legal aid, and support groups.

In the 1990s, a men's movement led by Professor Barry Chevannes and others at the Mona campus of the University of the West Indies took shape. Chevannes organized workshops for men throughout the island to foster male responsibility, to help men learn to express their emotions, and to discuss their fears about the challenges of fatherhood and partnerships with liberated women. Whereas in the 1980s the popular press featured numerous articles for women on acquiring ladylike mannerisms, newspapers in the 1990s featured the topic of "manhood" extensively. Coverage of the crisis of masculinity, the increase in male school dropouts, crime, and idleness reflected increasing discomfort with traditional notions of male dominance, the turmoil created by women's growing economic independence, and the need to develop new models of male responsibility. Since the benchmark of manhood has been to provide material support for children, men are expressing mounting frustration in their inability to find gainful employment, even though this objective has always presented a struggle for working-class men in particular. Men insist that they must have work to have women. Since women's opportunities are improving and they can afford to be more selective, tension between men and women is rising.

Shifting relations between men and women have also given rise to new mating practices. Adolescent girls increasingly pursue older men as sources of economic support, eschewing boys of their age by saying that "school boy have pocket change but big man have salary." At the same time, older men are seeking younger girls as part of the myth of the "virgin cure" for HIV. Unfortunately, these relationships are contributing to rising rates of HIV among adolescent girls. In recent years, economically successful single women, including higglers, have sought younger men for sexual satisfaction and status, keeping them in new clothes, lodging, and food. In sum, Jamaican gender relations are in flux, influenced by internal factors as well as transnationalism, industrialism, and globalization, producing a wide range of contradictory results: confusion over gender roles, increased opportunities, status, and independence for women, burgeoning tension between men and women, and a decline in perceptions of male productivity despite of their continued dominance in politics and the formal sector of employment.

REFERENCES

Austin-Broos, D. J. (1987). Pentecostals and Rastafarians: Cultural, political, and gender relations of two religious movements. *Social and Economic Studies*, *36*, 1–39.

Bailey, W. Branche, C., McGarrity, G., & Stuart, S. (1998). *Family and the quality of gender relations in the Caribbean*. Mona, Jamaica: Institute of Social and Economic Research, University of the West Indies.

Brody, E. B. (1974). Psychocultural aspects of contraceptive behavior in Jamaica. *Journal of Nervous and Mental Disease*, *159*, 108–119.

Chevannes, B. (1993) Sexual behaviour of Jamaicans: A literature review. *Social and Economic Studies*, *42*, 1–45.

Chevannes, B. (2001). *Learning to be a man: Culture, socialization and gender identity in five Caribbean communities*. Mona, Jamaica: University of the West Indies Press.

Cooper, C. (1995). *Noises in the blood: Orality, gender, and the "vulgar" body of Jamaican popular culture*. Durham, NC: Duke University Press.

Douglass, L. (1992). *The power of sentiment: Love, hierarchy and the Jamaican family elite*. Boulder, CO: Westview Press.

Fox, D. (1999). Masculinity and fatherhood re-examined: An ethnographic account of the contradictions of manhood in a rural Jamaican town. *Men and Masculinities*, *2*, 66–86.

Lake, O. (1994). The many voices of Rastafarian women: Sexual subordination in the midst of liberation. *New West Indian Guide*, *68*, 235–257.

McKay, L. (1993). Women's contribution to tourism in Negril, Jamaica. In J. Momsen (Ed.), *Women and change in the Caribbean* (pp. 278–286). Bloomington: Indiana University Press.

Roberts, G. W., & Sinclair, S. A. (1978). *Women in Jamaica: Patterns of reproduction and family*. Millwood, NY: KTO Press.

Sargent, C. F., & Harris, M. H.(1992). Gender ideology, childrearing, and child health in Jamaica. *American Ethnologist*, *19*, 523–537.

Senior, O. (1991). *Working miracles: Women's lives in the English-speaking Caribbean*. Bloomington: Indiana University Press.

Sobo, E. J. (1993). *One blood: The Jamaican body*. Albany, NY: State University of New York Press.

Wedenoja, W. (1989). Mothering and the practice of "balm" in Jamaica. In C. S. McClain (Ed.), *Women as healers: Cross-cultural perspectives* (pp. 76–97). New Brunswick, NJ: Rutgers University Press.

Kayapo

William H. Fisher

ALTERNATIVE NAMES

The Kayapo are also known as the Mebengokre, Northern Kayapo, Cayapo, Kaiapo, Mekranoti, Mekrãgnoti, Gorotire, Metuktire, Irã'ãmranhre, Txukarramãe, Xikrin, Kararaô, Gradáu, Gradaho, Tchikrin, Djore, Purucarus, and Chicrís.

LOCATION

The Kayapo are located in the states of Pará and Mato Grosso, Brazil.

CULTURAL OVERVIEW

People of the 16 different villages embraced by the encompassing label "Kayapo" or identified as one of the Kayapo subgroups above all refer to themselves as "Mebengokre" or "people of the watery depression." Population currently stands around 5,000 and has been on the increase for some two decades. The communities mentioned are also classified as Northern Kayapo to differentiate them from the Southern Kayapo.

For some 200 years Kayapo have moved steadily westward from the savannah regions in the state of Tocantins toward areas of tropical forest or forest–savannah margins. Large villages with thousands of residents are known historically. As with other Gê language family speakers, settlement residence alternated with treks involving groups of extended families. Subsistence depends on a range of techniques: collective and solitary hunting and fishing, collecting wild plant foods, and slash-and-burn horticulture. An opportunistic orientation that moves people to food resources predominates.

Kayapo settlements are composed of a ring of houses occupied by extended families built up through matri-uxorilocal residence. A men's house is commonly constructed upon the central plaza. Populations average several hundred but may range from under 100 to nearly 1,000. The village center comprises a ceremonial area where dancing and singing occurs almost daily. These performances are often rehearsals leading over weeks or months to a ceremonial climax of whatever festival is underway. That the Kayapo consider themselves to be part of a slowly unfolding ritual much, if not most, of the time seems to make them fairly unique.

Each village is politically autonomous, although bonds of kinship link individuals of different villages. Formal leadership positions exist in association with age grades and men's clubs. Prominent secular leaders are males who combine a number of attributes, including a knowledge of specialized speech and chants (*ben*) and persuasive and powerful oratorical ability. Leaders drawn from the unmarried men's age grade should be energetic and exemplary workers. Auxiliary women's groupings exist consisting of wives of associated men's organizations, with the wife of the male chief serving as female chief. The visibility of this role is low and appears more as a conceptual counterpart to men's activity and organization rather than a public leadership role. Nevertheless, without a respected wife who exercises her own influence over female public opinion, a man is considered unqualified to lead. Membership in age grades is calculated by social age rather than absolute age, which, in turn, is linked to physical and social maturity, marriage and birth of children, and eventually grandchildren.

Marriage is monogamous and divorce is common, although lifelong spouses are also common and may become extraordinarily close emotionally. Kinship terminology follows an Omaha pattern, but there are no descent groups. Pedigrees may extend back four or five generations, and names are endlessly recycled. Names, ceremonial ornaments, and privileges linked to a name are more important for tracing relationships between living persons than are deep genealogies. Genitors do not name their own children, who receive their ceremonial and nonceremonial names from a class of same-sex social mentors who include genitors' cross-sex siblings and ascending lineal relatives. Both males and females inherit formal friends from their father and this relationship may be inherited patrilineally.

CULTURAL CONSTRUCTION OF GENDER

Males and females are distinguished according to their different genitalia, as "penis ones" (*me my*) and "vagina ones" (*me ni*). However, human growth is not automatic and the social qualities and physical abilities that allow one to act as an adult man or woman are built up slowly, although transition from one age/gender category to another is abrupt. The formation of the fetus requires repeated intercourse and may involve different men. Different phases of the life cycle are signaled by passage to the next age grade. Each age grade carries distinct standards of proper food consumption, social behavior, including sexual behavior, and distinctive participation in economic and ritual activities. Toward the end of their lives, elderly men and women have acquired quite different knowledge but act in very similar ways and enjoy a similar relaxation of dietary rules and codes of etiquette. Attributes of gendered persons are also differentiated according to age. It is difficult to point to any attribute associated with genitalia that survives the abrupt age transitions unaltered.

Formerly, boys of 7 or 8 would leave their natal houses to sleep in a bachelor's dormitory or men's house; today they sleep in their natal residences as well. Men must marry out of their houses and also leave the village to hunt, make war, or to travel further afield—often today to Brazilian towns and cities. Males thus require specialized knowledge to control the eventual consequences of the supernatural threats to which they are exposed and the development of bodily abilities such as sureness of foot and piercing eyesight in order to be good hunters. New knowledge and abilities come burdened with food and behavioral taboos in order to be effective. The development of men is thought to require more time, effort, and guidance from elders than that of women. However, female bodily abilities and knowledge must also be cultivated in a fashion analogous to those of males. Kayapo cite examples of women hunters and travellers, including those who have made contact with far-flung societies from which they are said to have brought back valuable cultural knowledge. In short, whether male or female, Kayapo can only carry out activities proper to their gender by virtue of their own preparation

and self-transformation. Male assertions of superiority to women, when they occur, refer to socially developed qualities, such as greater propriety and self-restraint, rather than to natural endowments of manhood. As in other Amazonian societies, women do not necessarily acknowledge male superiority, and conflicts between men and women as groups are considered to be normal.

At birth, male and female infants have their ears pierced and a hole is made below a boy's lower lip. By adulthood Kayapo men may have progressively distended this opening to receive a lip disk. While the earlobe holes of both males and females are both distended, only men decorate these with earrings. After childhood, both males and females wear their hair long. Sexually active females traditionally shave the crown of their head, as do children of both sexes and men on the occasion of certain rituals and life crises. Hair is also cut by both sexes to mark mourning periods. Women paint children of both sexes with elaborate geometrical designs and adorn the lower cheeks of men and women with similarly elaborate genipap designs. Formerly, male dress, apart from body paint and ornaments such as bracelets, consisted of a conical penis sheath fitted over the foreskin; females wore belts around the waist. Today most women wear single-piece shifts, and males wear shorts; plastic flip-flops are commonly worn by everyone.

While the gendered attributes of persons shift with age, a stark gender opposition is imposed on the village layout: the public realm of the plaza is considered to be associated with maleness, while the ring of houses forming the circumference of the plaza is a female realm. There are some general behavioral differences characteristic of men and women: adult women keen both as a lament and in welcome, ceremonial speech is used only by adult males, there are some slight differences in male and female vocabulary, and females of any age should avoid contact with bows and arrows and firearms. However, during some life phases and life crises, males, too, should not handle firearms and do not speak publicly.

Bachelors and unmarried nubile women are generally thought to embody the height of sexual attractiveness. Pudginess is attractive in females and men greatly augment their ability to attract sexual partners if they have manufactured goods to distribute or are frequently successful as hunters or fishers. Characteristics such as intelligence are appreciated equally in males and females, and both males and females acquire specialized knowledge in the use of medicinal plants and both may become shamans. In summary, males and females are born with different genitalia but are formed from identical components—a physical substance shared with both male and female nuclear family relations, knowledge gained from both males or females, and a soul-essence that is unique to each person. Physical and social abilities must be developed in distinct ways in order to acquire characteristics proper to one's age/gender grade.

GENDER OVER THE LIFE CYCLE

Life stages are classified according to age/gender grades, and both males and females make cosmetic alterations or embellishments to the body proper to each grade. Codes of conduct and alimentary rules are also correlated with these social categories. Position in sibling birth order and personality differences are also cited in connection with the public persona, individual vigor, and prestige of different individuals.

The Socialization of Boys and Girls

Before they can walk unaided, infants are never left unattended. Babies are carried in a sling that allows access to the breast, which they are generally offered at the first signs of crying or discontent. Small children are allowed to crawl under close supervision. Children are highly desired and no preference is expressed for either gender. Ideally, a couple would alternate between boy and girl births.

Newborns of both sexes are called "suckling ones" (*kra-karà*) or simply "little ones" (*meprire*). Boy and girl infants are heavily adorned with red cotton bandoliers, cotton bands below the knees, and cotton wristbands and ankle bands, while their faces are covered with achiote and their bodies painted with an identical genipap motif. Parents appear to take delight in strong personalities irrespective of gender. After they learn to walk and speak, even more attention is lavished on both boys and girls; they receive yet more ornaments and have their head crowns shaven and decorated. This stage corresponds to weaning in some Kayapo villages. Bodies of boys and girls are painted with identical motifs which may be seen on adult women in some cases, while identical cheek motifs may be sported by adults and children of both sexes.

From about 3 to 8 years, boys are referred to as *mebôktire* and girls as are referred to as "big children" (*meprintire*). Children play in public space when outside their own household and unselfconsciously adopt postures they have observed all their lives; boys and girls tend to interact in groups that closely match their sex and age. Both genders may play raucous and energetic games, but boys are given little bows and arrows, fishlines and hooks, and model airplanes and whirligigs made of straw, and girls are given little baskets and baby slings. Girls begin to accompany their female relatives to the gardens, tend to smaller children, and carry small burdens, while boys are called on much less frequently to help. Children of both sexes are taught to stand up for themselves vigorously against bullies of both sexes; they may engage in open temper tantrums, and children as old as 7 or more may seek the solace of the breast if they are greatly troubled. All children are encouraged to respect their grandparents and others of their relationship category, called *ingêt* (male) and *kwatỳj* (female) (which includes MB (mother's brother), FZ (father's sister), and MBS (mother's brother's son)), and to choose to learn specific skills and knowledge from them. The senior relative in this relation, particularly of the same sex, should be the one to discipline the junior one, rather than the child's own parents. Parents comment favorably on childrens' signs of independence, such as the desire to sleep separately, although children are also encouraged to sleep with their grandparents from whom they learn tradition and special skills. Children are aware of the sexual activity of couples and unmarried girls who receive lovers in the close quarters of the house. Although boys and girls may remain unclothed, girls are taught to sit with their legs together. Boys who have already demonstrated a propensity to aggressiveness may be given medicines to develop bellicosity further. In general, steps are taken to make boys fierce (*akrê*) and to make girls tame (*uabô*), though individuals may display either quality.

Formerly, it was common for a *meprintire* girls to be betrothed to an older man, who, while taking other women as sexual partners, would occasionally sleep near the girl and give her presents, including meat, so that she would like him. When the girl reached an age appropriate for sexual relations, the marriage would be consumated. Although the girl was not yet fully able to assume the economic role of wife, the son-in-law was incorporated into the division of labor within the uxorilocal household under the direction of his wife's parents, toward whom he would show either deference or avoidance on proper occasions.

Before the onset of puberty, there are radical changes in the lives of both boys and girls. Around 8 years of age boys advance to the *meôkre* grade (the painted ones) and are inducted into the men's house. Here, younger boys are in close contact with older boys and bachelors to whom they listen attentively. They watch as older males slip away for trysts with women, and elders come at night to awaken them with stories or counsel in tradition. Although a boy returns to his natal house to eat, he no longer receives the almost unlimited attention and comfort afforded younger children. No longer is he painted by his mother, but by men. Girls at this age also shoulder more responsibility for subsistence and are less coddled. They begin to develop their own skills in body painting, practicing on dolls and playmates of the same age. The continuity in a girl's life can be seen in her body paint; she continues to be painted with motifs appropriate for children and continues to wear red cotton thread wrapped below the knees. However, *mekurêrê* girls older than about 8 have their hair cut and may begin to engage in sexual relations. They are not old enough to have husbands or to bear children.

Puberty and Adolescence

After a boy reaches puberty, he receives a penis sheath and becomes known as *menõrõnyre* (ones who sleep in a new way). At this time, crown hair, kept cropped since weaning or walking, may be grown out. This period marks the height of a male's independence from the domestic realm, since his life revolves around socializing with other bachelors, dancing, and generally being the energetic and visible emblem of village strength and unity, and he is not yet incorporated into a wife's household. While he accompanies older men in order to learn needed skills, he must not engage in many of their activities. He is susceptible to spiritual dangers of game and, although he often leads the way clearing the trail and gathering raw materials for adornment, such as sweet-scented inner bark, he should not discharge a firearm or eat many foods he will later consume freely. In short, his main task during this phase of his life is to develop physically, through correct adherence to food and behavioral restrictions, in order to develop "strong eyes" and knowledge. As a prospective husband he should learn to weave, among other things, a baby sling, basket, and ceremonial mat from buriti palm thatch. Young men should still have shame, or social reserve, in addressing the assembly of adult men and should be concerned with learning from adults rather than debating with them. Moreover,

their sexual activity heightens the shame they feel, particularly in the presence of their parents. *Menõrõnyre* may be scraped periodically with a comb made of dogfish teeth as a collective discipline of their age grade. Girls are not scraped in this way. However, an older female mentor of the boy may be scraped along with him. Stinging medicine is applied to the long scratches on arms, thighs, and calves to promote speed and strength. Boys knock down wasp nests with their bare hands and have their faces and arms smeared with the carbonized remains of burnt nests to cultivate fierceness.

No special recognition is afforded to defloration or a girl's first menstruation, which is thought to result from sexual activity. There are numerous accounts to support the conclusion that menstruation is thought to be anomalous or akin to illness and should be controlled through the regular use of medicines. When children are desired, other herbal medicines are used to activate fertility. A girl's readiness for child-bearing is signaled by painting with a distinctive motif, *mekrajtyk* (those with blackened thighs). She may receive lovers in the house at night. The shame felt by *menõrõnyre* of the sexual themes in the presence of their elders does not seem to afflict the young women age grade, and this is cited by some males as evidence of their lower level of sociality.

Attainment of Adulthood

The birth of a child represents the entrance into both a married state and adulthood. Either one or several fathers share the state of pregnancy (*metujarô*) with the mother. Once the umbilical cord falls, there are a series of public symbolic procedures involving both relatives and nonrelatives by which the new mother and father are reintegrated into full village life as *mekranyre* (those with new children). However, the postpartum taboo on the woman's sexual relations with her husband remains in force. In past times, it could extend up to 2 years. Nowadays, the norm seems to be several months. During this time, the man commonly takes on a *prõ krô'ã*, or substitute spouse.

The union of parental substance with that of their offspring and the association between what the parents ingest and the characteristics of the child that begins *in utero* is thought to be ongoing and reflected in the coordinated observances of parents on behalf of an ill or ritually honored child. On the other hand, foods off limits to the *menõrõrnyre*, such as certain fish, are perfectly acceptable to parents. Married men are able to hunt because they are better prepared than bachelors to deal with the supernatural dangers entailed in killing game. Men often know specific medicines to allow them to override the ill effects of prohibited species and for this reason have a greater potential range of diet than their spouses. However, men are expected to be generous suppliers of game and fish to their household.

Married women always have their own garden, since one of the obligations of their husbands is to clear forested areas and assist in preparation and sometimes planting of crops as well. A women is commonly assisted by her unmarried sisters or widowed mother in her garden. Widowed or single women may prevail on a lover to slash their garden. Game distribution is overseen by the house's senior woman.

Middle Age and Old Age

With the birth of three or four children, mother and fathers become incorporated in the *mekrakramtire* (those with many children grade). The social reserve and shame that have constrained a man in both the men's house and his wife's house begins to ease during this life stage, and he may become a public orator and intervene most vigorously in discussion in the men's council. He has probably sponsored a name ceremony for his child which enmeshes him in future obligations to provide food and support to others but also gains him recognition as a peacemaker. Wives of this grade have been ceremonial sponsors along with their husbands and also enjoy the respect accorded parents of honored children. With the birth of grandchildren and the gradual recognition of the diminuition of their own sexual potency, men and women become part of the *mebengêt* (social mentors) grade. As they cease to have young children of their own they are less susceptible to restrictions observed by newer parents. Men of this age are the butchers of large game, and both sexes begin to consume many foods considered deleterious to younger people. Social reserve may be flaunted. Old folks of both sexes make their opinions known, often vocally and to the discomfort of others. *Mebengêt* may also make jokes and assume postures of ridicule during solemn occasions. They are thought to be inept as learners but finally able to verbalize fully and demonstrate what they have learned from their own elders over the course of a lifetime. Men may become heralds during this life stage, exhorting the entire village in the early morning and at nightfall. Finally, some communities

insist on a terminological distinction between sexually inactive and very old men (*kubêngêt*) and women (*abêngêt*), presumably because their own gendered activity no longer serves to make this distinction.

PERSONALITY DIFFERENCES BY GENDER

Kayapo are accepting of a wide range of personality types. The fierceness displayed by men is felt to necessarily be constantly inculcated through magic, ritual, and oratory. Boys and young men constantly engage in verbal and physical contests of one-upmanship, quite differently from their female counterparts. However, by the time men are married, such open competitiveness is frowned upon. Men feel far more affected by rules of social reserve and requirements to act tough and, consequently, women show a more open and easy sociability with other women. Women of different houses, for example, will time their baths in the river so as to socialize together, although this also may act as an impediment to interruptions by menfolk. Every few days women will spend hours painting one another and also gather nightly to sit and chat on the village patio. Men are more openly relaxed outside the more formal constraining context of the village and enjoy nighttime socializing in the men's house precisely because interlocutors remain unseen in the darkness and may be answered with less reserve. In private contexts, both men and women are openly sentimental, particularly when discussing close kin relations. Men notably stress close friendships with age mates to a much greater extent than women.

GENDER-RELATED SOCIAL GROUPS

Social structure may be either male and female oriented depending on where one stands. The major foci of social life are, respectively, houses, or residence units, sharing common ritual and subsistence interests formed by groups of related women and in-marrying men, and the men's house, which is generally off-limits to women. Houses are exogamous and maintain their relative position within the village circle and also commonly during treks. Each has an area for joint cooking by female kin in a stone/earth oven.

The men's house serves as a sleeping place for bachelors and divorced or separated men. It is the site of sitting places for the various male age grades and men's clubs and the focus of male social life. Men may take meals in the men's house as well as in their residences. Decisions affecting the entire community are taken in the men's house.

GENDER ROLES IN ECONOMICS

Married couples are expected to maintain fields in which crops are grown, notably, corn, sweet potatoes, bananas, squash, yams, sweet manioc, and, today, bitter manioc. Females are in charge of harvesting and preparing food, including meat and fish provided by men. Both genders are extraordinarily capable of providing for their own needs without their complement over periods of time that may range to several months.

Various activities are carried out by each gender: males slash underbrush, fell trees, burn the garden area, hunt with bows and arrows and firearms in addition to clubs, and make weapons, basketry, ritual ornaments, household utensils, canoes and, nowadays, "craft" items for sale. They may also collect Brazil nuts, animal pelts, or other natural commodities for sale. Women prepare food in the stone/earth ovens, boil and sieve manioc, make salt from palm stalks, make cotton string (an essential item for ornaments), collect firewood, and plant, weed, and harvest gardens. Both genders cooperate in housebuilding, although men cut the logs needed for houses modeled after the Brazilian backwoods style. Formerly, women erected house structures. Both genders collect wild products, such as piqui, although males specialize in honey (even though many, such as the *menõrõny*, cannot eat it), palmito, bacaba, and assaí. Women tend to focus on other resources, such as wild legumes and chocolate and certain ants and grubs. Men collect stinging ants for use on hunting dogs as well as the feathers, resin, and eggshell used in ritual ornaments. Both men and women may fish with hook and line, although only men handle fish poisons. Men tend to roast food, although women may do so as well; women are susceptible to heated vapors and so will not toast manioc flour over an open fire, although they will participate in other steps of the procedure.

Tasks performed outside the household that involve many people are organized according to age grades. In making manioc flour, unmarried nubile girls may fetch water, bachelors fish for the entire work party, and elderly women split firewood, while younger mothers sieve manioc and collect tapioca starch, married men do the toasting, and men with many children feed manioc through an electric grinder. The least active contributors to subsistence are usually boys and young men (*meôkre* and *menõrõnyre*) who may rarely hunt, fish, or garden, concentrating instead on self-decoration, singing, and dancing.

PARENTAL AND OTHER CARETAKER ROLES

Although childcare falls most heavily on the mother, fathers may hold their small children although feeding and cleaning up are left to the mother. Adults are uniformly expansive and enthusiastic with children regardless of their sex. Once they are weaned, small children of both sexes may accompany their father to the men's house. The caretaker role extends to older siblings as well and encompasses a spiritual dimension because parents and siblings share the vital substance thought to make up part of a person and thus must act as custodians through behavioral restraints and alimentary practices. Children also have the benefit of co-resident mothers and fathers (MZ and MZH), and *ngêti* (MF and MB) and *kwatỳj* (MM, MMZ, FZ) both lavish special attention on their *tabdjwỳ* (reciprocal terms) with whom they come to be identified ceremonially. Wet nursing is common and grandmothers as well as mothers may nurse. Children have numerous *ngêti* and *kwatỳj* and, especially boys, are encouraged to cultivate these relationships, actively because through them they will acquire specialized knowledge and ceremonial valuables. Boys are also initiated into the men's house with the expectation that they will be mentored by older boys. The role of substitute father is prominent in men's house induction, and he may be an important teacher and mentor in a boy's life. Additionally, in arrangements of institutionalized spouse exchange, parents regard offspring of exchange partners as classificatory "children" and, while they may not observe taboos on their behalf, may show them familiar attention.

LEADERSHIP IN PUBLIC ARENAS

Although there is a tendency today for chiefs to inherit the role from their fathers, this is far from the rule, and leadership roles must still be achieved on the basis of special talent, ability, and energy even when succession is weighted in favor of a leader's offspring. Institutionalized leadership, with the exception of wives of chiefs who act as leaders of corresponding female age grades or women's clubs, is limited to males. These include *benad-jwyr* (speakers of ceremonial speech), ritual song leaders, scouts, including those who specialize in tracking specific enemy peoples, and *ngôkonbàri* (Xikrin) or *meôbadjwynh*—leaders of unmarried age grade activities. In the past, courageous raiders were acknowledged for their ability to abscond with goods or even prisoners. Although killing a human enemy or a jaguar is desired as a mark of valor, no special position accrued to a killer, although he did have to undergo a special ceremony on his return to the village. Heralds are also male. Elderly women may be highly respected and quite influential; however, they exercise their influence both through public pronouncement and more informal counsels, particularly with other women. Public oratory in the men's house, where consensus decisions chart the course for future action, is the prerogative of adult men.

GENDER AND RELIGION

As noted previously, both men and women play parallel roles in major great-name ceremonies; although the male versions are more extensive and complex, the names and rituals valuables transmitted in the respective ceremonies are considered equally prestigious. Besides names and ritual ornaments, females inherit the right to raise certain animals as pets, while men inherit the right to claim certain cuts of meat from game animals. When female names are celebrated, females are featured performers, and males take center stage when male children are honored. In other ceremonies, such as the babassu palm ceremony or the new corn ceremony, males also take the lead. Certain ceremonial roles, such as gourd rattle bearers, are limited to males. Men may also dress up as monkeys during certain rituals at which time they make many sexually suggestive and outrageous acts, often aimed at female onlookers. Only mature adult men chant ceremonial speeches which feature a specialized lexicon known only to a restricted number of specialists. The ritual knowledge of songs, names, and ornaments held by both men and, women is greatly valued and, in such matters, the less knowledgeable defer to the more knowledgeable regardless of gender. Both males and females are ritual

sponsors for the children involved and both contribute to gathering the necessary foodstuffs. The *kwatỳj* of honored children are expected to make themselves available sexually to male celebrants during the night of the ritual climax. Rituals may also feature collective sexual intercourse in which younger unmarried women maintain relations with married men and married women do the same with bachelors. One researcher claims to have documented spikes in the birthrate 9 months after great name ritual celebrations.

Although shamans do not have a role in collective ritual, they are considered to be important for the community. They learn new knowledge from outside the village through their contact with spirits. They are also important actors in military campaigns and may locate enemies from afar or provide means for warriors to instill fear in their enemies.

LEISURE, RECREATION, AND THE ARTS

Work and play are not neatly separated and a family outing to the garden to spend the day may be considered a leisure activity. Families may also sit together on mats under the night sky for an hour or two in the evening. Beyond such occasions, males and females do not socialize together. With the current demographic increase the number of young children clearly burden women with almost constant activity. Respite from work generally takes the form of a leisurely dip in the river, often while snacking on sweet potatoes, or when women socialize in front of their houses on the central patio after dark. Every adult woman is an accomplished body painter and has command of a number of motifs that express both socially correct classification of age/gender grade and life crisis state as well as personal style and flair. Every seventh or eighth day—or when the previous genipap application has faded away—adult women gather to paint each other's bodies. During these times men and even children are conspicuously absent and these are often gay occasions when much information is exchanged. Men's painting of their own bodies and women's painting of men is much more cursory; however, the painting of a child can take several hours. Women also raise pets (birds, monkeys, and even tapirs!), often as an inherited ceremonial privilege.

Hunting is valued both as a prestigious activity and also because it allows men to relax away from the formality and constraints of the village. Men do not hunt or go to the gardens daily, as do women, and they may spend idle time in conversation or doing nothing. While sitting at home or in the men's house they also weave baskets or other items and make weapons, such as clubs and bows and arrows, or ritual ornaments, such as mollusc shell necklaces or feather headdresses. Although such items have essential functions, they are also considered to be beautiful. The techniques for making them are considered essential male knowledge, but some men are noticeably more accomplished than others. It should be noted that to remain without doing anything in the village for an extended time invites gossip and reproach, mainly because to do nothing by oneself is considered antisocial. Although unmarried men seem to engage in less work than others, they make a great show of going around together and in this way avoid such accusations.

Relative Status of Men and Women

Males and females develop knowledge, skills, and bodily qualities that are expressed in different and complementary ways over the course of a lifetime. The arena of male activity—the forest and the world beyond the village and the public men's house—demands a rigorous and lengthy period of restrictions and activities that both men and women believe is more demanding than that to which women must be submitted. Men feel that they have earned a measure of superiority over women by virtue of a more developed and sustained formal decorum within the village and confrontation with dangers outside it. There is at least one myth attributing the invention of important ceremonies to women and the usurpation of these by men. However, public institutions are a major means through which men assert that male age/gender qualities are necessary for the reproduction of the community as a whole and thus on par with or superior to the biological fertility of females. Men coordinate activities that ensure that the younger men will learn the right skills, eat the right foods, and acquire the necessary knowledge for their further development. Women also do this for younger women, but usually in the domestic sphere or as a less ostentatious counterpart to public male activities. Men also defend the village militarily and from supernatural dangers though appropriate chants. The prestigious positions that are limited to males, principally that of chief or "true chanter of the *ben*" is associated with leadership of public institutions. Females and males

possess prestige by virtue of inherited wealth validated in great-name ceremonials, but male institutions alone provide a means of coalescing different kindreds (and cross-cutting them as well). Both sexes have a good deal of autonomy in the choice of spouse, and both girls and boys are warned that if they are lazy or incompetent no one will want them as a marriage partner.

Equally present, and expressed through customary forms, is an ongoing battle of the sexes that gives voice to the dissatisfactions felt and expressed collectively by both men and women. This may take the form of verbal duels or mutual ridicule between groups of men and women. Although adequacy of males and females in pursuit of their gender-specific pursuits is often called into question ("incompetent hunter!" "lazy gardener!"), the escalation of insults can lead to deprecation of masculine sexuality and attractiveness as lovers. Males counter in the same vein, but their barbs do not seem to have the same impact. Men are the ones who initiate violence, organizing mock raids during which women are terrorized or struck with prickly bromeliad leaves. However, women inevitably counterattack, often with firebrands. They may enlist their own children or *tabdjwỳ*, and after a male raid toddlers may be seen stolidly planted in the doorway of their house, minature warclub in hand, to block father's return home. In cases where they feel their interests slighted, women may also act collectively to withhold their labor and resources from activities organized by male age grades that demand a female complement of labor, such as the cultivation of a large garden that may require cuttings from women's domestic plots.

Clearly, Kayapo feel that they are treated in terms of a common status defined by gender, in addition to and apart from statuses of kinship, age, and ceremonial prestige. Status is relative, but both men and women may feel themselves to be the ones having their interests subordinated to their gender opposites. Both genders operate from different positions of strength—women as gardeners living in matri-uxorilocal residences within which food is shared and prepared, and men within the men's house and public sphere. It seems precisely because male assertions of superiority are so ineffective as ideology that men have attempted to make women fear them. The threat of gang rape has been reported by researchers—not as a punishment for any particular trepass but seemingly as an expression of male dissatisfaction with female behavior—and customarily girls are initiated into sex by older men, some reluctantly. The reason why accounts of the relative status of men and women continue to be differently described in the literature derives from the fact that either side may be temporarily ascendent in the ongoing war between the sexes. Collective conflict between males and females clearly affects the tenor of husband–wife and son-in-law–parents-in-law relations within the domestic units. The fierceness of adult men qualifies them for political and diplomatic preeminence but does not compel female cooperation.

SEXUALITY

Sexuality, like gender, is thought to be created through proper social activity, and men are thought to make a women's vaginal cavity into an appropriate organ for conception. Menarche, when it occurs, is thought to be the result of sexual activity. There is no regular sexual abstinence associated with menstrual periods. The literature is not clear on what contributes to the capacity of a boy to have sex beyond activities to ensure growth and maturity in general. The sexual act itself is instrumental for stimulating growth of young people of the *meprintire* and *menõrõnyre* grades, and boys are preferably initiated into sex by older women as are girls by older men. However, there are also beliefs expressed in myth that sexual contact between married women and bachelors may be dangerous to the latter. There is no doubt that older men may have self-interested motives to propagate this in order to clear the field of younger sexual rivals. However, unmarried adolescents of both sexes are expected to engage in sex. Males can easily slip out of the men's house at night, and relations may be facilitated for girls by having them bed down near the doorway of their residence where they can receive lovers while others sleep.

Males and females of all ages talk about sex in positive terms. Being attractive to the opposite sex is part of the motive for grooming and cleanliness. Medicines or charms may also be used to enhance attractiveness to the opposite sex. Pursuit of sexual liaisons precedes marriage and continues thereafter until desire subsides in the grandparent age grade. Any time a male and a female not sharing kin ties are alone together, intercourse is assumed to have occurred, and sexual tension exists whenever unrelated males and females co-mingle publicly. Sexual jealously is held to be a major cause of intravillage contention. As mentioned above, sexual liaisons are common during ceremonial climax and sexual intercourse

is required in some ritual contexts. Females commonly mark the arms and shoulders of their lovers (rather than their husbands) with scratches, indicating that passion may be heightened in extramarital trysts. Sexual relations outside marriage entail some form of gift from the male on each occasion. Women may inflate their demands if not presented with a gift at the time of the act. Married couples are expected to enjoy sex, but the post partum taboo when a woman (but not her spouse) is enjoined from sexual activity almost ensures that men will look for other sexual partners as well.

Modesty demands that men keep the glans penis covered (the scrotum and penis shaft may be exposed) and women should not sit with their legs open. Homosexual relations appear to be unknown between women, and although sexual fondling among bachelors is not uncommon, it appears to occur in the context of fantasizing about absent females.

COURTSHIP AND MARRIAGE

Young couples who are openly attentive to one another are assumed to be already married, even if they have yet to bear a child, because public courtship is nonexistent. Flirting, sexual liaisons, and gift-giving on the part of the male may all precede marriage. However, a prospective couple would not be able to spend significant time together before actual co-residence.

Public displays of affection between the sexes are not seen. Marriage is entered into freely by both parties. Extensive kinship relations and relatively small village size may reduce potential (i.e., unrelated) partners to a small number. Marriage may be preceded by exchanges of food between the houses of the potential spouses, and a prospective husband may be expected to show competence in weaving and hunting to the satisfaction of his in-laws. A daughter's mother is said to be particularly attentive to the qualities of potential partners for her offspring but cannot override her daughter's own wishes. The ceremony that openly marks the marriage relationship commemorates the birth of the first child rather than the initiation of co-residence. Second marriages need not be marked in any way other than a transfer of residence, a man usually moving to his wife's house.

Almost everyone gets married at least once during their life, although where a demographic balance exists, women outnumber men. Women who conceive a child when no man accepts paternity are designated by a specific term (*mekupry*). Although they are accommodated within extended family residences by virtue of kin ties, they generally gain a reputation for promiscuity and a dependence on the gifts they receive in return for sex. Widowed or divorced people are also accommodated within the extended family residences. There is no levirate or sororate, and a brother would only marry the sister of own brother's wife in exceptional circumstances.

HUSBAND–WIFE RELATIONSHIP

The husband–wife relationship is based on a complementary division of tasks between a husband and a wife, common stewardship over the mystical substance they share with their offspring, and overall compatibility between them and the wife's extended co-resident kin. Either party may initiate divorce if dissatisfied. Divorce is particularly frequent after the death of a child. Children almost always remain with the mother after divorce, but there are exceptions when the man may take them back to his natal household. Husbands may choose to spend their time outside the home, particularly in the men's house, and there is wide latitude for how closely couples share common meals or time together. In general, couples marry freely and are expected to like each other, but one may observe a range of emotional involvement. Each person makes decisions regarding his or her own sphere of activity, and jointly when both must be present. This means that a woman and, if co-resident, her mother as well have quite a bit to say about the distribution of food, including fish and game, and the comforts available to a husband in his home. The term *prõ* for W or and *mied* for H is used in reference to any sexual partner.

OTHER CROSS-SEX RELATIONSHIPS

Brothers and sisters ideally should transmit their great names, ceremonial inheritances, and knowledge to their siblings' offspring of the same sex. This entails continuous mutual obligations between siblings throughout their life. Although males leave their homes to be initiated into the men's house, they maintain an interest in the affairs of their sisters and may end up returning to their natal house, particularly in the case of divorce or death of their spouse.

A person should joke with the spouse of a same-sex formal friend toward while showing the latter formality and avoidance. The public joking generally focuses on ribald commentary on sexual comportment.

The relationship between an in-marrying husband and his mother-in-law carries a great deal of formality. While she may address him directly, he must channel any thoughts through his wife, avoid looking directly at her, being alone with her, etc.

Males have more opportunity to interact with their mothers, aunts, and grandmothers (*kwatỳj*) than girls do with their fathers, uncles, and grandfathers. This is because men are absent from home more during childhood when the lives of both girls and boys center around their residence. Consequently, men will cite what they have learned from their mothers (M, MZ) and *kwatỳj* (FZ, MM, FM, MBW), in addition to their fathers (F, FB) and *ngêti* (MB, MF, FF, MBS), while women cite knowledge, such as medicines, they have learned from their husband.

CHANGE IN ATTITUDES, BELIEFS, AND PRACTICES REGARDING GENDER

Several related changes are occurring in many Kayapo villages. Trekking is becoming curtailed to shorter time periods. With firearms, canoe travel, and cash and food coming in from outside, as well as opportunities to get outside the village for sightseeing and education, men are better able to meet their economic obligations and have access to resources independently of extensive kinship networks or the collective male activities organized out of the men's house. While these opportunities by and large do not exist for women, who continue to be dependent on domestic relations organized by related females, some females have begun to engage in new activities. Little girls are enthusiastic participants in schools for literacy and mathematics, where these have been established in villages. They have become operators of video cameras, and even sought opportunities to made beadwork or other items that can be sold outside the village. Young people may socialize more freely together and even on occasions set up "nightclubs" where they can dance to the sounds of Brazilian music.

There are more single mothers (*mekupry*) since there are fewer reasons for males to enter into marriage. When they do, they prefer to be less subservient to their in-laws and may often insist upon separate quarters for the couple and their children. Households also seek to be more autonomous economically, which generally entails more solitary and less collective work. The raising of boys in the men's house, where they were thoroughly inculcated with a distinct male ethos and pride in their fierceness to enemies and their own women alike, has given way to enculturation with less of a boarding-school hazing quality. Boys spend more time in their natal homes and are not so quick to assume fatherhood.

BIBLIOGRAPHY

Banner, H. (1952). A casa dos homens Gorotire. *Revista do Museu Paulista* (NS), *6*, 445–449.

Cohn, C. (2000). *A criança indígena: a concepção Xikrin de infância e aprendizado.* Unpublished master's dissertation, University of São Paulo, Brazil.

Dreyfus, S. (1963). *Les Kayapó du nord, état de Para-Brésil. Contribution à l'étude des Indiens Gé.* Paris: Mouton.

Fisher, W. H. (2001). Age-based genders among the Kayapo. In T. Gregor & D. Tuzin (Eds.), *Gender in Amazonia and Melanesia: an exploration of the comparative method* (pp. 115–140). Berkeley: University of California Press.

Lea, V. (1994). Gênero feminio Mebengôkre (Kayapó): desvelando representações desgastadas. *Cadernos Pagu, 3*, 85–116.

Lea, V. (1995). The houses of the Mebengokre (Kayapó) of central Brazil—A new door to their social organization. In J. Carsten & S. Hugh-Jones (Eds.), *About the house: Lévi-Strauss and beyond* (pp. 206–225). Cambridge, U.K.: Cambridge University Press.

Lea, V. (2002). Multiple paternity among the Mebengokre (*Kayapó, Jê*) of Central Brazil. In S. Beckerman & P. Valentine (Eds.), *Cultures of multiple fathers: The theory and practice of partible paternity in lowland South America* (pp. 105–122). Gainesville: University of Florida Press.

Murphy, I. I. (1992). *"And I, in my turn, will pass it on": Indigenous education among the Kayapo Amerindians of Central Brazil.* Unpublished doctoral dissertation, Department of Administrative and Policy Studies, School of Education, University of Pittsburgh, PA.

Turner, J. B. (1967). *Environment and cultural classification: A study of the Northern Kayapó.* Unpublished doctoral dissertation, Harvard University, Cambridge, MA.

Turner, T. S. (1980). The social skin. In J. Cherfas & R. Lewin (Eds.), *Not work alone: A cross-cultural view of activities superfluous to survival* (pp. 112–140). London: Maurice Temple Smith.

Turner, T. S. (1995). Social body and embodied subject: Bodiliness, subjectivity, and sociality among the Kayapo. *Cultural Anthropology, 10*(2), 143–170.

Verswijver, G. (1982). "Les femmes peintes," une cérémonie d'imposition de noms chez les Kayapó-Mekrãgnotí. *Bulletin de la Société Suisse des Américanistes, 46*, 41–59.

Verswijver, G. (Ed.). (1992). *Kaiapó Amazonia: The art of body decoration.* Gent: Snoeck-Ducaju & Zoon.

Vidal, L. (1977). *Morte e vida numa sociedade indígena Brasileira.* São Paulo, Brazil: Editora da Universidade de São Paulo.

Vidal, L. (1992). A pintura corporal e a arte gráfica entre os Kayapó–Xikrin do Cateté. In L. Vidal (Ed.), *Grafismo indígena: Estudos de antropologia estética* (pp. 143–189). São Paulo, Brazil: Livros Studio Nobel.

Werner, D. (1984). Child care and influence among the Mekranoti of Central Brazil. *Sex Roles, 10*(5/6), 395–404.

Werner, D. (1984). Paid sex specialists among the Mekranoti. *Journal of Anthropological Research, 40*(3), 394–405.

Kazakhs

Cynthia Werner

ALTERNATIVE NAMES

Kazakhs are also known as Kazak (alternative spelling) and as Kirgiz and Kirgiz-Kaisak (alternative names used by Russians until the 1920s).

LOCATION

Kazakhs can be found in Kazakhstan, a country that became an independent nation-state in 1991 when the Soviet Union dissolved. Kazakhstan is located in Central Asia, and shares borders with Russia, China, Kyrgyzstan, Uzbekistan, and Turkmenistan. Significant populations of Kazakhs also live in Russia, China, Kyrgyzstan, Uzbekistan, and Turkey.

CULTURAL OVERVIEW

The Kazakhs descend from nomadic Turkic and Mongol tribes who formerly occupied the Eurasian steppes. According to most sources, the Kazakhs emerged as a distinct ethnic group in the mid-15th century when a number of clans broke away from the Uzbek khanate. Over the centuries, Kazakh culture has been shaped by a nomadic pastoral economy, a tribal social structure, customary laws, a blend of Islamic and shamanic religious beliefs, and Russian and Soviet colonization.

The Kazakh economy was traditionally based on nomadic pastoralism, the seasonal migration of livestock herds to known pastures and water sources. The typical household had a herd that included sheep, horses, camels, cows, and goats. The nomadic economy influenced a gendered division of labor, where men were expected to care for the livestock and defend the territory while women cooked, cleaned, took care of children, served guests, and prepared textiles (Bacon, 1966).

The Kazakhs have a patrilineal tribal social structure. They are divided into three "hordes" (*zhuz*), which are further subdivided into a number of "tribes" or "clans" (*taipa* or *ru*), which are further segmented into tribal lineages (*ata* or *ru*).

Tribal leaders (*khans* and *bais*) had authority over families who lived within their territory and managed relations between tribal groups. Traditionally, conflicts over land, livestock, family, and kinship were resolved through either customary law (*adat*) or Islamic shar'ia law (Martin, 1996).

Islam was first brought to the territory that is now Kazakhstan by Arab conquerors in the 8th century, where archeological evidence shows that it took root among some of the sedentary peoples of the region. But it was much later, in the 15th and 16th centuries, that Sufi dervishes traveled across the steppes and converted many of the Kazakhs to Islam. Since many of the pre-Islamic practices remained predominant, Catherine the Great encouraged Tatar mullahs to provide Islamic education to the nomads, in the hope that it would "civilize" them. Although the Kazakhs have a Muslim identity, many of the characteristics associated with Muslim culture never took hold in Kazakhstan. For example, Kazakh women never wore veils that covered their faces and they do not practice seclusion. Further, a number of Islamic practices and beliefs have blended with pre-Islamic shamanic practices and beliefs (Michaels, 1997).

Russian influence over Kazakh culture begins with the 18th century when a military alliance was formed between a Kazakh khan and the Russian czar. The northern part of the Kazakh steppe increasingly came under Russian influence as the Russians established military outposts in the 19th century, and Russian peasants migrated there in the early 20th century. In 1920, Bolshevik revolutionaries gained control of the land and established administrative control over the region that is now known as Kazakhstan. From 1920 to 1991, the Soviet rulers attempted to transform many aspects of Kazakh culture in ways that conformed with communist ideology. Traditional gender relations, tribal structure, and the Islamic faith were all targets of social change (Bacon, 1966; Massell, 1974; Olcott, 1991).

In 1991, the Kazakh republic of the Soviet Union became an independent nation-state. The newly independent Republic of Kazakhstan is a multiethnic state, with sizable minority populations, including Russians, Ukrainians, Tatars, Uzbeks, Koreans, and Uighurs. Since independence, the revival of Kazakh traditional culture has been accompanied by less public and government support for measures that improve the status of women in society. Simultaneously, increased exposure to Western cultures has brought new fashions and attitudes that express a greater openness toward sexuality (Akiner, 1997; Bauer, Boschmann, & Green, 1997; Michaels, 1998).

CULTURAL CONSTRUCTION OF GENDER

The Kazakh culture recognizes male and female gender categories. There is a rigid distinction between male and female categories in terms of socialization, division of labor, and dress. Men and women dress differently. Men typically wear Western-style pants and shirts. Women typically wear modest dresses and skirts, but new modern fashions include feminine pants and pantsuits for urban women, and jeans and shorts for girls and younger women. The color red, associated with youth, is only worn by girls and young unmarried women. In rural regions of Kazakhstan, married women may wear a kerchief to symbolize their marital status.

While individual preferences vary regarding hair color, eye color, and other physical features, Kazakhs generally consider tall strong men to be more attractive than short weak men. Kazakhs generally consider women to be attractive if they are of average height with pale skin and long hair. Although robust women were preferred in the past, younger Kazakhs today are more likely to consider thin women to be beautiful.

Sexual preferences are not associated with visual clues. Most homosexuals try to conceal their sexual preferences, including through marriage to a person of the opposite sex.

GENDER OVER THE LIFE CYCLE

In the Kazakh language, there are general terms that refer to a "boy" (*ul bala*) and a "girl" (*qyz bala*), and there are more specific terms for several life stages. Kazakh infants of both sexes are known as *bope* until they are approximately 3 years old, at which point they become known as

toddlers, or *nares*. Around the age of 6, boys are referred to by the general term for boy (*ul bala* or simply *bala*), while girls are known by the general term for girl (*qyz*). By the time a girl becomes a *qyz*, she is expected to help with housework. Kazakhs believe that children reach puberty around the age of 14, at which point a boy is called a *zhigit* and a girl may be called a *boi zhetken*. The next life stage is marked by marriage, rather than the attainment of a certain age. Upon marriage, a girl is referred to as a young bride (*kelinshek*) and a boy becomes a young groom (*er zhigit*). A girl who does not marry by the age of 25 becomes known as an "older girl" (*qary qyz*). Around the age of 30, a married man is known as an *er kisi* and a married woman is known as an *aiyel*. Around the age of 60, a man becomes an old man (*kariya* or *shal*) and a woman becomes an old woman (*kariya* or *kampir*).

The transition from unmarried youth to married adult is the only transition that is publicly marked. A large wedding feast (*uilenu toi*) is held at the boy's house and, in some cases, a farewell feast for the girl (*qyz uzatu toi*) might also be held at the girl's house. The bride and groom are seated at a central stage at both events, where they are expected to stand up repeatedly as they are toasted by each of the wedding guests.

There are two other events that are publicly marked and represent important transitions, yet do not represent the transition from one named life stage to another. First, when a child takes his or her first step, the event is marked with a small family ritual known as the *tusau keser*, where a small rope symbolizing the cradle rope is connected to each of the child's legs and then ritually cut by a respected adult. Second, young boys are circumcised at the age of 3, 5, or 7. This event marks the moment a boy becomes a Muslim. A small ceremony is held on the day of the circumcision, and a large feast (*sundet toi*) is held as early as a month later.

Socialization of Boys and Girls

Kazakhs express a general preference for boy children, because boys have the cultural obligation to help their parents after they marry and boys pass on the family line. This cultural preference is illustrated by several Kazakh girl names, such as *Ulbolsyn* ("Let it be a boy") and *Ulzhan* ("boy's soul"), which indicate a sex preference for the following child. Although Kazakh families strongly desire at least one boy child, there is a preference to have a mix of boy and girl children, as girls are needed to help their mother with household chores.

Kazakh children do not have a single set of caretakers. Parents and grandparents play an important role in socialization, but in extended family households, aunts, uncles, older cousins, and older siblings may also help to socialize a child. According to Kazakh custom, a couple's first child is given to the man's parents to raise. Although this custom is not followed by all families, it is very common to encounter Kazakh children, especially firstborn children, who have been primarily raised by their grandparents, not their parents.

As infants, boys and girls are both traditionally swaddled and placed in a rocking cradle (*besik*), which makes it easy for older children to help care for them. Not all families use the cradle in contemporary Kazakhstan. Families who use the cradle may keep an infant in it for over a year. By the time an infant leaves the cradle, gender socialization becomes more noticeable. To begin, boys and girls play differently. Boys are allowed to run, chase, and wrestle each other, and they are taught to prefer masculine toys, such as cars and trucks. Girls are expected to play more quietly with toys and dolls.

Around the age of 5, boy children are circumcised and the occasion is celebrated by a large feast (*sundet toi*). From the Kazakh perspective, this occasion marks the moment a boy becomes a Muslim. In the Soviet period, the state advocated atheism and did not approve of circumcision, which was viewed as an unnecessary Muslim tradition. In practice, parents with strong affiliations to the Communist Party were less likely to circumcize their children, while other parents were likely to circumcize their sons secretly and hold a small family gathering to mark the occasion. Among Kazakhs, girl children are not circumcized and there is no comparable rite of passage.

Both boys and girls receive 11 years of coeducational public schooling. Families that can afford the additional expense send both boy and girl children to the university.

Although boys and girls may receive the same level of schooling, they are disciplined differently at home. Boys are disciplined or scolded less frequently than girls, who are often scolded for not behaving in a modest way and not helping with household work. While parents want their sons to be hard workers and to help around the house, they expect more help from their daughters. Kazakh parents believe that it is important for a young girl to learn how to help with all household chores and to behave modestly. Such qualities are necessary for a girl to find a good spouse and to have a successful marriage. Girls are expected to help with household work to such an extent that they are perceived negatively if they frequently leave the home for leisure activities, such as visiting friends. These expectations, which relate to a girl's honor and reputation, are much stronger in rural and southern regions of Kazakhstan, where traditional gender ideals have not changed as much as in urban and northern regions of Kazakhstan. In urban and northern regions of Kazakhstan, young girls have become more interested in personal appearance and leisure activities and less interested in household chores and sexual modesty (Michaels, 1998).

Boys and girls are introduced to sexuality in informal ways through friends and relatives, and more recently through global television programs and local print media. Boys often learn about sex by listening to older brothers and cousins talk about such things. Girls are less likely to learn about sex through conversation, and less likely to express an interest in sexuality owing to the cultural emphasis on female sexual modesty. On a girl's wedding day, the girl's sisters-in-law and married friends will take her aside and tell her about sex.

Puberty and Adolescence

At puberty, the general pattern of socialization continues, and the division between the sexes becomes even stronger. Boys, on the one hand, are allowed even greater social freedoms than before, though they are expected to help out with household labor. Girls, on the other hand, are more strictly disciplined than before, as parents are increasingly worried about their daughter's reputation within the community. (As will be discussed further in the "Sexuality" section, unmarried women are not supposed to have sex before marriage.) Girls are expected to help out with household chores and to behave modestly.

Attainment of Adulthood

Men and women are considered to be adults upon marriage. This is linguistically accentuated for women as the word for "girl" (*qyz*) is the same as the word for "virgin," and the word for "woman" (*aiyel*) is the same as the general word for "wife." A girl who does not marry by the age of 25 becomes known as an "older girl" (*qary qyz*).

Older girls work and socialize as adults, but they receive a hard time about their single status. Unmarried men (*boidaq zhigit*) also receive pressure to marry by the time they reach the age of 30.

Upon marriage, a woman takes on several new social roles. In addition to becoming a wife and an eventual mother, a married woman becomes a daughter-in-law (*kelin*). A good *kelin* is expected to respect her in-laws by providing unpaid household services for them. The expectations for daughters-in-law are higher if they are "in hand" (i.e., living in the same household). Nevertheless, expectations exist whether or not the young couple lives with the groom's parents. Further, the English term "daughter-in-law" is somewhat misleading as the social role of a *kelin* is not limited to a woman's relationship with her husband's parents. In other words, the services of a *kelin* can be requested by other relatives on her husband's side. For example, an older woman may invite any younger *kelin* married into her husband's patrilineal clan to come and help her prepare food for guests or to perform other tasks (Werner, in press a).

Married men and women are not expected to be physically or economically independent of the husband's parent's household. Some young couples live with the husband's parents, and almost all couples have some economic ties with their parents. At first, the economic ties might benefit the younger couple, but eventually the younger couple are expected to support the elderly couple.

Middle Age and Old Age

As men and women reach middle age, they become more economically independent. Instead of depending on others, they have several dependents, including children and elderly parents. In connection with this relative economic independence, middle-aged couples tend to have very active social lives. Compared with younger and older couples, middle-aged couples attend and host more feasts and dinner parties. This is one way that they maintain the strong social networks which are critical for household survival (Werner, 1998b). Middle-aged women increase their status when their sons marry and have children, and when their mother-in-law dies.

As men and women reach old age, there is a gradual shift toward economic and physical dependence on their grown children. The transition occurs as they retire and their health begins to fail. Although elderly men and women become more dependent on their children, they are highly respected by all members of society. Elderly men (*aqsaqal*), in particular, are respected for their knowledge and advice. Upon reaching old age, Kazakh men and women are more likely to observe Islamic rites, such as the daily prayers and fasting during the holy month of Ramadan. Although a few Kazakhs adhere to these practices throughout their lives, most consider these Islamic practices to be impractical until they reach old age and have more free time.

PERSONALITY DIFFERENCES BY GENDER

Kazakh women are socialized to act in a nurturing way toward children, guests, and elderly relatives. Women are the ones to care for hurt children and ill parents. Compared with men, Kazakh women are much more social and talkative around friends and guests. At the same time, women may act shyly and modestly toward strangers. Kazakh men, in comparison, are generally very confident and independent when it comes to dealing with outsiders, yet they are not as communicative as women when it comes to dealing with personal relationships. Kazakh men are socialized to become the dominant spouse, the dominant parent, and eventually the dominant head of the household. They express this dominance by making important decisions and commanding others to fulfill their requests.

GENDER-RELATED SOCIAL GROUPS

As explained in the "Cultural Overview," Kazakh society has both patrilocal residence and patrilineal descent. Upon birth, individuals automatically become members of their father's tribal lineage, tribe, and horde. Upon marriage, a woman moves to a residence controlled by another tribal lineage and contributes labor to this new tribal lineage, though she remains a member of her father's lineage. The patrilineal tribes and lineages are loosely associated with territorial divisions and still have importance in contemporary Kazakh culture. A person in a position of power, for example, has some moral responsibility to help other members of the same tribe or tribal lineage. Therefore it is easier to live in a region where one's lineage is a dominant group (Werner, 1998a). Tribal affiliation is also important when it comes to marriage. Kazakhs are not supposed to marry a relative on the father's side who is less than seven generations removed. In practice, Kazakhs marry outside their immediate tribal lineage to ensure that they do not marry a close patrilineal relative (Werner, in press b).

There are no important nonkin associations for males or females in Kazakh society.

GENDER ROLES IN ECONOMICS

Women's household chores include a number of daily tasks: caring for children, preparing meals, serving tea to guests, cleaning the house, washing clothes, and arranging the daily bedding. Many women also bake their own bread, prepare a variety of dairy products, and sew clothes for their family. Meanwhile, the men help with domestic work by buying groceries and helping with childcare. In rural areas, where there is more household work, women also milk the cows and horses and work in the household garden, and men also care for livestock and help with the garden work. Compared with men, Kazakh women have very little leisure time at home. In order to complete their household chores, many women rely on the help of their children and their daughters-in-law. For children, the boundaries between "female" and "male" household chores are much more flexible. With the exception of food preparation and clothes washing, boys are known to help out with household chores, especially in households that have a shortage of female labor. However, the expectations for boys' help are lower than those for girls' help (Werner, in press a).

Women also work hard to maintain household networks by serving guests, helping others serve guests, and preparing gifts for various occasions. With hospitality as one of the central elements of Kazakh culture, households frequently host dinner parties to socialize with friends and they occasionally sponsor large feasts to celebrate new marriages and male circumcision. These events are enjoyed by women, yet they also burden women with additional responsibilities. Gift exchange is another aspect of women's role in household networking. Different occasions call for different gifts, and women are responsible for selecting and presenting most gifts on behalf of their household (Werner, 1998b, in press a).

In traditional Kazakh society, craft specializations were strictly divided by gender. Women sewed clothing,

wove rugs, and made wool and other textiles. Men made ceramic objects, leather objects, and boots (Bacon, 1966).

In modern Kazakh society, there are also gendered patterns for occupational specializations. On the one hand, both men and women work as doctors, teachers, economists, and agricultural workers. On the other hand, women dominate certain occupations, such as day-care workers, shopkeepers, secretaries, nurses, and janitors. In urban centers, women are more likely to be employed as translators and administrative assistants for foreign businesses. There are a few positions that are rarely, if ever, filled by women: policemen, firemen, and military recruits. In addition, the chief positions in any business or government office are usually held by men (Bauer et al., 1997).

Both men and women sell goods in local marketplaces. In the post-Soviet period, as unemployment increases and the availability of consumer goods increases, the number of market vendors has increased dramatically (Bauer et al., 1997). Women dominate the sale of cloth, clothing, and food products, while men are exclusively involved with the sale of livestock although they can also be found selling clothes and food products. Gender stereotypes suggest that women are better at market trade because they have the patience to sit in the bazaar, the skills to persuade others verbally, and the ability to resist friends and relatives who request cash loans. While many merchants buy and sell goods close to home, some merchants travel to distant marketplaces, sometimes in foreign countries, to buy and sell their wares. In some cases, male and female merchants live apart from their families for weeks or months (Werner, in press a).

According to the laws of Kazakhstan, both men and women can buy, sell, and own property, including livestock. In practice, property is more likely to be in the husband's name.

PARENTAL AND OTHER CARETAKER ROLES

A variety of individuals play a parenting role in the life of a child. Mothers are the primary nurturers. They spend the most time with the children, they socialize children to know what is right and wrong, they provide children with tender hugs and encouragement, and they care for children when they are ill. Fathers play a more distant parenting role. They pay less attention to the child on a daily basis, but their advice, admonitions, and praise carry more authority from the child's perspective. Grandparents also play an important role in the socialization of a child. Grandparents are generally expected to indulge and spoil their grandchildren. In some cases, they take on a more serious role. According to Kazakh custom, the first child is given to the father's parents to be raised. This custom is followed by some families. In these cases, the grandparents tend to be more lenient than the parents toward the child. Aunts, uncles, and older siblings also play a parenting role by scolding younger relatives when they do something wrong and giving them orders to help with household chores.

LEADERSHIP IN PUBLIC ARENAS

Traditionally, men always dominated leadership roles in Kazakh society. At all levels of tribal organization, only men served as leaders. Although tribal divisions do not have the same political importance as they did in the past, men still serve as informal tribal leaders.

Through Soviet affirmative action policies, Kazakh women started to take on leadership roles in the modern political system. As a general rule, women have successfully worked as middle-level managers, especially in the educational and welfare sectors of the government, but they have had more difficulty reaching upper-level positions. Though women can participate in the military, this is rare and female leadership in the military is practically nonexistent. The number of women occupying political positions of power has decreased in the post-Soviet period (Bauer et al., 1997). At the same time, however, women have become disproportionately represented in the growing number of nongovernmental organizations (NGOs), many of which receive funding from the international aid community. Women have also taken on leadership roles in business, establishing and operating their own businesses, and organizing through an association for businesswomen. Finally, a number of Kazakh women have served as leaders for the growing number of charitable funds.

GENDER AND RELIGION

The Kazakhs have a Muslim identity, though their religious beliefs and practices include pre-Islamic elements that involve shamanism and ancestor worship (Michaels, 1997). There are no gendered orders in Kazakh society. Among Kazakhs, it is extremely rare for a woman to serve as mullah, or Islamic prayer leader. However, women frequently receive a calling to be a traditional healer (*tauyp* or *emshi*) (Privratsky, 2001).

Kazakhs believe that the spiritual world entails a three-tiered hierarchy. Allah, or God, is a male at the top of the hierarchy. The second level consists of good and evil spirits, which are primarily female. The third level consists of ancestor-spirits, which are both male and female.

LEISURE, RECREATION, AND THE ARTS

In general, men have more leisure time than women. Teenagers and youth of both sexes enjoy going to discos, bars, and cafés. There are more opportunities for those activities in urban areas. On occasion, they might enjoy nature by going to a park or a lake for a picnic. Grown men spend their leisure time in a variety of ways. In rural areas, they go to the livestock bazaar to socialize with other men, they visit other men's homes, and they play horse sports such as *kokpar* (a polo-like game played with a goat carcass). In urban areas, men play billiards, play sports (especially basketball and soccer), and go to the sauna. In comparison, women have almost no leisure time because there is always more housework to do. Women's leisurely pursuits include visiting other people's homes, going shopping, and taking the children to the park. Certain leisure activities, such as the livestock bazaar and the *kokpar* game, are for men only.

RELATIVE STATUS OF MEN AND WOMEN

Kazakh men have more status and authority than Kazakh women. At the household level, men make the most important decisions, such as whether to purchase an expensive item, whether to send a child to the university, and whether a child's suitor would make an acceptable spouse. Men also have the authority to make decisions regarding important household resources. However, all these decisions are usually discussed between husband and wife, so women do have an influence on major decisions. Control over individual income varies from one household to the next; in some households all income is pooled, while in others individuals retain control over some of their income.

A Kazakh woman's sexuality is controlled by men. Before marriage, her father and brothers monitor her comings and goings to ensure that she does not engage in premarital sex and reprimand her if she does not behave in a sexually modest way. In traditional Kazakh society, fathers also decided who would marry their daughters. Kazakh women today have more influence over their marriage, but most marriages still involve final consent from the girl's parents. After marriage, a woman's husband controls her sexuality, as he has the right to demand sex from his wife. In contrast, men's sexuality is much less controlled. Men are not expected to be sexually modest, and they are not expected to fulfill the sexual demands of their wives. To a certain extent, though, their sexuality is controlled by their parents who still play an influential role in who a boy chooses to marry. Only rarely would a young man marry a girl without his parent's approval. Although girls generally marry with their parent's consent, they are more likely to marry without their father's consent, particularly if the bride is "kidnapped," with or without her consent, by the groom (Werner, in press b), as described below in the section on "Courtship and Marriage."

SEXUALITY

Kazakh men and women believe that sex is natural and healthy, in addition to being important for reproductive purposes. They believe that people who do not have regular sex may experience physical and psychological side effects, such as headaches, bad moods, and aggressive behavior. The only time that sex is considered to be dangerous is during the first 40 days after the birth of a child. Although sex is considered to be important, many Kazakh women are reluctant to discuss their sexual preferences with their husbands.

Attitudes towards premarital and extramarital sex differ for males and females. Women are expected to refrain from premarital sex, though not all do so in practice. Men do not experience any negative social consequences for having premarital sex. Extramarital sex is considered to be morally wrong for either sex, though there is less stigma attached to men who have extramarital affairs.

Sexual modesty is especially important for Kazakh women. There is a tension in Kazakh society between older generations, who believe sexual modesty is very important, and younger generations who are influenced by Western images of sexuality. Teenage girls and unmarried women, especially in urban areas, often act and dress in ways that are considered to be "sexy."

Cross-dressing is a rare and surreptitious practice in Kazakh society. Similarly, Kazakh society does not look favorably toward male or female homosexuality, which is generally viewed as unnatural and dirty. Female homosexuality is considered to be more aberrant than male homosexuality. Nevertheless, some Kazakh men and women identify as "gay" and "lesbian" respectively, and gay bars can be found in large urban centers.

COURTSHIP AND MARRIAGE

Traditionally, Kazakh marriages were usually arranged by parents when the bride and groom were still young children. The bride and groom might not have met more than once or twice before the wedding (Argynbaev, 1978). Patterns of courtship and marriage changed dramatically in the Soviet period, in part due to the state's efforts to reduce gender inequality. Grown men and women receive lots of pressure to marry, and only a small minority of people never marry.

In the contemporary period, marriages are formed in a variety of ways that reflect both the pre-Soviet past and the Soviet legacy. Typically, young couples either meet in school or at university or they are introduced to each other through friends and relatives. Couples often date for several months before the topic of marriage comes up. Parents often influence who their children decide to marry by initiating certain introductions and offering their consent. The amount of influence that the parents have varies from one family to the next. Physical attraction and love are important considerations for the young couple, while parents are more likely to consider the status of the other family, the bride's ability to do housework, and the groom's ability to provide for the future. A Kazakh man is unlikely to marry a woman without his parent's consent.

There are three general paths to marriage in Kazakhstan. First, there is a modern version of the arranged marriage (*quda tusu*), where the bride and groom have as much, or more, input in the marriage decision as their parents. In addition to giving their consent, the parents are expected to deal with the formalities of "arranging" the marriage, which involves a series of exchanges between the new in-laws. Second, some marriages are formed when the groom kidnaps the bride (*alyp qashu*). This path to marriage is very common in the southern regions of Kazakhstan, and almost nonexistent in the northern regions. The Kazakh word for bride kidnapping (*alyp qashu*, literally "to take and run") is a general term used to refer to both consensual and nonconsensual bride kidnappings. Bride kidnapping varies from case to case in terms of the level of consent and the primary motive for kidnapping. Brides who are kidnapped without their consent generally choose to stay, rather than to return home with a tarnished reputation. The third alternative is for a couple to get married in a simpler fashion with an official yet simple ceremony at the civil registry and perhaps a small celebration at home (Werner, in press b).

Most marriages are celebrated with a series of feasts and events, the order of which varies from one marriage to the next. Both sets of in-laws hold a "matchmaker" or "in-law" party (*qudalyq*) in honor of their new relatives. These parties involve numerous exchanges of food and gifts between the immediate in-laws and their core relatives and friends. A "face-opening ceremony" (*betashar*) is held at the groom's house, as a formal introduction of the bride to the groom's family and social network. During the ceremony, the bride stands with her face veiled next to two other women who married into this kin group. A man playing the *dombyra*, a guitar-like instrument with two strings, sings out each guest's name. When their name is called, each guest walks toward the bride and puts a small amount of money in a jar as the bride bows her head in greeting. At the end of the ceremony, the veil is removed and the bride begins her new life as a wife and daughter-in-law (Werner, in press b). The girl's farewell party (*qyz uzatu toi*) is an optional event that takes place at the bride's house. These ceremonies range from an intimate family dinner at home to a large feast with several hundred guests. At the end of a meal, the girl is escorted to the groom's house by the groom and other family members. It is customary for the farewell to be accompanied by ritual wailing.

The wedding feast (*uilenu toi*) is a large family feast sponsored by the groom's family. Several hundred guests are invited to the feast, including the bride's family and friends and the groom's family and friends. In rural regions, the wedding feast is usually held at home. In urban areas, the wedding feast may take place in a restaurant (Werner, 1998a, 1998b). The Islamic marriage covenant (*neke qiyar*) is a small ceremony performed by a mullah at the groom's house. The mullah recites verses from the Qur'an, asks the couple to confess their faith, has the couple and the witnesses drink from a bowl of water (in which two coins have been placed), and then gives his blessing (Privratsky, 2001). A civil ceremony (*ZAGS registratsiya*) is held at a local administrative building or marriage hall. This brief ceremony, directed by a state official, ensures that the couple are legally married. After the ceremony, an entourage of young people travel in cars with wedding ribbons to nearby scenic locations and take numerous photographs.

Legally, divorce can be initiated by the man or the woman. In practice, however, divorce is usually initiated by the man because there are fewer consequences for a divorced man than for a divorced woman. There are a variety of acceptable reasons for a man to initiate a divorce: the wife is unable to bear children, she is a bad housekeeper, she does not get along well with her in-laws, he is in love with somebody else, or he suspects her of infidelity. Women are more likely to initiate divorce in situations where the husband drinks excessively, physically abuses her, or does not provide for the family. Before resorting to divorce, a Kazakh man must consider his parent's opinion and the personal difficulty of living without his children. If the woman is considered to be a good wife, mother, and daughter-in-law, his parents will encourage him to stay in the marriage. If she is considered to be a bad wife, mother, and daughter-in-law, his parents will likely support his decision to divorce. A Kazakh women has additional things to consider before she divorces. She must consider where she will live after the divorce, how she will cover the expenses for herself and her child, and how she will remarry. Many women return to their parent's home after a divorce, but parents do not always welcome them with open arms. Children always stay with their mother, which makes it more difficult economically for women to seek a divorce. Remarriage is possible for both sexes, but there is much less stigma attached to divorced men and therefore remarriage is easier for them.

Widows and widowers can remarry. Young widows are much more likely to remarry than older widows. Widowers, on the other hand, are more likely to remarry regardless of their age, because Kazakhs believe men need a woman to help them with housework. Both widows and widowers are more likely to remarry somebody who was previously married.

Husband–Wife Relationship

Ideally, Kazakh husbands and wives live together in a relationship characterized by mutual affection and respect. Kazakh husbands and wives eat together with other family members and any guests. Married couples always have their own private bedroom in which they sleep together. Infants may sleep in the same room. Couples spend a lot of time together, though men leave the house more often to socialize with friends. Couples vary in regard to whether they make decisions together or not.

Polygamy is illegal in Kazakhstan, though it did exist in the pre-Soviet past. Among the older generation, it is not uncommon to find an occasional polygamous marriage.

Other Cross-Sex Relationships

Brothers and male cousins have a protective relationship with their sisters. In addition, a teasing relationship exist between a girl or woman and her sister's husband. Both sides in this relationship tease each other verbally.

References

Akiner, S. (1997). Between tradition and modernity: The dilemma facing contemporary Central Asian women. In M. Buckley (Ed.), *Post-Soviet women: From the Baltic to Central Asia* (pp. 261–304). Cambridge, U.K.: Cambridge University Press.

Argynbaev, Kh. (1978). Marriage and marriage rites among the Kazakhs in the 19th and early 20th centuries. In W. Weissleder (Ed.), *The nomadic alternative: Modes and models of interaction in the African–Asian deserts and steppes* (pp. 331–341). The Hague, The Netherlands: Mouton.

Bacon, E. (1966). *Central Asians under Russian rule: A study in culture change*. Ithaca, NY: Cornell University Press.

Bauer, A., Boschmann, N., & Green, D. (1997). *Women and gender relations in Kazakstan*. Manila, Philippines: Asian Development Bank.

Martin, V. (1996). *Law and custom in the steppe: Middle horde kazakh judicial practices and Russian colonial rule, 1868–1898*. Unpublished doctoral dissertation, University of Southern California, Los Angeles, CA.

Massell, G. J. (1974). *The Surrogate proletariat: Moslem women and revolutionary strategies in Soviet Central Asia, 1919–1929*. Princeton, NJ: Princeton University Press.

Michaels, P. (1997). *Shamans and surgeons: The politics of health care in Soviet Kazakstan, 1928–1941*. Unpublished doctoral dissertation, University of North Carolina, Durham, NC.

Michaels, P. (1998). Kazak women: Living the heritage of a unique past. In H. L. Bodman & N. Tohidi (Eds.), *Women in Muslim societies: Diversity within unity* (pp. 187–202). Boulder, CO: Lynne Rienner.

Olcott, M. B. (1991). Women and society in Central Asia. In W. Fierman (Ed.), *Soviet Central Asia: The failed transformation* (pp. 235–254). Boulder, CO: Westview Press.

Privratsky, B. (2001). *Muslim Turkistan: Kazak religion and collective memory*. London Curzon Press.

Werner, C. (1998a). Household networks and the security of mutual indebtedness in rural Kazakhstan. *Central Asian Survey, 17,* 597–612.

Werner, C. (1998b). Women and the art of household networking in rural Kazakhstan. *Islamic Quarterly, 41,* 52–68.

Werner, C. (in press a). Feminizing the new silk road: Women traders in rural Kazakhstan. In C. Nechemias, K. Kuehnast, & N. Popson (Eds.), *Post-Soviet women encountering transition: Nation-building, economic survival, and civic activism*. Baltimore, MD: Johns Hopkins University Press.

Werner, C. (in press b). Women, marriage, and the Nation-State: The rise of nonconsensual bride kidnapping in Post-Soviet Kazakhstan. In P. J. Luong (Ed.), Transformations of Central Asian states: From Soviet rule to independence. Ithaca, NY: Cornell University Press.

Kuna

James Howe

ALTERNATIVE NAMES

The Kuna (or San Blas Kuna) call themselves Tule (Dule), a word that also means "people," "person," or "indigenous person," although they also use the name Kuna.

LOCATION

The Kuna live along the eastern Caribbean shore of Panama on the coast of San Blas, as well as in and around the cities of Panama and Colón. Other smaller Kuna populations, who are not considered in this article, live in the interior of eastern Panama and northwest Colombia.

CULTURAL OVERVIEW

During the 17th and 18th centuries, the Kuna, then a riverine and forest population in the Darién region of eastern Panama, engaged in intermittent conflict with Spanish colonial authorities while cooperating with Northern European pirates and traders. During a century of peace beginning in the late 18th century, most of the Kuna moved to the northern Caribbean coast of San Blas, and between the middle 19th and early 20th centuries they continued out onto nearby islands.

Today the coastal Kuna inhabit some 50 communities—six on the shore, two upriver, and the rest on coral islets. They grow plantains and bananas, corn, rice, and root crops on the mainland, raise coconuts for sale on the shore and uninhabited islands, and meet their protein needs mostly from the sea. Since 1938 the coast has been a legally recognized indigenous reserve, now called the Comarca de Kuna Yala. It has been governed since 1945 by three "big chiefs" (*sagla dummagan*) or *caciques* and the semiannual Kuna General Congress. As of the year 2000, there were 31,000 Kuna in Kuna Yala or San Blas, and 24,000 in urban Panama (Dirección de Estadística y Censo, 2001).[1]

CULTURAL CONSTRUCTION OF GENDER

The Kuna strongly differentiate man (*machered*) and woman (*ome*) as cultural categories, and they say that many things in the universe, such as panpipes and buildings, come in male–female pairs. The roles and spheres of influence of the two genders are strongly differentiated, though men and women converse and interact frequently with little ceremony or deference on either side, tempering the undeniable but moderate subordination of women in Kuna society.

Male and female dress is strongly differentiated. In the late 19th and early 20th century men wore distinctively cut home-made pants and shirts, gold earrings, bowler hats, and, in the 19th century, long hair. Today they wear store-bought shirts and pants, with baseball caps and other assorted hats for work, and in the case of senior men, fedoras for village meetings.

Women's dress changed radically during the 19th century. A small strip of sewn designs at the waist of a blue blouse expanded to become a reverse-appliqué blouse with complex colorful designs, called a *mola*, today a form of indigenous art sold throughout Europe and the Americas. Kuna women wear red and yellow headcloths and blue, green, and white wraparound skirts, both manufactured abroad for the indigenous trade. Their forearms and lower legs are tightly wrapped with rows of beadwork, and they wear large gold rings in the nasal septum, gold earrings, and chestpieces, and necklaces of silver coins, shells, pods, and beads.

Today, at the beginning of the 21st century, a few villages enforce the wearing of traditional women's dress, but many others leave it to individual choice (see Tice, 1995, pp. 81–82). Probably a majority of girls are now growing up wearing slacks, shorts, and skirts, but a surprising number of women still wear *mola* at least some of the time, even in the city, and overall female dress remains a key marker of Kuna identity.

GENDER OVER THE LIFE CYCLE

The Kuna express a strong desire for both male and female children, and Kuna leaders traditionally urged their followers to *dula omeloge*, "increase the membership." A couple with only male or only female children may take medicine to increase their chances of having a child of the opposite sex or will adopt or foster a child.[2]

Socialization of Boys and Girls

A baby (*goe, gwarugwa* "newborn") of either gender receives a great deal of attention and physical affection.[3] Infants are nursed on demand, and they are often carried around and sung to by older sisters and other female housemates as well as by their mothers. Children of any age are almost never struck or spanked, though as they grow older they may be disciplined with shame or harsh words, and they receive less physical affection than before.

When female babies are a few days old, they undergo a small ritual in which their ear lobes and nasal septum are pierced and small pieces of string tied in the holes. Traditionally, parents would mark the piercing by a village-wide celebration (*ikko inna*) with drinking of cane beer, though this ritual has almost disappeared. Today some parents sponsor a long puberty ceremony (*inna suit*) for a young prepubertal daughter, usually as a stratagem to space out the considerable costs of providing these ceremonies for several female children (see below).

In other respects, males and females begin to be treated in significantly different ways when they are old enough to get around easily on their own. Young girls, who traditionally begin to wear little *mola* blouses as soon as they can walk, and soon thereafter skirts and headcloths, are kept close to home. (Today, children of both sexes often start with factory-made underpants and tops.) As they grow older, girls are called on to carry their younger siblings and sing them lullabies, and eventually they begin to help a little with other household work (see Hatley, 1976).

Boys, in contrast, enjoy a great deal of freedom to roam around the village flying kites, catching birds, swimming, fishing off docks, and raising hell; during the first half of the 20th century they went naked or wore shirts but no pants. Sometimes beginning with diminutive canoes of their own, they soon graduate to more serious fishing and eventually to helping in the forest. In the past boys were toughened and made industrious through the bites of leaf-cutter ants and the application of stinging nettles; the latter was also used as a punishment for both adults and unruly boys.

Today, the experiences of male and female children converge more than before, since both typically complete kindergarten and several years of primary school.[4] Boys and girls should be periodically admonished and counseled by village leaders as well as their parents, and traditionally both are administered medicine baths and drinks to make them hard workers, good students, and, in the case of girls, expert *mola* makers.

Puberty and Adolescence

Puberty is the stage at which boys begin to work seriously in the forest with their fathers and brothers, and, during the early 20th century, to put on long pants for the first time. Many also go away for a year or more of migrant labor, and today a large minority continue their schooling through secondary or university levels (see below). As incipient adults, these "youths" (*sapingana*) are exhorted to act like a Kuna man (*Dule machered*) by working hard and defending their people, and pieces of a past warrior ethos surface in, for instance, performances in which pairs of young men dance with stinging nettles grinding between them. Traditionally, many youths would become village constables (*sualibgana*) and within a few years begin apprenticeships in ritual.

Coming of age is much more strongly marked for females. As a young girl approaches puberty, she is called a *dungu*, from the verb *dungue*, "to grow." From her first menses until marriage or loss of virginity, she is a *yaagwa*, "maiden." The kin term for daughter also changes at puberty, from *bunolo* to *sisgwa*.

When a girl has her first period (*sergue*, "to become mature"), her father announces the event in euphemistic language to the village men, who arrive at her house the following day to build a ritual enclosure (*surba emakke*) in which she is isolated. During the next 3 days, she is repeatedly bathed in seawater, her hair is cut short for the first time, and she is painted black with the juice of a plant (*Genipa americana*). The sequence ends with a community-wide feast.

Over the next few years her parents sponsor two puberty ceremonies in her honor, both called *inna* after the *chicha* or cane beer which participants consume (see Prestán Simón, 1975, pp. 135–230). A 1 day affair called *inna mutiki*, "night *chicha*" used to follow within a couple of weeks after the rituals of first menstruation, but today it is more likely to come last and to be understood as compensation to the village for its efforts in the other puberty ceremonies. The *inna suit* or "long *chicha*," which takes up to 4 days to complete, entails performance of a lengthy chant cycle and numerous component rituals, as well as feasting, dancing, drinking, and merrymaking by villagers. A long Kuna name is chosen for the maiden, and her hair is cut short again. Otherwise, she spends much of the ceremony isolated outside in an enclosure and is more or less ignored.

In recent decades, some girls have received only a single short chicha (called an *inna mutiki dummad*), and some parents avoid the major expense of puberty ritual altogether, especially for daughters who chose to wear Panamanian clothes, merely serving a hot drink to the community to mark the occasion. However, amid the general decline of ritual in recent decades, villages continue to hold a good many chichas.

Today quite a few boys and girls continue on to higher educational levels, though boys are favored. According to the year 2000 national census (Dirección de Estadística y Censo, 2001), 7,272 males and 4,735 females had completed some secondary school, while 906 males and 457 females had attended university. Several dozen individuals have pursued advanced degrees abroad.

Attainment of Adulthood

A girl is considered a full adult woman (*ome*) when she marries and has her first child, which often occurs during her middle teenage years. A boy becomes a man (*machered*) when he is enrolled on the work lists for village labor, and when he marries and has a child.

Middle Age and Old Age

Kuna men and women typically reach the height of their influence, respect, and mastery in middle age and early old age. If all goes well, a woman will have daughters and granddaughters; she will be female household head, midwife, and respected senior woman. A man will be household head, senior ritualist, and perhaps village leader. An individual who has gotten old (*serredgusa*) deserves leisure and support from his or her children and sons-in-law, though in fact many work hard into advanced old age.

PERSONALITY DIFFERENCES BY GENDER

No serious culture and personality studies have been carried out among the Kuna. As a matter of gender stereotypes, men say that women are in general unruly, argumentative, and prone to gossip and quarreling—a male accused of lying or spreading stories may be berated for not acting like a Kuna man (*Dule machered*) (Howe, 1986, p. 231). Women are expected to express emotion, especially during puberty ceremonies and wailing for the dead (Howe & Hirschfeld, 1981). Men, in contrast, are supposed to mourn with stoic reserve and, in the case of political leaders, to maintain a mask of restrained calm in public situations. According to Sherzer (1987, p. 103), "differences between Kuna men's and women's speech are relatively slight" in everyday conversation, though men perform several genres of ceremonial discourse generally closed to women.

GENDER-RELATED SOCIAL GROUPS

Despite the claims of many naive observers, the Kuna do not maintain unilineal descent groups or descent reckoning of any sort, and kinship is thoroughly bilateral. The primary kin-based social group is the uxorilocal or matrilocal household, governed by the rule that upon marrying a man goes to live with his wife. In recent decades households have averaged somewhere in the range of eight to ten members (Howe, 1985; Tice, 1995, p. 117), but earlier in the century they were quite a bit larger (Chapin, 1983, p. 472). Mothers and coresident adult daughters, who work together daily, can be seen as a consanguineal household core, but (Helms [1976] to the contrary) in-married males, except in their first tentative years of marriage, are full members, and the senior male, just like his wife, is seen as progenitor as well as household head.

Village communal labor (which varies considerably from one island to the next) is organized along single-gender lines. Male groups build homes, wharves, public buildings, and airstrips; they work in village-owned stores and coconut groves; and they provide sugar cane, corn, bananas, fish, and other items for communal rituals. Women (often loosely supervised by male task leaders) sweep the streets, tend store, serve refreshments to male workers, and prepare food and drink for feasts and rituals.

Within each village the Kuna maintain an array of voluntary organizations, often called *sociedades*, which are devoted to land-clearing, fishing, cropping of coconuts and subsistence crops, running communal stores, and other purposes. Though single-sex groups outnumber those with mixed membership, the effective units in many nominally all-male *sociedades* are husband–wife pairs. For the last 30 years a women's organization for marketing *molas* has fostered female leadership and organization.

GENDER ROLES IN ECONOMICS

Until well into the 19th century, the Kuna followed much the same division of labor as other lowland South American groups: men cut and burned off the forest, and women planted, weeded, and harvested. In roughly the same period that the Kuna moved down to the shore and out onto the islands (see above), men began to take over most agricultural labor—possibly because of the longer distances between home and fields, the great weight of the cash and subsistence staples (coconuts and plantains), male fears for women's safety, and increased labor inputs by women into their clothing (see Brown, 1970; Tice, 1995, pp. 36–38).[5]

Today agricultural labor is overtly recognized as a male domain. A young woman is told at marriage that she has acquired a machete or hand, and men are repeatedly admonished that it is a world of work, in which they must feed their children by raising plants (Salcedo, 1980).[6] Women still participate in some activities, especially at the eastern end of the coast (see Tice, 1995, pp. 115–177); they go with their husbands or with other women to cut bananas and to fetch coconuts, kindling wood, crabs, crayfish, river snails, and tree fruit in season. Out of choice or necessity, a very few women do more, but in almost all subsistence tasks males predominate.

Men and women carry loads very differently. Women bear baskets, bags, bunches of coconuts, and other burdens over their shoulders on their backs (except when they lug them short distances in the way that suitcases are carried), while men fasten them to either end of a pole balanced on a shoulder.

On the water, women very seldom run outboards and only occasionally help their husbands with sailing, but they readily paddle canoes, often visiting the closest mainland river with other women to wash clothes and fetch water. Trips to the river have been important occasions for female socializing (as have all-woman funeral meals at village graveyards), though more than 20 communities have built aqueducts to bring fresh water from the mainland, drastically reducing women's off-island work.[7]

Fishing is heavily gendered as a male activity—a newborn is often announced either as a "fisherman" (*ua soed*) or a "water filler" (*dii baled*)—though quite a few women go out fishing once in a while. Women used to help in catching sea turtles as they laid their eggs on beaches (once a significant source of cash income), but only men netted turtles in the sea, as is the case today for hunting, lobster diving, and catching octoupi used to sell.

The home is seen as the woman's domain, and even more so the kitchen, a smaller structure behind the main sleeping house. Men sometimes help in small ways, by watching children or stirring a pot for a few moments, but they seldom or never sweep, cook, scrub clothes, or fetch wash water from on-island wells (see Tice, 1995, pp. 125, 147). Both men and women husk coconuts. Women spend hours preparing food, especially in making drinks from corn, banana, cacao, and sugar cane (now largely replaced by coffee, cocoa, and Kool-Aid), and in cooking the staple stew based on fish, coconut, and bananas or plantains (for details, see Prestán Simón, 1975, pp. 49–50).

As a key element in gender interdependence, the Kuna insist that a wife or female kinswoman should meet a returning man at the water's edge to help him pull up and unload his canoe and (if their house is some distance away) to carry home its contents. According to Kuna theory, men and women exchange raw fish and produce for cooked food, and, once foodstuffs have passed into women's hands, it is for them to redistribute as they wish (Salcedo, 1980, pp. 66–68). Interhousehold food exchange and hospitality are overtly recognized as key symbols of community and ethnic solidarity, though by the late 20th century fish and bananas had entered the village cash economy, and gift exchange of food had fallen off sharply.

In the field of handicrafts, men make firefans and baskets (a highly gendered activity), fashion utensils of gourds, and carve implements and curing figures of wood. House construction is a male skill, as is canoe building (a semispecialized occupation). Until the middle decades of the 20th century women spun cotton and wove hammocks, and Nordenskiöld, Pérez Kantule, and Wassén, (1938, pp. 38–39) note that both men and women once made pottery, probably of different sorts. Men used to make pants and shirts on hand-cranked sewing machines, but needlework is otherwise a quintessentially female activity—with the notable exception that in many villages a handful of "womanish" (*omegid*) homosexual men sew (but do not wear) *molas*.

Although fields are initially cleared by men, both sons and daughters inherit, in roughly equal proportions. Some farms are turned over to adult children or assigned to them for later inheritance, but often at least a few parcels are held back by aged parents until they die. Although a man does not inherit from his wife's mother or father, he is highly conscious that his children will do so, and in the meanwhile he typically works his spouse's fields together with his own as, in effect, a lifetime joint estate.

The senior male in a household is often referred to as the *negibed* "master/owner of the house," but if he and his wife divorce, he moves out and she keeps the dwelling. In the normal developmental cycle, junior couples hive off in turn, usually because of quarrels or overcrowding, and at the deaths of the senior husband and wife, the last remaining junior couple takes the house. Modern homes with cement walls and composition roofs are in many cases now being inherited by testamentary disposition.

For a long time the elaborate costume of Kuna women has represented a significant expense for fathers and husbands, but in the 1960s and 1970s *molas* also began to bring in income, as a national and international market developed for blouses and blouse panels (see Tice, 1995, pp. 56–75). Today, in addition to selling used *mola* panels, women make others just to sell to daytrippers, cruise ship passengers, and middle-men who feed the national and international market. The importance of *mola* income to household economies has further increased since the 1980s and 1990s, as blighted palms and international market shifts have drastically reduced returns from the coconut trade. A women's *mola* cooperative (Salvador, 1997; Swain, 1978, pp. 174–182; Tice, 1995, pp. 99–114), though it controls only a fraction of the market, has proved crucial in helping women organize and receive better returns for their labor.

Kuna men have shipped out as sailors since at least the 19th century, and in the 20th century increasing numbers went away for long periods to work in banana plantations, urban restaurants, and U.S. army bases in the Canal Zone. (A few land-poor youths also seek work as agricultural laborers in other Kuna villages.) In recent years men and women with secondary and university educations have secured salaried positions in the city, though unemployment is high and men are favored. For less educated indigenous women, urban money-making opportunities other than *mola* sewing are scarce. Inside San Blas, Kuna men and women have worked as teachers in roughly equal numbers, and (with a tilt towards males) in other government jobs (see Swain, 1978, p. 111; Tice, 1995, p. 53). Holloman (1969, p. 132) recorded 245 such posts in 1967. In the village economy, women, teenage boys, and a few adult men tend radios and airstrips for tiny wages, men work on cargo boats run by five to ten of the villages, and males and females participate in family businesses such as stores, bread-baking, and (for a wealthy minority) tourist enterprises. Both men and women deal with village stores and the crews of Colombian merchant vessels in selling coconuts and buying manufactured goods, and women (especially at the Western end of the coast, where most cruise ships visit) sell *molas* to tourists. However, most women have been reluctant to speak Spanish, even if they have attended school, and many of the Colombian sailors know a little Kuna.

Concerning household finances, this author's data, mostly from the 1970s, indicate that in traditional households with significant income from coconuts, each couple pooled cash in its own box, over which the wife had considerable say, and that the senior couple covered a great part of household expenses, even for their married daughters and grandchildren (cf. Holloman, 1969, p. 176; Tice, 1995, pp. 132, 151). Tice (1995, p. 176) writes that in recent years "Women individually control their own income from *mola* sales," and that men active in lobster diving often fail to devote cash returns to family needs.

PARENTAL AND OTHER CARETAKER ROLES

The Kuna place great emphasis on the mother's role, portraying her as the one person who will always look out for and defend her children. In daily life, female siblings, coresident aunts and cousins, grandparents, and fathers often take turns caring for children, and in properly functioning households, it is expected that fathers and grandparents will provide materially for their dependents.

However, only mothers are thought to give love and care unconditionally.

Leadership in Public Arenas

Men dominate Kuna politics. Each village maintains a hierarchy of offices, with several politico–religious chiefs, secondary officers called *argar*, and village constables, as well as specialized positions for house building and other tasks; some now have a secular administrative chief as well (Howe, 1986). Since the 1980s a few of the largest and most sophisticated islands have instituted women's meetings or elected women as *argar* or administrative chief, though not so far as traditional chief. Two women have run unsuccessfully for the national assembly; the daughter of a famous chief briefly served as governor or intendente of Kuna Yala, and women have played leading roles in establishing at least one urban settlement (De Gerdes, 1995; Tice, 1995, p. 51). In Kuna Yala, women also make their feelings known on key issues, such as the election of a new village leader, and a few regional women's meetings have been held. Nonetheless, the vast majority of office-holders and participants in decision-making, at both the village and regional level, are male.

Until recently most men also participated extensively in ritual, spending years or decades establishing names as puberty chanters, medicinalists, or singers of curing chants (see Chapin, 1987; Nordenskiöld et al., 1938; Sherzer, 1987). One ritual specialty, that of puberty hair-cutter, is reserved for women. Seers or *neles*, who are born into their role, can be male or female, and the tiny handful of women who actually practice as *nele* are also free to master other ritual specialties. Much more significantly, senior women play important but less publicly recognized roles as midwives, funeral mourners, cooks and organizers of village feasts, and curers' wives. The latter, as Chapin (1983, pp. 172–178) shows, actually do much of the work of diagnosis and treatment.

Gender and Religion

Kuna religion, which embodies the assumptions of Kuna gender roles, is carried on primarily by village chiefs called *saila*, who chant to their assembled followers several times a week in a gathering house (see Howe, 1986; Sherzer, 1987). (Today in some villages men and women only meet separately, and attendance has fallen off.) The deities are a married couple: Great Mother, who inspires devotion from the Kuna, was put in place as the earth by the more powerful and fearsome Great Father, who animated her trees and rivers and counseled her on their functions. Individual humans go through a cosmic life-cycle, sent to earth by a celestial midwife Muu (another incarnation of Great Mother), and returning at death to their heavenly parents in "Father's Place" above.

Among the many named actors in Kuna mythology or sacred history, the great majority (other than heroes' wives) are male. In one way or another, the few exceptions reinforce traditional assumptions about gender. They include Gikatiryai, who taught women their crafts and duties; Nagagiryai, who taught designs for *molas*; a female seer who, by inadvertently causing the death of eight successive husbands, led to the dispersal of the proto-Kuna; and a young girl menaced by vampire peoples, embodying the fragility of Kuna ethnicity. Even the notable star-woman Inanatili, who outwrestled her future husband, came to earth to marry and to teach women lullabies and mourning (Howe & Hirschfeld, 1981).

The Kuna feel that all people need frequent counseling on their behavior, and, according to men, none more than women. Often addressed condescendingly in chiefly chants and spoken admonishments as girls (*siamarye*), women are reminded to keep their houses clean, care for their families, and avoid gossip and arguments.

The puberty ceremonies mentioned above celebrate female maturation and offer prominent roles to a few women. Moreover, the occult symbolism of the puberty chant cycle deals with female sexuality and reproduction (Prestán Simón, 1975, pp. 135–230), as do the inner secrets of some curing chants. Here as elsewhere, however, male ritualists predominate, and they pay more attention to each other and the crowd at the *inna* than to the girl for whom the ceremony is given. Moreover, the symbolism could arguably be taken as a male attempt to tame or appropriate female procreative power.

Through the early 20th century, gender roles and many other practices of daily life were hedged around by a profusion of taboos (*ised*) (see Prestán Simón, 1975, pp. 29, 50, 86, 130–131). Today, except in a few areas such as childbirth, these taboos have lapsed, and no ethnographic account exists showing convincingly how they once worked.

LEISURE, RECREATION, AND THE ARTS

Both men and women work hard, but except in cases of special need or hardship, they enjoy daily leisure as well as occasional days off. Women take periodic breaks throughout the day, men take a longer free period after their return home, most often in mid-afternoon, and both are released in the evening from all but minor household tasks. Men and women spend a great deal of time in conversation (in both same-gender and mixed groupings), and both visit friends and kin in other households. Late afternoon visiting, however, has been strongly associated with men, who make several stops on their peregrinations to be given drinks and (in the past) fed meals. Teenage boys—and more recently girls—devote afternoon hours to basketball and volleyball, and in many communities Sunday is now a day of rest or light work.

At sunset and into the evening, adolescents cruise the streets, something they would have been strongly discouraged from doing in the past. Men chat, play dominoes, and sometimes have a beer on the porches of stores and homes. Until recently, almost everyone would attend sacred and secular village gatherings, women on alternate nights and occasional mornings, men almost every night. In the past, men also devoted a great deal of time in the evening or late at night to learning and practicing ritual, and the more ambitious among them would make extended trips to learn away from home. Today, however, apprenticeship has almost ceased.

Women, especially the young and middle-aged, devote much of their time free from other tasks to sewing, to the extent that one of the calls to singing gatherings is "Go sew *molas!*" (*Mormaynamaloe!*). Salvador (1997, pp. 168–170; see also Tice, 1995, p. 124) notes that older women often make it possible for juniors to sew by taking on the most time-consuming household tasks. For some resource- and worker-poor households, *mola* sewing has become a demanding and nearly full-time occupation (Tice, 1995). Almost all women sew *molas*, but only a few are known for cutting top-quality designs.

Every few weeks or months, people stop work to attend a puberty ceremony in their own or a neighboring village. Men and women sit at opposite ends of the *innanega* or chicha house, though they also mix and converse in passing. Both drink heavily of the cane beer (*inna*) and both get drunk, though men are more likely to continue for long periods with purchased rum and aguardiente. (Men also drink much more frequently and heavily than women during national holidays.) In two episodes during the long 4-day ceremonies, men and women dance, both separately and together. Since World War II, several islands have created secular dance troupes (*noga gope*) based loosely on puberty dancing, with practices and performances in the afternoon or evening.

Although women have their own forms of singing (lullabies and mourning), men predominate in the verbal arts. In the realm of material art, the woman's sewn *mola* blouse receives wide recognition at home (chiefs chant that needle and cloth are women's paper and ink) and even more in the wider world. During the 1920s, a program by the Panamanian government to eliminate nose-rings and leg-bindings highlighted the importance of women's dress as an ethnic marker, and today *molas*—and the women who wear them—are widely taken as key symbols of both Kuna and Panamanian identity.

RELATIVE STATUS OF MEN AND WOMEN

In an early ethnographic study of Kuna female gender, Reina Torres wrote that "within her culture, the Cuna woman occupies a truly exceptional place. During all her life she is the object of the greatest consideration, flattery, and respect" (Torres de Ianello, 1957, p. 3). Torres' opinion has been echoed by many observers since then, especially naive amateurs, who typically describe Kuna society as a matriarchy. Although few social scientists today feel comfortable making such sweeping claims about gender (see Swain, 1978, pp. 43–75), one can say that Kuna women do indeed receive respect from men, mixed with some condescension and even a little scorn. Moreover, the consideration mentioned by Torres constrains as well as protects women

Overall assessments of the Kuna gender hierarchy depend to a great extent on judgments about the significance of art and dress. Kuna women are preoccupied with beauty and fashion—with changing designs in tradecloth skirts and headcloths, new ways of wearing headcloths, expensive gold jewelry, and innovations in blouse form as well as *mola* motifs—all of which might at one time have struck some feminists as a diversion or form of false consciousness. Salvador (1997), on the other hand, speaks for most observers of Kuna society in praising the ensemble of Kuna women's dress as well as *molas* in particular as a notable form of cultural expression.

Men and women are traditionally most equal within the domestic sphere, especially the senior couple in a household, who work in close cooperation. As mothers, women receive devotion from their children. Although women no longer do much agricultural labor, their domestic work is highly valued, they own land and houses, and since the late 20th century they have been making major contributions to household income, though they are often exploited by foreign *mola* buyers and Kuna middle-men.

Women are most subordinate in the public sphere. Men fill most political and ritual roles, and they take the lion's share of power and recognition, to the extent that women's names were often not remembered or known, even by relatives.[8] Male protectiveness has also constrained and confined women, who until very recently were not allowed to travel away from home without a husband or male kinsman—or at all.

In the village gatherings men work to rein in the conduct of women, whom they depict in their speeches as unruly and difficult (see Howe, 1986, pp. 229–233). But such attempts at control ultimately extend to everyone's behavior, including their own, and in the adjudication of disputes and quarrels, senior men enforce the rights (as they understand them) as well as the obligations of women and junior males. Villages vary widely today in their rigor, from those that attempt, for instance, to prohibit divorce and cut off rumors and quarrels, to others that have more or less given up on social control. Quite a few communities have tried to discipline the behavior of members resident in Colón or Panama City, but with only mixed success, and it is in urban settings that Kuna women, especially educated women, have gained the greatest freedom.[9]

Overall, though women use the weapons of the weak to undermine male control, they have seldom challenged public patriarchy directly except in the city and a in few of the most sophisticated island communities. On the other hand, they have great influence in the domestic sphere, and in the game of love (see below) they are as active as men. Perhaps most important, in the small interactions of daily life, the egalitarian ethos of Kuna society overrides gender hierarchy, as men and women speak their minds in the most frank, straightforward, and undeferential manner.

SEXUALITY

In an early ethnography, Stout (1947, pp. 38–39) depicted the Kuna as prudish and straight-laced, which is quite misleading. It is true that adults use euphemisms to discuss childbirth and sexuality, and public speeches condemning moral transgressions can be self-righteous, but in private the Kuna are quite libidinous. They often joke about sex, finding it amusing as well as enjoyable, and women in particular can be quite earthy, especially when intoxicated or in single-gender groups on the mainland. To describe themselves in this context, the Kuna often use the Spanish word *vivo,* "lively."

Traditionally the Kuna have tried to hide the facts of life from preadolescent children. (The author's experience suggests they had little success, even in the 1970s.) Women wear loose-fitting clothes during pregnancy, and they give birth in absolute silence, either in an enclosed corner of a house or more often in a special birth hut—today, they frequently retire to a village maternity clinic.

As noted above, preadolescent and adolescent girls were in the past guarded and isolated, and they married soon after their puberty ceremonies, leaving little room for premarital experimentation (something far from being the case today). Adulterous affairs, on the other hand, have been quite common, according to the experience of ethnographers and other observers since the 1960s, and older informants, speaking frankly, say that earlier generations were even livelier (see also Nordenskiöld et al., 1938, p. 32). Although men are thought to be more aggressive and likely to take the initiative, it is recognized that both men and women enjoy sex, and that both bear responsibility for their actions.

As for marital relations, young couples enjoy little privacy, except in the first weeks of marriage, during which traditionally they slept inside a temporary enclosure. Kuna sleeping houses are large undivided one-room structures filled with hammocks, and movement in one hammock can be felt in others and heard in the creaking of timbers. Young couples are encouraged to visit family coconut groves on the mainland for intercourse. They also slip outside in the dark or arrange to meet at home when the house is empty. In recent decades many houses have been partitioned, and couples may be allowed to build satellite sleeping huts. Moreover, migrant laborers often bring home beds. Nonetheless, marital sex can be as difficult to arrange as adultery.

No serious study has been carried out of Kuna sexuality. The one informant who spoke to the author on sexual practices said that couples often had intercourse with a man sitting on a low stool, so that they could move apart quickly if surprised. (Kuna women's wrap-around skirts come on and off easily.)

Kuna women often wear headcloths in public, pulling them around their faces in bright sun, in the gathering house, in mourning, or in situations in which they feel shy or wish to preserve their modesty and dignity. Women go bareheaded at home, and today young women do so even in public. When washing clothes at the river or near their cookhouses, or at home before dawn and late at night, women often strip to the waist, and men used to bathe naked outside, with their genitals tucked between their legs. Although women should not touch medicines or engage in sexual relations during menstruation, restrictions on menstruating women are otherwise light.

Kuna men take pains to shield Kuna women from life's dangers, especially against sexual threats by outsiders. As Swain (1978, p. 123) notes, "The message of male protector, dealing with the outside world, and female progenitrix maintaining the home, are strongly communicated as ideal Cuna forms." Intense struggles between the Kuna and Panamanian policemen in the early 1920s pivoted on issues of sexual access and intermarriage, and it is only recently that a very few Kuna have begun to marry outside their own ethnic group.

A handful of overtly homosexual and effeminate men, called *omegid*, "womanish, like women," or more slightingly, *amma* (a word that in other contexts means "aunt" or "female genitals"), are found in many villages. Many sew *molas*, and a few even belong to the women's *mola* cooperative, but they do not wear female dress (see Tice, 1995, pp. 59, 72–75). They are generally accepted in Kuna society, although the author has recently heard them denounced in a regional meeting for allegedly spreading the AIDS epidemic. As in much of Latin America, heterosexual males may sometimes have sex with homosexuals without risking much shame so long as they take the dominant role.

COURTSHIP AND MARRIAGE

As noted above, girls were married soon after puberty, but boys stayed single until the age of 18 or 20. As unmarried youths, boys were expected to work with their fathers as well as clearing and planting fields of their own. Matches were secretly prearranged by the senior generation, with the bride's parents most often taking the initiative. In a form of marriage by capture called "the dragging" (*gagaleged*), the groom would be surprised and carried off forcibly to be thrown in the hammock of the bride chosen for him. (A young man who objected strongly

could flee for a few months to another island.) Then and now, sons-in-law have worked for their parents-in-law for as long as they remain married, though they return frequently, often daily, to their natal households, and they continue to work with their fathers and brothers on family lands.

The dominance of the senior generation eroded sharply over the course of the 20th century. Although the dragging ritual continues in many villages, children and adolescents see each other every day in school, young people flirt and talk in the street, couples typically choose each other, and quite a few girls become pregnant before marrying (see Bonilla, 2000). Young married men still work for their in-laws, but they break free sooner than in the past, and many go off to the city for paid work, leaving their wives and children to be fed by the wife's father, or else, in recent years, taking their families with them to the city while their children are of school age. The percentage of unmarried, divorced, and abandoned mothers in Kuna Yala has risen to alarming levels in recent years (see Tice, 1995, pp. 118, 128–131, 150–152, 166–174).

HUSBAND–WIFE RELATIONSHIP

Kuna often ask, rhetorically, who you should save if your wife and mother are drowning—the answer is your mother, who is irreplaceable, whereas a new wife can be found "like changing clothes" (*mol ogwaedyobi*). Ethnographers have observed considerable instability in early marriages; estranged husbands often return home temporarily to their natal households, and divorce is common. Informants' accounts suggest that this was also the case in the late 19th and early 20th centuries (see Holloman, 1969, pp. 166–168; Nordenskiöld et al., 1938, pp. 31–32): if a young man returned to his wife after three separations, his father-in-law was supposed to hit his head against a housepost, to impart the essence of the post's stability as well as punishing him.

But the Kuna also lay great store by the marriage tie and, over time, couples who stay together very often develop strong affectionate relationships. Along with their children they form a unit within the household in terms of expense allocation, quarrels with other couples, and potential formation of new households. The senior man and wife work together closely in managing household labor, and many examples of strong lifelong attachments can be observed. When Panama achieved independence in 1903, the regional chief Inanaginya urged his followers to stay with Colombia by comparing their national affiliation with an old and mutually beneficial marriage.

OTHER CROSS-SEX RELATIONSHIPS

Rules and expectations for behavior between kin, whether same or opposite sex, are not strongly codified, except in the case of parents, grandparents, and children. Relations among adult siblings are often partly shaped by seniority, which is linguistically marked in same-sex sibling terms. Brothers should ideally look out for their sisters, and in general the relationship between siblings (*gwenadgan*) is projected as the model not only for kin relations as a whole, but for community and ethnic solidarity as well. It is expected that kin who are or have been coresident will be closer than those who have not. Overall, however, relations between kin depend primarily on individual likes and dislikes, as the Kuna themselves point out.

CHANGES IN ATTITUDES, BELIEFS, AND PRACTICES REGARDING GENDER

The extensive changes in Kuna gender roles discussed throughout this article can be summarized in the following terms:

1. a shift in the 19th century to male agricultural labor and the elaboration of women's dress;
2. through the 20th century, the spread of schooling for both boys and girls, and weakening control by the senior generation of marriage and household labor;
3. since the 1960s, the growth of an international market for women's handicrafts, and since the 1980s, increasing dependence on women's cash income;
4. since the late 1960s, the growth of a female-controlled handicraft cooperative;
5. in the late 20th century, the spread of feminist ideals, especially among educated Kuna, and the opening up of salaried employment for some women as well as men;
6. the great movement of Kuna to urban Panama in recent years.

NOTES

1. As of the year 2000, there were, in addition, 1,700 Kuna in the Darién region of eastern Panama and another 1,400 scattered through western Panama (Dirección de Estadística y Censo, 2001).

2. In the early 20th century midwives often buried infants born deformed or albino (the Kuna have the highest rate of albinism in the world), but there does not seem to have been any differential infanticide favoring male or female children.
3. Some mothers play with their infant sons' penises while nursing them.
4. Out of a total population of 49,143 over the age of 4 in the year 2000, 4,794 males and 8,696 females were without any schooling, reflecting a past gender bias. Numbers for those who had completed some grade school (9,859 vs. 9,643) and who had completed sixth grade (3,818 vs. 3,453) were essentially equal (Dirección de Estadística y Censo, 2001). See below on higher educational levels.
5. Kuna oral history takes note of this change. Brown's (1980) pioneering article, based on secondary sources, has a skewed chronology. Among the Colombian Kuna the old division of labor still held at least as recently as the 1970s. My data suggest provisionally that the San Blas Kuna went through a transitional stage in which both men and women worked in the fields. Tice (1995, pp. 115–177) has detailed contemporary comparisons from different subregions.
6. By the end of the 20th century agricultural production had diminished in much of Kuna Yala.
7. On some islands far from shore or on which women now work intensively sewing *molas* for sale (see Tice, 1995, p. 124), men fetch all or most of the water from the mainland.
8. Some of my male informants could not remember the names of close female relatives, who were identified by kin terms or as so-and-so's wife. Today, however, as both men and women take Hispanic and anglophone names, women are more widely known by name.
9. On the other hand, women who move to the city with their families in search of better schools for their children may find themselves working at home in greater isolation and with weaker support systems than in the islands, though the situation is undoubtedly somewhat better for the several thousand people living in all-Kuna settlements around Colón and Panama City.

REFERENCES

Bonilla, A. (2000, March 18). El matrimonio kuna. Trasfondo, *La Prensa* (Panama), p. 6A.

Brown, J. K. (1970). Sex division of labor among the San Blas Cuna. *Anthropological Quarterly, 43,* 57–63.

Chapin, N. M. (1983). *Curing among the San Blas Kuna of Panama.* Unpublished doctoral dissertation, University of Arizona, Tucson, AZ.

De Gerdes, M. L. (1995). *Constructing kuna identity through verbal art in the urban context.* Unpublished doctoral dissertation, University of Texas, Austin, TX.

Dirección de Estadística y Censo, Gobierno de Panamá (2001). *Censos nacionales de población y vivienda, 14 de Mayo de 2000: Vol. 2, Población.*

Hatley, N. B. (1976). Cooperativism and enculturation among the Cuna Indians of San Blas. In J. Wilbert (Ed.), *Enculturation in Latin America: An anthology* (UCLA Latin American Studies Series no. 37, pp. 67–94). Los Angeles: University of California.

Helms, M. W. (1976). Domestic organization in eastern Central America: the San Blas Cuna, Miskito, and Black Carib compared. *Western Canadian Journal of Anthropology*, 6, 133–163.

Holloman (1969). *Developmental change in San Blas*. Unpublished doctoral dissertation. Northwestern University, Evanston, IL.

Howe, J. (1985). Marriage and domestic organization among the San Blas Cuna, In W. D'Arcy & M. Correa (Eds.), *The botany and natural history of Panama* (pp. 317–331). St Louis, MO: Missouri Botanical Garden.

Howe, J. (1986). *The Kuna gathering: Contemporary village politics in Panama*. Austin: University of Texas Press.

Howe, J., & Hirschfeld, L. A. (1981). The star girls' descent: a myth about men, women, matrilocality, and singing. *Journal of American Folklore*, 94, 292–322.

Nordenskiöld, E., Pérez Kantule, R., & Wassén, S. H. (Ed.). (1938). *An historical and ethnographical survey of the Cuna Indians* (Comparative Ethnographical Studies 10) Göteborg, Sweden: Etnografiska Museum.

Prestán Simón, A. (1975). *El uso de la chicha y la sociedad kuna* (Ediciones Especiales 72). Mexico: Instituto Indigenista Interamericana.

Salcedo, G. (1980). Un consejo matrimonial, In J. Howe, N. M. Chapin, & J. Sherzer (Eds.), *Cantos y oraciones del congreso Cuna* (pp. 54–72). Panamá: Editorial Universitaria.

Salvador, M. L. (1997). Looking back: Contemporary Kuna women's arts. In M. L. Salvador (Ed.), *The art of being Kuna: Layers of meaning among the Kuna of Panama* (pp. 151–210.). Los Angeles: U.C.L.A. Fowler Museum of Cultural History.

Sherzer, J. (1987). A diversity of voices: Men's and women's speech in ethnographic perspective, In S. U. Philips, S. Steele, & C. Tanz (Eds.), *Language, gender, and sex in comparative perspective* (Studies in the Social and Cultural Foundations of Language No. 4, pp. 95–120). Cambridge, U.K.: Cambridge University Press.

Stout, D. B. (1947). *San Blas Cuna acculturation: An introduction.* New York: Viking Fund.

Swain, M. B. (1978). *Ailigandi women: continuity and change in Cuna female identity*. Unpublished doctoral dissertation, University of Washington, Seattle, WA.

Tice, K. E. (1995). *Kuna crafts, gender, and the global economy.* Austin: University of Texas Press.

Torres de Ianello [Torres de Araúz], R. (1957). *La mujer cuna de Panamá* (Ediciones Especiales). Prestán Simón, Mexico: Instituto Indigenista Interamericano.

Kyrgyz

Kathleen Kuehnast

ALTERNATIVE NAMES

The Kyrgyz are also known as the Kara-Kirgiz and the Alatau Kirgiz.

LOCATION

A land-locked country, Kyrgyzstan is located in Central Asia between the latitudes 39°N and 43°N. Kyrgyzstan borders the Chinese People's Republic to its east. On its other borders are three newly independent states, the countries of Kazakhstan to its north, Tajikistan to the southwest, and Uzbekistan on its western border. The country occupies 198,500 km², and only about 7% of its land is arable. Its climate offers extreme conditions of harsh cold winters (−23°C) and hot, dry summers (+41°C).

Referred to as the "little Switzerland of Central Asia," Kyrgyzstan is located amid the Pamir and Tien Shan mountain ranges, which are among some of the highest in the world, with the tallest peak being Mount Pobeda at 7,439 m. The second-largest mountain lake in the world, and one of the most transparent, Lake Issyk Kul (Kyrgyz for warm lake), is located in the northeastern part of Kyrgyzstan at 1,607 m above sea level and has brackish water that never freezes. Kyrgyzstan lies in a highly active seismic region.

CULTURAL OVERVIEW

The Kyrgyz (over 2 million) are primarily found in one of the recently independent countries of the former Soviet Union, the Kyrgyz Republic (or Kyrgyzstan). To understand the Kyrgyz and their construction of gender, it is useful to mention their diverse historical predicaments during the past 150 years. Until the 1920s, the Kyrgyz were a seminomadic group, thought to have originated in the Yenisei River region in northern Siberia around 900 CE. Throughout the last millennium, the Kyrgyz, along with other nomadic groups, traveled vast distances from the eastern shores of the Aral Sea to the western border of China and south to Afghanistan for the purpose of herding their sheep and horses. Although the Kyrgyz cultural patterns resemble those of the nomadic tribes of Central Asia, nevertheless some among them became sedentary, especially in the southern areas of the country. Here mosques and *madrassas* (religious schools) were constructed in the 12th century. Among the northern tribes, the nomadic Kyrgyz did not significantly convert to Islam until the early 19th century.

Between 1925 and 1991, the Kyrgyz experienced intensive Soviet collectivization. This change had a major impact not only on their livelihood, but also on their family structure and kinship patterns. Prior to 1925, women were primarily illiterate. By the mid-1930s, female literacy rates had reached 35%, and by the early 1990s there was complete literacy of men and women.

It should be noted that among the Central Asian ethnic groups, the Kyrgyz and the Kazakh of Kazakhstan are more closely related in terms of their language, cultural practices, and kinship structures than any of the other major groups (Tajiks, Turkmen, or Uzbeks).

CULTURAL CONSTRUCTION OF GENDER

Gender is recognized by the Kyrgyz through two categories—men and women, or male and female. The two categories are manifested in cultural norms and domestic practices that divide societal responsibilities by gender. In contemporary Kyrgyz culture, both men and women are accustomed to modern dress; thus their clothing tends to be more European or Western than traditional Muslim cloaks or any sort of veiling. In rural areas, some women wear scarves to cover their head, which is seen as a display of modesty, especially among married women. Few women are veiled, as is customary in many religious Muslim countries. In urban centers, women commonly wear facial make-up, particularly on their eyes, lips, and cheeks. Differentiation is age related in regard to visual appearances. Young women are considered more attractive if they allow their hair to grow long. There are fewer expectations for men's visual appearance, except that they should maintain a sense of cleanliness in dress; despite Muslim influence, most Kyrgyz men are clean-shaven.

During pre-Soviet times, the Kyrgyz lived in a structure called a yurt, which was divided into female and male spaces. To the left of the entryway is a space designated for men (*er jak*); this includes a space for saddles and other horse-riding implements. The right is considered the women's side (*epchi jak*), an area separated by a *chiy* (screen), where domestic items such as pots and utensils were kept.

The Kyrgyz have traditionally practiced arranged marriages along tribal lines, and thus individuals had very little say in their actual marriages. Commonly though, young women under the age of 18 years were considered more attractive or "marriageable," since great importance is placed in Kyrgyz culture on the ability to bear children—thus, the younger the bride, the higher the likelihood of many children.

GENDER OVER THE LIFE CYCLE

The Kyrgyz recognize the following events as important lifestyle passages and publicly mark each event: birth, the first steps of a child, circumcision of a boy, engagement, marriage, retirement, and death. Birthday celebrations are a recent phenomenon, since prior to sovietization birth dates were never recorded or registered. For most Kyrgyz over the age of 75 years (in the year 2000), the date and year of their birth are usually an approximation.

The Kyrgyz names for life cycle stages are as follows: *balalyk*, childhood; *ospurum*, teenager; *jashtyk/ jash ubak*, youth; *tolgonchak*, mature age; *karylyk*, old age. In addition, the names for life cycle events are different for males and females. Male stages: *bala*, boy; *jigit*, young man; *jetilgen chak*, man; *chal*, elderly man. Female stages: *kyz*, girl; *selki*, young woman; *ajal*, woman; *kempir*, elderly woman.

Socialization of Boys and Girls

Boys and girls in Kyrgyz society are reared differently from infancy through childhood by parents and others, including extended family members, other kin, neighbors, and peers. The birth of a boy is considered more of a celebration for a family than the birth of a girl, but the difference in response is marginal. In part, boys are preferred over girls because they are socially ordained to care for their parents, whereas girls move away from their natal home once they are married. The eldest male is expected to live in the parents' home upon marriage. The youngest male child in the family is responsible for caring for the parents when they are old. Thus the responsibilities and obligations of male children to their natal family are greater than those of female children, who are expected to care for their husband's parents.

Different expectations exist for Kyrgyz girls and boys in the domestic sphere. Boys are expected to have a more leisurely childhood, to play with other boys, to ride horses, to hunt, and to learn to be a man, whereas girls at a young age are given household responsibilities, including cooking, cleaning, sewing, and caring for younger children or elderly adults, as part of their training to be a woman.

The primary caretakers among the Kyrgyz are often the parents or grandparents. Both prior to and during the Soviet period, the extended-family living pattern usually meant that three generations lived together in one dwelling. Sometimes this would include aunts and uncles of the married couple. Grandparents are highly revered and cared for, since many grandchildren actually have a stronger bond with them than with their own parents. Grandparents or an aunt or uncle often take part in the instruction and discipline of children. Boys and girls are disciplined differently; at times girls are more severely disciplined for misbehaviors, since the expectation for their acting appropriately and modestly is much higher than for young boys. Girls and boys learn informally about sexuality and courting rituals.

During the Soviet period, coeducation for girls and boys was normalized. Nevertheless, there were different expectations for performance in schools. In reviewing standardized texts for elementary education, illustrations often equate women with the domestic sphere and men with heavy labor. This is somewhat ironic, since Soviet women were among the most active worldwide in the labor force. Often it was said that women must carry a "double burden," that of both domestic and public work.

Because many of the Kyrgyz customary practices are highly influenced by Muslim customs, it is expected that male children should be circumcised by the age of 5 or 7 years of age (preferably in an odd year rather than an even year). It is generally considered that the earlier the boy is circumcised, the better, since it takes less time for recovery. Even though circumcision was considered illegal by the Soviets, many Kyrgyz boys were nevertheless circumcised following Muslim practices. In some parts of Kyrgyzstan, circumcision was performed symbolically, and the penis of the child was only touched with a knife.

Puberty and Adolescence

The period of adolescence is recognized by the Kyrgyz, but has only been emphasized in the last century under the Soviet educational system. Except for moving from elementary education into higher grades, schools are the most formalized vehicles for marking this period of time. As mentioned above, adolescent girls are seen as attractive for marriage. Under Soviet law, the legal age for marriage changed from 9 to 16 years of age for girls and from 16 to 18 years for boys.

One of the more recent concerns of adolescent women (*kyz*) today is the revival of the old practice of *kyz ala kachuu* or bride-stealing, which is when a young man abducts a young woman from her home or off the street for the purpose of marrying her. This practice can be found among various ethnic groups throughout Central Asia and the Caucasus. In the rural regions, bride-stealing has long been a common feature of some marriage agreements. Even though it is considered illegal, perpetrators are rarely brought to court, since such actions bring shame to the young bride's family. Furthermore, social norms dictate that stolen brides are expected to capitulate so as not to bring shame upon their relatives. Once a young woman is stolen, she is married that day, so she loses her virginity, leaving her little choice but to stay in her new predicament. The Kyrgyz have a saying that refers to this situation, "*Tash tüshkön jerinde oor*" ("Let the stone lie where it has fallen").

Attainment of Adulthood

The most significant rite of passage indicating a transition from boyhood to manhood and from girlhood to womanhood is marriage, and secondly, giving birth to a child. The latter is particularly important for recognizing a woman as a full-fledged adult, no matter how old she is when she gives birth to her first child.

Middle Age and Old Age

The life cycles of middle-aged and elderly adults have changed dramatically in the last decade, as a result of the declining economic conditions in the country. Many who had looked forward to retirement at 50 years (for women) and 55 years (for men) find themselves working in the informal market instead of enjoying their leisure time. The elderly, many of whom are women, find that the social safety net once in place during the Soviet period is no longer there, and they have few options but to depend on their children for day-to-day assistance.

PERSONALITY DIFFERENCES BY GENDER

Men and women in Kyrgyz society are in many ways far more interdependent in their behaviors than many other Central Asian groups. In part, their nomadic heritage allowed for a much more egalitarian division of roles. While men took the herds to the higher pastures, women were in charge of the home front. As a result, this legacy still permeates domestic arrangements among the Kyrgyz. Women are recognized to be in charge of all issues related to the home and family. This is not just care giving behaviors but also decision-making behaviors. Both Kyrgyz men and women tend to be highly nurturing of their children, which reflects the overall value of children in the society. A young child is readily cared for by his or her father (or grandfather), as much as by his or her mother. Although there are many customary practices that favor male dominance in the society, there is a general mythology that the Kyrgyz share, that at one time the Kyrgyz were a matriarchal tribe, where women had equal or greater power than men. Reflecting this belief system is the general mild manner of the men and the strong presence of capable women. Sometimes stereotypes are communicated that Kyrgyz women are hardworking and Kyrgyz men are lazy. Historically speaking, the Kyrgyz have been significantly influenced by the Soviet egalitarian gender ideals, as well as by the more Islamic gender ideals of powerful men and cloistered women.

GENDER-RELATED SOCIAL GROUPS

Ideal gender types and realities often do not coincide, and in the case of the Kyrgyz many of the Soviet and post-Soviet social institutions were structured around men.

Although many women made significant advancements in politics, economics and medicine, the reality is that women do not have as many opportunities, nor do they receive equal pay.

Much of Kyrgyz society is geared toward the male, including marriage residence, which is exogamous, or living near or with the husband's family. Kin groups are formed through patrilineal lineage system or *bir atanyng baldary*—seven generations of Kyrgyz patrilineal family. Prior to Soviet collectivization, the economic demands of pastoral nomadism required alliances among the Kyrgyz patrilineal kinship groups (*ayils*) in order to maintain grazing pastures and water rights for their horses, sheep, and cattle. One way of solidifying economic relationships with neighboring tribes was through arranged exogamous marriages. Agreements between two groups to exchange their daughters (*kuda söök*) formed the foundation of economic relations that often lasted for several generations, since wives had to be taken from the same *söök* (bones) as their mothers. Members of these two groups were expected to assist one another. They shared grazing lands and protected each other's animals from raids made by neighboring tribes. Often marriages were arranged between tribal groups prior to the birth of children (*bel kuda*). Betrothal of small children who were still in their cradles was called *beshik kuda*. Agreements between the *kuda söök* were honored even in the event of a death, when the customary law of levirate required a brother or a relative to marry the widow.

In Kyrgyz society, social structures tend to be separated by gender. Whether it is a social club, a business association, or a wedding party, men and women tend to seek their own sex for social affiliation.

GENDER ROLES IN ECONOMICS

The division of labor between men and women in making a living, household and domestic work, and occupational specialization is fairly well defined. Despite 70 years of living under Soviet rule, Kyrgyz women are still expected to maintain the household and domestic work, while at the same time having a job outside the home. Men are less likely to perform domestic duties. During the Soviet period, women participated in nearly all labor arenas, except heavy industrial work. Today both men and women are involved in informal trade and entrepreneurial activities, in part due to the economic problems in the

region. Women have dominated the "shuttle trade" markets, in which they travel to nearby countries and buy up goods and sell them in Kyrgyzstan at local markets. This is primarily because women seem to be less harassed then men at customs or border stops. Thus, women have gained a significant niche in the market. More and more, men who are from rural villages are moving to the urban centers to find work. This has had a major impact on families, leaving many women to be single parents raising many children, as well as maintaining gardens for household food reserves. Although women are legally able to inherit land, customary law sometimes prohibits them from actually gaining the property.

PARENTAL AND OTHER CARETAKER ROLES

Parental roles are not necessarily preordained in Kyrgyz culture, since birth parents do not always raise their child. Occasionally, extended family members, grandparents, or aunts and uncles play a more day-to-day role in parenting than the actual birth parents. Grandmothers are particularly counted on as a primary caregiver of young children, and many Kyrgyz have closer relationships with their respective grandparents than they do with their own parents. In some instances, the first-born child born of an eldest son is given to the parents in what is called *amanat*. The relationship between the "gifted" child and the aging grandparents is seen as reciprocal, because the child assists the grandparents' household but in turn the grandparents help preserve Kyrgyz traditions by passing their knowledge on to the child. In most cases the child is well aware of the fact that his grandparents are not his biological parents, but nevertheless calls them by the names *ata* (father) and *ene* (mother), and calls his own father and mother "older brother" and "older sister."

During the Soviet period, parental roles shifted from family members to state institutions. By the mid-1950s, the number of *detskii sad* (kindergartens) reached an all-time high as children's centers were set up throughout the urban and rural regions in Kyrgyzstan to care for their children. Every collective farm had its programs where children resided for weeks at a time, while parents worked long hours during the peak seasons of planting and harvesting. The childcare centers addressed one part of postwar economic issues—it helped to free women in order to increase their productivity. Because of the type of laborious work done by the most physically capable, the parents of young children were rarely available to raise their offspring. It was the grandparents who often nurtured language skills, social values, shared stories, and kept alive various traditions for the young children.

Today the difficult economic predicament means that, typically, both parents work outside the home. Sometimes a niece or a cousin lives with and cares for the younger children of their relatives, or else an older sibling is placed in charge of the younger brothers or sisters.

Both mothers and fathers are much more indulgent of young boys then of young girls. Physical affection is much more common with infants or toddlers than with older children. Children are not necessarily indulged, but instead they are considered a part of the household structure and are expected to contribute to ensuring that the household runs effectively. Children often have many responsibilities, particularly the girls in a family. Both mothers and fathers expect more from a female child. A daughter is engaged in some sort of household work at a very young age, whereas a young boy is often left to play on his own rather than asked to participate in household duties.

LEADERSHIP IN PUBLIC ARENAS

During the past 10 years of national independence, women's leadership in Kyrgyzstan has declined in the public arenas, in part because the quotas for women in government ended with the Soviet era. Since then, women have found that the most viable opportunities for them are found in newly formed nongovernmental organizations, where they have proven to be extremely active. Nevertheless, it is useful to consider that, among the Kyrgyz, there is a mythology or a belief system that the Kyrgyz were once a matriarchal tribe, and that women were expected to be good warriors, fine horseback riders, and excellent statesmen. In this light, Kyrgyz women are sometimes a part of local government institutions, such as village councils (*aiyl okmotu*), but these women tend to be older and have garnered a great deal of respect in the village community.

GENDER AND RELIGION

The Kyrgyz are highly syncretic in their approach to religion. They combine traditions of animism, shamanism, and Islam into their daily lives. The legend of *Umay Ene*, a female deer, tells what happened that when the forest burned (in Siberia) and only one child survived, who was raised by *Umay Ene*. Considered to be the grandmother of all Kyrgyz and the spirit who protects children and animals, many women pray to *Umay Ene*. When shamans (many of whom are women) perform a healing on a child they often say, "It is not my hand but the hand of *Umay Ene* who heals." During the harvest or when cattle and sheep gave birth to calves and lambs, the Kyrgyz say "*Umay Ene's breast gives us milk*." Female Kyrgyz shamans also officiate at life cycle celebrations, such as birth and marriage, and conduct funeral services, but central to their role in the Kyrgyz community is the performance of public and private healing rituals. These usually include the chanting of Muslim prayers, as well as prayers to the deceased or to animal spirits. Infertility and chronic pain are typical reasons for seeking out a shaman. Shamanism, which predates Islam by hundreds of years, survived the Islamic conversion of the Kyrgyz because Sufism, the predominant missionary sect of Islam among the Kyrgyz, was extremely porous and incorporated the shamanistic practices into its Islamic rituals.

The resurgence of Islam during the 1990s in Central Asia has given rise to many men becoming more active in religious practices. In some of the southern regions of Kyrgyzstan it has also meant that the *otines*, the female Muslim clergy, have been given added importance in their role as teachers in the villages (Fathi, 1997). Within the Islamic community, *otines* oversee the religious education of females from birth to adulthood and also conduct religious rituals for births, marriages, and funerals.

LEISURE, RECREATION, AND THE ARTS

The Kyrgyz have many celebrations (*toi*). Both men and women are intricately involved in preparing for such events, which incorporate leisure and recreation, as well as an expression of the arts for them. Elaborate displays of food and energetic sports, such as wrestling, horse racing, and a form of polo, are all a part of making a celebration successful. At the heart of most events is the storytelling and music. The Kyrgyz are renowned for their epic poem, *The Manas*, a story of a medieval warrior who battles his enemies and brings pride to the Kyrgyz tribes. Both men and women sing and play musical instruments, but dancing is not customary among the Kyrgyz. The Soviets introduced formalized dance movements to the Kyrgyz, but these were not based on cultural practices. The Soviets also introduced chess, which is a popular past-time for men. Segregation in leisure time is voluntary and based on years of the separation of women and men due to their respective work and household duties. Women often work cooperatively on making a *shyrdak* (felted carpet) or weaving a *chiy* (woven reed screen).

RELATIVE STATUS OF MEN AND WOMEN

Men and women in Kyrgyz society have differential authority, rights, and privileges. As mentioned above, the nomadic traditions and the sovietization of the Kyrgyz contributed to the relative egalitarian status between the sexes, especially when compared with other Central Asian groups. Nevertheless, overall men have more status in Kyrgyz society, both formally and informally, except for the domestic concerns, where women are given much more control in decision-making. Men and women are both able to inherit land, but in most instances it goes to a male child of the woman. Kyrgyz women work outside the home and, in these instances, are often in control of the income they make. Studies have shown that most of women's income goes to support the household. As women grow older, and become mothers-in-law, their status increases. It is usually the young daughter-in-law (*kelin*) who has the lowest status in a household. She is expected to do whatever her husband and his mother and father tell her to do. In some instances, domestic violence is not perpetrated by the husband against his wife, but by the mother-in-law physically abusing the young *kelin*.

SEXUALITY

Attitudes toward sexuality in Kyrgyz society are generally natural and healthy, but highly private and modest. Attitudes toward practices of premarital sex and extramarital sex differ for males and females. It is generally expected that men might have premarital and extramarital sex, but it is not necessarily accepted, especially by women. There are definite negative attitudes for women having premarital or extramarital sex, but nevertheless it does occur. To some degree, as men and women age there is more acceptance about extramarital sex, but neither gender expects it in their own marriage. In other words it is done, illicitly. Little expression of sexuality is allowed in childhood, and it depends to some extent on whether a child is growing up in an urban or rural environment; the latter is a little more relaxed about innocent experimenting.

Modesty is shown by women who cover their hair or wear a scarf, especially after marriage. In more traditional regions, it is considered immodest for a woman or a man to show their legs, but this is changing as Western influences infiltrate the younger generation. Overall, the Kyrgyz have very few outward expressions of cross-sex identification, nor are male and female homosexuality publicly acknowledged, although it does exist.

Sexuality is also perceived in relationship to producing children. During the intensive Soviet campaign after World War II, Kyrgyz women were encouraged to produce larger families. This campaign was embraced wholeheartedly by the Kyrgyz, since children are considered a sign of great prosperity as well as security for one's old age. The pressure placed on a Kyrgyz woman to have a large family has always been great, since the fertility of a woman—especially the birth of sons—is considered a sign of good fortune for an extended family (Tabyshalieva, 1997).

COURTSHIP AND MARRIAGE

Several different patterns of male–female courtship and marriage exist among the Kyrgyz. Among rural populations, a more traditional approach toward courtship exists, which often includes some aspects of arranged marriage. In pre-Soviet times, marriages were often arranged between tribal groups prior to the birth of children (*bel kuda*). Betrothal of small children who were still in their cradles was called *beshik kuda*. Agreements between the *kuda söök* were honored even in the event of a death, when the customary law of levirate required a brother or a relative to marry the widow. Today, matchmakers are still used and usually attempt to link families together. Although such arranged marriages were illegal, during the Soviet period, as were the payments of brideprice (*kalym*) and dowry (*sep*), these practices continued throughout the last century and are being revived in the post-Soviet society.

Among more urban Kyrgyz, marriages are the result of a young man and woman deciding on such a union.

Such an approach resembles many modern marriages. They usually seek out a judge to perform the ceremony and, more recently, many are also seeking the blessing of a mullah (Islamic cleric).

Upon marriage, a young couple is often given "guardian parents" for the newly married (*ökül apa* and *ökül ata*—authorized or entrusted mother and father). The parents of the groom arrange for an established married couple to act as sponsors, confidants, and mentors to a newly married couple. It is understood to be a very private and confidential relationship, but it was also kept very private during the Soviet period because it had once been considered anticommunist to have an *ökül apa* and *ökül ata*. According to the tradition, after the *ökül* parents have been identified, contact with them is up to the young couple. If there is no contact, then it is considered a formal process and no gifts are exchanged. But if the young couple seek out the *ökül* parents then the relationship has two aims. One is to provide a good model for the couple, and the second is to make contacts stronger between families, since they are not blood relatives.

HUSBAND–WIFE RELATIONSHIP

The husband–wife relationship among the Kyrgyz is characterized generally by duty and a quiet respect; affection is primarily given to their offspring. They tend to approach their marriage as team members; they rarely display public affection or hostility. The relationship is considered private. Husbands and wives often eat together with their family, sleep together, spend time visiting their respective extended families together, and often make decisions together. There is a fairly defined division of labor when it comes to household tasks and family concerns.

Polygyny occasionally occurs, when a man takes a second wife, but it is unofficial as it is not legal in Kyrgyzstan. In instances where polygyny does take place, Islamic codes are put into effect; the first wife has more status than the second, but it is expected that both wives must be given similar resources to support their respective children. If a marriage is not satisfactory, divorce is often the result and can be initiated by either the husband or the wife. The children typically stay with the mother, but the husband can also seek custody. In pre-Soviet marriages, children of a divorce would go to the husband's relatives.

OTHER CROSS-SEX RELATIONSHIPS

These relationships are discussed under various categories above. The most significant relationship outside marriage is the grandparent–grandchild relationship.

CHANGE IN ATTITUDES, BELIEFS, AND PRACTICES REGARDING GENDER

During the post-Soviet period from 1991 to the present, Kyrgyz society has experienced a confluence of different and contrasting ideologies. Although societal change affects all age cohorts, it certainly affects each group differently. The younger generation is less influenced by gender and sexual egalitarian ideals from the Soviet period, but instead find themselves confronted by two highly contradictory ideals of men and women, that of conservative Islam and that of Western media. These very different approaches to sexuality and gender roles leave a highly contradictory situation in which to examine Kyrgyz norms definitively. The gendered expectations of the middle-aged cohort have been shaped by years of Soviet education, in which men and women were professed to be equal, and in which many of the laws attempted to bring more equality to the sexes. Among older Kyrgyz, gender and sexuality have remnants of pre-Soviet ideals and highly traditional approaches, as well as Soviet expectations that women should participate actively in society.

BIBLIOGRAPHY

Abramzon, S. M. (1978). Family-group, family, and individual property categories among nomads. In W. Weissleder (Ed.), *The nomadic alternative: Modes and models of interaction in the African–Asian deserts and steppes* (pp. 179–188). The Hague, The Netherlands: Mouton.

Akmataliev, A. (1993). *Baba saltiy, ene adebi* [Traditions of fathers, customs of mothers]. Bishkek, Kyrgyzstan: Balasagiyn.

Bauer, A., Boschmann, N., Green, D., & Kuehnast, K. (1998). *A generation at risk. children in the Central Asian republics of Kazakstan and Kyrgyzstan*. Manila, Philippines: Asian Development Bank.

Buckley, M. (1997). Victims and agents: gender in post-Soviet States. In M. Buckley (Ed.), *Post-Soviet women: From the Baltic to Central Asia* (pp. 3–16). Cambridge, U.K.: Cambridge University Press.

Carlson, B. A. (1994). The condition of children in the countries of the Former Soviet Union (FSU): A statistical review. *Journal of Development Studies*, *31*(1), 1–16.

Dunn, S. P., & Dunn, E. (1967). Soviet regime and native culture in Central Asia and Kazakhstan: The major peoples. *Current Anthropology, 8*(3), 147–208.

Fathi, H. (1997). Otines: the unknown women clerics of Central Asian Islam. *Central Asian Survey, 16*(1), 27–43.

Gorsuch, A. E. (1996). "A woman is not a man": The culture of gender and generation in Soviet Russia, 1921–1928. *Slavic Review, 55*(3), 638–660.

Kenenbaeva, K., Tabyshalieva, A., & Karasaeva, A. (1995). Current status of women of Kyrgyzstan. In E. Shukurov (Ed.), *Women of Kyrgyzstan: Tradition and new reality* (pp. 75–89). Bishkek, Kyrgyzstan: Ychkyn.

Kuehnast, K. (1997). *The stone must lie where it has fallen*: Dilemmas of gender and generation in post-Soviet Kyrgyzstan. Doctoral dissertation, University of Minnesota (UMI No.).

Kuehnast, K. (2000). Coming of age in post-Soviet Central Asia: Dilemmas and challenges facing youth and children. *Demokratizatsiya, 8*(2), 186–198.

Rosenhan, M. S. (1978). Images of male and female children in children's readers. In D. Atkinson, A. Dallin, & G. W. Lapidus (Eds.), *Women in Russia* (pp. 292–305). London: Harvester Press.

Tabyshalieva, A. (1997). Women of Central Asia and the fertility cult. *Anthropology and Archeology of Eurasia, 36*(2), 45–62.

Tolmacheva, M. A. (1993).The Muslim woman in Soviet Central Asia. *Central Asian Survey, 12*(4), 531–548.

Zhdanko, T. A. (1978). Ethnic communities with survivals of clan and tribal structure in Central Asia and Kazakhstan in the nineteenth and early twentieth centuries. In W. Weissleder (Ed.), *The nomadic alternative: Modes and Models of interaction in the African–Asian deserts and steppes* (pp. 179–188). The Hague, The Netherlands: Mouton.